Montgomery's
AUDITING
Twelfth Edition

Montgomery's
AUDITING
Twelfth Edition

VINCENT M. O'REILLY, CPA
Distinguished Senior Lecturer, Carroll School of Management, Boston College
Retired Executive Vice Chairman, Professional Practice and Service Quality,
Coopers & Lybrand L.L.P.

PATRICK J. McDONNELL, CPA
Vice Chairman, Business Assurance, Coopers & Lybrand L.L.P.

BARRY N. WINOGRAD, CPA
Director, Business Assurance Services, Coopers & Lybrand L.L.P.

JAMES S. GERSON, CPA
Director, Audit Policy and Quality, Coopers & Lybrand L.L.P.
Vice Chair, Auditing Standards Board of the
American Institute of Certified Public Accountants

HENRY R. JAENICKE, Ph.D., CPA
C.D. Clarkson Professor of Accounting,
College of Business and Administration,
Drexel University

JOHN WILEY & SONS, INC.
New York   Chichester   Weinheim   Brisbane
Singapore   Toronto

Published by John Wiley & Sons, Inc.

Published simultaneously in Canada.

This publication is designed to provide accurate and authoritative information in regard to the subject matter covered. It is sold with the understanding that the publisher is not engaged in rendering legal, accounting, or other professional services. If legal advice or other expert assistance is required, the services of a competent professional person should be sought.

Library of Congress Cataloging-in-Publication Data:

ISBN 0-471-14063-5

Printed in the United States of America.

10 9 8 7 6 5 4 3 2 1

About the Authors

Vincent M. O'Reilly, CPA, is a co-author of the eleventh edition of this book. He is the retired Executive Vice Chairman, Professional Practice and Service Quality, and was a member of the Management Committee of Coopers & Lybrand L.L.P. Previously he was Deputy Chairman, Accounting and Auditing. He is currently Distinguished Senior Lecturer at the Carroll School of Management at Boston College. He received the 1997 John J. McCloy Award from the Public Oversight Board of the AICPA's SEC Practice Section for his outstanding contributions to audit excellence.

Patrick J. McDonnell, CPA, is Vice Chairman, Business Assurance, and a member of the Management Committee of Coopers & Lybrand L.L.P. He chairs Coopers & Lybrand's International Accounting and Auditing Board. He was formerly Vice Chairman, Client Service, and Managing Partner responsible for the Midwest operations of Coopers & Lybrand. He was a member of the AICPA's Special Committee on Assurance Services.

Barry N. Winograd, CPA, is Director, Business Assurance Services, at Coopers & Lybrand L.L.P. and is responsible for the Firm's audit service methodologies and related training. In this role, he has overseen the development and implementation of the Firm's Global Total Engagement Quality methodology. He also serves major clients in the financial services industry, providing audit services, as well as special services in the areas of internal control, derivatives, and acquisitions. He was a member of the AICPA's Special Committee on Financial Reporting.

James S. Gerson, CPA, is Director, Audit Policy and Quality, at Coopers & Lybrand L.L.P. In that role, he has responsibility for developing audit policies and practices, including support materials for the practice, as well as responsibility for risk management and quality control. He is Vice Chair of the Auditing Standards Board of the AICPA. He also is a member of the SECPS Peer Review Committee. Previously he served on the Financial Reporting Coordinating Committee and the Employee Benefit Plans Committee of the AICPA.

Henry R. Jaenicke, Ph.D. and CPA, is the C.D. Clarkson Professor of Accounting at Drexel University and a co-author of the tenth and eleventh editions of this book. He was the principal research consultant to the Commission on Auditors' Responsibilities and authored the commission's research study on *The*

Effect of Litigation on Independent Auditors. He won the American Accounting Association's Wildman Medal for his FASB research study, *Survey of Present Practices in Recognizing Revenues, Expenses, Gains, and Losses.* He also is co-author of *Evaluating Internal Control*, published by John Wiley & Sons, and of *Accounting for Museum Collections and Contributions of Collection Items*, published by the American Association of Museums.

Historical Perspective

Robert H. Montgomery (1872–1953) together with William M. Lybrand (1867–1960), Adam Ross (1869–1929), and T. Edward Ross (1867–1963) founded the firm of Lybrand, Ross Bros. & Montgomery (now Coopers & Lybrand L.L.P.) in 1898, two years after the first CPA law was passed. The four had for some time previously practiced public accounting in Philadelphia.

Montgomery was a prolific writer and leader of his profession. He was instrumental in the organization of what is now the American Institute of Certified Public Accountants and served as its president. Earlier, he also taught at Columbia University, New York University, and the University of Pennsylvania.[1] He saw the need for a practical book on auditing and in 1905 and 1909 published American editions of Dicksee's *Auditing,* a British work. Noting the radical departure of American practice from Dicksee's work, however, he wrote the first American book on the subject, *Auditing: Theory and Practice,* in 1912. Ten subsequent editions followed from 1916 through 1990. For the seventh edition, co-authors Alvin R. Jennings and Norman J. Lenhart joined him and the book was renamed *Montgomery's Auditing.* The eighth edition, published after his death, was co-authored by Norman J. Lenhart and Philip L. Defliese in 1957. The ninth edition, published in 1975, was co-authored by Philip L. Defliese, Kenneth P. Johnson, and Roderick K. Macleod. The tenth edition, co-authored by Jerry D. Sullivan, Richard A. Gnospelius, Philip L. Defliese, and Henry R. Jaenicke, was published in 1985; a college version (adapted for classroom use) also was begun at this time. The eleventh edition, co-authored by Vincent M. O'Reilly, Murray B. Hirsch, Philip L. Defliese, and Henry R. Jaenicke, was published in 1990; it too had a college version. Comparisons of the various editions reveal the development of accounting and auditing in the United States.

In 1956, in recognition of the growing needs of international practice, Cooper Bros. & Co. in the United Kingdom and other countries (founded in 1854), MacDonald Currie & Co. in Canada (founded in 1910), and Lybrand, Ross Bros. & Montgomery joined as member firms of what is now Coopers & Lybrand International. The Coopers & Lybrand name was adopted worldwide in 1973. Dropping the Montgomery name from a firm that had so long celebrated his contributions was not easy. The continued association of the Montgomery name, however, with his major contribution to the literature of the profession is a proper tribute to his memory.

---

[1]For a full account of Montgomery's contributions, see his autobiography, *Fifty Years of Accountancy* (New York: The Ronald Press Co., 1939).

Preface

Each of the previous editions of this book has commented on the nature of change affecting the audit process. Most concluded that the rate of change was quite dramatic. Of late, however, the nature of the changes seems to have been more in the methodology of applying well-founded principles than in revising the basic underpinnings of the profession.

The ten generally accepted auditing standards have remained largely as they were. The most significant additional elucidation in recent years has been the further clarification of the auditor's responsibility for considering fraud in a financial statement audit. The attention given to this subject is testimony to the continuing presence of a gap between what users of financial statements expect from auditors and what auditors have been supplying. We have not heard the last word on this subject by any means.

Despite the stability of auditing standards, we appear to be entering a new phase of dramatic change for the profession. The basic value of the core service of the profession is under challenge. The profession's structure is changing in ways that some believe could undermine the most critical attribute of auditors—their independence. Moreover, the high status that U.S. auditing standards have earned in the commercial marketplace is beginning to be replaced by a growing recognition that allegiance to internationally established auditing standards ultimately may become the norm.

Still, we believe that the profession's core service—audits conducted in accordance with generally accepted auditing standards of financial statements prepared in conformity with generally accepted accounting principles—continues to be valuable because of the credibility that audit assurance imparts to the information provided by management in financial statements. And we also believe that the profession is still held in high regard by readers of those financial statements. A key component in providing investor confidence in capital markets is the confirming role of audited financial information as a periodic check on the information flow entering the marketplace.

Furthermore, as much as some might criticize the profession's shift into other services and question the value of auditing historical information, it is interesting to note that others, and in fact some of the profession's critics, are calling on auditors to provide even more information about the entities that they audit. There is growing recognition that auditors are well-positioned to learn about their clients and should be able to use that information to improve the governance of those entities.

Despite these changes, the basic audit concepts and objectives remain largely unchanged. They have evolved to a high level and do not need major revision. Still, as entities become more and more dependent on computerized processing for generating and processing transactional information, and as the pressure on auditors to accomplish their tasks effectively and efficiently continues to increase, auditing focus and techniques must change.

The increasing need to understand and assess internal control in the course of audits, and the continuing importance of understanding the industry in which the entity operates and of understanding and evaluating the accounting judgments and estimates made by the entity's management, are major influences on the approach taken in this edition. We trust that it will bring value to the reader, much as auditors in general are encouraged to bring value to their clients and the users of the financial and other information they report on.

We acknowledge with thanks the permission granted to us by the American Institute of Certified Public Accountants, the Canadian Institute of Chartered Accountants, and The Institute of Internal Auditors to quote or paraphrase passages from their publications. Copies of the complete documents can be obtained from those organizations.

This book represents the efforts and ideas of many people. The following individuals, presently or formerly associated with Coopers & Lybrand L.L.P., contributed to various portions of the book: Sander Abernathy, James B. Alfano, Alan M. Bangser, Kelly A. Barnes, Michael E. Barrett, Dennis D. Bartolucci, Carina B. Canedo, Clark L. Bernard, Bhaskar H. Bhave, John T. Buckley, Ted Chambers, Kenneth R. Chatelain, Joseph S. Cohen, Kenneth E. Dakdduk, John Dalton, John C. Davis, William J. Davis, Ralph Deacetis, Larry D. DeBower, Robert L. DeNormandie, Raymond L. Dever, Nelson W. Dittmar, Ellis M. Dunkum, David S. East, Stephen D. Eddy, Patrice Edmonds, Frederick J. Elmy, Robert Ernst, Joseph B. Feiten, Martin J. Fiscus, Robert T. Forrester, John J. Gillen, Richard A. Gnospelius, Timothy J. Gordon, Richard P. Graff, Lynford E. Graham, Jr., Richard S. Greenberg, Gregory T. Grobstein, Bjorn Hanson, James F. Harrington, Kevin P. Hassan, Robert H. Herz, Robert B. Hetler, W. Jeffrey Hoover, Nicholas L. Iacuzio, Claes Janzon, Dennis R. Jennings, William Jewell, Robert A. Jinkins, Jeffrey L. Johanns, Michael A. Johns.

Also, Martin Kehoe, John A. Konawalik, Gregory H. Kozich, Michelle R. Krupa, Frederick R. Kruse, Martin M. Leahy, Todd J. Lifson, Stephen J. Lis, John P. Lombardi, John J. Lynch, Rocco J. Maggiotto, Ronald T. Maheu, Donald J. Markey, John P. Marra, John A. Mattie, C. Michael Mayer, Richard C. Maynard, Bernard P. Morgan, Margaret M. Morgan, Patricia F. Obermaier, Frank C. Olmsted, Jerry A. O'Neil, Rajan Parmeswar, Marnie Pease, Gregory Peterson, Joseph P. Petito, David Prinzivalli, Beth Rawson, Walter G. Ricciardi, Paul Allan Schott, Henry J. Schultzel, Kimberly H. Smith, Press C. Southworth, Richard M. Steinberg, Ann M. Thornburg, Carl O. Thorsen, Steven J. Toups, Jill R. Tregillis, Denise M. Tyson, Robert W. Uek, Lee Ann C. Underwood, Randall J. Vitray, Howard A. Weiser, Allen J. Weltmann, Sandra Ormsby Wheeler, Kenneth D. Williams, David W. Wilson, Raymond L. Wilson, Ray E. Winborne, Martha F. Zelsman, Donna M. Zianni.

We owe a special acknowledgment to Myra D. Cleary, who was the senior editor of the book and managed the administrative aspects of its creation. In that role, she endeavored, by editing and rewriting the manuscript, to shape it into a coherent work. To all those individuals, and any who were inadvertently omitted, go not only our thanks, but also the usual absolution from blame for errors and omissions.

Finally, we would like to dedicate this edition to Philip L. Defliese, past chairman of Coopers & Lybrand and co-author of the eighth, ninth, tenth, and eleventh editions of this book. He was a dedicated educator, standard setter, and leader of the profession. He will be missed.

V.M.O.
P.J.M.
B.N.W.
J.S.G.
H.R.J.

Contents

CHAPTER 3   AUDITING STANDARDS AND PROFESSIONAL CONDUCT   3·1

PART 2   THEORY AND CONCEPTS

CHAPTER 6   THE AUDIT PROCESS   6·1

CHAPTER 13   AUDITING THE REVENUE CYCLE   13·1

CHAPTER 14   AUDITING THE PURCHASING CYCLE   14·1

CHAPTER 15   SUBSTANTIVE TESTS   15·1

PART 3   AUDITING SPECIFIC ACCOUNTS

CHAPTER 17   AUDITING CASH AND CASH EQUIVALENTS   17·1

CHAPTER 18   AUDITING ACCOUNTS RECEIVABLE AND RELATED REVENUE CYCLE ACCOUNTS   18·1

CHAPTER 23 AUDITING ACCOUNTS PAYABLE AND RELATED PURCHASING CYCLE ACCOUNTS   23·1

CHAPTER 24   AUDITING INCOME TAXES   24·1

CHAPTER 25   AUDITING DEBT AND EQUITY   25·1

CHAPTER 26   AUDITING FINANCIAL STATEMENT DISCLOSURES   26·1

PART 4   COMPLETING THE WORK AND REPORTING THE RESULTS

CHAPTER 27   COMPLETING THE AUDIT   27·1

CHAPTER 28   REPORTING ON AUDITED FINANCIAL STATEMENTS   28·1

CHAPTER 29   OTHER REPORTING SITUATIONS RELATED TO AUDITS   29·1

CHAPTER 32   COMPLIANCE AUDITING   32·1

PART 5   AUDITING SPECIALIZED INDUSTRIES

CHAPTER 33   AUDITING BANKS AND SAVINGS
INSTITUTIONS   33·1

CHAPTER 38   AUDITING GOVERNMENTAL UNITS   38·1

CHAPTER 39   AUDITING HEALTH CARE ORGANIZATIONS   39·1

CHAPTER 42   AUDITING INVESTMENT COMPANIES   42·1

CHAPTER 49   AUDITING SECURITIES AND COMMODITIES BROKER-DEALERS   49·1

Abbreviations and References

Abbreviations

References in this book to names of organizations, committees, and publications often are abbreviated, as follows (abbreviations used in Part 5 of the book are excluded):

AAA	American Accounting Association
AcSEC	Accounting Standards Executive Committee
AAER	Accounting and Auditing Enforcement Release
AICPA	American Institute of Certified Public Accountants
ALI	American Law Institute
APB	Accounting Principles Board
ARB	Accounting Research Bulletin
ASB	Auditing Standards Board
ASR	Accounting Series Release
EITF	Emerging Issues Task Force
FASB	Financial Accounting Standards Board
FRR	Financial Reporting Release
GAO	General Accounting Office
GASB	Governmental Accounting Standards Board
IAPC	International Auditing Practices Committee
IFAC	International Federation of Accountants
IIA	Institute of Internal Auditors
IRS	Internal Revenue Service
SAB	Staff Accounting Bulletin
SAP	Statement on Auditing Procedure
SAS	Statement on Auditing Standards
SEC	Securities and Exchange Commission
SFAS	Statement of Financial Accounting Standards
SOP	Statement of Position
SQCS	Statement on Quality Control Standards
SSARS	Statement on Standards for Accounting and Review Services
SSAE	Statement on Standards for Attestation Engagements

References

References in this book to AICPA and FASB pronouncements are current as of September 30, 1997. In addition to citations to original AICPA or FASB pronouncements (or later codifications, where applicable), second references are provided wherever possible. For pronouncements contained in *AICPA Professional Standards*, second references are to the appropriate section in that publication. Second references for accounting pronouncements are to the *Current Text* of FASB Accounting Standards; however, all quotations from the accounting literature are taken from the original pronouncements.

PART 1

The Audit Environment

1

An Overview of Auditing

The principal subject of this book is auditing and the auditing profession—what auditors do when they perform an audit and the institutional framework within which the practice of auditing takes place. An understanding of what an audit is and how it is performed helps in understanding the social function of an audit and the professional responsibilities auditors assume when they fill that function. To understand the background and logic behind the methods and techniques auditors use and the care they exercise in conducting an audit, one also must understand the environment and institutions within which an audit occurs. Knowing what constitutes an audit performed with due professional care and why particular auditing procedures are followed enables the auditor to adapt to changing circumstances in order to meet social, legal, and professional responsibilities. An auditor who understands the theory and concepts of auditing is more effective and efficient than an auditor who does not have that understanding.

1.1   TYPES OF ASSURANCE SERVICES

Auditors examine representations of others (that is, information prepared by others) and provide assurance about the reliability of those representations to people who use them in making business decisions. Providing that assurance, even if it is after the information is first made available to users, adds to the usefulness of the information, and this is what makes the service valuable. Traditionally, the information that auditors have provided assurance about was in the form of historical financial statements. As the reputation and professionalism of certified public accountants (CPAs) grew, they increasingly were requested to provide assurance on representations other than historical financial statements. As a result, auditing has evolved into a broader profession that involves providing assurance on many kinds of information, not just historical financial statements. CPAs today provide assurance on such kinds of information as the effectiveness of an entity's internal control, reports on its operations and performance, descriptions of computer software, and assertions about compliance with statutory, regulatory, and contractual requirements. While this book is concerned primarily with audits of historical financial statements, it also covers many other assurance services provided by CPAs in public practice.

Assurance services have been defined broadly by the AICPA Special Committee on Assurance Services as "independent professional services that improve the quality of information, or its context, for decision makers." The assurance services that CPAs provide, which are discussed in greater detail in Chapter 2, fall into several categories:

- Audits, which include financial audits, compliance audits, and performance audits
- Reviews of financial information, which provide less assurance than audits
- Attestation engagements, in which the auditor expresses a written conclusion about the reliability of another party's written assertion
- Other assurance services that do not fall within the profession's strict definitions of audits, reviews, or attestation engagements, but that also provide assurance about the reliability of information

Another service performed by CPAs that is related to assurance services but does not result in the expression of assurance is a compilation. A compilation consists of presenting information in the form of financial statements without expressing any opinion on that information.

1.2   DEFINITION OF AUDITING

Different types of audits and the purposes of audits have evolved over many years, and this evolution is still taking place. Accordingly, auditing should be defined broadly enough to cover the various types and purposes of audits. The definition of auditing that appeared in *A Statement of Basic Auditing Concepts*, published in 1973 by the American Accounting Association (AAA) Committee on Basic Auditing Concepts, embraces both the process and purpose of auditing.

> Auditing is a systematic process of objectively obtaining and evaluating evidence regarding assertions about economic actions and events to ascertain the degree of correspondence between those assertions and established criteria and communicating the results to interested users. (p. 2)

The AAA Committee noted that its definition of auditing was intentionally quite broad to cover "the many different purposes for which an audit might be conducted and the variety of subject matter that might be focused on in a specific audit engagement" (p. 2). In fact, the definition is broad enough to encompass attestation services and possibly even other assurance services. The following discussion of each key phrase in the definition is couched primarily in the context of an audit of the financial statements of a business entity, usually referred to as a financial audit.

(a)   Assertions About Economic Actions and Events

The assertions of management that are embodied in a set of financial statements are the subject matter of an audit of those statements. For example, the item "inventories . . . $5,426,000" in a balance sheet of a manufacturing entity embodies the following assertions, among others: The inventories physically exist; they are held for sale or use in operations; they include all products and materials; $5,426,000 is the lower of their cost or market value (as both terms are defined under generally accepted accounting principles); they are properly classified on the balance sheet; and appropriate disclosures related to inventories have been made, such as their major categories and amounts pledged or assigned. Comparable assertions are embodied in all the other specific items and amounts in financial statements. Those assertions can be conveniently grouped into a few broad categories, which are discussed in Chapter 6. Chapters 17 through 25 explain how those assertions apply to specific accounts in financial statements.

The assertions are made by the preparer of the financial statements—management—and communicated to the readers of the statements; they are not assertions by the auditor. The auditor's responsibility is to express an opinion on management's assertions in the context of the financial statements taken as a whole, and to communicate that opinion to the readers in the form of the auditor's report. Similar assertions are also the subject matter of compliance and performance audits.

Since the subject matter of auditing usually is information about economic actions and events, assertions must be quantifiable to be auditable. Building costs are quantifiable, as is the number of stock options outstanding; the morale of employees is not. Information that is quantifiable is also generally verifiable; information that is not verifiable is by definition not auditable. Information is verifiable if it "provides results that would be substantially duplicated by independent measures using the same measurement methods" (Accounting Principles Board Statement No. 4, para. 90).

(b) Degree of Correspondence Between Assertions and Established Criteria

Everything that takes place during an audit has one primary objective: the formation of an opinion by the auditor on the assertions about economic actions and events that have been audited. The auditor's opinion will specify how well those assertions conform to established criteria or standards. In financial audits, generally accepted accounting principles (GAAP) are the established criteria against which the assertions are measured; GAAP require that inventories exist and be owned by the entity before they can be included among its assets. If the inventories exist and are owned by the reporting entity, and if the other assertions implicit in the item "inventories . . . $5,426,000" also conform to generally accepted accounting principles, the auditor will conclude that there is complete correspondence between those assertions and established criteria.

GAAP are, for the most part, explicit and precisely defined, as are the criteria for comprehensive bases of accounting other than GAAP. (See the discussions of the meaning of fair presentation in conformity with GAAP in Chapter 28 and of reporting on other bases of accounting in Chapter 29.) The same may be true in the case of many compliance audits. For example, the criteria against which assertions relating to adherence to the terms of a specific contract are measured are the provisions stated in that contract. In other instances, such as a performance audit of an entity's capital budgeting system, the criteria are far less precise and are generally ill defined. In those situations, the auditor and the client will have to agree on the criteria to be used, and those criteria should be explicitly stated in the auditor's report. (See the discussion of established and stated criteria in Chapter 31, "Attestation Engagements.")

(c) Objectively Obtaining and Evaluating Evidence

In essence, auditing consists of obtaining and evaluating evidence that will support the auditor's opinion that the assertions conform to established criteria. "The types of evidence obtained and the criteria employed to evaluate evidence may vary from audit to audit, but all audits center on the process of obtaining and evaluating evidence" (*A Statement of Basic Auditing Concepts*, p. 2). In a financial audit, for example, evidence about the degree of correspondence between assertions in the financial statements and generally accepted accounting principles consists of underlying accounting data (such as journals, ledgers, and files) and corroborating information (such as invoices, checks, and information obtained by inquiry, observation, physical inspection of assets, and correspondence with third parties). To continue with the inventory example, the auditor may examine purchase contracts or paid invoices to ascertain that the entity owns the inventory, observe an inventory count to determine that it exists, and retotal the perpetual inventory ledger to ascertain the mathematical accuracy of the dollar amount of inventory reported on the balance sheet.

The auditor also must interpret and evaluate the evidence obtained before reaching the conclusion that the assertions conform to objective criteria. The judgments required are often extremely difficult and call for significant analytical and interpretive skills. For example, judging whether inventories are properly valued at the lower of cost or market requires the auditor to understand and evaluate how the entity determined cost. This may be particularly difficult if sophisticated last-in, first-out costing methods are used or if a standard cost system is employed, to cite just two examples. That same inventory valuation assertion also requires the auditor to evaluate how management determined replacement cost, estimated selling price, and normal profit margins in the course of ascertaining market value. Finally, the auditor must evaluate whether provisions for losses on obsolete and slow-moving items are adequate. Conclusive evidence is rarely available to support these judgments, but they are crucial to an audit of financial statements. The different types of evidence used in a financial statement audit and criteria for evaluating the evidence are discussed in Chapter 6.

The definition of auditing specifies that the process of obtaining and evaluating evidence must be carried out objectively. Objectivity in the process of obtaining and evaluating evidence is not the same as objectivity of the evidence itself. Objectivity of evidence relates to how useful the evidence will be in achieving the auditor's purpose, a matter that is discussed in Chapter 6. Objectivity of the process refers to the auditor's ability to maintain an impartial attitude in selecting and evaluating evidence. That impartial attitude is part of the concept of auditor independence, which is discussed at length in Chapter 3.

(d) Systematic Process

The word "systematic" implies that planning the audit and formulating an audit strategy are important parts of the audit process. Moreover, evidence should be selected and evaluated in relation to specific audit objectives, many of which are interrelated. This requires the auditor to make many decisions in the course of planning and performing an audit.

A Statement of Basic Auditing Concepts notes that the phrase "systematic process" suggests that "auditing is based, in part at least, on the discipline and philosophy of scientific method" (p. 2). Most auditors, however, do not think of themselves as applying the scientific method, probably because the term implies a more highly structured method of inquiry than is possible or even desirable in most audits. Certainly, an audit should be founded on a carefully conceived audit strategy, but that strategy is subject to extensive modification during an audit as the auditor obtains and evaluates evidence relating to specific assertions about the various, often interrelated components of financial statements.

(e) Communicating the Results to Interested Users

The end and aim of all audits is a report that communicates to the reader the degree to which management's assertions meet the agreed-upon criteria. In an audit of financial statements, the communication, called an auditor's report, states the conclusions reached on whether or not the financial statements conform to generally accepted accounting principles in all material respects. (This kind of report is discussed at length in Chapter 28.) In other types of audits, the auditor similarly reports the findings to interested parties. Thus, the definition of auditing includes the reporting phase, when the auditor communicates an opinion or evaluation to interested parties, as well as the investigative phase, when the auditor obtains and evaluates evidence to form that opinion or evaluation.

(f) Relationship Between Accounting and Auditing

It should be clear from the definition of auditing and the references to various types of possible audits that there *need not* be any relationship between auditing and accounting. Virtually any information that is quantifiable and verifiable can be audited, as long as the auditor and the auditee agree on the criteria to be used as the basis for determining the degree of correspondence. For example, an auditor for the United States General Accounting Office may be requested to audit the effectiveness of a particular airplane. The criteria for measuring effectiveness, which will have to be agreed on before the audit takes place, will most likely be concerned with speed, acceleration, cruising altitude, number and type of armaments, and so on. None of these criteria involve accounting data.

The subject matter of most audits, however, and all financial audits, is usually accounting data that is contained in the books, records, and financial statements of the audited entity. The assertions about economic actions and events that the auditor is concerned with are often assertions about accounting transactions and the resulting account balances. The established criteria that accounting assertions ordinarily are measured by are generally accepted accounting principles. Thus, while an accountant need not be knowledgeable about auditing, an auditor must be knowledgeable about accounting. The accounting process creates financial statements and other useful information; auditing generally does not create accounting data or other information. Rather, auditing enhances the value of the information created by the accounting process by critically evaluating that information and communicating the resulting opinion to interested parties.

1.3   ORIGINS AND EARLY HISTORY OF AUDITING[1]

Historians believe that record keeping originated about 4000 B.C., when ancient civilizations in the Near East began to establish organized governments and businesses. From the beginning, governments were concerned with accounting for receipts and disbursements and collecting taxes. An integral part of this concern was establishing controls, including audits, to reduce errors and fraud on the part of incompetent or dishonest officials. Several "modern" forms of internal control are described in the Bible, which is generally viewed as covering the period between 1800 B.C. and A.D. 95, and the explanation of the logic behind instituting controls—that if employees have

---

[1] Much of the material in this section is based on Richard Brown, *A History of Accounting and Accountants* (Edinburgh: T. C. and E. C. Jack, 1905); and Michael Chatfield, *A History of Accounting Thought*, rev. ed. (Huntington, NY: Robert E. Kreiger Publishing Company, 1977).

an opportunity to steal they may take advantage of it—reflects the same professional skepticism expected of auditors today. Specifically, the Bible discusses dual custody of assets, the need for competent and honest employees, restricted access, and segregation of duties.

The government accounting system of the Zhao dynasty (1122–256 B.C.) in China included an elaborate budgetary process and audits of all government departments. In fifth-century B.C. Athens, the popular Assembly controlled the receipt and disbursement of public funds. The public finance system included government auditors who examined the records of all officeholders at the expiration of their terms. In the private sector, managers of estates conducted audits of the accounts. Public finance in the Roman Republic was under control of the Senate, and public accounts were examined by a staff of auditors supervised by the treasurer. The Romans maintained segregation of duties between the officials who authorized taxes and expenditures and those who handled receipts and payments, and, like the Greeks, devised an elaborate system of checks and counterchecks.

The oldest surviving accounting records and references to audits in English-speaking countries are those of the Exchequers of England and Scotland, which date back to 1130. There are references to auditors and auditing in the thirteenth century in both England and Italy, and a French work on estate management written in the same century recommends an annual audit of the accounts. The City of London was audited at least as early as the 1200s, and in the early fourteenth century auditors were among the elected officials. From that time on, there is extensive evidence that the value of audits was widely recognized and that the accounts of municipalities, private landholdings, and craft guilds were audited regularly.

The early audits in Great Britain were of two types. Audits of cities and towns were held publicly before the governing officials and citizens and consisted of the auditors' hearing the accounts[2] read by the treasurer. Similarly, audits of guilds were heard before the membership. By the middle of the sixteenth century, auditors of cities often annotated the accounts with phrases such as "heard by the auditors undersigned." Reporting by auditors can be traced to this preliminary form of "audit certificate." The second type of audit involved a detailed examination of the "charge and discharge" accounts maintained by the financial officers of large manors, followed by a "declaration of audit," that is, an oral report before the lord of the manor and the council. Typically, the auditor was a member of the manorial council, and thus was the precursor of the modern internal auditor.

Both types of audits performed in Great Britain before the seventeenth century were directed primarily at ensuring the accountability of funds entrusted to public or private officials. Those audits were not designed to test the quality of the accounts, except insofar as inaccuracies might point to the existence of fraud. The economic changes between 1600 and 1800—which saw the growth of towns in place of manors, and factories in place of guilds, and the beginning of widespread commerce—introduced new accounting concerns. These focused on the ownership of property and the calculation of profits and losses in a business sense. Auditing also began to evolve from a listening process to a close examination of written records and testing of supporting evidence. At the end of the seventeenth century, the first law was enacted (in Scot-

---

[2] The practice of "hearing the accounts," which originated in the days when few people could read, continued until the seventeenth century. The word "audit," in fact, derives from the Latin word for a hearing.

land) prohibiting certain officials from serving as auditors of a town, thus introducing the modern notion of auditor independence to the Western world.

Despite these advances in auditing practices, it was not until well into the nineteenth century—which brought the construction of railways and the growth of insurance companies, banks, and other joint-stock companies—that the professional auditor became an important part of the business scene. The railroad industry in the United States was among the first employers of internal auditors. By the latter part of the nineteenth century, so-called traveling auditors visited widely dispersed ticket agencies to evaluate management's accountability for assets and its reporting systems.

1.4   HISTORICAL DEVELOPMENT OF EXTERNAL AUDITING IN THE UNITED STATES[3]

The development of external auditing in this country owes much to the various Companies Acts enacted in Britain during the second half of the nineteenth century. Before 1850, audits were a minor part of an accountant's practice and were not performed routinely. When they were performed, they were viewed as a way to make managers and directors accountable to absentee stockholders for the stewardship of assets. The auditor's primary objective was the detection of fraud. Moreover, there were no standards governing what the examination should consist of or the qualifications of those performing it. The Companies Acts aimed to establish auditing and reporting standards, beginning with the 1845 Act, which required that one or more of a company's stockholders be appointed to audit the balance sheet but did not address the issues of qualifications or responsibilities. The Companies Acts of 1855–1856 removed the requirement that auditors had to be stockholders and thus gave companies the option of engaging an external auditor. In addition, a petition by 20 percent of the stockholders could compel a company to appoint an external auditor. This was the first step toward compulsory independent audits. The Act of 1862 included a detailed description of an audit examination, as well as the first standard form of the auditor's report. It took until 1900, however, for annual audits to become mandatory for all limited companies. Standards for qualification of auditors, however, along with accounting and disclosure requirements, were not incorporated into British regulations until the twentieth century. The first comprehensive text on auditing, *Auditing: A Practical Manual for Auditors,* by Lawrence R. Dicksee, was published in England in 1892.

Independent audits in the United States up to the turn of the twentieth century were modeled on British practices. The audit work consisted of detailed scrutinies of clerical data relating to the balance sheet. Robert H. Montgomery, in the first edition of this book, called the early American audits "bookkeeper audits," and he estimated that three quarters of the audit time was spent on footings and postings. Since there were no statutory requirements for audits in America, and since most audits were performed by auditors from Britain who were sent by British investors in U.S. companies, the profession grew slowly at first. Only a small amount of auditing literature was

[3] A more comprehensive history of American auditing appears in C. A. Moyer, "Early Developments in American Auditing," *The Accounting Review* (January 1951), pp. 3–8.

published in the United States prior to the 1900s. H. J. Mettenheim's 16-page work entitled *Auditor's Guide* (1869) contained suggestions for preventing fraud and instructions for auditing cash. *Science of Accounts* by G. P. Greer, published in 1882, described auditing procedures for various accounts; significantly, those procedures included gathering evidence from outside the books. In 1905 and again in 1909, Montgomery published American editions of *Dicksee's Auditing*, and in 1912, recognizing the departures of U.S. practice from the British, he wrote the first American auditing book, *Auditing: Theory and Practice*, subsequently to be retitled *Montgomery's Auditing*.

Gradually, American audits evolved into "test audits" as procedures were adapted to rapidly expanding American business, which considered British-style detailed checking of footings and postings too time-consuming and expensive. In addition to increased use of testing methods, auditors began to obtain evidence from outside entities' records as a means of examining transactions. Because of investors' concerns, they began to pay closer attention to the valuations of assets and liabilities. These developments reflected a broadening of audit objectives beyond checking clerical accuracy and detecting fraud. Independent auditing in the modern sense was emerging in the United States, motivated largely by the demands of creditors, especially banks, for reliable financial information on which to base credit decisions.

Financial statement users in the early years of the twentieth century continued to focus on the balance sheet as the primary indicator of an entity's health, and, for the most part, auditors emphasized the balance sheet in their work. The first U.S. authoritative auditing pronouncement, prepared by the American Institute of Accountants [now the American Institute of Certified Public Accountants (AICPA)] at the request of the Federal Trade Commission, was published in 1917 and referred to "balance-sheet audits." A revised pamphlet was published in 1929, under the title "Verification of Financial Statements." Although the pamphlet still emphasized the balance sheet audit, it discussed income statement accounts in detail, thus reflecting the growing interest in results of operations. The 1929 pamphlet also covered reporting practices and stressed reliance on internal control.

The 1936 edition of the pamphlet was entitled "Examination of Financial Statements by Independent Public Accountants." The use of the word "examination" rather than "verification" indicated the fundamental changes in auditing theory and practice that had occurred by that time. In 1936 it generally was acknowledged that the independent auditor's function was more accurately described as an examination (i.e., auditing by testing selected items) than a verification, which implies a detailed audit of all data. In addition, the 1936 revision reflects an early use of the term "*independent* public accountants" in the professional auditing literature. This revision was influenced by a number of significant events of the previous few years, most notably the AICPA's collaboration with the New York Stock Exchange in an effort to improve reporting standards and the enactment of the Securities Act of 1933 and the Securities Exchange Act of 1934, which required listed companies to file audited financial statements.

The modern era of audit standard-setting began in 1939, when the AICPA created the Committee on Auditing Procedure and that committee issued the first Statement on Auditing Procedure (SAP). Fifty-four SAPs were issued through 1972, at which time the name of the committee was changed to the Auditing Standards Executive Committee (later renamed the Auditing Standards Board), which codified all the SAPs in Statement on Auditing Standards (SAS) No. 1; that series of statements continues to the present.

Beginning in the 1970s, the responsibilities and performance of auditors became the subject of increased public interest. The 1970s and 1980s were marked by a succession of alleged audit failures, followed by congressional hearings, the creation of special commissions to determine the role and responsibilities of auditors, the conclusion that a gap (referred to as the "expectation gap" and discussed in more detail in Section 1.6, Continuing Efforts to Meet Users' Needs) existed between the public's perception of what an audit was supposed to do and the limitations of the actual audit process, and heightened activity by the Auditing Standards Board (ASB) to help close, or at least narrow, the expectation gap. Professional studies of auditor responsibilities and the promulgation of new auditing standards have continued in the 1990s in an ongoing effort to reconcile users' expectations and auditors' professional responsibilities, as discussed later in the chapter.

The nature of auditing has evolved in response to business, professional, regulatory, and other events, as well as to changes in the public's perceptions and expectations. Auditing is clearly an evolutionary process, which will continue in response to further changes in the social, legal, and business environment, and in users' expectations, which are similarly dynamic and change over time. Certain key events in the evolution of auditing are highlighted in Figure 1.1.

Figure 1.1   Historical Perspective of Auditing—Key Events

Date	Event
c. 4000 B.C.	First audits of tax collections in Babylonia
1800 B.C.–A.D. 95	Biblical references to internal controls and surprise audits
c. 1130	Audits of revenue and expenditures by Exchequers of England and Scotland
c. 1200	City of London audited
1500s	Manorial accounts audited by member of council—precursor of internal auditor
Mid-1500s	City accounts annotated by auditors—preliminary form of "audit certificate"
Late 1600s	Earliest law prohibiting town officials from serving as auditors—first notion of auditor independence
1845–1900	First auditing and reporting standards established by British Companies Acts
1854	First professional charter to Scottish Institute—creation of the "Chartered Accountant" (CA) designation
Late 1800s	Internal auditors employed by U.S. railroad companies
1887	American Institute of Accountants (now American Institute of Certified Public Accountants) established

Figure 1.1   *(Continued)*

Date	Event
1892	Publication of *Dicksee's Auditing: A Practical Manual for Auditors*
1896	First CPA law (in New York State)—creation of the CPA designation
1899	First woman CPA (Christine Ross)
1900	Annual audits made compulsory for limited companies in Britain
1905–1912	Publication of Montgomery's editions of *Dicksee's Auditing*, and of the first edition of *Montgomery's Auditing*
Early 1900s	Evolution of U.S. audits from "detailed" audits to "test" audits
1917	First U.S. authoritative auditing pronouncement published by American Institute of Accountants
1921	General Accounting Office (GAO) created by the Budget and Accounting Act
1933 and 1934	Passage of the federal securities acts
1936	Revised auditing pronouncement entitled "Examination of Financial Statements by Independent Public Accountants"
1939	First Statement on Auditing Procedure issued
1941	Institute of Internal Auditors (IIA) founded
1948	Ten "generally accepted auditing standards" adopted by AICPA membership
1961	Publication of *The Philosophy of Auditing* by Mautz and Sharaf
1972	First Statement on Auditing Standards, *Codification of Auditing Standards and Procedures*, issued
Mid-1970s	Congressional hearings on the accounting profession
1977	Division for CPA Firms created by AICPA; member firms required to undergo peer review
1978	*Report, Conclusions, and Recommendations* of the Commission on Auditors' Responsibilities (Cohen Commission)
Mid-1980s	Congressional hearings on the accounting profession
1986	First Statement on Standards for Attestation Engagements issued
1987	Report of the National Commission on Fraudulent Financial Reporting (Treadway Commission)
1988	Nine "expectation gap" Statements on Auditing Standards issued by Auditing Standards Board
1992	*Internal Control—Integrated Framework* by the Committee of Sponsoring Organizations of the Treadway Commission (COSO)
1993	Report of the Public Oversight Board, *In the Public Interest*
1994	Report of the Advisory Panel on Auditor Independence, *Strengthening the Professionalism of the Independent Auditor*
1996	Report of the General Accounting Office, *The Accounting Profession, Major Issues: Progress and Concerns*
1997	Creation of the Independence Standards Board

1.5   ROLE OF INDEPENDENT AUDITS

The social purpose that independent audits serve today has been concisely stated by the Financial Accounting Standards Board in Statement of Financial Accounting Concepts No. 1, *Objectives of Financial Reporting by Business Enterprises*, as follows:

> The effectiveness of individuals, enterprises, markets, and government in allocating scarce resources among competing uses is enhanced if those who make economic decisions have information that reflects the relative standing and performance of business enterprises to assist them in evaluating alternative courses of action and the expected returns, costs, and risks of each. . . . Independent auditors commonly examine or review financial statements and perhaps other information, and both those who provide and those who use that information often view an independent auditor's opinion as enhancing the reliability or credibility of the information. (para. 16)

By providing an independent, external perspective, an audit enhances the credibility of financial information, and thus reduces the information risk to financial statement users. "Information risk" is the risk that information, in this case information contained in financial reports, is incorrect. Information risk is distinguishable from business risk, which is the risk that, even with correct information, the return on an investment will be less than expected because of some unforeseen circumstance or event. Investors and creditors demand, and the market pays, a return for assuming risk. Reducing the information risk in financial information reduces the risk premium that must be paid by an entity. This lowers the audited entity's cost of capital, thereby promoting the efficient allocation of scarce economic resources among competing uses. Of course, audits are not the only way to reduce information risk. Accounting standard-setting bodies in both the public sector (the Securities and Exchange Commission) and the private sector (the Financial Accounting Standards Board and the Governmental Accounting Standards Board) promote uniformity of accounting measurement principles and full disclosure of relevant financial information.

There has been considerable research over the years on the value of annual financial statements to investment and credit decision makers. That research, with its focus on the "efficient market hypothesis," seems to suggest that annual financial statements have little effect on security prices. Information is available to investors in the financial press and from investment analysts and is acted on before the annual financial statements are published. There is widespread agreement, however, that *audited* financial statements do have "information content," that is, they contain *new* information merely by virtue of their having been audited. The Commission on Auditors' Responsibilities, also known as the Cohen Commission, after its chairman, Manuel C. Cohen, concluded that "audited financial statements provide a means of confirming or correcting the information received earlier by the market. In effect, the audited statements help to assure the efficiency of the market by limiting the life of inaccurate information or by deterring its dissemination."[4]

In addition to the credibility dimension, the AAA Committee on Basic Auditing Concepts considered the control dimension as another aspect of the value an audit adds to financial information.

[4] *Report, Conclusions, and Recommendations*, 1978, p. 6.

The addition of the audit function serves as a *control* over the quality of information because:

1. It provides an independent check on the accounting information against established criteria presumably reflecting the user's needs and desires.

2. It motivates the preparer of the information to carry out the accounting process under his control in a way that conforms to the user's criteria since he (the preparer) knows his efforts will be subjected to independent, expert review.[5]

The motivational aspect of an audit has long been recognized: Knowing that an audit will be performed is a strong deterrent to disseminating erroneous information.

(a) Demand for Audits of Financial Statements

Several groups or organizations have the power or authority to require that specific entities be audited. (The authors are not suggesting that without those specific requirements audits would not occur. As just noted, a market demand for audits also arises out of a desire to reap the benefits of reduced information risk.) The demand for audits comes from creditors and potential creditors, the SEC and the various stock exchanges acting on behalf of actual and potential investors, and government agencies that require nonbusiness entities to file audited financial statements.

Lending institutions, such as banks and insurance companies, frequently want audited financial statements of borrowers and prospective borrowers. Other creditors, such as vendors, may request audited financial statements to help them make credit and lending decisions. All of those organizations may want audited financial statements throughout the life of the credit or loan agreement. To a great extent, audits are performed because lenders and creditors demand them. In addition, the Securities Act of 1933 and the Securities Exchange Act of 1934 require that companies (with several exceptions) that issue securities to the public or seek to have their securities publicly traded on the various securities exchanges and in the securities market must file audited financial statements with the SEC. Since 1933, the New York Stock Exchange has required independently audited financial statements to be filed with listing applications and to be published annually after a security has been listed for trading on the exchange.

An additional benefit from financial statement audits is that the entity's board of directors and management often are provided with information about the entity's internal control. Auditors are required to inform the audit committee (or its equivalent) about significant deficiencies in the design or operation of internal control that come to their attention in the course of an audit. In practice, auditors often extend that communication to include less significant deficiencies as well, along with suggestions for improving internal control. The latter communication is ordinarily in writing, although it is customary to review its contents with management before the document, known as either a "management letter" or an "internal control letter," is finalized. The management letter is provided as a service and is an important by-product of an audit.

---

[5] *A Statement of Basic Auditing Concepts*, 1973, p. 13.

Performing an audit also gives the auditor substantial knowledge of the entity's business and financial operations. That knowledge often enables the auditor to provide other, nonaudit services, such as advice about tax planning and employee benefits.

(b) Expectations of Users of Financial Information

The National Commission on Fraudulent Financial Reporting, also known as the Treadway Commission, after its chairman, James C. Treadway, Jr., stated that:

> The financial statements are first and foremost the responsibility of the management of the reporting entity. But the independent public accountant plays a crucial role in the financial reporting process.

> Users of financial statements expect auditors to bring to the reporting process technical competence, integrity, independence, and objectivity. Users also expect auditors to search for and detect material misstatements, whether intentional or unintentional, and to prevent the issuance of misleading financial statements.[6]

Survey research reported in Canada by the Macdonald Commission indicated, however, that:

> The public at large and even some quite sophisticated members of the financial community have only a vague understanding of the responsibilities undertaken and work done by the auditor. To the public it is the end result, the financial disclosure, that is important. The auditor is quite likely to be the first to be blamed for errors or inadequacies in financial disclosure almost without regard to his or her audit responsibility.[7]

The Canadian survey results parallel those of earlier surveys taken in the United States and other countries, and are confirmed by views expressed in Congress, in the media, and in the report of the Treadway Commission.

Inaccurate or misleading financial reporting happens in one of two ways. First, financial statements or other financial information may be misstated unintentionally because of errors in processing or recording transactions (such as failure to record an authorized sale that actually took place) or because of incorrect judgments in interpreting facts or presenting them in conformity with GAAP. For example, management may truly believe a particular lease is an operating lease when, in fact, under GAAP it should be classified as a capital lease.

Second, the financial reporting may be deficient because of deliberate financial statement misrepresentations by management or because assets have been stolen or otherwise misappropriated and the loss not properly shown in the financial statements. Examples of these types of fraud are, respectively, the deliberate recording of sales that never occurred, and the undiscovered theft of customers' remittances.

The public's concern about being misinformed by financial statements stems from an awareness of the inherent potential conflict of interest between preparers and

---

[6] *Report of the National Commission on Fraudulent Financial Reporting* (Treadway Commission), 1987, p. 49.

[7] *Report of the Commission to Study the Public's Expectations of Audits* (Macdonald Commission) (Toronto: Canadian Institute of Chartered Accountants, 1988), p. 11.

users of financial statements. This is not to say that there is or must be a conflict of interest; nor does it suggest that managements are dishonest. It merely suggests that preparers may have certain biases in preparing financial information, as do those who use the information. Audits have a restraining influence in that auditors serve as independent third-party intermediaries between preparers and users of financial information.

(c) Addressing User Expectations

In performing audits aimed at meeting financial statement users' expectations, independent auditors perform two functions. One of them is serving as an expert gatherer and evaluator of evidence to corroborate the completeness, genuineness, and arithmetical accuracy of the information presented in the financial statements. For example, the item "accounts receivable—trade" shown in a balance sheet implies that the accounts receivable exist, that the entity owns them, and that all existing and owned trade accounts receivable are included in the total. It also implies that the computations behind the amount shown are mechanically accurate—that is, the arithmetic involved in preparing customer invoices, posting the invoice amounts to individual customer accounts, and summarizing the individual accounts was done correctly—and that the effects of transactions with nontrade debtors (e.g., entity officers and other related parties) have not been included. An auditor will obtain and evaluate evidence to corroborate those assertions.

The auditor's other function involves management's assertions concerning financial statement disclosures and valuations in conformity with generally accepted accounting principles. To make the financial statements useful or, at a minimum, ensure that they are not misleading, certain disclosures about the accounts receivable may be necessary. Also, generally accepted accounting principles require that accounts receivable be valued net of appropriate allowances, such as for uncollectible accounts and returns. Deciding what to disclose and estimating the necessary allowances require the financial statement preparer to exercise considerable judgment. An integral part of the auditor's function is to interpret the facts supporting the preparer's judgments and evaluate the judgments made. To do this, the auditor must have a thorough understanding of the entity's business as well as of generally accepted accounting principles.

Over the years, the evidence-gathering function has become less important and the interpreting/evaluating function more so. This is not to suggest that the former is unimportant or that it is not time-consuming, but merely that the more judgmental aspect of the audit has taken on greater significance. In part, this has resulted from management's increasing success, given advances in technology, in developing controls that ensure mechanically correct accounting information. Auditors often find it more efficient to test the entity's internal control to obtain evidence that it is designed and operating effectively than to test the output of the accounting system. Another reason for this change in audit emphasis is the proliferation of complex and innovative transactions and the need to evaluate how management has chosen to account for them. Still another reason is the increase in both the number and level of specificity of accounting standards, especially disclosure requirements. These all demand increased time and effort from the auditor to obtain the facts defining the underlying substance—rather than merely the legal form—of the transactions and evaluate the judgments management made in accounting for them.

(d)   Limitations of Auditing

No audit provides complete assurance that the financial statements are free from material misstatement. Misstatements can exist in audited financial statements even though the audit was performed according to generally accepted auditing standards, principally because of the limitations of both the accounting and auditing processes.

For example, financial statements reflect numerous accounting estimates whose measurement is inherently uncertain and dependent on the outcome of future events. To the extent that the accuracy of accounting information is dependent on an unpredictable future event, the information may be inaccurate. An audit of that information cannot make it more accurate, for an auditor cannot add certainty that does not exist.

Moreover, accounting measurement principles frequently provide more than one way to account for a given transaction or event. For example, there are several acceptable ways of accounting for the flow of inventory costs through an entity and for the depreciation of tangible assets. Neither the authoritative accounting literature nor logic supports one alternative over another. This flexibility of generally accepted accounting principles allows entities to influence the financial information they present. Also, reasonable financial statement preparers and auditors can disagree about the interpretation and application of accounting principles.

In addition to limitations imposed by the existing accounting framework, there are limitations imposed by management's decisions about the accounting procedures and controls to use in processing transactions. Management makes decisions, based largely on weighing costs and benefits, about the design of controls. No cost-effective internal control can provide absolute assurance that management's financial reporting objectives will be met with 100 percent accuracy.

Similarly, the audit process itself and auditing technology limit the assurance that can be attained from an audit. Ideally, an auditor would like to have sufficient first-hand evidence to provide absolute assurance about every assertion implicit in a set of financial statements, but that is usually impracticable if not impossible. For one thing, even if that goal could be achieved, it probably would not be worth the cost, to either the entity or the financial statement user. Accordingly, in corroborating an assertion about an account balance or a class of transactions, the auditor often will examine less than 100 percent of the items involved. Moreover, the auditor cannot audit the results of events and transactions that were never recorded. If controls to ensure the completeness of processing and recording data are nonexistent or ineffective, it may be impossible to audit some aspects of the financial statements or even the statements as a whole. In addition, the need for judgment and the fact that much of the evidence available to the auditor is persuasive, rather than conclusive, preclude the auditor from attaining absolute assurance. Lastly, the characteristics of fraud—for example, concealment and falsified documents—also may lead to a material misstatement going undetected.

Generally accepted auditing standards recognize these limitations by requiring only that the auditor obtain sufficient evidence to provide a reasonable basis for forming an opinion on the financial statements. The auditor's standard report acknowl-edges this by stating that auditing standards "require that we plan and perform the audit to obtain reasonable assurance about whether the financial statements are free of material misstatement."

1.6 CONTINUING EFFORTS TO MEET USERS' NEEDS

The limitations of auditing are generally well known to auditors, but not to most users of audited financial information. In addition, because of the mistaken assumption by some that fraudulent financial reporting (and, by implication, an audit failure) is in-volved whenever there is a business failure, the public may perceive the quality of au-ditor performance as lower than it actually is. As a result, the public's expectations for audits exceed its perception of auditors' performance.

The Macdonald Commission, in its report cited earlier, described the expectation gap between the public's expectations from audits and the public's perception of what audits actually provide as consisting of a standards gap and a performance gap. As shown in Fig-ure 1.2, the standards gap represents public expectations that go beyond existing audit-ing and accounting standards. The performance gap represents public perceptions that auditor performance falls short of what is required by existing standards.

The Macdonald Commission Report notes that

The emphasis in this diagram [Figure 1.2] is on public expectations and public percep-tions. Those expectations may or may not be reasonable, and those perceptions may or may not be realistic. . . . If the public has reasonable expectations not met by existing pro-fessional standards (line segment B to C) or the profession's performance falls short of its standards (line segment C to D), then it can and should act to improve standards or improve performance. On the other hand, if the problem is that the public's expectations are unreasonable (line segment A to B) or its perceptions of performance are mistaken

Figure 1.2 Components of the Expectation Gap

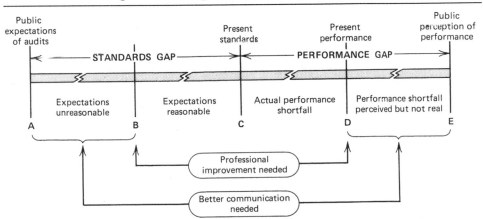

Source: Reprinted, with permission, from *Report of the Commission to Study the Public's Expectations of Audits,* 1988, The Canadian Institute of Chartered Accountants, Toronto, Canada, p. 6. Any changes to the origi-nal material are the sole responsibility of the authors and/or John Wiley & Sons, Inc., and have not been re-viewed by or endorsed by the CICA.

(line segment D to E), then the logical course is to attempt to improve public under-standing. Should that not be feasible, the profession must be prepared to cope with the consequences.[8]

Over the past two decades, numerous efforts have been made to reduce the actual performance shortfall. These efforts have come from several directions. This book de-tails, particularly in Chapters 3 and 4, steps taken to maintain the level of audit qual-ity, and sanctions imposed when audit failures do occur. As noted below, in 1988, the ASB issued nine authoritative auditing pronouncements designed to narrow the ex-pectation gap by raising performance and reporting standards. Since then, additional pronouncements have been issued to address, among other things, auditors' respon-sibilities with respect to internal control and fraud. Those standards, as well as oth-ers, are discussed throughout the book, starting in Chapter 4.

(a)   Studies, Proposals, and Recommendations

In 1977, the House Subcommittee on Oversight and Investigations of the Committee on Interstate and Foreign Commerce (Moss Subcommittee) issued a report on its study of federal regulatory agencies under its jurisdiction. Most of the Moss Subcom-mittee's recommendations were for actions to be taken by the SEC, but one related to communicating to shareholders and the public more detailed disclosure of illegal and questionable activities by corporations. The following year, the Senate Subcommittee on Reports, Accounting, and Management of the Committee on Government Opera-tions (Metcalf Subcommittee) issued its report, which contained a number of recom-mendations directed to the accounting profession. Among them were recommenda-tions relating to the organization of accounting firms and quality reviews of their practice, the reporting of illegal or questionable activities, the detection of manage-ment fraud, and expansion of the description of the audit process in the auditor's re-port.

The Cohen Commission, cited earlier, published a number of recommendations for reducing the gap it identified between the performance of auditors and the ex-pectations of financial statement users. Those recommendations included clarifying the auditor's responsibility for detecting fraud, extending responsibilities relating to the detection and disclosure of illegal acts beyond the requirements of the then re-cently issued SAS No. 17, expanding the consideration of internal control as part of a financial statement audit, and improving the auditor's communication with users by revising reporting requirements, including reporting on uncertainties. Other recom-mendations related to auditor independence, education and professional develop-ment, the process of establishing auditing standards, and ways to enhance regulation of the profession so as to maintain the quality of audit practice. Many, though not all, of the Cohen Commission's recommendations have been acted on by the profession in the years since its report was issued.

The Treadway Commission report was discussed earlier in this chapter. It set forth a number of recommendations directed at different groups, including public accoun-tants, for deterring fraudulent financial reporting. Among the recommendations for public accountants were increasing the auditor's responsibilities to assess the poten-

---

[8] *Report of the Commission to Study the Public's Expectations of Audits*, op. cit., pp. 6–7.

tial for fraudulent financial reporting and to design tests to detect it, improving quality assurance programs, and changing the wording of the standard auditor's report to clarify the auditor's responsibilities.

In 1993, the Public Oversight Board (POB) of the AICPA's SEC Practice Section (SECPS) issued its Special Report, *In the Public Interest: Issues Confronting the Accounting Profession*, which contained recommendations directed to a number of parties, including accounting firms. The POB's recommendations for accounting firms focused on the importance of exercising professional skepticism, the need for additional guidance on assessing the likelihood of management fraud, and the reporting of suspected illegal acts by management. The POB also recommended expanding the responsibilities of firms, the peer review process, and the SECPS Quality Control Inquiry Committee with respect to investigating and learning from alleged audit failures. In 1994, the Advisory Panel on Auditor Independence issued its Report to the POB entitled *Strengthening the Professionalism of the Independent Auditor*, which offered suggestions for enhancing auditors' independence and professionalism.

The report of the AICPA Special Committee on Financial Reporting, *Improving Business Reporting—A Customer Focus: Meeting the Information Needs of Investors and Creditors*, recommended in 1994 that a comprehensive model of business reporting be developed that would be responsive to users' needs for information, and that auditors be willing to provide assurance on any information encompassed by the new model. These recommendations highlighted users' needs for auditor involvement in a wide range of financial information.

(b) Profession's Responses to Recommendations

Many of the recommendations noted above are repeated in the reports of one study after another, lending increased credibility to them. A large number of them have been acted on by the profession, some in more than one way and by more than one party, and the debate over others continues.

(i) Auditing Standards.   In 1977, the ASB issued SAS No. 16 and No. 17 to provide guidance on the auditor's responsibilities for detecting and reporting errors and irregularities, and illegal acts by clients. Those statements were superseded in 1988 by SAS No. 53 and No. 54, respectively. As discussed in detail in Chapter 4, in 1997, SAS No. 82, *Consideration of Fraud in a Financial Statement Audit* (AU Section 316), superseded SAS No. 53. SAS No. 82 contains detailed guidance on risk factors that auditors should consider in assessing whether financial statements may be materially misstated because of fraudulent acts. As noted above, the need for improved guidance on auditors' responsibilities in the areas of detecting and reporting fraud and illegal acts by clients was a recurrent theme in the studies described.

The nine so-called expectation gap standards were issued in 1988. In addition to SAS Nos. 53 and 54, they included SAS No. 55 on internal control, SAS No. 58 on reporting on audited financial statements, and standards on analytical procedures, auditing accounting estimates, going concern considerations, communication of internal control related matters, and communicating with audit committees. In 1995, SAS No. 55 was superseded by SAS No. 78, reflecting changes in thinking about what auditors' responsibility for internal control should be as part of a financial statement audit and how that responsibility can best be met. Also in 1995, SAS No. 58 was amended by SAS No. 79, which changed the way the presence of uncertainties is communicated to financial statement users. Both of those topics were included in the Cohen Commission's conclusions about areas where changes in auditing standards were needed. The ASB's continual efforts to revise and refine its standards points to the dynamic nature of auditing and of the standards that govern the conduct of audits.

(ii) Reporting on Internal Control.   Another area where some commentators believe an expectation gap continues to exist involves public reporting on an entity's internal control. Several study groups and professional organizations have recommended that entity management issue a report to shareholders that includes an assessment of the entity's internal control. In 1988, the SEC issued proposed rules that would have required registrants to include a report of management's responsibilities for internal control in annual reports to shareholders and annual filings with the SEC, but would not have required explicit auditor reporting on internal control or on management's report thereon. Many reservations were expressed about the proposed rules, however, and the SEC withdrew them in 1992. Beginning in 1993, managements of insured depository institutions with $500 million or more in total assets were required by the Federal Deposit Insurance Corporation Improvement Act of 1991 (FDICIA) to report on internal control over financial reporting and to obtain auditor attestations to those reports.

In 1992, the Committee of Sponsoring Organizations of the Treadway Commission (COSO) issued a report entitled *Internal Control—Integrated Framework*, authored by Coopers & Lybrand L.L.P., which set forth a definition of, criteria for evaluating, and guidelines for management reporting on internal control. In 1993, the ASB issued Statement on Standards for Attestation Engagements (SSAE) No. 2, *Reporting on an Entity's Internal Control Over Financial Reporting*, providing guidance for performing and reporting on engagements to attest to management's report on internal control; that standard was amended in 1995 by SSAE No. 6. The development of standards covering attest services relating to internal control was responsive to the recommendation—made by the Cohen Commission, Treadway Commission, POB, and AICPA Board of Directors—calling for auditor association with management's report. A common thread woven through the profession's position on reporting on internal control is that the responsibilities of the CPA and of entity management should be clearly delineated: Management is the asserter; the CPA reports on management's assertions.

In contrast to those who advocate *required* reporting on internal control by management and the auditor, there are some who contend that existing laws such as the Foreign Corrupt Practices Act (see Chapter 9) and the 1933 and 1934 Securities Acts provide for adequate sanctions and accountability for internal control and financial reporting for all SEC registrants. Additionally, they point to the COSO report as a private-sector initiative that can be expected to bring about improvement in the internal control area and further encourage *voluntary* reporting. They note that there may be significant costs, particularly to smaller entities, of engaging auditors to attest to management reports on internal control, and question whether the benefits to users outweigh those costs. Accordingly, they oppose any legislative or regulatory attempts to mandate management reporting on internal control and accompanying auditor attestation.

(iii) Strengthening the Self-Regulatory System.   In 1977, the AICPA established the Division for CPA Firms, consisting of the SEC Practice Section (SECPS) and the Private Companies Practice Section (PCPS), and instituted a peer review program for member firms. At the same time, the Institute also created the Public Oversight Board to oversee the activities of the SECPS. Membership in SECPS is now required for firms that audit public companies; other firms are required to participate in an alternative AICPA peer review program. The AICPA has quality control standards that govern a firm's audit practice and a disciplinary system for both individual members and member firms.

(c)   Issues Awaiting Resolution

In 1996, the General Accounting Office (GAO) issued a report, *The Accounting Profession, Major Issues: Progress and Concerns*, which resulted from its review of recommendations made and actions taken between 1972 and 1995 to improve accounting and auditing standards and the performance of independent audits of public companies. While acknowledging that the profession had been responsive to recommendations for changes, the GAO concluded that several issues remained to be addressed, among them the continued existence of an expectation gap in the areas of responsibility for the detection of fraud and for reporting on the effectiveness of internal control. As noted earlier and discussed at length in Chapter 4, in 1997 the ASB issued SAS No. 82, *Consideration of Fraud in a Financial Statement Audit* (AU Section 316), which contains detailed guidance on factors that auditors should consider in assessing the risk that financial statements may be materially misstated because of fraud.

Although SAS No. 82 includes risk factors relating to the absence of controls, and states that the auditor should consider those factors in assessing the risk that assets may have been misappropriated, at the time of this writing auditors are not required to assess internal control specifically to form an opinion on its effectiveness in preventing or detecting fraud. Noting that effective internal control is a main line of defense in preventing or detecting fraud, the GAO recommended that auditors' responsibilities for assessing internal control should be expanded. The report states, "Performing a full evaluation of internal controls would provide greater assurance of detecting and preventing significant fraud and thereby more effectively address the expectation gap."[9]

The GAO also cited ongoing concerns about auditor independence, although it acknowledged the steps that have been taken by both the profession and regulators and legislators to strengthen auditor independence. Among steps taken by the profession, the report cites the Rules on independence and conflicts of interest in the Code of Professional Conduct, the SECPS prohibition against performing certain management advisory services for audit clients and the requirement to report to the audit committee fees received for management advisory services performed, and the requirements of SAS Nos. 60 and 61 to communicate to the audit committee internal control deficiencies and matters such as disagreements with management, consultations with other accountants, and difficulties in dealing with management in connection with an

---

[9] *The Accounting Profession, Major Issues: Progress and Concerns* (Washington, DC: United States General Accounting Office, 1996), p. 11.

audit. In 1997, the Independence Standards Board (ISB) was created as a separate body to establish independence standards for audits of public entities.

The GAO report also noted regulatory and legislative efforts to enhance auditor independence: the SEC's requirement that disagreements between the auditor and management of public companies be disclosed upon the resignation or dismissal of the auditor, the FDICIA requirements relating to the formation and activities of audit committees of banks regulated under the Federal Deposit Insurance Act, and the Private Securities Litigation Reform Act of 1995, which requires auditors of public companies to notify the SEC of material illegal acts that are not reported by the companies.

Regarding the possible effect on independence of performing consulting services, an issue that has been studied and debated by many groups, the GAO expressed agreement with the conclusions of the Cohen Commission, Treadway Commission, and Advisory Panel on Auditor Independence, all of which failed to find evidence that providing consulting services impairs auditor independence. The GAO noted, however, that concerns about auditor independence may escalate as accounting firms continue to expand their services beyond traditional audit services. The GAO endorsed the proposals of the Advisory Panel that auditors view the entity's board of directors, not management, as the client and that auditors communicate directly with the board and its audit committee concerning the selection of accounting principles and the financial reporting process. In the GAO's view, these measures would enhance auditor independence and also, if as a result the board assumed greater responsibility for overseeing the effectiveness of internal control, might lead to an increase in reporting on internal control.

Clearer definitions of the roles and responsibilities of an entity's management, board of directors, and audit committee in the financial reporting process and of the auditor's relationship with each of those groups would benefit both auditors and users of financial information and would help narrow the expectation gap. Generally at present, management selects the auditors, and many auditors consider management to be the client. The Advisory Panel on Auditor Independence pointed out that this relationship can constrain the auditor's open communication with the board and audit committee and that this situation is detrimental to the audit process. As noted above, the Advisory Panel recommended that the board, as the shareholders' representative, should be considered the client. The Advisory Panel stated that "assisting the board in its fiduciary mission is the essence of the auditor's own obligation to the public— and the hallmark of the auditor's professionalism."[10] Any measure that enhances the auditor's professionalism cannot help but narrow the expectation gap.

---

[10] *Strengthening the Professionalism of the Independent Auditor* (New York: Public Oversight Board, 1994), p. 20.

2

Organization and Structure of the Auditing Profession

2.1 TYPES OF ASSURANCE SERVICES

Although the focus of this book is on audits of historical financial statements, the auditing profession provides other types of assurance services, some of which are described in this section. Some of these services continue to be referred to as "audits," while others—particularly some of the newer ones—are called "attest engagements." Still other services in which CPAs provide assurance to their clients and others are referred to in this book as "other assurance services."

(a) Financial Audits

In a financial audit, an auditor seeks evidence about assertions related mainly to financial information, usually contained in a set of financial statements or some component thereof. The established criteria against which that financial information is measured are generally accepted accounting principles or some other specified basis of accounting (such as might be stipulated in a rental agreement). Generally, the information will be used by parties other than the management of the entity that prepared it. Sometimes, however, the information is intended to be used primarily by management for internal decision-making purposes. In that event, it may include nonfinancial as well as financial data. While most often financial audits are associated with independent auditors whose work results in an opinion on financial statements, both internal auditors and government auditors also perform financial audits, often in conjunction with compliance or performance audits.

(b) Compliance Audits

Compliance audits are intended to determine whether an entity has complied with specified policies, procedures, laws, regulations, or contracts that affect operations or reports. Examples of compliance audits include auditing a tax return by an Internal Revenue Service agent, auditing components of financial statements to determine compliance with a bond indenture, auditing a researcher's expenditures under a government grant to determine compliance with the terms of the grant, and auditing an entity's hiring policies to determine whether it has complied with the Equal Employment Opportunity Act. As with all audits, a compliance audit requires established criteria (such as those contained in a law or regulation) to measure the relevant assertions against. Compliance audits are performed by independent auditors and by internal and government auditors (often as part of a performance audit).

If a policy, contract, law, or regulation has a direct and material effect on the entity's financial statements, determining the extent of compliance with it usually will be an integral part of a financial statement audit.[1] For example, an auditor reviews an entity's conformity with the restrictive covenants in a long-term debt agreement to ascertain that a violation of the covenant has not made the entire bond issue due and payable at the lender's option, which might require that the debt be reclassified

---

[1] Statement on Auditing Standards No. 54, *Illegal Acts by Clients* (AU Section 317), indicates that a law or regulation has a direct effect on financial statements if it relates to financial and accounting matters. It cites as an example (in paragraph 5) a tax law that affects the entity's tax liability and the amount recognized as tax expense.

as a current liability. Independent auditors do not, however, plan their audits of financial statements to provide assurance about an entity's compliance with policies, contracts, laws, and regulations that do not have a direct and material effect on the financial statements. Chapter 4 describes the auditor's responsibilities when a possible illegal act is detected. Compliance audits are discussed further in Chapter 32.

(c) Performance Audits

Performance audits, also referred to as operational audits, include economy and efficiency audits and program audits. *Government Auditing Standards*, issued by the U.S. General Accounting Office and revised most recently in 1994, defines those audits as follows:

> Economy and efficiency audits include determining (1) whether the entity is acquiring, protecting, and using its resources (such as personnel, property, and space) economically and efficiently, (2) the causes of inefficiencies or uneconomical practices, and (3) whether the entity has complied with laws and regulations concerning matters of economy and efficiency.
>
> Program audits include determining (1) the extent to which the desired results or benefits established by the legislature or other authorizing body are being achieved, (2) the effectiveness of organizations, programs, activities, or functions, and (3) whether the entity has complied with significant laws and regulations applicable to the program.

Using resources economically means achieving a specified output or performance level at the lowest possible cost. An entity that met or exceeded the specified level at the lowest cost would be using its resources economically. Using resources efficiently means attaining the highest possible output or performance level at a specified cost. If output or performance can be increased without incurring additional costs, the implication is that a more efficient use of resources is possible. The achievement of desired results or benefits refers to the extent to which a program meets objectives and goals that are proper, suitable, or relevant. Results that are consistent with established objectives and goals indicate that the program is being carried out effectively.

Objectives and goals may be established by federal or state legislatures or granting agencies, or they may be set by an entity's management. As noted in Chapter the subject matter of auditing usually is quantifiable information about economic transactions and events. Some quantifiable objectives and goals may not relate to economic actions and events, however, which raises the question of whether their evaluation falls within the definition of auditing. For example, in an audit of program results a study of prison system, program objectives and goals almost surely will not be in terms of economic actions or events; instead, they may be stated in terms number of prisoners rehabilitated and released, the number of repeat offenders, or the percentage of prison capacity utilized. While such program audits may stretch the definition of auditing, they are widely performed, particularly ment auditors, and are almost always referred to as audits.

(d) Reviews of Financial Information

A review engagement consists of applying certain limited procedures statements as a basis for expressing limited assurance that there modifications that should be made to them. That limited assurance is less than the assurance provided by an audit.

(e) Attest Engagements

An attest engagement is defined in Statement on Standards for Attestation Engagements, *Attestation Standards* (AT Section 100.01), as "one in which a practitioner is engaged to issue or does issue a written communication that expresses a conclusion about the reliability of a written assertion that is the responsibility of another party." The scope of services covered by this definition is similar, if not identical, to that in the American Accounting Association's definition of auditing, which was discussed in Chapter 1. Examples of attest services include testing and reporting on representations about the characteristics of computer software, investment performance statistics, internal control, prospective financial information, and historical occupancy data for hospitals.

The profession has not yet reached a consensus about which services should be called audits and which attest engagements. For the foreseeable future, however, it is clear that attest services related to historical financial statements will continue to be called audits. Also, the term "attest engagement" will be limited to an engagement in which the practitioner issues a *written* opinion about a *written* assertion.

(f) Other Assurance Services

Many of the services CPAs in public practice currently perform do not fall into any of the categories previously described. These services—as well as new services that are not being provided currently—are best described as "other assurance services." They may include providing assurance on performance measures, such as the effectiveness of health care providers, or on an entity's compliance with its human resource policies or operating policies. The AICPA Special Committee on Assurance Services considered the potential scope of assurance services, which the Committee defined broadly as "independent professional services that improve the quality of information, or its context, for decision makers," and identified and developed detailed business plans for six new assurance services. Those services are risk assessment, business performance measurement, information systems reliability, electronic commerce, health care performance measurement, and assessing the quality of providers of elder care. In addition, the Committee considered, but did not develop business plans for, seven other assurance services.

2.2 TYPES OF AUDITORS

Auditors can be classified into three three categories: independent, internal, and government.

Independent auditors, also referred to as external auditors, and frequently as CPAs, CPAs in public practice, public accountants, or "outside" auditors, are never owners or employees of the entity that retains them to perform an audit, although they receive a fee for their services. Independent auditors perform financial statement audits to meet the needs of investors and creditors and the requirements of regulatory bodies like the Securities and Exchange Commission (SEC). The audits typically result in an opinion on whether the financial statements are fairly stated, in all material respects, in conformity with generally accepted accounting principles. Occasionally, CPAs perform compliance and performance audits. Increasingly, they perform attest engagements and provide other assurance services.

Internal auditors are employed by the entity they audit. The Institute of Internal Auditors has defined internal auditing as "an independent appraisal function established within an organization to examine and evaluate its activities as a service to the organization. The objective of internal auditing is to assist members of the organization in the effective discharge of their responsibilities. . . . The internal auditing department is an integral part of the organization and functions under the policies established by management and the board [of directors]."[2] The primary function of internal auditors is to examine their entity's internal control and evaluate how adequate and effective it is. In performing that function, internal auditors often conduct performance (or operational) audits that are broadly designed to accomplish financial and compliance audit objectives as well.

The independence of internal auditors is different from that of independent (i.e., external) auditors. Internal auditors' independence comes from their organizational status—essentially, their function and to whom they report—and their objectivity. For external auditors, independence derives instead from the absence of any obligation to or financial interest in the entity they were retained to audit, its management, or its owners.

Government auditors are employed by agencies of federal, state, and local governments. When the audit is of the government agency or department that employs the auditors, they function as internal auditors; when they audit recipients of government funds (including other government agencies), they act as external auditors. For example, auditors employed by the U.S. Department of Agriculture may audit the internal operations of that department; they also may audit the economy, efficiency, and program results of research funded by the Department of Agriculture but performed by others, such as colleges and universities. Most audits performed by government auditors are performance audits of economy, efficiency, and programs, which include determining whether the entity being audited has complied with laws and regulations concerning economy and efficiency as well as those applicable to the program. Some audits, such as those by the Internal Revenue Service, are performed almost exclusively for compliance purposes.

There are many different groups of government auditors; virtually every level of government and every government agency has its own auditors. One group in particular warrants further discussion—the General Accounting Office (GAO). A nonpolitical agency headed by the Comptroller General of the United States, it was created by and reports directly to Congress. The GAO has the authority to audit virtually every federal agency and expenditure. The GAO formulated the notion of and standards for economy, efficiency, and program audits, which are the major part of its activities.

2.3 ORGANIZATION OF AN ACCOUNTING FIRM

Accounting firms range in size from an individual CPA in business as a sole practitioner to large firms with an international practice, hundreds of offices worldwide,

---

[2] *Standards for the Professional Practice of Internal Auditing* (The Institute of Internal Auditors, Inc., 1978), p. 1.

and thousands of partners and employees. In between these two extremes are numerous small and medium-sized firms of professional accountants. In general, the larger firms offer a broader range of services than do the smaller ones. The majority of medium-sized and large accounting firms are multicapability firms, meaning that they serve clients in several major practice areas, including assurance, taxation, consulting, and human resources advisory services. Although the structure of individual firms varies, it is possible to make some generalizations about the services typically offered by the majority of accounting firms.

(a) Assurance Services

The most basic practice area of a CPA firm, assurance services consist primarily of performing independent audits of entities' financial statements. CPAs also perform reviews, engagements based on agreed-upon procedures, attest engagements, and other assurance services.

(i) Audits. An audit requires personnel with a blend of skills and technical expertise. For example, if the engagement is extremely complex technically, the audit team may require members who have industry expertise, a high level of knowledge of computer systems, tax expertise, and the ability to understand difficult actuarial computations. A team with such expertise frequently will find and recommend ways to improve the entity's financial and operating policies, a client service that is derived from the audit process.

In addition to audits, accounting firms generally offer a number of audit-related services, either in conjunction with an audit or as separate engagements. One of these services is a communication to management containing recommendations for improvements in internal control relating to financial reporting and other matters, such as comments on operating efficiencies and profitability. Additional audit-related services include acquisition audits of entities that clients are contemplating acquiring, and issuing letters reporting whether an entity is in compliance with the covenants of debt instruments.

(ii) Reviews. CPAs also perform review services. Review services for nonpublic entities are defined by the American Institute of Certified Public Accountants (AICPA) in the first of a series of Statements on Standards for Accounting and Review Services (SSARSs). Those statements resulted from the AICPA's recognition of the need for professional services that are less than an audit, but that provide some assurance about the reliability of a nonpublic entity's financial statements. Reviews are discussed further in Chapter 30.

(iii) Agreed-Upon Procedures Engagements. Accountants sometimes are engaged to perform agreed-upon procedures to specified elements, accounts, or items of a financial statement. In these engagements, the parties agree on the procedures to be performed, and use of the resulting report is limited to those parties. These agreed-upon procedures engagements are discussed further in Chapter 30. Other types of agreed-upon procedures engagements fall under the attestation standards and are discussed in Chapter 31.

(iv) Attest Engagements. In an attest engagement, the accountant provides written assurance about an assertion or assertions made by another party. The definition of an attest engagement is broad and covers a variety of assertions. For example, an accountant may be engaged to examine or review, and report on insurance claims data or enrollment and attendance data for a college. While attest engagements typically are undertaken by audit personnel, at times they are performed by personnel specializing in some of the "nonassurance services" offered by accounting firms, as described below. (Attest engagements are described further in Chapter 31.)

(v) Other Assurance Services.   In an engagement to provide assurance services beyond those currently defined in the authoritative professional literature, the objective is to improve the quality of information, or its context, for decision makers. Since the particular set of information that is used by a specific decision maker to make a specific decision will vary with the circumstances, the assurance provider must be able to identify what information is relevant and determine how and when to develop and present that information to the decision maker. The AICPA plans to develop measurement and reporting criteria to assist the assurance provider that will be sufficiently broad so that they can be customized to fill the needs of individual decision makers. While assurance services may be undertaken by audit personnel, they also may be performed by personnel specializing in some of the "nonassurance services" offered by accounting firms, as described below, particularly since those individuals may have the competencies appropriate for providing those services.

(b)   Nonassurance Services

Accounting firms provide nonassurance services to their clients in the form of compilations, tax services, and consulting services.

(i) Compilations.   A service performed by CPAs that is related to assurance services but does not result in the expression of assurance is a compilation. A compilation consists of presenting information in the form of financial statements without expressing any opinion on them. Compilations are discussed further in Chapter 30.

(ii) Tax Services.   A major service provided by accounting firms is in the area of taxation—tax and business planning and compliance services offered to businesses and individuals. Tax services offered to businesses by accounting firms cover a broad spectrum, including preparing federal, state, and local tax returns; advising on merger or acquisition approaches to minimize taxes and on structuring operations to take advantage of tax opportunities; and reviewing tax returns for compliance with applicable laws and regulations. Services to individuals include tax, financial, and estate planning.

A firm's tax practice often includes one or more special service groups that address complex issues related to taxation. For instance, some accounting firms maintain support groups composed of senior tax professionals who monitor new tax laws, regulations, rulings, cases, and other related developments and communicate this specialized knowledge to the rest of the firm. Many firms employ lawyers and engineers to advise clients on tax aspects of various transactions. Other groups that combine both tax and financial accounting expertise may be established to provide tax services relating to state and local tax matters; mergers, acquisitions, divestitures, sales of businesses, and related financing transactions; specialized industries that are affected by legislative, regulatory, and judicial proceedings; and international tax developments that concern multinational entities.

(iii) Consulting Services.   Consulting services, sometimes called management advisory or management consulting services, are offered in several diversified areas, such as strategic planning, finance, inventory and supply, transportation, computerization, and human resources. For example, professionals working in the consulting practice of an accounting firm may undertake work and make recommendations to an entity's management in one or more of the following areas:

- Establishing long-range strategic planning programs
- Analyzing and improving administration—organization, methods, procedures, and productivity
- Developing information technology strategy, equipment and software evaluation and selection, and telecommunications network and security evaluation
- Designing and implementing information systems
- Applying techniques, such as just-in-time inventory planning, to improve profitability
- Improving materials controls, from consumer goods sales forecasting to manufacturing planning and control

Human resources advisory professionals employed by accounting firms can advise clients about:

- Planning executive compensation arrangements, conducting salary surveys, and devising wage programs
- Designing employee benefit and profit-sharing plans, performing annual actuarial valuations, and implementing health care, life, and disability insurance programs
- Communicating benefits and compensation policies to employees
- Developing benefits and compensation administration systems
- Determining compliance with government reporting requirements

Those consultants also may provide technical support to audit engagement teams.

(c) Firm Structure

It is difficult to generalize about the organization of accounting firms because each one has its own structure and no two are exactly alike. Some multioffice firms are organized by groups or regions, with one partner assigned overall responsibility for the practice offices in each group or region. The group or regional partners may report to a number of vice chairmen or other designated partners. Each practice office is headed by a partner, often called the managing partner or partner in charge of the office, who is responsible for day-to-day operations. Within each practice office, there may be separate units for assurance services, tax, consulting, and perhaps one or more specialized practice areas. In addition to professional personnel, each practice office may have an administrative staff to handle personnel management, including recruiting, and to support the office's accounting and reporting function.

In addition to their practice offices, many large accounting firms have a number of specialized departments, usually organized as part of a national office, that provide support to the practice. Examples of such resource groups are industry specialization, marketing and planning, professional education, and accounting and auditing policy setting, research, and consulting. Firms that practice in different countries are further organized under an international structure usually governed by a committee of representatives from the various member firms or geographic areas.

(d) Audit Engagement Team

Each audit is staffed by a team headed by a partner who signs the audit report and is ultimately responsible for the audit and its results. Especially on large or complex engagements, there may be more than one partner, or the partner may delegate many functions to one or more managers; however, one partner retains responsibility for the quality of the audit and thus should be actively involved in its planning and in evaluating the results, as documented and summarized by the members of the engagement team. The team usually includes a manager (or more than one on a large engagement) and other personnel with varying degrees of experience and professional expertise and competence. Firms establish staff classifications through which employees progress and policies that set forth the responsibilities of audit personnel on each level. While these responsibilities vary from one firm to another, the typical functions and duties of each classification can be described generally.

(i) Partner.   The partner has primary responsibility for accounting and auditing services and is usually the direct contact with the client. The partner is responsible for all decisions made in the course of the engagement, including those about the scope of services, the audit strategy, and the resolution of significant accounting and auditing issues. In short, the partner is responsible for ensuring that the audit has been planned, conducted, and reported on in accordance with the firm's policies and professional standards. As noted in Chapter 3, firms that are members of the SEC Practice Section of the AICPA's Division for CPA Firms are required to assign a second, or concurring review, partner on SEC engagements to provide additional assurance that those objectives are achieved. Because of the perceived benefits of such additional partner review, many firms assign a concurring review partner to other engagements as well.

The concurring review partner on an engagement generally assesses the audit strategy, including auditing procedures to be performed in sensitive or high-risk areas, and may suggest additional matters to be addressed or recommend ways of enhancing audit efficiency. He or she reviews the draft audit report, related financial information and disclosures, and, where applicable, published reports and filings to be made with the Securities and Exchange Commission (SEC) and other regulatory bodies. In some circumstances, the review may be more detailed and include inquiring of members of the engagement team and reviewing working papers to determine that the scope of auditing procedures and related documentation comply with the firm's policies and professional standards.

(ii) Manager. Under the direction of a partner, a manager is responsible for administering all aspects of an engagement, including planning and coordinating activities with the entity's personnel, delegating duties to team members, coaching them, supervising and reviewing their work, controlling engagement time and expenses, and overseeing billings and collections. A manager is expected to have attained a degree of technical competence in accounting and auditing sufficient to ensure that an audit complies with all applicable professional standards and firm policies. The manager is also responsible for keeping the partner informed of all significant developments throughout the audit. Among other things, the manager often is delegated the responsibility for reviewing proposed changes in the audit program, the report to management covering internal control related matters, the financial statements first in draft form and then in final form, and the working papers documenting the engagement.

(iii) Other Personnel. An experienced accountant, sometimes called the field team leader or in-charge accountant, is responsible, under the manager's direction, for the overall quality, timeliness, and efficiency of the fieldwork in an audit. This involves assisting the manager with administrative matters during the planning phase of the engagement as well as during and after the fieldwork. During the fieldwork, this individual is responsible for understanding the entity's business, industry, and internal control; identifying inherent risks; assessing control risk; reviewing working papers prepared by other engagement team personnel; drafting the report on internal control related matters and the proposed audit report; and preparing a summary of audit findings, sometimes called critical issues, for the manager's and partner's attention.

Less experienced personnel are responsible for completing assigned tasks under supervision. Their assignments, which vary with the size and complexity of the engagement, generally include preparing documentation of the understanding of the entity's business and its internal control, performing various types of auditing procedures and documenting the results, and keeping higher-level personnel informed of all findings.

2.4 ORGANIZATION OF THE AUDITING PROFESSION

The auditing profession in the United States has formed numerous voluntary groups with various purposes, among them the AICPA, state societies or institutes of CPAs, and The Institute of Internal Auditors, all of which have broadly based memberships. In addition, there are more specialized organizations of government auditors, computer auditors, teachers of auditing, and internal auditors with particular industry interests. The designation "Certified Public Accountant" is granted by state boards of accountancy, discussed in the next section of this chapter.

(a) American Institute of CPAs

The mission of the AICPA is "to provide members with the resources, information, and leadership that enable them to provide valuable services in the highest professional manner to benefit the public as well as employers and clients." About 40 percent of the AICPA's approximately 330,000 members, all of whom are required to be CPAs, are in public practice either with CPA firms or as sole practitioners. (The rest are in business and industry, government, or education, or are retired.) The AICPA provides a broad range of services to members, including continuing professional education, technical accounting and auditing assistance, auditing standard setting, self-regulation of the profession, and assistance in managing an accounting practice.

Ultimate authority over the AICPA is vested in its Council. Its 23-member Board of Directors, which includes three non-Institute members who represent the public, administers resources and sets policy. Pronouncements in the form of technical and ethical standards are issued by senior technical committees composed of Institute members in public practice and, to some extent, in industry, government, and academe. Those committees and the pronouncements they issue are shown in Figure 2.1.

In addition, the AICPA has four voluntary member sections that individuals with special interests may join: tax, personal financial planning, management consulting

Figure 2.1   Pronouncements Issued by AICPA Senior Technical Committees

Senior Technical Committee	Public Statements Issued or Reviewed
Accounting and Review Services Committee	Statements on Standards for Accounting and Review Services,[a] and Interpretations Statements on Standards for Attestation Engagements[a]
Accounting Standards Executive Committee	Statements of Position Practice Bulletins Audit and Accounting Guides
AICPA Peer Review Board	Standards for Performing and Reporting on Peer Reviews
Auditing Standards Board	Statements on Auditing Standards,[a] and Interpretations Statements on Standards for Attestation Engagements,[a] and Interpretations Statements on Quality Control Standards Statements of Position Audit and Accounting Guides Auditing Procedures Studies Notices to Practitioners
Management Consulting Services Executive Committee	Statements on Standards for Consulting Services[a] Statements on Standards for Attestation Engagements[a]
Personal Financial Planning Executive Committee	Statements on Responsibilities in Personal Financial Planning Practice
Professional Ethics Executive Committee	Interpretations of Rules of Conduct[a] Ethics Rulings[a]
Tax Executive Committee	Statements on Responsibilities in Tax Practice

[a] The Rules of the AICPA Code of Professional Conduct and implementing resolutions of Council require AICPA members to comply with standards contained in these pronouncements; departures therefrom must be justified by those members who do not follow them.

services, and information technology. (There is also a Division for CPA Firms, composed of an SEC Practice Section and a Private Companies Practice Section, that CPA firms may join. The Division for CPA Firms is discussed in Chapter 3.) Non-CPAs employed by CPA firms and meeting other eligibility requirements may join one or more of the AICPA's member sections, but not the AICPA itself, as Section Associates and receive the same member section benefits as CPA members. Individuals who have passed the Uniform CPA Examination, but have not received their CPA certificates because they have not completed their experience requirements, may become AICPA Associates. College students and recent graduates who have not yet passed the CPA examination may become Student Affiliates. Chartered accountants and CPAs who are members of associations belonging to the International Federation of Accountants (IFAC) and who do not hold a CPA certificate issued by a U.S. jurisdiction may join the AICPA as International Associates.

The AICPA provides educational programs covering a wide range of technical and professional subjects of interest to members in public practice, business, teaching, and government. The Institute also publishes the *Journal of Accountancy* and *The Tax Adviser* monthly, which are available to nonmembers as well as members; several newsletters of interest to practicing members; and numerous pamphlets, reports, and studies. The Institute's Board of Examiners prepares and grades the semiannual CPA examinations on behalf of the 50 states and other licensing jurisdictions. Through its Professional Ethics Division, the AICPA issues Interpretations of the Principles and Rules of the Code of Professional Conduct, investigates complaints against members regarding unethical practices, and assists in investigating and presenting ethics cases referred to the Joint Trial Board.

(b)   State Societies of CPAs

In addition to belonging to the AICPA, most CPAs belong to a state society of CPAs. The purpose of the state societies is also to improve the profession and help their members better serve the public interest. To accomplish this, the state societies offer members continuing professional education courses, provide consultation services, maintain liaison with members of state legislatures and relevant administrative agencies of state governments, publish professional journals, clarify and enforce professional technical and ethical standards, and provide other services to members, such as various types of group insurance. Members of a state society are automatically members of a specific local chapter within the state, which holds regular meetings and coordinates its activities with those of the state society.

(c)   Institute of Internal Auditors

The Institute of Internal Auditors (IIA) was formed to promote the professionalism and education of internal auditors. The organization has more than 58,000 members in 224 affiliates throughout the world. It has developed professional standards and a code of ethics, and has identified a common body of practitioner knowledge. The Institute sponsors training seminars, conferences, research, and books and other publications, including a bimonthly journal entitled *The Internal Auditor*. The Institute's

Board of Directors and other international committees set Institute policy. The IIA offers a certification program leading to the professional designation of Certified Internal Auditor (CIA).

(d) Other Organizations

Auditors with specialized interests have formed various organizations, usually with more precisely defined objectives than the broadly based AICPA and IIA. Among those groups are computer, insurance company, government, and bank auditors. Members of the American Accounting Association who are interested in auditing research and teaching have established an Auditing Section of the Association, which publishes *Auditing: A Journal of Practice & Theory*. Membership in some of these organizations is limited to auditors practicing in a specific field or industry.

2.5 PROFESSIONAL CERTIFICATION AND LICENSING

The main professional designations relating to the practice of auditing are Certified Public Accountant, Certified Internal Auditor, Certified Information Systems Auditor, and Certified Fraud Examiner.

(a) Certified Public Accountant (CPA)

Starting in 1896, the various states have licensed and regulated individuals who have met specified education, experience, and examination requirements and who hold themselves out to the public as CPAs. Accountancy laws governing the licensing of professional accountants and establishing state boards of accountancy to administer and enforce them have been enacted in all 50 states, the District of Columbia, Guam, Puerto Rico, and the U.S. Virgin Islands. Only individuals who pass the CPA examination and meet the education and experience requirements of their state boards are granted a license to practice by the state and are entitled to use the designation Certified Public Accountant or CPA. The CPA certificate is granted to qualified candidates to ensure the professional competence of those who offer their services to the public as professional accountants.

The semiannual, two-day CPA examination is prepared by the Board of Examiners of the AICPA and is given uniformly throughout the 54 United States licensing jurisdictions in May and November. The examination currently consists of the following four sections:

- *Business Law and Professional Responsibilities*: tests the candidate's knowledge of a CPA's professional responsibilities and of the legal implications of business transactions, particularly as they relate to accounting and auditing
- *Auditing*: tests the candidate's knowledge of auditing standards and procedures, and the skills necessary to apply them in auditing and other attestation engagements provided by CPAs
- *Accounting and Reporting—Taxation, Managerial, and Governmental and Not-for-Profit*

Organizations: tests the candidate's knowledge of principles and procedures for federal taxation, managerial accounting, and accounting for governmental and not-for-profit organizations, and the skills needed to apply them

- *Financial Accounting and Reporting*: tests the candidate's knowledge of authoritative accounting pronouncements for business entities and the skills necessary to apply them

Some states may require candidates to be tested in other subjects as well, most commonly professional ethics.

All state boards of accountancy use the AICPA Uniform CPA Examination and Advisory Grading Service. Even though the papers are graded by the AICPA, the state boards are responsible for the quality, composition, and grading of the examination and for licensing individuals, and thus may review the Institute's grading. Education and experience requirements differ from state to state. Although in some states individuals receive a CPA certificate on passing the examination, most states require a period of experience before they issue a license to practice.

Additional information concerning a state's regulations and requirements can be obtained from the following sources:

- The appropriate state education department or state board of accountancy
- National Association of State Boards of Accountancy, 380 Lexington Avenue, New York, NY 10168-0002
- American Institute of Certified Public Accountants, 1211 Avenue of the Americas, New York, NY 10036-8775
- The appropriate state society of certified public accountants

Publications that may have information about the CPA examination and state accountancy laws include:

- *Information for Uniform CPA Examination Candidates*, published by the American Institute of Certified Public Accountants
- *Digest of State Accountancy Laws and State Board Regulations*, which includes a listing of the state boards of accountancy, published by the National Association of State Boards of Accountancy and the AICPA

(b) Certified Fraud Examiner (CFE)

The Association of Certified Fraud Examiners, established in 1988, prepares and administers the Uniform CFE Examination, which tests candidates' knowledge of financial transactions, conducting investigations, legal aspects of fraud, and criminology and ethics. The CFE program is an accreditation, not a licensing, program. The CFE designation indicates that its holder has demonstrated expertise in resolving allegations of fraud, obtaining evidence, testifying to findings, and assisting in the detection and prevention of fraud and white-collar crime. CFEs must meet specified CPE requirements and adhere to the Association's Code of Professional Ethics and bylaws. Additional information about the experience and education requirements for the CFE examination can be obtained from the Association of Certified Fraud Examiners, 716 West Avenue, Austin, TX 78701.

(c) Certified Internal Auditor (CIA)

The Certified Internal Auditor examination measures technical competence in the practice of internal auditing and is administered by the Board of Regents of The Institute of Internal Auditors (IIA). The IIA's Director of Professional Practices is responsible for preparing, administering, and grading the examination within the guidelines established by IIA's Board of Regents and Board of Directors. The Certified Internal Auditor examination is open to internal auditors and others who have the required professional qualifications. To maintain the CIA designation, a holder of a CIA certificate must meet specific continuing professional education (CPE) requirements. The certificate confers professional recognition but does not include a license to practice. Because CIAs do not offer their services to the public, states do not license them. Additional information relating to the experience and education requirements for the CIA examination can be obtained from The Institute of Internal Auditors, 249 Maitland Avenue, Altamonte Springs, FL 32701-4201.

(d) Certified Information Systems Auditor (CISA)

The Certified Information Systems Auditor examination tests knowledge and skills in the various fields of EDP auditing and is administered by the Information Systems Audit and Control Association (ISACA). To retain certification, a CISA must meet certain CPE requirements or retake the examination. The CISA program is also one of professional recognition rather than state licensure. Additional information about the experience and education requirements for the CISA examination can be obtained from the ISACA, 3701 Algonquin Road, Suite 1010, Rolling Meadows, IL 60008.

2.6 ASSURANCE STANDARDS AND STANDARD-SETTING BODIES

Assurance standards, in the broadest sense, are guidelines for performing professionally responsible audits, attest engagements, and other assurance services. Several organizations have formulated such standards.

(a) Generally Accepted Auditing Standards

The membership of the AICPA approved and adopted ten broad statements collectively entitled "generally accepted auditing standards," often abbreviated as GAAS. Nine of them originally were adopted in 1948; the tenth was adopted some years later, but the basic principle had existed before. The standards have not changed basically since (although our understanding of several of them has changed significantly over the years and they have been amended to reflect that understanding and resulting changes in terminology). Of the ten standards, three are concerned with personal qualities that the auditor should possess (general standards), three with how an audit should be conducted (field work standards), and four with the form and content of the auditor's report (reporting standards). The ten GAAS are discussed in detail in Chapter 3.

The authority to amplify and interpret the ten GAAS resides in a senior technical committee of the AICPA. From 1939 to 1972, that committee was called the Committee on Auditing Procedure and issued 54 pronouncements called Statements on Auditing Procedure. The Committee on Auditing Procedure was replaced in 1972 by the Auditing Standards Executive Committee, and in 1978 the Auditing Standards Board (ASB) was formed to succeed the Executive Committee. The ASB is now responsible for promulgating auditing standards and procedures to be observed by AICPA members in accordance with the Institute's Code of Professional Conduct. The pronouncements of the Auditing Standards Executive Committee and the ASB are called Statements on Auditing Standards (SASs). They define the nature and extent of auditors' responsibilities and provide guidance to auditors in carrying out their duties. From 1972 through September 1997 the two committees issued 82 SASs. While statements issued by all three committees are technically amplifications and interpretations of the ten original GAAS, they and the ten GAAS are frequently referred to collectively as generally accepted auditing standards.

In addition to issuing SASs, the ASB approves for publication auditing interpretations of the SASs; the interpretations are prepared by the Audit Issues Task Force of the ASB. As they are issued, SASs, auditing interpretations, and other AICPA professional standards are incorporated in the AICPA's looseleaf service, *Professional Standards*, which results in a continuous codification of those pronouncements. Once a year, a bound version of the latest *AICPA Professional Standards* is published.

(h) International Auditing Standards

The desirability of developing more uniform auditing standards and practices worldwide has long been recognized and is gaining increasing support as international business continues to expand. Efforts to promote international uniformity in auditing standards were formally initiated in 1977, when representatives of approximately 50 countries, including the United States, established the International Federation of Accountants (IFAC). The broad objectives of IFAC, as stated in paragraph 2 of its Constitution, are "the development and enhancement of a coordinated worldwide accountancy profession with harmonized standards." IFAC's efforts are directed toward developing international technical, ethical, and educational guidelines for auditors, and reciprocal recognition of practitioners' qualifications.

Responsibility for developing and issuing exposure drafts and standards on generally accepted auditing practices and audit reports is vested in IFAC's International Auditing Practices Committee (IAPC); through September 1997 it has issued 30 International Standards on Auditing (ISAs), plus three others in its series entitled International Standards on Auditing/Related Services, all of which are codified in AU Section 8000 of *AICPA Professional Standards*. (The related services addressed by the standards are compilations, reviews, and agreed-upon procedures engagements.)

For the most part, the provisions of the standards coincide closely with comparable U.S. standards. Although the standards are not authoritative in the United States and are not covered by the AICPA Code of Professional Conduct, if a standard is intended to be issued that would deviate significantly from U.S. standards, the AICPA's Auditing Standards Board or Accounting and Review Services Committee considers ways of resolving the differences. In addition, the IAPC has issued ten International Auditing Practice Statements, which are intended to assist auditors in implementing the provisions of certain ISAs. This series of statements, which are codified in AU Section 10,000 of *AICPA Professional Standards*, does not have the same authority as the ISAs.

In 1990, IFAC issued the "Guideline on Ethics for the Accountancy Profession," which revised and codified its previous ethics pronouncements, consisting of a Statement of Principles, a series of notes explaining the intentions underlying the principles, guidance on implementing ethical standards, and guidelines for formulating ethical requirements. In issuing ethics guidelines, IFAC recognizes that implementation is affected by the legal, social, and economic conditions prevailing in individual countries. Nevertheless, the "Guideline on Ethics" was designed to serve as a prototype for an international code of business ethics.

In 1992, the International Organization of Securities Commissions (IOSCO) approved a resolution to recognize the ISAs for use in multinational reporting. In recommending that the IOSCO membership take that step, key members of IOSCO's Technical Committee, which reviewed the standards, concluded that they "represent a comprehensive set of auditing standards and that audits conducted in accordance with these standards could be relied upon by securities regulatory authorities for multinational reporting purposes." IOSCO has more than 100 members, including the U.S. SEC, although the SEC has not yet accepted the ISAs as a basis for reporting in the United States.

(c)   Role of the SEC and the Courts

The various federal acts that the SEC administers give it broad powers. Those powers probably include promulgating auditing standards and may extend even to prescribing specific steps to be followed by auditors of financial statements filed with the Commission. The Commission has, however, adopted the general policy of relying on the public accounting profession to establish auditing standards, largely because of the profession's willingness to address issues the SEC deems significant. The policy stated by the Commission in 1940 in Accounting Series Release No. 19 continues to be effective.

> Until experience should prove the contrary, we feel that this program is preferable to its alternative—the detailed prescription of the scope of and procedures to be followed in the audit for the various types of issuers of securities who file statements with us—and will allow for further consideration of varying audit procedures and for the development of different treatment for specific types of issuers.

This is not to suggest that the SEC has not or will not influence the development of auditing standards. Indeed, it has done so on several occasions and is likely to continue doing so. That influence takes essentially two forms: stimulating the ASB to issue a pronouncement when the Commission believes one is needed (as occurred with SAS No. 36, *Review of Interim Financial Information*) and informing the ASB of its views during the standard-setting process. The ASB must continually acknowledge the presence of the SEC throughout its deliberations, but must not sacrifice the independence and objectivity that are essential to its standard-setting function.

Despite numerous opportunities to interpret auditing standards when auditors have been the subject of litigation, only rarely have the courts failed to apply the profession's own auditing standards, and then it was primarily in areas involving reporting standards. Conformity with promulgated professional auditing standards has generally been an effective defense for auditors.

(d) Standards for Internal Auditing

The Institute of Internal Auditors in 1978 adopted a series of *Standards for the Professional Practice of Internal Auditing*. Those standards, which are reproduced in Figure 2.2, address the independence of internal auditors, their professional proficiency, the scope and performance of their work, and the management of internal auditing departments. The IIA standards differ somewhat in their philosophy from the AICPA standards for external auditors in that the former represent the practice of internal auditing as it *should be*, whereas to a large extent SASs represent the Auditing Standards Board's view of the consensus among practitioners—what is "generally accepted." That difference should not be exaggerated, however; the IIA standards are

Figure 2.2   Summary of General and Specific Standards for the Professional Practice of Internal Auditing

100   **INDEPENDENCE—Internal auditors should be independent of the activities they audit.**
    110   *Organizational Status*—The organizational status of the internal auditing department should be sufficient to permit the accomplishment of its audit responsibilities.
    120   *Objectivity*—Internal auditors should be objective in performing audits.

200   **PROFESSIONAL PROFICIENCY—Internal audits should be performed with proficiency and due professional care.**
    The Internal Auditing Department
    210   *Staffing*—The internal auditing department should provide assurance that the technical proficiency and educational background of internal auditors are appropriate for the audits to be performed.
    220   *Knowledge, Skills, and Disciplines*—The internal auditing department should possess or should obtain the knowledge, skills, and disciplines needed to carry out its audit responsibilities.
    230   *Supervision*—The internal auditing department should provide assurance that internal audits are properly supervised.
    The Internal Auditor
    240   *Compliance with Standards of Conduct*—Internal auditors should comply with professional standards of conduct.
    250   *Knowledge, Skills, and Disciplines*—Internal auditors should possess the knowledge, skills, and disciplines essential to the performance of internal audits.
    260   *Human Relations and Communications*—Internal auditors should be skilled in dealing with people and in communicating effectively.
    270   *Continuing Education*—Internal auditors should maintain their technical competence through continuing education.
    280   *Due Professional Care*—Internal auditors should exercise due professional care in performing internal audits.

Figure 2.2   (Continued)

300   **SCOPE OF WORK—The scope of the internal audit should encompass the examination and evaluation of the adequacy and effectiveness of the organization's system of internal control and the quality of performance in carrying out assigned responsibilities.**

310   *Reliability and Integrity of Information*—Internal auditors should review the reliability and integrity of financial and operating information and the means used to identify, measure, classify, and report such information.

320   *Compliance with Policies, Plans, Procedures, Laws, and Regulations*— Internal auditors should review the systems established to ensure compliance with those policies, plans, procedures, laws, and regulations which could have a significant impact on operations and reports and should determine whether the organization is in compliance.

330   *Safeguarding of Assets*—Internal auditors should review the means of safeguarding assets and, as appropriate, verify the existence of such assets.

340   *Economical and Efficient Use of Resources*—Internal auditors should appraise the economy and efficiency with which resources are employed.

350   *Accomplishments of Established Objectives and Goals for Operations or Programs*—Internal auditors should review operations or programs to ascertain whether results are consistent with established objectives and goals and whether the operations or programs are being carried out as planned.

400   **PERFORMANCE OF AUDIT WORK—Audit work should include planning the audit, examining and evaluating information, communicating results, and following up.**

410   *Planning the Audit*—Internal auditors should plan each audit.

420   *Examining and Evaluating Information*—Internal auditors should collect, analyze, interpret, and document information to support audit results.

430   *Communicating Results*—Internal auditors should report the results of their audit work.

440   *Following Up*—Internal auditors should follow up to ascertain that appropriate action is taken on reported audit findings.

500   **MANAGEMENT OF THE INTERNAL AUDITING DEPARTMENT—The director of internal auditing should properly manage the internal auditing department.**

510   *Purpose, Authority, and Responsibility*—The director of internal auditing should have a statement of purpose, authority, and responsibility for the internal auditing department.

520   *Planning*—The director of internal auditing should establish plans to carry out the responsibilities of the internal auditing department.

530   *Policies and Procedures*—The director of internal auditing should provide written policies and procedures to guide the audit staff.

540   *Personnel Management and Development*—The director of internal auditing should establish a program for selecting and developing the human resources of the internal auditing department.

550   *External Auditors*—The director of internal auditing should coordinate internal and external audit efforts.

560   *Quality Assurance*—The director of internal auditing should establish and maintain a quality assurance program to evaluate the operations of the internal auditing department.

Source: From *Standards for the Professional Practice of Internal Auditing.* Copyright 1997 by The Institute of Internal Auditors, Inc. 249 Maitland Avenue, Altamonte Springs, Florida 32710-4201 U.S.A. Reprinted with permission.

also a consensus, but of the best of practice rather than of what is minimally acceptable. The IIA periodically issues Statements on Internal Auditing Standards to provide guidance on issues of interest to internal auditors.

(e)   Standards for Government Auditing

The Comptroller General of the United States, who heads the General Accounting Office, the largest employer of government auditors in the United States, has issued a set of *Government Auditing Standards*, popularly referred to as the "Yellow Book." The standards were first published in 1972 and have been revised several times since then, most recently in 1994. Adherence to the standards is required for audits not only of federal organizations, programs, activities, and functions but also of federal funds received by nonprofit organizations and other nongovernmental entities. The standards should be followed for state and local government audits performed by government auditors or CPAs, and several state and local audit agencies also have adopted them. The standards incorporate the AICPA's auditing standards, in some cases expanding on them, and are compatible with the standards issued by the IIA.

The standards define two types of government audits: financial audits (which include financial statements and financial-related audits) and performance audits (which include economy and efficiency audits and program audits). The standards consist of general standards, including independence and due professional care, and field work and reporting standards; they are discussed further in Chapters 32 and 38.

(f)   Attestation Standards

In 1986, the AICPA's ASB and its Accounting and Review Services Committee (ARSC) jointly issued Statement on Standards for Attestation Engagements (SSAE), *Attestation Standards* (AT Section 100), the first in a series of statements on such engagements. (The AICPA's Management Consulting Services Executive Committee also is authorized to issue SSAEs.) The attestation standards provide guidance and establish a broad framework for performing and reporting on attest services generally. The standards do not supersede any existing SASs or other authoritative standards, but are a natural extension of the ten GAAS. Because of their breadth, the attestation standards serve as a basis for establishing interpretive standards for a wide range of services, while at the same time setting reasonable boundaries around the attest function. As of September 1997, six SSAEs have been issued. They are discussed in Chapter 31.

(g)   Statements on Standards for Accounting and Review Services

Statements on Standards for Accounting and Review Services (SSARSs) are issued by the ARSC to provide guidelines for performing and reporting on review and compilation engagements. The SSARSs, and related interpretations, establish performance standards for these engagements, and specify and illustrate the appropriate reporting in various circumstances. Seven SSARSs have been issued as of September 1997. They are discussed in Chapter 30.

3

Auditing Standards and Professional Conduct

All professions have technical and ethical standards to guide members in carrying out their duties and in their relationships with the various groups with which they come in contact. Also, all professions have means for enforcing those standards. Compliance with the public accounting profession's technical and ethical standards is enforced through various mechanisms created by the American Institute of Certified Public Accountants (AICPA) and by state societies of CPAs, state boards of accountancy, the Securities and Exchange Commission (SEC), the courts, and accounting firms themselves.

3.1 AUDITING AS A PROFESSION

While various writers and organizations have different criteria for defining an activity as a profession, there seems to be widespread agreement that the following characteristics must be present:

1. Formal recognition of professional status by means of a license issued by a government body after admission standards have been met
2. A body of specialized knowledge, usually acquired through formal education
3. A code of ethics to provide standards of conduct, and a means of enforcing compliance with the code
4. Informal recognition and acceptance of professional status by the public, and public interest in the work performed
5. Recognition by the professionals of a social obligation beyond the service performed for a particular client

There can be little doubt that auditing has the attributes necessary to qualify as a profession. The privilege of practicing as a public accountant is limited by the statutes of the various states and territories to those who have been granted the designation of Certified Public Accountant (CPA) by a particular state or territory. The certification is granted only to those who have passed the CPA examination and, in most jurisdictions, who also have met specified education and experience requirements. At least in part because the CPA examination is uniform throughout all licensing jurisdictions and has a well-deserved reputation of being difficult, the public has come to expect a high level of expertise in accounting and auditing from a person who is a CPA.

The specialized knowledge of accounting and auditing that an auditor must have usually is acquired initially through an academic program at the undergraduate level, the graduate level, or both. The necessary knowledge is acquired also through on-the-job training and continuing education courses, sometimes to meet licensing or membership requirements of various bodies. For example, many states require an average of 40 hours of annual continuing education credits for CPAs to keep their license to practice; the AICPA's membership requirements also stipulate that members in public practice meet a similar level of professional education, with fewer credits required for members not in public practice. CPAs also must supplement their knowledge through an ongoing program of reading and self-study to keep current with new professional standards and stay abreast of economic and business issues.

As discussed later in this chapter, membership in the AICPA requires adherence to the Institute's Code of Professional Conduct. The Institute of Internal Auditors also has such a code, adherence to which is required of those internal auditors who have qualified as Certified Internal Auditors by virtue of having met examination, education, and experience requirements. The AICPA's Code of Professional Conduct and its enforcement are designed to ensure that CPAs who are members of the AICPA accept and achieve a high level of responsibility to the public, clients, and colleagues.

It is apparent that the public considers public accountancy a profession. Universities have established schools and programs of professional accountancy, and a mechanism is in place for separate accreditation of those programs by the American Assembly of Collegiate Schools of Business (AACSB). There is a high level of public interest in the work performed by CPAs, particularly auditing and, increasingly, other assurance services. It is unusual for someone other than a CPA to be asked to attest to financial or other information that will be disseminated outside the entity. Recently, the range of services performed by CPAs has broadened into areas not previously considered the domain of public accountancy, attracting attention both within the profession and among the public.

Lastly, it is clear that the profession has long recognized an obligation to the public at large that extends well beyond the services performed for a particular client. While auditors realize that they have an obligation or responsibility to the client that has retained them, they are also aware that their audience is much larger. Audited financial statements are read and used by many other groups—present and potential investors and creditors, suppliers, employees, customers, and government agencies. Testimony before legislative bodies at all levels of government and other less formal recommendations regarding tax laws, securities acts, and other relevant legislation have indicated a concern for the public interest that extends far beyond the parochial interests of auditors whose livelihood could be enhanced or diminished by the proposed legislation. Often, the positions an auditor takes publicly on such matters conflict with the specific interests of one or more clients, but professionals should place the interests of the public ahead of their own or those of a particular client.

The Public Oversight Board (POB) of the AICPA SEC Practice Section has addressed, in two separate reports,[1] issues of the accounting profession's responsibilities to the public vis-à-vis standard setting. In its 1993 report, the POB recommended that firms "take special care to ensure that their participation in the standard setting process is characterized by objectivity and professionalism." In 1994, the Advisory Panel counseled firms to be careful in how they communicate their views to standard setters, the SEC, clients, and the public at large. The Advisory Panel stated:

> Developing positions for submission to the FASB, the SEC, and AcSEC is part of an accounting firm's responsibility. Therefore, it is essential that the firm's internal organization and processes for developing those positions be insulated from undue pressure from or on behalf of clients. In addition, communications about firm positions on FASB proposals must be done in a judicious, professional way that does not appear to curry favor with clients or appear to be part of an organized campaign. Client-related motivations, or even the appearance thereof, in reaching or communicating accounting policy

---

[1] *In the Public Interest* (POB, 1993) and *Strengthening the Professionalism of the Independent Auditor* (Advisory Panel on Auditor Independence, 1994).

decisions can contribute to a decline in the integrity, objectivity, and professionalism of public accounting firms and in public respect for the profession.

3.2 GENERALLY ACCEPTED AUDITING STANDARDS

Professions set technical standards to ensure a specified minimum level of performance and quality, primarily because they recognize that the public has an interest in and relies on the work of professionals—and this is undoubtedly true for the auditing profession. Standards set the minimum level of performance and quality that auditors are expected, by their clients and the public, to achieve. In contrast to auditing procedures—which are steps to be performed and vary depending on factors unique to each audit, such as entity size, industry, accounting system, and other circumstances— standards are measures of the quality of performance. Auditing standards should be unvarying over a wide spectrum of audit engagements over long periods of time.

The balance between the exercise of professional judgment and the establishment of specific rules to guide professional conduct pervades every aspect of accounting and auditing. The auditing profession clearly has rejected the two extremes: On the one hand, "cookbook" rules are not and never will be sufficient to cover every possible combination of circumstances and thereby allow auditors to shed their responsibility to exercise professional judgment; on the other hand, a framework exists to provide guidance for exercising judgment in all significant aspects of audit practice. It is between the two extremes that tensions and controversies arise: for example, how much uniformity should be required in auditing practice versus how much flexibility should be permitted, or to what extent standard sample sizes and auditing procedures should be spelled out versus the extent to which an auditor's pragmatic judgments should be required. Although the specific subject matter of debate changes from time to time, it is likely that the philosophical debate itself will never be concluded. It should be noted that this same tension between rules and individual judgment pervades most professions.

The membership of the AICPA officially adopted ten generally accepted auditing standards (GAAS), nine of them in 1948 and the tenth some years later. AICPA pronouncements—Statements on Auditing Procedure and Statements on Auditing Standards—have amplified, modified, and interpreted the ten GAAS. Fifty-four Statements on Auditing Procedure (SAPs) were issued between 1939 and 1972; 82 Statements on Auditing Standards (SASs) have been issued since then, and others are in draft. Statement on Auditing Standards No. 1 codified the 54 SAPs; updated codifications of SAPs and SASs that are still effective are issued annually by the AICPA.

Practitioners and others who need to understand auditors' work and reports should be thoroughly familiar with the SASs, for they constitute the authoritative professional auditing literature. The ten generally accepted auditing standards—the source of all subsequent SAPs and SASs—are found in SAS No. 1 (AU Section 150 of *AICPA Professional Standards*), as follows:

General Standards

1. The audit is to be performed by a person or persons having adequate technical training and proficiency as an auditor.

2. In all matters relating to the assignment, an independence in mental attitude is to be maintained by the auditor or auditors.

3. Due professional care is to be exercised in the planning and performance of the audit and the preparation of the report.

Standards of Field Work

1. The work is to be adequately planned and assistants, if any, are to be properly supervised.

2. A sufficient understanding of internal control is to be obtained to plan the audit and to determine the nature, timing, and extent of tests to be performed.

3. Sufficient competent evidential matter is to be obtained through inspection, observation, inquiries, and confirmations to afford a reasonable basis for an opinion regarding the financial statements under audit.

Standards of Reporting

1. The report shall state whether the financial statements are presented in accordance with generally accepted accounting principles.

2. The report shall identify those circumstances in which such principles have not been consistently observed in the current period in relation to the preceding period.

3. Informative disclosures in the financial statements are to be regarded as reasonably adequate unless otherwise stated in the report.

4. The report shall either contain an expression of opinion regarding the financial statements, taken as a whole, or an assertion to the effect that an opinion cannot be expressed. When an overall opinion cannot be expressed, the reasons therefor should be stated. In all cases where an auditor's name is associated with financial statements, the report should contain a clear-cut indication of the character of the auditor's work, if any, and the degree of responsibility the auditor is taking.

(a) General Standards

The general standards relate to the qualifications of an auditor and the quality of the audit work. They are personal in nature and are distinct from the standards governing the performance of field work and reporting.

(i) Training and Proficiency.   The first general standard suggests that the auditor must have proper education and experience in the field of auditing to meet the profession's requirements for adequate training and proficiency. Training begins with formal education and continues with proper supervision and review on the job, as well as formal continuing professional education and self-study. Formal continuing education and self-study are necessary parts of this standard, especially as new developments in accounting, auditing, finance, data processing, taxes, and other aspects of business management continue to force change on practitioners. The need for formal continuing education and self-study, however, does not diminish the importance of on-the-job training, planned development of well-rounded experience, and adequate supervision and review in maintaining proficiency.

(ii) Independence.   The second general standard requires that the auditor not be biased toward the client. Furthermore, to safeguard the confidence of the public and users of financial statements in auditor independence, auditors must also be recognized as independent. SAS No. 1 (AU Section 220.03) provides the following amplification of this:

> To *be* independent, the auditor must be intellectually honest; to be *recognized* as independent, he must be free from any obligation to or interest in the client, its management, or its owners. For example, an independent auditor auditing a company of which he was also a director might be intellectually honest, but it is unlikely that the public would accept him as independent since he would be in effect auditing decisions which he had a part in making. Likewise, an auditor with a substantial financial interest in a company might be unbiased in expressing his opinion on the financial statements of the company, but the public would be reluctant to believe that he was unbiased. Independent auditors should not only be independent in fact; they should avoid situations that may lead outsiders to doubt their independence.

The distinction drawn in this quotation is often referred to as that of "independence in fact" contrasted with "independence in appearance." The former— intellectual honesty—cannot be ensured by rules or prohibitions. The latter—avoiding potentially compromising situations—can be, at least partially. To guard against any appearance or presumption of loss of independence, the AICPA has established specific rules on independence in its Code of Professional Conduct, as discussed in the next section of this chapter. Likewise, the SEC has emphasized the importance of independence and has issued rules relating to it.

(iii) Due Professional Care.   SAS No. 1 (AU Section 230.04) notes that due professional care relates to what independent auditors do and how well they do it. Due professional care imposes a responsibility on each person in an auditing firm to exercise the skills he or she possesses with reasonable care and diligence; due professional care also requires appropriate supervision and critical review of the work done and of the judgments made. For example, due professional care is not exercised if the auditor fails to corroborate representations of entity management that are significant to the financial statements, such as representations regarding the collectibility of long-outstanding accounts receivable.

Due professional care also entails the exercise of professional skepticism, especially when obtaining and evaluating evidence, including management's answers to audit inquiries. An auditor should neither assume that management is dishonest nor assume unquestioned honesty. Professional skepticism includes a questioning mind and a critical assessment of audit evidence. For example, the auditor may detect conditions or circumstances that indicate that a material misstatement could exist. Typically, these are conditions or circumstances that differ from the auditor's expectations; for example, errors are detected in an audit test that apparently were known to management but were not voluntarily disclosed to the auditor. Professional skepticism requires that when such indications appear, the auditor should reconsider the audit plan in order to obtain sufficient competent evidence that the financial statements are free of material misstatements.

(b) Standards of Field Work

The standards of field work cover planning and supervising the audit, understanding internal control, and obtaining audit evidence.

(i) Adequate Planning and Supervision.

Planning an audit engagement involves both technical and administrative considerations. The technical aspect of planning entails formulating an overall audit strategy for the engagement. Implementing the audit strategy includes numerous planning decisions of an administrative nature, such as scheduling the work, assigning personnel, and similar matters.

Early appointment of the auditor facilitates audit planning. In particular, it makes it possible to consider performing certain auditing procedures during the year rather than at year-end. This increases both audit efficiency and the likelihood of identifying problems at an early date. In the planning stage, analytical procedures are performed to help determine the nature, timing, and extent of other auditing procedures by identifying significant matters the auditor should address.

SAS No. 22, *Planning and Supervision* (AU Section 311.11), states that supervision involves directing the work of assistants and determining whether the objectives of that work were accomplished. On many engagements, as much as one-quarter of the total audit time is spent on supervision. The time is well spent, because the total audit time is likely to be much greater without effective supervision.

Supervision starts with assigning tasks and ensuring that each task and its objectives are understood. It continues with frequent discussions between supervisor and assistants for the purpose of both keeping informed, especially about significant problems encountered, and providing ongoing advice and direction to assistants. That means discussions among the partner, manager, and staff members on an engagement; on large audits, personal visits to many different groups and locations may be required. Supervision also entails dealing with differences of opinion among staff members concerning accounting and auditing issues. A final element of supervision is reviewing the completed work of assistants, discussing the review with them, and evaluating their performance.

(ii) Understanding Internal Control.

The importance of the second standard of field work has increased as the role of an entity's internal control in preventing and detecting fraud and error has received widespread recognition, as highly reliable computerized accounting systems have become available and widely used, and as auditors have become increasingly concerned with conducting efficient as well as effective audits. This standard requires the auditor to obtain a sufficient understanding of the entity's internal control to adequately plan the tests of transactions and account balances to be performed; the standard does not require that all controls, or even any of them, be tested *unless* the auditor plans to use the knowledge obtained from such tests to restrict the testing of transactions and account balances. Subsequent chapters discuss the components of internal control, how the auditor assesses it, and how that assessment affects the tests the auditor applies to account balances and underlying transactions.

(iii) Obtaining Competent Evidence. A detailed understanding of the third standard of field work is important to all phases of auditing. The standard covers both the competence and the sufficiency of evidence. The competence of evidence relates to its relevance and reliability; sufficiency depends on the amount of assurance the auditor believes is needed to support an opinion that the financial statements are not materially misstated.

(c) Standards of Reporting

Four standards of reporting govern this aspect of the audit effort.

(i) Adherence to Generally Accepted Accounting Principles. The auditor is required first to be thoroughly familiar with generally accepted accounting principles, and second to determine whether the financial statements reported on "present fairly" the entity's financial position, results of operations, and cash flows in conformity with those principles. Chapter 28, "Reporting on Audited Financial Statements," deals in depth with the auditor's reporting responsibilities relating to generally accepted accounting principles (GAAP) and fairness, and presents examples of appropriate auditors' reports in cases of departures from GAAP.

(ii) Consistency. The consistency standard requires the auditor to identify in the auditor's report circumstances in which GAAP have not been applied consistently from period to period. The objective is to ensure either that changes in accounting principles and methods of applying them do not materially affect the comparability of financial statements between periods or that the effect is disclosed.

(iii) Adequate Disclosure. The intent of the third standard of reporting is that issuers of financial statements and auditors have a responsibility to ensure that disclosures are adequate, regardless of whether a specific authoritative pronouncement covers the matter. It is thus the auditor's responsibility to identify matters of potential interest to users of the financial statements and to form a conclusion about whether and how they should be disclosed. If management does not make the necessary disclosures, the auditor should qualify his or her opinion on the financial statements.

(iv) Expression of Opinion. An auditor's report must be painstakingly precise in spelling out the opinion expressed. Leaving the meaning of an auditor's opinion open to readers' inferences is both inappropriate and dangerous. From the time of its adoption, the fourth standard of reporting has been accompanied by detailed recommendations for reporting in all conceivable circumstances. The intention of those detailed prescriptions is to ensure that all auditors use precisely the same words in the same circumstances to prevent misinterpretation of their opinions and the responsibility they assume.

3.3 AICPA CODE OF PROFESSIONAL CONDUCT

The Code of Professional Conduct of the American Institute of Certified Public Accountants covers both the profession's responsibility to the public and the CPA's responsibility to clients and colleagues. While the AICPA Code is directly enforceable only against individual members, in reality its applicability is much more pervasive. Most of the significant portions of the Code have been adopted by the various state societies or institutes of CPAs and in many cases also have been incorporated into state statutes or the regulations of state boards of accountancy that license CPAs to practice before the public. In effect, all of these organizations enforce ethical behavior by CPAs.

Codes of ethical conduct are not unique to the practice of accounting. All professionals, including doctors, lawyers, and actuaries, to name a few, have deemed it essential to promulgate codes of professional conduct and to establish means for ensuring their observance. Such codes define the type of behavior that the public has a right to expect from the professionals, and thereby enhance the public's confidence in the quality of professional services rendered.

Most codes of professional conduct, including the AICPA's, contain general ethical principles that are aspirational in character and represent the objectives toward which every member of the profession should strive. Usually, the codes also contain a set of specific, mandatory rules that state the minimum level of conduct the professional must maintain to avoid being subject to disciplinary action. In the past, some sections of many codes of conduct also had an ancillary effect of reducing competition, through prohibitions against advertising, solicitation of clients, and encroachment on the practice of a fellow professional. The courts have deemed such prohibitions to be illegal, however, and most professional associations, including the AICPA, have revised their codes to permit advertising and other forms of solicitation, so long as the professional does not seek to obtain clients by false, misleading, or deceptive advertising or other forms of solicitation.

The AICPA's ethical standards fall into four categories: Principles, Rules, Interpretations of the Rules, and Ethics Rulings. The Principles and Rules comprise the Code of Professional Conduct, the latest version of which was adopted by vote of the AICPA membership in 1988. The Principles express the basic tenets of ethical and professional conduct. The Rules consist of enforceable ethical standards to which AICPA members must adhere: Members must be prepared to justify departures from the Rules. Interpretations of the Rules have been adopted by the AICPA to provide guidelines on the scope and application of the Rules. Ethics Rulings summarize the application of the Rules and Interpretations to a particular set of factual circumstances. The Code as a whole is intended to provide guidance and rules for all AICPA members in the performance of their professional responsibilities, regardless of whether the members are in the public practice of accountancy, in industry, in government, or in academe. Some of the Rules, however, are specifically relevant and stated to be applicable only to CPAs in public practice.

The Preamble to the Principles of Professional Conduct emphasizes the professional's responsibility to the public, clients, and colleagues. The Principles of the Code of Professional Conduct are goal-oriented, describing general ideals accountants should aspire to, while the Rules set forth minimum levels of acceptable conduct. The high level of conduct for which CPAs should strive is embodied in the more philosophical Principles, which "call for an unswerving commitment to honorable behavior, even at the sacrifice of personal advantage."

The Principles of the Code are as follows:

Responsibilities. In carrying out their responsibilities as professionals, members should exercise sensitive professional and moral judgments in all their activities.

The Public Interest. Members should accept the obligation to act in a way that will serve the public interest, honor the public trust, and demonstrate commitment to professionalism.

Integrity. To maintain and broaden public confidence, members should perform all professional responsibilities with the highest sense of integrity.

Objectivity and Independence. A member should maintain objectivity and be free of conflicts of interest in discharging professional responsibilities. A member in public practice should be independent in fact and appearance when providing auditing and other attestation services.

Due Care. A member should observe the profession's technical and ethical standards, strive continually to improve competence and the quality of services, and discharge professional responsibility to the best of the member's ability.

Scope and Nature of Services. A member in public practice should observe the Principles of the Code of Professional Conduct in determining the scope and nature of services to be provided.

A discussion of each of the Rules, along with the related Interpretations and Rulings, follows.

(a) Independence, Integrity, and Objectivity

According to the Principles of the Code of Professional Conduct,

Integrity is an element of character fundamental to professional recognition. It is the quality from which the public trust derives and the benchmark against which a member must ultimately test all decisions.

Integrity also requires a member to observe the principles of objectivity and independence and of due care.

Objectivity is a state of mind, a quality that lends value to a member's services. It is a distinguishing feature of the profession. The principle of objectivity imposes the obligation to be impartial, intellectually honest, and free of conflicts of interest. Independence precludes relationships that may appear to impair a member's objectivity in rendering attestation services.

The importance of independence is indicated by the prevalence of the subject in the profession's authoritative literature. It is found not only in the Principles of the Code of Professional Conduct and Rule 101, but also in the corresponding rules of professional conduct of the various state societies and state regulatory agencies; in SAS No. 1 (AU Section 220) (discussed in an earlier section of this chapter); in Statement on Quality Control Standards No. 2, *System of Quality Control for a CPA Firm's Accounting and Auditing Practice* (QC Section 20); and in Rule 2-01 of SEC Regulation S-X. Independence enhances the auditor's ability to act with integrity and objectivity.

A further indication of the importance that the accounting profession accords independence is the formation in 1997 of the Independence Standards Board (ISB) to establish independence standards for audits of public entities. The ISB will operate within the AICPA and will be under the oversight of the SEC. At its inception, the ISB adopted the current guidance of the SEC relating to independence as its standards for those audits. To achieve its objectives, the ISB plans, among other things, to:

1. Develop a conceptual framework for independence
2. Promulgate standards and interpretations on matters involving auditor objectivity and independence
3. Develop a process for the consideration of emerging issues affecting independence

Rule 101 (Independence) states, "A member in public practice shall be independent in the performance of professional services as required by standards promulgated by bodies designated by Council." The services consist essentially of auditing and attestation services. The specific services that require independence are discussed below. Auditors, like practitioners in other professions, offer clients specialized technical skills and knowledge based on training and experience, but that is not all. Clients and others rely on auditors because of their belief in the auditors' professional integrity, independence, and objectivity. Clearly, the published opinion of an auditor has little value unless it rests unquestionably on those qualities. They are personal, inward qualities not susceptible to precise determination or definition, and are best maintained by the individual auditor's own conscience and the recognition that a professional's principal asset is a reputation for integrity, independence, and objectivity. It is also important to the public's confidence in an auditor's opinion that the auditor's respect for those qualities be as apparent as possible.

The Code of Professional Conduct, like SAS No. 1, emphasizes *appearing* to be independent as well as *being* independent. Both the accounting profession and the SEC have spelled out detailed prohibitions against those activities or relationships that might suggest or imply a possibility of lack of independence.

Interpretation 101–1 (ET Section 101.02) provides examples of situations that impair independence.

Interpretation of Rule 101. Independence shall be considered to be impaired if, for example, a member had any of the following transactions, interests, or relationships:

A. During the period of a professional engagement or at the time of expressing an opinion, a member or a member's firm

    1. Had or was committed to acquire any direct or material indirect financial interest in the enterprise.
    2. Was a trustee of any trust or executor or administrator of any estate if such trust or estate had or was committed to acquire any direct or material indirect financial interest in the enterprise.
    3. Had any joint, closely held business investment with the enterprise or with any officer, director, or principal stockholders thereof that was material in relation to the member's net worth or to the net worth of the member's firm.
    4. Had any loan to or from the enterprise or any officer, director, or principal stockholder of the enterprise except as specifically permitted in Interpretation 101–5.

B. During the period covered by the financial statements, during the period of the professional engagement, or at the time of expressing an opinion, a member or a member's firm

1. Was connected with the enterprise as a promoter, underwriter or voting trustee, as a director or officer, or in any capacity equivalent to that of a member of management or of an employee.
2. Was a trustee for any pension or profit-sharing trust of the enterprise.

The above examples are not intended to be all-inclusive.

Regulation S-X, Rule 2–01, "Qualifications of Accountants," specifies the SEC's independence requirements.

The Commission will not recognize any certified public accountant or public accountant as independent who is not in fact independent. For example, an accountant will be considered not independent with respect to any person or any of its parents, its subsidiaries, or other affiliates (1) in which, during the period of his professional engagement to examine the financial statements being reported on or at the date of his report, he, his firm, or a member of his firm had, or was committed to acquire, any direct financial interest or any material indirect financial interest; (2) with which, during the period of his professional engagement to examine the financial statements being reported on, at the date of his report or during the period covered by the financial statements, he, his firm, or a member of his firm was connected as a promoter, underwriter, voting trustee, director, officer, or employee. A firm's independence will not be deemed to be affected adversely where a former officer or employee of a particular person is employed by or becomes a partner, shareholder or other principal in the firm and such individual has completely disassociated himself from the person and its affiliates and does not participate in auditing financial statements of the person or its affiliates covering any period of his employment by the person. For the purposes of Rule 2–01 the term "member" means (i) all partners, shareholders, and other principals in the firm, (ii) any professional employee involved in providing any professional service to the person, its parents, subsidiaries, or other affiliates, and (iii) any professional employee having managerial responsibilities and located in the engagement office or other office of the firm which participates in a significant portion of the audit.

In determining whether an accountant may in fact be not independent with respect to a particular person, the Commission will give appropriate consideration to all relevant circumstances, including evidence bearing on all relationships between the accountant and that person or any affiliate thereof, and will not confine itself to the relationships existing in connection with the filing of reports with the Commission.

Many of the foregoing prohibitions reach extremes that might appear ridiculous to a nonprofessional, but they reflect the profession's concern about the appearance of independence. For example, no partner in an auditing firm or member of the partner's immediate family is permitted to own even one share of stock of a client or affiliated company or even to participate in an investment club that holds such shares, no matter what the individual's personal net worth, the size of the company, or the partner's distance from the actual audit work. As another example, an auditing firm may not have its employees' pension fund managed by an investment counselor that also manages a mutual fund client; even though there is no actual financial relationship, there might be an appearance of lack of independence. In addition, other Interpretations and Ethics Rulings under Rule 101 outline specific prohibitions in this area.

The AICPA's and SEC's prohibitions relating to independence are not entirely free of social costs. Weighing the costs and benefits of prohibitions on individual or firm conduct in order to enhance independence is a matter of public policy and social choice. The current independence rules indicate the importance that both the profession and the public attach to the auditor's independence, integrity, and objectivity.

(i) Accounting Services. Interpretation 101–3 (ET Section 101.05) permits members to provide bookkeeping or data processing services to clients only if the following requirements are met:

- The client's management must accept responsibility for the financial statements.
- The CPA must not assume the role of an employee or management of the client.
- The CPA must comply with applicable standards for audits, reviews, or compilations, i.e., must perform appropriate procedures regarding financial statements prepared from records that the CPA has maintained or processed.

The SEC has noted that an accountant's maintaining the records of an SEC registrant either manually or through automated means may be indicative of a lack of independence. (Many of the SEC's independence requirements extend to the entire period covered by the financial statements, which generally cover three years of operations and cash flows.)

(ii) Loans from Clients. As noted earlier, Interpretation 101–1 prohibits CPAs from having a loan to or from a client, with certain exceptions. Interpretation 101–5 (ET Section 101.07) specifies the types of loans from a financial institution client that would not be considered to impair the CPA's independence, as follows: (1) automobile loans and leases collateralized by the automobile, (2) loans of the surrender value under terms of an insurance policy, (3) borrowings fully collateralized by cash deposits at the same financial institution (e.g., "passbook loans"), and (4) credit cards and cash advances on checking accounts with an aggregate balance not paid currently of $5,000 or less. Also permitted are home mortgages, other secured loans (for which the value of the collateral must at all times exceed the balance of the loan), and loans not material to the CPA's net worth that (a) existed as of January 1, 1992, (b) were obtained before the lending financial institution became a client requiring independence, (c) were obtained from a financial institution for which independence was not required and were later sold to a client for which independence is required, or (d) were obtained from a firm's financial institution client requiring independence by a borrower before he or she became a member with respect to such client. Permitted loans must be kept current as to all terms and must have been obtained under the financial institution's normal lending procedures, terms, and requirements.

(iii) Family Relationships. Interpretation 101–9 (ET Section 101.11) addresses two categories of family relationships that may affect the independence of members. The first category comprises a member's spouse, dependent children, and any other dependent person living in the same household as or supported by the member. With the exception of employment meeting criteria specified in the Interpretation, the financial interests and business relationships of such individuals are ascribed to the member and thus are governed by Rule 101. The second category is nondependent close relatives, defined as nondependent children, brothers and sisters, grandparents, parents, parents-in-law, and the spouses of any of those individuals. Relatives in this category are not permitted to have a material financial interest or investment in or business relationship with a client of a member, nor may they hold a position with a client in which they can exercise significant influence over its operating, financial, or accounting policies.

(iv) Independence and Attest and Agreed-Upon Procedures Engagements. Statement on Standards for Attestation Engagements (SSAE), *Attestation Standards* (AT Section 100.22–.24), requires members to be independent in performing engagements covered by that Statement (and by extension, subsequently issued SSAEs), and AU Section 220 requires independence on the part of those performing engagements under the Statements on Auditing Standards. Interpretation 101–1, quoted earlier, provides guidance on the types of transactions, interests, and relationships that might impair a CPA's independence when he or she provides services covered by the above professional standards. Until recently, those services generally resulted in reports whose use was not restricted. Interpretation 101–11 (ET Section 101.13) provides guidance regarding independence for attestation engagements and for engagements under SAS No. 75, *Engagements to Apply Agreed-Upon Procedures to Specified Elements, Accounts, or Items of a Financial Statement* (AU Section 622), when the reports issued state that their use is restricted to identified parties and the CPA reasonably expects that the reports will be so restricted.

The Interpretation specifies the relationships between a CPA and the party responsible for an assertion in an attest engagement or for a specified element, account, or item of a financial statement that is the subject matter of an engagement under SAS No. 75 (defined as the responsible party) that would impair the CPA's independence. The prohibited relationships apply only to the engagement team (which is defined in the Interpretation) and their families, to partners or proprietors (and their families) located in an office performing a significant part of the engagement, and to certain individuals whose relationships with the subject matter or responsible party are known to members of the engagement team. In contrast, prohibited relationships in audit engagements apply to all members of the engagement team, all partners or proprietors in the accounting firm, and all managerial employees in an office that participates in a significant portion of the engagement. A major reason for the difference is that many attest and agreed-upon procedures engagements result in client relationships that are only temporary, rather than ongoing, as is usually the case, for example, with audit engagements.

(v) Extended Audit Services. Interpretation 101–13 (ET Section 101.15) establishes that the performance of extended audit services, such as assisting in the client's internal audit activities and performing audit services that go beyond the requirements of GAAS, does not impair independence, provided the CPA does not act or appear to act in the capacity of the client's management or employees. The Interpretation presents examples of activities that would be considered to impair independence because they constituted management functions or decision making. Among those activities are performing ongoing monitoring or control activities as part of the entity's internal control, and reporting to the board of directors or audit committee on behalf of the director of internal audit.

(vi) Past-Due Fees.   Ethics Ruling No. 52 (ET Section 191.103–.104) addresses the effect of past-due fees on the independence of a member's firm. The Ruling states that independence may be impaired if, when the current-year audit report is issued, billed or unbilled fees for professional services provided more than one year prior to the date of the report remain unpaid. The Ruling states that such unpaid fees assume the characteristics of a prohibited loan. (The SEC's rules in this regard are more restrictive than those of the AICPA.)

(vii) Conflicts of Interest.   Rule 101 on independence is applicable only to members in public practice. That Rule (and the Interpretations under it) are intended, according to the Principles of the Code of Professional Conduct, to preclude "relationships that may appear to impair a member's objectivity in rendering attestation services." Rule 102 is intended to prohibit members, whether or not in public practice, from subordinating their judgment to others when performing *any* professional service.

Rule 102 (Integrity and Objectivity) states

> In the performance of any professional service, a member shall maintain objectivity and integrity, shall be free of conflicts of interest, and shall not knowingly misrepresent facts or subordinate his or her judgment to others.

Interpretation 102–2 (ET Section 102.03) addresses conflicts of interest. This Interpretation states

> A conflict of interest may occur if a member performs a professional service for a client or employer and the member or his or her firm has a relationship with another person, entity, product, or service that could, in the member's professional judgment, be viewed by the client, employer, or other appropriate parties as impairing the member's objectivity. If the member believes that the professional service can be performed with objectivity, and the relationship is disclosed to and consent is obtained from such client, employer, or other appropriate parties, the rule shall not operate to prohibit the performance of the professional service. When making the disclosure, the member should consider Rule 301, *Confidential Client Information*.

> Certain professional engagements, such as audits, reviews, and other attest services, require independence. Independence impairments under rule 101, its interpretations, and rulings cannot be eliminated by such disclosure and consent.

(viii) Members Other than in Public Practice.   Interpretations 102–3 through 102–6 clarify that the requirements of Rule 102 regarding integrity and objectivity apply to all AICPA members performing professional services. Interpretation 102–3 concerns a member's obligations to an employer's external accountant; Interpretation 102–4 deals with circumstances where a member has a disagreement with a supervisor regarding the preparation of financial statements or the recording of transactions. In the latter instance, the member is required to take certain steps to ensure that the situation does not constitute a subordination of judgment, which is prohibited by Rule 102. Interpretation 102–5 establishes that Rule 102 applies to members performing educational services, and Interpretation 102–6 that the Rule applies to the performance of professional services involving client advocacy, such as tax or consulting services and supporting a client's position on an accounting issue before a regulatory agency.

(b) General and Technical Standards

The Rules require adherence to standards related to the conduct of the CPA's work.

(i) General Standards.   Rule 201 sets forth the following general standards:

A member shall comply with the following standards and with any interpretations thereof by bodies designated by Council.

A. *Professional Competence*. Undertake only those professional services that the member or the member's firm can reasonably expect to be completed with professional competence.

B. *Due Professional Care*. Exercise due professional care in the performance of professional services.

C. *Planning and Supervision*. Adequately plan and supervise the performance of professional services.

D. *Sufficient Relevant Data*. Obtain sufficient relevant data to afford a reasonable basis for conclusions or recommendations in relation to any professional services performed.

(ii) Technical Standards.   Rules 202 and 203 are as follows:

Compliance with standards. A member who performs auditing, review, compilation, management consulting, tax, or other professional services shall comply with standards promulgated by bodies designated by Council.

Accounting principles. A member shall not (1) express an opinion or state affirmatively that the financial statements or other financial data of any entity are presented in conformity with generally accepted accounting principles or (2) state that he or she is not aware of any material modifications that should be made to such statements or data in order for them to be in conformity with generally accepted accounting principles, if such statements or data contain any departure from an accounting principle promulgated by bodies designated by Council to establish such principles that has a material effect on the statements or data taken as a whole. If, however, the statements or data contain such a departure and the member can demonstrate that due to unusual circumstances the financial statements or data would otherwise have been misleading, the member can comply with the rule by describing the departure, its approximate effects, if practicable, and the reasons why compliance with the principle would result in a misleading statement.

Rules 202 and 203 were adopted to require compliance with the profession's practice standards and accounting principles. There is a strong presumption that adherence to accounting principles promulgated by the FASB and the Governmental Accounting Standards Board (GASB) will result in financial statements that are not misleading.

Rule 203 and Interpretation 203–1 also recognize that occasionally there may be unusual circumstances in which the literal application of pronouncements on accounting principles would have the effect of rendering financial statements misleading. In such unusual cases, the proper accounting treatment is one that will render the financial statements not misleading. Chapter 28 discusses the appropriate wording of the auditor's report in these circumstances.

Interpretation 203–4 emphasizes a member's responsibility for the preparation of financial statements in conformity with GAAP. It states that Rule 203 applies to all members and to all affirmative statements that financial statements or other financial data is presented in conformity with GAAP.

(c) Responsibilities to Clients

The Principles of the Code of Professional Conduct note that a CPA has responsibilities to clients as well as to the public. CPAs should serve their clients with competence and with regard for the clients' interests. They also must, however, maintain their obligation to the public as evidenced by their independence, integrity, and objectivity.

A fundamental responsibility of the CPA concerns the confidentiality of client information. Rule 301 states that "a member in public practice shall not disclose any confidential client information without the specific consent of the client." Members may, however, disclose certain information to the AICPA ethics division and state boards, or in connection with a practice-monitoring program, and may file complaints with state societies or boards of accountancy without violating client confidentiality, even if the complaint necessitates disclosing confidential client information without the specific consent of the client. CPAs may not, however, volunteer confidential client information to government agencies.

Interpretation 301–3 (ET Section 301.04) clarifies that Rule 301 does not prohibit the review of a CPA's professional practice in conjunction with a prospective purchase, sale, or merger. The Interpretation states that the CPA must take precautions to prevent the disclosure of any client information obtained by the reviewer, since such information is considered to be confidential.

On a related matter, several state licensing authorities have concluded that a peer review of an accounting firm, in which engagement documentation is reviewed by another accounting firm, violates client confidentiality. In response, some accounting firms are asking clients for advance notification of objections to a review of their information by another firm; the request is sometimes made in the engagement letter.

(i) Need for Confidentiality.   Both common sense and the independence concept dictate that the auditor, not the client, should decide what information the auditor needs to conduct an effective audit. That decision should not be influenced by a client's belief that certain information is confidential. An efficient and effective audit requires that the client have the necessary trust in the auditor to be extremely candid in supplying information. Therefore, the client must be assured of confidentiality and that, except for disclosures required by generally accepted accounting principles, information shared with the auditor will go no further without explicit permission.

Despite the profession's emphasis on confidentiality, executives of some entities are concerned about losing control of sensitive material through an auditor's staff. They may believe that certain material is so sensitive that they cannot be comfortable with an auditor's general assurances about the character and training of the audit staff. If access to the material is necessary to the auditor's opinion, the client's executives have no alternative but to grant access; if they wish to limit that access to specified individuals on the audit team, that condition should be respected. Although awareness of clients' sensibilities is important, the authors have observed that clients' fears generally tend to subside as the working relationship is strengthened, confidence grows, and mutually satisfactory arrangements are made.

(ii) Confidentiality versus Privilege.   Except as noted earlier, communications between the client and the auditor are confidential; that is, the auditor should not reveal the information contained in the communication without the client's permission. Under common law, however, that information is not privileged. Information is privileged if the client can prevent a court or government agency from gaining access to it through a summons or subpoena. Information given to an auditor by a client is often not privileged; it is subject to summons or subpoena in many jurisdictions, including the federal courts. (In those states where an auditor–client privilege does exist, it can be waived only by the client. While it exists for the client's benefit, it also serves to enhance full and honest disclosure between client and auditor.) Auditors and their professional organizations generally support clients' legal resistance to summonses and subpoenas to produce documents or other communications given to or received from their auditors, when it appears that there are legitimate reasons for maintaining confidentiality.

One particularly sensitive area involves the auditor's review of the client's analysis of the provision for income taxes. As a result of Internal Revenue Service subpoenas of auditors' tax provision working papers, and several lawsuits resulting from CPA firms' refusal to comply, many clients are reluctant to provide the auditor with such tax analyses. Regardless of a client's fears, however, the auditor must review sufficient evidential matter to conclude that the tax provision is adequate. Fortunately for the public as well as for the profession, the courts have placed significant limitations on the extent to which these working papers may be subpoenaed.

(iii) Insider Information.   Auditors and their staff have the same responsibilities as management for handling insider information: not to turn it to personal profit or to disclose it to others who may do so. Those responsibilities are clearly covered by the general injunctions of the Code of Professional Conduct: Independence forbids personal profit, and confidentiality forbids aiding others in that pursuit. The ways in which insider information may be used, even inadvertently, are many and subtle; society's heightened standards of accountability have focused attention on the responsibility of all insiders and others with access to inside information to use such information only for the benefit of the entity.

(iv) Problems Involving Confidentiality.   Some clients' fears that secrets will be passed on to competitors are so great that they refuse to engage an auditor whose clients include a competitor; others are satisfied with assurances that the staff on their engagement has no contact with a competitor's personnel. The price paid by a client for so high a degree of confidentiality is the loss of industry expertise that can be provided by auditors who are familiar with more than one company in an industry. Experience suggests that the risk of leakage of information that has competitive value is extremely slight.

A more difficult and quite common dilemma results if two of an auditor's clients do business with each other. For example, an auditor of a commercial bank is likely also to have clients among the bank's depositors and borrowers. Suppose the auditor observes the September 30 physical inventory of a company that is also a borrower at the client bank, and finds a substantial shortage. Under the terms of the company's loan agreement with the bank, audited financial statements are not due at the bank until the next March 31. The client understandably wants time to determine the cause of the shortage. What does the auditor do? This is a practical dilemma quite apart from problems of potential formal legal liability or expression of an opinion on either set of financial statements. On the one hand, the auditor must not use insider information from one client to profit by improving his or her relationship with the other client. On the other hand, it is absurd for the auditor to pretend not to know something that he or she does know. One party will be unhappy if the auditor does nothing; the other party will be upset if the auditor does anything.

Without the client's permission, the auditor cannot disclose confidential information obtained in the course of one engagement to another client. However, the auditor cannot issue a report if he or she has learned information from any source that indicates that the financial statements are not fairly stated in all material respects. Continuing with the example above, the first step is to attempt to obtain the permission of the client borrower to disclose the problem to the client bank. If that fails, it may be possible for the auditor to perform additional auditing procedures that will uncover the problem at the client bank. Without disclosing any confidential information to any party, the auditor may "uncover" the issue at the client bank and ensure that its financial statements are fairly stated before the report is issued.

Before information is publicly disclosed, however, the auditor needs to obtain and document all available pertinent facts, discuss them with the client, and evaluate their effect on the financial statements. All of this takes time, but the resulting delay in making the disclosure is justified: Disclosing information prematurely or inappropriately, that is, before it has been adequately investigated, may create more problems than it solves.

If the client's management refuses to disclose information that the auditor has concluded should be disclosed, the auditor must decide whether it is possible to continue to serve the client. The auditor may want to seek legal counsel in this situation. Usually the auditor will consider going to the board of directors, and in some cases to the SEC and the stock exchanges. Those are very serious steps, and whether to take them is as difficult a decision as an auditor can ever be called on to make. The auditor would risk even more serious problems, however, by favoring a client over other concerned parties. The courts have made clear, as indicated by the *Fund of Funds*[2] case, that an auditor who has reason to believe, from whatever source, that a client's financial statements are materially misstated cannot issue an unqualified opinion.

Another problem of confidentiality may result if a client that is considering acquiring another company engages its own auditor to audit that company. What happens to the auditor's findings and to whom is the duty of confidentiality owed? Common practice in those circumstances is to obtain written confirmations from the chief executives of both entities regarding the extent and limitations of the auditor's responsibilities to each. The confirmation letter to the company to be acquired often includes a statement that the auditor has no responsibility to that company other than the obvious requirement to act in a professional manner. Usually the confirmations

---

[2] *Fund of Funds, Ltd.* v. *Arthur Andersen & Co.*, 545 F. Supp. 1314 (S.D.N.Y. 1982).

approve delivering the findings to the acquiring company, but only after discussing them with the company to be acquired.

Auditors, for their part, are concerned about the confidentiality of their working papers and are reluctant to allow other parties access to them. Most auditors do grant such access to certain parties who request it for legitimate purposes, such as current or former clients who ask the auditor to make working papers available to a third party in connection with a potential transaction with lenders, buyers, or investors. In the latter situation, the auditor generally meets with the client to discuss the circumstances and provide the client the opportunity to review the working papers first, and requires written authorization from the client allowing the third party access and a letter of understanding from the third party. Some auditors specifically withhold from third parties working papers related to time and billing data and client continuance review documentation. Secondary auditors grant access to their working papers to a principal auditor who takes responsibility for the work of the secondary auditors and asks for access to relevant working papers; predecessor auditors allow a successor auditor access to their working papers. Finally, regulators may request access to working papers relating to an audit conducted under the *Government Auditing Standards* or a law, regulation, or contract that requires such access. Auditors are obligated to accede to those requests, but the auditor should seek the advice of legal counsel if a regulator requests access to particular working papers that does not seem relevant to the purpose of the investigation.

(d) Responsibilities to Colleagues

While there are currently no specific Rules governing a CPA's responsibility to colleagues, the Principles set forth the fundamental tenet of cooperation among members of the profession by stating that AICPA members should "cooperate with each other to improve the art of accounting, maintain the public's confidence, and carry out the profession's special responsibilities for self-governance."

(e) Other Responsibilities and Practices

(i) Acts Discreditable to the Profession. Rule 501 states: "A member shall not commit an act discreditable to the profession." Interpretations under Rule 501 (ET Section 501.01–.07) provide examples of specific acts that would be discreditable to the profession.

1. Retention of client records after a demand is made for them
2. Discrimination, including sexual and other forms of harassment, based on race, color, religion, sex, age, or national origin in hiring, promotion, or salary practices
3. Failure to follow governmental audit standards, guides, procedures, statutes, rules, and regulations (in addition to generally accepted auditing standards) that may be specified in an audit of government grants, government units, or other recipients of government monies if an engagement has been accepted under those conditions
4. Negligence in the preparation of financial statements or records (thus explicitly including CPAs who are not in public practice and who serve as preparers rather

than auditors of financial statements)

5. Failure to follow requirements (e.g., established standards, guides, rules, and regulations) of governmental or regulatory agencies in performing attest or similar services

6. Soliciting or disclosing CPA examination questions and answers

(ii) Form of Organization and Name.   Since 1991, CPAs have been allowed to practice public accounting in any organizational form permitted by state law or regulation, including a general corporation. Previously, Rule 505 restricted the form of practice to a proprietorship, partnership, or professional corporation. A major reason underlying the change was a belief that the previous rule restricted CPAs in limiting their individual liability exposure and their flexibility in responding to a dynamic business environment. Rule 505 now reads as follows:

> A member may practice public accounting only in a form of organization permitted by state law or regulation whose characteristics conform to resolutions of Council.

> A member shall not practice public accounting under a firm name that is misleading. Names of one or more past owners may be included in the firm name of a successor organization. Also, an owner surviving the death or withdrawal of all other owners may continue to practice under a name which includes the name of past owners for up to two years after becoming a sole practitioner.

> A firm may not designate itself as "Members of the American Institute of Certified Public Accountants" unless all of its owners are members of the Institute.

Appendix B to the Code contains a resolution of AICPA Council that specifies the characteristics that a firm or an organization must have to comply with Rule 505.[3] That resolution requires that a majority of the ownership of the firm must consist of CPAs; non-CPA owners must be actively engaged as firm members in providing services to the firm's clients as their principal occupation. A CPA must have ultimate responsibility for services provided by the firm. Non-CPA owners may not have final responsibility for attest or compilation engagements, may not hold themselves out as CPAs, must abide by the Code of Professional Conduct, and are subject to the same education and CPE requirements as AICPA members, but are not eligible for AICPA membership. State accountancy statutes and regulations of state boards of accountancy differ from state to state on these matters, and each state board must deal individually with specific issues as they arise.

---

[3] The characteristics specified in the resolution apply to a firm or an organization that performs (1) audits or other engagements in accordance with the Statements on Auditing Standards, (2) reviews or compilations of financial statements in accordance with the Statements on Standards for Accounting and Review Services, and (3) examinations of prospective financial information in accordance with the Statements on Standards for Attestation Engagements, or that holds itself out as a firm of certified public accountants or uses the term certified public accountant(s) or the designation CPA in connection with its name. The characteristics of all other firms or organizations may be whatever is legally permissible under applicable law or regulation.

(f) Marketing Professional Services

The marketing of professional services is addressed in three Rules. Rule 302 prohibits the performance of services for certain attest clients, and the preparation of tax returns (generally including amended returns) for any client, on a contingent fee basis; Rule 503 restricts the payment of commissions to or receipt of commissions from a client when the CPA also performs certain attest services for that client, and also requires disclosure of the acceptance or payment of referral fees and of permitted commissions; and Rule 502 sets restraints on advertising and solicitation. These Rules reflect the provisions of a final order issued by the Federal Trade Commission (FTC) in 1990, pursuant to an 1989 consent agreement with the AICPA.

Under the consent agreement, the AICPA agreed to cease and desist from enforcing some portions of its Code of Professional Conduct relating to contingent fees, commissions, referral fees, solicitation, advertising, and the use of trade names in designating a practice unit. As a result of the FTC agreement and order, the AICPA revised its Rules relating to those areas. Many state societies of CPAs and state boards of accountancy have adopted the AICPA Rules regarding commissions and contingent fees, and others are considering doing so.

(i) Contingent Fees, Commissions, and Referral Fees.
Rule 302 prohibits CPAs from performing any professional services for, or receiving, a contingent fee, if the CPA performs any of the following services for the client:

- An audit or review of financial statements
- A compilation of financial statements, when a third party can reasonably be expected to use the financial statements, and the compilation report does not disclose a lack of independence
- An examination of prospective financial information

The FTC order defines the above services as attest services. As used in the order, "attest services" do not include all the types of services described as attest services in the accounting and auditing literature. Excluded from the definition, for example, would be services involving prospective financial information other than an examination and any service (other than one involving prospective financial information) covered solely by the Statements on Standards for Attestation Engagements.

For purposes of Rule 302, fees are not considered contingent if they are fixed by courts or other public authorities or, in tax matters, if they are determined based on the results of judicial proceedings or the findings of government agencies. Interpretation 302–1 (ET Section 302.02) defines certain terms in the provisions of the Rule dealing with tax matters and provides examples of tax services that would and would not be permitted.

Rule 503 prohibits CPAs from accepting commissions for recommending or referring a product or service to a client, or recommending or referring a product or service to be supplied by a client, when the CPA performs attest services for that client, as that term is defined in the FTC order and explained previously. The Rule also requires that permitted commissions be disclosed to the party to whom the CPA recommends or refers a product or service to which the commission relates. Further, the acceptance of a referral fee for recommending or referring a potential client to a CPA or the payment of a referral fee to obtain a client must be disclosed to the client.

Under Rules 302 and 503, a CPA is precluded from performing attest services (as defined above) for a client during the period in which the CPA is engaged to render or performs services for a contingent fee or a commission, or receives a contingent fee or a commission. Further, a CPA may not provide the defined attest services if the engagement, performance, or receipt occurred during any period covered by the historical financial statements. For example, if a CPA was asked in February 1999 to audit financial statements as of December 31, 1996, 1997, and 1998, he or she could not accept the engagement if he or she had performed services for a contingent fee, or had received a contingent fee, during any of the years 1996, 1997, or 1998, or in the period from February 1999 until the issuance date of the audit report. This prohibition would apply even if the CPA, at the time of performing services or of receiving a contingent fee or commission, had no reason to expect to be asked to perform the audit.

(ii) Advertising and Other Forms of Solicitation.   Rule 502 on advertising and other forms of solicitation is as follows: "A member in public practice shall not seek to obtain clients by advertising or other forms of solicitation in a manner that is false, misleading, or deceptive. Solicitation by the use of coercion, over-reaching, or harassing conduct is prohibited." There are no other restrictions on advertising or other forms of solicitation.

3.4 INCENTIVES FOR MAINTAINING AUDIT QUALITY

(a) Introduction

Audit quality embraces the concepts of professional competence and the meeting or exceeding of professional standards (both technical and ethical) in expressing an opinion on audited financial statements, performing other attest services, being associated with unaudited financial statements, and providing other types of accounting services.

Audit quality proceeds primarily from a firm's enlightened self-interest and from the concept of integrity. The first step in ensuring the quality of a firm's accounting and auditing practice is to incorporate quality control measures into the audit itself— requirements, at the engagement level, for documentation, the use of practice aids, and reviews by various knowledgeable personnel. While each firm's specific policies concerning documentation, use of practice aids, consultation, and review, and its means of enforcing them, depend largely on its size, organizational structure, and style or philosophy of management, each of those elements must be present in one way or another. In addition to building audit quality into individual engagements as a means of achieving and maintaining a reputation for professional excellence, incentives for maintaining audit quality are provided through regulatory mechanisms and other means.

The regulatory mechanisms include both the self-regulatory system of the profession and the disciplinary systems provided by government agencies like the SEC and individual state boards of accountancy. The self-regulatory system of the profession imposes penalties for performance or conduct that departs from professional standards. In addition, the profession has developed recommendations for quality control systems to provide reasonable assurance that CPA firms conform with professional standards in the conduct of their accounting and auditing practices.

Furthermore, the AICPA requires members engaged in the practice of public accounting in the United States or its territories to practice as owners or employees of firms enrolled in an approved practice-monitoring program in order to retain their membership in the Institute. There are two approved practice-monitoring programs.

- The peer review program of the SEC Practice Section of the AICPA Division for CPA Firms
- The peer review program the AICPA has established in cooperation with state CPA societies

Both of those programs are discussed later in the chapter.

Other incentives for maintaining audit quality also exist. For one thing, firms are increasingly exposed to litigation in the conduct of their audit practices and to sanctions by the SEC. This subject is covered in detail in Chapter 5. In addition, clients, and particularly audit committees, are putting increasing pressure on firms to maintain high audit quality. Audit quality is also a significant factor in a firm's ability to attract and retain clients and high-caliber personnel. Furthermore, through the efforts of financial writers and other news media, there is increasing public awareness of a firm's image and of the events that shape it.

The remainder of this section describes the profession's quality control and practice-monitoring programs, and the disciplinary systems of the profession and the state boards of accountancy.

(b) Quality Controls

The objectives of quality control policies and procedures are to improve individual and firm performance and to ensure compliance with technical and ethical standards. The relationship of generally accepted auditing standards to quality control standards is discussed in SAS No. 25, *The Relationship of Generally Accepted Auditing Standards to Quality Control Standards* (AU Section 161.03).

> Generally accepted auditing standards relate to the conduct of individual audit engagements; quality control standards relate to the conduct of a firm's audit practice as a whole. Thus, generally accepted auditing standards and quality control standards are related, and the quality control policies and procedures that a firm adopts may affect both the conduct of individual audit engagements and the conduct of a firm's audit practice as a whole.

Statement on Quality Control Standards (SQCS) No. 2, *System of Quality Control for a CPA Firm's Accounting and Auditing Practice* (QC Section 20), requires CPA firms to have a system of quality control for its accounting and auditing practice, which is defined as all audit, attest, accounting and review, and other services for which standards have been established by the Auditing Standards Board or the Accounting and Review Services Committee under Rule 201 or 202 of the AICPA Code of Professional Conduct.

SQCS No. 2 describes five elements of quality control and notes that they are interrelated (e.g., a firm's hiring practices affect its policies relating to engagement performance).

1. *Independence, integrity, and objectivity.* Policies and procedures should be established to provide the firm with reasonable assurance that personnel maintain independence (both in fact and in appearance) in all circumstances requiring independence and perform all professional responsibilities with integrity and objectivity.

2. *Personnel management.* Personnel management encompasses hiring, assigning personnel to engagements, professional development, and advancement activities. Policies and procedures should be established to provide the firm with reasonable assurance that:

   • Those hired have the characteristics to enable them to perform competently

   • Work is assigned to personnel who have the required degree of technical training and proficiency. In assigning work, the nature and extent of supervision should be considered. Generally, the more competent and experienced the personnel assigned to an engagement, the less direct supervision is needed.

   • Personnel participate in continuing professional education, both general and industry-specific, and other professional development activities that will enable them to meet their assigned responsibilities and satisfy applicable continuing education requirements of the AICPA and regulatory agencies

   • Personnel selected for advancement are qualified to fulfill the responsibilities entailed

3. *Acceptance and continuance of clients.* Policies and procedures should be established for deciding whether to accept or continue a client relationship and whether to perform a specific engagement for a client. Such policies and procedures should provide the firm with reasonable assurance that the likelihood of being associated with a client whose management lacks integrity is minimized. Such policies and procedures also should provide reasonable assurance that the firm undertakes engagements only when it can reasonably expect to complete them with professional competence, and that it considers the risks associated with providing professional services in specific circumstances. Furthermore, to minimize the risk of misunderstandings about services to be provided, policies and procedures should call for obtaining an understanding with the client about the services.

4. *Engagement performance.* Policies and procedures should be established to provide the firm reasonable assurance that work performed meets applicable professional standards, regulatory requirements, and the firm's quality standards.

5. *Monitoring.* Policies and procedures should be established to provide the firm with reasonable assurance that the policies and procedures relating to the other elements of quality control are designed appropriately and applied effectively. Monitoring involves ongoing consideration of the:

   • Relevance and adequacy of the policies and procedures

   • Appropriateness of guidance materials and practice aids

   • Effectiveness of professional development activities

   • Compliance with policies and procedures

(i) Independence, Integrity, and Objectivity. Public accounting firms are required to be independent of clients for whom they perform attest services, such as audits. Thus, all of a CPA firm's professional personnel must adhere to applicable independence rules, regulations, interpretations, and rulings of the AICPA, state societies of CPAs, state boards of accountancy, state statutes, and, if applicable, the SEC and other regulatory agencies. Firms should communicate the independence policies and procedures to appropriate personnel and monitor compliance with them. Typically, one or more individuals will be designated to maintain and monitor a firm's independence policies and procedures.

Integrity is a personal attribute that encompasses honesty and candidness within the constraints of client confidentiality. Integrity requires that personnel not subordinate the public trust to client service, and not subordinate either client service or the public trust to personal gain and advantage. Objectivity is a state of mind and quality that adds value to services performed. It obligates professionals to be impartial, intellectually honest, and free of conflicts of interest. Integrity and objectivity are required by Rule 102 of the Code of Professional Conduct, discussed earlier.

(ii) Personnel Management. The proficiency of personnel is a key aspect of a firm's quality control system. Firm management should ensure that the firm is adequately staffed and that each staff level possesses the skills necessary to achieve the desired level of professional excellence. Supervision is usually exercised on an engagement-by-engagement basis, and it commonly depends on factors such as the nature of the service performed, including the complexity of the client's business; the size of the engagement team necessary to serve the client and the extent of the team's training; and the intended use of the financial statements (e.g., whether they will be included in an SEC document, or restricted to management's internal use only).

(iii) Acceptance and Continuance of Clients and Engagements. The element relating to accepting and retaining clients formalizes a long-standing practice by auditors of seeking to ascertain the reputation and business integrity of potential clients and evaluating relationships with existing clients as a means of protecting their own reputation and avoiding inadvertently accepting an audit of high or unknown risk. The extent of the inquiry varies with the circumstances. It will be informal and brief, for example, if the potential client is well known in the community or can be easily investigated through mutual business associates. In other instances, more extreme and formal inquiries are called for, as often happens with entities having new management or diverse private ownership, or those in industries or areas with which the auditor is relatively unfamiliar.

Sources of information that are useful in the investigation of a prospective client include:

- Recent financial statements, both annual and interim and both audited and unaudited
- Forms 8-K filed with the SEC, if the company is registered
- Predecessor auditors
- Outside legal counsel and bankers
- Regulatory authorities

- Investigatory or credit rating services
- Industry associations and publications
- Information available in the media

The investigation process should be ongoing and not end when the client is accepted. The auditor should be alert to changed circumstances that might call for reconsideration of the relationship with the client. For example, if an entity is purchased or its management is replaced by individuals unknown to the auditor, another investigation would be in order. This process applies as well to consideration of accepting a specific engagement for an entity that is already a client.

(iv) Engagement Performance.   These policies and procedures cover planning, performing, supervising, reviewing, documenting, and communicating the results of engagements. The extent to which policies and procedures in each of those areas apply to individual engagements is determined by engagement circumstances and the requirements of professional standards. Policies and procedures also are needed to provide reasonable assurance that personnel refer to professional literature and consult with others, as appropriate. Consultation with individuals in a firm, or outside of it, who have specialized expertise is appropriate when an auditing or accounting issue is complex or unusual. Examples are the application of newly issued technical pronouncements; industries with special accounting, auditing, or reporting requirements; emerging practice problems; choices among alternative GAAP when an accounting change is to be made; and filing requirements of regulatory agencies. The nature of a firm's consultation organization depends on, among other things, the size of the firm and the level of knowledge, the competence, and the judgment of the persons performing the work.

(v) Monitoring.   Monitoring is performed internally by individuals acting on behalf of the firm's management, as contrasted with peer reviews, discussed below, which are conducted by individuals not associated with the firm being reviewed. SQCS No. 3 (QC Section 30) provides guidance on implementing the monitoring element and notes that monitoring is enhanced by procedures that provide a means of identifying and communicating circumstances that may necessitate changes or the need to improve compliance with monitoring policies and procedures. Those policies may include inspection procedures, preissuance or postissuance review of certain engagements, determining corrective actions and improvements needed, appropriately communicating weaknesses in the system or in the level of understanding or compliance with it, follow-up to ensure that necessary modifications are made on a timely basis, and analyzing and assessing new professional pronouncements, results of independence confirmations, continuing professional education and other professional development activities undertaken by personnel, acceptance and continuance decisions, and interviews of personnel.

Inspection procedures make it possible for a firm to internally evaluate the adequacy of its quality control policies and procedures, how well personnel understand them, and the overall compliance with them. Based on its evaluation, a firm can consider revisions or clarifications that may be needed. While a peer review is not a substitute for monitoring, the objective of inspection procedures is similar to that of a peer review. Therefore, a firm's quality control policies and procedures may provide that a peer review conducted under standards established by the AICPA may substitute for inspection procedures for the period covered by the peer review.

In addition to the elements of quality control, QC Section 20 discusses the considerations that are relevant to administering the system. They are assigning responsibility for the design and maintenance of quality control policies and procedures, determining the manner and extent of communicating them to personnel, and determining the form and extent of documentation of the policies and procedures and of compliance with them.

(c) Practice-Monitoring Programs

(i) AICPA Division for CPA Firms. The AICPA Division for CPA Firms comprises two sections, one for SEC practice and the other for private company practice. The principal objective of each section is to improve the quality of CPA firms' practice by establishing requirements for member firms and an effective system of self-regulation. Following are requirements that have the most direct effect on audit quality.

Requirements common to both sections:

- Adhere to quality control standards established by the AICPA Auditing Standards Board
- Ensure that all professionals in the firm achieve at least the minimum hours of continuing professional education prescribed by the section
- Submit to peer reviews of the firm's accounting and auditing practice, as described in more detail below

Additional SEC Practice Section (SECPS) Requirements for All SEC Engagements[4]:

- Periodically rotate partners
- Have a partner other than the audit partner in charge review and concur with the audit report on the financial statements before it is issued
- Refrain from performing certain management advisory services. Such services include psychological testing; public opinion polls; merger and acquisition assistance for a finder's fee; recruitment for managerial, executive, or director positions; and, in certain situations, actuarial services to insurance companies.
- Communicate at least annually with the audit committee or, if there is no audit committee, with the board of directors (or its equivalent in a partnership) the total fees received from the client for management advisory services during the year under audit and a description of the types of such services rendered[5]
- Report to the Quality Control Inquiry Committee (described below) any litiga-

---

[4] The section's definition of an SEC engagement includes audits of certain banks and other lending institutions and certain sponsors or managers of investment funds, even though they are not registered with the SEC.

[5] In addition, SAS No. 61 requires auditors of SEC clients and other entities that have an audit committee or its equivalent to communicate certain other matters to the committee, as discussed in Chapter 4.

tion (including criminal indictments) against the firm or its personnel or any proceeding or investigation publicly announced by a regulatory agency that alleges deficiencies in the conduct of an audit of the financial statements or reporting thereon of a present or former SEC client. Any allegations made in such formal litigation, proceeding, or investigation that the firm or its personnel have violated the federal securities laws in connection with services other than audit services must also be reported.

- Notify the Chief Accountant of the SEC within five business days when the auditor–client relationship with an SEC registrant ceases (because the auditor has resigned, declined to stand for reelection, or been dismissed)

Member firms of SECPS are required to undergo peer reviews of their accounting and auditing practice every three years or at such additional times as designated by the SECPS Executive Committee. The reviews are conducted in accordance with review standards established by the SECPS Peer Review Committee, as discussed later. Member firms of the Private Companies Practice Section (PCPS) must submit to peer reviews of their accounting and auditing practice at least once every three years. The reviews are conducted in accordance with the AICPA *Standards for Performing and Reporting on Peer Reviews* (discussed later).

Each section is governed by an executive committee composed of representatives from member firms that establishes the section's general policies and oversees its activities. The Executive Committee of the SECPS also has a Peer Review Committee that administers its peer review program and a Quality Control Inquiry Committee established to identify corrective measures, if any, that should be taken by a member firm involved in a specific alleged audit failure. The activities of the SECPS are also subject to review by an independent Public Oversight Board that issues public reports.

(ii) SEC Practice Section Peer Review Program. Peer reviews must be conducted in conformity with the confidentiality requirements in the AICPA Code of Professional Conduct. (Rule 301 contains an exception that allows a peer review of a member's practice.) Information obtained concerning a reviewed firm or any of its clients is confidential and should not be disclosed by review team members to anyone not "associated with the review." (The Executive and Peer Review Committees and the Public Oversight Board are encompassed by the phrase "associated with the review.") While the AICPA Code of Professional Conduct does not deal specifically with independence in relationships between reviewers, reviewed firms, and clients of reviewed firms, the concepts of independence expressed in the Code are considered in regard to these relationships. The firm under review has the option of either having the Peer Review Committee appoint the review team or engaging another member firm to conduct the review; however, reciprocal reviews are not permitted.

The peer review team evaluates whether the reviewed firm's quality control system for its accounting and auditing practice met the objectives of the quality control standards established by the AICPA, whether it was complied with to provide reasonable assurance of conforming with professional standards, and whether the firm was in compliance with the membership requirements of the section. Some tests made by the review team are performed on a firmwide basis, others at the practice office level, and still others on an individual engagement basis. Although the review is of the firm's accounting and auditing practice, other segments, such as tax, are covered in the review (1) to the extent that personnel from those segments assist on accounting and auditing engagements, and (2) as to compliance with membership requirements. At the completion of the peer review, the review team furnishes the reviewed firm with a formal peer review report and, if applicable, a letter of comments on matters that may require action by the firm, both of which are available to the public. The SEC Practice Section reference manual presents an example of an unqualified peer review report, which is reproduced in Figure 3.1.

Figure 3.1   Unqualified Peer Review Report

[AICPA or Other Appropriate Letterhead]

September 15, 19__

To the Partners
Jones, Wilson & Co.

We have reviewed the system of quality control for the accounting and auditing practice of Jones, Wilson & Co. (the firm) in effect for the year ended June 30, 19__. Our review was conducted in conformity with standards for peer reviews promulgated by the peer review committee of the SEC Practice Section of the AICPA Division for CPA Firms (the section). We tested compliance with the firm's quality control policies and procedures (at the firm's executive office and at selected practice offices in the United States)* and with the membership requirements of the section to the extent we considered appropriate. These tests included the application of the firm's policies and procedures on selected accounting and auditing engagements. (We tested the supervision and control of portions of engagements performed outside the United States.)**

In performing our review, we have given consideration to the general characteristics of a system of quality control as described in quality control standards issued by the AICPA. Such a system should be appropriately comprehensive and suitably designed in relation to the firm's organizational structure, its policies, and the nature of its practice. Variance in individual performance can affect the degree of compliance with a firm's prescribed quality control policies and procedures. Therefore, adherence to all policies and procedures in every case may not be possible. (As is customary in a peer review, we are issuing a letter under this date that sets forth comments related to certain policies and procedures or compliance with them. None of these matters were considered to be of sufficient significance to affect the opinion expressed in this report.)***

In our opinion, the system of quality control for the accounting and auditing practice of Jones, Wilson & Co. in effect for the year ended June 30, 19__, met

Figure 3.1   *(Continued)*

---

the objectives of quality control standards established by the AICPA, and was being complied with during the year then ended to provide the firm with reasonable assurance of conforming with professional standards. Also, in our opinion, the firm was in conformity with the membership requirements of the section in all material respects.

————————————————

William Brown
Team Captain

or

Johnson & Co. [for review by a firm]

or

————————————————

John Doe [for review by an association or state society-sponsored review team]

---

* To be included, as appropriate, for reviews of multioffice firms.
** To be included for reviewed firms with offices, correspondents, or affiliates outside the United States. The wording should be tailored if the reviewed firm's use of correspondents or affiliates domestically is significant to the scope of the review.
*** To be included if the review team issues a letter of comments along with the unqualified report.

With respect to member firms with SEC clients, a procedure has been established to enable the SEC to make its own evaluation of whether the peer review process and the Public Oversight Board's oversight of it are adequate. The procedure permits the SEC access, during a limited period following the Peer Review Committee's acceptance of the peer review report, to defined areas of the peer review working papers, with appropriate safeguards to prevent the SEC from identifying the clients whose audit working papers were reviewed. After their review of the working papers on a specific peer review, the SEC representatives discuss with representatives of the Public Oversight Board and the Peer Review Committee any matters that they believe the committee should consider.

The following circumstances ordinarily would require a modified report:

- The scope of the review is limited by conditions that preclude the application of one or more review procedures considered necessary

- The system of quality control as designed fails to meet one or more applicable objectives of quality control standards established by the AICPA, resulting in a condition in which the firm did not have reasonable assurance of conforming with professional standards

- The degree of noncompliance with the reviewed firm's quality control policies and procedures was such that the reviewed firm did not have reasonable assurance of conforming with professional standards

- The reviewed firm did not comply with the membership requirements of the Section in all material respects

The objective of the letter of comments is to report to the reviewed firm matters that resulted in a modified report or matters that, while not resulting in a modified report, the review team believes created a condition in which there is more than a remote possibility that the firm would not conform with professional standards on accounting and auditing engagements. It is quite common for a letter of comments to accompany the peer review report. The letter should include appropriate comments regarding the design of the reviewed firm's system of quality control, its compliance with that system, and its compliance with the membership requirements of the Section. The review team also may communicate orally to senior management of the reviewed firm comments that were not deemed significant enough to be included in the letter of comments.

(iii) AICPA Peer Review Program.   The AICPA peer review program is designed for firms that are not members of the Division for CPA Firms or are members of the Division's Private Companies Practice Section. The AICPA program is similar to the program for members of the SECPS. There are some differences, however, between the two programs, particularly in the reporting requirements and distribution of review reports.

The standards for the AICPA peer review program:

- Provide distinctly different performance and reporting standards for two types of peer reviews—an on-site review for firms that examine historical or prospective financial statements or perform agreed-upon procedures engagements, and an off-site review for firms that issue compilation or review reports but perform no examinations of historical or prospective financial statements

- Provide guidance on general considerations applicable to all peer reviews

- Describe how review teams are formed and what qualifications they must possess

- Define the responsibilities of the review team, the reviewed firm, and the entity administering the review, and provide standards, procedures, and guidelines to be followed by each participant in the process

Reports and related letters of comments on peer reviews for firms that are members of the PCPS are made public; those for other firms are not.

(d) Disciplinary System

The AICPA (in conjunction with state societies of CPAs), state boards of accountancy, the courts, and the SEC may impose sanctions on individuals and firms for performance or conduct that violates professional standards or civil or criminal laws. The paragraphs that follow discuss disciplinary actions of the profession and state boards of accountancy; legal and other sanctions are covered in Chapter 5.

(i) Disciplinary System Within the Profession for Individuals. The AICPA's self-disciplinary mechanism for individual members consists of the Institute's Professional Ethics Division (the Division) and the Joint Trial Board.

The Division is responsible for interpreting the Code of Professional Conduct and proposing amendments to it. The Division is also responsible for investigating alleged violations of the Code for possible disciplinary or rehabilitative action, including hearings before panels of the Joint Trial Board. The Division may initiate an investigation on the basis of complaints from individuals, state societies of CPAs, or government agencies, or on the basis of information from news media, the SEC *Docket*, or the IRS *Bulletin*.

The Division can take the following types of disciplinary actions against individual members:

- A subcommittee of the Division may conclude that a prima facie violation of the Code of Professional Conduct or bylaws is not of sufficient gravity to warrant further formal action, and it may direct the member or members concerned to complete specified continuing professional education courses or to take other remedial or corrective action. There is no publication of that action in the Institute's principal membership periodical, *The CPA Letter*. The member has the right to reject this directive. If he or she does, the Executive Committee of the Division then will decide whether to bring the matter to a panel of the Joint Trial Board for a hearing.

- The Executive Committee of the Division may decide, usually on the recommendation of one of its subcommittees, that there is prima facie evidence of a violation of sufficient gravity to refer the case to a panel of the Joint Trial Board, which may result in suspension (with or without other remedial or corrective action) or expulsion from membership or public censure. Publication of the names of members found guilty of the charges is required.

The AICPA's bylaws provide for automatic termination of membership (with publication of name) if a member is convicted of (1) a crime punishable by imprisonment for more than one year, (2) the willful failure to file any income tax return that he or she is required to file as an individual taxpayer, (3) filing a false or fraudulent income tax return on the member's own or a client's behalf, or (4) the willful aiding in the preparation and presentation of a false and fraudulent income tax return of a client.

(ii) Disciplinary System Within the Profession for Firms. The Executive Committee of each section of the AICPA Division for CPA Firms has the authority to impose sanctions on member firms for failing to meet membership requirements, either on its own initiative or on the basis of recommendations from the applicable peer review committee. The following types of sanctions may be imposed on member firms:

- Corrective measures by the firm, including consideration by the firm of appropriate actions with respect to individual firm personnel
- Additional requirements for continuing professional education
- Accelerated or special peer reviews
- Admonishments, censures, or reprimands
- Monetary fines
- Suspension or expulsion from membership

(iii) State Boards of Accountancy.   A state board of accountancy is charged with enforcing laws that regulate the practice of public accounting in that state. Generally, a board has the power to revoke or suspend the certificates of CPAs; to revoke, suspend, or refuse to renew permits to practice; and to censure the holders of licenses or permits to practice.[6] Those penalties can be imposed for a wide variety of acts or omissions specified in accountancy laws. Several states also require the registration of firms, issue permits for firms to practice in the state, and have the power to revoke or suspend those permits. An increasing number of states have required firms to participate in "Positive Enforcement Programs"—a type of peer review—as a condition for practicing within those states.

3.5 ENHANCING THE INDEPENDENCE OF AUDITORS

Generally accepted auditing standards, the attestation standards, the AICPA Code of Professional Conduct, the SEC, and individual accounting firms require auditors to maintain an attitude of independence and prohibit certain relationships with clients.[7] Nevertheless, some people believe that there are potential threats to auditor independence because the client selects the auditor and pays the fee and because the auditor may undertake nonaudit or even nonassurance services for the client. Since auditors are often selected and paid, retained, or replaced at the sole discretion of the management on whose representations they are expected to report, many people believe that total professional independence is impossible. While total independence may be impossible, auditors are extremely conscious that their independence is vital and that they must preserve the standards of the profession for the sake of their own reputation.

The profession, the SEC, and responsible leaders of the financial community have recognized this alleged threat and have taken steps to deal with it. Some entities require that the selection and retention of auditors be ratified by the stockholders. In

---

[6] It should be noted that the AICPA has no such powers, since it does not issue certificates or permits to practice. AICPA disciplinary actions relate only to membership in the Institute.

[7] As discussed earlier in this chapter, Interpretation 101–11 of Rule 101 of the Code of Professional Conduct distinguishes the independence requirements appropriate for audit engagements and for attestation engagements that result in reports for general use from those appropriate for attest engagements and agreed-upon procedures engagements that result in reports for restricted use.

the case of entities whose securities are publicly traded, the SEC requires public notice of the termination of auditors, disclosure of any accounting or auditing disputes within two years between the client and the former auditor, and a letter from the former auditor concurring in such disclosure. Those are worthwhile steps, but they mitigate rather than eliminate the threat to auditor independence.

Another alleged threat to auditor independence arises from the increasingly diverse types of services provided to audit clients by public accounting firms. Such services include nonaudit services traditionally offered by public accounting firms, such as tax services (tax return preparation, tax planning advice, and representation before the IRS); management services, some that are related to accounting and auditing (such as advice on systems, controls, data processing, and cost accounting) and some that are not (for instance, market studies or studies of factory layout); and accounting services (such as compilations and reviews for nonpublic companies and advice on selection and application of accounting principles and the accounting implications of proposed management decisions). More and more, public accounting firms also provide various types of nonassurance services to audit clients. Currently, there is no general proscription by either the SEC or the AICPA against performing nonaudit (or nonassurance) services for audit clients. The SEC has at times in the past monitored such relationships and required their disclosure, and the AICPA Division for CPA Firms prohibits members of its SECPS from providing certain management advisory services.

In 1994, the Advisory Panel on Auditor Independence, which was appointed by the POB of the SECPS, published its report, *Strengthening the Professionalism of the Independent Auditor* (referred to as the Kirk Report, after the chairman of the Advisory Panel). The Advisory Panel addressed the need for additional or amended AICPA or SEC rules and regulations or legislation on auditor independence and concluded that none were necessary. The Advisory Panel did, however, conclude that the POB, SEC, and others should support proposals to enhance the independence of boards of directors and their accountability to shareholders, which in turn will strengthen the professionalism of auditors and add value to the independent audit. In that light, the Advisory Panel set forth a number of recommendations for enhancing the objectivity and professionalism of auditors. Some of those recommendations had been considered and evaluated by the Cohen Commission in its 1978 report and again by the Treadway Commission in its 1987 report. The Cohen and Treadway Commissions also set forth a number of other proposals to strengthen auditor independence, many of them aimed at protecting the auditor from management influence. The remainder of this chapter discusses and evaluates each of those recommendations and proposals.

Neither audit effectiveness nor audit efficiency would be strengthened if the auditor were isolated from client management. An auditor must work with management because management's active and positive cooperation is required in conducting an audit, and that in turn requires the auditor and management to have a high degree of confidence in one another. Yet auditor independence must be maintained despite the need for cooperation. Another difficulty auditors face in maintaining their independence is that they are members of a profit-making firm that depends on fees over which client management may exert considerable control. Several proposals have been set forth to increase the auditor's ability to resist pressure from management.

(a) Formation of Audit Committees

Over the years, a number of professional and regulatory bodies have suggested requiring entities to have audit committees of boards of directors as a means of reinforcing auditors' independence from management. The SEC endorsed the establishment of audit committees composed of outside directors in 1972 (ASR No. 123) and subsequently adopted nonbinding rules underscoring this commitment. The AICPA recommended as early as 1967 that audit committees be established for all publicly held companies. A special House subcommittee in 1976 also noted the desirability of audit committees. In 1978, the New York Stock Exchange mandated that domestic companies with listed securities establish audit committees made up entirely of outside directors; in 1979, the American Stock Exchange strongly recommended similar action. The Cohen Commission strongly endorsed the use of audit committees to recommend to shareholders the appointment of independent auditors and to evaluate the relationship between auditor and management. The Institute of Internal Auditors also endorsed the establishment of audit committees consisting of outside directors by both public companies and other organizations, such as not-for-profit and governmental bodies. The Treadway Commission recommended that the SEC require all public companies to establish audit committees composed solely of outside directors. It also provided guidance on how audit committees could serve as "informed, vigilant, and effective overseers of the financial reporting process and the company's internal controls."[8] Finally, in 1996, the National Association of Securities Dealers proposed that issuers in its SmallCap Market be required to have an audit committee consisting of a majority of outside directors.

Today, although not universally required, audit committees are an important part of our corporate structure. They oversee an entity's accounting and financial reporting policies and practices, help the board of directors fulfill its corporate reporting responsibilities, and help maintain a direct line of communication between the board and the entity's external and internal auditors. Although occasionally the entire board may turn to the independent auditors for assistance in reviewing the financial statements or other data, contact between the board and the auditors is generally through the audit committee.

Over the years, the AICPA and the New York Stock Exchange have issued general guidelines for audit committees but have not mandated specific duties, responsibilities, or activities. Since specific functions have not been prescribed for audit committees, their activities vary from one entity to the next. Effective committees, however, generally should perform at least the following:

- Recommend the appointment of the independent auditor and review the fee arrangements
- Review the proposed scope of the independent audit
- Communicate with the internal auditors and review their activities, effectiveness, and recommendations for improving the entity's internal control
- Review the financial statements and the results of the independent audit

---

[8] *Report of the National Commission on Fraudulent Financial Reporting* (Treadway Commission), 1987, p. 41.

- Review the report by management (discussed in Chapter 31) containing management's opinion on the effectiveness of the entity's internal control and the basis for that opinion
- Consider the selection of accounting policies
- Scrutinize the required communications from the independent auditor regarding deficiencies in the entity's internal control, weaknesses discovered in the course of the audit, and many other matters related to the audit (those communications are discussed in Chapter 4)
- Oversee or conduct special investigations or other functions on behalf of the board of directors

In the authors' opinion, the widespread establishment of audit committees of outside directors has been beneficial to management, directors, stockholders, and the auditing profession. Auditors and outside directors have common interests that are vastly strengthened by interaction between the two groups. An active and involved audit committee serves to protect corporate interests by overseeing the activities of the auditor and, at least to some extent in matters of financial reporting, entity management. An effective audit committee of outside directors demonstrates that all parties with responsibility for reliable financial reporting—management, the independent auditors, and the board of directors acting in an oversight capacity—are diligently carrying out their duties to the stockholders. An audit committee reinforces the auditor's independence, while the auditor provides an independent source of information to the directors; management's support of the relationship demonstrates a sense of accountability.

(b) Enhancing the Auditor's Responsibilities to the Board of Directors

The report of the Advisory Panel on Auditor Independence recommended that auditors, in discharging their responsibilities to evaluate an entity's selection and application of accounting principles, financial statement disclosures, and accounting estimates, view the board of directors, not management, as the client. The report added that this clarification of the auditor's relationship to the board would create a more balanced relationship between management and the auditor. The report states:

> As the shareholders' representative, the board is accountable to them for monitoring the company's performance in achieving its goals and plans. That accountability is discharged, in part, by ensuring that shareholders receive relevant and reliable information about the company performance and financial position. The board should expect the auditor to assist it in discharging that responsibility to the shareholders, and the auditor should assume the obligation to do so. (p. 16)

Moreover, the Kirk Report recommended that the auditor should communicate to the board of directors and audit committee his or her views on the appropriateness of the entity's accounting principles, clarity of financial disclosures, and degree of aggressiveness or conservatism of accounting principles and underlying estimates by management. Thus, the Advisory Panel would extend the auditor's present responsibility for evaluating the *acceptability* of accounting principles that the entity uses, to evaluating their *appropriateness*. The report sums up this recommendation as follows:

> The auditor would not only evaluate the company's compliance with generally accepted accounting principles but also express, to the audit committee and the board of directors, a qualitative judgment about the company's choices of principles, disclosures, and estimates. For years, the auditing standards have required the auditor to judge whether the accounting principles selected and applied are "appropriate in the circumstances." The standard to which the auditor has been held in making that judgment has been whether the selected principle falls within the range of acceptable practice. The Panel would hold the auditor to a different standard in communicating with the board of directors. (p. 19)

The Advisory Panel stated that its objective in setting forth this recommendation was to enhance the board's and audit committee's objectivity in considering management's choice of accounting principles and estimates. The Panel acknowledged that the recommended communication on the appropriateness of accounting principles, disclosures, and estimates will require the exercise of professional judgment. If such communication is required by the AICPA or the SEC, it would represent a significant extension of the auditor's present responsibilities.

(c) Communicating with Predecessor Auditors

SAS No. 7, *Communications Between Predecessor and Successor Auditors* (AU Section 315.01–.09), requires a successor auditor to attempt to communicate with the predecessor as part of the process of determining whether to accept an engagement. AU Section 315.06 outlines the procedures to be followed by a successor auditor.

> The successor auditor should make specific and reasonable inquiries of the predecessor regarding matters that the successor believes will assist him in determining whether to accept the engagement. His inquiries should include specific questions regarding, among other things, facts that might bear on the integrity of management; on disagreements with management as to accounting principles, auditing procedures, or other similarly significant matters; and on the predecessor's understanding as to the reasons for the change of auditors.

AU Section 315 indicates that the predecessor auditor is obligated to "respond promptly and fully" to any "reasonable" question, but it also recognizes that, in unusual situations such as when litigation is or may be involved, the predecessor may need to advise the successor that the response is limited. In that event, the successor auditor should consider whether the information obtained from all sources is adequate to support accepting the client. If the client refuses to allow the successor auditor to talk to the predecessor auditor, the successor auditor should also consider whether to accept the engagement.

After a successor auditor has been appointed, there are two occasions when communications between the predecessor and the successor auditors are appropriate. One reflects the successor's need to review the prior auditor's working papers, and the other arises if the successor believes that there is an error in the financial statements on which the predecessor auditor expressed an opinion.

Working papers are the property of the auditor who prepared them, who is under no compulsion to share them with a successor auditor. In the absence of unusual circumstances, however, such as litigation between the client and the predecessor auditor or amounts owed to the predecessor auditor by the client, predecessor auditors customarily allow successor auditors access to at least certain working papers. Generally, those are working papers that disclose the results of the audit work and contain information of accounting significance, but not proprietary information about the audit scope or design or about administrative matters. Some auditors may make available more working papers, but may require a successor auditor to sign a letter of understanding as to the use of the information before they will grant access to a broad range of working papers of audit significance. In addition, access to working papers should be granted to a successor auditor only at the request of or with the specific consent of the former client.

(d)   Scrutiny of Auditor Changes

Management sometimes threatens to dismiss the auditor when there is a disagreement on accounting principles. Management might then "shop around" for a more compliant auditor. Requiring auditor changes to be ratified by an audit committee is one way of relieving pressure on the auditor from management. Outside scrutiny of the dismissal of an auditor also inhibits the tendency to apply such pressure. The scrutiny of auditor changes has been enhanced by SEC requirements to disclose potential "opinion shopping" situations and disagreements between the client and the auditor when there is a change in auditors (as previously noted, auditors are required by SAS No. 61 to report disagreements to the audit committee or board of directors of SEC clients and other entities that have an audit committee or its equivalent, even when there has not been a change in auditors).

(i) Opinion Shopping.   An auditor may be asked by another accountant's client for professional advice on an accounting or auditing technical matter. In some situations, the client and its auditor may have disagreed about the matter in question. When the client's purpose in seeking another professional opinion is to find an accountant willing to support a proposed accounting treatment that would favor a particular reporting objective but that is not supported by the client's auditor, the practice is commonly referred to as "opinion shopping." SAS No. 50, *Reports on the Application of Accounting Principles* (AU Section 625), contains standards to be followed by an accountant who is asked to give an opinion on an accounting matter to another auditor's client (see discussion in Chapter 29).

The SEC has noted that the search for an auditor who would support a proposed accounting treatment may indicate an effort by management to avoid the requirement for an independent audit, and that an auditor's willingness to support a proposed accounting treatment that may frustrate reliable reporting may suggest a lack of professional skepticism and independence on the part of the auditor. The SEC requires disclosure of possible opinion shopping situations in connection with a change in auditors if the registrant consulted the newly engaged auditor within approximately two years before the engagement.[9] (The SEC rule specifies the matters covered by the consultation and the information required to be disclosed.)

---

[9] SEC Financial Reporting Release No. 31, April 7, 1988.

(ii) Disagreements with Clients.   Since 1971, the SEC has required disclosure in a timely Form 8-K filing of a change in auditors made by the registrant, including disclosure of certain disagreements between the registrant and the predecessor auditor during the two most recent fiscal years and any subsequent interim period. The predecessor auditor provides a letter, which is generally filed by the entity with its Form 8-K, either concurring with the entity's disclosures or setting forth any disagreements that were omitted or require further explanation. In addition, if the predecessor auditor objected to an accounting method or disclosure that had a material effect on the financial statements and the successor auditor agrees to it, Item 304 of Regulation S-K requires the registrant to disclose the disagreement and the effect on the financial statements that would have resulted if the method advocated by the former auditor had been followed.[10]

SEC Financial Reporting Release No. 31 clarified the meaning of the term "disagreements," identified certain "reportable events" that require the same disclosures as for disagreements, and specified the required disclosures for disagreements and reportable events. (As noted above, it also provided for disclosure of possible opinion shopping situations.)

The SEC rules emphasize that the term "disagreements" should be interpreted broadly to include any differences of opinion regarding accounting principles or practices, financial statement disclosure, or auditing scope or procedure that, if not resolved to the satisfaction of the former auditor, would have caused him or her to refer to the disagreement in the audit report. Further, the rules indicate that a disagreement means a difference of opinion, not necessarily an argument. Both disagreements that were resolved to the former auditor's satisfaction and those that were not are required to be reported. However, initial differences of opinion based on incomplete facts or preliminary information that were later resolved to the former auditor's satisfaction (before his or her dismissal or resignation) are not disagreements.

Certain other events also require the same disclosures as for disagreements, when there is a change in auditors (even if the registrant and the former auditor did not have a difference of opinion regarding the event). These reportable events include situations in which the former auditor advised the registrant that:

- Internal controls necessary for the registrant to develop reliable financial statements did not exist
- He or she was unwilling to rely on management's representations or be associated with the registrant's financial statements
- He or she would have had to significantly expand the scope of the audit and was not permitted to do so
- Information came to his or her attention that he or she has concluded materially affects the fairness or reliability of either a prior audit report or the under-

---

[10] SEC Financial Reporting Release No. 34, issued in March 1989, revised the SEC's rules with respect to the timing of Form 8-K filings relating to changes in auditors, as well as the required Regulation S-K disclosures.

lying financial statements, or the current financial statements, and, for whatever reason, the issue was not resolved

The registrant also must disclose whether:

- The former auditor resigned, declined to stand for reelection, or was dismissed
- The audit committee of the board of directors or the board discussed the subject matter of each disagreement or reportable event with the former auditor
- The registrant has authorized the former auditor to respond fully to the inquiries of the successor auditor regarding the subject matter of each disagreement or reportable event

As previously noted, members of the SECPS of the AICPA Division for CPA Firms must notify the Chief Accountant of the SEC within five business days when the auditor–client relationship with an SEC registrant ceases, regardless of whether the client has reported a change in auditors in a Form 8-K filing.

(e)   Rotation of Audit Personnel

To decrease the auditor's incentive for yielding to pressure from management, some people have proposed mandatory rotation of auditors, with a new auditor to be appointed every three to five years. Also, some argue that a new auditor would bring a fresh viewpoint to the engagement. Rotation would considerably increase audit costs, however, because of the start-up and learning time necessary on a new engagement. In addition, the Cohen Commission, noting that most cases of substandard performance by auditors were first- or second-year audits, stated, "Once an auditor becomes well acquainted with the operation of a client, audit risks are reduced" (p. 109).

Because of this, the Cohen Commission concluded that rotation of audit firms should not be required. The Commission also pointed out that the primary advantage of rotation—the fresh viewpoint—can be achieved if the personnel assigned to an engagement are systematically rotated.[11] This recommendation is reflected in the membership requirement of the SECPS of the AICPA Division for CPA Firms that the engagement partner on audits of SEC engagements be periodically rotated. (The National Association of Insurance Commissioners has since adopted a similar rule for insurance companies.) The SECPS reconsidered the mandatory rotation of firms in 1992 and decided against instituting such a policy. A 1994 report of the staff of the Office of the Chief Accountant of the SEC entitled *Staff Report on Auditor Independence* concurred with the Cohen Commission and SECPS finding about the costs versus benefits of mandatory rotation, and the Kirk Report expressed its agreement that mandatory rotation of audit firms is not needed in view of other safeguards, such as partner rotation and concurring partner review.

(f)   Transfer of the Audit Function to the Public Sector

In order to sever the ties between auditor and management, proposals have been made to have independent auditors approved, assigned, or compensated by a govern-

[11] *Report, Conclusions, and Recommendations*, 1978, pp. 108–9.

ment agency or by the stock exchanges or to have audits conducted by a group of government auditors. The Cohen Commission concluded that having auditors approved, assigned, or compensated by the government was not warranted either by the magnitude of deficiencies in present practice or by the promise of potential improvements. It also noted that the government may use accounting information to accomplish its own economic or political objectives, which suggests that increased government involvement in audits may well create problems of independence and objectivity.[12]

(g)   Auditor Selection of GAAP for Clients

Traditionally, management has had the primary responsibility for the financial statements, including selecting what accounting principles to use and what disclosures to make. Proposals have been made to require the auditor to assume those responsibilities. The authors believe that the present division of responsibility is sound and should not be changed. Management, with firsthand knowledge of what has occurred, should be responsible for ensuring that events and transactions are properly reported. Furthermore, management is in the best position to make the judgments and estimates necessary to prepare the financial statements, and the auditor is in the best position to challenge and evaluate those judgments and estimates.

Occasionally, an issue involving reporting standards or the application of generally accepted accounting principles becomes a "disagreement" between management and the auditor. Such disagreements are frequently resolved by the auditor's convincing management of the propriety of an accounting principle or the necessity and justification for a particular disclosure. If, however, the auditor is not successful, a qualification results. Probably the most effective way of avoiding this is for the client to seek the auditor's early involvement and consultation in the formative stages of nonroutine transactions. In that way, neither party is faced with an unavoidable accounting or auditing outcome that is unsatisfactory to the client.

The linkage between selecting accounting principles and accumulating and classifying accounting data is very close. If auditors were responsible for selecting accounting principles and disclosures, they would lose the independent evaluation function that they perform today. Auditors should use their expertise to advise and counsel management in preparing financial statements, with management retaining the ultimate responsibility for the presentation. As noted earlier, enhanced communication between the auditor and the board of directors about the appropriateness of the entity's accounting principles would enhance the auditor's independence.

(h)   Prohibition of Management Advisory Services

The potential adverse effect on auditor independence of performing management advisory services for audit clients has been debated for four decades. The Treadway Commission noted that:

> Some argue that the independent public accountant's performance of management advisory services improves the quality of audits. They claim that in the process of advising management the independent public accountant acquires a deeper understanding of the client's business. Many in the public accounting profession also maintain that benefits

---

[12] *Ibid.*, p. 105.

accrue to the audit process when the independent public accountant is already familiar with the company's operations.

Others believe that some management advisory services place independent public accountants in the role of management, add commercial pressures to the audit examination and, as a result, impair independence. These individuals also argue that, at the very least, the public accountant's performance of management advisory services raises the perception of impaired independence. (p. 43)

Like the Cohen Commission before it, the Treadway Commission reviewed previous studies of the issue and sponsored its own research study. Neither commission found any actual case in which an auditor's independence was compromised by providing management advisory services. The Treadway Commission cited several empirical studies, however, that indicated that "a substantial percentage of members of key public groups involved in the financial reporting process believe that performing certain management advisory services can impair a public auditor's objectivity and independence."[13]

The Treadway Commission concluded that the existence of that perception should not be ignored. It noted that members of the SECPS of the AICPA's Division for CPA Firms must disclose to the audit committee or board of directors the total fees received from an SEC audit client for management advisory services during the past year and a description of the types of such services rendered. The Treadway Commission recommended that the audit committee should oversee management judgments relating to management advisory services and the auditor's independence.

The *SEC Staff Report on Auditor Independence*, mentioned earlier, considered the impact of management advisory services on auditor independence and concluded that no changes in SEC rules and regulations were needed. Although the Kirk Report expressed agreement with the SEC staff, the Advisory Panel pointed out that auditing, unlike other services offered by public accounting firms, entails a public responsibility. The Advisory Panel recommended that accounting firms consider how the audit function can be enhanced and not submerged in large multiline public accounting/management consulting firms. The Kirk Report states:

Growing reliance on nonaudit services has the potential to compromise the objectivity or independence of the auditor by diverting firm leadership away from the public responsibility associated with the independent audit function, by allocating disproportionate resources to other lines of business within the firm, and by seeing the audit function as necessary just to get the benefit of being considered objective and to serve as an entrée to sell other services. (p. 9)

Since the publication of the Kirk Report in 1994, the number of nonaudit services offered by public accounting firms has increased and has expanded to include a wide array of nonassurance services as well, such as internal audit outsourcing and brokerage and investment advisory services. The U.S. General Accounting Office (GAO), in its 1996 report, *The Accounting Profession, Major Issues: Progress and Concerns*, noted that the continuing expansion of services offered by public accounting firms posed a concern about independence. The GAO observed, however:

[13] Treadway Commission, p. 44.

We continue to believe that measures that would limit auditor services or mandate changing auditors are outweighed by the value of continuity in conducting audits and the value of traditional consulting services. We believe the more reasonable action is the Kirk Panel's idea of bringing the independent auditor more into a direct working relationship with the board of directors and emphasizing the independent audit committee's roles as an overseer of the company's financial reporting process; a buffer between management and the auditor; and a representative of user interests in full, fair, and reliable financial reporting.

The GAO further noted efforts by the profession to strengthen auditor independence, as described throughout this chapter. These include requirements to report various matters—fees received for management advisory services and the types of services provided, disagreements with management, consultations with other accountants, difficulties encountered in performing the audit, and weaknesses in internal control—to the entity's audit committee. They also include the Rules and Interpretations of the Code of Professional Conduct that emphasize auditor independence and objectivity, and specifically cover the acceptance of consulting engagements. Finally, since the issuance of the GAO report, the Independence Standards Board, discussed earlier in the chapter, was formed to promulgate independence standards for audits of public entities.

4

Auditors' Professional Responsibility

4.1 PROFESSIONAL RESPONSIBILITY VERSUS LEGAL LIABILITY

The terms "auditors' responsibility" and "auditors' legal liability" often are confused by nonauditors. The distinction is subtle, yet it must be drawn in order for auditors and nonauditors to communicate with each other. This entire book, with the exception of Chapter 5, "Auditors' Legal Liability," is concerned with auditors' responsibilities.

An appropriate way of viewing the relationship between responsibility and liability is to think of "responsibilities" as synonymous with "professional duties," and "legal liabilities" as relating to society's means of enforcing adherence to those professional duties—that is, compliance with professional standards—and providing compensation to victims of wrongful conduct. The concept of auditor responsibility usually arises in two related contexts: responsibility for what, and to whom? Answers to both questions are found primarily in the technical and ethical standards of the public accounting profession; occasionally they are specified in state and federal statutes and court decisions. All of these sources provide guidance to auditors on how to conduct audits with due professional care and thus meet their professional responsibilities, and on the duties that auditors owe to their clients and third parties.

Chapter 3 described the various mechanisms the AICPA and state boards of accountancy have for maintaining the quality of audit practice. The legal process, discussed in Chapter 5, is another mechanism that helps ensure that auditors meet their responsibilities. Litigation and threats of litigation serve as enforcers of duties; they also help define auditors' responsibilities and, on rare occasions, create what some perceive to be new responsibilities. The Commission on Auditors' Responsibilities (Cohen Commission) noted that "court decisions are particularly useful [in defining auditors' responsibilities] because they involve consideration of competing theories of responsibility. However, they must be considered carefully because a decision is usually closely related to the facts of a particular case. Consequently, the language used in a particular decision may not be the best expression of the technical issues involved."[1] The outcome of a specific legal case also may not be a reliable indicator of auditors' responsibilities because it is often impossible to discern the rationale of a jury verdict, and appellate decisions often are clouded by procedural rules, such as the requirement that factual determinations not be disturbed.

4.2 RESPONDING TO PUBLIC EXPECTATIONS

To a great degree, auditors' responsibilities reflect the expectations of users of audited financial statements. Users expect an auditor to evaluate the accounting, recognition, measurement, and disclosure decisions made by management and decide whether the financial statements are free of material misstatement, either intentional or not. Auditors have long accepted the responsibility to design the audit to detect material unintentional misstatements in financial statements, which auditing literature refers to as *errors*. After all, if that is not a purpose of the audit, what is? The auditor's responsibility for designing audits to detect dishonest

<hr>

[1] *Report, Conclusions, and Recommendations*, 1978, p. 2.

ments in financial statements—what the auditing literature refers to as *fraud*—has been less clear over the years, mainly because of the difficulty, or even impossibility, of detecting skillfully contrived misstatements, particularly if any form of collusion is present.

Users' expectations of financial statement audits have been a concern of the profession for many years and have been the subject of several reports. In 1978, the Cohen Commission concluded that a gap, which quickly began to be referred to as the "expectation gap," existed between the performance of auditors and the expectations of financial statement users, and that, with certain exceptions, the users' expectations were generally reasonable. The Commission recommended a number of ways to respond to user expectations by clarifying and tightening auditing standards and improving communication of the auditor's role and work to the public. Many of those recommendations were acted on by the accounting profession, but some were either rejected or ignored.

By the mid-1980s, the expectation gap had been exacerbated by difficult economic times in certain industries and several notable bankruptcies traceable to questionable business practices or to management's lack of awareness of the risks it was incurring. Unfortunately, many investors mistakenly believe that a business failure equates with an audit failure. Also, highly publicized instances of fraudulent financial reporting and illegal corporate activities had raised questions about auditors' responsibility for detecting and reporting fraud and other illegalities, and also about the auditor's role in assessing an entity's controls that might prevent them. In addition, senior management, audit committees, and boards of directors of major corporations were expressing a desire for the independent auditor to provide them with more assistance in meeting their responsibilities for overseeing the corporate financial reporting process.

In response, the National Commission on Fraudulent Financial Reporting (Treadway Commission) was established under the sponsorship of the AICPA, the American Accounting Association, the Financial Executives Institute, The Institute of Internal Auditors, and the National Association of Accountants (now, the Institute of Management Accountants). The Commission's objectives were to develop initiatives for the prevention and detection of fraud and, in particular, to determine what the role of the independent auditor should be in detecting management fraud. The Treadway Commission's recommendations were published in October 1987. The five sponsoring organizations set up a committee—the Committee of Sponsoring Organizations (COSO)—to support implementation of those recommendations.

Partly in response to the Treadway recommendations, but also driven by other forces, the AICPA's Auditing Standards Board (ASB) issued a number of Statements on Auditing Standards (SASs) and Statements on Standards for Attestation Engagements (SSAEs) in the late 1980s. These pronouncements represented a major attempt to respond to the public's expectations of auditors and to the needs of senior management and corporate directors.

The financial press continued to report instances of material financial statement misstatements involving fraud through the early 1990s, especially frauds involving inventory. A 1993 report of the Public Oversight Board (POB) of the AICPA Practice Section made several recommendations aimed at enhancing auditors' abilities to detect fraud and suggested that standard setters provide guidance beyond what then existed in the SASs. In 1997, the ASB issued SAS No. 82, *Consideration of Fraud in a Financial Statement Audit* (AU Section 316). While SAS No. 82 did not change the auditor's responsibility to detect fraud, it is likely to increase the attention given to the risk of fraud because of its more prominent use of the term "fraud" (previously, the professional literature used the euphemism "irregularity" instead of "fraud") and its specification of procedures to assess the risk of fraud.

The authors of this book believe that the SASs and SSAEs that were issued to address the expectation gap, including SAS No. 82, respond in many significant respects to the needs of financial statement users, senior management and boards of directors, and the public. It is clear, however, that the issues surrounding the expectations of those groups do not simply concern auditor performance and responsibilities, but are far more complex. There are, for example, fundamental concerns about the accounting measurement and disclosure principles that enter into the preparation of financial statements, about business ethics and conduct, and about the responsibilities of corporate directors and management. The ASB can address only the auditor's performance and responsibilities. The authors believe it has done so in a way that will help to close the expectation gap and that is also responsive to many of the concerns of the Treadway Commission and the POB relating to auditors' responsibilities in performing an audit and communicating their findings.

4.3   RESPONSIBILITY FOR DETECTING ERROR, FRAUD, AND ILLEGAL ACTS

The authoritative auditing literature for many years reflected the view that auditors were not responsible for detecting financial statement misstatements (particularly fraud) unless the application of generally accepted auditing standards (GAAS) would result in such detection. Many financial statement users, however, believe that one of the primary purposes of an audit is to detect intentional misstatements in *all* circumstances. The Securities and Exchange Commission (SEC) has long taken the position that an audit can be expected to detect certain kinds of fraud, stating in Accounting Series Release (ASR) No. 19, "In the Matter of McKesson & Robbins, Inc.," issued in 1940:

> Moreover, we believe that, even in balance sheet examinations for corporations whose securities are held by the public, accountants can be expected to detect gross overstatements of assets and profits whether resulting from collusive fraud or otherwise. . . . We feel that the discovery of gross overstatements in the accounts is a major purpose of such an audit even though it be conceded that it might not disclose every minor defalcation.

(a)   AICPA Professional Requirements

Many commentators both inside and outside the accounting profession believe that until fairly recently, official pronouncements on auditors' responsibilities were broad, vague, and sometimes overly defensive and self-serving. However, the authoritative pronouncement on the auditor's responsibility to detect financial statement misstatements now explicitly states:

The auditor has a responsibility to plan and perform the audit to obtain reasonable assurance about whether the financial statements are free of material misstatement, whether caused by error or fraud. (AU Section 110.02)

Accordingly, the auditor is responsible for detecting *material* error and fraud, not *all* error and fraud. Moreover, materiality, which is discussed in Chapter 6, is measured in terms of the financial statements taken as a whole. The auditor's responsibility for detecting error and fraud thus acknowledges the context in which an audit is conducted, that is, that the purpose of an audit is to enable the auditor to express an opinion on the financial statements taken as a whole. A CPA also may be engaged specifically to determine whether a known misstatement is the result of fraud, or to determine whether an immaterial fraud exists. Those engagements are referred to as fraud examinations and are not covered by the professional auditing literature. The responsibilities discussed in this chapter relate solely to responsibilities to detect error and fraud in a financial statement audit.

SAS No. 47, *Audit Risk and Materiality in Conducting an Audit* (AU Section 312), which is discussed in Chapter 6, provides guidance to auditors in considering the risk that the financial statements are materially misstated because of either error or fraud. SAS No. 82 provides further guidance to auditors in discharging their professional responsibility related to fraud. Specifically, SAS No. 82:

- Describes the types of fraud pertinent to an audit and their characteristics
- Requires the auditor to specifically assess the risk of fraud that could result in a material misstatement of the financial statements, and provides categories of fraud risk factors that should be considered in the auditor's assessment
- Provides guidance on the effect that the auditor's fraud risk assessment should have on the auditing procedures to be performed
- Provides guidance on the evaluation of audit test results as they relate to the risk of fraud
- Requires the auditor to document in the working papers, when planning the audit, the assessment of the risk of fraud and how that assessment affects the auditing procedures, as well as any fraud risk factors identified during the audit and the auditor's response
- Provides guidance regarding the auditor's communication about fraud to management, the audit committee, and others

Generally accepted auditing standards require the auditor to plan and perform his or her work with due professional care. Due professional care, in turn, requires the auditor to exercise professional skepticism. (Due professional care and professional skepticism are discussed in Chapter 3.) The exercise of due care allows the auditor to obtain *reasonable assurance* that the financial statements are free of material misstatement. *Absolute assurance* is not attainable, in part because of the nature of audit evidence (which is discussed in Chapter 6) and in part because of the characteristics of fraud (discussed below). As a result, the due care standard makes it clear that the auditor is not an insurer or guarantor that the financial statements are free of material misstatement.

Since the auditor's opinion on the financial statements is based on the concept of obtaining reasonable assurance, the auditor is not an insurer and his or her report does not constitute a guarantee. Therefore, the subsequent discovery that a material misstatement, whether from error or fraud, exists in the financial statements does not, in and of itself, evidence (a) failure to obtain reasonable assurance, (b) inadequate planning, performance, or judgment, (c) the absence of due professional care, or (d) a failure to comply with generally accepted auditing standards. (AU Section 230.13)

A principal reason for this is that even a properly designed and executed audit may not detect material frauds, because of their multifaceted characteristics. For example, fraud may be concealed through forged or otherwise falsified documents. Auditors are not trained to authenticate signatures or documents, and as a result audits conducted in accordance with GAAS rarely involve authenticating signatures or documents. Fraud also may be concealed through collusion among management, employees, or third parties. Collusion may allow the creation of evidence that appears persuasive to the auditor, but that in fact is false, thereby making otherwise appropriate auditing procedures totally ineffective. As a result, auditing procedures that are effective for detecting an unintentional misstatement may be ineffective when the same misstatement is intentional, cleverly executed, or concealed through collusion.

(b) Error and Fraud and the Characteristics of Fraud

The terms "errors" and "fraud" are described in the professional literature.

The term *errors* refers to unintentional misstatements or omissions of amounts or disclosures in financial statements. Errors may involve—

- Mistakes in gathering or processing data from which financial statements are prepared.
- Unreasonable accounting estimates arising from oversight or misinterpretation of facts.
- Mistakes in the application of accounting principles relating to amount, classification, manner of presentation, or disclosure. (AU Section 312.06)

Fraud can cause two types of misstatements—misstatements arising from fraudulent financial reporting and misstatements arising from misappropriation of assets. The primary factor that distinguishes fraud from error is that the underlying action that results in the financial statement misstatement is intentional in the case of fraud and unintentional in the case of error.

Misstatements arising from fraudulent financial reporting are intentional misstatements or omissions of amounts or disclosures in financial statements to deceive financial statement users. Fraudulent financial reporting may involve acts such as the following:

- Manipulation, falsification, or alteration of accounting records or supporting documents from which financial statements are prepared.
- Misrepresentation in, or intentional omission from, the financial statements of events, transactions, or other significant information.
- Intentional misapplication of accounting principles relating to amounts, classification, manner of presentation, or disclosure. (AU Section 316.04)

Misstatements arising from misappropriation of assets (sometimes referred to as defalcation) involve the theft of an entity's assets where the effect of the theft causes the financial statements not to be presented in conformity with generally accepted accounting principles. Misappropriation can be accomplished in various ways, including embezzling receipts, stealing assets, or causing an entity to pay for goods or services not received. Misappropriation of assets may be accompanied by false or misleading records or documents and may involve one or more individuals among management, employees, or third parties. (AU Section 316.05)

Fraudulent financial reporting often is done to further a management goal, such as higher reported earnings, rather than for direct personal enrichment, although inappropriate bonuses and other forms of compensation may result from the misstated earnings. Fraudulent financial reporting is likely to have a significant effect on financial statements. It often involves the deliberate misapplication of accounting principles, such as premature revenue recognition, failure to provide for uncollectible accounts receivable, overstatement of inventory, failure to record liabilities, inadequate financial statement disclosures, and shifting expenses to future periods by capitalizing costs that should have been expensed.

Misappropriation of assets can take the form of the theft of cash, inventory, or other assets or the unauthorized use or sale of entity resources. This type of fraud is generally less significant to the financial statements than is fraudulent financial reporting. The concealment of defalcations can, of course, result in overstatements of assets (paid receivables reported as still due) or understatements of liabilities (cash misappropriated and reported as payments made). In many instances of defalcation, however, the financial statement misstatement is limited to the misclassification of expenses on the income statement; the balance sheet will not be misstated if the asset that has been misappropriated has been removed from the statement. (For example, inventory that was stolen may have been properly removed from the balance sheet but charged to cost of sales rather than to a loss account.)

Fraud usually involves the perception of some pressure or incentive by one or more individuals who are in a position to perpetrate fraud and a belief that an opportunity exists to commit fraud. An incentive to misappropriate assets may arise because of financial stress or an adverse relationship between the individual and the entity. Management may have an incentive to engage in fraudulent financial reporting to maintain reported levels of performance in the face of a declining market, the loss of significant customers, or obsolete inventory in order to maintain the price of the entity's stock or to avoid violating restrictive debt covenants. Opportunities to commit fraud include the absence of controls to prevent fraud or to detect it on a timely basis, and the ability to override or circumvent controls that do exist.

There is no important distinction between error and fraud in the auditor's responsibility to obtain reasonable assurance that the financial statements are free from material misstatement. There is a distinction, however, in how the auditor should respond to the two kinds of misstatements when they have been detected. Isolated, immaterial errors in processing data or applying GAAP are not significant to the audit. When fraud is detected, however, even if the dollar amount is immaterial to the financial statements, the auditor needs to consider the implications for the integrity of the entity's employees (and particularly the integrity of management) and the possible effect on other aspects of the audit.

(c)   Assessing the Risk of Fraud

Risk factors or other conditions may alert the auditor to the possibility that fraud may exist. Those factors may be related to particular account balances or classes of transactions, or they may have effects that are pervasive to the financial statements taken as a whole. As an example of the former, management that places undue emphasis on increased earnings may be disinclined to provide adequate allowances for uncollectible accounts receivable or unsalable inventory. To illustrate the latter, pressure on divisional executives to meet unrealistic budgets, or a downturn in the economy, may lead to recording sales in advance of shipments, nonrecognition of expenses, unreasonably low estimates of annual depreciation, or other means of artificially inflating income.

SAS No. 82 requires the auditor to assess the risk that the financial statements may be materially misstated due to fraud and to consider that assessment in designing the audit. (This assessment is necessary even if the auditor otherwise plans to assess control risk at maximum.[2])   The auditor should consider risk factors related to both fraudulent financial reporting and misappropriation of assets.

Risk factors that relate to fraudulent financial reporting may be grouped into three categories:

- *Risk factors relating to management's characteristics and influence over the control environment.* These factors pertain to management's abilities, pressures, and style, and its attitude toward internal control and the financial reporting process. Examples include:
  - A motivation to engage in fraudulent financial reporting because bonuses, stock options, or other incentives are tied to unduly aggressive earnings targets
  - Ineffective or inappropriate communication and support of values or ethics
  - High management or director turnover
  - Strained relationships with current or prior auditors
  - A history of securities law violations
- *Risk factors relating to industry conditions.* These factors involve the economic and regulatory environment in which the entity operates. Examples include:
  - A high level of competition, market saturation, or declining profits
  - Rapid changes in technology or rapid product obsolescence
  - New accounting, statutory, or regulatory requirements affecting financial stability or profitability
- *Risk factors relating to the entity's operating characteristics and financial stability.* These factors are related to the nature and complexity of the entity and its transactions, financial condition, and profitability. Examples include:
  - Inability to generate cash flows from operations along with high reported earnings

---

[2] Control risk is discussed in Chapter 6.

- Pressure for additional capital
- Significant accounting estimates involving unusually subjective judgments or uncertainties or that may change in the near term and in a way that would be financially disruptive
- Significant related party transactions
- An overly complex organizational structure
- High vulnerability to interest rate changes
- Threat of imminent bankruptcy or hostile takeover

Risk factors that relate to misappropriation of assets may be grouped into two categories:

- *Risk factors relating to the susceptibility of assets to misappropriation.* These are related to the nature of the entity's assets and the degree to which they are susceptible to theft. Examples include:
  - Large amounts of cash on hand
  - Small-size, high-value inventory
  - Easily marketable assets, such as bearer bonds or diamonds
- *Risk factors relating to controls.* These are related to the lack of controls designed to prevent or detect misappropriations. Examples include:
  - Inadequate supervision or management oversight
  - Deficient record keeping
  - Inappropriate segregation of duties
  - Poor physical safeguards over assets susceptible to misappropriation
  - Lack of mandatory vacations for key employees

The auditor may identify these risk factors at several stages during the audit: when performing client acceptance and retention procedures, during engagement planning, while obtaining an understanding of the entity's internal control, or while conducting field work. Also, the auditor's cumulative assessment of the risk of fraud may be affected by the identification of various conditions during the course of the audit, such as:

- Discrepancies in the accounting records because of unrecorded or unsupported transactions or last-minute significant "adjustments"
- Conflicting or missing documents
- Problems that arise in dealing with management, such as denial of access to records or employees, undue time pressures, and tips or complaints to the auditor about fraud

(d) Responding to the Risk of Fraud

The presence of one or more of these risk factors or conditions does not necessarily mean that material fraud is probable. However, when factors or conditions are present that increase the risk of material fraud, the auditor should respond to that higher risk. In some cases, the auditor's risk assessment might call for an overall response. For example, more experienced personnel could be assigned to the audit, the extent of procedures applied in particular areas (for example, the size of the sample in a particular test) could be increased, the type of procedure used could be changed to obtain evidence that is more persuasive than otherwise would have been appropriate (for example, confirming transactions with independent sources outside the entity instead of examining entity documentation), or the timing of certain tests could be changed to be closer to or at year-end. A higher risk also may call for changes in how the auditor exercises professional skepticism in conducting the audit, for example, when the auditor considers management's selection and application of accounting principles and when he or she determines whether control risk can be assessed below the maximum. (Professional skepticism is discussed in Chapter 3; the auditor's assessment of control risk is discussed in Chapter 12.)

The auditor also should consider how the presence of fraud risk factors and conditions may affect the audit of specific accounts, transactions, and assertions. For example, if there is a risk of fraudulent financial reporting involving improper revenue recognition, the auditor might confirm with customers the terms of contracts and the absence of side agreements that could affect the appropriate accounting, rather than confirming only the balances in customers' accounts, which otherwise might be the appropriate auditing procedure. As another example, the nature of the entity's business and the absence of appropriate controls may lead the auditor to conclude that there is a risk of misappropriation of material amounts of cash. In that situation, the auditor might determine that it is appropriate to count cash and other assets that can easily be converted into cash, such as securities, at year-end.

(e)   Evaluation of Test Results

Before the audit has been completed, the auditor should consider whether the accumulated results of all auditing procedures performed and conditions noted change the assessment of the risk of fraud that was made in planning the audit. If the risk assessment does change, the auditor should consider whether there is a need to perform additional or different procedures.

Chapter 27 (Section 27.5, Summarizing Misstatements and Evaluating the Audit Findings) discusses how the auditor processes and evaluates misstatements found during the audit, regardless of whether they are intentional (fraud) or unintentional (error). If a misstatement *is* or *may be*[3] the result of fraud, the auditor should:

- Consider the implications for other aspects of the audit—for example, the need to reconsider the effectiveness of the entity's internal control
- Discuss the matter and the approach to further investigation with a level of management that is above those involved, and with senior management
- Attempt to obtain further evidence to determine whether material fraud has occurred and, if it has, the effect on the financial statements

[3] SAS No. 82 notes that "intent is often difficult to determine, particularly in matters involving accounting estimates and the application of accounting principles." The *may be* threshold does not require the auditor to determine that fraud is *probable* before the responsibilities described in this section apply.

- Report to the audit committee fraud that involves senior management and fraud (even if not on the part of senior management) that causes the financial statements to be materially misstated
- Consider suggesting that management consult with legal counsel
- Consider withdrawing from the engagement

(f) Documentation Requirements

Chapter 7 discusses the purpose of audit working papers and provides guidance on what matters generally should be documented in working papers. SAS No. 82 specifies the required documentation of the auditor's assessment of the risk of fraud and the response to that assessment. The following matters should be documented in the working papers:

- Evidence of the performance of the risk assessment
- Specific risk factors identified as being present during the planning phase
- The response to those risk factors, individually or in combination
- Additional risk factors or other conditions identified during the course of the audit and any further responses to those risk factors and conditions

(g) Illegal Acts by Clients

Independent auditors have been responsible, to a certain extent, for the detection and disclosure of illegal or questionable acts by clients since 1977, when SAS No. 17, *Illegal Acts by Clients,* was issued. SAS No. 17 resulted, at least in part, from attention on the part of various government bodies, particularly the SEC, to illegal or questionable corporate acts, such as bribes, political payoffs, and kickbacks—usually made at least ostensibly for the benefit of the entity. In the 1980s, public attention once again focused on auditors' responsibilities with respect to clients that were alleged to have committed illegal acts; that attention led to the issuance in 1988 of SAS No. 54 (AU Section 317), which superseded SAS No. 17. Illegal acts by clients are violations of laws or government regulations, perpetrated by an entity or by management or employees acting on behalf of the entity; they do not include personal misconduct unrelated to the entity's business.

Some laws and regulations have a direct and material effect on the determination of amounts in financial statement line items. For example, tax laws affect the provision for income taxes and the related tax liability; federal laws and regulations may affect the amount of revenue that should be recognized under a government contract. The auditor, however, considers such laws and regulations from the perspective of their known relation to audit objectives and the corresponding financial statement assertions, rather than from the perspective of legality per se. The auditor's responsibility to detect misstatements resulting from illegal acts that have a direct and material effect on financial statement amounts is the same as for errors and fraud.

SAS No. 54 (AU Section 317.06) explains, however, that there is another class of illegal acts for which the auditor has far less detection responsibility.

Entities may be affected by many other laws or regulations, including those related to securities trading, occupational safety and health, food and drug administration, environmental protection, equal employment, and price-fixing or other antitrust violations. Generally, these laws and regulations relate more to an entity's operating aspects than to its financial and accounting aspects, and their financial statement effect is indirect. An auditor ordinarily does not have sufficient basis for recognizing possible violations of such laws and regulations. Their indirect effect is normally the result of the need to disclose a contingent liability because of the allegation or determination of illegality. For example, securities may be purchased or sold based on inside information. While the direct effects of the purchase or sale may be recorded appropriately, their indirect effect, the possible contingent liability for violating securities laws, may not be appropriately disclosed. Even when violations of such laws and regulations can have consequences material to the financial statements, the auditor may not become aware of the existence of the illegal act unless he is informed by the client, or there is evidence of a governmental agency investigation or enforcement proceeding in the records, documents, or other information normally inspected in an audit of financial statements.

The auditor should be aware of the possibility that these kinds of illegal acts may have occurred. Normally, an audit performed in accordance with generally accepted auditing standards does not include procedures specifically designed to detect these illegal acts. Only if specific information comes to the auditor's attention indicating that such acts might exist and might need to be disclosed in the financial statements, should the auditor apply procedures specifically directed to ascertaining whether such an illegal act has occurred. An audit conducted in accordance with generally accepted auditing standards provides no assurance that this type of illegal act will be detected or that any resultant contingent liabilities will be disclosed.

Procedures that otherwise would be applied, however, for the purpose of forming an opinion on the financial statements, may bring possible illegal acts to the auditor's attention. Such procedures include reading minutes of directors' meetings; inquiring of the entity's management and legal counsel concerning litigation, claims, and assessments; and performing tests of the various account balances. The auditor also may make inquiries of management concerning the entity's:

- Compliance with laws and regulations
- Policies relating to the prevention of illegal acts
- Communications to, and the receipt of representations from, its own management at appropriate levels of authority concerning compliance with laws and regulations. Those representations often include statements, signed annually by all levels of management, that they have not violated entity policy—which usually is defined to cover all of the actions proscribed by the Foreign Corrupt Practices Act (discussed in Chapter 9), as well as conflicts of interest—and that they are not aware of any such violations.

Finally, through the performance of procedures (including communication with attorneys) to determine the existence of loss contingencies, the auditor may uncover violations of laws.

Distinguishing between illegal acts that have a direct and material effect on financial statements and illegal acts whose financial statement effect is indirect can be difficult. Although SAS No. 54 gives examples of both types of illegal acts, it does not provide explicit guidance on determining which category an illegal act falls into. Direct-effect illegal acts relate to violations of laws and regulations that affect a line-item financial statement amount. An example of such laws and regulations is the tax code provisions that determine how an entity's tax liability is measured and presented in its financial statements. In contrast, failure to comply with tax code provisions relating to the filing of information has only an indirect effect on financial statements, namely, the requirement to disclose the contingent liability for tax penalties. Another example of a direct-effect illegal act would be violations of state usury laws when related regulations provide for the remedy of refunding excess interest charged.

4.4 REQUIRED AUDITOR COMMUNICATIONS

Auditors have responsibilities to communicate certain information or events in connection with their audit work. Some of those responsibilities are specified by professional standards; others are specified by statute. For example, various Statements on Auditing Standards require the auditor to communicate certain matters to the audit committee, or to determine that management has appropriately reported them. Those matters include material errors, frauds, and illegal acts, and significant deficiencies in the design or operation of internal control that the auditor becomes aware of in the course of the audit, including deficiencies related to the preparation of interim financial information. The SEC Practice Section of the AICPA Division for CPA Firms requires the auditor to communicate to the audit committee fees received for management advisory services. In addition, auditors usually acquire information in the course of an audit that may be helpful to the audit committee in meeting its responsibility for overseeing the entity's financial reporting process, including the audit itself, or to management in operating the business. Lastly, the Private Securities Litigation Reform Act of 1995 requires the auditor to notify the SEC of material illegal acts in certain circumstances.

(a) Responsibilities on Discovering an Error, Fraud, or Illegal Act

An auditor who becomes aware of an error or a possible fraud or illegal act should determine the potential effect on the financial statements being audited. The auditor should be aware of the sensitivity of these matters and the need for substantial evidence before making any allegations of fraud or illegal acts. If the auditor concludes that the financial statements are materially misstated, because of either errors or possible frauds or illegal acts, or that loss contingencies or the potential effects of an illegal act on the entity's operations are inadequately disclosed, he or she should insist that the statements be revised. If they are not, the auditor should express a qualified or an adverse opinion on the financial statements.

In addition, whenever the auditor has determined that there is evidence that a fraud may exist, he or she should bring the matter to the attention of management at a level high enough to be able to deal appropriately with it, including further investigation if considered necessary. This level should be at least one level above those involved. Fraud involving senior management and fraud that causes a material misstatement of the financial statements (whether involving senior management or others) should be reported to the audit committee. (The audit committee also may want to be informed about misappropriations perpetrated by lower-level employees.) The auditor also should determine that the audit committee has been informed about all illegal acts of which the auditor becomes aware, unless they are clearly inconsequential. If the auditor has identified fraud risk factors that represent deficiencies in the entity's internal control, those deficiencies also should be reported to senior management and the audit committee, as discussed later in the chapter.

Disclosure of frauds or illegal acts to parties other than the entity's senior management and its audit committee, however, ordinarily is not part of the auditor's responsibility (unless the matter affects the opinion on the financial statements), and would be precluded by the auditor's ethical and legal obligation of confidentiality. There are several circumstances, however, in which a duty to notify parties outside the entity may exist: (a) disclosure to the SEC when an auditor change is reported,[4] (b) disclosure to a successor auditor upon appropriate inquiry, (c) disclosure in response to a subpoena, (d) disclosure to a governmental agency in accordance with requirements for audits of entities that receive financial assistance from a governmental agency, and (e) disclosure to the SEC under the Private Securities Litigation Reform Act of 1995. Potential conflicts with the auditor's ethical and legal obligations for confidentiality may be complex. As a result, the auditor may wish to consult with legal counsel before discussing fraud or illegal acts with parties other than the client.

The auditor may not be able to determine the extent of a possible fraud and its effects on the financial statements. If the auditor is precluded by management from applying necessary procedures or is otherwise unable to conclude whether fraud may materially affect the financial statements, an opinion qualified because of a scope limitation or a disclaimer of opinion should be issued. The auditor also could be precluded by management from evaluating whether a possible illegal act is, in fact, illegal and material to the financial statements. In those instances, the auditor generally should disclaim an opinion on the financial statements. If, however, the auditor's inability to determine whether an act is illegal does not result from client-imposed restrictions, a scope qualification may be appropriate.

If the client refuses to accept the auditor's report as modified for the reasons described above, the auditor should withdraw from the engagement and indicate the reasons for withdrawal to the audit committee or board of directors. Withdrawal also might be appropriate in other circumstances, such as when the entity continues to retain a known perpetrator of fraud in a position with a significant role in the entity's internal control, or when it refuses to take remedial action the auditor considers appropriate when an illegal act has occurred. Withdrawal from an engagement would cause a change of auditors, which, for a publicly traded company, would trigger the SEC Form 8-K filing discussed in Chapter 3, thereby publicizing the reasons for the withdrawal.

(b)   Auditor "Whistleblowing"

In large part because of several well-publicized business failures, some of which required bailouts by the federal government, Congress and regulators became increas-

---

[4] As noted in Chapter 3, CPA firms that are members of the AICPA's SEC Practice Section have an obligation to notify the SEC when a firm has resigned, declined to stand for reelection, or been dismissed.

ingly concerned about auditors' responsibilities with respect to their clients' compliance with laws and regulations and about how instances of noncompliance were reported. Those concerns led to inclusion in the Private Securities Litigation Reform Act of 1995 (the Act) of a requirement for auditors of public companies to notify the SEC of material illegal acts when an entity's management and board of directors have failed to take timely and appropriate remedial action and have failed to comply with a requirement to notify the SEC of such inaction. In addition, the Act requires the auditor to use procedures in accordance with GAAS (as may be modified or supplemented by the SEC) that would provide reasonable assurance of detecting illegal acts that have a direct and material effect on an entity's financial statements, thereby codifying into law the requirements of SAS No. 54. It also codifies into law current professional requirements that the auditor identify related party transactions that either are material to the financial statements or require disclosure (see Chapters 8 and 26), and that the auditor evaluate whether there is substantial doubt about the entity's ability to continue as a going concern over the ensuing fiscal year (see Chapter 26).

The Act requires that if the auditor determines it is likely that an illegal act has occurred, he or she is required to:

- Determine and consider the possible effect of the illegal act on the entity's financial statements, including any contingent monetary effects, such as fines, penalties, and damages
- As soon as practicable, inform the appropriate level of the entity's management and ensure that the audit committee (or board of directors in the absence of an audit committee) is informed of the illegal act, unless it is clearly inconsequential

The auditor also is required to report, as soon as practicable, his or her conclusions directly to the entity's board of directors in circumstances where:

- The illegal act has a material effect on the financial statements
- Senior management has not taken, and the board of directors has not caused senior management to take, timely and appropriate remedial action with respect to the illegal act
- The failure to take remedial action is reasonably expected to warrant departure from a standard auditor's report or the auditor's resignation

On receipt of such a report by the board of directors, the entity is required to notify the SEC within one business day, with a copy of the notification sent to the auditor. If the auditor fails to receive such a notice within one day, he or she should either:

- Furnish the SEC with a copy of his or her report on the next business day following the failure to receive notice
- Resign from the engagement and furnish the SEC with a copy of his or her report (or the documentation of any oral report given) within one business day

With respect to the report made to the SEC, the Act specifies that no auditor will be held liable in a private action for any finding, conclusion, or statement made pursuant to its direct reporting provisions. Willful violations, however, are subject to SEC civil action.

(c) Communicating Internal Control Deficiencies

While management has primary responsibility for reliable financial reporting, the board of directors, generally acting through its audit committee (if there is one), is responsible for overseeing the financial reporting process. That responsibility can be carried out most effectively if the board or audit committee is informed of deficiencies in internal control that the auditor becomes aware of. Management also is usually interested in the auditor's observations about internal control deficiencies and ways of remedying them, and in suggestions the auditor may have for improving the entity's operations and profitability.

SAS No. 60, *Communication of Internal Control Related Matters Noted in an Audit* (AU Section 325.02), requires the auditor to communicate to the audit committee of the board of directors, or its equivalent, matters coming to his or her attention in the course of the audit that represent "significant deficiencies" in the design or operation of any of the components of internal control that could adversely affect the entity's ability to "record, process, summarize, and report financial data consistent with the assertions of management in the financial statements." The SAS refers to these matters as "reportable conditions," and expresses a preference that they be communicated in writing rather than orally. The SAS explicitly permits the auditor to comment on other matters that do not meet the criteria of *reportable conditions* but that the auditor deems to be of value to the audit committee, and those comments may be segregated from observations about reportable conditions.

Although the auditor is required to communicate reportable conditions only to the audit committee or its equivalent, the authors believe it is good practice to communicate such matters to management as well. If there is no audit committee or board of directors or the equivalent, the communication would be made only to management (which is likely to be an owner-manager) or to the party that engaged the auditor.

The auditor may come across matters other than reportable conditions in the course of an audit that would be helpful to management in carrying out its duties. These are matters that either may be below the threshold of significance for reporting to the audit committee, or may be financial and business suggestions that would enhance operational efficiency and profitability. The auditor usually discusses such matters with management and also may communicate them in writing.

It is good practice for the auditor to discuss all comments on internal control with management before drafting a written communication. If the auditor's understanding of controls was mistaken in some respect, discussing the comments will clarify the misunderstanding and save the auditor the embarrassment of discovering it later. In many instances, management's responses to the auditor's suggestions are included in the communication. The best time to discuss deficiencies in controls and related problems and to draft a written communication is at the conclusion of tests of controls. Ideally, that point occurs when both auditor and management have time to consider the auditor's findings. Preferably it should take place far enough before year-end to permit corrective action that could affect the auditor's remaining work.

The auditor has no obligation to extend the work that he or she otherwise would do in an audit in order to search for reportable conditions; there is merely an obligation to report those coming to his or her attention as a result of procedures that were performed. Many practitioners believe that reports on internal control that are based solely on what the auditor learns in the course of an audit are likely to be misunderstood or misinterpreted by the public at large, who may read into them a greater degree of assurance than is warranted. Accordingly, the SAS specifies that "the report should state that the communication is intended solely for the information and the use of the audit committee, management, and others within the organization" (AU Section 325.10). The report also may discuss the inherent limitations of internal control in general and the specific nature and extent of the auditor's consideration of controls.

A reportable condition may be of such magnitude as to be considered a *material weakness* in internal control. A material weakness is "a reportable condition in which the design or operation of one or more of the internal control components does not reduce to a relatively low level the risk that errors or . . . [fraud] in amounts that would be material in relation to the financial statements being audited may occur and not be detected within a timely period by employees in the normal course of performing their assigned functions" (AU Section 325.15). Although not required to do so, an auditor may choose to separately identify those reportable conditions that meet this definition. Or, if it is appropriate to do so, the auditor may state that none of the reportable conditions communicated were believed to be material weaknesses. However, the auditor should not issue a written representation that no reportable conditions were noted during the audit, because of the potential for misinterpretation of the limited degree of assurance that such a report would provide. Figure 4.1 presents an example of a report to an audit committee on internal control related matters.

The client may already be aware of the existence of reportable conditions related to the design or operation of controls, and may have decided to accept the accompanying degree of risk because of cost or other considerations. If the audit committee has acknowledged that it understands and has considered a deficiency and the related risks, the auditor need not continue to report the matter after it has been initially reported to the committee. Nevertheless, changes in management or in the audit committee, or merely the passage of time, may make repeated reporting of such matters appropriate and timely.

Many auditors believe that all recommendations for improvements in internal control that are communicated to any level of management should be brought to the attention of the audit committee. One way to do this would be to include a statement in the report to the audit committee that the auditor has, in a separate communication to management, made suggestions for internal control improvements that do not involve reportable conditions. A copy of that communication could also be sent to the audit committee.

As discussed previously, the auditor may report conditions noted during the audit that he or she believes will be helpful to management, but that do not reach the threshold level of a reportable condition. Similarly, management may request the auditor to be alert to certain matters that might not be considered reportable conditions and to submit a report on the findings. These agreed-upon arrangements, which may be particularly useful to the client, do not relieve the auditor of the basic responsibility to communicate reportable conditions.

Figure 4.1   Report on Internal Control Related Matters

April 12, 19XY

Audit Committee of the Board of Directors
ABC Manufacturing Co., Inc.
123 Industrial Road
Anytown, U.S.A. 12345

Members of the Audit Committee:

In planning and performing our audit of the financial statements of the ABC Manufacturing Co., Inc., for the year ended December 31, 19XX, we considered its internal control in order to determine our auditing procedures for the purpose of expressing our opinion on the financial statements and not to provide assurance on internal control. However, we noted certain matters involving internal control and its operation that we consider to be reportable conditions under standards established by the American Institute of Certified Public Accountants. Reportable conditions involve matters coming to our attention relating to significant deficiencies in the design or operation of controls that, in our judgment, could adversely affect the company's ability to record, process, summarize, and report financial data consistent with the assertions of management in the financial statements.

Access Controls to Data by Terminals Can Be Bypassed

At the present time, there is a critical "file protect" system that prohibits the access of production data by remote terminal users. Our review disclosed a method (special coding of a control card) by which this system can be bypassed and remote terminal users can access and/or alter financial data in computer files. Unauthorized access to data files can result in inaccurate financial data being reported by the systems or confidential data being available to unauthorized personnel. Management is currently studying various means of correcting this situation.

The Director of Internal Audit Reports to the Controller

The objectivity of the internal audit function is enhanced when the director of internal audit reports to an individual or group in the company with sufficient authority to promote independence, provide adequate consideration of findings and recommendations in audit reports, ensure that appropriate action is taken on audit recommendations, and resolve conflicts between internal auditors and various levels of management. At ABC Manufacturing Co., Inc., the director of internal audit for each subsidiary reports to the subsidiary controller; the corporate director of internal audit reports to the corporate controller. We believe that the directors' objectivity would be enhanced if they reported to the vice-president and treasurer of each subsidiary and the corporate vice-president and treasurer, respectively, with summaries of all internal audit reports presented to the audit committee of the board of directors.

Inadequate Systems for Preparing Consolidated Statements

The accounting department presently does not have sufficient staff to prepare consolidated reports of worldwide operations in time to meet the company's re-

Figure 4.1   *(Continued)*

quirements for preparing quarterly and year-end financial information. Those requirements presently are met, in part, through the assistance of both the internal auditors and ourselves. Preparing consolidated financial statements is not an appropriate service for either the internal or external auditors to provide. Financial management agrees with our reviews and is currently undertaking to add sufficient competent personnel and appropriate computer software to the accounting department to enable it to prepare consolidated quarterly and year-end financial statements on a timely basis.

This report is intended solely for the information and use of the audit committee, management, and others within the company.

Very truly yours,

Smith and Jones, CPAs

(d)   Other Communications with Audit Committees

SAS No. 61, *Communication With Audit Committees* (AU Section 380), requires the auditor to determine that certain additional matters related to the conduct of an audit are communicated—either by the auditor or by management—to those who have responsibility for financial reporting; generally, this means the audit committee. The required communications are applicable to all SEC engagements (as defined in Chapter 3) and to other entities that have an audit committee or equivalent group with formally designated oversight of the financial reporting process. Among the items that should be communicated are:

- The level of responsibility the auditor assumes under GAAS for the financial statements and for considering the entity's internal control (This is usually communicated in the engagement letter, discussed later.)
- Significant accounting policies that the entity has selected for new or unusual transactions, and changes in those policies
- The process management used to formulate particularly sensitive accounting estimates, and the basis for the auditor's conclusion that they were reasonable (see Chapter 15)
- Significant adjustments to the financial statements that resulted from the audit and that have a significant effect on the entity's financial reporting process (discussed in Chapter 27)
- The auditor's responsibility for other information in documents, such as annual reports to shareholders, containing audited financial statements [see the discussion in Chapter 28, Section 28.3(d), Material Inconsistency Between Financial Statements and Other Information Reported by Management]
- Disagreements with management over the application of accounting principles,

the scope of the audit, and the wording of the auditor's report (discussed in Chapter 3)

- The auditor's views on auditing and accounting matters that management consulted other auditors about (see the discussions in Chapters 3 and 29)

- Major issues regarding the application of accounting principles and auditing standards that the auditor and management discussed in connection with the auditor's initial or recurring retention

- Serious difficulties encountered in dealing with management related to the performance of the audit, such as unreasonable delays in permitting the start of the audit or in providing needed information, unreasonable timetables, or not making needed entity personnel available

Some of these matters should be discussed with the audit committee before the auditor's report is drafted, because the discussion may help the auditor form the appropriate conclusion about the financial statements. Others could occur after the report has been issued. The communication of recurring matters need not be repeated every year.

4.5 ENGAGEMENT LETTERS

Most auditors recognize the need to establish an understanding with the client regarding the objectives of the engagement, the responsibilities of both management and the auditor, and the limitations of the engagement. That understanding usually is documented in a written communication called an "engagement letter" (sometimes referred to as a "letter of arrangement").[5] Some auditors also include fee terms and other arrangements in the letter. Engagement letters typically include statements that document an understanding between the entity and the auditor that:

- The objective of the audit is an opinion on the financial statements

- Management is responsible for the financial statements

- Management is responsible for establishing and maintaining effective internal control over financial reporting

- Management is responsible for the entity's compliance with laws and regulations applicable to the entity's activities

- Management is responsible for making all financial records and related information available to the auditor

- Management will provide the auditor with a representation letter at the end of the audit (see Chapter 27)

- The auditor is responsible for conducting an audit in accordance with GAAS

- GAAS require the auditor to obtain reasonable, rather than absolute, assurance about whether the financial statements are free of material misstatement; as a result, a material misstatement may remain undetected

---

[5] At the time of this writing, the ASB has issued an exposure draft of an SAS that would require the auditor to establish an understanding with the client and document the understanding in the working papers, preferably through a written communication with the client.

- If the auditor is unable to complete the audit, he or she may decline to express an opinion or issue a report
- The auditor is required to understand the entity's internal control sufficiently to plan the audit, but the audit is not designed to provide assurance on internal control or to identify deficiencies in internal control
- The auditor is responsible for communicating deficiencies in internal control of which he or she becomes aware; additional communications are required by GAAS

Sometimes engagement letters also include the following:

- Arrangements regarding the conduct of the audit, such as its timing, the entity's assistance in the preparation of schedules, and the availability of documents
- Arrangements concerning the involvement of specialists and internal auditors
- Arrangements to be made with a predecessor auditor
- Fees and billing arrangements
- Limitations or other arrangements regarding the liability of the auditor or the client
- Conditions under which access to the auditor's working papers may be granted to others

A typical engagement letter is shown in Figure 4.2.

Figure 4.2   Typical Engagement Letter

[Date]

[Chief Financial Officer]
[Name of Entity]

Dear _____:

This letter of arrangement between [entity] and [auditor] sets forth the nature and scope of the services we will provide, [entity's] required involvement and assistance in support of our services, the related fee arrangements, and other terms and conditions designed to ensure that our professional services are performed to achieve the mutually agreed upon objectives of [entity]

SUMMARY OF SERVICES

We will audit the [consolidated] financial statements of [entity] as of and for the period ending _____, in accordance with generally accepted auditing standards. The objective of an audit is the expression of our opinion concerning whether the

Figure 4.2   *(Continued)*

financial statements present fairly, in all material respects, the financial position, results of operations, and cash flows of the [entity] in conformity with generally accepted accounting principles [other comprehensive basis of accounting]. We expect to deliver our report on or about _____. If, for any reason, we are unable to complete the audit, we may decline to issue a report as a result of this engagement.

In conjunction with your annual audit, we will perform a review of [entity's] unaudited [consolidated] quarterly financial statements and related data for each of the first three quarters in the year ending _____, before they are released. This review, which is substantially less in scope than an audit, will be conducted in accordance with standards established by the American Institute of Certified Public Accountants. We will report to you in writing each quarter on the results of our review. From time to time, we also will report any additional observations arising from our reviews that we believe are appropriate for your consideration.

[Where applicable, add: We also will read the other information included in the annual report to shareholders and consider whether such information, including the manner of its presentation, is materially inconsistent with information appearing in the financial statements.]

Any additional services that you may request, and that we agree to provide, will be the subject of separate written arrangements.

[*Details regarding terms and conditions of engagement and fee arrangements would be included here*]

LIMITATIONS OF THE AUDITING PROCESS

Our audit will include procedures designed to obtain reasonable assurance of detecting misstatements due to errors or fraud that are material to the financial statements. As you are aware, however, there are inherent limitations in the auditing process. For example, audits are based on the concept of selective testing of the data being examined and are, therefore, subject to the limitation that misstatements due to errors or fraud, if they exist, may not be detected. Also, because of the characteristics of fraud, including attempts at concealment through collusion and forgery, a properly designed and executed audit may not detect a material misstatement due to fraud.

Similarly, in performing our audit we will be aware of the possibility that illegal acts may have occurred. However, it should be recognized that our audit provides no assurance that illegal acts generally will be detected, and only reasonable assurance that illegal acts having a direct and material effect on the determination of financial statement amounts will be detected. We will inform you with respect to material errors and fraud, or illegal acts that come to our attention during the course of our audit.

Figure 4.2   *(Continued)*

RESPONSIBILITIES AS TO INTERNAL CONTROL

As a part of our audit, we will consider [entity's] internal control, as required by generally accepted auditing standards, sufficient to plan the audit and to determine the nature, timing, and extent of auditing procedures necessary for expressing our opinion concerning the financial statements. You recognize that the financial statements and the establishment and maintenance of effective internal control over financial reporting are the responsibility of management. Appropriate supervisory review procedures are necessary to provide reasonable assurance that adopted policies and prescribed procedures are adhered to and to identify errors and fraud or illegal acts. An audit is not designed to provide assurance on internal control. As part of our consideration of [entity's] internal control, however, we will inform you of matters that come to our attention that represent significant deficiencies in the design or operation of internal control.

REPRESENTATION FROM MANAGEMENT

Management is responsible for the fair presentation of the financial statements in conformity with generally accepted accounting principles, for making all financial records and related information available to us, and for identifying and ensuring that the entity complies with the laws and regulations applicable to its activities. At the conclusion of the engagement, [entity's] management will provide to us a representation letter that, among other things, addresses these matters and confirms certain representations made during the audit, including, to the best of their knowledge and belief, the absence of fraud involving management or those employees who have significant roles in the entity's internal control, or others where it could have a material effect on the financial statements.

COMMUNICATIONS

At the conclusion of the engagement, we will provide management [and the audit committee or others so designated], in a mutually agreeable format, our recommendations designed to help [entity] make improvements in its internal control and operations, and other matters that may come to our attention (see "Responsibilities as to Internal Control" above).

    As part of this engagement we will ensure that certain additional matters are communicated to the appropriate members of management and the audit committee [or others with equivalent authority]. Such matters include (1) the initial selection of and changes in significant accounting policies and their application; (2) the process used by management in formulating particularly sensitive accounting estimates and the basis for our conclusions regarding the reasonableness of those estimates; (3) audit adjustments that could, in our judgment, either individually or in the aggregate, have a significant effect on your financial reporting process; (4) any disagreements with management, whether or not satisfactorily

Figure 4.2 *(Continued)*

resolved, about matters that individually or in the aggregate could be significant to the financial statements or our report; (5) our views about matters that were the subject of management's consultation with other accountants about auditing and accounting matters; (6) major issues that were discussed with management in connection with the retention of our services, including, among other matters, any discussions regarding the application of accounting principles and auditing standards; and (7) serious difficulties that we encountered in dealing with management related to the performance of the audit.

ACCESS TO WORKING PAPERS

The working papers for this engagement are the property of [auditor] and constitute confidential information. Any requests for access to our working papers will be discussed with you prior to making them available to requesting parties.

SUBPOENAS

In the event we are requested or authorized by you or required by government regulation, subpoena, or other legal process to produce our working papers or our personnel as witnesses with respect to our engagement for you, you will, so long as we are not a party to the proceeding in which the information is sought, reimburse us for our professional time and expenses, as well as the fees and expenses of our counsel, incurred in responding to such a request.

* * * * * * * *

If the foregoing is in accordance with your understanding, please sign the copy of this letter in the space provided and return it to us. If you have any questions, please call _____ at _____.

Very truly yours,

5

Auditors' Legal Liability

Beyond the disciplinary system of the profession discussed in Chapter 3, auditors,[1] in common with other professionals, are subject to legal and other sanctions as a consequence of deficiencies, that is, failure to meet professional standards in the performance of their work. Unlike some other professionals, however, whose liability is limited to their clients and patients, independent auditors are also liable to growing numbers of nonclient third parties, mainly investors and creditors, who rely on audited financial statements in making decisions that expose them to substantial potential losses. As a result, auditors' exposure to possible loss is great, and the amount of potential loss is usually indeterminate at the time the audit is performed. This chapter examines auditors' civil liabilities to clients and third parties, as well as criminal liability and civil regulatory remedies. It starts with an overview of the American legal system.

5.1   OVERVIEW OF THE AMERICAN LEGAL SYSTEM

The American legal system consists of state and federal courts and administrative agencies. Auditors' legal liability under that system derives from both common and statutory law as applied by the courts and the rulings of administrative agencies. Common law evolves from judicial rulings on matters of law in specific cases. Statutory law may codify or change common law. Judicial interpretation of statutory law, in turn, leads to the development of case law precedents. This interaction permits the courts continually to redefine the auditor's role and duties. Administrative agencies, which are created by state legislatures and Congress, have the power to enact and enforce regulations affecting auditors.

(a)   Federal Courts

A court must have subject matter jurisdiction over a particular case and personal jurisdiction over a defendant in the case before it has the power to try the case. Generally, the subject matter jurisdiction of the federal courts is based on one of two concepts: diversity jurisdiction or federal question jurisdiction. The *diversity jurisdiction* of the federal courts is derived from the U.S. Constitution and was created to prevent prejudicial treatment of out-of-state litigants in state courts. Diversity jurisdiction exists when the parties to a lawsuit are from different states and the amount in controversy exceeds $75,000. For there to be diversity jurisdiction, none of the plaintiffs (the parties who brought the suit) can be citizens of the state of any of the defendants (the parties against whom the suit was brought). The citizenship of a corporation is based on its place of incorporation and its principal place of business; if they differ, it is considered a citizen of both states. The citizenship of a partnership is determined by the citizenship of its partners.

Federal question jurisdiction is present when a plaintiff asserts a right under the Constitution, a federal statute, or a federal regulation. Federal courts also have jurisdiction over claims brought by the United States.

In addition to subject matter jurisdiction, a court also must have *personal jurisdiction*

---

[1] In this chapter, the words "auditor" and "auditors" apply to both individuals, whether sole practitioners or employees of CPA firms, and auditing firms, unless otherwise specified or indicated by context.

over a defendant. Generally, if a defendant is present in a court's district, the court will have personal jurisdiction over the individual. Courts also have "long-arm" jurisdiction that applies when a person from outside the district provides services that cause injury within the district.

To hear a case, the court must have subject matter jurisdiction and personal jurisdiction over the defendants, and be a proper "venue," that is, an appropriate location for the trial. In general, cases based on diversity jurisdiction may be brought in the judicial district where all plaintiffs or all defendants reside or where the claim arose. Cases based on federal question jurisdiction may be brought where all defendants reside or where the claim arose. In rare circumstances, a court with subject matter jurisdiction, personal jurisdiction, and venue will transfer a case to a more convenient forum, such as where all the witnesses are located, under a doctrine known as *forum non conveniens*.

A defendant may raise any claim it has against the plaintiff in a counterclaim and may bring a related claim against nonparties in a third-party complaint. For example, if a company sued its auditor for failing to prevent an embezzlement loss, the auditor could counterclaim for fees owed by the company and could file a third-party claim against the embezzler.

(b) Administrative Agencies

Administrative agencies, such as the Securities and Exchange Commission (SEC), have the power, delegated by state legislatures and Congress, to enact and enforce regulations and punish violators of them. Thus, the SEC has the power to enact a regulation requiring auditors of companies registered with it to comply with generally accepted auditing standards (GAAS), investigate whether a violation of that regulation occurred, file a complaint against an alleged violator, decide the merits of the complaint, and determine the penalty for the violation. The judges employed by federal administrative agencies to decide complaints brought by the agency are referred to as administrative law judges.

Federal courts will overturn an administrative agency's decision only if the agency's action violates the Constitution or a statute, is arbitrary or capricious, or is not supported by the record created by the agency to support its decision. However, if there is conflicting evidence, the agency's decision will not be overturned by the courts.

(c) State Courts

State courts hear and decide legal disputes that a federal court may not have jurisdiction over. These disputes may involve state statutes, some of which parallel federal statutes, such as the federal securities laws, or common law.

Common law includes contract law, which concerns the enforcement of promises, and the law of torts, which involves the duty to not cause harm to others. The law of torts covers negligence, which is the failure to conform one's conduct to the standard of a reasonable person, and fraud, which is an intentional misstatement made for the purpose of monetary gain. Professional malpractice, the failure of a licensed professional to conform his or her conduct to professional standards, falls under the law of negligence. For auditors, professional standards are contained in generally accepted auditing standards. In almost all cases there must be evidence, typically from a licensed professional, that there has been a deviation from professional standards in order to support a charge of professional malpractice. Thus, unless a violation is so egregious that it would be obvious to a layperson, a plaintiff generally must retain an "expert" witness in order to prevail in a malpractice claim.

(d) Judicial Procedures

A civil case is brought by filing a complaint with a court; the complaint is served or delivered, with a summons, to the defendant. The summons is a document that tells the defendant he or she has been sued and must respond to the complaint. The complaint must contain a plain and concise statement of the facts and the legal theories that the plaintiff believes entitle him or her to relief.

Generally, the defendant files an answer to the complaint, admitting or denying each of the allegations in the complaint, or files a motion to dismiss the complaint or a motion for summary judgment. A motion to dismiss may accept the truth of the allegations but argue they are insufficient to entitle the plaintiff to relief. A motion to dismiss also may be based on deficiencies in the complaint. For example, allegations of fraud must be specific and particular, and the plaintiff's failure to detail facts in support of a charge of fraud is a basis for dismissal of a complaint. Deficiencies also include a lack of personal or subject matter jurisdiction.

A motion for summary judgment argues there is no genuine issue of material fact and the party filing the motion is entitled to dismissal or relief as a matter of law. Motions for summary judgment often are accompanied by documents or statements under oath, called affidavits. If the sworn statements or documents conflict on material issues, those issues must be resolved at trial, which may be before a jury if any party requests one. Before the trial, both parties to the dispute are entitled to discovery of all facts relevant to the dispute, including facts that may lead to relevant evidence.[2] The parties are required to produce documents and provide pretrial testimony under oath at depositions. The parties also may obtain subpoenas from the court to compel persons who are not parties to the lawsuit to provide documents or testimony at a deposition or at the trial.

The only relevant information not available to a litigant is information protected by a privilege, such as the attorney–client privilege. The attorney–client privilege protects confidential communications between a client and his or her attorney made for the purpose of obtaining legal advice. Courts also recognize an attorney work product privilege, which protects material that would provide insight into the attorney's theories on a legal dispute, such as a memorandum recording the attorney's assessment of the strengths or weaknesses of the case. Disclosure of privileged information to a third party, such as an accountant, may constitute a waiver of the privilege. Thus, there is tension between a client's obligation to disclose material information to its accountants and to the public, and the desire to protect privileged information from disclosure to its opponents in litigation. Many states recognize by statute an accountant–client privilege. However, federal courts do not recognize such a privilege in

---

[2] The Private Securities Litigation Reform Act of 1995, discussed later in this chapter, limits discovery in certain circumstances in federal securities fraud suits.

cases involving federal claims. In every state, with the possible exception of Illinois and Tennessee, the client may waive the privilege and obtain the accountant's files and testimony. (Clients also may waive the attorney–client privilege.)

At trial, the plaintiff has the burden of producing evidence in support of his or her claim and of persuading the fact finder of each element of the claim. Thus, the plaintiff must convince the fact finder—the jury, or the judge if there is no jury and the judge is serving as the fact finder—that it is more likely than not that the facts supporting his or her claim occurred.

The federal appellate courts and most state appellate courts generally will not review issues of law until there is a final ruling that resolves the entire case, such as dismissal of the case or a jury verdict. Moreover, the appellate courts will not disturb the fact finder's determination unless it is clearly erroneous or there was legal error—such as the exclusion of admissible evidence or an improper instruction to the jury on the applicable legal standards. Most court opinions that establish legal precedents are decisions on motions prior to trial or decisions on appeals of dismissals or jury verdicts.

5.2   LITIGATION EXPLOSION

Few lawsuits were brought against accountants prior to 1965. In the late 1960s, several court decisions signaled dramatic changes in the attitude of the courts and the expectations of the public concerning auditors' responsibilities and their legal liability to third parties. By the mid-1970s, hundreds of lawsuits were pending against accountants. Lawsuits against accountants received new impetus in the early 1980s, with jury awards of damages in the tens of millions of dollars, including an $80 million award in 1981. Such awards initiated a new wave of litigation against accountants.

Undoubtedly, auditors' legal liability is one of the most important issues currently facing the profession. In 1993, the latest year for which statistics are available, the out-of-pocket litigation costs of the six largest accounting firms, including insurance premiums, legal fees, and awards and settlements, was estimated to be $1 billion or 11.9 percent of their domestic accounting and auditing revenues. Jury awards against accounting firms reached their highest level in that year. One firm suffered a $338 million award over an allegedly faulty audit of a bank; the verdict, however, was set aside by the trial judge. In November 1996, the appellate court affirmed the trial judge's ruling and ordered a new trial.[3] In another case, purchasers of convertible debentures of a company that went bankrupt were able to obtain a jury award of $26 million in compensatory and $200 million in punitive damages against the company's former auditors. The matter was subsequently settled out of court for an undisclosed amount after the trial court set aside the verdict. The year 1992 also was marked by extremely large settlements, as illustrated by an accounting firm's $400 million settlement with federal banking regulators arising out of services performed for failed savings and loan institutions.

A number of factors have contributed to the increase in litigation against auditors, including technical legal developments that made legal remedies available to third parties (discussed in a later section), social changes that influenced the public's ex-

---

[3] *Standard Chartered PLC* v. *Price Waterhouse*, 229 Ariz. Adv. Rep. 26 (Ariz. App. 1996).

pectations of auditors and its willingness to assert claims (most notably, the growth of consumerism and the perception of auditors as "insurers" of the reliability of a company's financial statements), and what has been referred to as the savings and loan crisis.

The effect the litigation explosion may have on an accounting firm was dramatically illustrated when Laventhol & Horwath, a 75-year-old firm with 50 offices and $345.2 million in revenue in fiscal 1990, filed for bankruptcy in November 1990. Laventhol's failure was attributed to litigation problems, including 110 lawsuits pending at the time of bankruptcy and settlements in the amount of $30 million and $13 million in late 1989 and early 1990, which exceeded the firm's insurance coverage.

(a) Consumerism

It was inevitable with the passage of the federal securities laws in the early 1930s and the growth of the securities markets that investors and creditors would make increased use of audited financial statements. Paralleling this development has been the growth of an attitude that just as consumers of the products and services of American business are entitled to expect more from the products they buy than they did in the past, so too are investors and creditors, as consumers of financial information. When people's expectations are not met, they are increasingly likely to contact legal counsel, especially since many attorneys are willing to take cases on a contingency basis.

This attitude has been buttressed by the access that disappointed consumers of financial information have to far-reaching remedies, perhaps the most significant of which from the auditor's point of view is the class action lawsuit (discussed later in this chapter). The result of these developments has been a heightening of the public's expectations of auditors and their work, and a far greater willingness on the part of investors and creditors who relied on that work to seek recovery from auditors for losses suffered. Rightly or wrongly, many people believe auditors can act to prevent investor and creditor losses and are thus a logical choice to bear those losses.

(b) Auditors as "Insurers"

A second important influence on the legal environment is the public's perception of auditors as "guarantors" of the reliability of an entity's financial statements. The public, perhaps because of the perceived precision of financial statements and the prominence of the auditor's report accompanying them, often does not recognize that an entity's management has primary responsibility for its financial statements and that the auditor's role inherently involves numerous difficult judgments. (As noted elsewhere, the auditor's standard report adopted by the Auditing Standards Board in 1988 attempted to specifically address these user misperceptions.)

Thus, when the "guarantor" is viewed as a large, successful organization with substantial resources (including professional liability insurance), and frequently in troubled situations is also the only financially viable entity available to sue, it should not be surprising that auditors are looked to for their "deep pockets" and are sued by injured persons primarily because of their ability to pay, regardless of culpability. The fact that an auditor's fees for an engagement rarely bear any reasonable relationship to the auditor's potential liability, and that the auditor derived no "equity" benefit from the operations of the entity, seldom sways disappointed investor-plaintiffs from seeking to recover their losses from the auditor.

Substantial numbers of lawsuits against auditors alleging inadequacies in their professional services probably will continue to be a fact of life, at least for the foreseeable future. The nine auditing pronouncements issued in 1988 in an attempt to narrow the "expectation gap" and SAS No. 82 on the auditor's consideration of fraud, and other efforts by the profession to articulate its objectives, responsibilities, and the limitations of those responsibilities, may have an effect on the public's expectations and perception of auditors. In the meantime, an auditor's best protection against liability (in addition to adequate malpractice insurance, when available) is to avoid associating with entities that are likely to cause losses to investors or creditors, to do competent work, and to keep in mind an understanding of how the courts perceive the professional's role and responsibilities, as expressed in judicial rulings under common law and as codified in the securities laws.

(c) Savings and Loan Crisis

The savings and loan (S&L) crisis precipitated a large number of lawsuits by the government in the late 1980s and early 1990s, including 4,000 against accountants and their firms seeking an estimated $15 billion. Two forces worked against the accounting profession during that time: the sheer number of potential and actual S&L lawsuits that had to be defended against, and the possibility that because of the application of "joint and several liability" (discussed later in this chapter) an accounting firm could be held liable for all of the damages awarded to a plaintiff, a potentially catastrophic event, even though the firm's apportioned share of negligence may have been determined to have been small. As a result, accounting firms settled many of the cases involving failed S&Ls for significantly less than the initial claims. (The largest settlement by an accounting firm was for over $400 million.) Cumulatively, these payments had a significant effect on the profession. Insurance rates increased significantly in the late 1980s and many providers left the market. (It took until the late 1990s for this situation to begin to change.) Another result was that the profession has become more averse to taking on clients in risky industries due to increased liability risk, and many firms have dropped clients in such industries.

5.3 LIABILITY TO CLIENTS

An auditor's liability to a client is based on the direct contractual relationship between them, referred to as "privity," and on the law of torts. Under common law, a professional is liable to a client for breach of contract (e.g., an auditor's issuing an unqualified opinion without conducting an audit in accordance with GAAS when that has been contracted for) and also, under tort law, for ordinary negligence. Obviously, if an auditor is liable to a client for ordinary negligence, gross negligence and fraud on the part of the auditor are also grounds for liability to a client.

Most lawsuits by clients are brought on grounds of ordinary negligence, which is defined as the failure to exercise due professional care. For auditors, due professional care essentially means adhering to generally accepted auditing standards. Gross negligence is the lack of even slight care. The client may have a cause for action against the auditor if the financial statements contain a misrepresentation of a material fact—that is, a material error or fraud—that was not detected because of the auditor's failure to exercise due care, and that injured the client.

Suits by clients arise in a variety of contexts, but certain patterns are evident. Many instances of litigation against auditors involve the situation in which an audit does not detect an ongoing embezzlement by an employee of the client, and additional money is taken after the audit is completed. The client contends the losses occurring after the audit would have been prevented if the auditor had detected the embezzlement. A client also may contend that internal control deficiencies enabled losses to go undetected, and the auditor failed to bring such deficiencies to the attention of management.

Clients often have fidelity bond coverage to protect against such losses. In many circumstances, after a fidelity bond carrier pays on a loss, it becomes "subrogated" to the client's claim against the auditor, that is, it "steps into the shoes" of the client and may assert the client's rights.[4]

Clients also bring suits against their accountants in a variety of other contexts. For example, suits by clients may arise out of business acquisitions, when the accountant has performed a review prior to the acquisition. The purchase price may be based on the assets of the acquired entity as reflected by the financial statements. If the client determines later that the assets were overstated, a suit against the accountant may result. Clients also have sued when they discovered that certain divisions they thought were profitable based on the financial statements were actually losing money. The client contends it would have closed the unprofitable divisions had it known about the losses and thereby would have prevented additional injury.

A claim by a client for failing to detect an embezzlement scheme or an overstatement of assets or income is generally based on negligence. It is alleged the accountant failed to comply with professional standards; had such standards been followed, the subsequent losses would have been prevented. Since such a claim is brought by the client, privity is satisfied. The person who embezzled the money or who sold the business also is made a party to such litigation in most cases. By the time the loss is discovered, however, the embezzler has often spent the stolen funds and will be "judgment-proof," that is, will lack insurance or assets to collect a court judgment against. In addition, the seller may have been released from liability by the buyer as part of the sales contract.

Besides defending the quality of their audits, auditors also defend themselves in such cases by pointing to negligence on the part of officers and employees of the client—in selecting or supervising the embezzler or in evaluating the acquisition. This concept is known as contributory negligence. In addition, auditors point to management's primary responsibility for the financial statements and internal control. In states where contributory negligence is still the rule, proof of such negligence will completely bar the client's claim.

---

[4] In 1945, the predecessor of the American Institute of Certified Public Accountants reached an agreement with the industry trade group representing the surety bond companies. The agreement provided that accountants would encourage their clients to rely on fidelity bond coverage to protect themselves from losses from embezzlements. In exchange, a number of fidelity bond carriers agreed not to sue an accountant for failing to detect such losses unless they could first prove to an independent panel that the accountant was grossly negligent. A number of courts have enforced the agreement.

Today, however, most states follow the concept of comparative negligence, and the client's negligence will not bar the claim. Instead, it will be compared with any negligence of the auditor and any other defendant's liability on a percentage basis, and liability will be apportioned based on the parties' relative degrees of fault. Until recently, most of those states, however, also followed some form of the rule of joint and several liability, under which claimants can collect all or part of their damages from any defendant found liable, irrespective of that defendant's proportionate fault. In many cases, the other defendants are "judgment-proof" because they have few assets and no insurance, leaving the auditor, who usually has "deep pockets," responsible for all the damages awarded. An increasing number of states, however, have recognized the unfairness of "joint and several liability" and have replaced it with a "proportionate liability" rule, or some variation thereof, under which defendants are not required to pay more than their proportionate share of the claimant's losses.

Under what is often termed the *National Surety* doctrine, some states require that the negligence of the client must contribute to the accountant's failure to properly perform the audit before such negligence will constitute a defense under either the comparative or contributory negligence concept.[5] Under the *National Surety* doctrine, the accountant could not raise as a defense the fact that management negligently failed to discover an embezzlement scheme, because such negligence would not interfere with the conduct of the audit. However, if management failed to follow the auditor's recommendations about internal control, for example, the auditor would be able to raise the client's negligence as a defense. The client's negligence also could be raised as a defense if the client failed to provide material information to the auditor that would have had an effect on the scope of the audit—such as any suspicious acts by an employee that came to the attention of management or other employees.[6]

At some point, fraud by a client company may become so pervasive that it will bar any claim by the company against the accountant. In *Cenco Inc.* v. *Seidman & Seidman*,[7] managerial employees of the client engaged in a massive fraud that involved the overstatement of inventories. The inflated value of inventory increased the price of the company's stock, and enabled it to buy other companies cheaply, obtain overstated insurance recoveries for lost inventory, and borrow money at lower rates. The chairman and president were aware of the fraud, but seven of the nine members of the board were not. The company brought a negligence claim against the accountants for failing to detect the fraud. The court held that the company could not recover against the accountants "if the fraud permeates the top management of the company and if, moreover, the managers are not stealing from the company—that is, from its current stockholders—but instead are turning the company into an engine of theft against outsiders—creditors, prospective stockholders, insurers, etc."

An accounting firm may be liable for a loss resulting from an embezzlement, even if it provides only review or compilation services and does not conduct an audit. In *Robert Wooler Co.* v. *Fidelity Bank*,[8] the court held that the accounting firm, which had

---

[5] *National Surety Corp.* v. *Lybrand*, 256 A.D. 226 (N.Y. App. Div. 1939).

[6] In general, an employer is legally responsible for the negligent acts of an employee, but not for acts of intentional dishonesty for the personal benefit of the employee.

[7] 686 F.2d 449 (7th Cir.), *cert. denied*, 459 U.S. 880 (1982).

[8] 479 A.2d 1027 (Pa. App. 1984).

not performed an audit, nevertheless had an obligation "to warn its client of known deficiencies in the client's internal operating procedures which enhanced opportunities for employee defalcations." In *1136 Tenants' Corp.* v. *Max Rothenberg & Co.*,[9] an accountant engaged to perform nonaudit accounting services was liable for failing to inform the client of missing invoices, which enabled an employee's embezzlement to go unnoticed.

Auditors should try to avoid misunderstandings with clients about their responsibility for detecting errors or fraud and illegal acts. Because this is a sensitive area, most auditors discuss these matters with the entity's management and follow up with a written communication (generally referred to as an "engagement letter" and discussed and illustrated in Chapter 4) spelling out a mutual understanding of functions, objectives, and responsibilities regarding the audit. Such communications do not, however, relieve the auditor of legal liability for failing to exercise due professional care.

Potential liability also arises from the auditor's confidential relationship with a client. As discussed in Chapter 3, the auditor has a professional responsibility not to disclose confidential information obtained during an audit unless disclosure is required to fairly present the entity's financial information in conformity with generally accepted accounting principles. In *Fund of Funds, Ltd.* v. *Arthur Andersen & Co.*,[10] the auditors were found liable as a result of, among other things, failing to use information they obtained from another client to determine which of the two clients' financial statements accurately portrayed the facts of the same transaction. Thus, there may be a legal precedent for holding an auditor liable for not disclosing and using information obtained from services rendered to one client that is relevant to the audit of another client. The auditor's professional responsibility in this situation is discussed in Chapter 3.

5.4   CIVIL LIABILITY TO THIRD PARTIES UNDER COMMON LAW

Most civil suits brought by third parties against auditors under common law allege losses resulting from reliance on financial statements. Such suits arise when lenders or investors lose money on a loan to or an investment in a company and contend, with the benefit of hindsight, that the financial statements materially misstated the company's financial condition. Suits of this type have increased as a result of a number of judicial decisions beginning in the 1960s that expanded the class to whom the auditor owed a duty of care and also raised the level of care owed to third parties. Laws vary from state to state on whether an auditor may be liable for ordinary negligence to persons he or she might reasonably expect to rely on an audit opinion. Liability for gross negligence and fraud extends to all third parties.

(a) Privity of Contract Doctrine

Unlike the auditor–client relationship, there is no privity of contract between the auditor and third parties. Traditionally, claims by third parties under common law were

---

[9] 36 A.D.2d 804 (App. Div. 1971), *aff'd*, 281 N.E.2d 846 (N.Y. 1972).

[10] 545 F. Supp. 1314 (S.D.N.Y. 1982).

based on the law of torts, and only fraud, not ordinary negligence from failure to exercise due care, was considered a wrongful act by an auditor. The first case to test the privity of contract doctrine involving auditors in the United States was *Ultramares Corp.* v. *Touche*[11] in 1931. The plaintiff, without the defendant's knowledge, had relied on financial statements audited by the defendant to make loans to a company that later became insolvent. The plaintiff alleged that the auditors were guilty of negligence and fraudulent misrepresentation in not detecting fictitious amounts included in accounts receivable and accounts payable. The court upheld the doctrine of privity of contract as a limitation on the auditors' liability to the unforeseen third party for ordinary negligence, based, at least in part, on Judge Cardozo's reasoning that auditors' liability for negligence should not be extended to third parties because doing so would have the potential effect of deterring people from entering the profession, which would be detrimental to society. Cardozo described the consequences of extending the auditor's duty to third parties as follows:

> If liability for negligence exists, a thoughtless slip or blunder, the failure to detect a theft or forgery beneath the cover of deceptive entries, may expose accountants to a liability in an indeterminate amount for an indeterminate time to an indeterminate class. The hazards of a business conducted on these terms are so extreme as to enkindle doubt whether a flaw may not exist in an implication of a duty that exposes to these consequences.

(b) Primary Benefit Rule

Courts in some states, however, have attempted to increase the auditor's liability to third parties for ordinary negligence by undermining the privity doctrine. The first crack in the privity rule occurred in the *Ultramares* case itself with the formulation of the "primary benefit rule," which held that an auditor would be liable to a third party for ordinary negligence if the auditor knew that the audit was being performed for the primary benefit of a specifically identified third party. Before the mid-1960s, however, most third-party plaintiffs bringing suit against auditors pursuant to the primary benefit rule were not successful, even in cases in which the auditor knew specific persons might rely on the opinion. For example, in *State St. Trust Co.* v. *Ernst*[12] the auditor was found not liable to a lender for negligence, even though the auditor knew the particular lender intended to rely on the audited financial statements.

Further weakening of the privity of contract doctrine in cases of professionals' liability did not occur until 1963, 32 years after *Ultramares*. It began with a series of cases that represented an attack on the primary benefit rule. The *Hedley Byrne* case[13] was decided by the highest court of England, the House of Lords, in 1963. The case did not involve auditors, but a negligently stated accommodation credit report by a bank on which a third person relied, to his damage. In their opinions, the justices stated that "where there is a relationship equivalent to contract . . . , there is a duty of care." The court's finding, however, was intended to have somewhat limited application in that it extended the duty of care to only a restricted class of third parties, as in *Ultramares*.

---

[11] 255 N.Y. 170 (1931).

[12] 278 N.Y. 104 (1938).

[13] *Hedley Byrne & Co. Ltd.* v. *Heller & Partners, Ltd.*, 1964 A.C. 465 [1963] 2 *All E.R.* 575 (H.L. 1963).

(c)   Foreseen Third Parties

In 1965, the American Law Institute (ALI) issued its Second Restatement of the Law of Torts, a compendium of tort principles. Partly in reliance on *Hedley Byrne*, the ALI interpreted the law of negligent misrepresentations by professionals to third parties more broadly than before. The Restatement provides that an accountant is liable to a person who justifiably relies on false information when the accountant fails to exercise reasonable care in obtaining or communicating the information, if: (1) the loss is suffered "by the person or one of a limited group of persons for whose benefit and guidance . . . [the accountant] knows that the recipient intends to supply" the information; and (2) the loss is suffered "through reliance upon" the information in a transaction that the accountant knows the recipient intends the information to influence or in a substantially similar transaction. Thus, the Restatement extended liability to a member of a limited group that the accountant is aware will receive information that is provided with regard to a transaction the accountant is aware of or a substantially similar transaction. This can be described as a "foreseen" class of recipients, as opposed to a "foreseeable" class, defined as an unlimited class of persons not identified by the auditor who foreseeably may be expected to rely on information.

The distinction in the Restatement's interpretation of a professional's duty to third parties between *foreseen* and *foreseeable* persons is critical to an understanding of post-1965 legal decisions based on common law. In several significant cases, courts accepted the foreseen class concept of the Restatement. In *Rusch Factors, Inc.* v. *Levin*,[14] the court ruled that the auditor could be liable to the third-party plaintiff, a lender of the client, for negligence. In this case, the audit was performed at the specific request of the plaintiff-lender. In another case, *Rhode Island Hospital Trust National Bank* v. *Swartz, Bresenoff, Yavner & Jacobs*,[15] the court found the auditors liable for negligence to a foreseen party; the auditors knew that the plaintiff-bank required audited financial statements of the client, even though they did not know the specific identity of the plaintiff.

(d)   Foreseeable Third Parties

Until 1983, auditors' common law liability for negligence extended no further than foreseen third parties. In that year, the New Jersey Supreme Court ruled in a motion for partial summary judgment that an auditor has a duty to reasonably foreseeable but unidentifiable third-party users who may rely on financial statements for appropriate business purposes.[16] The plaintiffs had alleged that they relied on financial statements audited by the defendants in making an investment that subsequently proved to be worthless, after the financial statements were found to be misstated. The plaintiffs were not members of an identifiable group of users to whom the financial statements were intended to be furnished. In handing down the opinion, the court quoted the court's opinion in *Rusch Factors*, which questioned the wisdom of the *Ultramares* decision, as follows:

[14] 284 F. Supp. 85 (D.R.I. 1968).

[15] 482 F.2nd 1000 (4th Cir. 1973).

[16] *H. Rosenblum, Inc.* v. *Adler*, 93 N.J. 324 (1983).

Why should an innocent reliant party be forced to carry the weighty burden of an accountant's professional malpractice? Isn't the risk of loss more easily distributed and fairly spread by imposing it on the accounting profession, which can pass the cost of insuring against the risk onto its customers, who can in turn pass the cost onto the entire consuming public? Finally, wouldn't a rule of foreseeability elevate the cautionary techniques of the accounting profession?[17]

The court added its own belief that:

> When the independent auditor furnishes an opinion with no limitation in the certificate as to whom the company may disseminate the financial statements, he has a duty to all those whom that auditor should reasonably foresee as recipients from the company of the statements for its proper business purposes, provided that the recipients rely on the statements pursuant to those business purposes.

The key distinction between the Restatement rule and the liberalized standard recognized in New Jersey is the accountant's knowledge at the time the audit is performed with regard to who will be supplied with financial statements and for what purpose. Under the Restatement rule, the accountant must have been aware of a limited group of parties and the particular or a substantially similar transaction in which it was intended that a party would rely on the financial statements. For example, if a certain investor was considering purchasing a company, the accountant would have to have known about the investor's intended reliance on the financial statements in connection with the proposed purchase. Under the liberalized test, the accountant would be liable for negligence to an unforeseen investor with regard to an unexpected transaction if such an event was foreseeable.

Soon after the decision by the New Jersey Supreme Court in *Rosenblum*, the Wisconsin Supreme Court reached the same result in *Citizens State Bank* v. *Timm, Schmidt & Co.*[18] In the *Timm* case, the court stated that "the fundamental principle of Wisconsin negligence law is that a tortfeasor is fully liable for all foreseeable consequences of his act." The court rejected any policy consideration that might have justified a more restrictive rule of liability for accountants.

In 1985, however, the highest court in New York rigorously adhered to the *Ultramares* rule in *Credit Alliance Corp.* v. *Arthur Andersen & Co.*[19] The court in *Credit Alliance* set forth three "prerequisites that must be satisfied before accountants would be held liable in negligence to third parties who rely to their detriment on inaccurate financial reports: (1) the accountants must have been aware that the financial reports were to be used for a particular purpose or purposes; (2) in the furtherance of which a known party or parties was intended to rely; and (3) there must have been some conduct on the part of the accountants linking them to that party or parties, which evinces the accountants' understanding of that party or parties' reliance."

Since the decision in *Credit Alliance*, other state courts have taken various positions. In 1986, in *International Mortgage Co.* v. *John P. Butler Accountancy Corp.*[20] an intermediate

---

[17] *Rusch Factors, Inc.* v. *Levin*, 284 F. Supp. 85 (D.R.I. 1968).

[18] 113 Wis. 2d 376 (1983).

[19] 65 N.Y. 2d 536 (1985).

[20] 177 Cal. App. 3d 806 (1986).

appellate court in California rejected the New York rule and followed New Jersey and Wisconsin, holding that an accountant was liable to a lender for failing to detect that a preexisting mortgage was not reflected on a real estate firm's financial statements, even though the lender first contacted the real estate firm after the report was issued.

In 1988 the highest court in New York reaffirmed the test set forth in *Credit Alliance* and applied it in the context of a review of financial statements (see Chapter 30).[21] A year later, in *Law Offices of Lawrence J. Stockler, P.C.* v. *Rose*,[22] the Michigan Court of Appeals followed the Restatement test, holding that the accountant could be liable for negligence to the purchaser of a company that relied on the financial statements. In this case, the accountant was aware, at the time the report was issued, that the purchaser would rely on the financial statements for purposes of purchasing the company. The court rejected the "foreseeable" test followed by California, New Jersey, and Wisconsin on the following ground:

> The reasons for taking this more restricted approach in third party actions against the accountant have been a recognition that the financial statements themselves are the representations of the client (with the auditor's liability arising from the opinion rendered concerning the accuracy of the client's records) and the accountant's inability to control the distribution of the report or the content of some of the statements he is assessing.

In 1989 the Idaho and Nebraska supreme courts and the intermediate court of appeals in Florida adopted the *Ultramares* rule.[23]

In 1992, *International Mortgage* was overruled by the supreme court of California, which held in *Bily* v. *Arthur Young*[24] that in professional negligence cases, an accounting firm is liable only to its clients and not to third parties, such as investors or lenders, unless the third party can establish fraud or negligent misrepresentation. The court's rationale for adopting a new precedent was the prevention of liability out of proportion to fault. With this decision, which represented a significant victory for the accounting profession, California moved away from the foreseeability test, adopted by only a minority of the states, which would expose accountants to the broadest universe of potential claimants in professional negligence actions.

Since 1987 no additional states have adopted the foreseeability test. Additional states that decided to continue adhering to the *Ultramares* view are Alabama,[25] Alaska,[26] Maryland,[27] and Montana.[28] In addition to California, the following states adopted the Restatement approach: Florida,[29] Louisiana,[30] and West Virginia.[31]

---

[21] *William Iselin & Co.* v. *Mann Judd Landau*, 71 N.Y. 2d 420 (1988).

[22] 174 Mich. App. 14 (1989).

[23] *Idaho Bank & Trust Co.* v. *First Bancorp*, 115 Idaho 1082 (1989); *Citizens National Bank* v. *Kennedy & Coe*, 232 Neb. 477 (1989); *First Florida Bank* v. *Max Mitchell & Co.*, 541 So.2d 155 Fla. App. (1989).

[24] 834 P.2d 745 (Cal. 1992).

[25] *Colonial Bank* v. *Ridley & Schweigert*, 551 So.2d 390 (Ala. 1989).

[26] *Selden* v. *Burnett*, 754 P.2d 256 (Alaska 1988).

[27] *Tischler* v. *Baltimore Bancorp*, 801 F. Supp. 1493 (D. Md. 1992).

[28] *Thayer* v. *Hicks*, 793 P.2d 784 (Mont. 1990).

[29] *First Florida Bank* v. *Max Mitchell & Co.*, 558 So.2d 9 (Fla. 1990).

[30] *First National Bank of Commerce* v. *Monco Agency, Inc.*, 911 F.2d 1053 (5th Cir. 1990).

[31] *First National Bank* v. *Crawford*, 386 S.E.2d 310 (W. Va. 1989).

At the time of this writing, the following jurisdictions, in addition to those cited above, appear to be adhering to the *Ultramares* rule: Arkansas,[32] Delaware,[33] Indiana,[34] Kansas,[35] and Pennsylvania.[36] The following jurisdictions apparently are following the Restatement approach: Georgia,[37] Hawaii,[38] Iowa,[39] Minnesota,[40] Missouri,[41] New Hampshire,[42] New Mexico,[43] North Carolina,[44] Ohio,[45] Tennessee,[46] Texas,[47] and Washington.[48] The only court to join New Jersey and Wisconsin was the supreme court of Mississippi in 1987.[49] In that case the accountant provided a copy of the financial statements to a third party.

An interesting development on this issue occurred in 1987, when the Illinois legislature enacted a statute that codified the *Ultramares* rule.[50] Arkansas, Kansas, and Utah have since enacted similar statutes.[51] These statutes provide that accountants are not liable for negligence to anyone other than their clients, unless it can be established that the auditor knew of and acceded to third parties' reliance on the auditor's report. In addition, the Illinois and Arkansas statutes provide a mechanism by which accountants may limit their liability by formally identifying in writing to the third parties and the client the third parties they know to be relying on the report. That communication is known as a "privity letter." Finally, in 1995, New Jersey adopted a statute that rejected the standard set forth earlier in *Rosenblum*.[52] The law states that an accountant must specifically acknowledge a third party in order for privity to vest. In the case of a bank, the acknowledgment must be in writing. Wisconsin and Michigan also have adopted variations of the "acknowledgment" requirement. Thus, Mississippi remains the only state with a "foreseeability" type privity provision.

[32] *Robertson v. White*, 633 F. Supp. 954 (W.D. Ark. 1986).

[33] *McLean v. Alexander*, 599 F.2d 1190 (3d Cir. 1979).

[34] *Toro Co. v. Krouse, Kern & Co.*, 827 F.2d 155 (7th Cir. 1987).

[35] *Nortek, Inc. v. Alexander Grant & Co.*, 532 F.2d 1013 (10th Cir. 1974), *cert. denied*, 429 U.S. 1042 (1977).

[36] *Hartford Accident & Indemnity Co. v. Parente, Randolph, Orlando, Carey & Associates*, 642 F. Supp. 38 (M.D. Pa. 1985); *Pennine Resources, Inc. v. Dorwart Andrew & Co.*, 639 F. Supp. 1071 (E.D. Pa. 1986).

[37] *Badische Corp. v. Caylor*, 257 Ga. 131 (1987).

[38] *Chun v. Park*, 51 Haw. 462 (1969).

[39] *Pahre v. Auditor*, 422 N.W.2d 178 (Iowa 1988).

[40] *Bonhiver v. Graff*, 311 Minn. 111 (1976).

[41] *Lindner Fund v. Abney*, 770 S.W.2d 437 (Mo. App. 1989); *Aluma Craft Mfg. Co. v. Elmer Fox & Co.*, 493 S.W.2d 378 (Mo. App. 1973).

[42] *Spherex, Inc. v. Alexander Grant & Co.*, 122 N.H. 898 (1982).

[43] *Stotlar v. Hester*, 92 N.M. 26 (Ct. App. 1978).

[44] *Raritan River Steel Co. v. Cherry, Bekaert & Holland*, 322 N.C. 200 (1988).

[45] *BancOhio National Bank v. Schiesswohl*, 515 N.E.2d 997 (Ohio 1986).

[46] *Stinson v. Brand*, 738 S.W.2d 186 (Tenn. 1987).

[47] *Blue Bell, Inc. v. Peat, Marwick, Mitchell & Co.*, 715 S.W.2d 408 (Tex. Ct. App. Dallas 1986); *Shatterproof Glass Corp. v. James*, 466 S.W.2d 873 (Tex. Civ. App. 1971).

[48] *Haberman v. WPPSS*, 109 Wash. 2d 107 (1987).

[49] *Touche Ross & Company v. Commercial Union Insurance Co.*, 514 So.2d 315 (Miss. 1987).

[50] Ill. Rev. Stat. ch. 111 ¶ 5535.1 (1987).

[51] Ark. Stat. Ann. §16-114-302 (Supp. 1987); Kan. Stat. Ann. §1-402 (Supp. 1988); Utah Code Ann. §58-26-12 (Supp. 1990).

[52] NJ Stat. Ann. section 2A:53A-25.

The legislative changes to privity case law are largely attributable to the efforts of state CPA societies that have brought the issue before state legislatures. The legislatures, as compared with the courts that have considered the issue, are accustomed to dealing with broad public policy issues. The courts also are limited by having before them only a very narrow set of facts of a case, while the legislatures can consider a wide array of expert advice and views.

Some third parties have attempted to satisfy the privity requirement imposed by common law, such as *Credit Alliance*, or the above statutes by notifying the accountants in writing *after* the report has been issued that they are relying on it. Accountants have been advised to respond to such letters by communicating in writing that they were not aware at the time the report was issued that the parties would be relying on it.

(e)   Scienter Requirement

In addition to actions on the grounds of negligence, third parties may bring suit against auditors on the grounds of fraud or constructive fraud that is inferred from evidence of gross negligence. Constructive fraud differs from actual fraud in that the former involves the lack of a reasonable basis for believing that a representation is true, whereas the latter involves actual knowledge that a representation is false. Actions grounded in fraud (actual or constructive) require the plaintiff to prove some form of knowledge on the auditor's part of the falsity (or its equivalent) of a representation. This knowledge is commonly referred to as "scienter" and the requirement to prove it as the "scienter" requirement. Essentially, it is a requirement to prove an intent to injure. In some jurisdictions, scienter may be established by proof of any one of the following three elements:

1. Actual knowledge of the falsity of the representation
2. A lack of knowledge of the truth of the representation
3. A reckless disregard for the truth or falsity of the representation

Under common law, the distinction between negligence and fraud rests essentially on the requirement for scienter. If a jury were to find that the defendant-auditors expressed an unqualified opinion on the financial statements when they had no knowledge of the facts, and if this would support an allegation of fraud in other respects,[53] then liability for the tort of deceit (fraud) could extend to all injured third parties. Without scienter, the case would not involve fraud. The question of the requirement to prove scienter and the elements that constitute scienter are further explored in the discussion, later in the chapter, of the auditor's liability under Section 10(b) of the Securities Exchange Act of 1934 and related Rule 10b-5.

5.5   CIVIL LIABILITY TO THIRD PARTIES UNDER THE FEDERAL SECURITIES ACTS

The principal provisions of the federal securities acts that have determined the auditor's civil liability are Section 11 of the Securities Act of 1933 and Section 10(b) of the

---

[53] Those "other respects" include proof of false representation that was relied on by and caused damages to the plaintiff.

Securities Exchange Act of 1934 and related Rule 10b-5. Class action suits against auditors under the federal securities laws became common after 1966, when the procedural rules governing them were liberalized. Class actions are litigation in which one or a relatively small number of plaintiffs sue on behalf of a very large number of allegedly injured persons. One of the prerequisites of a class action is that the number of potential claimants is so large that it would be impracticable for each of them to sue individually. The dollar amount of potential liability in class actions can run into the hundreds of millions of dollars, thereby making the class action technique a formidable weapon.

(a) Securities Act of 1933

The Securities Act of 1933 regulates public offerings of securities and contains provisions intended to protect purchasers of securities. Section 11(a) reads, in part, as follows:

> In case any part of the registration statement . . . contained an untrue statement of a material fact or omitted to state a material fact required to be stated therein or necessary to make the statements therein not misleading, any person acquiring such security . . . may . . . sue . . . every accountant . . . who has with his consent been named as having . . . certified any part of the registration statement . . . with respect to the statement in such registration statement . . . which purports to have been . . . certified by him.

Thus, Section 11 of the Securities Act of 1933 imposes civil liability on auditors for misrepresentations or omissions of material facts in the financial statements and any other part of the registration statement reported on by the auditor. The measure of damages under the civil provisions of the 1933 Act is based on the difference between the amount the plaintiff paid for the security and either the market price at the time of the suit or, if the security was sold, the selling price.

Section 11 expands the elements of an auditor's liability to third parties beyond that of common law in the following significant ways:

1. Privity with the plaintiff is not a necessary element; unnamed third parties, that is, the purchasers of securities in a public offering, may sue auditors.
2. Liability to third parties does not require proof of fraud or gross negligence; ordinary negligence is a basis for liability.
3. The burden of proof of negligence is shifted from the plaintiff to the defendant. The plaintiff has to prove only a material misstatement of fact.
4. The auditor is held to a standard of care described as the exercise of "due diligence"—a reasonable investigation leading to a belief that the financial statements are neither false nor misleading.
5. The plaintiff need not prove reliance on the financial statements or the auditor's report on them, but the defendant-auditor will prevail if the plaintiff's knowledge of the "untruth or omission" is proved.

The first, and still the most significant, judicial interpretation of Section 11, *Escott*

v. *BarChris Construction Corp.*,[54] did not occur until 1968. The *BarChris* case was a class action against a bowling alley construction corporation that had issued debentures and subsequently declared bankruptcy, and against its auditors. The suit was brought by the purchasers of the debentures for damages sustained as a result of false statements and material omissions in the prospectus contained in the registration statement. The court ruled that the auditors were liable on the grounds that they had not met the minimum standard of "due diligence" in their review for subsequent events occurring to the effective date of the registration statement (required under the 1933 Act and known as a "keeping current" review) because the auditor performing the review failed to appropriately follow up management's answers to his inquiries.

A defense to a Section 11 action against auditors would require demonstrating that a reasonable investigation [defined in Section 11(c)] had been made and that the auditors had reasonable grounds for believing and did believe that the financial statements were true and not misleading. In the *BarChris* case, the court stated that "accountants should not be held to a higher standard than that recognized in their profession," but held that the individual accountant responsible for the keeping current review, who had little practical auditing experience, had not met even that standard. As a direct result of this case, professional standards governing auditing procedures in the subsequent period (described in Chapter 27) were made stricter, and auditing firms began to place more emphasis on staff members' knowledge of a client's business and industry.

A controversial aspect of the 1933 Act concerns the issues of reliance and causation. An auditor is liable to purchasers of securities who may not have relied on the financial statements or the auditor's opinion or who may not even have known of their existence. If the auditor can prove, however, that something other than the misleading financial statements caused the plaintiff's loss, the amount of loss related to those other factors is not recoverable. Section 11 thus provides a causation defense, but it clearly places the burden of proof on the defendant-auditor; it requires the defendant to prove that factors other than the misleading statements caused the loss (in whole or in part). The courts have rarely considered the causation defense in Section 11 cases against auditors because damages in such cases have usually been determined in out-of-court settlements, as happened in *BarChris*.

Before 1988, accountants were often charged with violating Section 12(2) of the 1933 Act. This statute imposes liability on any person who "offers or sells" a security "by means of a prospectus or oral communication, which contains an untrue statement of a material fact or omits to state a material fact necessary in order to make the statements, in the light of the circumstances under which they are made, not misleading." Some courts took the position that any party, including accountants, that provided "substantial assistance" in connection with a sale could be charged with violating the section. In 1988, the U.S. Supreme Court ruled in *Pinter* v. *Dahl*[55] that to be liable under Section 12 one had to be a "substantial factor" or "substantial participant" in a sale. In *Pinter*, the Court held that liability under Section 12 extended only to the person who successfully solicited the purchase.

---

[54] 283 F. Supp. 643 (S.D.N.Y. 1968).

[55] 108 S. Ct. 2063 (1988).

(b) Securities Exchange Act of 1934

Many more suits alleging civil liability against auditors have been brought under the Securities Exchange Act of 1934 than under the 1933 Act. The 1934 Act, which requires all companies whose securities are traded to file annual audited financial statements and quarterly and other financial information, regulates trading of securities and thus has broad applicability. Auditors' liability under the 1934 Act, however, is not as extensive as under the 1933 Act in the following significant respects:

- As established by the *Hochfelder* case (described below) in 1976, ordinary negligence is not a basis for liability to third parties under Section 10(b) and Rule 10b-5. Thus the auditor's liability to unforeseen third parties under the 1934 Act is essentially the same as it is under common law following *Ultramares* and *Credit Alliance*.

- The burden of proof of both reliance on the financial statements and causation (i.e., that the loss was caused by reliance on the statements, known as "proximate cause") rests with the plaintiff, as it does under common law.

On the other hand, the 1934 Act is accessible to both buyers and sellers of securities; Section 11 of the 1933 Act applies only to buyers.

Damages recoverable under the civil provisions of the 1934 Act are the plaintiff's "out of pocket" losses, determined by the difference between the contract price of the securities and their actual value on the date of the transaction. Actual value ordinarily is considered to be the market value on the date the misrepresentation or omission is discovered and rectified.

The majority of civil lawsuits against auditors have been based on Section 10(b) and Rule 10b-5. Their provisions apply to any purchase or sale of any security, and thus they can be used by a plaintiff with respect to both registered public offerings (also covered by the 1933 Act) and most other transactions in securities. Rule 10b-5 states, in part, that:

> It shall be unlawful for any person . . . (a) To employ any device, scheme, or artifice to defraud, (b) To make any untrue statement of a material fact or to omit to state a material fact necessary in order to make the statements made, in light of the circumstances under which they were made, not misleading, or (c) To engage in any act, practice, or course of business which operates or would operate as a fraud or deceit upon any person, in connection with the purchase or sale of any security.

Section 10(b) and Rule 10b-5 do not provide a good-faith defense; rather, the defendant must refute the specific charges brought by the plaintiff. On the other hand, in a Rule 10b-5 action, the burden of proof that the auditor acted fraudulently rests with the plaintiff; under Section 11 of the 1933 Act, the burden of proof that the auditor was not culpable rests with the defendant-auditor.

The SEC enacted Rule 10b-5 in 1942 as a disciplinary measure for its own use against those who act fraudulently with regard to the purchase or sale of securities. A series of judicial interpretations subsequently made the rule accessible to private claimants who were able to prove damages resulting from their reliance on financial statements containing misrepresentations or omissions. Unfortunately, Rule 10b-5 is not at all precise in defining standards for liability, and it does not include a due-diligence defense. Between the time of its enactment and the *Hochfelder* ruling in 1976 (discussed below), the courts interpreted the rule in disparate ways. Thus, in some jurisdictions auditors were found liable to third parties for ordinary negligence (absence of due diligence) in rendering their opinions; in other jurisdictions the courts held that an element of knowledge of the wrongful act or an intent to commit fraud (scienter) was required. Much of the controversy was resolved by the U.S. Supreme Court in 1976 with its decision in *Ernst & Ernst* v. *Hochfelder*.[56]

The complaint in *Hochfelder* charged that the auditors had violated Rule 10b-5 by their failure to conduct proper audits and thereby aided and abetted a fraud perpetrated by the president of a securities firm. The plaintiff's case rested on a charge of negligence and did not allege fraud or intentional misconduct on the part of the auditors. The Supreme Court ruled that a private suit for damages under Section 10(b) and Rule 10b-5 required an allegation of scienter. The Court's opinion stated, in part:

> When a statute speaks so specifically in terms of manipulation and deception, and of implementing devices and contrivances—the commonly understood terminology of intentional wrongdoing—and when its history reflects no more expansive intent, we are quite unwilling to extend the scope of the statute to negligent conduct.

It is important to note that this decision did not impose any general standard for liability under the federal securities laws. It applied specifically to Section 10(b) and Rule 10b-5. The negligence standard under the federal securities laws continues to apply to those sections where Congress expressly intended it to apply or where the courts have determined that imposing liability without scienter in the implied liability sections of the law is compatible with the overall structure and philosophy of the statutes. For example, a negligence standard is still applicable to liability under Section 11 of the 1933 Act.

The Court noted in *Hochfelder* that "in certain areas of the law, recklessness is considered to be a form of intentional conduct for purposes of imposing liability for some act." Thus, although the Court declined to address the question of reckless behavior in that case, most courts have since held that recklessness is sufficient to meet the scienter test.

In an action under Section 10(b), a buyer or seller of a security also must demonstrate reliance on the misstatement. This defense can be important in cases where the plaintiff did not know of the misstatement, such as when he or she never read the financial statements. One exception to the reliance requirement is the "fraud on the market" theory of liability, which the Supreme Court adopted in 1988 in *Basic, Inc.* v. *Levinson*.[57] This doctrine provides that a misstatement or omission that has a general effect on the market price of the security can result in liability, even without actual reliance by the plaintiff. The rule is based on the theory that the purchaser or seller relies on the integrity of the market price, which should reflect all relevant information available in the market. However, at least for the present, the doctrine is limited to securities traded on the national public markets, such as the New York or American Stock Exchange.

[56] 425 U.S. 185 (1976).
[57] 485 U.S. 224 (1988).

Prior to 1994, an auditor also could be held liable for aiding and abetting a violation of Section 10(b). For example, in *Roberts* v. *Peat, Marwick, Mitchell & Co.*,[58] the U.S. Court of Appeals for the Ninth Circuit ruled that an accounting firm could be liable for aiding and abetting a violation of Section 10(b). In that case the offering documents indicated that the accounting firm agreed to perform accounting services for the partnership, and the plaintiffs alleged that the firm knew that the documents were false and that it furthered the fraud by consenting to the inclusion of its name in the offering material. According to the court, "the investors relied on Peat, Marwick's reputation when deciding to invest and . . . they would not have invested had Peat, Marwick disclosed the alleged fraud." In 1994, the Supreme Court ruled that there was no cause of action for aiding and abetting a Rule 10b-5 violation.[59]

(c) Private Securities Litigation Reform Act of 1995

The Private Securities Litigation Reform Act of 1995 (the Reform Act) contains several provisions that have important implications for accountants' legal liability.[60] To withstand a defendant's motion of dismissal of a complaint brought in a securities fraud lawsuit, a plaintiff must allege facts from which a strong inference of fraudulent intent can be drawn; assertions such as that the financial statements are materially misstated and the auditor knew about the misstatement are not sufficient. In addition, if the defendant files a motion to dismiss, no discovery is permitted until the court has ruled on the motion. Thus, the plaintiff will not be able to obtain the auditors' working papers for use in alleging facts to avoid dismissal of the complaint.

The Reform Act also replaces the joint and several liability rule, discussed earlier, with a proportionate liability standard, under which defendants pay only their "fair share" of proportionate liability unless there has been an intentional violation of the securities laws. Under prior law, defendants could have been required to pay the entire amount of a loss, even if they were found to be responsible for only a small part of it.

(d) RICO

Beginning in the early 1980s, numerous suits were brought against accountants for violations of the Racketeer Influenced and Corrupt Organizations (RICO) statute of the Organized Crime Control Act of 1970. In general, RICO provides a remedy of triple damages and attorney's fees to any person injured by reason of the operation of an enterprise through "a pattern of racketeering." The statute defines a pattern of racketeering as two violations of a list of statutes, including mail fraud, wire fraud, and securities fraud. In 1989, the U.S. Supreme Court held that such a "pattern" of racketeering activities may be satisfied by a series of actions that are part of a single fraudulent scheme, thus opening the statute to widespread use.[61]

Although the statute, which provides a remedy to any victim of a common-law fraud, was designed to attack organized crime, courts have generally followed the lit-

---

[58] 857 F.2d 646 (9th Cir. 1988).

[59] *Central Denver Bank* v. *First Interstate Bank of Denver*, 511 U.S. 164 (1994).

[60] Other sections of the Reform Act are discussed in Chapter 4 of this book.

[61] *H. J. Inc.* v. *Northwestern Bell Telephone Co.*, 109 S. Ct. 2893 (1989).

eral language of the statute. Moreover, the Supreme Court has stated that there is no record that Congress intended its use to be limited to organized crime activities. The first RICO case to go to trial against an accountant resulted in a 1988 verdict against the accountant.[62] In 1993, however, the Supreme Court[63] limited the liability of outside professionals, such as accountants, under RICO in ruling that in order to be liable one must participate in the operation or management of the illegal enterprise itself; mere association through the provision of accounting or auditing services is not sufficient.

5.6   CRIMINAL LIABILITY

Violations of the securities acts that give rise to civil liability for association with misleading financial statements also subject auditors to criminal penalties (fines of up to $10,000 or imprisonment for not more than five years, or both) under Section 24 of the Securities Act of 1933 and Section 32 of the Securities Exchange Act of 1934 if the violations can be shown to be willful or intentional. Auditors also are exposed to criminal penalties under the federal mail fraud and conspiracy statutes.

Perhaps because of the availability of other legal remedies (including injunctions, administrative proceedings, and civil suits by third parties) and the absence of the element of personal gain, there have been few criminal actions against auditors. Four of the most widely publicized criminal prosecutions were *Continental Vending*,[64] *Four Seasons*,[65] *National Student Marketing*,[66] and *Equity Funding*,[67] which together produced the conviction of eight individuals. Those cases demonstrate that auditors' errors of judgment in not insisting on appropriate accounting, including adequate disclosure, of certain matters known to them may result in criminal liability in certain circumstances, even though no motive can be proved and no personal gain can be shown to have resulted.

John C. Burton, former Chief Accountant of the SEC, stated the Commission's position on bringing criminal charges against auditors:

> While virtually all Commission cases are civil in character, on rare occasions it is concluded that a case is sufficiently serious that it should be referred to the Department of Justice for consideration of criminal prosecution. Referrals in regard to accountants have only been made when the Commission and the staff believed that the evidence indicated that a professional accountant certified financial statements that he knew to be false when he reported on them. The Commission does not make criminal references in cases that it believes are simply matters of professional judgment even if the judgments appear to be bad ones.[68]

---

[62] *The Wall Street Journal*, May 9, 1988, p. 43. The case was settled for $15 million after the defendant said it would appeal a jury verdict in the amount of $60 million.

[63] *Reves* v. *Ernst & Young*, 113 S. Ct. 1163.

[64] *United States* v. *Simon*, 425 F.2d 796 (2d Cir. 1969), *cert. denied*, 397 U.S. 1006 (1970).

[65] *United States* v. *Clark*, 360 F. Supp. 936 (S.D.N.Y. 1973).

[66] *United States* v. *Natelli*, 527 F.2d 311 (2d Cir. 1975), *cert. denied*, 425 U.S. 934 (1976).

[67] *United States* v. *Weiner*, 578 F.2d 757 (9th Cir.), *cert. denied*, 439 U.S. 981 (1978).

[68] John C. Burton, "SEC Enforcement and Professional Accountants: Philosophy, Objectives and Approach," *Vanderbilt Law Review* 28 (January 1975), p. 28.

The consequences of criminal prosecution to an auditor may go beyond the obvious ones of the costs of defense and the resulting fines and imprisonment. A successful criminal prosecution may help to establish civil liability and generally will preclude the individual from continuing to practice as an auditor.

5.7   OTHER SEC SANCTIONS

Auditors are also subject under the federal securities acts to legal sanctions that do not involve criminal penalties or the payment of damages. The SEC, as the principal government regulatory agency charged with enforcing financial reporting standards, has two civil remedies available to it: civil injunctive actions and disciplinary (administrative) proceedings under Rule 2(e) of its Rules of Practice. Either remedy may be sought against an individual auditor or an entire firm.

The Securities Enforcement Remedies and Penny Stock Reform Act of 1990 substantially increased the SEC's enforcement powers and remedies. The Act empowers the SEC to issue "cease-and-desist" orders requiring compliance with the securities laws and possibly requiring a party to take affirmative action to avert future violations. Prior to the Act, the SEC was required to seek such relief as a party in federal court. The Act also authorizes the SEC to obtain monetary penalties in civil actions in federal court and in certain administrative proceedings of up to $500,000 for each violation.

(a)   Injunctive Proceedings

The SEC has the authority under Section 20 of the 1933 Act and Section 21 of the 1934 Act to initiate injunctive actions in the courts to restrain future violations of the provisions of those acts [including Section 10(b) of the 1934 Act]. Under currently prevailing standards, discussed below, such injunctions are available only against those the SEC can persuade a court are likely to violate the federal securities laws again if not enjoined. In a case tried in 1980, *Aaron* v. *SEC*,[69] the Supreme Court held that injunctions under Section 10(b) of the 1934 Act [and one subsection of Section 17(a) of the 1933 Act] require scienter.[70]

The consequences of an injunction may extend far beyond an admonition to obey the law in the future. The injunction can be useful to plaintiffs in subsequent civil suits for damages, and the person enjoined is exposed to civil and criminal contempt proceedings. Moreover, an injunction resulting from a consent decree, in which guilt is neither admitted nor denied, may require the auditor or firm to adopt and comply with certain procedures to prevent future violations.

Requests for permanent injunctions are tried publicly before a judge without a jury. Thus, the injunctions are granted or denied largely at the discretion of the trial judge. The SEC must prove not only that a violation of the securities laws has occurred but also that there is a reasonable likelihood that future violations will occur if an in-

---

[69] 446 U.S. 680 (1980).

[70] The Supreme Court decided, however, that injunctions under two other subsections of Section 17(a) do not require scienter.

junction is not imposed. For example, in *SEC* v. *Geotek*,[71] the court found there was no evidence of a past violation. The issue of what constitutes a "reasonable likelihood" of future violations remains unresolved. On the one hand, the courts tend to give great weight to the SEC's expert judgment of the immediate need for an injunction. On the other hand, however, in *SEC* v. *Bausch & Lomb, Inc.*,[72] the court ruled against enjoining the auditors, on the grounds of insufficient evidence that they were likely to commit further violations.

In a significant victory for the accounting profession, a federal court entered a judgment in favor of an accounting firm[73] in an SEC injunctive action for alleged violations of the antifraud provisions of the securities acts. The court handed down a highly stringent rule of liability. In order for the SEC to get an injunction against an accounting firm, the Commission must prove that the accounting firm's procedures were so deficient that the audit amounted to no audit at all or that the accounting judgments made were such that no reasonable accountant would have made the same decisions if confronted with the same facts.

(b)   Administrative [Rule 2(e)] Proceedings

Rule 2(e) of the SEC's Rules of Practice states that the Commission:

> May deny, temporarily or permanently, the privilege of appearing or practicing before it in any way to any person who is found . . . (i) not to possess the requisite qualifications to represent others, (ii) to be lacking in character or integrity or have engaged in unethical or improper professional conduct, or (iii) to have willfully violated or willfully aided and abetted the violation of any provision of the federal securities laws . . . or the rules and regulations thereunder.

Before 1989, proceedings under Rule 2(e) were generally conducted in private hearings. Such proceedings are now public, unless the SEC directs otherwise in a particular case. In addition, the resulting Accounting and Auditing Enforcement Releases, which set forth the SEC's allegations and the terms of settlement, attract a great deal of publicity. Rule 2(e) gives the SEC the explicit authority to suspend from appearing or practicing before it auditors who have been permanently enjoined from violation of the securities laws or convicted of a felony or of a misdemeanor involving immoral conduct.

Over the years, the SEC has devised imaginative, often sweeping sanctions against auditing firms under Rule 2(e), many of which involved agreements to institute new or improved control procedures and to subject those procedures to an independent compliance review. In the past, these sanctions were often announced in Accounting Series Releases (ASRs), and are now published in Accounting and Auditing Enforcement Releases (AAERs). Among the sanctions that have been imposed on accounting firms are the following:

1. Required a firm to conduct a study of the use of a specific accounting method and to establish guidelines for the firm's practice in this area [ASR No. 173 (July 2, 1975)]

---

[71] 426 F. Supp. 715 (N.D. Cal. 1976), *aff'd sub nom. SEC* v. *Arthur Young & Co.*, 590 F.2d 785 (9th Cir. 1979).
[72] 420 F. Supp. 1226 (S.D.N.Y. 1976), *aff'd*, 565 F.2d 8 (2d Cir. 1977).
[73] *SEC* v. *Price Waterhouse*, 797 F. Supp. 1217 (S.D.N.Y. 1992).

2. Required a firm to employ consultants to review and evaluate the firm's auditing procedures for publicly held companies [ASR No. 176 (July 22, 1975)]

3. Prohibited a firm from merging or combining practices with another accounting firm [ASR No. 196 (September 1, 1976)]

4. Prohibited a firm for 60 days from undertaking new engagements likely to result in filings with the SEC [ASR No. 209 (February 16, 1977)]

5. Required a firm to conduct or sponsor a research project relating to reliance on internal controls and to incorporate, to the extent deemed appropriate, the results into the firm's audit practice [ASR No. 241 (February 10, 1978)]

6. Censured a firm, other than following a permanent injunction or criminal conviction [ASR No. 248 (May 31, 1978)]

7. Required a firm to name a new managing partner of one of its offices [ASR No. 288 (February 26, 1981)]

8. Required a firm to create a Special Review Committee to review its audit practice, and required it to adopt and implement any and all recommendations of the committee [AAER No. 9 (June 30, 1983)]

9. Required a firm to emphasize audit documentation and revenue recognition in firm training programs [AAER No. 78 (October 10, 1985)]

10. Required that audit work on the firm's publicly held client must be reviewed by an independent auditor who is a member of the AICPA's SEC Practice Section and is approved by the SEC Office of the Chief Accountant; and that working papers must be made available to the SEC [AAER No. 86 (February 10, 1986)]

11. Required a CPA or his firm to join the AICPA's SEC Practice Section and receive an unqualified peer review report, and the CPA to take 50 hours of courses on GAAP and GAAS in each of two years [AAER No. 150 (September 3, 1987)]

SEC sanctions such as these generally are publicly disclosed and obviously can have a significant impact on a CPA firm's practice. Almost all recent Rule 2(e) proceedings, however, have involved consent decrees, in which the auditing firm neither denied nor admitted guilt.

Like all the other sanctions imposed on auditors, these raise the question of what standard of care the auditor must observe to avoid action under Rule 2(e). The grounds for SEC-imposed sanctions, including temporary or permanent suspension as well as the more innovative actions described above, fall into three categories.

1. A finding that the auditor lacked certain personal qualities, for example, character or integrity, or the qualifications to represent others

2. An adverse finding by a court, the SEC, or a state licensing body of actions involving something more than ordinary negligence

3. A finding by the Commission of unethical or improper professional conduct

Rule 2(e) proceedings following a permanent injunction fall into the second category, which generally requires either willful intent or an act so evidently reprehensible that it leads to criminal conviction or loss of license resulting from violation of the securities laws. The SEC believes, however, and the Supreme Court has agreed to some extent at least (see above), that ordinary negligence is sufficient for it to seek and obtain a civil injunction. The SEC's view was reinforced in August 1992 when it used its Rule 2(e) authority to bar two auditors accused of having negligently conducted an audit from appearing before the Commission for two years.[74] The U.S. Court of Appeals later remanded this case to the Commission for clarification of the basis for its ruling. In 1997, the Commission reaffirmed its authority to discipline an auditor for negligence, and the respondents have appealed to the circuit court again.

Some of the more innovative procedures required by the SEC in settlement of Rule 2(e) proceedings are evidence of the Commission's ability to create or influence specific professional standards. This has taken basically two forms:

1. Language in a proceeding indicating auditing responsibilities not prescribed by the profession. [An example is the view expressed in ASR No. 153 (1974) that successor auditors must review the work of predecessor auditors, and that a refusal by the client to permit the necessary communication should be grounds for rejecting the engagement. Professional literature at the time did not make predecessor–successor communications mandatory. Moreover, present standards, while requiring such communication, leave room for the exercise of professional judgment on the effect of a prospective client's forbidding such communication.]

2. Language in a consent decree requiring an auditing firm to develop specific auditing procedures not addressed in the professional literature. (An example is the auditing firm's consent in ASR No. 153 to develop and submit to the SEC procedures for the audit of related party transactions. An SAS on the subject did not exist at the time of ASR No. 153.)

As discussed in Chapter 2, traditionally the SEC has left the specific implementation and interpretation of GAAS to the auditing profession. At the least, Rule 2(e) proceedings and the accompanying consent decrees provide a vehicle for selective departure from that policy.

5.8 PROFESSION'S RESPONSES TO THE LITIGIOUS ENVIRONMENT

The litigious environment has encouraged the public accounting profession as a whole and individual firms to reexamine and strengthen auditing standards and ways of encouraging compliance with them. Since the increase in litigation against auditors, the AICPA has issued a great many authoritative auditing pronouncements and has twice revised its code of professional conduct. The Institute also has devoted considerable attention to the design and implementation of peer reviews of firms' quality controls. Individual firms have devoted increasingly more resources to their own policies and procedures for maintaining and raising the quality of practice.

[74] Accounting and Auditing Enforcement Release No. 412 (Aug. 26, 1992).

(a) Authoritative Pronouncements

Many of the Statements on Auditing Procedure (SAPs) and SASs were issued following audit failures that led to litigation. In addition, other auditing pronouncements originated from accounting pronouncements that, in turn, can be traced to alleged misconduct of one kind or another that led to litigation. For example, SAP No. 47, *Subsequent Events* (issued in 1971), and No. 49, *Letters for Underwriters* (issued in 1971 and superseded in 1993 by SAS No. 72, which was amended in 1995 by SAS No. 76), can be traced to the *BarChris* case, discussed earlier. SAS No. 7, *Communications Between Predecessor and Successor Auditors* (1975), was related to the *U.S. Financial*[75] case. The origin of SAP No. 44 (1971), *Reports Following a Pooling of Interests*, was Accounting Principles Board Opinion No. 16, *Business Combinations* (1970). This in turn had its source in the deterioration of accounting principles evidenced at least in part by litigation, like the *Westec*[76] case, that raised questions of the propriety of the accounting principles selected and applied to account for particular combinations. Moreover, a number of auditing pronouncements further refined or clarified previous pronouncements that were traceable to litigation involving auditors. For example, several subsequent pronouncements further clarified the auditor's responsibilities set forth in SAP No. 1, *Extensions of Auditing Procedure*, which had its source in the *McKesson & Robbins*[77] case.

Other auditing pronouncements, while not individually traceable to specific audit failures that led to litigation, represent part of the accounting profession's program to close the "expectation gap," discussed in Chapters 1 and 4, which had its roots in several audit failures and attendant litigation and investigations. SAS Nos. 53 through 61, issued in 1988, were all responsive to the issues underlying the expectation gap, namely, a series of business failures that revealed material misstatements in audited financial statements. In 1995, SAS No. 55 was amended by SAS No. 78, and SAS No. 58 was amended by SAS No. 79. SAS No. 82, *Consideration of Fraud in a Financial Statement Audit*, issued in 1997, superseded SAS No. 53. SAS No. 82 sets forth specific risk factors that auditors should consider in assessing whether financial statements may be materially misstated because of fraudulent acts. All of those pronouncements increased the auditor's responsibility to detect errors and fraud, sharpened the guidance on how to meet that heightened responsibility, and created new responsibilities to communicate both the existence of errors and fraud and the conditions that enabled them to occur.

(b) Increased Attention to Quality Control

Both the auditing profession and individual firms have recognized the need for more effective controls over the quality of audit practice. Statement on Quality Control Standards No. 2, *System of Quality Control for a CPA Firm's Accounting and Auditing Practice* (QC Section 20), issued in 1996, updated the requirements for CPA firms to have a system of quality control for its accounting and auditing practice. Efforts by the AICPA to improve and monitor the quality of audit practice are described in

---

[75] *In re U. S. Financial Securities Litigation*, 609 F.2d 411 (9th Cir 1979), *cert. denied*, 446 U.S. 929 (1980).

[76] *In re Westec Corp.*, 434 F.2d 195 (5th Cir. 1970).

[77] ASR No. 19, "In the Matter of McKesson & Robbins, Inc." (1940).

Chapter 3. Both the profession and the state boards of accountancy have disciplinary systems through which sanctions are imposed on auditing firms and individual auditors for violations of the Code of Professional Conduct and state accountancy laws. These self-regulatory measures are also discussed in Chapter 3.

Individual firms also have designed and implemented programs for monitoring their audit practices, including, among other things:

- Increased emphasis on policies and procedures for accepting and retaining clients
- Increased resources devoted to continuing education
- Institution of second-partner and interoffice reviews of working papers and reports
- Internal communications directed at both accounting and auditing issues
- Policy statements on internal quality control programs
- Engaging other auditing firms to conduct independent quality reviews
- Increased emphasis on research in auditing theory and applications, including the use of technology to enhance the quality of audit performance

The practice many auditing firms have adopted (even when it is not required[78]) of having a second-partner review of engagements has been traced directly to the *Continental Vending* case.[79] Second-partner reviews are discussed in Chapter 27. As mentioned earlier, most auditors follow the practice of setting forth the scope and inherent limitations of an audit in an engagement letter to the client's management. Many of the points covered in a typical engagement letter also are addressed in the representation letter from management, which SAS No. 19, *Client Representations* (AU Section 333), requires the auditor to obtain. As discussed in Chapter 27, management's representation letter provides written evidence of, among other matters, inquiries made by the auditor and management's responses to them. Both the engagement letter and the management representation letter may constitute important evidence in the event of a lawsuit.

(c)   Efforts to Reduce Exposure to Liability

It has been argued that the best protection against legal liability for both CPA firms and individual practitioners is meticulous adherence to the technical and ethical standards of the profession, and establishing and implementing policies and procedures designed to ensure that all audits are systematically planned and performed, that the work is done with a high degree of professional skepticism by people who understand the client's business circumstances, that appropriate evidence is obtained and objectively evaluated, and that all work done is carefully documented. These objectives are the underlying structure of the theory and practice of auditing described throughout this book.

---

[78] Members of the SEC Practice Section of the AICPA Division for CPA Firms are required to have second-partner reviews of SEC engagements.

[79] A. A. Sommer, Jr., "Legal Liability of Accountants," *Financial Executive* 42 (March 1974), p. 24.

Such actions may help ensure that only quality work is performed, but quality work is no longer sufficient to eliminate the auditor's exposure to liability. The environment in which CPAs practice has changed markedly in the past two decades, as has the relationship between quality work and liability. Litigation against accountants in private securities class action lawsuits often has been initiated to force a settlement, with little regard or even knowledge of the quality of work performed; this was one of the significant influences on Congress in passing the Reform Act, discussed earlier.

The increase in litigation is not unique to the accounting profession. Many businesses have sought repeal of laws that are being used to award significant damages. Aviation manufacturers were successful in getting Congress to shorten the statute of limitations in suits alleging defective airplanes. Product manufacturers are seeking limits on punitive damage awards at the federal level and in many states. Drug manufacturers seek use of an "FDA defense" in litigation involving their products.

The amount of compensation sought by plaintiffs, and awarded by judges and juries, also has increased to levels not experienced in the past. The application of joint and several liability and the awarding of significant punitive damages have had increasingly graver consequences for accountants. Just as Congress responded to perceived abuses of the federal statutes by enacting the Reform Act, there has been growing acknowledgment by state legislatures of inequities in the application of the joint and several liability concept and unrestrained punitive damage awards. Part of this legislative interest has resulted from the increased activity of the accounting profession in broad-based state legal liability or "tort reform" coalitions, and part is attributable to growing public concern over the loss of jobs and over the impact of liability laws on investment in technology and innovation.

One outcome of the increased litigation against the accounting profession has been the widespread use of liability-limiting forms of organization by CPA firms. Until the 1990s, the typical CPA firm was organized as a partnership in which each partner was personally liable for all of the debts of the partnership. If the debts of the partnership exceeded the net worth of the individual partners, the bankruptcy of the partnership could result in the bankruptcy of the individual partners as well.

Nearly every major accounting firm and many smaller firms now operate in some form of organization that limits the personal liability of owners. Largely as a result of efforts of the accounting profession, every jurisdiction (except, at the time of this writing, Vermont, Wyoming, the District of Columbia, and Puerto Rico) has authorized the creation of an entity known as a limited liability partnership (LLP) and its use by accountants. This entity combines the tax, organizational, and operational aspects of a general partnership with the personal liability aspects of a corporation, so that each LLP partner is personally liable only for his or her own negligent actions and those of someone under his or her direct supervision and control. LLP partners are not personally liable for the debts of the entity or of the other partners.

The accounting profession continues to view tort reform as a priority issue and continues to pursue legislation on both the federal and state level. At the federal level, the profession, along with associations representing the high technology, securities, and venture capitalist industries, supported amendments to the 1995 Reform Act that were introduced in Congress during 1997 that would create a uniform national standard for private securities class action lawsuits. (Because the Reform Act amended only federal securities statutes and case law, class action securities lawsuits against accounting firms have been filed in state courts that would be barred in the federal courts.)

On the state level, the profession continues to support business coalition-led efforts to change legal provisions in the areas of joint and several liability, punitive damages, and the statute of limitations. Between 1995 and 1997, tort reform bills were enacted in several states, including Illinois, Indiana, Michigan, New Jersey, Ohio, and Texas. During 1997, the accounting profession played a key role in opposing efforts to either roll back tort reform laws or repeal favorable legal liability case law in Maryland and Ohio. Accountants remain active in numerous other state tort reform initiatives that would significantly affect auditors' liability.

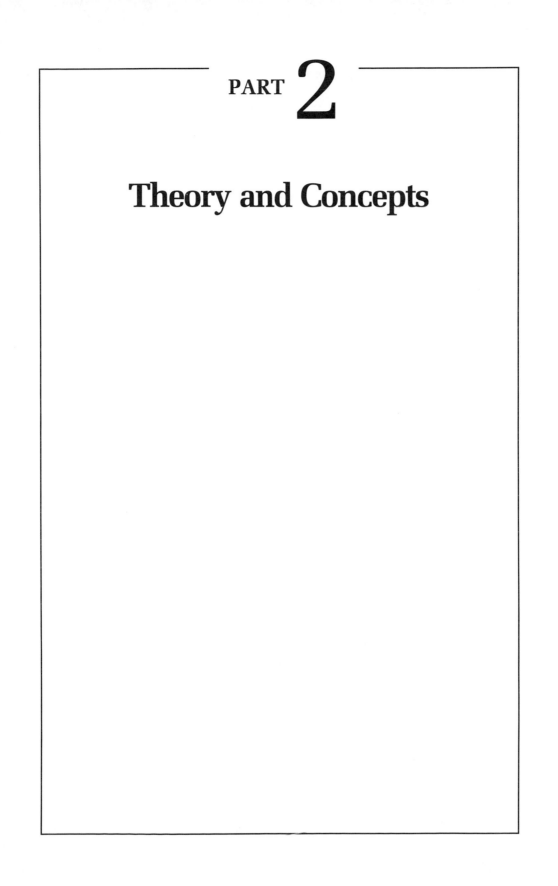

PART 2

Theory and Concepts

6

The Audit Process

Most of the auditor's work in forming an opinion on financial statements consists of obtaining and evaluating evidence about management's assertions that are embodied in those statements. To be able to express an opinion on financial statements, the auditor develops specific audit objectives related to those assertions and then designs and performs audit tests to obtain and evaluate evidence about whether the objectives have been achieved. Throughout the process, the auditor must make decisions about whether the evidence obtained is competent and sufficient for formulating an opinion.

This chapter explores the concepts of audit objectives, audit evidence, audit risk, and materiality, and presents an overall framework, based on those concepts, for viewing the audit process. The framework consists of a series of systematic steps that represent the various phases of the audit work, as determined by the audit objectives and evidence decisions, resulting in an audit that meets the requirements of professional standards. The steps are usually the same in every audit, but the types of tests performed and the evidence obtained vary with each engagement.

6.1   MANAGEMENT ASSERTIONS, AUDIT OBJECTIVES, AND AUDITING PROCEDURES

An entity's financial statements can be thought of as embodying a set of assertions by management. Statement on Auditing Standards (SAS) No. 31, *Evidential Matter*, as amended by SAS No. 80 (AU Section 326), groups financial statement assertions into the following broad categories:

- Existence or occurrence
- Completeness
- Rights and obligations
- Valuation or allocation
- Presentation and disclosure

The authors believe it is helpful to consider explicitly two additional categories of assertions that are implicit in the SAS No. 31 list, namely:

- Accuracy
- Cutoff

Assertions about existence relate to whether assets, liabilities, and ownership interests exist at a specific date. These assertions pertain to both physical items—such as inventory, plant and equipment, and cash—and accounts without physical substance, such as accounts receivable and accounts payable. Assertions about occurrence are concerned with whether recorded transactions, such as purchases and sales, represent economic events that actually occurred during a certain period.

Assertions about completeness pertain to whether all transactions and other events and circumstances that occurred during a specific period and should have been recognized in that period have in fact been recorded. For example, all purchases of goods and services should be recorded and included in the financial statements. The completeness assertion also states that all recognizable financial statement items are in fact included in the financial statements. For example, management asserts that accounts payable reported on the balance sheet include all such obligations of the entity.

Assertions about rights and obligations relate to whether assets are the rights, and liabilities are the obligations, of the entity at a given date. For example, the reporting of capitalized leases in the balance sheet is an assertion that the amount capitalized is the unamortized cost of rights to leased property and that the amount of the lease liability is the unamortized obligation of the entity.

Assertions about valuation or allocation pertain to whether financial statement items are recorded at appropriate amounts in conformity with generally accepted accounting principles (or another comprehensive basis of accounting). For example, the financial statements reflect an assertion that depreciation expense for the year and the carrying value of property, plant, and equipment are based on the systematic amortization of the carrying value of the assets, and that trade accounts receivable are stated at their net realizable value.

Assertions about presentation and disclosure relate to the proper classification, description, and disclosure of items in the financial statements; for example, that liabilities classified as long-term will not mature within one year, and that the accounting policy note to the financial statements includes the disclosures required by generally accepted accounting principles.

Assertions about accuracy relate to the mathematical correctness of recorded transactions that are reflected in the financial statements and the appropriate summarization and posting of those transactions to the general ledger. For example, the financial statements reflect an assertion that accounts payable reflect purchases of goods and services that are based on correct prices and quantities and on invoices that have been accurately computed.

Assertions about cutoff relate to the recording of transactions in the proper accounting period. For example, a check to a vendor that is mailed on December 31 should be recorded in December and not, through either oversight or intent, in January.

The professional literature is written in terms of financial statement assertions; auditors generally translate those assertions into audit objectives that they seek to achieve by performing auditing procedures. For each assertion embodied in each item in the financial statements, the auditor develops one or more corresponding audit objectives. Then the auditor designs procedures for obtaining sufficient competent evidential matter to either corroborate or contradict each assertion and thereby achieve the related audit objective or reveal a deficiency in the financial statements.

Figure 6.1 illustrates how auditors consider these seven broad categories of assertions in formulating audit objectives and designing auditing procedures to obtain evidence supporting them. In the figure, a single auditing procedure is linked to each stated audit objective. In an actual audit, a combination of auditing procedures generally will be necessary to achieve a single objective, and some auditing procedures will relate to more than one objective. For example, in addition to observing physical inventory counts by entity personnel to obtain evidence that inventories included in the balance sheet physically exist, the auditor also may confirm the existence and amount of inventories stored in public warehouses or with other custodians at locations outside the entity's premises. Moreover, observing inventory counts also pro-

Figure 6.1   Examples of Audit Objectives and Procedures

Management Assertion	Example of Audit Objective	Example of Auditing Procedure
Existence or occurrence	Inventories in the balance sheet physically exist.	Observe physical inventory counts by entity personnel.
Completeness	Sales revenues include all items shipped to customers.	Review the entity's periodic accounting for the numerical sequence of shipping documents and invoices.
Accuracy	Accounts receivable reflect sales transactions that are based on correct prices and quantities and are accurately computed.	Compare invoice prices with master price list and quantities with shipping records and customer's sales order; recalculate amounts on invoices.
Cutoff	Sales transactions are reported in the proper period.	Compare shipping dates with dates of journal entries for sales recorded in the last several days of the old year and the first several days of the new year.
Rights and obligations	Real estate in the balance sheet is owned by the entity.	Inspect deeds, purchase contracts, settlement papers, insurance policies, minutes, and related correspondence.
Valuation or allocation	Receivables are stated at net realizable value.	Review entity's aging of receivables to evaluate adequacy of allowance for uncollectible accounts.
Presentation and disclosure	Loss contingencies not required to be recorded are appropriately disclosed.	Inquire of the entity's lawyers concerning litigation, claims, and assessments and evaluate the related disclosures.

vides evidence that the inventory quantities include all products, materials, and supplies on hand (completeness objective). In addition, it provides evidence about other accounts and objectives (such as the existence of plant) and about certain aspects of the entity's internal control (such as how management operates the business, restrictions on access to storage facilities, and the competence of employees).

Relating the evidence obtained from auditing procedures to the audit objectives is an iterative process of accumulating, analyzing, and interpreting information in light of the auditor's expectations, past experience with the entity's management, generally accepted accounting principles, good management practices, and common sense. Procedures performed to meet one audit objective for one account frequently generate information that requires further action by the auditor to achieve that particular audit objective or other audit objectives related to that particular account or other accounts. Evidence that raises questions, for example, about recorded revenues also may raise questions about the adequacy of the allowance for inventory obsolescence, which in turn will require the auditor to accumulate and analyze additional evidence.

6.2   AUDIT EVIDENCE AND AUDIT TESTS

The third standard of field work states:

> Sufficient competent evidential matter is to be obtained through inspection, observation, inquiries, and confirmations to afford a reasonable basis for an opinion regarding the financial statements under audit. (AU Section 326.01)

The evidence necessary to either corroborate or contradict the assertions in the financial statements and thus provide the auditor with a reasonable basis for an opinion is obtained by designing and performing auditing procedures. This section of the chapter describes the various kinds of evidence that are available to the auditor and the types of procedures that the auditor performs to obtain it.

(a)   Types of Evidence

Evidential matter necessary to support the assertions in the financial statements consists of *underlying accounting data* and all *corroborating information* available to the auditor. Underlying evidence for the most part is available to the auditor from within the entity. It consists of the accounting data from which the financial statements are prepared, and includes journals, ledgers, and computer files; accounting manuals; and memoranda, worksheets, and spreadsheets supporting such items as cost allocations, computations, and reconciliations.

Corroborating evidence is information that supports the underlying evidence; generally it is available to the auditor from both the entity and outside sources. Entity sources include information closely related to accounting data, such as checks, electronic funds transfers, invoices, contracts, minutes of meetings, correspondence, written representations by knowledgeable employees, and information obtained by the auditor by inquiry of officers and employees and observation of employees at work. Additional types of corroborating evidence include confirmations of amounts due or assets held by third parties (such as customers and custodians), correspondence with experts such as attorneys and engineers, and physical examination or inspection of assets such as marketable securities and inventories.

Increasingly, both accounting data and corroborating information are in electronic form. Moreover, in some entities, various types of information may be available in electronic form only. For example, transactions may be processed electronically using Electronic Data Interchange systems, or documents may be scanned and converted into electronic images, and source documents may not be retained.

Examination of underlying accounting data, even if it is accessible to the auditor, is not sufficient by itself to meet the third standard of field work. The auditor must obtain satisfaction about the quality of the underlying evidence through corroborating evidence. For example, an auditor often finds it necessary to confirm open accounts receivable to support receivable balances in the accounts receivable subsidiary ledger. To cite another example, the auditor ordinarily should corroborate lists of inventory items counted by entity personnel, by observing the physical inventory counting procedures and making some test counts.

Auditors use various methods or procedures—inquiry, observation, inspecting and counting assets, confirmation, examination of documents and records, reperformance, and analytical procedures—to obtain sufficient competent evidential matter. How the evidence is classified is not very important; what is important is the auditor's ability to evaluate each kind of evidence in terms of its relevance and reliability, as discussed later in this chapter.

(i) Inquiry.   Inquiry means asking questions. The questions may be oral or written and may be directed to entity personnel or to third parties. At the planning stage of the audit, the auditor needs to develop an understanding of the entity's business and its internal control. One of the easiest ways to do this initially is through inquiry. (Later in the audit, the understanding is either corroborated or contradicted by the results of other procedures.) At various stages in the audit, the auditor may ask the entity's employees specific questions about matters arising in the course of the audit work. The auditor makes inquiries of management as part of evaluating accounting principles and estimates. Requesting a representation letter from management as to the recording of all known liabilities, the existence of contingent liabilities, and the existence and carrying value of inventory is a form of inquiry. The auditor also may inquire of third parties, such as the entity's outside legal counsel regarding legal matters, on matters outside the auditor's expertise. In all instances, the auditor's evaluation of responses is an integral part of the inquiry process.

(ii) Observation.   Observation involves direct visual viewing of employees in their work environment and of other facts and events. It is a useful technique that can be employed in many phases of an audit. The auditor should consider, however, that employees may not perform in the same way when the auditor is not present. At the beginning of the audit, the auditor may tour the entity's facilities as part of gaining an understanding of the business. That tour also may provide possible indications of slow-moving or obsolete goods. Observation of employees taking a physical inventory can provide firsthand knowledge to help the auditor assess the adequacy of the inventory taking. Watching employees whose functions have accounting significance perform their assigned tasks can help the auditor assess whether specific controls are being performed effectively.

(iii) Inspection and Counting of Assets.   The auditor may obtain evidence by inspecting or counting assets. For example, the auditor may count cash or marketable securities on hand to ascertain that the assets in the accounts actually exist and are accurately recorded.

(iv) Confirmation.   Confirmation involves obtaining a representation of a fact or condition from a third party, usually (and preferably) in writing. Examples are a confirmation from a bank of the amount on deposit or of a loan outstanding, or a confirmation from a customer of the existence of a receivable balance at a certain date. Auditors most often associate confirmations with cash (confirmation from a bank) and accounts receivable (confirmation from customers). Confirmation, however, has widespread applicability. Depending on the circumstances, virtually any transaction, event, or account balance can be confirmed with a third party. For example, creditors can confirm accounts and notes payable; both customers and creditors can confirm specific transactions and their terms; custodians can confirm securities held for others; insurance companies can confirm insurance premiums paid during the year and balances due at year-end, as well as borrowings on life insurance policies; transfer agents and registrars can confirm shares of stock outstanding; and trustees can confirm balances due under long-term borrowings and payments required and made under bond sinking fund requirements.

(v) Examination of Documents and Records. Examining documents and records includes reading, looking at supporting documentation, comparing, and reconciling. The auditor may read the minutes of the board of directors' meetings for authorization of new financing. The auditor may look at customer accounts to determine that all customers' sales invoices have been recorded, or may examine invoices, purchase orders, and receiving reports to ascertain that the charges to a particular asset or expense account are adequately supported. The auditor may look at evidence in the form of signatures or initials on a purchase invoice, indicating that the invoice has been compared, by appropriate personnel, with the corresponding purchase order and receiving report, and that the footings and extensions on the invoice have been recalculated. The auditor may compare vendor invoices with related receiving reports for evidence that merchandise has been received for bills rendered by creditors. The auditor may examine the reconciliation of accounts receivable subsidiary ledgers with control accounts.

(vi) Reperformance. Reperformance involves repeating, either in whole or in part, the same procedures performed by employees, particularly recalculations to ensure mathematical accuracy. Reperformance may involve some of the other techniques previously mentioned, such as comparing or counting. For example, comparing a vendor's invoice with the corresponding purchase order and receiving report, where there is evidence in the form of initials on a document that an employee previously made that comparison, is reperformance. Reperformance also may involve recounting some of the entity's physical inventory counts, recalculating the extensions and footings on sales invoices and inventory listings, repeating the calculations of depreciation expense, and reconstructing a bank reconciliation prepared by an employee. In addition, in evaluating management's accounting estimates and its choice and application of accounting principles, the auditor may reperform the processes followed by management.

(vii) Analytical Procedures. Analytical procedures are reasonableness tests of financial information made by studying and comparing relationships among data and trends in the data. Analytical procedures include scanning or scrutinizing accounting records, such as entries to an inventory control account for a period, looking for evidence of unusual amounts or unusual sources of input, which, if found, would be investigated further. Other examples of analytical procedures typically performed in an audit include fluctuation analyses, ratio analyses, comparisons of accounting data with operating data or budgets, and comparisons of recorded amounts with expectations developed by the auditor. Analytical procedures are performed early in the audit to help the auditor in planning other auditing procedures, during field work to obtain evidence about specific assertions and accounts, and at the end of the audit as an overall review of the financial statements.

(b) Competence of Evidential Matter

The third standard of field work requires the auditor to obtain evidential matter that is both competent and sufficient. To be competent, evidence must be both relevant and reliable.

To be relevant, evidence must affect the auditor's ability to accept or reject a specific financial statement assertion. The auditor reaches a conclusion on the financial statements taken as a whole through a series of judgments made throughout the audit about specific financial statement assertions. Each piece of evidence obtained is evaluated in terms of its usefulness either in corroborating or contradicting an assertion by management or in the auditor's evaluation of evidence obtained at other stages of the audit. Evidence is relevant to the extent that it serves either of those purposes.

An example or two will illustrate the concept of relevance of evidence. Confirming accounts receivable by requesting the entity's customers to inform the auditor about any differences between their records of amounts they owe the entity and the entity's records of open balances is a commonly performed auditing procedure. When considered in conjunction with other evidence, a signed confirmation returned to the auditor indicating agreement with the open balance can provide support for the management assertion that the account receivable exists and is not overstated. Confirmations, however, do not provide evidence about collectibility, completeness, or rights and obligations. A confirmed account may not be collectible because the debtor does not intend or is unable to pay; receivables may exist that have not been recorded and therefore cannot possibly be selected for confirmation; or the entity may have sold the receivables to another party and may merely be acting as a collection agent for that party. Similarly, physically inspecting and counting inventory gives the auditor evidence about its existence, but not about its valuation or about the entity's title to it.

Evidence also must be reliable if it is to be useful to the auditor. The Financial Accounting Standards Board definition of reliability is also appropriate in the context of audit evidence. Reliability is "the quality of information that assures that information is reasonably free from error and bias and faithfully represents what it purports to represent."[1] Synonyms for reliability are dependability and trustworthiness. The reliability of audit evidence is influenced by several factors.

- *Independence of the source.* Evidential matter obtained by the auditor from independent sources outside the entity being audited is usually more reliable than that from within the entity. Examples of evidence from independent sources include a confirmation from a state agency of the number of shares of common stock authorized to be issued, and a confirmation from a bank of a cash balance, a loan balance, or securities held as collateral. (The higher level of reliability that such evidence provides does not mean that errors in confirmations of this nature never occur.) In contrast, evidence arising from inquiries of entity personnel or from inspecting documents provided by management is usually considered less reliable from the auditor's viewpoint.

- *Qualifications of the source.* For audit evidence to be reliable, it must be obtained from people who are competent and have the qualifications to make the information free from error. (The independence-of-the-source criterion addresses the

[1] Statement of Financial Accounting Concepts No. 2, "Glossary of Terms."

possibility of deliberate errors in the evidence; the qualifications-of-the-source criterion addresses the possibility of unintentional errors in the evidence.) For instance, confirmations provided by businesses are usually more reliable than confirmations provided by individuals. Answers to inquiries about pending litigation from the entity's lawyers are usually more reliable than answers from persons not working in the legal department. The auditor should not necessarily assume that the higher a person's position in the entity, the better qualified that person is to provide evidence. The accounts payable clerk probably knows the true routine in the accounts payable section of the accounting department better than the controller does. Furthermore, auditors should challenge their own qualifications when evaluating evidence they have gathered. When inspecting or counting precious gems in a jeweler's inventory, for example, the auditor is probably not qualified to distinguish between diamonds and pieces of glass.

- *Internal control.* Underlying accounting data developed under satisfactory internal control is more reliable than similar data developed under less effective internal control. Also, the auditor does not accept management's description of the entity's internal control without corroboration. Instead, if the auditor plans to look to internal control as a source of audit evidence about specific financial statement assertions, he or she observes the activities of entity personnel and tests other aspects of internal control to determine that controls are operating effectively.

- *Nature of the evidence.* Evidence varies in the extent to which it is fact-based versus opinion-based. Evidence obtained by an auditor's direct, personal knowledge through counting, observing, calculating, or examining documents may be thought of as fact-based. Evidence based on the opinions of others, such as the opinion of an appraiser about the value of an asset acquired by the entity in a nonmonetary transaction, the opinion of a lawyer about the outcome of pending litigation, or the credit manager's opinion about the collectibility of outstanding receivables, may be thought of as opinion-based. Evidence that is opinion-based often requires more judgment by both the preparer (i.e., the appraiser, the lawyer, or the credit manager) and the auditor than does evidence that is fact-based and, therefore, may be less reliable than fact-based evidence. Sometimes, however, only opinion-based evidence is available to the auditor for evaluating a particular financial statement assertion.

The auditor's twofold goal in performing an audit in accordance with generally accepted auditing standards is to achieve the necessary assurance to support the audit opinion, and to perform the audit as efficiently as possible. Thus, in addition to considering the relevance and reliability of evidence, the auditor also must consider its availability, timeliness, and cost. Sometimes a desirable form of evidence is simply not available. For example, an auditor who is retained by the entity after its accounting year-end cannot be present to observe and test-count the ending inventory. Also, time constraints may not permit an auditor to consider a particular source of evidence. For example, confirming a foreign account receivable might delay the completion of the audit by weeks or even months. Different types of evidence have different costs associated with them, and the auditor must consider cost–benefit trade-offs.

Fortunately, auditors usually have available more than one source or method of obtaining evidence to corroborate a particular financial statement assertion. If one source or method is not practicable to use, often another can be substituted. For example, a customer who may not be able to confirm an account receivable balance may be able to confirm specific sales transactions and cash remittances. Or a more costly source of evidence may be substituted for a less costly source that is not as reliable. For instance, a petroleum engineer who is independent of the entity could be retained instead of the auditor's relying on engineers employed by the entity for estimates of proven oil reserves. The auditor should choose the type of evidence (corroborating evidence often is sought using more than one method) that achieves the audit objectives at the lowest cost.

(c)   Sufficiency of Evidential Matter

Determining the sufficiency of evidential matter is a question of deciding how much evidence is enough to obtain the reasonable assurance necessary to support the auditor's opinion. The sufficiency of evidence depends partly on the thoroughness of the auditor's search for it and partly on the auditor's ability to evaluate it objectively. For some auditing procedures, the amount of evidence needed corresponds precisely with the decision to use a certain procedure at all; that is, the auditor either performs or does not perform the procedure. For example, a decision to confirm the number of shares authorized by the state of incorporation is a decision to confirm *all* authorized shares. If the entity had numerous bank accounts, however, the auditor could confirm only some of the accounts with the banks. In that case, the question of sufficiency becomes one of determining the extent of testing. The extent of testing, including the use of sampling, is discussed in Chapters 15 and 16.

(d)   Types of Audit Tests

The evidence that the auditor obtains and the procedures for obtaining it described previously can also be classified according to the purpose for which the evidence is gathered. Viewed in terms of their purpose, most auditing procedures are either *tests of controls* or *substantive tests*. These two types of audit tests and their respective purposes are discussed at length in Chapters 12 and 15. They are described briefly here to set the stage for the overview of an audit that is presented later in this chapter. (Some auditing procedures—for example, procedures undertaken as part of obtaining an understanding of the entity's business and internal control and other planning activities, and procedures undertaken to obtain details of account balances—do not fit into these two categories. Most of those activities do not in themselves generate audit evidence; they must be undertaken, however, before useful evidence can be gathered.)[2]

Tests of controls are performed to provide the auditor with evidence about the effectiveness of the operation of internal control. That evidence, if it is obtained, supports an assessment of control risk that is below the maximum or low for one or more assertions (control risk is discussed later in this chapter). To illustrate a test of controls, consider the part of an entity's internal control in which the prices on vendors' invoices are matched by computer with prices on the corresponding purchase orders and an exception report is generated of invoices for which the prices do not match. Exceptions are then resolved by communication with the vendors and the corrected invoices are reprocessed. As evidence that this control activity has been performed, the

---

[2] In this book, the word "test" is restricted to the two types of tests mentioned above. The word "procedure" is used more broadly to describe any of the wide variety of activities performed on an audit, including tests of controls and substantive tests.

person following up on exceptions initials the exception report. To test the effectiveness of these procedures, the auditor may inspect the exception report for evidence of review and action by the employee. If that evidence is present and the invoices do not appear on the subsequent exception report, the auditor would conclude that the generation of the exception report and the subsequent follow-up operated effectively in that specific instance.

If tests of controls support an assessment of control risk that is below the maximum or low for one or more assertions, the assurance needed from substantive tests can be reduced. Substantive tests consist of *analytical procedures* and *tests of details* of transactions and account balances. Their purpose is to provide the auditor with evidence supporting management's assertions that are implicit in the financial statements or, conversely, to discover misstatements in the financial statements. Analytical procedures used as substantive tests are discussed in detail in Chapter 15. An example of a test of the details of transactions is the auditor's examination of underlying documents that support purchases, sales, and retirements of property, plant, and equipment during the year. The auditor examines the documents as a means of forming a conclusion about the assertions concerning existence, rights and obligations, and accuracy that are implicit in the property, plant, and equipment account reported in the balance sheet. An example of a test of details of an account balance is the confirming of accounts receivable in order to form a conclusion about their existence.

Other substantive auditing procedures include reading minutes of meetings of the board of directors and its important committees, obtaining letters from outside counsel regarding legal matters, and obtaining a letter of representation from management stating, among other matters, that it is responsible for the financial statements and that no material transactions have been omitted from the accounting records underlying the financial statements.

(e) Audit Evidence Decisions

The amount and kinds of evidence that the auditor decides are necessary to form an opinion on the financial statements taken as a whole, and the timing of procedures used to obtain the evidence, are matters of professional judgment. The auditor makes these decisions only after carefully considering the circumstances of a particular engagement and the various risks (discussed next) related to the audit. The goal in every audit should be to perform the work in an effective and efficient manner.

As discussed in Chapter 1, an auditor usually has to rely on evidence that is persuasive rather than conclusive. In deciding how much persuasive evidence is enough, by necessity the auditor must work within time constraints, considering the cost of obtaining evidence and evaluating the usefulness of the evidence obtained. In making these decisions, the auditor cannot ignore the risk of issuing an inappropriate opinion or justify omitting a particular test solely because it is difficult or expensive to perform. While an auditor is seldom convinced beyond *all* doubt with respect to the assertions embodied in the financial statements, he or she must achieve a high level of assurance about those assertions to support the opinion given.

In deciding the nature, timing, and extent of auditing procedures to be performed, the auditor can choose from a number of alternative strategies. For example, for some audit objectives for specific accounts, the auditor might decide to perform tests of controls. The tests would be designed to provide evidence that the accounting system from which the account balances were derived and other relevant controls were operating consistently and effectively, and would be combined with limited substantive tests of the account balances themselves. For other audit objectives or accounts, the auditor might decide to obtain evidence mainly from substantive tests. These decisions will be influenced by answers to such questions as: what are the principal risks of the entity's business; what are the significant account balances in the financial statements; is internal control satisfactory; and which approach provides the needed assurance most efficiently? These questions are not all-inclusive, but are indicative of the kinds of considerations and judgments the auditor must make.

6.3   AUDIT RISK

There is no practical way to reduce audit risk to zero. Generally accepted auditing standards, user expectations, and sound business practices require the auditor to design and perform auditing procedures that will permit expressing an opinion on the financial statements with a low risk that the opinion will be inappropriate. The complement of that risk is an expression of the level of assurance that the opinion will be appropriate. Stated another way, the auditor seeks to have a low risk that the opinion expressed is inappropriate, or a high level of assurance[3] that the financial statements are free from material misstatements (the concept of materiality is discussed later in this chapter). Obtaining audit assurance and limiting audit risk are alternative ways of looking at the same process.

The auditor varies the nature, timing, and extent of auditing procedures in response to his or her perception of risk. Thus, when risk is perceived to be high, more reliable evidence, procedures timed at or near the end of the period under audit, and larger sample sizes are common. Risk analysis also is used to balance the mix of tests of controls and substantive tests—both analytical procedures and tests of details—to achieve an efficient audit.

(a)   Overall Audit Risk

The term "overall audit risk" is used to describe the risk that the auditor will issue an inappropriate opinion. That opinion may be either that the financial statements taken as a whole are fairly stated when they are not, or that they are not fairly stated when they are.[4] For practical reasons, auditors are particularly attuned to the risk of issuing a "clean" opinion on materially misstated financial statements. It is unlikely that auditors would issue a qualified or an adverse opinion on fairly stated financial statements because the entity's concern over the adverse consequences of such opinions normally would result in additional study and investigation that would clear up

---

[3] The required high level of assurance is referred to in the professional literature as "reasonable assurance." Chapter 4 of this book discusses the concept of reasonable assurance.

[4] SAS No. 47 (AU Section 312.02) defines audit risk as "the risk that the auditor may unknowingly fail to appropriately modify his or her opinion on financial statements that are materially misstated." Even though this definition does not include the risk that the auditor might erroneously conclude that the financial statements are materially misstated when they are not, it logically follows that the auditor should obtain sufficient evidence to give the proper opinion in all circumstances.

the misperception. Nevertheless, both aspects of overall audit risk have cost implications for auditors.[5]

It is usually impracticable to consider overall audit risk in relation to the financial statements taken as a whole because particular account balances, groups of account balances, or related classes of transactions are likely to have different patterns of risk and the auditing procedures applied to them are likely to have different relative costs. It ordinarily is practicable, however, to consider audit risk for each assertion associated with each significant account, group of accounts, or class of transactions. The various audit risks for each assertion related to each account balance or group of account balances are then combined to represent overall audit risk.

The auditor's primary objective in conducting an audit is to limit audit risk in individual balances or classes of transactions so that, at the completion of the audit, overall audit risk is limited to a level sufficiently low—or conversely, that the level of assurance is sufficiently high—to permit the auditor to express an opinion on the financial statements taken as a whole. A secondary objective is to obtain the desired assurance as efficiently as possible.

(b)   The Components of Audit Risk

Audit risk at the account balance or class of transactions level has two components: the risk that the financial statements will contain misstatements (resulting from either errors or fraud) that are material, either individually or in the aggregate, and the risk that the auditor will not detect those misstatements through the performance of substantive tests (both analytical procedures and tests of details). The former risk is not under the auditor's control. The auditor identifies the risks that are associated with the entity and assesses the risk that its internal control will not prevent misstatements from reaching the financial statements or detect any that do; however, he or she cannot reduce or otherwise change the risks. The latter risk, called *detection risk*, is controlled by the auditor through the selection and performance of substantive tests directed at specific assertions relating to specific transactions and account balances. The auditor's assessment of the risk of the financial statements containing misstatements determines the level of detection risk he or she can accept and still restrict audit risk to an appropriately low level.

The risk that the financial statements will contain misstatements has two aspects: inherent risk and control risk. *Inherent risk* is the susceptibility of an account balance or a class of transactions to material misstatements, without consideration of internal

---

[5] SAS No. 47 (footnote to AU Section 312.02) notes that "in addition to audit risk, the auditor is also exposed to loss or injury to his or her professional practice from litigation, adverse publicity, or other events arising in connection with financial statements audited and reported on. This exposure is present even though the auditor has performed the audit in accordance with generally accepted auditing standards and has reported appropriately on those financial statements. Even if an auditor assesses this exposure as low, the auditor should not perform less extensive procedures than would otherwise be appropriate under generally accepted auditing standards." This exposure is one aspect of the risk an accountant faces in accepting any engagement to perform professional services. As indicated above, the auditor is required to assess audit risk independently of his or her evaluation of the exposure presented by an engagement to perform professional services.

control. That susceptibility may result from either conditions affecting the entity as a whole or characteristics of specific transactions or accounts. *Control risk* is the risk that the entity's internal control will not prevent material misstatements or detect on a timely basis any that do reach the financial statements. The auditor identifies inherent risks to determine areas where the risk of material misstatement may be high. In assessing control risk, the auditor obtains an understanding of the components of the entity's internal control and, if appropriate, tests them to determine whether, and to what extent, they are operating effectively and thus can be expected to prevent or detect misstatements. The evidence resulting from the tests of controls reduces the evidence the auditor needs from substantive tests of transactions and account balances to restrict audit risk to an acceptably low level. The auditor's assessment of control risk is the subject of Chapter 12.

In seeking to limit audit risk to a sufficiently low level, the level of detection risk the auditor can accept varies inversely with his or her assessment of the risk of the financial statements containing material misstatements. That is, the higher the perceived risk of material misstatements, the more assurance the auditor needs from substantive tests (i.e., the lower the acceptable level of detection risk) to limit audit risk, and vice versa. Similarly, given the assurance desired from substantive tests, the assurance the auditor needs from tests of details will vary inversely with the assurance obtained from analytical procedures.

Various combinations of audit effort devoted to risk assessment activities, analytical procedures, and tests of details can restrict audit risk to the same low level, but some combinations will be more efficient (i.e., less costly) than others. Based on his or her expectations about control risk, the auditor formulates an audit strategy that will, in a cost-effective manner, provide sufficient competent evidence to (1) confirm those expectations about control risk through the performance of tests of controls, and (2) reduce detection risk sufficiently, through the performance of substantive tests, to achieve a low level of audit risk.

Before issuing an unqualified opinion, the auditor should be satisfied that *overall* audit risk is appropriately low. As noted earlier, in considering overall audit risk, the individual audit risks for the various account balances and assertions are combined. To date, however, no single, simple, generally agreed-on mathematical approach to combining these risks has been developed. Nor has the profession been able to agree on what an appropriately low level of overall risk is. While the auditor may at times think in quantitative terms when considering alternative audit strategies and assessing risk, risk management ultimately requires seasoned judgment based on experience, training, and business sense. The way the audit results of each component of the financial statements are combined depends on how the auditor apportions materiality and combines risk.

Many attempts have been made to develop mathematically based risk assessment models, but there is no requirement that audit risk or its components be quantified. In fact, it may not be practicable to quantify the components of audit risk because of the large number of variables affecting them and the subjective nature of many of those variables. Accordingly, many auditors do not attempt to assign specific values to audit risk or its components. Normative models for apportioning materiality and combining risk for the financial statements taken as a whole have been a subject of academic research for some years, but do not seem likely to yield practical benefits in the foreseeable future.

(i) Inherent Risk.   Financial statements may be susceptible to misstatements because of a condition that exists at the macroeconomic, industry, or entity level, or by a characteristic of an account balance or a class of transactions. The auditor identifies those risks as a result of his or her understanding of the entity's business and industry, performing analytical procedures, studying prior years' audit results, and understanding the entity's transactions, their flow through the accounting system, and the account balances they generate. In assessing the risk that the financial statements may contain material misstatements, the auditor considers the inherent risks he or she has identified.

Some aspects of inherent risk are not limited to specific transactions or accounts but stem from factors that are more broadly related to the entity's business environment. These risks usually cannot be controlled by management; they include changes in general business conditions, new governmental regulations, and other economic factors such as a declining industry characterized by bankruptcies, other indications of financial distress, and a lack of financial flexibility, which might affect the realization of assets or incurrence of liabilities, or might influence entity management or other personnel to deliberately misstate financial statements. Conversely, overly rapid expansion (with or without concomitant demand) can create quality failures resulting in potential sales returns or unsalable inventory.

The audit objectives most likely to be affected by inherent risks relating to such macroeconomic, industry, or entity-wide factors are valuation or allocation, rights and obligations, and presentation and disclosure. Certain risks might have such a pervasive effect on the entity's financial statements as a whole as to warrant special audit attention. For example, a severe recession might lead to substantial doubt about an entity's ability to continue to operate as a going concern. The auditor's responsibility in this situation is described in Chapter 26 [Section 26.7(b), Going Concern Uncertainties].

While inherent risks stemming from external and entity-wide conditions cannot be controlled by the entity, the control environment set by management (the "tone at the top") and its monitoring of internal control to identify changes in circumstances affecting the entity can help ensure that the financial statements reflect the underlying economic realities that those conditions create. In addition, management may establish special control activities or perform special year-end procedures in response to inherent risks. Examples include special reviews of inventory obsolescence or of the provision for uncollectible accounts receivable.

Other aspects of inherent risk are peculiar to a specific class of transactions or account. The risk of misstatements is greater for some classes of transactions or accounts than for others. In general, transactions that require considerable accounting judgment by entity management are more likely than other transactions to produce errors. Similarly, some assets are more susceptible to theft than others; cash is more prone to misappropriation than are steel beams. Account balances derived from accounting estimates are more likely to be misstated than account balances composed of more factual data. The characteristics of accounts with generic titles differ from one entity to another and even within an entity. For example, not all inventories are the same. Consequently, in assessing risk, the auditor considers the characteristics of the specific items underlying the particular account. In some instances, the risks relate to whether the inventory exists; in other situations, the risks relate to its valuation.

Inherent risks related to specific transactions and accounts should be, and usually are, addressed by the entity's internal control. If so, and if based on efficiency considerations, the auditor plans to test the effectiveness of controls, then those inherent risks are considered in conjunction with the assessment of control risk relating to the transactions and accounts. For example, the auditor may determine in planning the audit that an asset (such as cash) with characteristics (liquidity and transferability) that make it extremely prone to theft, is nevertheless subject to extremely effective controls. In effect, management has designed specific controls in light of the asset's characteristics. In this environment the auditor may find it efficient to test how effectively the controls are operating. If they are effective, the auditor may be able to assess the risk of misappropriation—and thus the risk of a financial statement misstatement—as relatively low.

(ii) Control Risk.   There are likely to be errors in the financial reporting process that management does not detect because no affordable system of internal control can be 100 percent effective. In addition, it is not always practicable to subject all transactions to detailed scrutiny, and not all assertions are addressed to the same extent—either intentionally or otherwise—by controls. For example, discretionary bonuses and unusual transactions may not be subject to control activities; in addition, management override of established controls is always possible. Therefore, some risk normally is associated with every entity's internal control; entities with effective controls carry a relatively lower risk, those with less effective controls, a relatively higher risk.

The auditor may be able to obtain evidence—by testing the controls an entity applies to transactions and balances—that those controls are operating effectively. To the extent that such evidence is available and can be obtained efficiently, the auditor will be able to conclude that the risk of the financial statements containing misstatements is correspondingly lowered. For accounts and assertions that are not specifically addressed by controls, or if the auditor does not plan, for reasons of efficiency or otherwise, to test the effectiveness of controls, he or she will have to obtain all audit assurance for relevant accounts and assertions from substantive tests.

(iii) Detection Risk.   Detection risk is the possibility that misstatements in a material amount, either individually or cumulatively, will go undetected by substantive tests—both analytical procedures and tests of details. The auditor can perform different combinations of substantive tests to reduce detection risk related to a particular account and assertion. For example, the auditor may perform analytical procedures, tests of details, or a combination of the two; perform tests at year-end or at an interim date; test 100 percent of the items in an account balance or less than 100 percent by using sampling or other methods of testing less than an entire account balance. In deciding which procedures to perform, when to perform them, and the extent of testing, the auditor considers the competence and sufficiency of the evidence that can be obtained from various procedures. Using a combination of tests directed at a specific assertion for a specific account balance is generally more effective than using a single test, because analytical procedures and tests of details complement each other and thus are more powerful in combination.

Furthermore, since the two types of substantive tests are complementary, the assurance derived from one reduces proportionately the assurance the auditor needs from the other to reduce detection risk. For example, as a conceptual exercise—since generally accepted auditing standards require that some substantive tests be performed on all audits, regardless of the level of detection risk—suppose an auditor performs no tests of details or analytical procedures. If there is a misstatement in the financial statements, there is a 100 percent chance that it will not be detected (detection risk is 100 percent). Performing either tests of details or analytical procedures will reduce the likelihood that the misstatement will go undetected (detection risk). If both tests of details and analytical procedures are performed, the likelihood that neither procedure will detect the misstatement is less than if only one type of test is performed, because for the misstatement to go undetected by the auditor, *both* tests of details and analytical procedures must fail to detect it.

(iv) Sampling Risk.   In the context of drawing conclusions from performing auditing procedures, risks may be classified as either sampling or nonsampling risks, depending on whether sampling is used in determining the extent of testing. Sampling risk is the risk that, when an audit test is restricted to a sample, the conclusion reached from the test will differ from the conclusion that would have been reached if the same test had been applied to all items in the population. Sampling risk is discussed in Chapter 16.

(v) Nonsampling Risk.   Nonsampling risk encompasses all risks that are not specifically the result of sampling. Thus, nonsampling risk is the risk that any factor other than the size of the sample selected will cause the auditor to draw an incorrect conclusion about an account balance or about the operating effectiveness of a control. Examples of nonsampling risk are:

- Omitting necessary auditing procedures (e.g., failing to review board minutes)
- Applying auditing procedures improperly (e.g., giving confirmation requests to entity personnel for mailing)
- Applying auditing procedures to an inappropriate or incomplete population (e.g., excluding an entire class of purchases from the process of selecting a sample for substantive tests of the accuracy of recorded transactions and then concluding that all purchase transactions have been accurately recorded)
- Failing to recognize a deviation in a control when it is encountered in a test of controls
- Failing to detect that accounting recognition, measurement, or disclosure principles have been improperly selected or applied
- Failing to take action either in response to audit findings or because factors requiring attention have been overlooked

Analyses of past alleged audit failures indicate that such nonsampling risk factors as failure to understand the entity's business processes or risks, errors in interpreting accounting principles, mistakes in interpreting and applying auditing standards, and misstatements caused by management or employee fraud are among the most significant audit risk factors and sources of auditor liability. Nonsampling risk can be controlled by carefully planning the audit and maintaining high standards of audit quality. Quality standards address matters such as independence and professional development of staff, independent review of working papers, and supervision of the performance of auditing procedures. These are covered in detail in Chapter 3.

6.4 MATERIALITY

A concept of materiality is a practical necessity in both auditing and accounting. Allowing immaterial items to complicate and clutter the auditing process or financial statements is uneconomical and diverts users' attention from significant matters in the financial statements. Materiality judgments influence audit planning and, in the evaluation of audit results, are critical to determining whether the financial statements are fairly presented. Inherent in rendering an audit opinion is the recognition that financial statements cannot precisely or exactly present financial position, results of operations, and cash flows. Such precision is unattainable because of limitations in the accounting measurement process and constraints imposed by the audit process and auditing technology, as discussed in Chapter 1. The wording of the standard auditor's report explicitly recognizes this by stating that the financial statements are presented fairly *in all material respects.*

For the auditor, the consideration of materiality is a professional judgment made largely according to his or her perception of the needs of the users of the financial statements. In terms of users' needs, materiality is defined as "the magnitude of an omission or misstatement of accounting information that, in the light of surrounding circumstances, makes it probable that the judgment of a reasonable person relying on the information would have been changed or influenced by the omission or misstatement."[6] Ultimately, the users of financial statements determine what is material. There are many users, however, including shareholders, investors, creditors, regulators, financial analysts, labor unions, audit committees, and entity management, and each may have a different view of what is important. For example, investors rely on information to assess long-term prospects such as trends of cash flows and income; short-term creditors focus more on asset liquidity in the immediate future.

SEC Regulation S-X (Rule 1-02) defines materiality as follows:

> The term "material," when used to qualify a requirement for the furnishing of information as to any subject, limits the information required to those matters about which an average prudent investor ought reasonably to be informed.

This definition has been reinforced by court decisions such as the *BarChris* case[7] in which the judge clearly indicated that the materiality issue involved amounts he believed would motivate the "average prudent investor," not the average banker or security analyst. In developing a standard of materiality for a particular situation, other court cases refer to the "reasonable shareholder"[8]; FASB Concepts Statement No. 2, to the "reasonable person"; and an American Accounting Association publication, to

[6] Statement of Financial Accounting Concepts No. 2, *Qualitative Characteristics of Accounting Information.*

[7] *Escott* v. *BarChris Construction Corp.,* 283 F. Supp. 643 (S.D.N.Y. 1968).

[8] For example, TSC *Industries v. Northway, Inc.,* 44 U.S.L.W. 4852 (1976).

the "informed investor."[9] Thus, the consensus seems to be that materiality is influenced by the user, who may be informed, but is not necessarily sophisticated, about financial statements.

Materiality has both qualitative and quantitative aspects. A financial statement misstatement may be quantitatively immaterial, but may nevertheless have a material effect on the financial statements. SAS No. 47 (AU Section 312.11) cites as an example, "an illegal payment of an otherwise immaterial amount [that] could be material if there is a reasonable possibility that it could lead to a material contingent liability or a material loss of revenue." Moreover, such matters may have broad implications regarding the integrity of management, and thus may warrant further investigation. The auditor may need to assess the possible pervasiveness of the problem, reassess the effectiveness of internal control, and report the findings to an appropriate level of management. Similarly, qualitatively innocuous mistakes in the form of small unintentional errors can add up to quantitatively material dollar misstatements that would cause the auditor to qualify the opinion if adjustments were not made to the accounts. Materiality judgments also influence items that are or should be disclosed without directly affecting the financial statement amounts. Because of the dual influence of qualitative and quantitative factors in determining materiality, the concept is difficult to operationalize. It is not surprising that the profession has not been able to establish a single, agreed-on quantitative standard.

The assessment of materiality takes place throughout an audit, particularly during planning and when evaluating the results of auditing procedures. SAS No. 47 (AU Section 312.14) requires the auditor, in planning an engagement, to consider a "preliminary judgment about materiality levels for audit purposes." That preliminary judgment may include assessments of what constitutes materiality for significant captions in the balance sheet, income statement, and statement of cash flows individually, and for the financial statements taken as a whole. One purpose of this preliminary materiality judgment is to focus the auditor's attention on the more significant financial statement items while he or she is determining the audit strategy. The materiality levels established for a particular account balance or class of transactions are generally more stringent, in a quantitative sense, than overall materiality levels established for the financial statements taken as a whole. As a practical matter, SAS No. 47 indicates that the preliminary judgment about materiality for the financial statements taken as a whole is generally the smallest aggregate level of errors that could be considered material to any one of the financial statements (AU Section 312.19).

As an example of how an auditor might set materiality levels in planning the audit, he or she may consider misstatements aggregating less than $100,000 not to be material to net income, but may establish a higher materiality threshold for misstatements that affect only the balance sheet (such as misclassifications). This would be because the relatively higher magnitude of the balance sheet components might cause the $100,000 to be even less material to the balance sheet. Similarly, when planning procedures at the line item level (such as receivables or inventories), the auditor must consider that immaterial misstatements in separate line items might aggregate to a ma-

---

[9] *Accounting and Reporting Standards for Corporate Financial Statements* (Evanston, IL: American Accounting Association, 1957).

terial amount. Thus, auditing procedures in one area—for example, receivables—might have to be designed to detect income statement misstatements of much less than $100,000, because of possible misstatements in other areas of the balance sheet.

To perform an effective and efficient audit, the auditor must continually assess the results of procedures performed and repeatedly reevaluate whether, based on those results, the scope of procedures planned for the various accounts is adequate, or possibly excessive. For example, individually immaterial misstatements of certain expenses may aggregate to a material amount. As audit work progresses, the auditor may find that the individually immaterial misstatements do not offset each other but cause income to be overstated. In these circumstances, the auditor may need to adjust the scope of procedures for the expenses remaining to be examined in order to gain assurance that a material aggregate misstatement will be detected if it exists. It also may be necessary to apply additional procedures to areas that have already been audited.

New facts and circumstances also may change the amount the auditor considers material to individual financial statement line items or to the financial statements taken as a whole. For example, if adjustments are made to the accounts during the course of the audit, the parameters the auditor used to determine materiality in the planning stage (e.g., amounts for net income, revenues, and shareholders' equity) may change. By the end of the audit, materiality may be different than at the planning stage. An auditor who does not continually reassess materiality and audit scope as the engagement progresses assumes a greater risk of performing an inefficient or ineffective audit. Materiality assessments and audit planning should be viewed as dynamic, rather than static, auditing concepts.

To keep track of misstatements discovered through the various tests and other procedures performed during an audit and to help in drawing conclusions about their effect on the financial statements, the auditor often maintains a summary of potential audit adjustments. This summary assists the auditor in accumulating known misstatements found through audit tests, misstatements based on projections developed from sampling procedures, and misstatements relating to management's accounting estimates that the auditor believes are unreasonable. Ordinarily, management adjusts the records for many of the known misstatements. The auditor then considers the effect of the remaining unadjusted items on the financial statements. Sometimes the auditor believes that further adjustments are necessary for an unqualified opinion to be given. The summary also assists in ascertaining which financial statement is affected by the misstatements. The summary of adjustments is discussed in further detail and illustrated in Chapter 27 (Section 27.5, Summarizing Misstatements and Evaluating the Audit Findings).

6.5 THE STEPS IN AN AUDIT

The audit process can be viewed as depicted in Figure 6.2. The activities in the figure can be summarized as follows:

1. Carrying out engagement planning and management activities, including decisions to accept (or retain) the client and organizational and planning decisions
2. Obtaining information about the entity

Figure 6.2   Summary of the Audit Process

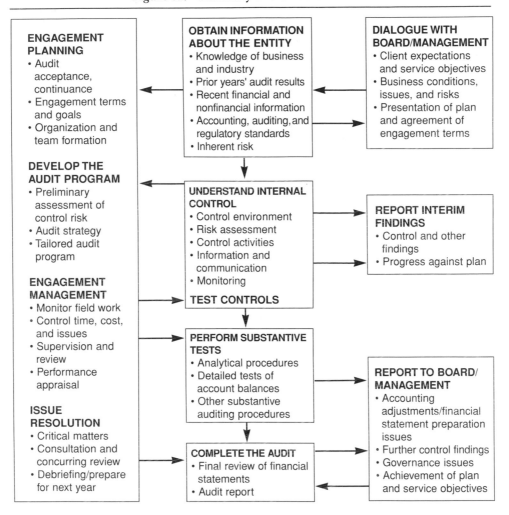

3. Understanding internal control

4. Assessing control risk and developing the audit strategy

5. Confirming the assessment of control risk by performing tests of controls

6. Developing the substantive test audit program

7. Performing substantive tests

8. Completing the audit, including performing final analytical and other procedures, and reviewing and evaluating the audit findings

9. Formulating the audit report and communicating findings

These steps are elaborated on below.

The work undertaken in each step varies from one audit to another and may vary from year to year for a given entity. Moreover, these phases of the audit seldom appear as separate, isolated, specifically identifiable activities. With the exception of the reporting phase of the audit process, all the steps involve activities that affect strategy decisions. Broadly speaking, the audit strategy is the approach to obtaining the necessary assurance, in relation to key audit areas, from tests of controls and substantive tests. Strategy considerations are most intense during the risk assessment activities and when the auditor evaluates the results of those activities and develops the audit program. The key strategy decision made is the extent to which tests of controls will be performed to reduce the assurance needed from substantive tests.

(a) Engagement Planning and Management

Before a new or recurring engagement is accepted, appropriate information is gathered and evaluated as a basis for deciding whether to accept or retain the client. Once the engagement has been accepted, the engagement terms and goals are established and agreed to. An important element of this is to understand the client's expectations so that the auditor can plan to meet or exceed them, within the context of the auditor's professional responsibilities. A number of timing considerations need to be discussed and settled, among them:

- Dates by which entity personnel will have assembled the data, records, and documents required by the auditor
- Date or dates on which the entity plans to physically count inventories or other assets
- Deadlines for issuing the report on the financial statements and any other audit-related reports
- Dates of the auditor's meetings with the audit committee of the board of directors

A number of organizational and planning decisions also need to be made, for example, decisions about using the work of internal auditors and specialists (such as actuaries and appraisers), using the work and reports of other auditing firms that have been engaged to audit one or more components of the entity, assigning staff, preparing time budgets, and other similar scheduling and administrative activities. In addition, opportunities to improve relations with management and the board of directors and to maximize the quality of client services may be identified at this stage of the audit. Engagement planning and management is discussed in Chapter 7.

(b) Obtaining Information About the Entity

At an early stage in the audit, the auditor obtains (or updates) information about the entity. This information is used to identify inherent risks and make preliminary materiality judgments as a basis, in part, for developing the audit strategy. Among other things, the auditor gathers information about:

- The nature, size, and organization of the entity and its operations
- Matters affecting the entity's business and industry, such as
  - The business environment
  - Legal and regulatory constraints and requirements

- Results of prior years' audits
- Significant accounts or groups of accounts and the interrelationships among significant financial and operating data
- Accounting and auditing standards of particular relevance to the entity

The information is obtained in a number of ways. The auditor may begin by consulting such materials as the entity's recent annual reports and interim earnings or other news releases; general business or industry publications; industry audit and accounting guides developed by the AICPA, the auditor's firm, and others; and trade association materials. Prior years' working papers and current correspondence files are also valuable sources of information. (For an initial engagement, the auditor may make inquiries and review preceding years' working papers of the predecessor auditor, if the entity has been audited in the past.) The auditor supplements this knowledge by interviewing officers and employees and others knowledgeable about and experienced in the industry. Additionally, the auditor typically reviews the entity's policy and procedures manuals; tours its major plants and offices; reads the minutes of recent meetings of the board of directors, its important committees, and the stockholders; reads relevant contracts and other agreements; and performs preliminary analytical procedures such as comparing the entity's significant financial and operating data with that of its competitors and analyzing relationships and trends in the data. Obtaining information about the entity is the topic of Chapter 8.

(c)   Understanding the Entity's Internal Control

Generally accepted auditing standards require the auditor to obtain and document an understanding of the entity's internal control sufficient to plan the audit. Internal control consists of five components: control environment, risk assessment, control activities, information and communication, and monitoring.

On a recurring engagement, the auditor focuses on aspects of internal control that have been added, have changed, or have assumed increased importance since the previous audit. The understanding must be sufficient for planning the audit, that is, for the auditor to identify and react to the risk of material misstatements in the financial statements and design appropriate substantive tests to detect them. In obtaining the understanding of the entity's internal control, the auditor identifies the critical points where significant misstatements could occur and determines whether controls to prevent or detect such misstatements have been designed and placed in operation. As a practical matter, especially on recurring engagements, the auditor often performs tests of controls concurrently with updating the understanding of the internal control components.

The auditor obtains (or updates) the understanding of the entity's internal control mainly through observing and inquiring of entity personnel, referring to relevant policy and procedures manuals, and inspecting books, records, forms, and reports. As a practical matter, the auditor generally does not "relearn" or redocument the entity's internal control each year. Most audits are recurring engagements, for which the auditor carries forward the knowledge and documentation developed in prior years and updates them for significant changes since the preceding year's audit. Most (if not all) of those changes generally come to the auditor's attention through continuing contact with the entity between one year's audit and the next.

To plan and control the audit and document his or her compliance with generally accepted auditing standards, the auditor needs a record of the information obtained. Some auditors document all the information in narrative form; others prefer to use narratives for general information about the control environment and risk assessment activities, and flowcharts, questionnaires, or other types of practice aids to describe the information system relevant to financial reporting and various controls. The extent to which the auditor documents the understanding of the various internal control components depends on whether there have been significant changes in matters affecting the entity, its business, or internal control since the preceding audit, as well as the planned assessment of control risk and the audit strategy contemplated. If the auditor is concerned that the documented understanding of the accounting system may be incorrect or incomplete, perhaps because of changes since the preceding audit, it may be efficient to trace one or a few representative transactions through the system (sometimes called a *transaction review* or *walkthrough*). Often, in documenting the understanding of the internal control components, the auditor records information that is useful in subsequent stages of the audit, especially for performing tests of controls. Chapter 9 presents an overview of internal control. Detailed discussions of the various components and of how the auditor obtains and documents an understanding of them are contained in Chapters 10 and 11.

(d) Assessing Control Risk and Developing the Audit Strategy

The auditor uses the information gathered so far—about the entity, including identified inherent risks, and about internal control—to evaluate whether controls have been properly designed to prevent errors or detect them on a timely basis, make a preliminary assessment of control risk, and develop, or refine, the audit strategy. Frequently, particularly on recurring engagements, the auditor formulates a major part of the audit strategy based on a presumption about the assessment of control risk, before the documentation and tests of controls have been completed for the current year. It often is practical and efficient to anticipate the control risk assessment and audit strategy early in the audit because the auditor then can document the understanding of internal control in a way that will facilitate the performance of tests of controls, if such tests are planned.

In formulating the audit strategy before completing the documentation and testing of controls, the auditor assumes that he or she already has an adequate understanding of the design (and its effectiveness) and the operation of the internal control components. On a new engagement, the basis for that assumption generally is derived from knowledge (which may be limited in scope) obtained through inquiries, observation, and inspection of documents, records, and reports undertaken in the course of developing the understanding of internal control, from any tests of controls performed at that time, and from review of the predecessor auditor's working papers. On a recurring engagement, that assumption is further supported by the prior year's audit experience, inquiries of knowledgeable entity personnel, and the general information gathered or updated about the entity and its industry.

If the auditor assesses control risk at maximum, no further internal control work is done, and the auditor designs substantive tests to gain all the assurance needed for all relevant audit objectives and account balances. If, on the other hand, the assessment is that control risk is below the maximum or low, the auditor considers whether, based on the work done so far, he or she believes it will be efficient to limit substantive tests of specific accounts directed to certain audit objectives. Ordinarily, the auditor concludes that substantive tests can be limited and formulates an audit strategy that calls for confirming the control risk assessment by performing tests of controls.

The basic audit strategy alternatives are either to perform tests of controls and thus limit substantive tests, or to perform substantive tests without significant restriction based on tests of controls. Usually, different strategies are adopted for different audit areas. That is, the auditor will plan to achieve one or more audit objectives for an account or a group of accounts principally by performing tests of controls and restricting substantive tests, while achieving other audit objectives principally or entirely by performing substantive tests. This flexibility also applies to different locations, subsidiaries, and components of business activities. The auditor's aim is to choose an audit strategy that will most efficiently limit audit risk—that is, the risk that he or she will unknowingly fail to modify the opinion appropriately if the financial statements are materially misstated—to a low level.

For a multilocation audit, the audit strategy also includes decisions about whether to limit the number of locations where auditing procedures are performed in a specific engagement. Based on the preliminary control risk assessment, the quality of the internal audit function, the materiality of various locations, and other factors, the auditor may decide to rotate the audit emphasis from year to year. This strategy may enhance audit efficiency and make a complex engagement less costly. The way to accomplish this varies with the circumstances of the engagement. Subject to audit risk considerations, the auditor may vary both the locations visited and the strategies employed at various locations. In a large multilocation engagement, often only a few, if any, locations are individually material to a specific account balance or class of transactions. The auditor must ensure, however, that each year's audit work is adequate to support the opinion on the financial statements for that year.

Regardless of the audit strategy chosen, auditors traditionally have focused more on audit objectives related to balance sheet accounts than on their income statement counterparts, since that is frequently the most efficient way to conduct an audit. Emphasizing balance sheet accounts is also conceptually sound: Balance sheet accounts represent the entity's economic resources and claims to those resources at a point in time, reflecting the cumulative effects of transactions and other events and circumstances on the entity. Income statement accounts reflect the entity's performance during a period between two points in time, measuring its revenues, expenses, gains, and losses that occurred during that period. Many income statement accounts are logically related to one or more balance sheet accounts. Often, evidence that helps achieve audit objectives for a balance sheet account also helps achieve corresponding audit objectives for an income statement account. For example, evidence about the completeness, accuracy, and existence of trade accounts receivable at the beginning and end of a period is also a source of assurance about the completeness, accuracy, and occurrence of sales transactions during the period.

The audit strategy selected for each audit area should be documented, including significant inherent risks identified and the audit implications of the control risk assessment. That documentation also should reflect certain other planning decisions, such as analyses to be prepared by entity personnel, the need to use the work of other auditing firms or specialists, and the effects of an internal audit function on the audit strategy. The audit strategy as initially determined should be reviewed, and revised if necessary, as the audit progresses and new information becomes available. As noted earlier, the auditor may design the substantive test audit program and plan and schedule the work before performing tests of controls. If tests of controls then indicate that aspects of internal control have not operated effectively throughout the period, the auditor may have to reassess the risk that account balances could be materially misstated, and revise the audit strategy accordingly. Control risk assessment and its effect on the audit strategy are discussed in Chapter 12. Determining and implementing the audit strategy for specific transaction cycles and account balances and disclosures is presented in Chapters 13, 14, and 17–26.

(e) Confirming the Assessment of Control Risk by Performing Tests of Controls

The auditor confirms a preliminary below-the-maximum or low control risk assessment by performing tests of controls designed to provide evidence about whether certain controls have operated effectively and continuously. The lower the assessed level of control risk, the less assurance is needed from substantive tests and the more they are restricted. The more substantive tests are restricted, the greater the auditor's need for evidence that misstatements that might be caused by control deficiencies or breakdowns will be prevented or detected in a timely manner. The auditor seeks that evidence by performing tests of controls and evaluating the results.

In performing tests of controls, the auditor is concerned about how activities were carried out, the consistency with which they were performed, and by whom they were carried out. Tests of controls may include inquiring of entity personnel who carry out activities, as well as others in a position to be aware of control breakdowns; observing how the activities are performed; examining records and documents for evidence that they have been carried out; and reperforming control activities by duplicating the actions of the entity's personnel.

Performing tests of controls is efficient only if the audit time and effort saved by limiting substantive testing exceed the time and effort spent in performing the tests of controls. Therefore, tests of controls generally are performed only when achieving the relevant audit objectives solely by substantive testing would require significant audit time and effort. The auditor should not automatically decide to perform tests of controls, even if it appears that they will provide the necessary evidence, without considering whether performing them will be efficient.

After performing tests of controls, the auditor considers whether controls operated as he or she previously understood. If they did not, but the assessment of control risk was nevertheless confirmed, the auditor amends the recorded understanding of internal control. If the control risk assessment was not confirmed by the tests of controls, the auditor amends the assessment and considers the implications for the audit strategy and the audit program, including how any deficiencies and breakdowns noted affect the risk that account balances could be materially misstated. The auditor also should discuss with appropriate entity personnel any significant deficiencies in the design of controls and any significant breakdowns in their operation. Performing tests of controls is discussed in Chapter 12. Tests of controls related to the revenue and purchasing cycles and to production transactions also are described in Chapters 13, 14, and 19, respectively.

(f)   Developing the Substantive Test Audit Program

The audit program reflects the audit strategy and sets out details about the nature, timing, and extent of substantive tests for each account or group of accounts in the financial statements. Decisions about those tests are based primarily on the auditor's assessment of the risk of material misstatement associated with the audit objectives relevant to each account balance and class of transactions. Those assessments, in turn, are based on the auditor's judgments about materiality, inherent risk, and control risk. Risk assessment decisions and materiality judgments should be reevaluated as the audit progresses to take account of any significant changes in facts or circumstances.

As explained in Chapter 1, the auditor typically tests less than 100 percent of the items in an account balance or class of transactions. Most auditors start with the presumption that it will not be necessary to perform substantive tests on every item that supports an account balance in the financial statements. From the understanding of internal control and from any tests of controls performed, the auditor usually has some evidence that management has established controls that reduce the risk of material misstatement, either in particular accounts or groups of accounts or in the financial statements as a whole, and that the controls are operating effectively. That evidence reduces the assurance needed from substantive tests. Substantive tests are the topic of Chapter 15, supplemented by the discussion of sampling in Chapter 16. Chapters 17–26 discuss substantive tests applicable to specific account balances and disclosures.

(g)   Performing Substantive Tests

In performing substantive tests, the auditor obtains, evaluates, and documents evidence to corroborate management's assertions embodied in the accounts and other information in the financial statements and related notes. The auditor's purpose in performing substantive tests is to gain assurance about whether the audit objectives corresponding to management's assertions have been achieved for account balances and classes of transactions. As discussed earlier in this chapter, substantive tests include analytical procedures and tests of details of account balances and transactions, with the assurance obtained from one reducing the assurance needed from the other.

Substantive tests also may provide evidence about internal control. For example, a misstatement discovered through a substantive test may, upon further investigation, be found to have resulted from a deficiency in internal control. In that situation, the auditor may have to reassess prior conclusions about internal control. Performing substantive tests of individual account balances and disclosures is discussed in Chapters 17–26.

(h)   Completing the Audit

After all the previous steps in the audit have been performed, the auditor performs final analytical and certain other procedures, such as reading minutes of recent board and committee meetings and obtaining representation letters. Then he or she makes final materiality judgments, summarizes misstatements and evaluates the audit findings, reviews the working papers, reviews the financial statement presentation and disclosures for adequacy, and considers events occurring after the balance sheet date. Those procedures require the exercise of considerable professional judgment and thus generally are performed by the senior members of the engagement team. Completing the audit is the topic of Chapter 27.

(i)   Formulating the Audit Report and Communicating Findings

Finally, the auditor prepares the audit report expressing an opinion on the financial statements and generally also communicates to management and the audit committee significant internal control deficiencies and other findings noted during the course of the audit. Some of these communications are required by professional standards, and others, reported to management in what often is called a "management letter," are provided as a service that adds further value to the audit engagement. In addition to this more formal reporting, at key stages throughout the audit, the auditor should contact management to discuss mutual expectations, as well as engagement planning and organizational issues. Audit reporting is covered in Chapters 28 and 29; other auditor communications are discussed in Chapter 4.

7

Engagement Planning and Management

The first standard of field work requires that the audit be adequately planned. Good management practices require that it be controlled to ensure that it is performed efficiently and on a timely basis, as well as in accordance with professional standards—that is, effectively. Engagement planning and management involve numerous planning decisions and ongoing activities for controlling all aspects of the performance of the audit to ensure that it is carried out effectively and efficiently.

From the time an engagement is first considered—even before it is accepted—until the results are summarized and evaluated at the end of the engagement, the auditor makes numerous decisions, which collectively constitute the plan for the engagement. Planning takes place throughout the engagement and includes various activities necessary to ensure that the audit is carried out effectively and efficiently. In the early stages of the engagement, planning entails determining whether to accept or continue with the client and establishing engagement terms and goals. Understanding the client's expectations and planning to meet or exceed them, within the context of the auditor's professional responsibilities, and communicating with the client regarding engagement arrangements and issues, facilitates the audit process.

Formulating the engagement plan also involves deciding such matters as whether to use the work of the entity's internal auditors, whether the assistance of a specialist is needed, and whether to use the work of other auditors who have audited any of the entity's components. The activities involved in planning the audit and the order in which they are done vary with the engagement; often the various activities overlap.

7.1   ACCEPTING OR RETAINING THE CLIENT

Before the auditor can begin to plan the details of the engagement, he or she must consider whether to accept or, for a recurring engagement, retain the client. Deciding whether to accept or continue with a client requires the exercise of professional skepticism and judgment about a variety of risks affecting both the entity and the auditor.

All entities face business risk, that is, the risk that they will not be profitable or will not remain a going concern. An entity with increased business risk may be more likely to engage in fraudulent financial reporting or be involved in unwarranted litigation than one not facing significant risks. Those factors may increase the auditor's business risk—in the form of the risk of potential litigation costs and damage to his or her reputation, and threats to fee realization—from association with the entity. In deciding whether to be associated with a client, the auditor also should consider factors that may increase audit risk. To manage the risks inherent in becoming or remaining associated with a client, audit firms usually establish procedures, in addition to those required by generally accepted auditing standards, to be performed before a new client is accepted or a recurring one retained. In the course of performing those procedures, much information about the entity is gathered, which forms the foundation of the auditor's knowledge about the entity's business.

In investigating a prospective client, a principal concern of the auditor is the integrity of members of the entity's management. Accordingly, auditors typically consider the general reputation of high ranking employees, such as executives and others with broad financial and operating influence, and influential directors and shareholders, as well as the entity itself. This may involve discussions with commercial and investment bankers and lawyers, and obtaining a Dun & Bradstreet report. Generally, auditors also obtain and read the most recent financial statements of a prospective client and communicate with the predecessor auditor, with emphasis on questions of management's integrity and the reason for the change in auditor. Other considerations in connection with investigating a prospective client include management's response to suggestions for improving internal control made by the predecessor auditor or the internal auditors, whether there are any independence issues, whether the auditor has personnel with the industry and other expertise to provide the desired service, and whether the entity's management is able and willing to pay an acceptable fee.

Today's rapidly changing business environment makes it necessary to reevaluate periodically, perhaps as often as annually, whether to continue to be associated with a client. The evaluation can point to risks stemming from changes affecting management's integrity, management practices, the entity's financial condition, or operational matters.

The Detection and Prevention of Fraud Task Force of the SEC Practice Section of the AICPA Division for CPA Firms has identified a number of factors that may indicate increased risk associated with an engagement and that auditors may want to consider in their decisions about client acceptance or continuance. The risks are categorized as either business risks of the entity, business risks of the auditor, or audit risks, and are shown in Figure 7.1.

7.2 CLIENT SERVICE AND COMMUNICATION

To an outsider, the practice of auditing often appears to consist mainly of comparing figures, examining documents, and reviewing financial statements, all of which involve little contact with people. In reality, however, auditing is concerned with the activities of people, for it is people who define the entity's control environment, monitor its controls, design accounting systems, keep accounting records, perform control activities, program computers to process accounting data, enter into contractual agreements, prepare financial statements, and engage auditors. Further, an audit is carried out on the entity's premises with the help of the entity's personnel, and ultimately, the auditor is responsible to people: the entity's board of directors, trustees, and stockholders. Auditing is, to a great extent, a process of dealing with people.

The auditor needs to develop and maintain a network of contacts at all levels in the entity. Depending on the type of information the auditor needs, he or she may obtain it most expeditiously from nonmanagement personnel, operating management, financial management, the chief executive officer, the chief financial officer, the internal auditors, or others. Lack of access to entity personnel—especially access to top management—may inhibit the auditor's ability to effectively complete the audit.

(a) Establishing Engagement Terms and Goals

After the decision to accept or retain a client has been made, the terms of the engagement have to be established with management. The first step is for the auditor to meet with the entity's management to discuss their expectations for the audit and areas of particular concern to them. This enhances engagement efficiency and im-

Figure 7.1   Risk Factors Associated with an Engagement

1. Entity's Business Risk
   • Management:
   –Engages in activities indicative of a lack of integrity.
   –Is prone to engage in speculative ventures or accept unusually high business risks.
   –Displays a poor attitude toward compliance with outside regulatory or legislative obligations.
   –Engages in complex transactions or innovative deals that make the determination of the effects on the financial statements difficult to assess or highly subjective.
   –Lacks a proven track record.
   –Is evasive, uncooperative or abusive to the audit team.
   • The Entity:
   –Has products that are new and unproven.
   –Depends on a limited number of customers or suppliers.
   –Is experiencing a deteriorating financial condition or liquidity crisis.
   –Is subject to uncertainties that raise substantial doubt about its ability to continue as a going concern.
   –Operates in countries where business practices are questionable.
   –Has an inadequate capital base or is highly leveraged.
   –Is experiencing difficulty in meeting restrictive debt covenants.
   –Generates negative cash flows from operations but reports operating profits.
   –Has publicly traded debt outstanding that is below investment grade.
   –Is a low tier firm in an emerging or maturing industry where weak competitors are exiting the market.
   –Is subject to unpredictable changes in price and availability of product inputs that cause significant variance in profitability.
   –Is vulnerable to rapidly changing technology.
   –Is investing cash from short-term borrowings in long-term assets.
   • The Industry:
   –Is undergoing rapid change.
   –Is subject to high competition, market saturation, product obsolescence, or declining demand.
   –Has high operating leverage demonstrated by high fixed costs and low variable costs.
   –Is highly cyclical or counter cyclical.
   –Has a low entry barrier.

   –Is facing regulations that will adversely impact profitability throughout the industry.

2. Auditor's Business Risk
   –The entity is prone to a high number of lawsuits or controversies.
   –There are frequent changes in the entity's auditors.
   –The entity plans to engage in an initial public offering or use the financial statements to engage in a debt or equity offering.
   –The financial statements will be used in connection with an acquisition or disposal of a business or segment.

3. Auditor's Audit Risk
   The auditor should follow SAS No. 47, *Audit Risk and Materiality in Conducting an Audit*, which provides guidance on the auditor's consideration of audit risk when planning and performing an audit of financial statements. Examples of factors that may increase audit risk include:
   –Operations that are dominated by a single individual.
   –Undue emphasis on achieving earnings per share; maintaining the market price of the company's stock; or meeting earnings projections.
   –Unreliable processes for making accounting estimates or questionable estimates by executives.
   –Unrealistic budget levels that encourage unrealistic objectives.
   –A high volume of significant year-end transactions.
   –Compensation based to a significant degree on reported earnings.
   –An unnecessarily complex corporate structure.
   –Prior-year financial statements that were restated for correction of an error or irregularity.
   –Attempts by management to reduce the scope of the audit.
   –Substantial litigation involving the entity's business practices.
   –Material weaknesses or other reportable conditions in the internal control structure.
   –Significant and unusually complex related party transactions.
   –Affiliates that are unaudited or audited by others.
   –Management espouses aggressive accounting principles.
   –Understaffed accounting department or inexperienced personnel.
   –Financial reports not prepared on a timely basis.

Source: AICPA Division for CPA Firms—SEC Practice Section, *Practice Alert*, September 1994. Copyright © 1994 by the American Institute of Certified Public Accountants, Inc.

proves relations with management. Understanding management's expectations and working with management to develop a plan that will meet them are essential to providing a high level of service and require that the auditor develop and maintain a knowledge of the entity's business, people, and needs; build and enhance professional relationships at all levels of the entity's organization (as discussed in a later section of this chapter); and manage all aspects of the engagement effectively. These practices not only facilitate meeting management's expectations and providing constructive business advice, but also enable the auditor to satisfy his or her professional responsibilities while at the same time managing the business risk associated with every audit. The terms of the engagement are set forth in the engagement letter to management, as discussed in Chapter 4.

Certain planning details almost inevitably need to be discussed with management and agreed on before the work begins. These include determining what schedules and analyses the entity's staff will be requested to prepare and other ways entity personnel can assist the auditor, and whether to use the work of the internal auditors. A number of key dates also have to be established, such as the dates on which the entity plans to physically count inventories or other assets; dates by which entity personnel will have assembled the data, records, and documents required by the auditor; dates of the auditor's meetings with the audit committee; and the deadlines for issuing the report on the financial statements and any other audit-related reports. It may be desirable (for example, in order to avoid misunderstandings) to confirm these matters in writing.

Based on the discussions with management, the auditor establishes a timetable for completing the principal segments of the audit work. The entity's scheduling requirements, for example, when personnel will be available to provide required assistance in performing certain procedures, should be considered in establishing the timetable. The timetable determines, to a large extent, the way in which the engagement will be conducted, as well as providing a basis for exercising control over its conduct. The degree of detail included in the timetable will depend on engagement size and complexity.

If any significant changes in planned procedures are made, they normally should be communicated to management as soon as they occur, in writing or orally, as appropriate. This assists in identifying responsibility for time overruns, which may help ensure recovery of resultant costs.

(b)   Working with Management and Other Personnel

As discussed above, the auditor should consult with management about their expectations for the audit so that these expectations can be considered in formulating the terms and goals for the engagement. The auditor also should discuss the plans for the engagement with management, primarily to establish timetables and assignments. The auditor is then more likely to receive data from the entity and access to personnel when they are needed. Careful, cooperative planning does not compromise the auditor's independence or responsibility for determining audit scope. The auditor always retains that responsibility, but management can facilitate the process.

Even in the best-planned, smoothest running engagement, an auditor needs to ask many questions and make many requests of the entity's employees. Employees also may help the auditor directly by preparing schedules and analyses, searching files, accumulating data, processing accounts receivable confirmations (under the auditor's control), and making computers and computer files accessible to the auditor for testing purposes. Clearly, courtesy and consideration are required, and the auditor should minimize the number and duration of interruptions.

Operating management can be a valuable source of information to the auditor. For example, in a manufacturing business, the production manager may be able to provide information relevant to the amounts of the allowances for inventory valuation and obsolescence; in a retail business, buyers can often provide this information.

(i) Chief Executive Officer.   It is important for the auditor to establish and maintain meaningful contact with the chief executive officer (CEO). Such contact leads to the development of a professional relationship in which both parties are comfortable discussing relevant issues with each other. For example, the CEO may consult the auditor about a contemplated acquisition or other transaction, or the auditor may contact the CEO to discuss observations made during the audit concerning operating or financial matters.

(ii) Chief Financial Officer.   An auditor who is broadly experienced and has a good understanding of the entity is inevitably a valuable adjunct to the chief financial officer (CFO). The auditor can contribute expertise in accounting and financial reporting drawn from experience with other entities and can provide an objective point of view. In addition, the auditor is a source of informed, knowledgeable comments on events and decisions facing the CFO. As with the CEO, the auditor should foster a professional relationship with the CFO that includes open lines of communication.

(iii) Head of Internal Audit.   In the interests of audit efficiency, the auditor tries to coordinate the overall audit work with the internal auditors as far as possible. This involves meeting with the head of internal audit to discuss the scope of work done by the internal auditors and, as discussed earlier in the chapter, to consider whether the auditor can use that work, the rotation of certain audit coverage, the sharing of working papers, the exchange of audit reports, and communications with management.

(iv) Staff.   In all but the smallest audits, an auditor will be involved with a number of the entity's employees, including computer and accounting staff, who are involved in issues directly or indirectly related to accounting and auditing. The range of possible issues covers the whole spectrum of business activity and could involve merger negotiations, labor contracts, lease or purchase decisions, fair trade laws, or environmental issues, to name a few. The auditor should be asked to review and approve the accounting treatment of proposed transactions before the fact rather than afterward. Because of their expertise and experience, auditors frequently can offer suggestions for improvements.

(c)   Working with Audit Committees and Boards of Directors

(i) Audit Committees.   Audit committees of outside directors are now an integral part of the American corporate structure, appearing not only in large organizations but also in smaller businesses and in not-for-profit organizations. Chapter 3 describes the role of audit committees in enhancing independence; it also discusses the responsibilities typically undertaken by audit committees.

Statement on Auditing Standards (SAS) No. 61, *Communication With Audit Committees* (AU Section 380), requires the auditor to determine that certain matters related to the conduct of an audit are communicated to those who have responsibility for oversight of the financial reporting process. This requirement applies only to audits of entities that either have an audit committee (or otherwise have formally delegated oversight of the financial reporting process to a group equivalent to an audit committee, such as a finance or budget committee) or are SEC registrants. If an SEC registrant does not have an audit committee (for example, a recently formed entity that has not yet formed an audit committee), the communication should be made to the board of directors. SAS No. 61 further states that matters may be communicated by either the auditor or management, and that the communication may be oral or written. The matters that must be communicated are described in Chapter 4.

SAS No. 61 underscores the importance of audit committees in overseeing the financial reporting process and facilitating communication between the full board of directors and the auditor. The matters required to be communicated help the audit committee understand the reasonable, but not absolute, assurance the audit provides. The communication also aids the committee in its oversight of management's activities. Although the requirements of SAS No. 61 apply only to audits of entities that have an audit committee (or its equivalent, such as a finance or budget committee) or are SEC registrants, the authors believe this communication should be made on all audit engagements. The auditor could communicate with the board of directors of other entities when there is no audit committee or its equivalent, or, if there is no board of directors, with the owner-manager.

(ii) Boards of Directors.   In the normal course of events, contact between the board of directors and the auditor is generally through the audit committee. Because the SEC requires a majority of the members of a registrant's board of directors to sign its annual report on Form 10-K, however, the entire board may turn to the auditor for assistance in reviewing the financial statements and other financial data contained in the 10-K. Some auditors routinely provide the board with fairly detailed reports describing the nature and extent of their involvement with the entity and relevant observations. In addition, if an SEC registrant does not have an audit committee or its equivalent, the communication required by SAS No. 61 is generally directed to the board.

(iii) Stockholder Meetings.   While there is no professional or regulatory requirement that the auditor attend the annual stockholders' meeting, auditors generally attend when invited to do so. This is particularly appropriate if the stockholders vote to ratify the selection of the auditor. The auditor should be prepared to answer questions regarding the CPA firm, the audit just concluded, and the financial statements. The auditor also can help management prepare for the meeting.

7.3 USING THE WORK OF OTHERS

(a) Internal Auditors

In some entities, internal auditors operate with virtually no restrictions and report to the board of directors or audit committee on a wide range of matters. In other entities, they may be more limited in their duties and may not enjoy full organizational independence. Internal auditors can operate in a variety of ways. They may:

- Perform specific controls, focusing heavily on activities like surprise cash counts and inventory counts
- Function as part of the monitoring component of the entity's internal control, that is, examining and assessing aspects of other internal control components
- Have broad responsibility for evaluating compliance with company policies and practices
- Conduct financial, compliance, and operational audits (described in Chapter 2)
- Carry out special projects or be responsible for specific aspects of internal control

AU Section 319.38 includes the internal audit function as part of an entity's internal control, specifically, one aspect of the monitoring component, by which management assesses, on an ongoing basis, the quality of the other aspects of internal control. For example, an entity may have established a control that calls for an employee to perform bank reconciliations. The internal auditor might evaluate how well the reconciliation process is designed and whether it is effectively performed by the employee, and report on it to management. In some entities, internal auditors perform the reconciliations as part of their review of cash disbursements procedures, which is one way of providing for separation of duties between employees who handle cash disbursements and those who perform reconciliations. In this instance, however, the internal auditors are performing a control activity rather than monitoring its performance.

SAS No. 65, *The Auditor's Consideration of the Internal Audit Function in an Audit of Financial Statements* (AU Section 322), specifies that as part of obtaining an understanding of internal control, the auditor should obtain an understanding of the internal audit function sufficient to identify those internal audit activities that are relevant to planning the audit. The auditor ordinarily can obtain the necessary understanding through inquiries of appropriate management and internal audit personnel. Principal areas of inquiry may include:

- The charter, mission statement, or similar directive from management or the board of directors, and the goals and objectives established for the internal audit function
- The level or position of the person or persons within the organization to whom the internal auditors report, for instance, whether there is access to the board of directors or audit committee
- The specific responsibilities assigned to the internal auditors
- Whether the internal audit function adheres to the standards for the professional practice of internal auditing developed by The Institute of Internal Auditors
- The internal audit plan, including the nature, timing, and extent of work
- The extent, if any, to which the internal auditors' access to records, documentation, and personnel is restricted

If the auditor determines that internal audit activities are not relevant to the financial statement audit, no further consideration of the function is required. If the internal audit activities are relevant to the audit, and it is efficient to consider the work of the internal auditors, the auditor should:

- Assess the competence and objectivity of the internal auditors
- Determine the effect of internal audit work on the audit strategy
- Consider the extent to which the internal audit work affects auditing procedures
- Evaluate and test the effectiveness of the internal auditors' work

In assessing the competence and objectivity of the internal auditors, the auditor should consider information obtained or updated from prior years and from discussions with management, as well as the results of any recent external review of the internal audit function. The following factors are relevant to an assessment of competence:

- Education level and professional experience. For example, if the circumstances require tests of computer controls, the internal auditors should have an adequate knowledge of computer audit techniques.
- Professional certification of internal auditors and requirements for continuing education.
- Internal audit policies, programs, and procedures.
- Practices regarding assignment of internal auditors. For example, internal auditors may possess different types of skills, which should be consistent with their work assignments.
- Supervision and review of the internal auditors' activities. For example, the work carried out by the internal auditors should be supervised by senior internal audit personnel.
- Quality of working paper documentation, including the adequacy of evidence of the work done by the internal auditors.
- Quality of reports and recommendations, and the nature and frequency of, and response to, reports issued by the internal auditors.
- Hiring, training, performance evaluation, and consultation practices of the internal auditors.

Even though internal auditors are not independent of the entity, they should maintain objectivity. When assessing objectivity, the auditor should pay particular attention to the nature of internal audit work in areas that are sensitive or entail a high level of subjective judgment. The need for objectivity is critical in such areas. Factors that should be considered are policies prohibiting internal auditors from auditing areas where there may be a conflict of interest and the organizational status of the internal audit function.

If the auditor determines that the competence and objectivity of the internal audit function are sufficient, he or she should then consider how the internal auditors' work may affect such audit areas as obtaining an understanding of the entity's internal control, assessing control risk, and performing substantive tests. The internal auditors may perform procedures in all those areas that will provide useful information to the auditor. In many entities, the internal auditors review, assess, and monitor internal controls; the results of that work may be useful to the auditor in gathering information about the design of controls and about whether they have been placed in operation.

The auditor also may consider the internal auditors' work in assessing the risk of material misstatement at both the financial statement level and the account balance or class-of-transactions level. That work may consist of performing tests of controls at selected locations or of testing controls directed at specific financial statement assertions. The auditor may be able to reduce the number of locations at which he or she performs auditing procedures or to change the nature, timing, and extent of testing relating to a particular audit objective. Finally, the internal auditors may perform procedures that provide direct evidence about specific account balances and that the auditor may consider in determining the audit assurance needed from substantive tests directed at relevant audit objectives.

When considering the extent to which internal audit work may affect the procedures otherwise considered necessary, the auditor should keep the following in mind:

- Evidence obtained through the auditor's direct personal knowledge, including observation, inspection, examination of evidence, and reperformance, is generally more persuasive than information obtained indirectly.

- The responsibility to report on the financial statements is solely the auditor's and cannot be shared with the internal auditors.

- Judgments concerning control risk, materiality, sufficiency of testing, and evaluation of significant accounting estimates must be those of the auditor.

In determining the extent of the effect of the internal auditors' work, the auditor considers the risk of material misstatements in the financial statements. The auditor also considers the materiality of financial statement amounts and the degree of subjectivity involved in evaluating the audit evidence supporting the assertions. As the materiality of financial statement amounts increases and either the risk of material misstatement or the degree of subjectivity increases, the auditor's need to perform his or her own audit tests increases. Conversely, as these factors decrease, the need for the auditor to perform his or her own tests decreases. For example, if the risk of material misstatement is assessed at low, the auditor may decide, after considering the results of internal audit work, that additional testing is not necessary. On the other hand, for significant accounts or assertions where the risk of material misstatement or the degree of subjectivity is relatively high, the auditor should not use the internal auditors' work without directly performing sufficient additional procedures to reduce audit risk to an acceptable level. Examples of assertions that might require direct testing by the auditor are those relating to valuations based on accounting estimates and to the existence and disclosure of uncertainties, subsequent events, and related party transactions.

The auditor should evaluate and test the effectiveness of internal audit work that will affect the nature, timing, and extent of auditing procedures. The extent of the evaluation and testing procedures is a matter of professional judgment, based on the extent of the effect of internal audit work on the audit. The auditor may wish to consider:

- The results of the assessment of internal auditors' competence and objectivity
- The nature of the internal auditors' work that was considered in developing the audit strategy
- The extent to which the internal auditors' work affects the audit strategy and the significance of the assertions or accounts to which the work relates
- The degree to which the internal auditors' findings and conclusions correlate with the auditor's own findings and conclusions in other areas

In designing the procedures to be used in making the evaluation, the auditor should consider whether:

- The scope of the internal auditors' work is appropriate for the role of the internal audit function in the particular entity
- The internal audit programs are adequate
- The work performed is adequately documented in working papers
- Conclusions are appropriate in the circumstances
- Reports are consistent with the results of the work performed
- Supervision and review within the internal audit function appear to have been appropriately carried out

The auditor should test the internal auditors' work by either reperforming some tests of controls, transactions, or balances examined by the internal auditors, or by testing similar controls, transactions, or balances not examined by them. The auditor should compare the results of his or her tests with the results of the internal auditors' work.

Regardless of whether the auditor believes that internal audit activities are relevant to the audit, liaison with internal audit is generally desirable to keep the auditor informed of developments that may have audit implications. Liaison with internal audit also is important in terms of meeting management's expectations and enhancing client relationships.

If the auditor determines that the internal auditors are performing relevant audit work that is expected to have an effect on his or her procedures, the two auditor groups should coordinate their work. Techniques that may be useful to the auditor in coordinating audit work include:

- Holding regularly scheduled coordination meetings
- Preparing integrated testing programs
- Sharing some of the more complex (as opposed to routine) audit tasks
- Reviewing internal audit programs before the internal audit work is performed
- Reviewing audit reports
- Discussing possible accounting and auditing issues

- Making joint presentations to the audit committee or board of directors
- Providing the internal auditors with audit software and training

Because the auditing techniques used by the two auditor groups are often similar, sometimes the auditor can use audit documentation prepared by the internal auditors rather than prepare the data independently. For example, flowcharts and systems diagrams prepared by the internal auditors also may serve the auditor's purposes, especially when they follow standard formats. To facilitate coordination and integration of audit efforts, it may be beneficial for the two auditor groups to create and maintain a common user file of certain working papers, such as descriptions of the internal control components. If this is done, the auditor should have sufficient control over the common file to ensure the integrity of his or her working papers.

The effectiveness of coordination with internal audit is enhanced if it takes place before the internal auditors finalize their plans for the year, since the auditor must assume responsibility for the overall scope of the audit, including determining the effect of internal audit work on the audit strategy. This effectiveness may be impeded if internal audit planning precedes the auditor's planning. For example, the internal auditors may develop their annual plan based on the entity's forthcoming fiscal year, whereas the auditor generally determines the audit strategy after the year has commenced. In this case, the internal auditors might be encouraged to use a planning cycle that coincides with, or follows, the external audit planning cycle; this could involve using a planning year other than the entity's fiscal year.

(b) Specialists

In considering evidence to corroborate management's assertions, an auditor occasionally may encounter a matter that requires special expertise. The auditor cannot be expected to have or develop the expertise of a person in another profession or occupation and thus may decide to arrange for a specialist to help obtain competent evidential matter. Special skill or experience may be required in situations where matters are complex or subjective and are potentially material in relation to the financial statements. The need for a specialist should be established early in the audit, so that the necessary arrangements can be made on a timely basis.

Specialists may be used on a recurring basis or only for special matters. An actuary ordinarily will be engaged to perform certain calculations in determining employee benefit plan costs. An appraiser may be used to establish fair market value of real estate collateralizing bank loans. Lawyers may be used as specialists in matters other than litigation, claims, or assessments. Petroleum engineers may be used to estimate oil reserves, and gemologists to appraise precious gems.

The auditor should be satisfied with the competence, reputation, and standing of the specialist in the particular field. The specialist's competence may be demonstrated by professional certification, license, or other formal recognition. Peers or others familiar with the specialist's work may be able to vouch for the individual's reputation and standing. The auditor also should consider whether the specialist has a relationship with the entity. As indicated in paragraph 11 of SAS No. 73, *Using the Work of a Specialist* (AU Section 336.11), "When a specialist does not have a relationship with the client, the specialist's work will ordinarily provide the auditor with greater assurance of reliability." Specialists are not required to be independent in the same sense as auditors are; however, if a relationship exists, the auditor should assess the risk of the relationship impairing the specialist's objectivity. If the auditor believes the specialist's objectivity might be impaired, the auditor should perform additional procedures with respect to some or all of the specialist's assumptions, methods, or findings to ascertain that the findings are not unreasonable, or should engage another specialist for that purpose.

The work of a specialist may be used as an auditing procedure to obtain competent evidential matter, but it is not sufficient in itself. Additional auditing procedures should be performed to meet the requirements of particular circumstances. The procedures should not duplicate any of the specialist's work, but are generally needed to corroborate accounting data that entity personnel provide to the specialist (e.g., employee census data supplied to an actuary). The specialist is responsible for the appropriateness, reasonableness, and application of any methods or assumptions used. The auditor must understand the methods or assumptions used, however, to determine whether the specialist's findings are suitable for corroborating the related information in the financial statements. The auditor is not required to conclude that the specialist's findings are reasonable, only that they are not unreasonable. For example, an appraisal of real estate owned may indicate a 25 percent increase in fair market value over the previous year. This finding would appear to be unreasonable if current market conditions generally indicated a decline in values of comparable real estate during the same period. An auditor who believes that a specialist's findings are unreasonable should perform additional procedures, including inquiry of the specialist.

If the auditor is not able to resolve a matter after performing additional procedures, he or she should consider obtaining the opinion of another specialist. An unresolved matter will result in a qualified opinion or a disclaimer of opinion because the inability to obtain sufficient competent evidential matter constitutes a scope limitation [paragraphs 22 and 23 of SAS No. 79, *Amendment to Statement on Auditing Standards No. 58*, Reports on Audited Financial Statements (AU Sections 508.22 and .23)].

SAS No. 73 specifies that the work or findings of the specialist should not be referred to in the auditor's report unless, as a result of the specialist's report or findings, the auditor decides to add explanatory language to the standard report or depart from an unqualified opinion. Reference to and identification of the specialist may be made if the auditor believes this will enable users to better understand the reason for the explanatory language or the departure from an unqualified opinion. The authors believe that if the auditor refers to the report or findings of a specialist by name or in general terms, the specialist should be made aware of the reference and requested to provide a letter indicating agreement to the reference to his or her work.

(c) Other Auditors

In reporting on the financial statements of an entity or group of entities, an auditor may use the work and report of other auditors who have audited one or more components (subsidiaries or divisions) of the entity or group. Other auditors also may be used to carry out part of an engagement on grounds of efficiency. Physical distance and language barriers among components of an entity also may be overcome most economically through these arrangements. When more than one auditor is involved in the engagement, one must serve as principal auditor. Determining who is the principal auditor involves considering, among other things, the relative materiality of the portions of the entire engagement performed by each auditor and the auditor's overall knowledge of the engagement. Those considerations usually lead to a conclusion that the auditor of the parent company is the principal auditor. The principal auditor should establish communication links with other auditors involved in the engagement. Timetables, procedures to be performed, and the type of report needed by the principal auditor should be communicated early in the audit.

Even though each auditor has individual responsibility for the work performed and the opinion rendered, the principal auditor should apply certain procedures in order to be able to use another auditor's report and express an opinion on the overall financial statements. SAS No. 1 (AU Section 543) contains guidelines about what procedures should be performed. They include inquiring about the other auditor's professional reputation and ascertaining that the other auditor is independent, is aware of the intended use of the financial statements and report, is familiar with GAAP, GAAS, and other (e.g., SEC) reporting requirements, and has been informed about matters affecting the elimination of intercompany transactions and the uniformity of accounting principles among the components. In addition, the principal auditor may request the other auditor to read "other information" that may accompany the financial statements, for the purposes discussed in Chapter 28.

When another auditor's work is used, the principal auditor's opinion may or may not refer to the other auditor's involvement. That issue is discussed in Chapter 28, "Reporting on Audited Financial Statements." If the decision is not to refer to the other auditor, in addition to the procedures mentioned above, the principal auditor may review the other auditor's audit programs or working papers, read summaries of the work performed and conclusions reached by the other auditor, or attend key meetings between the other auditor and management. The principal auditor also may visit the other auditor's premises or obtain written representations about various matters. The need for such steps should be considered early in the audit and continually reviewed.

7.4   MANAGING THE ENGAGEMENT

Managing an engagement involves controlling the performance of all activities so that the audit both meets generally accepted auditing standards and is performed efficiently and within management's time expectations. Evaluating engagement performance against the plan on an ongoing basis helps to ensure that the engagement goals will be achieved and provides a basis for identifying ways to improve efficiency. The progress of the work should be monitored in relation to the established timetable and budget and appropriate action taken to correct the causes of any unnecessary deviations from plans or unfavorable variations from budget. Engagement management also includes staffing the engagement and monitoring its progress by supervising and reviewing the work of subordinates to ensure that the audit is performed in accordance with the approved audit strategy and professional standards.

(a)   Engagement Control

Monitoring and controlling engagement time effectively are important aspects of engagement control. Time management includes developing a timetable for the work, preparing time budgets, scheduling and reporting time, negotiating fees, and billing. The complexity of audits of multilocation and multinational companies makes detailed time and expense budgets particularly critical to the timely and efficient conduct of those engagements. In monitoring time, the auditor is concerned with the timely and accurate recording of hours spent on the job by the engagement team, estimates of time necessary to complete the auditing procedures, and comparisons of actual hours with budgeted hours. Effective time management can help the auditor identify causes of unfavorable time variances as they occur and take timely corrective action.

A time budget should be prepared for the different audit tasks and the different levels of personnel assigned to them. The amount of detail to be included in the time budget will vary with the size of the engagement. Sometimes preliminary time budgets are prepared at an early stage and revised, if necessary, when the detailed audit strategy is determined. Budgets help keep the work within management's and the auditor's time expectations and are the basis for establishing the audit fee. The budgets should cover all the different tasks and levels of personnel to be employed on the engagement. Tasks should be sufficiently segmented so that they can be addressed in relatively short periods, thereby enabling staff members to manage their time efficiently.

Both during the field work and at the end of the audit, time and expense overruns should be evaluated. If they were caused by inefficiencies, the evaluation can help ensure that they will not be repeated in the following year; if they were caused by the entity's management or personnel, the auditor will have support for additional billing. If overruns were caused by the discovery of errors or fraud, the evaluation serves as a reminder to the auditor to determine that the matter has been handled properly. Finally, the evaluation helps ensure that next year's budget and proposed audit fee changes will be realistic and also promotes more efficient use of staff.

Computers can contribute to efficient engagement management, particularly in planning, budgeting, and scheduling. Extremely time-consuming when performed manually, these tasks can be expedited considerably by software such as calculation worksheets, or spreadsheets. Once a spreadsheet is set up, the user can input and change data, conditions, and formulas, and the results are recalculated automatically.

The use of word processing to prepare letters and documents from standard templates, including letters of arrangement and representation letters, confirmation requests, financial reports, audit programs, and audit reports, is now widespread. Accounting firms also use computers in a number of other ways to enhance the efficiency of their practices. Some of these computer applications are:

Automated working papers. In addition to maintaining documents in word processing libraries, engagement management can be enhanced by the use of automated working papers, audit programs, and reports. Other aspects include the use of retrieval software to search authoritative literature on-line, and communications to stay in touch with the audit team and entity management. Accounting firms are increasingly automating their audits, to the point where it is expected that the use of notebook computers with such programs will replace the audit bags of documents that all auditors used to carry.

Audit statistics. In performing analytical procedures on the entity's financial results, the auditor often makes comparisons with industry results. Industry statistics and key business ratios can be collected and maintained on computer files.

Electronic mail. Electronic mail has the benefits of speed and ease of response. It can be sent by telecommunications systems to and from geographically disparate locations, thereby improving communications within a firm.

Software also can facilitate the effective use of, and control over, audit resources by determining the cost of assigned staff and evaluating alternatives, allocating staff and available chargeable hours to assignments, and scheduling staff by engagement, tasks to be performed, expected utilization, and available hours. Many accounting firms have management information systems to record budgets and time charges, facilitate prompt billing and revenue collection, and produce management and exception reports, such as staff utilization rates and overdue accounts. In some firms this processing is done on a centralized basis. Accounting firms will probably follow the trend in the business community toward decentralizing systems using mini- or microcomputers at the local level that process local data and then input results to, and retrieve reports from, the central processing site(s).

(b) Staffing the Engagement

Personnel for the engagement must be identified and assigned. Assigning staff to an engagement generally involves consideration of the technical complexity of the engagement, the necessity of industry expertise, the continuity of the engagement team, personnel career development, and staff commitments to other engagements. Some audit firms have policies relating to the rotation of staff among engagements for the purpose of promoting the professional development of individual staff members; such policies should be considered in staffing decisions. In addition, as noted in Chapter 3, the periodic rotation of engagement partners is required by the SEC Practice Section of the AICPA Division for CPA Firms on SEC engagements, and by the National Association of Insurance Commissioners on insurance company engagements. Staff availability and cost considerations sometimes lead to adjustments in the timing of certain procedures and other planning decisions.

Assignments and engagement plans have to be communicated to staff. Personnel to whom work is delegated should be told what their responsibilities are, what objectives their procedures are meant to achieve, and when their work should be completed within the overall audit timetable. It is a good management practice to hold an informal meeting with staff prior to the beginning of fieldwork to discuss planning decisions, including significant risks and issues identified, details of the current-year audit program, and goals, objectives, and management's expectations (including deadlines). Staff also should be informed of matters that may affect the nature, timing, and extent of auditing procedures, such as the nature of the entity's business and possible accounting and auditing problems.

If the entity uses computers in significant accounting applications, the engagement team may need specialized audit skills. AU Section 311.10 specifies that if the work of a professional with such skills (whether a member of the engagement team or an outside professional) is used, the auditor must have sufficient computer-related knowledge to communicate audit objectives to that professional, evaluate whether the procedures he or she applies meet the auditor's objectives, and determine how the results of those procedures affect the nature, timing, and extent of other planned auditing procedures.

(c) Supervision and Review

Supervision and review are essential parts of managing an engagement. Engagement control, including time management, is directly enhanced by procedures to ensure that the engagement team members receive adequate and appropriate supervision. In addition to the staff meeting, the auditor in charge of the field team should meet with each staff member before the person begins work on an audit area. The purpose of this meeting is to ensure that the person understands the procedures to be performed (through a review of the detailed audit program for the area) and the issues relevant to the area, as well as the auditor's goals and expectations, such as the deadline and budget for the area. Communication with all personnel involved on the engagement may be usefully supplemented by periodic progress meetings. Supervision includes ongoing monitoring of the work to ensure that staff members appear to have the necessary skills to carry out their assigned tasks, that they appear to understand their instructions, and that the work is being carried out in accordance with the plan and the audit program.

Supervision also entails comparing the completed work with established timetables and budgets, training and coaching, and identifying differences in professional judgment among personnel and referring them to the appropriate level for resolution, as well as directly reviewing the work performed, as recorded in the working papers. The working papers are the auditor's record of the work done on an audit and the conclusions reached on significant matters. Statement on Auditing Standards No. 41, *Working Papers* (AU Section 339), specifies that the auditor should prepare and maintain working papers. The following section contains a detailed discussion of working papers; reviewing working papers is discussed in Chapter 27.

Efficient review of working papers and other documentation contributes to effective engagement control. Review of working papers is more efficient if the reviewer looks through the working papers in the presence of the staff member who prepared them, as soon as possible after their completion. That way, queries raised during the review process can be addressed directly and without delay, and followed up promptly. In any event, issues raised should be resolved before the engagement is finalized and the audit opinion issued. The review process can be made more efficient if each working paper is reviewed in detail by only one reviewer. It is ordinarily feasible to do this, except in high-risk or highly judgmental areas, such as valuation accounts, significant reserves, or other accounts based on management estimates, where additional reviews may be necessary.

7.5 WORKING PAPERS

Working papers help the auditor in planning, controlling, and supervising the work. More specifically, the working papers document:

- The understanding of the entity's business, including inherent risks identified
- The understanding of the entity's internal control
- The evaluation of the effectiveness of the design of controls
- The audit strategy decisions

- Tests of controls performed and the basis for the conclusion about whether controls are operating effectively

- Substantive tests applied to transactions, account balances, and other information presented in the financial statements

- The supervision and review of the work of any assistants

- The resolution of exceptions and unusual matters

- Recommendations for improving internal control, as noted throughout the engagement

- Support for the auditor's opinion on the financial statements[1]

In addition, the working papers provide information needed for SEC reports, tax returns, and reports to other government agencies, and they serve as a source of information for succeeding audits.

Working papers are the property of the auditor and are not a substitute for the entity's accounting records. (In some cases, as an accommodation to management, working papers are transmitted to management to be used as a substitute for a record that entity personnel would otherwise prepare.) The auditor should adopt reasonable procedures for the safekeeping and retention of working papers long enough to meet his or her own practice needs and to satisfy any pertinent legal requirements for records retention.

Audit documentation software packages are available that automate some of the labor-intensive tasks associated with auditing financial statements, including footing the trial balance and financial statements, ensuring the arithmetical accuracy and consistency of account groupings, and listing relevant financial statement ratios for subsequent analysis. Documentation programs also can be used to prepare opening and closing trial balances, lead schedules showing current- and prior-period information, financial statements, and other working papers. Software can be used to produce and format reports to be used as audit working papers. Auditors can use documentation software packages, instead of preparing working papers, to document the use of other audit software. The audit software packages are often designed to be used on the auditor's notebook computer at the entity's office, a practice that is becoming increasingly common.

(a)   Form and Content of Working Papers

Working papers include audit programs, grouped account schedules, lead schedules, analyses, memoranda, letters of confirmation, copies or representative abstracts of entity documents, narratives, flowcharts, questionnaires, and various other forms and practice aids. They may be handwritten, typewritten, or in the form of computer printouts or data stored on electronic media. Often, portions of working papers are prepared by entity personnel according to auditor-determined specifications; the auditor should, of course, test the accuracy of those working papers.

The *content* of working papers generally cannot be standardized. Certain types of working papers, however, do lend themselves to standardization, such as a summary

---

[1] As noted in footnote 3 to AU Section 339.01, however, "there is no intention to imply that the auditor would be precluded from supporting his report by other means in addition to working papers."

of accounts receivable confirmation coverage and results. Working papers should be legible, complete, readily understandable, and designed to fit the circumstances and needs of the auditor for the particular engagement and subject matter under audit.

Unnecessary or irrelevant working papers that do not serve a useful purpose should not be prepared. If such working papers are inadvertently prepared, they generally should not be kept. Although the content of working papers varies with the engagement, there are several advantages to adopting a standardized approach to their *format*. A standardized approach facilitates the systematic organization of working papers for use during an engagement, enhances their ready access for reference or review, and aids in their orderly filing for future reference. Thus, every working paper should be titled, dated, and initialed by the preparer at the time the work is performed.

Every working paper should contain an explanation of the procedures followed (unless the information is included elsewhere in the working papers, such as in an audit program) and the results of those procedures. Figure 7.2 shows a working paper that illustrates this. Sometimes the procedures are obvious from the computations or other data recorded; sometimes a narrative explanation (or reference to an audit program step containing the explanation) is required. When an explanation is required, it is frequently placed at the end of the working paper and assigned a symbol or "tick mark," which is placed next to the appropriate item (generally a dollar amount) in the body of the working paper. For example, a working paper listing the details of notes receivable at a particular date may have the letter "E" after the details of each note, with the following explanation at the end of the working paper: "E=note examined," meaning that the auditor physically inspected the notes. Some auditors use a standardized set of symbols to document procedures.

Each working paper or set of working papers covering an audit objective should contain a clear record of all work performed. This record should include an explanation of exceptions noted by the auditor as a result of the procedures performed and identification of proposed adjustments to account balances. Language such as "are fairly stated" and "appear to be fairly stated" should be avoided, however, because the conclusion could be misinterpreted as having been reached in the context of the financial statements taken as a whole. That inference would be inappropriate and unsupportable, since the conclusion is based on only a portion of the work done during the audit of the overall financial statements.

Most working papers contain quantitative information. Some working papers, however, are prepared based on inquiry or observation procedures and contain no quantitative information. For example, the auditor may inquire of management about the existence of transactions with related parties or observe the physical condition of inventory during the entity's year-end inventory count. In these instances, the auditor should prepare working papers that clearly document the inquiries made, the personnel involved, any tests resulting from the inquiry, or a description of the condition observed and the conclusion reached.

(b) Working Paper Organization

There are no rigid guidelines for organizing a set of audit working papers. What follows should be viewed as general guidance that is subject to substantial modification by individual auditors and firms.

Figure 7.2   Sample Working Paper

Client:	Cooper's Cabinets
Year End:	12/31/00
Subject:	Interest Receivable
Working Paper No. 63-4	

Description	Quantity/ Par Value	Beg. Int. Rec.	Int. earned	Interest Received	Ending Int. Rec.
B ⟶		P	A		cf
T-Bill 7% matures 2002	3,000,000	0	52,500.00	0	52,500.00
T-Bill 7% matures 2002	2,056,500	0	35,989.00	0	35,989.00
RJR Nabisco - 8.75% matures 2004	4,000,000	0	87,500.00	0	87,500.00
Gen. Motors CARS 11.5% matures 2003	4,000,000 C	0	115,000.00	0	115,000.00
Maxus 8.5% matures 2008	2,000,000	0	42,500.00	0	42,500.00
Ralston Purina 9.5% matures 2016	1,000,000	0	23,750.00	0	23,750.00
Revlon 10% matures 2010	520,000	0	13,000.00	0	13,000.00
TOTALS		0 ff	370,239 ff	0 ff	370,239 ff
				I/S	T/B

Legend

A - Recalculated interest earned as par value x interest rate x period (portion of year). Note: all securities pay interest on 6/30 and 12/31. All securities were acquired on 10/1/00 with the proceeds of a public offering.

B - To ensure completeness and accuracy, agreed description, par value and interest rate to the investment detail w/p's which are matched one for one to the broker confirms for completeness and accuracy.

C - Investigated unusually high interest rate and the nature of the security, which is an asset-backed obligation. See working paper 63-6 for further discussion.

cf - Cross-footed

ff - Footed

I/S -Traced to income statement

P - Compared to prior period

T/B - Traced to trial balance

Detailed working papers are often summarized through the use of lead schedules for each financial statement caption. This technique provides an overview of an entire audit area for the preparer, as well as for reviewers. In addition, a lead schedule enables a reviewer to look at as much or as little detail as is considered necessary in the circumstances.

Detailed support for lead schedules or other summary working papers is often filed behind the summary in order of relative significance or other meaningful sequence. There should always be an easy-to-follow trail between the detailed working papers and the amounts in the financial statements. Each working paper should be able to stand on its own; that is, it should be complete and understandable in itself. Reference may be made to other working papers to document audit findings. Cross-referencing of working papers should be specific rather than general. The "to–from" technique is used to make the "direction" of referencing apparent; that is, it shows which number is the source and which is the summary (see Figure 7.3).

(c) Typical Working Papers

As suggested above, the variety of conditions encountered in practice generates a wide variety of working papers. In addition, they may be in very different forms, ranging from paper to computer files of varying sophistication. Nevertheless, some types of working papers have common characteristics, whatever their form, which are explained in this section of the chapter.

(i) Grouped Accounts Schedule. A schedule of grouped accounts is usually the key working paper in many audits because it is the one where data from all the underlying working papers is integrated, referenced, and summarized into the amounts appearing in the financial statements. There are a number of ways to prepare a schedule of grouped accounts and each of them has its advantages. Often it is prepared in a form that compares the current figures with those of the previous period. It may be prepared in balance sheet and income statement order, with subtotals for classifications of accounts. Adjustments made by management as a result of the audit and financial statement reclassification entries are shown in additional columns. The schedule is usually cross-referenced to supporting working papers.

(ii) Other Schedules and Analyses. Auditing procedures are documented on a variety of schedules and analyses, as well as in narrative form.

Tests of controls may be documented in narrative form by describing what tests were performed and which controls were tested. Sometimes a test of controls requires preparing a list of items to be extracted from the files or compared with data in another location. If so, the schedule or listing prepared can serve as the working paper. In some instances, tests of controls are documented on the same form— for example, a questionnaire—as the recorded understanding of the controls.

Substantive tests of details most often are evidenced by some kind of analysis; the form depends on the nature of the auditing procedures performed. For example, the working papers might include an analysis showing the composition of the ending balance in a particular account, or perhaps a summary of the account. They

Figure 7.3 Working Paper Organization

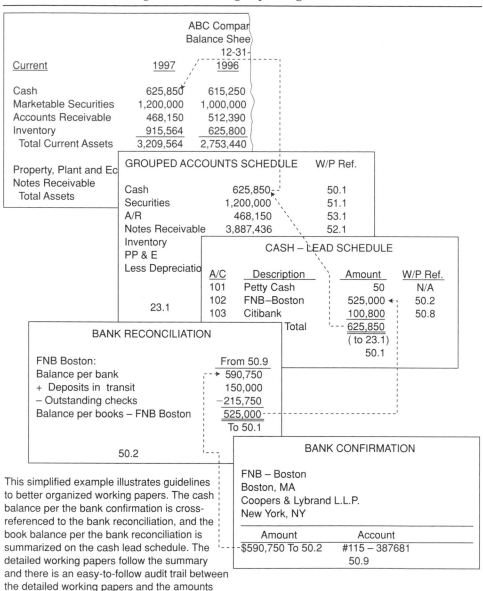

ABC Compar
Balance Shee
12-31-

Current	1997	1996
Cash	625,850	615,250
Marketable Securities	1,200,000	1,000,000
Accounts Receivable	468,150	512,390
Inventory	915,564	625,800
Total Current Assets	3,209,564	2,753,440

Property, Plant and Ec
Notes Receivable
  Total Assets

GROUPED ACCOUNTS SCHEDULE   W/P Ref.

Cash	625,850	50.1
Securities	1,200,000	51.1
A/R	468,150	53.1
Notes Receivable	3,887,436	52.1
Inventory		
PP & E		
Less Depreciatio		

23.1

CASH – LEAD SCHEDULE

A/C	Description	Amount	W/P Ref.
101	Petty Cash	50	N/A
102	FNB–Boston	525,000	50.2
103	Citibank	100,800	50.8
	Total	625,850	50.1
		(to 23.1)	

BANK RECONCILIATION

	From 50.9
FNB Boston:	
Balance per bank	590,750
+ Deposits in transit	150,000
− Outstanding checks	−215,750
Balance per books – FNB Boston	525,000
	To 50.1

50.2

BANK CONFIRMATION

FNB – Boston
Boston, MA
Coopers & Lybrand L.L.P.
New York, NY

Amount	Account
$590,750 To 50.2	#115 – 387681
	50.9

This simplified example illustrates guidelines to better organized working papers. The cash balance per the bank confirmation is cross-referenced to the bank reconciliation, and the book balance per the bank reconciliation is summarized on the cash lead schedule. The detailed working papers follow the summary and there is an easy-to-follow audit trail between the detailed working papers and the amounts reflected in the financial statements.

also might include an analysis of the activity in the particular account for the period, showing the beginning balance, a summary of the transactions during the period (logically classified so that relationships with related accounts are apparent), and the ending balance. The working papers should present both the account information and an indication of what evidence was examined and what other auditing procedures were performed. Sometimes the dollar amount or the percentage of the total tested also is shown.

Analytical procedures involve a study and comparison of relationships among data; they are often evidenced by computations the auditor makes as part of the comparison. The working paper evidence usually consists of a narrative description of the procedures, their results, and further investigation of matters identified as having a significant effect on the audit.

(iii) Documentation of Significant Issues.   Significant issues, such as technical or engagement management questions, errors discovered by procedures performed, or unusual matters that arise during the audit, should be documented. Issues may be matters from the previous year that are appropriate to be readdressed in the current audit, risks identified during the client acceptance or continuance process, risks identified at the planning stage, exceptions arising from the audit work, or other matters warranting further attention. Documentation of significant issues should include the steps taken to resolve them (such as additional auditing procedures, consultation with management, the auditor's own research and reasoning), the people who were involved in the resolution, and the resulting conclusions. It is undesirable simply to check off a question or record a cryptic answer such as "cleared." Explanations of significant issues should be complete and conclusive.

(iv) Permanent Working Papers.   Working papers for recurring engagements usually contain files that are carried forward from preceding years' audits; these are

Figure 7.4   Common Working Paper Deficiencies

- Working paper not initialed and dated by preparer or reviewer.
- Working paper not properly titled to indicate client and purpose.
- Cross-referencing too general; reviewer unable to find referenced working papers.
- Reason for cross-referencing missing or not apparent.
- Tick marks appearing on the working paper without a descriptive legend.
- Purpose of working paper not apparent; no explanation given.
- Working papers sloppy, cluttered, or illegible.
- Exceptions or unusual items not properly explained or evaluated.
- Working paper content illogical.
- Amounts not in agreement with trial balance.
- Poor quality, illegible photocopy placed in the working papers.
- Detailed explanation given for insignificant items or differences, for which a simple notation, such as "Amounts insignificant; no audit work deemed necessary," would be sufficient.
- Arrangement of working papers not logical.
- Too much reliance placed on the prior year's working papers, resulting in a lack of focus on unusual items or changes in significant account balances.
- Preparing a working paper because a working paper prepared by entity personnel was not in the exact format preferred by the auditor.
- Nature of auditing procedures performed not described fully and clearly.
- Use of similar tick marks to denote different procedures.

often referred to as permanent files. These files should include data having continuing use and not subject to frequent change. Examples of such data include copies or abstracts of the certificate of incorporation, bylaws, bond and note indentures, union agreements, important contracts having historical significance, organization charts, the entity's accounting procedures, key personnel, and location of plants. The file also may include activity schedules not maintained by the entity, for example, schedules of future amortization or depreciation (sometimes referred to as lapse schedules), and analyses and other working papers that have historical significance, such as analyses of various capital accounts. Audit programs, descriptions of the accounting system, flowcharts, and questionnaires or other documentation of internal control also are often kept in the permanent files.

(d) Common Working Paper Deficiencies

Deficiencies in working papers often result in confusion and wasted time at several stages—carrying out auditing procedures, assisting new staff in the following year's audit, and reconstructing at a later date the work performed and judgments made. Those deficiencies are generally discovered during the working paper review process, which is discussed in Chapter 27. Some of the more common working paper deficiencies are listed in Figure 7.4.

8

Obtaining Information About the Entity

The auditor needs an understanding of various aspects of the entity and its business in order to determine the auditing procedures to be performed, their timing, and their extent. Much of the information that forms the understanding is general and relates to the nature of the entity's business, the industry it operates in (including legal and regulatory requirements peculiar to the industry), the processes management has implemented to meet entity objectives, the significant accounts in the entity's financial statements, the accounting policies and practices used by management, and interrelationships among entity financial and operating data. Based on that understanding, the auditor identifies inherent risks associated with the entity. Those risks, in turn, affect the auditing procedures to be performed. The auditor also makes preliminary determinations as to materiality.

On a new engagement, gathering information about the entity can be a lengthy, detailed process, which may be aided by reference to a predecessor auditor's files, as discussed later in the chapter. For a recurring engagement, much of the general information about the entity is available from prior years' working papers and needs only to be updated, not gathered all over again. Both entity personnel and the auditor should be careful not to treat changed circumstances perfunctorily. An entity's personnel can easily forget changes that took place during the year because they have become routine by the time the auditor makes inquiries; the auditor can easily treat significant changes as trivial if their implications are not considered thoroughly. An auditor approaching a recurring engagement should remember that changed conditions can make last year's understanding of the entity and the risks associated with it obsolete and a misleading guide to the nature and extent of the procedures required. The auditor should review changed circumstances and update his or her understanding before designing auditing procedures.

Information about the entity's business and industry, recent financial information, familiarity with the results of prior years' work, and a knowledge of applicable accounting, auditing, and regulatory standards are useful for identifying inherent risks and the controls management may have implemented in response to those risks. The relevant information is diverse, obtained from many sources, and documented in a number of places in the audit working papers. Most of the information-gathering procedures are performed during the early stages of the audit; however, the auditor is likely to obtain additional information about the entity throughout the engagement and should consider that information in determining the nature, timing, and extent of auditing procedures. In gathering information about the entity, as well as at other stages in the audit, matters may arise that require research in order to acquire information needed for the decision-making process.

8.1 OBTAINING KNOWLEDGE OF THE ENTITY'S BUSINESS AND INDUSTRY

To a large extent, entities' operations will respond to the structure and dynamics of the industry or industries in which they do business. The auditor should become familiar with those industry characteristics, with trends in the industry, and with the entity's position in the industry. Industry conditions that can affect an entity include its market share and relative size, industry practices such as the use of quantity discounts and consignment sales, and competition from other industries. If the entity has significant activities in more than one industry, the auditor should obtain information about each industry.

To be effective, the various day-to-day operational processes must be responsive to the dynamics of the industry in which the entity operates. Broadly, business processes consist of a combination of interrelated activities, decisions, information, and resources designed to accomplish the entity's objectives. Business processes cut across functional, unit, and geographical boundaries. Identifying an entity's business processes can be considered in terms of the following questions: What does the entity do and how does it do it?

An entity's business processes include the means by which it sets guidelines and directives for managing the business as a whole, the methods it uses for delivering products and services and managing customer relationships, and the various functions, such as financing and investing activities, that support and facilitate the operation of the business. Examples are new product development, which may, depending on the entity and its industry, include research activities; production planning, which may be complex and involve constructing new facilities; analyzing market needs, projecting demand, and considering competitors; arranging financing for operations; purchasing materials, including establishing relationships with suppliers; manufacturing products; and distributing and marketing products or services.

Information about the business and its processes that is particularly relevant to the auditor includes product lines, sources and methods of supply, marketing and distribution methods (including major customers), sources of financing, and production methods. The auditor also should obtain information about the locations and relative size of operating plants, divisions, and subsidiaries, and the extent to which management is decentralized. The auditor's understanding of the entity's business processes helps in identifying risks associated with the entity's operations and methods of doing business and may facilitate the design of appropriate auditing procedures.

The auditor also should learn about economic conditions that affect the entity's business and industry. Economic conditions affect the continuing ability to generate and collect revenues, operate profitably, and provide a return to investors. Unfavorable economic conditions may raise questions about whether the entity's assets are recoverable, how its liabilities should be measured, and, ultimately, whether it can remain in business. Unfavorable economic conditions also may increase the likelihood of intentional financial statement misrepresentations.

The auditor can obtain entity and industry information from a variety of sources, including government statistics; economic, financial, industry, and trade journals; publications and brochures written by the entity; internal audit reports, where applicable; and reports prepared on the entity, its competitors, or its industry by underwriters, merchant bankers, and securities dealers and analysts. Increasingly, on-line computer services and proprietary data bases are becoming a source for such information. In some instances, relevant information may be available in regulatory or examination reports, supervisory correspondence, and similar materials from applicable regulatory agencies. If regulatory examinations are in process, the auditor may attend (as an observer) closing conferences between the examiner and the entity. Finally, the auditor learns about the entity and its industry through discussions with management.

8.2 REVIEWING PRIOR YEARS' AUDIT WORK

The knowledge the auditor obtains from reviewing prior years' audit work assists in determining the likelihood of material misstatements with respect to individual account balances or classes of transactions, thereby affecting the current year's risk assessment and the level of assurance required from substantive tests. For example, if no new inherent risks have been identified and the entity's internal control has not changed, and few deviations from prescribed policies and procedures were found in prior years, the auditor may not need to make significant changes in the audit strategy and audit program. While generally it is necessary to review only the working papers from the immediate prior year, information relating to several prior years may be useful in designing the current year's tests, particularly with respect to the degree of change in and operating effectiveness of internal control.

Working papers from prior years that are useful to review contain financial information, the understanding of the entity's business and industry, control risk assessments, documentation of significant accounting and auditing matters, and specific references to the sources (or causes) of adjustments made to the financial statements. The auditor also should review the effectiveness and efficiency of the prior year's engagement to identify auditing procedures that should be continued, expanded, reduced, or eliminated in order to enhance the quality and efficiency of the current audit and client service plan.

For a new engagement, much of the needed information may be available from a review of the predecessor auditor's working papers. As noted in Chapter 3, predecessor auditors generally make at least certain of their working papers accessible to successor auditors. Ordinarily, a review of the prior-year working papers will provide factual information about the entity's internal control, analyses of certain balance sheet accounts, details relating to contingencies and commitments, and summaries of proposed audit adjustments. Support for the predecessor auditor's assessment of audit risk, including the risk of management misrepresentation, and control risk assessments also can be found in the working papers, as well as evidence about key audit issues identified in prior years, their resolution, and the results of tests of controls and substantive tests.

If it is not possible to review a predecessor's working papers, the auditor may obtain an understanding of opening balances and related accounting principles by performing the following procedures:

1. Comparing the totals of the entity's detailed account listings with control accounts (particularly for accounts receivable, inventory, fixed assets, and cash), performing analytical procedures, reviewing the results of physical inventories conducted by the entity, reviewing reconciliations of the general ledger to the financial statements (including adjusting, consolidating, and elimination entries), and performing other procedures relating to major opening balances.

2. Performing procedures relating to activity during the current year designed to provide additional evidence about opening balances. This may be particularly effective with respect to debt, capital stock, deferred taxes, and certain accruals, such as for income taxes and interest payable.

3. Reviewing significant unusual transactions, particularly those occurring in the early part of the current year, to determine whether they are recorded in the correct period or represent potential adjustments to the prior-year financial statements. Examples include large inventory adjustments; receivable write-offs, returns, and allowances; and deferred charge write-offs.

4. Reviewing accounting policies in effect in the prior year and their application. Areas requiring particular attention include revenue recognition and deferral of costs, and the basis for significant valuation allowances and accruals.

5. Considering any loss contingencies that may have existed. This information would be available from copies of the prior-year attorneys' letters and from any correspondence from taxing authorities.

8.3 GATHERING AND ANALYZING RECENT FINANCIAL INFORMATION

In order to highlight new developments in the business, to identify which account balances and classes of transactions are material and which are immaterial, and to identify relationships among accounts, the auditor should review recent financial statements and other available financial as well as nonfinancial information and performance indicators. In addition, comparing recent financial information with prior-year data and budgets for the current year can alert the auditor to favorable or unfavorable operating trends, significant deviations from expected results, recent financing or investment activities, and other changes in the entity's business. The auditor also can apply ratio and trend analyses to interim data or compare interim account balances with prior-year balances. The auditor's knowledge about the entity's business and industry assists in designing analytical procedures.

Statement on Auditing Standards (SAS) No. 56, *Analytical Procedures* (AU Section 329), requires the auditor to use analytical procedures in planning the audit for the purpose of identifying matters to be considered in determining the audit strategy. Analytical procedures are especially helpful in pointing out unusual or unexpected relationships, which may indicate material misstatements in specific account balances, or inherent risks such as declining liquidity or poor operating performance, which may have a pervasive effect on the financial statements. Also, comparing the entity's financial results with those of other entities in its industry group as a whole may be a useful way to determine whether its performance is consistent with that of other similar entities. Information compiled by services like Dun & Bradstreet, Robert Morris Associates, or Standard & Poor's can give the auditor standard "benchmarks" against which to measure performance. Increasingly, auditors are using computers to access such information from public data bases. The nature and extent of analytical procedures depend on how large and complex the business is and what financial information is available.

In addition to financial data, analytical procedures used in planning the audit are sometimes based on relationships between financial and nonfinancial information, particularly for entities in industries in which an "average" rate has meaning. For example, in the retail industry, comparing an entity's sales per square foot in the current year with that of the prior year would provide an indication of changes in the business and, based on the auditor's knowledge of industry trends in retail sales, may suggest areas on which to focus during the audit.

The auditor's primary focus in performing analytical procedures as part of the process of planning other audit tests is to identify specific risks early in the audit. Unusual or unexpected balances or relationships among data aggregated at a high level, such as financial statement line items or major components thereof, can point to accounts that are subject to specific risks. The auditor then can plan the nature, timing, and extent of auditing procedures to obtain evidence about those accounts and also can consider the implications of the risks for other accounts. Analytical procedures performed early in the audit also may highlight unfavorable trends or other issues that may raise questions about the entity's ability to continue as a going concern.

8.4   UPDATING KNOWLEDGE OF APPLICABLE ACCOUNTING, AUDITING, AND REGULATORY STANDARDS

The auditor's understanding of the business aids in understanding issues related to accounting recognition, measurement, and disclosure principles. In light of his or her knowledge of such principles, the auditor should evaluate whether the entity's accounting policies and practices are appropriate for the processes management uses in conducting the business. If any accounting policies or practices were changed during the current year, the auditor should determine whether it was in response to changes in business processes or in accounting or regulatory standards, or to better reflect operating results, and should consider the possible implications for the audit.

The auditor should identify any accounting or auditing standards that warrant special attention in the current year, such as standards that have become applicable or have taken on increased significance because of changes in the entity's business or because of significant, unusual, or nonrecurring transactions. Management may not be aware that such standards apply to the entity's financial statements or may not fully understand how to apply the standards. New or changed regulatory standards may have a similar impact on the financial statements. The auditor should consider discussing such standards with management at the earliest possible date so that any necessary action can be taken on a timely basis.

8.5   CONSIDERING THE ENTITY'S RISK MANAGEMENT POLICIES

All entities face risks in achieving their goals. Profits—or, in a not-for-profit environment, the achievement of other operating objectives—are the result, at least in part, of the assumption of those risks. Risk results from the chance that entity activities (financial, production, and marketing) will not turn out as planned. Sound management entails assessing risks, deciding which ones to assume, and then instituting policies and procedures to control and reduce those risks as much as possible. As discussed in Chapter 9 (see Section 9.1, Definition and Components of Internal Control), risk assessment and management is a component of an entity's internal control. The auditor should understand the entity's risk assessment and management policies both as part of his or her responsibilities to understand the entity's internal control and as part of the process of identifying inherent risks.

The broader aspects of risk assessment and management are discussed in Chapter 9. This section discusses one aspect of that topic, namely, the risks that entities face from losses of assets from casualties or theft and from the incurring of liabilities as the result of injury to individuals, damage to their business or property, or damage to the environment. For example, an entity's premises or property may be vandalized or destroyed by fire; its products may malfunction, causing hardships to customers; or its employees may injure themselves at work. Some of those risks may expose the entity to potentially bankrupting losses of business or assets or incurrence of liabilities.

A major concern of the auditor is how management identifies the occurrence of an event that requires recording a liability for an estimated loss in conformity with Statement of Financial Accounting Standards (SFAS) No. 5, *Accounting for Contingencies* (Accounting Standards Section C59). Most entities, either formally or informally, analyze their exposure to such risks and decide which they are willing to accept, which they are not, and the most appropriate means of avoiding or transferring risks in the latter group. In addition, entities have potential exposure from unintentional violations of laws or regulations, such as those regarding occupational safety and health, the environment, or equal employment. The auditor should be aware that such violations also could create the need to record a liability. (The auditor's responsibility for detecting and communicating illegal acts by clients is discussed in Chapter 4; accounting standards for recognizing and disclosing contingent liabilities are discussed in Chapter 26 [see Section 26.7(a), Contingencies].

Entities that choose to deal with the analysis of risk on a formal basis usually establish a risk management function that is responsible for designing an insurance program flexible enough to consider changing conditions and circumstances in the entity's business operations. The risk management function identifies risks and potential loss exposures facing the entity and designs ways to manage them. Purchasing insurance coverage through insurance underwriters is the most common practice. One alternative is the establishment of self-insurance trusts from which claims are paid, and another is to self-insure without the establishment of a trust or other means of segregating assets. (Self-insurance as a method of risk management is discussed in Chapter 20.) Management should periodically review the appropriateness of the entity's risk management policies, considering changes in the entity's operations, such as the opening of new facilities, that may necessitate changes in insurance coverage.

Insurance programs relate, in some way, to almost every phase of an entity's operations. Thus, the risk management function—or insurance group, as it is sometimes called—coordinates its activities with managers throughout the entity to determine the types and amounts of coverage required. The insurance group's records need to be current and reflect all appropriate information to ensure that all material risks are considered. The insurance group also reviews billings received for accuracy of rates charged and the coverage provided.

8.6   IDENTIFYING RELATED PARTY TRANSACTIONS

In understanding the entity's business, the auditor has a specific responsibility to consider relationships and transactions with related parties. SFAS No. 57, *Related Party Disclosures* (Accounting Standards Section R36), sets forth disclosure requirements with regard to related parties and contains (in Section R36.406) the following definition of related parties:

> Affiliates of the enterprise; entities for which investments are accounted for by the equity method by the enterprise; trusts for the benefit of employees, such as pension and

profit-sharing trusts that are managed by or under the trusteeship of management; principal owners of the enterprise; its management; members of the immediate families of principal owners of the enterprise and its management; and other parties with which the enterprise may deal if one party controls or can significantly influence the management or operating policies of the other to an extent that one of the transacting parties might be prevented from fully pursuing its own separate interests. Another party also is a related party if it can significantly influence the management or operating policies of the transacting parties or if it has an ownership interest in one of the transacting parties and can significantly influence the other to an extent that one or more of the transacting parties might be prevented from fully pursuing its own separate interests.

The terms "affiliates," "control," "immediate family," "management," and "principal owners" are further defined in SFAS No. 57.

Under AU Section 334, *Related Parties*, the auditor has the responsibility to understand the entity's business activities well enough to evaluate whether disclosures regarding related parties are appropriate, including the propriety of any management representations that related party transactions took place at terms equivalent to arm's-length transactions. AU Section 334 sets forth specific auditing procedures the auditor should consider in determining the existence of related parties, procedures to help identify material transactions with related parties, and procedures the auditor should consider when examining any related party transactions identified.

Management has the ultimate responsibility for identifying, recording, and disclosing related party transactions, and the auditor should obtain specific representation from management that it is aware of, and has fulfilled, that responsibility. The auditor's procedures, however, should extend beyond inquiry of, and obtaining such representations from, management. The auditor also should review other potential sources of information, such as proxy material, stockholder listings, and minutes of meetings of the board of directors and executive or operating committees. As far as possible, the auditor should identify related parties at the beginning of the audit and distribute their names to all members of the engagement team, including those responsible for auditing other divisions or subsidiaries. This will help them identify related party transactions in the course of their work. The auditor should assess management's procedures for identifying related parties and transactions to determine the nature and extent of auditing procedures necessary to identify such transactions.

8.7   IDENTIFYING INHERENT RISKS

As discussed in Chapter 6, inherent risks result from conditions that exist at the macroeconomic, industry, and entity level and also from the characteristics of the entity's transactions and related account balances. Inherent risks that originate at the entity-wide level or outside the entity generally are not addressed by specific accounting procedures and control activities. In fact, it usually is not possible to exercise control over such inherent risks, which may relate to changes in the general business environment, government regulations, and other economic factors. However, if an entity's internal control includes an effective control environment and risk assessment function, this provides evidence of management's ability to react to changes in inherent risks on a timely basis.

As might be expected, information about inherent risks stemming from external conditions comes mostly from outside sources, including business and trade publications. To a large extent, the auditor identifies macroeconomic and industry conditions from his or her general knowledge about business and about current economic and political developments. An awareness of risks associated with the entity or its industry also comes from understanding the business processes used by the entity and the conditions prevalent in the industry, and from reviewing prior-year working papers.

In contrast to those types of inherent risks, management designs controls in response to the particular characteristics of its classes of transactions and account balances. Therefore, inherent risks that are related to those characteristics often are addressed by specific aspects of internal control, including accounting procedures and control activities. These inherent risks ordinarily are considered in conjunction with the assessment of control risk, which is covered in Chapter 12. Inherent risks associated with specific types of transactions and account balances are identified not only in the course of obtaining an understanding of the entity's business processes and industry conditions, and reviewing prior-year working papers, but also from analyzing financial information and the auditor's familiarity with relevant accounting standards.

The auditor considers both aspects of inherent risk in determining the auditing procedures to be performed. Inherent risks may be identified at any time during the audit; the implications of risks identified later in the audit, after the audit program has been designed, should be considered and the planned tests modified appropriately.

8.8 MAKING PRELIMINARY MATERIALITY JUDGMENTS

As noted in Chapter 6, SAS No. 47, *Audit Risk and Materiality in Conducting an Audit* (AU Section 312.14), requires the auditor to consider a "preliminary judgment about materiality levels" in planning an engagement. Preliminary judgments about materiality are based on a review of recent financial information and prior years' annual and interim reports, as well as on the auditor's knowledge of the entity's business and industry. Those preliminary judgments focus the auditor's attention on the more significant financial statement items and thus assist in determining the nature, timing, and extent of auditing procedures to be performed. Materiality is discussed in detail in Chapter 6.

8.9 RESEARCHING AUDITING ISSUES

The profession has set high standards for the technical and ethical conduct of CPAs. Many of those standards establish precise requirements for auditor performance in a variety of circumstances. In meeting their obligation under those standards, auditors need to become familiar with the requirements of the 10 generally accepted auditing standards (GAAS) and the related Statements on Auditing Standards; in addition, often they need to refer to other professional literature for guidance on interpreting and adhering to GAAS.

Generally accepted auditing standards serve a dual purpose: They implicitly require an auditor to be aware of all pertinent literature—the first general standard—and they serve as a first level of research to resolve auditing issues. For example, an auditor may be confronted for the first time with the need to issue a letter for under-writers on an engagement that includes filing the auditor's report with the Securities and Exchange Commission (SEC) under the Securities Act of 1933. The accepted form and content of the letter, as well as important suggestions for procedures to fol-low and cautions to observe, can be researched readily in SAS No. 72, *Letters for Under-writers and Certain Other Requesting Parties*, as amended by SAS No. 76 (AU Section 634).

The auditor also should be familiar with AICPA auditing interpretations. Inter-pretations are not as authoritative as Statements on Auditing Standards, because they are not subject to due process, but they are issued by the Audit Issues Task Force of the Auditing Standards Board (ASB) of the AICPA (with review by the ASB) to pro-vide timely guidance on the application of Statements on Auditing Standards, and CPAs may have to justify departures from auditing interpretations. Thus, if faced with an auditing question with respect to, for example, related party transactions (dealt with in AU Section 334), the auditor would consult interpretations in AU Sec-tion 9334 for additional guidance.

An auditor who does not have prior experience in an industry may be engaged to audit an entity in that industry. The auditor should, among other considerations, de-termine whether a relevant industry audit and accounting guide has been issued by the AICPA. For example, an auditor engaged by an investment company should read the latest edition of the audit and accounting guide for that industry. The guides have authoritative status similar to that of auditing interpretations. Chapters 33–49 of this book also may be helpful.

Auditors sometimes need to research issues in the latest authoritative accounting pronouncements in order to determine whether the assertions in financial statements are in conformity with generally accepted accounting principles (GAAP). Chapter 28 of this book discusses sources of GAAP and the hierarchy of GAAP in SAS No. 69, *The Meaning of* Present Fairly in Conformity With Generally Accepted Accounting Principles *in the Independent Auditor's Report* (AU Section 411). If appropriate, the audi-tor also should consult SEC rules and interpretive releases.

Auditors also should be familiar with the latest edition of *Accounting Trends and Tech-niques*, published by the AICPA. Issues of disclosure and presentation can be re-searched readily in this publication. It also contains wording of auditor's reports in un-usual situations. While the publication is nonauthoritative, it includes examples from recent practice and its use can serve to demonstrate an auditor's diligence.

An auditor may be faced with a question regarding independence, which is an eth-ical consideration. In that case, he or she should refer to the AICPA's Code of Profes-sional Conduct and similar pronouncements of the relevant state society, state board of accountancy, and the SEC.

Other research sources that the auditor may consult include:

- Statements of Position (SOPs) of the AICPA's Auditing Standards Division, which revise or clarify recommendations in industry audit and accounting guides. SOPs are published as separate documents and are also included in reprints of audit guides and in the AICPA's *Technical Practice Aids*.

- Notices to Practitioners issued by the AICPA's Auditing Standards Division, which are published in *The CPA Letter*, a semimonthly news report published by the AICPA. Notices to Practitioners disseminate important information quickly.

- AICPA Audit Risk Alerts, issued annually to inform auditors of changes in the industry economic, regulatory, legislative, accounting, and auditing environment.

- SECPS Practice Alerts, prepared by the Professional Issues Task Force of the AICPA's SEC Practice Section to provide information to help improve the efficiency and effectiveness of audit practice.

- Auditing Procedures Studies, which address various areas of practice, such as auditing emerging businesses and applying confirmation procedures.

- Publications of federal agencies that provide guidance for audits of entities under their jurisdiction. Examples are the U.S. General Accounting Office's *Government Auditing Standards, 1994 Revision* (the "Yellow Book") and the SEC's Financial Reporting Releases and Accounting and Auditing Enforcement Releases.

- Periodicals, such as the *Journal of Accountancy* and *The CPA Journal*, which contain practical guidance on interpreting and applying auditing pronouncements. These journals also report on the publication of accounting and auditing pronouncements and other research materials.

Thus, a substantial body of authoritative and nonauthoritative literature exists to help auditors resolve issues concerning auditing standards and procedures. In practice, most auditors are familiar with these sources and refer to them frequently. Practitioners and firms should receive, review, and maintain all authoritative pronouncements and interpretations as well as other professional literature—such as industry audit and accounting guides—for reference purposes. Larger firms maintain research departments for consultation.

Not all issues encountered, however, can be researched so readily. Many state societies of CPAs and the AICPA offer technical services to assist in research, or a local university may be of help. These organizations, as well as many firms, often use computer-assisted research sources; some firms also have their own research data bases. An auditor also may consult relevant trade associations or fellow practitioners with appropriate backgrounds and experience.

When a question is identified, the auditor must clarify the related issues, develop an approach to obtaining research assistance, evaluate the material uncovered as to relevance and authoritative status, and reach a conclusion. For engagement efficiency and good client relations, issues should be identified early, so that the time spent resolving them does not unduly delay completion of the audit.

9

Overview of Internal Control

An entity's internal control consists of five interrelated components: the control environment, risk assessment, control activities, information and communication, and monitoring. The components include processes, policies, procedures, methods, records, and other means designed and implemented by management to enable the entity to generate reliable financial information, comply with applicable laws and regulations, and promote operational efficiency.

9.1   DEFINITION AND COMPONENTS OF INTERNAL CONTROL

Statement on Auditing Standards (SAS) No. 78, *Consideration of Internal Control in a Financial Statement Audit: An Amendment to SAS No. 55* (AU Section 319),[1] defines internal control as:

> A process—effected by an entity's board of directors, management, and other personnel—designed to provide reasonable assurance regarding the achievement of objectives in the following categories: (a) reliability of financial reporting, (b) effectiveness and efficiency of operations, and (c) compliance with applicable laws and regulations. (para. 6)

This definition, with its specification of different categories of objectives, is intended to meet the needs of different parties—senior management, board members, independent accountants, internal auditors, other business personnel, legislators and regulators, and educators—who have an interest in internal control. Accommodating such diverse groups necessarily leads to a broad definition and the inclusion of a wide range of controls to meet the varying objectives. While these objectives are distinct, they overlap. Generally, even though many controls may address more than one objective, controls often tend to relate more closely to one of the objectives than to the others. As discussed in more detail later, the auditor's primary concern is with the effect of internal control on the reliability of financial reporting.

AU Section 319 describes internal control as comprising five components that are necessary for the objectives to be achieved: the control environment, risk assessment, control activities, information and communication, and monitoring. The control en-

---

[1] SAS No. 78 amended SAS No. 55 to reflect the definition and components of internal control contained in *Internal Control—Integrated Framework*, which was published in 1992 by the Committee of Sponsoring Organizations of the Treadway Commission (COSO). COSO was formed to support implementation of the recommendations in the 1987 report of the National Commission on Fraudulent Financial Reporting, commonly referred to as the Treadway Commission, that its sponsoring organizations—the American Accounting Association, the American Institute of Certified Public Accountants, the Financial Executives Institute, the Institute of Internal Auditors, and the Institute of Management Accountants (formerly the National Association of Accountants)—work together to integrate the diverse internal control concepts and definitions then prevalent, and to develop a common reference point for considering internal control.

COSO commissioned Coopers & Lybrand L.L.P. to conduct a study to develop practical, broadly accepted criteria for establishing internal control and evaluating its effectiveness. *Internal Control—Integrated Framework*, which resulted from the study and often is referred to as the COSO Report, had two objectives:

1. To establish a common definition of internal control that would serve the needs of different parties.

2. To provide a standard against which business and other entities—large or small, in the public or private sector, for profit or not—could assess their control systems and determine how to improve them.

vironment is the foundation for all the other components. Risk assessment and control activities are performed as means of achieving the entity's objectives. Information needed to meet the entity's various objectives is generated and communicated throughout the entity, in all directions. Finally, the entire process is monitored. The division of controls into five components is a practical construct that facilitates discussion of the topic. From the auditor's perspective, what is important is not the classification of controls into particular components, but whether a specific aspect of internal control affects financial statement assertions or the auditor's ability to form judgments about those assertions.

Lastly, internal control can be considered in relation to the entity as a whole, or to any operating unit or business function. The relationships between categories of objectives, the components of internal control, and the entity are shown in Figure 9.1.

The *control environment* comprises the attitudes, abilities, awareness, and actions of an entity's personnel, especially its management, as they affect the overall operation and control of the business. In the words of the National Commission on Fraudulent Financial Reporting (Treadway Commission), it is the "tone at the top." The control environment represents the collective effect of various factors [described in detail in Chapter 10, Section 10.1(a), Control Environment] on the effectiveness of specific controls. Management's actions in enforcing the entity's code of conduct, for example, would be one aspect of the control environment.

Risk assessment refers to management's process of identifying, analyzing, and managing risks that affect the achievement of its objectives. As discussed in Chapter 10 [Section 10.1(b), Management's Risk Assessment], risks may be presented by internal or external events and circumstances, such as changes in an entity's operating en-

Figure 9.1   Relationship Between Objectives and Components

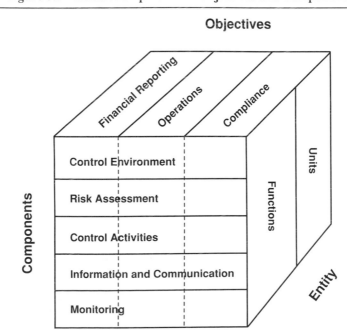

vironment, new information systems, or new lines of business. In general, risks that might affect the financial statements as a whole are more closely related to operations than to financial reporting and are not addressed by controls directed to financial reporting objectives. Risks that affect specific financial statement assertions, and therefore are relevant to financial reporting, usually are addressed by specific control activities designed by management to meet financial reporting objectives. The auditor considers those risks in conjunction with understanding and assessing control activities, as described in detail in Chapter 11.

Control activities are the policies and procedures that help ensure that necessary actions are taken to address risks to the achievement of the entity's objectives. Control activities have various objectives and are applied at different organizational levels. Control activities that are relevant to an entity's objectives regarding the reliability of financial reporting can be considered as falling into one of two categories: application controls (consisting of transaction processing controls, file maintenance controls, and asset protection controls) and computer controls. These categories of control activities are discussed briefly in this chapter and in more detail in Chapter 11 (see Section 11.1, Control Activities).

The *information and communication* component encompasses the identification and flow of information within an entity in a way that enables people to perform their roles and discharge their responsibilities. The accounting system is the part of the information system that is most directly relevant to financial reporting objectives. The accounting system consists of the procedures established, including electronic means, to transmit, process, maintain, and access information, as well as the documents produced as a result of those procedures. These procedures and documents help management operate the business effectively and enable it to prepare reliable financial statements. For example, the way in which a purchase transaction is initially recorded and posted to ledger accounts is part of the accounting system. The accounting system is discussed in detail in Chapter 10 [see Section 10.1(d)(i), The Accounting System].

Monitoring relates to management's process for assessing the quality of the entity's internal control. The objective of monitoring activities is to determine whether an entity's internal control is operating as intended and is modified when necessary. Monitoring controls may be exercised at the entity level or at lower levels, such as at the cycle or transaction level (discussed later). Monitoring is discussed further in Chapters 10 and 11 [see Sections 10.1(c), Monitoring, and 11.2, Monitoring Controls].

The five components of internal control are applicable to all entities, but how they are configured within an entity will depend on several factors, among them:

- The entity's size
- Its organization and ownership characteristics
- The nature of its business
- The diversity and complexity of its operations
- Its methods of transmitting, processing, maintaining, and accessing information
- Applicable legal and regulatory requirements

Small and mid-sized entities may have less formal controls than those found in larger entities. This often is appropriate, because management of such entities frequently is closely involved in all aspects of the business, including financial reporting. In these circumstances, there may be less need for documented accounting procedures or formal control activities. The control environment, or "tone at the top," may be conveyed informally by management's example, without a written code of conduct. On the other hand, some smaller entities may engage in sophisticated transactions, such as trading in derivatives, or may be subject to certain legal or regulatory requirements. These circumstances might warrant more formal controls to ensure that applicable objectives are met.

Auditors have long recognized the inherent limitations on the effectiveness of internal control. AU Section 319 notes the following factors that may reduce or eliminate the effectiveness of controls:

- Faulty judgment in decision making or mistakes in application on the part of a person responsible for establishing or performing a control
- Collusion among individuals, circumventing controls whose effectiveness depends on segregation of duties
- Management override of controls

In view of these as well as cost limitations, internal control can provide reasonable, but not absolute, assurance that its objectives will be accomplished. This is recognized by AU Section 319, the Foreign Corrupt Practices Act of 1977, and sound financial management. Management will always have to make economic judgments about relative benefits and costs. AU Section 319 expresses it in this way:

> The cost of an entity's internal control should not exceed the benefits that are expected to be derived. Although the cost–benefit relationship is a primary criterion that should be considered in designing internal control, the precise measurement of costs and benefits usually is not possible. Accordingly, management makes both quantitative and qualitative estimates and judgments in evaluating the cost–benefit relationship. (para. 17)

9.2　RELEVANCE OF AN ENTITY'S INTERNAL CONTROL TO AN AUDIT

The auditor's responsibility regarding an entity's internal control is formalized in the second standard of field work, stated in paragraph .01 of AU Section 319, as follows:

> A sufficient understanding of internal control is to be obtained to plan the audit and to determine the nature, timing, and extent of tests to be performed.

In addition, as discussed in Chapter 6, the auditor assesses control risk to determine the acceptable level of detection risk with respect to the items in the entity's financial statements. In assessing control risk, the auditor is most concerned with controls that affect the reliability of financial statement assertions. Other controls, however, also may be relevant to an audit. For example, controls over production statistics that are used by the auditor in certain analytical procedures have audit relevance, even though the information itself is not part of the financial statements. Controls that address an entity's compliance with the regulations of an oversight agency may be relevant to the audit if failure to comply could have a direct and material effect on the financial statements.

The relationship of internal control to assertions may be either direct or indirect. The degree of directness of the relationship determines, in part, how likely a specific control is to have an effect on a particular assertion for a specific account balance or class of transactions. For example, accounting for the numerical sequence of sales invoices (a control activity) directly addresses the completeness assertion for accounts receivable and sales, while management's review of monthly sales reports prepared from data generated by the accounting system (a monitoring control) has a less direct effect on the assertion regarding the completeness of those account balances. As explained in Chapter 11 (see Section 11.2, Monitoring Controls), however, management's review of operating reports or similar data produced by the system may indirectly provide evidence about the reliability of financial information.

Controls established to protect or safeguard assets against unauthorized acquisition, use, or disposition often meet both financial reporting and operational objectives. The auditor's consideration of such controls generally is limited to controls that are relevant to reliable financial reporting. Restricting access to files containing payroll data is likely to be relevant to a financial audit, for example, whereas controls over excessive use of materials in an entity's manufacturing process generally are not.

Most controls that relate to the effectiveness and efficiency of various management decision-making processes are not relevant to an audit and need not be included in the auditor's understanding of internal control or assessment of control risk. Although auditors have no responsibility to do so, they often report observations about those controls as a client service when they make such observations in the course of an audit. For example, an auditor who noticed that excess cash was kept in non-interest-bearing accounts might suggest that entity personnel reexamine how often cash is moved into investment accounts.

As discussed in Chapter 6, the accounts and disclosures in the financial statements represent various assertions by entity management. For each assertion embodied in each item in the financial statements, the auditor develops one or more corresponding *audit objectives* and then designs auditing procedures to ascertain whether the objectives have been met. Of the seven categories of assertions or audit objectives described in Chapter 6, existence/occurrence, completeness, and accuracy (and sometimes cutoff and valuation) often can be achieved, to varying degrees, by obtaining evidence that related financial reporting *control objectives* are met by an entity's internal control, particularly its accounting procedures and control activities. To the extent that the auditor concludes that the control objectives are achieved for classes of transactions or transaction cycles, he or she can restrict substantive tests directed at relevant audit objectives for the related account balances.

9.3 TRANSACTION CYCLES AND CONTROL OBJECTIVES

The approach to internal control described in this book views certain business processes, or segments thereof, in terms of "cycles" into which related transactions can be conveniently grouped and for which specific accounting procedures and control activities are established by an entity's management.[2] Each cycle typically comprises several transaction classes that vary with the particular business. For example, sales of goods and services, cash receipts, and customer returns may be three distinct transaction classes making up the revenue cycle. Each class of transactions may be further divided by specific type of transaction; for instance, sales of goods and services may be subdivided into cash sales and credit sales, or into foreign sales and domestic sales. Transaction classes are distinguished from each other primarily by differences in the accounting procedures and control activities applied to them.

Two major transaction cycles are identified in this book and discussed in detail in Chapters 13 and 14. They are the revenue and purchasing cycles, and may be described as follows:[3]

> *Revenue Cycle*: transactions relating to generating and collecting revenue, and related controls applied to such activities as recording sales orders, shipping, and cash collection.
>
> *Purchasing Cycle*: transactions relating to purchases and payments, and related controls applied to such activities as ordering and receiving purchases, payroll functions, and cash disbursements.

The essence of a cycle is the path by which each class of transactions flows through the accounting system, and the nature of control activities applied. The auditor considers each transaction class to determine whether appropriate accounting procedures and control activities have been designed and are operating effectively to achieve their intended financial reporting control objectives. As discussed later in this chapter, to the extent that the auditor obtains evidence to support a belief that those objectives are met, he or she will be able to restrict substantive tests aimed at the existence/occurrence, completeness, and accuracy (and sometimes cutoff and valuation) of account balances that are part of a transaction cycle.

(a) Control Objectives

For a specific class of transactions, control objectives that are relevant to financial reporting relate to:

- Processing transactions
- Maintaining files on which those transactions and related data are stored
- Protecting assets against loss from errors and fraud

---

[2] The FASB defines a "transaction" as "an external event involving transfer of something of value . . . between two (or more) entities" (Statement of Financial Accounting Concepts No. 6, para. 137). The term is used more broadly in this book to include all events and circumstances that require accounting recognition. In the context of computerized systems, the term is used even more broadly to encompass any change to the computerized records.

[3] Other transaction cycles—for example, producing goods for sale—may be identified, if the entity has designed specific control activities unique to classes of transactions.

(i) Processing Transactions.   Three control objectives relate to the processing of individual types of transactions. They are:

Authorization: all recorded transactions represent economic events that actually occurred and relate to the entity, and were approved by designated personnel. Typical control activities include authorization by an appropriate individual and exception reporting (for example, reporting employees working more than a given number of hours in a week, with subsequent review and follow-up by a responsible official).

Completeness of input: all transactions that occurred are initially entered into the accounting records and accepted for processing. Relevant control activities include, for example, computer matching of transactions to other data within the system, a computer check of the sequence of document numbers, and one-for-one checking of source documents to data entered into the system, with appropriate reporting of exceptions, subsequent review, and follow-up in each case.

Accuracy of input: transactions are initially recorded at the correct amount, in the appropriate account, and on a timely basis. Control activities designed to ensure completeness of input, for example, one-for-one checking, also may ensure accuracy of input. Specific control activities to achieve accuracy include edit checks (such as matching a customer number input at a terminal to the customer master file, followed by the system displaying the customer name on the screen for visual checking) and batching source documents and controlling the batch totals.

(ii) Maintaining Files.   Three control objectives relate to the maintenance of files on which transactions are stored. These objectives, which relate to a transaction cycle as a whole, are:

Integrity of standing data: changes to standing data (for example, the selling price master file) are authorized and accurately and completely input and standing data, once input, is not changed without authorization. For example, the marketing department authorizes price changes and then reviews the selling price master file to determine that the changes have been accurately and completely input.

Completeness and accuracy of update: all transactions input and accepted for processing are updated to the appropriate data file and the update is accurate. Relevant control activities include control totals, which may be manual batch totals reconciled to updated file totals, and computerized accounting procedures that calculate sales invoices from a transaction file of goods shipped.

Completeness and accuracy of accumulated data: once data is updated to a file, the data remains correct on the file until it is properly removed. An example of a control activity related to this objective is the periodic reconciliation of subsidiary ledgers to general ledger control accounts.

(iii) Protecting Assets.   An additional control objective relates to protecting assets:

Asset protection: assets are protected against loss from errors and fraud (particularly misappropriation) in the processing of transactions and the handling of related assets.[4] Examples of relevant control activities are physical controls that restrict access to physical inventories and related documents, and segregation of duties between personnel authorized to purchase assets and those authorized to disburse cash.

Loss of assets through *errors* is prevented or detected by appropriate transaction processing and file maintenance controls and by segregation of duties among employees. Loss of assets through *fraud* is prevented or detected by physical controls, such as locked storage areas; segregation of duties among employees; and restricted access to documents that can be used to transfer assets, such as purchase orders and checks, to confidential (proprietary) data, and to the means, such as computer programs and data files, of effecting unauthorized amendments of data.[5]

(b) Computer Controls

Many control activities require employees to use and respond to computer-generated data. For controls to be effective, the data needs to be accurate and complete. That is, the control activities relevant to financial reporting usually are dependent on programmed accounting procedures or programmed control procedures (i.e., procedures that are carried out by computer). Accordingly, the effectiveness of those controls, and the resultant achievement of the control objectives described above, often depends on the effectiveness of another group of controls, referred to as computer controls or general controls.

Computer controls can be classified into four categories:

1. *Changes to applications*: controls designed to ensure that changes to computer programs are designed appropriately and implemented effectively. These controls relate to program amendments, rather than to entire applications, and ensure that amendments are properly designed, tested, and implemented.

2. *Development and implementation*: controls over the development and implementation of new or significantly enhanced applications, intended to ensure that programmed procedures are appropriately designed and effectively implemented. These controls include controls over the original design of systems, the testing and documentation of programs and systems, and procedures for putting approved programs into use and transferring data held in the prior applications.

---

[4] This objective is limited to losses related to processing transactions and handling assets. It does not include loss of assets arising from management's operating decisions, such as selling a product that proves to be unprofitable, incurring expenditures that turn out to be unnecessary, authorizing what proves to be unproductive research or ineffective advertising, and, in a retail business, accepting some level of pilferage by customers.

[5] Paragraph 9 of the Appendix to SAS No. 78 (AU Section 319.84) notes that the extent to which controls designed to prevent theft of assets (i.e., loss resulting from fraud in processing transactions or handling assets) are relevant to the reliability of financial statements, and therefore to the audit, depends on the circumstances, such as whether assets are highly susceptible to misappropriation.

3. *Computer security*: controls designed to restrict access to the computer system, programs, and data. The entity may restrict access through a combination of access controls applied at various levels.

4. *Computer operations*: controls designed to ensure that data is processed to the correct file, recovery from processing failures is possible, and programs are properly scheduled, set up, and executed.

(c) Specific Control Objectives: An Example

Conceptually, the seven control objectives described above fit every entity and apply to all transactions into which it enters (and the related files and assets), regardless of the specific control activities established to achieve them. In practice, however, auditors usually consider control objectives only as they apply to major classes of transactions, such as sales, purchases, cash receipts, and cash disbursements. Those are generally the high-volume transactions within transaction cycles. In addition, certain entities may enter into other high-volume transactions, depending on the nature of their business.

In applying the seven control objectives described earlier to a class of transactions, the auditor develops control objectives tailored to the specific class of transactions. As an example, Figure 9.2 identifies the control objectives for credit sales transactions processed by computer in the revenue cycle.

Figure 9.2   Control Objectives for Credit Sales Transactions

Control Objective	Specific Control Objective for Credit Sales Transactions in a Computerized Accounting System
Authorization	All recorded sales transactions represent actual shipments of goods or rendering of services to nonfictitious customers of the entity and are approved by responsible personnel.
Completeness of input	All credit sales transactions are input and accepted for processing.
Accuracy of input	Sales are correctly recorded as to amounts, quantities, dates, and customers in the proper period; are accurately converted into computer-readable form; and are accurately input to the computer.
Integrity of standing data	All changes to the selling price master file and the customer master file are authorized and input accurately and completely.
Completeness and accuracy of update	The sales and accounts receivable data files are accurately updated by all sales transaction data input and accepted for processing.
Completeness and accuracy of accumulated data	Data in the accounts receivable subsidiary ledgers and the general ledger control account remains correct until authorized changes in the data are made.
Asset protection	Only authorized personnel have access to accounts receivable records and other data stored on files; the same employee does not receive cash and also record the receipts.

9.4   RELATIONSHIP BETWEEN CONTROL RISK AND THE ACHIEVEMENT OF AUDIT OBJECTIVES

As discussed earlier in this chapter, the auditor assesses control risk to determine the acceptable level of detection risk for the various audit objectives with respect to the account balances in the entity's financial statements. While the auditor may assess control risk at the maximum level for some audit objectives, often it is possible to assess control risk below the maximum or at low for certain audit objectives by performing tests that provide evidence that controls are operating effectively. (The term *below the maximum* is used in this book to refer to a range of assessments lower than maximum, but not *low*.) The auditor then can limit the substantive tests applied to account balances for those audit objectives. For example, if the auditor is satisfied, based on the results of tests performed in assessing control risk for the revenue cycle, that control activities related to sales transactions are adequate to ensure that all authorized shipments of products, and only authorized shipments, are accurately billed and recorded, the auditor can reduce substantive tests related to the completeness, accuracy, and existence/occurrence of sales and the related charges to accounts receivable.

As a practical matter, in determining the assurance needed from substantive tests directed at the completeness, accuracy, and existence/occurrence objectives (and sometimes the cutoff and valuation objectives) for particular account balances, the auditor considers the *overall* assessment of control risk for the relevant class of transactions or transaction cycle—not *individual* control objectives. To the extent that the auditor concludes that one or more control objectives are not being met for a class of transactions or transaction cycle, he or she will not have assurance that the audit objectives of completeness, accuracy, and existence/occurrence of related account balances have been met. (If the auditor does not have evidence of effective control activities that address cutoffs and accounting estimates, he or she also will have no assurance that the cutoff and valuation objectives have been achieved.) In practice, the auditor determines what could go wrong in processing specific transactions or in their maintenance on files as a result of an absent or ineffective control activity (i.e., a control objective not being achieved); considers how that could affect the completeness, accuracy, and existence/occurrence (and, to a lesser extent, cutoff and valuation) objectives; and then designs and performs substantive tests to detect possible financial statement misstatements that could arise as a result of the control deficiency.

If a control objective at a particular stage of processing is not achieved, the data generated at that and subsequent stages of processing, as well as information derived from the data, may not be reliable in one or more respects. It may reflect events and transactions that did not occur, it may be incomplete, it may be mathematically inaccurate, or it may reflect assets or liabilities that do not exist. The auditor needs to consider the control objectives of authorization, completeness of input, and accuracy of input whenever data is entered into the system, and whether the absence of control activities designed to address the control objectives relating to the maintenance of files (integrity of standing data, completeness and accuracy of update, and completeness and accuracy of accumulated data) at each stage of processing could result in a material financial statement misstatement. Accordingly, it is not sufficient simply to identify and test one or more control activities somewhere in the system related to a particular control objective. Absent or ineffective control activities relating to updating or to accumulated data at any stage of processing could result in a financial statement misstatement.

Control activities to ensure completeness of input may have an especially significant effect on the conduct of an audit. Auditors often find it particularly difficult to obtain sufficient evidence regarding the completeness of transaction recording. Because the control objectives of accuracy of input and authorization are concerned mainly with *recorded* transactions and balances, the auditor usually can obtain sufficient evidence about their accuracy and occurrence or existence, even if control activities are inadequate, by performing substantive tests of those balances or of the underlying transactions, such as examining supporting documentation and reperforming accounting procedures.

When assessing the completeness of transaction processing and the resultant accounting records, however, the auditor is concerned with the possibility of *unrecorded* transactions, for which there is usually no evidence. For instance, if prenumbered documents are used to record transactions, the auditor can account for the numerical sequence of documents and thus obtain evidence that all transactions for which a prenumbered document was prepared have been recorded. However, this will not detect unrecorded transactions if documents were not prepared for all transactions. The auditor should therefore pay particular attention to control activities designed to ensure that all transactions are recorded on a document, for example, a requirement that a shipping document be prepared before a storeroom clerk releases merchandise for shipment.

As discussed in earlier chapters of this book, usually an auditor has to rely on evidence that is persuasive rather than conclusive. This is particularly true for evidence supporting the completeness of recording of transactions that have occurred. In most instances, persuasive evidence about completeness can be obtained, but in extreme circumstances where completeness control activities are absent or particularly ineffective, the auditor should question the auditability of the accounting records. Not all classes of transactions of a particular entity may be auditable; at the extreme, the significance of unauditable classes of transactions may be so great as to make the entity as a whole unauditable.

The absence of adequate control activities to protect assets and records affects the timing and extent of substantive tests. For example, the absence of adequate control activities to limit physical access to inventories may mean that a complete inventory count must be performed at the balance sheet date, even if other control activities applied to the inventory records are adequate. This is because, in the absence of control activities to protect the inventory, the auditor would have no assurance that unrecorded additions or deletions—whether approved or not—did not occur in the period between an interim count date and year-end.

9.5   MANAGEMENT'S RESPONSIBILITY FOR INTERNAL CONTROL UNDER THE FOREIGN CORRUPT PRACTICES ACT

Changes in the business and legal environment, in particular the Foreign Corrupt Practices Act of 1977 (the Act), have magnified the importance of internal control to management. The Act, which amended the Securities Exchange Act of 1934, has two parts: One deals with specific acts and penalties associated with certain corrupt practices; the second, with standards relating to internal accounting controls (i.e., control activities).

(a) Illegal Payments

The Act prohibits any domestic company—or its officers, directors, employees, agents, or stockholders—from paying or offering to pay a foreign official to obtain, retain, or direct business to any person, except for payments made to expedite a routine governmental action. Specifically, the law prohibits payments to foreign officials, political parties, and candidates for the purpose of obtaining or retaining business by influencing any act or decision of foreign parties in their official capacity, or by inducing such foreign parties to use their influence with a foreign government to sway any act or decision of such government. This section of the Act applies to virtually all U.S. businesses, and noncompliance with its provisions, as amended in 1988, can result in fines of up to $2 million for corporations and up to $100,000 for individuals who willfully participate in the bribery of a foreign official. Violators also may be subject to imprisonment for up to five years.

(b) Internal Accounting Control

The section of the Act that addresses internal accounting control imposes additional legal obligations on publicly held companies. Failure by such companies to maintain appropriate books and records and internal accounting controls violates the Securities Exchange Act of 1934. In addition, the 1988 amendments to the Act imposed criminal liability for failing to comply with the internal accounting control provisions if an individual knowingly circumvents or knowingly fails to implement a system of internal accounting controls or knowingly falsifies any book, record, or account.

Specifically, the Foreign Corrupt Practices Act establishes a legal requirement that every SEC registrant:

(A) Make and keep books, records and accounts, which, in reasonable detail, accurately and fairly reflect the transactions and dispositions of the assets of the issuer; and

(B) Devise and maintain a system of internal accounting controls sufficient to provide reasonable assurances that the following four objectives are met:

   (i) transactions are executed in accordance with management's general or specific authorization;

   (ii) transactions are recorded as necessary (I) to permit preparation of financial statements in conformity with generally accepted accounting principles or any other criteria applicable to such statements, and (II) to maintain accountability for assets;

   (iii) access to assets is permitted only in accordance with management's general or specific authorization; and

   (iv) the recorded accountability for assets is compared with the existing assets at reasonable intervals and appropriate action is taken with respect to any differences.

The requirements in (B) are compatible with the control objectives discussed earlier in this chapter. [The language dealing with internal accounting control was taken directly from the relevant authoritative auditing literature (AU Section 320) in effect when the Act was drafted. AU Section 320 was superseded by SAS No. 55, subsequently amended by SAS No. 78.] The 1988 amendments to the Act clarified the terms *reasonable detail* and *reasonable assurances* by describing them as the level of detail and degree of assurance that would satisfy prudent officials in the conduct of their own affairs.

It is clear from the legislative history of the Act that Congress' primary intent was to prevent corrupt payments to foreign officials, and that the requirements for accurate books and records and for internal accounting controls were intended mainly to help accomplish that objective. But those requirements are considerably more extensive, since they cover all transactions, not only those related to illegal foreign payments. The SEC has enforced these provisions of the law in connection with domestic improprieties as well as with illegal foreign payments.

While the Act has necessitated more direct management involvement in designing and maintaining internal control, it does not specifically affect the auditor's responsibility. The auditor's responsibility with respect to internal control remains as prescribed by the second standard of field work in AU Section 319. This was explicitly articulated in an AICPA interpretation dealing with illegal acts by clients, which noted that the Foreign Corrupt Practices Act created new responsibilities for *companies* subject to the Securities Exchange Act of 1934, but not for their *auditors*.

9.6 FEDERAL SENTENCING GUIDELINES FOR ORGANIZATIONS

In late 1991, the United States Sentencing Commission issued Federal Sentencing Guidelines (the Guidelines) for judges to use in sentencing organizations convicted for crimes committed by their employees and agents, even if the organization was unaware of, or did not approve, an illegal act. The Guidelines affect all organizations and cover violations of federal employment, antitrust, securities, and contract laws, as well as crimes such as wire and mail fraud, commercial bribery, money laundering, and kickbacks.

Under the Guidelines, guilty organizations face fines that can reach hundreds of millions of dollars, depending on the severity of the crime and the culpability of the organization. Fines can be greatly reduced, however, if the organization shows that it had established an "effective program to prevent and detect violations of law" prior to the occurrence of an illegal act. A business is considered to have an effective program if it has exercised due diligence in seeking to prevent and detect criminal conduct. The Guidelines list the following seven steps that demonstrate the exercise of due diligence by an organization:

1. Establishing compliance standards and procedures for employees and other agents that are reasonably capable of reducing the potential of criminal conduct

2. Assigning to specific, high-level individual(s) within the organization the over-all responsibility for overseeing compliance with the established standards and procedures

3. Using due care not to delegate substantial discretionary authority to individuals whom the organization knows (or should know) have a propensity to engage in illegal activities

4. Taking steps to communicate the compliance standards and procedures effectively to all employees and agents (e.g., by requiring participation in training programs and by disseminating publications that explain in a practical manner what is required)

5. Taking reasonable steps to achieve compliance with these standards. These steps may include the use of monitoring or auditing systems designed to detect criminal conduct and implementing and publicizing a reporting system for employees and agents to report criminal conduct by others within the organization without fear of retribution

6. Enforcing the standards consistently through appropriate disciplinary mechanisms, including, as appropriate, discipline of individuals responsible for the failure to detect an offense

7. Taking all reasonable steps, after the detection of an offense, to respond appropriately and to prevent similar offenses in the future

These steps include many of the controls described earlier in this chapter and discussed in greater detail in the COSO Report. That report, with its guidance on evaluating an organization's compliance with relevant laws and regulations, can provide an appropriate methodology for determining whether an organization has an effective program to prevent and detect violations of law.

10

Understanding Entity-Level Controls

Controls that are relevant to financial reporting are applied at various levels in an entity. Controls in some components, such as the control environment, operate at a high level within an entity and thus have an impact on many or all account balances. Other controls are applied at successively lower levels and relate to increasingly more detailed processes and activities. Some of those controls are applied to a cycle or an entire class of transactions in a cycle, and have an effect on the account balances derived from related transactions. Others, specifically control activities, operate at even lower, more detailed levels and tend to be focused on individual applications within transaction cycles and to affect specific account balances and audit objectives. The latter controls are most relevant when the auditor plans to assess control risk at low. Understanding the entity-level aspects of internal control is discussed in this chapter, and understanding control activities and aspects of monitoring that relate to a cycle or transactions in a cycle in Chapter 11 (see Section 11.3, Developing the Understanding). Chapter 12 covers assessing control risk and testing controls, at all levels, to confirm the assessment (see Section 12.5, Documenting the Assessment of Control Risk and Tests of Controls).

Figure 10.1 depicts the process by which the auditor obtains an understanding of internal control and assesses control risk. The flowchart shows the various decisions the auditor makes and their consequences for the audit strategy. The steps in the flowchart are explained in the following sections of this chapter and in Chapters 11 and 12.

10.1 · DEVELOPING THE UNDERSTANDING

The second standard of field work specifically requires the auditor to obtain a sufficient understanding of the entity's internal control for planning purposes. A sufficient understanding of internal control is one that when considered together with other information about the entity, such as that from prior years' experience, enables the auditor to evaluate whether controls are effectively designed, identify misstatements that could occur because of any design deficiencies, consider the risk of such misstatements occurring, and design appropriate substantive tests to detect them. Statement on Auditing Standards (SAS) No. 78, *Consideration of Internal Control in a Financial Statement Audit: An Amendment of SAS No. 55* (AU Section 319), points out that while internal control is relevant to both the entity as a whole and its individual operating units or business functions, it may not be necessary for the auditor to obtain an understanding of internal control related to each of the entity's operating units or business functions. An audit guide to the SAS, *Consideration of Internal Control in a Financial Statement Audit*, issued by the AICPA's Control Risk Audit Guide Revision Task Force illustrates how auditors might apply the provisions of the SAS in determining an audit strategy that might be used for entities of various sizes, including obtaining the necessary understanding of internal control.

Meeting the second standard of field work requires the auditor to develop an understanding of relevant controls in the various components, regardless of the planned control risk assessment. It may not be necessary for the auditor to understand control activities when control risk is assessed at maximum or below the maximum, because in those circumstances no tests of control activities will be performed. The auditor should, however, consider whether an understanding of any specific control activities is necessary in order to design substantive tests.

Figure 10.1   Understanding Internal Control and Its Audit Implications

UNDERSTAND ENTITY-LEVEL CONTROL COMPONENTS:

1. Control Environment
2. Management's Risk Assessment
3. Information and Communication
4. Monitoring[a]

UNDERSTAND ACCOUNTING SYSTEM AND COMPUTER ENVIRONMENT

EVALUATE EFFECTIVENESS OF DESIGN

MAKE PRELIMINARY ASSESSMENT OF CONTROL RISK

Maximum control risk	Below the maximum control risk	Low control risk
No further understanding needed	Obtain understanding of activity-level monitoring controls; evaluate effectiveness of design	Obtain understanding of control activities; evaluate effectiveness of design
No tests of controls performed	Test entity-level controls and activity-level monitoring controls to confirm assessment[b]	Test entity-level controls and control activities to confirm assessment[b]
Design substantive tests to gain high assurance	Design substantive tests to gain moderate assurance	Design substantive tests to gain low assurance

[a] Includes performance reviews, which are classified as control activities in SAS No. 78. See footnote 2 in Chapter 11.

[b] On recurring engagements, certain tests of controls may be performed at the same time as updating the understanding, based on the planned assessment of control risk.

In developing the understanding of internal control, the auditor determines the *design* of relevant controls, that is, how they are supposed to operate, and whether they have been *placed in operation*, that is, whether the entity is actually using them. The auditor's objective in understanding controls is not to obtain evidence about whether they are *operating* effectively; evidence about the effective operation of controls is obtained by testing the controls, which is discussed in Chapter 12 (see Section 12.3, Performing Tests of Controls). Often, however, the auditor obtains some evidence about operating effectiveness as a result of performing procedures aimed at developing the understanding, because those procedures are similar to procedures used in testing controls. The auditor considers that evidence when determining the tests of controls to perform in order to be able to restrict substantive tests directed at certain audit objectives and account balances.

The understanding of internal control required for audit planning (that is, for identifying and reacting to the risk of material misstatements) is obtained by considering previous experience with the entity, reviewing prior-year audit results, making inquiries of entity personnel and observing them in the performance of their duties, and examining descriptions of procedures and other appropriate documentation prepared by the entity's personnel. As explained in Chapter 6, observation involves direct viewing of employees in the work environment. Inquiry (interviewing) entails asking specific questions of the entity's management and employees, which may be done informally or in formal interviews. Interviewing is one of the most effective ways to gain an initial understanding of the entity's internal control. The auditor examines records (either manual or electronic), documents, reconciliations, and reports for evidence that a procedure has been properly applied. The specific procedures the auditor performs to obtain the necessary understanding of internal control, and the extent to which they are performed on a particular audit, vary according to the entity's size and complexity, the auditor's previous experience with the entity, the particular control, and the entity's documentation.

Reviewing prior years' audit results can help the auditor determine the likelihood of material misstatements in account balances in the current year. For example, if the control environment was found to be effective in prior years and there have been no changes in the people and procedures that generate information management uses to monitor business processes, the auditor should consider this when planning substantive tests of accounts requiring management estimates and judgments.

As a result of prior years' experience with the entity, the auditor usually has some idea, before beginning to update the understanding of internal control, of the level at which control risk will be assessed in the current audit. In some cases, the nature and extent of procedures performed in updating the understanding may be affected by the control risk assessment at which the auditor expects to arrive. For example, if the auditor expects to test controls to be able to assess control risk at low for certain account balances, he or she may perform more procedures and document the results more thoroughly in updating the understanding than if he or she expects to not test controls and assess control risk at maximum.

(a) Control Environment

An entity's management can foster an environment that encourages control consciousness on the part of employees and contributes to the quality of the other components of internal control. Such a control environment "has a pervasive influence on the way [an entity's] business activities are structured, objectives established and risks assessed. It also influences control activities, information and communication systems, and monitoring activities."[1] AU Section 319 describes the control environment as the foundation for all other components of internal control and states that it may either mitigate the risk of fraud by management or, conversely, reduce the effectiveness of the other components.

Knowledge about the control environment enables the auditor to determine (1) whether it appears to be conducive to maintaining effective internal control, and (2) whether it minimizes the incentives and opportunities for management to deliberately distort the financial statements. Understanding the control environment also

---

[1] *Internal Control—Integrated Framework* (New York: Committee of Sponsoring Organizations of the Treadway Commission, 1992), Framework volume, p. 19.

gives the auditor an indication of management's and the board of directors' attitudes toward control and their approach to directing the business. In developing the understanding, the auditor should consider the controls management establishes, as well as whether management's actions demonstrate adherence to the substance of those controls.

Various factors that contribute to an entity's control environment can have a pervasive effect on the management assertions underlying the financial statements. These factors typically include:

- Management's integrity and ethical values
- The entity's commitment to competence
- The composition and activities of the board of directors or audit committee
- Management's philosophy and operating style
- The organizational structure
- The assignment of authority and responsibility
- Human resource policies and practices

The following paragraphs discuss each of these factors and indicate their relevance to the audit.

(i) Integrity and Ethical Values. Management's integrity and ethical values are a primary element of the control environment and have a pervasive effect on the other control components. If management establishes ethical standards, communicates them within the entity, and reinforces them by its own example, it will establish an environment that is conducive to ethical behavior. In such an environment, personnel will be less likely to engage in dishonest or illegal acts, especially if management removes or reduces incentives to do so. Management's integrity and ethical values may be indirectly reflected in events such as frequent turnover of operating management personnel, possibly resulting from senior management's overemphasis on unreasonable operating or financial goals, for example, making a significant portion of operating management's compensation contingent on meeting those goals. This type of pressure to meet unreasonable expectations also may encourage management to intentionally misstate financial information.

Management's attitude regarding standards of ethical behavior is reflected in its establishment and enforcement of a formal or informal code of conduct. By demonstrating its own compliance with this code, management sets an example for employees to follow. Management further communicates its expectations by the way it monitors employees' behavior and reacts to violations of the code.

(ii) Commitment to Competence. For an entity to have an effective control environment, employees must have the knowledge and skills needed to carry out their job responsibilities. If they do not have the competence required to understand what is expected of them and to do it capably, they will make mistakes that may lead to out-of-control situations. Management should be committed to recruiting and retaining employees capable of performing at the requisite level of competence and to providing appropriate training.

(iii) Composition and Activities of the Board of Directors and Committees. The effectiveness of the board of directors and committees, especially the audit committee, is an important factor in the control environment. The more effective the board and audit committee are in overseeing the entity's accounting and financial reporting policies and practices, the less likely management is to have the opportunity to misappropriate resources, involve the entity in illegal acts, subject the entity or its assets to inordinate risk, or materially misstate financial information. The effectiveness of the board of directors and audit committee is influenced by whether board members are independent from management, how frequently the board and the audit committee hold meetings, and how well they analyze relevant accounting and financial information and raise difficult questions with management. In addition, the presence of an audit committee that fosters a direct line of communication between the board and the external and internal auditors is a further indication that the board of directors is monitoring management appropriately.

(iv) Management's Philosophy and Operating Style. Management expresses its philosophy and operating style through its attitudes toward a broad range of matters, including taking and monitoring business risks, reporting financial information, how conservative or aggressive it is in selecting accounting principles from among acceptable alternatives, its approach to developing accounting estimates, and its attitude toward the information processing and accounting functions. If management is dominated by one or a few individuals, their philosophy and operating style are likely to have a particularly significant influence on the control environment.

How candidly management discusses matters with the auditor, whether management previously has tried to materially misstate financial information, and whether there are frequent disputes over the application of accounting principles are other direct indications of management's philosophy and operating style.

The attitudes and attributes of management that characterize its philosophy and operating style have a significant impact on both the entity's ability to maintain effective control and the likelihood of attempts by management to deliberately distort the financial statements. Accordingly, the auditor needs to identify and understand those attitudes and attributes. Because they are subjective, it may take more judgment and experience on the part of the auditor to understand them than any of the other factors.

(v) Organizational Structure. All business entities have an organizational structure within which their operations are planned, executed, controlled, and monitored. Defining key areas of responsibility and establishing appropriate lines of reporting are significant aspects of the organizational structure. For example, the director of internal audit should report to a higher level of authority than the individuals responsible for the areas under audit. Without the appropriate line of reporting, the internal audit department's work, including recommendations for corrective action, may lack objectivity. In addition, the organizational structure should indicate a separation of responsibilities among employees so that an individual is not in a position to both commit and conceal errors or fraud.

(vi) Assignment of Authority and Responsibility.   To ensure that the activities of the business are properly carried out, individuals within the entity must have an adequate understanding of the entity's objectives and of their authority and responsibilities for meeting those objectives. Adequately communicating expectations to personnel and monitoring their achievement help to ensure that the business will be run properly. Policies governing the delegation of authority, responsibilities, and reporting relationships must be effectively communicated to employees.

Considering whether the methods used to assign and communicate authority and responsibilities, including ethical responsibilities, are appropriate will help the auditor judge whether personnel understand their responsibilities and therefore can be expected to carry them out properly. If management does not effectively communicate its expectations, employees may not comply with controls.

(vii) Human Resource Policies and Practices.   To operate effectively, the entity needs appropriate policies and procedures for hiring, training, supervising, and evaluating employees to ensure that they have sufficient knowledge and experience to carry out their assigned responsibilities. There must be a sufficient number of employees and the employees must have adequate equipment. The entity's human resource policies and practices should be directed toward achieving those goals. For example, the proper functioning of computer operations and processing depends on personnel with appropriate skills and on adequate computer equipment to meet the entity's processing needs. Training should include communication of roles and responsibilities, which often is accomplished through training sessions and seminars. Basing promotions on performance appraisals reinforces the entity's commitment to rewarding employees' performance.

If the auditor concludes that the entity's human resource policies and practices appear to be adequate, the personnel who operate the accounting system and perform control activities are likely to be competent. That, in turn, reduces the likelihood that financial information will contain misstatements.

(b) Management's Risk Assessment

All entities face a variety of risks by being in business, requiring management to determine how much risk should be accepted and to take steps to maintain risk within these levels. In assessing risks, management is concerned with risks to all of the entity's objectives. In the narrower context of financial reporting objectives, risk assessment entails management's identification, analysis, and handling of risks that affect the entity's ability to record, process, summarize, and report financial data consistent with management's assertions in the financial statements. This process of management's risk assessment should be distinguished from the auditor's assessment of the risk of issuing an inappropriate opinion on the entity's financial statements.

The auditor's understanding of the entity's risk assessment should encompass management's process for dealing with risks related to financial reporting objectives. This entails how management estimates the significance of various risks, evaluates the likelihood that they will occur, and determines the actions to address them. In some circumstances, management may not take action to address an identified risk, but may decide to accept the risk because the cost of avoiding it is disproportionately high or for other reasons. As a practical matter, auditors generally consider management's risk assessment relating to financial reporting objectives in conjunction with obtaining or updating the understanding of the control activities that management has established to address the risks it has identified. The auditor's understanding of control activities is discussed in Chapter 11.

Risks that threaten an entity's ability to achieve its objectives come from a variety of sources, both external and internal, such as:

Changes in the Regulatory and Operating Environment: changes in the regulations to which the entity is subject or in its operating environment can expose it to new and different risks, including those that result from increased competition and pressure to contain costs.

New Personnel: new personnel who are responsible for aspects of internal control may have different views about how to establish and implement controls. In effecting changes to bring the controls in line with their views, they may fail to understand the reasons for certain old policies and procedures and may eliminate them, thereby opening the entity to risks that it previously addressed. Also, new employees may not understand procedures fully and consequently may not comply with them effectively.

New or Changed Information Systems: controls that were designed to be carried out in the presence of a particular information system and that were effective under that system may no longer be effective if the system is replaced or significantly revised. If management continues to rely on them to meet its information needs, erroneous data could be produced.

Rapid Growth: rapidly expanding operations may outstrip the ability of controls to keep pace, resulting in an increased risk of situations slipping out of control.

New Technology: new technologies introduced into the entity's production processes or information systems may call for different controls. If this is not recognized and controls are not redesigned to fit the new technology, the systems may generate errors and fail to detect them.

New Lines, Products, or Activities: if an entity begins doing business in new areas or enters into transactions with which it is unfamiliar, its controls may no longer be effective and may need to be changed.

Corporate Restructurings: corporate restructurings may entail cutbacks in staff and changes in how employees are supervised. They also may result in changes in work assignments and thus affect the segregation of duties between employees, which could invalidate the effectiveness of other controls.

Foreign Operations: the risks associated with foreign operations often differ from those of domestic operations. Entering into or expanding foreign operations may create new risks that existing controls do not address adequately.

Accounting Pronouncements: management's adoption of new accounting principles or changes in accounting principles may present risks affecting the reliability of financial reporting.

(c)   Monitoring

Business processes are dynamic, changing, sometimes rapidly and at other times more moderately, in reaction to market and other economic conditions. An entity makes decisions continually that affect its internal control. It may enter into new types of transactions, hire different people, and set new objectives for the business. Controls that were designed for a particular set of circumstances may no longer be appropriate if those circumstances change. Even without major changes, the effectiveness with which controls are applied may deteriorate over time. For these reasons, internal control requires monitoring to ensure that it continues to operate in accordance with management's objectives and expectations. The auditor needs to understand sufficiently how management oversees, or monitors, controls relating to financial reporting, including the system for implementing corrective actions in response to problems or other situations.

Monitoring is the process by which management assesses the design and operation of the other control components to determine that they continue to be appropriate for the entity's risks. It also entails acting to address any problems noted. Monitoring activities may be either ongoing, such as regular management and supervisory activities designed to oversee whether the entity's financial reporting control objectives are being achieved, and reliable financial information is thereby being produced, or periodic, such as an evaluation made for the specific purpose of assessing the effectiveness of controls.

Ongoing aspects of monitoring may be exercised at the entity level or the cycle or transaction level. The latter monitoring controls are discussed in Chapter 11 (see Section 11.2, Monitoring Controls) in conjunction with control activities, to which they are closely related. As explained in that chapter, some of these monitoring controls are designed to ensure that control activities operate effectively. Others, while not established primarily for that purpose, indirectly contribute to that objective. At the entity level, senior management monitors the business by reviewing reports of divisional and subsidiary operations and taking actions needed to meet the entity's financial reporting objectives.

Internal auditors or other personnel who perform similar functions contribute to the monitoring process on a periodic basis. Their activities focus on the design and operation of controls, and they identify deficiencies in controls and recommend improvements. Outside parties that deal with an entity also contribute to its monitoring function to some extent. For instance, customers who question amounts billed to them or regulators that furnish feedback based on their oversight activities provide information that management uses in monitoring an entity's internal control.

(d)   Information and Communication

All active businesses have some form of information system to identify and control the flow of data relating to transactions and resources in a way that enables personnel to carry out their roles and responsibilities. An entity's information system consists of the various means used to transmit, process, maintain, and access both data related to the transactions it generates and the activities, such as production processes, in which it engages, and information about external events, such as economic information relating to changing demands of the marketplace, materials used in the entity's operations, the competitive environment, and legislative and regulatory initiatives.

For internal control to be effective, individuals must have a clear understanding of their roles and responsibilities. That includes knowledge of how their activities relate to activities others perform and the chain of command for reporting exceptions. Open lines of communication are needed if exceptions are to be reported appropriately and acted upon effectively. Management communicates information through policy manuals, accounting and financial reporting procedures manuals, and other written directives. Communication also can be oral and by example.

The accounting system is a major part of the information system and consists of the methods and records used to record, process, summarize, and report transactions and other events and circumstances and to maintain accountability for related assets and liabilities. The accounting system is the part of the information system that functions at the level of specific activities and relates most directly to the entity's financial reporting objectives. In those respects, it is closely related to control activities, which are discussed in Chapter 11. This discussion of the accounting system is presented in this chapter, however, to emphasize that the accounting system is part of the information and communication component, and that an understanding of the accounting system is required for planning purposes on all audits, regardless of the assessment of control risk.

(i) The Accounting System.   Accounting systems often are integrated with other information systems. These types of systems generate information used for both accounting and management decision-making purposes. An example is an accounting system that generates both cost accounting information used for product pricing and external financial reporting, and an information system to provide executives with related data for internal financial and operational decision-making purposes.

An effective accounting system includes appropriate methods and records to:

1. Identify and record all authorized transactions
2. Describe each transaction on a timely basis and in sufficient detail to classify it properly for financial reporting
3. Measure the monetary value of the transaction so that it can be recorded in the financial statements
4. Determine when the transaction occurred, to ensure that it is recorded in the proper accounting period
5. Present the transaction and related disclosures properly in the financial statements

Virtually all accounting systems are computerized, but in varying degrees. In many systems, computers execute most accounting procedures, but certain procedures are performed manually, particularly the initiation of transactions, which may take place at locations where terminals are not available. In some systems, all accounting procedures are computerized, including the generation of transactions. Examples of computer-generated transactions include standard month-end journal entries (and appropriate reversing entries in the subsequent month) and the payment of recurring operating expenditures (such as rents and royalties). Computerized accounting procedures are referred to as *programmed accounting procedures.* As discussed in Chapter 11 (see Section 11.1, Control Activities), control activities that often are an integral part of the accounting system also consist of both programmed and manual procedures.

While almost all businesses use computerized systems, they may limit the use of such systems to processing transactions that are part of a cycle. As described in Chapter 9 (see Section 9.3, Transaction Cycles and Control Objectives), a cycle is made up of classes of similar transactions that an entity enters into in large numbers in operating its business, making it practical to automate their processing. Most often, entities purchase packaged systems for common applications, such as sales and accounts receivable, purchases and accounts payable, and payroll processing, if the volume of transactions is high enough to warrant using such systems. Some entities, particularly very large ones, may develop their own programs for those and other, specialized applications. Many entities do not have computerized systems for processing less common transactions, and process them manually. For example, an entity, such as a museum, whose principal revenue is from cash sales of admissions, might use a computerized system for those revenues, but might not computerize the processing of occasional revenue transactions, such as sales of equipment or the receipt of pledges, that result in receivables. The discussion of accounting systems in this chapter assumes the use of computerized systems (which may include certain manual functions) for an entity's major, recurring transactions. It also recognizes that unusual or infrequently occurring transactions are likely to be processed manually.

Two principal types of data are used by the accounting system: *standing data* (also called *master file data*) and *transaction data*. Standing data is data of a permanent or semipermanent nature used repeatedly during processing. This type of data includes rates of pay used to calculate salaries and customer credit limits used to decide whether to accept customer orders. Transaction data is data that relates to an individual transaction, such as the number of hours a particular employee works in a particular week, which is used to calculate that person's salary. Errors in standing data are likely to be of greater significance than errors in transaction data because errors in standing data will affect many transactions until they are corrected. In most systems, standing data is reviewed only when originally set up on files and not each time it is used.

Conceptually, the accounting system is separate from control activities, which are discussed in Chapter 11 (see Section 11.1, Control Activities). However, it generally is not practical to separate the contribution of the accounting system toward achieving the financial reporting control objectives (described in Chapter 9, Section 9.3, Transaction Cycles and Control Objectives) from that of the control activities that are applied to the transactions that flow through the accounting system. That is because the appropriateness of control activities depends on the attributes of the accounting system, such as the means of processing transactions, the volume of transactions, and the level of the system's sophistication. A simple accounting system and a sophisticated one may both contribute toward meeting the entity's control objectives, if the controls each system applies to transactions processed are appropriate to that system.

For example, in an accounting system for processing sales invoices, control activities to achieve completeness of input for sales and accounts receivable generally might include computer matching of computer-generated shipping documents to an outstanding sales order file and sales transaction file, the generation of an exception report by the computer if there are mismatches, and appropriate investigation and follow-up. In a system where manual procedures are performed before transactions are entered into the computer, such as where shipments are recorded manually on shipping documents from which invoices subsequently are prepared, the same objective might be met by prenumbering the shipping documents and accounting for their numerical sequence, with investigation and follow-up of missing or unmatched items. The attributes of the accounting system, particularly the extent to which it is computerized, determine the appropriateness of the control activities in each instance. Control activities are discussed in Chapter 11.

(ii) The Computer Environment.   Computerized systems and their configurations, along with the way that the computer function is organized, constitute the *computer environment*, also frequently called the *information technology* (IT) *environment*. Computer environments vary widely from one entity to another. Even when the same type of computers from the same vendor are used, there is an almost infinite variety of combinations of types of peripheral devices, software options, telecommunications networks, and application software.

The computer environment is a major factor in the entity's transaction processing. Early systems printed out all of the results of processing, so that the auditor frequently obtained detailed printouts (hardcopy) that included the calculations performed, data used, and all exceptions and rejections, and then reperformed the programmed accounting procedures to gain evidence of the accuracy of computer-generated data. Since this in essence bypassed the computer, it was called "auditing around the computer." Today, auditing this way is close to impossible because of the large volume of transactions and the number of locations where processing may take place. Modern systems rarely print out calculations in detail, and many systems do not have hardcopy source documents and do not generate all output in hardcopy form.

The usual method of conducting an audit today is to use the computer to test computer controls or to use software to test programmed accounting and control procedures. Originally called "auditing through the computer," this technique is essential in modern processing systems. It entails audit strategy decisions about whether and to what extent to test controls, and about the nature, timing, and extent of substantive tests of computer-generated data. In addition, the auditor can use computer software to perform many tests that would be too time-consuming and perhaps not even possible to do manually, which is referred to as "auditing with the computer."

The auditor needs an understanding of key computer applications (including whether they are developed in-house or purchased), the hardware and software used to process financially significant transactions, and the implications of that information for the audit. The auditor also needs to understand the organization of the IT function. All of this information serves as a basis for ascertaining the likelihood that the entity has appropriate computer controls and determining whether audit software can be used.

(1) Hardware.   Computers basically consist of a central processing unit (CPU), internal storage (memory) and external storage, input/output devices, and other peripheral

equipment. External storage can be on magnetic tape, disk, or optical disk (CD-ROM). Input/output devices consist mainly of terminals with screens and keyboards, and printers for hardcopy output. Other input devices include scanners, wireless hand-held units (commonly used by package delivery systems), barcode readers, point-of-sale registers, optical character readers, mark sense readers, and light guns.

Other peripheral equipment includes telecommunications devices such as modems, which translate digital computer signals into analog form for transmission over phone lines and re-translate them at the other end. (Totally digital networks preclude the need for modems, since the data is transmitted and received digitally.) Other devices include bridges, routers, multiplexors, and controllers, which handle complex communications requirements, directing information to the appropriate part of the system or computer.

(2) Software.   The programs that run the system and direct its operations are collectively called *system software*. System software includes the operating system, which directs internal operations and makes it possible for specific application software programs to run. Among other components of system software are utilities (which include report generators and powerful editors used to write or change programs and data on file), telecommunications software, file and program access control software, and database management systems.

Originally, almost all application software was written in-house, created specifically for each application program, such as accounts receivable or payroll, to accomplish particular tasks. Some entities, particularly large ones, still develop custom-designed applications in-house, depending on how specialized their processing needs are. Such applications are developed by system analysts and programmers, who should follow a standard system development methodology intended to ensure that applications are appropriate, adequately controlled, and completed on time and within budget, and meet management and user needs.

Because developing system software is expensive and time-consuming, vendors have designed standard applications, referred to as purchased systems or packaged software. Most entities use packages as an alternative to developing their own software. Depending on the vendor, purchased systems are available with or without *source code*, which is the instructions written in high-level languages that programmers use. Source code needs to be "compiled" or translated into machine language or *object code* modules (the 0s and 1s of binary digits) and linked (i.e., strung together to form a complete load module, ready for processing) by link-editors so that the computer can execute it. If the vendor does not make the source code available to users, they cannot easily make changes to the programs.

Users can, however, change some program functions through other methods, such as selecting from among various options or employing "user exits," which allow the insertion of user programming in certain locations. Options are customizing features that vendors include to make their systems more efficient by allowing users to tailor the software to their own needs without having to rewrite it. The use of options, along with other types of flexibility built into purchased applications, is now so extensive that some application packages are referred to as "environments" and in effect provide each user with a customized application.

Applications may be processed by a number of computers linked in local area networks (LANs) and in wide area networks (WANs). These systems are referred to as client/server application packages. Users have client computers, usually PCs or notebooks, which make requests for processing. The servers, which are often powerful workstations, accept those requests and direct them to the appropriate system or computer for processing. In some cases processing is totally local; in others it is spread across several locations. Since the applications are split into various modules that are distributed across many computers, the user does not know where the processing actually takes place.

(3) Database Management Systems.   Database management systems (DBMSs) eliminate much of the redundancy of data that exists when each program requires its own file structure. In a standard file structure, each program has data available to it in files designed specifically for that program. (A file consists of records, which in turn contain data fields or elements.) For example, in a payroll system, the payroll program uses an employee master file containing a record for each employee, with data fields for employee name, number, social security number, address, and pay rate. In such an environment, the human resources department has another program, with its own file that duplicates much of the information held in the payroll system. In a DBMS, on the other hand, all data elements are held in a central data base and are called on as required by the particular application program. In the foregoing example, a "human resources data base" would contain employee data elements used by the payroll, human resources, and other applicable departments.

(4) Organization of the IT Function.   The organization of the IT function depends largely on the extent and type of computer processing, the number of employees, and the control techniques used. A number of IT functions need to be performed, regardless of the size and complexity of an entity's IT installation. Some may be performed by a separate group of employees. Some or even most of them may be outsourced, depending on the number and technical sophistication of an entity's employees. Others may be performed by accounting department personnel.

> *Information systems management*: develops long-range plans and directs application development and computer operations.
>
> *System analysis*: designs systems, prepares specifications for programmers, and serves as intermediary between users and programmers.
>
> *Programming*: develops logic, writes computer programs, and prepares supporting documentation.
>
> *Technical support*: selects, implements, and maintains system software, including operating systems, network software, and DBMS. (Vendors may provide technical support for their software.)
>
> *Database administration*: designs, implements, and maintains the data base and data dictionary that reside in the DBMS.
>
> *Network management or administration*: manages the operation of the communication networks (including network utilization, routing, and problem management).
>
> *Computer operations*: operates computers in accordance with manual and computer-generated instructions.
>
> *Data entry operations*: converts data into machine-readable form primarily using terminals, or enters data using PCs or workstations.

Data control: maintains control over the completeness, accuracy, and distribution of input and output.

Security administration: controls security over the system, including the use of access controls and maintenance of user IDs and associated password files.

Tape library: receives, maintains, and issues magnetic media files (data and programs) on tapes or disks and maintains system libraries.

How duties are segregated within the IT and accounting functions is an important aspect of internal control. To the extent possible, different people should perform the aforementioned functions. For example, programmers should not have the ability to access programs actually in use. In general, the more sophisticated the system and the larger the installation, the greater the opportunity to segregate incompatible functions. In small entities, the same person may perform more than one function, which can present control problems with respect to incompatible duties, such as when one person does almost all the work related to the operation of a departmental computer.

Segregation of duties also involves separating incompatible functions outside of IT. This can be accomplished by permitting—normally via user IDs and passwords—user departments to access only the functions required to perform their jobs. For example, if the payroll and human resources departments are among the users of a common data base, the payroll clerk should be able to access only the program that generates paychecks, while an employee from human resources should be able to access only the program that processes changes in pay status.

(5) *Decentralized and Distributed Data Processing.* The earliest computerized operations took place in centralized departments to which organizational users submitted jobs for processing. Requests for new and changed application systems also were submitted to this department. Personnel in the department designed, developed, operated, and maintained all of the entity's application systems. As the number of requests, together with the complexity of the systems, increased, many user departments sought alternatives to a centralized function, which often was perceived to be unresponsive to user needs.

At the same time, advances in technology led to smaller, more powerful, and less expensive computer systems, which increasing numbers of users began to buy and install throughout the entity, particularly at the departmental level. This was followed very quickly by "end user computing" or EUC, resulting from the widespread availability and use of computers. In EUC, processing was dispersed throughout the entity, and users tended to make their own hardware and software selections, often at huge organizational costs. EUC was followed in turn by organizationally directed computer use, which is referred to as *decentralized or distributed data processing or computing*. In this type of processing, the systems are decentralized by design, and a support network is provided.

Decentralized systems and distributed systems can be distinguished primarily by the extent of integration of the systems. Decentralized computing tends to be less integrated than distributed processing. In a decentralized environment, departmental computers generally operate independently of a centralized computer. In a distributed system, there is usually a coordinating facility responsible for unifying all computers, together with software, communications, and database technology, into an entity-wide information system.

(iii) Understanding the Accounting System and the Computer Environment.

An understanding of the flow of transactions through the accounting system gives the auditor a general knowledge of the various classes of transactions, their volume and typical dollar values, and the procedures for authorizing, executing, initially recording, and subsequently processing them. Information about how the computer environment affects the transmission, processing, and maintenance of information and access to it, in turn, enables the auditor to identify the significant IT accounting applications and understand such matters as:

- The mode in which they operate (such as batch, on-line or real-time, or centralized computer or client/server)
- What accounting functions they perform (the principal programmed accounting procedures)
- Who operates them (including the relationships among users, operators, and programmers)
- How significant data used in processing those applications originates (for example, whether it is entered through remote terminals or extracted from previously generated data files)
- The significant data files generated or updated by the processing
- Information about reports produced—when and how they are produced, when and to whom they are distributed, and how they are used
- Whether entity personnel who use the information generated by the system would be likely to detect and report potential errors in data underlying the financial statements

In addition to understanding the accounting system, the auditor should understand other aspects of the information system that have implications for financial reporting, such as the generation of operations-related reports that management relies on for making decisions that affect financial reporting objectives as well as operational objectives. The auditor also needs to understand management's methods of communicating with personnel concerning their responsibilities and management's expectations in the area of financial reporting.

The auditor does not have to understand every detail of processing in the accounting system. An overview of the system generally is sufficient for the auditor to identify significant classes of transactions and related account balances, and significant accounting records, supporting documents, and reports. The understanding also should enable the auditor to consider the reliability of the accounting and financial reporting process as a basis for preparing financial statements. This will enable the auditor to become aware of how misstatements might occur and their significance, and to identify key reports used to prepare the financial statements or to monitor the business and how those reports are generated. Finally, the auditor needs an understanding sufficient to discuss transactions and reports with entity management and the staff who process the transactions and generate the reports.

In a recurring engagement, much of the relevant information about the accounting system is already available in the prior years' working papers. Although the auditor should use this information as much as possible, it should be reviewed and updated each year. In addition to the review of prior-year working papers, the auditor might want to look at the entity's procedures manuals covering accounting procedures and related control activities. The auditor also might decide to trace one or a few transactions of each relevant class of transactions completely through the system (referred to as a "transaction review" or a "walkthrough") to develop a more complete understanding of the accounting procedures performed.

10.2   EVALUATING DESIGN EFFECTIVENESS

After obtaining an understanding of controls sufficient to plan the audit, the auditor evaluates the effectiveness of their design to determine whether they could, if they operated effectively, achieve the objectives for which they were established.[2] The auditor considers that evaluation in arriving at a preliminary assessment of control risk, which then will be confirmed through tests of controls, as discussed in Chapter 12 (see Section 12.3, Performing Tests of Controls).

Effective design relates to whether one or more controls in place are appropriate to prevent or detect material misstatements with respect to specific audit objectives. The auditor evaluates design effectiveness by considering whether the control is designed so that it could, if it operated effectively, achieve the objective for which it was established. The auditor also should consider whether the design of controls is appropriate for the objectives of the entity's business, the characteristics of the industry, and the detailed activities and risks of the business.

To illustrate the concept of design effectiveness, assume that the auditor has ascertained, as part of understanding the monitoring component, that the internal auditors review bank reconciliations as part of their review of controls over cash disbursements. The auditor may have observed the internal auditors reviewing the reconciliations and determined that they are competent and that they report control deficiencies and breakdowns to the head of internal audit as prescribed. However, the auditor also may have learned that the head of internal audit reports to the controller, who approves the payment of invoices for major purchases of equipment, and that the head of internal audit has no access to a more senior level of management or to the board of directors or its audit committee. The auditor would conclude that the organizational structure relating to the internal audit function was ineffective and that this aspect of the monitoring component did not sufficiently reduce the risk that payments could be made for fictitious purchases and the cash diverted to an individual's personal use. The auditor would have to consider this risk in assessing control risk with respect to cash and fixed assets.

---

[2] In describing how the auditor evaluates design effectiveness, the authors are following the approach taken in Statement on Standards for Attestation Engagements No. 6, *Reporting on an Entity's Internal Control Over Financial Reporting: An Amendment to Statement on Standards for Attestation Engagements No. 2*, rather than AU Section 319, which includes the consideration of design effectiveness with that of operating effectiveness and indicates that both are assessed through performing tests of controls.

10.3   APPLICATION TO SMALL AND MID-SIZED ENTITIES

All entities, regardless of size, have internal control objectives, including financial reporting objectives, but the ways in which an entity ensures that its internal control objectives are met vary according to its size and organization. In smaller entities, financial reporting objectives may be implied rather than explicitly stated, and they may be implemented differently in small and mid-sized entities than in larger ones. For example, the appropriateness of an entity's organizational structure—whether it is centralized or decentralized—depends, in part, on the size and nature of the entity. A highly structured arrangement, including formal documentation of reporting lines and responsibilities, may be appropriate for a larger entity, but could impede the necessary flow of information and thus be inappropriate in a smaller entity, such as an owner-operated business. The auditor should judge the effectiveness of the entity's controls in light of its size and organizational structure.

Methods of disseminating information within an entity also will vary with its size. For example, ways of communicating in large entities include written codes of conduct, job descriptions, policy bulletins, and operating manuals. In smaller entities, codes of conduct may be implicit in the operating style of the owner-manager. Smaller owner-managed entities also may not have audit committees composed of outside directors, but the lack of independent directors may not affect the control risk assessment in such entities. Similarly, the process management uses to assess risks may be less formal in smaller entities than in large ones.

Information and communication systems in small and mid-sized entities also tend to be less formal than in larger ones. In situations where management is closely involved in day-to-day operations, there may not be a need for sophisticated records and procedures, such as a formal credit checking policy or competitive bidding process. Effective communication may not require formal channels and written documentation, but may be achieved by more casual means.

The accounting system that is appropriate for a particular entity will vary according to the entity's size. Smaller entities generally do not need formal accounting systems to the same extent as larger ones, and often their systems do not include extensive accounting procedures, sophisticated records, or elaborate control activities. Effective management involvement in the operation of the system may compensate for the lack of those features.

The objectivity with which management carries out reviews, such as reviews and analyses of sales reports, is particularly important in audits of small businesses that are dominated by owner-managers or others who have the authority to establish policies and make decisions about how to pursue business objectives. On the one hand, owner-manager reviews may enhance internal control because of the close attention with which they are carried out. They also may provide an additional level of segregation of duties in the accounting function. On the other hand, if there is no level of review above that of management (such as a review by nonmanagement members of the board of directors), the contribution of management reviews to internal control may be limited by a possible lack of objectivity. This would be particularly true if management's objectives regarding the financial statements did not coincide with those of the auditor—as would be the case if management's primary concern were maximizing (or minimizing) reported earnings rather than fair presentation in conformity with GAAP.

10.4 DOCUMENTING THE UNDERSTANDING AND EVALUATION OF DESIGN

Professional standards require the auditor to document the understanding of the components of internal control. Professional standards do not specify the form and extent of documentation, and thus the documentation will vary with the size and complexity of the entity and the nature of its controls. In general, the more complex the controls, the more detailed the documentation will be. The control risk audit guide, mentioned earlier, includes examples of various forms of documentation—narratives, flowcharts, and questionnaires—that can be used in recording the understanding of internal control. Often the understanding of internal control components is documented together with the assessment of control risk and tests of controls, as discussed in Chapter 12 (see Section 12.5, Documenting the Assessment of Control Risk and Tests of Controls).

Auditors sometimes document the assessment of the entity-level components on a form that lists the various factors that make up those components and provides space for the auditor's comments and conclusions about each factor. Figure 10.2 illustrates part of such a form for the control environment, dealing with integrity and ethical values.

The documentation of accounting systems that process financially significant transactions usually includes a record of the significant classes of transactions and principal accounting procedures, files, ledgers, and reports. It may be in the form of narratives, diagrams of the inputs and outputs of the system, or flowcharts. A systems diagram may show, for each significant type of transaction, the sources of data processed by the system and the documents and reports that have accounting or control significance. Flowcharts are symbolic diagrams that show procedures in graphic form and thus make it easy to understand and communicate information. Commonly used flowcharting symbols are depicted and explained in Figure 10.3.

Auditors frequently document accounting systems on a type of flowchart called an *overview flowchart*, which illustrates the flow of significant classes of transactions from initiation, through processing, to the reports generated by the system, including those that are used to update the general ledger. An overview flowchart displays, normally on one or two pages, the accounting system for a transaction cycle in summary form. It provides the auditor with information about the nature of transactions that flow through the system. An overview flowchart should depict the principal features of the accounting system, including the following:

1. The nature and source of significant transactions
2. The key processes and flow of significant transactions
3. Principal files or ledgers supporting account balances and the processes by which they are updated

Figure 10.2   Assessment of Control Environment

Area for assessment	Comments
Integrity and ethical values Management should convey the message that integrity and ethical values within the organization cannot be compromised, and employees should receive and understand that message. Management should continually demonstrate, through words and actions, a commitment to high ethical standards and proper working practices. *Consider, for example, the following points of focus:* • *Existence and implementation of codes of conduct and other policies regarding acceptable business practice, conflicts of interest, or expected standards of ethical and moral behavior, and their communication throughout the organization.* • *Establishment of the "tone at the top" and extent of its communication throughout the organization.* • *Candor in dealings with employees, suppliers, customers, investors, creditors, insurers, competitors, and auditors (e.g., whether management conducts business in an ethical manner and insists that others do so, or pays little attention to ethical issues).* • *Appropriateness of remedial action taken in response to departures from approved policies and procedures or violation of the code of conduct, and the extent to which remedial action is communicated or otherwise becomes known throughout the entity.* • *Legal actions brought or threatened against management or the entity.* • *Attitudes toward "housekeeping," for example, adequacy of the maintenance of facilities and equipment, organization of work areas, storage sites, inventory, files, records, etc.*	
Audit implications and/or management letter comments:	

4. Reports produced that have accounting significance, their frequency and distribution, and the files from which they are derived

Each of those features is described below with reference to the revenue cycle accounting system flowcharted in Figure 10.4.

Nature and source of significant transactions: the significant transactions flowcharted for the revenue cycle are customer sales and cash receipts. Other revenue cycle transactions outside the main flow of information, such as adjustments to accounts receivable and standing data amendments, would be described in a supplementary narrative to the flowchart. The flowchart shows that customer sales transactions originate with the input of sales orders from customers and the au-

Figure 10.3   Flowcharting Symbols

Symbols Applicable to All Accounting Systems

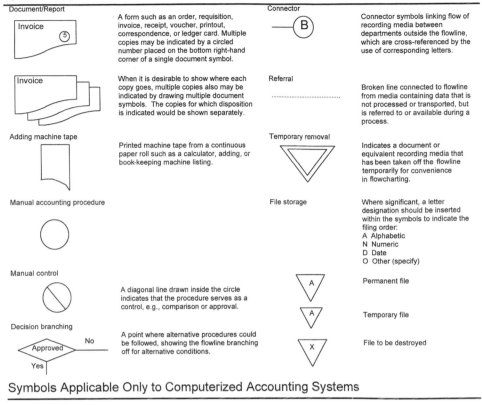

Document/Report

Invoice

⑤

A form such as an order, requisition, invoice, receipt, voucher, printout, correspondence, or ledger card. Multiple copies may be indicated by a circled number placed on the bottom right-hand corner of a single document symbol.

Connector

B

Connector symbols linking flow of recording media between departments outside the flowline, which are cross-referenced by the use of corresponding letters.

Invoice

When it is desirable to show where each copy goes, multiple copies also may be indicated by drawing multiple document symbols. The copies for which disposition is indicated would be shown separately.

Referral

....

Broken line connected to flowline from media containing data that is not processed or transported, but is referred to or available during a process.

Adding machine tape

Printed machine tape from a continuous paper roll such as a calculator, adding, or book-keeping machine listing.

Temporary removal

Indicates a document or equivalent recording media that has been taken off the flowline temporarily for convenience in flowcharting.

Manual accounting procedure

File storage

Where significant, a letter designation should be inserted within the symbols to indicate the filing order:
A Alphabetic
N Numeric
D Date
O Other (specify)

Manual control

A diagonal line drawn inside the circle indicates that the procedure serves as a control, e.g., comparison or approval.

A

Permanent file

A

Temporary file

Decision branching

Approved — No

Yes

A point where alternative procedures could be followed, showing the flowline branching off for alternative conditions.

X

File to be destroyed

Symbols Applicable Only to Computerized Accounting Systems

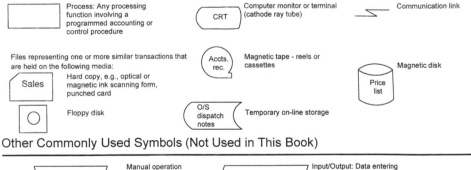

Process: Any processing function involving a programmed accounting or control procedure

CRT

Computer monitor or terminal (cathode ray tube)

Communication link

Files representing one or more similar transactions that are held on the following media:

Sales

Hard copy, e.g., optical or magnetic ink scanning form, punched card

Accts. rec.

Magnetic tape - reels or cassettes

Price list

Magnetic disk

Floppy disk

O/S dispatch notes

Temporary on-line storage

Other Commonly Used Symbols (Not Used in This Book)

Manual operation

Input/Output: Data entering or leaving a computerized system

Figure 10.4 Overview Flowchart

Entity: _Alpha Corporation_   Date: _____

Application: _Revenue Cycle_   Prepared by: _A. N. Auditor_

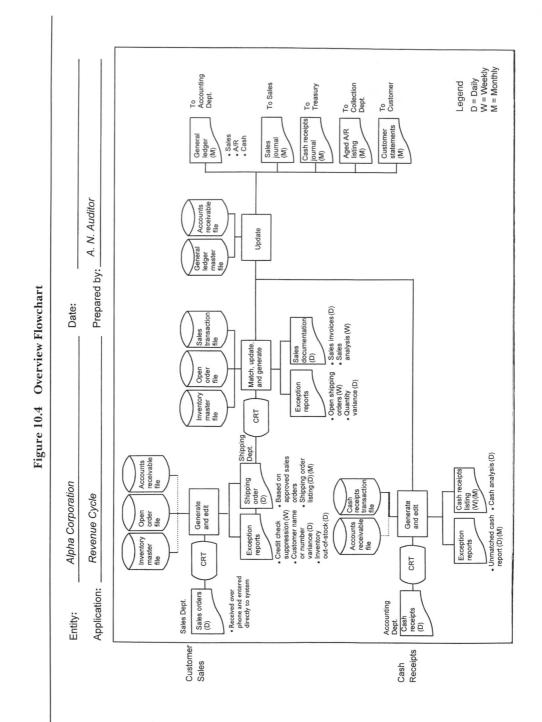

tomatic generation and further processing of shipping orders. This information helps the auditor identify what source documents to use in designing substantive tests and where in the processing of customer sales controls addressing completeness of input might be performed.

Key processes and flow of significant transactions: the flowchart shows how sales transactions flow from initiation (when the sales order is received over the phone and recorded on a sales order document), through processing (when the sales order is input to the system and used in connection with standing data to generate a shipping order and sales invoice), to updating relevant accounting files and producing the ultimate reports from the system (the general ledger, sales journal, and aged accounts receivable listing). Also shown are the processes, called editing and matching, that compare sales orders and shipping orders with data on file to determine whether there are exceptions that must be cleared by someone authorized to do so, before processing can continue. This information helps the auditor understand how certain key files are updated and reports produced, so that he or she can design substantive tests or identify related control activities.

Principal files or ledgers supporting account balances and the processes by which they are updated: the flowchart shows the principal file supporting the accounts receivable balance (the accounts receivable file) and how it is updated (e.g., by accessing data on the sales and cash receipts transaction files). This information helps the auditor identify key files that should be subjected to substantive tests. It also helps identify key files that should be subject to control activities and therefore be considered when testing the effectiveness of controls.

Reports produced that have accounting significance, their frequency and distribution, and the files from which they are derived: the flowchart shows how accounting reports (e.g., the aged accounts receivable listing and the general ledger) are produced, where they are distributed and how frequently, and from which files they were derived (the accounts receivable and general ledger master files). This information helps the auditor identify reports to use in designing substantive tests. The flowchart also shows how and when exception reports are produced. This helps identify documents management may use in exercising monitoring controls.

The degree of detail required in an overview flowchart varies, depending on the entity's accounting system and whether the auditor plans to test the effectiveness of control activities or of monitoring controls. While the overview flowchart is used primarily to document the accounting system, it also may be a convenient place to document the design of key control activities or of monitoring controls, particularly if the auditor does not plan to test those controls as part of the process of assessing control risk. Often key control activities that must be understood in order to design efficient substantive tests will be included on the flowchart, such as matching shipping documents to invoices to ensure the completeness of recorded sales, and procedures relating to physical inventory counts. On the other hand, if the auditor plans to test control activities, they will be documented on other forms (discussed in Chapter 11) and generally will not be indicated on the overview flowchart. In any event, an overview flowchart should contain sufficient information to facilitate the design of substantive tests.

Figure 10.5   Computer Environment Form

Changes to applications	YES	NO
1.1 Can the entity make changes to the program code related to audit-significant computer programs (i.e., does the entity have in-house developed software or access to the source code for vendor developed packages)?		
1.2 Have there been any changes to any audit-significant computer programs during the period other than vendor installed updates (e.g., in-house enhancements, vendor changes for entity specifications, bug fixes, etc.)?		

Development and implementation	YES	NO
2.1 Have any audit-significant computer programs been developed and/or implemented during the period, including new vendor packages?		
2.2 Have any audit-significant computer programs been in the process of development and/or implementation during the period, including new vendor packages?		

Flowcharts are appropriate for all engagements, regardless of size or complexity. On many recurring engagements, flowcharts already will have been prepared; they should be reviewed and updated annually and used as long as they continue to be relevant. A complete redrawing of flowcharts annually is usually unnecessary unless the underlying procedures have changed or previous amendments have impaired a flowchart's clarity. Supporting documentation—such as copies of (or extracts from) accounting records, procedures manuals, and filled-in specimen forms or documents—should be cross-referenced to the flowcharts and filed with them.

The auditor also should understand and record information about computer hardware and software used in financially significant applications. Some auditors document the relevant information on a form designed to record, concisely and in one place, the organization of the IT function, the hardware and software in use, the configuration of the network, and the details of the application environment, such as packages used, type of processing, access security software, and so on. Part of such a form is illustrated in Figure 10.5.

To facilitate the consideration of the effect of deficiencies in the design of controls on the nature, timing, and extent of substantive tests, auditors often prepare a working paper that summarizes those deficiencies. The working paper is also useful in preparing the communication to management on control deficiencies (discussed in Chapter 4). In some auditing firms, the working paper consists of a questionnaire or checklist setting out considerations that typically are relevant to the various types of controls. The working paper documentation often includes a description of the deficiency and its possible effect on the financial statements, identification of material misstatements that could result, and an explanation of the audit response, including any amendment to planned tests.

11

Understanding
Activity-Level Controls

Chapter 10 discussed internal control as it applies to the entity as a whole and to transactions, cycles, and transaction classes within cycles at higher, less detailed levels. This chapter focuses on control activities, that is, those controls that directly address specific account balances and audit objectives, and on monitoring controls that operate at the cycle or transaction level (in contrast to the entity level). Control activities and these lower-level monitoring controls, together with the accounting system [as discussed in Section 10.1(d)(i), The Accounting System], operate at the activity level; that is, they relate to specific business processes and related transactions and accounts. Accordingly, they affect an entity's financial reporting objectives more directly than do controls that operate at higher, less detailed levels. This chapter describes the different categories of control activities that typically are part of an entity's internal control, as well as lower-level monitoring controls (often referred to herein simply as monitoring controls), and how the auditor develops an understanding of them.

When the auditor plans to assess control risk at low, he or she is likely to consider the entity's financial reporting objectives with respect to account balances that are part of a transaction cycle in terms of specific control objectives [described in Section 9.3(a), Control Objectives] to be met by internal control, rather than in terms of the management assertions or audit objectives of existence/occurrence, completeness, and accuracy. Even though in evaluating whether the entity has met the control objectives, the auditor considers all the components taken together, the focus is on the *control activities* component. This is because, of all the control components, control activities operate at the lowest, most detailed level. The auditor considers whether management has designed and placed in operation control activities that, if they operate effectively, will achieve the control objectives. Evidence that control activities are operating effectively, which is obtained by performing tests of controls (discussed in Section 12.3, Performing Tests of Controls), will enable the auditor to significantly restrict substantive tests aimed at the existence/occurrence, completeness, and accuracy of account balances that are part of a transaction cycle.[1]

When the auditor plans to assess control risk below the maximum (i.e., not at low), the focus is likely to be on monitoring controls that operate at the cycle or transaction level, rather than on control activities. Evidence about the effective operation of these lower-level monitoring controls often is sufficient to enable the auditor to restrict substantive tests to some extent, but not by as much as evidence about the effective operation of control activities would permit. This is because monitoring controls operate at a higher level than do control activities and therefore do not provide as much evidence about the existence/occurrence, completeness, and accuracy of account balances as do control activities.

11.1 CONTROL ACTIVITIES

In contrast to the other internal control components, which usually relate to all transactions into which an entity enters, control activities generally are established only for high-volume or high-risk classes of transactions. The design of control activities is in-

---

[1] Entities sometimes institute control activities that, if designed and operating effectively, may permit restricting substantive tests aimed at the cutoff objective. Similarly, controls over the completeness and accuracy of data that underlies accounting estimates may allow the auditor to restrict substantive tests of that data.

fluenced by the size, complexity, and nature of the business as well as by the nature of the entity's internal control as a whole, particularly its computer environment. For instance, a large entity usually establishes formal approved vendor or customer lists, credit policies, and controls over computer security. A small entity may not always need such controls to meet its financial reporting objectives.

Management designs and implements control activities at various stages and data-processing levels. Some of those activities are applied directly to transactions, files, and data, and are referred to as *application controls*. Application controls include *transaction processing controls* and *file maintenance controls*. Transaction processing controls are established to ensure that the entity meets its control objectives related to individual transactions. The achievement of control objectives related to data stored on files is ensured through file maintenance controls, which are applied to transaction cycles as a whole rather than to individual transactions. Application controls also include other control activities—referred to as *asset protection controls*—that address the physical security of related assets and records and the segregation of duties among employees. *Computer controls* do not relate to specific transactions or files but have a pervasive effect on an entire transaction cycle(s) or on the entity as a whole, because the ability of other control activities to achieve the control objectives depends on their functioning. [The term *information processing controls* sometimes encompasses both application controls and computer controls. Computer controls sometimes are referred to as *general controls* or *information technology* (IT) *controls*.] Figure 11.1 shows the different categories of control activities.

Control activities usually involve a combination of *programmed control procedures* by which the computer generates reports, and manual operations that are applied to those reports. For example, before a vendor's invoice is paid on its due date, a computer program may match all open invoices due on that date with the file of open receiving reports. If there is a match, the computer removes both the invoices and the receiving reports from their respective files, puts them into a paid invoice file, and prints out the vendor's check. If there is no match, either because there is no receiving report or because the data on the receiving report differs from the data on the invoice, the computer does not print out the check but instead prints out an exception report of invoices due for which no receiving report exists or for which the data on the two documents does not agree. An accounting supervisor reviews and clears the exception report by determining that, in fact, the goods have not been received and no receiving report should have been created, or that the data otherwise does not agree and the vendor should not be paid.

In the example above, the computerized matching and the generation of the exception report are programmed control procedures; the review and clearing of the exception report is a manual control activity. Both operations are necessary to achieve the control objective—in this case, that all payments to vendors are authorized. In addition, computer controls are necessary to ensure that the programmed control procedures (as well as programmed accounting procedures) are appropriately implemented and operated, and that only authorized changes can be made to programs and data. Otherwise there can be no assurance that the exception report is accurate and complete.

An entity's control activities should address the various control objectives that it must meet in order to generate reliable financial information. Of the seven control objectives defined in Chapter 9 [Section 9.3(a), Control Objectives], three (authorization, completeness of input, and accuracy of input) are met by transaction processing controls; three (integrity of standing data, completeness and accuracy of up-

Figure 11.1   Categories of Control Activities

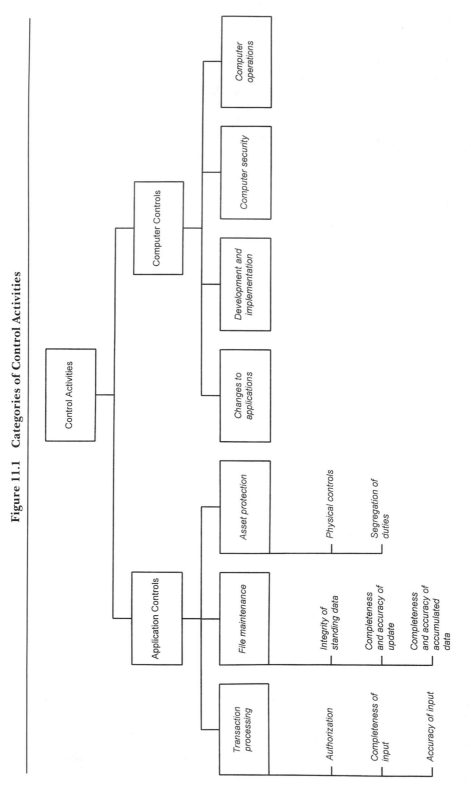

date, and completeness and accuracy of accumulated data) are met by file maintenance controls; and one (protecting assets) is met by controls that restrict access to
assets and records and segregate duties among employees. To be effective, control activities must cover the entire processing system from the initial recording of transactions to their ultimate recording and storage in manual ledgers or computer files. Collectively, the control activities that achieve the seven control objectives ensure that all
transactions that occurred are authorized and are recorded completely and accurately, that errors in execution or recording are detected as soon as possible, that
recorded accounting data is appropriately maintained on computer files and in
ledgers, and that assets and related records are protected. The achievement of those
control objectives depends on computer controls, to the extent that the entity's operations are computerized, and is facilitated by monitoring controls, such as supervision
and management reviews.

(a) Transaction Processing Controls

The following paragraphs discuss different control activities that achieve the control
objectives related to transaction processing.

(i) Authorization.   Recorded transactions can be controlled in various ways to ensure that they represent actual economic events. The most elementary way to do this
is to require transactions to be approved by persons with the authority to do so. Controls to ensure authorization may be built into the system so that transactions are automatically tested against predetermined expectations; exceptions are then reviewed
by someone who is authorized to approve them. Controls to ensure that the system
does not record fictitious transactions include segregating responsibilities for processing transactions (such as credit sales) from responsibilities for corresponding with
other parties to the transaction (such as mailing monthly statements and opening
customer correspondence).

Typical authorization techniques include approval by an appropriate level of management, exception reporting (such as reporting employees working more than a
given number of hours in a week, with a subsequent management review), computer
matching to authorized standing or transaction data (e.g., matching customers' orders to authorized credit limits or matching goods received to authorized purchase orders), and procedures that restrict access to programs and data files to authorized
users. A manager can give approval on-line by inputting an appropriate password and
authorization code at a terminal. Except for manual authorization, the effectiveness
of the above techniques is likely to depend on the operation of programmed control
procedures and on the security procedures applied to files, as discussed later in this
chapter.

Some authorization controls are designed to ensure that only transactions that actually occurred are recorded, and that no transactions are recorded more than once.
For example:

- Accounting procedures normally are established to record goods received on receiving reports, and goods shipped on shipping reports. Control activities designed to ensure the authorization of these transactions include inspecting the

related goods to determine that their description, condition, and quantities are correct and comparing that information with data on sales and vendors' invoices. (Any significant discrepancies noted also should be investigated and resolved if these control activities are to be effective.)

- Canceling the voucher and related documents supporting a purchase transaction at the time of payment prevents their being recorded a second time and being reused to support a duplicate payment or a payment for a nonexistent purchase.

Other authorization controls are designed to ensure that personnel approve individual transactions in accordance with established guidelines. Such authorization can be general or specific. A general authorization may take the form of giving a department or function permission to enter into transactions against some budgeted amount. Budget approval for a capital expenditure, for instance, in effect serves as authorization for expenditures up to the budgeted amount. Another example, from the retail industry, is the "open to buy" concept in which a buyer is authorized to buy merchandise up to a specified amount. A specific authorization, on the other hand, would grant permission to a person to enter into a specific transaction, for example, to buy a specific amount of raw material needed to produce a made-to-order item. Increasingly, controls to ensure the authorization of transactions are automated by specifying in advance the conditions under which a transaction will be automatically authorized and executed. For example, a production order can be automatically authorized when the available amount of an inventory item falls to a predetermined point. Even in nonautomated systems, general authorizations may accomplish the same objective.

(ii) Completeness of Input.   Completeness of input controls are designed to ensure that all transactions are initially input to the accounting system and accepted for processing. The initial recording of transactions may involve manual procedures performed before transactions are entered into the computer, although in many systems, transactions are input at terminals as they occur, with no prior manual recording. In the former instance, controls are designed to ensure that all transactions that occur are entered on a control document (e.g., a receiving report or shipping advice) and then recorded. Without adequate completeness of input controls, it is possible for documents to be lost or misplaced, and this could result in a failure to record transactions that occurred. (Controls also should be established for correcting and resubmitting rejected items.) Examples of controls designed to ensure completeness of input are described below:

- Numbering all transactions as soon as they originate (or, preferably, prenumbering them) and then accounting for all the transactions after they have been processed. Numbering documents is an accounting procedure; the control activity is the act of reviewing to see that all numbered documents complete the expected processing. A technique known as a computer sequence check can be used to have the computer ascertain that the sequence of serially numbered documents is maintained and report missing or duplicate numbers for manual investigation. The possibility of purposeful or accidental errors in the numbering process diminishes if the numerical sequence is printed in advance on the forms. If the risk of error or misuse is not considered significant, the numbering may be originated simultaneously with the document.

- Determining that all data is processed by using "control totals." Grouping source documents at the input stage and establishing a control total over the group can accomplish this goal. The control activity involves comparing the control total with the total entered and accepted for processing, and identifying and correcting errors that caused differences. (The comparison can be done manually or by computer.) The assumption is that the processing is correct if the two totals agree. There is, of course, a possibility of one error exactly offsetting another error or omission, but the possibility is slight.

- Matching data from different sources. Examples are computer matches of transactions input to other data within the system (such as matching the receipt of goods to the open purchase order file), and periodic reviews, either manually or by computer, of unmatched documents (such as receiving reports or vendors' invoices) and the investigation of long-outstanding items to ascertain that a document has not been lost in the processing.

Completeness of input controls are also necessary to ensure that information is correctly summarized and financial reports are properly prepared for both internal and external purposes. Such controls are particularly important if general ledger entries come from sources other than books of original entry. For example, it is relatively easy to ascertain the completeness of postings to the general ledger for sales transactions if the postings come directly from the summarized totals in the sales journal. A simple review to ensure that there are 12 monthly postings in the general ledger may suffice. If, however, general ledger entries arise from other sources as well, additional control activities may be necessary to ensure that all transactions are summarized and posted. Using standard journal entry numbers, with reviews to determine that all appropriate standard journal entries are present, may facilitate achieving this control objective.

(iii) Accuracy of Input. Accuracy of input controls are necessary to ensure that each transaction is recorded at the correct amount, in the right account, and on a timely basis. Although the controls usually are applied mainly to key financial data that directly affects balances in the financial statements, they also may be applied to reference data such as customer number or invoice date.

Controls over accuracy of input include the generation and review of exception reports resulting from matching transaction data to data already on file. For instance, before cash receipts from customers are credited to their accounts, they may be matched to specific sales charged to the customers' accounts and an exception report of unmatched receipts may be generated. One purpose of the match and the exception report may be to ensure that the full amount of specific invoices is collected—an operational control. Matching receipts to sales on the accounts receivable file and follow-up of the exception report, however, also provide evidence of the accuracy of the sales transactions.

Control activities to ensure that transactions are recorded on a timely basis are also essential to achieve the accuracy of input objective. This objective requires procedures to establish the date when a transaction occurred. (Those procedures also help to ensure a proper "cutoff," that is, that transactions are recorded and reported in the proper accounting period.) As an example, goods received are inspected and recorded at the time of their receipt. Usually, the receiving records are matched to related vendors' invoices as part of a subsequent control to ensure the timely recording of transactions.

Certain techniques used to ensure completeness of input also may ensure accuracy of input of some types of data. Examples of such techniques are one-for-one comparison, establishing control totals for certain data, and computer matching of data from different sources. Specific techniques to achieve accuracy usually include a wide range of edit checks, many of which may be carried out directly at terminals as transactions are input. These edit checks depend on programmed control procedures, like matching a customer number input at a terminal to the customer master file, followed by display of the customer name on the screen for visual checking.

(b)   File Maintenance Controls

Three types of control activities achieve control objectives related to the maintenance of data on files. They are described below.

(i) Integrity of Standing Data.   Controls that address integrity of standing data are designed to ensure that changes to standing data contained on files are authorized and accurately and completely input. For example, only the credit department should be able to change master files containing customer credit limits, and only with the manager's approval. Similarly, changes to the sales price master file should require the approval of an appropriate manager before they are input, and the accuracy and completeness of the changes should be reviewed after the file has been updated. One-for-one comparisons may be used when dealing with standing data because of the limited volume of changes and the importance of the data. An example is comparing changes in wage rates used to calculate employees' salaries with an approved listing of wage rate changes.

(ii) Completeness and Accuracy of Update.   Controls that address completeness and accuracy of update are designed to ensure that all transaction data input and accepted for processing updates the appropriate data file and that the update is accurate. For example, in the revenue cycle, it is necessary to ensure that the sales and accounts receivable files are accurately updated by the amount of each day's sales. Controls also should address the completeness and accuracy of the update of computer-generated data, including calculations and summarizations of transaction data that are carried out by programmed accounting procedures as the data is processed. A computer, for instance, may calculate and prepare sales invoices from a transaction file of goods shipped; similarly, the invoices may be summarized automatically for posting to the accounts receivable control account.

In some cases, the completeness of input and accuracy of input controls also might control completeness and accuracy of update. Examples are a one-for-one comparison carried out on a report produced after updating or, where updating takes place at the same time as input, a sequence check carried out on an updated file. Alternatively, some form of control total is used to ensure completeness and accuracy of update, such as computer-generated totals and control records that report out-of-balance situations.

(iii) Completeness and Accuracy of Accumulated Data.   Controls that address completeness and accuracy of accumulated data ensure that data that has been updated to a file continues to be correct until it is removed in an authorized manner. Examples of techniques for ensuring the completeness and accuracy of accumulated data are reconciling the accounts receivable detail ledger to the general ledger, matching cash receipts to the accounts receivable file, and reconciling an inventory count to the recorded inventory. If controls to ensure completeness and accuracy of accumulated data are absent or ineffective, the files may be incomplete or inaccurate, or may contain unauthorized data. If an entity failed to periodically reconcile subsidiary ledgers to the general ledger control account, for instance, misstatements could exist in either the control account or the detailed accounts.

Some control activities that achieve one or more transaction processing control objectives also address completeness and accuracy of accumulated data. For example, matching cash receipts to the accounts receivable file is performed mainly to ensure that cash receipts are posted accurately, but it also serves to ensure that all unpaid accounts receivable remain on the file and the details of individual accounts (customer name, invoice number, and dollar amount) remain accurate. That matching procedure, or other similar procedures, would be likely to disclose errors in files if any disruption in transaction processing occurred, although the errors might not be revealed on a timely basis.

As an illustration of how account balances could be misstated if control activities relating to completeness and accuracy of accumulated data were not effective, assume that during the year an entity disposed of some spoiled raw materials. The quantities disposed of were removed from the detailed perpetual inventory records, but the control account inadvertently was not adjusted. In this situation, an adequate transaction processing control over raw material disposal was not sufficient to prevent misstatement of the inventory balance. Controls addressing completeness and accuracy of accumulated data, such as reconciling the perpetual inventory records to the control account and investigating differences, also would have been necessary. And if the materials disposed of were not removed from either the detailed perpetual inventory records *or* the control account, neither one would properly reflect the existing assets. Physically counting the inventory, reconciling the count to the accounting records, and investigating differences would be the appropriate control activities.

(c)   Asset Protection Controls

Asset protection controls consist of physical controls and arrangements that divide responsibilities in ways that the same people do not perform accounting procedures or control activities and also handle assets.

(i) Physical Controls.   Physical controls are implemented to secure assets and records and are based on restricting access to authorized personnel. Examples are securing locations where assets are stored and restricting access to documents, such as shipping orders, that are used to authorize asset movements. To prevent theft or simply well-intended activity not consistent with established policies and procedures, it is necessary to restrict access to anything that could be used to initiate or process a transaction. Physical controls are most commonly considered in connection with negotiable assets—cash, securities, and sometimes inventory and other items easily convertible to cash or personal use. The concept of limited access applies equally to the books and records and the means of altering them, such as unused forms, unissued checks, check signature plates, files, and ledgers.

In their simplest form, physical controls include such things as a safe, a vault, a locked door, a storeroom with a custodian, a guarded fence, or other means of preventing unauthorized persons from gaining access to assets and records. Control activities also should protect assets and records from physical harm such as accidental destruction, deterioration, or simply being mislaid.

(ii) Segregation of Duties.   If internal control is to be effective, there needs to be an adequate division of responsibilities among those who perform accounting procedures or control activities and those who handle assets. This segregation of duties consists of assigning different people to authorize a particular class of transactions, perform control activities when the transactions are processed, monitor those activities, maintain the related accounting records, and handle the related assets. Such arrangements reduce the risk of error and limit opportunities to misappropriate assets or conceal other intentional misrepresentations in the financial statements. For example, to reduce the risk of error, management may establish procedures for the review and approval of monthly reconciliations of a control account by someone who did not perform the reconciliations.

Segregation of duties also serves as a deterrent to fraud or concealment of error because of the need to recruit another individual's cooperation (collusion) to conceal it. For example, separating responsibility for physical assets from responsibility for the related record keeping is a significant control mechanism over the fraudulent conversion of the assets. Similarly, the treasurer who signs checks should not be able to make entries in the disbursements records and thereby hide unauthorized disbursements. Control is even further enhanced if neither the treasurer nor the bookkeeper is responsible for periodically reconciling the bank account and taking appropriate action if there are any differences. For the same reason, personnel responsible for authorizing and inputting changes to sensitive standing data should not also be responsible for processing related transaction data.

In smaller entities, certain types of control activities may not be relevant or may be performed in a less formal way. Smaller entities tend to have less formal accounting systems, and the related control activities are tailored to the characteristics of the processing system. In particular, because they have fewer employees, it may be difficult for smaller entities to effect segregation of duties; however, management oversight of incompatible activities often can compensate for the lack of adequate segregation of duties.

(d) Computer Controls

The consistency with which programmed procedures process data is one of the benefits of the computer and is made possible in part by computer controls. If the programmed procedures are subject to adequate computer controls, their performance should not vary. Accordingly, random errors, which might occur in a manual accounting system, are virtually nonexistent in a computerized system.

As noted earlier, application controls consist of a combination of programmed control procedures and manual controls, called *user controls*. Programmed control procedures typically generate reports (known as exception reports) of instances when the computer is unable to complete the prescribed operation. The effectiveness of application controls thus depends on two things. First, there must be adequate computer controls to ensure the effectiveness of the programmed procedures, or there will be no assurance that the exception reports are accurate and complete. Second, a user control, which commonly consists of the follow-up of items in exception reports, is also necessary.

There are four categories of computer controls.

1. *Changes to applications*: If computer programs are developed internally or are developed by others to the entity's specifications, controls are necessary to ensure that changes to those programs are designed appropriately and implemented effectively. These controls relate to program amendments, rather than to entire applications, and ensure that amendments are properly designed, tested, and implemented.

2. *Development and implementation*: Whether software is developed in-house or purchased, controls over the development and implementation of new or significantly enhanced applications also are necessary. These controls are designed to ensure the appropriate design and effective implementation of programmed procedures relating to the original design of systems, the testing and documentation of programs and systems, and putting approved programs into use and transferring data held in the prior applications.

3. *Computer security*: Access to the computer system, programs, and data should be restricted. Restricted access generally is accomplished through a combination of access controls applied at various levels in the entity.

4. *Computer operations*: Controls should ensure that data is processed to the correct file, recovery from processing failures is possible, and programs are properly scheduled, set up, and executed. Controls over computer operations relate to system functions and therefore can affect both programmed procedures and data files.

(i) Changes to Applications. Controls over changes to applications developed internally or to the entity's specifications, also known as maintenance or change controls, should ensure that amendments to existing applications are appropriately designed, tested, approved, incorporated within the application, and updated to the live program files, and that change requests are handled appropriately.

Program changes vary in complexity, ranging from relatively simple changes in editing procedures to major overhauls of large systems. Requests for changes are formalized and include enough details to facilitate authorization and to enable the changes to be designed. Testing of the changed program follows a process similar to that for new systems (discussed next), and changes are approved appropriately before implementation.

Typically, the following procedures are involved when changes are made to applications:

- System change requests are approved and communicated to information technology (IT) personnel, generally on a standard change request form
- A cost–benefit analysis is performed
- Approved changes are tracked throughout the process, by an appropriate change management process
- The final design of changes is reviewed and approved by both user and IT management
- All changes, including those initiated within IT, are tested appropriately, and test results are reviewed and approved by user and IT management
- Implementation of tested changes is approved by the requester
- IT functions affected by the changes are notified, for example, computer operations and database administration
- Documentation (such as operations runbooks, user manuals, program narratives, and system descriptions) is prepared or updated
- Appropriate quality control and quality assurance steps are performed throughout the process

Controls also ensure that each system has an "owner." An owner is the individual or department user of the system with the authority to request (or approve) changes in the system. It is important to identify ownership for purposes of assigning responsibility, such as for approving the system or addressing errors in data. IT management should ensure that the owner requests all changes. In larger entities, because of the complexity and interrelationship of systems, often a user committee reviews and co-ordinates changes.

Once IT receives and accepts a request, detailed specifications describing the requested change are developed by IT personnel (e.g., programming, database administration, or telecommunications specialists). When the changes are extensive, these specifications and the related project plan should include the same types of considerations as those for new systems (discussed later).

Procedures should be established to prevent users from inappropriately bypassing formal change procedures by initiating program changes through direct contact with programmers. This can lead to unauthorized changes, inappropriate installation dates, inadequate testing, and inconsistent application of accounting principles. In addition, IT personnel should inform users of proposed program changes, even ones that are viewed as purely technical matters that users cannot comprehend and will not be affected by, such as modifications and file reorganizations, changes from tape to disk, and optimizing restart procedures. All such changes should be communicated to users appropriately. Although users may defer in-depth technical review to IT management, they should be aware that the system is being modified so that they can determine whether their input or output data or other areas will be affected.

(ii) Development and Implementation.   Development and implementation controls help guard against financially significant errors in new applications. The procedures cover the authorization and design of new applications, testing of new application programs, and procedures for putting approved programs into use; they apply to both internally developed and vendor-supplied applications. In the latter situation, the principal concerns are limited to the original selection of the package, any modifications required to the package, and the testing and implementation of the package in the entity's environment.

Quality control and quality assurance procedures should be applied to all systems under development. In a large environment with a lot of development activity, there should be a formal quality control committee, with direct access to senior management. This is necessary for appropriate follow-up on issues created by or within the development process.

(1) System Design and Program Development or Acquisition.   Controls for program development ensure that appropriate programmed procedures are designed and coded in computer language and that the system includes the appropriate user controls. The development process involves a feasibility study and cost–benefit analysis, which serve as the basis for general design requirements. The requirements are converted into detailed system specifications. When a system is being purchased, these controls ensure that the appropriate specifications are developed and the acquisition process is controlled to ensure that the package selected meets the entity's needs.

Once detailed specifications have been developed and approved by both the user and system or program developers, which may be done in modules or for the system as a whole, programming can begin. Computer programs are generated in a variety of ways, ranging from purchasing or customizing application software packages to writing programs in-house, which may involve the use of prototyping, computer-assisted software engineering (CASE), and code generation tools. In any event, the programs should be documented in enough detail to facilitate subsequent testing, appropriate future modifications, and training of personnel.

(2) Program and System Testing.   Testing normally occurs in three distinct stages: program testing, system testing, and parallel running.

Program testing consists of verifying the logic of individual programs, usually through *desk checking* and computer processing of *test data*. Desk checking involves determining visually that the program coding is consistent with the program specifications; it is generally done by a programmer other than the one who wrote the code. Desk checking normally is performed in conjunction with computer processing of hypothetical test data. Test data is designed to cover all elements of data in all classes of transactions that the system might encounter and for which input specifications exist.

System testing consists of determining that the programs are logically compatible with each other and do not have an adverse impact on the system as a whole. Processing test data is the principal technique used in system testing; adjustments and reruns continue until all observed logic failures have been corrected. The user and system analysts are the principal parties involved in the system testing process; programmers primarily correct program errors.

Parallel running involves operating the system under conditions that approximate the anticipated "live" environment, while the old system continues to operate. Results of operating the new system are compared with those of the old system, with appropriate follow-up of inconsistencies. Parallel running is a means of testing the logic, programming, and implementation of a complete system, including all user controls. One of its objectives is to confirm the system's ability to cope with actual conditions and volumes of transactions. A manager may review and approve operating and user instructions as part of the parallel running process, or this may be done as part of the final acceptance procedures.

(3) Cataloguing.   Cataloguing is the process of incorporating computer programs into various program libraries, which may contain programs in source code, object code, or load module form. *Source code* or language refers to the high-level computer languages that programmers use (such as COBOL). *Object code*, also known as object modules, is the output of the compiler in machine code or language. Ordinarily, a programmer writes in source language form, which is then incorporated into a test source library. Subsequently, the computer compiles or interprets the program into an object module and catalogues it into a test library. To be executable, the various object modules that make up a program are coordinated in a process called link-editing. This process creates the *executable* or *load module* that the computer actually uses for program execution.

Program testing is performed using the program in a *test library*. After a program has been completely tested and approved, the test source program is transferred to the production source library. The program in the production source library is used for cataloguing into the *production library*. This ensures that the production program is completely equivalent to the tested and approved source program.

It is important that cataloguing be controlled effectively. For example, it is preferable for programmers to have access to the test library only, and for testing and documentation to be completed before programs are incorporated into production libraries. At an appropriate cutoff point, with appropriate approvals, a formal procedure transfers programs from test to production status.

(4) Conversion.   Conversion of data files may be necessary when a computerized system replaces a manual system or an existing computerized system, or an existing computerized system is significantly enhanced and the existing files need to be "rebuilt." To ensure that newly created or converted data files contain correct data, entities develop a conversion plan, which generally covers:

- Design of the conversion process
- Documentation of any data conversion programs to be written
- Techniques to test the results of conversion (e.g., file balancing, one-to-one comparisons)
- Conversion timetable
- Assignment of user and data processing responsibilities

IT management involved in the process (e.g., the database administrator and other programming project leaders) and user management (or a designee) review and approve the plan.

Normally, the conversion plan is designed to ensure that:

- Specifications for all master files and transaction files to be converted or created are identified
- Specifications for new files are reviewed and approved by appropriate user and IT management
- Specifications for each new file are compared with those of existing files to determine the effect of any format changes to existing fields, new fields needed as a result of the new or modified system, and existing fields that will be eliminated from the converted files
- Techniques are designed and responsibilities assigned to ensure that the newly created data files are complete and accurate
- Data created for new files is appropriately reviewed and approved before being input to those files, for example, by one-for-one checks

Appropriate user and IT management review and approve the final results of the conversion process.

(iii) Computer Security.   Security controls are necessary to restrict access to data maintained on computers, computer programs, and computers themselves. Security controls over data are designed to protect data from unauthorized access that could result in their modification, disclosure, or destruction or that could inappropriately move assets, like cash or inventory, by manipulating data or processing unauthorized transactions. Security procedures are particularly important for standing data, since it is used repeatedly in processing transactions and may not be reviewed often enough to ensure timely identification of errors. Security procedures also are necessary to protect files from accidental destruction or erasure. Further, security control procedures can help enforce division of duties by limiting the system functions, applications, or access to data to specific users. The extent of security needed depends on the sensitivity of the entity's data, the characteristics of the related assets, and the effectiveness of other controls.

Security procedures usually involve techniques that restrict access to, use of, and ability to change data files to authorized users and ensure that the level of access is consistent with the users' responsibilities. The principal techniques are logical or software protections available in both application and system software (discussed later), and physical security controls. Physical security controls cover access to computer terminals, PCs, and data files stored off-line. On-line networked environments provide many users access to data files, and thus physical security controls are not sufficient to control program and data file security. System software, particularly access control software (such as ACF2, RACF, or TopSecret) generally protects both programs and data files in on-line environments. Generally, a combination of different access controls is used to control data file and program security. In addition, software used to maintain libraries of computer programs on file sometimes includes security features. Although security aspects often are built into applications and provide some protection, normally access control software is also necessary.

The software normally requires users to enter passwords, which reference tables of permissions that define the access rights of individuals. Where passwords are in use, procedures are required to ensure that they are appropriately selected, kept secret, changed regularly, and removed immediately upon termination or transfer of the employee.

In the absence of security controls, the entity could be subject to the risk of defalcations or management fraud from unauthorized program changes or manipulation of data representing the assets of the entity. In on-line environments, knowledgeable users might be able to access program files, increasing the risk that unauthorized changes may be made to programs in order to misappropriate assets and modify reporting routines to conceal the misappropriations. The risk of unauthorized amendment of programs generally is lower where the entity uses vendor-supplied packages and the user does not have access to the source code that would allow changes to the program. However, there is still the risk of unauthorized changes to options within purchased systems.

Security procedures also are necessary for system maintenance programs, such as for correcting data files after a processing failure. These programs, commonly referred to as utility programs, often can make changes directly to programs or data, frequently without leaving any record of the changes. Communications software and database management packages often have password facilities, but these are rarely as strong as access control software.

Security procedures normally address such matters as:

- The classification scheme for information stored on computers or located outside of data processing, including security categories (e.g., research, accounting, marketing) and security levels (e.g., top secret, confidential, internal use only, unclassified)

- The data in each information class and individuals or functions authorized to use it, and control and protection requirements

- The types or classes of sensitive assets and the potential threats and protection requirements for each

- The responsibilities of management, security administration, resource owners, computer operations, system users, and internal auditors

- The consequences of noncompliance with policies and procedures

- Any security implementation plan

Where packaged application systems are in use, data file access controls may be defined in option tables. The permissions or privileges defined within the tables should be created by the user departments according to job function, and implemented by a security officer or administration function within IT. The information in the tables is the responsibility of the user departments, although the actual implementation and maintenance usually are not.

(iv) Computer Operations.   Computer operations controls ensure the use of correct data files, including their correct version, and provide recovery procedures for processing failures; they also help ensure that programmed procedures are applied consistently. Computer operations procedures cover both processing of data and IT department operations, and can be applied at the central location, local installations, or both.

Procedures to ensure the use of correct data files include software checking of information on files and, less frequently, manual checks of external file labels by operators. Control over recovery from processing failures requires that data be copied regularly as backup, that processing status at the time of failure can be established, and that proper recovery take place. Procedures that schedule jobs for processing, set them up, and execute them ensure the consistent operation of programmed procedures. Procedures also cover the actions of computer operators, such as supervision and review of their work. In on-line, real-time systems, data files normally are available to users at all times, so that relatively little operator intervention is required; in those systems, system software largely controls operations. In batch systems, operators group jobs into job streams and set them up with the required files. Since more operator intervention is required, computer operations controls may be of greater concern in these systems.

(1) Computer Processing Procedures.   The computer operations department or function usually controls the day-to-day functioning of hardware and software. In many entities, it is assisted by a production control department. Computer operations is responsible for the physical running of the computer system (e.g., mounting files and printer forms and making decisions about computer hardware, such as whether to discontinue using a device in the event of a failure). The production control department is responsible for job scheduling and setup.

Production control normally uses a job scheduling system and a tape management system to control the submission of jobs to the computer and ensure that the correct files are used for those jobs. Production control includes standards (e.g., job classes, use of tape and disk storage devices, printer classes, routing of output) for developing or updating run instructions for new or modified systems. Those standards consider time constraints and processing sequences that apply to each system. Effective controls for implementing and modifying systems (discussed earlier) normally include review and approval of operating parameters and job schedules by application owners and production control or computer operations management.

In client/server environments and other distributed systems, computer operations are more difficult to control. The increasingly distributed nature of applications and data makes it harder to apply controls on a centralized basis than it was in the past.

In some data processing installations, job scheduling, setup, and execution are not controlled by software or a production control department; instead, they are controlled manually. In those environments, computer operations supervisors or other computer operations management should supervise manual procedures.

(2) Backup and Recovery Procedures.   In the event of a computer failure, backup arrangements are necessary so that the recovery of production programs, system software, and data files does not introduce errors into the system. The principal techniques that can be employed are:

- A facility for restarting at an intermediate stage of processing, for use if programs are intentionally or unintentionally terminated before their normal ending, or for backing out transactions that were not processed completely before the termination

- A system to copy or store master files and associated transaction data, which makes it possible to restore files lost or damaged during disruption

- Procedures to ensure that copies of operating instructions, run instructions, and other documentation are available if originals are lost

- Formal instructions for resuming processing or transferring it to other locations, usually called a contingency plan

(3) System Software.   System software controls ensure that system software is properly implemented, maintained, and protected from unauthorized changes. System software consists of various programs that direct computer functions, allowing the applications to run. System software includes the operating system, utilities, sorts, compilers, file management systems, library management packages, time-sharing software, telecommunications software, job accounting software, database management systems (DBMSs), and security software packages.

System software is acquired from computer or software vendors, rather than written by the user. Controls relate to selecting and implementing the appropriate options within the software, including vendor-supplied amendments or "fixes," and to security and backup.

Controls for implementing system software are similar to those for other packaged systems, except that a technical support group (e.g., system programmers) performs the work, not application programmers. The "owners" are the management of various data processing functions, such as the database administrator, security administrator, and network or telecommunications administrator.

If an entity's technical support group develops some aspects of system software or adds functions to vendor-supplied system software (by making use of "exit" routines), it should follow appropriate system design procedures. When a vendor supplies system software, the user tests the integration of a particular package into the existing environment, including the selection of options and any subroutines the technical support group added via exits.

Maintenance of system software deals primarily with changes supplied by the vendor. On extremely rare occasions, the user may modify system software. All such modifications should be controlled in much the same way as changes to application programs. The vendor periodically modifies vendor-supplied system software and introduces the modifications as new programs or amendments to existing programs. New or amended system software is tested to ensure that it operates as intended within the entity's data processing environment. Tests of system software that interacts with application programs, such as the operating system, simulate the production environment. Normally, those tests involve running the system software with copies of proven application programs to identify anomalies associated with the modified system software.

In many entities, neither the technical expertise nor the tools exist to make amendments to system software. This is often true of the operating system, which is provided by the vendor in a low-level code like machine code or microcode, or in code built into the computer. In those circumstances, the risk of unauthorized amendments to the system software is minimal. Where the technical expertise and tools do exist to change the system software, entities establish controls similar to those for the security of application programs. The technical support group is generally smaller than the application programming group, giving individual system programmers a greater opportunity to become familiar with a broader array of system software. The technical support group needs access to system software not only to perform routine maintenance but also in the event of processing failures and other emergencies. Consequently, entities normally enforce division of duties to prevent technical support personnel from obtaining a detailed understanding of the applications processed and of user controls for key files and transactions in those applications. Also, the work of technical support staff should be supervised closely.

11.2 MONITORING CONTROLS

As discussed in Chapter 10 [Section 10.1(c), Monitoring] in the context of monitoring at the entity level, internal control includes activities whose purpose is to assess the functioning of other controls. On the activity level, many monitoring controls consist of management and supervisory activities designed to oversee whether control activities are operating effectively to ensure the reliability of financial information. These monitoring controls may relate to the financial reporting function as a whole; to the processing of transactions, maintenance of files, or protection of assets in one or more transaction cycles; or to the operation of the computer function.

Monitoring controls that relate to applications and to protecting assets enhance the effectiveness of control activities in achieving relevant control objectives, although the monitoring controls, even if they are directed at applications in a specific transaction cycle, do not in themselves provide evidence that control objectives are achieved, as they are not focused at a low enough level. For example, a controller who reviewed the reconciliation of subsidiary ledgers to the related control accounts most likely would notice errors made in processing transactions and maintaining files. The absence of reconciling items would provide some evidence that transactions were processed and files maintained effectively, although neither the reconciliation nor the controller's review of it would prevent errors from occurring in the first place. Some monitoring controls, particularly those involving the supervision of others, are designed specifically to oversee accounting procedures and control activities. Such supervisory actions lower the risk that accounting procedures and control activities may not function at all times as designed.

Monitoring controls over the computer function include management's tracking of open requests for changes to applications, how requests are prioritized, and whether users are satisfied with changes made; monitoring of the development (or acquisition) and implementation of new applications; overseeing the effectiveness of measures taken (e.g., the implementation of access controls) to control security risks; and monitoring various facets of computer operations, such as system availability, data processed against incorrect files, job failures, and reruns. For instance, an IT manager should review and approve the adequacy of procedures for implementing and testing program changes.

Other monitoring controls (sometimes called *management reviews* or *performance reviews*[2]) are a byproduct of management's reviews and analyses of reports or other data the accounting system produces, made primarily for operational purposes, such as a sales manager's review and analysis of a report of monthly sales activity. Managers of various functions within an entity review reports of the performance of the activities for which they are responsible, analyze the results, and take appropriate investigative and corrective actions. Such management reviews may be based on various performance indicators such as comparisons of actual performance to budgets, forecasts, or prior-period results, or on relationships of data from different sources. The data may be either financial or operational; if management follows up on unexpected results generated from financial reporting systems, the analysis of performance indicators may serve financial reporting control purposes as well as operational purposes.

Although management or performance reviews are not designed specifically to oversee the operation of accounting procedures and related control activities, management's use of data in operating reports may detect material misstatements that those controls should have prevented or detected. In this way, these monitoring controls help ensure that errors that do occur will be detected on a timely basis and thus provide some evidence about the effectiveness of accounting procedures and control activities.

Following are examples of how management's operational reviews and analyses can provide evidence that indicates that an entity's internal control is effective:

- A sales manager's review of a report of sales revenue and comparison with the volume of goods known to have been shipped, would indicate whether reported sales appear reasonable. The manager's judgment that the sales figure is reasonable would provide some evidence of the correctness of financial information the *accounting system* generated.

- Management generally would notice failures to bill for goods shipped or services rendered through the adverse effect on profitability; and overbillings for goods shipped or services rendered by unfavorable reactions from customers, including nonpayment of excess billings. The lack of such events would provide some evidence of the effectiveness of *application controls*.

- A supervisor's knowledge that attempted computer security violations are reported promptly would provide some evidence that *computer controls* are operating effectively.

The usefulness of management reviews in providing evidence about the effectiveness of accounting procedures and control activities depends on:

- The competence of the individuals reviewing the reports. They should have an adequate level of business knowledge and technical expertise and be familiar with the entity's operations.

---

[2] In SAS No. 78, performance reviews are classified as a category of control activities. Many monitoring controls are closely related to control activities and illustrate particularly well the interrelatedness of the internal control components and the fact that what is important is whether controls achieve the objectives for which they were established, not how they are categorized.

- The authority of the individuals performing the reviews to take corrective action. They should be adequately positioned within the entity to act effectively.

- The objectivity of the individuals performing the reviews. The individuals should be independent of those who perform the work, both functionally (that is, there should be adequate segregation of duties) and motivationally (for example, an officer's review might be of less value from the auditor's standpoint if the officer's compensation is based on operating results being reviewed).

11.3 DEVELOPING THE UNDERSTANDING

AU Section 319 requires the auditor to obtain a sufficient understanding of each of the five components of the entity's internal control to plan the audit—that is, to make a preliminary, or planned, assessment of control risk for each significant class of transactions and account balance and to design substantive tests that reduce to an acceptable level the risk that material misstatements will not be detected.[3] AU Section 319 explicitly states that audit planning ordinarily does not require an understanding of control activities related to each account balance or to every relevant audit objective. The extent of the understanding of the components of internal control, particularly control activities, that is necessary to plan the audit varies with the preliminary, or planned, assessment of control risk.

In general, the higher the planned assessment of control risk, the less the need to understand and document control activities. Some of the control activities that achieve the various control objectives may be closely related to aspects of other internal control components, particularly the accounting system. In addition, control activities, both application and computer controls, often are subject to monitoring controls. Accordingly, the auditor is likely to obtain some information about the presence or absence of control activities as part of obtaining an understanding of the other components. The auditor should consider that information in determining what additional understanding, if any, of control activities is necessary to plan the audit. On the other hand, an understanding of certain control activities may be helpful in understanding the accounting system, and the auditor may want to obtain such an understanding for that purpose. The following paragraphs present a logical and efficient approach, under varying preliminary assessments of control risk, to meeting the requirement of AU Section 319 to understand the entity's control activities.

If the auditor plans to assess control risk *at the maximum*, it may be sufficient to document information about the presence or absence of control activities that the auditor obtained as part of understanding the other components. Since no controls will be tested as a basis for restricting substantive tests, it is not necessary to expand the understanding to include the design of application and computer control activities (or of monitoring controls that are exercised at the activity level) and whether they have been placed in operation. It may be prudent in these circumstances, however, for the auditor to understand the entity's physical controls and its arrangements for segre-

---

[3] In practice, auditors may not develop an understanding of specific control activities until after they have made a preliminary assessment that control risk is at low. As noted later, however, in the course of developing an understanding of controls in the other components, the auditor usually acquires some understanding about control activities.

gating duties, since a principal purpose of these controls is the prevention or detection of fraud.

If control risk is preliminarily assessed *below the maximum* for one or more transaction cycles, the auditor also should obtain an understanding of and document the design of relevant monitoring controls over both applications and computer functioning, and determine that they have been placed in operation. The specific monitoring controls over computer functioning that the auditor needs to understand will be determined by the characteristics of the entity's computer environment and by whether various events occurred during the year, such as the development or acquisition of new programs or amendment of existing ones. Those considerations are discussed later in the chapter in connection with the auditor's understanding of computer controls when control risk is assessed at low.

Understanding monitoring controls may help the auditor to identify control objectives that are not being met and to consider the related audit implications. In some circumstances, the auditor's understanding may lead to a conclusion that monitoring controls are inadequate to support a below-the-maximum assessment. If the auditor still believes that it would be efficient to assess control risk below the maximum, he or she may develop an understanding of application or computer controls that compensate for the absent or ineffective monitoring controls, and thus be able to achieve the desired assessment.

Finally, if control risk is preliminarily assessed at *low*, the auditor should obtain an understanding of and document the design of application controls and computer controls designed to achieve all relevant control objectives and determine that they have been placed in operation. Those procedures will help the auditor design and perform tests of those controls to confirm the assessment, as discussed in Chapter 12 (Section 12.3, Performing Tests of Controls). When the planned control risk assessment is low, it is not necessary for the auditor to develop an understanding of activity-level monitoring controls, although such an understanding may be helpful in identifying application and computer controls and in understanding how management oversees the operation of the business.

The extent to which an understanding of the various categories of computer controls is necessary depends on whether the entity implemented new computer programs or amended existing ones during the year, whether entity personnel have the ability to make changes to computer programs or to computer operations, and how security over programs and data is maintained. If the entity did not develop or implement programs, the auditor does not need to understand controls over new programs. If programs were not amended (other than vendor-installed updates), and the entity does not develop its own software and does not have access to the source code in purchased programs used to process financially significant data, it is not necessary to understand controls over changes to applications. If entity personnel cannot change programmed procedures, there have not been operating problems during the year, and the loss of systems or data would not cause irreparable damage to the entity, it generally would not be necessary for the auditor to understand controls over computer operations. Finally, it would not be necessary to understand security controls if:

- Authorization controls do not depend on computer security, such as user IDs and passwords
- Restricted access to assets and records does not depend on computer security

- Computer systems do not contain confidential data whose disclosure could present an audit risk

- Controls over changes to application programs do not depend on restricted access to the system

However, it would be rare for computer operations and computer security not to require some attention from the auditor.

11.4 EVALUATING DESIGN EFFECTIVENESS

As discussed in Chapter 10, after obtaining the understanding of controls, the auditor evaluates the effectiveness of their design to determine whether they could, if they operated effectively, achieve the objectives for which they were established.[4] When the auditor plans to assess control risk at low, and thus has obtained an understanding of control activities, he or she considers whether those controls are appropriately designed to prevent or detect material misstatements with respect to specific audit objectives and account balances. In evaluating the design effectiveness of control activities, the auditor should consider whether the controls are designed to ensure that transactions are authorized and are processed completely and accurately; that data remains reliable throughout all stages of the transaction cycle, both processing and maintenance on files; and that assets are protected against theft and other unauthorized actions.

For instance, the auditor may have determined, as part of understanding control activities related to the production cycle, that an inventory storage facility is kept locked at all times and requires the use of a magnetic card for entry. Moreover, only a limited number of employees, whose responsibilities involve handling inventory, are issued cards. However, in the course of obtaining the understanding of controls, the auditor observed that the door to the storage area remained unlocked for two minutes after a card had been used for entry, leaving ample time for an unauthorized person to enter without using a card. In this case, the auditor would conclude that the design of the card entry system was defective and that there was a risk of undetected theft of inventory, and therefore a risk of misstatement of the financial statements.[5]

When the auditor plans to assess control risk below the maximum, and has obtained an understanding of monitoring controls, the next step is to consider the extent to which, based on the design of those controls, they can be expected to enhance the effectiveness of related control activities or to detect misstatements that may occur because of the lack or ineffectiveness of control activities.

---

[4] In describing how the auditor evaluates design effectiveness, the authors are following the approach in Statement on Standards for Attestation Engagements No. 6, *Reporting on an Entity's Internal Control Over Financial Reporting: An Amendment to Statement on Standards for Attestation Engagements No. 2*, rather than AU Section 319, which includes the consideration of design effectiveness with that of operating effectiveness and indicates that both are assessed through performing tests of controls.

[5] Paragraph 9 of the Appendix to SAS No. 78 (AU Section 319.84) notes that the extent to which controls designed to prevent theft of assets are relevant to the reliability of financial statements, and therefore to the audit, depends on the circumstances, such as whether assets are highly susceptible to misappropriation.

11.5   APPLICATION TO SMALL AND MID-SIZED ENTITIES

In small and mid-sized entities, control activities and monitoring controls may be less formal than in larger entities. In addition, management's hands-on involvement in business operations and close review of operating and performance reports often obviate the need for control activities that are typically part of a larger entity's internal control. Some smaller entities may not have a sufficient number of employees to effect appropriate segregation of duties and may have to rely on an owner-manager's direct supervision of the performance of incompatible functions. In addition, computer controls in smaller entities may be informal and not well-documented, and the number and expertise of computer personnel may be limited. Controls relating to computer security, in particular, may be deficient. The managers' use of information generated by computerized systems, in light of their direct knowledge of the business, may compensate for this situation.

11.6   DOCUMENTING THE UNDERSTANDING AND EVALUATION OF DESIGN

As noted in Chapter 10 (Section 10.4, Documenting the Understanding and Evaluation of Design), professional standards require the auditor to document the understanding of the internal control components, but do not specify the form and extent of documentation. Thus, the documentation will vary with the size and complexity of the entity and the nature of its internal control. In addition, the auditor may document, in the same place or on separate working papers, the evaluation of the design effectiveness of controls. In general, the more complex the internal control components, the more detailed the documentation will be.

This section presents several alternative formats for documenting the auditor's understanding of control activities and monitoring controls, provides examples, and explains when each could be used. The AICPA audit guide to SAS No. 78, *Consideration of Internal Control in a Financial Statement Audit*, also provides guidance on documenting the understanding of controls. Individual auditors and firms often express a preference for one type of documentation by means of their internal policy pronouncements and the practice aids (for example, forms, checklists, and questionnaires) they provide, which may be either required or optional. Regardless of the type of documentation the auditor uses, it must provide a means for recording in the working papers a description of the relevant controls.

The auditor should reconsider the recorded understanding of control activities and monitoring controls during subsequent stages of the audit, particularly after performing tests of controls and substantive tests. Substantive tests may disclose departures from or deficiencies in prescribed controls. In that event, the documentation should be amended to reflect the new information.

Controls typically are documented by narratives, flowcharts, control matrices, questionnaires, or other forms designed for this purpose. The same or different forms of documentation can be used for application and computer control activities and for application and computer monitoring controls.

(a) Narratives

While many auditors prefer flowcharting as the means of documenting the design of the accounting system and related control activities, narratives are often useful and, particularly where internal control is unsophisticated, may be more cost-effective. When the auditor uses narratives, they should contain all relevant information.

(b) Flowcharts

Control activities are sometimes documented on a flowchart, often called a *systems flowchart*, that depicts, for each significant class of transactions, the path of a transaction from its inception (that is, the point where the transaction first enters the accounting system) to the update of the general ledger. It provides, in a convenient form, a combined description of the accounting system and related control activities and contains information necessary for the auditor to design tests of those control activities. A systems flowchart typically contains, for each significant class of transactions:

1. The details of significant accounting procedures and control activities, including segregation of duties and monitoring activities
2. The job titles of the personnel performing the activities
3. The frequency of the operation of the activities

The information usually is organized by area of responsibility within the system. Depending on the responsibilities involved, an organizational unit may vary from a large department (such as a sales department) to one individual (the credit manager). The names of the organizational units through which the transactions flow should be shown at the top of the flowchart. The flow of transactions usually is from top left to bottom right. Control activities may be marked on the flowchart by a diagonal line inside a procedure symbol and may include a narrative supplement noting the nature of the control activity (e.g., "approval").

Systems flowcharts need not be excessively detailed, as only significant activities should be depicted. One or more accounting procedures and related control activities may be depicted by one symbol, with a narrative explanation of each significant activity provided separately on the flowchart. This normally makes it possible to show each transaction cycle on one or two pages. An illustration of part of a systems flowchart for the sales order and billing portions of a revenue cycle is provided in Figure 11.2.

(c) Control Matrices

Some auditors capture information about the principal control activities and any apparent deficiencies in them (such as omitted activities) through the use of control matrices. Control matrices may be designed to record control activities related to transaction processing, file maintenance, asset protection, or any other relevant types of activities. A control matrix might describe the principal control activities designed to meet specific control objectives and might serve as an aid in understanding those ac-

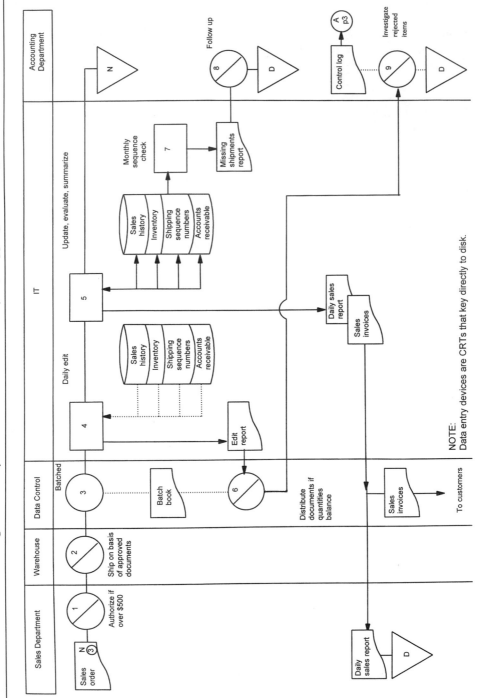

Figure 11.2   Systems Flowchart: Revenue Cycle, Shipping and Billing

11·26

Figure 11.3   Revenue Cycle: Record of Application Controls

Part A: Transaction-Level Controls - Sales of Goods and Services		
Control Objective	**What control activities address the control objective?**	**w/p ref***
1.1a Authorization: Recorded sales transactions represent actual sales to nonfictitious customers and are approved. *Consider, for example, the following points of focus:* - *What prevents or detects sales to fictitious customers?* - *How are sales terms and prices approved?* - *How are customers' credit limits controlled?*		
1.2a Completeness of Input: Authorized sales transactions are input and accepted for processing. *Consider, for example, the following points of focus:* - *What ensures that work orders or shipments of goods are input for processing?* - *What ensures that a sales invoice is generated for every shipment or work order?* - *What prevents duplicate recording of sales?*		
1.3a Accuracy of Input: Sales transactions are accurately recorded as to amounts, quantities, dates, and customers and in the proper period. *Consider, for example, the following points of focus:* - *What ensures that the price and amount of the sale are correct?* - *What ensures that sales are recorded in the proper period?* - *What ensures that what is invoiced represents the actual goods shipped or services rendered?*		

* Cross-reference to the working paper where the tests of controls have been performed.

tivities and designing tests of controls. In some situations, it may serve as a substitute for an internal control questionnaire or other similar form of documentation, as discussed below.

(d)   Internal Control Questionnaires

Since control objectives and the means of achieving them are much the same from one entity to another, some auditors find it efficient to design an internal control questionnaire (ICQ) to document control activities on all or most engagements. The questionnaire is usually divided into transaction cycles that cover the main transaction flows, and is organized in terms of the control objectives that control activities should achieve at each stage of processing. If systems flowcharts have been prepared, the information contained in them should be used, as much as possible, in completing the ICQ. Questionnaires also can be used to document monitoring controls and are convenient means of documenting the control activities or monitoring controls that the auditor intends to test.

The questionnaire may be more or less open-ended. For example, it may merely direct the auditor to consider what control activities might be in place to achieve each control objective, or it may identify and list specific control activities that typically are found relating to each control objective. Similarly, an ICQ for monitoring controls may be suggestive of the types of controls that could exist, or may describe specific monitoring controls.

The questions in the latter, more close-ended type of questionnaire are usually phrased so that they may be answered "Yes" or "No" to indicate, respectively, the presence or absence of a control. If a question does not apply to a specific entity or location, the appropriate response is N/A (not applicable). The questions in an ICQ for control activities are sometimes further subdivided between:

1. Those that seek information concerning *accounting procedures* that are not in themselves control activities, but that form the basis for the exercise of control activities

2. Those that seek to determine whether *control activities* are present

Frequently, the questions also indicate the type of control activity being addressed: transaction processing, file maintenance, asset protection, or computer. While it is not necessary to have this degree of subdivision for an ICQ to be effective, it may allow for a better understanding of the entity's internal control and is helpful in designing both tests of controls and substantive tests.

A more open-ended form of questionnaire might, for example, be organized by control objective and list for each objective a number of points that an auditor should consider, sometimes referred to as "points of focus," in thinking about how the objective is achieved. The auditor would then record the control activities that address the control objective. Control activities should be described in sufficient detail to support the auditor's conclusion as to whether the control appears to be effectively designed. Part of such a form appears in Figure 11.3 for the transaction processing control objectives relating to sales.

12

Assessing Control Risk and Developing the Audit Strategy

Both Statement on Auditing Standards (SAS) No. 47 (AU Section 312) and No. 55, as amended by SAS No. 78 (AU Section 319), require the auditor to assess control risk to determine what level of detection risk is acceptable in an audit. Assessing control risk is defined in AU Section 319.47 as the "process of evaluating the effectiveness of an entity's internal control in preventing or detecting material misstatements in the financial statements."

To be effective, internal control must be designed effectively and must operate effectively. *Design effectiveness*, which was discussed in Chapters 10 and 11 (Sections 10.2 and 11.4, Evaluating Design Effectiveness), relates to whether a control is suitably designed to prevent or detect material misstatements in specific financial statement assertions. The auditor evaluates the effectiveness of the design of a control in conjunction with obtaining the understanding of internal control. *Operating effectiveness* relates to how a control was applied, whether it has been consistently applied throughout the period, and who applied it. (In the context of the operation of controls, the term operating effectiveness incorporates the concept of consistent, or continuous, operation.) For example, an entity's internal control may include an effectively designed system for reporting past-due accounts receivable, but if the reports are not acted on in a timely manner, the control is not operating effectively. To obtain evidence of the effective operation of controls, the auditor carries out tests of the controls.

Control risk should be assessed in terms of financial statement assertions and corresponding audit objectives, which means that the auditor should consider controls in terms of how they contribute to the achievement of those objectives. The assessment of control risk takes into consideration controls in all five components of internal control, since they collectively address the entity's financial statement assertions. As noted in Chapter 9, the controls in those components are interrelated. For example, some aspects of the control environment affect the entity's ability to maintain an effective accounting system and control activities, others affect management's ability to make the informed judgments and estimates necessary to prepare financial statements, and still others affect the entity's ability to ensure that controls remain appropriate to changing conditions over time and restrict the opportunity for management fraud. The auditor considers all those controls both individually and collectively in assessing the extent to which they contribute to meeting the entity's financial reporting objectives.

The effect of controls on the achievement of financial statement assertions or audit objectives tends to vary with the control component. Some components, such as the control environment and certain monitoring activities, may have a pervasive effect on many account balances and classes of transactions, and on how those accounts and transactions are audited. For example, the conclusion that an entity has a decentralized organizational structure with an effective internal audit function that reports to top, centralized management, may affect the auditor's decision about the number of locations at which to perform auditing procedures or whether to perform certain procedures in some locations at an interim date. Control activities, related accounting procedures, and activity-level monitoring controls, on the other hand, are applied at lower, more detailed levels and have more direct effects on specific account balances.

12.1 PRELIMINARY ASSESSMENT OF CONTROL RISK

Based on the understanding of the various components of internal control, the evaluation of the effectiveness of their design, evidence of the effectiveness of their operation obtained concurrently with developing the understanding, and efficiency considerations (discussed later), the auditor makes a preliminary assessment of control risk. The preliminary assessment is the level of control risk the auditor *expects* will be supported by evidence that will be obtained from performing tests of controls.

As a practical matter, the auditor usually tests some controls, particularly with respect to the entity-level components, concurrently with developing the understanding of internal control. For example, on a recurring engagement where the auditor intends to test controls, he or she may update the understanding of controls and test them simultaneously because it is efficient to do so. Even on a new engagement, procedures directed at obtaining the understanding of controls also may produce evidence about their effective operation.

AU Section 319.59 cites the following procedures as an example of tests of controls performed concurrently with obtaining the understanding: inquiry about management's use of budgets, observing management's comparison of monthly budgets with actual expenses, and inspecting reports of the investigation of variances between budgeted and actual amounts. Although those auditing procedures are directed at ascertaining the design of the entity's budgeting policies and whether they have been placed in operation, the procedures also may provide evidence about the effectiveness of their operation in detecting material misstatements in classifying expenses. This evidence will influence the auditor's assessment of control risk for the presentation and disclosure objective relating to expenses in the income statement.

Another example of how procedures performed in obtaining the required understanding of controls also can provide evidence of their effective operation involves segregation of duties. In the course of understanding the accounting system, the auditor usually observes whether responsibilities for cash receipts and deposits are adequately segregated. In doing this, the auditor will at the same time obtain evidence about how effectively the separation procedure is operating. This evidence will influence the auditor's assessment of control risk for, in this instance, the existence objective relating to cash.

The auditor may make a preliminary assessment of control risk at the *maximum* level (that is, 100 percent) for all or certain audit objectives and proceed directly to substantive tests to obtain assurance for those audit objectives. In this instance, the auditor assumes that control risk is 100 percent and does not seek evidence to refute that assumption. In assessing control risk at the maximum, the auditor expects either that evidence to support a lower assessment is not available or that it would not be efficient to test controls to obtain the evidence. In either case, all of the auditor's assurance that relevant audit objectives have been met must come from substantive tests.

In most situations, however, the auditor has obtained, from procedures performed in understanding controls, evidence that supports a preliminary assessment of control risk for certain audit objectives and account balances that is below the maximum level. The term *below the maximum* refers to a range of assessments lower than maximum, but not *low*. That range can be thought of as a continuum along which control risk may be placed according to the auditor's professional judgment about the control components, particularly the control environment, including the organization of the finance and financial reporting functions; the accounting system, including the computer environment; and monitoring activities. The auditor also considers prior experience with the entity in arriving at that judgment. A below-the-maximum assessment indicates that only moderate assurance that relevant audit objectives have been met is needed from substantive tests. That level of assurance, however, ordinarily will require that the auditor perform substantive tests of details.

In some situations, the auditor may believe that a combination of tests of controls performed in obtaining or updating the understanding and additional tests that will be performed, will provide sufficient evidence to support an assessment of control risk at *low*. Low control risk describes an assessment that the risk of material misstatement is sufficiently low that the level of assurance required from substantive tests is also low, in which case substantive tests may be restricted to analytical procedures.

12.2 DEVELOPING THE AUDIT STRATEGY

The preliminary assessment of control risk is the basis for the audit strategy. Developing the audit strategy involves making detailed decisions about the specific auditing procedures to be performed to obtain the necessary assurance about each audit objective for each account balance in the financial statements. Those decisions are based mainly on the auditor's judgment about what evidence of the effective operation of controls is likely to be available and about the efficiency of testing controls in a particular transaction cycle. In making those determinations, the auditor considers information about the entity's business and industry (including inherent risks), the understanding of internal control and its audit implications, materiality judgments, and the cost of performing various types of auditing procedures.

As noted in Chapter 9 (Section 9.4, Relationship between Control Risk and the Achievement of Audit Objectives), in assessing control risk for specific account balances within a transaction cycle, or major transaction class within a cycle, the auditor generally assesses control risk for the audit objectives of *completeness*, *accuracy*, and *existence/occurrence* together. This is because it would be unusual for controls applied to a transaction cycle or class of transactions within a cycle to address one of those objectives to the exclusion of the others or to be effective with respect to one and not the others. Accordingly, the assessment of control risk is likely to be the same for the three objectives.

If the auditor has assessed control risk at maximum, no controls will be tested and all audit assurance will come from substantive tests. If, as is more common, the preliminary assessment is below the maximum or low, the auditor will extend the understanding of controls to include activity-level monitoring controls or control activities, evaluate the effectiveness of their design, and perform tests of controls (beyond any tests performed concurrently with developing the understanding of controls) to confirm the preliminary assessment.

If the planned control risk assessment is below the maximum, but not low, the auditor expects to obtain a moderate amount of assurance about the completeness, accuracy, and existence/occurrence audit objectives for systems-derived accounts, that is, accounts derived from a major class of transactions in a transaction cycle, by obtaining evidence of the effective design and operation of the entity-level controls, the accounting system, and activity-level monitoring controls. However, those controls do not sufficiently address the control objectives related to transactions and files and to protecting assets, and therefore the auditor should perform substantive tests of details to gain the remaining assurance necessary with respect to the completeness, accuracy, and existence/occurrence of related accounts.

If the planned control risk assessment is low, the auditor achieves assurance for the completeness, accuracy, and existence/occurrence audit objectives for systems-derived accounts mainly by obtaining evidence of the effective design and operation of the accounting system and related control activities. Substantive tests of details can be reduced significantly or possibly even eliminated. To determine whether the completeness, accuracy, and existence/occurrence audit objectives have been met, the auditor considers whether the entity has met the control objectives related to transactions and files and to protecting assets. [Those control objectives are defined in Chapter 9, Section 9.3(a), Control Objectives, and described in detail in Chapter 11, Section 11.1, Control Activities.] Evidence of effective design and operation that indicates that the control objectives relevant to a particular transaction cycle have been met, supports the auditor's preliminary assessment of control risk at low.

The auditor may assess control risk below the maximum or at low even if a control objective has not been achieved because of a missing or ineffective control, but only if he or she ascertains the effect of the unmet control objective on the financial statements. Any unmet control objective for a significant systems-derived account or class of transactions has the potential to result in a material misstatement of the financial statements. Accordingly, if there is an unmet control objective, the auditor should design and perform a substantive test of details to respond to any resulting risk of material misstatement and determine whether such misstatements have occurred. The combination of tests of controls and substantive tests, including those performed in response to unmet control objectives, provides the assurance the auditor needs about the audit objectives of completeness, accuracy, and existence/occurrence.

An entity's control activities often are not designed to prevent or detect material misstatements related to the audit objectives of *cutoff* and *valuation*. Similarly, control activities generally do not address the risk of misstatements related to the audit objectives of *rights and obligations* and *presentation and disclosure*. Therefore, the auditor needs to design substantive tests to gain assurance about those objectives for all accounts, regardless of the control risk assessment. However, control activities may reduce the risk of material misstatement in the underlying data used in making accounting valuations and estimates. Monitoring controls also might identify material errors in cutoffs, valuations, and estimates. Accordingly, the auditor may find it efficient to test those controls as a means of determining that the underlying data is accurate and complete.

(a) Tailoring Tests of Controls to the Preliminary Assessment

The preliminary assessment of control risk is the principal determinant of which controls the auditor will test. The lower the assessed level of control risk, the greater the need for evidence that controls are operating effectively to prevent misstatements from reaching the financial statements or to detect them in a timely manner.

If the preliminary assessment of control risk is below the maximum, but not low, tests of controls may be limited to *entity-level controls* and *activity-level monitoring controls*. In those circumstances, tests of controls performed concurrently with developing the understanding of controls may provide sufficient evidence to support the below-the-maximum assessment, and further tests of controls may not be necessary.

Provided that the entity-level controls and activity-level monitoring controls are effective, it generally is not necessary to test control activities when control risk is assessed below the maximum. If, however, monitoring controls are not effective enough on their own to support the planned restriction of substantive tests, and if it is efficient to do so, the auditor may test relevant control activities that compensate for absent or ineffective monitoring controls, or, as noted earlier, design a specific substantive test to detect misstatements that might result. Based on the results of all the tests, the auditor makes a judgment about where along the below-the-maximum continuum control risk falls. The assessment of control risk along the continuum will affect the extent of substantive tests, as discussed in Chapter 15 [Section 15.2(c), Extent of Testing].

Tests of controls performed concurrently with developing the understanding of controls ordinarily are not directed at control activities and thus do not provide sufficient evidence to support an assessment of control risk at low. To assess control risk at low, the auditor needs to test the operating effectiveness of specific *application and computer control activities*.

Tests of control activities are necessary to support a low control risk assessment because control activities (and related accounting procedures) are applied at lower, more detailed levels and have more direct effects on specific audit objectives and account balances within transaction cycles than do controls that are part of the other components. For instance, controls established to ensure that all items reported on a receiving report log are included in accounts payable in the correct amounts, relate directly to the completeness and accuracy of accounts payable. In situations where tests of control activities support a low control risk assessment, it may not be necessary to test activity-level monitoring controls.

Effectively designed and operating control activities can provide assurance that material misstatements in the accounting records will be *prevented*. Monitoring controls provide less assurance than control activities and by themselves may help ensure only that a misstatement will be *detected* after it has occurred. For example, management's regular review for credit control purposes of an aged receivables listing and follow-up of late items should detect incorrect underlying information. In conjunction with other controls in the revenue cycle, such a review may give the auditor sufficient evidence to assess control risk below the maximum, but not at low. This will allow the auditor to restrict detailed substantive tests of receivables, but not to eliminate them entirely.

Because tests of control activities usually require more audit effort than tests of controls in the other components, tests of control activities generally are not performed unless the auditor has determined that evidence to support a low control risk assessment for the completeness, accuracy, and existence/occurrence audit objectives for an account balance or class of transactions is available and can be obtained efficiently. In those circumstances, the auditor may be able to eliminate or significantly curtail substantive tests of details relating to those objectives. AU Section 319 (para. .81) cautions that regardless of the assessed level of control risk, some substantive tests should be performed for significant account balances and classes of transactions. The authors believe, however, that if the auditor assesses the risk of material misstatement related to completeness, accuracy, and existence/occurrence for a significant account balance or class of transactions at low, it ordinarily is not necessary to direct substantive tests specifically to those audit objectives.

As a practical matter, tests of control activities and activity-level monitoring controls performed when the audit strategy is to assess control risk at low or below the maximum normally are restricted to major transaction classes, because other transactions are relatively low volume and the related accounts can be audited more efficiently by substantive tests. Also, when the planned assessment of control risk is low, the auditor usually tests accounting procedures in conjunction with related control activities.

The auditor sometimes may believe evidence of the effective operation of certain key control activities is necessary in order to design substantive tests with respect to a particular audit objective, regardless of the preliminary assessment of control risk. The auditor then plans, at an early stage, to test the effectiveness of those control activities. Even if the results of such tests are not expected to support a low control risk assessment, they may affect the nature, timing, and extent of substantive tests. Examples of such key control activities are physical inventory cycle count procedures, which the auditor might test to help establish the accuracy of inventory quantities, and cash reconciliations, tests of which might help establish the accuracy of the cash account balance.

Decisions about testing control activities and assessing control risk in a computerized environment typically focus first on computer controls, because they ensure the effectiveness of programmed control procedures, and then on application controls. Evidence that computer controls are operating effectively gives the auditor some assurance that the data the system processes and stores is complete, accurate, and protected against unauthorized change. Only after obtaining this assurance would the auditor test the application controls to determine whether they meet the control objectives related to the authorization, completeness, and accuracy of transactions and files, and to the protection of assets.

The auditor determines which categories of computer controls to test primarily by considering the characteristics of the entity's computer environment, as discussed in Chapter 10 [Section 10.1(d)(ii), The Computer Environment]. The auditor also considers the risk of errors versus the risk of fraud, the programmed control procedures applied to transactions and files, and the control objectives those procedures address. The effectiveness of application controls that meet the authorization, completeness, and accuracy control objectives depends on computer controls relating to development and implementation, changes to applications, and computer operations. The asset protection control objective is met, at least in part, by security controls, particularly access controls, as well as by an appropriate division of duties.

The auditor typically does not test programmed control procedures unless the audit strategy includes tests of related computer controls. This is because it is not likely to be efficient to obtain evidence of the effectiveness of programmed control procedures by testing those procedures themselves. Also, the reliability of programmed procedures may be in question if the computer controls are inadequate or untested. In these circumstances, it usually would be more efficient to obtain the necessary assurance from substantive tests. There may be some circumstances in which the auditor does not test computer controls, but nevertheless wishes to test the effective operation of programmed *accounting* procedures directly. Those tests will be costly because of the sheer volume of such procedures in a typical computerized accounting system, although the use of software might facilitate the testing. Testing techniques using audit software are described in Chapter 15 [Section 15.2(d), Using Computer Audit Techniques to Perform Substantive Tests].

One of the following audit strategies usually results with respect to computer controls:

- The auditor tests all relevant categories of computer controls and the results support a conclusion that they ensure the effectiveness of application controls that address all relevant control objectives. The auditor then tests the application controls.

- The results of tests of computer controls indicate that they ensure the effectiveness of application controls that address the authorization, completeness, and accuracy of transaction processing and file maintenance; however, evidence of the effectiveness of computer security controls is not available or not efficient to obtain. In this situation, the auditor assesses the risk of financial statement misstatements associated with the security of data and assets by considering such factors as the susceptibility of relevant assets to theft, the sensitivity of stored data, and the adequacy and interrelationship of other relevant components of internal control. Often, the auditor will not be able to obtain evidence that the asset protection objective is met and will design substantive tests to provide the required assurance that related audit objectives have been achieved (principally the existence of assets and the classification of expenses and losses).

- The auditor determines that the computer controls are not effective or that testing them would be inefficient and assesses control risk and designs the audit strategy to call for few tests of controls and more assurance from substantive tests.

(b) Efficiency Considerations

Testing controls in order to restrict substantive tests is efficient only if the audit effort (or "cost") of performing those tests is less than the audit effort entailed in performing the substantive tests that would be required if the auditor did not test controls. (Cost includes more than the number of hours of auditor time; it also involves staffing considerations and the level of support required and likely to be available from the entity.) AU Section 319.62 discusses audit efficiency considerations as follows:

> In considering efficiency, the auditor recognizes that additional evidential matter that supports . . . [an] assessed level of control risk for an assertion would result in less audit effort for the substantive tests of that assertion. The auditor weighs the increase in audit effort associated with the additional tests of controls [beyond those performed concurrently with obtaining the understanding] that is necessary to obtain such evidential matter against the resulting decrease in audit effort associated with the reduced substantive tests. When the auditor concludes it is inefficient to obtain additional evidential matter for specific assertions, the auditor uses the assessed level of control risk

based on the understanding of internal control in planning the substantive tests for those assertions.

The auditor usually decides that it would *not* be efficient to perform tests of controls in a particular transaction cycle when one or more of the following circumstances are present:

1. Volumes of transactions are low, or the characteristics of account balances make substantive tests relatively easy to apply.
2. The particular application is based on a manual accounting system.
3. The necessary tests would entail testing a large number of controls, as might be the case, for example, if computer controls do not ensure the effectiveness of programmed control procedures in a computerized system.

In these circumstances, the auditor would likely design and perform substantive tests for all relevant audit objectives and account balances in a particular transaction cycle, taking into consideration materiality and the results of risk assessment activities already carried out.

For large entities with pervasive, complex, and integrated computerized systems, it may be readily apparent that testing controls in all transaction cycles is an efficient strategy. In fact, in entities that transmit, process, maintain, or access significant financial information electronically, it may not be feasible or possible to achieve certain audit objectives by performing only substantive tests. Other entities, whether large or smaller, may have relatively complex computerized accounting systems, but the number and expertise of computer personnel may be limited. In other instances, there may be extensive application controls, but some computer controls may be informal and not well-documented. There are frequently deficiencies in controls related to computer security, although some of these deficiencies may be mitigated if the entity uses purchased accounting packages for which the source code is not readily available (that is, the entity's personnel are effectively unable to amend the programs). On these types of engagements it is often more difficult for the auditor to decide whether testing controls is an efficient strategy.

Management's expectations and requirements also affect audit strategy decisions. For example:

- Management may request the auditor to assess internal control in greater depth than might be considered necessary for audit purposes, or additional responsibilities relating to internal control may arise because the entity is subject to special regulatory or other requirements. In those circumstances, the auditor may acquire a more detailed understanding of internal control than otherwise would have been necessary. This, in turn, may make it efficient to perform tests of controls and restrict substantive tests.

- Management may require the audit report shortly after year-end, leading the auditor to decide to perform substantive tests of details at an interim date rather than at year-end. Tests of controls may be an efficient and effective way of obtaining assurance that the risk of material misstatement is acceptably low during the period between the early testing date and year-end.

12.3 PERFORMING TESTS OF CONTROLS

As noted earlier, on most engagements, the auditor obtains some evidence about the effective operation of entity-level controls and activity-level monitoring controls as a result of procedures performed in developing the understanding of internal control. That evidence often allows the auditor to assess control risk somewhere along the below-the-maximum continuum. To lower the assessment of control risk further (either along the below-the-maximum continuum or to low), the auditor will need to perform additional tests of controls.

(a) Sources of Evidence and Techniques Used to Test Controls

The evidence necessary to support a specific assessment of control risk is a matter of auditor judgment and influences the auditor's decisions about the specific tests to perform, the techniques to use, when to perform the tests, and how much testing to do. In making those determinations, the auditor should consider the source of evidence, its timeliness, and whether related evidence exists.

The techniques used in testing controls are observation, inquiry of entity personnel, examination of documents and records (both manual and electronic), and, in some cases, reperformance of the application of procedures. (With the exception of reperformance, the techniques used to test controls are the same as those used to obtain the understanding of controls, as described in Chapter 11, Section 11.3, Developing the Understanding.)

The procedures used in testing controls should be sufficiently comprehensive to support the control risk assessment. For example, if the auditor inquires about a sales manager's review and investigation of a report of invoices with unusually high or low gross margins, merely asking the sales manager whether he or she investigates discrepancies is likely to be inadequate. In this case, appropriate questions might include the following:

- How is the report reviewed?
- Are there particular situations to which the manager's attention is directed?
- Is every report reviewed?
- How long does the review take?
- How are the items on the report investigated?
- Are all items investigated?
- What sorts of problems cause these exceptions?
- Are those problems recurring?
- Are those problems being eliminated?
- How is it ensured that every report is received?
- Are the reports ever not produced, or do reports ever have no entries on them?
- How often are the reports reviewed?
- Were there any periods in which these reports were not reviewed?

- Who reviews these reports in the absence of the person who normally has that responsibility?
- Has anything ever occurred to suggest that the report is not reliable?

During the inquiry process, the auditor should apply professional skepticism and, wherever possible, corroborate the resulting explanations by inspecting procedures manuals and reports or other similar documents. The auditor also may make corroborative inquiries of individuals other than those implementing the controls. Although the auditor can acquire relevant information by making appropriate inquiries, AU Section 319.69 states that inquiry alone generally does not provide sufficient evidence to support a conclusion about whether a specific control activity is effective. Accordingly, if the auditor believes a control activity may have a significant effect in supporting a low control risk assessment for a specific audit objective, he or she usually should perform tests in addition to inquiry to obtain sufficient evidence that the control is operating effectively.

There may be no documentation of the operation of some controls, such as certain arrangements for segregating duties. In that event, evidence may be obtained through observation. In general, evidence the auditor obtains directly, such as by observation, is more reliable than that obtained indirectly, such as by inquiry. However, this must be weighed against the possibility that the observed control may not be performed in the same way when the auditor is not present.

For manual aspects of internal control (such as the follow-up of items contained in computer-generated exception reports), the auditor should examine documents and records of the application when they may reasonably be expected to exist (for example, there may be written explanations, check marks, or other indications of performance on a copy of a report used in applying a control). The auditor generally examines documentation of the performance of monitoring controls such as supervision and reviews. The lack of reports or documents that the auditor typically would expect a control to generate may indicate that the control is not operating effectively, even though it may be designed effectively.

Tests based on observation, inquiry, and examination of documents and records often provide sufficient evidence about the operating effectiveness of a control. That is, these tests provide evidence of how the control was applied, whether it was applied consistently throughout the period, and the person(s) who applied it. However, in some instances, the auditor also may have to reperform the application of a control to obtain adequate evidence that it is operating effectively. When the auditor believes a control is so significant that further evidence of its effectiveness is necessary, it is appropriate to reperform its application. For example, a bank's control designed to ensure the completeness and accuracy of updating a standing data file of interest rates may entail comparing authorized changes in interest rates with the data on the file after the changes have been input. That control may be so significant to the accuracy of interest charged to loan customers that the auditor may wish to reperform the comparison a few times to gain additional evidence that it is operating as prescribed. If extensive reperformance of controls is likely to be necessary, the auditor should reconsider whether it is efficient to perform tests of controls in order to restrict the scope of substantive testing.

(b) Timeliness of Evidence

If observation is used as a test of controls, the auditor should consider that the evidence obtained from that test is relevant only to the time when the observation took place. Accordingly, the evidence may not be sufficient to assess effectiveness for untested periods. In that situation, the auditor may decide to perform other tests of controls to obtain evidence about whether the control was operating during the entire period under audit. For instance, the auditor may observe cycle counting of inventory at a point in time and examine documents used to record the counts made during other time periods.

In considering evidence to support the assessment of control risk in the current year, the auditor may consider prior-year audit evidence. In determining whether such evidence is relevant to the current audit, the auditor should consider the audit objective involved, the specific controls, the extent to which they were tested in prior years, the results of the tests of controls, and the evidence about the operation of controls that the auditor may expect from substantive tests in the current audit (see the later discussion of dual-purpose tests). The auditor should obtain information currently about whether changes in internal control have occurred and, if so, their nature and extent. All of these considerations may support either increasing or decreasing the evidence necessary in the current period.

(c) Continuous Operation of Controls

When assessing whether tests of controls support the planned restriction of substantive tests, the auditor needs to determine that relevant controls have operated continuously during the period. Manually applied controls are prone to random failures. When assessing those controls, the auditor should obtain evidence of their application for events occurring at different places and at different times during the period. These tests need not be extensive. In some situations, tests of monitoring controls may provide evidence that underlying manually performed application controls operated continuously. The extent of testing will depend on factors such as the frequency (e.g., daily, monthly) of reports, the number of people exercising the control, and the number of locations at which the control is exercised. For example, if a control is the review of a monthly report by personnel at multiple locations, the auditor might examine reports covering several months at each of the locations.

Spreading tests throughout the period is not always necessary to obtain evidence about continuous operation. For instance, if a control involves reviewing and following up an exception report that is cumulative, transactions or circumstances meeting specified criteria continue to be reported and reviewed as long as the criteria are met (examples would be reports of "goods shipped but not billed" or "goods received but not invoiced"). For such controls, tests that provide evidence that a control operated effectively at a point in time also will provide evidence about the operation of the underlying accounting procedures throughout the period up to that point in time.

Programmed accounting and control procedures are not subject to random failures or deterioration over time, provided that relevant computer controls are operating effectively. If the auditor has tested the computer controls and found them to be operating effectively, this provides evidence that programmed accounting and control procedures operated continuously throughout the period. In addition, users of information affected by controls would notice control breakdowns and report them to appropriate levels of management. Thus, the auditor can sometimes obtain indirect evidence, from the ongoing operation of business activities, that controls operated continuously.

(d)   Testing Computer Controls

The auditor's purpose in testing computer controls is the same as in testing application controls, namely, to test the effectiveness of the controls as a basis for restricting substantive tests. The same techniques are used in testing both kinds of controls, that is, inquiry, observation, examination of evidence, and, where appropriate, reperformance. The auditor may be able to use software, however, to assist in performing the tests of computer controls.

Two trends have affected the way the auditor approaches testing computer controls. First, as noted in Chapter 10 [Section 10.1(d)(ii) The Computer Environment], many IT functions are moving from centralized processing toward decentralized or fully distributed client/server systems. Second, where large centralized systems still exist, their size and complexity are increasing. While some computer controls are still common to all applications, application-specific procedures are growing more prevalent. For example, the applications for each major user may be supported by different system analysis and programming functions, which may be subject to different controls. In that situation, the auditor would have to test controls for applications in each area.

In some sophisticated computer environments, computer software can help the auditor test the entity's computer controls. For instance, user controls for reviewing and authorizing proposed changes to programs may be performed on-line without creating any hardcopy documentation. The auditor can use software to reperform such controls. Although software can facilitate such tests of controls involving reperformance, the auditor still should consider carefully whether it might be more efficient to perform substantive tests than to reperform computer controls. Generally, computer controls are not reperformed often since it is difficult to reproduce for testing purposes the conditions under which the controls operate.

(e)   Dual-Purpose Tests

Tests of controls normally precede substantive tests because the results of tests of controls affect the auditor's decision about the nature, timing, and extent of substantive tests. Sometimes, however, for greater audit efficiency, the two types of tests may be performed simultaneously using the same document or record. For instance, the auditor may use the same accounts receivable balances selected for confirmation (a substantive test) to determine that the customers' files contain documents showing that the sales orders were appropriately approved (a test of controls). Moreover, a test of controls may provide evidence about dollar errors in the accounts. Also, a substantive test may provide evidence about internal control if no errors were found as a result of the substantive test or if errors that were found were investigated and determined to be the result of a control deficiency.

(f)   Interrelationship of Evidence

In assessing control risk for a specific audit objective, the auditor should consider evidence in its entirety. Evidence provided by tests of one component of internal control should be considered in relation to evidence about the other components. Evidence produced by different tests of controls should be considered in combination. Evidence from various tests that supports the same conclusion is more reliable than evidence resulting from a single test. When audit evidence from more than one source leads to different conclusions, however, the auditor should reconsider the original assessment. For example, if tests of the control environment and monitoring activities indicate that controls should prevent or detect unauthorized changes in a computer program, but tests of the operation of the program reveal that unauthorized changes were made and were not detected, the auditor would reassess the conclusion about the control environment.

(g)   Evaluating the Results of Tests of Controls

The auditor should review the results of the tests of controls and consider whether the planned assessed level of control risk has been attained. If the auditor finds that the risk of material misstatement for particular audit objectives is higher than originally expected, he or she will have to reconsider the assurance needed from substantive tests.

   If the tests of controls reveal a departure from or breakdown in prescribed controls, the auditor should consider its cause and document the conclusions reached. What amendments need to be made to planned substantive tests will depend in part on the reasons for the departure. For instance, the appropriate audit response to control breakdowns should be different if the cause was a poorly trained clerk who substituted for a highly trained clerk during the latter's three-week vacation than if the breakdown resulted from incompetent work or ineffective supervision throughout the year.

   Depending on the nature of the control, if a departure or breakdown is corrected long enough before year-end, and this is confirmed by appropriate tests, normally no amendment to other audit tests will be necessary. Departures from and breakdowns in controls should be considered for reporting to management, as discussed in Chapter 4, and the documentation of internal control should be amended as required. Also as noted in Chapter 4, the auditor should consider whether any departures from and breakdowns in controls appear to be unintentional or intentional. Intentional departures or breakdowns might be an indication of fraud; in that event, the auditor should consider the implications for the integrity of management and employees and for other aspects of the audit.

   In evaluating the effectiveness of controls, the auditor considers all the control components taken together. The various components contribute to internal control in different ways. The entity-level components must be effective for internal control as a whole to be effective. If the auditor concludes that internal control as it relates to the entity as a whole is effective, there is a lower risk that other, lower-level aspects of internal control will be overridden or bypassed and that misstatements may occur. That conclusion helps the auditor determine the nature, timing, and extent of other auditing procedures, including both tests of activity-level monitoring controls and of control activities, and substantive tests.

If the auditor concludes that the control environment and the monitoring component are not conducive to the maintenance of the other control components or that they do not minimize sufficiently the incentives and opportunities for management to override controls or intentionally misrepresent the financial statements, he or she will need to consider whether appropriate substantive tests can be designed to address the increased risk of both errors and fraud, and, in particular, the possibility of management fraud. The assessment may identify issues relating to the reliability and integrity of management that should be considered in the conduct of the audit. In some cases, these issues may result in the need to reevaluate the client relationship. In addition, the auditor may identify matters that should be brought to the attention of senior management or the audit committee.

12.4 EFFECT OF AN ENTITY'S USE OF A SERVICE ORGANIZATION

An entity may use a service organization, such as a data processing center, to record certain transactions, process data, or even execute transactions and maintain the related accounting records and assets, such as securities. Transactions may flow through an accounting system that is, wholly or partially, separate from the entity's, and the auditor may find it necessary or efficient in assessing the entity's internal control to consider procedures that the service organization performs. To do that, the auditor may obtain a report prepared by the service organization's auditor (referred to as the service auditor) covering the processing of transactions at the service organization.

SAS No. 70, *Reports on the Processing of Transactions by Service Organizations*, as amended (AU Section 324), provides guidance on the factors an auditor (referred to as the user auditor) should consider when auditing the financial statements of an entity that uses a service organization to process certain transactions. (SAS No. 70 also provides guidance on the responsibilities of the service auditor who issues a report on the processing of transactions by a service organization for use by user auditors, as discussed in Chapter 29.) The user auditor should consider the effect of the service organization on the entity's internal control and the availability of evidence about the entity's internal control that is necessary to plan the audit, assess control risk, and perform substantive tests. SAS No. 70 provides guidance on the auditor's use of either of the two reports (described next) that service auditors may provide. In deciding to obtain a report of either type from a service auditor, the user auditor should consider the features of the service organization's controls and their relationship to the entity's internal control.

An entity may use a service organization in connection with recording transactions and processing related data, or in connection with executing transactions and maintaining the related accountability. In the former situation, the user auditor often considers it necessary, in order to obtain a sufficient understanding of the flow of transactions to plan the audit, to obtain a service auditor's *report on controls placed in operation*. This report contains a description of the service organization's controls that may be relevant to a user's internal control, states whether such controls have been placed in operation as of a specific date, and states whether they are suitably designed to achieve specified control objectives. In many instances, the report identifies input documents, key files processed, and reports generated. Even if a service auditor's report is not available, the user auditor may be able to obtain or update the necessary understanding of processing at the service organization by reviewing documentation maintained at the entity's premises, inquiring of employees about the service organization's processing, performing substantive tests to obtain information about the nature of processing at the service organization, or visiting the service organization.

If the service organization executes transactions and maintains the related accountability, the accounting procedures and control activities that are essential to achieving one or more of the entity's control objectives will most likely be located in whole or in part at the service organization. If the user auditor plans to assess control risk below the maximum or at low, he or she ordinarily will find it necessary to obtain a service auditor's *report on controls placed in operation and tests of operating effectiveness*. This report includes all of the items contained in the report described in the previous paragraph, and in addition describes the tests performed and states whether the controls tested were operating with sufficient effectiveness to provide reasonable, but not absolute, assurance that the related control objectives were achieved during the specified period. The user auditor will, however, need to determine that the service auditor has addressed all control objectives of interest. Even if such a report is not available, it may be possible to support an assessment below the maximum, provided the entity has sufficient controls over data (e.g., payroll information) input to the service organization and data (e.g., payroll checks and records) generated by it.

SAS No. 70 requires an auditor who uses a service auditor's report that contains an opinion on the design or the operating effectiveness of controls to make inquiries about the service auditor's professional reputation, unless that information is already known. If the service auditor's report covers tests of controls, the user auditor also should consider the length of time that has elapsed from the end of the period covered by those tests to the entity's year-end. If the elapsed time is significant, the user auditor might inquire as to whether entity personnel are aware—from their knowledge of changes in contract provisions, discussions with service organization personnel, differences in output reports, or changes in input data—of changes in the service organization's system. If they are, the user auditor might request management's permission to contact the service organization or its auditor to obtain an understanding of the changes and the effect they may have on the control risk assessment. The user auditor also might compare the service organization's output data during the intervening period with similar output data for an earlier period(s) for evidence of design changes in the system or fluctuations in volume or dollar amounts. If management is unable to explain these fluctuations, the auditor could ask management's permission to discuss the matter with the service organization or its auditor. After reviewing the service auditor's report, the user auditor may decide that additional auditing procedures are necessary. In that event, he or she may ask management to request the service organization to have its auditor expand the scope of the testing performed. If the user auditor is unable to obtain the necessary evidence, it usually will be necessary to visit the service organization and perform appropriate tests of controls in effect there.

12.5   DOCUMENTING THE ASSESSMENT OF CONTROL RISK AND TESTS OF CONTROLS

Professional standards require the auditor to document the basis for the conclusions reached concerning the control risk assessment for specific audit objectives related to the account balances and classes of transactions reflected in the financial statements. (For audit objectives for which control risk is assessed at maximum, however, SAS No. 78 specifies that only the conclusion itself need be documented; the basis for the conclusion does not have to be documented.) Similar to documentation of the understanding of internal control, the nature and extent of the documentation of the basis for the conclusions will vary according to the control risk assessment and the nature of the entity's internal control and its documentation.

Chapters 10 and 11 present several alternative formats for documenting the understanding of accounting procedures, monitoring controls, and control activities; provide examples; and explain when each could be used. The auditor may document the assessment of control risk and the tests of controls performed to confirm the assessment using the same forms as were used for documenting the understanding or using different ones; that will depend on individual auditor or firm preference. Regardless of the type of documentation the auditor uses, it must provide a means for recording in the working papers a description of the relevant controls and any tests the auditor performed to assess how effectively they operate.

The choice of documentation depends on such factors as the type of test (for example, observing that a control is performed versus reperforming it) and the policies of the particular CPA firm. For some tests of controls, it is efficient to record the test on the same form as the understanding. Alternatively, separate working papers could be used to document the tests; this method is particularly useful when a test consists of examining evidence of a control's operation (such as authorization of payroll changes by department heads and personnel managers) or reperformance of a control (such as reperforming, at year-end, the entity's monthly follow-up of all unmatched cash receipts included in a suspense account, for evidence that the receipts were credited to the proper account).

Some auditing firms have designed forms for both recording the understanding of controls and documenting the results of tests of those controls. The form may be organized like an ICQ [described in Chapter 11, Section 11.6(d), Internal Control Questionnaires]; that is, it may be divided into sections by control objectives and list under each control objective questions related to control activities that achieve that objective and related monitoring controls. The auditor indicates a "Yes" or "No" answer to each question and describes, either directly on the form or on an attached working paper, the relevant controls and the tests of controls. A question or blank space may follow each section that prompts the auditor to draw an overall conclusion about whether the controls, taken as a whole, are operating effectively and to document the reasons for the conclusion.

Regardless of the form used to document tests of controls, relevant information about the nature, timing, and extent of tests should be recorded in enough detail to support the auditor's conclusion about whether the controls are operating effectively. That generally includes a description of the tests performed, the entity personnel interviewed, and any documents examined or observations made to corroborate the inquiries, as well as any exceptions and how they were cleared or their audit implications. Since in most circumstances only one or a few items are examined, extensive documentation, such as that normally required in sampling applications, is unnecessary. Rather, only the items selected for testing and the results of the test need to be documented. An illustration of a form used to record tests of controls is presented in Figure 12.1.

It is often helpful for the auditor to prepare a document summarizing the deficiencies found in the operation of controls. Some auditors document operating deficiencies on the same working paper as deficiencies in the design of controls, as discussed in Chapter 10 (Section 10.4, Documenting the Understanding and Evaluation of Design); other auditors use different forms of documentation for the different types of deficiencies. Whatever form of documentation is used, it permits the auditor to consider the effect of deficiencies on planned substantive tests. It also facilitates preparing the communication on control deficiencies (discussed in Chapter 4). The working paper documentation usually includes a description of the nature of the deficiency and its possible effect on the financial statements, a decision on whether the

Figure 12.1   Record of Test

Entity

Year ended

Application Cycle

Revenue

Purchasing

Inventory

Other:

Control activity: **W/P-ref:**

Computer Section

Change to Applications

Development/Implementation

Computer Security

Computer Operations

Personnel interviewed and dates:

Documents examined or observations made to corroborate inquiry:

Note: Be alert for previously unidentified weaknesses in segregation of duties that could increase control risk. In other words, be alert for situations where the effect of this control could be mitigated by the same person performing an incompatible control function.

deficiency could result in material misstatement in the financial statements and the justification for this decision, and an explanation of the audit response to the deficiency, including any amendment to the nature, timing, or extent of substantive tests. The documentation should be amended whenever the auditor finds pertinent information in the course of the audit, whether by performing tests of controls or substantive tests.

13

Auditing the Revenue Cycle

The audit of accounts in the revenue cycle (e.g., sales, sales returns and allowances, service revenue, accounts receivable and related allowance accounts, deferred revenues, and cash) usually consists of a combination of substantive tests and tests of controls to support an assessment of control risk that is below the maximum or at low. Rarely would the audit of revenue cycle accounts consist solely of substantive tests—in most entities, revenue transactions are sufficiently numerous that management installs the necessary controls and the auditor finds it efficient to test them as a basis for restricting substantive tests.

This chapter covers the process by which the auditor determines the strategy for auditing the revenue cycle. It describes typical revenue transactions, the accounting systems for processing them, and the monitoring and control activities applied to the transactions. It also discusses the conditions under which the auditor will be able to arrive at a preliminary assessment of control risk that is below the maximum or at low and the controls that ordinarily should be tested under various control risk assessments. Chapter 18 describes the nature, timing, and extent of substantive tests of revenue cycle accounts that would be appropriate under the alternative risk assessments of maximum, below the maximum, and low.

Revenue transactions that are completed within a relatively short time—when sale, delivery of product or rendering of service, and collection occur within a few weeks or months of each other—are the most common revenue transactions and are the subject of this chapter and Chapter 18. The focus of both chapters is on revenues generated by an entity's principal operations. Ancillary revenues, such as dividends, interest, and rent, are discussed in Chapters 21 and 22. Chapter 18 also discusses substantive tests for several specific types of revenue transactions that various entities may confront.

13.1   TYPICAL TRANSACTIONS AND CONTROLS

The revenue cycle in most entities can be divided into three typical classes of transactions:

- Sales of goods and services
- Payments received for goods and services
- Goods returned by and claims received from customers

(a)   Sales of Goods and Services

The process of selling goods and services generally includes the following activities:

- Receiving and recording customers' orders
- Authorizing credit terms and shipments
- Confirming orders
- Executing shipping orders for goods or work orders for the performance of services
- Recording the shipments or services performed

In considering the accounting system that processes revenue transactions and the monitoring and control activities applied to them, the auditor is interested mainly in controls to ensure that all sales transactions that actually occurred are authorized and are recorded accurately; that is, that the entity's controls achieve the seven control objectives described in Chapters 9 and 11. Those control objectives are closely related to the audit objectives of completeness, accuracy, and existence/occurrence of revenue cycle accounts, particularly sales and accounts receivable. Other controls, while not directly related to those audit objectives, also may be of interest to the auditor. For example, the fact that credit checks are performed may provide evidence the auditor can use to evaluate whether the allowance for uncollectible accounts is adequate, which affects the valuation audit objective for accounts receivable.

The paragraphs that follow describe the various activities involved in the sale of goods, and the controls typically applied in processing the transactions. Some of the activities described in this section also apply to sales of services, while others, like requisitioning, packing, and shipping, do not. To the extent that the processes are similar for both goods and services, the discussion of controls applies to sales of services as well.

(i) Receiving and Recording Customers' Orders.

For the selling entity, receipt of a customer's order, either by mail, telephone, fax, or other electronic means, starts the revenue cycle. When customer orders are received, they may be logged in a sales order record or similar document, recorded on prenumbered forms, batched for further processing, or entered directly into a computer.

An open order file typically is generated when orders are input. Completeness of input of orders may be ensured by numerical sequencing or controlling batch totals. Completeness of processing of sales orders is then controlled by subsequently matching shipments against open orders and deleting fully processed orders from the open order file. Controls designed to ensure completeness of input of customer orders—for example, the use of batch controls—also may help ensure that orders were input accurately.

The objective of controls over customer orders when they are received is to ensure that all orders received are considered for shipment. Although the absence or ineffectiveness of such controls would not result in financial statement misstatements, the auditor may be interested in the procedures applied to sales orders before shipping orders (described below) are generated. Those procedures may indicate, for example, that management coordinates inventory requirements and production orders with product demand. They also may help ensure that all shipments are recorded; for example, the periodic review and follow-up of open orders should identify shipments that have not yet been recorded, as well as orders not yet shipped.

(ii) Authorizing Credit Terms and Shipments.

Management typically establishes procedures to determine how much credit to extend to customers, communicates the information appropriately, revises it periodically, and monitors adherence to established credit limits. In some entities that perform the credit approval function manually, customers' orders are sent to the credit department before they are recorded. In other entities, authorization takes place after orders have been recorded. Procedures for authorizing credit limits, other terms, and sales prices vary among entities, but certain practices are similar in most credit departments. Orders from repeat customers with a good record of payment, unless in excess of authorized credit limits, usually are processed routinely. Periodically, the credit department determines, by referring to published sources or requesting audited financial statements, that customers' financial condition has not deteriorated. The same means are used to ascertain new customers' creditworthiness. Many entities establish minimum sales order amounts before a credit check will be performed and credit extended. In any event, credit approval usually is evidenced in writing by the credit manager or other designated individual.

Where the authorization process is computerized, the input of sales orders generates a computer match of relevant customer order information to the customer master file that includes predetermined credit limits and other terms, and to the sales price master file. If an order is in excess of the customer's limit or is for a customer not on the system, or if the sales terms or price is outside predetermined limits, a shipping or production order will not be generated and the sales order may not be accepted for further processing. Instead, an exception report will be produced for follow-up by an appropriate individual. In some systems, the computer also matches sales orders against an inventory master file to ascertain whether the goods are on hand to fill the order. The integrity of standing data is achieved by limiting changes to the customer master file to credit department personnel, and changes to the sales price master file to marketing personnel. The completeness and accuracy of changes to those files are reviewed after the files have been updated.

After all necessary approvals have been obtained, the shipment of goods or the production order is authorized. When the goods are available for shipping, a shipping order is automatically generated. The authorization process usually is subject to a monitoring control over the initial entry of and changes to standing data such as predetermined credit limits, terms, and sales prices.

(iii) Confirming Orders.   Inaccurately transcribed or lost orders can cause customer dissatisfaction and loss of revenues. To avoid errors or misunderstandings, many entities confirm orders with customers. This procedure may entail simply a telephone call or sending the customer a copy of the internally prepared sales order form or a computer-generated confirmation form. In many entities, the substantial cost of changing or canceling an order after it has been processed makes the confirmation procedure a sound business practice; in other entities, however, order processing time is so short that confirming orders is not practicable.

(iv) Executing Shipping Orders.   The steps in executing an order for goods are usually requisitioning, packing, and shipping. The instructions for all of those steps may be prepared on one form, or several different forms may be used. If considerable work is involved in execution, such as fabrication to a customer's specifications, it may be necessary to prepare execution instructions in several stages. For items that are manufactured specifically for customers, work orders may be generated and a file of open work orders maintained for follow-up. For other items, customers' orders may be requisitioned from finished goods inventory, from the factory by means of a production order, or from suppliers by means of a purchase order. The shipping orders usually are then matched against the inventory master file to determine whether the inventory exists to fill the order, or this match may have been done when the orders were received, as mentioned earlier.

In some entities, a copy of the authorized sales order or a shipping order is used to instruct the various departments involved in physically executing shipments and to evidence the actual shipments. In other entities, a "picking list" is generated, possibly by computer, and used by the warehouse or production department to gather and prepare orders for shipment. A packing slip or a bill of lading may be used by the shipping department in packing and shipping orders. Whatever form is used to document shipments, it will show the quantity shipped and the initials of the various people responsible for executing the shipment and the dates of their performance. Each department needs enough copies of the instructions to enable it to both advise other relevant departments of its action and retain evidence of performance in its own files.

Completeness of recording shipments may be ensured by accounting for the numerical sequence of shipping orders or prenumbered bills of lading. An exception report listing outstanding shipping orders would identify authorized orders not yet input as shipped. Executed shipping orders usually are matched to the open shipping order file to ensure that shipments input to the sales transaction file (and inventory master file) contain the quantities that were shipped.

(v) Recording Shipments and Billing Customers. The recording of shipments generally initiates the formal recording of sales transactions for accounting purposes. The input of executed shipping orders to the sales transaction file automatically generates a sales invoice. The controls of matching executed shipping orders to the open order file, as previously discussed, and of inputting executed shipping orders only when appropriate supporting documentation (for instance, initialed and dated shipping orders or bills of lading) exists, are designed to ensure the complete and accurate recording of accounts receivable.

Since the sales transaction file is the basis for recording sales and accounts receivable, controls to ensure the complete and accurate pricing of all invoices are imperative. Numerical sequencing generally is used for individual invoices; control totals are used for posting to the accounts receivable control account; the sales transaction file is used for posting to the detailed accounts receivable listing (the accounts receivable subledger or subsidiary ledger). Many systems produce "missing item," or exception, reports of items like open shipping orders or missing bill of lading numbers, with investigation of unmatched items by a person independent of the shipping and invoicing functions. Batch totals also can be used, for example, total units shipped and total units invoiced. The investigation and resolution process is documented and periodically reviewed by supervisory personnel. Management's review of sales reports (a monitoring control) is also a source of evidence that sales are recorded accurately and completely.

The final activity in a sales transaction is updating the general ledger accounts receivable control account and the detailed accounts receivable listing. There may be a matching procedure to ensure the completeness and accuracy of updating if the control account and detailed account are updated separately. It is also necessary to ensure the completeness and accuracy of accumulated data, specifically, that the accounts receivable control account and the detailed accounts receivable listing continue to be in agreement between postings, or transaction updates. A file maintenance control commonly used to ensure this is the periodic comparison of the detailed accounts receivable listing with the general ledger control account by a person independent of the invoicing and cash receipts functions, with supervisory review of the comparison.

An inadequately designed or ineffective accounting system or control activities for invoicing and updating the accounts can result in critical misstatements. For example:

- Goods shipped but not invoiced could cause an understatement of revenues and accounts receivable
- Unauthorized transactions could be recorded, causing a possibly uncollectible account
- Errors on invoices could go undetected, causing an under- or overstatement of revenues and receivables
- Errors in recording transactions in the control accounts and subsidiary ledgers could result in the misstatement of related balances (Errors or delays in posting also could affect the collectibility of receivables)

Customers' complaints about recurring errors also could adversely affect their confidence in the entity.

(vi) Variations in Typical Sales Transactions.   The activities described above are usually necessary, to the extent that they apply, in all sales transactions. Following are some common examples of variations in those activities.

In over-the-counter retail sales, the above activities may be condensed into a short personal encounter. The customer orders orally and the clerk accepts the order, reviewing authorized sales terms and often determining the customer's credit standing within the entity or at a financial institution, like the issuer of a credit card, via a remote access computer terminal. The sales slip combines all the paperwork, sometimes including the stock withdrawal notice and possibly the reorder notice (or the tag removed from the goods may serve those purposes); the clerk physically executes the sale; the customer pays or the sales slip is forwarded to the billing department or the financial institution for invoicing. The control consists of accounting for the prenumbered sales slips or the cash register tapes and following up on missing items.

In contract sales, there may be requests for proposals, bid preparation, bidding, and extended contract negotiations.

In providing continuing services, such as electric or telephone services, most of the activities described above are performed once for each customer and execution is continuous thereafter until the customer either cancels the service or fails to pay for it. The revenue process from rents, royalties, and interest is similar. A procedure for periodic reporting of the amount of service delivered is needed to initiate billing.

In transportation services, billing and collection may come before physical execution and at a different time from the receipt, authorization, and confirmation of the order. A customer buys a ticket or a token and uses it at a later time.

(b) Payments Received for Goods and Services

Payments received for goods and services generally include the following activities:

- Receiving the cash and depositing it in the bank
- Comparing amounts remitted with recorded amounts
- Authorizing discounts and allowances
- Recording cash receipts, discounts, and allowances

(i) Receiving the Cash and Depositing It in the Bank.   Cash may be received by entity personnel or directly by the bank. Asset protection is a significant control objective in the receipt stage. Controls related to this objective will differ depending on whether cash is received by the bank or by the entity. Other controls applied to cash receipts are similar, regardless of where cash is received.

When cash is received by the entity through the mail, it is usually in the form of checks. Currency or checks may be received over the counter, by collectors, or by salespeople. Customer remittances received by the bank generally are through a lockbox or a wire transfer.

A lockbox system is a service offered by many banks to reduce cash transit time, thus increasing funds available to the entity. Customers send their remittances to a post office box under control of the bank, which records the deposits and furnishes the entity with the details. A lockbox provides improved protection of cash receipts because entity personnel do not have access to them.

When funds are remitted by wire transfer, no currency or checks are involved. The customer provides details of the transfer (amount and bank account numbers) to its bank, which then executes the transfer. The receiving bank (the bank used by the entity) notifies the entity of the details of the transfer. Wire transfers normally are used only when large sums of money are being remitted. Cash transit time is significantly reduced; in fact, the funds normally are available the same day the transfer is made. As with a lockbox, protection of cash receipts is improved because entity personnel do not have access to them.

When cash is received through a lockbox or wire transfer, the bank provides some form of detail of the deposit. This may be remittance advices, statement stubs, or other correspondence from customers; alternatively, it may be a manual or electronic listing showing customers' names, amounts, and invoices being paid. This detail is used later to record cash receipts and to ensure their complete and accurate processing.

Cash received by the entity by mail is normally delivered from the mail room to an individual (e.g., a cashier) responsible for listing the receipts, endorsing checks, and preparing a deposit ticket. Listing (or, as it is frequently called, "prelisting") the cash receipts is the first step in establishing control over them. The listing usually includes names, amounts, and the invoices being paid (the customer's bill stub is commonly used for that purpose). Over-the-counter receipts may be listed on cash register tapes or counter sales slips prepared in the presence of customers; cash received from collectors or salespeople and not accompanied by listings also is listed upon receipt. Like the bank's detail of deposits, the entity's cash receipts listing is used later to ensure the complete and accurate processing of cash receipts. Preparing the listing of receipts and accounting for the numerical sequence by an individual independent of other cash functions address asset protection, completeness, and accuracy of cash receipts.

Controls to ensure protection of cash received by the entity include endorsing checks as soon as they are received and promptly depositing them in a bank account. Typically, an endorsement stamp including the notation "For Deposit Only" is used, and each day's cash receipts are deposited intact and without delay by an individual independent of other cash functions. Items not suitable for immediate deposit, like postdated checks or checks containing errors, typically are listed separately from the items ready for deposit, and later the two lists are reconciled with the deposit.

Often, cash is received from more than one source and at various times during the day. If more than one list or batch of cash receipts is prepared in a day, they usually are identified, for example, by batch number. Lists of receipts are totaled, usually at least daily, and the totals are compared with the corresponding deposit slip totals. If receipts flow from a number of sources, such as branch offices, collection departments, cash registers, lockboxes, and wire transfers, typically a control form or checklist is used to highlight missing entries and ensure the prompt reporting and inclusion of receipts from all locations daily. Deposit or collection items charged back by a bank as uncollectible generally are delivered to and investigated by someone who has no responsibility for either handling or recording cash.

(ii) Comparing Amounts Remitted with Recorded Amounts. A comparison of cash remittances with accounts receivable balances ensures that the entity and its customer agree on the details of the invoice(s) being paid as well as the total amount. An exception report is then generated listing all cash receipts that could not be matched against an open invoice on the accounts receivable file. The comparison identifies credits taken for sales returns or allowances and whether they were authorized. The comparison also discloses whether discounts taken by customers were within the discount period, whether the receipt was applied to the appropriate customer's account, and whether there are any potential disputes about amounts due. It also identifies cash receipts that were inaccurately input or that should not be applied against accounts receivable, for example, receipts from transactions outside the revenue cycle (such as the sale of a fixed asset). In addition, errors in the updating of sales to the accounts receivable file may be identified. For example, if certain sales were not updated to the accounts receivable file, investigation of the unmatched cash receipt would identify the error. Discrepancies are investigated and documentation of the resolution and any necessary corrections is reviewed by supervisory personnel.

(iii) Authorizing Discounts and Allowances. Discounts and allowances represent noncash reductions of the recorded invoice and receivable amounts. Discounts taken by customers are reviewed to ascertain that they are within the stated terms and for the proper amount. In some entities, discounts are routine, and the approval and recording function is well systematized. The discount terms and amount may be matched against the invoice or a master file containing discount information, at the time the cash receipt is input. An exception report of unauthorized discounts taken is generated for follow-up, investigation, and necessary corrections.

Allowances, on the other hand, are less frequent, more difficult to ascertain, and often based on evaluations of customer complaints. Allowances generally are controlled by policies specifying who may authorize them and under what conditions. Forms and reporting procedures are used to establish prompt authorization, approval, and documentation of allowances. Investigation of uncollected receivables may reveal unrecorded allowances.

Nonroutine discounts and allowances taken by customers usually are approved by supervisory personnel independent of those who receive cash and maintain the accounts receivable subsidiary ledger. Documentation of approval ordinarily is noted on prenumbered credit memos whose numerical sequence is reviewed for missing numbers to ensure completeness of input.

(iv) Recording Cash Receipts, Discounts, and Allowances.   Cash receipts may be recorded before being compared with invoices, after any discounts or allowances taken have been approved, or at the same time as the comparison and identification of any discounts or allowances taken. In any event, the process of recording cash receipts is the same. The detailed lists prepared when the cash is received normally are used as source documents for inputting cash receipts. If the bank provides details of lockbox receipts in electronic form, such as magnetic tape, inputting receipts may entail merely loading the tape onto the computer for processing. Typically a daily cash receipts report is generated, listing all receipts input. Once entered, the total cash receipts recorded for the day usually are reconciled to the original listings or batch totals and to authenticated duplicate deposit slips or other bank notices. This reconciliation, normally performed by an individual independent of those who enter the receipts, ensures that all cash receipts have been entered.

The final activity in processing payments for goods and services is updating the general ledger. In a manual system, the totals in the cash receipts journal and approved journal entries for discounts and allowances are posted to the general ledger periodically (usually monthly). When these transactions are processed by computer, the cash receipts file (which also may contain authorized discounts) is used to update the general ledger. The detailed accounts receivable file is relieved when the cash receipts and discounts are input and accepted for processing. Allowances and discounts, when not part of the routine transaction processing, normally are input separately and update the detailed accounts receivable file, if accepted for processing. Numerically sequenced credit memos are generated and the credit memo file is updated. This file is then used to update the general ledger.

Posting to the detailed accounts receivable ledger generally is performed by people independent of cash functions; the general ledger ordinarily is posted by computer or by someone other than the person who updates the accounts receivable subsidiary ledger or file. This segregation of duties meets both authorization and accuracy objectives. Typically its effectiveness is ensured by periodic reconciliation of the general ledger to the detailed accounts receivable ledger. Periodic mailing of customer statements also helps ensure that all cash receipts, discounts, and allowances have been recorded accurately.

(c) Goods Returned by and Claims Received from Customers

The third class of transactions in the revenue cycle is the processing of returns and claims. These transactions often are less well controlled than sales or cash receipts transactions: Returns and claims are likely to be sporadic and lacking in common characteristics. Accordingly, establishing control over them as early as possible enhances the achievement of the completeness, accuracy, and authorization control objectives. Since returned goods represent an asset to the entity, many of the controls described in Chapter 14 for receiving goods are relevant.

Typically, goods returned by customers and the processing of claims are handled in the following steps:

- Receiving and accepting goods or claims
- Preparing receiving reports
- Reviewing claims
- Authorizing credits
- Preparing and mailing credit memos
- Recording returns and claims

(i) Receiving and Accepting Goods or Claims.   The receiving department handles goods returned for credit. Returned goods may go through the same receiving routine as other receipts of goods (discussed in Chapter 14) or may be processed through a separate receiving area, inspection procedure, and paperwork system. In either case, counting, inspecting, and noting quantities and condition serve as a basis for later determining the credit to give the customer and whether the goods need repair or can be placed back in stock.

(ii) Preparing Receiving Reports.   Receiving reports typically are used for documenting and establishing control over goods returned. Generally, they are completed when goods are received. They commonly are prepared on prenumbered reports by the receiving department, which is independent of the shipping function. All pertinent data is recorded for later processing. If appropriate, reports may be completed in the presence of the customer to ensure that all customer complaints are recognized. The subsequent control of accounting for the numerical sequence and investigating missing or duplicate receiving reports is performed by people independent of the shipping and receiving functions and is designed to ensure that all goods returned are recorded.

(iii) Reviewing Claims.   After goods have been received and recorded by the receiving department, the related claims are reviewed by a customer service department that is independent of the receiving function. This procedure establishes the authenticity of claims and determines the amount of credit, if any, to be granted. Sometimes the customer service department prepares credit memos for approval by the credit, sales, and accounting departments. In other entities, the results of the inspection and review are noted directly on the receiving reports and forwarded to the three departments.

(iv) Authorizing Credits. The sales department generally is responsible for final authorization of credits. This approval is based on receiving reports and careful independent and documented inspection of goods, and is evidenced on the receiving and inspection reports. Credit memos initiated by the sales department usually are independently reviewed.

(v) Preparing and Mailing Credit Memos. Credit memos generally are prepared only on the basis of authorized receiving and inspection reports, by individuals (preferably in the sales department) other than those who receive cash and record accounts receivable. Credit memos are usually in numerical sequence, and quantities, terms, prices, and extensions are reviewed for accuracy, by someone other than the preparer, before mailing. Listings of credit memos issued, containing all pertinent data, normally are prepared to support the appropriate journal entry and for posting the accounts receivable subsidiary ledger. Credits for returned goods may be processed in the same way as allowances. Approved receiving reports may be used as source documents for computing the credits. Numerically sequenced credit memos are generated, and the accounts receivable file and credit memo file updated.

(vi) Recording Returns and Claims. There is a natural inclination to delay the processing of returns and claims; periodic review of the open file of receiving reports is a useful procedure for identifying unprocessed claims. Understanding the reason for returns may help management determine whether they are a symptom of a problem, such as defective production or a malfunctioning order entry system. In addition, achievement of the completeness control objective is enhanced by accounting for the numerical sequence of recorded credit memos, with appropriate follow-up of duplicate or missing items.

(d) Monitoring Controls

As indicated in Chapter 10, management requires reliable financial information to operate the entity. In some situations, management reviews information generated by the accounting system and oversees the performance of control activities established to provide that information. Those monitoring controls were discussed earlier in the chapter in conjunction with related control activities. In other situations, discussed in this section, management evaluates such information in the course of reviewing and analyzing reports for the purpose of monitoring the entity's operations. Evidence that management makes those reviews, often referred to as performance reviews, can provide some assurance to the auditor of the reliability of financial information.

High-level managers—including sales, production, and financial personnel—typically review key performance indicators, such as sales volume, sales returns, gross profit, and other financial ratios. They compare sales with information accumulated from outside the accounting system, such as budgets, forecasts, and production volume statistics, as well as prior periods' performance indicators. Credit and financial management may monitor credit risk by reviewing the accounts receivable aging schedule and data such as the number and value of accounts exceeding their credit limit, the number and value of rejected orders, and the number and value of accounts written off as uncollectible. Credit and sales managers also may monitor information about new customers, billing complaints, and sales transactions with unusual quantities or prices. The controller typically reviews the periodic reconciliation of the accounts receivable subsidiary ledger to the control account to determine that it is being performed adequately and on a timely basis.

13.2 DETERMINING THE AUDIT STRATEGY

As discussed in Chapter 6, the key audit strategy decision the auditor makes for each significant account balance is whether to perform tests of controls to support a below-the-maximum or low assessment of control risk for specific audit objectives. The auditor frequently tests an entity's controls in the revenue cycle to obtain evidence of their effective operation as a basis for reducing the assurance needed from substantive tests directed at the completeness, accuracy, and existence/occurrence audit objectives. If the entity has implemented controls designed to achieve proper cutoff at year-end, the auditor also may decide to test them in conjunction with other tests of controls. Similarly, there may be satisfactory controls, which the auditor can test, with respect to the completeness and accuracy of the data underlying the estimates that are related to the valuation objective. With those exceptions, the auditor generally achieves the remaining audit objectives by performing substantive tests designed after considering the entity's inherent risks and his or her understanding of controls.

(a) Developing the Understanding of Controls

As discussed in Chapter 11, the auditor is required, at a minimum, to obtain an understanding of the entity's internal control sufficient to plan the audit. This understanding, together with the auditor's evaluation of the effectiveness of the design of controls, is used to identify the types of misstatements that might occur and the risk of their occurring, and to design substantive tests. The understanding is obtained, or updated, by considering previous experience with the entity, reviewing prior-year audit results, interviewing entity personnel, observing them as they perform their duties, reviewing descriptions of policies and procedures prepared by entity personnel, and inspecting documents and records.

In addition to information about how entity-level controls affect the revenue cycle, the predominant means of processing transactions (manually or by computer), the level of the system's sophistication, and other general characteristics of internal control, the auditor should consider the following types of information, as appropriate, related to the revenue cycle:

- The entity's main source(s) of revenues
- The volume and dollar amount of sales and the number of customers
- The usual terms of sales, which would determine when it is proper to record revenue
- The usual credit and discount terms
- The flow of revenue cycle transactions through the accounting system

If the auditor plans to assess control risk at maximum, an understanding of the above aspects of internal control generally is sufficient to plan the audit. If, however, as is typical, the auditor's planned assessment of control risk for revenue cycle accounts is below the maximum or low, he or she will need to understand controls at a more detailed level as a basis for testing them. If the auditor plans to assess control risk below the maximum, he or she will extend the understanding of controls to include such monitoring controls as management reviews of sales reports, supervision of employees who investigate items on exception reports, and the other monitoring controls described earlier in the chapter; and consider the extent to which they can be expected to detect misstatements of revenue cycle accounts. The auditor will then test those controls, and perhaps also certain entity-level controls, to obtain evidence of their effective operation to support the below-the-maximum assessment.

The procedures performed for the purpose of obtaining or updating the understanding of controls may serve as tests of controls as well, if they provide evidence that controls are operating effectively. Such tests of controls, particularly if they include tests of monitoring controls, often provide evidence to support an assessment of control risk that is below the maximum for the completeness, accuracy, and existence/occurrence audit objectives. For example, when inquiring about management's review of sales reports (a monitoring control), the auditor also may observe personnel performing the review or examine reports or documents that provide evidence of the review. If, after considering the level of detail reviewed and the likelihood that the reviewer would detect a material misstatement, the auditor concludes that the management review is operating effectively, it provides some evidence with respect to the completeness and accuracy of sales.

To support an assessment of control risk at low, the tests of controls performed should include tests of control activities. That is because control activities explicitly address control objectives and have direct effects on specific audit objectives and account balances. Thus, evidence that control activities, along with controls in the other components, are operating effectively supports an assessment that all the components of internal control interacting together reduce to a low level the risk that control objectives will not be achieved.

If the auditor plans to assess control risk at low, he or she will develop an understanding of the application and computer controls relating to sales orders, shipping documents, invoices, and cash collections, and the extent to which duties are segregated among the people performing accounting procedures and control activities. The auditor considers whether those controls have been placed in operation and are appropriately designed to achieve their objectives, and whether evidence of their effective operation is likely to be available and efficient to obtain. If so, the auditor will test the controls to obtain evidence that they meet the control objectives relating to account balances and transactions in the revenue cycle. (The control objectives are defined in Chapter 9 and discussed further in Chapter 11.) That evidence will provide the auditor with assurance about specific audit objectives related to systems-derived accounts in the revenue cycle—usually, completeness, accuracy, and existence/occurrence of accounts receivable and sales.

(b) Audit Strategy Decisions—An Illustration

Professional judgment is needed to assess risks and translate that assessment into the various decisions that constitute the audit strategy. Following is a description of the testing decisions an auditor might make in developing an appropriate audit strategy for the revenue cycle.

The entity is a manufacturer with a strong control environment and a well-developed computerized accounting system for sales and cash receipts. Application software, which was developed in-house and is fully integrated with other financial modules, supports all revenue cycle processing. Computer controls are strong in all areas, including development and implementation of new systems and computer security. The volume of transactions is high and involves many products.

Customer orders are received by mail; a customer service representative enters the order information from the customer's purchase order: the customer's name and address, item, quantity, and price. The system then automatically performs several operations, checking for customer authenticity, inventory quantities, prices, discounts, and credit authorization. The computer generates a sales order, which is entered on a backlog report. The shipping manager accesses the backlog report daily and, by "tagging" the orders to be shipped that day, creates a shipping list. Orders are prepared in the stockroom from the shipping list and sent to the shipping department, which stages each order and closes out the sales order. This removes the order from the backlog report. The shipping manager also reviews the backlog report each day to ensure that all orders tagged for shipment the previous day were recorded that day and are, therefore, no longer on the report.

When the sales order is closed, the packing slip and address labels are printed automatically and matched to the products and the products are shipped. The system also uses the closed sales order file to update the inventory, cost of sales, sales, and accounts receivable files. An invoice is printed automatically and mailed. The computer totals and prints out the orders received each day; this information is used by sales managers to track performance and anticipate sales volumes. Customer statements are sent out monthly.

Customer payments are remitted to a lockbox. The bank provides on-line access to all collection information, ranging from daily batch totals to the detailed information on individual cash receipts. The bank sends the entity, by overnight delivery, copies of all the checks and remittance advices (which are carbon copies of invoices) received each day. A clerk inputs the cash receipts information from the copies of the checks and remittance advices; the computer matches each cash receipt to the open invoice file. Cash receipts are reconciled to the bank deposits daily and the credit manager reviews the reconciliations each week. Cash receipts are posted to the accounts receivable and cash receipts files daily. Controls also have been designed and placed in operation over returns, allowances, and write-offs.

Customer standing data is printed and distributed to sales representatives periodically for their review. Changes to customer standing data are initiated and approved principally by the sales representatives and are closely supervised by the credit manager. Changes to standing price data are generated by the marketing department and approved by financial management. The entire price list is reviewed and updated annually, in conjunction with the process of developing and approving the budget.

At the end of the month, the credit department reconciles the computer-generated accounts receivable aging schedule to the general ledger; the reconciliation is reviewed by both the credit manager and the controller. Monitoring controls also include the sales and production managers' review of sales and production reports and the financial statements and their identification of any unexpected results.

In these circumstances, based on his or her understanding of internal control and any tests of controls performed concurrently with obtaining the understanding, the auditor probably would initially assess control risk at low. He or she would then perform additional tests of controls, including tests of computer controls, to obtain evidence that the controls were operating effectively and achieving the control objectives described in Chapter 9. The nature, timing, and extent of substantive tests of details that would be appropriate when control risk is assessed at low are described in Chapter 18.

As indicated in Chapter 9, for systems-derived accounts, the auditor meets the audit objectives of completeness, accuracy, and existence/occurrence, usually as a group, by determining that the transaction-level control objectives (authorization, accuracy of input, and completeness of input) and the cycle-level control objectives (completeness and accuracy of updating, completeness and accuracy of accumulated data, integrity of standing data, and restricted access to assets and records) have been achieved. Even if the auditor concludes that not all of the control objectives have been met, however, it may be more efficient, depending on the circumstances, to assess control risk at low and perform certain substantive tests directed at detecting misstatements that could have resulted from the unmet control objectives. What is necessary is for the auditor to achieve all audit objectives, either by developing a basis for concluding that the risk of material misstatement of related accounts is low or by performing substantive tests of those accounts.

For example, the shipping manager's daily review of the backlog report is a significant completeness control whose objective is to ensure that all shipments are updated to the system, which includes the sales order being removed from the backlog report. If, as a result of performing tests of that control, the auditor determined that the shipping manager did not review the backlog report, the auditor might continue to assess control risk at low, but should consider reviewing the backlog report as a substantive test at year-end to look for long-outstanding sales orders that actually may have been shipped.

On the other hand, suppose that the entity's procedures permitted sales orders to be created based on sales representatives' phone calls. When orders were received from customers not already in the customer standing data file, customer service clerks would have password access to add the customers to the file on-line. As a result, recorded sales might include amounts that were not actual sales to nonfictitious customers. Also, as noted in the description of the entity's revenue cycle, the packing slip is matched by the shipping clerk to the products shipped. This procedure ensures that the recorded sale (which contains the same information as on the packing slip) and the invoiced amounts are based on the goods actually shipped. Its absence could result in inaccurate or nonexistent accounts receivable and sales.

In these circumstances, the auditor might conclude that control risk should be assessed below the maximum, but not at low. In that event, he or she might extend the understanding of internal control to include monitoring controls over revenue transactions and test those controls to confirm the below-the-maximum assessment. The auditor would not, however, develop an understanding of control activities or test them. It would be necessary, as indicated in Chapter 18, to confirm accounts receivable. Other substantive tests might include matching a selection of invoices to bills of lading signed by the shipping agent. (A large number of credit memos might indicate

Figure 13.1 Sales of Goods and Services

	Control Objectives		
	Transaction Processing		
	Authorization	*Completeness of Input*	*Accuracy of Input*
Specific Control Objectives	All recorded sales transactions represent actual shipments of goods or rendering of services to nonfictitious customers of the entity and are approved.	All sales transactions are input and accepted for processing.	Sales are correctly recorded as to amounts, quantities, dates, and customers; are recorded in the proper period; and are accurately input to the computer.
Examples of Control Activities	Reporting and resolving orders rejected because customers, prices, or credit or other terms were not contained on, or were outside the pre-established limits on, customer and price master files. Approving new customers on the files or transaction-specific customer information, such as shipping address or billing address.	Accounting for the numerical sequence of shipping or work orders input to the computer. Determining that a sales invoice was generated for each executed shipping or work order. Reporting and resolving missing, unmatched, or duplicate shipping orders or invoices by individuals independent of shipping functions. Reporting and resolving long-outstanding items on the open shipping or work order file. Resolving reports of executed shipping and work orders rejected as not matching against the open file by individuals independent of shipping functions.	Completeness of input controls for shipping or work orders also address the accuracy of input for quantities and descriptions. Mailing of customer statements, and investigating and resolving disputes or inquiries, by individuals independent of the invoicing function.

Figure 13.1 *(Continued)*

Control Objectives

| | *File Maintenance* | | |
Integrity of Standing Data	*Completeness and Accuracy of Updating*	*Completeness and Accuracy of Accumulated Data*	*Asset Protection*
All changes to standing data are authorized and accurately input.	All sales transactions input and accepted for processing are accurately updated to the sales and accounts receivable files.	The integrity of individual accounts receivable in the subsidiary ledger and the general ledger accounts receivable and sales accounts, after sales transactions have been accumulated in them, is preserved.	Only authorized personnel have access to accounts receivable records or data stored on them, including standing data.
Approving changes to master files for customers, terms, and credit limits. Approving changes to master file for sales prices.	Comparing total sales input with the total updated to the sales and accounts receivable files.	Balancing of the subsidiary ledger (previous balance plus sales less receipts, compared with the current total). Reconciling the subsidiary ledger to the control account in the general ledger. Reporting and resolving discrepancies.	Restricting access to accounts receivable files and files used in processing receivables.

Figure 13.2   Payments Received for Goods and Services

	Control Objectives		
	Transaction Processing		
	Authorization	*Completeness of Input*	*Accruacy of Input*
Specific Control Objectives	All cash receipts from customers are approved for application against specified invoices.	All payments received are input and accepted for processing.	Receipts are correctly recorded as to amounts, dates, and customers; are recorded in the proper period; and are accurately input to the computer.
Examples of Control Activities	Reporting and resolving differences as to the appropriate invoice being paid. Reporting and resolving differences as to the amount of the receipt and the amount of the invoice.	Prelisting of cash received. Comparing bank advices (e.g., validated deposit slip) with the total of the prelistings and the total receipts input, by individuals independent of receiving, prelisting, or recording cash receipts. Investigation of past-due receivables by individuals independent of receiving or recording cash receipts.	Reporting and resolving cash receipts not matched against an unpaid invoice on the accounts receivable subsidiary ledger by individuals independent of other receipt functions. Mailing of customer statements, and investigating and resolving disputes or inquiries, by individuals independent of receiving or recording cash receipts, posting to the accounts receivable subsidiary ledger, or authorizing write-offs of receivables.

Figure 13.2 *(Continued)*

Control Objectives

*File Maintenance**

Completeness and Accuracy of Updating	*Completeness and Accuracy of Accumulated Data*	*Asset Protection*
All receipts input and accepted for processing are accurately updated to the cash receipts and accounts receivable files.	The integrity of individual accounts receivable in the subsidiary ledger and the general ledger accounts receivable and cash accounts, after receipts have been updated to them, is preserved.	Only authorized personnel have access to receipts and accounts receivable records or data stored on them, including standing data. Receipts are promptly deposited in the entity's bank account.
Comparing total cash input with the totals updated to the cash receipts and accounts receivable files.	Same control activities as described in Figure 13.1, "Sales of Goods and Services."	Receiving and prelisting cash by individuals independent of recording cash receipts.
	Reconciling the bank statement to the general ledger cash account by personnel independent of receiving and recording cash receipts (and of accounts payable and cash disbursements functions).	Restrictive endorsement of checks on receipt.
		Deposit of receipts intact daily.
		Individuals involved in the receipt and deposit function are not authorized check signers.
		Restricted access to accounts receivable files and files used in processing cash receipts.

* Integrity of standing data is covered in Figure 13.1, "Sales of Goods and Services."

that shipping errors were prevalent. Actual shipping errors should result in book-to-physical adjustments as a result of the year-end physical inventory.)

(c)   Tests of Controls to Support a Low Control Risk Assessment

If the auditor plans to assess control risk at low for accounts that are part of the revenue cycle, such as accounts receivable, cash, and sales, he or she will test the application controls over revenue transactions. In addition, the auditor will need evidence of the effectiveness of computer controls that affect those accounts and transactions. (Computer controls are discussed in Chapter 11, and tests of those controls in Chapter 12.) Specific control objectives and typical application controls that address sales of goods and services, and payments received for them are described in Figures 13.1 and 13.2, respectively. The accounting system assumed to be in operation in the figures is a sophisticated computerized system.

As discussed in Chapter 12, the tests of controls that the auditor would perform include an appropriate combination of inquiring about the entity's control activities, observing that they have been placed in operation, and examining evidence that they are operating effectively. Also as discussed in Chapter 12, reperformance may be used in tests of controls, but if that becomes necessary, the auditor usually determines that it is more efficient to perform substantive tests.

The third class of transactions in the revenue cycle, goods returned by and claims received from customers, is usually less significant than sales and payments received. Accordingly, tests of control activities generally are not performed. If return transactions were significant, however, the auditor might perform tests of controls such as the following:

Inquire about and observe:
- Controls designed to ensure that all goods returned by customers are appropriately documented
- Procedures for accounting for the numerical sequence of documents supporting goods returned by customers, claims made, and credit memos, including the way errors are investigated and resolved
- Procedures for authorizing adjustments to the account

Examine the following documents or reports to support inquiries and observations:
- Receiving reports
- Credit memos
- Exception reports for missing or duplicate items

When performing tests of controls, the auditor should be aware of audit objectives other than completeness, accuracy, and existence/occurrence that may be affected by those tests. An audit objective frequently considered when testing controls in the revenue cycle is valuation. When tests of controls are performed, the auditor usually tests credit department approval procedures; the results of those tests help in evaluating the entity's allowance for uncollectible accounts. For example, amounts due from sales made to potentially high-credit-risk customers close to year-end would be classified as "current" in the accounts receivable aged trial balance, which normally would not indicate a potential collection problem. In the absence of controls over granting credit, however, the auditor may consider it necessary to test the collectibility of "current" receivables. The auditor might do this by extending the review of collections in the post-balance-sheet period.

In evaluating the results of tests of control activities (including tests of computer controls), the auditor considers whether the entity's internal control, taken as a whole, is appropriately designed to achieve the control objectives and is operating effectively. This will determine whether the low control risk assessment was attained for specific accounts and audit objectives and, thus, whether the auditor can restrict substantive testing as planned. Results differing from those anticipated when developing the audit strategy require the auditor to reconsider the nature, timing, and extent of planned substantive tests—not only for revenue cycle accounts, but also for other accounts that may be affected. For example, ineffective control activities to ensure completeness of recorded sales also may affect inventory and cost of sales.

14

Auditing the Purchasing Cycle

The purchasing cycle consists of the acquisition of goods and services in exchange for cash or promises to pay cash. The audit of accounts in the purchasing cycle (e.g., purchases of merchandise or raw materials, various expenses, accounts payable, and cash) usually consists of a combination of substantive tests and tests of controls to support an assessment of control risk that is below the maximum or at low. Rarely would the audit of purchasing cycle accounts consist solely of substantive tests—in most entities, expenditures and cash disbursements are sufficiently numerous that management installs the necessary controls and the auditor finds it efficient to test them as a basis for restricting substantive tests.

This chapter covers the process by which the auditor determines the strategy for auditing the purchasing cycle. It describes typical purchases of goods and services, the accounting system for processing them, and the monitoring and control activities applied to the transactions. It also discusses the conditions under which the auditor will be able to arrive at a preliminary assessment of control risk that is below the maximum or at low and the controls that ordinarily should be tested under various control risk assessments. Chapter 23 describes the nature, timing, and extent of substantive tests of purchasing cycle accounts that would be appropriate under the alternative risk assessments of maximum, below the maximum, and low.

The purchasing cycle is part of the larger "expenditure cycle" that comprises all transactions in which assets are produced or acquired, expenses are incurred, and payments are made to discharge liabilities incurred. Since the expenditure cycle is too broad to be covered in a single chapter and because it is usually more efficient to divide the cycle into more manageable segments when performing an audit, the expenditure cycle is discussed in several chapters. The discussion in this chapter is limited to transactions involving purchases of and payments for goods and services generally, including human resources, since it is often those transactions that are sufficiently numerous to warrant the installation of control activities directed at all control objectives. Expenditures that present specific auditing issues are covered elsewhere. Inventories and cost of sales are discussed in Chapter 19; prepayments and accruals, including employee benefit expense, in Chapter 20; property, plant, and equipment and related accounts, in Chapter 22; income tax accounts, in Chapter 24; and loss contingencies, in Chapter 26.

14.1   TYPICAL TRANSACTIONS AND CONTROLS

The purchasing cycle in most entities can be divided into three typical classes of transactions:

- Acquisition of goods and services
- Payments made for goods and services
- Goods returned to suppliers

Conceptually, payrolls are part of the purchasing cycle, but the related controls are somewhat unique. Accordingly, two additional classes of transactions are often identified:

- Payroll processing
- Payment of wages

(a) Acquisition of Goods and Services

The process of acquiring goods and services includes the following steps:

- Determining needs
- Ordering
- Receiving, inspecting, and accepting goods
- Storing or using goods
- Recording the goods or services purchased

In considering the accounting system that processes purchasing transactions and the monitoring and control activities applied to them, the auditor is interested mainly in controls to ensure that all purchase transactions that actually occurred are authorized and are recorded accurately; that is, that the entity's controls achieve the seven control objectives described in Chapters 9 and 11. Those control objectives are closely related to the audit objectives of completeness, accuracy, and existence/occurrence of purchasing cycle accounts, particularly purchases and accounts payable. Other controls, while not directly related to those audit objectives, also may be of interest to the auditor. For example, management reviews of open purchase orders may generate reports the auditor can use in evaluating whether there are unrealized losses on open purchase commitments, which affects the valuation audit objective.

The paragraphs that follow describe the various activities involved in the purchase of goods and services, and the controls typically applied in processing the transactions. Some of the activities described in this section also apply to purchases of services, while others, like receiving, inspecting, storing, and using, do not. To the extent that the processes are similar for both goods and services, the discussion of controls applies to purchases of services as well.

(i) Determining Needs.   The purchasing cycle starts when someone identifies a need, which may occur in several different ways. For example:

- Raw material inventory replenishment needs may be determined by a person or automatically when stock on hand reaches a reorder point or when a bill of materials for a job order is prepared. Some computerized systems may identify needs by reference to records of quantities on hand or production orders and simultaneously execute some of the steps in the purchasing process, for example, selecting vendors and preparing purchase orders. In certain systems, raw material needs are identified and the order is placed with the vendor without any human intervention; the entity's computer communicates directly with the vendor's computer.
- Needs for occasional goods and services are identified and described by the user, usually on a requisition form that is then approved by the person with authority over the user's department or the particular type of purchase.
- The need for some services that are provided on a recurring basis by the same vendor, such as utilities, telephone, periodicals, or maintenance services, usually is determined initially and thereafter is provided continuously until the end of

the contract period or until it is determined that the service is no longer needed or a different supplier is selected.

- Determining the need for specialized services, like insurance, advertising, and legal and auditing services, is ordinarily the responsibility of designated individuals.
- Needs for fixed assets usually are identified by a capital budgeting process.

Controls over requisitions typically include review and authorization by an appropriate individual and accounting for the numerical sequence of prenumbered requisition forms. Those controls are designed to ensure that only necessary goods and services are ordered and that all items requisitioned are actually ordered. While the purpose of these procedures is more closely related to management's decision making than to financial statement assertions, the controls may have an effect on certain financial statement accounts. For example, if review and authorization procedures for requisitions are absent or ineffective, inventory may become overstocked and eventually obsolete, thereby reducing its value.

(ii) Ordering. In most large entities, specially trained purchasing agents rather than personnel from user departments determine sources, negotiate terms, and place orders. Controls over vendor selection and ongoing monitoring can affect both accounts payable and inventory. A separate purchasing function can lower the entity's cost and enhance control over purchases by providing a division of duties.

Accumulating requisitions before purchase orders are placed requires specialized skills and experience to group items most efficiently, concentrate orders to obtain volume discounts while also maintaining multiple sources of supply, solicit bids effectively, negotiate schedules for vendor production and storage prior to delivery, and generally get the best possible prices and services. Absent or ineffective controls in this area are often difficult to quantify, because the cost of inefficient purchasing is generally not measurable, although ineffective controls usually result in an increase in the cost of items acquired.

When the purchasing department receives a requisition, typically it first determines that the amount and type of goods or services being requisitioned have been approved by an individual with the appropriate authority. The requisition then serves as the source document for inputting the order. The requisition information is input and matched against vendor, price, and (if applicable) inventory master files to assist in vendor selection, evaluating quoted prices, and determining the accuracy of product numbers or descriptions. The integrity of vendor standing data is achieved by limiting changes to the vendor master file to purchasing personnel. The completeness and accuracy of changes to the file are reviewed after the file has been updated.

After all of the specific information about the purchase, such as time and method of delivery, specifications for materials, and quantity and price, have been determined, a purchase order is generated and the open purchase order file is updated. The purchase order authorizes a vendor to deliver goods or services and bill on specified terms, and also authorizes the receiving department to accept the goods described. Since purchase orders authorize the execution of transactions, their issuance is usually well controlled. Typically, access to unissued purchase orders is restricted to prevent unauthorized personnel from initiating purchase transactions. Vendors may not be aware of or may not verify whether orders are placed by authorized individuals. While this may not have a financial statement impact, it could result in overstocking or the purchase of unnecessary items. Prenumbering purchase orders and subsequently accounting for the numerical sequence help ensure that entity personnel are aware of all open purchase commitments. That awareness is necessary to ensure that appropriate provisions for losses on purchase commitments are recorded.

Controls over the accuracy and authorization of purchase orders typically include comparing them with requisition forms and reviewing them for approval by an authorized individual. These procedures are performed before orders are placed with vendors. An additional control over the accuracy of orders may be giving requisitioners copies of the purchase orders for them to review for conformity with their expectations. Purchase orders with small dollar amounts or routine characteristics may be subjected to a less detailed review.

Some specialized goods and services cannot be handled by a purchasing department because the technical and performance requirements are too specialized or in some cases cannot be specified in advance. For example, the purchase of property and casualty insurance generally requires an insurance risk analysis. This analysis and the subsequent negotiations with an independent insurance agent or broker require special skill and training. Such specialized purchases must be negotiated directly between representatives of the responsible department and the vendor. Bypassing the purchasing department is likely to be a persistent and sometimes highly sensitive problem for most entities because of the conflict between the need for controls that a centralized purchasing function can provide and the desires of individual users, who may believe they can get better quality and service by dealing directly with vendors. Deciding where to draw the line between operating autonomy and centralized purchasing varies from entity to entity, but even in entities with highly centralized purchasing functions, some specialized services are allowed to bypass them. In those situations, control activities typically include requirements that agreements be in writing, goods be approved on receipt, and the user approve the invoices.

(iii) Receiving, Inspecting, and Accepting Goods.   In many entities, the volume of receiving is so large that the receiving function is carried out in a specially organized department separate from the requisitioning, purchasing, and accounting departments. A separate receiving department enhances control over purchases by providing segregation of duties.

The receiving function typically inspects goods for conformity with specifications on purchase orders. Quantities are verified by counting, weighing, or measuring. To improve the likelihood that receiving personnel will determine quantities independently, some systems provide for omitting quantities from the copy of the purchase order sent to the receiving department or, in a computerized system, restricting receiving personnel's access to quantity information on the open order file. The receivers also determine the quality of goods as far as possible, including whether there is shipping damage. Inspection of incoming goods is an essential control activity for management's purposes. Laboratory or technical analysis of goods may be necessary in some cases to determine that their quality meets specifications. This requires specialized technical skills and is usually assigned to an appropriately staffed inspection department.

The purchasing and accounting departments are notified of the receipt and acceptance of shipments. Receiving personnel generally document receipts on a receiving report, a packing slip sent with the goods by the vendor, or a copy of the purchase order. The information provided includes vendor, date received, quantity and condition of goods received, and sometimes the carrier. The document is signed by whoever received the goods. The receiver may input the information directly into the system, which then updates the open purchase order file, indicating that all or a portion of the order was received; generates a receiving report and an open receiving report file; and sometimes also updates the perpetual inventory file. Receipts that cannot be matched with an open purchase order may not be accepted by the receiving department; if they are accepted, they are reported on an exception report for investigation and follow-up, which typically are performed by accounting personnel. Receiving reports are generally prenumbered and their numerical sequence is subsequently accounted for. This control is designed to ensure that goods received are reported completely and on a timely basis to prevent understatement of accounts payable and costs or inventory.

Services and some goods do not arrive through the receiving department but are received directly by users. While formal procedures may be prescribed for users to originate receiving reports, more often the vendor's invoice for the service or goods is forwarded to the user for approval and acknowledgment of receipt.

(iv) Storing or Using.   Goods received through the receiving department are forwarded to the appropriate location for storage or use. Controls over storing purchased goods and issuing them to production are covered in Chapter 19, "Auditing Inventories and Cost of Sales."

(v) Recording.   An asset or expense and the related liability most often are recorded by people independent of the ordering and receiving functions on the basis of a vendor's invoice that has been matched to an approved purchase order, and of evidence that goods were received or services performed. In some systems, perpetual inventory records are posted when the receiving department inputs the receipt; alternatively, the accounting department may post the inventory records using a copy of the receiving report. Receiving reports not matched with invoices at the end of a period should generate an entry to record a liability for goods received but not billed.

Failure to apply controls to vendors' invoices as soon as they are received is a common internal control deficiency, particularly if many invoices must be routed for approval to operating personnel whose main interests are directed elsewhere. The resulting delay in recording invoices may, depending on the accounting system and related controls, cause accounts payable and the related asset or expense accounts to be misstated and may result in the loss of discounts for prompt payment. (A large number of unmatched invoices or receiving reports that have not been approved and recorded may indicate deficiencies, breakdowns, or delays in the procedures for processing and approving invoices.)

Invoices may not be specifically approved, but may be recorded based on the authorization of the related purchase orders and on evidence that receiving reports are properly matched to purchase orders. The invoices would then be matched to the open receiving report file; invoices that did not match would be reported on an exception report and updated to a temporary file of unmatched invoices.

Once invoices have been authorized for recording, the transactions are recorded in a purchases journal and are then summarized and posted. The account distribution is reviewed and entered (sometimes an initial account distribution is noted on the purchase order) to prevent transactions from being misclassified. Cutoff procedures to ensure that invoices are recorded in the proper period include reviewing the receiving report file, with attention to the dates goods were received.

The process of authorizing invoices for recording may be reviewed and approved by supervisors. Alternatively, invoices may be approved by supervisors when checks for payment are prepared or when they are signed. Supervisory review and approval are sometimes performed on only a representative sample of vendors' invoices or on specific types of invoices, most commonly if the entity has a large volume of low-dollar-value transactions and effective controls.

File maintenance controls consist primarily of reconciliations of accounts payable subsidiary ledgers to control accounts, with supervisory review of the reconciliations. The resolution of errors detected by the reconciliation and review processes also is adequately supervised. Segregating the duties of those who approve invoices, post the detailed inventory and accounts payable records, maintain control accounts, perform the reconciliations and supervisory reviews, and resolve errors also enhances the effectiveness of controls.

(b) Payments Made for Goods and Services

Controls relating to the cash disbursements process—the second transaction class in the purchasing cycle—are intended to ensure that no unauthorized payments are made, that accurate records are made of each payment, and that unclaimed checks are adequately identified, controlled, and ultimately voided. Other controls, more closely related to management decisions than to financial statement assertions, are designed to ensure that all liabilities are paid in ways that meet cash flow and vendor relationship objectives, including taking all available discounts for timely payment.

To prevent unauthorized payments, approvals are required for all requests for payment, and invoices and receiving documents are canceled after the related checks have been signed, so that those documents cannot be submitted for processing again. Controls to accomplish those objectives are enhanced if there is segregation of duties between those who prepare checks and those who originate requests for payment. The check signer should have evidence, at the time the check is signed, that the payment has been authorized. The system may prevent checks from being printed unless the invoice matches the appropriate purchase files. Asset protection controls require the signer to mail or handle signed checks in a way that makes them inaccessible to the people who authorize or process payments; unissued checks are safeguarded, and spoiled checks are mutilated or otherwise controlled.

If the number of employees is limited and the same person performs duties that are incompatible from a strict internal control viewpoint, some measure of control can be achieved by involving the supervisor in the processing. For example, sometimes the same person records payments to vendors and draws the checks. In this situation, the supervisor who signs the checks might require that all supporting evidence accompany the checks presented for signature and might assign someone other than the processor to cancel the supporting documents and mail the checks directly to the vendors.

Checks are drawn specifically to the order of the creditors being paid or to custodians of imprest funds being reimbursed, not to "cash" or "bearer." Drawing checks to the order of a specific entity or individual limits their negotiability and provides an acknowledgment of receipt through payees' endorsements.

Countersignatures are an effective control only if each signer makes an independent examination of checks and supporting documents. Although a countersignature affixed with proper understanding and discharge of assigned responsibility provides effective control, signature by a single employee after careful examination of supporting documents offers greater protection than superficial countersignatures, which create an illusion of control and could result in reliance by one person on functions not performed by another.

Controls to ensure that all acknowledged liabilities are paid in time to take advantage of cash discounts, promote good relations with suppliers, and maintain the entity's credit rating are more closely related to management's decision making than to financial statement assertions. Timely payments are ensured by periodic reviews of files of unmatched receiving reports and invoices and by the aging of open accounts payable.

Complete and accurate recording of payments is controlled by prenumbering checks, maintaining a detailed check register, accounting for the numerical sequence of checks entered in the register, and comparing paid checks returned by the bank with the check register as part of the periodic reconciliation of cash in banks. After appropriate inquiry into the reasons for long-outstanding checks, payment is stopped at the bank and the accounts are adjusted either to reverse the original entries or to record the items in a separate liability account.

Supervision of the cash disbursements process is provided by the check signer's review of supporting documentation, the review of bank reconciliations, and the reconciliation and review of the accounts payable trial balance.

(c) Goods Returned to Suppliers

Every credit due an entity because goods are returned or an allowance is negotiated is an asset equivalent to a receivable, although its recording is usually different, as discussed below. It is important, therefore, that these claims be adequately controlled, even though they are likely to be nonroutine and infrequent. Many entities also have policies and procedures for processing their own internally generated debit memos.

Returns for credit must be prepared for shipment to the vendor; the shipping department usually has procedures for notifying the accounts payable and purchasing departments at the time items are returned. Controls similar to those used for sales can be used, for example, requiring all shipping documents and supporting materials to be accompanied by a numerically controlled debit memo, usually prepared by the purchasing department and recorded in a debit memo journal by the accounting department. (Chapter 13, "Auditing the Revenue Cycle," discusses those controls.) Control of freight claims usually can be achieved in a similar manner.

When a credit memo is received from a vendor, it is matched to the related debit memo, if any, shipping documents, or other relevant internally generated documents.

Quantities returned, prices, dates, vendor's name, extensions, and footings are compared by personnel independent of the purchasing, shipping, and inventory control functions. If the entity has formal debit memo procedures, credits and claims often are deducted immediately from the next vendor payment without waiting for a vendor credit memo.

Claims for allowances, adjustments, and occasional returns that are not subject to the above procedures are subject to some control for notifying the accounting and purchasing departments of a dispute or claim due. Since there are no positive means for controlling compliance with that type of procedure, knowledgeable personnel throughout the entity are periodically asked about the existence of outstanding claims or allowances.

Even though they represent a valid asset, vendor credit memos or internally generated debit memos usually are not recorded as receivables, but rather are recorded as reductions of the payable to the vendor because a legal right of offset ordinarily exists in such instances. If this offsetting results in a debit balance in a vendor payable account, the debit balance may be recorded as a receivable. Vendor debit balances usually are not reclassified unless the total amount of such accounts is material. If they are reclassified because they are material, it is necessary to consider appropriate allowances for collectibility, because the debit balances may arise from vendors who no longer do business with the entity.

(d) Payroll Processing

Payroll processing is the one function most likely to have similar characteristics from one entity to another, which is one reason that payroll processing is the service most commonly offered by data processing service organizations. Over the years, payroll transaction processing has become increasingly systematized and generally well controlled. The typical payroll transaction is distinguished from other purchasing cycle transactions by the withholding of amounts to cover various types of employee obligations (for example, taxes and insurance premiums) and by different control activities.

Payroll processing includes:

- Authorizing employment
- Recording time worked or output produced
- Calculating gross pay and deductions

(i) Authorizing Employment. Documents authorizing employment are prepared independently of the prospective employee's immediate supervisor and those responsible for preparing the payroll. Preferred practice is to lodge that responsibility in the human resources department, which, in the formal hiring process, creates records authorizing employment, rate of pay, and payroll deductions. The human resources department also prepares pay rate changes and employee termination notices.

The employment records contain data of a permanent or semipermanent nature, which is referred to as standing data. Standing data, such as employee name, social security number, rate of pay, authorized deductions, and tax exemptions, is used for calculating gross pay and deductions each time a payroll is processed. Consequently, errors in standing data are usually more significant than errors in data relating to a single pay period (referred to as transaction data), such as hours worked. The completeness, accuracy, and authorization of standing data, which is not changed frequently, should be controlled by periodic review by the human resources department of recorded payroll standing data and of changes thereto.

(ii) Recording Time Worked or Output Produced.   Evidence of performance of services (including overtime) is produced in the form of time reports or clock cards, which should be controlled by supervisory review and approval. If pay is based on production quantity rather than time, as with piecework or commissions, the quantity should be similarly approved and reconciled to recorded production or sales data.

(iii) Calculating Gross Pay and Deductions.   Calculating gross pay and deductions involves matching the transaction data (that is, the records of time or output for the payroll period) and standing data for each employee. The payroll should be approved by an appropriate individual based on evidence that the relevant control activities have been performed. An appropriate individual reviews the gross payroll and deductions for reasonableness and approves the amounts. The self-interest of employees and their ready access to the human resources department also act to limit the risk of underpayment. Normally, the risk of overpayment is reduced by specifying the maximum amount of a payroll check or establishing payroll grade levels with maximum salaries for each level. Control is also facilitated by comparing payroll costs with standards or budgets or by reconciling payroll costs to production cost or job order records.

Accounting distribution for financial statement purposes ordinarily is not difficult to control because the wages of most employees are charged to the same account from one period to another. Detailed cost accounting systems may call for distributing the total amount among cost centers; in those cases, control over the completeness of the distribution usually is exercised by comparing the amount distributed with the total payroll. The accuracy of the distribution is ensured by investigating differences revealed by variance analyses.

The computation of payroll deductions is governed either by statute (in the case of payroll taxes) or contract (union agreement, group insurance contract, or agency agreements with charitable organizations or credit unions). The authorization to deduct amounts from an employee's pay is given by the individual in writing and ordinarily is obtained and maintained by the human resources department. Cumulative records of deductions are required for each employee. Controls over payments of withheld amounts are similar to those for payments of recorded accounts payable.

As previously noted, many entities contract with data processing service organizations for the actual calculation of gross pay and deductions, based on appropriately approved standing and transaction data. If this is done, the output from the service organization should be reviewed in the same manner as discussed earlier. (See Chapter 12 for a discussion of the auditor's responsibilities in this situation.)

In most entities, the recognized advantages of segregation of duties in payroll processing are not difficult to achieve. The duties of the human resources and accounting departments are separated, and the person who approves time records is independent of both departments. All of those functions are separate from the handling of payroll checks or cash, as discussed below.

(e) Payment of Wages

Payment of the net payroll amount may be accomplished by check, direct deposit into the employee's bank account, or, in increasingly rare instances, cash payment. Approval of payroll checks, which are often prepared as an integral part of the payroll calculation, usually includes comparing the total of all checks with the total of the payroll summary. Segregation of duties related to payroll disbursements made by check should be the same as for other cash disbursements. It is especially important to segregate duties if the checks are distributed rather than mailed. For example, employees' checks should be distributed by people who do not have responsibility for preparing or approving the payroll.[1]

Unclaimed wages are listed at once, safeguarded, investigated with the human resources department to determine the existence of the employees, and returned to cash if unclaimed within a short time.

(f) Monitoring Controls

As indicated in Chapter 10, management requires reliable financial information to operate the entity. In some situations, management reviews information generated by the accounting system and oversees the performance of control activities established to provide that information. Those monitoring controls were discussed earlier in the chapter in conjunction with related control activities. In other situations, discussed in this section, management evaluates such information in the course of reviewing and analyzing reports for the purpose of monitoring the entity's operations. Evidence that management makes those reviews, often referred to as performance reviews, can provide some assurance to the auditor of the reliability of financial information.

High-level managers—including production and financial personnel—typically review key performance indicators, such as gross profit and other financial ratios. They compare expenses with information accumulated from outside the accounting system, such as production and cash budgets, as well as prior periods' performance indicators. Purchasing managers also may monitor information about new vendors, long-outstanding purchase orders, and purchase transactions with unusual quantities or prices. The controller typically reviews the periodic reconciliation of the accounts payable subsidiary ledger to the control account to determine that it is being performed adequately and on a timely basis. The controller also may monitor monthly accounts payable cutoff procedures and any necessary adjusting entries, and may analyze accrued expenses to ensure that all liabilities and expenses have been recorded. Management may monitor payroll expense by reviewing production reports containing performance indicators such as full-time employee equivalents, average hourly pay rates, and payroll expense per standard unit of measure, for example, payroll expense per patient-day in a hospital. Nonproduction management may receive monthly expense analyses that include payroll expenses, which can be compared with infor-

---

[1] Internal auditors may observe a payroll distribution to provide assurance that payments are not made to nonexistent personnel. At one time, it was not uncommon for external auditors to perform the same test, but except for special "fraud audits," it rarely is done today.

mation accumulated from outside the accounting system, such as departmental budgets and past performance indicators.

14.2 DETERMINING THE AUDIT STRATEGY

As discussed in Chapter 6, the key audit strategy decision the auditor makes for each significant account balance is whether to perform tests of controls to support a below-the-maximum or low assessment of control risk for specific audit objectives. The auditor frequently tests an entity's controls in the purchasing cycle to obtain evidence of their effective operation as a basis for reducing the assurance needed from substantive tests directed at the completeness, accuracy, and existence/occurrence audit objectives. If the entity has implemented controls designed to achieve proper cutoff at year-end, the auditor also may decide to test them in conjunction with other tests of controls. Similarly, there may be satisfactory controls, which the auditor can test, with respect to the completeness and accuracy of the data underlying the estimates that are related to the valuation objective. With those exceptions, the auditor generally achieves the remaining audit objectives by performing substantive tests designed after considering the entity's inherent risks and his or her understanding of controls.

(a) Developing the Understanding of Controls

As discussed in Chapter 11, the auditor is required, at a minimum, to obtain an understanding of the entity's internal control sufficient to plan the audit. This understanding, along with the auditor's evaluation of the effectiveness of the design of controls, is used to identify the types of misstatements that might occur and the risk of their occurring, and to design substantive tests. The understanding is obtained, or updated, by considering previous experience with the entity, reviewing prior-year audit results, interviewing entity personnel, observing them as they perform their duties, reviewing descriptions of policies and procedures prepared by entity personnel, and inspecting documents and records.

In addition to information about how entity-level controls affect the purchasing cycle, the predominant means of processing transactions (manually or by computer), the level of the system's sophistication, and other general characteristics of internal control, the auditor should consider the following types of information, as appropriate, related to the purchasing cycle:

- The volume, dollar amount, and types of purchases, and the number of vendors the entity buys from
- The flow of purchasing cycle transactions through the accounting system

If the auditor plans to assess control risk at maximum, an understanding of the above aspects of internal control generally is sufficient to plan the audit. If, however, as is typical, the auditor's planned assessment of control risk for purchasing cycle accounts is below the maximum or low, he or she will need to understand controls at a more detailed level as a basis for testing them. If the auditor plans to assess control risk below the maximum, he or she will extend the understanding of controls to include such monitoring controls as management reviews of operating expenses, supervision of employees who investigate items on exception reports, and the other monitoring controls described earlier in the chapter, and consider the extent to which they can be expected to detect misstatements of purchasing cycle accounts. The auditor will then test those controls, and perhaps also certain entity-level controls, to obtain evidence of their effective operation to support the below-the-maximum assessment.

The procedures performed for the purpose of obtaining or updating the understanding of controls may serve as tests of controls as well, if they provide evidence that controls are operating effectively. Such tests of controls, particularly if they include tests of monitoring controls, often provide evidence to support an assessment of control risk that is below the maximum for the completeness, accuracy, and existence/occurrence audit objectives. For example, when inquiring about management's review of operating expenses (a monitoring control), the auditor also may observe personnel performing the review or examine reports or documents that provide evidence of the review. If, after considering the level of detail reviewed and the likelihood that the reviewer would detect a material misstatement, the auditor concludes that the management review is operating effectively, it provides some evidence with respect to the completeness and accuracy of expenses.

To support an assessment of control risk at low, the tests of controls performed should include tests of control activities. That is because control activities explicitly address control objectives and have direct effects on specific audit objectives and account balances. Thus, evidence that control activities, along with controls in the other components, are operating effectively supports an assessment that all the components of internal control interacting together reduce to a low level the risk that control objectives will not be achieved.

If the auditor plans to assess control risk at low, he or she will develop an understanding of the application and computer controls relating to purchase orders, receiving documents, invoices, and cash disbursements, and the extent to which duties are segregated among the people performing accounting procedures and control activities. The auditor considers whether those controls have been placed in operation and are appropriately designed to achieve their objectives, and whether evidence of their effective operation is likely to be available and efficient to obtain. If so, the auditor will test the controls to obtain evidence that they meet the control objectives relating to account balances and transactions in the purchasing cycle. (The control objectives are defined in Chapter 9 and discussed further in Chapter 11.) That evidence will provide the auditor with assurance about specific audit objectives related to systems-derived accounts in the purchasing cycle—usually, completeness, accuracy, and existence/occurrence of accounts payable, purchases, and various expenses.

(b)   Audit Strategy Decisions—An Illustration

Professional judgment is needed to assess risks and translate that assessment into the various decisions that constitute the audit strategy. The following is a description of the testing decisions an auditor might make in developing an appropriate audit strategy for the purchasing cycle.

The entity is a manufacturer with a strong control environment and a well-developed computerized accounting system for purchases and cash disbursements. Application software, which was developed in-house and is fully integrated with other financial modules, supports all purchasing cycle processing. Computer controls are strong in all areas, including development and implementation of new systems and computer security. The volume of transactions is high and involves many different types of raw materials and services.

The entity's authorization procedures vary depending on the nature of the purchase. Raw materials, fixed assets, and significant service contracts are authorized via the "purchase order" process; recurring expenses and services under $1,000 are authorized via the "direct payment" process.

Under the purchase order process, manually prepared purchase requisitions, which include the accounting distribution, are reviewed and signed by a department manager authorized to approve requisitions above specified amounts. Purchasing department clerks prepare purchase orders, using data from the approved requisitions and standard vendor numbers, and forward them to the vendors. Only purchasing department personnel have computer access to create purchase orders. The general ledger distribution is reviewed by the purchasing department clerk, who compares the distribution per the requisition to the chart of accounts prepared by the controller. A purchasing department clerk prints a daily purchase order detail and reviews it line-by-line for obvious input errors.

To enhance efficiency, certain recurring expenses and services under $1,000 do not require authorized purchase requisitions but instead are controlled through the direct payment process. In this process, disbursements clerks require oral approval from department managers before the clerks prepare vouchers for invoices that are not authorized with a purchase requisition and purchase order. After obtaining approval from a department manager, the disbursements clerks input the purchase information based on the invoice; price, quantity, and vendor are confirmed orally with the purchasing department when the invoice is approved for payment. The accounting distribution also is obtained from the purchasing department at that time. The disbursements clerks review the accounting distribution, using the chart of accounts prepared by the controller, to ensure that the invoice is posted to the correct account. The controller tracks monthly expenses to detect unusual trends.

Receiving information is input to the receiving report file by receiving clerks directly from the packing slip, without reference to the open purchase order file. The computer automatically performs an on-line match to the open purchase order file and provides an audible signal to the clerks if there is a mismatch of part number or quantity; the clerks then review the packing slip to ensure that the amounts input were correct. A "mismatch report" is prepared listing all goods received that do not match the open purchase order file. A purchasing supervisor manages the mismatch resolution process by reviewing the mismatch report each week and communicating with the purchasing department clerks. The supervisor reviews the report for input errors, unusual amounts, trends with certain vendors or departments, as well as the volume of mismatches, and documents the review by initialing and dating the report. The purchasing supervisor also reviews the open purchase order report to detect long-outstanding purchase orders and contacts vendors and the requisitioning departments to take the necessary corrective action. Partial shipments and fixed asset purchases are not described in this illustration, but they also are subject to appropriate controls.

Invoices are received by the accounts payable department, where they are input by clerks who (alone) have password access; those clerks do not have access to perform other purchasing cycle functions. The computer will accept only vendors that are in the vendor standing data file; invoices from nonapproved vendors are posted to a "problem invoice report." The clerks perform an on-line match between the invoice and the receiving report file to determine that all invoiced goods were received; that match also detects input of incorrect quantities and vendors. The system will not allow an invoice to be matched to the same receiving report twice; the system also will not accept an invoice number twice for input. At the same time, the invoice price is matched to the open purchase order file to detect incorrect pricing. All mismatches are posted to the problem invoice report and are followed through and resolved daily. The appropriate asset or expense account is charged and accounts payable credited when invoices are vouchered.

An accrual for uninvoiced receipts is posted to a separate general ledger account each month (with the offset posted to inventory). The accrual is posted directly from an uninvoiced receipts report, obtained from the receiving report file, with prices from the open purchase order file. The controller reviews the entry before it is posted. Invoices for services are also under appropriate controls.

The accounts payable supervisor reviews the problem invoice report monthly to ensure that items on the report are resolved on a timely basis, to note any unusual items, and to consider whether the volume of activity on the report is within expectations. The controller reviews items on the report monthly and prepares an entry to ensure that the liabilities are captured on a timely basis. Each vendor statement is compared line by line with the vendor's account on the aged accounts payable file to detect discrepancies, which are then corrected over the phone with vendors. The accounts payable supervisor reviews all vendor statements after their clerical review to ensure that the latter reviews are being performed and to identify old outstanding items that might suggest a problem in processing.

Cash disbursements are processed by a disbursements clerk, who is supervised by the disbursements supervisor. Only the clerk and the supervisor have password access to authorize payments. The clerk has no other access; the supervisor has full access for all purchasing functions except for creating purchase orders.

Invoices are selected for payment based on their invoice date and the agreed payment terms with particular vendors, as maintained on the vendor standing data file. Before preparing the checks, the disbursements supervisor prints out a listing of vendor names and amounts to be paid, which is reviewed for reasonableness, after which the checks are printed. The computer updates the accounts payable file and posts the check totals to the cash disbursements file daily. Unissued checks and the check signing plate are secured; only the disbursements supervisor has physical access to them. Controls also have been designed and placed in operation over purchase returns and allowances and the related credits received from vendors.

Changes to vendor standing data—including vendor number, name, address, and payment terms—are processed weekly. Only one clerk and supervisor are authorized to make changes. Purchasing and operating department managers may request the addition of new vendors or changes to existing vendors. The accounts payable supervisor approves all changes prior to input.

The general ledger is updated monthly, based on the accumulation of daily activity used to update the accounts payable file. The accounts payable file is reconciled monthly to the general ledger control account by an accounts payable clerk, and is reviewed by the accounts payable supervisor. Monthly closing procedures include a one-

Figure 14.1   Acquisitions of Goods and Services

	Control Objectives		
	Transaction Processing		
	Authorization	Completeness of Input	Accuracy of Input
Specific Control Objectives	All recorded purchase transactions represent actual receipts of goods and services and are approved.	All purchase transactions are input and accepted for processing.	Purchases are correctly recorded as to amounts, quantities, dates, vendors, and general ledger account; are recorded in the proper period; and are accurately input to the computer.
Examples of Control Activities	Approval of requisitions and purchase orders. Matching invoices for goods and services received to receiving reports and purchase orders by individuals independent of purchasing and receiving functions. Reporting and resolving invoices and receiving reports that do not match against approved purchase orders.	Accounting for the numerical sequence of requisitions and purchase orders input to the computer. Reporting and resolving missing or duplicate items by individuals independent of receiving and purchasing functions. Reporting and resolving long-outstanding items on the aged open purchase order file, and receipts and invoices rejected as not matching against the open purchase order file. Accounting for the numerical sequence of receiving reports. Reporting and resolving missing or duplicate items by individuals independent of receiving and cash disbursements functions.	Counting, where appropriate, and inspecting goods received, by personnel independent of purchase and accounting functions. Completeness of input controls for purchase orders also address the accuracy of input for vendor, prices, and descriptions; completeness of input controls for receiving reports also address the accuracy of input for date, quantities, and descriptions. Reporting and resolving unmatched items by individuals independent of receiving and purchasing functions. Review of account classifications.

Figure 14.1   *(Continued)*

Control Objectives

File Maintenance

Integrity of Standing Data	Completeness and Accuracy of Updating	Completeness and Accuracy of Accumulated Data	Asset Protection
All changes to standing data are authorized and accurately input.	All purchase transactions input and accepted for processing are accurately updated to the general ledger and accounts payable files.	The integrity of individual accounts payable in the subsidiary ledger and the general ledger accounts, after purchase transactions have been accumulated in them, is preserved.	Only authorized personnel have access to accounts payable records and data stored on them.
Approving changes to vendor master files for name, address, and payment terms.	Comparing total purchases input with the total updated to the purchases and accounts payable files.	Balancing of the subsidiary ledger (previous balance plus purchases less payments compared with the current total). Reconciling the subsidiary ledger to the control account in the general ledger, reporting and resolving discrepancies.	Restricting access to accounts payable files and files used in processing payables.

Figure 14.2 Payments Made for Goods and Services

| | *Control Objectives* | | |
| | *Transaction Processing* | | |
	Authorization	*Completeness of Input*	*Accuracy of Input*
Specific Control Objectives	All cash disbursements are for actual purchases of goods and services and are approved.	All payments made are input and accepted for processing.	Disbursements are correctly recorded as to amounts, dates, and payees; are recorded in the proper period; and are accurately input to the computer.
Examples of Control Activities	Approving payment (before checks are signed) by officials independent of purchasing, receiving, and accounts payable functions. Examination by signatory, at time of signing checks, of supporting documentation (e.g., invoices, receiving reports, purchase orders). Canceling supporting documentation to prevent resubmission for payment.	Accounting for the numerical sequence of checks, both used and unused. Reporting and investigating missing or duplicate checks. Reporting and investigating long-outstanding checks by individuals independent of accounts payable and cash disbursements functions.	Matching disbursements records against accounts payable/open invoice files. Reporting and resolving differences by individuals independent of accounts payable and cash disbursements functions.

Figure 14.2 *(Continued)*

Control Objectives

---

*File Maintenance**

Completeness and Accuracy of Updating	*Completeness and Accuracy of Accumulated Data*	*Asset Protection*
All disbursements input and accepted for processing are accurately updated to the cash disbursements and accounts payable files.	The integrity of individual accounts payable in the subsidiary ledger and the general ledger accounts, after purchase transactions have been updated to them, is preserved.	Only authorized personnel have access to cash, unissued checks, and accounts payable files or data stored on them.
Comparing total disbursements input with the totals updated to the cash disbursements and accounts payable files.	Same control activities as described in Figure 14.1, "Acquisitions of Goods and Services."	Mailing of checks by individuals independent of recording accounts payable.
	Reconciling the bank statement to the general ledger cash account by personnel independent of accounts payable and cash disbursements functions (and receiving and recording cash receipts).	Authorized check signers are independent of cash receipts functions.
		Physically protecting mechanical check signers and signature plates.
		Restricting access to accounts payable files and files used in processing cash disbursements.

---

* Integrity of standing data usually is not relevant to payments made for goods and services.

Figure 14.3   Calculating and Recording Payroll

	Control Objectives		
	Transaction Processing		
	Authorization	*Completeness of Input*	*Accuracy of Input*
Specific Control Objectives	All recorded transactions for employee wages are for actual services performed and are approved.	All employee wages for services performed are input and accepted for processing.	Employee wages are correctly recorded as to wage rate, hours, and time period; are properly calculated as to gross wages, withholdings, and net pay; are recorded to the correct general ledger accounts; and are accurately input to the computer.
Examples of Control Activities	Approving processing of pay for employees with hours in excess of a predetermined limit.	Comparing total hours (in batch form) with total hours input to the computer.	Completeness of input controls for total hours also address the accuracy of input.
	Approving changes to master files for new employees and deleted employees.	Reporting and investigating employees on master file for whom no hours worked have been input.	Matching employee data to comparable master file data—employee name, number, and so on. Reporting and investigating mismatched items.
			Reporting hours worked in excess of a predetermined limit.

Figure 14.3   *(Continued)*

Control Objectives

| | *File Maintenance* | | |
Integrity of Standing Data	*Completeness and Accuracy of Updating*	*Completeness and Accuracy of Accumulated Data*	*Asset Protection*
All changes to standing data are authorized and accurately input.	All employee wage transactions input and accepted for processing are accurately updated to the payroll register and individual payroll files.	The integrity of the individual employee payroll records and the payroll summary and general ledger accounts for payroll withholdings is preserved.	Only authorized personnel have access to payroll files and data stored on them, including standing data.
Approving changes to master files for wage and salary rates and individual personnel data.	Comparing total hours and number of employees input with the totals updated to the payroll register.	Reconciling the employee subsidiary ledger to the control accounts in the general ledger; reporting and resolving discrepancies.	Restricting access to payroll files and data stored on them. Distribution of checks by persons independent of recording and approving the payroll. Physically protecting mechanical check signers and signature plates.

week accrual period in which invoices related to the prior month are "posted back"; quarterly and year-end procedures cover two weeks. The chief financial officer, controller, and department managers all review the monthly financial statements to ensure that all activity, including purchases, is included. At year-end, the controller also monitors invoices received after the normal two-week cutoff period for significant items. Monitoring controls also include the production manager's review of production reports and the financial statements and identification of any unexpected results. Financial management reviews a detailed revenue and expense analysis monthly and also compares monthly cash disbursements and cash balances with budgeted amounts.

In these circumstances, based on the understanding of internal control and any tests of controls performed concurrently with obtaining the understanding, the auditor probably would initially assess control risk at low. He or she would then perform additional tests of controls, including tests of computer controls, to obtain evidence that the controls were operating effectively and achieving the control objectives described in Chapter 9. The nature, timing, and extent of substantive tests of details that would be appropriate when control risk is assessed at low for the purchasing cycle are described in Chapter 23.

As indicated in Chapter 9, for systems-derived accounts, the auditor meets the audit objectives of completeness, accuracy, and existence/occurrence, usually as a group, by determining that the transaction-level control objectives (authorization, completeness of input, and accuracy of input) and the cycle-level control objectives (completeness and accuracy of updating, completeness and accuracy of accumulated data, integrity of standing data, and restricted access to assets and records) have been achieved. Even if the auditor concludes that not all of the control objectives have been met, however, it may be more efficient, depending on the circumstances, to assess control risk at low and perform certain substantive tests directed at detecting misstatements that could have resulted from the unmet control objectives. What is necessary is for the auditor to achieve all audit objectives, either by developing a basis for concluding that the risk of material misstatement of related accounts is low or by performing substantive tests of those accounts.

For example, in this environment, the two-week, year-end closing process is a significant completeness control whose objective is to ensure that all acquisitions of goods and services are recorded in the proper period and that there are no unrecorded liabilities at year-end. If the auditor determined that the year-end closing process did not adequately address purchases of services made under the "direct payment" process, the auditor might continue to assess control risk at low, but should consider making specific inquiries of the controller to determine whether he or she monitored invoices received after the normal two-week cutoff period and specifically to assess the accrual for direct payment invoices received after year-end, as substantive tests at year-end.

On the other hand, suppose that the entity's procedures did not generate an uninvoiced receipts report and did not include other controls to prevent goods that have been ordered and received from going unrecorded. As a result, assets, expenses, and accounts payable might be incomplete. In this situation, based on the understanding of internal control and any tests of controls performed concurrently with obtaining the understanding, the auditor probably would not be able to assess control risk at low. He or she might then assess control risk below the maximum, extend the understanding to include monitoring controls over purchasing transactions, and test those controls to confirm the below-the-maximum assessment. The auditor would not, however, develop an understanding of control activities or test them. Substantive tests of details, described in Chapter 23, would be directed at all assertions and probably would be performed as of year-end. Chapter 23 discusses substantive tests specifically directed at the completeness of accounts payable and related accounts. Chapter 23 also discusses the extent of testing that is appropriate with a below-the-maximum control risk assessment.

(c)   Tests of Controls to Support a Low Control Risk Assessment

If the auditor plans to assess control risk for accounts that are part of the purchasing cycle, such as accounts payable, cash, and purchases, at low, he or she will test the application controls over purchasing transactions. In addition, the auditor will need evidence of the effectiveness of computer controls that affect those accounts and transactions. (Computer controls are discussed in Chapter 11, and tests of those controls in Chapter 12.) Specific control objectives and typical application controls that address the acquisition of goods and services, payments made for them, and calculating and recording payroll[2] are described in Figures 14.1, 14.2, and 14.3, respectively. The accounting system assumed to be in operation in the figures is a sophisticated computerized system.

As discussed in Chapter 12, the tests of controls that the auditor would perform include an appropriate combination of inquiring about the entity's control activities, observing that they have been placed in operation, and examining evidence that they are operating effectively. Also as discussed in Chapter 12, reperformance may be used in tests of controls, but if that becomes necessary, the auditor usually determines that it is more efficient to perform substantive tests.

In evaluating the results of tests of control activities (including tests of computer controls), the auditor considers whether the entity's internal control, taken as a whole, is appropriately designed to achieve the control objectives and is operating effectively. This will determine whether the low assessment of control risk was attained for specific accounts and audit objectives and, thus, whether the auditor can restrict substantive testing as planned. Results differing from those anticipated when developing the audit strategy require the auditor to reconsider the nature, timing, and extent of planned substantive tests—not only for purchasing cycle accounts, but also for other accounts that may be affected. For example, ineffective control activities to ensure completeness of recorded purchases also may affect inventory and cost of sales.

---

[2] Even if an entity has controls over calculating and recording payroll that would support an assessment of control risk at low, the auditor often will find it more efficient to audit payroll expenditures through substantive test analytical procedures. Substantive tests of salaries, wages, accrued payroll, and related liabilities are discussed in Chapter 23.

15

Substantive Tests

As stated in earlier chapters of this book, the primary purpose of an audit is the expression of an opinion on whether the entity's financial statements are presented fairly, in all material respects, in conformity with generally accepted accounting principles. The auditor needs a high level of assurance that the opinion is appropriate; that is, audit risk must be limited to a low level. Audit risk was defined in Chapter 6 as consisting of the risk (comprising inherent and control risks) of the financial statements containing a material misstatement and the risk, known as detection risk, of not detecting a material misstatement in the financial statements. The auditor identifies inherent risks associated with the entity and assesses control risk as a basis for determining the audit strategy, and controls detection risk by performing substantive tests to gain the necessary assurance regarding the various assertions embodied in the financial statements. The audit strategy for each significant class of transactions or related account balance will depend on the auditor's judgment both about how effectively relevant controls are designed and operating and about whether it is more efficient to test the controls or to test the account balances themselves. The auditor *may* choose to obtain evidence entirely from substantive tests of account balances and transactions, but, as stated in AU Section 319.81, *may not* choose to omit substantive tests entirely for *all* of the assertions (and corresponding audit objectives) relevant to significant account balances or transaction classes.

Substantive tests consist of tests of details of account balances and related transactions, and analytical procedures.[1] Generally, a combination of these procedures are performed in auditing a specific account balance or class of transactions. The nature, timing, and extent of the substantive tests to be performed to meet specific audit objectives for each account balance and class of transactions are determined by:

1. The type of account involved
2. The information about the entity obtained or updated for the purpose of making preliminary judgments about materiality and identifying inherent risks
3. The assessment of control risk
4. The auditor's judgment about the most efficient and effective combination of auditing procedures

The effect of those factors on the selection of substantive tests—and on the timing and the extent of those tests—is described later in this chapter.

Assessing how much assurance can be attained from a particular substantive test is a matter of professional judgment and cannot be specified without knowledge of the full context in which the test is to be performed. This chapter describes many substantive tests. Auditors rarely perform all of them on an engagement. Instead, after considering the evidence obtained from tests of controls and other risk assessment activities, an auditor selects the specific tests, for each audit objective relevant to each

---

[1] Some auditors treat certain procedures—principally reading minutes of meetings of the board of directors and its important committees and obtaining letters from lawyers regarding legal matters and letters of representation from management—as a third type of substantive tests, sometimes called "other auditing procedures" or "other substantive tests." Those procedures are discussed in this chapter and in Chapter 27.

financial statement account and disclosure, that will provide the evidence necessary in the particular circumstances.

The key to selecting appropriate substantive tests is the auditor's understanding of management's assertions and the corresponding audit objectives. The auditor identifies specific audit objectives for each significant account balance and designs auditing procedures to provide the necessary assurance that those objectives have been achieved. Figure 15.1 illustrates the audit objectives that may be applicable to an entity's trade accounts receivable and sales, and provides examples (which are not intended to cover all circumstances) of substantive tests of details the auditor may perform to satisfy the objectives.

15.1   SUBSTANTIVE TEST STRATEGY DECISIONS

(a)   Types of Accounts

The nature, timing, and extent of substantive tests appropriate for a particular audit objective and account vary with the type of account. Accounts may be classified into three types:

1. Accounts that are derived from a major class of transactions within a transaction cycle that typically involves high volumes of transactions. Examples are cash, accounts receivable, inventory, accounts payable, purchases, salaries and wages, and sales. These are referred to in this book as *systems-derived accounts*. As explained in Chapter 9 (Section 9.3, Transaction Cycles and Control Objectives), the transactions that generate these accounts are commonly subjected to control activities that address control objectives relating to processing transactions, maintaining files, and protecting assets. Decisions about whether the audit strategy for these accounts should include tests of controls generally are related to whether that would be the most efficient way to achieve the existence/occurrence, completeness, and accuracy audit objectives.

2. Accounts that reflect internal allocations of revenues or expenses over time through the accrual, deferral, or amortization of assets or liabilities. Examples of such accounts include accrued receivables and payables, deferred charges and credits, machinery and equipment, and asset valuation and estimated liability accounts. These accounts often require management to exercise judgment in determining the period or method of allocation and also in selecting and applying accounting measurement and recognition principles. While the transactions and accumulated data that form the basis for these accounts are sometimes subjected to control activities, it is usually more efficient not to test controls related to these accounts.

3. Accounts that typically reflect a relatively small number of material transactions in an accounting period. Examples of these accounts include long-term investments, bonds payable, land and buildings, and contributed capital accounts. Balances in these accounts often are carried forward unchanged from one year to the next. Because transactions affecting these accounts occur infrequently, control activities may not be established to address control objectives relating to processing transactions, maintaining files, and protecting assets. Even when the transactions affecting these

Figure 15.1 Audit Objectives for Trade Accounts Receivable and Sales

Audit Objective	Specific Audit Objectives for Trade Accounts Receivable and Sales	Illustrative Substantive Tests of Details[a]
Completeness	Trade accounts receivable represent all amounts owed to the entity at the balance sheet date arising from sales transactions. All shipments made and services rendered during the period covered by the financial statements and all returns and allowances are reflected in the financial statements.	Compare records of goods shipped and services performed with recorded transactions.
Accuracy	Sales transactions are based on correct prices and quantities and are accurately computed and classified in the appropriate general ledger and accounts receivable subsidiary ledger accounts. The accounts receivable subsidiary ledger is mathematically correct and agrees with the general ledger.	Compare amounts on shipping documents and invoices with supporting documents and recorded transactions. (Confirmation of customers' accounts to some extent also indicates the accuracy of the balances.) Using audit software, calculate invoice amounts and total the accounts receivable subsidiary ledger.
Existence/ Occurrence	Recorded accounts receivable represent amounts owed to the entity at the balance sheet date. Recorded sales transactions represent goods actually shipped or services actually rendered during the period covered by the financial statements.	Confirm customers' accounts, investigate any discrepancies reported or questions raised, and determine whether any adjustments are necessary.
Cutoff	Sales transactions, cash receipts, and returns and allowances are recorded in the proper period.	Perform cutoff tests: (a) Determine that sales invoices are recorded as sales in the proper period by comparing the related records of goods shipped and services performed with recorded sales for several days before and after year-end. (b) Determine that credit memos are recorded in the proper period by examining the related records of returns and claims from customers for several days before and after year-end.

(*Continues*)

Figure 15.1 *(Continued)*

Audit Objective	Specific Audit Objectives for Trade Accounts Receivable and Sales	Illustrative Substantive Tests of Details[a]
Valuation/Allocation	Accounts receivable are stated at net realizable value (i.e., net of appropriate allowances for uncollectible accounts, discounts, returns, and similar items). Revenue is recognized only when appropriate accounting recognition and measurement criteria are met.	Determine whether the allowance for uncollectible accounts is adequate by reviewing the aged trial balances, discussing the allowance and composition of the receivable balance with management, and identifying significant old receivables and receivables in dispute or changes in the collectibility of current receivables. Review cash collections after the balance sheet date and examine related remittance advices or other supporting documentation to ascertain that payments relate to the balance that was due at the balance sheet date. Determine the adequacy of collateral, if any. Review relevant credit file information, such as customer financial data and correspondence. Discuss all significant potentially uncollectible accounts with management. Determine that revenue has been recognized in conformity with GAAP.
Rights and Obligations	Accounts receivable are legal rights of the entity at the balance sheet date (i.e., customer accounts that have been sold or factored are excluded from the accounts receivable balance).	Make inquiries and read agreements relating to the possible sale of receivables that the entity continues to service.
Presentation and Disclosure	Accounts receivable, sales, and related accounts are properly described and classified in the financial statements. Accounts receivable pledged as collateral are properly disclosed. Concentrations of credit risk arising from accounts receivable are properly disclosed.	Identify liens, security interests, and assets pledged as loan collateral by reviewing debt and lease agreements; confirmation replies, particularly from financial institutions; and minutes of directors' meetings. Inquire of management about those items and about concentrations of credit risk that need to be disclosed.

[a]Analytical procedures, such as analysis of monthly sales trends compared with prior years and budget, also may be designed to provide assurance relating to audit objectives for trade accounts receivable and sales.

accounts are subject to control activities, testing controls usually is not an efficient audit strategy.

(b) Effect of Control Risk Assessment

The assessment of control risk affects the nature, timing, and extent of substantive tests directed at the existence/occurrence, completeness, and accuracy (and sometimes cutoff and valuation) audit objectives for account balances derived from transactions commonly subjected to control activities or monitoring controls that operate at the level of transaction cycles or classes of transactions (i.e., systems-derived accounts). In assessing control risk the auditor generally considers existence/occurrence, completeness, and accuracy together for the accounts within a particular transaction cycle. Based on the assessment of control risk, the auditor often is able to conclude that the risk of material misstatement, and therefore the level of assurance required from substantive tests, with respect to those objectives for systems-derived accounts is lower than for other audit objectives. This conclusion generally is based on the following:

1. Existence/occurrence, completeness, and accuracy often are addressed by controls whose operating effectiveness can be tested

2. The fact that computer processing is not subject to random error further reduces the risk of material misstatement, particularly with respect to accuracy and, to a lesser extent, completeness

3. Existence/occurrence, completeness, and accuracy normally are not affected by management's subjective judgments and estimates

Although controls generally address the existence/occurrence objective, it is the audit objective most at risk with respect to fraud. Segregation of duties, physical controls, computer security controls, and controls over the authorization of transactions are particularly relevant to the existence/occurrence objective. Since management or employee fraud usually involves both deliberate circumvention of controls and an attempt to conceal the result, the auditor may need to perform substantive tests of details for existence/occurrence, regardless of the control risk assessment.

For accounts other than systems-derived accounts, control activities may not address the risks associated with existence/occurrence, completeness, and accuracy, although aspects of the control environment and accounting system may affect the achievement of those audit objectives. Even though an entity may have control activities to ensure a proper cutoff of purchases, sales, cash receipts, and cash disbursements, the auditor generally finds it more efficient not to test controls with respect to the cutoff objective but instead to obtain evidence primarily from substantive tests.

It usually is not possible to derive significant evidence from internal control in relation to the audit objectives of valuation, rights and obligations, and presentation and disclosure for any type of account. This is because those objectives generally are not addressed by control activities, although control activities may address the existence/occurrence, completeness, and accuracy of data that management uses in making valuation and disclosure judgments, such as annual depreciation of plant and equipment. Management's judgments and estimates that are related to the valuation, rights and obligations, and presentation and disclosure objectives, can be complex and may not be free from bias. Many entities do not have the professional expertise within their organization to deal completely with the many issues relating to these objectives. The impact of inherent risks and assessments of the control environment—notably the competence of financial accounting personnel and the quality of management reviews of financial information—are particularly relevant to these objectives. Even in large, well-managed entities, however, the auditor rarely is able to assess the risk of material misstatement with respect to valuation, rights and obligations, and presentation and disclosure at low and should always seek a high level of assurance from substantive tests directed to these objectives.

(c)   Nature of Substantive Tests Under Varying Risk Assessments

(i) Substantive Tests That Provide High Assurance.
Assessing control risk at maximum for a specific audit objective for a particular account means that all audit assurance, within the context of materiality, will be derived from substantive tests, primarily tests of details. As noted above, that is often the only feasible or the most efficient audit strategy for all audit objectives for non-systems-derived accounts and for the valuation, rights and obligations, and presentation and disclosure audit objectives for systems-derived accounts. Assurance with respect to rights and obligations and the selection of accounting principles can be obtained only by considering the substance of specific transactions and other events and circumstances that affect the entity and the appropriateness of the accounting recognition, measurement, and disclosure principles that the entity has selected and applied to reflect them. While analytical procedures can be good detectors of changes in accounting principles, they will not alert the auditor to a misstatement resulting from an incorrect accounting principle that remains unchanged.

For accounts involving the accrual, deferral, or amortization of revenues and expenses, analytical procedures and reperformance of computations usually provide the necessary assurance about accuracy. Assurance about existence/occurrence and completeness with respect to transactions that give rise to those accounts usually is obtained, to the extent necessary, by means of substantive tests of details. For accounts involving balances that are carried forward from one year to the next, the auditor may obtain evidence regarding the existence/occurrence, completeness, and accuracy objectives by examining the details underlying the transactions in the accounts, reperforming calculations on selected transactions, and performing analytical procedures. Assurance with respect to existence for certain of those accounts may be obtained by confirmation or, in situations where the theft of assets is a significant risk, inspection of assets. In certain entities the recorded transactions that affect these accounts are subject to control activities; if so, the auditor should consider this fact as part of the risk assessment activities.

(ii) Substantive Tests That Provide Moderate to Low Assurance.
For the existence/occurrence, completeness, and accuracy objectives (and sometimes cutoff and valuation) for systems-derived accounts, assessing control risk below the maximum makes it possible to restrict the substantive tests required to obtain the necessary audit assurance. For those audit objectives, substantive testing normally consists of a

combination of analytical procedures and tests of details. Tests of details generally can be restricted to a level that provides low to moderate assurance. The level of assurance necessary will take into consideration inherent risks identified and will depend largely on the assessment of control risk; that is, whether it is closer to maximum or to low. If control risk is assessed toward the upper end of the continuum (closer to maximum), the auditor should seek to obtain moderate assurance from substantive tests of details. If control risk is assessed at the lower end of the continuum (closer to low), the auditor may restrict the level of substantive tests of details to provide low assurance. If it is effective and efficient to assess control risk at low for existence/occurrence, completeness, and accuracy for systems-derived accounts, the auditor may restrict substantive tests for those objectives and accounts mainly to appropriate analytical procedures.

Often the auditor determines that it is efficient to perform tests of details to obtain all necessary assurance about the cutoff objective, even if control activities address cutoff for systems-derived accounts, such as purchases, sales, cash receipts, and cash disbursements. Some entities, however, have well-designed cutoff controls, and in those instances it may be efficient to assess control risk below the maximum for the cutoff objective and perform a combination of tests of details and analytical procedures to obtain the necessary additional assurance. Furthermore, tests of transaction processing controls also may provide some evidence regarding the cutoff objective.

(iii) Tests of Income Statement Accounts. As noted in Chapter 6, auditors traditionally have focused more on audit objectives related to balance sheet accounts than income statement accounts, for both practical and conceptual reasons. Frequently, that is the most efficient way to conduct an audit and is also conceptually sound. For some systems-derived income statement accounts, tests of details directed at an audit objective for a balance sheet account may provide the necessary assurance regarding the same audit objective for the related income statement account. For example, tests of details directed at completeness of accounts receivable may include matching shipping documents with invoices and eventually with entries in the general ledger. These tests also provide assurance regarding the completeness of revenue. However, the auditor should consider whether the extent of testing, which in this example was designed to test the balance sheet account, also satisfies the income statement account. If not, the auditor may extend the tests of details or perform an analytical procedure directed at revenue (see Chapter 18) to obtain the necessary additional assurance.

Many income statement accounts are related to balance sheet accounts and may be audited as described above. Examples include purchases/accounts payable, provision for bad debts/allowance for doubtful accounts, insurance expense/prepaid insurance, and interest expense/accrued interest. Some income statement accounts are directly related to other income statement accounts and may be effectively audited by performing analytical procedures. For instance, there is often a direct relationship between sales commissions and revenue. Still other income statement accounts are not directly related to other accounts, either in the balance sheet or income statement, such as legal expense, and, if material, should be audited by tests of details.

(iv) The Effect of Efficiency Considerations and Availability of Evidence on Decisions About Testing. In determining the nature of substantive tests, the auditor considers both the level of assurance required and the efficiency with which evidence can be obtained. While analytical procedures commonly provide an efficient means of obtaining assurance, tests of details, although often less efficient, typically provide a higher level of assurance. As discussed earlier, in designing and performing substantive tests the auditor should consider the relationship among accounts and the likelihood that evidence obtained about one or more audit objectives with respect to a particular account balance or class of transactions also may provide assurance about other account balances or classes of transactions.

When designing substantive tests, the auditor should consider the information available within the entity and the reviews and other procedures that management performs. For example, management often uses key performance indicators and budgetary and other operating information to monitor the entity's operations. Management's review of this information may disclose potential material misstatements in the financial statements, may provide evidence of the effectiveness of the accounting system and control activities, and may be useful in designing substantive tests.

Entity personnel typically perform procedures at year-end, for purposes of financial statement preparation, that are not performed at other times during the year. Examples of such procedures are periodic or cycle inventory counts, preparation of year-end accruals, and comparisons with third-party evidence, such as comparing loans with loan certificates, reconciliations of cash, or reconciliations of suppliers' statements. When considering the risk of financial statement misstatement and designing substantive tests, the auditor also should consider any special controls management may have instituted over these procedures. However, misstatement amounts experienced in prior years may not be indicative of current conditions unless the processing procedures and specially instituted controls have remained in effect from one year to the next. For example, an entity that does not maintain a perpetual inventory system may price its inventory at year-end based on recent purchases (first-in, first-out basis). Without assessing special activities relating to the pricing of inventory, the auditor would have no basis for concluding that the current year's inventory pricing does not contain a material misstatement, regardless of prior year experience.

Understanding how accounting procedures and, in some cases, related control activities affect an account balance usually helps in designing substantive tests. The auditor may have obtained this information with respect to systems-derived accounts when obtaining an understanding of the entity's internal control and should consider the need to obtain such an understanding for other accounts as well. For instance, the auditor may obtain an understanding of the prepaid insurance account through inquiry and might test a few transactions to corroborate the responses to the inquiry; those tests also would provide evidence of a substantive nature. The results of these procedures would determine whether further substantive tests were necessary; whether they should be analytical procedures, tests of details, or both; and their extent.

15.2 SUBSTANTIVE TESTS OF DETAILS

(a) Techniques Used to Perform Tests of Details

Substantive tests of details of transactions and account balances or of other information in the financial statements normally involve the techniques of inquiry, observation, examining documents and records, reperformance, inspecting assets, and confirmation. The following paragraphs describe each of these and suggest how they relate to the seven audit objectives.

Frequently, one of the auditor's first steps in testing an account balance or class of transactions is to make *inquiries* of entity management and employees; the responses are then corroborated by other tests. At various stages in the audit, discussions with management or employees and subsequent follow-up may bring errors to the auditor's attention. As an example, the auditor inquires about management's plans as part of considering the entity's ability to continue as a going concern, as discussed in Chapter 26. In addition, the auditor obtains letters from the entity's lawyers regarding legal matters and letters of representation from management concerning, among other matters, the recording of known liabilities, the existence of contingent liabilities, and the existence and carrying value of inventory. Inquiries may provide evidence about many audit objectives, depending on the specific accounts or transactions involved. Lawyers' and management representation letters provide assurance relating to rights and obligations, and presentation and disclosure. These letters are discussed further in Chapter 27.

The auditor may *observe* the entity's employees as they perform various tasks, like counting inventory. The auditor's observation of how the entity conducts a physical inventory can provide firsthand knowledge of the accuracy and completeness of the inventory count.

The auditor often *examines documents or records* supporting a transaction or item in the financial statements. Depending on the direction of a test involving examining documentation, the test may provide assurance either that recorded transactions occurred and related assets or liabilities exist (existence/occurrence), or that all transactions that occurred were recorded (completeness). For instance, the auditor may select particular accounts payable and examine the underlying purchase orders, invoices, and receiving reports to determine that recorded accounts payable are for items that were ordered and received. Examining documentation supporting recorded amounts is a test for existence/occurrence, and sometimes is known as vouching. Going in the opposite direction, the auditor may select shipping documents, compare them with the related sales invoices, and compare the details on those documents with entries in the sales journal and general ledger. The purpose of that test would be to obtain assurance about completeness, that is, that all goods shipped were billed and recorded. Examining documents that indicate that transactions have occurred and determining that the transactions have been recorded in the accounts sometimes is known as tracing. Examining documentation related to transactions recorded shortly before and after the entity's year-end provides assurance about the cutoff objective. The auditor normally examines documents to obtain evidence that employees have performed all prescribed procedures, reperforms those procedures (on a test basis, if appropriate), and determines that no aspects of the transaction appear unreasonable (such as a supplier's invoice not addressed to the entity). That evidence may have been generated wholly or partly outside the entity (such as suppliers' invoices, customers' orders, signed contracts) or by the entity itself (such as purchase orders, receiving reports, marketing plans). If external evidence is available, it usually is considered more reliable than internal evidence.

If entity personnel compare accounting records with physical assets, such as inventory, or with documents, such as invoices, the auditor may be able to use these comparisons and their documentation in performing substantive tests. That is, the auditor may choose to test the entity's matching procedures, which is what typically happens during the physical inventory count, rather than perform similar or duplicative procedures. If the entity's internal control includes supervision or reviews of those comparisons, the auditor, as part of the substantive tests, may examine the documentation of those monitoring controls to obtain evidence that they operated effectively (alternatively, the auditor may have done this in assessing control risk). As an example, the auditor's tests of the physical inventory count ordinarily would include tests of the activities of personnel who supervise the employees who do the actual counting. In addition, management's review of reports, which is an aspect of monitoring that the auditor often tests in assessing control risk, also can serve as the basis for a substantive test, depending on the type of report involved. For instance, management's review of reports of write-offs or dispositions of obsolete inventory could be one source of evidence that the financial statements do not reflect inventory carried at more than its net realizable value.

One specific form of internal documentation the auditor reads at various stages in the audit is minutes of meetings of the board of directors and its important committees. Reading the minutes enables the auditor to examine the board's approval of the significant corporate actions for which such approval is required and to determine whether significant decisions that affect the basic financial statements or require disclosure in the notes have been dealt with properly. The auditor should be satisfied that management has provided copies of minutes of all meetings held during the period, including meetings held after year-end but prior to the report date.

The auditor may *reperform*, usually on a test basis, procedures performed by employees, primarily to determine that a transaction was accurately accounted for. Reperformance of computations, such as of a reconciliation, also provides some assurance about the existence of the account balance (in the case of a reconciliation, cash). Many account balances represent the result of a computation or an accumulation of computations. To substantiate the accuracy of such an account balance, the auditor often reperforms some or all of the detailed computations or otherwise makes an overall evaluation of the balance. If judgment is the basis of a computation, such as in the valuation of accounts receivable, the auditor reperforming the computation also should understand and evaluate the reasoning process underlying the judgment. For example, if the provision for uncollectible accounts is based on a formula (giving appropriate consideration to past experience) related to the age of the receivables, the auditor should consider the reasonableness of the formula as well as reperform the mathematical calculations. (The auditor also would perform other procedures regarding the collectibility of accounts receivable in reviewing the adequacy of the provision for uncollectible accounts.)

Inspecting assets involves counting or examining physical items represented by accounts in the financial statements. A typical example of inspection, combined with observation, is the tests of employees' counting procedures and recounting of some of the counts during a physical inventory. Other items subject to inspection (which the auditor may count or examine directly) include cash, marketable securities, and property, plant, and equipment. Inspecting assets is a principal source of assurance about their existence and about the accuracy of the related accounts, and may provide some assurance about completeness, that is, that all items counted were recorded, and about valuation, that is, that inventory is not obsolete.

Confirmation consists of obtaining and evaluating a direct communication from a third party in response to a request for information about a specific item affecting one or more financial statement assertions. As noted in Chapter 6, evidence obtained from sources independent of the entity usually is more reliable than that from parties within the entity. Thus, if the auditor seeks greater assurance about a financial statement assertion from substantive tests, for example, because the assessed level of control risk is at or close to maximum, or because a transaction is unusual or complex, he or she is likely to request confirmations from outside parties instead of or in addition to examining documents or making inquiries of entity personnel. Although confirmations may provide assurance relating to any of the audit objectives, they do not address all objectives equally well. In general, and depending on their design, confirmations tend to be more effective in providing evidence about existence/occurrence, rights and obligations, and, to a somewhat lesser extent, accuracy and cutoff than about valuation and completeness.

Confirmation requests should be tailored to specific audit objectives, circumstances, information sought, and respondents. In designing confirmation requests, the auditor should consider the types of information respondents can be expected to be able to confirm, which is largely a function of their accounting and information systems. For instance, a customer may not be able to confirm the total balance owed, but may be able to confirm individual transactions. To determine what information is relevant to the purpose of the confirmation, the auditor needs to understand the entity's transactions; often details of transactions can be confirmed in addition to amounts. Confirmation requests should be directed to individuals who are believed to be knowledgeable about the specific items to be confirmed. For instance, if an auditor seeks to confirm the terms of and balances outstanding under a major contract between the entity and a supplier, the confirmation request might be addressed to the executive handling the entity's account.

Many substantive tests of the details of transactions and account balances involve procedures, such as examining documents or reperforming calculations, that are the same as the procedures used in testing controls. This is not surprising; whether a particular procedure is a test of controls or a substantive test depends not on the procedure itself, but on the purpose for which it is performed. For example, reviewing the entity's bank reconciliation could be a test of entity personnel's performance of periodic reconciliations of the cash account (a test of controls); the auditor's reconciliation at year-end would be a substantive test of the accuracy and existence of the cash balance. As a general rule, tests of details of transactions that are subject to controls are tests of controls; tests of details of ending balances of balance sheet accounts are substantive tests. Regardless of the purpose of a particular test, however, many tests provide evidence that serves the other purpose as well.

(b)   Timing of Tests of Details

It is often desirable to perform tests of details before year-end (early substantive testing), particularly if management wants the audit to be completed shortly after year-end. This may be done in appropriate circumstances without impairing the effectiveness of the audit, although before doing so the auditor should assess the difficulty of controlling the incremental audit risk. AU Section 313.04-.07 discusses factors that the auditor should consider prior to performing tests of details before year-end.

If early substantive testing is done, the auditor will have to obtain satisfaction that, for the balances tested early, the risk of material misstatement is low during the intervening period between the early testing date and year-end. Generally, the auditor obtains that satisfaction by testing relevant controls during the intervening period.[2] Such tests of controls might include reviewing reconciliations of individual ledger balances to control accounts and investigating any unusual items in the reconciliations. The auditor also should perform analytical and other substantive procedures, as described later, to obtain assurance about the recording of transactions during the intervening period.

In certain circumstances, the auditor might obtain satisfaction about transactions during the intervening period by examining evidence of the operation of special controls in effect for that period. As an example, management's review of sales transactions recorded around year-end, performed to ensure a proper cutoff, also would provide some evidence about the existence and accuracy of sales recorded after an early accounts receivable confirmation.

If the auditor performs early substantive testing, the balances tested early should be linked to year-end balances by one or more of the following procedures, as appropriate in light of the assessment of control risk:

- Reviewing key performance indicators and management information for unexpected variations in account balances at the balance sheet date, and investigating any material fluctuations in account balances and any unusual activity since the time of the early substantive tests

- Scanning entries in the relevant general ledger accounts (including control accounts) or reviewing summaries of recorded transactions to determine whether any expected entries have been omitted and whether the entries appear to be reasonable in relation to the normal level of activity

- Reviewing any special activities the entity has carried out on the year-end figures

- Reviewing reconciliations of individual ledger balances to control accounts, and investigating any unusual items in the reconciliations

- Ensuring that any relevant matters brought forward from the early substantive testing date have been satisfactorily resolved

- Reassessing any valuation accounts (e.g., allowance for uncollectible accounts) in light of the latest available information

In most instances, early substantive testing is not appropriate unless the auditor has obtained evidence, through tests of controls, that controls related to transactions

---

[2] AU Section 313.05 states that "assessing control risk at below the maximum is not required in order to have a reasonable basis for extending audit conclusions from an interim date to the balance-sheet date; however, if the auditor assesses control risk at the maximum during the remaining period, he should consider whether the effectiveness of certain of the substantive tests to cover that period will be impaired." The authors believe an auditor would rarely have the required "reasonable basis" if control risk was assessed at maximum. However, it also would be rare for an auditor to assess control risk at maximum for the existence/occurrence, completeness, and accuracy audit objectives for systems-derived accounts.

and account balances tested early are effective, that is, unless control risk has been assessed below the maximum or at low. In addition, early substantive testing usually is not done for all assertions relating to an account balance. For example, the existence of accounts receivable may be confirmed at an early date, but their valuation tested at year-end. In particular, if control activities necessary to protect assets (such as inventories) from theft are ineffective, early substantive testing (such as observing early physical inventory counts) normally is not appropriate, because the auditor will be unable to obtain evidence that those assets were protected in the intervening period, and will therefore not have evidence about their existence at year-end.

Significant changes in the entity's circumstances after the date of early substantive testing may require the auditor to perform additional procedures. To avoid unnecessary work, the auditor should consider the possibility of such changes when determining the auditing procedures to be performed. AU Section 313 contains the authoritative guidance on performing substantive tests before the balance sheet date.

(c) Extent of Testing

In the first edition of this book, published in 1912, Montgomery recognized as an "obvious conclusion" the notion that "no audit can or should embrace a complete verification of all the transactions of the period under review."[3] If for every procedure the auditor selected for obtaining evidence, or even if for a few of those procedures, he or she were to examine every item that could possibly be selected for examination, it would be virtually impossible to complete an audit on a timely basis, not to mention at a reasonable cost. Neither the entity's management nor the public expects the auditor to examine every transaction. Consequently, the auditor is continually faced with the question: How much testing is enough?

The auditor's preliminary judgments about materiality and the assessment of control risk are the primary factors in determining the extent of substantive testing. If the auditor seeks a low level of assurance about an account balance (that is, is willing to accept a relatively high level of detection risk), substantive tests might consist solely of analytical procedures, limited substantive tests of details, or a combination of the two. The limited substantive tests of details might, for example, consist of examining one or a few items in the account balance, the purpose of which would be to confirm the risk assessment.

Some tests of details, such as a recomputation of an accrued liability, cannot be applied to less than an entire account balance. In addition, other accounts, because of their nature, usually are examined 100 percent. For example, in performing a bank reconciliation, the auditor tests all of the details (e.g., all outstanding checks). Also, the auditor confirms with the stock transfer agent all shares of stock issued and outstanding. In other cases, the efficiency and effectiveness of audit testing can be increased by selecting certain items or accounts for 100 percent examination because of the high risk of material misstatement. For instance, in testing the accrual for executive vacation pay that the president's secretary computed, the auditor might recompute each executive's pay.

---

[3] R. H. Montgomery, *Auditing Theory and Practice* (New York: Ronald Press, 1912), p. 81.

In many instances, however, it may not be efficient to subject all items that make up an account balance or class of transactions to substantive tests of details. When an auditing procedure will be applied to less than 100 percent of the population of an account balance or class of transactions, the auditor faces a choice about which method to use in determining the items to be examined: high-value testing, "accept-reject" testing, or sampling.

(i) High-Value Testing. In high-value testing, an auditor examines sufficient items with high-dollar values in an account balance or class of transactions so that the remaining amount is immaterial and need not be tested. Alternatively, the risk of material misstatement in the items not included in the high-value testing may be reduced to a low level by using other auditing procedures; for example, analytical procedures using scanning techniques or sampling procedures (discussed below and in Chapter 16). For example, if accounts receivable consisted of six accounts aggregating 85 percent of the account balance and 50 accounts making up the remaining 15 percent, the auditor might confirm all six high-value accounts positively and apply analytical procedures to the account as a whole or scan the portion not tested. The working papers should document the auditor's planning considerations in high-value testing, the procedures performed, and the results of and conclusions drawn from the tests.

(ii) Accept–Reject Testing. In some situations, an auditor may use a testing method known as accept–reject testing. While this method is similar to sampling in some respects, it differs from sampling in that sampling involves the projection of a misstatement amount but accept–reject testing does not. In place of projection, the auditor either "accepts" that the test objective has been achieved because the test yields no or negligible misstatements, or "rejects" the test because it yields more than negligible misstatements. If the test is "rejected," additional audit testing is carried out (after ensuring that the source of the misstatement has been identified and the account has been adjusted) to achieve the test objective. Following are some examples of accept–reject applications when the projection of a misstatement amount is not practicable:

1. The addition of a listing of accounts receivable may be tested by adding only certain pages. If no misstatements are found, the auditor may accept the test and conclude that the account balance is accurately totaled. On the other hand, if a misstatement is found, the auditor normally rejects the account balance and asks entity personnel to retotal it.

2. A population of bank reconciliations may be accepted or rejected on the basis of testing only some of the reconciliations. Projecting a dollar amount of misstatement to a population of bank reconciliations would be meaningless, as would projecting a misstatement amount in addition on one page in a listing to the entire listing.

3. In performing substantive tests of inventory counts, the auditor may make test counts of the various count teams and would likely accept the work of count teams that produced accurate counts. If a team's counting was found to be inaccurate, the auditor might reject its work and require the area that team counted to be entirely recounted.

If misstatements are detected through the application of such procedures, the auditor is unlikely to be able to project the misstatements to the entire population, and as a result generally changes either the nature or the extent of the planned auditing procedures to obtain the required assurance about the entire population.

The working papers should document the auditor's planning considerations in accept–reject testing, the methods by which the items to be tested were selected, and the conclusions drawn from the tests.

(iii) Sampling. In sampling, an auditor projects a misstatement amount to the entire account balance or class of transactions from which the sample was selected, in order to form a conclusion about the population. Whether sampling is appropriate depends on the objective of the test, the technique that best achieves that objective, and the level of assurance required from the test. The auditor usually makes the decision to use sampling as a basis for selecting and evaluating evidence after specific auditing procedures have been selected for use in obtaining evidence. For example, the decision to examine vendor invoices to obtain assurance about the existence and accuracy of accounts payable usually precedes the decision to use sampling to select the invoices for examination.

Following are examples of substantive tests that often involve sampling:

- Selecting accounts receivable balances or transactions for confirmation
- Selecting accounts payable balances or transactions for the purpose of examining underlying documentation and reperforming calculations to establish the existence and accuracy of accounts payable
- Price-testing selected inventory items to establish the accuracy of cost or valuation at the lower of cost or market
- Selecting and independently counting items from the entity's perpetual inventory records for the purpose of testing the existence and accuracy of the inventory quantities (where the entity carries out cycle counts of inventory items and makes necessary adjustments to the perpetual records)

In developing a sample, the auditor considers the level of assurance required from the test. Statement on Auditing Standards (SAS) No. 39, *Audit Sampling* (AU Section 350), includes a model that demonstrates mathematically what auditors know intuitively: As more assurance is obtained from one source, less assurance is required from other sources. The model also allows the auditor to express levels of assurance numerically, which may be useful as a confirmation of the thought process in designing substantive tests, including those using sampling, to obtain the required level of assurance. As discussed earlier, if control risk has been assessed below the maximum but not at low, the level of assurance required from substantive tests usually can be obtained from a combination of analytical procedures and tests of details, often using sampling. The level of assurance sought from the sampling application, and thus its design, depend on where along the below-the-maximum continuum the risk assessment falls and the nature and results of any analytical procedures performed. The model also demonstrates how a small change in one of these factors, such as the level of assurance obtained from analytical procedures, has a significant effect on the design of the sample that will be needed. This points to the need to consider cost–benefit relationships when determining the nature and extent of substantive tests, including analytical procedures.

Using and documenting sampling in performing auditing procedures is the topic of Chapter 16.

(d) Using Computer Audit Techniques to Perform Substantive Tests

In a computerized system, an auditor can perform many substantive tests most efficiently using audit software. Auditing with the computer can increase efficiency by mechanizing auditing procedures and enabling the auditor to test large numbers of transactions. Software is available, or the auditor can develop it, to test transactions, master file and reference data, historical data, programs, and activity logs—in fact, almost any information that is stored in a computerized system. The auditor also can perform various auditing procedures—including analytical procedures and tests of details—with the help of audit software designed specifically for that purpose.

The auditor can use the same software tools in more than one testing technique; in certain circumstances these tools also can be used in performing tests of controls. Sometimes a combination of different types of software is required to meet a single audit objective. Audit software can assist in calculating, summarizing, selecting, sorting, and comparing data, and producing reports to the auditor's specifications. Sometimes, such as when an auditor uses generalized audit software packages (discussed later), the same software can access and process data. For example, the auditor can use software to examine all data on a file, to identify data that meets a particular condition (e.g., a total of debtors' balances that exceed their credit limits), and to print out selected data, like the results of tests or items selected for investigation.

Software tools that the auditor can use to access and process data include generalized audit software packages, application audit software packages, customized audit software, inquiry programs, report generators, and other system utility software and service aids.

(i) Generalized Audit Software Packages.   The most widely used computer-assisted audit techniques employ generalized software packages specifically designed for audit purposes. Audit tasks performed on entity files include totaling a file, identifying exceptions, selecting items for manual review, and formatting reports. Generalized audit software helps the auditor carry out those tasks on a variety of files at different installations. Its use eliminates much of the work involved in writing individual computer programs to accomplish those functions.

To use audit software, the auditor defines what computer configuration the program is to be run on and which files to use. Simplified procedural statements or parameters control the program logic. The software normally has special functions to facilitate using the program to generate the kind of audit evidence and documentation desired. These include report formatting (page numbering, page breaking, column placement, and headings), totaling and subtotaling data, automatic production of processing statistics (number of records read and processed, and number of positive, negative, and zero-value records), and sorting and summarizing data.

Whenever the auditor uses the entity's data files in performing tests, the files should be backed up so that the entity's data cannot be lost or altered inadvertently.

In general, it is not advisable to use the entity's "live" production files in audit testing for that and other reasons. It is preferable to use copies of such files, outside of the normal processing cycle, or dummy transactions that are readily identifiable and easy to remove.

Generalized audit software packages permit programs for specific applications to be developed in a relatively short time by people with limited programming skills. The use of generalized packages also reduces the auditor's reliance on the entity's staff, although their assistance is usually required to install the package and develop instructions to operate it. The main disadvantage of generalized packages is that there are usually limitations on the number and structure of files that the user can access. Often the auditor can overcome those limitations by using a generalized audit software package in combination with customized software or utilities.

(ii) Application Audit Software Packages.   Certain auditing procedures and requirements are so similar from one audit to another that the same programs can be applied with only minor changes, even though the data files vary. Some auditing firms have developed application audit software packages to achieve common audit objectives in several areas, like accounts receivable, accounts payable, and payroll. For instance, an auditor may use application audit software to analyze the accounts receivable ledger by age, select items for audit testing, produce confirmation letters, and match subsequent collections received. To run the software, the auditor converts the data files into a compatible format, determines the appropriate parameters, and executes the software. Some audit tests are unique to certain industries and to applications within those industries; some firms have also developed packages for these specialized areas.

(iii) Customized Audit Software.   Although generalized and application software packages are useful in many situations, the auditor may need to develop customized software for special needs. For example, software packages may not be available for the entity's computer, the output required may be very specialized, or the computations and data handling may be particularly intricate. In those circumstances, the auditor may use the computer languages available on the entity's system to develop customized audit software. In addition, many generalized audit software packages allow the integration of additional routines into the software, affording increased flexibility and wider applicability.

(iv) Inquiry Programs.   When available, standard data inquiry (or interrogation) programs, which extract or display data without updating or otherwise changing it, can be economical audit tools. Relatively simple interrogation methods exist for many smaller computers, and are often built into larger database management systems. A disadvantage of using inquiry programs is that they are often unique to a particular computer or database, which means that the auditor will have to read manuals and learn the particular program.

(v) Report Generators.   Report generators are versatile utilities that auditors can use to obtain data from the system in specified forms that meet their specific needs. These utilities can generate a variety of reports, including reports on database contents.

A major advantage of report generators is that the auditor can request data initially and then progressively refine the request, focusing on more specific areas of interest. Report generators originally were designed to report on system functions, and auditors also can use them in this way to produce listings of system privileges and similar data.

(vi) Systems Utility Software and Service Aids.   Computer manufacturers and software vendors provide systems utilities and service aids to perform limited, predefined tasks. Utilities and service aids normally are used to enhance system functioning or for programming. Utilities may be necessary to set up and execute computerized auditing procedures. Some utilities can substitute for procedures that generalized audit software or specially written programs otherwise would perform. The auditor can use utilities to examine processing activity, interrogate data, and test programs and operational procedures. For example, one utility can copy and rearrange sequential files; another can extract particular records from one file and create a subset file for audit testing.

(e) Substantive Tests of Programmed Accounting Procedures

If the auditor needs evidence of the effective operation of programmed accounting procedures, it can be obtained by testing those procedures directly throughout the period, generally using various types of audit software. (In certain circumstances, manual techniques are appropriate, as discussed later.) As noted in Chapter 12 [Section 12.3(d), Testing Computer Controls], however, testing specific programmed procedures is costly and the auditor usually chooses an alternative audit strategy. Therefore, only a brief description of some of the techniques used for testing programs is presented here.

(i) Flowcharting Programs.   This software helps the auditor understand the programmed procedures by producing flowcharts and other documentation of the program under analysis. Lists of commands and data names in the program can be generated and are often helpful in program code analysis (described below).

(ii) Program Tracing and Mapping.   These techniques involve processing test data through application programs and are used primarily by programmers when developing and testing programs. Program tracing identifies the actual steps executed; program mapping identifies any unexecuted program instructions. Auditors use these techniques only occasionally because of the technical skills needed to analyze the results.

(iii) Program Code Analysis.   This technique involves analyzing computer programs. Its main purpose is to confirm the existence of programmed procedures in a program or series of programs. Program code analysis consists of:

- Identifying the program to be examined, by reference to the entity's documentation.
- Selecting the form of code to be examined, which is normally the source code. The auditor must know the programming language and make sure that the source version examined is the same version as the production program in use.

- Analyzing the selected coding. It is usually difficult to follow another person's coding, but adherence to programming standards may simplify this task. Software aids, such as flowcharting programs, can produce additional documentation. In subsequent periods, comparison programs can be used to indicate changes.

(iv) Test Data and Integrated Test Facility.   The test data method tests the entity's transaction processing controls. The audit software tools discussed earlier test actual entity data; in the test data method, entity programs process test data. The output of the processing is then compared with predetermined results.

There are two methods of running test data:

- Test data can be processed using the entity's operational programs (but separately from the entity's data), using either copies of master files or dummy files set up for testing purposes
- Test data can be included in the entity's regular data processing, with a manager's approval

The latter method is referred to as an Integrated Test Facility (ITF). If specific records on the master files are reserved or created for this purpose and consistently processed during testing at regularly established intervals, an ITF is also referred to as "Base Case System Evaluation."

(v) Manual Testing.   The auditor can use manual techniques for testing programmed procedures if adequate visible evidence is available. Data that must be tested to test the programmed procedures can be voluminous, however, making manual testing techniques impractical and inefficient. Although some visible evidence of the operation of programmed procedures is usually available, the results of processing rarely are printed out in detail. Instead, totals and analyses are printed out without supporting details, thus rendering it impossible for the auditor to determine the correctness of a total or an analysis. Exception reports and rejection listings that are produced do not provide evidence that all items that should have been reported or rejected were properly treated. In those instances, the auditor can request and sometimes obtain reports generated specifically to meet audit needs.

Sometimes visible evidence that the system does not readily provide can be recreated. Methods to achieve this are known collectively as "manual simulation techniques" and include:

- Reassembling processed data into the same condition that existed when the programmed procedure was applied (e.g., reassembling batches of sales invoices to test the batch totals posted to the sales ledger control account)
- Using current data before computer processing (e.g., testing the additions of batches before they are sent for processing, to determine that accurate batch totals are established to control subsequent processing)
- Selecting a small number of items from those submitted for processing and processing them in a separate run (e.g., splitting a batch into two batches, one large

and one small, processing the small batch separately, and agreeing the resulting computer-produced total to manually precalculated results)

- Simulating a condition that will produce a report if the programmed procedure is working properly (e.g., altering a batch total to an incorrect figure so that the batch should be rejected, or withholding a document to see whether it is reported as missing); this approach requires careful planning and coordination with user departments

- Requesting a special printout of items processed (e.g., a listing of sales invoices included in a sales total produced by the computer)

Manual tests cannot be performed if visible evidence of the operation of a programmed procedure neither exists nor can be produced, and the appropriate condition cannot be simulated. This often occurs in systems where transactions are entered directly through terminals without source documents.

15.3   ANALYTICAL PROCEDURES

Analytical procedures are an integral part of the audit process. They are reasonableness tests of account balances and classes of transactions and, as stated in SAS No. 56, *Analytical Procedures* (AU Section 329.02), "consist of evaluations of financial information made by a study of plausible relationships among both financial and nonfinancial data." Examples of analytical procedures routinely performed in an audit include fluctuation analyses, ratio analyses, comparisons of financial statements, and scanning accounting records for unusual entries or entries that do not meet the auditor's expectations. SAS No. 56 requires analytical procedures to be used in the planning and overall review stages of the audit, as discussed in Chapters 8 and 27 (Sections 8.3, Gathering and Analyzing Recent Financial Information, and 27.1, Analytical Procedures), respectively, and encourages their use as substantive tests to provide assurance with respect to specific audit objectives for particular account balances or classes of transactions. Analytical procedures, together with tests of controls and substantive tests of details of transactions and balances, provide the evidential matter required by the third standard of field work.[4]

(a)   Developing Expectations

The basic premise underlying analytical procedures is that relationships among data may reasonably be expected to exist and continue in the absence of known conditions to the contrary. Examples of those conditions include specific unusual transactions or events, accounting changes, business changes, random fluctuations, and errors or fraud. Changes in relationships among data in the absence of conditions known to the auditor could suggest that the financial statements were misstated because of unknown errors or fraud.

In performing analytical procedures, the auditor first develops expectations of recorded amounts or ratios derived therefrom, by considering plausible relationships

[4] Analytical procedures also are used in complying with professional standards in connection with various reports on unaudited financial information, as discussed in Chapter 30.

among data. The bases for the auditor's expectations are knowledge obtained about the entity's business, the industry in which it operates, and inherent risks related to the entity broadly and to its specific account balances and classes of transactions. The auditor then compares the expectations with the recorded amounts or ratios. The comparisons may be simple or complex, and may involve single or multiple relationships.

Typically, the auditor uses the following sources of information, either individually or in combination, in developing expectations:

- Financial information of comparable prior periods, adjusted for known current changes. For example, an expectation of current year's sales might be formed from the prior period's sales adjusted for known price and volume increases. That expectation would then be compared with the current period's recorded sales.

- Anticipated results. For instance, an auditor could develop expectations from budgets, forecasts, and extrapolations of interim results, which would then be compared with recorded results.

- Relationships among elements of financial information within the period. For example, an expectation of commission expense in relation to sales could be developed from an auditor's knowledge of the entity's commission policies and then compared with the relationship between recorded commission expense and recorded sales.

- Information regarding the industry in which the entity operates. For instance, expectations of gross margins could be developed from industry-wide statistics for particular product lines.

- Relationships between financial information and relevant nonfinancial information. For example, an auditor might develop expectations concerning available square footage related to revenue in a retail operation, labor hours related to labor costs, average rent related to rent revenue, or number of properties related to real estate tax expense.

Unexpected relationships or other items that appear to be unusual should be investigated if the auditor believes they indicate matters that may have implications for the audit. In investigating unusual items, the auditor generally considers them in light of the information obtained about the entity and its business, and makes inquiries of management. The auditor then seeks additional evidence to corroborate management's replies. Analytical procedures are effective only if the auditor exercises skepticism in evaluating management's explanations of unexpected results and seeks relevant and reliable evidence to support those explanations.

(b) Using Analytical Procedures to Achieve Audit Objectives

A major decision the auditor makes in designing substantive tests is whether to perform an analytical procedure, a test of details, or a combination of the two. That decision is based on the auditor's judgment about the expected effectiveness and efficiency of available procedures, considering the total assurance sought from substantive tests with respect to a specific audit objective for a particular account balance or class of transactions. In many situations, it is possible to design analytical procedures that, when considered in combination with other auditing procedures, will provide relatively high levels of assurance, so that the auditor will need less assurance from other substantive tests. In designing and performing both analytical procedures and tests of details, the auditor should consider the relationship among accounts and the likelihood that evidence obtained about one or more audit objectives with respect to a particular account balance or class of transactions also may provide assurance about other account balances or classes of transactions.

The effectiveness and efficiency of an analytical procedure in identifying potential errors or fraud depends on, among other things, (a) the plausibility and predictability of the relationship among the data analyzed, (b) the availability and reliability of the data used to develop the expectation, (c) the precision of the expectation, and (d) the nature of the account balances or classes of transactions and the particular audit objectives.

(i) Plausibility and Predictability of the Relationship.   It is important for the auditor to understand what makes relationships among data plausible. Data sets sometimes appear to be related when they are not, which could lead the auditor to erroneous conclusions. Relationships in a stable environment are usually more predictable than relationships in a dynamic or unstable environment. Relationships among income statement accounts tend to be more predictable since they represent transactions over a period of time, whereas relationships among balance sheet accounts tend to be less predictable because a balance at a point in time may be subject to many random influences. Relationships involving transactions subject to management discretion are usually less predictable; for example, management may influence the timing of maintenance or advertising expenditures.

(ii) Availability and Reliability of the Data Used to Develop the Expectation.   The availability of the necessary data to develop expectations for a particular assertion will vary. SAS No. 56 notes, as an example, that for some entities expected sales might be developed from production statistics or from square feet of selling space as a means of testing the completeness of sales. For other entities, however, data relevant to that assertion may not be readily available, and it may be more effective or efficient to perform substantive tests of details on the entity's shipping records.

The auditor also should consider whether the underlying financial and nonfinancial data used to develop the expectation is reliable. In considering the likelihood of misstatements in such data, the auditor considers, among other things, knowledge obtained during previous audits, the assessment of control risk, and the results of tests of details of account balances and transactions. How reliable data used in analytical procedures must be depends on how much assurance the auditor desires from the procedure. For instance, in analytical procedures used in planning the audit, untested industry data may be appropriate for developing an expectation about the level of business activity. Expectations developed using information from a variety of independent sources may be more reliable than expectations developed using data from a single source.

(iii) Precision of the Expectation.   The precision of the expectation depends on, among other things, how thoroughly the auditor considers the factors that affect the amount being audited, and the level of detail of the data used to develop the expectation.

Many factors affect financial relationships. For example, prices, volume, and product mix may affect sales, each of which, in turn, may be affected by a number of factors. In developing expectations, the auditor should consider the factors that might have a significant impact on the relationship. The more assurance desired from analytical procedures, the more thoroughly the auditor should consider factors affecting the relationship.

Analytical procedures based on expectations developed at a more detailed level have a greater chance of detecting misstatements of a given amount—and thus provide greater assurance—than do broader comparisons. Comparisons of monthly amounts may be more effective than those of annual amounts, and comparisons by location or lines of business may be more effective than entity-wide comparisons. What level of detail is appropriate may be influenced by the nature of the entity, its size and complexity, and the level of detail available in its records. Generally, the possibility that offsetting factors could obscure material misstatements increases as an entity's operations become more complex and more diversified. For example, the auditor's expectations regarding profit margins on sales in a diversified business will be more precise if they are based on an analysis using disaggregated data, such as gross profit margin by facility or product line, rather than on an analysis of the consolidated gross profit margin.

(iv) Nature of the Account Balance and Audit Objective. For some accounts, analytical procedures may be the most effective means for achieving certain audit objectives and sometimes may be the only procedure performed. For example, in some situations, two common analytical procedures, comparing the allowance for uncollectible accounts as a percentage of accounts receivable and as a percentage of overdue receivables with expectations developed from similar percentages for prior years, might provide sufficient evidence with respect to the valuation objective for accounts receivable. (In other situations, some substantive tests of details, such as investigating specific overdue items, also might be done.) Or, in auditing accrued payroll at year-end, the auditor may test the reasonableness of the accrual by multiplying the gross pay for the weekly, semimonthly, and monthly payrolls by the ratio of days accrued at year-end to the total number of days for the pay periods. Analytical procedures may be particularly effective when potential misstatements would not be detectable by examining details of transactions, especially when the relevant audit objective is the completeness of recorded transactions. As discussed in Chapter 18, analytical procedures commonly are directed at revenue because of the significance of that account and its relationships to other income statement accounts.

On the other hand, examining documentation (a test of details) may be the most appropriate means of obtaining assurance regarding the accuracy of fixed asset additions. In obtaining assurance regarding the accuracy of depreciation expense, a combination of analytical procedures and tests of details (such as recalculation of individually significant amounts) may be appropriate. Like other auditing procedures, analytical procedures that are directed specifically at one or more audit objectives for a particular account balance or class of transactions may simultaneously address other accounts or objectives as well; the auditor should consider this when deciding how to obtain the necessary assurance for a particular account or objective.

(v) Analytical Procedures Software.   Software can be used to calculate absolute dollar and percentage changes, ratios, and trends, and to highlight significant changes, allowing the auditor to concentrate on evaluating the differences and obtaining explanations for them. This software is available on microcomputers, or by using utilities or software packages on minicomputers and mainframes. Increasingly, auditors use computers to compare entity data with industry data using public databases and microcomputer software. Software can perform virtually all of the analytical techniques discussed in this chapter.

(c)   Other Considerations in Using Analytical Procedures

The auditor may choose to use analytical procedures to help determine sample size, to stratify a population, or to assist in the design of other substantive tests. In determining the sample size necessary for auditing procedures related to inventory obsolescence, for example, the auditor may examine the change in inventory turnover rates for various components of inventory to decide which inventory items require more attention. Analytical procedures provide corroborative evidence about the accounting treatment of transactions and balances, and also can be good detectors of changes in accounting principles, but of course they will not alert the auditor to a misstatement if an inappropriate accounting principle remains unchanged. Analytical procedures may be particularly useful in helping the auditor to identify transactions that have not been recorded. Similarly, as discussed earlier, if the auditor performs substantive tests of details before year-end, analytical procedures can often provide evidence about the recording of transactions in the period between early testing and year-end.

   The results of analytical procedures may possibly lead the auditor to extend testing. For example, the auditor might calculate the number of days' sales outstanding and observe that it had increased significantly, and management's explanation of that trend might not be adequate. In those circumstances, the auditor might decide to confirm more customer accounts than planned and to confirm them at the end of the year to ensure that fictitious receivables did not exist. The auditor also might expand tests for collectibility to ensure that the allowance for uncollectible accounts was adequate.

   Scanning can be a particularly effective analytical procedure, provided the auditor has a thorough understanding of the account or schedule in question and the types of misstatements that could occur. For instance, in scanning an inventory listing, the auditor needs to know how the listing is categorized (that is, what items have been grouped together) and what constitutes a reasonable set of parameters for both quantity and price for each group. A larger than expected quantity of an inventory item might indicate an error in transferring information from the count sheets to the listing, or it might be indicative of slow-moving merchandise that needs to be considered in the valuation allowance. In addition, the auditor would investigate any price that was unexpectedly high or low. Similarly, an auditor scanning accounts receivable would be alert to negative amounts that might indicate the misapplication of cash or incomplete recording of sales, and also would watch for account balances with related parties. Scanning a listing of monthly charges to expense accounts can alert the auditor to abnormal items that may reflect errors. Scanning also may be used to test the remaining portion of an account balance after the auditor has examined several large items that constitute a significant portion of the balance.

Analytical procedures may be performed using monetary amounts, physical quantities, ratios, or percentages; they may be applied to overall financial information of the entity, to financial information of components such as subsidiaries or divisions, and to individual elements of financial information. Some auditors have developed specialized software programs to extract appropriate entity data from computer files and perform standardized procedures. Other software packages require the auditor to input data to a computer, which processes the data and generates analytical reports.

Many performance reviews carried out by management are based on the use of analytical techniques to identify unusual transactions, balances, or relationships on a timely basis. Examples of data that may be subject to these reviews include operating budgets and results, sales analyses, inventory turnover and obsolescence reports, cash flow analyses, and forecasts. The auditor may identify such reviews when obtaining an understanding of the entity's internal control. Depending on the relevance and reliability of the reviews and of the underlying data, the information generated may be useful to the auditor in performing analytical procedures.

15.4   TESTING ACCOUNTING JUDGMENTS AND ESTIMATES

The auditor has a responsibility to evaluate the accounting judgments and estimates that management makes. The substantive tests to do this consist of a combination of tests of details and analytical procedures.

(a)   Evaluating Accounting Judgments

The auditor's responsibility entails more than merely substantiating facts about specific transactions and other events and circumstances in order to achieve specific audit objectives for relevant accounts. The auditor also is responsible for evaluating how management has translated those facts into appropriate accounting presentations. Audit failures may result from the auditor's failure to evaluate the application of generally accepted accounting principles (GAAP), even when all of the relevant facts are available.

The possibility that financial statement misstatements may result from the intentional or unintentional misapplication of GAAP is a pervasive aspect of audit risk. Accordingly, it should be kept in mind at all times during the audit, not only when performing substantive tests directed at the valuation, rights and obligations, and presentation and disclosure objectives.

The auditor should evaluate the selection and application of accounting principles. The evaluation should include accounting judgments to address the risk that GAAP could be misapplied, intentionally or unintentionally, with respect to how transactions are accounted for and measured and how they are presented and disclosed in the financial statements. The auditor's evaluation of the selection and application of GAAP requires consideration of the entity's environment, the industry involved, economic conditions, and numerous other intangible factors. Meeting that responsibility requires an extensive knowledge of accounting principles and of the ways in which they should be applied to produce financial statements that reflect, in all material respects, the substance of the entity's transactions and present a picture of the entity that is not misleading.

(b) Auditing Accounting Estimates

Achieving the valuation objective for many accounts requires the auditor to evaluate accounting estimates. Accounting estimates are financial statement approximations that are necessary because the measurement of an account is uncertain until the outcome of future events becomes known, or because relevant data concerning past events cannot be accumulated on a timely, cost-effective basis. Examples of the first type of accounting estimates include uncollectible receivables, obsolete inventory, useful lives of equipment, actuarial assumptions in employee benefit plans, and warranty claims. Examples of the second type of accounting estimates include allocating passenger ticket revenues to airlines other than those issuing the tickets, and telephone company revenues from long distance calls involving more than one company. SAS No. 57, *Auditing Accounting Estimates* (AU Section 342), provides guidance to the auditor in auditing both types of estimates.

Management is responsible for making the necessary accounting estimates; the auditor is responsible for evaluating their reasonableness. Even when management's estimating process involves competent personnel using relevant and reliable data and the most likely assumptions about the factors that affect an accounting estimate, the subjectivity that enters into those estimates introduces the potential for bias. As a result, the auditor should evaluate accounting estimates with an attitude of professional skepticism. The auditor's objective in evaluating accounting estimates is to obtain sufficient competent evidence to provide reasonable assurance that all material accounting estimates have been developed, are reasonable, and are presented and disclosed in conformity with GAAP.

In evaluating the reasonableness of an estimate, the auditor should use one or a combination of three basic approaches.

1. Review and test the process management used to develop the estimate
2. Independently develop an expectation of the estimate to corroborate the reasonableness of management's estimate
3. Review events or transactions occurring after the date of the financial statements (but before the audit is completed) that provide an actual amount to compare with the estimate

When following the first of these approaches, the auditor should:

- Understand the process management established to develop each significant accounting estimate
- Assess control risk related to management's process for developing the estimate
- Identify and evaluate the key factors and assumptions management used to formulate the estimate, concentrating on those key factors and assumptions that are:
  - Material to the estimate

- Sensitive to variations
- Deviations from historical patterns
- Subjective, and therefore susceptible to misstatement and bias
- Assess the reliability of the underlying data that enters into the estimate
- Determine that the calculations used to translate the underlying data and assumptions into the accounting estimate are accurate

The first two and last two of the above steps do not need further clarification as they involve procedures that are discussed throughout the book. However, procedures helpful in identifying and evaluating the key factors and assumptions are unique to auditing accounting estimates. They may involve some or all of the following steps:

- Identifying the sources of information that management used to formulate the assumptions and considering, based on information obtained from other audit tests, whether the information is relevant, reliable, and sufficient for the purpose
- Considering whether there are additional key factors or alternative assumptions
- Evaluating whether the assumptions are consistent with one another, with the supporting data, and with relevant historical data
- Analyzing historical data used in developing the assumptions to assess whether it is comparable and consistent with data of the period under audit, and determining whether it is sufficiently reliable
- Considering whether changes in the business or industry or in other facts or circumstances may cause factors different from those considered in the past to become significant to the accounting estimate
- Reviewing available documentation of the assumptions used in developing the accounting estimate and inquiring about any other relevant plans, goals, and objectives of the entity; and considering their relationship to the assumptions
- Considering using the work of a specialist [SAS No. 73, *Using the Work of a Specialist* (AU Section 336)]

15.5 EVALUATING THE RESULTS OF SUBSTANTIVE TESTS

When misstatements are found as a result of substantive tests, the auditor should ascertain the reason for them and consider the implications with respect to the entity's internal control. Misstatements may lead the auditor to reconsider the understanding of internal control and the control risk assessment. For example, control risk relating to accounts receivable may have been assessed at low with respect to the recording of sales and customer receipts; however, positive confirmation requests indicate numerous unexpected misstatements. Upon further review, the auditor discovers that an unauthorized program change occurred during the year—a control deficiency not previously identified in assessing control risk. The auditor should reconsider the understanding of computer controls and the assessment of control risk, and amend the relevant documentation of the understanding of computer controls and control risk assessment.

If the nature or frequency of misstatements indicates the possibility of significant misstatement in the account balance in which they were found or in related account balances, the auditor should consider the implications for the audit strategy and the audit opinion and take appropriate action.[5] Possible auditor actions include:

- Asking management to adjust for all or some of the known and projected misstatements

- Asking management to perform additional work to determine whether there are additional misstatements in the account balance

- Extending the planned auditing procedures to obtain additional evidence about misstatements or to demonstrate that the account balance is not materially misstated.[6] In determining whether additional evidence is necessary, the auditor should consider the effect of evidence obtained from substantive tests (including analytical procedures) of other accounts and audit objectives as well as evidence from tests directed specifically at the account and audit objective under consideration

- Concluding that the financial statements are materially misstated and modifying the audit report accordingly

As explained in Chapter 27 (Section 27.5, Summarizing Misstatements and Evaluating the Audit Findings), auditors often maintain a summary of misstatements of various types (known misstatements, amounts projected from sampling applications, and unreasonable accounting estimates) found as a result of their auditing procedures. At the completion of the audit, the summary is evaluated to determine whether adjustments to account balances are necessary before the auditor can conclude that the financial statements are presented fairly, in all material respects, in conformity with generally accepted accounting principles.

15.6   DEVELOPING THE AUDIT PROGRAM

Auditing procedures are compiled into a document referred to as an audit program. An audit program is a list of steps to be performed in the course of an audit. It typically specifies the nature, timing, and extent of the audit work, aids in scheduling and assigning the work, guards against possible omissions and duplications, and provides part of the documentation of the work done. An audit program is necessary for adequate planning and supervision of an engagement under the first standard of field work and is required by SAS No. 22, *Planning and Supervision* (AU Section 311).

---

[5] If the auditor determines that the cause of an adjustment is or may be the result of fraud, he or she should evaluate the probable implications, even if the effect of the adjustment is not material to the financial statements. Chapter 4 discusses the auditor's responsibility when there are indications that financial statement fraud may have occurred.

[6] If the auditor found the misstatements by applying sampling, extended sampling of the same population usually would not be cost effective and most likely other auditing procedures would have to be designed. For example, additional tests might "target" high-misstatement segments of the original test population.

The auditor should revise the audit program as new information is obtained during the audit.

The audit program should be organized in a way that provides for the efficient performance of the procedures listed. More specifically, the program should be organized so that when an auditor examines a particular document, as many of the planned auditing procedures as possible are performed. For instance, assume that one auditing procedure calls for examining vendor invoices for initials indicating that the invoice was reviewed for mathematical accuracy and matched to a purchase order and receiving document, and that another auditing procedure calls for examining vendor invoices for evidence that they were authorized for payment. Combining these auditing procedures into one audit program step will enhance audit efficiency. Since the authors believe that audit programs should be tailored to the specific circumstances of individual entities, a "complete" audit program as such is not presented in this book, although specific tests of controls and substantive tests are presented and discussed throughout the book in the context of auditing the various transaction cycles and account balances.

Auditors differ over the degree of detail that an audit program should include. Some auditors believe that an audit program should be as general as possible and that someone wanting to know what detailed audit steps were performed can find that information by looking at the working papers that report the results of the audit tests. Such an audit program might, for example, include the step, "Perform tests of controls applied to shipments." Other auditors believe that the audit program should be as detailed and specific as possible. The advantage of this is that two people reading the audit program would perform exactly the same audit tests on the same number of transactions or balances. An audit program that reflected this attitude might contain the step, "Examine 75 shipping documents for signature of individual authorized to release merchandise from warehouse." If this approach is used, care should be taken not to eliminate judgment from the audit process and make that process somewhat mechanical. Either approach may be consistent with an efficient and effective audit as long as the work is planned and supervised appropriately for the particular type of audit program, and the education and training of the auditor performing the procedures are adequate to enable the individual to make the necessary judgments.

16

The Use of Audit Sampling

Chapter 15 noted that sampling is one method of selecting the items to be examined when an auditing procedure will be applied to only a portion of the population of an account balance or class of transactions. Statement on Auditing Standards (SAS) No. 39, *Audit Sampling* (AU Section 350.01), provides a formal definition of audit sampling: "Audit sampling is the application of an audit procedure to less than 100 percent of the items within an account balance or class of transactions for the purpose of evaluating some characteristic of the balance or class."

Based on the results of applying an auditing procedure to a representative sample of items, the auditor can make an inference (by projecting or extrapolating the sample results) about the entire population from which the sample was selected. SAS No. 39 requires that the auditor select items in such a way that the sample can be expected to be representative of the population. After performing the necessary auditing procedures, the auditor is required to project the sample results to the population. When evaluating whether the financial statements as a whole may be materially misstated, the auditor should aggregate all projected misstatements (discussed later) determined from sampling applications and other likely misstatements[1] determined from nonsampling procedures.

Auditors use sampling in both tests of controls and substantive tests. It is especially useful when the auditor's selection of items to be tested is drawn from a large population and the auditor has no specific knowledge about the characteristics of that population, such as the frequency, size, and direction of misstatements. For example, accounts receivable, inventory, and accounts payable balances could be overstated or understated as a result of using incorrect quantities or prices or because of errors in posting or arithmetical extensions and footings.

16.1 AUDIT RISK AND SAMPLING

Having decided that a particular auditing procedure will be applied to a sample of an audit population, the auditor should then determine the minimum sample size that is needed to control audit risk—the risk of an undetected material misstatement in the financial statements. That risk was discussed in Chapter 6 in the context of formulating the audit strategy on an overall basis. How that discussion relates to sampling is explained here.

(a) Defining the Population

The first step in applying sampling is to identify and characterize the population from which the sample will be taken. The sample results can be used to make inferences only about the population from which the sample was drawn. Accordingly, the population should be restricted to items in the balance or class of transactions that are relevant to the objectives of the test. SAS No. 39 (AU Section 350.17) requires the auditor to "determine that the population from which he draws the sample is ap-

---

[1] In addition to projected misstatement, likely misstatement includes known misstatements specifically identified by the auditor in nonsampling procedures and differences between unreasonable estimates in the financial statements and the closest reasonable amount in a range of acceptable amounts. (These concepts are discussed further in Chapter 27.)

propriate for the specific audit objective. For example, an auditor would not be able to detect understatements of an account due to omitted items by sampling the recorded items. An appropriate sampling plan for detecting such understatements would involve selecting from a source in which the omitted items are included."[2]

(b) Sampling Risk

There is a risk—consisting of sampling risk and nonsampling risk—that the auditor may reach incorrect conclusions when performing either tests of controls or substantive tests of details. Sampling risk is the risk that, when an audit test is restricted to a sample, the conclusion reached from the test will differ from the conclusion that would have been reached if the same test had been applied to all items in the population. It is the chance that the test will indicate that a control is operating effectively or an account is not materially misstated when the opposite is true, or that the control is not operating effectively or an account is materially misstated when the opposite is true. Sampling risk also can be viewed as the complement of the desired level of assurance from a particular sample. Thus, if the auditor seeks a high level of assurance from a test, a low sampling risk should be specified. Sampling risk is inversely related to sample size (i.e., with all other factors remaining the same, the larger the sample, the lower the sampling risk).

Sampling risk has the following aspects:

1. In the context of tests of controls, the *risk of assessing control risk too low* is the risk that the auditor will conclude, based on the sample, that the control is operating more effectively than it actually is.[3] The *risk of assessing control risk too high* is the risk that the auditor will conclude, based on the sample, that the control is operating less effectively than it actually is.[4]

2. In the context of substantive tests of account balances, the *risk of incorrect acceptance* is the risk that the auditor will conclude, based on a sample, that the recorded account balance is not materially misstated when examination of every item in the population would reveal that it is materially misstated.[5] The *risk of incorrect rejection* is the risk that the auditor will conclude, based on a sample, that the recorded account balance is materially misstated when examination of every item in the population would reveal that it is not materially misstated.[6]

---

[2] In general, audit sampling (or any testing) directed at a recorded balance will not provide assurance as to the completeness of the balance. To test the completeness of an account balance (e.g., accounts receivable), it is often necessary to test some other source that includes the potentially omitted items (e.g., the shipping log).

[3] SAS No. 39 (AU Section 350.12) describes this risk as the risk that the auditor will conclude, based on a sample, that the assessed level of control risk is less than the true operating effectiveness of the control. This type of risk is sometimes referred to in the statistical literature as the *beta* risk.

[4] SAS No. 39 (AU Section 350.12) describes this risk as the risk that the auditor will conclude, based on a sample, that the assessed level of control risk is greater than the true operating effectiveness of the control. This type of risk is sometimes referred to in the statistical literature as the *alpha* risk.

[5] This risk is sometimes referred to in the statistical literature as the *beta* risk.

[6] This risk is sometimes referred to in the statistical literature as the *alpha* risk.

The risks of assessing control risk too high and of incorrect rejection relate primarily to audit efficiency. For example, if the auditor initially concludes, based on an evaluation of an audit sample, that an account balance is materially misstated when it is not, performing additional auditing procedures and considering other audit evidence ordinarily would lead the auditor to the correct audit conclusion. Similarly, if the auditor's evaluation of a sample leads to a higher assessed level of control risk for an assertion than is necessary, substantive tests are likely to be increased to compensate for the perceived internal control ineffectiveness. Although the audit might be less efficient in those circumstances, it would nevertheless be effective.

The risks of incorrect acceptance and of assessing control risk too low are of greater concern to the auditor, since they relate directly to the effectiveness of an audit in detecting material misstatements. It is thus necessary to ensure that the extent of testing (sample size) is adequate to keep those risks from exceeding acceptable levels. The complement of the risks of assessing control risk too low and of incorrect acceptance—the desired level of assurance—sometimes is referred to as the "reliability" or "confidence level." For instance, an auditor's willingness to accept a 5 percent risk of assessing control risk too low for a test of a particular control also could be expressed as seeking a confidence level of 95 percent.

(c) Nonsampling Risk

Nonsampling risk encompasses all risks that are not specifically the result of sampling; that is, the risk that any factor other than the size of the sample selected will cause the auditor to draw an incorrect conclusion about an account balance or about the operating effectiveness of a control. Nonsampling risk is discussed in detail in Chapter 6.

16.2 DETERMINANTS OF SAMPLE SIZE

To plan a sampling application, an auditor must consider three factors: how much risk can be accepted that the sample results will be misleading (the acceptable level of sampling risk), how much of a deviation or misstatement can be accepted (tolerable deviation rate or misstatement amount), and how much of a deviation or misstatement there might be in the population (expected deviation rate or misstatement amount). The auditor then determines an appropriate sample size, either by applying statistical sampling techniques that incorporate those factors, or on a nonstatistical[7] basis by applying professional judgment in considering each factor's relative impact on sample size. The population size is sometimes important to the statistical computations, but when the population is large (e.g., over 2,000 items), the effect on the computations is often minimal. For small samples taken from large populations, the population size has the least influence of all the relevant factors on sample size. Planning a sampling application requires the auditor to develop the sampling strategy thoroughly before the testing begins.

---

[7] The term "nonstatistical sampling" is used in SAS No. 39 to describe what many auditors refer to as "judgmental sampling." Statistical sampling procedures involve the exercise of substantial amounts of audit judgment, as, of course, does nonstatistical sampling.

SAS No. 39 requires that, before sampling, the auditor remove from the population for 100 percent examination those items for which, based on auditor judgment, potential misstatements could individually equal or exceed tolerable misstatements. Those items are not considered as sample items and are removed for both efficiency and effectiveness reasons. In some circumstances, the auditor may be able to achieve high dollar coverage of the population by examining a relatively small number of items, and by doing so may reduce the risk of an undetected material misstatement to an acceptably low level. Examining items to achieve a specified level of dollar coverage is not sampling. If the risk of a material misstatement is reduced to an acceptably low level by nonsampling procedures, sampling the remaining items may not be necessary.

Auditing procedures that are appropriate to the audit objective for which the sample was selected should be applied to each sample item selected. In some circumstances, the auditor may not be able to apply the planned procedure to one or more sample items, often because supporting documents are missing. If considering the unexamined items to be misstated would not change the evaluation of the sample results, no further auditing procedures need be applied. If, however, considering the unexamined items to be misstated *would* affect the overall evaluation of the results of the tests performed on the sample, the auditor should consider alternative procedures that would provide further evidence on which to base a conclusion. One alternative is to expand the sample so that the unexamined items become insignificant; however, replacement of the unexamined items is inappropriate.

In other cases, supporting documents may have been voided or may not have the characteristic that is being tested. If documents have been properly voided, they are not treated as sample items. Documents that do not have the characteristic being tested are not included as sample items for that characteristic. In these situations, it may be necessary to increase the size of the initial sample to meet the sample size requirements for the test.

(a) Acceptable Level of Sampling Risk

The auditor determines the acceptable level of sampling risk after considering the evidence obtained from other procedures performed on the account or control being tested. For example, if an auditor has assessed control risk at low, then a high level of detection risk with a high accompanying sampling risk (smaller sample size) is acceptable for related substantive tests of details. On the other hand, if the auditor has assessed control risk at or close to maximum, then a low sampling risk (large sample size) is necessary for related substantive tests of details. Very low levels of sampling risk normally are attainable only with very large sample sizes (i.e., several hundred items).

(b) Tolerable Deviation Rate or Misstatement Amount

The *tolerable deviation rate* (usually shortened to "tolerable rate") is the rate of deviation from a prescribed control that can be found to exist, as a result of performing tests of controls, without causing the auditor to either revise the assessed level of control risk or modify planned substantive tests.[8] The *tolerable misstatement amount* (usually shortened to "tolerable misstatement") is the amount of dollar misstatement in an account balance that may be discovered as a result of performing a substantive test of details and not require performing other auditing procedures or affect the auditor's opinion on the financial statements. For substantive test samples, the tolerable misstatement cannot be larger than the smaller of the materiality amount for the individual item or for the financial statements taken as a whole (which is the smaller of balance sheet or income statement materiality). For example, if balance sheet materiality is $200,000 and income statement materiality is $100,000, the tolerable misstatement should be no larger than $100,000 or the materiality amount for the individual item, if smaller. Materiality is discussed in Chapter 6.

The chance of the true misstatement in every sampling application equaling tolerable misstatement is remote, and thus auditors normally plan auditing procedures so that the sum of the individual tolerable misstatements exceeds the amount considered "tolerable" (material) for the financial statements as a whole. In other words, the auditor usually sets tolerable misstatement for an account balance somewhere between overall materiality and a proportional allocation of overall tolerable misstatement to that account.

As the tolerable rate or misstatement amount increases, the sample size required to achieve the auditor's objective at a given level of sampling risk (or of its complement, reliability) decreases. (This conclusion is derived from the sample size table for statistical samples, Table 16.1, on page 16.14; the same concept applies to nonstatistical samples.) Thus, with all other factors remaining the same, sample size can be almost halved if the tolerable rate or misstatement amount is doubled (e.g., from 5 percent to 10 percent) at a confidence level of 95 percent with an expected deviation rate or misstatement amount (discussed later) of one-half of 1 percent. For tests of controls using statistical sampling, the examples in SAS No. 39 suggest a range of possible tolerable deviation rates between 5 percent and 10 percent. No such guidelines can be given for substantive tests, however, since an auditor must determine tolerable misstatement for a specific account judgmentally based on a number of factors—overall materiality, account balance materiality, and type and amount of individual items within an account balance—that are not precisely definable. For example, if inventory has a larger account balance than accounts receivable, then inventory may be allocated a larger tolerable misstatement than accounts receivable.

Designing a sample with a high tolerable rate or misstatement amount may produce evidence that is too imprecise to support a conclusion at a low risk level about the effective operation of a control or the absence of a material misstatement. Also, a large sample generally can detect both frequent and infrequent deviations or misstatements that aggregate to a material amount, but a small sample can be relied on to detect only frequent deviations or misstatements. At the extreme, some items in an account may individually be so material or may have such a high likelihood of misstatement that the auditor should be unwilling to accept any sampling risk; those items should not be sampled but should be examined 100 percent.

---

[8] Some auditors use the term "tolerable misstatement rate" instead of "tolerable deviation rate." Although an ineffective control *may* cause financial statement misstatements, it does not necessarily do so. Thus, the word "deviation" is used in this book in referring to a departure from a prescribed control.

(c) Expected Deviation Rate or Misstatement Amount

Expected deviation rate or misstatement amount also has an impact on sample size. As the expected rate or amount increases, the sample size necessary to meet the auditor's specified sampling risk at a given tolerable deviation rate or misstatement amount increases as well. The auditor's specification of the expected deviation rate or misstatement amount in the population to be sampled should be his or her best estimate of the true deviation rate or misstatement amount in that population. Auditors commonly use the results of prior years' tests of controls to estimate the expected deviation rate; if those results are not available, a small preliminary sample from the current year's population can be used for that purpose, or the auditor's "best guess" can be used. The estimate need not be exact, since it affects only the determination of sample size and not the auditor's evaluation of sample results. Unless the expected deviation rate is "low" (e.g., 1 percent or less) for a test of controls, it is often more efficient not to test controls and instead design substantive tests to obtain the required audit assurance.

In a statistical sampling context, the relationship between the increase in expected deviation rate or misstatement amount and the increase in sample size is not proportionate. Sample size increases significantly as the expected deviation rate or misstatement amount approaches the tolerable deviation rate or misstatement amount. For example, if the auditor estimates the expected deviation rate at 1 percent for a particular test of controls and specifies a tolerable deviation rate of 5 percent at a 95 percent confidence level (5 percent risk of assessing control risk too low), the appropriate minimum statistical sample size is 95. If, given the same circumstances, the expected deviation rate was estimated at 3 percent, the sample size would be 370. (This can be seen by referring to Table 16.1 on page 16.14.) When the expected deviation rate approaches the tolerable deviation rate, very large sample sizes are often necessary. On the other hand, if the auditor sets an expected deviation rate that is below the true deviation rate, the sample is likely not to be large enough to support, at the desired level of reliability, a conclusion that the true deviation rate does not exceed the tolerable deviation rate.

Figures 16.1 and 16.2 summarize the effect of the factors discussed previously on sample size.

Figure 16.1 Factors Influencing Sample Size in a Test of Controls

	Conditions Leading to	
	Smaller Sample Size	*Larger Sample Size*
Desired assessed level of control risk	Higher	Lower
Expected deviation rate	Lower	Higher
Tolerable deviation rate	Higher	Lower
Number of items in population	Virtually no effect on sample size unless population is very small (fewer than 2,000 items)	

Figure 16.2   Factors Influencing Sample Size in a Substantive Test of Details

	Conditions Leading to	
	Smaller Sample Size	Larger Sample Size
Assessed level of control risk	Lower	Higher
Stratification[a]	Greater	Lesser
Expected misstatement:		
Size of expected individual misstatement	Smaller	Larger
Frequency and aggregate amount of expected misstatement	Lower	Higher[b]
Tolerable misstatement	Higher	Lower
Assurance from other substantive tests (e.g., analytical procedures)	Significant	Little or none
Number of items in population	Virtually no effect on sample size unless population is very small (fewer than 2,000 items)	

[a] Stratification is the separation of population items into groups or strata on the basis of some characteristic related to the specific audit objective.

[b] If the auditor's assessment of the amount of expected misstatement exceeds an acceptable level of materiality, it may be inadvisable to perform the test on a sample basis.

16.3   CHOOSING STATISTICAL OR NONSTATISTICAL METHODS

SAS No. 39 explicitly recognizes that both statistical and nonstatistical approaches to audit sampling, when properly applied, can provide sufficient evidential matter. Moreover, the guidance in SAS No. 39 applies equally to both approaches. Both approaches have advantages and disadvantages that the auditor should consider.

Statistical sampling has two defining characteristics. It uses a random selection procedure and the results of the tests are evaluated using statistical methods. The major advantages of statistical sampling are the opportunity to determine the minimum sample size necessary to meet the objectives of audit tests and the opportunity to express the results quantitatively. In statistical sampling, sampling risk can be measured in quantitative terms and objectively evaluated and controlled. This is because the process of determining the appropriate sample size entails specifying a level of reliability[9] and a desired degree of precision.[10]

[9] As noted on page 16.5, reliability may be thought of as the auditor's level of assurance or confidence—expressed as a percentage—that the statistical results provide correct information about the true population value. A 95 percent reliability level is considered a high level of audit assurance for substantive tests of details. If control risk is assessed below the maximum or at low, or if additional assurance is obtained from other substantive tests such as analytical procedures, the auditor often designs a substantive test sample at a level below 95 percent.

[10] Precision may be defined as the difference between the rates or amounts specified for tolerable misstatement and expected misstatement (both of which were explained on pages 16.6–16.8) in planning a sample. For example, if tolerable misstatement is set at 5 percent and expected misstatement is set at 1 percent, the desired precision of the test is 4 percent. In some types of sampling, such as attributes sampling used in tests of controls, precision is stated in terms of a rate of occurrence (e.g., 5 percent). In other types, such as variables sampling used in substantive tests of details, it is expressed as a dollar amount (e.g., $25,000). SAS No. 39 uses the concepts of "tolerable misstatement" and "allowance for sampling risk" instead of precision.

There are also disadvantages to using statistical sampling, however, and they can result in practical problems that might make the use of statistical techniques less efficient than nonstatistical sampling procedures. For instance, the statistical sampler *must* use random sample selection techniques, which can be more time-consuming than the unsystematic (haphazard) techniques available to the nonstatistical sampler. In selecting a random sample, the auditor may have practical problems establishing a correlation between a table or computer printout of random numbers and the population under audit. For example, an auditor who plans to use random number selection of unpaid invoices in the audit of accounts receivable may face a population that consists of invoices held at three different locations, with the invoice numbers assigned at each location without regard to the numbers assigned at the other locations. Not only will problems arise from missing numbers in the population as a result of paid invoices, but duplicate numbers also could exist because of the lack of coordination among locations in assigning invoice numbers. Thus, the auditor might have to renumber the population in order to use random number selection.

The use of specialized audit software to extract a sample from a population stored in machine-readable form may greatly reduce the costs of selecting a statistical sample. When an auditor uses appropriate audit software, statistical samples may not be more costly than nonstatistical samples. As a result, the availability of computerized sample selection and evaluation programs is often a deciding factor in determining whether it is efficient to use statistical sampling techniques. Before deciding whether to use a statistical sampling procedure in a particular circumstance, the auditor should make a cost–benefit analysis, weighing the additional costs of determining sample size, extracting the sample, and evaluating the results using appropriate formulas against the benefits of knowing the reliability and precision associated with the sample results.

As a result of these considerations, nonstatistical sampling generally is used on most audits. In special circumstances, however, statistical sampling may be the preferred approach. In high-risk audit situations, the additional information obtainable from using statistical sampling for sensitive accounts such as inventory and accounts receivable may warrant its use. Engagements other than audits of financial statements also may call for more controlled procedures and objectively quantifiable results. For example, an accountant may be engaged specifically to determine the accuracy of processing claims between two parties, with the expectation that excess payments will be repaid. In this case, the additional objectivity of statistical techniques may be worth the additional cost. Other engagements may involve evaluation of the accuracy of a database or a pool of costs. Government audit agencies, state sales tax auditors, and the Internal Revenue Service routinely use statistical sampling in estimating compliance with statutes and regulations.

Statistical sampling applications, in both tests of controls and substantive tests, are particularly well-suited to assistance from audit software. Using software reduces the need to make calculations manually and relieves the auditor of the need to understand fully some of the mathematical methods and concepts involved in sampling.

A number of statistical sampling software packages are available to the auditor, some of which require almost no understanding of statistics. Most such packages support a limited number of statistical methodologies—usually those the accounting firm that developed the software uses most frequently. Other packages provide a wider selection of statistical methods, permitting the auditor to select the method best suited to the objective under consideration.

16.4   STATISTICAL TESTS OF CONTROLS

A statistical technique called *attributes sampling* that deals with proportions and rates may be used for tests of controls. Attributes sampling techniques are used to estimate the true proportion (not dollar value) of an attribute in a population. The auditor should carefully define the attribute being measured—such as proper approval of an invoice for payment—because the person who examines each sample item must have criteria for determining whether the sample item possesses that attribute or not. The sample results are then projected to the population and statistical computations made to measure the precision and reliability associated with the sample results. In tests of controls, departures from prescribed controls (i.e., deviations) generally are measured in rates of incidence. For example, in a sample of 50 disbursement checks, the absence of evidence of proper authorization of 1 check generally is expressed as a 2 percent sample deviation rate (1/50). Since the control either operates or not, percentages are a convenient way to express sample test results.

The true deviation rate in the population is likely to be higher or lower than the rate found in a sample. The statistical sampler can make a statement about how high the true deviation rate could be, at a given level of reliability. For example, an auditor, having evaluated a statistical sample, could state: One deviation was found in a random sample of 50 items (a 2 percent deviation rate); thus, there is a 90 percent level of reliability (10 percent sampling risk) that the true deviation rate in the population is less than 8 percent.

In the authors' view, a mathematical statement of risk based on statistical attributes sampling often has limited applicability in assessing the effectiveness of a control in a typical engagement. Since statistical procedures (e.g., formal random selection) introduce additional expense, and statistical and nonstatistical procedures may provide essentially equivalent audit information, the extra expense is rarely justified. Additionally, because of the existence of other, corroborative sources of audit evidence and the interrelatedness of many auditing procedures, a single test is rarely the sole source of audit evidence about whether a control is operating effectively. Furthermore, even after assessing the operating effectiveness of a control statistically, the auditor must still exercise judgment to determine whether, and to what extent, the control affects the assessment of control risk. As noted in Chapter 12 [Section 12.3(f), Interrelationship of Evidence], the assessment of control risk for a specific audit objective should be based on evidence provided by tests of controls in their entirety. The statistical measurement of sampling risk associated with a test of controls does not diminish the need to consider the interrelationships among the components of internal control.

(a)   Basic Concepts of Attributes Sampling

If the true deviation rate in a population were known, the auditor could compute the exact (discrete) probability of obtaining a specific sample result (such as 1 deviation in a sample of 50 items). The auditor does not, however, know the true deviation rate and thus can only infer what it could be, based on sample results. Because the auditor samples from a finite population and removes each item from the population as it is sampled (i.e., sampled items are not replaced), the auditor should use the appropriate statistical formulas to compute the reliability and precision of the sample results.

To illustrate the attributes sampling technique, consider a simple example in which the true population deviation rate is known. The example is later varied to resemble more closely a realistic audit situation. Assume the following:

Population	=	1,000 invoices
Properly approved invoices	=	950 items
Improperly approved invoices	=	50 items

The attribute being measured by the auditor is the approval of invoices for payment. In assessing the approval control, the auditor might use the following decision rule: If no deviations were found in a sample of five items, the control would be considered effective, but if one or more deviations were found in the sample (a 20 percent or more sample deviation rate), the control would not be considered effective. (Small sample sizes are used to illustrate the concepts and computations and are not indicative of suggested sample sizes.) What is the chance the auditor would find no deviations in a random sample of five items from this population?

If the auditor takes a sample of five invoices from the population, one item at a time, there will be 950 chances out of the total population of 1,000 of drawing a properly approved invoice as the first sample item. If the first invoice was properly approved and is not placed back into the population, there will be 949 properly approved invoices out of the total of 999 items in the population available for the second draw. The probability of a sample of five invoices from this population containing no deviations is:

$$\frac{950}{1,000} \times \frac{949}{999} \times \frac{948}{998} \times \frac{947}{997} \times \frac{946}{996} = .7734$$

That is, there is a 77 percent chance of finding no deviations in a sample of five items when the true deviation rate in the population is 5 percent (50/1,000).[11]

Ordinarily, the auditor would not know the true deviation rate in the population. Assume that the auditor would not consider the control to be operating effectively if he or she believed that the true deviation rate exceeded 5 percent. In other words, a 5 percent deviation rate is "tolerable," but a greater deviation rate is not. In this case, having drawn a sample of five invoices, all of which were found to be properly ap-

[11] The calculations in this example follow the principles of the hypergeometric formula, which is the proper general formula for computing probabilities in this situation and can be found in most introductory statistics books. In certain circumstances, calculations using the binomial and Poisson probability distributions can yield approximations close to the exact hypergeometric probabilities. Normal distribution theory, however, is often inappropriate for attributes sampling in auditing because it approximates the hypergeometric probabilities only when deviation rates are between 30 and 70 percent. Generally, much lower deviation rates are found in audit populations. The mean-per-unit estimation technique, discussed later in this chapter, is an appropriate application of normal distribution theory.

proved, the auditor would be accepting a 77 percent sampling risk (the risk of assessing control risk too low, as defined in SAS No. 39) that the true deviation rate might not be acceptable, even if no deviations were found in the sample of five items. The complement of the sampling risk (100 percent − 77 percent = 23 percent) is the reliability level of the test. Stated another way, the auditor obtained from the sample of five items a 23 percent level of reliability that the true deviation rate does not exceed 5 percent.

Increasing the sample size will reduce the sampling risk and thus increase the reliability of the test. For instance, if one more item were added to the sample, the sampling risk would be reduced from 77 percent to 73 percent (.7734 × 945/995 = .7345). To achieve a 90 percent reliability level (10 percent sampling risk) for the conclusion that the true deviation rate does not exceed 5 percent, a sample of approximately 45 items would be required, with no exceptions noted. Thus, by setting a tolerable deviation rate (5 percent) and a reliability level (90 percent) in the planning stage of the sampling application, the auditor could estimate, using statistical formulas, the minimum required sample size (45) to satisfy a stated audit objective.

The relationship among reliability, tolerable deviation rate, and sample size is particularly significant. For a given sample size (e.g., 60) and a tolerable deviation rate (e.g., 5 percent), only a certain level of reliability (in this case, 95 percent) can be obtained. To obtain a higher level of reliability or to be able to set a lower tolerable deviation rate (or both), the sample size must be increased. That is the price that the auditor must pay to reduce the risk of assessing control risk too low (the *beta* risk).

The auditor also may buy "insurance" that the sample will not contain so many deviations that control risk will be assessed too high (the *alpha* risk). This insurance is bought at the cost of a larger sample size. To control this risk (i.e., the risk that the sample will indicate that the deviation rate in the population may be unacceptable when, in reality, it is acceptable), the auditor should take a larger sample. By specifying a conservative (higher) expected deviation rate, the auditor protects somewhat against concluding that controls are operating less effectively than they actually are when one or more deviations appear in the sample. Another way to control this risk is for the auditor to specify an acceptable deviation rate, lower than the tolerable deviation rate, at which the risk of assessing control risk too high is to be controlled, and a reliability level commensurate with that specified risk. For instance, the auditor may wish to be able to conclude at a 90 percent reliability level (10 percent risk) that the true deviation rate does not exceed the tolerable deviation rate of 5 percent, and also may wish to be assured at an 80 percent reliability level that, if the population deviation rate is actually 2 percent (the lower acceptable deviation rate), the sample results will not include so many deviations that they will lead to the conclusion that the population may contain an unacceptable deviation rate, that is, more than 5 percent. The closer the lower acceptable rate is set to the tolerable rate, and the higher the associated reliability level is set, the larger will be the sample size necessary to protect against the risk of assessing control risk too high. In practice, controlling that risk at a meaningful level is often inefficient, given the significant flexibility available to the auditor in designing additional substantive tests when sample results indicate that control risk may be higher than was anticipated. Controlling this risk is covered in more advanced statistical sampling discussions.

(b) Determining Sample Sizes in Statistical Attributes Tests

When designing an attributes test, the auditor should decide if it is necessary to estimate the range within which the true deviation rate lies (i.e., whether upper and lower deviation limits are relevant) or if it is sufficient to test whether the true deviation rate either exceeds or falls below a certain tolerable level. (For example, the auditor may need to know only whether the true deviation rate exceeds the tolerable rate.) A sample in which the auditor is concerned with both the upper and lower limits is evaluated on a two-sided basis; if only one limit is of interest, the sample is evaluated on a one-sided basis. A possible conclusion for a two-sided estimate is that the auditor can be 95 percent assured that the true deviation rate is between 2 percent and 8 percent. A possible conclusion for a one-sided test is that the auditor can be 95 percent assured that the true deviation rate is not greater than 8 percent. Usually the auditor needs assurance only that the true deviation rate does not exceed the tolerable rate. Knowing the lower limit of the true rate would not add to the audit usefulness of the information from a sample.

If the auditor needs only a one-sided evaluation, the sample should be designed accordingly. One-sided testing is more efficient than two-sided testing because it is generally possible to use a smaller sample size to meet the same reliability level and tolerable deviation rate for one-sided tests than for two-sided estimates. Most standard attributes tables and some computer programs designed for audit use assume a one-sided testing plan. If a two-sided plan is desired, the documentation for the one-sided computer program or table usually explains how to make the conversion.

Table 16.1 is an abbreviated table for sample sizes at the 95 percent reliability level. To use the table, the auditor specifies a tolerable deviation rate and an expected population deviation rate, and locates the column for the tolerable rate along the top of the table and the row for the expected rate along the left side of the table. The intersection of the row and column indicates the minimum necessary sample size. For instance, if the tolerable rate is 6 percent and the expected rate is 1 percent, the minimum sample size is 80 items.

Table 16.1   Determination of Sample Size (Reliability = 95%)

Expected Deviation Rate (Percent)	Tolerable Deviation Rate (Percent)											
	1	2	3	4	5	6	7	8	9	10	12	14
0.00	300	150	100	75	60	50	45	40	35	30	25	20
0.50		320	160	120	95	80	70	60	55	50	40	35
1.0			260	160	95	80	70	60	55	50	40	35
2.0				300	190	130	90	80	70	50	40	35
3.0					370	200	130	95	85	65	55	35
4.0						430	230	150	100	90	65	45
5.0							480	240	160	120	75	55
6.0									270	180	100	65
7.0										300	130	85
8.0											200	100

Reliability levels for tests of controls are generally set high (e.g., as high as 90 percent or 95 percent) if the test is the auditor's primary source of evidence about whether a control is operating effectively. However, lower reliability levels usually are warranted, because the auditor ordinarily will obtain additional evidence about the operating effectiveness of the control through extensive observation and inquiries, tests of related controls, and examination of the control aspects of sample items selected for substantive tests. Tolerable deviation rates of between 5 and 10 percent are common; the more critical the control and the more likely that a deviation will cause a financial statement misstatement, the lower the tolerable deviation rate should be set. Appendix A contains tables for determining sample size in statistical attributes sampling at reliability levels of 60, 80, 90, and 95 percent. Because of rounding in those and other tables, however, the auditor should consider using computer software to determine the most efficient sample size. Computer programs may be particularly helpful in determining sample sizes in situations not covered by tables or where the population size is small, requiring more precise computations than are possible using tables.

(c)   Selecting the Sample

An auditor should select a statistical sample randomly, regardless of whether it is expensive, inconvenient, or time-consuming to do so. (A nonstatistical sample does not have to be selected randomly; however, knowing how to select a true random sample may help an auditor using nonstatistical sampling to select a representative sample.) Random sample selection is any method of selection in which every item (element) in the population has an equal (or, more technically, calculable) probability of being included in the sample. The two most common methods of achieving a random sample are random number selection and systematic selection.

For random number selection, the auditor needs a source of random numbers, such as random number tables or a computer program for generating random numbers, and a scheme establishing a one-to-one correspondence between each random number selected and a particular population item. The correspondence scheme is simple if the documents are numbered and can be retrieved based on the numbers. If documents are unnumbered or are filed other than numerically, the auditor may have to assign sequential numbers to them. If it is not easy to make the numbers correspond, or the auditor cannot determine the size of the population, it may be difficult to conclude that the population is complete.

In systematic sample selection, the auditor calculates a sampling interval (n) by dividing population size by sample size, randomly identifies a starting point between 1 and n, and then methodically selects every nth item in the entire population to be sampled. Alternatively, the auditor may use multiple random starts to overcome any possible nonrandomness in the population arrangement and to avoid potential criticism about the randomness of a sampling population. Using computer programs to generate random numbers or batch programs to select items randomly is often an efficient way of selecting specific items for examination.

Often the auditor finds it efficient to perform more than one test of controls using the same sample. For example, the auditor may wish to test, using a reliability level of 95 percent, an expected deviation rate of 1 percent, and a tolerable deviation rate of 8 percent, a control that entity personnel apply to ensure the mathematical accuracy of cash disbursement vouchers. Using Table 16.1, the auditor can determine that the appropriate sample size is 60. If a sample of 80 disbursements had already been selected to test a control relating to authorization, the auditor could randomly (or systematically) select 60 items from the initial 80 items for purposes of testing the control relating to mathematical accuracy. Or, the auditor may perform both tests using 80 items (the larger of the two sample sizes) when it is not too costly to do so.

(d) Evaluating Statistical Attributes Sample Results

After the auditor performs the auditing procedures, the results must be evaluated, using mathematical formulas, tables, or computer programs, to determine the upper (and, if desired, lower) deviation rate limits for a specified reliability level, based on the sample results. To determine the upper limit on the deviation rate, the auditor must have four pieces of information:

- The reliability level (which is selected judgmentally)
- The sample size
- The number of observed deviations in the sample
- The population size

Table 16.2 is an abbreviated table for evaluating sample results at a desired reliability level of 95 percent in a large population. The sample size is located along the left column and the number of deviations found in the sample is located along the sample size row. The achieved upper deviation rate limit is read from the top of the column. The auditor compares this with the tolerable deviation rate to determine whether the objective of the test has been met. Alternatively, some auditors may seek to know the

Table 16.2   Evaluation of Results Based on Number of Observed Deviations (Reliability = 95%)

Sample Size	Achieved Upper Deviation Rate Limit (Percent)											
	1	2	3	4	5	6	7	8	9	10	12	14
30										0		
35									0			1
40								0			1	
45							0				1	2
50						0				1		2
55						0			1		2	3
60				0				1			2	3
65				0				1		2	3	4
70				0			1		2		3	4
75				0			1		2		4	5
80				0		1		2		3	4	5
85				0		1		2	3		5	6
90				0		1	2		3	4	5	6
95				0	1		2	3		4	5	7
100			0		1		2	3	4		6	8

achieved reliability of the test for a fixed tolerable deviation rate; this would require using several tables for varying reliability levels. Appendix B contains tables for evaluating sample results in attributes sampling at reliability levels of 60, 80, 90, and 95 percent.

Continuing with the earlier example, suppose in the test of 80 disbursement checks for proper authorization, 1 deviation was found. By using Table 16.2, the auditor determines an upper deviation rate limit of 6 percent. If the tolerable rate is 6 percent, the objective of the test has been met. If, however, 2 deviations were found in the test of disbursement vouchers for mathematical accuracy, from a sample of 60 items, the upper deviation rate limit would be 12 percent, which would exceed the specified tolerable deviation rate of 8 percent. In this instance, the auditor does not have the assurance sought from the test, and control risk should be assessed at a higher level than originally anticipated.

(e) Discovery Sampling

Discovery sampling is a special application of attributes sampling and is useful when the attribute being tested is of such critical importance that a single exception in the sample may have audit significance. This single instance is a "red flag" that indicates the existence of a problem or a need for further investigation. Some examples of significant attributes are:

- Inaccuracies in an inventory of securities held in trust
- Fraudulent transactions
- Illegal payments
- Circumvented controls
- Fictitious employees

When setting a discovery sample size, the auditor determines how many items to examine to obtain assurance at a high level of reliability (e.g., 95 percent) that, if the true deviation rate in the population is at some low level (e.g., 1 percent), one or more instances will be found in the sample. Since the attribute being examined is critical, auditors often use high reliability levels (95 percent or above) and low "tolerable" deviation rates (less than 5 percent). The procedure for determining sample size is the same for discovery sampling as for attributes sampling in general, except that since the auditor expects no deviations, the expected deviation rate is assumed to be zero. To find an appropriate sample size, the auditor may use tables or computer programs. For example, in a population of over 10,000 items, the auditor would require a sample of 300 items to be assured at a 95 percent reliability level that if the population incidence was 1 percent or more, 1 instance would appear in the sample (see Table 16.1).

Evaluating discovery sampling results is straightforward. If no instances of the critical attribute appear in the sample, the auditor has the assurance specified when the sample was designed. No evaluation tables or computer programs are necessary.

Although discovery sampling has been described in terms of tests of controls, the auditor may use any random sample of items—whether selected for tests of controls or for substantive testing—to gain assurance that a deviation from or an instance of a defined critical attribute would have appeared in the sample under certain conditions. For instance, in a random sample of 300 accounts receivable selected for confirmation from a population of 2,000 or more, the auditor may use computer programs or standard tables to determine that, at a 95 percent level of reliability, the sample would have contained at least 1 instance of a fictitious receivable if 1 percent of the items in the population were fictitious.

(f)   Sequential Sampling

In the previous discussion of attributes sampling, the sample was designed using a sampling plan of a fixed size. Another form of attributes sampling is sequential sampling, in which the auditor selects the sample in several stages, using computer programs or tables specifically designed for sequential sampling to determine the sample size for each stage. After selecting items in the first stage of the sample and performing tests, the auditor evaluates the results and either (1) concludes that the sample meets or does not meet the criteria for reliability and tolerable deviation rate, and discontinues sampling, or (2) determines that a conclusion cannot be reached and selects and evaluates additional items (this is the second stage of the process). The sampling continues until a decision is ultimately reached. The auditor may design sequential plans to include any number of stages. The risk of assessing control risk too high may or may not be specifically controlled, and the sample sizes at each stage may vary; for example, some plans have larger initial sample sizes and smaller second-stage sizes, while others have smaller initial sample sizes and larger second-stage sample sizes. Regardless of the plan adopted, the auditor must follow the rules established for the plan to obtain the desired level of assurance.

An excerpt of a two-stage sequential sampling plan is presented in Table 16.3. The sampling plan was designed for a 95 percent level of reliability. By following the decision rules, the auditor will be able to determine whether the specified criteria have been met or not. In the illustration, the auditor stops testing after the first-stage sample if no deviations or if two or more deviations are found, but goes on to the second stage if one deviation is found. Separate sample evaluation tables are unnecessary, because the decision rules are an integral part of the sampling plan. Appendix C contains tables for two-stage sequential sampling plans at reliability levels of 80, 85, 90, and 95 percent.

A sequential plan allows the auditor to examine additional sample items if an unexpected deviation is found in the sample (thus controlling the risk of assessing control risk too high), or to stop the work after examining a small number of items if no deviations are found in the first sample. Thus, it may be efficient for the auditor to use a sequential sampling plan if a zero or very low deviation rate is expected or if it is difficult to estimate an expected deviation rate. In a fixed sample plan, if unfavorable results were obtained from the first sample, the auditor would be precluded from simply extending the sample and evaluating the combined results using a fixed sample table as though they were a single sample. To evaluate the results of a sequential plan properly, the exact plan and all the decision rules must be specified before the sample sizes are determined.

Table 16.3 **Two-Stage Sequential Sampling Plan (Reliability = 95%)**

Tolerable Deviation Rate (Percent)	Initial Sample Size	Second-Stage Sample Size
10	31	23
9	34	29
8	39	30
7	45	33
6	53	38
5	65	42

	Decision Rules		
	No Deviations	*One Deviation*	*Two or More Deviations*
Initial sample	Stop—achieved goal	Go to next stage	Stop—failed
Second stage	Stop—achieved goal	Stop—failed	Stop—failed

16.5 STATISTICAL SUBSTANTIVE TESTING

A group of statistical techniques called *variables sampling* can be used in substantive testing. Variables sampling techniques are used to estimate the true dollar value of a population or the total misstatement amount in the population and thereby permit the auditor to conclude that a recorded balance is not materially misstated. Since variables techniques deal with dollar values, their use in substantive testing is common. Although a variety of variables techniques may be used, two—monetary unit sampling and stratified mean-per-unit sampling—are particularly effective in auditing and are used widely. Two others—difference and ratio estimation techniques—are also effective in certain circumstances.

From a statistical variables sampling test, the following type of conclusion can usually be drawn: The amount of population misstatement projected from the sample is $20,000. The auditor can state with a 95 percent level of reliability, however, that the true amount of misstatement in the population is between $10,000 and $30,000. This means that the direct projection, or point estimate, of the misstatement in this account or class of transactions is $20,000, but the true misstatement amount at a 95 percent level of reliability may be anywhere between $10,000 and $30,000. The auditor should decide whether a $30,000 misstatement would be material to the account or class of transactions being examined. If it is not material, the auditor may conclude, exclusive of the results of other tests, that there is a 95 percent reliability level that no material misstatement exists in the population. If an amount less than $30,000 but greater than $20,000 could be material, the auditor's assurance that a material misstatement does not exist is reduced to less than a 95 percent level of reliability. After considering the results of this and all other tests, if the auditor still does not have reasonable assurance that the account or class is not materially misstated, he or she may have to perform additional auditing procedures.

Some variables techniques project sample results in terms of audited amounts; others project sample results in terms of the amount of misstatement—or difference (recorded amount minus audited amount)—as in the foregoing case. If the results are in terms of the misstatement amount, the auditor should add to or subtract from the total recorded amount to produce an estimate of the total audited amount.

(a) Applying Variables Sampling

An auditor using variables sampling relies on statistical theory (including the necessary auditor judgments to apply that theory) to draw conclusions about whether material misstatement exists in the population sampled. In general, variables sampling may be an efficient sampling approach in any of the following situations:

- The population consists of a large number of items
- High dollar coverage cannot be achieved by examining an economical number of items
- The auditor is unable to determine which specific items in the population should be examined to meet the audit objectives
- The auditor desires a quantitative evaluation of sampling risk from the audit test, as might be appropriate in an unusually high-risk situation

As in attributes sampling, the auditor can buy "insurance" against concluding that the population may be materially misstated when examining all items in the population would reveal that the population was not materially misstated—the *alpha* risk. Controlling this risk requires the auditor to increase the sample size, which is determined by setting an acceptable, less than material, amount of misstatement and an associated reliability level.

(b) Monetary Unit Sampling (MUS)

In this statistical technique, the individual monetary unit in the population (i.e., the dollar) is the sampling unit. Thus, the sample is composed of random dollars, not random items, in the population. When a particular dollar is identified for examination, the auditor examines the entire item or transaction of which the identified dollar is a part and determines an audited value for the entire transaction. The ratio of the misstatement amount, if any, found in the transaction to the recorded amount is used to "taint" the sample dollar. For example, a recorded transaction value of $200 with an audited value of $150 yields a 25 percent tainting of the identified dollar. This tainted dollar information is used to project a point estimate of the misstatement and create an upper (and, if desired, a lower) misstatement limit at a specified reliability level.

Since in monetary unit sampling the auditor randomly selects the sample from a population of dollars, large-value transactions have more chances of being selected and are more likely to enter the sample than are small-value transactions. Consequently, a transaction containing an understatement would have relatively fewer chances of selection than would a properly stated transaction or a transaction containing an overstatement. MUS is one of the variables sampling evaluation methods that utilizes a probability-proportional-to-size (PPS) sample selection technique. This selection method is often appropriate in an audit, because large-value transactions are often of greater concern to auditors than small-value transactions.[12] Common applications where MUS may be an effective audit tool include:

- Selecting accounts for confirmation of receivables
- Testing the pricing of inventory
- Determining the accuracy of recorded amounts of fixed assets
- Selecting employees for payroll tests

There are both advantages and disadvantages to MUS. Some of its advantages are:

- The sample sizes used with MUS are generally efficient
- It is usually easy to apply
- It is an effective statistical technique for substantiating that an expected low-misstatement population is not materially misstated

The disadvantages of MUS are:

- The population must be cumulatively totaled so that random dollars can be identified
- It is less likely to detect understated balances than overstated ones
- It cannot select zero-value items for examination
- Either credit balance items must be sampled as a separate population or the selection of sample items must be based on the absolute recorded value of the population items

(i) Determining Sample Size. Determining sample size for an MUS sample is similar to the method used for attributes sampling in tests of controls. The auditor should specify the dollar value of the population, a level of reliability, a maximum tolerable misstatement rate expressed as a percentage of the dollar value of the population, and an expected misstatement rate expressed as a percentage of the dollar value of the population. The auditor may use the same tables or computer programs as for attributes sampling to determine sample size.

For instance, assume that accounts receivable has a balance of $1,000,000 as of the confirmation date and the auditor has specified a reliability level of 95 percent. If the maximum tolerable misstatement amount is $50,000, the maximum tolerable misstatement rate is 5 percent ($50,000/$1,000,000). If the expected misstatement amount is $10,000, the expected misstatement rate is 1 percent ($10,000/$1,000,000). Using Table 16.1, the auditor can determine that the sample size is 95. Before determining sample size, the auditor should consider whether any population items exceed the maximum tolerable misstatement amount—in this case, $50,000. Any items in excess of that amount should be segregated from the population for 100 percent examination, and their value should be subtracted from the total population value.

---

[12] Stratification can be used with an item-based sample selection method to accomplish a similar objective. Stratification is discussed later in this chapter in connection with mean-per-unit estimation.

(ii) Selecting the Sample.   To determine which items in the population contain the selected dollar units, the population is cumulatively totaled by item. If the records are computerized, those totals should be easy to obtain; however, if the records are manual, this process may be time-consuming. The auditor can then select the MUS sample using random or systematic selection to identify unique dollars in the cumulatively subtotaled population, resulting in a random selection of dollar units from the population since each item has a chance of selection proportional to its dollar value.

The most common method of MUS sample selection is systematic selection with at least one random starting point between $1 and the sampling interval (the population value divided by sample size—in the illustration, $1,000,000 divided by 95, or $10,526). When using systematic selection, the auditor is assured that all items in the population greater in value than the sampling interval will be selected; those items should be treated as items selected for 100 percent examination, because there is no chance that they will not be selected. Alternatively, the auditor may remove these large-value items from the population before selecting the sample items, reducing the population by the dollar value of the items removed.

(iii) Evaluating MUS Results.   After selecting the sample, the auditor applies the planned auditing procedures to the sample items, determines an audited value for each item examined, and evaluates the results. The first step in the evaluation is to calculate the "tainting" of the misstatements the auditor found in the sample. The tainting is determined by computing the ratio of each misstatement amount found in the sample items to the recorded amount.[13] To continue with the earlier illustration of accounts receivable confirmations, the three misstatements in Figure 16.3 are assumed to have been found in a population of $1,000,000 from which a sample of 95 items had been chosen.

The next step is to calculate the projected misstatement for the population. This is done by dividing the sum of the individual tainting factors by the sample size, in this case (.40 + .10 + .05)/95, or .0058, and multiplying the result by the population amount ($1,000,000), yielding the point estimate of the misstatement amount, in this case $5,800. [Had all three errors been 100 percent tainted—that is, had the audited amounts been zero in each case—the point estimate of the misstatement amount for the population would have been $31,579, derived as follows: ([1.00 + 1.00 + 1.00]/95) × $1,000,000.]

The last step is to compute an upper misstatement dollar limit. This requires two calculations. First, the auditor uses the table for evaluating the results of an attributes sample to calculate an upper misstatement rate limit for three misstatements in a sample of 95 items at a 95 percent reliability level.[14] Since the misstatements were

---

[13] Misstatement amounts found in sample items are those differences between recorded values and audited values that the auditor determines, after applying auditing procedures to the sample items, are in fact misstatements. For example, a response to a confirmation request might indicate that the recorded balance of an account receivable is incorrect because the balance had been paid before the confirmation was received. The auditor should determine whether a payment for that amount was in fact received within several days of the mailing of the confirmation. If it was, the audited value of the customer's balance and the recorded value would be in agreement as of the date of the confirmation and no misstatement would exist.

[14] More precise results may be obtained by using other tables or computer programs that are less subject to rounding errors than are the attributes evaluation tables. Another method of computing the upper misstatement dollar limit that uses a different set of tables is illustrated in the AICPA audit and accounting guide, *Audit Sampling* (New York: AICPA, 1983).

Figure 16.3   Calculation of Misstatement-Tainting Amounts

| | Amount | | | |
Error	Recorded	Audited	Difference	Tainting
1	$100	$ 60	$40	.40
2	200	180	20	.10
3	80	76	4	.05

not 100 percent taintings, the auditor can obtain a more precise upper misstatement rate limit by using a "building block" approach, that is, by multiplying the increment in the upper misstatement rate limit for each misstatement by the individual tainting factors and adding the products to calculate the upper misstatement rate limit, as illustrated in Figure 16.4.

For conservatism, the misstatements are arranged in descending order according to the size of the tainting. Also, an allowance for possible, but unfound, misstatements is labeled "0" and is conservatively assigned a tainting of 1.00. (This allows for the possibility that misstatements existed in the population, even if no misstatements had been found in the sample.) Next, the auditor converts the upper misstatement rate limit to a dollar amount by multiplying it by the total population amount, in this case $1,000,000 × .0465, or $46,500. [Had all three misstatements been 100 percent tainted misstatements, the auditor would have used the attributes evaluation table (Table 16.2) to determine an upper misstatement rate limit of 8 percent, which would have been converted directly to dollars by multiplying it by the population dollar amount ($1,000,000 × 8%, or $80,000).]

In the foregoing example, the auditor can conclude that, at a 95 percent level of reliability, the true amount of misstatement in the population is less than $46,500.[15] The auditor then compares this upper misstatement dollar limit of $46,500 with the tolerable misstatement amount used in determining the sample size, $50,000. If at the specified reliability level the tolerable misstatement is greater than the upper misstatement dollar limit, the results support accepting the recorded amount as not being materially misstated. If at the specified reliability level the tolerable misstatement is less than the upper misstatement dollar limit, the true population misstatement amount could exceed the tolerable misstatement.[16] When the tolerable misstatement initially is significantly below the upper misstatement dollar limit (i.e., there is a higher than desired sampling risk that the true misstatement amount may exceed the tolerable misstatement), the auditor should recalculate the upper misstatement dollar limit at successively lower reliability levels until the tolerable misstatement and upper misstatement dollar limit are approximately equal, to determine the additional risk implied by the test results. This may help the auditor choose among several possible courses of action, which are discussed in Chapter 15 (Section 15.5, Evaluating the Results of Substantive Tests).

[15] Other ways to state this conclusion are as follows: (1) the auditor is 95 percent confident that the true amount of the population is at least $1,000,000 − $46,500, or $953,500; (2) the auditor is 95 percent confident that the true amount of misstatement in the population is not more than $5,800 + $40,700.

[16] If at the specified reliability level the tolerable misstatement is also less than the point estimate, there is a high risk (greater than 50 percent) of misstatement.

Figure 16.4   Calculation of Upper Misstatement Rate Limit

Number of Misstatements	Upper Misstatement Rate Limit[a]	Increment	Tainting	Product
0	.04	.04	1.00	.0400
1	.05	.01	.40	.0040
2	.07	.02	.10	.0020
3	.08	.01	.05	.0005
		Upper misstatement rate limit		.0465

[a] Determined by reference to Table 16.2, "Evaluation of Results Based on Number of Observed Deviations (Reliability = 95%)," on p. 16.16.

(iv) Considering Other Techniques.   Although it would be cost effective to be able to use one variables technique in all audit situations, the auditor should be knowledgeable about several techniques in order to choose the technique that will yield the most precise and relevant statistical results in a particular sampling application. For example, some audit tests, such as those involving samples from accounts payable, have as their specific objective to detect and evaluate understated amounts within the population of recorded accounts. In other cases, such as some inventory pricing tests, a number of understatements may be expected, even if the primary audit objective is to detect and evaluate overstatements. Because MUS is more likely to detect overstatements, its use may not be desirable in situations in which understatements are suspected. Furthermore, MUS methods of evaluating understatements found in the sample and methods that suggest netting them with overstatements in the sample remain an area of controversy and require further research. MUS also may sometimes be less efficient than other statistical techniques in situations where expected misstatement rates are high.

The following techniques are based on normal distribution theory. Although their use in auditing has diminished as a result of advancements in MUS technology, they remain important and effective techniques.

(c)   Mean-Per-Unit Estimation

In the mean-per-unit (MPU) technique, the auditor selects a random sample of accounts or items from the population and, using the audited values of the sample items or balances, projects the average (or mean) value of the audited sample values to the population to create a population point estimate. For example, if the auditor selected a sample of 50 items from a population of 10,000 items and found their average audited value to be $20.25, the point estimate of the population amount would be $202,500 ($20.25 × 10,000). The auditor would have very little confidence, however, that the point estimate of $202,500 was the true population amount. An auditor can express confidence only in terms of the upper and lower precision limits that are determined in a statistical test. If upper and lower precision[17] limits have been calcu-

---

[17] SAS No. 39 uses the term "allowance for sampling risk" rather than "precision."

lated, the auditor can make the following type of statement: I am 95 percent confident that the true amount of the population falls within the interval of $202,500 plus or minus 10 percent (or, plus or minus $20,250).

One advantage of MPU is that it can be used on populations that do not have detailed recorded amounts. For instance, it may be used to estimate the audited value of an inventory where only quantity information is recorded. Although MPU can be an effective technique in a wide variety of audit situations (such as those in which expected misstatement rates might be either low or high and those in which understatement is as likely as overstatement), the large sample sizes necessary to achieve the precision that the auditor commonly seeks in many audit tests may not always make it the most efficient statistical technique to use, unless the auditor stratifies the population, as explained later in this chapter.

A key factor in determining how close the point estimate of the population value will be to the true population value is the degree of variability (also referred to as dispersion) in the population. For example, if the average audited value of $20.25 in the foregoing example was developed from 50 invoices that were each valued at exactly $20.25, the auditor would intuitively be more comfortable with the point estimate than if the sample revealed 20 zero-value items, 20 items valued at $1.00, and 10 items valued at $99.25. Statistical computations of the upper and lower precision limits for the population (or misstatement) amount at a given level of reliability take into consideration the observed variability in the sample data. The more variable the sample data, the wider the range between the upper and lower precision limits will be (i.e., precision deteriorates as variability increases).

Because of the key role that sample values and their variability play in determining the point estimate and upper and lower precision limits, the sample should be as representative of the population as possible. The auditor cannot rely on very small samples to provide representative sample values, since the selection of one or several unusually large or small items in the sample would significantly affect the point estimate.

(i) Basic MPU Concepts.   SAS No. 39 requires the auditor to project sample results to the population as a basis for considering whether material misstatement exists in the population. In meeting this requirement, the auditor uses the information obtained from a sample to estimate the extent of misstatement in the population or the true value of the population.

To make statistical inferences about the dollar value or misstatements in a population from a sample, the auditor must compute the sample mean and the sample standard deviation. For instance, an auditor, not knowing the audited values of the population of 10,000 accounts receivable, might take a random sample of 100 items totaling $3,318.73. The sample mean is computed by dividing $3,318.73 by 100, to get $33.19, which is multiplied by the number of items in the population ($33.19 × 10,000) to compute an estimate, or projection, of the total value of the population ($331,900).

It is extremely unusual for any one sample mean to be exactly the same as the true mean in the population. Each different random sample of items from the population would most likely yield a different sample mean. For audit purposes, it is desirable for the sample mean to be close to the true mean. This is accomplished by both taking a representative sample from the population and choosing an adequate sample size.

A second measure that must be computed for the mean-per-unit technique is the sample standard deviation, which is a measure of the variability of particular item values around the mean value of the sample and, as discussed later, is used to compute the statistical results from the sample. In a sample whose values are very close to each other, and thus to the mean, the standard deviation will be very small. If there are both very large and very small values in the sample, however, the standard deviation will be larger. The sample standard deviation is computed using the following formula:

$$\text{Sample standard deviation} = \sqrt{\frac{\text{Sum of squared differences between sample audited values and mean value}}{\text{Sample size} - 1}}$$

(ii) Applying the Concepts. Figure 16.5 illustrates the calculation of a sample standard deviation. The example assumes that a sample of 100 items drawn from a population of 10,000 items produced a sample mean of $33.19.

The individual sample audited values are listed in Column (1). Column (2) shows the average or mean value of the sample items, and Column (3), the differences between the individual audited sample values and the mean value. In Column (4), the differences are squared and totaled. [The differences are squared to keep them from netting out to zero, as they do in Column (3).] The total of the squared differences is divided by the sample size minus one, and the square root of the result is taken, giving the standard deviation of the sample, in this case $27.729.

The calculations involved in computing the standard deviation can be confusing, but it is important that the auditor grasp the mathematical relationships involved. The standard deviation decreases as the variability of the sample values around the mean value decreases (holding sample size constant), and it also decreases as the sample size increases (holding the variability constant). (As mentioned earlier, very small sample sizes generally do not give reliable information about the total population, because small samples sometimes contain one or more items that are unrepresentative of the population and that can significantly distort the point estimate of the population value and the calculations of variability among items.)

Figure 16.5   Calculation of a Sample Standard Deviation

Sample Observation	(1) Audited Value	(2) Mean Value	(3) Difference	(4) Difference Squared
1	$ 80.29	$33.19	$47.10	$ 2,218.41
2	6.97	33.19	−26.22	687.49
•	•	•	•	•
•	•	•	•	•
•	•	•	•	•
100	10.30	33.19	−22.89	523.95
Totals	$3,318.73			$76,120.85

$$\sqrt{\frac{\$76,120.85}{100 - 1}} = \$27.729$$

The standard deviation (a sample statistic) is used to compute the standard error (a statistic related to the population value). The standard error, in turn, determines the upper and lower precision limits of the point estimate of the population value, which in this example is $331,900 (mean value of $33.19 × population size of 10,000 items). The standard error is the population size multiplied by the sample standard deviation divided by the square root of the sample size,[18] as follows:

$$\text{Standard error} = \frac{10,000 \times \$27.729}{\sqrt{100}} = \$27,729$$

The auditor can then compute the upper and lower precision limits by multiplying the standard error ($27,729) by a reliability factor (discussed later) appropriate for the desired level of reliability (e.g., the factor for 95 percent reliability is 1.96; for 90 percent reliability, 1.64), and calculating an interval on either side (plus or minus) of the projected population value [in this example, $331,900 ± (1.96 × $27,729)]. The conclusion, at a 95 percent reliability level, is that the lower precision limit is $277,551 and the upper precision limit is $386,249.

The statistical sampling results can be summarized by the statement that the total population amount is between $277,551 and $386,249 with 95 percent reliability. Thus, there is only a 5 percent risk (the complement of reliability) that the true value falls outside this range. SAS No. 39 refers to this risk for substantive test sampling applications as the risk of incorrect acceptance. If the true value of the population can be in the interval between $277,551 and $386,249 without causing the auditor to conclude that material misstatement exists in the population, then the auditor can say with 95 percent confidence that no material misstatement exists in this population. The limits are of primary importance when an auditor employs MPU sampling. Point estimates are less important; they are used to compute the interval, or limits, on the population value. A reliability percentage can be associated only with computed upper and lower precision limits. No statistical statement or reliability level can be associated with point estimates.

In the preceding calculations, a 95 percent reliability level has been used. Sampling results, especially in the audit environment, do not always require a 95 percent level of reliability. Auditors often have information in addition to their sample results that they can rely on in reaching audit conclusions, and thus a reliability level of less than 95 percent frequently is appropriate for audit applications. The Appendix to SAS No. 39 contains an illustration leading to a substantive test sampling application with a desired reliability level of less than 50 percent. For practical purposes, if sampling is such a minor element in the auditor's strategy or if the sampling effort is minimal, it is rarely economical to perform a statistical procedure to be able to measure precisely the reliability of the sample.

---

[18] The sample standard deviation also should be multiplied by a finite population correction factor

$$\left(\sqrt{1 - \frac{\text{size of sample}}{\text{size of population}}} \right)$$ when computing the standard error. However, when the sample size is small relative

to the population (less than 10 percent), the factor has little influence on the computations. For many audit sampling applications this factor will not be significant and therefore is not illustrated in this chapter.

Figure 16.6   Normal Distribution

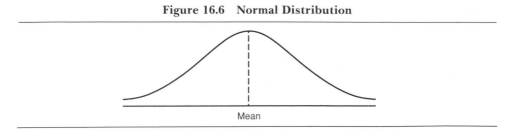

Mean

(iii) Reliability Factors.   The concept of reliability factors, as illustrated earlier, is derived from statistical theory based on the known mathematical properties of the normal, or bell-shape, distribution. The theory is that if repeated large samples from the population are taken and the frequency distribution of the point estimates of the population value from each sample is plotted (with the values along the horizontal axis and the frequency along the vertical axis), the distribution of the point estimates would create the distribution commonly referred to as the normal distribution. The normal, or bell-shape, distribution is illustrated in Figure 16.6.

The properties of the normal distribution that are used in the MPU technique have the following effect: If repeated samples were taken from the population and a point estimate of the population value from each sample was computed, 68 percent of the point estimates would lie at less than 1 standard error on either side of the true population value and 95 percent of the point estimates would lie at less than 1.96 standard errors on either side of the true population value. That result is adapted to fit the audit situation (i.e., the auditor takes a single sample and makes inferences about the true population value from that sample). Thus, the auditor can determine, at a particular reliability level, upper and lower precision limits between which the true population value is expected to lie.

Reliability factors associated with different reliability levels are shown in Figure 16.7. Thus, if the auditor wanted to evaluate sample results at a 90 percent level of reliability and if a two-sided evaluation was appropriate (see subsequent discussion), the standard error would be multiplied by 1.645 to measure the allowance for sampling risk, or precision. Similarly, for a 99 percent reliability level, the auditor would multiply the standard error by 2.576 to measure the allowance for sampling risk.

When designing a statistical test, the auditor should consider whether a two-sided estimate is necessary, or whether a one-sided test is sufficient to determine whether

Figure 16.7   Factors for Different Reliability Levels

Two-Sided Evaluation		*One-Sided Evaluation*	
Reliability	*Factor*	*Reliability*	*Factor*
60%	.842	60%	.253
70%	1.036	70%	.524
80%	1.282	80%	.842
85%	1.440	85%	1.036
90%	1.645	90%	1.282
95%	1.960	95%	1.645
99%	2.576	99%	2.326

the true value either exceeds or falls below a certain tolerable level. By designing a one-sided evaluation, the auditor may be able to draw the desired conclusion using a smaller sample size than a two-sided evaluation would require. Alternatively, for the same sample size and reliability level, a one-sided evaluation yields greater precision (a smaller allowance for sampling risk). For example, the auditor may use statistical techniques in lieu of determining exact amounts for inventory values. In that event, the auditor may desire a two-sided estimate, using the "plus and minus" as a benchmark for evaluating the precision of the sample result. However, when the auditor assesses the principal risk as either overstatement or understatement, such as in evaluating accounts receivable (in which the principal risk is generally overstatement), a one-sided test may be sufficient for audit purposes. The auditor may apply other procedures (e.g., analytical procedures) to assess the risk of understatement.

(iv) Stratified Mean-Per-Unit Estimation.   One method of improving the precision of the mean-per-unit technique without increasing the sample size is to stratify the population and sample each stratum independently. In stratification, the auditor segments the population into groups of items that are likely to be close to each other in audited value. After the mean and standard error in each stratum have been calculated, the auditor can combine the results for the individual strata to create an overall estimate. The first several strata dramatically reduce the required sample size (or reduce the allowance for sampling risk for the same sample size). Although increasing the number of strata generally improves the precision of the estimate (or reduces the required sample size necessary to achieve a specific precision), diminishing returns and other factors often lead the auditor to use between three and ten strata in most circumstances.

Research has shown the stratified mean-per-unit technique to be a very effective audit tool. It can be used in suspected low-misstatement and high-misstatement situations and, with the use of a sufficient number of strata, often can result in relatively efficient sample sizes. Since, unlike MUS, the technique requires a random selection of items, zero (recorded) value items have a chance for selection. The technique can be equally effective for evaluating overstatements and understatements of recorded values and net misstatement amounts.

Despite the advantages of stratified MPU, however, there are a number of significant constraints on its efficiency. Stratifying the population often requires reorganizing the underlying data, which, unless there is extensive computer assistance in data manipulation and sample selection, can be expensive. To compute the sample size required to meet the auditor's objectives, estimates of the variability among audited values need to be developed. Since estimates are somewhat difficult to develop, auditors often use the recorded values to estimate the necessary sample size and then include a safety factor (add extra sample items to the computed sample size). If the auditor performed a statistical application in the prior year, past experience is often a useful guide in estimating variability.

The following paragraphs summarize the steps required to apply stratified mean-per-unit estimation. Some of the steps in the evaluation process require the use of computations discussed earlier in the chapter. The steps are as follows:

1. Determine the number of strata to be used
2. Determine stratum boundaries (the high and low population values for each stratum)

3. Determine an appropriate overall sample size

4. Allocate the overall sample size to the individual strata

5. Randomly select the sample items from each stratum

6. Perform auditing procedures to determine an audited value for each sample item

7. Compute an overall point estimate (projection) of the population value

8. Compute the overall upper and lower precision limits at the desired reliability level

As previously indicated, between three and ten strata are generally sufficient to meet audit objectives efficiently. A number of formulas (or judgment) can be used to satisfy steps 2, 3, and 4. One formula option for steps 2 and 4 determines stratum boundaries so that each stratum contains an approximately equal proportion of population dollars, and allocates sample size so that each stratum is allocated approximately the same sample size. Another option attempts to minimize the overall sample size by determining stratum boundaries and allocating sample size in such a way that the overall standard error is minimized.[19] As a rule of thumb, the auditor should plan for at least 20 to 25 items in each stratum so that representative results for each stratum are more likely. The computations in steps 3 and 4 are often based on recorded values or small preliminary samples from the population. [As noted, because these figures may not be exactly representative of the final sample audited values, the auditor may want to add a "cushion" (10 percent is common) to the computed stratum sample sizes to ensure that the desired precision of the sample will be achieved.] Computer software can be designed to accomplish steps 2 through 5, 7, and 8 with a minimum of effort on the auditor's part, except for supplying the key judgments or information (such as reliability, precision, population size, and other options). Computer software can efficiently analyze a population, stratify it, determine sample sizes, allocate them to different strata, select a valid random sample from each stratum, and evaluate sample results. In this, as well as in other statistical sampling applications, manual computations of the formulas are often unnecessary and inefficient, given the current availability of computer software.

To evaluate the results of a stratified sample, the auditor calculates a sample mean, sample standard deviation, point estimate, and standard error for each stratum, and finally combines the results from the individual strata (steps 7 and 8). The combined (overall) point estimate is simply the sum of the individual point estimates. The auditor computes the combined standard error as the square root of the sum of the squared individual standard errors.

To illustrate, assume the following facts:

	Stratum 1	Stratum 2
Population	4,000	1,200
Sample size	50	50
Sample mean	$343.19	$989.91
Standard deviation	$21.98	$85.42
Point estimate	$1,372,760	$1,187,892
Standard error	$12,434	$14,496

[19] For more details, see Donald M. Roberts, *Statistical Auditing* (New York: AICPA, 1978).

Based on these facts, the results of the two strata can be combined as follows:

1. Combining of sample results
   (a) Point estimate = $1,372,760 + $1,187,892 = $2,560,652
   (b) (Standard error)^2 = $154,604,356 + $210,134,016 = $364,738,372

$$\text{Standard error} = \sqrt{\$364,738,372} = \$19,098$$

2. Calculation of two-sided precision limits and total audited amount, 95% reliability

$$\$2,560,652 \pm 1.96\ (\$19,098)$$
$$\$2,560,652 \pm \$37,432$$

3. Summary of misstatement limits

Recorded value	$2,787,200	$2,787,200
Lower precision limit	2,523,220	
Upper precision limit		2,598,084
Misstatement limits	$ 263,980	$ 189,116

Although the recorded value lies outside the computed precision limits of $2,523,220 and $2,598,084, the auditor may be able to accept it if the difference between the recorded value ($2,787,200) and the farthest limit ($2,523,220) is not material. Another way to arrive at the same conclusion is to compare the computed upper misstatement limit ($263,980) with the tolerable misstatement amount used in planning the sample. Even if the sample supports accepting the recorded amount, the auditor may propose an adjustment of the accounts for misstatements found in the sample as well as misstatements identified as a result of other procedures performed on the account.

(d) Difference and Ratio Estimation

Difference and ratio estimation techniques are other variables sampling techniques also based on random item selection. They have many features in common with mean-per-unit sampling and can be used in stratified or unstratified populations, but are most effective when stratification is employed. These techniques have long been used in audit tests because of their apparent ability to generate precise results with relatively small sample sizes. Research has demonstrated, however, that they may not be dependable (i.e., the auditor may believe the sample yielded a 95 percent level of reliability when it actually yielded a lower reliability) in populations with low misstatement rates or when used in unstratified form with small sample sizes.[20] For this reason, their use is recommended only when an auditor expects high misstatement rates, such as in some inventory pricing situations (even if the misstatement rates are high, the amounts may still be small and offsetting) or for conversions of inventory bases (such as first-in, first-out to last-in, first-out conversions in which each

[20] See John Neter and James K. Loebbecke, *Behavior of Major Statistical Estimators in Sampling Accounting Populations*, Auditing Research Monograph No. 2 (New York: AICPA, 1975).

item can be expected to show a "difference"). Either technique can be used in tests for both overstatements and understatements. Whether one technique is superior to the other in producing a more precise estimate depends on the characteristics of the misstatements found in the sample.

The computations used in these techniques are based on the differences between the recorded and audited amounts of the sample items. The techniques require estimating a standard deviation and, if stratification is used, employ similar formulas for obtaining stratum limits and combining them to obtain overall limits.

In the difference estimation approach, the auditor calculates the point estimate of the population misstatement amount (or difference) by computing the average sample misstatement and multiplying it by the number of items in the population. In the ratio approach, the point estimate of the population value is based on the ratio of the audited amount to the recorded amount of the sample items. In both approaches, the auditor should ascertain that the sample contains differences that are representative of those in the population. Unlike mean-per-unit sampling, difference and ratio estimation techniques require that each population item have a recorded amount.

These techniques are most effective if the auditor expects many small differences between the recorded and audited amounts of the sample items. As a rule of thumb, 20 or more differences are considered sufficient. If no differences are found in the sample, these techniques are not used to evaluate the sample findings. Other statistical procedures are available to evaluate the precision of the sample results and to evaluate the upper limit on the possible misstatement amount that could still exist in the population.

An example of how an auditor might evaluate a sample using difference estimation at a 95 percent reliability level and with two-sided limits is summarized here.

1. Assumed facts

    (a) Population

Size	100,000
Amount	$1,700,000

    (b) Sample

Size	100
Audited amount	$1,500
Recorded amount	$1,600
Difference amount	−$100
Mean difference	−$1
Standard deviation of sample differences[21]	$2

2. Calculations

    (a) Point estimate of difference

    Population size × mean difference

    $100,000 \times -\$1 = -\$100,000$

---

[21] The standard deviation of sample differences is a measure of variability of *differences* between recorded values and audit values around the mean of those *differences*. In the earlier discussion of MPU estimation, the sample standard deviation was a measure of variability of audited *values* around the mean of those *values*.

(b) Standard error

$$\frac{\text{Population size} \times \text{standard deviation of sample differences}}{\text{Square root of sample size}}$$

$$\frac{100,000 \times \$2}{\sqrt{100}} = \$20,000$$

(c) Upper and lower error limits

Point estimate ± standard error × reliability factor

$100,000 \pm \$20,000 \times 1.96$

$100,000 \pm \$39,200$

Thus, the true amount of misstatement is indicated as falling between \$60,800 and \$139,200 at a 95 percent reliability level. Provided these possible misstatement amounts do not exceed the tolerable misstatement for the account, the auditor may be able to conclude at the desired reliability level that the balance is not materially misstated.

An example of a ratio estimation computation is not presented, but the calculations would be similar to those for difference estimation. The ratio technique point estimate is based on a ratio of the audited sample values to the recorded sample values, and the precision is calculated by measuring the variability of the sample ratios, using a computational formula.[22] Using the foregoing example, the ratio technique point estimate of the projected misstatement amount would be

$\$1,500/\$1,600 \times \$1,700,000 = \$1,593,750$

$\$1,700,000 - \$1,593,750 = \$106,250$

The difference estimation technique is often more precise when all the differences found in the sample are of a similar amount and are not related to the recorded values for the items containing the misstatements. The ratio estimation technique may be more precise when the differences in the sample are roughly proportional to the recorded values of the items containing the misstatements (i.e., when large items contain the large differences and small items contain the small differences).

---

[22] One such computational formula to measure the variability of the sample ratios (i.e., the standard deviation [SD_R] for an unstratified ratio estimator) is

$$SD_R = \sqrt{\frac{\Sigma x_i^2 + \hat{R}^2 \Sigma y_i^2 - 2_{\hat{R}} \Sigma x_i y_i}{n-1}}$$

where:

x_i = individual sample audited values

y_i = individual sample recorded values

$\hat{R}$ = the computed overall sample ratio $\left(\dfrac{\Sigma x_i}{\Sigma y_i} \right)$

n = sample size

Σ = summation

16.6 NONSTATISTICAL SAMPLING

The auditor faces the same decisions in applying both nonstatistical and statistical sampling, namely, determining an appropriate sample size, selecting the sample, performing the tests, and evaluating the results. This section provides guidance to the auditor in applying nonstatistical sampling techniques. Much of that guidance is, of course, based on statistical sampling principles and techniques.

(a) Determining Sample Size

If the sampling application involves nonstatistical sampling, only the most general guidance can be given regarding the appropriate sample size in different circumstances. No rule of thumb is appropriate for all applications. Many auditors, in an effort to provide some uniformity among nonstatistical sampling applications throughout their practice, have developed more specific guidance for nonstatistical sampling applications, in some cases based on sample sizes used in similar circumstances on other engagements, and in other cases based on statistical sampling concepts and technology.[23]

The following guidance represents the authors' views on determining appropriate sample sizes in nonstatistical applications, also based in part on experience and in part on conclusions reached in statistical sampling applications. This discussion, however, is clearly only one approach to providing guidance for the auditor's judgment process.

Some auditors establish a minimum sample size for tests of controls (e.g., 20 items) because they believe that there is some amount of testing below which the assessment of control risk will be unaffected. In determining an appropriate sample size for substantive tests of details, the auditor should consider the effect on sample size of the various factors discussed earlier in this chapter, namely, sampling risk, tolerable misstatement, expected misstatement, and the characteristics of the population. Of key importance is the level of assurance (sampling risk) required, which is based on all procedures (risk assessment activities, other substantive tests of details, and analytical procedures) performed to achieve a specific audit objective.

Sample sizes may reach levels (for example, sample sizes of 250) above which little additional audit assurance results from a few additional sample items (that is, a practical limit above which diminishing returns limit the audit assurance obtainable from additional sample items). An auditor contemplating selection of more than 250 items for a nonstatistical sample should either consider using statistical sampling to increase the efficiency and effectiveness of the sampling application or ascertain that the cost–benefit trade-off of sampling versus other auditing procedures has been fully as-

---

[23] Auditors sometimes refer to sampling tables to confirm the reasonableness of judgmentally determined sample sizes (see Appendices A and B). When doing so, they should be aware that such tables were designed for attributes sampling and do not consider the variable characteristics of substantive test items or the mitigating effect of stratifying the population to enhance audit efficiency. Only highly homogeneous populations have characteristics similar to those of populations tested using attributes sampling. Accordingly, if the auditor uses tables to corroborate a judgmentally determined sample size and if the population lacks homogeneity, he or she should consider stratification to achieve a greater degree of homogeneity in each stratum.

sessed. Experience demonstrates that in many audit situations, statistical samples of fewer than 250 items will achieve the audit objectives.

(b) Selecting Representative Samples

Whenever sampling is used in an audit, SAS No. 39 requires that sample items be selected in such a way that they can be expected to be representative of the population from which they are drawn. The dictionary defines "representative" as "typical of a group or class." If each item in a population or subpopulation has a chance (not necessarily an equal chance) of being selected, the resulting sample is potentially representative of the characteristics contained in the population or subpopulation. For example, an auditor cannot rely on a sample to be representative if it consists of one or a few blocks of items in sequence (such as all items in a particular time period, on a particular page, or in a particular alphabetical section of a ledger) or if it is not drawn from the whole population. As another example, sample items that are used to evaluate the reasonableness of an entity's entire accounts receivable balance should be selected from the details of that entire balance, so that each item in the population has a chance of being selected. Conversely, sample items that are used exclusively to evaluate balances outstanding for more than 90 days should be potentially representative of that group of balances, but may not necessarily be representative of the entire accounts receivable balance. Other procedures or a separate sample may be necessary to draw conclusions about the remainder of the receivables.

The auditor may achieve representative samples through either unsystematic, systematic, or dollar-weighted selection techniques. In the first two methods, the population may be stratified or unstratified. Unsystematic sample selection (sometimes referred to as haphazard sample selection) attempts to avoid personal bias in selecting items for testing. It is called haphazard selection because auditors intend it to approximate random sample selection; the term does not imply any element of carelessness. Personal bias toward selecting certain items can affect it, however, such as a subconscious tendency to favor items in a particular location on each page or never to pick the first or last items in a listing. In its purest hypothetical form, unsystematic selection would involve blindfolded selection from a thoroughly mixed pile of all the records. More commonly, an auditor will choose a number of items from throughout the ledger or other records, after gaining satisfaction about the completeness of the population from which the sample is selected.

The only difference between the nonstatistical and statistical sampler's use of systematic sample selection is that the nonstatistical sampler often does not specifically identify a random starting point. Systematic selection is currently a commonly used nonstatistical sample selection method and in all likelihood will continue to be, because it is usually a cost-effective approach to extracting a potentially representative sample.

For substantive tests of details, an auditor can reduce sampling risk without increasing sample size by stratifying the population by size or nature in order to permit different intensities of sampling for different strata. This technique may be used effectively to help ensure representative samples in either statistical or nonstatistical sampling applications. Often the auditor can use strata already inherent in the entity's data (e.g., location or product line). The sample sizes would vary in accordance with the auditor's assessment of the risk of material misstatement associated with each stratum; that is, a larger number of sample items should be apportioned to those strata in which the auditor has assessed a higher risk of material misstatement. Either systematic or unsystematic selection methods can be used with a stratified population.

Dollar-weighted selection techniques can lead to sample sizes that are nearly as efficient as those used with stratified techniques. Dollar-weighted selection is similar to the unsystematic method except that the auditor judgmentally "weights" the selection of sample items based on their recorded amount, giving more weight to items with large recorded values. (This should not be confused with 100 percent examination of items above a specified dollar level and a sample of other items, or with a formal stratification plan.)[24]

(c)   Evaluating Sample Results

Regardless of whether statistical or nonstatistical techniques are applied, the auditor should extrapolate (project) the sample results to the whole population. Because conclusions based on sample results apply only to the population from which the sample items were drawn, it is important that the auditor carefully define the population (i.e., the aggregate of items about which information is desired) and keep it in mind when evaluating the sample results. For example, the auditor cannot support conclusions about accurate pricing of the entire raw materials inventory on the basis of a sample selected only from raw materials used in producing one of several products.

(i)   Tests of Controls.   Sample results for tests of controls are appropriately stated as deviation rates, which are determined by dividing the number of sample deviations by the sample size. The deviation rate in the sample is the best estimate of the deviation rate in the population from which the sample was selected.

The auditor should follow up on identified deviations from controls to determine if they are "isolated incidents," such as a clerk's being on vacation, or indications of a possible control deficiency. Isolated incidents should always be included as sample deviations and projected to the population; the auditor should evaluate their impact on the assessment of control risk carefully. If the projected deviation rate exceeds the tolerable rate, the auditor should reconsider the control risk assessment. Either a single instance of a control deficiency (e.g., circumvention of a control) or the aggregate effect of a number of instances (whether "isolated" or not) may be sufficient to change the assessed level of control risk.

Random deviations in the operation of application controls should be infrequent in computerized systems. Errors are more commonly introduced by incorrectly specified or implemented system changes. Often, the identification of a deviation or error in a system leads to the identification and correction of all other similar deviations or errors. Once an error has been identified, the entity generally makes a system change to prevent further misstatements.

(ii)   Substantive Tests.   There are several acceptable methods of projecting the impact of dollar misstatements in a substantive test sample to the population. In the

[24] For a discussion of dollar-weighted sample selection, see page 16.22.

ratio approach, the auditor determines the projected population misstatement by multiplying the total dollar amount of the population by a misstatement rate obtained by dividing the total dollar amount of sample misstatements by the total dollar amount of the sample, as follows:

$$\underset{\text{(population amount)}}{\$1,000,000} \times \frac{\$100 \text{ (sample misstatements)}}{\$1,000 \text{ (sample amount)}} = \underset{\text{population misstatement}}{\$100,000 \text{ (projected}}$$

In the *average-difference approach*, the total number of items in the population is multiplied by the average misstatement amount obtained by dividing the total dollar amount of sample misstatements by the number of sample items, as follows:

$$\underset{\text{(population items)}}{15,000} \times \frac{\$1,000 \text{ (sample misstatements)}}{140 \text{ (sample items)}} = \underset{\text{population misstatement)}}{\$107,143 \text{ (projected}}$$

The ratio approach is generally the more appropriate technique when the misstatement amounts are roughly proportional to the recorded values of the sample items (i.e., the larger dollar misstatements are from the larger sample items). The average-difference approach is more appropriate when the misstatement amounts are disproportionate to the recorded values of the sample items (e.g., large items have small dollar misstatements and small items have large dollar misstatements, or the dollar misstatements are all about the same size regardless of recorded amount).

Another acceptable (but infrequently used) method is the *projection-of-average-audit-value approach*. This approach is used, for example, to construct a balance sheet value for inventory if recorded values are not available and only quantity (not price) information can be obtained from the records.[25] This approach also may be most appropriate if there are recorded amounts but the general ledger control account does not agree with the sum of the individual recorded amounts. In the average-audit-value approach, the total number of items in the population is multiplied by the quotient obtained by dividing the total "audited" dollar amount of the sample items by the number of sample items, as follows:

$$150,000 \text{(population items)} \times \frac{\$900 \text{ (total sample audited value)}}{150 \text{ (sample items)}} = \underset{\text{population amount)}}{\$900,000 \text{ (projected}}$$

In this technique, the misstatement projection is the difference between the recorded and projected population dollar amounts.

Other methods of projection also may be appropriate. It is important to remember that different projection techniques often result in different projected misstatement amounts. Auditors may find the ratio approach useful for a wide variety of situations, but no one method of projecting the misstatement is necessarily "better" than the others in all circumstances.

To ascertain the total projected misstatement for the account balance being examined, the projected misstatement from the sample results should be added to any

---

[25] Statistical samples generally are employed in developing estimated inventory amounts for financial reporting or tax reporting purposes.

known misstatements discovered as a result of nonsampling procedures performed, such as misstatements identified in 100 percent examinations of selected items or from high-dollar-coverage tests. Since, by definition, the dollar amount of the projection of sample results already includes the sample misstatements found, those misstatements should not be separately added to the projected misstatement. Similarly, misstatements affecting the account balance that the auditor found in related tests of controls also should not be separately added to the projected misstatement.

An auditor using stratification in the sampling plan should project the results for each stratum separately and then add the stratum projections to determine the projected misstatement for the account or class of transactions being examined.

The auditor should compare the projected misstatement obtained from sampling procedures and other likely misstatements with the tolerable misstatement. (If the tolerable misstatement was not quantified for purposes of determining sample size, the auditor may find it useful to use overall financial statement materiality or some smaller amount for this comparison.) Even if the projected misstatement from sampling procedures plus other likely misstatements are less than tolerable misstatement—the misstatement the auditor can accept before modifying the opinion—the auditor should record the projected misstatement on a working paper that summarizes misstatements and potential adjustments, discussed in Chapter 27 (Section 27.5, Summarizing Misstatements and Evaluating the Audit Findings), to determine whether all likely misstatements discovered during the audit equal or exceed the auditor's determination of materiality. The auditor also should evaluate the nature of the misstatements and discuss them with management. In some circumstances it may be practical for entity personnel to review the remaining population for items having characteristics similar to those in the sample that were found to contain misstatements. When adjustments are made to the recorded balance, the related projected misstatement should be reduced by the amount of the adjustments. For example, if the auditor calculated a projected overstatement of $20,000 in an inventory balance based on misstatements found in the sample, but by investigating a few instances of a particular problem was able to identify $11,000 of overstatement that management agreed to record as an adjustment to the recorded inventory balance, the projected misstatement would be reduced to $9,000.

If the projected misstatement from sampling combined with other likely misstatements is greater than the tolerable misstatement (or financial statement materiality), the auditor should consider the implications for the audit strategy and opinion, and take appropriate action. Possible auditor actions are discussed in Chapter 15 (Section 15.5, Evaluating the Results of Substantive Tests).

(iii) Allowance for Sampling Risk.   Even if the projected misstatement amount or deviation rate is less than the tolerable misstatement amount or deviation rate, the auditor still should consider the risk that the true misstatement amount or deviation rate in the population exceeds the tolerable amount or rate. Thus, an allowance for sampling risk, defined as a margin for inaccuracy or imprecision in the sample result, must be determined. (The concept is similar to "precision," a term defined earlier in connection with statistical sampling applications.) When statistical sampling is applied, the auditor computes the allowance for sampling risk. However, the nonstatistical sampler must rely on rules of thumb and judgment to consider the allowance for sampling risk. For instance, assume that the tolerable misstatement in an account balance of $2,000,000 is $80,000 and that the total projected misstatement based on an appropriately sized sample is $20,000. A statistical test might result in a computed precision of plus or minus $40,000 for a specified level of reliability, such as 95 percent. Since the projected misstatement (i.e., $20,000) plus the allowance for sampling risk (i.e., $40,000) does not exceed the tolerable misstatement, the auditor may conclude that there is an acceptably low sampling risk (i.e., 5 percent, the complement of the 95 percent reliability level) that the true population misstatement does not exceed the tolerable misstatement. In part because of the difference between the $20,000 projected misstatement and the $80,000 tolerable misstatement, the nonstatistical sampler, not knowing the exact precision, would make a judgment that he or she may be reasonably assured that there is an acceptably low sampling risk that the true monetary misstatement in the population exceeds the tolerable misstatement. On the other hand, if the total projected misstatement approaches or exceeds the tolerable misstatement, the auditor may conclude that there is a high sampling risk that the true monetary misstatement in the population exceeds the tolerable misstatement.

A possible rule of thumb for the nonstatistical sampler when considering an allowance for sampling risk is: If the deviation rate or number or amount of misstatements actually identified in the sample does not exceed the expected rate or misstatement used in determining an appropriate sample size, the auditor generally can conclude that the risk that the true deviation rate or misstatement amount exceeds the tolerable rate or amount is consistent with the risk considered acceptable when the sample was initially planned. For example, if an auditor performing a test of controls had established expected and tolerable deviation rates of 1 percent and 5 percent, respectively, a deviation rate approximating 1 percent would be a satisfactory result consistent with the risk considered acceptable when the sample was planned. Conversely, if the deviation rate identified in the sample exceeds the expected deviation rate used in determining the sample size, the auditor generally should conclude that there is a higher-than-planned sampling risk that the true rate exceeds the tolerable rate.

If, based on this rule of thumb, the auditor concludes that there is an unacceptably high risk that the true deviation rate or misstatement amount in the population exceeds the tolerable deviation rate or misstatement amount, appropriate action is necessary. For tests of controls, the auditor should consider revising the control risk assessment. For substantive tests, the auditor's possible actions are the same as those—discussed in the preceding section—appropriate when projected misstatement exceeds tolerable misstatement. In using this rule of thumb for substantive tests, the auditor may encounter situations in which the acceptability of the achieved sampling risk for a particular account balance or class of transactions is not clear—for example, if the sampling risk indicated by the sample only slightly exceeds the level the auditor originally desired from the test, and other auditing procedures have not yet been applied to the account or related accounts. In these cases, the auditor should consider deferring further action until the aggregation and evaluation of misstatements for the remaining areas in the financial statements have been completed. That topic is discussed in Chapter 27 (see Section 27.5, Summarizing Misstatements and Evaluating the Audit Findings).

16.7 DOCUMENTING AUDIT SAMPLING

Documentation of the sampling applications used on an audit must satisfy the professional standards for working papers promulgated in Statement on Auditing Standards No. 41, *Working Papers* (AU Section 339). Working paper documentation of auditing procedures is discussed in Chapter 7 of this book. The documentation should relate to planning the sampling application, performing it, and evaluating the results. Figure 16.8 identifies and categorizes information that the auditor should document.

Figure 16.8   Summary of Audit Sampling Documentation

	Documentation Needed	
Type of Information	*Related to Planning the Sample*	*Related to Performing and Evaluating the Results of the Sample*
Objective and description of test	X	
Definition of misstatements (deviations)	X	
Population:		
1. Definition	X	
2. Description of how completeness was ensured	X	
3. Identification of items for 100 percent examination, if any	X	
Sample size determination factors:		
1. Degree of assurance/sampling risk	X	
2. Tolerable misstatement	X	
3. Expected misstatement	X	
4. Other factors, if any	X	
Sample size, including how determined	X	
Description of sample selection methods, including stratification	X	
Evaluation of sample results:		
1. Projection of misstatements		X
2. Aggregation with items examined 100 percent		X
3. Investigation of misstatement sources (causes)		X
4. Consideration of allowance for sampling risk		X
5. Conclusion on test		X
Aggregation with other test results and consideration of overall allowance for sampling risk		X

Appendix A:
TABLES FOR DETERMINING SAMPLE SIZE: ATTRIBUTES SAMPLING

Reliability Levels of 60, 80, 90, and 95 Percent

Appendix A: Table 1   Determination of Sample Size (Reliability = 60%)

Expected Deviation Rate (Percent)	Tolerable Deviation Rate (Percent)														
	1	2	3	4	5	6	7	8	9	10	12	14	16	18	20
0.00	95	50	35	25	20	15	15	15	10	10	10	10	10	5	5
0.50	310	110	70	55	40	35	30	25	25	20	20	15	15	15	10
1.0		160	70	55	40	35	30	25	25	20	20	15	15	15	10
2.0			140	80	40	35	30	25	25	20	20	15	15	15	10
3.0				140	65	55	30	25	25	20	20	15	15	15	10
4.0					150	70	45	25	25	20	20	15	15	15	10
5.0						140	60	40	35	20	20	15	15	15	10
6.0							150	65	50	35	30	15	15	15	10
7.0								160	70	45	30	15	15	15	10
8.0									170	75	35	25	20	15	10
9.0										180	45	25	20	15	10
10.0											70	30	20	20	10

Appendix A: Table 2   Determination of Sample Size (Reliability = 80%)

Expected Deviation Rate (Percent)	Tolerable Deviation Rate (Percent)														
	1	2	3	4	5	6	7	8	9	10	12	14	16	18	20
0.00	170	80	55	40	35	30	25	20	20	20	15	15	10	10	10
0.50		150	100	75	60	50	45	40	35	30	25	25	20	20	15
1.0		280	100	75	60	50	45	40	35	30	25	25	20	20	15
2.0			340	140	85	50	45	40	35	30	25	25	20	20	15
3.0				400	160	95	60	55	35	30	25	25	20	20	15
4.0					450	150	95	70	50	45	25	25	20	20	15
5.0						500	180	100	60	55	35	30	20	20	15
6.0								190	100	70	45	30	30	20	15
7.0									200	120	55	40	30	25	15
8.0										230	75	50	35	25	25
9.0											130	55	45	30	25
10.0											240	80	50	30	30

Note: These tables are designed for one-sided tests. To determine the relevant table to use for two-sided estimation, double the one-sided test table indicated sampling risk. For example, the 95 percent reliability table implies a 5 percent sampling risk; doubling the sampling risk to 10 percent indicates that this table also can be used for a 90 percent reliability two-sided estimation sample.

Appendix A: Table 3   Determination of Sample Size (Reliability = 90%)

Expected Deviation Rate (Percent)	Tolerable Deviation Rate (Percent)														
	1	2	3	4	5	6	7	8	9	10	12	14	16	18	20
0.00	230	120	80	60	45	40	35	30	25	25	20	20	15	15	15
0.50		200	130	100	80	65	55	50	45	40	35	30	25	25	20
1.0		400	180	100	80	65	55	50	45	40	35	30	25	25	20
2.0				200	140	90	75	50	45	40	35	30	25	25	20
3.0					240	140	95	65	60	55	35	30	25	25	20
4.0						280	150	100	75	65	45	40	25	25	20
5.0							320	160	120	80	55	40	35	30	20
6.0								350	190	120	65	50	35	30	25
7.0									390	200	100	60	40	30	25
8.0										420	140	75	50	40	25
9.0											230	100	65	45	35
10.0											480	150	80	50	40

Appendix A: Table 4   Determination of Sample Size (Reliability = 95%)

Expected Deviation Rate (Percent)	Tolerable Deviation Rate (Percent)														
	1	2	3	4	5	6	7	8	9	10	12	14	16	18	20
0.00	300	150	100	75	60	50	45	40	35	30	25	20	20	20	15
0.50		320	160	120	95	80	70	60	55	50	40	35	30	25	25
1.0			260	160	95	80	70	60	55	50	40	35	30	25	25
2.0				300	190	130	90	80	70	50	40	35	30	25	25
3.0					370	200	130	95	85	65	55	35	30	25	25
4.0						430	230	150	100	90	65	45	40	25	25
5.0							480	240	160	120	75	55	40	35	30
6.0									270	180	100	65	50	35	30
7.0										300	130	85	55	45	40
8.0											200	100	75	50	40
9.0											350	150	90	65	45
10.0												220	120	70	50

Appendix B:
TABLES FOR EVALUATING SAMPLE RESULTS: ATTRIBUTES SAMPLING
Reliability Levels of 60, 80, 90, and 95 Percent

Appendix B: Table 1   Evaluation of Results Based on Number of Observed Deviations (Reliability = 60%)

Sample Size	*Achieved Upper Deviation Rate Limit (Percent)*																
	1	*2*	*3*	*4*	*5*	*6*	*7*	*8*	*9*	*10*	*12*	*14*	*16*	*18*	*20*	*25*	*30*
5														0			
10									0						1		2
15						0						1			2		3
20					0					1			2			3	4
25				0				1				2		3		5	6
30				0			1			2	3		4			6	7
35			0			1			2		3	4	5			7	9
40			0		1				2		3	4	5	6		8	10
45			0		1			2		3	4	5	6	7		10	12
50		0		1			2		3		4	5	6	7	8	11	13
55		0		1		2		3		4	5	6	7	8	9	12	15
60		0		1		2	3		4		5	7	8	9	10	13	16
65		0		1	2		3		4	5	6	7	8	10	11	14	18
70		0	1		2	3		4	5		7	8	9	11	12	16	19
75		0	1		2	3	4		5	6	7	9	10	12	13	17	20
80		0	1	2		3	4	5		6	8	9	11	12	14	18	22
85		0	1	2	3		4	5	6	7	8	10	12	13	15	19	24
90		0	1	2	3	4	5		6	7	9	11	13	14	16	21	25
95	0		1	2	3	4	5	6	7	8	9	12	13	15	17	22	26
100	0		1	2	3	4	5	6	7	8	10	12	14	16	18	23	28
110	0	1	2	3	4	5	6	7	8	9	11	14	16	18	20	25	31
120	0	1	2	3	4	6	7	8	9	10	12	15	17	19	22	28	34
130	0	1	2	3	4	6	7	8	10	11	14	16	19	21	24	30	37
140	0	1	3	4	5	7	8	9	11	12	15	17	20	23	26	33	40
150	0	1	3	4	5	7	9	10	11	13	16	19	22	25	28	35	43
160	0	2	3	5	6	8	9	11	12	14	17	20	24	26	30	38	45
170	0	2	3	5	7	8	10	12	13	15	19	22	25	29	32	40	48
180	0	2	4	5	7	9	11	13	14	16	19	23	26	30	34	42	51
190	0	2	4	6	8	9	11	13	15	17	21	25	28	32	36	45	54
200	1	2	4	6	8	10	12	14	16	18	22	26	30	34	37	47	58
210	1	3	5	7	9	11	13	15	17	19	23	27	32	36	39	50	61
220	1	3	5	7	9	11	14	15	18	20	24	28	33	37	41	52	64
230	1	3	5	7	10	12	14	16	18	21	26	30	34	39	43	55	67
240	1	3	5	8	10	13	15	17	20	22	26	32	36	41	45	58	70
250	1	3	6	8	10	13	16	18	20	23	28	32	37	42	47	60	73
260	1	3	6	8	11	13	16	19	21	24	29	34	39	45	49	63	76
270	1	4	6	9	11	14	17	20	22	25	30	35	41	46	51	65	79
280	1	4	7	9	12	15	17	20	23	26	32	37	43	48	54	68	82
290	1	4	7	10	12	16	18	21	24	27	32	39	44	49	56	70	85
300	1	4	7	10	13	16	19	22	25	28	33	40	45	51	58	73	88

Note: Only upper deviation limits are obtainable using these tables.

Appendix B: Table 2   Evaluation of Results Based on Number of Observed Deviations (Reliability = 80%)

Sample Size	\\ *Achieved Upper Deviation Rate Limit (Percent)* ||||||||||||||||| 1	2	3	4	5	6	7	8	9	10	12	14	16	18	20	25	30
5																	0
10														0			1
15											0					1	2
20									0				1			2	3
25							0				1			2		3	5
30						0				1		2		3		4	6
35					0				1		2		3		4	6	7
40				0				1			2	3	4		5	7	9
45				0			1			2	3	4		5	6	8	10
50				0		1				2	3	4	5	6	7	9	11
55			0			1		2			3	4	5	6	7	10	13
60			0		1			2		3	4	5	6	7	8	11	14
65			0		1			2		3	5	6	7	8	9	12	15
70			0		1		2		3	4	5	6	8	9	10	13	17
75			0	1			2		3	4	6	7	8	10	11	15	18
80		0		1		2	3		4	5	6	8	9	10	12	16	20
85		0		1		2	3		4	5	7	8	10	11	13	17	21
90		0		1	2	3	4		5	6	7	9	10	12	14	18	22
95		0		1	2	3	4		5	6	8	9	11	13	15	19	24
100		0	1		2	3	4		5	6	8	10	12	14	16	20	25
110		0	1	2	3		4	5	6	7	9	11	13	15	17	23	28
120		0	1	2	3	4	5	6	7	8	10	13	15	17	19	25	31
130		0	1	2	3	4	6	7	8	9	11	14	16	19	21	27	34
140		0	2	3	4	5	6	8	9	10	13	15	18	20	23	30	36
150		1	2	3	4	6	7	8	10	11	14	16	19	22	25	32	39
160	0	1	2	3	5	6	7	9	10	12	15	18	21	24	27	34	42
170	0	1	2	4	5	7	8	10	11	13	16	19	22	25	29	37	45
180	0	1	3	4	6	7	9	10	12	14	17	20	24	27	30	39	48
190	0	1	3	4	6	8	9	11	13	14	18	22	25	29	32	41	51
200	0	1	3	5	6	8	10	12	14	15	19	23	27	30	34	44	54
210	0	2	3	5	7	9	11	13	15	16	20	24	28	32	36	46	56
220	0	2	4	5	7	9	11	13	15	17	21	25	30	34	38	49	59
230	0	2	4	6	8	10	12	14	16	18	22	27	31	35	40	51	62
240	0	2	4	6	8	10	12	15	17	19	24	28	33	37	42	53	65
250	0	2	4	6	9	11	13	16	18	20	25	29	34	39	44	56	68
260	0	2	5	7	9	11	14	16	19	21	26	31	36	41	46	58	71
270	0	3	5	7	9	12	14	17	20	22	27	32	37	42	47	60	74
280	0	3	5	8	10	12	15	18	20	23	28	33	39	44	49	63	77
290	1	3	5	8	10	13	16	19	21	24	29	35	40	46	51	65	79
300	1	3	6	8	11	14	16	19	22	25	30	36	42	47	53	68	82

Appendix B: Table 3   Evaluation of Results Based on Number of Observed Deviations (Reliability = 90%)

Sample Size	Achieved Upper Deviation Rate Limit (Percent)																
	1	2	3	4	5	6	7	8	9	10	12	14	16	18	20	25	30
5																	
10																0	
15													0			1	
20											0				1	2	
25									0				1		2	3	4
30								0				1		2		4	5
35							0				1		2		3	5	6
40						0				1		2	3		4	6	7
45					0				1		2		3	4	5	7	9
50					0			1			2	3	4	5		8	10
55					0	1				2	3		4	5	6	9	11
60				0		1			2		3	4	5	6	7	10	13
65				0		1		2		3	4	5	6	7	8	11	14
70				0		1		2		3	4	5	6	8	9	12	15
75			0			1	2		3		4	6	7	8	10	13	16
80			0		1		2		3	4	5	6	8	9	10	14	18
85			0		1		2	3		4	5	7	8	10	11	15	19
90			0		1	2		3	4		6	7	9	11	12	16	20
95			0	1		2	3		4	5	6	8	10	11	13	17	22
100			0	1		2	3	4	5		7	9	10	12	14	19	23
110			0	1	2	3		4	5	6	8	10	12	14	16	21	26
120		0		1	2	3	4	5	6	7	9	11	13	15	17	23	29
130		0	1	2		3	4	6	7	8	10	12	15	17	19	25	31
140		0	1	2	3	4	5	6	7	9	11	13	16	18	21	27	34
150		0	1	2	3	4	6	7	8	9	12	15	17	20	23	30	37
160		0	1	2	4	5	6	8	9	10	13	16	19	22	25	32	40
170		0	1	3	4	5	7	8	10	11	14	17	20	23	26	34	42
180		0	2	3	4	6	7	9	11	12	15	18	22	25	28	37	45
190		1	2	3	5	6	8	10	11	13	16	20	23	26	30	39	48
200		1	2	4	5	7	8	10	12	14	17	21	24	28	32	41	51
210		1	2	4	6	7	9	11	13	15	18	22	26	30	34	44	54
220		1	3	4	6	8	10	12	14	15	19	23	27	31	35	46	56
230		1	3	5	6	8	10	12	14	16	20	25	29	33	37	48	59
240		1	3	5	7	9	11	13	15	17	21	26	30	35	39	50	62
250	0	1	3	5	7	9	11	14	16	18	23	27	32	36	41	53	65
260	0	2	4	6	8	10	12	15	17	19	24	28	33	38	43	55	68
270	0	2	4	6	8	10	13	15	18	20	25	30	35	40	45	57	70
280	0	2	4	6	8	11	13	16	18	21	26	31	36	41	47	60	73
290	0	2	4	7	9	11	14	17	19	22	27	32	37	43	48	62	76
300	0	2	4	7	9	12	14	17	20	22	28	33	39	45	50	64	79

Appendix B: Table 4   Evaluation of Results Based on Number of Observed Deviations (Reliability = 95%)

Sample Size	Achieved Upper Deviation Rate Limit (Percent)																
	1	2	3	4	5	6	7	8	9	10	12	14	16	18	20	25	30
5																	
10																	0
15															0		1
20												0				1	2
25											0			1		2	3
30										0		1			2	3	4
35									0			1		2		4	5
40								0			1		2		3	5	6
45							0				1	2		3	4	6	8
50						0				1		2	3	4	5	7	9
55						0			1		2	3	4		5	8	10
60				0			1				2	3	4	5	6	9	11
65				0			1			2	3	4	5	6	7	10	13
70				0		1			2		3	4	5	7	8	11	14
75			0			1			2		4	5	6	7	8	12	15
80				0		1		2		3	4	5	7	8	9	13	16
85				0		1		2	3		5	6	7	9	10	14	18
90				0		1		2	3	4	5	6	8	9	11	15	19
95				0	1		2	3		4	5	7	9	10	12	16	20
100			0		1		2	3	4		6	8	9	11	13	17	22
110		0		1		2		3	4	5	7	9	10	12	14	19	24
120		0		1		2	3	4	5	6	8	10	12	14	16	21	27
130		0	1	2		3	4	5	6	7	9	11	13	15	18	24	30
140		0	1	2		3	4	5	6	7	10	12	14	17	19	26	32
150	0		1	2		4	5	6	7	8	11	13	16	18	21	28	35
160		0	1	2	3	4	5	7	8	9	12	14	17	20	23	30	38
170		0	1	2	3	4	6	7	9	10	13	16	19	22	25	32	40
180		0	1	2	3	5	6	8	9	11	14	17	20	23	26	35	43
190		0	1	3	4	5	7	8	10	11	15	18	21	25	28	37	46
200		0	1	3	4	6	7	9	11	12	16	19	23	26	30	39	48
210		0	2	3	5	6	8	10	12	13	17	20	24	28	32	41	51
220		0	2	3	5	7	8	10	12	14	18	22	25	29	33	44	54
230		1	2	4	5	7	9	11	13	15	19	23	27	31	35	46	57
240		1	2	4	6	8	10	12	14	16	20	24	28	33	37	48	59
250		1	2	4	6	8	10	12	15	16	21	25	30	34	39	50	62
260		1	3	5	7	9	11	13	15	17	22	26	31	36	41	53	65
270		1	3	5	7	9	11	14	16	18	23	28	33	37	42	55	68
280		1	3	5	7	10	12	14	17	19	24	29	34	39	44	57	71
290	0	1	3	6	8	10	12	15	18	20	25	30	35	41	46	60	73
300	0	1	4	6	8	11	13	16	18	21	26	31	37	42	48	62	76

Appendix C:
TABLES FOR TWO-STAGE SEQUENTIAL SAMPLING PLANS: ATTRIBUTES SAMPLING

Reliability Levels of 80, 85, 90, and 95 Percent

Appendix C: Table 1   Two-Stage Sequential Sampling Plan (Reliability = 80%)

Tolerable Deviation Rate (Percent)	Initial Sample Size	Second-Stage Sample Size
10	17	22
9	19	24
8	21	30
7	24	36
6	29	36
5	35	43
4	46	45
3	62	59
2	97	77

Appendix C: Table 2   Two-Stage Sequential Sampling Plan (Reliability = 85%)

Tolerable Deviation Rate (Percent)	Initial Sample Size	Second-Stage Sample Size
10	20	22
9	22	26
8	25	29
7	29	31
6	34	37
5	41	44
4	54	45
3	71	65
2	113	79

Appendix C: Table 3   Two-Stage Sequential Sampling Plan (Reliability = 90%)

Tolerable Deviation Rate (Percent)	Initial Sample Size	Second-Stage Sample Size
10	23	29
9	26	30
8	30	30
7	35	32
6	41	38
5	51	39
4	64	49
3	89	56
2	133	87

Appendix C: Table 4   Two-Stage Sequential Sampling Plan (Reliability = 95%)

Tolerable Deviation Rate (Percent)	Initial Sample Size	Second-Stage Sample Size
10	31	23
9	34	29
8	39	30
7	45	33
6	53	38
5	65	42
4	84	46
3	113	60
2	169	94

Decision Rules for Two-Stage Sequential Sampling Plans

	No Deviations	One Deviation	Two or More Deviations
Initial sample	Stop—achieved goal	Go to next stage	Stop—failed
Second stage	Stop—achieved goal	Stop—failed	Stop—failed

PART **3**

Auditing Specific Accounts

17

Auditing Cash and Cash Equivalents

Cash includes cash on hand and balances with financial institutions that are immediately available for any purpose. Cash equivalents are short-term, highly liquid investments, such as money market funds, time deposits, commercial paper, certificates of deposit, and similar types of deposits. They are readily convertible to known amounts of cash and generally mature within three months of their date of purchase.

17.1   AUDIT OBJECTIVES

Figure 17.1 describes specific audit objectives related to cash and cash equivalents.

17.2   TYPICAL TRANSACTIONS AND CONTROLS

The balance in the cash account results from cash receipts and cash disbursements. The principal source of cash receipts is collections from customers; those transactions are part of the revenue cycle, which was discussed in depth in Chapter 13. Other sources of cash are the issuance of debt and equity (Chapter 25); the sale of property, plant, and equipment (Chapter 22); and revenues from investments (Chapter 21). The principal

Figure 17.1   Audit Objectives for Cash and Cash Equivalents

Completeness	All cash and cash equivalents on hand at the balance sheet date are included in the financial statements.
	All cash receipts and disbursements that occurred during the period are recorded.
Accuracy	Amounts reported for cash and cash equivalents on hand at the end of the period are accurate.
	Cash receipts and disbursements are accurately recorded.
Existence/Occurrence	Recorded cash and cash equivalents exist.
	Recorded cash transactions represent receipts and disbursements that actually occurred during the period covered by the financial statements.
Cutoff	Cash receipts, disbursements, and transfers between bank accounts are recorded in the proper period.
Valuation/Allocation	All items properly included as part of cash are realizable in the amounts stated; for example, foreign currency on hand or on deposit in foreign countries is properly stated.
Rights and Obligations	The entity has legal title and ownership rights to cash and cash equivalents.
Presentation and Disclosure	Cash restricted as to availability or use is properly identified and disclosed.
	Cash equivalents pledged as collateral or otherwise restricted are properly identified and disclosed.

use of cash is to pay for purchases of goods and services, which are part of the purchasing cycle, discussed in Chapter 14. Other uses of cash are to purchase property, plant, and equipment (Chapter 22); repay long-term borrowing and acquire treasury stock (Chapter 25); and pay interest and dividends (Chapter 25). Purchases and sales of securities, either as part of the entity's cash management procedures (described below) or to accomplish other objectives, also can represent significant uses and sources of cash. Lastly, cash receipts and disbursements may be generated by nonrecurring transactions, such as the sale of a segment of the business.

Management ordinarily institutes appropriate controls in each of the control components to address the completeness, accuracy, and authorization of cash transactions, as well as appropriate segregation of duties and physical controls with respect to cash transactions. Those controls are described in the chapters noted above and are not repeated here. Management generally also institutes controls to achieve the file maintenance objectives and to safeguard cash once it has been recorded. Segregation of duties, custodial controls, and timely bank reconciliations are particularly significant because cash represents the highest form of liquidity and is so easily transferable. The remainder of this section focuses on those controls.

(a)   Disbursements of Currency

Disbursements made in currency from petty cash funds are normally for advances, freight bills, and other minor expenditures. Sometimes wages and salaries are paid in currency. An entity usually achieves asset protection of funds used for currency disbursements by keeping the relevant fund (or funds) on an imprest system under which the sum of unexpended cash and paid vouchers equals the fixed amount in the fund. Imprest bank accounts for payroll and branch office local expenditures sometimes function like petty cash funds.

(b)   Reconciliation of Bank Accounts and Cash Transactions

Periodic reconciliations of amounts recorded in the entity's cash accounts to amounts shown on bank statements are key control activities to meet the asset protection objective for cash. The reconciliation procedure will be more effective if, in addition to reconciling the balances, the detailed items listed on the bank statement are reconciled to the detailed items recorded in the accounts during the period covered by the bank statement. This ensures that all items recorded in the accounts, including offsetting items within receipts or disbursements, also are recorded on the bank statement and vice versa. This type of reconciliation is referred to as a "proof of cash," and is described in detail later in this chapter.

(c)   Segregation of Duties

Effective segregation of duties requires that the person responsible for reconciling bank balances to account balances not have functions relating to cash receipts, cash disbursements, or preparing or approving vouchers for payment. It also requires that the person performing the reconciliation obtain the bank statements directly from the bank and make specific comparisons, like comparing paid checks and other debits and credits listed on the bank statement with entries in the accounts, examining checks for signatures and endorsements, and reconciling bank transfers.

(d) Cash Management

Entities have certain objectives for managing their cash. A universal objective is to generate maximum earnings, consistent with the risks involved, by investing or otherwise using cash, including concentrating it in deposits that "earn" the most in banking relations and bankers' services. Management's use of the cash records to monitor the entity's financing needs and cash management strategies may also contribute toward meeting financial reporting control objectives for cash.

A principal tool of cash management is cash forecasting and budgeting, that is, trying to plan, in as much detail and as far ahead as possible, what receipts can be expected and what disbursements will be required. The objective is to schedule as precisely as possible the amount and timing of borrowings and of cash available for temporary investments. Doing this requires accurate daily calculations of balances, transfers, commitments, and the maturity of cash equivalents and temporary investments, which often leads to effective controls relating to cash. Variations from budget are reported to a cash manager who scrutinizes them closely. If the manager is independent of the handling of and accounting for cash, these reviews may be an effective monitoring activity.

Good cash management requires controls for (1) evaluating the risk and return of different kinds of cash equivalents and temporary investments, and (2) making the actual investment decisions. The treasury function in many entities has become increasingly sophisticated in response to the rapidly growing number of complex financial instruments for investing available cash for periods ranging from overnight to several months. The risks and returns associated with those instruments vary widely and may be difficult to understand and analyze. Management must understand the risks and returns, however, both to make informed investment decisions and to apply appropriate accounting measurement and disclosure principles. Finally, treasury management also entails decisions about who should authorize and execute cash management transactions. Sometimes the transactions are initiated automatically, such as by overnight sweeps of cash balances into money market instruments; sometimes they are discretionary on the part of cash managers; and sometimes senior-level management authorization is required.

Another objective of effective cash management is to bring receipts under managerial control as quickly as possible, which depends on fast and accurate processing, including daily bank deposits, lockbox systems, wire transfers, and one-way depository bank accounts. Effective cash management also calls for close attention to invoices in process to make sure payments are timed to use cash resources most effectively.

17.3 DETERMINING THE AUDIT STRATEGY

The remainder of this chapter is generally based on the assumption that the auditor, through the appropriate combination of risk assessment activities and substantive tests performed in other segments of the audit, will have reduced audit risk to an appropriately low level with regard to the completeness, accuracy, and existence/occurrence of cash receipts from customers, cash disbursements to vendors, and cash management and other cash transactions. (If deemed necessary as a result of inherent risks identified and the assessment of control risk, the auditor should obtain further assurance about the accuracy of cash records and the completeness and occurrence of cash transactions by tracing receipts and disbursements to the cash account, on a test basis if appropriate.) Accordingly, the following discussions of audit strategy and substantive tests focus on auditing the cash account on the balance sheet.

(a) Risk Factors and Materiality

Because cash and cash equivalents are so liquid and transferable, the risk of theft is greater than for any other asset. Accordingly, the auditor focuses on how responsive controls, particularly those relating to asset protection and segregation of duties, are to that inherent risk characteristic.

Failure to detect cash defalcations is, at a minimum, frequently a source of embarrassment to the auditor. Often, it may be the basis for litigation, particularly if it involves material fraud that a plaintiff contends the auditor should have detected following a testing plan that gave appropriate consideration to the inherent risk associated with cash and the entity's response to that risk. Cash defalcations may result in nonexistent assets being reported on the balance sheet, which would be the case if a theft was not concealed and the cash account not reduced by the amount stolen. Often, however, cash defalcations are concealed by unauthorized charges to income statement accounts, resulting in an appropriate balance sheet presentation for cash, but an income statement containing misclassified or fictitious expenses, along with possibly deficient disclosures.

Meeting the cutoff objective with respect to cash receipts from customers and disbursements to vendors is important to prevent end-of-period "window dressing" of working capital accounts. Recording bank transfers in the wrong period also could be indicative of a defalcation, as discussed under Bank Transfer Schedule later in this chapter.

In considering materiality, the auditor should determine the volume and value of cash transactions and the locations and approximate amounts of all cash funds, bank accounts, cash equivalents, and other negotiable assets. (The auditor also should inquire whether cash or securities in the entity's possession include property of other organizations, such as an employees' association, or entity property not recorded in the accounts, such as unclaimed wages and employees' savings.) This information will reveal the actual size of the cash account and enable the auditor to assess its significance in relation to the entity's financial position.

(b) Assessment of Control Risk

The auditor ordinarily will have gained an understanding of how well duties involving recording and handling cash are segregated, as well as other aspects of internal control relating to cash transactions, when auditing the revenue and purchasing cycles. The auditor now needs to assess whether the entity has effective asset protection and segregation of duties to safeguard cash balances, and has established effective controls—mainly reconciliations—to meet the file maintenance objectives relating to cash.

The nature, timing, and extent of substantive tests of cash and cash equivalents are strongly influenced by the auditor's identification of inherent risks and assessment of control risk. For example, the auditor may merely review employee-prepared bank reconciliations, rather than independently perform one or more reconciliations, if he or she has obtained evidence that bank reconciliations are performed regularly and effectively and there is proper segregation of duties within the various cash functions. The effectiveness of control activities also affects the timing of substantive tests. For example, public companies often have early earnings release dates, so that the auditor may wish to perform early substantive tests of cash. If the auditor has tested segregation of duties and asset protection control activities and found them to be effective, they may provide evidence that the control objectives are met in the period between the early testing date and year-end. When performing substantive tests before the balance sheet date, the auditor should consider the factors discussed in Chapter 15 [Section 15.2(b), Timing of Tests of Details].

If the auditor plans to assess control risk at low for the audit objectives of completeness, accuracy, and existence/occurrence in both the revenue and purchasing cycles, ordinarily there should be no need to perform tests of details of cash records. Such tests may be necessary, however, if there is a risk that employees would intentionally misstate details in the bank reconciliations or there is a lack of division of duties, and this, together with other factors (such as the absence of key control activities), leads the auditor to believe there may be a risk of fraud. (If there is a lack of division of duties or other risk of fraud, the auditor also may consider obtaining year-end bank statements and original supporting documents, such as canceled checks, directly from the bank.)

Other controls may affect the nature and extent of substantive tests. For example, management personnel or the internal auditors may receive monthly bank statements directly from the banks, review the statements for unusual transactions, and examine the signatures on the returned checks. Those procedures provide the auditor with additional evidence of the effectiveness of internal control regarding cash. In addition, the auditor may test monitoring activities that management performs as part of determining the entity's financing needs and cash management strategies, which ordinarily will reduce the assurance needed from substantive tests.

In the past, many auditors spent an inordinate amount of time applying detailed auditing procedures to cash—such as reviewing or reperforming bank reconciliations at one or more dates, performing one or more independent reconciliations, and examining every cash receipt and disbursement and supporting documents for one or more months. If controls relating to cash are not designed and operating effectively, such detailed auditing procedures may be necessary to provide reasonable assurance about the cash account. Over the years, however, those procedures increasingly have taken on the character of extended rather than routine auditing procedures, and are performed only if the auditor suspects a material misstatement of the cash balance and is unable to obtain sufficient evidence by other means to either affirm or allay that suspicion.

17.4   SUBSTANTIVE TESTS

This section describes substantive tests for auditing cash balances,[1] which fall into the following categories:

- Testing the completeness, accuracy, and existence of ending balances
  - Confirming balances and other information with banks and other financial institutions
  - Preparing, reviewing, or testing bank reconciliations
  - Cash counts
- Testing bank transfer cutoff
- Reviewing restrictions on cash balances and related disclosures

Analytical procedures that can be applied to cash and cash equivalents are limited, primarily because those accounts have few relationships with other accounts. Analytical procedures generally would not be helpful in identifying significant risks related to cash or in flagging potential misstatements in cash or cash equivalents.

(a)   Confirming Account Balance Information with Financial Institutions

The auditor confirms account balances (both loan balances and deposit accounts) at year-end by direct correspondence with financial institutions. This may include accounts closed during the year. Requests to financial institutions for confirmation of both deposit and loan account balances should be made using the Standard Form to Confirm Account Balance Information with Financial Institutions, which was approved by the AICPA, the American Bankers Association, and the Bank Administration Institute in 1990. The form is shown in Figure 17.2.

The auditor mails the original and duplicate of the confirmation form to the financial institution; the institution signs one copy and returns it to the auditor and retains the other. The confirmation procedure can be expedited if the financial institution receives the confirmation form before the confirmation date and at least two weeks before a reply is required. The exact name and number of the accounts to be confirmed should be prelisted on the form.

Before the current form was adopted, other transactions and arrangements with financial institutions, including contingent liabilities, compensating balances, and lines of credit, were confirmed using the same form that was used to confirm account balances. With the increase in the number and variety of services financial institutions provide and the number of different people in positions to confirm various items, combining requests for confirmation of different items on one form became impractical. As a result, the AICPA Auditing Standards Division developed three illustrative letters for use in confirming transactions other than account balances. Those letters are discussed and illustrated in Chapter 25 [Section 25.4(e)(i), Confirming Contingent Liabilities, Compen-

---

[1] Auditing procedures for investments, discussed in Chapter 21, may be appropriate for auditing certain cash equivalents.

Figure 17.2   Standard Financial Institution Confirmation Form

STANDARD FORM TO CONFIRM ACCOUNT
BALANCE INFORMATION WITH FINANCIAL INSTITUTIONS

ORIGINAL
To be mailed to accountant

CUSTOMER NAME

We have provided to our accountants the following information as of

the close of business on _____ , 19____ .
regarding our deposit and loan balances. Please confirm the accuracy
of the information, noting any exceptions to the information provided.
If the balances have been left blank, please complete this form by
furnishing the balance in the appropriate space below.* Although we
do not request nor expect you to conduct a comprehensive, detailed
search of your records, if during the process of completing this confirmation additional information about other deposit and loan accounts
we may have with you comes to your attention, please include such
information below. Please use the enclosed envelope to return the
form directly to our accountants.

Financial
Institution's
Name and
Address

1. At the close of business on the date listed above, our records indicated the following deposit balance(s):

ACCOUNT NAME	ACCOUNT NO.	INTEREST RATE	BALANCE*

2. We were directly liable to the financial institution for loans at the close of business on the date listed above as follows:

ACCOUNT NO./ DESCRIPTION	BALANCE*	DATE DUE	INTEREST RATE	DATE THROUGH WHICH INTEREST IS PAID	DESCRIPTION OF COLLATERAL

_____
(Customer's Authorized Signature)

_____
(Date)

The information presented above by the customer is in agreement with our records. Although we have not conducted a
comprehensive, detailed search of our records, no other deposit or loan accounts have come to our attention except as noted below.

_____
(Financial Institution Authorized Signature)

_____
(Date)

_____
(Title)

EXCEPTIONS AND/OR COMMENTS

Please return this form directly to our accountants: [   ]

* Ordinarily, balances are intentionally left blank if they are not
available at the time the form is prepared.   [   ]

D451 5951

Approved 1990 by American Bankers Association, American Institute of Certified Public Accountants and Bank Administration
Institute. Additional forms available from: AICPA—Harborside Financial Center, 201 Plaza Three, Order Department, Jersey City,
NJ, 07311-3881

sating Balances, Lines of Credit, and Other Arrangements]. Using the revised standard confirmation form for account balances and the letter form of confirmation for other transactions with financial institutions enables the auditor to direct requests for specific information to the appropriate recipients.

(b) Bank Reconciliations

As noted earlier, the reconciliation of bank accounts, and the appropriate division of duties with respect to cash balances and transactions, are key control activities. The auditor's assessment of the effectiveness of employees' reconciliations determines the nature, timing, and extent of many of the substantive tests of cash. The adequacy of the accounting system, the competence of employees doing the reconciliations, and the segregation of duties are the major factors in that assessment. The more effective the auditor finds the reconciliations to be, that is, the lower the assessed level of control risk, the less detailed the auditor's reconciliation procedures have to be. Those procedures may range from simply reviewing employee reconciliations at year-end, if control risk has been assessed at low, to performing independent reconciliations covering the entire year using the proof of cash form (discussed later). Generally, performing proof of cash reconciliations for the entire year is considered necessary only in special situations, such as when a defalcation is believed to have occurred. Between those two extremes, the auditor may review and test the reconciliations, or may perform independent reconciliations at year-end (either using the proof of cash form or not). The various audit approaches to bank reconciliations are described below.

(i) Review of Entity's Reconciliations. If the auditor has assessed control risk at low, then merely reviewing the entity's reconciliations at year-end may be appropriate. The steps in reviewing an entity's bank reconciliations are:

1. Obtain copies of the reconciliations and test their mathematical accuracy.
2. Trace the book balances on the reconciliations to the general ledger balance. This generally will require using a summary of the individual cash account balances in the general ledger account.
3. Scan the bank reconciliations for significant unusual reconciling items and adjustments, and obtain evidence to support them by inquiry or examination of appropriate documents.

(ii) Review and Test of Entity's Reconciliations. In addition to the review procedures described above, the auditor may decide to test the supporting documentation for the entity's year-end bank reconciliations. Generally, it is necessary to obtain and test only the year-end bank reconciliations. If there is inadequate division of duties between persons responsible for reconciling cash accounts, processing cash receipts and disbursements, and approving checks for payment, it may be appropriate to obtain bank reconciliations for earlier periods and review the resolution of unusual reconciling items. If the entity maintains several bank accounts and controls are adequate, it may be appropriate to select a sample of accounts to review; at least one account should be tested for each bank with which the entity does business.

The extent of the auditor's review of the year-end bank reconciliations and tests of underlying documentation also depends on the discipline with which employees reconcile and control cash accounts and the degree of scrutiny of cash control activities by individuals who are independent of day-to-day cash processing. In addition, depending on these same considerations, the auditor might ask management to request that the bank send directly to the auditor a bank statement and related canceled checks for the "cutoff period" (usually a week or two immediately following the balance sheet date) or for the following month. Alternatively, the auditor may use the entity's bank statement for the following month, if the reconciliation is tested at an interim date.

In addition to steps 1 and 2 above, the procedures below typically are involved in tests of the entity's reconciliations. These procedures assume that the testing is performed as of the balance sheet date and that cutoff statements for a reasonable period after the balance sheet date are obtained from the bank.

1. Determine that paid checks, deposits, and debit and credit advices appearing on the cutoff bank statements and issued on or before the balance sheet date appear on the year-end reconciliations.

2. Trace to the cash disbursements records outstanding checks listed on bank reconciliations but not returned with the cutoff statements.

3. Trace deposits in transit on the bank reconciliations to the cutoff bank statements and the cash receipts records, and determine whether there are any unusual delays between the date received per the books and the date deposited per the bank statements.

4. Trace other reconciling items to supporting documentation and entries in the cash records.

5. Investigate old or unusual reconciling items. If checks remain uncashed after a specified period of time, the reason should be determined and the amounts either restored to the cash account or disposed of according to state escheat law.

6. Determine the exact nature of items on the year-end bank statements not accounted for by the reconciliation procedures, such as debits or credits followed by offsetting entries of identical amounts that appear to be, or are represented by entity personnel to be, bank errors and corrections not so coded. If information in the entity's records is inadequate, clarification should be requested from the bank. In these circumstances, the auditor should consider performing a "proof of cash" reconciliation (described below) if the entity's reconciliation process does not include one.

Some entities experiencing cash flow difficulties follow a practice of preparing, recording, and then "holding" checks and releasing them as cash balances become available. Management may believe it is easier to "hold" the checks than to void them and replace them when cash becomes available. Although the entity should be urged to prepare checks only when they can be released, the auditor may encounter this situation when checks are routinely prepared by computer based on predetermined invoice due dates entered at the time invoices are processed.

Accordingly, the auditor should inquire whether any checks drawn before year-end were released after year-end and should consider obtaining the numbers of the last checks written for the current fiscal year. If the amount of "held" checks is potentially significant at the balance sheet date, the auditor should plan to examine them at that date and subsequently determine that the amount of such checks has been reinstated by appropriate adjusting entries in the cash account (and related liability accounts) at that date.

(iii) Independent "Proof of Cash" Reconciliations. A proof of cash reconciliation (also known as a "four-column reconciliation") summarizes and controls the examination of cash records for a selected period. An advantage of the proof of cash is that it reconciles balances at the beginning and end of the period and, with little additional effort, also reconciles transactions recorded in the accounts during the period to those reflected on the bank statement. An auditor preparing a proof of cash is thus able to "prove" the propriety of recorded transactions in the accounts to an independent source (the bank statement). The auditor can describe any other audit tests applied to the receipts, disbursements, or balances on the form. A proof of cash working paper is illustrated in Figure 17.3.

A proof of cash reconciliation involves performing the steps described above for reviewing and testing reconciliations (which may or may not be in the form of a proof of cash), plus the procedures described below. Procedures already performed need not be repeated.

1. Enter the totals from the bank statement on the proof of cash form.
2. Obtain the entity's reconciliation as of the close of the preceding period and compare balances shown on that reconciliation with the corresponding amounts shown by the accounts and the bank statement; substantiate outstanding checks at the close of the preceding period by examining paid checks returned by the bank in the current period and investigating any still outstanding; and substantiate deposits in transit and other reconciling items at the close of the preceding period by referring to the current bank statement, bank notifications of charges and credits, and other supporting documents.
3. Compare daily totals of recorded cash receipts shown in the cash journal with daily deposits appearing on the bank statement. If there are time lags between the receipt, recording, and depositing of collections, investigate any that appear unreasonable in light of the entity's usual practices. (Delay in depositing receipts constitutes inefficient cash management and exposes cash items on hand to risk of loss or misuse, such as "lapping" collections of accounts receivable—a method of continuously concealing a defalcation by crediting later collections to accounts whose collections were not previously recorded.) Enter unmatched cash receipts items or deposit items on the proof of cash form.
4. Compare paid checks returned with the bank statement with the disbursements records for check number, date, payee, and amount. The comparison determines not only which checks have not cleared the bank during the period but also that dates, payees, and amounts of disbursements as shown by the paid checks agree with recorded disbursements. List checks outstanding at the end of the period, foot the list, and enter the total on the proof of cash form.
5. Account for all checks issued in the sequence between the first and last checks drawn on the bank account during the period.

Figure 17.3 Proof of Cash

XYZ Corporation
Proof of Cash - Month of December
12/31/XX

	Balance Beginning of period	Receipts	Disbursements	Balance End of period
Per bank statement	31,268 A	42,687 A	46,560 A	27,395 C,F,A
Deposits in transit:				
Beginning	1,000 T	(1,000)		
End		2,000		2,000 T
Outstanding checks:				
Beginning	(3,917)		(2,817) O	(1,100) Y
End			3,460	(3,460) O
Unrecorded charges and credits				
Collection from customer				
on note, credited by bank				
during period, entered on books				
after end of period		(2,078)		(2,078) CM
Per Books	28,351 A	41,609 A	47,203 A	22,757 A
	F	F	F	F
Audit adjusting entry #1:				
Collection of customer note				2,078
Per books as adjusted				24,835
				F

Legend of auditing procedures:
F   Footed & crossfooted
A   Agreed with amounts shown on bank statement/books
C   Balance confirmed with bank; see bank confirmation on W/P ___
T   Traced to subsequent bank statement
O   Checks cleared on subsequent bank statement
Y   Check #895 dated 11/27/XX for $1,100 is still outstanding
    Examined purchase order, receiving report, and vendor invoice.
    The purchase made and paid by this check appears proper.
    No adjusting entry proposed.
CM Examined bank credit memo

6. Determine that the reconciliation foots and cross-foots. All items appearing in either of the balance columns and bank errors corrected in the same period also must appear appropriately in either the receipts or disbursements column (as additions or subtractions) so that both activity and balances are reconciled. A later entry in the accounts that apparently offsets an item in a reconciliation is not necessarily proof of its correctness. The propriety of reconciling items or adjusting entries is not established merely by the fact that including them makes it possible to reconcile the balances.

7. Compare deposits in transit and outstanding checks revealed by the reconciliation with a subsequent bank statement and accompanying paid checks. Substantiate checks outstanding at the date of the reconciliation that are not returned with the subsequent bank statement, if material in amount, by referring to properly approved vouchers or other available documents.

As noted earlier, the auditor may, in special situations, consider it necessary to perform proof of cash reconciliations throughout the year. In that event, following up reconciling items (step 7 above) ordinarily would not be required, because the auditor would have tested the entity's procedures in that area in step 2.

(c) Count of Cash on Hand

Cash funds on hand, normally constituting one or more petty cash funds, are seldom significant in relation to the overall cash balance, except in certain industries such as retail stores, banks, and casinos. Therefore, auditors generally do not perform substantive tests of the year-end balance of cash on hand. Nevertheless, they may wish to perform tests of control activities relating to the day-to-day operation of cash funds to obtain evidence that the activity in the funds has been authorized and is completely and accurately recorded. Ineffective control activities could result in improperly classified expenses in the income statement

Some circumstances require physical counting of currency and other cash items on hand. If cash on hand and undeposited receipts are significant in relation to the overall cash balance, or if transactions executed with cash on hand are material, individually or in the aggregate, cash should be counted. The auditor also should consider the adequacy of the controls over processing these types of transactions, particularly custody controls and division of duties between persons responsible for recording transactions and for custody of cash.

If the auditor concludes that a cash count is required, it ordinarily should be done at year-end and be coordinated with the examination or confirmation of negotiable assets such as marketable securities, notes receivable, and collateral held as security for loans to others. In addition, the auditor should take appropriate steps to ensure that a cash shortage at a particular location cannot be concealed by the conversion of negotiable assets or the transfer of cash from another location. If simultaneous physical examination of negotiable assets on hand is not practicable, the auditor should establish control over all such assets to avoid the possibility of a shortage in one group being covered up by other assets already examined. Less active negotiable assets—such as notes receivable and marketable securities—may be counted in advance and placed under seal until all counts are completed. Occasionally it is necessary to permit movement of assets under seal; the auditor should control and record all such transactions. Totals of funds and other negotiable assets counted or confirmed should be reconciled to general ledger controlling accounts as of the date of the examination.

An auditor should not assume responsibility for custody of cash or negotiable assets in a physical count, but should insist on continuous attendance by a representative of the entity while those assets are being examined. After the count has been completed, the entity's representative should acknowledge its accuracy. Auditors should never count funds in the absence (even if temporary) of the custodian, and should always obtain a written acknowledgment from the entity's representative that the funds were returned intact. If the count discloses an overage or shortage in the fund, the auditor should ask for a recount and acknowledgment by the entity's representative of the accuracy of the count.

(d) Bank Transfer Schedule

To ensure there has been a proper cutoff at year-end, the auditor should determine whether significant transfers of funds occurred among the entity's various bank accounts near the balance sheet date. All transfers of funds within the entity should be considered—whether among branches, divisions, or affiliates—to make sure that cash is not "double counted" in two or more bank accounts and that "kiting" (explained below) has not occurred. The auditor should determine that (1) each transaction represented as a transfer is in fact an authorized transfer; (2) debits and credits representing transfers of cash are recorded in the same period; and (3) the funds are actually deposited in the receiving bank in the appropriate period.

Kiting is a way of concealing a cash shortage caused by a defalcation, such as misappropriating cash receipts, that was perpetrated previously. It involves the careful and deliberate use of the "float" (the time necessary for a check to clear the bank it was drawn on). Kiting is effected by drawing a check on one bank, depositing it in another bank just before year-end so that the deposit appears on the bank statement, and not recording the transfer in the cash receipts or cash disbursements journals until after year-end. The float period will cause the check not to clear the bank it was drawn on until after year-end, and the amount transferred is included in the balances of both bank accounts. Since the transfer is not recorded as a receipt or a disbursement until the following year, it will not appear as an outstanding check or a deposit in transit on the reconciliation of either bank account. The effect is to increase receipts per the bank statement; if the misappropriation of cash receipts and the kiting take place in the same period, receipts per the bank statement will agree with receipts per the cash receipts journal at the date of the bank reconciliation. (If the misappropriation of cash receipts occurs in the period before the kiting, a proof of cash may also reveal the kiting.) Kiting requires that the transfer process be repeated continually until the misappropriated funds have been restored.[2]

A bank transfer schedule is an efficient and effective tool that assists the auditor in determining that all transfers of funds among bank accounts near the balance sheet date are recorded in the proper accounting period, that cash has not been double-counted, and that there is no apparent kiting. The schedule should indicate, for each transfer, the date the check effecting the transfer was recorded as a cash disbursement, the date it was recorded as a cash receipt, the date it cleared the bank it was drawn on, and the date it cleared the bank in which it was deposited. The list of bank transfers should be compiled from both originating documents (paid checks or bank advices) returned with the subsequent bank statement and the cash receipts and disbursements records. A bank transfer schedule is illustrated in Figure 17.4.

The dates on the bank transfer schedule should be obtained from the cash records and the dates on the check showing when it was received by the bank in which it was deposited and when it was canceled by the bank on which it was drawn. The date the check was recorded as a disbursement should be compared with the date it was recorded as a receipt; the dates should be the same. If they are not and the entries are in different fiscal years, an adjusting entry may be necessary to prevent double-counting

---

[2] Banks and other financial institutions use the term "kiting" in a wider sense, to include writing checks against inadequate funds with the intent of depositing sufficient funds later, but before the checks clear the bank.

Figure 17.4 Bank Transfer Schedule

Check Number	Disbursement (Transfer Out)		Receipt (Transfer In)	
	Date Recorded in Books	Date Paid by Bank	Date Recorded in Books	Date Received by Bank
A	12/28/96	01/03/97	12/28/96	12/29/96
B	12/29/96	01/05/97	12/29/96	01/03/97
C	12/29/96	01/03/97	01/02/97	01/02/97
D	01/02/97	01/05/97	01/02/97	12/29/96
E	01/04/97	01/10/97	01/04/97	01/08/97

of cash, depending on the offsetting debit or credit to the entry that was made in the year being audited. Then, for each transfer, the bank dates (paid and cleared) should be compared with the corresponding dates the transaction was recorded in the books (received and disbursed). If those dates are in different accounting periods, the transfer should appear on the bank reconciliation as a reconciling item—an outstanding check if the check cleared the disbursing bank in a later period than it was recorded, and a deposit in transit if it cleared the receiving bank in a later period than the receipt was recorded. Lastly, unusually long time lags between dates recorded and dates cleared should be investigated for possible holding of checks at year-end—a cutoff problem.

In Figure 17.4, there are no double-counting problems with the transfers involving checks A, B, and E because the transfer out of one bank account was recorded in the same period as the transfer into the other bank account. Transfers A and B should appear as outstanding checks on the reconciliation of the disbursing bank's account. Transfer B should also appear as a deposit in transit on the reconciliation of the receiving bank's account. Transfer E should not affect either the books or the reconciliations, because it occurred in the following year and all dates are in the same accounting period.

The other transfers in the figure require further analysis. Transfer C should appear on the reconciliation of the disbursing bank's account as an outstanding check at December 31, 1996. If it does, the balance per the books will not be in error. If it does not, the total of outstanding checks will be understated and the balance per the books will be overstated, possibly covering up an unrecorded check drawn on that account that already cleared the bank. (The transfer should also appear as an adjustment to the balance in the receiving bank to ensure that the cash is included in that account as of December 31.) The auditor also should inform management that the failure to record both the disbursement and the receipt in the same period is a control deficiency.

Transfer D is an example of possible kiting. That transfer should appear as an outstanding check on the reconciliation of the disbursing bank's account; it should also appear as a recording error (an omitted disbursement) on the reconciliation. If kiting were taking place, it is unlikely that the preparer of the reconciliation would be aware that a check was outstanding that should be included on the outstanding check list; nor would the person doing the kiting call the "recording error" to anyone's attention. The funds transferred would thus be counted twice—once in the bank account on which the check was drawn and once again in the account in which it was deposited. Transfer D would result in a misstatement, though not from kiting, if the delay in recording was the result of an oversight or an attempt to conceal an overdraft at the bank.

(e) Reviewing Financial Statement Presentation and Related Disclosures

The auditor should review the evidence previously obtained and, if necessary, perform further procedures to ensure that cash and cash equivalents are presented appropriately in the financial statements and that all appropriate disclosures related to cash have been made. The increased attention being focused on cash management has raised questions about the appropriate balance sheet treatment of cash equivalents, bank overdrafts, outstanding checks and drafts, and restricted cash balances. Bank confirmations, responses to inquiry letters, loan agreements, minutes of board of directors' meetings, and bond indentures may indicate restrictions on the availability or use of cash that should be disclosed. Inquiries of management also may indicate the need for disclosures of cash balances that are restricted or the property of others. (If the latter, the related liability should be recorded.) If the entity has substantial funds in other countries or in foreign currencies, the auditor should determine whether there are any restrictions on their availability and that appropriate disclosures have been made.

(i) Cash Equivalents.   The cash caption on the balance sheet should include cash on hand and balances with financial institutions that are immediately available for any purpose, and cash equivalents. Statement of Financial Accounting Standards No. 95, *Statement of Cash Flows* (Accounting Standards Section C25), defines cash equivalents as short-term, highly liquid investments that are readily convertible to known amounts of cash and are so near their maturity (generally within three months) at the date of purchase that they present an insignificant risk of changes in value because of changes in interest rates. The entity's policy for determining which items are treated as cash equivalents should be disclosed, either parenthetically or in the notes. Other temporary investments that because of size or maturity are not considered readily available should not be included as cash equivalents.

(ii) Bank Overdrafts.   There are two types of bank overdrafts.

> *Book*: in which checks have been issued for more than the book balance in the account on which they were drawn but, because of outstanding checks, the bank's records show a positive balance.

> *Actual*: in which the bank has paid out more funds than are in the account.

If an actual overdraft is the bank's method of temporarily lending funds to an entity, the overdraft should *not* be offset against other cash balances (with either the same or a different bank), but should be classified as a liability.

For financial statement purposes, overdrafts are determined based on book balances. A book overdraft in one bank account may properly be offset only against positive *unrestricted* book balances in the same bank, with appropriate disclosure of the netting. Negative balances in other cash accounts should be classified as liabilities.

(iii) Outstanding Checks and Drafts.   Checks that have not been released at the end of an accounting period should not be considered outstanding, that is, should not be deducted from the cash balance. Drafts payable on demand that have been issued and are outstanding at the end of an accounting period should be netted against the cash balance because they are similar in substance to outstanding checks. However, the legal distinctions between drafts and checks make it also acceptable to present drafts payable as liabilities, with disclosure of the amount.

(iv) Restricted Cash.   The auditor should review special inquiry letters, loan agreements, minutes, bond indentures, and other relevant documents to determine if there are any restrictions on the availability or use of cash. Cash sometimes includes balances with trustees, such as sinking funds, or other amounts not immediately available, for example, those restricted to uses other than current operations, designated for acquisition or construction of noncurrent assets, or segregated for the liquidation of long-term debt. Restrictions are considered effective if the entity clearly intends to observe them, even though the funds are not actually set aside in special bank accounts. The facts pertaining to those balances should be adequately disclosed, and the amounts should be properly classified as current or noncurrent. Sometimes cash balances are the property of others, in which case a related liability should have been recorded.

Entities often maintain compensating balances with banks to support their outstanding borrowings or to ensure future credit availability. Balances maintained under agreements that contractually restrict the use of the funds should be segregated on the balance sheet and classified as current or noncurrent depending on whether the related debt is short- or long-term. In addition, the Securities and Exchange Commission requires additional disclosures of compensating balances[3] maintained under formal and informal arrangements.

---

[3] SEC Accounting Series Release No. 148 defines compensating balances as "that portion of any demand deposit (or any time deposit or certificate of deposit) maintained by a corporation which constitutes support for existing borrowing arrangements of the corporation with a lending institution. Such arrangements would include both outstanding borrowings and the assurance of future credit availability."

18

Auditing Accounts Receivable and Related Revenue Cycle Accounts

This chapter discusses substantive tests that the auditor may use to achieve the audit objectives related to revenue cycle accounts, principally accounts receivable and revenues. The audit strategy that determines the nature, timing, and extent of substantive tests for each account balance and class of transactions in the revenue cycle is based primarily on the auditor's identification of inherent risks and assessment of materiality and control risk relating to specific audit objectives, and on efficiency considerations.

18.1   AUDIT OBJECTIVES

Specific audit objectives applicable to accounts in the revenue cycle are described in Figure 18.1.

18.2   IDENTIFYING INHERENT RISKS

As discussed in Chapter 8, the auditor obtains or updates information about various aspects of the entity and its business in order to identify inherent risks. Receivables and related revenues are more likely to be overstated or nonexistent than understated or incomplete because attempts to improve financial statement presentation may involve inadequate management consideration of valuation allowances that reduce the carrying amount of receivables to their net realizable value, or the recognition of revenue transactions before they have been realized. Therefore, substantive tests in the revenue cycle concentrate on seeking evidence about the existence, accuracy, and valuation of receivables, although the possibility that receivables are incomplete or otherwise understated is not ignored.

The auditor should understand the entity's customer base for its various lines of business, its credit and collection policies, how changes in its lines of business and its credit and collection policies are managed, and their impact on inherent risk. A significant element of inherent risk in auditing receivables and revenues is that they may be overstated through improper revenue recognition methods, caused by recording transactions that did not occur, improper cutoffs, or the inappropriate selection of accounting principles—errors or fraud related to the *existence/occurrence, cutoff,* and *valuation* objectives.

Some revenue recognition issues involve accounting for unusual or complex transactions; others involve improper accounting for routine transactions. The auditor should be concerned about revenue transactions that the entity has entered into that include contingent sales agreements, customer rights of return, repurchase agreements, or other "special" terms that call into question the collectibility of the receivable and even the entity's legal rights to the revenue. The possibility of misapplication of generally accepted accounting principles (GAAP) increases when those revenue transactions are with related parties. The auditor should pay particular attention to large or unusual transactions recorded at or near year-end. Figure 18.2 provides examples of improper and unusual revenue transactions.

Many audit failures have been caused by the auditor not sufficiently understanding the nature of the entity's business and the substance of unusual or complex trans-

Figure 18.1   Audit Objectives for Revenue Cycle Accounts

Completeness	Accounts receivable represent all amounts owed to the entity at the balance sheet date arising from revenue transactions.
	Unearned revenues represent all amounts received for which shipments have not been made and services have not been rendered.
	All shipments made and services rendered during the period covered by the financial statements and all returns and allowances are reflected in the financial statements.
Accuracy	Revenue transactions are based on correct prices and quantities and are accurately computed and classified in the appropriate general ledger and accounts receivable subsidiary ledger accounts.
	The accounts receivable subsidiary ledger is mathematically correct and agrees with the general ledger.
	Unearned revenues represent the correct amount received for shipments to be made or services to be rendered in future periods.
Existence/Occurrence	Recorded accounts receivable represent amounts owed to the entity at the balance sheet date.
	Unearned revenues represent amounts received by the entity for future sales transactions.
	Recorded revenue transactions represent goods actually shipped or services actually rendered during the period covered by the financial statements.
Cutoff	Revenue transactions, cash receipts, and returns and allowances are recorded in the proper period.
Valuation/Allocation	Accounts receivable are stated at net realizable value (that is, net of appropriate allowances for uncollectible accounts, discounts, returns, and similar items).
	Revenue is recognized only when appropriate accounting recognition and measurement criteria are met.
Rights and Obligations	Accounts receivable are legal rights of the entity at the balance sheet date (that is, customer accounts that have been sold or factored are excluded from the accounts receivable balance).
	Unearned revenues reflect amounts received for which the entity is obligated to provide future shipments or services.
Presentation and Disclosure	Accounts receivable, revenues, unearned revenues, and related accounts are properly described and classified in the financial statements.
	Accounts receivable pledged as collateral are properly disclosed.
	Concentrations of credit risk arising from accounts receivable are properly disclosed.

actions it enters into. Detecting, understanding, and evaluating those transactions is particularly difficult if management deliberately withholds information from the auditor. Understanding the entity's industry and the transactions it enters into is an essential first step in determining the proper accounting for and reporting of these types of transactions.

Figure 18.2   Examples of Improper and Unusual Revenue Transactions

---

- Sales in which the customer's obligation to pay for the merchandise/service depends on:
  –receipt of financing from another (third) party;
  –resale to another (third) party (i.e., consignment sale);
  –fulfillment by the seller of material unsatisfied conditions; or
  –final acceptance by the customer following an evaluation period.

- Sales in which substantial uncertainty exists about either collectibility or the seller's ability to comply with performance guarantees.

- Sales that require substantial continuing vendor involvement after delivery of merchandise (e.g., software sales requiring installation, debugging, extensive modifications, other significant support commitments, etc.).

- Shipments to and held by a freight forwarder pending return to the company for required customer modifications.

- Sales of merchandise shipped in advance of the scheduled shipment date without the customer's agreement or assent.

- Pre-invoicing of goods in process of being assembled or invoicing prior to, or in the absence of, actual shipment.

- Shipments made after the end of the period (i.e., books kept open to record revenue for products shipped after period end).

- Transactions involving the application of the percentage-of-completion method of accounting. (There have been instances in which overly optimistic percentage-of-completion estimates were used, reasonably dependable estimates could not be made or a historical basis for making estimates did not exist.)

- Sales not based on actual (firm) orders to buy.

- Shipments made on cancelled or duplicate orders.

- Shipments made to a warehouse or other intermediary location without the instruction of the customer.

- Sales billed to customers prior to delivery and held by the seller ("bill and hold" or "ship in place" sales). (There have been cases in which payments have not been required for a lengthy period and cases in which delivery to the customer never took place.)

- Sales on terms that do not comply with the company's normal policies.

- Transactions with related parties.

- Barter transactions.

- Significant, unusual transactions near year-end.

- Partial shipments when the portion not shipped is a critical component of the product (e.g., shipment of computer peripherals without the central processing unit).

Source: Practice Alert No. 95-1, *Revenue Recognition Issues,* issued by the Professional Issues Task Force of the SEC Practice Section of the AICPA Division for CPA Firms, January 1995. Copyright © 1995 by the American Institute of Certified Public Accountants, Inc.

18.3 ANALYTICAL PROCEDURES

Analytical procedures may be particularly useful in identifying unusual transactions and balances that may represent specific risks relevant to auditing receivables and revenues. Analytical procedures frequently highlight relationships between accounts and risks not otherwise apparent during the risk assessment phase of an audit. As discussed in Chapter 8, analytical procedures are a required part of planning; their use at an early stage in an audit often results in more informed strategy decisions. The procedures discussed in this section, however, also can be applied in the substantive testing and final review stages of an audit.

Scanning the detailed list of accounts receivable and investigating significant unusual items, such as credit balances, are analytical procedures that are particularly relevant to auditing receivables and revenues. Scanning the accounts receivable listing can be an effective means of identifying unusual audit risks associated with receivables and revenues. For example, the existence of credit balances in accounts receivable may indicate the failure to record sales transactions or the misapplication of cash receipts; unusually small balances may indicate inaccurate billing procedures. When deciding whether to scan the detailed listing of accounts receivable, the auditor considers whether credit balances could be significant and the entity's internal control, particularly monitoring controls. For example, if the credit manager or others scrutinize the listing on a regular basis, the likelihood of unusual balances may be decreased.

The auditor typically performs analytical procedures specifically directed at revenue for two reasons. First, understanding how revenue is generated and the major influences on revenue provides a better understanding of the entity's business and an improved opportunity to identify matters pertinent to the audit strategy. Second, analytical procedures can provide evidence that neither revenue nor the resulting accounts receivable are materially misstated, which should affect the extent to which substantive tests of details of those accounts are performed. In addition, since revenue often bears a direct relationship to other items in the income statement, once the auditor has sufficient evidence—from analytical procedures or other tests—that revenue has not been misstated, revenue can be used as a variable in developing other analytical procedures, for example, a gross profit analysis.

Analytical procedures are helpful in providing assurance that sales and accounts receivable are neither understated nor overstated. Tests of the reasonableness of recorded sales and analytical comparisons of accounts and relationships may provide assurance about completeness of sales and receivables. In addition, if there are no or only a few instances where perpetual inventory quantities must be reduced as a result of the physical count, this indicates that all sales (and, presumably, the related receivables) were recorded. In these circumstances, the risk of unbilled or unrecorded receivables may be sufficiently reduced so that analytical procedures may provide most of the additional assurance needed about the completeness of recorded revenues and receivables.

The design of revenue-based analytical procedures may take different forms and can vary from one industry to another or among entities. Analytical procedures, for example, can indicate trends in sales, returns, and collections of receivables that may assist the auditor in identifying possible financial statement misstatements. A common revenue analytical procedure is the comparison of sales for a quarter with the previous quarter and with the same quarter of the previous year. The explanation of variances derived from this procedure, built up over a period of years, provides the auditor with a valuable source of information upon which to develop expectations. Studies have shown that in using this method of obtaining data, an effective procedure is to update revenue data through part of the current year (such as three quarters) and develop an estimate (an expectation) for the remainder of the year. These studies also show that the analytical procedure is more effective if an expectation is developed in advance and compared with the recorded amount of revenue, as opposed to analyzing the recorded revenue in the absence of a previously developed expectation.

Relationships among revenue accounts and between revenue and other accounts also can be reviewed and compared with those of prior periods and those anticipated in budgets or forecasts. Those relationships include the ratios of accounts receivable to sales, various allowance accounts to sales, and cost of goods sold to sales. It also may be useful to relate sales of certain product lines to one another. Ratios, and the balances in the accounts themselves, can be compared from month to month and with the corresponding period of the prior year. Trends and fluctuations (seasonal and other) should be noted and explanations sought for unusual patterns. Sometimes sales can be related to units sold or produced and the trend of an "average unit price" examined.

In some industries, effective revenue-based analytical procedures include reasonableness tests based on operating data. For example, a hotel's room revenue can be compared with an expectation derived from multiplying estimated occupancy by the average room rate. The hotel's occupancy rate can also be compared with industry occupancy data. Similarly, the retail industry uses sales per square foot as a benchmark. For a particular location, a calculation of sales per square foot that appears to be too high or too low may indicate a potential misstatement of recorded revenue. To cite other examples, the auditor can usually substantiate dues, tuition, and similar revenues rather easily by comparing receipts with membership or registration records. Sometimes the substantiation can be done on an overall basis: number of members or students multiplied by annual dues or tuition. In the services industries, there is often independently generated statistical data, such as numbers of rooms cleaned, beds made, meals served, and the like, that can be used to corroborate service revenue.

The auditor should consider management's performance of analytical procedures as part of its monitoring controls. The auditor may obtain an understanding of the procedures performed by management and consider using their results to supplement his or her own analytical procedures. Management typically reviews various internal sales and budgetary reports and data, such as the following:

- Actual sales compared with historical trends and budgets or forecasts
- Actual gross margins compared with historical trends and budgets
- Actual write-offs, credit memos, and other noncash reductions of receivables compared with budgets and historical information
- Accounts receivable aging
- Unfilled sales commitments

Management's review of reports such as these may help identify material misstatements in the processing of sales transactions. For example, investigation of significant differences between reported sales and budgeted and historical sales could identify incomplete updating of shipments to the general ledger.

The way management responds to the auditor's inquiries resulting from analytical procedures also may give some indication of the quality of the entity's control environment. For example, prompt, logical, and meaningful answers to questions about fluctuations in gross margins from the prior to the current year would provide some indication, in the absence of evidence to the contrary, that the entity's management is "in control" and that the accounting system and control activities appear to be functioning as intended. Analytical procedures, however, also may indicate trends, even in well-controlled entities, that may lead the auditor to extend substantive tests; for example, trends that raise questions about the collectibility of accounts receivable.

18.4   SUBSTANTIVE TESTS OF DETAILS

Substantive tests of details applied to revenue cycle accounts are directed principally to accounts receivable. The assurance needed for income statement accounts usually is obtained from a combination of tests of controls, analytical procedures, and substantive tests of details applied to balance sheet accounts. The remainder of this section describes substantive tests of details that could be performed with respect to accounts receivable. The tests that are actually selected, as well as their timing and extent, will depend on the auditor's assessment of control risk, as well as his or her identification of inherent risks and assessment of materiality. It would be highly unusual for all of the procedures described in the remainder of this section to be applied in a particular audit.

(a)   Control Risk Assessment and the Nature, Timing, and Extent of Substantive Tests

The auditor is required to obtain an understanding of the entity's internal control sufficient to plan the audit. The auditor also should assess control risk for the assertions embodied in the financial statements—in this case, the assertions related to receivables and revenue. The understanding and assessment are used to identify the types of misstatements that might occur and the controls that may reduce them, and, based on that information, to determine the nature, timing, and extent of substantive tests. Obtaining the understanding and assessing control risk for accounts in the revenue cycle are discussed in Chapter 13.

The auditor achieves the audit objectives related to revenue cycle accounts by performing substantive tests or a combination of substantive tests and tests of controls. The auditor frequently tests controls to obtain evidence of their effective operation as a basis for reducing the assurance needed from substantive tests directed at the completeness, accuracy, and existence/occurrence audit objectives. Chapter 13 presents an illustration of the strategy decisions an auditor might make in auditing the revenue cycle.

Before performing substantive tests on accounts receivable and related valuation accounts, the auditor needs assurance that the detailed list of accounts receivable in the subsidiary ledger (usually referred to as the accounts receivable trial balance) contains all sales transactions that remain uncollected at year-end and reconciles to the related control account in the general ledger. If the results of tests of controls provide sufficient evidence about the completeness of the trial balance, substantive tests of the completeness of accounts receivable generally will be limited to analytical procedures. Also, when control risk has been assessed at low, or when the accounting system is reliable because secure packaged software is used, it should not be necessary to test the mathematical accuracy of the detailed list. The auditor should consider the possibility, however, that information from the detailed list could be suppressed, either during the report writing process or subsequent to its printing.

Normally, entity personnel routinely compare the general ledger control account balance with the total of individual accounts receivable, investigate discrepancies between the two, and make appropriate adjustments. The auditor should trace the totals on the trial balance to the general ledger and determine that all reconciling items are appropriate. Reconciling items may indicate potential material misstatements resulting from, among other things, cutoff problems, unusual transactions, or breakdowns in internal control.

The auditor also may examine support for adjustments made throughout the year in reconciling detailed accounts receivable to the control account to obtain assurance that those adjustments are properly authorized and are not fictitious. In deciding whether to perform this test, the auditor should consider whether there is appropriate division of duties and whether differences disclosed by the reconciliation of the subsidiary ledger to the control account are investigated appropriately and corrected on a timely basis. If these procedures are not in effect, or if there is a lack of division of duties between individuals responsible for initiating and recording sales and related transactions, receiving and recording cash receipts, maintaining the accounting records, and reconciling the detailed records to the control account, the risk of misstatement is increased and the auditor should perform this test. In some entities, however, entries to the control account may be numerous, and it may not be necessary to evaluate all of them. The auditor should focus attention on those entries arising from the reconciliation process, by reviewing the client's reconciliations, identifying unusual adjustments, reviewing authorizations (when appropriate), and tracing the adjustments to supporting documentation and the general ledger.

If the auditor has assessed control risk for revenues and receivables at low for the audit objectives of completeness, accuracy, and existence/occurrence, substantive tests addressing those objectives may be limited to analytical procedures, except possibly for the need to confirm some accounts receivable. No detailed tests of transactions supporting the completeness and accuracy of revenue transactions need be performed, and, as discussed below, it may not be necessary to send confirmations to customers to achieve the existence objective.

If the auditor has assessed control risk for revenues and receivables below the maximum for the audit objectives of completeness, accuracy, and existence/occurrence, it will be necessary to confirm accounts receivable (existence/occurrence). It also will be necessary to obtain evidence that management has implemented procedures to ensure that all shipments and services are invoiced (completeness) and that those procedures have operated as prescribed. The auditor also will need assurance from substantive tests that the amounts on invoices underlying the detailed listing of accounts receivable are mathematically accurate and priced correctly (accuracy). That assurance can come from tests of the supporting documentation for those invoices, from confirming accounts receivable, from analytical procedures, or from a combination of those tests. When control risk has been assessed below the maximum, the auditor should establish the extent of testing so as to obtain a moderate to low level of assurance that the audit objectives of completeness, accuracy, and existence/occurrence are achieved. The auditor also should consider whether evidence obtained from tests directed at one audit objective is relevant to other audit objectives as well. For example, the confirmation of accounts receivable is directed toward the existence/occurrence audit objective, but also provides some evidence about accuracy.

In the unlikely event that the auditor has assessed control risk for revenues and receivables at maximum for the audit objectives of completeness, accuracy, and existence/occurrence, it will be necessary, in addition to confirming accounts receivable (existence/occurrence), to obtain evidence that management has implemented procedures to ensure that all shipments and services are invoiced and recorded (completeness) and that those procedures have operated as prescribed. (In the absence of such procedures, the auditor should consider tracing the details of shipping documents to the related invoices and related accounting records.) The auditor also should test the supporting documentation for invoices underlying the detailed listing of accounts receivable to determine that the amounts on the invoices are mathematically accurate and priced correctly (accuracy). When control risk has been assessed at maximum, the auditor should establish the extent of testing so as to obtain a high level of assurance that the audit objectives of completeness, accuracy, and existence/occurrence are achieved. As mentioned earlier, the auditor also should consider whether evidence obtained from tests directed at one audit objective is relevant to other audit objectives as well.

The auditor usually performs substantive tests of details to achieve the cutoff objective because entities frequently do not establish control activities designed to achieve a proper cutoff throughout the year. In some situations, however, control activities may address cutoff, or management may implement special controls at year-end, which the auditor may decide to test. Also, controls designed to ensure completeness of input and update may be effective in ensuring that transactions are recorded in the proper period. For example, the design of the accounting system itself may reduce control risk for cutoff. Nevertheless, it is usually more efficient for the auditor to perform substantive tests of details to achieve the cutoff objective. In determining the extent of those tests, the auditor should consider such factors as control activities directed at cutoff, the assessment of control risk, the type and frequency of cutoff errors found in prior years, and the assurance expected from other related substantive tests, such as tests for existence and completeness.

There may be satisfactory controls, which the auditor may have tested, with respect to the data underlying the estimates that are related to the valuation objective. The entity's control activities generally do not address management's subjective judgments and estimates, however, nor do they generally address the audit objectives of rights and obligations and presentation and disclosure. The risks of material misstatements associated with these objectives are, therefore, normally higher than the risks related to other audit objectives. The auditor generally achieves those audit objectives by performing substantive tests, supplemented by evidence obtained through identifying inherent risks and assessing the entity's internal control. For example, the auditor's awareness of an economic decline in an industry in which the entity has many customers may cause concern about the valuation audit objective for accounts receivable.

(i) Early Substantive Testing.   When control risk is assessed below the maximum or at low, the auditor often performs substantive tests related to completeness, accuracy, and existence/occurrence at an interim date—before the balance sheet date—and then performs various procedures to support the existence, completeness, and accuracy of customer balances at the balance sheet date. In those circumstances, a major concern is whether control activities will ensure the existence and accuracy of customer balances at the balance sheet date. In this regard, the auditor considers the effectiveness of controls relating to authorization for the shipment of goods and performance of services; prices and terms of sale; division of duties between the sales, invoicing, cash receipts, and shipping functions; reconciliation of detailed records to the accounts receivable control account; and errors found through confirmations and other procedures in prior years.

At the balance sheet date, the auditor considers the results of testing at the early date and the risk of material misstatement for the completeness, accuracy, and existence/occurrence objectives in the intervening period—the period between the date of the early substantive testing and the balance sheet date. This may involve inquiry, observation, and, when appropriate, examination of evidence of the operation of the information system and related control activities during the intervening period, examining evidence of the operation of special procedures established for the intervening period, or performing substantive tests of the details of transactions in the intervening period.

Even when control risk is assessed at maximum, the auditor may be able to obtain sufficient evidence to provide a reasonable basis for extending audit conclusions from an interim date to the balance sheet date. Performing early substantive testing is not likely to be efficient when control risk is at maximum, however, because of the extent of testing that likely will be required in the intervening period.

(b) Cutoff Tests of Shipments and Collections

Cutoff tests are intended to ascertain that all transactions have been recorded in the proper period. Improper cutoffs may result from errors or from intentional recording of sales in an improper period because of bonus arrangements, sales quotas, royalty agreements, income tax considerations, or other reasons. In the absence of controls directed toward cutoff, the sooner accounts are closed after year-end, the greater the likelihood that there will be unrecorded sales invoices. Thus, examining files of unmatched shipping documents and unrecorded invoices, the sales journal, the cash receipts journal, and other relevant records for a period after year-end is a common auditing procedure.

If the basic transaction documents are in numerical sequence, the auditor can note the number of the last shipping report and the last sales invoice recorded and also compare the date of the last entry in the cash receipts journal with the date those receipts were deposited in the bank. The auditor may examine perpetual inventory records, the sales journal, and the listing of unmatched shipping documents for evidence that goods sold and shipped before year-end have been removed from inventory and that sales and accounts receivable have been recognized. The auditor should apply the same procedures to obtain assurance that sales, shipments, and cash receipts applicable to the following year were not recorded in the year under audit. If the basic transaction documents are not prenumbered, it may be necessary to examine supporting documents for transactions with near year-end dates and large amounts. To obtain sufficient evidence that the cutoff was properly made, the documents would be selected from the sales journal, cash receipts journal, perpetual inventory records, and shipping records both before and after the cutoff date. Similar procedures should be applied to returns and claims from customers to determine that they are recorded in the proper period.

Cutoff tests of shipments are usually coordinated with the auditor's observation of the physical inventory count. When physical inventories are taken at a date other than year-end, it is important that shipment cutoff tests be made at the same date, as well as at year end. Cutoff errors are compounded when perpetual inventory records and the general ledger inventory account are adjusted for differences between book and physical amounts (see Chapter 19, "Auditing Inventories and Cost of Sales").

(c) Confirming Accounts Receivable

One of the most widely used substantive tests for determining the existence and, to a lesser extent, the accuracy of accounts receivable is direct confirmation by the auditor with customers, commonly referred to as "confirmation." Confirmation by the auditor of individual sales transactions or accounts receivable balances by direct communication with customers is one of only a few procedures that are designated as generally accepted auditing procedures.

Confirmation of receivables has been required by the profession since 1939, when Statement on Auditing Procedure No. 1 was adopted by the AICPA as a direct result of the McKesson & Robbins fraud. In the intervening years, confirmation of receivables has been the subject of extensive authoritative and other professional pronouncements, the most recent of which is Statement on Auditing Standards (SAS) No. 67, The Confirmation Process (AU Section 330) SAS No. 67 —the first authoritative professional pronouncement to provide guidance on using and evaluating confirmations generally retains the designation of confirmation of accounts receivable generally accepted auditing procedure; states that there is a presumption that in the absence of a limited number of circumstances (noted below), the auditor will confirmations of receivables; and requires documentation of a decision not to confirmations. Confirmations are not required if accounts receivable are im if the confirmation procedure would not be effective, or if the auditor's assessment of control risk is low, and this assessment, taken in conjunction with any inherent risks and evidence expected to be provided by analytical procedures substantive tests of details, is sufficient to reduce audit risk to an acceptable for applicable financial statement assertions. The assertion most by confirmation is existence, so an auditor would not be able to justify not confirming receivables if the assessed level of risk was other than low for the existence assertion.

As noted in Chapter 15, however, while confirmation produces evidence about the existence and (to some extent) the accuracy of accounts receivable, other procedures are needed to establish their collectibility. The most direct evidence regarding collectibility of receivables is subsequent customer payments. Those payments also provide reliable evidence about existence and accuracy, because it is highly unlikely that a customer will pay a balance that is not owed or is overstated. Only the accuracy of the date the sale took place is not substantiated by a subsequent customer payment. Confirmation may, however, reveal the improper application of customer payments to older, disputed invoices, perhaps to conceal an unfavorable aging schedule. In practice, the auditor often uses a combination of confirmation, examination of subsequent customer payments, and other procedures to test the existence and accuracy of accounts receivable.

The auditor must make a decision regarding the confirmation date. If there was no deadline for the entity to issue financial statements, confirming at year-end would be most effective. In today's business environment, however, there is usually a deadline, and accordingly the auditor often confirms receivables (and performs many other auditing procedures as well) at an earlier date. If early substantive testing is done, the auditor will need evidence that the risk of material misstatement occurring is sufficiently low during the intervening period, as discussed above and in Chapter 15.

Substantive tests sometimes provide evidence about control activities, if errors or fraud disclosed by those tests are investigated and found to result from a control deficiency or breakdown. Specifically, confirmation procedures may provide evidence of the effectiveness of internal control with respect to the revenue cycle. Many auditors consider receivable confirmations as a source of evidence about the effectiveness of the controls as well as a source of evidence about the existence and accuracy of accounts receivable.

(d) Confirmation Procedures

The auditor should compare the detailed list of accounts receivable with the general ledger account, should test the mathematical accuracy of the trial balance (which often is done using audit software) or test computer controls for evidence that the trial balance is mathematically accurate, and should determine that reconciling items between the control account and subsidiary ledger are appropriate.

(i) Selecting Accounts for Confirmation.   Depending on the audit strategy and the results of tests of controls, the auditor should decide whether to confirm all or only part of the accounts and, if the latter, the basis for selecting them. In determining the sample size and selecting the specific accounts to be confirmed, the auditor should follow the guidance provided in Chapters 15 and 16. (Guidance for extrapolating confirmation results to a conclusion about the total accounts receivable balance, where appropriate, is also presented in Chapter 16.) The selection should exclude debtors from whom replies to requests for confirmation cannot reasonably be expected, such as certain governmental agencies, foreign concerns, and some large industrial and commercial entities that use an open invoice or decentralized accounts payable processing system that makes confirmation impracticable.

The auditor should consider confirming accounts that appear unusual. Accounts with zero or credit balances also should be considered for confirmation. A credit balance suggests the possibility of an incorrect entry, especially if controls are not effective.

Accounts and notes receivable that have been discounted or pledged should be confirmed with lenders, so that any unrecorded liability or contingency will be brought to the auditor's attention. This procedure helps the auditor achieve the audit objectives of rights and obligations, and presentation and disclosure. If receivables have been discounted or pledged, confirming them with lenders does not preclude an auditor from requesting confirmation from the debtors as well, particularly if the entity is responsible for collections. (See Chapter 25 for a discussion of confirming contingent liabilities with financial institutions.)

To preserve the integrity of the confirmation process, the auditor should control the selection, preparation, mailing, and return of the confirmations. If management does not wish statements or confirmation requests to be sent to certain debtors, the auditor should be satisfied that there is an adequate reason before agreeing to omit them. If such accounts are material, the auditor should use alternative procedures (discussed below) to test their existence and accuracy. If the results of the alternative procedures are satisfactory, management's request not to confirm directly would not be considered a scope limitation (discussed in Chapter 28).

Replies to confirmation requests are sometimes difficult to obtain if a debtor's accounts payable processing is decentralized or uses an open invoice system, which is increasingly the case in a number of governmental departments and agencies as well as many large industrial and commercial entities. In an open invoice system, the debtor processes invoices individually and does not summarize them by vendor. Therefore, the debtor can identify whether or not an individual invoice has been paid, but cannot determine the total amount owed to any particular vendor. In many instances, however, such difficulties can be overcome, for example, by supplying details of the balance to be confirmed, such as invoice dates, numbers (including customer purchase order number), and amounts, or by confirming specific transactions rather than an account balance. In addition, respondents that cannot confirm balances of installment loans may be able to confirm the original loan amounts, the amount of their payments, and other terms of their loans.

The auditor often can make effective use of an entity's computerized accounts receivable system. Sample selection can be programmed and the files of detail accounts searched automatically, lists and analyses can be prepared, and the confirmation requests can be printed. General purpose computer programs designed to aid in the confirmation process are available and are discussed in Chapter 15.

(ii) Designing the Confirmation Request.   Confirmation requests may be made by means of sticker or rubber stamp affixed to customer statements or by a separate letter; the letter form may be used if statements are not ordinarily sent at the time confirmations are requested or if statements are not mailed to customers. It should be noted that the request is worded as coming from the entity. Even though the auditor drafts the request, prepares it, and selects the accounts, all confirmation requests (and any subsequent correspondence) should be made in the entity's name because the relationship exists between the entity and the customer (or the entity and the creditor, when liabilities are being confirmed).

(iii) Positive vs. Negative Forms.   There are two types of confirmation request— the positive form and the negative form. The positive form either states the information about which confirmation is requested and asks the respondent to indicate agreement or nonagreement, or requests the recipient to fill in the information. (The type of positive form in which the recipient is asked to fill in the information, called a blank form, may provide greater assurance about the information confirmed, but also may generate lower response rates.) The negative form of confirmation requests a response only if the recipient disagrees with the information provided.

Positive confirmations may be used for all accounts, a sample of accounts, or selected accounts, such as those with larger balances, those representing unusual or isolated transactions, or others for which an auditor needs greater assurance of existence and accuracy. The positive form of confirmation is called for if there are indications that a substantial number of accounts may be in dispute or inaccurate or if the individual receivable balances are unusually large or arise from sales to a few major customers. Obtaining and evaluating positive confirmations constitutes a substantive test of details of transactions and balances, and provides direct evidence about one or more financial statement assertions.

Experience has shown that a form of positive request, whether made by letter or a sticker affixed to the statement, that requires a minimum of effort on the part of the recipient produces more responses. The letter form, illustrated in Figure 18.3, is designed so that when the amount shown agrees with the debtor's records, the individual need only sign in the space provided and return the letter in the envelope enclosed with the request.

If statements of accounts prepared by the entity are to be used for positive confirmation requests, they may be sent in duplicate, with an appropriately worded request (often imprinted on the statement) that the debtor acknowledge the correctness of the statement by returning the duplicate, duly signed, directly to the auditor. A variation is the use of a monthly statement in which the balance and the name of the debtor appear in two places, separated by perforations. One part may be torn off, signed by the debtor, and returned directly to the auditor. Replies to positive requests may be facilitated if the auditor furnishes the details of the individual items included in the balances, usually by providing a copy of the detailed customer statement. That may be particularly helpful if the debtor's accounting system does not readily permit identification of account balances.

Positive confirmations provide audit evidence only when responses are received. Second requests, and sometimes third requests by registered mail, should be sent to parties from whom replies were not received. SAS No. 67 requires the auditor to apply alternative procedures to accounts for which responses to positive confirmation requests were not received, unless considering them as 100 percent misstatements would not affect the auditor's decision about the receivables balance and provided that he or she has not identified unusual qualitative factors or systematic attributes related to the nonresponses. The particular alternative procedures to be applied would vary with the circumstances and might include (a) comparing subsequent remittances credited to accounts receivable with remittance advices or other documents

Figure 18.3   Positive Confirmation Letter

[Name and Address of Debtor]

Dear Sirs:

In accordance with the request of our auditors [name and address of auditors], we ask that you kindly confirm to them your indebtedness to us at [date] which, according to our records, amounted to [amount].

If the amount shown is in agreement with your records, please so indicate by signing in the space provided below and return this letter directly to our auditors in the enclosed envelope. Your prompt compliance will facilitate the examination of our accounts.

If the amount is not in agreement with your records, please inform our auditors directly of the amount shown by your records, with full details of differences.

Remittances should not be sent to the auditors.

Very truly yours,

[Name of Entity]

The above stated amount is correct as of [date].

_____

[Debtor of Entity]

_____

[Title or Position]

---

to determine that payments relate to the account balance and (b) examining shipping documents, copies of sales invoices, customer sales orders, and other relevant correspondence supporting the unpaid portion of the account balance. Such procedures also would be appropriate when confirmation of account balances would be ineffective because of the likelihood that debtors would not respond or likely would not take care in developing their responses.

The negative form of confirmation is most frequently used for entities with a large number of low-value balances, as may occur in certain specialized industries, for example, financial institutions, utilities, and retail operations. Unreturned negative confirmations do not provide explicit evidence that the intended party received the request and determined that the information was correct. Accordingly, negative confirmations should be used only when the risk of material misstatement has been assessed as low. Unreturned negative confirmations can, however, provide indirect evidence supporting a belief that receivables are not materially misstated, if the auditor has sent out a large number of confirmations drawn from a large population and none or only a few are returned. Evidence provided by nonresponses to negative confirmation requests selected from a large population is similar to evidence from an analytical procedure that does not indicate a departure from the auditor's expectations.

The auditor should consider the audit effect of information contained on returned negative confirmations, which may provide direct evidence about financial statement assertions. Negative confirmations may generate responses indicating misstatements, especially if such misstatements are widespread in a large population and if requests are sent to a large proportion of the population. In those circumstances, negative confirmations may identify an unanticipated problem and thereby assist the auditor in assessing conclusions already reached and in determining whether additional evidence is needed. In this respect also, negative confirmations function similarly to analytical procedures used as substantive tests.

Negative confirmation requests may be returned by the post office with the notation "addressee unknown." Such requests may raise questions about the existence of the third parties and thus point out an unexpected problem. The auditor should follow up on such situations to determine the underlying cause, in much the same way as he or she would respond to an analytical procedure that indicated a problem where none was expected.

Because negative confirmations do not provide evidence that unreturned requests were received and reviewed by the intended parties, misstatements detected by evaluating returned confirmations cannot be projected to the entire population and cannot be used as a basis for determining the dollar amount of misstatement in the account as a whole. Responses indicating misstatements require the performance of additional tests of details to determine the nature and amount of misstatement in the account.

(iv) Processing Confirmation Requests.   After selecting the accounts for confirmation, the auditor should observe the following procedures in processing the requests, regardless of their form:

- Names, addresses, and amounts shown on statements of accounts selected for confirmation or on the confirmation letter should be compared with the debtors' accounts and reviewed for reasonableness.

- The auditor should maintain control over confirmations until they are mailed; this does not preclude obtaining assistance from appropriate entity personnel, under the auditor's supervision.

- Requests for confirmation, together with postage paid return envelopes addressed to the auditor, should be mailed in envelopes showing the auditor's address as the return address. If management objects to using the auditor's address, returns may be addressed to the entity at a post office box controlled by the auditor; the post office should be directed to forward mail to the auditor after the box is surrendered.

- All requests should be mailed by the auditor; the entity's mail room may be used for mechanical processing under the control of the auditor, who should deposit the completed requests at the post office.

- Undelivered requests returned by the post office should be investigated, corrected addresses obtained, and the requests remailed by the auditor.

The purpose of those procedures is not so much to protect against possible fraud on the part of the entity (although that possibility is clearly implied) as to preserve the integrity of the confirmation procedure. The audit evidence obtained from confirmation is less reliable if there is the possibility of accidental or purposeful interference with direct communication with debtors; the auditor should take all reasonable steps to minimize that possibility.

Respondents may use nontraditional media in replying to confirmation requests, such as electronic or facsimile responses, or may respond orally. In these circumstances, the auditor may need additional evidence to support a conclusion that the confirmations are reliable. For example, it is difficult to determine the source of facsimile responses; therefore, the auditor should consider steps such as calling the purported respondent to substantiate the source and contents of the confirmation and requesting the respondent to mail the original confirmation directly to the auditor. Oral confirmations should be documented in the working papers; if the information confirmed orally is significant, the auditor should request that it be provided directly to him or her in writing.

It is impracticable for an auditor to determine the genuineness or authenticity of signatures on replies to confirmation requests. If there are appropriate controls, particularly with respect to the acceptance of customer orders, and if the auditor has considered the reasonableness of the addresses on the confirmations, signature authenticity usually is not a concern. If, however, the auditor has determined that the risk of material misstatement in a particular customer account is high, an officer of the debtor should be asked to sign the confirmation reply. The auditor may then wish to communicate with that officer by telephone or other means to corroborate the authenticity of the confirmation.

(v) Evaluating the Results of Confirmation Procedures.   Exceptions disclosed by the confirmation process should be carefully scrutinized. The auditor should evaluate all exceptions and decide whether they represent isolated situations or indicate a pattern of disputed sales or payments involving more than one customer. Debtors' responses indicating that payments were sent but not recorded by the entity may signal misappropriations of cash and "lapping" of receivables (discussed below). If so, the situation should be thoroughly investigated to determine the amount of the misappropriation, and receivables should be reduced (since the entity received the payment) and a loss recorded in the amount of the misappropriation. In addition, the auditor should bring the matter to management's attention and should consider its effect on other auditing procedures.

In many instances, differences reported by debtors on accounts receivable confirmation requests do not have audit significance. Those differences are generally the result of either payments in transit at the confirmation date or delays in recording goods received by the debtor. The auditor should corroborate debtor assertions involving those kinds of differences by examining the cash receipts records and remittance advices for debtor payments received after the confirmation date to determine that the payments were for receivables existing at the confirmation date, and by examining bills of lading or other evidence of shipment. (Differences that are appropriately reconciled in this manner are not exceptions.) Other reported exceptions, usually involving small amounts, may result from disputes over allowances, discounts, shipping charges, or returned merchandise. These exceptions are usually neither material in amount nor indicative of serious deficiencies in internal control. After the auditor has made a copy or other record for control purposes, investigation of replies may be turned over to a responsible employee whose regular responsibilities do not involve cash, receivables, or credit functions. The auditor should review the employee's findings and, if considered necessary, perform additional procedures to substantiate the balance.

The auditor should evaluate all the evidence provided by the confirmations and any alternative procedures performed and determine whether sufficient evidence has been obtained for all applicable audit objectives. In making that evaluation, the auditor should consider the reliability of the evidence gathered; the nature of any exceptions, including their implications (both quantitative and qualitative); the evidence provided by other procedures; and whether additional evidence is needed. If the evidence provided by confirmations and other procedures is not sufficient, the auditor should request additional confirmations or extend other tests of details or analytical procedures.

(e)   Lapping

Lapping is a way of concealing a cash shortage by manipulating credits to the accounts receivable subsidiary ledger. To accomplish lapping, an employee must have access to incoming cash receipts, the cash receipts records, and the detailed accounts receivable records. Accordingly, if there is not appropriate segregation of duties, the auditor should consider the possibility of lapping.

Lapping is perpetrated in the following manner: An employee receives a customer's payment on an account receivable and misappropriates the cash, recording neither the cash receipt nor the reduction of the customer's account. Subsequent cash collections from another customer are later credited to the customer from whom the original collection was misappropriated, to prevent that customer's paid account from appearing as outstanding for more than a short time. Lapping is made easier when customers make periodic payments on their accounts, particularly in round amounts, rather than pay for specific invoices. Even if customers designate that remittances apply to specific invoices, the difference in amount between the second customer's remittance and the amount misappropriated from the first customer's remittance can be concealed by depositing additional cash if the subsequent payment is smaller or by making an additional credit to the first account, or even another account, if the subsequent payment is larger. Obviously, the lapping must continue indefinitely or until the cash shortage is replenished. Accordingly, the auditor should inquire about employees who are rarely absent from work or who do not take vacations that would require someone else to perform their work.

Control activities that should prevent or detect lapping include proper segregation of duties, required vacations for personnel responsible for handling cash and posting credits to customer accounts, mailing monthly statements to customers that show all activity in the accounts by dates, and reviewing entries to customers' accounts for unusual amounts.

The confirmation process, including careful attention to explanations for delays in posting remittances when a customer states that the amount to be confirmed was paid before the confirmation date, should reveal lapping if it is present. If lapping is strongly suspected, the auditor may want to perform additional procedures. For example, comparing customer remittance advices with credits in the accounts receivable subsidiary ledger, individual amounts on deposit slips with individual amounts posted to the cash receipts records, and individual amounts in the cash receipts records with credits to individual customer accounts (in each case, scrutinizing the dates of the entry or posting) also may uncover lapping. The auditor should be aware, however, of the possibility of altered bank deposit slips and may wish to confirm the accuracy of individual deposit slips with banks.

(f) Tests of Valuation

To achieve the valuation audit objective, the auditor should review the collectibility of receivable balances to determine that the allowance for uncollectible accounts is adequate, that is, that receivables are stated at their net realizable value as of the balance sheet date. Before making the review, the auditor should determine whether the method of estimating the allowance is reasonable and consistent with prior years and, if so, whether any current business or economic conditions might make the method inappropriate in the current year. For example, if estimates of the allowance for uncollectible accounts are based on the historical relationship of write-offs to total sales (percent of sales method), a significant economic downturn may require a revision of the historical percentage. That same circumstance also may make it inappropriate to develop an allowance for uncollectible accounts by applying historical percentages to groupings of an aged trial balance. For example, usually only a small percentage of accounts receivable less than 30 days old become uncollectible; however, a larger percentage of those balances may have to be considered in developing the allowance if the customer mix has changed in a time of economic distress.

(i) Reviewing the Aged Trial Balance.   The usual starting point for an auditor's tests of valuation is an aged trial balance. Entity personnel should prepare periodic aging analyses as a routine procedure; if that is not done, the auditor should ask that one be prepared. The auditor may be able to provide the entity with a general purpose computer program for aging accounts receivable. The auditor should compare the total shown on the analysis with the total receivables in the ledger and should obtain an understanding of how the aging analysis was prepared. If it is produced by a computer software package, the auditor needs to know what options in the software are used. (This may be done during tests of controls.) Depending on the auditor's risk assessment, he or she may need to trace amounts from the aging schedule to supporting documents to establish the reliability of the aging. In deciding whether to test the reliability of the aging, the auditor should consider the reliability of the system generating the aging schedule (for instance, whether secure packaged software is used), the control risk assessment, the reliability of the aging in prior years, and the activities of the credit department and others in scrutinizing the aging.

In reviewing an aging analysis, the most obvious aspect to evaluate is the number and dollar amount of overdue accounts. The auditor should probe more deeply than that, however, and scrutinize a number of accounts closely for evidence that might indicate collectibility problems. The auditor's purpose in inquiring into those matters is not to judge the collectibility of each individual account examined, but to gather evidence that the investigation and evaluation of individual accounts (usually performed by the credit manager) were adequate and that the overall allowance for uncollectible accounts is reasonable.

The auditor should review past-due receivable balances and other unusual balances with the credit manager to obtain information on which to base an opinion regarding their collectibility. Files of correspondence with collection agents and debtors should be examined. Past experience in collecting overdue accounts should be used as a guide in deciding the probable collectibility of current balances. Changes in the number and size of overdue accounts and possible changes in business conditions affecting collectibility should be discussed with the credit manager. As a result of those reviews and discussions, the auditor should understand the basis for the estimate of the allowance for uncollectible accounts and be able to judge whether the allowance is reasonable. Auditing accounting estimates is discussed further in Chapter 15.

(ii) Early Tests of Valuation. Detailed evaluation of the adequacy of the allowance for uncollectible accounts often is carried out at the balance sheet date, since it is at this time that the auditor has the most current information for valuation judgments. In entities where accounts receivable result from routine recurring transactions and where operations are not subject to cyclical variations or other market influences, however, it may be appropriate to make those judgments before the balance sheet date and then update them. In those circumstances, at the balance sheet date, the auditor should evaluate the adequacy of the allowance by reviewing developments in material long overdue, unusual, or disputed accounts; performing analytical procedures; considering any deterioration in the aged list of customer accounts that may have occurred since the early substantive testing date; and considering whether to trace amounts from the aging schedule to supporting documents to determine the reliability of the aging schedule.

(iii) Other Procedures Related to the Valuation Objective. The auditor also should scan revenue and receivable transactions after the balance sheet date, including sales, cash receipts, discounts allowed, rebates, returns, and write-offs. Those transactions—or their absence or an unusual increase or decrease in them—may reveal abnormal conditions affecting valuation at the balance sheet date. Events after the close of the fiscal period are often the best proof of whether the receivable balances at the balance sheet date are actually what they purport to be. Approvals for notes and accounts receivable written off during the year should be examined.

Notes receivable, whether past due or current, may themselves signal doubtful collectibility if they were received for overdue accounts receivable. The origin of notes should be determined because current notes may sometimes represent renewals of matured notes. If usual trade practice is to obtain notes from debtors of poor credit standing, the collectibility of the notes should be considered in the same way as other receivables. The collectibility of notes that collateral has been pledged against may depend on the value of the collateral. If the collectibility of significant collateralized notes is in question, the auditor may find it desirable to have an independent appraiser value the collateral.

The auditor should be particularly attentive to unusual, complex, and large revenue transactions that the entity has entered into, particularly those recorded at or near year-end, to evaluate whether recognition principles have been appropriately and consistently applied. (See the discussion earlier in this chapter.) The auditor also should perform analytical procedures in the overall review stage of the audit, as required by SAS No. 56, *Analytical Procedures* (AU Section 329).

(g) Tests of Rights and Obligations, and Presentation and Disclosure

Receivables from affiliates, directors, officers, and employees should be reviewed to determine that they have been properly authorized and are actually what they purport to be. If loans have been made over a long period of time, past experience often provides evidence of the debtors' intentions. It is good practice to review those receivable accounts even though they appear to have been settled before the balance sheet date, especially to see whether the loans were renewed after the balance sheet date. Receivables that in fact represent advances or loans should be segregated and so described. Receivables are financial instruments, and required disclosures include information about financial instruments that have off-balance sheet risk and with concentrations of credit risk. (Disclosures of financial instruments are considered further in Chapter 26.)

Proper recognition and presentation and disclosure of accounts receivable also require that liens, security interests, and accounts receivable pledged as loan collateral, assigned, or factored be identified. Accordingly, the auditor should review debt and lease agreements; confirmation replies, particularly from financial institutions; and minutes of directors' meetings. The auditor also should inquire of management about those items.

Throughout the audit, the auditor should be alert for transactions or issues that affect the audit objectives of rights and obligations and presentation and disclosure. The auditor considers all evidence related to other audit objectives in determining whether the recorded receivables are the legal rights of the entity and all necessary disclosures have been made. Many of the "other procedures" (described above) used to test valuation also address these audit objectives. In particular, examination of correspondence from third parties and other documentation may provide evidence related to the rights and obligations objective.

(h) Other Substantive Tests

When control risk has been assessed at maximum or below the maximum, the auditor may consider it advisable to test the details of revenue transactions by comparing, on a test basis, billings, shipping documents, and other data with recorded amounts in accounts receivable. Those comparisons help to achieve the completeness and accuracy objectives, and, if made for a period immediately before and after the fiscal year-end, also help determine that a proper sales cutoff was made. Other substantive tests that provide assurance about the completeness of invoicing of goods shipped and recording of goods invoiced include analytical procedures applied to revenue cycle accounts, plus an analysis of the size and direction of adjustments to recorded inventory quantities as a result of the physical inventory count.

The auditor usually examines credit memos issued during a period after the close of the fiscal year to determine that reported sales were not inflated by recording unauthorized sales in one year and issuing credit memos to eliminate them in the next year, and that proper provision was made in the year under audit for any such credit memos and for applicable discounts, returns, and allowances. The auditor should be alert for sales under terms permitting customers to return unsold merchandise.

If the auditor finds that consigned goods are treated as sales and included in receivable balances, with a resulting anticipation of profits, unsold goods in the hands of consignees (which should be confirmed) should be adjusted to the basis of like items in the merchandise inventory and reclassified as inventory. If the goods appear to be salable at an adequate profit margin, related charges, such as freight paid by the consignor, may be added to the inventory costs.

The auditor should read sales contracts with selling agents and other agreements affecting receivables to become aware of matters such as title to accounts receivable, time of billings, method or time of payments, commissions, and special discounts or rebates.

Recorded transactions underlying receivables other than trade accounts—such as debit balances in accounts payable, claims, and advances—should be reviewed; the auditor should note supporting evidence for the transactions. The auditor also should precisely identify the accounts as a basis for determining the extent of testing and for evaluating their collectibility and their classification in the balance sheet. Confirmations should be obtained by direct communication with debtors to the extent considered reasonable and practicable. Although receivables other than trade accounts may not be significant in amount, if they are not subject to adequate controls, they may require relatively more extensive substantive testing than trade receivables.

The auditor should determine that drafts sent for collection are recorded in the accounts, either separately as drafts receivable or included in accounts receivable. The auditor also should inquire of the banks where drafts have been deposited for collection or from which loans or advances on account of foreign shipments have been obtained, to learn whether drafts have been pledged against loans or advances. Drafts in the hands of collection agents should be confirmed and their status determined as of the balance sheet date. Since the auditor cannot always use the usual confirmation procedures to substantiate receivable balances from foreign debtors, the existence of drafts may provide evidence about those balances.

18.5 AUDITING PROCEDURES: SPECIAL CONSIDERATIONS FOR PARTICULAR TYPES OF REVENUES

For the most part, the auditing procedures described so far in this chapter are adaptable to the great variety of circumstances encountered in practice. One auditing procedure may take on greater significance than another, or certain procedures may be used more extensively, but on the whole auditing procedures for many accounts in the revenue cycle are basically similar. Some of the more common revenue sources that require emphasis on particular procedures are the following:

- Cash sales
- Interest, rents, and similar fixed payments for the use of property
- Royalties, production payments, and similar variable revenues
- Gifts and donations
- Deferred income or unearned revenue
- Revenues from long-term contracts

Chapter 21 discusses auditing procedures for income from marketable securities and other investments.

(a) Cash Sales

If cash sales are significant, control activities that address asset safeguarding are especially important. Cash sales are characteristic of relatively small unit value goods, which often are easily converted to cash and at the same time are difficult to keep under strict physical and accounting control. In many situations involving cash sales, segregating duties between access to merchandise and access to cash receipts is difficult, if not impossible, and management often will devise creative controls to compensate for this. Often, those procedures involve bringing the customer into the entity's control system, possibly by creating incentives for the customer to demand a receipt for amounts paid (which is generated only when the sale is recorded), perhaps to qualify for a prize or premium or to support a later merchandise return or exchange. Control over cash after it has been received and recorded is discussed in Chapter 17.

(b) Interest, Rents, and Similar Fixed Payments
for the Use of Property

Revenues from fixed payments usually can be substantiated fairly easily by an overall computation of amounts due and a comparison with amounts recorded. Usually, the entity prepares a list of the properties, loans, and so on, and the related income; the auditor should test the list by examining leases, loan agreements, and similar contractual bases for revenues, noting and evaluating all special terms that have financial statement implications. The auditor also may assess control activities directed at the receipt and recording of revenues, including measures for controlling and accounting for the vacancy rate in rental properties, and should note and evaluate delinquencies and arrearages and their implications for realization of the related assets. Some or all significant loans receivable should be confirmed; the auditor also may wish to confirm leases and similar contractual obligations.

In particular, the auditor will be concerned about audit risk relating to revenue and cash flow from leased assets owned by a lessor. In obtaining an understanding of internal control and assessing control risk relating to leases, the auditor should focus on the completeness and accuracy of recorded revenue. This may require evaluating how management arrived at the salvage value of leased property. For example, if a lessor leases a newly manufactured piece of equipment for a period of ten years, management may be required, depending on the equipment and the terms of the lease, to estimate the value of the equipment at the end of the ten years in order to record revenue from the transaction properly. In this situation, the auditor would need to know how management estimated salvage value and what factors it considered.

The auditor of the lessor also is concerned with the audit objective of existence. Since the leased asset is not on the lessor's premises, the auditor is unable to determine its existence and condition by physical inspection. Most often the auditor will achieve the existence objective by direct confirmation with the lessee and by applying analytical procedures. The auditor should obtain evidence that the accounting classification, measurement, and disclosure requirements for lessors, as specified in Statement of Financial Accounting Standards No. 13 and related pronouncements (Accounting Standards Section L10), have been followed. Lease transactions are discussed in Chapter 22.

(c)   Royalties, Production Payments, and Similar Variable Revenues

Many kinds of revenues are based on a stipulated variable, such as production or sales. Usually, the buyer of a right subject to variable payments for its use is required to report to the seller from time to time the amount of the variable and the computation of the resulting payment. If the amount of revenue is not significant, most entities simply accept the payer's statement after a superficial scrutiny for reasonableness. In that event, the auditor can do much the same, by examining the agreement on which the payment is based, comparing receipts with those of the prior year, and possibly requesting confirmation that all amounts due have been reported and paid. If amounts are significant, contracts usually provide for an independent audit of the accounting for the variable, either by the seller's auditor or by an independent auditor acceptable to the seller. Satisfactory audit reports on the payments ordinarily provide reasonable assurance that the related revenues are complete. Such reports on parts of a financial statement are discussed and illustrated in Chapter 29.

(d)   Gifts and Donations

Accountability for donations can be a problem because they rarely are covered by contract and they lack a delivery of goods or services to provide evidence that the revenue is due. If gifts are received centrally—as in development offices of colleges, hospitals, museums, and similar institutions—reasonably effective control activities can be established: properly supervised opening of mail and recording of receipts; segregation of duties among handling, acknowledging, and recording; and early accountability through means such as issuing prenumbered receipt forms that also serve as documentation for tax purposes. The auditor can test those controls in the same way as those over cash receipts in a for-profit entity.

If donations are received by numerous volunteers—as in many agencies financed by "annual drives"—internal control may be ineffective if management feels it is impolitic or impossible to ask volunteers to conform to otherwise appropriate controls. In those cases, a scope limitation exists (see the discussion in Chapter 28). The auditor should note the scope limitation in the audit report and state that he or she cannot express an opinion that all donations were recorded, and that the report covers only recorded receipts.

It is possible, however, to establish adequate controls for volunteer solicitations, as the methods used in many United Way drives have proven. Solicitation forms are prepared in advance, and their issuance to volunteers, processing, and return are controlled. The possibility of abuse is thus minimized, though not eliminated. When those controls are in effect, the auditor can test them and usually obtain reasonable assurance that gift revenue is complete.

(e) Deferred Income or Unearned Revenue

Sometimes the accounting system provides trial balances of detailed items supporting deferred income or unearned revenue balances, for example, students' advance payments of tuition. In those cases, the auditor can obtain the necessary assurance by reviewing the trial balance and comparing it with the control account, and examining individual items.

More often, transactions flowing through unearned revenue accounts are not controlled in detail. The input to the account may be on one basis—for example, ticket sales or subscription receipts—and the relief of the account may be on a different basis—a statistical measure of service delivered such as revenue per passenger mile or per issue delivered. In those cases, the entity makes a periodic analysis or "inventory" of the account balance. That inventory consists of scrutinizing the detail of underlying data, for example, of subscription records or of transportation tickets subsequently "lifted." It often can be an extremely arduous and time-consuming effort, comparable in many ways to physically counting inventories. For that reason, the date selected is usually based on practicality and convenience, and seldom coincides with the fiscal year-end.

The auditor's observation of and participation in the analysis should be similar to the observation and testing of physical inventory procedures. The auditor should observe and test the entity's procedures and evaluate the results. If controls appear adequate and the resulting adjustment of the account balance is small enough to indicate that the method of relieving the account is reasonably accurate, the auditor can be satisfied with applying analytical procedures to activity and balances between the test date and year-end.

Often, management believes that an unearned revenue "inventory" is impossible or prohibitively expensive. For a transit company, for example, the unearned revenue balance represents tokens in the hands of the public, and there is no way—short of changing the token—to identify those bought before a given date. If management cannot or will not substantiate the balance, neither can the auditor. The auditor can, nevertheless, usually obtain reasonable assurance that the balance is fairly stated in relation to the financial statements as a whole, by paying particular attention to tests of controls that provide evidence that all revenue commitments sold—tickets, tokens, subscriptions, and the like—are controlled and promptly recorded and that amounts transferred from unearned to earned revenue are accurately and consistently computed and well controlled, and by considering the relationship between the balance and the pattern of sales and service activity and investigating changes in the ratio. As long as transfers to revenue for estimates of lost and unused items are made on a conservative basis, the auditor can conclude that the amount is biased toward overstating the liability for service to be rendered.

(f) Revenues from Long-Term Contracts

Audit evidence for revenues from long-term contracts is obtained from confirmations and the various means management uses to monitor and control fulfillment of contract terms and the allocation of revenues to fiscal periods. Management should provide the auditor with an analysis of each contract and subsequent amendments. In many instances, an analysis prepared for management purposes will suffice, but in others an analysis will have to be prepared especially for audit purposes. Depending on the size and significance of the contracts, the auditor can compare the analysis with underlying data, including the contract itself, and review the accounting for costs incurred to date, the estimates of cost to complete each contract, and the amounts of revenue recorded in the period under audit. Such reviews should be done with operating personnel responsible for performance, as well as accounting and financial personnel.

Revenues from long-term contracts are usually accounted for by the percentage-of-completion method. The auditor's primary objective is to obtain evidence about the reasonableness of management's estimate of the degree of completion of the contract. That estimate may be made by relating costs incurred to date to the estimated total cost to complete the contract (the cost-to-cost method), by obtaining an architect's or engineer's estimate of the state of completion, or by physical measurement (usually accompanied by the auditor's observation) of the stage of completion, such as the number of production units completed. Further discussion of auditing accounting estimates is presented in Chapter 15.

After reviewing the entity's documentation supporting the estimated total cost to complete a project, the auditor should compare the estimate with the contract price. If the estimated total cost to satisfy contract requirements exceeds the total contract price, a loss usually should be recognized. The auditor also should review the financial statement presentation, including disclosures, for conformity with the recommendations for long-term contracts found in the latest edition of the AICPA audit and accounting guide, *Construction Contractors*.

It also is usually necessary to test other accounts related to long-term contracts, such as progress billings and advance payments. Accordingly, the auditor should perform, as appropriate in the circumstances, the procedures related to billings, collections, and receivables that were discussed earlier in this chapter. Further discussion of auditing long-term contracts is presented in Chapter 35.

18.6 SPECIAL AUDITING CONSIDERATIONS FOR NOTES AND OTHER RECEIVABLES

Notes and other receivables often result from transactions that do not occur in the ordinary course of business, for example, sales of assets or lines of business, lessors' net investment in direct financing and sales-type leases, and advances to directors, officers, and employees. Notes receivable also may be received for overdue accounts receivable or as renewals of matured notes.

The auditor usually performs substantive tests of details for assurance about notes and other receivable balances, rather than tests of controls, because these accounts usually consist of a low volume of transactions and often arise from unusual events. If the auditor judges that the risk of misstatement from these transactions could be material to the financial statements, either individually or in the aggregate, evidence about their accuracy (including the accuracy of interest received during the period and accrued interest receivable at the end of the period) should be obtained by analyzing the accounts in detail and examining documentation to support either the current year's activity or the year-end balance, depending on whether the account balance was carried forward from the prior year or turned over within the period. The auditor also usually performs substantive tests related to the existence of notes and other receivables. Audit assurance can be obtained by confirming individual accounts, by examining supporting documentation, or by examining cash collections subsequent to the balance sheet date. When the account balance is a note receivable, confirmation is the preferred procedure because it may highlight changes in the terms of the note and often can be performed more efficiently than the other procedures. Tests for valuation of notes receivable were discussed earlier in this chapter.

19

Auditing Inventories and Cost of Sales

Inventories and cost of sales, which can be considered part of the inventory cycle, are often among the most significant and difficult areas in auditing. Service-based entities as well as manufacturers, retailers, and wholesalers maintain significant amounts of inventory. The auditor's primary objective in this area is to gather evidence to support management's assertions about the existence, ownership, pricing, and valuation of inventory.

This chapter is written primarily from the perspective of a manufacturing entity. Much of the discussion, however, applies to other types of entities as well, like retailers and wholesalers that purchase and hold inventory for future sale, and various types of service organizations that consume inventory in the process of generating revenues.

The inventory cycle deals with the production, storage, and shipment of inventory. The term "inventory" is used to refer to items held for sale, in process of production, or to be converted or consumed in the production of goods or services. Inventory is usually characterized as either merchandise, raw materials, work in process, or finished goods. Merchandise refers to goods acquired for resale by dealers, who incur little or no additional cost preparing them for resale. Raw materials are items or commodities converted or consumed in the production process. Work in process represents products in intermediate stages of production. Finished goods represent the end products of the manufacturing process. Both finished goods and work in process normally have material, labor, and overhead components. The classification of inventory depends on the entity holding it and the nature of its operations. For example, coil steel is a finished product to a steel mill, but a raw material to an appliance manufacturer.

Cost of sales (also called cost of goods sold) includes all costs directly associated with purchasing and producing goods sold. Material costs assignable to inventory include merchandise, raw materials, and component parts used in the production process or purchased for resale, net of purchase returns, discounts, and other allowances. All direct costs incurred in the purchasing process, like inbound transportation (freight in), duties and taxes, and warehousing, are also included. In complex procurement systems that are expensive to operate, a separate purchasing overhead account may be maintained and included in material costs.

Other costs associated with production include direct labor and related costs, like employee benefits, and manufacturing overhead. Manufacturing overhead comprises costs that cannot be directly assigned to specific units of production but nonetheless are directly associated with the production process, for example, indirect labor, supervision, occupancy costs, utilities, repairs and maintenance, and depreciation. Operating supplies and other materials that do not become parts of products, like oils for lubricating machinery, normally are also included in overhead.

Cost of sales may include additional items such as losses from writing inventories down to market value, royalties paid for the right to manufacture a product or use a patented process or equipment, and amortization of preproduction and tooling costs. Cost of sales often is reduced by sales of by-products and the disposal value of scrap. Estimated costs of warranties, guarantees, and other commitments for future expenditures usually are included in cost of sales, although sometimes they are included in other expense categories. (The term "operating expenses" is sometimes used to describe costs and expenses incurred in generating revenues from the sale of services.)

19.1 AUDIT OBJECTIVES

Specific audit objectives applicable to inventories and cost of sales are described in Figure 19.1.

Figure 19.1 Audit Objectives for Inventory and Cost of Sales

Completeness	Inventories represent all raw materials, work in process, and finished goods that the entity owns, including those on hand, in transit, or on the premises of others. All shipments (and returns) of goods during the period covered by the financial statements are reflected in cost of sales.
Accuracy	The detailed perpetual inventory records are mathematically correct and agree with the general ledger inventory control account. Costs associated with inventories have been properly classified and accumulated. Cost of sales is based on correct costs and quantities, is properly summarized and posted to the cost of sales and inventory control accounts, and, if appropriate, is credited in the perpetual inventory records.
Existence/Occurrence	Recorded inventories physically exist in salable condition and represent property held for sale in the ordinary course of business. Recorded cost of sales represents goods shipped during the period covered by the financial statements.
Cutoff	Production costs incurred and charged to work in process, transfers to finished goods, and cost of sales (and returns) are recorded in the proper period.
Valuation/Allocation	Costs associated with inventory and cost of sales are determined and accumulated using generally accepted accounting principles consistently applied. Inventories (including slow-moving and obsolete items) are stated at not more than their net realizable value.
Rights and Obligations	The entity has legal title or ownership rights to the inventory; inventory excludes goods that are the property of others or have been billed to customers.
Presentation and Disclosure	Inventories and cost of sales are properly described and classified in the financial statements. All encumbrances against inventory are adequately disclosed.

19.2 TYPICAL INVENTORY TRANSACTIONS AND CONTROLS

There are essentially two major kinds of cost accounting systems—a job order system, in which goods are made in the quantities and to the specifications called for by a particular order, and a process system, in which goods are produced repetitively according to a schedule. Among the transactions typically found in the inventory cycle of either system are issuing raw materials for use in production, allocating labor and overhead costs, computing piecework and incentive pay, receiving materials directly into production, processing customers' materials, and transferring completed products to inventory. The inventory cycle also includes controls over storing raw materials, component parts, and finished goods, and over shipping goods produced.

There are numerous combinations and sequences that may occur in connection with producing goods for sale and storing raw materials and finished goods. The operating processes, accounting procedures, and control activities associated with production appear in many forms because of the technological diversity of modern manufacturing operations. The discussion in this chapter of typical transactions, accounting systems, and control activities provides only a generalized suggestion of the kinds of conditions that may be encountered in the three major types of transactions in the inventory cycle:

- Producing goods for sale
- Storing raw materials (including component parts) and finished goods
- Shipping goods produced

(a) Producing Goods for Sale

The process of producing goods for sale generally includes the following activities:

- Identifying production needs, and planning and scheduling production
- Producing goods
- Accounting for production costs
- Accounting for work in process

In considering the accounting system through which inventory transactions are processed and the control activities applied to them, the auditor is interested primarily in procedures to ensure that incurred production costs are authorized and are completely and accurately recorded and accumulated; that is, that the transaction processing and file maintenance control objectives are met. Those control objectives are closely related to the audit objectives of completeness, accuracy, and existence of accounts that are part of the inventory cycle—most significantly, raw materials, work-in-process, and finished goods inventories, and cost of sales. Other aspects of internal control, while not directly related to those audit objectives, also may be of interest to the auditor. For example, the fact that production is carefully planned to meet anticipated sales may provide evidence the auditor can use in evaluating the adequacy of the allowance for obsolete inventory, which affects the valuation audit objective relating to inventory.

Controls over the production process are important to management for operational reasons also, because errors in production and inventory data can result in wrong decisions. For example, inaccurate inventory records can result in poor purchasing or production planning decisions. Overstocking can lead to higher inventory carrying costs and a greater risk of obsolescence; understocking can lead to stock-outs, production downtime, and lost sales. Effective procedures to control inventory levels also reduce the probability of errors in accounting data and other data used by management in running the business, thereby contributing to operating effectiveness.

(i) Identifying Production Needs, and Planning and Scheduling Production. In a process system that produces finished goods inventory, identifying production needs may be an integral part of the system and may be accomplished by evaluating existing inventory levels in relation to sales projections. The need may be signaled by a periodic matching of physical or recorded inventory levels against a predetermined minimum. Computerized inventory records offer the opportunity for sophisticated forecasting and modeling computations.

After a need has been identified, a production requisition is initiated, which, after review and approval, becomes the authorization to produce. Product specifications and time and cost estimates usually are developed as part of the production planning and scheduling process. In particular, cost estimates give management a basis for informed scrutiny of actual costs. The result of planning and scheduling is a production order: the detailed execution instructions listing the operations and the desired results.

Poor product specifications (as well as poor inspection procedures) can cause rework, unsalable goods, or returned merchandise. Poor estimates and poor scheduling can give rise to excess cost in inventory, especially overruns on contracts. An auditor who understands the role of planning and scheduling in the production process will be able to assess the inherent and control risks associated with inventory and cost of sales more effectively.

(ii) Producing Goods.   Raw materials may be moved into the production process on the basis of a document (like an authorized bill of materials supporting an approved production order, an approved materials requisition, or a report of production orders scheduled to start) or electronically when an authorized production order is entered into the system. In either event, an appropriately authorized document or file should be created to account for the movement of materials, for both operational and accounting purposes. Often these documents or files may serve as authorization to update the perpetual inventory records for issues of materials to production. The documents, which are usually prenumbered, are accounted for or open files are reviewed periodically as part of procedures to ascertain that all transactions have been processed and recorded. If material is ordered directly for production, the production order, sometimes supported by an accompanying purchase order, alerts those concerned to the expected delivery date.

Setup time for machines used in the production process may or may not be accounted for separately, depending on management's informational needs. Tools and dies are sometimes charged as direct costs, particularly in job order production systems in which tools are likely to have been designed especially for a particular order and sometimes are paid for by the customer. Most often, though, tools and dies are capitalized because they can be reused on other work or production runs at other times. Usually, documents are prepared to record these processing steps: a time report or job ticket for the setup time and an issues slip or production order for the tool requirements. The documents are then reviewed and approved by supervisory personnel.

Measuring production quantities is a problem in a great many operations. Both production managers and cost accountants want accurate production counts, but in many cases the large number of units, the inaccuracy of measuring devices, and the problems of distinguishing between acceptable and unacceptable units make it difficult or uneconomical to measure production precisely.

Production often is inspected at several stages and levels. Operators inspect for signs of problems as they complete their work; supervisors may inspect output on a test basis. There may be specialists in quality control, or it may be necessary to employ the special skills and equipment of a laboratory to test the quality of production. Control activities related to measuring and inspecting production output provide evidence of the salability of the inventory and the level of warranty costs that may be incurred after the sale.

(iii) Accounting for Production Costs.

The accounting aspects of the inventory cycle are manifested in the entity's cost accounting system. Cost accounting systems employed by manufacturing concerns vary widely and range from very simple systems, which account for ending inventory balances annually, to very well-developed standard cost systems, which account for all materials handling, production in process, and completed production, and generate analyses of related variances from predetermined standard costs. A well-developed cost system should provide the details of transfers between raw materials and work in process and between work in process and finished goods, and of the distribution and accumulation of material, labor, and overhead costs by cost centers, job orders, or production runs.

Depending on the structure of the cost accounting system, raw materials may be charged to a job order or to a materials usage account in a process system. If a standard cost system is used, materials may be charged to production at standard quantities and prices, with resulting variances between standard and actual costs subsequently allocated to inventory and cost of sales.

Issues of raw materials may be recorded from a report of production orders scheduled to start, which is compared with production orders reported as actually started, or from raw materials storeroom issue slips whose numerical sequence is accounted for. Occasionally, especially in computerized systems, raw materials usage may be measured by periodically—usually monthly—pricing the ending raw materials inventory and adjusting the account balance through a charge to production.

The total cost of production payroll is accounted for through the purchasing cycle (covered in Chapter 14). Payroll costs are distributed to detailed cost accounts from payroll records or production reports. The aggregate labor cost distributed to production or other expense accounts is reconciled to a control total from the payroll records to ensure that all labor costs have been allocated to either job order or departmental expense accounts. The system may provide detailed accounts for idle time, waiting time, setup time, cleanup time, rework time, and so on. When a standard cost system is used, production labor is computed at standard rates and hours and, by comparison with actual costs, labor rate and efficiency variances are produced.

Many different kinds of costs enter into overhead and they are accumulated in descriptive accounts as charges originate. The basis for charging overhead to job orders, departments, or work-in-process inventory is usually some measure of activity, such as direct labor hours or dollars. There are likely to be different overhead rates for different departments, based on accounting or engineering studies. Entries to record overhead absorption may be originated as a separate accounting procedure, but most often they are integrated with entries for the data—payroll or materials usage—on which the absorption rate is based.

In a standard cost system, overhead may be charged through several intermediate accounts before eventually ending up in work in process, finished goods, and cost of sales to produce price, efficiency, and volume variances for management purposes. Overabsorbed overhead is removed from inventories to prevent stating them in excess of actual cost; underabsorbed overhead is generally allocated to inventories, unless it arises from costs that are written off as incurred. Some entities establish and allocate separate overheads for materials handling (purchasing, receiving, inspecting, and storing), as distinguished from manufacturing overhead, when those costs are significant.

Inventory standing data includes descriptive information about purchased and manufactured items and standard costs. The integrity of that data is achieved by limiting the ability to make changes to the inventory master file and standard costs to appropriate purchasing and manufacturing personnel.

Production rejected as a result of inspection is reported for cost accounting purposes. Sometimes the time spent reworking faulty items to meet specifications also is reported separately. Minimizing the amount of scrap and rework is an important operational objective; identifying and accounting for the cost of scrap and rework help achieve that objective. Once scrap has been created, it is subject to custodial controls and disposed of in a way that maximizes cost recovery and thereby minimizes production costs. Cost accounting is improved if scrap is identified with the operations or products creating it, but that is often impossible.

(iv) Accounting for Work in Process. Movement of production between departments during the manufacturing process is reported for operational purposes, but may or may not be recorded for accounting purposes. Work in process is credited and finished goods are charged when production is complete, on the basis of completed production orders, inspection reports, or finished goods receiving tickets that have been authorized. In addition, most entities have procedures for documenting evidence of inspection according to quality control standards.

Physical inventory counts of work in process are often difficult because a great many items in many different stages of completion must be identified. Goods may be scattered or in hoppers, vats, or pipelines where access, observation, or measurement is difficult, or they may be in the hands of outside processors. Adequate production management, however, requires that someone know the location and stage of completion of each item. The more difficult controlling production is, the more essential it is to have a means of ensuring that excess or "lost" costs do not build up in the work-in-process account.

(b) Storing Raw Materials and Finished Goods

Raw materials and component parts are accounted for and controlled from the time of their receipt through their use in the manufacturing process. Accomplishing this includes protecting the inventory by restricting access to authorized personnel, issuing materials to production only upon proper authorization, crediting the perpetual inventory records for issuances to production, and periodically counting materials on hand and agreeing the results to those records. Receiving raw materials and updating perpetual inventory records are covered in Chapter 14. Issuing raw materials to production was discussed in Section 19.2(a)(ii).

After production has been completed and has passed final inspection, it goes either to a warehouse or to a storage area to await shipment to customers. The notice to production management may be a copy of the completed production order, or it may be an inspection report or a warehouse receiving report. The completeness of charges to finished goods is controlled by accounting for the numerical sequence of production or receiving reports.

The primary control activities relating to inventories in most entities are physical counts of quantities on hand and periodic reconciliations to perpetual inventory records or general ledger balances. Perpetual inventory records of varying degrees of sophistication are found in practice. Some entities maintain perpetual records that reflect both inventory quantities and costs; others keep perpetual records in quantities only. Entities with simple operations and relatively few inventory items frequently do not maintain perpetual records at all.

Physical inventories are part of effective internal control. In entities with effective controls, a physical inventory is taken at least annually and sometimes more often, depending on the type of business, the nature and value of the inventory, and the effectiveness of internal control. The term "physical inventory" includes not only physically counting items, but also translating the quantities into dollars, summarizing the dollars, and comparing the results with the accounts. A complete count of the inventory of an entity, plant, or department may be made at one time while operations are suspended (sometimes referred to as a wall-to-wall inventory) or, if perpetual inventory records are maintained and other conditions are satisfactory, periodic counts of selected items may be made at various times during the year (known as a cycle count inventory). In the latter instance, all items in the inventory generally are counted at least once each year. Sometimes both types of inventory-taking are used. Since the two methods involve somewhat different techniques, they are discussed separately below.

(i) Inventories Taken at One Time.   Taking a complete inventory requires the cooperation of production, accounting, and storekeeping personnel since it often involves suspending or significantly reducing production, shipping, and receiving operations, and physically rearranging inventory to facilitate counting. Often an inventory committee is organized, consisting of management representatives of production departments, the controller's office, the general or cost accounting department, the shipping and receiving departments, the internal audit department, and the auditors. It is usually desirable for someone from production management to assume responsibility for rearranging the inventory and making available and training employees who are familiar with it to assist in the physical inventory procedures.

Inventory that has been marked with a scannable bar code can be counted using electronic scanners; this has become a common practice for retailers. In this environment, the inventory counts can be summarized and transferred to other records more quickly and accurately than is possible using nonelectronic means.

In many cases, entities use their own employees to count inventory because they are familiar with the items and locations, and they cannot perform their usual work routine while a count is in process. Because of the difficulty in counting the wide assortment of merchandise in retail stores, however, third-party counting services are frequently used. These vendors provide the advantage of large numbers of counters, and often use the most current information technology to capture the count electronically. Such services also can complete the count of most stores in four to six hours, thus minimizing the period in which the store may be closed to customers.

A physical inventory may be taken during the vacation period for factory employees, when production is stopped for some other reason, at a time when inventories are at a low level, at year-end, or at a convenient month-end prior to the balance sheet date. Inventory-taking before the balance sheet date is advisable, however, only if there are adequate controls to safeguard the inventory and to control and document inventory movements between the physical inventory and balance sheet dates.

The counts may be made by production, clerical, or accounting personnel; storekeepers; internal auditors; or an outside inventory service. Count teams often include at least one individual from the production department. Such an arrangement provides an added degree of control while utilizing the production department employees' familiarity with the inventory. However the initial counting is organized, the counts are verified. Some entities have a complete recount made by independent teams. Others assign production supervisors or internal auditors to make random test counts. These test counts are documented to provide adequate evidence of their performance and to establish responsibility for them.

An almost invariable requirement for a good physical inventory is preparing a written program in advance. An effective program includes instructions about how to:

1. Physically arrange the inventory in a way that simplifies the counts
2. Identify and describe the inventory properly, including stage of completion and condition, when appropriate
3. Segregate or properly identify slow-moving, obsolete, or damaged goods
4. Identify and list inventory belonging to others
5. Numerically control inventory tags or sheets
6. Record and verify individual counts
7. Obtain a proper cutoff of receipts, shipments, and interdepartmental movements, and the related documentation
8. Determine and list goods in the hands of others
9. Correct errors discovered as a result of the counts

In addition to instructions for controlling and recording the inventory, the program should include instructions to the accounting department for summarizing quantities, costing (pricing), extending (multiplying quantity by price), and summarizing the priced inventory. To ensure that the book-to-physical adjustment is computed accurately, the program should include reconciling the perpetual records to the general ledger as of the date of the physical inventory. Special procedures may be required for consignments in or out, goods in transit, and goods in public warehouses or at branches. Adequate supervision helps to ensure that procedures for arranging and counting the inventory, pricing, and summarizing the counts are properly followed.

The mechanics of counting vary. Seldom, if ever, can all individual items in an inventory be seen and counted; often they are in the packages or cartons they were purchased or are to be shipped in, or are located in bins or stockpiles in large numbers that cannot be physically weighed or counted. General practice is to count a reasonable number of items; some packages are opened and some items inspected, particularly if there are any unusual circumstances.

Differences between physical and recorded inventories are investigated and the possibility of leakage or pilferage needs to be considered. The records may be right and the count wrong; significant adjustments are not made without a thorough investigation.

(ii) Cycle Counts.   The inventory counting process can be disruptive to an entity. It often requires the cessation of normal business activities during the count because the movement of items during the count can affect its accuracy and because the entity's employees often are used to perform the count. To minimize the business disruption, cycle counts can be used. A cycle count involves the counting of a portion of inventory on a continuous basis. Over the course of a year, each item in inventory is subjected to a count at least once. In order to use cycle count procedures, an entity must have reliable controls to achieve a good cutoff on receipts and shipments. Without this, differences between the book and physical inventories can result from the timing between physical changes in the quantities of inventory and the recording of those changes in the perpetual inventory records.

Cycle counts may be made if there are adequate perpetual inventory records and controls over physical inventory movements and cutoff. Procedures used in making periodic counts differ from those for inventories taken at one time. Rather than large numbers of production and other personnel rearranging and counting all the inventory in a plant, periodic counts usually are made by relatively small groups of employees who are independent of the accounting function and who soon become expert at counting inventories.

Cycle count results are reported to accounting personnel and compared with the perpetual inventory records. Discrepancies between them are identified, investigated, and resolved. Discrepancies may result from improper physical counts, clerical errors, cutoff problems, and improper inputting of transactions. Identifying and correcting the causes of discrepancies are important aspects of a cycle counting system. Procedures to ensure the accuracy of cycle counts are similar to those used in wall-to-wall counts. When periodic counts are made and found to be reliable, the perpetual records may serve as the equivalent of a complete physical inventory and are priced, extended, and summarized for comparison with general ledger accounts at or near year-end.

(iii) Inventories in Public Warehouses.   Control activities generally include a preliminary investigation and continuing evaluation of the performance of the custodian of a public warehouse. Statement on Auditing Standards (SAS) No. 1, as amended by SAS No. 43 (AU Section 901.26-.27), suggests the following:

Consideration of the business reputation and financial standing of the warehouseman.

Inspection of the physical facilities.

Inquiries as to the warehouseman's internal controls and whether the warehouseman holds goods for his own account.

Inquiries as to type and adequacy of the warehouseman's insurance.

Inquiries as to government or other licensing and bonding requirements and the nature, extent, and results of any inspection by government or other agencies.

Review of the warehouseman's financial statements and related reports of independent auditors.

Review and update [of] the information developed from the investigation described above.

Physical counts (or test counts) of the goods, wherever practicable and reasonable (may not be practicable in the case of fungible goods).

Reconcilement of quantities shown on statements received from the warehouseman with the owner's records.

(iv) Other Inventories Not on the Premises.   Other inventories not on the premises normally include inventories on consignment, in the hands of processors or suppliers, and at branches. Those classifications of inventory are carried in separate accounts supported by perpetual records. Control activities may include review of monthly inventory and activity reports, confirmation, and periodic physical counts. Controls over receipts and shipments are similar to those over inventory on the premises, even though receipts and shipments may be in memorandum form only. To avoid possible duplication, special attention is given to goods in transit.

(v) Inventories Belonging to Others.   Many entities receive material purchased by their customers, process it in various ways, and hold it pending further instructions. All inventory belonging to others needs to be clearly identified and physically segregated to avoid erroneously including it in the inventory counts. If the amount is significant and the activity frequent, perpetual records are maintained. Records of the property of others generally are maintained carefully, particularly if the items are similar to or commingled with inventory the entity owns. The items also are counted to establish accountability to the owner.

(vi) Items Charged Off, But Physically on Hand.   Frequently, certain types of supplies, such as small tools, are charged to expense as purchased or classified as prepaid expenses. Those items are kept under physical protection; unissued items are subject to requisitioning procedures similar to those for other inventories. Items of doubtful value written off, but on hand, are segregated and protected until they are disposed of. Scrap and defective items that can be utilized in some manner or sold as seconds are subject to similar controls. Periodic physical inventories of such items are taken.

(c)   Shipping Goods Produced

When finished goods are shipped to customers, the transfer of costs from the finished goods account to cost of sales (if the detailed perpetual records reflect both inventory quantities and costs) is based on executed shipping orders. The process of executing orders and recording shipments and related control activities are described in Chapter 13. As discussed there, the complete and accurate recording of accounts receivable and sales is ensured by requiring appropriate supporting documentation before executed shipping orders are input to the sales transaction file. Simultaneously inputting those orders to the cost of sales transaction file (if perpetual records reflect both inventory quantities and costs) ensures the complete recording of charges to cost of sales and the reduction of finished goods inventory. Periodically, the detailed perpetual inventory records are adjusted to agree with physical counts and are costed (if only unit records are kept) and aggregated, and any difference between their total and the control account balance is charged to cost of sales. Significant or recurring differences are investigated to determine their causes and corrective action is taken as necessary.

19.3   DETERMINING THE AUDIT STRATEGY

The audit strategy for inventories and cost of sales is based primarily on the auditor's identification of inherent risks and assessment of control risk related to specific audit objectives, and on efficiency considerations. The auditor achieves the audit objectives discussed earlier by performing substantive tests or a combination of substantive tests and tests of controls.

The auditor frequently tests an entity's control activities to obtain evidence of their effective operation as a basis for significantly reducing the assurance needed from substantive tests directed at the accuracy objective. The existence/occurrence objective is achieved principally through observing the entity's inventory counting procedures, and the completeness objective is achieved by ascertaining that the count is complete and that all items counted are included in the detailed inventory listing. The cutoff objective for cost of sales typically is achieved concurrently with the cutoff objective for sales, as described in Chapter 18. The auditor generally achieves the remaining audit objectives (including cutoff of goods received) by performing substantive tests, supplemented by the evidence obtained through identifying the entity's inherent risks and assessing the other components of internal control. For example, the auditor's awareness of an economic decline in the industry may cause concern about the salability of inventory and hence its valuation.

The underlying data supporting inventory valuation is derived mainly from the purchasing cycle, described in Chapter 14. If tests of controls for purchase and payroll transactions produce evidence that the related accounting data is reliable, it can be relied on for inventory valuation purposes as well, often with little additional testing. This is particularly true if tests of controls in the purchasing cycle are planned and performed with the inventory cycle audit objectives in mind as well. For example, tests of controls of payroll can be expanded easily to include the distribution of labor costs to specific production lots or units in the perpetual inventory records. This may provide evidence about the accuracy of unit costs reflected in the perpetual inventory records as a basis for pricing the inventory.

(a)   Inherent Risk Factors and Materiality

As discussed in Part 2 of this book, the auditor obtains or updates information about the entity's business and industry as a basis for identifying inherent risks and assessing control risk. The audit risks associated with inventories vary based on the nature of an entity's inventory and its materiality to the financial statements. For example, there is a high level of inherent risk associated with inventories like precious metals or gems that have relatively high value and can be easily converted to cash. Accordingly, such inventories require control activities that are commensurate with that risk. Or, in estimating net realizable value, there is a higher level of risk associated with a product that must meet very strict technical standards or composition requirements than with a commodity that is generally acceptable to many potential users. Other factors that might create inherent risks include the kinds of judgments that enter into the inventory valuation (e.g., judgments about inventory obsolescence); the susceptibility of major products to technological obsolescence, spoilage, or changes in demand; and the availability of materials critical to the production process, the number of vendors able to supply such materials, the price stability of the materials, and the ability of the entity to pass along price increases to its customers.

(b)   Analytical Procedures

Analytical procedures often highlight relationships between accounts and reveal risks not otherwise apparent during the risk assessment phase of the audit. As discussed in Chapter 8, analytical procedures are a required part of audit planning. Their use at an early stage in the audit often results in more informed strategy decisions.

Analytical procedures can, for example, indicate trends that may help the auditor assess risk. Such trends may involve:

- The relationship among the components of production cost
- Production usage and price variances
- Finished goods inventory turnover (the ratio of cost of sales to average finished goods inventory)

The auditor should review those relationships and compare them with those of prior periods and those anticipated in budgets or forecasts. The ratios and the account balances themselves often are compared from month to month and with the corresponding period of the prior year. The auditor should note trends and fluctuations (seasonal and other) and seek explanations for unusual patterns. These analytical procedures may indicate areas that should be inquired about further, and may indicate the need to modify planned substantive tests of details.

Management typically reviews and analyzes key performance indicators to monitor inventory transactions and balances, and the auditor should consider using those analyses to supplement his or her own analytical procedures. Those performance indicators may include various production and inventory reports, like the following:

- Actual production and inventory levels in relation to historical trends and budgets or forecasts
- Material, labor, and overhead standard cost variances
- Actual gross margins compared with historical trends and budgets
- Trends in inventory turnover ratios
- Write-offs of excess, obsolete, slow-moving, and otherwise unsalable inventory and other write-downs compared with budgets and historical data
- Trends in inventory valuation and obsolescence write-offs

Those procedures may help identify material misstatements in processing or recording production costs or cost of sales. For example, investigating significant differences between reported and budgeted production costs could identify incomplete recording of production costs in the general ledger.

The way management responds to the auditor's inquiries resulting from analytical procedures may give some indication of the quality of the control environment. For example, prompt, logical, and meaningful answers to questions about fluctuations in inventory turnover ratios from the prior to the current year would provide some indication, in the absence of evidence to the contrary, that management is "in control" and that the accounting procedures and control activities appear to be functioning as intended. Analytical procedures, however, also may indicate trends, even in well-controlled entities, that may lead the auditor to extend substantive tests; for example, trends that raise questions about the realizability of recorded inventory values. Analytical procedures performed as substantive tests are discussed later in this chapter.

(c) Assessment of Control Risk

The auditor is required, at a minimum, to obtain an understanding of the entity's internal control sufficient to plan the audit. This understanding, together with the auditor's evaluation of the effectiveness of the design of controls, is used to identify the types of misstatements that might occur and the risk of their occurring, and to design substantive tests. The understanding is obtained or updated by considering previous experience with the entity, reviewing prior-year audit results, interviewing entity personnel, observing personnel as they perform their duties, reviewing entity-prepared descriptions of accounting procedures and control activities, and inspecting documents and records.

In addition to information regarding the control environment, other entity-level components of internal control, and how transactions are processed, the auditor should consider the cost accounting system, how well it reflects the actual production process, and how it reports the production costs incurred, the application of overhead, and the transfer of production costs to finished goods inventory and cost of sales; the accounting methods used to value inventory; and current-year production cost variances from standards or budgets. The auditor also should obtain an understanding of control activities applied to producing and shipping goods and storing raw materials and finished goods inventories, and how duties are segregated in performing those activities.

In the course of obtaining the understanding of internal control, the auditor will have obtained evidence to support a preliminary assessment of the extent to which controls have been properly designed and are operating effectively. That evidence ordinarily would enable the auditor to assess control risk below the maximum or at low for one or more audit objectives. For example, when inquiring about management's review of production reports (a monitoring control), the auditor also may observe the performance of the review or examine reports or documents that provide evidence of the review. If operating effectively, management's review provides some evidence with respect to the completeness and accuracy of costs charged to production. The auditor considers the level of detail reviewed and whether the individual performing the review would be likely to detect a material misstatement.

(d) Performing Tests of Controls

The auditor may seek additional evidence of the effectiveness of control activities to support an assessment of control risk at low if he or she believes that such evidence is likely to be available and efficient to obtain. If so, the auditor usually would perform tests of controls directed at specific audit objectives—commonly, completeness, accuracy, and existence/occurrence of inventory, production costs, and cost of sales—as a basis for restricting the nature and extent of substantive testing.

Whether to perform tests of controls in the inventory cycle should be determined separately for producing and storing goods, for each segment of the inventory (raw materials, work in process, and finished goods), and for the price and quantity components of inventory values. For example, the auditor may decide to obtain assurance about the quantity of items on hand by observing and testing the physical count of the items. The auditor may decide, however, that controls over pricing the inventory appear to be effective enough to warrant testing them and that it would be efficient to do so.

Although audit strategy decisions always must be tailored to specific circumstances, it is possible to make some general observations about what conditions might lead the auditor to either perform or not perform tests of controls. Such tests are likely to be effective and efficient if the understanding of internal control indicated that management had installed:

- Effective production planning, budgeting, and management information systems
- Effective computer controls as well as transaction processing and file maintenance controls for production and inventory
- Adequate segregation of duties between personnel who produce and store inventory and those responsible for the related accounting, and between personnel who store inventory and those responsible for receiving and shipping
- Adequate physical controls for all significant inventories

- A policy of taking physical inventories regularly to ensure the existence, accuracy, and salable condition of recorded inventories

- An effective accounting system and related control activities for accumulating all production costs and properly allocating them to inventory

- Adequate controls to ensure proper cutoffs in the receiving and shipping departments

Specific control objectives and examples of control activities applicable to producing goods for sale and storing inventory and for inventory costing are presented in Figures 19.2 and 19.3. The accounting system assumed to be in operation in the figures is a sophisticated computerized system. As discussed in Chapter 12, the tests of controls that the auditor would perform include an appropriate combination of inquiring about the entity's control activities, observing that they have been placed in operation, and examining evidence that they are operating effectively. Also, as discussed in Chapter 12, reperformance may be used in tests of controls; but if that becomes necessary, the auditor usually determines that it is more efficient to perform substantive tests. In addition to testing application controls, the auditor also would need evidence of the effectiveness of computer controls in order to assess control risk at low.

When performing tests of controls, the auditor should be aware of audit objectives other than completeness, accuracy, existence/occurrence, and cutoff that may be affected by those tests. For example, the auditor frequently considers the valuation objective when testing controls in the inventory cycle. Tests of the entity's procedures for pricing inventory components used in production are performed primarily to obtain evidence of the accuracy of the costs. The results of those tests, however, also will help the auditor determine whether the inventory is valued in accordance with the entity's inventory pricing method. For example, if the entity uses the first-in, first-out (FIFO) method of pricing inventory, the auditor could determine from testing the procedures used in charging costs during the various stages of production, whether finished goods are valued according to the FIFO assumption.

Highly developed cost systems often generate data that provides the details of:

- Transfers between raw materials and work in process and between work in process and finished goods

- Distribution of material, labor, and overhead expenses to cost centers, job orders, or production runs

- Stages of completion of work in process

- Variance accounts (in standard cost systems) identifying differences between actual and standard

- Differences between actual and budgeted costs

In addition to providing information about variances or differences between actual and budgeted amounts, an effective cost accounting system usually generates reports that analyze and explain that data. If management reviews these reports, the auditor may examine evidence of the reviews, including management's explanations for variances.

In evaluating the results of tests of controls (including tests of computer controls), the auditor considers whether the control activities, taken as a whole, are appropriately designed to achieve the control objectives and are operating effectively. This will determine whether the preliminary assessment of control risk has been confirmed for specific accounts and audit objectives and, thus, whether the auditor can significantly restrict substantive testing. Results differing from those anticipated require the auditor to reconsider the nature, timing, and extent of planned substantive tests, not only for inventory cycle accounts, but also for other accounts that may be affected. For example, ineffective control activities to ensure completeness of recorded shipments to customers may affect sales revenue as well as inventory and cost of sales.

(e) Early Substantive Testing

When control risk is assessed below the maximum or at low, the auditor often performs substantive tests related to completeness, accuracy, and existence/occurrence at an interim date—before the balance sheet date—and then performs various procedures to support the existence, completeness, and accuracy of inventory at the balance sheet date. In those circumstances, a major concern is whether controls will ensure the existence of inventory at the balance sheet date. In considering whether to perform early substantive tests of inventory quantities, the auditor considers the nature of the inventory, such as the ease with which it can be converted to cash; the management information system and management's review of available information in controlling the business; risk assessments made for the revenue and purchasing cycles; physical controls; and the division of duties between (a) the production and storage functions and the accounting department, and (b) the storage and the shipping and receiving functions.

At the balance sheet date, the auditor considers the results of testing at the early date and the risk of material misstatement for the completeness, accuracy, and existence/occurrence objectives in the intervening period between the date of the early substantive testing and the balance sheet date. This may involve inquiry, observation, and, when appropriate, examining evidence of the operation of the information system and related control activities during the intervening period, examining evidence of the operation of special procedures established for the intervening period, or performing substantive tests of the details of transactions in the intervening period.

Even when control risk is assessed at the maximum, the auditor may be able to obtain sufficient evidence to provide a reasonable basis for extending audit conclusions from an interim date to the balance sheet date. Performing early substantive testing when control risk is at maximum is not likely to be efficient, however, because of the extent of testing that will likely be required in the intervening period.

19.4 SUBSTANTIVE TESTS

If the auditor has assessed control risk for some or all production cycle accounts at low for the audit objectives of completeness, accuracy, and existence/occurrence, substantive tests addressing those audit objectives may, except for the need to observe physical inventory counts, be limited to analytical procedures. The auditor also will

Figure 19.2   Producing Goods for Sale and Storing Inventory

	Control Objectives		
	Transaction Processing		
	Authorization	Completeness of Input	Accuracy of Input
Specific Control Objectives	Inventory movements represent actual activity and are approved.	Inventory movements of material into production and transfers of production within work in process and to and from finished goods are input and accepted for processing.	Inventory movements are accurately recorded as to quantities and descriptions and are recorded in the proper period.
Examples of Control Activities	Approval of materials, labor, overhead charged to production, and transfers within work in process and to finished goods. Review of materials requisitions and labor distribution by department and/or job number. Release of finished goods only on the basis of approved shipping orders. Approval of adjustments to perpetual inventory records.	Accounting for the numerical sequence of requisitions of materials and component parts issued to and returned from production. Reporting and resolving missing or duplicate (unmatched) items by personnel independent of the materials handling function. Accounting for the numerical sequence of production reports or other records of finished production and transfers within work in process; reconciliation of those reports to quantities recorded, including investigation and resolution of missing documents and differences. Review and approval of monthly summarizing entries. Accounting for the numerical sequence of shipping orders.	Completeness of input control activities for missing or duplicate materials requisitions, records of labor and overhead charges, and transfers within work in process and to and from finished goods also address the accuracy of input for the fields matched or reconciled. Review of period-end cutoff procedures by personnel other than those who maintain related perpetual inventory or other accounting records or safeguard inventories. Reporting and resolving production costs and inventory transfers recorded in the wrong period.

Figure 19.2   *(Continued)*

Control Objectives

File Maintenance*		
Completeness and Accuracy of Updating	*Completeness and Accuracy of Accumulated Data*	*Asset Protection*
Inventory movements input are accurately updated to the raw materials, work-in-process, and finished goods files.	The integrity of the perpetual inventory records, after production costs have been accumulated in them, is preserved and they are relieved only upon sale or authorized adjustment.	Only authorized personnel have access to raw materials, work-in-process, and finished goods inventories and the related accounting records, including standing data.
Comparing total costs input with the total updated to the raw materials, work-in-process, and finished goods files.	Counting raw materials, work-in-process, and finished goods inventories; reconciling and adjusting the perpetual records to the physical counts.	Adequate physical control activities to prevent unauthorized access to inventories and related documents (requisitions, production reports) and inventory files and files used in processing production activity.
		Adequate segregation of duties between the maintenance of inventory records and the physical handling of inventory.

* Integrity of standing data is covered in Figure 19.3, "Inventory Costing."

Figure 19.3   Inventory Costing

| | ***Control Objectives**** | | |
| | *Transaction Processing* | | |
	Authorization	*Completeness of Input*	*Accuracy of Input*
Specific Control Objectives	Inventoried material, labor, and overhead costs reflect production charges that are approved.	Inventory costs are input and accepted for processing.	Charges to production for materials, labor, and overhead, and transfers within work in process and transfers of completed production to finished goods, are correctly recorded in the proper period as to quantities, descriptions, amounts, and dates in the general ledger control accounts and perpetual inventory records.
Examples of Control Activities	Approval of standard costs, overhead application rates, and allocation of production costs.	Reconciliation of records of labor and overhead charges to payrolls and overhead costs incurred, including reporting and resolving differences. Accounting for the numerical sequence of production reports or other records of finished production and transfers within work in process.	Completeness of input control activities for reconciliation of costs incurred to payrolls and overhead costs incurred also address the accuracy of input for the fields matched. Counting work-in-process and finished goods inventories and reconciling to the perpetual records. Reporting adjustments to the perpetual inventory records as a result of inventory counts.

*Asset protection is covered in Figure 19.2, "Producing Goods for Sale and Storing Inventory."

Figure 19.3   *(Continued)*

Control Objectives

File Maintenance

Integrity of Standing Data	*Completeness and Accuracy of Updating*	*Completeness and Accuracy of Accumulated Data*
All changes to standing data are authorized and accurately input.	All inventory costs are accurately updated to the inventory files.	The integrity of the inventory accounts, after production of inventory has been accumulated in them, is preserved and they are relieved only upon sale or authorized adjustment.
Establishing standing data for new inventory items by purchasing and production personnel and review and approval by purchasing and production supervisors.	Completeness and accuracy of updating control activities for producing goods for sale and storing inventory also ensure that the total inventory costs input and applied to quantities are equal to the amounts updated to the inventory file and general ledger accounts.	Balancing of the raw materials, work-in-process, and finished goods records (previous balance plus additions less transfers out, compared with the current total). Reconciling the perpetual records to the general ledger control accounts and approving adjustments, by personnel other than those responsible for maintaining related perpetual records or for safeguarding inventories.

consider the relevance to those audit objectives of evidence obtained from tests directed at other audit objectives and other accounts. For example, tests that provide evidence of the completeness of accounts payable also provide some evidence about the existence and accuracy of raw materials inventory. The auditor seldom assesses control risk at low for the cutoff, valuation, rights and obligations, and presentation and disclosure objectives, and therefore generally performs substantive tests of details for these objectives. (As noted earlier, cutoff tests for cost of sales typically are performed concurrently with cutoff tests for sales.)

(a) Observation of Physical Inventories

Since the *McKesson & Robbins* case precipitated the issue in 1939, the observation of physical inventories has been a required auditing procedure and one of the principal substantive tests of inventories. For a long time after 1939, auditors were expected to make voluminous and extensive test counts, sometimes virtually taking the physical inventory side-by-side with the entity's employees. In recent years, the emphasis has shifted to observation and testing of the procedures for the physical counts. In any event, both auditor and management should keep in mind that the entity is responsible for inventory quantities; the auditor's responsibility is to observe and evaluate the entity's procedures and results.

The official position of the profession is stated in SAS No. 1 (AU Section 331.09), as follows:

> It is ordinarily necessary for the independent auditor to be present at the time of count and, by suitable observation, tests, and inquiries, satisfy himself respecting the effectiveness of the methods of inventory-taking and the measure of reliance which may be placed upon the client's representations about the quantities and physical condition of the inventories.

AU Section 331.12 goes on to state:

> When the independent auditor has not satisfied himself as to inventories in the possession of the client through the procedures [of a physical count], tests of the accounting records alone will not be sufficient for him to become satisfied as to quantities; it will always be necessary for the auditor to make, or observe, some physical counts of the inventory and apply appropriate tests of intervening transactions.

(i) Planning the Inventory Observation.   Management has the primary responsibility for planning and taking the physical inventory. Because of the auditor's participation, however, the planning should be a joint effort. Management and the auditor should agree on the timing of the inventory after considering the following factors: The inventory should be counted at year-end if it is subject to significant volatility of movement or quantities, or if controls over accounting for movement are ineffective. If those controls are effective, the count can be taken before year-end or, if the entity uses cycle counts, on a staggered basis throughout the year. If the inventory is taken at one time, both management and auditor usually prefer a month in the last quarter of the fiscal year. Unless the entity has effective control activities that address proper cutoff, the auditor should discourage management from taking inventories of different departments (especially sequential work-in-process departments) over a period of several days, because double-counting of inventory could result. Alternative control activities to prevent double-counting are rarely cost-effective.

The auditor should determine the various locations of inventory, which will require an understanding of the nature of the business. For example, businesses with traveling sales and delivery operations may have inventories in various vehicles; in businesses that rebuild products for resale, components of those products may be at remote locations or in the hands of third parties for refurbishing.

The auditor should review and comment on the written instructions or memorandum of inventory plans. Often the management personnel responsible for the inventory hold one or more instructional meetings with those who are to supervise the inventory-taking. The auditor's presence at the meetings usually facilitates the plans for observing the inventory.

The auditor also should identify the inventory count teams and determine whether they include persons able to identify the nature and quality of the inventory and persons from departments that have no responsibility for the custody, movement, or recording of the inventory. If such persons are not part of the count team, the auditor should consider whether the planned extent of work is sufficient to ensure that a complete and accurate count is achieved and that slow-moving, obsolete, and damaged inventory is adequately identified. (Counters normally should not have knowledge of, or access to, inventory quantities shown in the perpetual records. If counters do have access to such information, which may occur if inventory is stored in many locations and the counters must locate the items, a checker should be assigned to observe the counters' procedures and to perform recounts as necessary.)

The need for a large number of auditors to be present is naturally greater if a complete physical inventory is taken at one time than if cycle counts or staggered inventories are taken. Audit staffing requirements must be determined based on the timing of inventories at various locations, the difficulty of observing them, and the number of counting teams the entity uses.

(ii) Observing the Physical Inventory.   The auditor should keep in mind the objectives of observing a physical inventory: to ascertain that the inventory exists and to observe that the count and description of the inventory and its condition are accurate and properly recorded. An auditor is neither a taker of inventory nor an expert appraiser of inventory quality, quantities, or condition; nonetheless, he or she cannot neglect the intelligent application of common sense. Well-arranged inventory is more likely to be accurately counted than is poorly arranged inventory. Signs of age and neglect are often obvious, for example, dust on cartons or rust and corrosion of containers, and they naturally raise questions about the inventory's usefulness and salability. The condition of the inventory is particularly important if the product must meet strict technical specifications. For example, in the aerospace industry, a metal part may have to possess specific size, weight, and shape characteristics, as well as conform to standards for a particular alloy mix. Failure to meet the specifications in the smallest way can mean that the part should be valued as scrap. Before observing the inventory, the auditor should know enough about the business to be able to recognize, at least in broad terms, the product under observation and the measures appropriate for determining its quality and condition. Thus, although an auditor should spend some time examining the inventory being counted, management, and everyone else concerned, should recognize that the auditor is not acting as an expert appraiser.

The auditor should spend most of the time observing the entity's procedures in operation. The diligence and proficiency of the counters (and count checkers, if applicable) should be noted: how carefully they count, weigh, and measure; how well they identify and describe the inventory; what methods they use to make sure no items are omitted or duplicated. The auditor also should observe whether supervisory personnel are present, how planned recounting procedures are executed, whether cutoff procedures are performed, how inventory count documents are controlled, how individual areas or departments are controlled and "cleared," and whether instructions are followed.

The auditor should make some test counts, both to confirm the accuracy of employees' counting and to record corroborative evidence of the existence of the inventory for later tracing to the inventory summarization. Recorded counts should be selected and recounted by the auditor to test their accuracy; in addition, inventory items should be selected and independently counted and compared with quantities recorded by employees. This provides evidence that all items on hand are accurately included in the recorded counts.

The auditor must use judgment in determining how many test counts to perform, considering, among other things, inventory with special characteristics such as high value or susceptibility to theft, the adequacy of the entity's controls over counting, and the expertise and diligence of individuals making the counts. In the absence of specific reasons to do otherwise, the auditor usually performs a small number of test counts in relation to the total number of items in the inventory. Sampling ordinarily is not appropriate for determining the extent of test counts because the auditor does not intend to project an error. This is an accept–reject application; if the auditor's counts disclose an unacceptable number of errors in a particular location, entity employees ordinarily would recount the inventory.

As part of the review of plans and observation of the physical inventory procedures, the auditor should note and evaluate the procedures followed in separately identifying and counting items moved from place to place (such as from department to department or from receiving area to storage area) and goods on hand belonging to others, such as consignments, bailments, goods on approval, and property of customers returned for repair or held awaiting delivery instructions. All items belonging to others should be counted and recorded separately, both because they should be subject to control and to preclude their mistaken or purposeful substitution for the entity's inventory.

Adequately identifying work in process, especially its stage of completion, is likely to be difficult and may be impossible without a bill of materials or similar document. Production or operating personnel must be able to identify items in process and their condition or stage of completion in order to control the production process, and so they should be able to do so for physical count purposes as well. If they cannot, the auditor may find a number of practical ways to deal with the problems of identifying and valuing work in process. On the basis of experience and common sense, the auditor can make assumptions that clearly cannot be materially in error: Goods in a given department can be assumed to have passed through an average stage of completion; the variety of goods in a given department can be assumed to be of an average size, formula, or character; tote boxes, bales, or coils can be assumed to be of an average weight.

(iii) Cycle Counts.   All procedures applicable to wall-to-wall physical inventory observation can be readily adapted to cycle count observation. The auditor can review the cycle counting schedules, plans, and instructions, and observe the physical arrangement and condition of the inventory, and the diligence and proficiency of the inventory count teams in counting and identifying inventory, controlling records of test counts, preventing omissions or duplications, and identifying and segregating slow-moving, obsolete, or damaged goods. Because the entire inventory is not being counted at one time, the auditor must take steps to ensure that the items counted are properly identified. The auditor can make a few test counts either independently or with the count teams, and can observe and, if desired, participate in reconciling the counts to perpetual records and investigating differences.

Effective cycle counting depends on effective control activities related to inventory quantities and timely recording throughout the production process. Having tested the effectiveness of the procedures for controlling inventory quantities and related cycle counting, the auditor can choose to observe and test physical inventory procedures at any convenient time, including, if necessary, before or after the period under audit.

The auditor also needs evidence that the cycle counting procedures observed were functioning before and can be expected to function after they were observed, and that they are applied to substantially all inventory items. A formal schedule of counts and specific assignments (covering both personnel to perform the counts and supervisory responsibility) is preferable. Many entities, however, operate under a loose policy of counting all items at least once a year and assign the counting to the stockkeepers to do as time allows. In those instances, the auditor can review worksheets, entries in the perpetual inventory records, and other evidence of the regularity of test counting, and can evaluate the results. Evidence of proper count procedures includes frequent counting; absence of substantial differences between counts and records over a period of time (but the presence of some insubstantial differences would be expected); adequate cutoff of receipts, shipments, and transfers (at the date of each count); quality of investigation of differences that occur (including segregation of duties between personnel performing initial counts and those investigating differences); and quality of storeroom housekeeping and inventory identification.

(iv) Difficult Inventories.   Certain types of material—for example, logs in a river, piles of coal and scrap metal, vats of chemicals—by their nature may be difficult to count, and an auditor may have to use ingenuity to substantiate quantities on hand. Measurement of a pile of metals may be difficult for a number of reasons: The pile may have sunk into the ground to an unknown depth; the metals may be of varying weights, precluding the use of an average; or the pile may be of uneven density. The quality of chemicals and similar materials may be impossible to determine without specialized knowledge, and the auditor may find it necessary to draw samples from various levels of holding tanks and send them for independent analysis. Frauds have been perpetrated by substituting water for materials stored in tanks.

Entities sometimes use photographic surveys, engineering studies, and similar specialized techniques to take physical inventories, and an auditor can observe how carefully they are conducted. In such situations, the auditor should consider the need for an expert or specialist to help take or evaluate the inventory. Guidance on the use of specialists is contained in Chapter 7.

In some circumstances, the auditor may be guided by the entity's system of handling receipts and disbursements from the piles. For example, the entity may use a pile rotation or exhaustion system, in which material received is placed on piles other than the one being drawn down. When a pile is exhausted, errors in the accounts are disclosed. If the pile rotation system functions satisfactorily, the auditor may consider using the accounting records, to a certain extent, as a source of evidence.

(v) Alternative Procedures If Observation of Physical Inventories Is Not Practicable. The auditor should not decide lightly that observation of inventories is impracticable or impossible. If the entity does not or cannot take a physical inventory, however, or if the auditor cannot be present at the inventory-taking, he or she may be able to form an opinion regarding the reasonableness of inventory quantities by applying alternative procedures. Those alternative procedures might include examining other physical evidence that may be tantamount to observing the physical count. For example, if the auditor is engaged after the physical inventory has been taken, subsequent physical tests (before or after year-end) may be a satisfactory substitute for observing the inventory-taking. The auditor also may examine written instructions for the inventory-taking, review the original tags or sheets, and make suitable tests of the summarization.

The auditor should always examine or observe some physical evidence of the existence of the inventory and make appropriate tests of intervening transactions or control activities performed on them. If, on the basis of those tests, the auditor is satisfied that inventories are fairly stated, he or she is in a position to express an unqualified opinion. On the other hand, there may be no practicable substitute for observation of inventory-taking, and an auditor may have to express a qualified opinion or disclaimer, depending on the materiality of the inventories and on whether the failure to observe was unavoidable or resulted from management's decision to limit the scope of the audit.

Sometimes procedures for substantiating beginning inventories must be based on examining other accounting documents and records. For example, in an initial audit the auditor generally will not have observed the physical inventory at the previous year-end, which is a principal factor in determining cost of sales for the current year. If reputable independent accountants expressed an unqualified opinion on the prior year statements, a successor auditor may accept that opinion and perhaps may review the predecessor auditor's working papers supporting the prior-year balance. If an audit was made for the preceding year, the auditor may be able to obtain reasonable assurance about the beginning inventories through expanded tests of counting records in order to be able to express an opinion on the current year of operations, provided he or she has been able to obtain sufficient physical evidence of the existence of the ending inventory. An auditor who is unable to form an opinion on the opening inventory may decide to qualify the audit opinion or disclaim an opinion with respect to results of operations for the year under audit.

Expanded tests of the accounting records may consist of a detailed physical inventory reports and summaries, including review and testing of cutoff data, examination of perpetual inventory records and production records, and review of individual product and overall gross profit percentages. In connection with the latter procedures, cost accumulations for selected inventory items should be tested and significant changes in unit costs directly traced to factors such as technological changes, mass buying economies and freight rate "breaks," changes in labor costs, and changes in overhead rates. Changes in gross profit percentages should be further related to changes in unit sales prices and changes in the profitability of the sales mix, if applicable.

Initial audits involving filings with the Securities and Exchange Commission present problems because audited income statements are required for three years. Despite the inherent difficulties in reporting on inventories of earlier years, the auditor must obtain reasonable assurance about the prior years' inventories through appropriate alternative auditing procedures if an unqualified opinion is to be issued.

(b) Testing Ownership and Cutoff

The auditor should determine that the entity holds title to the inventories. In many cases, this is relatively straightforward. Theoretically, the accounting for purchases and sales in transit at year-end is determined by the FOB terms (shipping point or destination), which determine title. Unless financial statements would otherwise be misleading, however, the legal test of title is often disregarded based on materiality considerations: Purchases are generally recorded when received, and sales when shipped. Auditing procedures related to the recording of purchases and sales in the proper period are discussed in Chapters 23 and 18, respectively.

The primary focus for determining ownership is on proper control of receiving and shipping activities and cutoffs at year-end and, if different, at the physical inventory date. Control over sales cutoff at an early physical inventory date is particularly important because sales cutoff errors at that date—as compared with year-end—are compounded when perpetual inventory records and control account balances are adjusted for differences between recorded and physical inventory. Since cutoff errors correct themselves in the following period when the sales and costs of sales are recorded in the normal course of transaction processing, a reduction of inventory and increase in cost of sales, if goods were shipped before the physical count but not recorded until after the physical count, will be recorded twice. The effect in that situation is to misstate gross profit by the full cost of the inventory involved in the cutoff error. On the other hand, a sales cutoff error at year-end (when the physical inventory has been taken at an earlier date) will result in a misstatement of gross profit only to the extent of the gross profit on the sale.[1]

At the time of the inventory observation, the auditor should visit the receiving and shipping departments, record the last receiving and shipping document numbers, and ascertain that each department has been informed that no receipts after or shipments before the cutoff date should be included in inventory. The auditor should review the

[1] Cutoff errors involving receipt of goods at the physical inventory date also misstate gross profit by the full cost of the inventory involved. Cutoff errors involving receipt of goods at year-end (when the physical inventory has been taken at an earlier date) have no effect on gross profit, except in the rare situation in which the merchandise also was sold.

records of those departments after the inventory date and compare the last receiving and shipping numbers with accounting department records to ensure that a proper cutoff was achieved. Special care should be taken to control the movement of inventory when manufacturing operations are not suspended during the physical inventory.

Some of the cutoff tests described above may involve sampling applications. In those cases, sample size should reflect the level of assurance needed by the auditor with respect to the cutoff objective, which in turn reflects the assessment of control risk. For example, if control risk is assessed at the maximum, perhaps because the entity's control activities do not address cutoff, the auditor should establish the extent of testing to obtain a high level of assurance that the cutoff objective has been achieved. If control risk is assessed below the maximum, the level of assurance needed can range from moderate to low.

If there are consignment inventories, inventories in public warehouses, or customer inventories, auditing procedures must be expanded. Inventory held by others should be substantiated by direct confirmation in writing with the custodians. If such inventory is material, the auditor should apply one or more of the following procedures, in accordance with SAS No. 1, as amended by SAS No. 43 (AU Section 331.14), to obtain reasonable assurance with respect to the existence of the inventory:

a. Test the owner's procedures for investigating the warehouseman and evaluating the warehouseman's performance.

b. Obtain an independent accountant's report on the warehouseman's control procedures relevant to custody of goods and, if applicable, pledging of receipts, or apply alternative procedures at the warehouse to gain reasonable assurance that information received from the warehouseman is reliable.

c. Observe physical counts of the goods, if practicable and reasonable.

d. If warehouse receipts have been pledged as collateral, confirm with lenders pertinent details of the pledged receipts (on a test basis, if appropriate).

If merchandise is billed to customers and held for them, care must be exercised to exclude that merchandise from inventory and to determine that the customers have authorized billing before delivery. The auditor also needs to be sure that title has passed and that there are no unusual terms that call into question the collectibility of the receivable or the entity's legal right to the revenue. Goods belonging to customers or others should be counted and, if significant in amount, should be confirmed with their owners. The auditor should be alert to the possibility of such goods and should make certain that the entity has a system for controlling the goods and that they are properly identified and segregated.

The auditor also should be alert for liens and encumbrances against the inventories. These are normally evident from reading minutes and agreements, or as a result of confirmations with lenders relating to loans or loan agreements. It may be necessary to investigate whether additional liens and encumbrances have been filed with state or local governmental authorities.

(c) Inventory Costing and Summarization

Inventory costing and summarization may be based on the physical inventory results or the perpetual inventory records (if those records have been determined to be reliable); in either case, the results are compared with the recorded amounts. The procedures performed in testing the summarization of the physical inventory quantities are as follows:

1. The inventory tags are tested to determine that all tags used for the physical counts and only those tags are included in the physical inventory summaries. The auditor also should ascertain that tags voided during the physical count have been properly accounted for. If count sheets were used for recording physical inventory results, the auditor should ascertain that unused spaces were not filled in after the physical count was completed.

2. The inventory summaries are compared with the auditor's record of counts and with the count sheets or tags; conversions and summarizations of units are tested.

3. Quantities are compared with perpetual records, if they exist, on a test basis, and differences and how the entity disposed of them are reviewed; this is particularly important when inventories are taken prior to year-end and perpetual records will be the basis for year-end inventory valuation.

4. Cutoff procedures are tested.

5. Customers' materials on hand and inventories in the hands of others are confirmed.

6. Unit costs are traced to and from the detailed priced inventory listings; the appropriateness of the unit costs is determined by reference to suppliers' invoices when necessary.

7. Raw materials, labor, and overhead costs to be applied to inventories are tested to determine that they are reasonably computed in accordance with an acceptable and consistent accounting method.

8. The multiplication of prices and inventory quantities and the resulting footings and summarizations are tested.

How extensively the auditor performs each of the above procedures depends on his or her knowledge of and experience with the entity, information obtained when observing the physical inventory count, understanding of internal control, and the results of any tests of controls performed. For example, if control risk has been assessed at low for the audit objective of accuracy, it will not be necessary to perform substantive tests of details of the costing of raw materials and purchased parts, the mathematical accuracy of the detailed priced inventory listings, or the allocation of material, labor, and overhead costs to work in process and finished goods. In other cases, the auditor should test the accuracy of inventory costing, including determining that standard costs approximate actual costs and that standard cost variances are allocated to the appropriate inventory accounts and to cost of goods sold, to provide a level of assurance commensurate with an assessment of control risk at maximum or below the maximum. Errors noted when testing the costing and summarization should be given particular consideration in assessing whether the entity's procedures are effective and whether additional testing is necessary.

In testing the costing of merchandise inventories and inventories of simple manufacturing operations, the auditor often can relate costs directly to specific vendor invoices and labor summaries. For example, for merchandising operations in which goods are purchased for resale, the cost of inventory can be determined by reference to appropriate purchase invoices. In simple manufacturing operations, the allocation of material costs, direct labor, and overhead to inventory may be straightforward. For such operations, it may be most efficient to substantively test the assigned costs.

In more complex manufacturing operations, evaluating material, labor, and overhead allocations may be more difficult. An example is the manufacturing operation of a steel mill where the raw materials ore, coal, and limestone are converted into finished steel of various types. Allocating costs is less objective and requires an understanding of process costing and an in-depth knowledge of the manufacturing process. It may be difficult for the auditor to obtain assurance regarding the costing of inventory without obtaining some evidence that the procedures for product costing and tracking inventory through the various stages of completion are effective.

Accountants have long recognized the conceptual problems associated with allocating overhead to work in process based on activity such as direct labor hours or dollars. Changes in the manufacturing environment—in particular, increased automation and computerization, reduced levels of inventories of raw materials and component parts through the use of just-in-time techniques, and direct labor becoming a smaller portion of production costs—have called into question the appropriateness of commonly used overhead allocation bases. Some entities have considered new techniques to generate cost accounting data that both better reflects the results of management's decisions and produces financial statements acceptable for financial reporting purposes. The auditor should consider the overhead allocation methods to ensure that they generate inventory and cost of sales values that are in conformity with GAAP appropriate to the entity's circumstances, and that those methods are not merely routine or mechanical applications of traditional techniques that do not reflect the entity's manufacturing environment.

The accounting method used to price inventory also affects the substantive tests to be performed. The differences in the procedures used under different valuation methods relate mainly to the sources of cost information and the mechanics of the pricing calculations. For example, pricing tests of inventory valued on a FIFO basis normally include a comparison of costs to most recent invoice prices for purchased merchandise and most recent unit production costs for manufactured goods. Pricing tests of last-in, first-out (LIFO) inventories normally include procedures to test consistency of base-year prices between years, comparisons of base-year costs for new items with current-year costs, recalculation of indices used to value current-year LIFO increments, and an overall review of the accuracy of the LIFO application.

LIFO presents opportunities, not available under other inventory costing methods, for the entity to manage earnings. Those opportunities often involve transactions, usually entered into near year-end, that would charge portions of the beginning inventory to cost of sales or, depending on management's reporting objectives, prevent a liquidation of the beginning inventory from being charged to cost of sales. Management could accomplish these income-managing objectives by entering into accommodation purchases or sales that, pursuant to an undisclosed resale agreement, would later be reversed. The auditor should be alert to the possibility of such transactions, which may be discovered by scanning the records for unusual transactions early in the next accounting period, particularly transactions with known related parties.

(d) Inventory Valuation

Generally accepted accounting principles require that inventories be reported at the lower of historical cost (using an acceptable flow-of-cost assumption) or market. "Market" is current replacement cost by either purchase or production, except that market may not exceed net realizable value (estimated selling price minus costs of completion and disposal) or be lower than net realizable value reduced by the normal profit margin. (Net realizable value frequently is referred to as the "ceiling," and net realizable value reduced by the normal profit margin frequently is referred to as the "floor.")

To achieve the valuation objective for inventories, the auditor should test the inventory costing as indicated earlier, and also should:

- Review and test procedures for identifying obsolete or slow-moving items
- Review the costing of damaged or obsolete items to determine that the assigned value does not exceed net realizable value
- Review and test the determination of market prices to determine whether market is lower than cost

In making valuation judgments, the auditor should consider the knowledge obtained about the entity's business and industry, the control environment, financial and operating information, and other information that could affect the valuation of inventories, for example:

- Technological advances that could render inventories obsolete
- The sufficiency and reliability of management information for testing valuation
- New product lines and future marketing forecasts and plans
- The entity's competitive position in the marketplace for its products
- Economic conditions
- The political stability of foreign governments
- Regulatory trends in domestic and foreign jurisdictions

In reviewing for obsolete items in inventory, the auditor should consider not only finished goods but also work in process and raw materials that will eventually become finished goods. The auditor may compare quantities with those in previous inventories on a test basis to identify slow-moving items or abnormally large or small balances. Comparing inventory quantities with sales forecasts is an effective test for obsolete items. Reviews of usage records can provide further indications of slow-moving items. If the entity does not maintain perpetual records, the auditor may examine purchase orders or production orders to determine how recently certain items of inventory were acquired. Many entities have formulas or rules of thumb that translate overall judgments on obsolete inventory into practical detailed applications, like all items over a year's supply, all items that have not moved within six months, or all items bearing certain identifying numbers with regard to date or class of product. The auditor must review whether the rules are realistic and comprehensive enough as well as whether they are fully and accurately applied. In addition to reviewing and testing the rules, the auditor must evaluate, based on an understanding of the business, whether, for each segment of the inventory, market conditions might raise questions about its realizability in the normal course of operations. The auditor also may inquire of sales and marketing executives about the salability of the inventories. Past experience can be the best guide to the net realizable value of items that must be disposed of at salvage prices. When certain finished goods are declared obsolete (or severe markdowns are required), related raw materials and work-in-process inventories (unless usable for other products) also may need to be written down.

Testing the application of the lower of cost or market principle is one of the more difficult and subjective aspects of the audit. In most situations, the auditor's identification of inherent risks, combined with the assessment of control risk, is particularly important in determining the extent of substantive testing. For example, if the risk of defective production or of the acceptance of incoming shipments of defective merchandise is high, the auditor may need to expand testing of the condition of inventories. Management usually applies the lower of cost or market test on an exception basis when a problem is identified. Accordingly, the auditor has limited opportunity to test control activities in this area. The greater audit risk is that not all problems have been identified, not that an identified problem may lead to a misstatement in the financial statements.

This risk may be mitigated by performing analytical procedures, including evaluating the trend in certain key indicators, such as historical inventory write-offs and returns, and inventory reserve balances in total and as a percentage of inventory. Key ratios (e.g., inventory turnover, days sales in inventory) also may highlight unfavorable trends that warrant additional auditing procedures.

The auditor should test the calculation of net realizable value of individual or major groups of products. Estimated selling prices may be compared with recent sales invoices—or preferably with the latest customer orders—and evaluated for possible trends in prices. Estimated costs of completion and disposal may be tested for reasonableness by an overall computation. The auditor ordinarily need not determine the value of inventory at reproduction or replacement costs if there is acceptable evidence that, for individual products or groups of products, the range between net realizable value and the market floor is not great. If it is significant, however, the auditor may test replacement costs by reference to cost records, current invoices, or purchase contracts. Reproduction costs may be tested in a similar manner, supplemented by discussions with production and accounting employees.

(e) Auditing Cost of Sales

In planning the audit, the auditor often views the income statement as the residual effect of changes in the balance sheet. The primary focus is on auditing balance sheet accounts at the beginning and end of the year. The audit opinion on results of operations, however, requires that the auditor perform auditing procedures to obtain satisfaction that transactions are properly accounted for and classified in the income statement.

Substantive tests of cost of sales are usually limited for two reasons. First, the audit plan is likely to include tests of controls relating to inventory movements and costing. Second, if the auditor performs substantive tests of the beginning and ending inventory balances and obtains evidence about the completeness, accuracy, and authorization of purchases of goods and services (including their proper classification) by testing controls that are part of the purchasing cycle, he or she has significant amounts of evidence about the "residual" cost of sales figure. Accordingly, substantive tests of cost of sales normally can be limited to analytical procedures that test the proper classification of costs by focusing on expected or traditional relationships among various components of cost of sales, and obtaining explanations for fluctuations in expense account balances. Often overhead and other variances also are analyzed as part of substantive tests of cost of sales. Typical analytical procedures are discussed later in this section.

If results of the above procedures indicate that additional evidence is needed to support the cost of sales balance, the auditor also may examine selected invoices for material and overhead costs and test the allocation of payroll costs, together with testing the summarization of detailed amounts in the account balances that enter into cost of sales. The auditor probably would perform analytical procedures as well.

(f) Purchase Commitments

Losses from purchase commitments may arise in connection with commodity purchases, forward transactions, or purchase commitments in excess of short-term requirements. If material losses could arise from unfulfilled purchase commitments, the auditor should identify the commitments and assess the potential need for a loss provision. This may be accomplished by examining open purchase order records, inquiring of employees who make purchase commitments, or requesting major suppliers to provide details of any purchase commitments outstanding at year-end. If there is doubt regarding whether all commitments have been identified, it may be appropriate to review suppliers' invoices and receiving reports for a period after year-end for evidence of purchases above prevailing prices or in quantities exceeding current requirements (by reviewing perpetual inventory records for evidence of goods that are slow-moving or obsolete), which may indicate unfavorable purchase commitments at year-end. Also, since major purchase commitments generally require the approval of the board of directors, examining minutes of board meetings may be helpful in discovering such commitments. Chapter 27 contains an illustration of the statement about purchase commitments that should be included in the management representation letter.

(g) Analytical Procedures

Auditing inventories challenges an auditor's knowledge and analytical skills more than almost any other audit activity. The better the auditor understands the entity's business, its operating problems, and the market and other economic conditions it operates in, the greater the ability to determine that the inventory is fairly stated in conformity with generally accepted accounting principles. That understanding can be applied to specific judgments in designing analytical procedures.

Both internal and external data is abundantly available for designing and testing statistical, ratio, and other kinds of analyses. The auditor should make every effort to use analytical procedures unique to the business, but only on the basis of a thorough understanding. The following paragraphs describe only those analytical procedures that are likely to apply to most inventories.

If standard cost systems or budgetary systems produce variance reports, the system has, in effect, performed a large part of the analytical procedure by identifying the variances. The auditor can then read the variance reports carefully and analyze reasons for variances. If variances are small, the auditor can infer that standards approximate actual costs and can significantly reduce price testing.

The auditor may compare purchases, usage reports, and production costs from month to month, and investigate and obtain explanations for fluctuations. Significant ratios may be computed and compared from month to month and with the prior year. The ratio of cost of sales to inventory and the gross profit ratio are universally considered informative. They must be used with caution in a period of changing prices, however, as results under FIFO will differ, perhaps significantly, from those under LIFO. In a great many industries, the computation of the ratio of total units to total value—that is, average unit cost—is valid and informative, but if the mix of unit costs is likely to vary substantially, explaining fluctuations in average unit costs may not be cost-effective. If they are valid, average unit costs can be computed for sales, purchases, and inventory balances. Analytical procedures based on product lines are likely to produce more precise expectations against which to compare data based on recorded amounts.

If available, sales forecasts and marketing plans can provide important information about salability and net realizable value of inventories. For example, marketing plans for a new line can effectively render obsolete an inventory that otherwise appears salable at normal profit margins. Sales forecasts and marketing plans, however, often are not well organized or in written form, and thus the auditor must take care not to waste time searching for material that is nonexistent or inconclusive. An auditor who has an adequate understanding of the entity will know what to expect and of whom to inquire.

Analytical procedures should be particularly intensive between an interim inventory date and year-end. Often the audit effort during this period is directed primarily toward tests of controls, with minimal substantive testing of intervening activity or the year-end balance. Analytical procedures provide an excellent means of identifying changes in conditions that may require additional substantive tests or, in conjunction with the results of related tests of controls and other substantive tests, of providing the needed assurance regarding the year-end balances.

(h) Management Representation Letter

It is standard practice for the auditor to request management to include certain matters relating to inventory in the representation letter. The focus of the letter is on judgments made by management in the financial accounting process; the letter includes representations relating to agreements to repurchase inventory or the absence thereof, net realizable value judgments, pledging of assets, and the nature of significant inventory purchase commitments. Management representation letters are discussed in Chapter 27.

20

Auditing Prepayments and Accruals

Prepayments are assets, most often in the form of services (but sometimes goods such as stationery and supplies), that have been acquired as part of the purchasing cycle but that apply to future periods or to the production of future revenues—for example, unexpired insurance, rent paid in advance, and prepaid taxes other than those on income. There is little conceptual difference between prepayments and assets like inventories, plant and equipment, and intangibles: All are expected to benefit future periods. Prepayments often are assumed to be less readily realizable than inventory or equipment, but there are significant exceptions; it may be easier to realize cash from the contractual right to cancel an insurance policy than on a custom-built, single-purpose structure.

Prepayments consist of prepaid expenses and deferred charges; the distinction is based mainly on whether the asset is current or noncurrent. How precisely that distinction is made depends on custom and materiality considerations. Prepaid insurance, for example, and many types of deposits do not expire and are not realized within one year or the entity's operating cycle, but traditionally are classified as current. The prepaid expense account is seldom material to the financial statements, and noncurrent items that are not material are included in prepaid expenses for convenience. If deferred costs (such as debt issuance costs) are material and will expire over several years, they are properly classified as noncurrent deferred charges.

Accruals, often referred to as accrued expenses, are items for which a service or benefit has been received and for which the related liability is acknowledged and reasonably determinable, but that are not yet payable (either because of the terms of the commitment or because the invoice has not been received). Some accrued liabilities accrue with the passage of time—for example, interest, rent, and property taxes—or with some service or activity, for example, payrolls, pensions, vacation pay, royalties, sales commissions, and payroll taxes. Others—for example, accrued environmental remediation costs—are accrued when it is probable that a liability has been incurred and the amount of the loss can be reasonably estimated. Deferred credits (such as unearned revenue and deferred income accounts) result from the receipt of revenues in advance of the related delivery of goods or services and are discussed in Chapter 18.

Agency obligations, such as payroll withholdings and deductions and sales tax collections, are funds collected for others for which accountability must be maintained until the funds are turned over at the required time to the agency for whom they are held in trust. Those obligations result from transactions that are part of the purchasing cycle, discussed in Chapter 14, and the revenue cycle, discussed in Chapter 13.

Many similarities exist among prepaid expenses, accrued liabilities, and agency obligations and among the underlying transactions that affect these accounts. For example, similar types of transactions may result in prepaid insurance or accrued insurance expense; the same is true for rent and property taxes. Items such as insurance premiums and various deposits often are held as agency obligations. All three categories of accounts frequently are subjected to similar types of controls and the general audit approach employed is also similar.

Other prepayments and accruals, such as those for pension and other postretirement benefits, are estimates that are highly dependent on assumptions and usually are prepared by specialists, such as actuaries. The audit approach for those accounts focuses on determining the reasonableness of those estimates and on using the work of specialists.

20.1   AUDIT OBJECTIVES

The auditor should approach prepayments and accruals with the view that liabilities are more likely to be understated or omitted from the accounts than overstated and, conversely, assets are more likely to be overstated than understated. Therefore, audit objectives should focus on ascertaining that prepaid assets are not overstated and that accrued liabilities are not understated, but without ignoring the possibility that the opposite may occur.

In specifying audit objectives for prepaid assets, the auditor should focus on obtaining reasonable assurance that:

- All amounts reported as assets were acquired in authorized transactions and were properly recorded at the time of acquisition (existence/occurrence, accuracy)
- The balance of the expenditure carried forward relates to future periods or can be reasonably expected to be recovered from future income (valuation or allocation)
- The basis of amortization is reasonable and consistent with prior years (valuation or allocation)
- Related expenses are properly classified (presentation and disclosure)

Principal audit objectives related to accrued liabilities are to obtain reasonable assurance that:

- All material accrued expenses, agency obligations, and other liabilities existing at the balance sheet date have been authorized, recorded, and properly measured (completeness, existence/occurrence, accuracy, and valuation or allocation)
- Related expenses have been recognized and properly measured on a consistent basis (valuation or allocation)

20.2   INTERNAL CONTROL

Chapter 14 discusses the acquisition of goods and services and the controls to which such expenditures usually are subjected. The transactions that give rise to prepayments and accruals often originate and are processed and controlled in the same way as transactions for other goods and services. Other prepayments and accruals, particularly those that are based on assumptions and estimates prepared by specialists such as actuaries, are not the result of transactions that are considered part of the purchasing cycle and, therefore, may not be subject to extensive control activities.

Control activities are applied to recurring prepaid expenses, accrued liabilities, agency accounts, and other liabilities to ensure timely recording of the required entries. Those activities are necessary because of the method of procuring many prepaid and accrued expense items. Recurring services such as utilities and rents, after initial identification, are provided continuously without further request. Specialized services, such as insurance, legal, advertising, and auditing services, also are frequently rendered on an ongoing basis. Real estate and property taxes are assessed and paid according to the taxing authority's fiscal year, and must be properly allocated to the entity's interim accounting periods. Systematic recording of accruals and amortization is best ensured by making standard monthly journal entries, approved by appropriate personnel.

After a prepaid expense has been recorded, further monitoring is required to ensure that it is amortized properly and that the unamortized balance does not exceed the value of the future benefit. If the expenditure initially was charged directly to an expense account, the appropriate amount (i.e., the portion deemed applicable to future periods) is removed from the expense account at the end of each accounting period and recorded as an asset.

Control activities for recurring prepayments, accruals, and the related expense accounts frequently include maintaining detailed files for expenditures like insurance, rent, and commissions, or schedules that are cross-referenced to the related supporting documents and contain pertinent information like cost, starting date, period covered, and amount to be expensed or accrued each period. The account balances and amortization computations are subjected to periodic monitoring activities. Some liability and agency accounts are treated as part of the purchasing cycle and are subjected to related accounting procedures and control activities. That may be the case for payroll withholdings, customers' deposits, and commissions payable.

20.3   DETERMINING THE AUDIT STRATEGY

The auditor may obtain the required understanding of internal control with respect to systems-derived prepaid and accrued accounts as part of auditing the purchasing cycle. Although the assessment of control risk for these accounts is strongly influenced by the assessed level of control risk for the purchasing cycle, the audit strategy for prepaid and accrued accounts usually emphasizes substantive tests of year-end account balances, largely because of efficiency considerations. In this regard, Statement on Auditing Standards (SAS) No. 78, *Consideration of Internal Control in a Financial Statement Audit: An Amendment of SAS No. 55* (AU Section 319), recognizes that "ordinarily audit planning does not require an understanding of the control activities related to each account balance, transaction class, and disclosure component in the financial statements or to every assertion relevant to them" (para. 33). Also, a single test may serve to both substantiate a prepaid or an accrued account balance and test the related control activities. Moreover, since substantive tests of balance sheet accounts at the beginning and end of a period also tend to provide assurance about the related expense accounts, it is both conceptually sound and efficient for the auditor to focus on substantive testing of the balance sheet accounts.

In formulating the audit strategy for systems-derived prepaid and accrued accounts, the auditor considers the nature and materiality of the specific accounts, the desired timing of their examination, and inherent risks that have been identified. The auditor might perform tests of controls relating to prepayments and accruals on an engagement involving an extremely fast year-end report release or publication of financial data by a large, well-controlled entity. Those tests would focus on control activities addressing the accuracy and authorization of prepayments, and the completeness of accruals.

The auditor often reviews and analyzes the composition of prepayments and accruals at an interim date. It is ordinarily more efficient, however, to perform other substantive tests at the balance sheet date, unless there are year-end time constraints that make early testing desirable. Early substantive testing requires the auditor to consider alternative means of obtaining the necessary audit assurance at the balance sheet date. In many cases, this is accomplished by updating the substantive tests performed at an interim date. In other situations, the auditor may perform tests of controls during the intervening period. Even in these cases, however, the auditor would be likely, at a minimum, to review the year-end account balances for reasonableness.

In determining the extent of substantive tests, the auditor should consider the inherent risk that the account may be materially misstated. Two key aspects of this risk are how liquid an asset is and the extent to which judgment enters into determining the account balance. Since prepayments by their nature are not particularly liquid, this usually is not a significant factor. Also, little judgment may be required for many of the recurring expenses that are amortized or accrued on a time basis, such as rent, insurance, and interest.

The materiality of prepaid asset and accrued liability accounts also may be a significant consideration in determining the extent of substantive tests. Some prepayments and accruals are insignificant, and an auditor may consider it sufficient simply to compare the balance with the corresponding balance in the prior period and scan the current-period activity. On the other hand, since auditing prepayments and accruals often affords insight into certain controls in the purchasing cycle and therefore may contribute to an auditor's understanding of internal control, some auditors scrutinize individual accrued and prepaid accounts even though the balances are insignificant.

Furthermore, while an individual prepaid account may not be significant to the balance sheet, an understanding of the content of the account may alert the auditor to a potential misstatement that could have a material effect on the financial statements. This is especially true of the prepaid insurance account. An understanding of the manner in which the entity manages risk, in particular the types of insurance coverage it maintains, may make the auditor aware of uninsured risks or unrecorded liabilities.

In many circumstances, the same auditor audits the financial statements of both the entity that provides pension and other employee benefits (i.e., the employer) and the related benefit plans themselves. When designing the nature, extent, and timing of auditing procedures for financial statement amounts recorded in accordance with Statement of Financial Accounting Standards (SFAS) Nos. 87 and 106, the auditor should not only base materiality judgments on the employer's financial statements, but also consider expected materiality to the plan's financial statements. Considering plan materiality when auditing the employer's financial statements can help avoid later adjustments to amounts in the plan's financial statements.

20.4 SUBSTANTIVE TESTS

Substantive testing usually consists of examining the contractual, statutory, or other basis for prepayments and accruals; examining documentation that supports additions to the accounts; ascertaining that the method of calculating periodic amortization or accrual is appropriate; and recomputing the amortization or accrual and the account balance. For many accrued liabilities and some prepaid expenses, the accrual or prepayment is based on an estimate of a liability or a future benefit that cannot be determined precisely. In that case, the basis and rationale for the estimate should be reviewed, compared with prior experience, and evaluated in the light of related circumstances. The related expense account usually is audited (at least in part) in connection with the aforementioned amortization or accrual.

The balances of agency accounts should be supported by trial balances of the detailed amounts. Based on materiality and risk assessment, the auditor should consider the need for substantive tests directed at the completeness and accuracy of agency accounts.

Prepaid expense and accrued liability balances often consist of routine recurring allocations of expenses between periods. When this is the case, the auditor often can obtain the necessary assurance about the accuracy of the account balance by recomputing it or applying analytical procedures, without performing a detailed analysis of the activity in the account. Thus, in some cases, analytical procedures are the principal or even the only substantive tests performed on prepaid and accrued accounts. Balances in those and related expense accounts should be compared with the prior-year balance sheet and income statement amounts. The underlying causes of trends, fluctuations, and unusual transactions should be evaluated for their implications for other accounts. If they exist, variance reports and analyses of actual costs and expenses compared with budgeted amounts also may be examined.

In a stable business, predictable relationships often exist among certain accounts, and changes in those relationships may signal conditions requiring accounting recognition. The auditor should compute pertinent ratios and compare them with corresponding ones for prior periods. For example, comparing selling expense with sales might lead the auditor to discover sales commissions that should be but were not accrued. Unexplained changes in ratios involving revenue and expense accounts may indicate possible misstatements of related prepayments and accruals.

Analytical procedures applied to related expense accounts can provide additional assurance about the reasonableness of prepayments and accruals. The auditor may review expense account activity for missing or unusual entries that may indicate unrecorded liabilities or the failure to amortize prepayments. Substantive tests of details normally are not performed on expense account balances unless the controls are extremely ineffective or the auditor wants additional assurance in high-risk or sensitive areas (such as legal expense).

(a)   Accrued Pension Costs

To ascertain that the liability for pension costs and the related expense have been determined in conformity with generally accepted accounting principles (GAAP), as set forth in SFAS No. 87, *Employers' Accounting for Pensions* (Accounting Standards Section P16), the auditor must understand the contractual and other arrangements giving rise to pension costs and be aware of the requirements of the Employee Retirement Income Security Act of 1974 (ERISA).[1] SFAS No. 87 prescribes precisely the way to

---

[1] Auditing pension plans is discussed in Chapter 34.

calculate pension costs. The significance of pension costs to most entities, and the effect of a possible misstatement of them on the financial statements, often calls for substantive testing. The extent of testing will depend on the auditor's risk assessment and on materiality considerations.

Many of the basic calculations required by SFAS No. 87 are actuarial calculations that should be considered the work of a specialist, and the auditor should apply the provisions of SAS No. 73, *Using the Work of a Specialist* (AU Section 336), in auditing those amounts. This does not require the auditor to reperform the actuary's calculations. Rather, the auditor needs to be satisfied that the assumptions provided by the entity and the methods used by the actuary are reasonable and in conformity with GAAP. It is particularly important for the auditor to understand the reasons for fluctuations in pension information from one period to the next, for example, changes in the settlement rate assumption, the methods and time periods for amortizing gains and losses, prior service cost, and the transition amount.

Under SAS No. 73, the auditor should obtain an understanding with the entity and the actuary about the nature of the actuary's work. This understanding should cover:

- The objectives and scope of the actuary's work
- The actuary's representations regarding his or her relationship, if any, to the entity
- The methods and assumptions to be used
- A comparison of those methods and assumptions with the ones used in the preceding period
- The appropriateness of using the actuary's findings to corroborate the representations in the financial statements
- The form and content of the actuary's report needed by the auditor

SAS No. 73 requires the auditor to evaluate the actuary's qualifications, reputation, and experience. The auditor also is required to make appropriate tests of the census data and other information the entity provided to the actuary. Those tests include confirming directly with the actuary the information provided by the entity and used by the actuary and reconciling that information to the entity's payroll and other records.

In examining actuarially determined amounts, the auditor should be satisfied that the assumptions provided by the entity and the methods used by the actuary conform with the provisions of SFAS No. 87. The auditor should not rely on an actuary's conclusion about whether the actuarially computed amounts conform with GAAP; such a conclusion requires a skilled and experience-based knowledge of accounting principles. The auditor should inquire of management or the actuary about unusual or unexpected shifts from the prior period in components of pension cost or benefit obligation. Analytical techniques can be effective audit tools when performed with an appropriate understanding of the methodologies prescribed in SFAS No. 87, the entity's activities, and the characteristics of its work force.

Other suggested procedures are set forth below. They are not intended to be all-inclusive or to apply to all situations. Selecting auditing procedures appropriate for a particular situation is a matter of judgment.

- Identify the entity's pension plans, and obtain an understanding of the nature, coverage, and other relevant matters pertaining to each plan.

- Compare pension cost and related balance sheet and disclosure amounts and other information with the prior year for reasonableness and changes affecting comparability. Trace amounts to the actuary's report and to any supporting schedules or working papers used in connection with other auditing procedures.

- Evaluate compliance with ERISA (see below).

- Determine whether plan asset and obligation amounts have been computed as of the measurement date and whether plan assets have been measured in conformity with GAAP. Investments are generally measured at fair value, except that certain contracts with insurance companies may be measured at their contract value, as discussed in SFAS No. 110 (Accounting Standards Section Pe5).

- Examine the entity's records to determine that the basic data (e.g., size, age, and sex distribution of the work force) used by the actuary is appropriate and that employees ultimately entitled to participate in the plan have been included in the actuarial calculations. Trace (normally in summary form) the employee data tested to the actuary's report or confirm it directly with the actuary.

- Review the actuary's report to determine whether all plan terms have been properly reflected in it and that the actuarial cost method is appropriate.

- Determine whether pension cost and related amounts have been computed on a consistent basis and recognized and disclosed in conformity with GAAP.

- Review the period from the measurement date to the entity's year-end (and beyond, to the extent necessary) to determine whether any significant events (e.g., changes in plan provisions) have occurred that would materially affect the computation of the provision for pension costs. If such events have occurred, consult with the actuary and obtain an estimate of the dollar effect on the provision.

(i) Auditing Insured Plans.   The auditor needs to determine the nature of the arrangement between the employer and the insurance company. In some arrangements, an insurance company unconditionally undertakes a legal obligation to provide specified benefits to specific individuals in return for a fixed consideration or premium. For example, the insurance company sells a nonparticipating annuity and assumes the risks and rewards associated with the benefit obligation and the assets transferred. On the other hand, in participating annuity arrangements, the employer participates in the experience of the insurance company, whereby the insurance company typically pays dividends to the purchaser, effectively reducing the employer's cost. Many variations of such contracts exist.

Auditing procedures for annuity contracts normally involve examining the contract or insurance company dividend and premium statements. If the annuity is a participating annuity, the participation right should be recognized, at cost, as an asset at its inception. The cost is determined by comparing the participating annuity contract with equivalent contracts without participation rights. In subsequent periods, the auditor should ascertain whether fair value can be reasonably determined and, if it cannot, should review the method used to amortize the cost of the participation right.

(ii) ERISA-Related Procedures. In reading minutes of meetings of the entity's board of directors and pertinent committees, and in performing other auditing procedures, the auditor should be alert to any evidence that a pension plan may potentially be terminated. In addition, the auditor may wish to inquire of management about the possibility of a plan termination. If there is more than a remote possibility, the auditor should ensure that appropriate entries are recorded or disclosures made in the financial statements.

The auditor should obtain evidence that the entity is in compliance with ERISA (the Act), since noncompliance may have an impact on the financial statements. In addition to funding requirements, the Act requires compliance in the areas of plan design, reporting and disclosure, fiduciary responsibilities, and record keeping. Determining compliance with the Act is a legal matter; the auditor therefore customarily relies on inquiries of the actuary, plan trustees, and the entity's and the plan's legal counsel for those determinations, as well as obtaining a representation from the entity as part of the management representation letter.

(b) Other Postretirement Benefit Obligations

The provisions of SFAS No. 106, *Employers' Accounting for Postretirement Benefits Other Than Pensions* (Accounting Standards Section P40), are similar in many respects to those of SFAS No. 87, *Employers' Accounting for Pensions* (Accounting Standards Section P16), and SFAS No. 88, *Employers' Accounting for Settlements and Curtailments of Defined Benefit Pension Plans and for Termination Benefits* (Accounting Standards Section P16). SFAS No. 106, however, addresses matters unique to nonpension postretirement benefits and provides recognition, measurement, and disclosure requirements related to those benefits.[2]

As SFAS No. 106 notes, "to the extent the promise to provide pension benefits and the promise to provide postretirement benefits are similar, the provisions of this Statement are similar to those prescribed by Statements 87 and 88; different accounting treatment is prescribed only when the Board has concluded that there is a compelling reason for different treatment." Thus, auditing procedures for postretirement benefit costs and obligations are similar to those for pension costs and obligations, although there are some distinctions.

(i) Accounting for the Substantive Plan. SFAS No. 106 requires that the accounting reflect the substantive terms of the postretirement benefit plan as understood by the employer and its employees. The substantive plan, however, may not be reflected in the terms described in the written plan. For example, a past practice of regularly increasing benefits or changing the cost-sharing provisions of the plan (e.g., deductibles, coinsurance provisions, or retiree contributions) may indicate that the substantive plan differs from the written plan.

An employer's cost-sharing policy will constitute the cost-sharing provisions of the substantive plan if either of the following conditions exist:

1. The employer has a past practice of either (1) maintaining a consistent level of cost sharing with its retirees or (2) consistently increasing or decreasing its

---

[2] While SFAS No. 106 applies to all health and welfare postretirement benefits other than pensions, its main focus is on retiree health benefits because of their high cost and complexity of measurement.

share of the cost of benefits by changing retirees' or active plan participants' contributions, deductibles, coinsurance provisions, out-of-pocket limitations, and so forth, in accordance with the employer's established cost-sharing policy.

2. The employer has the ability, and has communicated to affected plan participants its intent, to institute different cost-sharing provisions at a specified time or when certain conditions exist (e.g., when health care cost increases exceed a certain level).

SFAS No. 106 provides little guidance as to what constitutes a past practice of consistently maintaining or changing the cost-sharing provisions.

In reviewing the employer's determination of the substantive plan, the auditor might, in addition to reading the plan document and its amendments and the actuary's report, perform a variety of procedures, including making inquiries of management and reviewing past changes to cost-sharing provisions and communications to employees and retirees.

(ii) Actuarial Assumptions.   SFAS No. 106 describes a number of actuarial assumptions that should be considered in measuring an employer's postretirement health care obligation. Similar to a pension valuation, a retiree health valuation includes such assumptions as employee turnover, retirement age, and mortality. Certain assumptions that are made in a pension plan, however, may have a more significant effect in measuring retiree health care obligations. For example, assumptions about early retirement are less significant for a pension valuation because when an employee retires early, pension payments generally are reduced to reflect the longer time period over which payments will be made. Retiree health care costs simply would be incurred for a longer time period, however, if an employee retires early. Furthermore, the employer's portion of health care costs for retirees younger than age 65 usually is significantly higher than that for retirees age 65 or older since, in most cases, Medicare provides coverage only beginning at age 65.

Measuring the obligation for postretirement health care benefits requires employers to make assumptions about the amount and timing of benefits expected to be paid in the future. In estimating the amount of future payments, employers need to consider various factors, including historical claims cost by age, health care cost trend rates, and medical coverage to be provided by governmental authorities and others. Many of the calculations required by SFAS No. 106 are actuarial calculations that should be considered the work of a specialist, and the auditor should apply the provisions of SAS No. 73, *Using the Work of a Specialist* (AU Section 336). Auditing these amounts is similar to auditing accrued pension costs, as discussed above.

In circumstances in which the auditor's testing of actuarial assumptions calls for corresponding directly with the actuary, the auditor may choose to use a standard confirmation request letter developed by the AICPA.[3] Although the scope of SFAS No. 106 encompasses postretirement benefits other than health care, this letter was designed for postretirement health care benefits. Letters to actuaries, if any, that value

[3] This letter appeared in the November 1992 *Journal of Accountancy*, pp. 93–98. It has been reproduced in Richard M. Steinberg, Ronald J. Murray, and Harold Dankner, *Pensions and Other Employee Benefits: A Financial Reporting and ERISA Compliance Guide*, 4th ed. (New York: John Wiley & Sons, 1993), pp. 390–395.

other postretirement benefits, such as life insurance, tuition, legal services, and day care and housing subsidies, should be appropriately modified.

Much of the information used by the actuary to measure the obligation is often maintained and provided by the employer or by a third-party administrator (TPA). Such information includes historical claims cost and participants' age, sex, and dates of birth and hire. The auditor usually can test much of this information in conjunction with the testing required when auditing the pension plan obligation, except for historical claims cost, which usually will be the subject of separate audit focus.

In some circumstances, the claims cost experience of other employers—derived from data maintained by insurers, actuarial firms, or benefit consultants and adjusted as necessary for differing demographics—can be used to develop relevant cost information. If such third-party data is used, the auditor should consider its reasonableness and relevance to the employer's circumstances.

Employers often have information on net claims paid rather than on gross eligible charges. SFAS No. 106 allows calculations based on net claims cost, provided such amounts are appropriately adjusted to reflect the plan's cost-sharing provisions.

(c) Postemployment Benefit Obligations

SFAS No. 112, *Employers' Accounting for Postemployment Benefits* (Accounting Standards Section P32), provides standards for accounting for and reporting the estimated cost of benefits provided by an employer to former or inactive employees after employment but before retirement (postemployment benefits).

(i) Types of Postemployment Benefits Offered by Employers.
Employers may offer a variety of benefits to former or inactive employees after employment but before retirement, and to such employees' beneficiaries and covered dependents. Inactive employees are those who are not currently rendering service to the employer but have not been terminated, such as those who have been laid off or those on disability leave, regardless of whether they are expected to return to active status.

These benefits may include, but are not limited to, salary continuation, supplemental unemployment benefits, severance benefits, disability-related benefits (including worker's compensation), job training and counseling, and continuation of benefits such as health care and life insurance. Such benefits may be paid in cash or in kind, immediately upon cessation of active employment or over a specified period of time.

The auditor needs to gain an understanding of the benefits the entity offers and how they are accounted for. In particular, the auditor should ascertain whether management has appropriately identified benefits to which SFAS No. 112 applies. This determination can be difficult at times. For instance, some employers consider permanently disabled employees to be retired at the date of disability and therefore include certain benefits under their pension plan (accounted for under SFAS No. 87) and include health care benefits under their postretirement medical plan (accounted for under SFAS No. 106). Other employers do not consider a permanently disabled employee to be retired when he or she becomes disabled.

(ii) Accounting Requirements.
SFAS No. 112 requires recognition of postemployment costs on an accrual basis. Under the statement, employers should recognize

the obligation to provide postemployment benefits in accordance with SFAS No. 43, *Accounting for Compensated Absences* (Accounting Standards Section C44), if:

- The obligation is attributable to employees' services already rendered
- Employees' rights to the benefits accumulate over time
- Payment of the benefits is probable
- The amount of the benefits can be reasonably estimated

If these four conditions are not met, the employer should account for postemployment benefits when it is probable that a liability has been incurred and the amount can be reasonably estimated, in accordance with SFAS No. 5, *Accounting for Contingencies*. If an obligation for postemployment benefits is not accrued in accordance with SFAS No. 5 or No. 43 only because the amount cannot be reasonably estimated, the financial statements are required to disclose that fact.

SFAS No. 112 provides little guidance or examples for determining whether the criteria in SFAS No. 5 or No. 43 apply to a particular benefit program. In many circumstances, the auditor will need to evaluate and review documentation supporting the policies and intent of management's plans. For instance, when assessing whether payment of benefits for severance and layoff benefits under SFAS No. 43 is probable, the auditor may review memoranda or minutes of meetings that substantiate management's plans for work force reductions.

The statement also contains little specific guidance on measuring postemployment obligations and expense. However, it does indicate that discounting is permitted (but not required). It also suggests that employers may look to SFAS Nos. 87 and 106 for guidance on measurement issues to the extent that similar issues apply to postretirement and postemployment benefits, although delayed recognition of the transition obligation would not be appropriate for postemployment benefits.

(iii) Auditing Postemployment Benefits.   In many respects, the procedures for auditing employee postemployment benefit costs and obligations are similar to those for auditing postretirement benefits under SFAS No. 106, including reviewing the appropriateness of actuarial assumptions about the amount and timing of benefits, and personnel data, such as the employer's records of employees' salaries and employment terms. Auditing procedures should therefore be coordinated with work performed in connection with auditing postretirement benefits or, in some circumstances, auditing pension benefits.

(d)   Environmental Liabilities

A large number of entities in a wide variety of industries are affected by environmental laws and regulations—primarily the Resource Conservation and Recovery Act of 1976 (RCRA) and the Comprehensive Environmental Response, Compensation and Liability Act of 1980 (CERCLA, also known as Superfund)—governing (1) responsibility for ongoing hazardous waste management and pollution control, and (2) the remediation of historical hazardous waste sites. This section discusses accounting and auditing aspects of environmental remediation costs that are created by the threat that a claim, an assessment, or litigation may be asserted.

To date, the Environmental Protection Agency (EPA) has identified thousands of polluted sites, the most seriously contaminated of which are graded for their toxicity and danger to the public. The EPA also may initiate cleanup efforts at the sites and may seek to recover so-called "response costs," which are costs incurred by the government in overseeing and studying remediation, from entities that are determined to have contributed to the pollution. The most polluted sites—currently over 1,000—are placed on a National Priority List (NPL). The EPA has estimated that cleanup might cost an average of $25–$50 million per site, with the most troublesome sites costing more than $1 billion to remediate.

Through the Superfund legislation, the EPA is empowered to seek recovery from any entity (commonly referred to as a potentially responsible party, or PRP) that ever owned or operated a contaminated site or generated or transported hazardous materials to a site. Cleanup costs of Superfund sites represent a potentially significant liability for entities in industries such as chemicals, primary metals, electroplating, textiles, petroleum refining, rubber, and plastics. Banks, insurers, and real estate developers also may be at risk in their dealings with manufacturers and their contaminated properties. Subsequent owners as well as parent companies of PRPs may be potentially liable for cleanup costs.

In identifying a hazardous waste site, the EPA determines the people or entities that have some connection with the property. Under Superfund, PRPs can be held responsible for remediation costs for any one of five reasons:

1. They may be the current owners or operators of the property
2. They may have been owners or operators of the property at the time the hazardous substances were deposited
3. They may be, or may have been, the generators of the hazardous substances deposited at the property
4. They may have transported the hazardous substances to the property
5. They may have arranged for treatment or disposal of an entity's hazardous substances at another entity's facility

If the parties originally responsible for the contamination are financially insolvent or no longer exist, the responsibility falls on all other PRPs. That could be the present or former property owner or operator, even if that party had no part in contaminating the site.

The EPA on occasion requires payment of response costs, as well as legal fees expended. In addition to remediation and response costs, any responsible party also may be liable for natural resource damages for each release of hazardous substances. The EPA rarely has assessed damages, but if it does the potential cost could be sizable and could exceed the response costs.

Given the joint and several nature of the liability imposed by Superfund, large entities may find themselves facing response costs far greater than their proportionate share of the waste would otherwise indicate. Once a PRP has incurred response costs or reimbursed the government under a cost recovery suit, however, that party can identify other PRPs who also have some connection with the site, and can initiate a private party cost recovery action. Corrective action cleanups under RCRA are similar to those under Superfund; however, under RCRA there usually are no other parties involved against which cost recovery actions can be brought because the corrective actions typically involve entity-owned and operated facilities.

A number of publicly held companies have reported significant income statement charges for environmental cleanup costs. The list of entities recording and disclosing these charges is expected to grow, as government authorities continue to evaluate hazardous waste sites, and as entities complete cost estimates and engineering studies related to environmental cleanup. In addition, a number of lawsuits have been filed in which shareholders claim to have been financially damaged by corporations that failed to disclose environmental problems. As a result, entities are under pressure to take a hard and realistic look at their operations for potential exposure.

(i) Accounting Requirements.   Statement of Position (SOP) 96-1, *Environmental Remediation Liabilities*, provides accounting guidance for cleanup costs incurred under Superfund and other pollution control laws and regulations. It requires environmental remediation liabilities to be accrued when the criteria of SFAS No. 5, *Accounting for Contingencies* (discussed in Chapter 26), are met, and includes benchmarks to aid in the determination of when such liabilities should be recognized. It provides guidance on the recognition, measurement, display, and disclosure of environmental remediation liabilities. The SOP also includes a nonauthoritative section on pollution control and environmental remediation liability laws and regulations.

The SOP provides guidance only on accounting for environmental *remediation* liabilities; it does not provide guidance on accounting for pollution control costs with respect to current operations, for costs of future site restoration or closure that are required on the cessation of operations or sale of facilities, or for environmental remediation undertaken at the sole discretion of management. Also, it does not provide guidance on recognizing liabilities of insurance companies for unpaid environmental cleanup-related claims or address asset impairment issues.

The SOP incorporates, and thus effectively supersedes, the guidance in EITF Issue 93-5, *Accounting for Environmental Liabilities*. EITF Issue 89-13, *Accounting for the Cost of Asbestos Removal*, and Issue 90-8, *Capitalization of Costs to Treat Environmental Contamination*, are reprinted in the SOP and continue to be applicable. SEC Staff Accounting Bulletin (SAB) No. 92 continues to be applicable to SEC registrants and also is reproduced in the SOP.

(ii) Auditing Environmental Remediation Liabilities.   The SOP also provides guidance on auditing environmental remediation liabilities. It discusses audit objectives, assessment of audit risk, substantive auditing procedures, reviewing and testing the process used by management to develop the estimate of remediation liabilities, developing an independent expectation of the estimate, using the work of a specialist, auditing potential recoveries, inquiries of an entity's lawyer, management representations, assessing disclosure, evaluation of audit test results, communication with audit committees, and reporting considerations.

Exposures to environmental liabilities represent loss contingencies that constitute an uncertainty. Contingencies and uncertainties are discussed in Chapter 26. The guidance in AU Section 508.29–32, *Reports on Audited Financial Statements* (which is discussed in Chapter 28), should be followed in evaluating the effect, if any, of the uncertainty on the auditor's report. As indicated in Chapter 28, the auditor should distinguish between situations involving uncertainties and those involving scope limitations. In the latter case, the auditor may need to qualify or disclaim an opinion.

When performing risk assessment activities, auditors should consider the possibility of material environmental liabilities and should plan the audit accordingly. When identifying inherent risks, auditors should take into account the entity's industry, which may be particularly susceptible to environmental issues; the nature of its operations and manufacturing or other processes; and real estate holdings that may represent environmental risks. Auditors should discuss with entity management the steps it has taken to identify all exposures to environmental risks and should consider obtaining representations about estimates and disclosures of environmental remediation liabilities and contingencies in the management representation letter, which is discussed in Chapter 27. The auditor also should request information about environmental remediation matters in the letter of inquiry sent to the entity's legal counsel, which also is discussed in Chapter 27.

If an entity has established an estimate for an environmental liability, the auditor needs to determine the reasonableness of the estimate. This involves gaining an understanding of the method management used to develop the estimate, which in turn requires that the auditor become familiar with the remediation process used or planned for cleaning up contaminated areas. This understanding will help the auditor select the appropriate procedures for evaluating the reasonableness of management's estimate.

As discussed in Chapter 15, according to SAS No. 57, *Auditing Accounting Estimates* (AU Section 342), when auditing estimates, auditors should use one or a combination of the following approaches:

- Review and test the process used by management to develop the estimate
- Develop an independent expectation of the estimate to corroborate the reasonableness of management's estimate
- Review subsequent events or transactions occurring prior to completion of field work

Typically, auditors use either of the first two approaches, or a combination thereof, for auditing the estimate of environmental cleanup costs. In reviewing and testing management's estimating process, the auditor should consider the following procedures specific to environmental costs, in addition to those used for auditing accounting estimates in general:

- Understand management's process for developing its estimate
- Obtain supporting detail for the estimate and review the underlying assumptions
- Ensure that the estimate includes costs for all phases of remediation
- Review the assumptions surrounding third-party involvement (such as other PRPs and insurance coverage)
- If necessary, review the remediation process and cost estimates with appropriate specialists and evaluate their credentials

(e)   Self-Insurance Arrangements

Self-insurance (sometimes referred to as "no insurance") is a method of risk management in which the entity retains some risk of loss rather than pay a third party (i.e., an insurance company) to assume the risk. The amount of risk that an entity retains will vary depending on the nature of the risk and other considerations, such as the cost of insurance versus the monetary exposure if a loss had to be absorbed. Self-insurance may be combined with purchased insurance; for example, an entity may opt to self-insure small losses and purchase insurance (umbrella coverage) to protect against major losses. Moreover, some forms of purchased insurance result in the entity retaining some risk of loss, which also is a form of self-insurance.

A captive insurance company is an entity created and controlled by a parent entity for the main purpose of providing insurance for the parent. If risk is underwritten through this device, the auditor should understand the specialized accounting and auditing issues associated with a captive insurance company, and consider performing some or all of the following procedures:

- Assess the economic viability of the insurance captive
- Review its audited financial statements and actuarial loss reserve certifications
- Determine whether the captive underwrites insurance for third parties (e.g., reinsurers and other insurance providers). If so, review agreements to ensure the propriety of coverage limits, periods covered, and premium and loss activity
- Determine that the captive has the proper legal status in the country of its domicile
- Assess the appropriateness of the captive's reserves for estimated losses from asserted and unasserted claims, ensuring that reserves are consistent with industry practices

In retrospectively rated (as contrasted with guaranteed cost) policies, an estimated or deposit premium is paid to the insurance company at the inception of the contract period. The deposit premium consists of a minimum premium plus an amount for estimated claims. During the term of the policy, the deposit premium is adjusted, subject to any minimum and maximum premium limitations of the contract, based on the insured's claims experience. Auditors normally review retrospectively rated policy agreements, noting specific terms that affect premium adjustments (such as experience and claims periods and the methodology for calculating adjustments) to determine whether an additional premium liability should be recorded at the balance sheet date.

Claims-made insurance is a type of insurance that covers damage claims presented to the insurance company during the policy period. This form of coverage differs from the more traditional, occurrence-based coverage, which covers damages that occur (regardless of when the claims are presented for reimbursement) during the policy period. The major difference between the two versions of liability coverage is the event that activates or triggers the coverage. If a claims-made policy is not continually renewed or if "tail coverage" (that is, coverage for future periods) is not obtained when the policy is discontinued, an entity will be uninsured for claims reported to the insurance company after the termination of the policy, regardless of when the incidents occurred. Accordingly, the entity may need to accrue a liability at the balance sheet date for incurred but not reported claims that will be reported after the claims-made policy expires.

The auditor also should determine whether additional accruals for losses or unpaid deductibles are necessary as a result, for example, of cancellation of policies previously in force or changes in deductibles for new types of coverage.

When auditing entities using self-insurance arrangements, the auditor should consider factors such as the following:

- Types of insurance policies in force
- Actual or potential uninsured loss exposure from claims that could be filed after the expiration of a claims-made policy
- Cancellation of any significant policies previously in force
- Purchase of new policies with terms that are significantly different from previous policies (e.g., deductibles)
- Whether the entity changed the form of its insurance policies from occurrence to claims-made or from guaranteed costs to retrospectively rated
- Whether any prior insurers are insolvent, in rehabilitation, or of questionable solvency

If the entity has some form of self-insurance, the auditor will want to ensure that the liability for self-insurance claims is properly reported in the balance sheet. This includes determining whether all liabilities for self-insured occurrences through the balance sheet date have been considered. When an estimated accrual is made for the amount of a probable loss, the accrued amount should be the most likely amount in a range. If no amount in the range is more likely than any other, the minimum amount should be accrued. If the amount of the loss cannot be reasonably estimated, the nature of the contingency should be disclosed. The program of self-insurance coverage and the basis for any loss accruals also should be adequately disclosed in the financial statements.

When auditing entities with self-insurance liabilities, auditors should consider performing the following procedures:

- Review the amount of insurance coverage, if any, the type of coverage (claims-made or occurrence), the deductible provisions, and other relevant factors to determine the level of risk that is retained by the entity. Consider the financial viability of the insurance carrier
- Test the accuracy and completeness of the entity's incident reporting and monitoring system
- Review and test the method of estimating incurred but not reported (IBNR) claims
- Review actuarial reports used to estimate the liability for self-insurance claims, including the IBNR claims. Determine the extent of reliance on actuaries in accordance with SAS No. 73, *Using the Work of a Specialist* (AU Section 336)
- Determine the extent to which entity-relevant industry data is used to estimate the number, frequency, and loss value of reported and unreported incidents

- Determine that a liability is recorded for any additional premium that may be owed for retrospectively rated policies
- Review prior estimates and historical loss experience
- Review the appropriateness of disclosures related to self-insurance

(f) Substantive Tests of Other Prepayments and Accruals

(i) Prepaid Insurance. Most well-controlled entities maintain an insurance register that indicates, for each policy, the insurance company, policy number, type and amount of coverage, policy dates, premium, prepayments, expense for the period, and any coinsurance provision. From this register or from the insurance policies themselves, a schedule of prepaid insurance should be prepared, preferably by the entity's staff. The auditor should test the data shown on the schedule and examine insurance policies and vouchers supporting premiums. In addition, the auditor should note beneficiaries and evidence of liens on the insured property.

If original insurance policies are not available for inspection, the auditor should determine the reason. Since lenders often retain insurance policies on property that collateralizes loans, the absence of policies may indicate the existence of liens on the property. The auditor should request management to obtain the policies (or copies of them) and should examine them. Depending on his or her assessment of control risk, the auditor may request confirmations from the insurance companies or brokers.

Prepaid liability and compensation insurance, if premiums are based on payrolls, may be compared with payrolls to determine that charges to expense appear proper. Premiums due may exceed advance payments so that at the end of a period there may be a liability rather than a prepayment. Total prepaid insurance per the insurance register or schedule of prepaid insurance should be compared with the general ledger.

An auditor usually is not an expert in determining insurable values and has no responsibility for management's decisions concerning insuring risks and coverage, but may render helpful service by calling attention to differences among the amount of coverage, the insurable value (if available), and the recorded amount of insured property.

(ii) Prepaid and Accrued Property Taxes. The auditor should determine that the amount of prepaid taxes is actually an expense applicable to future periods, and should refer to local tax bills and laws because state and local tax statutes vary widely in their proration provisions. The related expense account should be analyzed and compared with prior years' accounts. Since taxes generally are computed by multiplying a base by a rate, the auditor can analyze the two components and seek explanations for fluctuations.

(iii) Prepaid and Accrued Commissions. The auditor should investigate whether prepaid or accrued commissions are proper. If commission expense is material, the auditor may wish to examine contracts with salespeople or obtain from management an authoritative statement of the employment terms. He or she may review sales reports, commission records, or other evidence of commissions earned, or may trace amounts in sales reports to commission records and cash records. If there are many salespeople, the auditor may, depending on his or her risk assessment, limit the examination to only a few accounts or to the entries for only a limited period. Transactions in the last month of the period may be reviewed to determine that commissions have been allocated to the proper period. The auditor should be satisfied that prepayments will be matched with revenues of future periods and are not current-period compensation. If amounts are significant, the auditor should consider confirming directly with salespeople the amounts due them and the commissions they earned during the year, and should test—for example, by applying commission rates against sales—the overall reasonableness of commission expense for the year. If there is a subsidiary ledger for prepaid or accrued commission accounts, the auditor should compare the balance of the general ledger account with the trial balance of the subsidiary ledger and investigate any differences.

(iv) Travel and Other Advances. Advances to employees for expenses may be tested by examining cash disbursements, expense reports, and cash receipts. If employees are advanced amounts as working funds on an imprest basis, the auditor may examine reimbursements in the month following the end of the period to determine whether material expenditures prior to the end of the period have been reimbursed. The auditor may review related entries after period-end to determine whether any should have been recorded in the period under audit. Advances may be confirmed by correspondence with employees. The general ledger account should be compared with the subsidiary ledger and differences investigated; the individual balances may be aged and long outstanding balances scrutinized. The auditor should identify unusual advances to officers and examine evidence that they were authorized.

(v) Accrued Professional Fees. The auditor should consider including in the audit inquiry letters to lawyers a request for the amounts of unpaid or unbilled charges, which can then be compared with the recorded liability.

(vi) Bonuses and Profit-Sharing Plans. Amounts due officers and employees under bonus or profit-sharing plans become a liability in the period during which the profits are earned. The auditor should determine that the liability is computed in accordance with the authorization and the plans in effect. If the exact amount of the liability cannot be determined until a later date, it must be estimated at the balance sheet date.

(vii) Unpaid Dividends. The auditor should recompute the liability for cash dividends declared but unpaid at the balance sheet date by multiplying the number of shares outstanding at the date of record by the rate of the dividend declared.

Frequently stockholders cannot be reached and dividend checks may be returned by the post office. The liability for unclaimed dividends may remain undischarged for some time, and the auditor may examine evidence to support charges and credits to the account.

Many large corporations, particularly those that have numerous stockholders or bondholders, turn over to fiscal agents the details of dividend or bond interest payments. Under those arrangements, the corporations usually consider their dividend or interest obligations discharged when they deposit the amount of the aggregate required payments with the fiscal agent. In those circumstances, the auditor is not concerned with unpaid dividend checks or uncashed bond coupons, which become obligations of the agent.

(viii) Compensated Absences.   SFAS No. 43, *Accounting for Compensated Absences* (Accounting Standards Section C44), requires that a liability be accrued for vacation benefits earned but not yet taken by employees. SFAS No. 43 generally does not, however, require a liability to be accrued for nonvesting sick pay, holidays, and other similar benefits until employees are actually absent.

The auditor should determine the method used to accrue vacation pay and accumulated vested sick pay, consider whether the method is appropriate and consistent with prior years, and recompute or test the recorded amounts. If vacation periods are based on length of service, the entity normally prepares a detailed computation of the accrued liability. The auditor should review the computation method used and test the accuracy of the computation. If a detailed computation is not available for testing, the auditor should estimate the amount of the accrual on an overall basis.

(ix) Royalties Payable.   In evaluating the amount of royalties payable, the auditor should examine royalty and licensing contracts and extract important provisions for the permanent files. He or she should try to determine from a royalty contract whether the payments are actually royalties or whether, in fact, they represent payments for the purchase of a patent or other asset covered by the agreement. If the contract is in reality a purchase agreement, the asset and liability should be recognized at the date of the contract, and depreciation or amortization of the asset should be charged to expense. If provisions of a royalty contract are not clear, the auditor should request a legal interpretation of ambiguous provisions.

Many contracts provide for a minimum royalty payment regardless of whether a liability for royalties accrues on a unit basis. If royalty payments are based on sales, the auditor may compare computations with recorded sales; statements of royalties due may be tested to substantiate recorded amounts. If royalty payments are based on the quantity or value of goods produced rather than on sales, the auditor should review documents on file supporting amounts accrued and test the underlying data. If accounting records are not kept in sufficient detail to furnish the required information, it may be necessary to analyze production records.

If lessors or vendors possess the only data on which royalties are based, statements of liability under royalty agreements may be secured from them. A request for confirmation may produce evidence of important differences in interpretation of contract provisions.

(x) Provisions for Warranty Costs.   Through inquiry and reading contracts and similar documents, the auditor should obtain an understanding of the entity's warranty policies as a first step in evaluating whether the estimated liability for warranty claims is adequate. Auditing procedures in this area commonly include examining documentation supporting open warranty claims, reviewing claims settled after the balance sheet date, and considering past activity in the account in the light of relevant changes (such as new products or changes in warranty periods)—all for the purpose of determining whether the estimated liability at the balance sheet date is adequate. The auditor also should apply the procedures discussed in Chapter 15 (Section 15.4, Testing Accounting Judgments and Estimates).

(xi) Suspense Debits and Credits.   Every chart of accounts contains a place for debit and credit items whose final accounting has not been determined. The person responsible may not have decided which expense account should be charged; the job order, cost center, or subaccount may not have been opened yet; or there may be some other unresolved question about the handling or propriety of the item. Although most suspense debit and credit accounts may be quite active during the year, all material issues should be resolved by year-end. The auditor should understand the nature of suspense items and how they arose, since their existence, even at an interim date, could indicate a deficiency in internal control.

The auditor may want to test balances at an interim date, however, and inquire into the disposition of items. This may contribute considerably to understanding the kinds of accounting problems that can occur and their implications for the auditor's risk assessment. In the rare instance of balances remaining at the end of the year, the auditor should age the items and inquire into the reasons why the proper distribution has not been determined. Particularly in the case of suspense debits, an entity commonly and understandably often wishes to carry in the balance sheet disputed items that someone in management "just doesn't want to give up on." If those debits are significant, the auditor needs evidence that they are likely to have a realizable value or to benefit future operations, and are therefore properly classified as assets.

21

Auditing Investments in Debt and Equity Securities and Related Income

"Investments," as used in this chapter, is a broad term used to describe nonoperating, income-producing assets of a nonfinancial commercial or industrial entity that are held either as a means of using excess cash or to accomplish some specified purpose. (Investments held by banks, insurance companies, investment companies, and securities and commodities broker-dealers are covered in Chapters 33, 41, 42, and 49, respectively.) Often, the description of investments in the financial statements gives further insight into the specific reasons they are held. Readers of financial statements should look at classifications, descriptions in captions, and descriptive notes to determine the nature and purpose of an entity's investments and management's intent in holding them. Income statement accounts related to investments include interest income, dividend income, gains or losses, and earnings or losses from investments accounted for by the equity method. (Changes in the fair value of available-for-sale securities are reflected in the equity section of the balance sheet.)

This chapter addresses investments in debt and equity securities (hereinafter referred to as "investments") and related income. The term "security" is defined in Statement of Financial Accounting Standards (SFAS) No. 115, *Accounting for Certain Investments in Debt and Equity Securities* (Accounting Standards Section I80), as are the terms "equity security" and "debt security." [1]

---

[1] The following definitions appear in Appendix C, "Glossary," of SFAS No. 115:

> [A security is] a share, participation, or other interest in property or in an enterprise of the issuer or an obligation of the issuer that (a) either is represented by an instrument issued in bearer or registered form or, if not represented by an instrument, is registered in books maintained to record transfers by or on behalf of the issuer, (b) is of a type commonly dealt in on securities exchanges or markets or, when represented by an instrument, is commonly recognized in any area in which it is issued or dealt in as a medium for investment, and (c) either is one of a class or series or by its terms is divisible into a class or series of shares, participations, interests, or obligations.

> [A debt security is] any security representing a creditor relationship with an enterprise. It also includes (a) preferred stock that by its terms either must be redeemed by the issuing enterprise or is redeemable at the option of the investor and (b) a collateralized mortgage obligation (CMO) (or other instrument) that is issued in equity form but is required to be accounted for as a nonequity instrument regardless of how that instrument is classified (that is, whether equity or debt) in the issuer's statement of financial position. However, it excludes option contracts, financial futures contracts, forward contracts, and lease contracts.

> - Thus, the term *debt security* includes, among other items, U. S. Treasury securities, U. S. government agency securities, municipal securities, corporate bonds, convertible debt, commercial paper, all securitized debt instruments, such as CMOs and real estate mortgage investment conduits (REMICs), and interest-only and principal-only strips.

> - Trade accounts receivable arising from sales on credit by industrial or commercial enterprises and loans receivable arising from consumer, commercial, and real estate mortgage lending activities of financial institutions are examples of receivables that do not meet the definition of *security*; thus, those receivables are not debt securities (unless they have been securitized, in which case they would meet the definition).

> [An equity security is] any security representing an ownership interest in an enterprise (for example, common, preferred, or other capital stock) or the right to acquire (for example, warrants, rights, and call options) or dispose of (for example, put options) an ownership interest in an enterprise at fixed or determinable prices. However, the term does not include convertible debt or preferred stock that by its terms either must be redeemed by the issuing enterprise or is redeemable at the option of the investor.

21.1   AUDIT OBJECTIVES

Specific audit objectives applicable to investments and income from investments are described in Figure 21.1.

21.2   TYPICAL INVESTMENT TRANSACTIONS AND CONTROLS

The steps involved in processing investment activities by commercial and industrial entities are more likely to be similar from one entity to another than in many other areas of business operations. They are often rather formal and well organized, whether the purpose is short-term investment of temporary excess cash, long-term investment, or investment for purposes of affiliation or control. The activities begin with selection and authorization of an investment; subsequent steps are acquisition, safeguarding, accounting for income, valuation, and disposition.

Management normally is aware of and monitors the amounts of funds available for investment as well as the future need for funds. In addition, many controls related to investment activities are administered directly by management.

(a)   Selection and Authorization

If investment activities are not significant, the selection and authorization of investments generally are specifically delegated to an executive officer, often the treasurer. If the activities are significant, they usually are overseen by top officers or by the board of directors itself, although investment transactions may be initiated automatically, for example, by overnight sweeps of cash balances into money market instruments, or by portfolio managers who manage discretionary accounts. Often an investment committee of officers or directors employs an investment advisor to whom it delegates the authority to make specific decisions about investment acquisitions and dispositions. Ultimately, however, the responsibility for investment decisions rests with management and the board of directors.

Control activities for selecting investments include formulating policies for the appropriate level of risk to be assumed, authorization by the board (either for specific investments or in the form of a general authorization to an officer or advisor to make investment decisions within specified parameters), and high-level management review and explicit approval of specific investment decisions before they are executed.

(b)   Acquisition

Controls over the acquisition process in general, for example, authorization for the disbursement of funds, are discussed in Chapter 14. The following discussion relates to additional control activities that are specific to the acquisition of investments.

Investments often are acquired through financial institutions that deal in formal markets. Typically, control activities include some form of approved acquisition list, which may include maximum prices, minimum yields, and minimum credit ratings. In an entity with effective controls, the approved list would reflect management's assessment of the risks inherent in various types of securities and the returns they gen-

Figure 21.1   Audit Objectives for Investments in Debt and Equity Securities and Related Income

Completeness	All investments owned by the entity at the balance sheet date are included in the financial statements.
	All investment income, including gains and losses, that should be recognized during the period covered by the financial statements is reflected in the financial statements; accrued investment income represents all amounts earned but not received at the balance sheet date.
Accuracy	Investments on hand at the end of the period and investment transactions that occurred during the period are based on correct prices and are accurately computed.
	Income from investments, including realized and unrealized gains and losses, is accurately reflected in the financial statements.
Existence/Occurrence	Recorded investments exist at the balance sheet date.
	Recorded investment transactions represent acquisitions and dispositions that actually occurred during the period covered by the financial statements.
	Recorded investment income, including recognized gains and losses, represent earnings and losses that actually occurred during the period covered by the financial statements.
Cutoff	Investment transactions and income from investments are recorded in the proper period.
Valuation	The accounting policies adopted by the entity for particular types of investments are in conformity with generally accepted accounting principles.
	The values at which investments are carried in the financial statements are in conformity with generally accepted accounting principles.
	All investment income, including realized and unrealized gains and losses that should be recognized, has been recognized.
Rights and Obligations	The entity has legal title to investments.
	There are no undisclosed encumbrances against the entity's investments.
Presentation and Disclosure	Investments are properly classified.
	All required disclosures related to investments and investment income have been made.
	Investments pledged as collateral or otherwise restricted are appropriately disclosed.

erate. Acquisitions of investments that do not have readily determinable fair values are almost always unique events, even if a fairly large number of units is acquired at one time, such as acquisitions of nonmarketable equity securities or of real estate for an endowment fund or investment portfolio. Selecting investments and negotiating acquisition terms are likely to be delegated to an investment specialist; high-level management review and approval are required before investment decisions are executed.

(c) Safeguarding Investments

Physical protection of securities is vital because many of them are readily negotiable; moreover, documents evidencing legal ownership have value even if securities are not readily negotiable. Therefore, physical controls and segregation of duties are particularly important for investments. Securities generally are kept in a vault or safe deposit box, or entrusted to a financial institution for safekeeping. The custodian and other personnel who have access to the securities should be independent of the functions of authorizing investment transactions, keeping investment records, handling cash, and maintaining the general ledger; preferably, each of those employees should be independent of all the others.

If securities are kept in a safe deposit box at a bank or in a vault on the premises, the number of people with authorized access should be kept to a minimum, but it is preferable for two people to be present whenever the box is opened. A safe deposit box is an effective means of protection, because a bank's provisions for physical security and procedures for restricting and controlling access to the vault are normally more extensive than most commercial and industrial entities are able to maintain

Other control activities for investments generally include periodically inspecting and counting securities for which delivery has been taken, reconciling the count to the general ledger, and investigating differences. Those procedures should be performed by people other than those responsible for authorizing and executing transactions and maintaining custody of the securities. Even if securities have been entrusted to a financial institution for safekeeping, or exist in electronic notation (book entry) form, the entity still needs to maintain records of transactions and balances and to periodically reconcile the records with those of the custodian.

(d) Accounting for Income

Chapter 13 discusses controls over incoming receipts; those controls are applicable to the processing of income from dividends and interest received directly by an entity.

Accounting for income from publicly traded marketable securities is usually straightforward: Interest is accrued periodically and dividends are recorded as received (or when the shares first trade "ex-dividend"). Published records of interest, dividends, and other distributions are compared with recorded income periodically to ensure that all income has been received on a timely basis. That procedure is more effective if it is exercised by a person other than those responsible for initially recording investments and cash receipts from investment income. If an investment is accounted for on the equity method, copies of financial statements of the investee are needed to determine the appropriate earnings or losses to record.

(e)   Valuation of Investments

Periodic valuation of investments is necessary for management decision-making purposes; it also is required so that fair value can be determined for financial statement purposes. If investments are few, have readily determinable fair values, and are not significant to an entity's operations, the valuation process sometimes is performed informally by the officer responsible for investments. If investments are significant, the valuation should be formally executed and documented. The frequency of valuation depends on the amount of investment activity and how often financial statements are issued. (Some active investment portfolios are under virtually continual valuation.)

(f)   Disposition

Dispositions of investments are usually subject to many of the same controls that are in place for acquisitions. Controls over the receipt and processing of proceeds from dispositions are discussed in Chapter 13.

(g)   Records of Investments

An investment ledger is desirable regardless of the size of a portfolio. The ledger generally contains an account for each investment, which is described completely: full title of the issue; number of shares or face value; certificate numbers (if the entity takes delivery of the securities); interest or dividend rate; maturities or other features such as call, conversion, or collateral; cost; and required amortization of premium or discount. If the tax basis is different from the book basis, the former also may be noted in the investment ledger account. The detail of the investment ledger is reconciled periodically to the general ledger control account.

(h)   Controls over Complex Financial Instruments

Additional controls over assessing and monitoring the risks associated with sophisticated and complex financial instruments, including derivatives, often are established in addition to those that apply to investment transactions generally.[2]

Management should establish an overall, entity-wide policy defining the objectives for entering into transactions involving financial instruments with off-balance-sheet credit or market risk or concentrations of credit risk.[3] The policy should cover selecting broker-dealers, portfolio managers, or investment advisors and limits on investments in particular financial instruments or particular industries, counterparties, and traders. Policies also should ensure that, when appropriate, the entity has obtained adequate collateral (both initially and on an ongoing basis). Policies should also address controls over securities in the possession of others that serve to collateralize borrowings and other transactions. These policies should be approved by the board of directors.

---

[2] Audit tests related to investments in sophisticated financial instruments are discussed later in this chapter. Disclosure requirements for derivatives are discussed in Chapter 26.

[3] These risks are discussed later in this chapter and in Chapter 26.

Transactions should be monitored on a regular basis and procedures should be in place to react to risks that have exceeded what management wishes to bear. Formal procedures should be established to monitor the economic health of counterparties (issuers). Appropriate levels of management reporting should be put in place. Procedures also should exist to segregate duties effectively among individuals responsible for making investment and credit decisions, custody of securities, disbursing and receiving funds, record keeping, confirmation of positions, and performing reconciliations.

21.3 DETERMINING THE AUDIT STRATEGY

In many commercial and industrial entities, the investment portfolio is not significant to the financial statements, and efficiency considerations often lead the auditor to adopt a strategy that emphasizes substantive testing. In some situations, however, the auditor may choose to perform tests of controls as a basis for reducing the assurance needed from substantive tests.

The assurance needed from substantive tests reflects in part the auditor's identification of inherent risks associated with the entity's particular types of investments. Identifying those risks, which have both accounting and auditing implications, is especially important if the entity's investment portfolio includes sophisticated, complex financial instruments whose terms and risks may not be widely understood. In addition to the risk of theft or physical loss of the securities, risks associated with investments are composed of information risk, market risk, and credit risk.

- *Information risk* is the possibility that the investor will be misinformed about or misunderstand the terms or the underlying economic substance of an investment, including the expected return. This can result in incorrect pricing and valuation of securities, inappropriate accounting for investment income, and unrealistic expectations about the investment's market and credit risk.

- *Market risk* is the possibility that future changes in interest rates, foreign exchange rates, or commodity or other prices may reduce the value of an investment.

- *Credit risk* is the possibility that the issuer of a debt security may fail to make interest and principal payments or otherwise perform according to the terms of the debt instrument.

The decision whether to perform tests of controls also reflects the auditor's understanding and assessment of controls that management has created in response to those risks. Those controls should (1) ensure that the personnel authorized to enter into investment transactions are competent, (2) require that written contracts specify the rights and obligations inherent in the investment transaction, (3) establish trading limits, (4) require reviews of investment transactions by competent personnel, (5) require periodic evaluation of market risk, credit risk, and the risk of physical loss, and (6) separate the responsibilities for authorizing, entering into, and accounting for investment transactions.

As mentioned earlier, many of the controls over investments are exercised directly by management. While management's close attention to investment transactions can be an effective aspect of internal control, the auditor should be alert for potential abuses and override. Other key aspects of internal control are arrangements for physical security and segregation of duties. These usually are the focus of tests of controls, if the auditor decides to perform them. In addition, the auditor may obtain evidence of the effectiveness of certain controls (such as those relating to depositing incoming receipts or disbursing funds) in connection with auditing the revenue and purchasing cycles, as discussed in Chapters 13 and 14.

Tests of controls over investment activities also may focus on acquisition, custody, and disposal. For example, the auditor may perform tests of controls of authorization of investment transactions and safeguarding of investments to obtain evidence that recorded investments exist and are owned at the balance sheet date. If those controls are found to be in place and operating effectively, the auditor may decide to reduce year-end confirmations (see below) or to perform them before year-end. Conversely, if those activities are absent or ineffective, the auditor may need to perform 100 percent confirmation at year-end. The auditor also may test controls over recording investment income to obtain evidence of its accuracy.

21.4 SUBSTANTIVE TESTS

This section discusses tests of existence, ownership, accuracy, and completeness; appropriateness of accounting policies; carrying values; investment income; and classification and presentation. (The auditor usually obtains evidence about cutoff of investment transactions through tests of existence, accuracy, and completeness.) The section concludes with tests related to investments in sophisticated financial instruments. Statement on Auditing Standards (SAS) No. 81, *Auditing Investments* (AU Section 332), provides further guidance concerning substantive tests related to auditing investments.

The auditor ordinarily obtains or prepares a detailed list of investments, including current-period transactions and related investment income. The list should be traced to the general ledger and tested for mathematical accuracy. The auditor should examine brokers' advices and internal authorizations for investments acquired and disposed of during the period, test the accuracy of investment income, and ascertain that all transactions were recorded in the proper period, based on the "trade date" rather than the "settlement date." (In determining the extent of such tests, the auditor should consider the adequacy of the entity's or the custodian's controls, the type and frequency of errors in prior years, and the materiality of the amounts involved.) Accrued interest receivable at the end of the period should be tested by recomputation or the application of analytical procedures. Evidence about the completeness of investments can be obtained by reviewing fluctuations in investment income, as well as by considering evidence obtained in other tests, such as security counts or confirmations of amounts with third parties.

The auditor should review the investment balances for reasonableness and review current-period activity for large or unusual journal entries. The latter may indicate potential misstatements from errors in recording acquisitions and dispositions of investments, improper accounting for changes in fair value, or inappropriate classification decisions.

(a)   Existence, Ownership, Accuracy, and Completeness

Establishing the existence (in either certificate form, electronic or "book entry" form, or a custodial account) and ownership of investments is paramount to the audit process, particularly because many securities are readily negotiable. Evidence of the existence and ownership of investments, as well as some assurance about the accuracy and completeness of the investment accounts, normally is obtained by confirmation or inspection. The auditor should agree the securities confirmed or inspected to the entity's detailed records. Whether these procedures are performed at year-end or at an interim date will be based on the auditor's assessment of control risk and on efficiency considerations.

(i)   Counting Securities.   The list of securities owned (and those held as collateral or for safekeeping) at the date of the count should include the following information: aggregate principal amount of bonds and notes; number of shares of stock; denomination of bonds or par value, if any, of stocks; maturity dates of bonds; and interest and preferred stock dividend rates. If available, information about the location of the securities usually is included on the list. The auditor examines the securities and compares them with the list. This process normally provides the auditor with evidence about controls; for example, an accurate security list, proper endorsement or evidence of ownership on the securities, proper division of duties between custodian and record keeper, adequate physical safeguards (such as use of a bank's safe deposit vault), and requirements that two people be present for access to the securities are all indications of effective internal control.

The auditor should maintain control over the securities from the start of the count until it has been completed, the results have been compared with the list of securities, and all exceptions have been investigated to the extent possible at the time. Responsible officers or employees should be present during the count to reduce the possibility of later questions about the handling of securities, and should acknowledge, in writing, the return of the securities intact upon conclusion of the count.

In the process of counting the securities, the auditor also should examine them. Although auditors are not qualified to assume responsibility for the genuineness or authenticity of certificates or instruments representing investments, they should be alert to the possibility of forged certificates. If any certificates appear to be unusual and if the auditor is unable to establish their authenticity by examining purchase documents, income records, or similar items, the security should be confirmed with the issuer or transfer agent.

Insurance companies and similar institutional investors often have in their portfolios registered instruments in large denominations that may have been reduced below face amount by partial payments. The auditor should confirm the amount of those instruments outstanding with the issuer, if it appears they do not have to be presented to the issuer or an agent for endorsement or reissue at the time a partial payment is received.

The auditor should note that stock certificates and registered bonds are in the name of the entity or an accredited nominee or, if they are not, that certificates are appropriately endorsed or accompanied by powers of attorney. Bonds with interest coupons should be examined to determine that coupons not yet due have not been detached. If coupons presently coming due are not attached to the bonds, the auditor should ask where they are and either inspect them or confirm them with the holders. Likewise, explanations should be obtained and evaluated for any coupons past due that are attached and have not been presented for payment. Interest in default should be noted in the working papers for consideration in connection with the audit of accrued income and carrying amounts of investments.

The auditor should investigate reasons for differences between the count and the list of securities. Certain types of differences are normal and expected, for example, securities held by others and securities in transit (unsettled transactions). The holders of securities in other locations should be identified and requests for confirmation sent. In-transit items should be related to recent transactions; outgoing in-transit items should be confirmed with recipients. Securities received through the mail for a few days following the date of the count should be examined to substantiate items in transit. Once the auditor is satisfied that all items on the security list have been counted or their location elsewhere has been confirmed and all differences have been reconciled, he or she may "release" control over securities.

The auditor should not overlook the possibility of substitutions. If, for example, examinations are being made of one or more trust accounts handled by the same trustee, securities in all accounts should be counted at the same time. Similarly, if different auditors are employed to examine several accounts, they should make their counts simultaneously. Otherwise, material shortages may be concealed by temporary transfers from accounts whose securities are not being counted. Securities owned or held as collateral or for safekeeping also should be counted simultaneously with cash funds and cash equivalents, undeposited receipts, notes receivable, and other negotiable assets if there is a possibility of substitution of one item for another.

(ii) Counts of Large Portfolios.   If an investment portfolio is relatively large and active (as in banks, insurance companies, investment companies, and broker-dealers), the count of securities may be a major undertaking requiring extensive planning, precise execution, and a large staff of auditors. The following matters should be considered in conjunction with those applicable to counts of small portfolios.

In counts of large portfolios, the auditor should make every effort to plan the count most expeditiously and also to institute the necessary controls with minimum inconvenience to entity personnel. Especially if a "surprise" count is made without prior notice, the auditor should ascertain the location of all securities, establish controls at various points necessary to record movements of securities, and plan the sequence of the count.

A properly controlled plan may consist of stationing an auditor—the "control" auditor—at each location to observe and record movements of securities, while other auditors perform the actual count. Bags, boxes, safes, or whole rooms may be sealed to be counted later. (The purpose of seals is to provide assurance to the auditor that no one has had access to the sealed items.)

If securities must be moved before the count is completed, the control auditor should observe the withdrawal or deposit, determine the reason for withdrawals, and record the transactions in the working papers. If securities that have already been counted must be removed to be mailed to correspondents, brokers, transfer agents, or others, they should be recorded and controlled until they are turned over to the postal authorities. Relatively inactive securities may be counted and placed under seal in advance of the main count or may be placed under seal and counted after the more active items have been examined.

The usual counting procedure is for the control auditor to release batches of securities to the counting auditors, keeping a record of batches released. The counting auditors count each issue of securities and call off the count to an auditor holding the security list. If the count and the list do not agree, the issue is recounted, sometimes by a different person, until the count agrees with the listed amount or it is determined that a difference exists.

(iii) Confirmation of Securities Not on Hand.   Items on the list of securities owned at the count date but not counted should be confirmed with the holders. If an entity's entire portfolio is held by a custodian, confirmation procedures usually take the place of the security count.

Items not on hand ordinarily include securities held by banks as collateral for loans, securities left with broker-dealers as custodians for safekeeping, securities with transfer agents, securities that exist on computerized files in "book entry" form, and, if the entity is a broker-dealer, items with other brokers on loan or awaiting delivery. The auditor should determine the location of those securities at the examination date, the appropriate responsible person acting as custodian, and the reasons they are held by the custodian. (If the securities are held by people or entities unknown to the auditor, he or she may consider it necessary to consider the creditworthiness of the third party or even inspect the securities physically rather than confirm them.) In examining the accounts of financial institutions, the auditor also should confirm contracts for the purchase or sale of securities on a "when issued" basis.

If the entire portfolio of securities is held in custody by a well-known, reliable, independent financial institution, the custodian should be requested to furnish directly to the auditor a list of securities held at the examination date. The confirmation request also should ask whether the entity has clear title to the securities. The auditor should compare the list with the security records and account for differences noted. It is sometimes desirable to corroborate the custodian's confirmation by counting the securities, for example, if the portfolio is large in relation to the custodian's assets or if the auditor seeks assurance about the adequacy of the custodian's procedures. A letter from the custodian's auditor addressing its internal control also can provide that assurance. Joint counts with other auditors having a similar interest are possible. [See the discussion in Chapter 12 (Section 12.4, Effect of an Entity's Use of a Service Organization) of the auditor's responsibilities under SAS No. 70, *Reports on the Processing of Transactions by Service Organizations* (AU Section 324).]

If securities are in the custody of an affiliate or are under the control of a person or group of people who take an active part in the entity's management, the auditor is not justified in relying solely on written confirmation from the custodian. Instead, the auditing procedures outlined above for counting securities under management's control should be followed.

(b)   Tests of the Appropriateness of Accounting Policies

The auditor should determine whether the accounting policies adopted by a particular entity for its investments in debt and equity securities are appropriate and that the investments have been classified into the proper category. Both the entity's industry and the type of investment determine the accounting policy that the entity should select for determining the classification and valuation of investments in debt and equity securities.

Some entities, such as state and local government entities, follow standards issued by the Government Accounting Standards Board and certain pronouncements of the AICPA (discussed in Chapter 38 of this book). Some entities, such as brokers and dealers in securities, not-for-profit organizations, employee benefit plans, and investment companies follow specialized accounting practices, some of which are discussed in FASB and AICPA publications and in various chapters of this book. The auditor should ascertain whether the accounting policies followed by such entities conform to the appropriate guidance.

Entities other than those described in the preceding paragraph are required to follow the guidance in SFAS No. 115, *Accounting for Certain Investments in Debt and Equity Securities* (Accounting Standards Section I80), when accounting for certain types of investments. Other investments held by those entities may require the application of the cost or equity method of accounting.

(i) Investments Accounted for Under SFAS No. 115.   Under SFAS No. 115, at the date of acquisition, debt securities should be classified into held-to-maturity, trading, or available-for-sale categories; equity securities that have readily determinable fair values should be classified into either trading or available-for-sale categories. The appropriateness of the classification should be reassessed at each reporting date.

Investments in debt securities should be classified as held-to-maturity only if the entity has the positive intent and ability to hold the securities to maturity, which is distinct from a mere absence of an intent to sell. The held-to-maturity category should not include debt securities that may be sold in response to changes in market interest rates, the security's prepayment risk, the entity's liquidity needs, foreign exchange risk, tax planning strategies, or other similar factors. Classification as held-to-maturity would be considered inappropriate, however, if a security is sold or transferred for circumstances or reasons other than those specified in SFAS No. 115. Trading securities (both debt and equity) are bought principally for the purpose of selling them in the near term. They are generally held for only a short period of time and are acquired with the objective of generating profits on short-term differences in price. All investments within the scope of SFAS No. 115 that are neither held-to-maturity nor acquired for trading purposes are classified as available-for-sale.

For entities presenting a classified balance sheet, all trading securities should be shown as current assets. All other securities should be shown as either current or noncurrent according to the provisions of Chapter 3A of Accounting Research Bulletin (ARB) No. 43 (Accounting Standards Section B05). (ARB No. 43 specifies that the term *current assets* designates assets that are reasonably expected to be realized in cash or sold or consumed in one year or during the normal operating cycle of the business, whichever is longer.)

The appropriate classification of investments in debt and equity securities depends on management's intent in purchasing and holding the investment, the entity's actual investment activities, and, in the case of certain debt securities, the entity's ability to hold the securities to their maturity. Accordingly, the auditor needs to understand the process that management uses to classify investments.

The auditor should examine evidence of management's intent related to investments—such as records of investment strategies, instructions to portfolio managers, and minutes of meetings of the board of directors or the investment committee of the board. When considering the entity's investment activities, sales of investments classified in the held-to-maturity category (for reasons other than those in paragraphs 8 and 11 of SFAS No. 115) should cause the auditor to question the appropriateness of management's classification of other investments remaining in that category, as well as future classifications of investments into that category. In evaluating the entity's ability to hold a debt security to maturity, the auditor may consider such factors as the entity's financial position, known working capital requirements, operating results, cash flow projections or forecasts, and debt agreements and other contractual obligations. Ordinarily the auditor also should obtain written representations from management about its intent and, with respect to held-to-maturity securities, the entity's ability to hold them to maturity. Management representation letters are discussed in Chapter 27.

(ii) Investments Accounted for at Cost.
Investments in equity securities that do not have readily determinable fair values are not within the scope of SFAS No. 115. Unless those investments are accounted for under the equity method or represent investments in consolidated subsidiaries, they should be accounted for at cost. Other investments, such as investments in real estate, partnership interests, and oil and gas interests, should also be accounted for at cost; these types of investments are not discussed in this chapter.

(iii) Investments Accounted for Using the Equity Method.
Investments may represent holdings of securities for purposes of control, affiliation, or financing of entities related to the investor's operations. Those investments, which should be classified as noncurrent assets, may require using the equity method of accounting, as discussed in Accounting Principles Board (APB) Opinion No. 18, *The Equity Method of Accounting for Investments in Common Stock* (Accounting Standards Section I82). (SFAS No. 115 does not apply to investments in equity securities accounted for under the equity method or to investments in consolidated subsidiaries.)

The equity method is appropriate for accounting for investments in (a) corporate joint ventures and (b) common stock of unconsolidated subsidiaries and other investments of 50 percent or less of the voting stock of the investee corporation if the investor has the ability to exercise significant influence over operating and financial policies of the investee. According to APB Opinion No. 18, an investment of 20 percent or more of the voting stock of an investee should lead to a presumption that, in the absence of evidence to the contrary, an investor has the ability to exercise significant influence over an investee. If it is clear that the investor exercises significant influence, the equity method is required even if less than 20 percent is owned.

The auditor should consider evidence related to the degree of influence or control the entity can exercise over an investee, to evaluate whether the equity method of accounting or consolidation is appropriate in the circumstances. In addition, the auditor should exercise appropriate professional care to ensure that transactions involving investments are accounted for in accordance with their substance, regardless of their form.

If there are investments accounted for by the equity method and if the investee is audited by other auditors, the auditor will have to use the report of the investee's auditors to be able to report on the investor's equity in the investee's underlying net assets and its share of the investee's earnings or losses and other transactions. This places the auditor in the position of a principal auditor who is using the work and reports of other auditors. The work and reports of other auditors also may serve as evidence with respect to investments carried at amortized cost or at fair value, which similarly would place the auditor in the position of a principal auditor. The procedures to be followed in those instances are discussed in Chapter 7; reporting aspects of using the work and reports of other auditors are discussed in Chapter 28.

(c)   Tests of Carrying Values

The valuation of investments varies with the type of security and any specialized industry practices.

(i) Amortized Cost.   Cost is the amount paid for an investment at the date of acquisition and includes such items as commissions and fees, but not accrued interest. If securities are received as gifts (which occurs most commonly in not-for-profit institutions), cost is the fair value as of the date of the gift.

Debt securities normally are acquired at a premium or discount, depending on the stated interest rate on the security compared with the market interest rate at the date of acquisition. For debt securities classified as held-to-maturity, the premium or discount should be amortized over the remaining life of the investment, using the effective interest method. Unless there is a decline in value that is other than temporary, held-to-maturity debt securities should be carried at amortized cost.

Cost of securities purchased and proceeds from securities sold normally are supported by brokers' advices. The auditor should examine these documents to substantiate the basis for recording those transactions. The auditor also may confirm the purchase price of the security with the issuer or custodian, as appropriate, and recompute any discount accretion or premium amortization. Additionally, the auditor should review management's method of determining cost (first-in, first-out, average, or specific identification) of securities sold and ascertain that it is consistent during the year and with prior years.

(ii) Fair Value.   Under SFAS No. 115, investments in debt securities that are not classified as held-to-maturity (that is, those that are classified as trading securities and available-for-sale securities) should be measured at fair value. All investments in equity securities that have readily determinable fair values (as defined in the statement), except for investments accounted for under the equity method and investments in consolidated subsidiaries, also should be measured at fair value. Changes in fair value (that is, unrealized holding gains and losses) of trading securities are recognized in the income statement; changes in fair value of available-for-sale securities are reported in other comprehensive income until realized, except for write-downs for other-than-temporary impairments, which are reported in the income statement.

(Some entities with specialized accounting practices, such as brokers and dealers in securities, investment companies, and defined benefit pension plans, recognize all changes in fair value in income or its equivalent, but those entities are excluded from the scope of SFAS No. 115.) SFAS No. 115 also provides guidance on accounting for transfers of securities between categories.

If investments are carried at fair value (or if fair value is disclosed for investments carried at cost), the auditor should obtain evidence corroborating the fair values using market quotations from published sources when available, or from broker-dealers who make markets in particular securities. If market quotations are not available, estimates of fair value frequently can be obtained from broker-dealers or other third parties based on their proprietary models, or from entity management, based on internally developed or acquired models. The auditor should consider the applicability of SAS No. 70, *Reports on the Processing of Transactions by Service Organizations* (AU Section 324), and SAS No. 73, *Using the Work of a Specialist* (AU Section 336), when fair value estimates are obtained from broker-dealers and other third parties.

If management has estimated fair value using a valuation model, the auditor should assess the appropriateness of the model and determine that management's assumptions are reasonable and appropriately supported. (In some circumstances, it may be necessary to involve a specialist in assessing the entity's fair value estimates and related models.) The auditor also should determine that the entity has made appropriate disclosures about the methods and assumptions used to estimate fair values. The auditor should not function as an appraiser, however, or substitute his or her judgment for that of the entity's management.

Investments in debt securities may be collateralized by various types of property, which may be an important factor in considering fair value and collectibility of the investment. In that situation, the auditor should obtain and evaluate evidence about the existence and transferability of the collateral and its fair value.

(iii) Equity Method. Under the equity method, an investment is recorded at cost at the date of acquisition and is then adjusted each period for the investor's appropriate share of earnings, losses, and other changes in shareholders' equity of the investee corporation. The investor's share of earnings and losses should be adjusted for the accounting effects of the difference between cost and the investor's share of the underlying book value at the acquisition date. If the investor is not obligated to make further advances or investments, the carrying value of the investment ordinarily should not be reduced below zero as a result of investee losses.

The investor's share of the investee's results of operations should be based on data from the investee's most recent reliable financial statements, which may be audited year-end statements or unaudited interim statements. If audited statements are used and there is a time lag, for example, three months, between the reporting dates of the investor and investee, the lag should be consistent from year to year. If the most recent reliable financial statements of the investee are unaudited interim statements as of the same date as the investor's year-end, the auditor should apply auditing procedures to those statements in light of the materiality of the investment in relation to the investor's financial statements. If audited financial statements of an investee over which the investor has significant influence cannot be obtained, which may happen particularly for foreign investees, a scope limitation may be present that, depending on materiality, could result in a qualified opinion or a disclaimer. (See the discussion and examples of scope limitations in Chapter 28.) The refusal of an investee to furnish financial data to the investor, however, is evidence (but not necessarily conclusive evidence) that the investor does not have the ability to exercise significant influence over the investee as to justify the use of the equity method.

The auditor should read available interim financial statements of the investee and inquire of the investor about events and transactions of the investee between the date of its financial statements and the date of the audit report on the investor's financial statements. Through such procedures, the auditor also should ascertain whether there were any material events or transactions subsequent to the date of the investee's financial statements.

(iv) Impairment.   Generally accepted accounting principles require management to determine whether a decline in fair value below the amortized cost of available-for-sale or held-to-maturity securities is other than temporary as of the date of the financial statements. Accordingly, the auditor should evaluate whether management has considered relevant information in determining whether an other-than-temporary impairment condition exists. SAS No. 81 (para. 32) provides examples of factors that may indicate an other-than-temporary impairment condition:

- Fair value is significantly below cost.
- The decline in fair value is attributable to specific adverse conditions affecting a particular investment.
- The decline in fair value is attributable to specific conditions, such as conditions in an industry or geographic area.
- Management does not possess both the intent and the ability to hold the investment for a period of time sufficient to allow for any anticipated recovery in fair value.
- The decline in fair value has existed for an extended period of time.
- A debt security has been down-graded by a rating agency.
- The financial condition of the issuer has deteriorated.
- Dividends have been reduced or eliminated, or scheduled interest payments on debt securities have not been made.

(d)   Tests of Investment Income

The auditor should determine that all income earned has been appropriately recorded and either collected or recognized as a receivable, and that all accrued income receivable has in fact been earned. The auditor usually obtains evidence about investment income and collection dates by referring to dates of purchase and disposal of investments, interest rates, and published dividend records. Interest should not be accrued on debt securities unless its collectibility is probable; previously accrued interest in arrears should be evaluated for collectibility and written off if it does not appear probable that it will be collected.

In testing income from investments, the auditor often can perform analytical procedures, for example, analyzing the rate of return or gross investment income on a month-to-month or quarter-to-quarter basis, or comparing income with budgeted or prior-year data. Fluctuations in investment income that do not conform to the auditor's expectations would indicate that recorded investments might not exist, that investments exist that have not been recorded, or that recorded income is inaccurate. (Analytical procedures, however, generally are not relevant for achieving other audit objectives with respect to investments.)

(e) Tests of Classification, Presentation, and Disclosure

The auditor should determine that investments have been classified into the proper categories—held-to-maturity, trading, and available-for-sale. The auditor also should determine that the investments are properly classified between the current and noncurrent categories, if the balance sheet is so classified. The auditor should ascertain that the financial statements contain all required disclosures regarding investment carrying values and realized and unrealized gains and losses. In addition, minutes, confirmation replies, loan agreements, bond indentures, and other appropriate documents should be reviewed to determine whether investments have been pledged as collateral or whether there is evidence of commitments to acquire or dispose of investments, both of which may require disclosures.

(f) Tests Related to Investments in Sophisticated Financial Instruments

More and more, entities are managing their available cash in ways that try to achieve the highest rates of return for a given level of acceptable risk. One result has been the increasing use of innovative, sophisticated, and often complex financial instruments to generate investment income. The proliferation and relatively short "shelf lives" of such investments make describing all of them and providing guidance for auditing them a most formidable task—far beyond the scope of this book.

The guidance that follows is, therefore, extremely generic. It applies to all investments and should be considered in addition to the procedures discussed earlier in this chapter. The suggested guidance should, of course, be tailored to risks associated with the specific types of investments being audited. (Guidance on auditing some of these kinds of investments is also presented in Chapter 49, "Auditing Securities and Commodities Broker-Dealers.") The auditor should always consider the substance of the transaction, not its form, and should consult with experts, as appropriate in the circumstances.

1. Review the records for transactions involving purchases and sales of investments in financial instruments of all types.
2. Develop an understanding of the nature of each financial instrument the entity has invested in, including the terms of individual transactions.
3. For each type of instrument, determine the appropriate accounting measurement and recognition principles. Review management's documentation describing the methodology, underlying assumptions, and calculations that support the valuation of each type of instrument. Determine whether the valuation principles, assumptions, and methods are appropriate.

4. Identify the risks associated with each instrument and evaluate how those risks affect the realizability of the investment. Those risks include (a) the risk that the issuer of the instrument or the counterparty to the investment transaction will be unable to make payment or otherwise complete the transaction at its scheduled maturity, and (b) the risk that fluctuations in interest rates, foreign exchange rates, or commodity prices may change the underlying value of the investment.

5. Count or confirm securities delivered to the investor or its agent, as appropriate.

6. Confirm transaction details with relevant counterparties.

7. Determine where securities not transferred to the investor or its agent are being held and confirm their existence and the custodian's legal obligation to the investor.

8. Consider whether it is desirable to (a) obtain a report from the custodian's auditor on the custodian's internal control with respect to securities held in safekeeping, (b) request that specific tests be performed by that auditor, or (c) personally perform such tests.

9. Evaluate the appropriateness of the financial statement classification and disclosure of investment transactions and the degree of risk involved in them.

Chapter 26 discusses disclosure of information about financial instruments, including derivatives, and provides guidance for auditing those disclosures.

22

Auditing Property, Plant, and Equipment, and Intangible Assets and Deferred Charges

Most entities use property, plant, and equipment in the process of generating revenues. The term "property, plant, and equipment" generally refers to noncurrent tangible assets, including those held under capital leases, that an entity uses to create and distribute its goods and services. The term "fixed assets" also is used (although not as much as in the past) to describe the property, plant, and equipment accounts. Related accounts that are audited in the same manner as property, plant, and equipment are leasehold improvements and construction in progress.

Many entities also incur expenditures for the acquisition of noncurrent intangible assets. Some "intangible assets" are specifically identifiable, such as patents, franchises, and trademarks, and have lives established by law, regulation, or contract. Other intangible assets cannot be specifically identified. The most common unidentifiable intangible asset typically is called "goodwill," which is the excess of the purchase price paid for a business over the sum of its identifiable net assets. Certain other expenditures are recorded as intangible assets or "deferred charges," because the expenditures are considered to benefit future operations and are not regarded as current expenses or losses.

Accounting principles require the cost of plant and equipment and intangible assets to be allocated on a rational and systematic basis over the periods benefited. Various depreciation or amortization methods are utilized to allocate the net cost of an asset (acquisition cost less estimated recoverable salvage value) over the period of benefit.

Expenditures to maintain or improve property, plant, and equipment are normal following their acquisition. A major audit consideration is whether such expenditures should be accounted for as expenses of the current period or reflected on the balance sheet as an increase in the carrying value of the asset. As a general rule, an expenditure should be capitalized if it benefits future periods by extending the useful or productive life of the asset. The distinction between the two categories of expenditures frequently is not clear-cut. Entities usually have stated policies defining which expenditures are to be capitalized, and the auditor needs to determine whether the policies are appropriate and are being complied with.

This chapter presents the objectives of auditing property, plant, and equipment and intangible assets and deferred charges, and describes typical transactions and related control activities. Controls over purchases and cash disbursements and related tests of controls were covered as part of the purchasing cycle in Chapter 14. Many of the controls over ordering, receiving, paying for, and recording property, plant, and equipment purchases may be similar to those for purchases in general. This chapter focuses on control activities normally not associated with the purchasing cycle, such as those relating to the completeness and accuracy of files containing property, plant, and equipment balances; to the protection of assets; and to authorization for acquisitions and sales of assets. The chapter also discusses the audit strategy for property, plant, and equipment and other noncurrent asset accounts, based on the auditor's risk assessment; that is followed by specific substantive tests that may be used in auditing property transactions and related account balances.

22.1 AUDIT OBJECTIVES

(a) Property, Plant, and Equipment

Figure 22.1 describes specific audit objectives applicable to property, plant, and equipment and related accounts.

Figure 22.1   Audit Objectives for Property, Plant, and Equipment

Completeness	All property, plant, and equipment owned by the entity at the balance sheet date are included in the financial statements.
Accuracy	Additions to and disposals of property, plant, and equipment and current-period depreciation are accurately recorded.
Existence/Occurrence	Property, plant, and equipment recorded in the accounts physically exist.
	Recorded additions to and disposals of property, plant, and equipment actually occurred and were properly authorized.
Cutoff	Property, plant, and equipment transactions were recorded in the proper period.
Valuation/Allocation	No material items were charged to expense that should have been capitalized, or vice versa.
	The cost or other basis of property, plant, and equipment is appropriate.
	Appropriate methods of depreciation were properly and consistently applied to all items of property, plant, and equipment that should be depreciated.
	The carrying value of property, plant, and equipment is appropriate in periods subsequent to acquisition, considering such factors as utilization, geographic location, laws and regulations, and technological changes.
Rights and Obligations	Property, plant, and equipment recorded in the accounts are owned or leased under capital leases.[a]
Presentation and Disclosure	Property, plant, and equipment pledged as collateral are identified and disclosed, along with other necessary disclosures.

[a]Audit objectives relating specifically to leased assets are discussed under Capital Leases later in this chapter.

(b)   Intangible Assets and Deferred Charges

Figure 22.2 describes specific audit objectives applicable to intangible assets and deferred charges.

22.2   TYPICAL TRANSACTIONS AND CONTROLS

(a)   Authorization of Expenditures

The acquisition of property usually requires a major use of funds, and the board of directors often approves the capital budget for property acquisitions. Some entities use

Figure 22.2   Audit Objectives for Intangible Assets and Deferred Charges

Completeness	All intangible assets and deferred charges that should be recognized as assets are included in the financial statements.
Accuracy	Intangible assets and deferred charges, and the current-period amortization of those accounts, are accurately calculated.
Existence/Occurrence	Recorded additions to and disposals of intangible assets and deferred charges actually occurred and were properly authorized.
Cutoff	Transactions involving intangible assets and deferred charges were recorded in the proper period.
Valuation/Allocation	The recorded amounts of intangible assets and deferred charges represent appropriate valuations.
	Intangible assets are being amortized on a consistent basis over the estimated periods of benefit.
	The carrying value of intangible assets has been reduced for any permanent decline in value.
	Deferred charges represent expenditures that are appropriately deferred to future periods.
	The basis for amortizing deferred charges is reasonable.
Rights and Obligations	The entity has ownership rights to recorded intangible assets and deferred charges.
Presentation and Disclosure	Appropriate disclosures have been made regarding intangible assets and deferred charges.

well-developed techniques of capital budgeting to evaluate the economic feasibility of proposed acquisitions, both large and small. Other entities are less formal and more subjective and judgmental in their analysis. The extent of economic justification required depends on the management style and preferences of those responsible for authorizing acquisitions of property and the significance of the expenditure.

Controls over property acquisitions usually call for a formal written request and specify the extent of economic justification that must accompany it, including the reasons for the expenditure and the estimated amount. This information is necessary to give those who authorize expenditures a meaningful basis for evaluating them. In most entities, purchases are initiated only on the basis of appropriate authorizations. There are often several levels of authorization, which may be set based on predetermined amounts; the larger the expenditure, the higher the level of authorization.

Expenditures may be authorized on an ad hoc basis as requests are received, but it is preferable to compile them in a capital budget for formal review and approval. Sometimes a capital budget enumerates specific acquisitions, but most often it has to be prepared far in advance and thus necessarily consists of estimates or aggregates of probable acquisitions. When a capital budget has been approved, it becomes the authorization for the purchasing or other department to execute acquisition transactions. Thereafter, the people responsible for the various segments of the capital budget authorize specific transactions.

Documents authorizing acquisitions typically are subject to numerical control. Usually, the entity also maintains records of purchase commitments. Written records are necessary to determine that transactions are executed in accordance with the authorization. One common system is to assign a "construction work order" number or "appropriation" number to each authorization, even if no construction is involved. Often, control totals of "commitments" and "construction work in progress" are supported by holding files of open work orders, which can be reconciled periodically to the control total.

Actual expenditures for property, plant, and equipment and other noncurrent assets are compared with the authorized requests; approval by the person who originally approved the estimated expenditure is required for expenditures that exceed amounts initially authorized. Control is further enhanced if approvals are obtained before overruns are incurred and if the accounting treatment of overruns also is approved.

If an expenditure is for the replacement of an existing asset, controls are necessary to ensure that the related retirement or disposal is recorded accurately. A procedure for identifying assets that are no longer in use or are being replaced helps ensure that assets disposed of or no longer in use are recorded properly as retirements. For example, an entity's procedures might require that all accounting entries related to a capital project be summarized and approved each quarter; the approval process might include comparing the summarization with the written approval for the replacement, which would detect a failure to record a retirement. Other control activities for property, plant, and equipment expenditures, such as recording vendors' invoices, preparing and signing checks, and recording them in the general ledger, are normally the same as for other purchases.

As part of authorizing expenditures, a designated official should approve the allocation between assets and expenses. The allocation should be based on the account classification in the approved written request. Someone independent of the person who prepared the initial coding should review account classifications of expenditures.

(b) Receipt and Installation

Routine or recurring acquisitions usually are processed through the normal purchasing procedures and are subject to the control activities described in Chapter 14 in connection with purchases in general. Specialists in engineering or contract negotiation may handle larger or technically specialized acquisitions. In either event, controls over acquisitions of property, plant, and equipment are designed to ensure that purchases are recorded in the general ledger and in the detailed property records. Controls over returned property, review and approval of invoices and related documentation, and authorization controls over entries in the detailed property records are as important in property purchases as in purchases of inventory or services.

Acquisitions that are complex or specialized enough to be the responsibility of a separate department generally are subject to specialized controls. Control over large-scale procurement has become a highly developed art, and managing the business process of "procurement" or "contract management" has become a profession in its own right. This discussion can only touch in the most general way on the kinds of control activities that may be found in practice.

A contract, including all specifications, usually is reviewed for completeness; the more detailed the initial specifications, the less the risk of costly unforeseen variations. The contract spells out the range of tolerable deviation from the specified standards and specifies the time of delivery and quality of performance. Since higher quality or closer tolerances are almost always more costly, contracts are best reviewed by a team comprising different skills and points of view: purchasing specialists, engineers, production personnel, lawyers, and cost accountants.

During construction, acquisition, or installation, a specified employee supervises step-by-step compliance by the contractor with the terms of the contract. Sometimes an outside specialist, like an architect, may supervise the contractor's compliance; other projects may require the full-time attention of one or more of the purchaser's executives or employees. Formal procedures generally exist for testing and accepting an acquisition, and compliance with them is documented and reviewed before the acquisition is legally accepted and final payment made.

Costs of acquisitions are accumulated in work order ledgers containing information relative to purchases, payments to contractors, and "in-house" labor and overhead. Accumulated costs are balanced to the control account periodically and compared with the authorized expenditure.

Acquisitions of small dollar value items, with a cost of less than $200, for example, may be expensed routinely even though the item is properly capitalizable. Such a policy is followed to reduce the clerical effort involved in maintaining detailed records for many small dollar value items. Materiality, however, should be determined on the basis of the aggregate of these small dollar items. Otherwise, a department that is authorized to purchase and expense components below the $200 limit could purchase components as replacement parts and use them to construct an asset at a cost of $2,000 that would not have been approved.

(c) Existence of Assets

Assets representing the balances included in the detailed property records generally undergo inspection periodically, and, if appropriate, documents of title are examined at reasonable intervals. These procedures will be more effective if they are carried out by people other than those who have custody of the assets, maintain the detailed records, and have custody of the documents of title. Typically, assets that are highly susceptible to theft, loss, or abnormal damage are physically inspected at least annually. Inspection of other assets on a periodic basis may be adequate unless there is an unusual amount of activity in the property accounts and the individual assets are replaced frequently.

Periodic physical inspection of individual assets by entity personnel is an effective means of avoiding misstatement of the property accounts by including assets that have disappeared or become unusable, or excluding items on hand but not recorded. The inspection entails determining both the existence of the asset and whether it is in current use and good condition.

(d)   Property, Plant, and Equipment Records

Property, plant, and equipment control accounts usually are supported by subsidiary ledgers for the following classifications of assets: land; buildings; leasehold improvements; machinery and equipment; furniture and fixtures; office equipment; motor vehicles; property, plant, and equipment leased or loaned to or from third parties; other property, plant, and equipment; and other noncurrent assets. Each subsidiary ledger consists of a detailed record for each asset in that class; records are kept for all items in use, including fully depreciated assets. The record for each item usually includes a description of the asset, its location, date of purchase or construction, identifying (voucher or work order) number, cost (including capitalized interest), depreciation or amortization method, salvage value, depreciation or amortization for the period, and accumulated depreciation or amortization. Often those records also show maintenance and repair history.

The subsidiary ledgers need to have sufficient information for individual assets to be identified, and their cost and accumulated depreciation or amortization to be reconciled to the respective control accounts. Marking the assets with identifying numbers and recording the numbers is one means of doing this. Alternatively, the accounting records may contain detailed descriptions of the individual assets, including, for example, manufacturer's serial numbers, which would allow ready identification of specific assets.

The subsidiary ledgers are updated regularly for the cost of additions and disposals and depreciation for the period, and are reconciled to the general ledger control accounts at least annually. Differences disclosed by the reconciliations are investigated, and a designated official reviews and approves the results before any adjustments are made.

Detailed records for property leased to or from other entities also are maintained. Those records include description, location, identifying number, and owner, and provide a complete record of leased assets. In the case of assets leased from others, the records allow the entity to distinguish such assets from assets it owns. In addition, records for leased property contain details of purchase options, renewal options, implicit interest rates, fair values of the items being leased, and other information necessary to account for the leases properly. Copies or extracts of lease agreements—both those of the entity as lessee and those of the entity as lessor—normally are retained with the entity's property records.

(e)   Records of Use, Maintenance, and Repairs

The entity keeps records of the use and maintenance history of equipment. The amount of use affects the amount of maintenance necessary, and the maintenance history indicates the kinds of repairs that may be expected and how much maintenance costs increase as the equipment is used. In some industries, regulatory agencies require records of usage, maintenance, and repairs. Rentals for many kinds of leased property are based partly on the amount of use (e.g., mileage for automobiles, units produced for machines, or hours of service for computers). Usage records that serve accounting purposes should be maintained and controlled carefully.

Accounting records and control activities related to use of equipment are usually very simple. Generally, they include policies for rates and methods of depreciation, depletion, and amortization; forms or schedules for computing data for entries and often a standard journal entry for recording them; and procedures for periodically reconciling the subsidiary ledgers to control accounts, reviewing differences, and adjusting recorded amounts.

(f)   Disposition of Property, Plant, and Equipment

Controls over dispositions of property, plant, and equipment are important to all entities, not only to preserve accurate records but also to make sure that assets are safeguarded and residual and salvage values effectively realized. Perhaps the most effective controls over dispositions are a work order system to document and account for retirements, restricted access to the property, and division of duties between those responsible for assets; those authorized to move, remove, or otherwise work on them; and those authorized to approve construction or removal work orders. Those arrangements would prevent the person responsible for property from releasing it without a properly authorized work order. A plant engineer or someone similarly responsible and knowledgeable would review retirement work orders and evaluate the reason given for the disposition, the estimated cost of removal, and the estimated recovery from scrap or salvage.

As with major acquisitions, an appropriate level of management approves significant dispositions of property. Dollar guidelines may be established for the level of management required to authorize a disposition. Very large dispositions, such as an operating plant, major product line, or large pieces of property or machinery, may require approval by the board of directors. A frequently encountered intermediate stage of control between little or none at all and a well-systematized and monitored system consists of a written policy calling for documentation of removals and dispositions. That policy would be supported by detailed records of assets on hand and comparisons of the records with periodic inventories, at least for movable and salable items.

(g)   Intangible Assets and Deferred Charges

An entity's controls for intangible assets and deferred charges are normally similar to those for tangible property. Effective controls over intangible assets and deferred charges generally include:

- A policy specifying the kinds of expenditures that are deferrable, and amortization methods and rates
- Proper authorization of related entries
- Periodic reviews of balances, realizable values, and deferral policy by responsible officials

22.3   DETERMINING THE AUDIT STRATEGY

The audit strategy for property, plant, and equipment is based primarily on the auditor's identification of inherent risks and assessment of control risk related to specific audit objectives, and on efficiency considerations. The auditor achieves the audit objectives discussed earlier through substantive tests or a combination of substantive tests and tests of controls.

The auditor may meet some of the audit objectives for property, plant, and equipment through procedures performed in connection with other aspects of the audit or tests of other accounts. For example, the pledging of property, plant, and equipment is generally discovered through reading and analyzing loan documents and minutes of meetings of the board of directors or other management groups. Property acquired under capital leases may be determined by reading minutes and analyzing lease or rental expense accounts. Similarly, the auditor may determine the continued existence of recorded property, plant, and equipment (though often not specifically or explicitly) as he or she moves about the facilities in the course of observing physical inventories and performing other audit tasks.

Other objectives are achieved through specific tests of controls and substantive tests of balances. For example, the auditor may perform tests of controls of additions and of disposals or retirements of property, plant, and equipment, and may examine appropriate documents for selected additions and retirements. Similarly, auditors often review charges to repair and maintenance accounts for items that should have been capitalized, and test the calculation and summarization of depreciation.

Determining the cost or other basis used to record property, plant, and equipment usually presents few problems because most assets are acquired individually in short-term credit transactions. The auditor must exercise judgment, however, about the appropriate cost in situations involving business combinations, self-constructed assets, capitalized leases, and nonmonetary transactions. While they are not usually a major audit concern, the auditor must be alert for changes in laws or general business conditions that might make it impossible to recover the remaining costs of property through revenue generated or outright sale. Also, the auditor should be aware of conditions that might require reevaluation of the remaining depreciable lives of property, plant, and equipment.

Auditing intangible assets and deferred charges is often uncomplicated because of the limited number of transactions generally found in these accounts, and accordingly is given relatively little attention in this chapter. The auditor should, however, determine that the carrying value of those assets can be fully recovered, that there has not been a permanent impairment of their value, and that the remaining period of amortization is appropriate.

(a)   Inherent Risk Factors

Among the most important procedures the auditor performs to identify inherent risks are learning about the entity's operations and economic environment, and correlating developments in those areas with activity in the property accounts. The auditor should be sure to understand the business reasons for additions and retirements and whether trends in operations or in the environment are likely to affect the values at which property is carried in the accounts.

The auditor should visit and tour the main plants perhaps once a year and smaller plants less frequently. One among several reasons for making a tour is to observe the existence and condition of the plant. Other evidence of matters affecting the property accounts can be found in the minutes of directors' and executive committee meetings.

The auditor also should inquire routinely of entity personnel about past or prospective changes in operations that might affect the property accounts.

Further, the auditor should consider the general business environment of the entity, including industry characteristics, and the nature of its property. In certain circumstances, it may be appropriate to extend substantive tests. For instance:

- If the auditor has reason to think that management may be attempting to inflate profits and thus may have capitalized items that should have been expensed, particular scrutiny should be given to additions of such items of property, plant, and equipment.

- If the entity's equipment is both mobile and readily marketable and hence could be easily misappropriated, the auditor should focus particularly on the authorization of disposals and substantiating the existence of the equipment.

- If the entity had, for the first time, construction in progress and had not designed a proper cost accumulation system, the auditor should extend procedures directed at construction costs.

(b) Analytical Procedures

Analytical procedures often highlight relationships between accounts and reveal risks not otherwise apparent during the risk assessment phase of the audit. As discussed in Chapter 8 (Section 8.3, Gathering and Analyzing Recent Financial Information), analytical procedures are a required part of audit planning. Their use at an early stage in the audit often results in more informed strategy decisions.

The auditor should compare the total amount of additions with budgeted amounts and, in light of what is known about the business, identify major individual additions and disposals, review gains and losses on disposals, and review the reasonableness of the depreciation expense for the year. Balances of asset, accumulated depreciation and amortization, and related expense accounts should be compared with the prior year and, if possible, month to month to identify fluctuations and unusual entries requiring explanation. In some industries, it may be possible to correlate income with the related asset. These analytical procedures may indicate areas that should be inquired about further, and may indicate the need to modify planned substantive tests of details.

Management typically reviews and analyzes key performance indicators to monitor property and equipment transactions, and the auditor should consider using those analyses to supplement his or her own analytical procedures. Those performance indicators may include information about capital project requests, actual capital expenditures, retirements, and depreciation expense. Management also may compare property and equipment activity with independently accumulated information, such as budgets and past performance indicators. Those procedures may help identify material misstatements in processing or recording plant and equipment activity. For example, investigating significant differences between reported and budgeted capital expenditures could identify incomplete recording of construction costs in the general ledger.

The way management responds to the auditor's inquiries resulting from analytical procedures may give some indication of the quality of the control environment. For example, prompt, logical, and meaningful answers to questions about differences between recorded and budgeted capital expenditures would provide some indication, in the absence of evidence to the contrary, that management is "in control" and that accounting procedures and control activities appear to be functioning as intended. Analytical procedures, however, also may indicate trends, even in well-controlled entities, that may lead the auditor to extend substantive tests; for example, trends that raise questions about the impairment of recorded asset values.

(c)   Assessment of Control Risk

The auditor is required, at a minimum, to obtain an understanding of the entity's internal control sufficient to plan the audit. This understanding, together with the auditor's evaluation of the effectiveness of the design of controls, is used to identify the types of misstatements that might occur and the risk of their occurring, and to design substantive tests. The understanding is obtained or updated by considering previous experience with the entity, reviewing prior year audit results, interviewing entity personnel, observing personnel as they perform their duties, reviewing entity-prepared descriptions of accounting procedures and control activities, and inspecting documents and records.

In the course of obtaining the understanding of internal control, the auditor will have obtained evidence to support a preliminary assessment of the extent to which controls have been designed and are operating effectively. That evidence ordinarily would enable the auditor to assess control risk below the maximum or at low for one or more audit objectives. The auditor may seek additional evidence of the effectiveness of control activities to support an assessment of control risk at low, if he or she believes that such evidence is likely to be available and efficient to obtain. If so, the auditor usually would perform tests of controls as a basis for further modifying the nature and extent of substantive testing.

It is generally more efficient to develop an audit strategy for property, plant, and equipment that emphasizes substantive tests rather than tests of control activities. Exceptions occur in highly capital-intensive entities that have a large volume of property transactions. For example, utilities generally have an effective accounting system and related control activities for processing and recording property transactions, most of which are for the acquisition or repair of utility properties. Even when the audit strategy is to emphasize substantive tests of the property and intangible asset accounts, the nature, timing, and extent of those tests are directly related to the auditor's understanding of internal control and assessment of control risk.

The auditor's decision whether to perform tests of controls is based primarily on efficiency considerations. The auditor may decide, for example, that performing mainly substantive tests would be more efficient, even if it is likely that control risk could be assessed at low. Such a conclusion might be appropriate if few assets are involved and they are generally high-value items, as commonly occurs. In those instances, the time required to perform tests of controls might be greater than the time required to substantively test the account balances. Or, if the property accounts are relatively immaterial, only limited substantive testing may be appropriate.

In other circumstances, such as a large entity with a centralized property department to control all aspects of acquisition, disposal, and record keeping, the auditor may decide that performing tests of controls is likely to be efficient. Previous chapters discussed tests of controls of other purchase and sales transactions; many of those tests will provide the auditor with evidence about the effectiveness of controls pertaining to certain aspects of property, plant, and equipment and other noncurrent asset transactions as well. However, controls relating to the purchase or sale of property, plant, and equipment often differ from those for other purchase and sales transactions. For example, different authorization procedures may be in effect, such as approval by the board of directors, or different procedures for verifying the receipt of equipment may be prescribed, for example, examination by the engineering department. Also, certain control activities, such as those related to disposals or retirements, are often unique to the property accounts and may not be covered by tests of controls in the revenue and purchasing cycles.

The paragraphs that follow describe some of the tests of control activities that an auditor may perform to test the effectiveness of internal control as it relates to the property accounts.

Tests of controls may be performed to provide evidence of the effectiveness of the entity's control activities for ensuring that all expenditures have been authorized. If only purchases over a predetermined amount require written authorization, the auditor should evaluate whether the specified amount is reasonable; if it is too high, material unauthorized expenditures could occur. The auditor should examine selected authorizations to determine whether those who approve expenditures have adequate details to allow them to make reasonable judgments. The auditor also might test management's review of the account classifications of expenditures. Testing the procedures for accumulating costs and comparing the costs with authorized expenditures also will provide evidence that recorded acquisitions were properly authorized and that both the accumulated costs and the authorized expenditures were completely and accurately input.

The auditor also may test control activities that ensure that disposals were appropriately accounted for. The auditor might test the activities that ensure that the proper level of management approved all retirements, that all costs and related accumulated depreciation associated with retirements were included in the retirement entry, and that all retirements were accurately recorded in the proper period.

Tests of controls with respect to depreciation rates may include examining evidence of authorized depreciation rates and changes in them. Also, the auditor may examine evidence that all property and equipment accounts have an assigned depreciation rate and that all depreciation rates and changes are accurately and completely input.

Tests of controls with respect to physical protection of assets generally include observation and examining documents such as reports on the results of a physical inspection, including evidence of appropriate adjustments to the accounting records. The auditor also might observe part or all of the physical inspection and examine signatures or initials of the person who independently supervised the inspection. If there are confirmations or other correspondence regarding title documents, the auditor also should examine this documentation.

Tests of controls may include examining documents and records to determine whether the descriptions or the identification system used in the property records is adequate. The auditor also should examine records of leased assets to determine their adequacy. In addition, the auditor may examine or reperform the entity's reconciliation of the subsidiary ledgers to the general ledger and examine evidence of the appropriate review and approval of differences.

If the entity has established control activities that the auditor has tested, it is not necessary to test the details of property, plant, and equipment and related accumulated depreciation accounts, unless there are unexpected fluctuations in the account balances between years or unusual risk factors have been identified. If tests of controls support an assessment of control risk at low, substantive tests of details of the property, plant, and equipment accounts during the year normally are restricted to:

- Reperforming or reviewing the control account reconciliation
- Testing major additions and disposals for authorization and accuracy
- Reviewing the reasonableness of the depreciation calculation for the year and the consistency of the method used with that of the prior year

If controls over expenditures for other noncurrent assets appear to be effective, and if management periodically reviews controls over recording and retaining such assets, the auditor may be able to perform tests of controls to obtain evidence of their effectiveness. Such tests of controls might include inspecting reports or other records evidencing the review of intangible assets and deferred charges by management.

In deciding the audit strategy for intangible assets and deferred charges, the auditor should recognize that judgments about whether to defer costs to future periods, what amortization periods are appropriate, and how to determine realizable values, are all highly subjective. For this reason, the auditor needs to evaluate the environment in which decisions about recording such assets are made, and whether those matters are reviewed at an appropriate level. In particular, the auditor should be satisfied that expenditures that should be expensed currently are not deferred to future periods to improve the profit position of an entity experiencing an economic downturn, and that the reverse does not occur as a means of normalizing or minimizing income to achieve other entity objectives.

(d) Early Substantive Testing

There are many occasions when staffing efficiency, reporting deadlines, or other factors prompt the auditor to perform substantive tests of property and other noncurrent asset accounts before year-end. Early testing may be appropriate, if the entity has effective controls over transaction processing during the period between the early testing date and year-end. The auditor also should consider controls over physical security of assets and, in some circumstances, segregation of duties. On the other hand, substantive tests are likely to be performed at year-end if relevant controls are not effective (e.g., if the detailed property or depreciation records are not adequately maintained).

Even if the auditor decides to perform substantive tests at year-end, as often happens when property, plant, and equipment comprise a few items of high individual value, completing some of the work before year-end is often desirable. For instance, purchases and dispositions of property, plant, and equipment during the first ten months of the year could be tested before year-end and the details recorded on a working paper for completion and assessment at year-end. The auditor generally performs much of the testing of other noncurrent assets, such as deferred charges, before year-end because the account balances frequently are adjusted only for periodic amortization. In those instances, only an evaluation of the carrying value of the asset may be necessary at year-end. Chapter 15 [Section 15.2(b), Timing of Tests of Details] discusses more fully the factors that should enter into decisions about early substantive testing.

22.4 SUBSTANTIVE TESTS

Many of the substantive tests described below can be recorded on a "Summary of Property, Plant, & Equipment & Accumulated Depreciation," frequently referred to as a "lead schedule," an example of which is shown in Figure 22.3. An auditor may prepare similar schedules for intangible assets and deferred charges.

(a) Examination of Opening Balances and Prior Year's Transactions

If financial statements are being audited for the first time, the auditor should decide to what extent it is necessary to examine property and other noncurrent asset accounts before the beginning of the year or years under audit. Since assets acquired in prior years and related accumulated depreciation are likely to be significant in the current balance sheet and income statement, the auditor should have a basis for believing that both are fairly stated in conformity with generally accepted accounting principles (GAAP).

If other independent auditors have audited and reported on financial statements for earlier years, reviewing the other auditors' working papers and the entity's records should be sufficient to provide the necessary understanding of the accounting principles, policies, and methods employed. In some cases—for example, if no audit was made in earlier years or if the predecessor auditor does not permit his or her work to be reviewed—the successor auditor's work should be a combination of analytical procedures and substantive tests of details. Available property records should be reviewed in enough depth to give the auditor an understanding of the accounting principles used and the consistency with which they were applied. The auditor may prepare or obtain analyses summarizing the annual changes in the asset and depreciation accounts and may examine evidence to support major additions and reductions. In particular, unusual items should be investigated to learn of revaluations or other major adjustments. The auditor should pay particular attention to property acquired by issuing common stock or exchanging other property. In an initial engagement, the auditor makes numerous historical analyses—such as of long-term debt, capital stock, additional paid-in capital, retained earnings, and minutes of directors' meetings. The auditor should be alert for matters in those analyses that affect property, plant, and equipment and other noncurrent asset accounts.

(b) Existence and Ownership of Assets

In an initial engagement, the auditor should seek evidence that tangible and intangible assets exist and are, in fact, the entity's property. If the entity's record keeping is

Figure 22.3   Property, Plant, and Equipment Lead Schedule

ACE Enterprises, Inc.
Summary of Property, Plant, & Equipment & Accumulated Depreciation
12/31/9X

Classification	Balance at Beginning of period	Additions	Disposals	Other	Balance at End of period
Cost	A	B		C	A
Buildings	10,745,986.43 T	98,723.66	9,161.31 D	(3,347.83)	10,832,200.95 TB
Machinery & Equipment	2,088,816.57 T	337,937.01	1,962.22 E		2,424,791.36 TB
Furniture & Fixtures	58,077.06 T	6,684.91		3,347.83	68,109.80 TB
	12,892,880.06	443,345.58	11,123.53	0.00	13,325,102.11
	F	F	F	F	F
Accumulated Depreciation					
	A	G		C	A
Buildings	3,007,975.34 T	214,929.27	9,161.31 D	(167.35)	3,213,575.95 TB
Machinery & Equipment	743,567.95 T	104,549.57	1,758.46 E		846,359.06 TB
Furniture & Fixtures	18,521.18 T	5,927.33		167.35	24,615.86 TB
	3,770,064.47	325,406.17	10,919.77	0.00	4,084,550.87
	F	F	F	F	F

Legend:

T - Traced to prior year workpapers
F - Footed & crossfooted
TB - Agreed to trial balance
A - Agreed to fixed asset subsidiary ledger
B - Supported by detail listing of fixed asset additions
     See workpapers _____ to _____ where additions were vouched
C - Reclassification for light fixtures erroneously classified as building
D - Write off obsolete and scrapped items
E - Sale of miscellaneous M&E - no further audit work deemed necessary
G - See workpapers _____ to _____ where reasonableness of entity's calculation
     of depreciation was tested using the firm's computer audit program for estimating depreciation

adequate, deeds, purchase contracts, and other evidence of ownership will be on file and retrievable. Sometimes, however, those documents get mislaid over the years as successive generations of management come and go and files are moved, rearranged, or culled. If no other evidence can be found, the auditor can ask management to seek representations from counsel concerning legal title to properties.

On subsequent audits, tests directed at the existence and ownership of property, plant, and equipment, and intangible assets and deferred charges normally consist of reviewing the entity's procedures for maintaining detailed records and for periodically comparing those records with the assets themselves, and examining selected additions, disposals, and allocations during the year. If the entity's detailed records are accurate, and if the auditor has tested control activities (including physical inspection) related to existence and ownership of property, plant, and equipment, substantive tests can be limited to reviews of selected major additions and disposals and periodic allocations.

If the entity periodically compares its detailed records with the actual assets but the auditor has not tested those procedures, the procedures set forth below should be carried out as of the date selected for testing:

- Review the procedures for conducting the physical inspection and comparison
- Consider whether to observe those procedures
- Review the actions taken to investigate discrepancies disclosed and to propose necessary adjustments to the records

The auditor should determine that a person who is independent of the custody of the assets and of maintaining the detailed property records compares the assets with the records. If the comparison is performed by a person who has custodial responsibility for or other access to the assets, the auditor should consider testing the comparison more extensively.

The comparison of the accounting records with the assets themselves also should be used to determine whether the carrying value of property, plant, and equipment requires adjustment because the assets are no longer in use or in good condition. The auditor should review the comparison to determine if obsolete or damaged assets on hand have been included and whether these assets are carried at an amount in excess of what can be recovered through revenue generated or outright sale.

If the entity does not compare assets with the accounting records, the auditor should consider requesting management to perform a complete or partial comparison, depending on such factors as susceptibility to loss, theft, or destruction. Alternatively, the auditor may make the comparison, although that may be a very inefficient use of audit time. If equipment is easily damaged, lost, stolen, or subject to personal use, such as in the case of small tools, the auditor should determine if the depreciation rate considers those factors and, if not, should consider physically inspecting such assets, if material.

In many instances, the auditor may obtain evidence of the existence and condition of a major portion of the entity's property, plant, and equipment through observation during physical inventory observations or routine plant tours. Other evidence also may be available regarding the existence of major property items; for example, continued sales of specific products provide evidence that the assets used to produce the products still exist and operate effectively. Conversely, discontinuance of a product or product line should raise questions as to the carrying value of the related production facilities. Continued full occupancy of a hotel facility, for example, also might provide evidence regarding the existence and condition of the furniture and equipment used in the facility and might preclude the need for an annual physical inspection of those assets. The auditor should consider, however, the risk of material misstatements arising in the property accounts if incorrect conclusions are drawn.

If the entity leases assets to others, the auditor should review the contractual and other arrangements and consider procedures to ascertain their physical existence and ownership. The auditor also should consider the appropriateness of the accounting policies and the adequacy of the accounting system and control activities, particularly physical controls that may include periodic inspection of leased assets.

In selecting procedures for substantiating the existence and ownership of real property, if transactions are usually few and of high value, the auditor should consider inspecting documents of title (or confirming that such documents are held by proper custodians—normally banks or other lending institutions) for all or a substantial portion of the properties, to ascertain that the entity has valid title and has not pledged the assets as collateral. In addition, the auditor may examine title insurance policies, confirm with title insurance companies, or, in some cases, examine recorded deeds. Schedules of property covered by casualty insurance policies may be compared with recorded assets, as may schedules used for property tax records. The auditor should review documentation and confirmations relating to notes payable and long-term debt for indications of assets that have been pledged as collateral. These procedures normally are performed at the balance sheet date.

(c) Acquisition of Assets

Substantive tests of property, plant, and equipment additions normally include the following (the extent of testing depends on the assessed level of control risk):

- Examining properly authorized agreements, architects' certificates, deeds, invoices, and other documents. For a purchase of land and buildings as a complete unit, the auditor should test the purchase price by comparing the data with the purchase agreement. For self-constructed assets, the auditor should consider the appropriateness of the accounting policies followed for capitalizing costs and the evidence supporting overhead and other cost allocations requiring judgments and estimates.

- Examining work orders and other supporting documentation for the entity's own materials and labor. The auditor should review the percentage added for overhead to ensure that only factory overhead, as appropriate, has been allocated to the addition.

- Reviewing the minutes of meetings of the board of directors or other committees to determine whether major additions were authorized appropriately.

Evaluating whether additions were appropriately approved should be based on the auditor's understanding of the authorization procedures and the level of the individuals authorized to approve acquisitions. If written authorizations are not obtained, the entity may acquire unneeded assets or capitalize portions of cost overruns that should be expensed. The approval process may not be adequate if authorizations do not include the reason for the expenditure, the estimated amount, the allocation between capital expenditures and charges to current operations, and procedures for comparing estimated amounts with actual expenditures. If these are lacking, the auditor should consider expanding the substantive tests, for example, by reviewing with senior management the usefulness of assets acquired during the year or reasons for budget overruns, to ensure that the recorded additions are appropriate.

(d) Disposition of Assets

The auditor should test entries removing assets from the accounts by examining evidence of approval, comparing acquisition cost with underlying records, recomputing accumulated depreciation and the resulting gain or loss, and evaluating the reasonableness of removal costs and recovery from scrap or salvage. If there is a properly controlled work order system or if the entity disposes of numerous assets at the same time, as in the case of a sale or an abandonment of a plant, the auditor usually can test the entries using a sample of the individual transactions.

As with acquisitions of assets, the auditor also should be familiar with the procedures for recording dispositions and with the levels of the people who approve them. If the procedures for recording new assets that replace existing assets do not identify the related retirement or disposal, the auditor may need to expand the testing of asset dispositions. The auditor should review additions for the year to determine if they are replacements for other assets and, if so, should ascertain that the replaced asset has been correctly accounted for. Also, the auditor should review miscellaneous income accounts for evidence of sales or disposals of assets.

(e) Classification of Expenditures

If tests of controls provide evidence that control activities for classifying expenditures between capital expenditures and current-period expenses are effective, the auditor may limit testing of classifications to scanning the charges to repair and maintenance accounts for significant or unusual items, reviewing fluctuations, and other substantive tests of additions. Ordinarily, however, the auditor performs further substantive tests, on at least a limited basis, even if control risk has been assessed at low. Those tests may include:

- Reviewing capitalizations, disposals, and repair and maintenance expense for reasonableness in relation to budgets and to the previous year, and obtaining explanations for any large or unusual fluctuations
- Reviewing whether all major additions and disposals during the year are classified properly
- Reviewing significant charges to repair and maintenance expense

Reviewing fluctuations in the repair and maintenance accounts and examining charges to these accounts to determine whether amounts should be capitalized provides evidence about the completeness of property, plant, and equipment. The auditor might vary the extent of the tests noted above depending on whether management approves the classification of expenditures.

As noted earlier in this chapter, an entity routinely may expense the cost of small-dollar items to reduce the clerical effort involved in maintaining detailed asset records. In reviewing charges to repair and maintenance accounts, the auditor should consider whether such items in the aggregate could have a material effect on the financial statements. Also, the auditor should recognize that determining whether an expenditure should be capitalized or charged to current operations may be subjective and highly judgmental. Even in an entity with effective controls, differences of opinion may arise over the nature and proper recording of a particular expenditure.

(f) Capital Leases

The discussion so far in this chapter has generally centered around transactions in which property, plant, and equipment are acquired by outright purchase. Often, however, the rights to such assets are obtained through lease transactions, which, together with the related accounting, can be highly sophisticated and complex. Although much of this chapter is equally applicable to purchased and leased assets, the auditor should consider the unique aspects of lease transactions. Detailed coverage of the various types of lease transactions and related accounting standards, however, is beyond the scope of this book.

In most entities, controls relating to the acquisition of property apply equally to purchases and leases. For example, a requirement for approval at a certain level for purchases of property over a specified amount typically applies to leases as well. If such a policy does not exist, the auditor should take this into consideration when obtaining an understanding of internal control and assessing risk.

For the auditor, the most important differences between purchase and lease transactions are those that deal with the audit objectives of rights and obligations, valuation, and presentation and disclosure. In a purchase transaction, the entity acquires title to the property and generally is not restricted in how it may use the property. In a lease transaction, the entity does not own the property and may use it only in the manner specified in the lease agreement. For instance, the lessee may be precluded by terms of the lease agreement from improving, modifying, or moving the property. In addition, the lessee will have use of the property only as long as the requirements of the lease agreement are met. Typically, the lessee has an obligation to make timely payments to the lessor, maintain the property, and, in many cases, pay taxes and insurance. In planning the engagement, the auditor should consider procedures that will identify material leases and provide assurance that the lessee is fulfilling its obligations under the agreement.

Obtaining assurance about proper valuation under GAAP and presentation and disclosure of lease transactions is more difficult. To properly evaluate the lessee's choice of accounting measurement and disclosure principles, the auditor needs to understand the lease transaction and the appropriate accounting treatment. In some instances, the documentation may not be sufficient for the auditor to evaluate the transaction, as in a case where the auditor cannot determine from the entity's records the interest rates implicit in the lease. In these instances, the auditor should arrange with management to obtain the necessary information directly from the lessor.

The specific measurement and disclosure requirements for accounting for leases are described in Statement of Financial Accounting Standards (SFAS) No. 13, *Accounting for Leases*, and related pronouncements (Accounting Standards Section L10). In general, lease transactions that have specified characteristics (capital leases) are required to be recorded by the lessee as if the lease resulted in acquiring property and incurring long-term debt. Assets acquired under capital leases are subject to the same accounting rules as other property, and the audit objectives related to assets acquired under capital leases are identical to those for other property, plant, and equipment accounts.

Because an entity may have lease obligations that do not meet the capitalization criteria, or may not have identified all leases that meet the criteria, the auditor should be familiar with those criteria and design auditing procedures to ensure that lease transactions have been properly classified. Analysis of lease expense accounts generally will help the auditor identify significant leasing transactions. The auditor ordinarily should examine records of leased assets, lease agreements, and other data related to leases capitalized during the period, to determine that they were properly classified and valued. The auditor also should review documents supporting rentals classified as operating leases to determine that they, too, were properly classified. Auditing procedures frequently required to evaluate the financial statement presentation of capital leases include reviewing the terms of individual leases; determining and evaluating the fair value, residual value, and estimated economic life of leased property; evaluating interest rate assumptions; and analyzing income tax considerations.

Because of the almost unlimited variety of leasing transactions, the complexity of lease computations, and the judgmental factors involved in assessing whether the audit evidence is appropriate, the auditor's review of leases may require more judgment than substantive tests of other property, plant, and equipment accounts. Often, the auditor of a lessee is presented with information that was obtained from the lessor and purports to support classification as an operating lease. The auditor should independently determine the classification in light of the facts and circumstances of the particular engagement. The auditor may need to use the services of specialists to review the fair value of property and estimated residual value under lease agreements. Finally, some leasing transactions are so complicated that often the auditor should look at a series of transactions and agreements to determine their economic substance—a process requiring much more judgment and experience than simply applying the criteria of SFAS No. 13.

(g) Constructed Assets—Interest Capitalization

The historical cost of acquiring an asset includes the costs of bringing it to the condition and location of its intended use. If that will take time, SFAS No. 34, *Capitalization of Interest Cost*, paragraph 6 (Accounting Standards Section I67.102), states that the related interest cost incurred during that period is a part of the historical cost of acquiring the asset.

In evaluating the amounts of interest capitalized, the auditor should determine that:

- Interest cost is being incurred
- The interest rate used is proper
- The average expenditures on which interest is capitalized have required the payment of cash, transfer of assets, or creation of a liability on which interest costs are incurred
- The activities necessary to get the asset ready for its intended use have been in progress throughout the period for which interest is capitalized

Determining the proper rate to use for capitalization can be simple if the expenditures are financed by a specific borrowing incurred for that purpose or by a specific working capital line of credit. If an outside party that is constructing the asset finances the expenditures, the auditor should determine whether the stated interest rate is the appropriate interest rate as specified by Accounting Principles Board (APB) Opinion No. 21, *Interest on Receivables and Payables* (Accounting Standards Section I69); if it is not, the auditor should consider the need for imputing interest at a fair rate. If specific borrowings cannot be identified, the auditor should use judgment in reviewing and testing the entity's determination of the appropriate weighted average interest rate, using the guidelines of SFAS No. 34. In making this judgment, the auditor should keep in mind that the objective is a reasonable measure of the interest cost incurred in acquiring the asset that otherwise would have been avoided. For example, the auditor may exclude certain borrowings that have been outstanding for a long time and bear interest at a rate not in line with current market conditions, like industrial bond issues relating to other assets.

Capitalization rates are to be applied to expenditures that have required the payment of cash, transfer of assets, or recognition of a liability on which interest is incurred. As a practical matter, monthly capitalized costs of an asset under construction often are used as an approximation of actual expenditures. In evaluating the reasonableness of this practice, the auditor might want to consider the average time to liquidate trade payables. If outsiders are constructing the asset, the auditor should be alert for material retainages withheld from progress payments until construction is completed.

Often the auditor can determine that activities necessary to get the asset ready for its intended use are in progress by observing a steady stream of expenditures over the construction period. The term "activities" is construed broadly to include all steps required to prepare the asset for its intended use, including administrative and technical activities during the preconstruction stage. Brief interruptions in activities, externally imposed interruptions, and delays inherent in the acquisition process do not require cessation of interest capitalization.

The capitalization period ends when the asset is substantially complete and ready for its intended use. The auditor should be aware that in a complex construction project, certain segments may be completed and become productive before completion of the entire project.

Other costs incurred on constructed assets that are properly capitalizable include costs to modify an asset for its intended use and costs of operating machinery during the testing phase of installation. Any revenue received from the sale of salvage materials or test production should reduce the capitalized costs. Interest income, however, should not be offset against capitalized costs except in the specific situation allowed by SFAS No. 62, *Capitalization of Interest Cost in Situations Involving Certain Tax-Exempt Borrowings and Certain Gifts and Grants* (Accounting Standards Section I67.116A-B), which amended SFAS No. 34.

(h) Depreciation and Salvage Values

Substantive testing of depreciation accounts should start with a review of the entity's methods and policies. Policies preferably should be systematically documented, but if they are not, the auditor can infer them from the computations and worksheets of prior and current years. Depreciation rates, salvage values, and useful lives may be compared with those in general use by similar entities. The auditor should test computations of depreciation expense, which in many cases may be accomplished by making approximations on an overall basis.

The auditor should consider the reasonableness of useful lives and whether known factors require reducing or extending the lives of any categories of plant assets. This can be accomplished by observing the pattern of gains and losses on disposition; consistent gains or consistent losses could suggest that the lives used are too short or too long or that salvage values used are inappropriate. For assets depreciated on the composite method, the auditor should review the relationship of the balances of allowance accounts to those of asset accounts. Ratios are, of course, affected by the pattern of additions, but after an auditor allows for unusually high or low additions in certain years, a significant upward or downward trend in the ratio of an allowance account to a related asset account should indicate whether useful lives are too short or too long. If either seems possible, an analysis of actual useful lives is necessary.

The auditor also should be aware of changing business conditions that might suggest the need to revise the estimated remaining lives of assets upward or downward for purposes of future depreciation charges. For example, leasehold improvements are depreciated over the estimated useful life of the improvements or over the original term of the lease, whichever is shorter, without regard to renewal options until those options are actually exercised or it becomes obvious they will be exercised. Significant expenditures for additional improvements with a life considerably longer than the remaining original lease might indicate management's intention to exercise a renewal option. Conversely, the auditor might learn that management intends to replace within the next two years computer equipment with a remaining depreciable life of four years. In these situations, the auditor should assess management's justification for changing or not changing the remaining depreciable life.

In practice, estimated lives, salvage values, and depreciation methods, once established for particular assets, commonly are not reviewed, by either management or the auditor, unless events or circumstances arise that call them into question. Auditors usually do not have the expertise to evaluate the remaining life of an asset and generally rely on other experts when necessary. Formal, in-depth reviews usually are made only for tax purposes, as part of acquisition reviews, or in industries in which depreciation has a significant effect on earnings, such as equipment leasing. The auditor's risk assessment process should include determining whether such an evaluation is appropriate.

If the reasonableness of the depreciation charges cannot be determined by making approximations on an overall basis for each class of assets, the auditor should test the individual computations and the balances in the subsidiary ledgers, compare the totals with the control account, and investigate any difference at year-end.

(i)   Other Substantive Tests

Information about the property accounts can be gathered from many different sources, especially the auditor's knowledge of the entity's operations and business environment. The auditor can correlate developments in those areas with activity in the property accounts and can consider the business reasons for additions and retirements and whether trends in operations or in the industry are likely to affect the values of property carried in the accounts. The auditor can perform several other procedures to gather additional evidence about the property accounts. For example, the auditor could:

- Visit and tour the main plants probably once a year and smaller plants less frequently. One among several reasons for making a tour is to observe the existence and condition of the plant.

- Examine the minutes of directors' meetings and executive committee meetings for matters affecting the property accounts.

- Review documentation and confirmations relating to notes payable and long-term debt for indications of assets that have been pledged as collateral.

- If there were any foreign currency property transactions during the year or balances at year-end, determine whether they were translated at appropriate rates.

- If the entity has several departments, subsidiaries, or affiliates, determine whether profits on transfers or sales within the group have been recognized that should be eliminated from the property accounts.

- Routinely inquire of entity personnel encountered in the course of the audit about past or prospective changes in operations that might affect the property accounts.

- Compare balances of asset, allowance, and expense accounts with the prior year and, if possible, month to month, to identify fluctuations and unusual entries calling for inquiry and explanation.

(j)   Intangible Assets and Deferred Charges

Intangible assets and deferred charges often involve the capitalization of amounts that are amortized over a number of future periods. The auditor usually tests the accuracy and existence/occurrence of capitalized amounts in the period in which they are incurred. In subsequent years, if there have been no additions, the auditor usually needs only to test the accuracy of amounts amortized or written off in the current period. Occasionally, it may be desirable to confirm the existence of material intangible assets (other than goodwill) by direct correspondence with attorneys or grantors of royalties, licenses, franchises, copyrights, or patents. Large or unusual journal entries may indicate potential material misstatements resulting from, among other things, improper application of accounting principles, errors in recording acquisitions and dispositions, and improper accounting for write-downs.

Analytical procedures may be an efficient and effective way of testing current-period amortization of intangibles and deferred charges. The auditor should judge the reasonableness of amortization expense in the light of the entity's operations, established amortization policies, and activity in the asset accounts during the period. Examples of analytical procedures include reviewing fluctuations in amounts compared with prior years; independently calculating an estimated expense for individual accounts; or, if the expense is a function of earned revenues, as may be the case for certain franchises or deferred costs, relating the expense to revenues earned during the period.

Substantiating the valuation of intangible assets requires extensive judgment on the auditor's part. Documentation for an account balance seldom provides conclusive evidence of value. Figure 22.4 illustrates some common types of intangible assets, bases for determining cost, and typical amortization periods.

Figure 22.4   Intangible Assets

Asset	Basis for Determining Cost	Amortization Period[a]
Patents	Cost of purchased patents; legal costs incurred in connection with successfully defending a patent suit (Costs of developing patents are generally expensed as incurred.)	Estimated period of benefits or 17 years (the legal life of a patent), whichever is less
Copyrights	Expenditures for government fees, attorneys' fees, and expenses (As with patents, research and development costs involved should be expensed as incurred.)	Estimated period of benefit or life of author plus 50 years (the legal life of a copyright), whichever is less
Trademarks, brands, and trade names	Expenditures for attorneys' fees, registration fees, and other expenditures identifiable with acquisition	Estimated period of use, but not more than 40 years
Franchises	Purchase price, including legal fees and similar costs	Estimated period of benefit, but not more than 40 years
Covenants not to compete	Purchase price or allocated purchase price in the case of a business combination	Specified term of the covenant, but not more than 40 years
Goodwill acquired	The excess of cost of the acquired enterprise over the sum of the amounts assigned to identifiable assets (tangible and intangible) acquired less liabilities assumed	Estimated period of benefit, but not more than 40 years
Intangible assets generally	Cost of intangible assets acquired from others (Costs to develop intangible assets that are not specifically identifiable are expensed as incurred.)	Estimated period of benefits, but not more than 40 years

[a]APB Opinion No. 17, which was issued in 1970, established that the amortization period for intangible assets with indeterminate lives should not exceed 40 years. The Securities and Exchange Commission has challenged the appropriateness of the amortization period used by registrants in particular circumstances.

(k) Carrying Values

Property, plant, and equipment, intangibles, and deferred charges generally are recorded at cost, which includes all expenditures necessary to acquire an asset and make it ready for its intended use, including freight and taxes. Determining whether the entity has appropriately capitalized costs requires the auditor to have extensive expertise in evaluating the selection and application of accounting principles for asset acquisitions.

Through depreciation and amortization, the cost of those assets is allocated to the periods in which the assets are used. Depreciable and amortizable assets are, in effect, "realized" in the normal course of business by charging depreciation and amortization to income, and thus provision for further reductions in their carrying amounts may be necessary only if future income from them is unlikely to equal or exceed their carrying amounts.

SFAS No. 121, *Accounting for the Impairment of Long-Lived Assets and for Long-Lived Assets to Be Disposed Of* (Accounting Standards Section I08), requires that long-lived and certain identifiable intangible assets to be held and used by an entity be reviewed for impairment whenever events or changes in circumstances indicate that the assets' carrying amount may not be recoverable. (Statement No. 121 excludes certain intangible assets from its scope, for example, financial instruments, long-term customer relationships of a financial institution, mortgage and other servicing rights, deferred policy acquisition costs, and deferred tax assets.)

In reviewing for recoverability, the entity should estimate future (undiscounted) cash flows from the use and eventual disposition of the assets. If the sum of those future cash flows is less than the asset's carrying amount, the assets should be written down and a loss recognized. The loss should be based on the fair value of assets expected to be held and used and on the fair value less cost to sell of assets to be disposed of, except for assets that are part of a segment of a business that will be disposed of in accordance with APB Opinion No. 30 (Accounting Standards Section I13), in which case the loss should be based on the assets' net realizable value. ("Fair value less cost to sell" requires that the expected net proceeds be discounted; "net realizable value" does not.)

SFAS No. 121 provides examples of situations that indicate that the recoverability of the carrying amount of an asset should be assessed. A change in general business conditions or in the area where property is located may indicate that carrying values may not be fully recoverable. On occasion, adverse conditions are so prevalent as to be obvious: idle plant or excess capacity; a depressed or deteriorating neighborhood, region, or industry; continuing losses. Other indications of potential inability to recover carrying values may be dramatic changes in the way an asset is used, changes in laws regulating environmental matters, a forecast of long-term losses from operations, and costs exceeding original expectations for acquiring or constructing an asset.

SFAS No. 121 provides guidance on estimating the expected future cash flows, including the grouping of assets that generate those cash flows, that are necessary to determine whether an impairment loss should be recognized. The statement also provides guidance on determining the fair value of an asset, which enters into the measurement of the loss.

If all or part of an asset grouping being tested for recoverability was part of a business combination accounted for as a purchase, the statement requires that the goodwill that arose in the transaction be included as part of the asset grouping in determining recoverability or be allocated on a pro rata basis. Goodwill not identified with impaired assets should be accounted for under APB Opinion No. 17.

If property previously used in operations is expected to be sold, its carrying amount should be written down to, but not below, net realizable value. The auditor should evaluate the circumstances surrounding the intended sale of significant assets or plant, to determine that the entity has made the distinction required by APB Opinion No. 30 (Accounting Standards Section I13) between a disposal of a segment of a business and the sale of significant assets. If the transaction is accounted for as the disposal of a segment of a business, the auditor also should review the treatment of expected operating income or losses from the measurement date to the disposal date. If expected income is used to offset other losses on the disposal, the auditor should take particular care in evaluating the methods and assumptions used to calculate the income amount. Finally, the auditor should consider whether the evaluation of the carrying value of specific productive assets or segments also has implications for evaluating the entity as a "going concern," as indicated by SAS No. 59 (AU Section 341) and discussed further in Chapter 26.

Except for recognizing impairments, fair values are not generally accepted as a basis for carrying values of property. There are other exceptions, however, such as reorganizations, quasi-reorganizations, the allocation of a basket purchase price, and other occasions when the consideration given to acquire assets has no objectively determinable value, such as a purchase of assets for common stock that has no readily determinable fair value. Fair values also are used for determining carrying amounts of donated property, assets acquired in certain nonmonetary transactions, and troubled debt restructurings. Property, plant, and equipment acquired in a transaction that must be accounted for by the purchase method are valued at fair value at the date of acquisition. Often, the amounts are determined by an appraisal performed at that time.

An independent appraiser usually performs the appraisal. The auditor should obtain satisfaction concerning the professional qualifications and reputation of the appraiser by inquiry or other procedures, as appropriate. The auditor also should understand the methods or assumptions the appraiser used to determine the assigned values, as required by SAS No. 73, *Using the Work of a Specialist* (AU Section 336). Based on knowledge of the entity's business and industry, the auditor should determine whether the values the appraiser assigned are appropriate for use in the financial statements. (Appraisal reports on the value of assets are among the most subjective and sensitive specialist reports that an auditor uses. SAS No. 73, discussed in Chapter 7, provides guidance on the auditor's use of the work of a specialist.) In applying SAS No. 73 to the work of a real estate appraiser, the auditor may consider the guidance in the AICPA audit and accounting guide, *Guide for the Use of Real Estate Appraisal Information*. This guide also helps the auditor understand the real estate appraisal process and how to use real estate appraisal information. While the majority of items purchased may be for use on an ongoing basis, management may intend to hold other items for resale or to use them only temporarily. In that case, the auditor should ensure that the assigned values do not exceed net realizable values.

(l)   Income Tax Considerations

In planning and performing auditing procedures for the property, plant, and equipment and other noncurrent asset accounts, the auditor should consider the interrelationship of those accounts and various income tax accounts. Many amounts used in determining periodic income tax accruals and deferred taxes are computed from the property and other noncurrent asset records.

The Tax Reform Act of 1986 modified the Accelerated Cost Recovery System (ACRS) established by the Economic Recovery Tax Act of 1981. Generally accepted accounting principles require that plant and equipment be depreciated over their expected useful lives. The useful life categories provided under the ACRS guidelines, however, generally do not conform with the actual expected useful lives of the assets to which they apply. If the effect of the difference between depreciation based on ACRS lives and depreciation based on actual expected lives on current or future financial statements is material, using ACRS depreciation for financial reporting purposes is not acceptable. For many businesses, this necessitates a second set of depreciation records for income tax purposes.

With the passage of the Tax Reform Act of 1986, a corporate alternative minimum tax (AMT) was introduced. In determining the AMT income, depreciation calculations are made under the Alternative Depreciation System and then additional depreciation calculations are necessary to determine AMT income. Thus, entities may be required to maintain as many as four sets of depreciation records (i.e., financial reporting, regular tax, and two for AMT) and possibly more, depending on whether an entity is subject to taxation in other jurisdictions.

Interest capitalization policies and the treatment of lease payments also may differ for financial reporting and income tax purposes. As stated above, SFAS No. 34 (Accounting Standards Section I67) requires that interest be capitalized during the acquisition period as part of the historical cost of acquiring certain property, plant, and equipment. The amount of interest capitalized for income tax purposes, however, probably will differ from that used for financial reporting, resulting in different book and tax bases for individual assets. Also, certain leasing transactions are recorded for financial statement purposes as assets acquired under capital leases, while for income tax purposes they may be treated as operating leases.

For transactions that result in different accounting for financial statement and income tax purposes, the auditor should identify the differences and consider them in planning the audit. The relationship of the property accounts to the income tax accounts generally requires close coordination of auditing procedures in the two areas. In reviewing the temporary differences between book and tax bases, the auditor may need to perform separate tests to substantiate the tax basis balances as well as the financial statement balances.

23

Auditing Accounts Payable and Related Purchasing Cycle Accounts

This chapter discusses substantive tests that the auditor may use to achieve the audit objectives related to purchasing cycle accounts, principally accounts payable and related costs and expenses. The audit strategy that determines the nature, timing, and extent of substantive tests for each account balance and class of transactions in the purchasing cycle is based primarily on the auditor's identification of inherent risks and assessment of materiality and control risk relating to specific audit objectives, and on efficiency considerations.

23.1   AUDIT OBJECTIVES

Specific audit objectives applicable to accounts in the purchasing cycle are described in Figure 23.1.

23.2   IDENTIFYING INHERENT RISKS

As discussed in Chapter 8, the auditor obtains or updates information about various aspects of the entity and its business in order to identify inherent risks. Liabilities and related expenses are more likely to be understated or omitted from the accounts than overstated, because the account balances usually consist of items that have been scrutinized and acknowledged before being recorded and because attempts to improve financial statement presentation may involve a failure to recognize valid liabilities and expenses. Therefore, substantive tests in the purchasing cycle concentrate heavily on seeking evidence of omitted or understated liabilities, although the possibility of overstatement is not ignored.

23.3   ANALYTICAL PROCEDURES

Analytical procedures frequently highlight relationships between accounts and risks not otherwise apparent during the risk assessment phase of the audit. As discussed in Chapter 8, analytical procedures are a required part of planning; their use at an early stage in the audit often results in more informed strategy decisions. The procedures discussed in this section, however, also can be applied in the substantive testing and final review stages of an audit.

Scanning the detailed list of accounts payable and investigating significant unusual items, such as debit balances and old unpaid invoices, are analytical procedures that are particularly relevant to auditing payables and purchases. Scanning the accounts payable listing can be an effective means of identifying unusual audit risks associated with payables and purchases. For example, the existence of old unpaid invoices or uncleared debit advices may indicate disputes with suppliers or the inclusion of invalid invoices. When deciding whether to scan the detailed listing of accounts payable, the auditor considers whether debit balances could be significant and the entity's internal controls, particularly monitoring controls. For example, if management reviews the accounts payable listing for purposes of managing cash flow or reviewing budgets, the likelihood of unusual balances may be decreased.

Figure 23.1   Audit Objectives for Purchasing Cycle Accounts

Completeness	Accounts payable represent all amounts owed by the entity at the balance sheet date arising from the purchase of goods and services.
	All goods and services received, less goods returned, during the period covered by the financial statements are reflected in the financial statements.
	All employee wages for services performed during the period covered by the financial statements are reflected in the financial statements; accrued payroll represents all amounts owed to employees at the balance sheet date.
Accuracy	Purchase transactions are based on correct prices and quantities and are accurately computed and classified in the appropriate general ledger and accounts payable subsidiary ledger accounts.
	The accounts payable subsidiary ledger is mathematically correct and agrees with the general ledger.
	All payroll amounts are based on correct wage rates and hours, and are accurately computed, summarized, and classified in the appropriate general ledger accounts.
Existence/Occurrence	Recorded accounts payable represent amounts owed by the entity at the balance sheet date.
	Recorded purchase transactions represent goods and services actually received during the period covered by the financial statements.
	Recorded payroll transactions represent wages for services actually performed during the period covered by the financial statements.
Cutoff	Purchase transactions, accounts payable, returns, and payroll transactions are recorded in the proper period.
Valuation/Allocation	Accounts payable and accrued payroll are stated at the correct amounts the entity owes.
	All expenses and losses applicable to the period have been recognized, including unrealized losses on unfavorable purchase commitments.
Rights and Obligations	Accounts payable and accrued payroll are legal obligations of the entity at the balance sheet date.
Presentation and Disclosure	Accounts payable, accrued payroll, and expenses are properly described and classified in the financial statements.
	Loss contingencies related to purchase commitments are properly disclosed.

Analytical procedures can indicate trends in expenses that may assist the auditor in assessing risk. Relationships among expense accounts and between expense and other accounts should be reviewed and compared with those of prior periods and those anticipated in budgets or forecasts. The account balances themselves often are compared from month to month and with the corresponding period of the prior year. Trends and fluctuations (seasonal and other) should be noted and explanations sought for unusual patterns.

The auditor should consider management's performance of analytical procedures as part of its monitoring controls. The auditor may obtain an understanding of the procedures performed by management and consider using their results to supplement his or her own analytical procedures. Management typically reviews various internal expense and budgetary reports and data, such as the following:

- Actual gross profit compared with historical trends and budgets or forecasts
- Actual expenses, including payroll, compared with historical trends and budgets
- Trends of returns and debit memos
- Accounts payable aging
- Open purchase commitments

Management's review of reports such as these may help identify material misstatements in the processing of purchase transactions. For example, investigation of significant differences between reported expenses and budgeted and historical expenses could identify incomplete updating of invoices to the general ledger.

The way management responds to the auditor's inquiries resulting from analytical procedures may give some indication of the quality of the entity's control environment. For example, prompt, logical, and meaningful answers to questions about differences between current-year expenses and budgeted amounts as of an interim date or corresponding prior-year amounts would provide some indication, in the absence of evidence to the contrary, that the entity's management is "in control" and that the accounting system and control activities appear to be functioning as intended. Analytical procedures, however, also may indicate trends, even in well-controlled entities, that may lead the auditor to extend substantive tests.

23.4 SUBSTANTIVE TESTS OF DETAILS

Substantive tests of details applied to purchasing cycle accounts are directed principally to accounts payable. The assurance needed for income statement accounts usually is obtained from a combination of tests of controls, analytical procedures, and substantive tests of details applied to balance sheet accounts. The remainder of this section describes substantive tests of details that could be performed with respect to accounts payable. The tests that actually are selected, as well as their timing and extent, will depend on the auditor's assessment of control risk, as well as his or her identification of inherent risks and assessment of materiality. It would be highly unusual for all of the procedures described in the remainder of this section to be applied in a particular audit.

(a) Control Risk Assessment and the Nature, Timing, and Extent of Substantive Tests

The auditor is required to obtain an understanding of the entity's internal control sufficient to plan the audit; the auditor also should assess control risk for the assertions embodied in the financial statements—in this case, the assertions related to payables and related expenses. The understanding and the assessment are used to identify the types of misstatements that might occur and the controls that may reduce the likelihood of their occurrence. Based on that information, the auditor determines the nature, timing, and extent of substantive tests. Obtaining the understanding and assessing control risk for accounts in the purchasing cycle are discussed in Chapter 14.

The auditor achieves the audit objectives related to purchasing cycle accounts by performing substantive tests or a combination of substantive tests and tests of controls. The auditor frequently tests controls to obtain evidence of their effective operation as a basis for reducing the assurance needed from substantive tests directed at the completeness, accuracy, and existence/occurrence audit objectives. Chapter 14 presents an illustration of the strategy decisions an auditor might make in auditing the purchasing cycle.

Before performing substantive tests on accounts payable, the auditor needs assurance that the detailed list of accounts payable in the subsidiary ledger (usually referred to as the accounts payable trial balance) contains all purchase transactions that remain unpaid at year-end and reconciles to the related control account in the general ledger. If the results of tests of controls provide sufficient evidence about the completeness of the trial balance, substantive tests of the completeness of accounts payable generally will be limited to analytical procedures. Also, when control risk has been assessed at low, or when the accounting system is reliable because secure packaged software is used, it should not be necessary to test the mathematical accuracy of the detailed list. The auditor should consider the possibility, however, that information from the detailed list could be suppressed, either during the report writing process or subsequent to its printing.

Normally, entity personnel routinely compare the general ledger control account balance with the total of individual accounts payable, investigate discrepancies between the two, and make appropriate adjustments. The auditor should trace the trial balance total to the general ledger and determine that all reconciling items are appropriate. Reconciling items may indicate potential material misstatements resulting from, among other things, cutoff problems, unusual transactions, or internal control breakdowns.

The auditor also may examine support for adjustments made throughout the year in reconciling detailed accounts payable to the control account to obtain assurance that those adjustments were properly authorized and posted to the control account. In deciding whether to perform this test, the auditor should consider whether there is appropriate division of duties and whether differences disclosed by the reconciliation of the subsidiary ledger to the control account are appropriately investigated and corrected on a timely basis. If these procedures are not in effect, or if there is a lack of division of duties between individuals responsible for initiating and recording purchases and related transactions, recording cash disbursements, maintaining the accounting records, and reconciling the detailed records to the control account, the risk of misstatement is increased and the auditor should perform this test. In some entities, however, entries to the control account may be numerous, and it may not be necessary to evaluate all of them. The auditor should focus attention on those entries arising from the reconciliation process by reviewing the reconciliations, identifying unusual adjustments, reviewing authorizations (when appropriate), and tracing the adjustments to supporting documentation and the general ledger.

If the auditor has assessed control risk for purchases and accounts payable at low for the audit objectives of completeness, accuracy, and existence/occurrence, substantive tests addressing those objectives may be limited to analytical procedures. No detailed tests of transactions supporting the completeness and accuracy of purchases of goods and services need be performed.

If the auditor has assessed control risk for purchases and accounts payable below the maximum for the audit objectives of completeness, accuracy, and existence/ occurrence, it will be necessary to obtain evidence that the entity has implemented procedures to ensure that all purchases are recorded (completeness) and that those procedures have operated as prescribed. The auditor also should examine disbursements records for a period after the balance sheet date, choosing items on the basis of high-dollar coverage. The auditor also will need assurance from substantive tests about the accuracy and existence of accounts payable on the detailed listing. When control risk has been assessed below the maximum, the auditor should establish the extent of testing so as to obtain a moderate to low level of assurance that the audit objectives of completeness, accuracy, and existence/occurrence are achieved. The auditor also should consider whether evidence obtained from tests directed at one audit objective is relevant to other audit objectives as well.

In the unlikely event that the auditor has assessed control risk for purchases and accounts payable at maximum for the audit objectives of completeness, accuracy, and existence/occurrence, it will again be necessary to obtain evidence that all purchases are recorded (completeness). To establish completeness of accounts payable, the auditor should examine disbursements records for the period after the balance sheet date and files of unmatched receiving reports, purchase orders, and vendor invoices and files of pending claims and credits for returned goods, as described below. The auditor also should trace selected liabilities on the accounts payable listing to supporting documentation and to disbursements records to determine that the liability exists at the balance sheet date (existence/occurrence) and is accurately recorded (accuracy). When control risk has been assessed at maximum, the auditor should establish the extent of testing so as to obtain a high level of assurance that the audit objectives of completeness, accuracy, and existence/occurrence are achieved. The auditor also should consider whether evidence obtained from tests directed at one audit objective is relevant to other audit objectives as well.

The auditor usually performs substantive tests of details to achieve the cutoff objective because entities frequently do not establish control activities designed to achieve a proper cutoff throughout the year. In some situations, however, control activities may address cutoff, or management may implement special controls at year-end, which the auditor may decide to test. Also, controls designed to ensure completeness of input and update may be effective in ensuring that transactions are recorded in the proper period. For example, the design of the accounting system itself may reduce control risk for cutoff. Nevertheless, it is usually more efficient for the auditor to perform substantive tests of details to achieve the cutoff objective. In determining the extent of those tests, the auditor should consider such factors as control activities directed at cutoff, the assessment of control risk, the type and frequency of cutoff errors found in prior years, and the assurance expected from other related substantive tests, such as tests for existence and completeness.

Control risk is seldom assessed at low with respect to the valuation, rights and obligations, and presentation and disclosure objectives, and therefore substantive tests of details usually are performed for these objectives if they are applicable.

(i) Early Substantive Testing.   When control risk is assessed below the maximum or at low, the auditor often performs substantive tests related to completeness, accuracy, and existence/occurrence at an interim date—before the balance sheet date—and then performs various procedures to support the existence, completeness, and accuracy of vendor balances at the balance sheet date. In those circumstances, a major concern is whether controls will ensure the completeness of accounts payable at the balance sheet date. In this regard, the auditor considers whether the entity reconciles detailed records to the control account; has properly established division of duties between initiation, recording, and payment of accounts payable; and properly records goods and services received and not invoiced.

At the balance sheet date, the auditor considers the results of testing at the early date and the risk of material misstatement for the completeness, accuracy, and existence/occurrence objectives in the intervening period—the period between the date of the early substantive testing and the balance sheet date. This may involve inquiry, observation, and, when appropriate, examining evidence of the operation of the information system and related control activities during the intervening period, examining evidence of the operation of special procedures established for the intervening period, or performing substantive tests of the details of transactions in the intervening period.

Even when control risk is assessed at maximum, the auditor may be able to obtain sufficient evidence to provide a reasonable basis for extending audit conclusions from an interim date to the balance sheet date. Performing early substantive testing when control risk is at maximum is not likely to be efficient, however, because of the extent of testing that likely will be required in the intervening period.

(b) Cutoff Tests of Purchases

Cutoff tests are intended to ascertain that all transactions have been recorded in the proper period. In the absence of control activities directed toward cutoff, the sooner the accounts are closed after year-end, the greater the likelihood that there will be unrecorded vendors' invoices. Thus, examining files of unmatched receiving reports and unrecorded invoices, the purchases journal, the cash disbursements journal, and other relevant records for a period after year-end is a common auditing procedure. (Cutoff tests of the receipt of goods and recording of inventory usually are coordinated with the auditor's observation of the entity's physical inventory count.)

If the basic transaction documents are in numerical sequence, the auditor can note the number of the last receiving report and the last check issued (or other basic transaction documents) prior to year-end. The auditor can examine perpetual inventory records, the year-end accounts payable trial balance, and the listing of unmatched receiving reports to determine whether goods received at or near year-end are included. Similarly, the last check issued can be traced to the cash disbursements records and the list of outstanding checks in the bank reconciliation. The auditor should apply the same procedures to obtain assurance that receipts and invoices applicable to the following year were not recorded in the current year. If the basic transaction documents are not prenumbered, it may be necessary to examine relevant documents, with emphasis on transaction dates and large amounts, selected from the various sources both before and after the cutoff date, to obtain sufficient evidence that the cutoff was properly made.

(c) Accounts Payable

Tests of the completeness of accounts payable involve reviewing the disbursements records after the balance sheet date and determining whether selected invoices, debit memoranda, or other items in those records relate to the period before the balance sheet date and should be recorded as of that date. Other tests of completeness include examining files of unmatched receiving reports, purchase orders, and vendors' invoices and files of pending claims and credits for returned goods to determine that the liability for goods and services received and credits for valid claims and returns are properly recorded.

Substantive tests directed at the existence and accuracy of recorded accounts payable normally consist of:

- Tracing selected entries in the accounts payable subsidiary ledger to subsequent cash disbursements or other supporting documents, such as vendors' invoices; examining evidence that personnel have matched all invoices to purchase orders and receiving reports; and reperforming the matching procedure (on a test basis if appropriate) to determine that all aspects of the transaction appear reasonable (e.g., that suppliers' invoices are addressed to the entity).

- Tracing adjusting items in the reconciliation of the subsidiary ledger to the control account to appropriate supporting documentation. The auditor also should test the mathematical accuracy of the accounts payable subsidiary ledger or trial balance and the reconciliation.

- Investigating the underlying causes of debit balances in accounts payable. These balances may represent overpayments or duplicate payments; if so, the auditor should consider whether they are collectible and should be reclassified. They also may represent purchases that were not recorded but were nevertheless paid; in that event, the auditor should ascertain why the purchases were not recorded.

Confirmation of accounts payable balances does not have the widespread acceptance as a substantive test that confirmation of accounts receivable has. Confirmation provides evidence principally about the existence of assets and liabilities, not about completeness, which is typically a source of greater audit risk for liabilities. Evidence about the existence of payables usually is obtained through tests of control activities related to ordering and receiving goods and recording invoices, through analytical procedures, and through the substantive tests discussed above. Only rarely is confirmation an effective or efficient means of obtaining the necessary assurance that accounts payable have been properly authorized and recorded. Reviewing disbursements records subsequent to year-end addresses the completeness of payables. (Confirming a few payables as a test of controls, however, may provide the auditor with useful evidence about the effective operation of controls over the completeness, accuracy, and proper cutoff of purchases from and disbursements to vendors, but the procedure is rarely used.) In unusual circumstances, confirmation (as a substantive test) may be called for if there are deficiencies in controls or if the results of other substantive tests indicate that payables may be incomplete or otherwise misstated. If undertaken, the confirmation procedure is similar to that described in Chapter 18 for confirming accounts receivable, except that an additional step of circularizing known suppliers with zero balances may be included. In extreme situations, if the auditor is still not satisfied as to possible unrecorded liabilities or the accuracy of recorded balances, the entity may be requested to deliver the mail, unopened, to the auditor daily for a reasonable period after year-end, so that the auditor can search for vendors' invoices and statements applicable to the year under audit.

Losses from purchase commitments may arise in connection with commodity purchases, forward transactions, or purchase commitments in excess of short-term requirements. If material losses could arise from unfulfilled purchase commitments, the commitments should be identified and the auditor should assess the potential need for a loss provision. This may be accomplished by examining open purchase order records, inquiring of employees who make purchase commitments, or requesting major suppliers to provide details of purchase commitments outstanding as of year-end. If the auditor is uncertain whether all commitments have been identified, it may be appropriate to review suppliers' invoices and receiving reports for a period after year-end for evidence of purchases above prevailing prices or in quantities in excess of current requirements (determined by reviewing perpetual inventory records for evidence of goods that are slow-moving or obsolete), which may indicate unfavorable purchase commitments at year-end. Also, since major purchase commitments generally require the approval of the board of directors, examining minutes of board meetings may help the auditor discover such purchase commitments. Chapter 27 illustrates the statement about purchase commitments that should be included in the representation letter.

(d) Salaries, Wages, and Payroll Taxes

Substantive tests directed at the completeness and accuracy of accrued payroll and related liabilities consist primarily of analytical procedures and examining the subsequent payment of the liability in the following year. The auditor should obtain an analysis of accrued salaries and wages and test its mathematical accuracy; totals should be agreed to the payroll records. If the entity has recorded an estimate (for example, by prorating the payroll for the overlapping period) rather than an exact computation, the appropriateness and consistency with prior years of the method of estimating should be ascertained. The auditor also should review the general ledger accounts relating to payroll expense. Analytical procedures can be helpful in this regard; for instance, the number of employees and the average salary per employee can be compared with the prior year. Any material unusual entries, unusual fluctuations in normal recurring entries in the payroll summaries, and payroll amounts capitalized in fixed asset accounts should be investigated. Substantive tests of details normally are not performed on payroll expense account balances unless controls are extremely ineffective or the results of other procedures, primarily analytical procedures, indicate the need for additional assurance from detail testing.

Based on materiality and risk assessment, the auditor may examine subsequent payments of agency obligations. Comparing current year-end balances with those of the prior year may indicate unusual items. For accounts like unclaimed wages, the auditor should examine and test a trial balance reconciling the details to a control account and should scrutinize the underlying details for unusual items. If old unclaimed wages have been written off, potential liability under state escheat or unclaimed property laws should be considered.

Accrued commissions should be substantiated by examining sales reports submitted by sales personnel, commission schedules, and contracts with sales personnel. If accrued commissions are significant, the auditor should consider confirming amounts due and commissions earned during the year directly with sales personnel. The overall reasonableness of commission expenses for the year may be tested by multiplying commission rates by sales.

The year-end liability for vacation pay, sick pay, and other compensated absences should be reviewed for compliance with Statement of Financial Accounting Standards (SFAS) No. 43, *Accounting for Compensated Absences* (Accounting Standards Section C44). If vacation periods are based on length of service, normally the entity prepares a detailed computation of the accrued liability. The auditor should review the method used and the computation to determine that the amount accrued is appropriate.

A published statement of policy may create liabilities for rights that accrue to employees even without formal labor contracts. Opinion of counsel may sometimes be necessary to determine whether there is a legal liability at the balance sheet date. Contracts and policies of that nature do not always indicate clearly whether employees' rights accrue ratably over a period or come into existence in their entirety at a specific date. The auditor also should be alert for possible liabilities arising from employee benefits so customary as to constitute an implied promise. Sick pay, severance pay, and some kinds of bonuses and pensions are examples.

(e) Costs and Expenses

Audit evidence with respect to the income statement is based mainly on auditing procedures applied to balance sheet accounts, correlation of amounts on the income statement with balances on the balance sheet, analytical procedures such as the review of performance indicators, and, where applicable, tests of controls. If control risk has not been assessed at low, procedures like correlating income statement amounts with balances in the balance sheet become more important. Many income statement items can be correlated with balance sheet accounts, such as interest with loan balances. In addition, the auditor can assess the reasonableness of the amounts, for example, by comparing the percentage of selling, general, and administrative expenses in relation to sales from period to period. Computer software can facilitate these tests.

When the procedures outlined above have been completed, there may still be income statement accounts about which the auditor needs further assurance. Tests should be designed to provide such assurance, which normally concerns one of two types of matters. If further assurance is needed about the occurrence or accuracy of specific expense accounts (like travel expense or maintenance expense), the auditor should request or prepare an analysis of the account in question or, at least, of the material items in it, and examine supporting documentation for enough items to gain assurance that there is no material misstatement. For example, the auditor may obtain a list of employees with expense accounts and make appropriate tests to determine whether all expenses have been reported and recorded in the accounts in the proper period, and may test related post-balance sheet entries to determine whether a proper cutoff was made.

If the auditor is concerned about the possibility of misstatement associated with a particular type of transaction rather than with particular account balances (as might be the case when controls over certain types of payments are ineffective), the areas in the expense accounts that might be affected should be isolated. For example, if certain payments are supported by receiving reports and other payments are not, the auditor need perform substantive tests only for the payments that are not supported by receiving reports. In this situation, the auditor would select a sufficient number of accounts that might be misstated and examine them to the extent necessary to obtain assurance that no material misstatement had occurred.

(f)   Searching for Unrecorded Liabilities

In addition to the specific substantive tests described above, the auditor typically performs procedures designed to detect other unrecorded liabilities, like insurance claims and other loss contingencies, as well as receives a letter of representation from management and a letter from the entity's counsel. Those topics are covered in detail in Chapter 27. The remainder of this section describes other procedures the auditor should perform to detect unrecorded liabilities.

The auditor should read minutes of meetings of stockholders, directors, and appropriate committees for the period under audit and up to the date of the audit report. Those minutes may reveal contracts, commitments, and other matters requiring investigation. The auditor also should examine contracts, loan agreements, leases, correspondence from taxing or other governmental agencies, and similar documents. Reviewing such documents may disclose unrecorded liabilities as of the balance sheet date.

One of the auditor's most difficult tasks is identifying liabilities for which no direct reference appears in the accounts. Clues to those obligations may be discovered in unexpected places, and the auditor should be constantly alert for them. For example:

- The auditor should review responses to bank confirmation requests in addition to analyzing interest expense to determine whether there are any unrecorded bank loans.

- Responses to requests for confirmation of bank loans may list as collateral, securities or other assets that do not appear in the records. They may be borrowed from affiliated entities or others.

- Manufacturers of machinery and equipment often sell their products at prices that include cost of installation. The auditor should determine that the estimated cost of completing the installation of equipment sold has been recorded in the same period as the sale of the equipment.

In a decentralized environment, the possibility of unrecorded liabilities may be more significant than in a centralized environment and may warrant a procedure for formal inquiry of department heads, supervisors, and others regarding knowledge of unprocessed invoices, unrecorded commitments, or contingent liabilities. This procedure may apply in a loosely controlled centralized environment as well.

The auditor should take a broad look at the entity's operations to determine whether all types of expenses and related liabilities, if any, that are expected have been recorded and appear to be reasonable. Familiarity with the entity's operations should disclose whether such items as royalties, commissions, interest, consignments, and the myriad of taxes most entities are subject to have been properly recorded.

The search for unrecorded liabilities cannot, of course, bring to light liabilities that have been deliberately withheld from the auditor's attention. The auditor's responsibility regarding fraud and illegal acts is discussed in Chapter 4. The receipt of a representation letter, as discussed in Chapter 27, does not relieve the auditor of professional responsibilities in this area.

Finally, transactions with affiliated entities often are not conducted on the same basis as transactions with outsiders; thus, they deserve special attention from the auditor. For example, charges for services rendered may not be billed on a timely basis. Whenever feasible, the auditor should review a reconciliation of the amount due to or from an affiliate by reference to both sets of records. If this cannot be done, the balance should be confirmed.

24

Auditing Income Taxes

Income tax differs from other costs and expenses because it is largely a dependent variable, based on revenue received and costs and expenses incurred by an entity. Management often is able to control the timing and amount of tax payments by controlling the related underlying transactions, particularly in closely held entities where minimizing taxes currently payable is often a significant management objective.

The issues associated with accounting for income taxes fall principally into two broad categories: determining the tax provision in the income statement and the timing of its payment. Those two issues complicate presentation of the current tax liability and deferred tax accounts on the balance sheet and the expense on the income statement. The actual liability is difficult to determine because of the complexities of federal and state tax statutes and regulations. The accounting is complicated further by the number and variety of differences between generally accepted accounting principles (GAAP) and the treatment permitted or required by tax laws and related rulings and regulations of the various taxing jurisdictions to which an entity is subject. For multinational entities, income taxes levied in foreign countries under the laws and regulations of those countries also must be evaluated to determine their treatment under U.S. accounting pronouncements.

Accounting for income taxes is governed principally by Statement of Financial Accounting Standards (SFAS) No. 109, *Accounting for Income Taxes* (Accounting Standards Section I27). The basic principles of SFAS No. 109 are summarized as follows:

- A current tax liability or asset is recognized for estimated taxes payable or refundable on the current year's tax returns
- A deferred tax liability or asset is recognized for the estimated future tax effects attributable to temporary differences and carryforwards, including operating loss carryforwards
- All measurements are based on regular tax rates and provisions of the enacted tax law; the effects of anticipated changes in tax laws or rates are not considered
- The amount of deferred tax assets is reduced, if applicable, by any tax benefits that, based on available evidence, are not expected to be realized

SFAS No. 109 requires that deferred tax assets be recognized for all temporary differences that will result in deductible amounts in future years and for carryforwards and then evaluated for realization based on available evidence. A valuation allowance is necessary if it is "more likely than not" (defined as a likelihood of greater than 50 percent) that some portion of or all deferred tax assets will not be realized. That determination is based on evidence concerning the sources of taxable income that may be available to realize future tax benefits. SFAS No. 109 specifies the four sources that may be available for that purpose; they are discussed later in this chapter.

24.1 AUDIT OBJECTIVES

The objectives in auditing income tax accounts are to obtain reasonable assurance that all tax liabilities (or refunds receivable), tax provisions, and deferred tax accounts (including the valuation allowance) are included in the financial statements; that they are properly measured, classified, and described; and that all necessary disclosures are made in the financial statements. The basic auditing procedures are to test the accuracy of the computation of the current and deferred tax liability or asset accounts and the charge or credit to expense for the period. This requires that the auditor determine that the underlying data is complete and accurate. The amounts involved are likely to be significant, and the issues affecting them numerous, complex, and often debatable. The discussion that follows suggests some of the specific objectives the auditor should meet in auditing income taxes.

In addition to obtaining reasonable assurance that the tax liability accounts accurately reflect the entity's current tax obligations (including interest and penalty charges, which should be accounted for separately from the tax expense and liability accounts), the auditor should determine that the entity has provided for probable loss contingencies that are reasonably estimable. Such contingencies may result from existing disagreements with taxing authorities or from the possibility that future disagreements may arise over positions an entity takes in its current tax return that the Internal Revenue Service (IRS) may interpret differently. Guidance for dealing with contingencies of this nature is contained in SFAS No. 5, *Accounting for Contingencies* (Accounting Standards Section C59). Further, the auditor should obtain reasonable assurance that deferred tax liabilities and assets are classified properly as to current and noncurrent amounts. The auditor also should determine that the total tax provision in the income statement is classified properly as to currently payable and deferred amounts. In addition, the auditor should ascertain that the tax effects of extraordinary items, discontinued operations, changes in accounting principles, and items that are charged or credited directly to shareholders' equity accounts have been properly calculated and reflected in the income statement.

Required disclosures under SFAS No. 109 vary according to whether the entity is a public or a nonpublic enterprise. Tax exposures not provided for in the financial statements but requiring disclosure under SFAS No. 5 also should be disclosed in the notes to the financial statements. In addition, public companies are subject to specific disclosure requirements of the Securities and Exchange Commission.

The efficiency of the audit of income tax accounts can be enhanced by collecting, in the course of examining other accounts, data that may be useful in examining the tax accrual. Examples include collecting tax depreciation data when auditing fixed asset accounts, and gathering officer compensation data when testing the payroll accounts. The auditor should analyze significant nonrecurring transactions to determine their impact on the tax accrual. Equally important from a client service standpoint, the auditor should be alert to tax planning and tax savings opportunities, and can help management plan transactions to result in the most favorable tax treatment.

24.2 TYPICAL TRANSACTIONS AND CONTROLS

(a) Typical Transactions

The tax transaction cycle consists of obtaining and summarizing the appropriate data, calculating the income tax effects, and disbursing the required tax payments at the appropriate time. Most tax compliance systems are organized according to the timing requirements of taxing authorities. A reminder list, often called a "tax calendar," helps control the filing of required tax returns and the timing of payments. A tax specialist usually computes tax amounts, which a financial officer then authorizes. The appropriate determination and recording of income tax expense and the related balance sheet accounts depend on proper recognition of the tax consequences of transactions for financial statement purposes, which may differ in many instances from the consequences reported on the tax returns. Internal control for income tax matters, therefore, may be sophisticated and complex.

(b) Internal Control

Even though the audit strategy for income tax accounts usually emphasizes substantive testing, it is important to recognize that a separate tax transaction cycle and related controls exist in most entities. It is the auditor's responsibility to obtain an understanding of internal control relating to tax transactions and to identify situations where tests of controls might be appropriate. The three key functions over which controls usually are established are tax planning, compliance, and recording. If the auditor tests the controls and finds them effective, it may be possible to adjust the timing and extent of substantive tests.

(i) Tax Planning. Adequate control of income tax expense requires extensive advance planning. This begins with management's setting financial objectives for a given period and considering the effect of taxes on those goals. Then tax transactions are scheduled and specific decisions made to minimize the tax liability and plan for the consequent cash disbursements. Cash flow implications significantly influence tax planning in many cases.

Tax planning is facilitated and in part controlled by checklists of compliance requirements (due dates, elections to be made, information requirements, legislative activity, and the like), alternatives and opportunities, and open issues. It is particularly important for entities to keep records of past decisions having future tax implications. In making decisions about the tax treatments of transactions, entities need to consider not only future business plans but also the ongoing tax implications of past elections and differences between accounting and tax recording of transactions.

Tax specialists, both the entity's employees and external consultants and auditors, are usually involved in the planning effort. They maintain reminder lists or checklists of tax savings opportunities, which are used to ensure that the entity properly avails itself of deductions, exemptions, deferrals, and elections permitted by the law. Tax savings opportunities are reviewed and the checklists prepared, usually early in the fiscal year, and definitely before year-end so that any necessary actions can be completed during the year.

The requirement in SFAS No. 109 for a valuation allowance for deferred tax assets that are not expected to be realized has increased the significance of tax planning. Tax planning strategies are one of the possible sources of taxable income specified in the statement as available to realize benefits for deductible temporary differences and carryforwards. SFAS No. 109 defines tax planning strategies as prudent and feasible actions that an entity might not take ordinarily but would take to prevent a carryforward from expiring unused and that would result in the realization of deferred tax assets.

(ii) Tax Compliance.   Control over compliance with income tax requirements is necessary both to minimize liability for those taxes and for accounting purposes, especially when an entity is subject to multiple taxing jurisdictions. Many entities have designed and established well-controlled compliance systems in recognition of this fact; those systems usually cover other taxes—such as property, sales, and payroll—as well as income taxes.

The actual preparation of tax returns and compliance with tax laws may be a full-time task for a staff of specialists in a large entity, or it may be delegated to an outside professional, like a certified public accountant, lawyer, or tax specialist. Smaller entities generally rely on outside professionals for tax services. Gathering the necessary information, planning and preparing returns, and payment of tax are generally systematized, subject to supervision, and overseen by a financial officer of the entity, who also reviews the details supporting the financial statement balances.

(iii) Recording Tax Transactions.   Once taxes have been appropriately planned, statutory compliance determined, and payments either disbursed or estimated, the entity must record tax transactions. Recording taxes is complicated by differences in recognizing transactions for accounting purposes and for tax purposes and by the estimation process that is part of determining the tax liability. Therefore, effective procedures for controlling entries to tax accounts are essential. All tax liability and asset accounts should be reconciled periodically to underlying detailed schedules or subsidiary ledgers. Appropriate computations should support the current and deferred liability and asset accounts.

To evaluate the appropriateness of the income tax liability, the entity's tax specialist may prepare an analysis of the alternatives and uncertainties that might affect the liability for the current and prior years. That analysis may then be discussed with the auditor and one or more external tax specialists. Once the alternatives and uncertainties have been sufficiently explored and understood, management is in a position to determine the amount of accrued tax liability that most reasonably represents their probable outcome, consistent with the guidance provided in SFAS No. 5.

Management should delegate the responsibility for authorizing entries in the various income tax accounts to one official. Because of differences in recording transactions for accounting and tax purposes, confusion often arises about the amounts and timely recording of monthly tax entries. The responsibility may rest with either an accountant or a tax specialist. The key point is that all entries are reviewed, reconciled, and controlled monthly in a consistent manner.

24.3 DETERMINING THE AUDIT STRATEGY

(a) Risk Factors

Income tax has long been one of the most significant items in financial statements. Most often the expense and the current and deferred liability are material to fair presentation of the financial statements. Thus, a misstatement of tax accounts may result in a material misstatement of the financial statements taken as a whole. Misstatements of income taxes can result from the incorrect calculation of taxable income, which affects the tax provision and net income, or from the inappropriate treatment of temporary differences, which affects the balance sheet classification of the tax liability but not the tax provision or net income. In determining an appropriate audit strategy for income taxes, the auditor should identify inherent risks and assess control risk associated with the tax accounts.

Income tax recorded in the accounts is always an estimate—or more properly the sum of a large number of estimates. For purposes of timely preparation of financial statements, estimates of amounts that ultimately will be reflected in the tax returns usually must be made before the returns themselves are prepared. Also, revenue agents' examinations often extend over several years, and informal and formal discussions of the resulting findings over several more years. It is common to have a number of taxable years "open" for review at one time. Meanwhile, judgments have to be made at least annually of the adequacy of the current and deferred tax liability. Entities must make those judgments with great care and attention to detail, often with assistance from their auditors and tax counsel.

The requirement in SFAS No. 109 for a valuation allowance for deferred tax assets not expected to be realized increases the risk involved in auditing the deferred tax asset account. Management must consider both positive and negative evidence concerning the realizability of deferred tax assets; the more negative evidence that exists, the more positive evidence will be necessary to support a conclusion that a valuation allowance is not needed. SFAS No. 109 cites examples of negative evidence that must be overcome to justify not recording a valuation allowance. As the weight of negative evidence increases, the need for positive evidence increases, as do the amount of evidential matter and extent of audit testing required.

Lastly, the appropriate tax treatment of many transactions is simply not clear, particularly because of the numerous changes in the tax laws and regulations in recent years and the proliferation of court decisions affecting the interpretation of those laws. In making the necessary estimates in the face of all these uncertainties, some managements take an "aggressive" stance, while others are more "conservative." An aggressive position regarding tax estimates does not necessarily suggest questionable business ethics or a desire to portray the entity in an unrealistically favorable light; rather, it may reflect sound business judgment—a desire to postpone cash outflows as long as legally possible. However, the auditor should consider the degree of management's aggressiveness in this area.

(b) Assessment of Control Risk

As previously noted, taxes usually are audited through substantive tests; however, in some entities internal control may be effective enough to allow the auditor to limit substantive tests or to perform certain substantive tests at an interim date. How much the auditor can limit substantive tests depends on the identification of inherent risks and the assessment of control risk. In particular, the following attributes of internal control may enable the auditor to reduce substantive tests:

- Reconciliation of tax account balances to supporting detail (like tax returns and summaries of differences between taxable income and accounting income)

- Supervision of those reconciliations and the supporting detail
- Management reviews of tax-related matters, as described below

Other factors that typically indicate the presence of effective controls are:

- Assigning responsibility for tax planning, return preparation, and follow-up to competent officials
- If subsidiaries maintain separate tax departments, coordination among them with respect to overall corporate planning
- A satisfactory system of reporting by branches, divisions, or subsidiaries
- A practice of obtaining competent outside advice, as warranted, on significant tax questions before and after major transactions are entered into
- Well-prepared and readily accessible historical tax material
- Maintaining records of adequate follow-up of due dates, payment dates, claims for refund, revenue agent adjustments, and coordination of federal and state taxes

There are several reasons why auditors usually take a substantive testing approach to income tax accounts. First, transactions in the tax accounts are not numerous and each one may be significant. The auditor may decide to substantively test each significant account balance and not test controls at all. In addition to being effective, in most instances this approach is also most efficient. Second, most significant tax decisions require a high degree of subjective analysis. The thought processes and research required to determine the appropriate accounting are difficult to test and often the auditor would need to duplicate them, at least in part. Finally, as required by Accounting Principles Board Opinion No. 28, *Interim Financial Reporting* (Accounting Standards Section I73), the recording of tax expense, liabilities, and deferred taxes throughout the year is based on an estimate of the effective tax rate expected to apply for the full year. At year-end, final tax estimates are recorded based on actual results. The year-end determination logically becomes the focal point for testing tax account balances.

As noted earlier, the effectiveness of an entity's internal control may have an impact on the extent and timing of substantive tests. Additionally, even if control activities have not been tested, it may be appropriate for the auditor to perform some substantive tests before year-end, especially when reconciling the prior-year tax return to the opening tax liability accounts, reviewing revenue agents' examinations, and examining records of estimated tax payments. On the other hand, identifying and testing differences between taxable income and accounting income are more likely to be done early only if control activities are effective.

The existence of management reviews of income taxes also may affect the audit strategy. If the tax aspects of transactions are well-planned and periodically monitored by qualified personnel (such as through reviews of effective tax rates and comparisons with budgets), and if those procedures can be assessed as adequate, this may allow the auditor to decrease emphasis on identifying the tax implications of transactions. On the other hand, the auditor probably would increase substantive testing if management did not employ a tax specialist, but focused on taxes only when preparing tax returns.

24.4 SUBSTANTIVE TESTS

The auditor should review the tax returns and related correspondence for all "open" years (for a recurring engagement this means reviewing the most recent year and updating the understanding of earlier years). Often the review can be combined with the auditor's participation in the preparation of the prior year's tax return or the technical review of the entity's preparation. If a revenue agent's examination is in process, the auditor should request from management reports and memoranda related to the examination and should review and evaluate any issues set forth in them. The auditor also should ask management about any other adjustments proposed by the agent. The auditor should determine whether the status of "open" tax years has been affected by extensions of the statute of limitations granted by the entity.

An auditor is expected to have sufficient knowledge of the major taxing statutes to be able to evaluate the accrued liabilities for the various taxes to which an entity is subject. Accordingly, on a recurring engagement, the auditor should review changes in the tax laws and regulations and court decisions since the preceding audit and consider whether they apply to the entity. It is extremely important that the auditor have sufficient expertise in tax matters to resolve all questions that arise; how much a tax specialist needs to be involved in the audit varies with the circumstances.

(a) Summary Account Analysis

As the starting point in the audit of the tax accounts and to provide an orderly framework for testing, the auditor usually requests analyses of the tax accounts for the year. The analyses may be prepared as of an interim date and later updated to year-end, and should show, for each kind of tax (including each type of deferred tax) and for each year still "open," the beginning balance, accruals, payments, transfers or adjustments, and the ending balance.

The auditor can then review the analyses, examine documents supporting transactions (to determine their existence or occurrence), and determine that prior-year overpayments and underpayments are identified properly (completeness), that deferred taxes are identified and computed properly (completeness and valuation), and that amounts currently payable are identified and scheduled for payment on the due dates (completeness and presentation). The appropriateness of the tax and accounting principles used and the mechanics of their application also should be substantiated (valuation). The level of detail the auditor examines in support of account balances and the extent to which normal business transactions (generated from other transaction cycles) are reviewed will depend on the auditor's risk identification and assessment activities and the materiality of the accounts.

Often the auditor obtains or prepares a comparative summary of income and other tax account balances, ascertains that the summary is mathematically accurate, agrees the totals to the general ledger trial balance and the previous year's working papers, and traces significant reconciling items to supporting documentation.

(b) Income Tax Payments and Refunds

The auditor should test tax payments by examining assessment notices, correspondence with taxing authorities, canceled checks, and receipts, if available. The auditor should ascertain whether the entity paid appropriate estimated taxes during the year and examine support for refunds received. In addition, the auditor should determine that assessments were reviewed before payments were made and that the payments were made on the due dates. If interest has been charged for late payment of tax, the auditor should ascertain the period of charge and review the calculations. The auditor also should compare taxes payable or refundable as shown on the tax returns filed for the previous year with the amounts recorded for that year and ascertain that any necessary accounting adjustments have been made. The auditor should prepare a schedule of carryover items from prior years and consider the current impact of the items.

(c) Income Tax Expense, Deferred Taxes, and Related Disclosures

The auditor should obtain or prepare a schedule showing the computation of the tax provision. The current and deferred tax liability accounts should be tested against the current and deferred tax computation. As mentioned earlier, it is normally efficient to gather the information required to prepare or review tax computations during the course of audit work on other accounts. Such information includes differences in tax and financial statement bases of many asset and liability accounts. For example, the auditor can assemble basis differences when reviewing book and tax depreciation during the audit of fixed assets. The auditor should scrutinize tax credits (such as foreign tax credits) and deductions (such as accelerated depreciation) based on special provisions of the law and test them for compliance with the Internal Revenue Code. The auditor should test the mathematical accuracy of the schedule and determine that it includes consideration of all matters affecting the computation of income taxes currently payable or refundable. Beginning and ending balances should be traced to the summary of income taxes payable, and significant reconciling items should be traced to supporting documentation.

The schedule supporting the tax calculations should include a reconciliation of accounting income to taxable income; differences should be individually identified. The auditor should analyze the effective tax rate and account for differences between the statutory rate and the effective rate. In addition, if differences are significant, the auditor may review their nature and amounts for propriety and consistency with the prior year, agree amounts to supporting documentation in the working papers, and determine that the differences are accounted for properly.

The auditor should determine that the entity has complied with requirements related to special tax status that it may have claimed. For example, favorable tax treatment may be available to certain entities, like not-for-profit entities, real estate investment trusts, financial institutions, S Corporations, regulated investment companies, and Foreign Sales Corporations (FSCs). If the entity claims status as one of those or similar types of entities, the auditor should ascertain that it has in fact met the relevant eligibility requirements. Similarly, the auditor should test for compliance with federal tax documentation requirements regarding material travel and entertainment expenditures, expenditures for charitable purposes, and other similar deductions.

In addition, the auditor should inquire about the status of all IRS examinations, examine revenue agents' reports for their effect on the prior and current years' tax provisions and financial statements (including necessary disclosures), and review the status of all tax disagreements. Adjustments to tax provisions for a previous year determined as a result of examinations by taxing authorities should be tested by examining the previous year's computations and any related correspondence. The auditor also should identify other tax matters that could be challenged and consider whether additional penalties may be assessed and, if so, whether they should be accrued.

The auditor should evaluate the adequacy of financial statement disclosures relating to income taxes as well as the propriety of the principles used to recognize and measure income taxes. Disclosures of accounting changes and significant uncertainties related to tax issues (discussed below) may be particularly sensitive matters. In addition, auditors of public companies must consider SEC disclosure requirements.

(d) Deferred Tax Asset Valuation Allowance

Under SFAS No. 109, the auditor should evaluate the reasonableness of management's determination of the valuation allowance (if any) needed for deferred tax assets not expected to be realized. Future realization of deferred tax assets ultimately depends on sufficient taxable income of the appropriate type (e.g., ordinary income or capital gains) within the carryback or carryforward periods stipulated by the tax law. SFAS No. 109 specifies the four sources of taxable income that may be available to realize a future tax benefit for deductible temporary differences and carryforwards:

- Taxable income in prior carryback years
- Taxable income from reversals of existing taxable temporary differences
- Taxable income from tax planning strategies that would be implemented, if necessary, to avoid losing the benefit of a deferred tax asset
- Expected future taxable income, exclusive of reversing temporary differences and carryforwards

The auditor should follow the guidance in Statement on Auditing Standards No. 57, *Auditing Accounting Estimates* (AU Section 342), in considering management's conclusion about the need for and amount of the valuation allowance.

The four sources of taxable income above are listed in order of the objectivity of the evidence they provide. SFAS No. 109 states that "the weight given to the potential effect of negative and positive evidence should be commensurate with the extent to which it can be objectively verified." The first two sources of taxable income are more objective and thus are more competent forms of evidential matter than the last two and ordinarily should be considered first in evaluating the realizability of deferred tax assets. If a deferred tax asset cannot be fully realized from carrybacks or reversals of temporary differences, tax planning strategies should be considered next. Finally, future taxable income, the least objective source, should be considered. If an analysis of future taxable income is the basis for a valuation allowance, management has primary responsibility for preparing the analysis, which should include all major underlying assumptions. The auditor should consider whether management has an objective basis for the analysis and should determine that the major assumptions are supported appropriately, especially those that are sensitive or susceptible to change, or inconsistent with historical trends. Concluding that a valuation allowance is not necessary based on future taxable income will be difficult, for example, when there is negative evidence such as cumulative losses in recent years.

Reaching a conclusion about the realizability of deferred tax assets and the valuation allowance may require the evaluation of large amounts of both positive and negative evidence that is of necessity surrounded by much uncertainty because it involves the occurrence or nonoccurrence of future events. Management must exercise judgment in weighing both types of evidence and their potential impact on the need for an allowance. If there is substantial negative evidence, the authors believe that a forecast of future taxable income by itself will not provide sufficient positive evidence to outweigh the negative evidence and support a conclusion that no valuation allowance is needed.

(e) Estimated and Contingent Liabilities

It is often necessary to provide in the accounts for possible additional liability that might result from revenue agents' examinations of the current year's and prior years' returns. Although such liability may not become payable for a long time, it should be included in the tax liability and the provision for income taxes in the income statement, in accordance with SFAS No. 5. Prior-year estimates of tax provisions should be reassessed based on recent IRS or court decisions or interpretations. The amount of any "cushion" should be supported by a detailed listing of possible tax questions and potential liabilities. The auditor should evaluate the propriety of contingent amounts and assess the adequacy of the tax accrual in light of all pending tax matters.

The auditor, by exercising judgment and consulting tax specialists, should reach a conclusion about each of the issues affecting the tax liability. While the function of a tax specialist may end with the estimate of the liability, the auditor's responsibility goes further. The auditor should evaluate the adequacy of the evidence supporting the decisions made—whether any data or matters affecting taxes have been overlooked and whether the evidence is adequate in the circumstances. If the treatment and disclosure of taxes in the financial statements depend significantly on the intentions of management, it is generally appropriate to obtain written representation of those intentions in the representation letter. For example, evidence of management's intentions may be necessary to support a decision to provide or not to provide for taxes on the undistributed earnings of subsidiaries. Also, evidence must be present to support the tax basis of assets purchased in an acquisition in which the purchase price must be allocated.

The auditor's need to obtain sufficient competent evidence to support the income tax accrual has several implications. First, a mere statement of management's intentions that might affect the tax accrual is insufficient evidence. Management must have specific plans that the auditor can evaluate to determine that they are reasonable and feasible. Second, restrictions on the auditor's access to information necessary to audit the tax accrual, possibly out of concern over IRS access to tax accrual working papers, may constitute a scope limitation and affect the auditor's ability to issue an unqualified opinion. [See an auditing interpretation of Section 326, *Evidential Matter* (AU Section 9326.06–.12), and the further discussion of IRS access to tax accrual working papers in Chapter 3.] Third, the opinion of the entity's outside or in-house legal counsel on the adequacy of the tax accrual is not sufficient competent evidence to support an opinion on the financial statements. According to the auditing interpretation of Section 326 (AU Section 9326.13–.17), the auditor should not rely on a specialist in another discipline if the auditor possesses the necessary competence to assess the matter.

The auditor should consider the working paper documentation necessary to support the portion of the tax accrual that relates to contingent items. The working papers should contain sufficient documentation to demonstrate compliance with generally accepted auditing standards and that the tax accrual was prepared in conformity with GAAP. As a minimum, the working papers should document the scope of the work the auditor performed and the conclusion reached regarding the adequacy of the tax accrual and should identify issues involving risk and exposure and the related dollar amounts. The auditor's professional judgment must determine the level of documentation of the tax accrual, including the accrual for contingencies, based on the facts and circumstances of the particular situation.

Documentation of the provision for income taxes has become a particularly sensitive area as a result of the 1984 U.S. Supreme Court ruling that an entity's tax accrual working papers prepared by independent auditors may be subject to IRS summonses.[1] Guidelines subsequently issued by the IRS, however, allow auditors' tax accrual working papers to be subpoenaed only if the relevant information is not available from the entity's records. Since there is no such restriction with regard to other working papers, the authors believe that tax accrual working papers should not be included with or filed with tax return or tax planning working papers. Each of the three sets of working papers should contain documentation appropriate to the purpose of the working papers, and cross-referencing between sets of working papers should be avoided.

(f) Foreign, State, and Local Taxes

Accruals for foreign, state, and local income taxes (including franchise taxes based on income) are reviewed in much the same way as federal income tax accruals. The auditor should obtain or prepare an analysis for the year of deferred and accrued foreign, state, and local income taxes, showing the computation of the provisions for the current year. He or she should test the mathematical accuracy of the analysis and trace applicable amounts to the general ledger, trial balance, and prior year's working papers. Significant reconciling items should be traced to supporting documentation. Support for payments made and refunds received during the year should be examined. The auditor also should compare the liability per the returns filed for the preceding year, the estimated liability recorded for that year, and the payments made to discharge that liability; evaluate the reasons for any differences; and determine that they have been appropriately accounted for.

---

[1] *United States* v. *Arthur Young & Company*, 465 U.S. 805 (1984).

All foreign, state, and local tax examinations should be reviewed, and the auditor should determine that appropriate provisions have been made for unresolved assessments. The auditor should evaluate the exposure for unpaid taxes and consider the adequacy of provisions for taxes and interest for prior years. Similarly, the auditor should determine whether the entity has filed amended returns to reflect the effect of federal tax assessments or payments.

25

Auditing Debt and Equity

The traditional distinction between debt and equity is clear in most businesses. Equity arises from owners' invested funds plus earnings retained and reinvested; debt is the result of borrowing funds for specific periods, both short- and long-term, although the individual loans are often renewed indefinitely. The distinctions among debt, equity, and other financing arrangements are often blurred, however. It is more realistic to view various debt, equity, lease, and other contractual arrangements as an array of alternatives that financial managers use to enhance the entity's earnings record as well as its financial strength. Common stock is as much a financing instrument as bank loans, and convertible debt may have as many equity characteristics as preferred stock. Financial managers may adjust the legal characteristics of an instrument, whether formally designated as debt or equity, to achieve a desired (or required) balance between protecting principal and income and sharing the risks and rewards of ownership. Financial instruments may be designed to reconcile an entity's need for financial resources at minimal cost with investors' preferences for safety and rewards. The result is a virtually continuous spectrum of financing instruments, ranging from straight borrowing to borrowing with equity features, borrowing with variable income features, stock with preferences as to income and principal, common stock, and even promises of future stock. The Securities and Exchange Commission (SEC) and the Internal Revenue Service from time to time have addressed the distinctions among debt, equity, and other financing arrangements, and the subject continues to be of interest to those agencies and to auditors and users of financial statements.

The amount, type, and classification of financing appearing in an entity's balance sheet are of concern to investors, lenders, bond rating agencies, and others who influence the supply of financial resources. It is therefore important to financial management. Over the years, a great deal of ingenuity has gone into designing financing that looks like something else, like disguising what were actually asset acquisitions as off-balance-sheet operating lease transactions. The Financial Accounting Standards Board (FASB) and its Emerging Issues Task Force (EITF) have since addressed many of those transactions, but auditors should constantly be alert to discern the substance of each transaction. If form is allowed to rule over substance, one or more audit objectives may not be achieved.

Transactions and accounts related to debt and equity include lessee accounting for capital leases, interest expense, debt discount and premium, early extinguishment of debt (including gain or loss thereon), debt defeasance, troubled debt restructuring, product financing arrangements, cash and stock dividends, stock splits, stock warrants, options and purchase plans, and treasury stock transactions. Many of these transactions and accounts involve special accounting measurement, presentation, and disclosure principles that require particular audit attention. Other matters with audit implications include short-term debt expected to be refinanced, debt covenants, compensating balance arrangements, debt conversion features, mandatory stock redemption requirements, and stock conversion features.

25.1 AUDIT OBJECTIVES

Figure 25.1 describes specific audit objectives applicable to debt and equity transactions and accounts. The application of these objectives to specific accounts varies depending on the nature of the debt and equity instruments and the related accounts.

Figure 25.1   Audit Objectives for Debt and Equity

Completeness	All obligations for notes payable, long-term debt, and capitalized leases and all equity accounts have been identified and are included in the financial statements.
	All off-balance-sheet obligations (e.g., operating leases, product financing arrangements, take-or-pay contracts, and throughput contracts) have been identified and considered for inclusion or disclosure in the financial statements.
Accuracy	Interest, discounts, premiums, dividends, and other debt-related and equity-related transactions and accounts have been accurately calculated.
Existence/Occurrence	All debt and equity accounts, transactions, and other changes in those accounts have been properly authorized.
Cutoff	All debt and equity transactions were recorded in the proper period.
Valuation/Allocation	All obligations for notes payable, long-term debt, and capitalized leases and all equity accounts are properly valued.
Rights and Obligations	All debt and equity accounts represent obligations of the entity or ownership rights in the entity.
	All terms, requirements, instructions, commitments, and other debt-related and equity-related matters have been identified and complied with.
Presentation and Disclosure	All obligations for notes payable, long-term debt, and capitalized leases and all equity accounts are properly classified, described, and disclosed.
	Interest, discounts, premiums, dividends, and other debt-related and equity-related transactions and accounts are properly classified, described, and disclosed.
	All terms, requirements, instructions, commitments, and other debt-related and equity-related matters are disclosed, as appropriate.

Most of the audit objectives included in the figure are self-explanatory; however, three issues related to presentation and disclosure merit further comment.

The question of whether particular assets and liabilities may be offset or "netted" usually arises when an asset is held for the purpose of settling a specific liability or when a debt is incurred to finance a specific asset. As a general rule, assets and liabilities should not be offset unless they are exclusively related to each other. Assets can be used for other purposes, and debts are a lien on all assets as well as those specifically pledged. Furthermore, paragraph 7 of Accounting Principles Board (APB) Opinion No. 10 states that "it is a general principle of accounting that the offsetting of assets and liabilities in the balance sheet is improper except where a right of setoff exists." FASB Interpretation No. 39, *Offsetting of Amounts Related to Certain Contracts*, defines the term "right of setoff" as a debtor's legal right, by contract or otherwise, to discharge all or a portion of the debt owed to another party by applying against the debt an amount that the other party owes to the debtor. A right of setoff exists only when all of the following conditions are met:

- Each of two parties owes the other determinable amounts
- The reporting party has the right to set off the amount owed with the amount the other party owes
- The reporting party intends to set off the debt
- The right of setoff is legally enforceable

The interpretation addresses the applicability of the general principle to various types of contracts in various circumstances.

Various commitments customarily are given and received in negotiating long-term financing and are included in formal debt covenants. Typical debt covenants include agreements to maintain a minimum level of working capital or net assets; to maintain adequate insurance; to maintain property, sometimes through specified additions to maintenance funds; to restrict dividends; not to pledge or mortgage certain property or to restrict the use of proceeds from its sale; to restrict leasing, borrowing, mergers, and the issuance or repurchase of other types of securities; to restrict the use of the proceeds from issuing the debt; to accumulate funds for repayment through a sinking fund; and to render reports and financial statements on specified dates. Such covenants are intended to protect the interests of securityholders, and failure to comply may be an event of default, which may give the securityholders the right to demand immediate repayment and perhaps other rights as well. Such covenants also may be important factors in encouraging or inhibiting changes in financial structure, selecting accounting principles, and adopting new accounting principles.

Statement of Financial Accounting Standards No. 129, *Disclosure of Information About Capital Structure* (Accounting Standards Section C24), contains disclosure requirements about the capital structure of entities (both public and nonpublic) that have issued securities. Those disclosures should include a brief discussion of rights and privileges for securities outstanding, including dividend and liquidation preferences, participation rights, call prices and dates, conversion or exercise prices or rates and pertinent dates, sinking-fund requirements, unusual voting rights, and significant terms of contracts to issue additional shares. The number of shares issued on conversion, exercise, or satisfaction of required conditions during at least the most recent annual fiscal period and any subsequent interim period presented also should be disclosed. In addition, companies that issue stock with liquidation preferences or redeemable stock should disclose all pertinent characteristics of those securities. The use of disclosure checklists to assist the auditor in achieving the presentation and disclosure audit objective generally is discussed in Chapter 26.

25.2 TYPICAL TRANSACTIONS AND CONTROLS

Financing transactions are likely to be relatively simple. Often, authorizing a transaction, executing it, and recording it each involve only one step. The preparation for authorization and execution, however, may be lengthy and complex; the study of whether to enter into a long-term financing transaction may take months, and once it has been decided, the time lawyers, accountants, investment bankers, and the entity's personnel expend in preparing to execute the transaction may be tremendous.

Since an entity's financing activities entail issuing legal obligations—both debt and equity—in exchange for cash or other property, control over authorization for issuance is critical. In almost all entities, the board of directors specifically and explicitly authorizes financing transactions. In fact, many legal jurisdictions, investment bankers, and institutional investors require board authorization. The board may authorize a type of financing and a maximum amount in general terms and then delegate the authority to execute the details to a financial officer, but the significance of financing transactions requires that the board assume direct and explicit responsibility for their authorization. The importance of financing and the commitments made to obtain it ensure close attention by top management.

In the typical business that executes no more than half a dozen financing transactions in a year, controls consist of a detailed review of transactions before they are executed and follow-up by the authorizing board or chief financial officer. In other entities the volume of activity may be greater, and a formalized accounting system and control activities may exist. The entity may act as its own registrar of bonds and stock, and may disburse its own interest and dividends. Alternatively, the volume of transactions may be great enough to justify using a registrar, transfer agent, and paying agent. If the volume of transactions is large enough, authorizing transactions and issuing instruments may be systematized. For example, new stock certificates may be issued routinely on receipt of cash or a corresponding number of old certificates. Control totals are computed for instruments issued and recorded, and the propriety of each transaction is subject to supervisory review. In view of the relatively high value and negotiability of many financing instruments, the expensive control activity of detailed review of each transaction is often considered worthwhile. Whether or not that review takes place, close monitoring of transaction activity and related controls is essential.

Some entities have developed variations of basic financing transactions to serve particular purposes. These variations include dividend reinvestment plans, in which dividends may be accumulated for a stockholder's account and additional shares purchased from the funds; "certificateless" plans, in which records on a file replace the cumbersome handling of certificates; and plans for the purchase of stock on an installment basis. Each of them, however voluminous the related data, involves a relatively simple accounting system. An account is maintained for each participating stockholder; additions and reductions are authorized and recorded; the subsidiary ledger accounts are periodically reconciled to the control account; and statements of the accounts are sent to stockholders.

The authorization and issuing of financing instruments are documented, both by executing the instrument itself and by initiating a record of it, for example, a register listing each item issued. Reacquired instruments are canceled and appropriately filed; the canceled instrument serves as documentation of reacquisition. Subsidiary ledgers are reconciled periodically to control accounts; the reconciliations account for all unissued, issued, and canceled financing instruments.

Issuing securities to the public is highly regulated by the SEC pursuant to the Securities Act of 1933 and by the "Blue Sky" laws of the various states. Subsequent securities trading is also regulated by the SEC under the Securities Exchange Act of 1934 and by the various stock exchanges. Monitoring compliance with the various regulations is primarily a legal function and normally is supervised by legal counsel. The entity's accounting department and its independent auditors, however, perform vital roles in preparing and auditing financial statements and other data required to comply with the regulations.

Interest payments are authorized in the broad sense by the terms of the financing instrument; specific payments are approved by a responsible officer. Dividends must be formally declared by the board of directors. Usually, the total interest installment or total dividend is deposited in an imprest fund, and disbursements are then subject to the same controls as other cash disbursements. If interest is paid by redeeming coupons detached from bonds, the coupons received are canceled and retained.

Interest and dividends unclaimed for a reasonable period are accounted for according to state law, which may permit writing them off by reversing the original accounting entry or may require that they be turned over to the state or continue to be carried as a liability. In either case, unclaimed items are identified and removed from the active accounts.

Reacquired financing instruments are generally subject to the same controls as negotiable instruments held as assets. They are kept under restricted access, counted periodically, and reconciled to a control account. Physical movement into or out of the "treasury" is also controlled by limiting access to authorized individuals.

The detailed task of accounting for and controlling ledgers of bondholders and stockholders and paying interest and dividends is most often delegated to independent registrars and transfer agents. The independent agents take over the control operations, but the entity's responsibility remains the same. Therefore, if independent agents are used, the entity maintains control accounts, requests periodic reports from the agents, and compares the reports with the accounts.

Controls over warrants and options are similar to those for the financing instruments themselves: careful authorization, restricted access to unexecuted documents, a record of activity, a ledger of outstanding balances, and periodic reconciliation of the ledger to control accounts.

Control activities to ensure that all rental payments required under leases are made consist of reminder lists, often in the form of a register of leases by payment due date. The information required for financial disclosures may be incorporated in the lease register or maintained separately in the department responsible for leases.

Compliance with commitments made in connection with financing is most commonly controlled by a reminder list, which is often maintained by the office of the treasurer, the official most likely to be responsible for financing activity. It also may rest in the office of the secretary, the office of legal counsel, or the controller's department.

Most transactions affecting retained earnings and paid-in capital accounts occur as an integral part of some other major transaction: stock issues, retirements or conversions, or dividend payments. Accordingly, the key control activities are those applied to the major transaction. An event giving rise to any other kind of entry in these accounts would be unusual and would call for authorization by the board of directors.

25.3 DETERMINING THE AUDIT STRATEGY

Additional responsibilities beyond performing the audit in accordance with generally accepted auditing standards may arise from client requests or because the entity is required to conform with special requirements. This might apply when an entity has equity securities that are subject to regulatory requirements or debt securities requiring compliance with covenants and restrictions.

The entity's timetable for releasing the financial statements also may affect the audit strategy. For example, the need to complete the audit early may require a different audit strategy than would have been selected without the time constraint. Timing of substantive tests is discussed in Chapter 15 [Section 15.2(b), Timing of Tests of Details].

(a) Risk Factors

The auditor needs a sufficient understanding of the entity's industry and business and its internal control to identify risk factors that could affect the audit strategy. Of particular importance are the level of debt and equity financing activity and the individuals responsible for, and procedures governing, the issuance of debt and equity instruments and the execution of leases and other financing arrangements. Other risks could result from the large amount of judgment that may be needed to determine the appropriate accounting principles for recording unusual or complex debt and equity transactions, the size of individual transactions, the volume of debt and equity transactions, and the relative significance of the debt and equity accounts.

(b) Assessment of Control Risk

Because of the significance of debt and equity accounts to an entity, management usually monitors them closely. In assessing control risk, the auditor should consider the effect of management's close attention to debt and equity transactions and accounts. In practice, however, since all the transactions for a year often can be examined fairly easily, it is frequently not efficient for the auditor to test controls. In these circumstances, the auditor's basis for the opinion comes from the detailed examination of transactions. On the other hand, in situations where financing activity is extensive, the auditor may consider it efficient to test controls to attain a low assessed level of control risk and restrict substantive tests of details.

25.4 SUBSTANTIVE TESTS

The following discussion applies to all kinds of financing transactions unless clearly inapplicable in the context or specified in the discussion. A convenient way to document substantive tests of the various kinds of financing transactions and accounts is an account analysis working paper, that is, a list of the notes, debt issues, or equities outstanding at the beginning of a period, and the additions, reductions, and outstanding amounts at the end of the period. Often the list can be carried forward from year to year if changes are infrequent. It may incorporate all pertinent information about the financing instruments, or that information may be summarized separately. The auditor should compare the list with the accounts and reconcile the total to the general ledger. The list also can be used to document other audit tests.

(a) Analytical Procedures

The most basic analytical procedures performed on debt and equity accounts are reasonableness tests of the amount of dividends paid, calculated by multiplying the number of shares outstanding on the dividend declaration date by the per share amount of the dividend, and of interest paid on bonds, calculated by multiplying the amount of debt outstanding by the stated interest rate. Analytical procedures are a particularly effective way of testing accrued interest payable at year-end. In addition, the auditor may analyze fluctuations in account balances compared with budgets, amounts for the prior year(s), amounts subjected to substantive tests at an interim date, and any other appropriate base figures, and evaluate the results for reasonableness in relation to other financial information and the auditor's own knowledge of the business.

(b) Tests of Details

Tests of details of debt and equity transactions and balances for accuracy and existence/occurrence consist of obtaining confirmations from third parties, reperforming computations, and examining documents and records. Some examples are:

Confirmations: debt payable and terms with holder; outstanding stock with holder and registrar; authorized stock with the Secretary of State of the state in which the entity is incorporated; treasury stock with safekeeping agent; and dividend and interest payments with disbursing agent

Reperformance of computations: debt discount or premium, interest, gains or losses on debt extinguishment, stock issuances and purchases, and dividends

Examining documents and records: debt and stock issuances and retirements, and interest and dividend payments to registrar; unissued debt and stock instruments (as partial substantiation of the completeness of recorded outstanding instruments)

(c) Extent of Tests

The extent of substantive testing depends on a number of factors, the most important of which generally are the assessed level of control risk, the nature and materiality of account balances, and the degree to which account balances are interrelated. Also, some tests by their nature, such as confirming outstanding shares of stock with the registrar, do not present extent-of-testing issues. As noted previously, it is generally efficient to audit debt and equity transactions and accounts through substantive tests. In these circumstances, the extent of substantive testing is greater than if a low assessed level of control risk had been attained through tests of controls.

Generally, debt and equity accounts are material and are not directly related to other accounts, although there are some relationships between debt and asset levels, debt and interest expense, and equity and dividends. Although recording debt and equity transactions normally requires little judgment, the instruments generally are easily transferable, and transactions are material. Typically, these factors call for increased testing.

(d) Other Procedures

Other procedures of a more general nature include reading articles of incorporation and minutes of meetings of the board of directors and its committees, and obtaining letters from lawyers about legal matters and letters of representation from management. The latter two topics are discussed in Chapter 27 (Section 27.3, Lawyers' Letters, and 27.4, Management Representations).

(i) Minutes of Meetings.   Reading the minutes of meetings of the board of directors and its committees enables the auditor to examine the board's approval of significant financing activities and to determine whether decisions affecting the financial statements (including required disclosures) have been handled properly. The auditor should be satisfied that copies of minutes of all meetings held during the period have been obtained as well as copies or drafts of minutes of all meetings held from the date of the financial statements through the end of field work.

(ii) Articles of Incorporation.   The articles of incorporation contain information about the classes of stock the entity can issue and the number of authorized shares in each class. Once this information is obtained, it can be kept in a permanent file; the articles of incorporation need not be read each year.

(e) Tests of Specific Debt and Equity Accounts

The auditor should trace authorization for all types of financing to a vote of the board of directors. If the directors have delegated authority for the details of financing, individual transactions should be traced to the authorizing officer's signature.

The auditor should read financing instruments carefully to be sure that the financing is properly classified and described in the financial statements. The instruments should be examined for commitments, which often accompany financing arrangements, and evidence of rights given or received, which might require accounting recognition and/or disclosure. For example, specific SEC rules govern the classification of preferred stock with mandatory redemption requirements or whose redemption is outside the control of the issuer. Regulation S–X, Rule 5–02–28, requires such stock to be included under a separate caption outside the stockholders' equity section of the balance sheet. Often an instrument is designed to achieve a desired accounting and tax result; it is good practice for the entity to seek the auditor's interpretation of accounting and disclosure implications of financing instruments before they are executed. Once the accounting and disclosure implications have been analyzed and understood, it is usually possible to set up a worksheet that can be carried forward from year to year for computing and documenting compliance with pertinent commitments and covenants.

If financing is in the form of a lease, the terms must be evaluated to determine whether it should be accounted for as an operating or a capital lease. If leases are capitalized, the auditor should test computations of the carrying amounts of assets and debt, and compare the terms with the underlying lease contract. Chapter 22 [Section 22.4(f), Capital Leases] discusses lease transactions.

The auditor should trace the recording of cash receipts and payments from financing and related activities into the accounts and compare those transactions with the authorization and terms of the instrument for timing and amount. Paid notes should be examined for evidence of proper authorization, documentation, and cancellation; the mathematical accuracy of interest expense, accrued interest, and dividends declared should be tested; in some circumstances, the auditor may recompute the amounts.

The auditor often confirms outstanding balances and terms, usually at year-end, with holders of notes and issuers of lines of credit, trustees under bond and debenture indentures, and registrars and transfer agents for stock issues. Authorized stock often must be recorded with the Secretary of State in the state of incorporation, and the auditor may request confirmation from that office. Treasury stock should be confirmed with the custodian, or, if there is no custodian, the auditor should examine the certificates in the presence of entity personnel.

If several types of financing are outstanding, the auditor should compare transactions in each with restrictions and provisions of the others. Bond and note indentures may restrict dividend payments; dividends on common stock may be affected by the rights of preferred stockholders or their rights may change with changes in capital structure or retained earnings accounts; certain transactions may require the consent of holders of senior securities, and so on. It is essential that management determine and the auditor review the restrictive provisions of the various agreements and determine that the most restrictive debt covenants are disclosed.

The auditor should review and test the reconciliation of detailed stock ledgers to the control account. Accounting for unissued, issued, and canceled certificates should be similarly tested.

The auditor may reperform computations of shares reserved for issuance on exercise of options and warrants or conversion of convertible securities and of the basis for valuing stock dividends and splits. In testing those computations, the auditor should pay close attention to the interrelated effects of one issue on another and on the total amount of each issue authorized and outstanding. The accuracy of accounting for warrants, options, and conversion privileges exercised can often be reviewed by an overall computation based on the terms of the related instruments.

If the interest rate of a financing instrument is not clearly the going market rate for that type of instrument at time of issuance, the auditor should evaluate the reasonableness of the interest rate in terms of the requirements of Accounting Principles Board Opinion No. 21, *Interest on Receivables and Payables* (Accounting Standards Section I69), and document the evaluation in the working papers. If the interest rate must be imputed, the documentation for the imputed rate may be carried forward from year to year.

If a financing instrument is issued for property other than cash, the auditor should review the terms of the transaction, basis for recording, and evidence of approval by the board of directors. Usually, a transaction of that kind is significant enough for the auditor to have been involved in management's planning of the transaction. In that event, there is ample opportunity for the auditor to suggest the appropriate basis for recording the property received and the kind of documentation that should be retained to support it.

(i) Confirming Contingent Liabilities, Compensating Balances, Lines of Credit, and Other Arrangements. Auditors typically confirm the entity's arrangements with financial institutions by requesting that management send letters to specific officials of those institutions who are knowledgeable about the particular transactions or arrangements. The kinds of arrangements that auditors may confirm, usually at year-end, include compensating balances, lines of credit, and arrangements that may create contingent liabilities, such as oral and written guarantees, commitments to purchase foreign currencies, repurchase or reverse repurchase agreements, and letters of credit. In addition, the auditor may ask management to request information about automatic investment services, bank acceptances, cash management services, futures and forward contracts, interest rate or loan swaps, loan agreements and related covenants, and other transactions or arrangements. The AICPA Auditing Standards Division has developed—and the American Bankers Association and Bank Administration Institute have approved—three illustrative letters for use in confirming transactions and arrangements with financial institutions involving contingent liabilities, compensating balances, and lines of credit. These letters are illustrated in Figures 25.2 through 25.4. Letters for use in confirming other transactions, arrangements, or information will have to be tailored to the specific item about which the auditor requests confirmation.

(ii) Debt Covenant Violations.   Debt agreements often contain covenants or provisions requiring the borrower to meet certain standards (e.g., maintaining specified levels of working capital, net assets, income, and property insurance) and to provide the lender with periodic information. These provisions are referred to as positive covenants. Positive covenants also may require the borrower to provide the lender with periodic financial statements, market values of pledged properties, or other internally generated reports. In addition, the borrower is often required to comply with various negative covenants (like limitations on capital expenditures, officers' salaries, dividends, leasing, borrowing, merging, and issuing or repurchasing other types of securities) and to present its financial statements in accordance with GAAP. Some debt agreements may contain cross-default provisions, which could result in acceleration of the lender's right of repayment because of default under or violation of other agreements. Violations of covenants or provisions, unless waived by the lender, usually require the borrower to classify the debt obligation as a current liability.[1]

Furthermore, some long-term debt agreements may include subjective acceleration clauses. These clauses typically state that the lender may accelerate the scheduled maturities of the obligation under conditions that are not objectively determinable. For example, a clause of this nature may state that if a material adverse change occurs in the borrower's financial condition or operations, the full amount of the obligation will become due on demand. In these circumstances, if the borrower incurs significant losses or experiences liquidity problems, the obligation probably should be classified as a current liability, because the borrower would be deemed to be in violation of this covenant. The auditor should consider consulting legal counsel in this situation. Guidance with respect to subjective acceleration clauses is provided in FASB Technical Bulletin No. 79-3, *Subjective Acceleration Clauses in Long-Term Debt Agreements* (Accounting Standards Section B05.501–503).

As previously mentioned, long-term debt obligations that will become callable by the lender or due on demand because of the borrower's violation of a debt covenant or

---

[1] Requests for the auditor to provide explicit assurance about the entity's compliance with contractual agreements are discussed in Chapter 29, "Other Reporting Situations Related to Audits."

Figure 25.2   Illustrative Letter for Confirmation of Contingent Liabilities

(Date)

Financial Institution Official*
First United Bank
Anytown, USA 00000

Dear Financial Institution Official:

In connection with an audit of the financial statements of (name of customer) as of (balance-sheet date) and for the (period) then ended, we have advised our independent auditors of the information listed below, which we believe is a complete and accurate description of our contingent liabilities, including oral and written guarantees, with your financial institution. Although we do not request nor expect you to conduct a comprehensive, detailed search of your records, if during the process of completing this confirmation additional information about other contingent liabilities, including oral and written guarantees, between (name of customer) and your financial institution comes to your attention, please include such information below.

Name of Maker	Date of Note	Due Date	Current Balance

Interest Rate	Date Through Which Interest Is Paid	Description of Collateral	Description of Purpose of Note

Information related to oral and written guarantees is as follows:

_____
_____
_____
_____

Please confirm whether the information about contingent liabilities presented above is correct by signing below and returning this directly to our independent auditors (name and address of CPA firm).

Sincerely,

(Name of Customer)

_____

By: _____
         (Authorized Signature)

*This letter should be addressed to a financial institution official who is responsible for the financial institution's relationship with the client or is knowledgeable about the transactions or arrangements. Some financial institutions centralize this function by assigning responsibility for responding to confirmation requests to a separate function. Independent auditors should ascertain the appropriate recipient.

Figure 25.2   *(Continued)*

Dear CPA Firm:

The above information listing contingent liabilities, including oral and written guarantees, agrees with the records of this financial institution.* Although we have not conducted a comprehensive, detailed search of our records, no information about other contingent liabilities, including oral and written guarantees, came to our attention. [Note exceptions below or in an attached letter.]

_____

_____

_____

_____

_____

(Name of Financial Institution)

By: _____ _____

(Officer and Title)   (Date)

*If applicable, comments similar to the following may be added to the confirmation reply by the financial institution. This confirmation does not relate to arrangements, if any, with other branches or affiliates of this financial institution. Information should be sought separately from such branches or affiliates with which any such arrangements might exist.

provision at the balance sheet date, or because of failure to cure the violation within a specified grace period, may need to be classified as current liabilities. Guidance in this area is contained in SFAS No. 78, *Classification of Obligations That Are Callable by the Creditor*, and FASB Technical Bulletin No. 79-3 (Accounting Standards Section B05); and EITF Issue No. 86-30, *Classification of Obligations When a Violation Is Waived by the Creditor*.

The auditor should test for compliance with debt covenants at all applicable dates during the year (recognizing, of course, the effect of any grace periods within which a violation could be cured). For example, some debt covenants may require the borrower to maintain a minimum amount of working capital at the end of each specified interim period as well as at year-end. The auditor should obtain written waivers of conditions of noncompliance of debt covenants directly from the responsible lending officers. It is not appropriate for the auditor to rely solely on management's written or oral representations or representations from the client's legal counsel that lenders have waived the violations. In reviewing a waiver of debt covenant violations to determine whether the liability should be classified as current or long-term, the auditor should obtain assurance that the waiver is unconditional for a period greater than one year from the balance sheet date and that it specifically and appropriately addresses each event of noncompliance.

In addition, some debt covenants may apply to a party other than the borrower. For example, the borrower may be a subsidiary whose debt agreement contains

Figure 25.3   Illustrative Letter for Confirmation of Compensating Balances

(Date)

Financial Institution Official*
First United Bank
Anytown, USA 00000

Dear Financial Institution Official:

In connection with an audit of the financial statements of (name of customer) as of (balance-sheet date) and for the (period) then ended, we have advised our independent auditors that as of the close of business on (balance-sheet date) there (were) (were not) compensating balance arrangements as described in our agreement dated (date). Although we do not request nor expect you to conduct a comprehensive, detailed search of your records, if during the process of completing this confirmation additional information about other compensating balance arrangements between (name of customer) and your financial institution comes to your attention, please include such information below. Withdrawal by (name of customer) of the compensating balance (was) (was not) legally restricted at (date). The terms of the compensating balance arrangements at (date) were:

EXAMPLES:
1. The Company has been expected to maintain an average compensating balance of 20 percent of its average loan outstanding, as determined from the financial institution's ledger records adjusted for estimated average uncollected funds.
2. The Company has been expected to maintain an average compensating balance of $100,000 during the year, as determined from the financial institution's ledger records without adjustment for uncollected funds.
3. The Company has been expected to maintain a compensating balance, as determined from the financial institution's ledger records without adjustment for uncollected funds, of 15 percent of its outstanding loans plus 10 percent of its unused line of credit.
4. The Company has been expected to maintain as a compensating balance noninterest bearing time deposits of 10 percent of its outstanding loans.

In determining compliance with compensating balance arrangements, the Company uses a factor for uncollected funds of _____ (business) (calendar) days.[1]

There (were the following) (were no) changes in the compensating balance arrangements during the (period) and subsequently through the date of this letter.

* This letter should be addressed to a financial institution official who is responsible for the financial institution's relationship with the client or is knowledgeable about the compensating balance arrangements. Some financial institutions centralize this function by assigning responsibility for responding to confirmation requests to a separate function. Independent auditors should ascertain the appropriate recipient.

[1] Not applicable if compensating balances are based on the financial institution's ledger records without adjustment for uncollected funds. If some other method is used for determining collected funds for compensating balance purposes, the method used should be described.

Figure 25.3 *(Continued)*

The Company (was) (was not) in compliance with the compensating balance arrangements during the (period) and subsequently through the date of this letter.

There (were the following) (were no) sanctions (applied or imminent) by the financial institution because of noncompliance with compensating balance arrangements.[2]

During the (period), and subsequently through the date of this letter, (no) (the following) compensating balances were maintained by the Company at the financial institution on behalf of an affiliate, director, officer, or any other third party and (no) (the following) third party maintained compensating balances at the bank on behalf of the Company. (Withdrawal of such compensating balances (was) (was not) legally restricted.)

Please confirm whether the information about compensating balances presented above is correct by signing below, and returning this letter directly to our independent auditors (name and address of CPA Firm).

Sincerely,

(Name of Customer)

_____

By: _____
           (Authorized Signature)

_____

Dear CPA Firm:

The above information regarding the compensating balance arrangements with this financial institution agrees with the records of this financial institution.* Although we have not conducted a comprehensive, detailed search of our records, no information about other compensating balance arrangements came to our attention. [Note exceptions below or in an attached letter.]

_____
_____
_____
_____

                                    _____
                                    (Name of Financial Institution)

                          By: _____ _____
                                    (Officer and Title)   (Date)

[2] Applicable only if the financial institution has applied sanctions during the (period) or notified the Company that sanctions may be applied. Indicate details.

* If applicable, comments similar to the following may be added to the confirmation reply by the financial institution: This confirmation does not relate to arrangements, if any, with other branches or affiliates of this financial institution. Information should be sought separately from such branches or affiliates with which any such arrangements might exist.

Figure 25.4   Illustrative Letter for Confirmation of Lines of Credit

(Date)

Financial Institution Official*
First United Bank
Anytown, USA 00000

Dear Financial Institution Official:

In connection with an audit of the financial statements of (name of customer) as of (balance-sheet date) and for the (period) then ended, we have advised our independent auditors of the information listed below, which we believe is a complete and accurate description of our line of credit from your financial institution as of the close of business on (balance-sheet date). Although we do not request nor expect you to conduct a comprehensive, detailed search of your records, if during the process of completing this confirmation additional information about other lines of credit from your financial institution comes to your attention, please include such information below.

The Company has available at the financial institution a line of credit totaling (amount). The current terms of the line of credit are contained in the letter dated (date). The related debt outstanding at the close of business on (date) was $(amount).

The amount of unused line of credit, subject to the terms of the related letter, at (date) was $(amount).

Interest rate at the close of business on (date) was _____%.

Compensating balance arrangements are_____
_____
_____
_____
_____

This line of credit supports commercial paper (or other borrowing arrangements) as described below:
_____
_____
_____
_____

*This letter should be addressed to a financial institution official who is responsible for the financial institution's relationship with the client or is knowledgeable about the lines of credit. Some financial institutions centralize this function by assigning responsibility for responding to confirmation requests to a separate function. Independent auditors should ascertain the appropriate recipient.

Figure 25.4   *(Continued)*

Please confirm whether the information about lines of credit presented above is correct by signing below and returning this letter directly to our independent auditors (name and address of CPA Firm).

Sincerely,

(Name of Customer)

_____

By: _____
        (Authorized Signature)

Dear CPA Firm:

The above information regarding the line of credit arrangements agrees with the records of this financial institution.* Although we have not conducted a comprehensive, detailed search of our records, no information about other lines of credit came to our attention. [Note exceptions below or in attached letter.]

_____

_____

_____

                                    _____
                                    (Name of Financial Institution)

                        By: _____ _____
                              (Officer and Title)   (Date)

*If applicable, comments similar to the following may be added to the confirmation reply by the financial institution: This confirmation does not relate to arrangements, if any, with other branches or affiliates of this financial institution. Information should be sought separately from such branches or affiliates with which any such arrangements might exist.

---

covenants requiring the parent company to maintain a minimum net worth or restricting transactions between the parent and subsidiary. In these instances, the auditor should obtain written representation from the parent company and its auditor that the applicable debt covenants have been complied with. If provisions or covenants of debt agreements are unclear, the auditor should ask management to request the lenders to provide a written interpretation of the item or items in question.

(iii) Stockholders' Equity.   Since analyses of stockholders' equity accounts appear in the financial statements and are subject to detailed scrutiny by security analysts and others, the auditor ordinarily should perform detailed substantive tests of changes in those accounts. Some entries, like appropriations of retained earnings, are simply traced to the board of directors' authorization. Other entries summarize a large volume of individual transactions and can be tested by means of an overall computation based on the authorizing instrument or vote of the directors. Still other entries—the most common example is the exercise of stock options that were granted in the past at various times and prices—are an aggregation of unique transactions and are best audited by examining the underlying authorization of the transactions and reperforming the calculations, as well as reconciling beginning and ending balances with the activity for the year. Each type of entry should be evaluated for compliance with loan agreements or other restrictive covenants or commitments.

The auditor should review the terms of outstanding stock subscriptions and perform enough tests of activity and balances to obtain reasonable assurance that they are being complied with. Outstanding stock subscriptions receivable preferably should be confirmed. Such receivables (whether for shares already issued or to be issued) typically are deducted from capital stock issued or subscribed, as appropriate, and additional paid-in capital; this accounting is required for SEC registrants. In addition, the EITF has concluded that reporting the receivable as an asset is appropriate only in limited circumstances in which there is substantial evidence of the ability and intent to pay within a reasonably short period.

(iv) Dividends.   The auditor should determine whether cash dividends, stock dividends and splits (including reverse splits), dividends payable in scrip, and dividends payable in assets other than cash have been properly accounted for. This requires determining whether the intentions of the board, as indicated in the resolutions authorizing dividends, are properly reflected in the financial statements.

In making the above determinations, the auditor should be aware of the distinction between stock dividends and stock splits. Accounting Research Bulletin (ARB) No. 43, Chapter 7B (Accounting Standards Section C20), provides guidance on the appropriate accounting. Generally, a distribution of less than 20 to 25 percent of the previously outstanding shares should be accounted for as a stock dividend by transferring an amount equal to the fair value of the stock dividend from retained earnings to the appropriate paid-in capital accounts. The SEC specifically requires distributions of less than 25 percent of the previously outstanding shares to be accounted for as stock dividends; distributions exceeding 25 percent should be accounted for as stock splits and do not affect retained earnings except as specified by state laws, unless the distributions appear to be part of a program of recurring distributions designed to mislead shareholders.

In the authors' opinion, the time to determine the fair value of the stock dividend shares and to make the appropriate transfer from retained earnings is the date the stock dividend is declared rather than the ex-dividend date or payment date. In computing the fair value of the shares to be issued, consideration may be given to the dilutive effect of the additional shares on market value. One way to recognize the dilutive effect is to divide the market value of a present share by one plus the stock dividend percentage to obtain the fair value of each share to be issued in the stock dividend. An alternative is to request management to obtain an investment banker's opinion of fair value appropriate for the stock dividend.

Covenants of debentures and other debt instruments often restrict the payment of cash dividends in some way (e.g., to earnings subsequent to the date of the instrument). The auditor should ascertain that dividend declarations do not exceed the amount of retained earnings available for dividends, and that the amount of unrestricted retained earnings has been calculated in accordance with the debt covenants or other restrictions and has been appropriately disclosed.

Holders of noncumulative preferred stock ordinarily have no claim to dividends in a year when the amount of the dividends has not been earned, except possibly when dividends earned in a prior year have been withheld improperly. Dividends paid on common stock may have encroached on the rights of holders of noncumulative preferred stock. An auditor who discovers that situation should bring the matter to the attention of appropriate management personnel and suggest that counsel be consulted about a possible liability to holders of noncumulative preferred stock.

In the event of a stock dividend or split, the auditor should ascertain that the capital stock authorization is not exceeded and that shares reserved for stock options and conversions of other issues have been considered.

(v) Partnership Capital. In auditing partnership financial statements, the auditor should read the partnership agreement. Ordinarily those agreements not only show the basis for sharing profits and losses but also often call for special allocations of different components of net income (like cash flows and depreciation) or contain provisions about fixed amounts of capital to be maintained by the various partners, loans by partners in certain circumstances, interest on partners' capital and loans, limitations on withdrawals, and similar matters. The auditor should analyze and substantiate changes in partnership capital between balance sheet dates and determine whether allocations and computations are in accordance with the partnership agreement.

Some partnerships conduct business without written partnership agreements. In those circumstances, the auditor should inquire whether the partners understand the bases on which the accounts are kept, particularly with respect to distributions of profits and losses and interest on partners' capital. If there are few partners, it may be appropriate to ask all partners to sign the financial statements on which the partners' accounts appear or, alternatively, to confirm the balances in their accounts. The required management representation letter (discussed in Chapter 27) may serve in lieu of those procedures.

(vi) Initial Audits. In an initial audit, the auditor should review the corporation's charter or certificate of incorporation, bylaws, and all pertinent amendments. How extensively the auditor reviews prior years' minutes of meetings of the board of directors and stockholders, other documents, and capital stock accounts depends on the circumstances and whether the financial statements were audited previously.

The auditor also should analyze the additional paid-in capital and retained earnings accounts from the corporation's inception to determine whether all entries were in conformity with GAAP then prevailing. If, however, previous audits have been made, the procedures may be limited to a review of analyses made by the predecessor auditors. The auditor also should review entries in those accounts for consistency of treatment from year to year. The analyses of additional paid-in capital accounts should segregate the balances by classes of stock outstanding.

(vii) Permanent Files. The auditor should include in the permanent working paper files information about the kinds of stock authorized, the number of shares of each authorized, par or stated values, provisions concerning dividend rates, redemption values, priority rights to dividends and in liquidation, cumulative or noncumulative rights to dividends, participation or conversion privileges, and other pertinent data. The auditor also should retain the analyses of additional paid-in capital and retained earnings in the permanent files so that changes in the current year may be compared readily with those in previous years.

26

Auditing Financial Statement Disclosures

ـ of the auditor's work in obtaining and evaluating evidence about whether a set of financial statements is presented fairly in conformity with generally accepted accounting principles is done as part of the audit of specific transaction cycles and accounts. Some aspects of financial statement presentation, however, are more pervasive and cannot be associated conveniently with specific cycles or accounts. This chapter discusses auditing considerations related to certain required financial statement disclosures that are not covered elsewhere because they are not related to specific transaction cycles and accounts.

As discussed in Chapter 6, management assertions that are embodied in financial statement components include those related to presentation and disclosure. Statement on Auditing Standards (SAS) No. 31, *Evidential Matter* (AU Section 326), notes that "assertions about presentation and disclosure deal with whether particular components of the financial statements are properly classified, described, and disclosed." The auditor's responsibility for the adequacy of disclosures derives from the third generally accepted auditing standard applicable to reporting, which states: "Informative disclosures in the financial statements are to be regarded as reasonably adequate unless otherwise stated in the report" [SAS No. 1 (AU Section 150.02)]. That standard is discussed, in general terms, in SAS No. 32, *Adequacy of Disclosure in Financial Statements* (AU Section 431). SAS No. 32 requires material matters regarding the financial statements to be disclosed in the statements themselves or in notes to the statements; if they are not, the auditor should express a qualified or an adverse opinion and should, if practicable, provide the information in the auditor's report. The auditor's reporting responsibilities with regard to inadequate disclosures are discussed in Chapter 28.

With the continuing proliferation of accounting standards in recent years, many auditors, including sole practitioners, have adopted checklists—often computerized—as a means of enhancing overall quality control and furthering staff development. Disclosure checklists can deal adequately with specifically required disclosures and serve as a "memory jogger"; they can, if properly prepared, also assist the auditor in meeting the standard of informative disclosure. Of course, the auditor's level of skill and judgment and his or her knowledge of the entity's business and industry obtained during the audit are the ultimate resources available to meet the disclosure standard.

Some auditors have developed separate disclosure checklists for companies subject to SEC reporting requirements and those that are not. Further, separate checklists may be prepared for certain specialized industries, such as banking, insurance, government units, and colleges and universities. A typical arrangement would be to have a series of questions covering all aspects of the financial statements in one column; specific references to the relevant authoritative pronouncement or the auditing firm's preferences in another column (by necessity, the requirements can only be generally stated in the checklist, but the references can make it easier to prepare and review the checklist); and an indication, in a third column, of whether the item is applicable, and, if so, whether it has been complied with. Space should be allowed for notes or calculations of amounts to demonstrate how materiality considerations entered into disclosure decisions. A completed checklist for an audit can document in one place all reporting and disclosure considerations.

If checklists are used by an auditing firm, it is desirable that a clear statement be appended setting forth the firm's policy on whether they are mandatory for all engagements, only for certain specified engagements, or simply to be used as practice aids. Disclosure checklists should be updated periodically and also should indicate the date produced so that authoritative pronouncements after that date will be considered.

26.1   CONTROLS RELATING TO FINANCIAL STATEMENT DISCLOSURES

The auditor's responsibilities with respect to auditing information contained in notes to financial statements are the same as those with respect to the basic financial statements (with the exception of unaudited information and supplementary disclosures). The information in many disclosures often is prepared by personnel not involved in or familiar with the entity's accounting functions and is not subject to the same type or degree of control as the information used in preparing the basic financial statements

The auditor, as a first step, should understand and evaluate the controls relating to the preparation of financial statement disclosures. Obviously, the controls appropriate in each situation depend on the nature and complexity of the disclosures themselves, as well as the degree to which the information is derived from, and therefore subject to the controls relating to, the formal accounting records. The following are examples of controls that usually are appropriate:

1. Written procedures should be maintained with respect to the accumulation of data used in financial statement disclosures. These procedures should describe what information is needed, the sources from which it is to be obtained, and the functions or personnel who are responsible for its accumulation.

2. Controls should be developed to ensure the completeness and accuracy of data accumulated from sources not subject to control activities applied to the accounting records. For example, the amount of employee debt guaranteed by an employer usually is obtained by aggregating the amounts of individual loans from the loan documents. An appropriate way to control accuracy would be to maintain a list, by employee and by loan payment date, so the amount of debt outstanding can be tested readily for arithmetical accuracy. An appropriate completeness control would be reconciling the total debt outstanding from this list to the amount of loans repaid during the year and amount of new loans guaranteed.

3. If information is supplied by outside specialists such as actuaries, attorneys, geologists, or engineers, formal procedures should be in place for requesting the information at the appropriate time and for providing the specialists with the information necessary for them to complete their work in a timely manner. Any data supplied to specialists should be subject to the completeness and accuracy controls discussed above.

4. Financial statement disclosures (usually, a complete set of statements, including notes) should be distributed to the management of various functions within the entity for their review to determine the adequacy of overall informative content with respect to any disclosures relating to their functions. For example, appropriate people in the employee benefits or human resources department should review the postretirement plan disclosures to determine the accuracy of the plan descriptions and reasonableness of the actuarial data contained therein.

rnal control over the preparation of financial statement disclosures affects the extent of the auditor's testing of the information. The amount of judgment required in determining what constitutes adequate informative disclosures means that no internal control system, however effective, can ensure that all appropriate disclosures are made. Therefore, the auditor should make an evaluation of the disclosures contained in the statements for each period, using the knowledge of the entity and its business and industry and all the specific information obtained during the audit, as well as technical knowledge of reporting and disclosure standards and the latest changes thereto.

26.2 DISCLOSURE OF ACCOUNTING POLICIES

To understand the financial statements, users must have information regarding the accounting policies followed by the reporting entity. APB Opinion No. 22, *Disclosure of Accounting Policies* (Accounting Standards Section A10), calls for disclosure of "all significant accounting policies," and specifically those policies that influence the accounting periods for which revenues and costs are included in the results of operations. In evaluating the entity's accounting policy disclosures, the auditor should consider the following questions:

- Is there an alternative generally accepted accounting principle or method that would be suitable in lieu of the policy being followed?
- Is the accounting policy currently in use peculiar to the industry in which the entity operates?
- Is the current accounting policy or its application unusual or innovative?

If the answer to any of these questions is yes, and the accounting policy has a material effect on the entity's financial position, results of operations, or cash flows, the policy should be disclosed.

The evaluation of materiality should be based on the effect of the accounting policy in use on financial position, results of operations, or cash flows, and not on whether the application of an alternative policy would produce a materially different result in the current year. In many cases, a comparison with the effects of an acceptable alternative policy would be impracticable. The existence of an alternative policy is not a pertinent consideration unless it would be acceptable for the specific application. The existence of an alternative policy that might be considered preferable to the policy in use, however, is a strong argument for disclosure. If disclosure of a particular policy is considered necessary, there is no requirement to refer to alternative accounting principles or to make comparisons with alternatives. The information called for is limited to a description of the policy in use.

The term "peculiar to an industry," used in APB Opinion No. 22 in defining criteria for disclosures, should be interpreted broadly to include transactions with characteristics that have led to the development of special accounting policies. Leasing, for example, cuts across many industry lines. Special accounting policies have been developed to consider the economic characteristics of these transactions, and such policies should be disclosed.

Evaluating the need to disclose policies with respect to transactions that are nonrecurring or that recur infrequently requires judgment. Generally, accounting policies covering nonrecurring or infrequently recurring transactions need be disclosed only for those years in which amounts relating to such transactions are included in the financial statements presented, unless disclosure of information is necessary to ensure that the financial statements are not misleading.

APB Opinion No. 22 expresses a preference for a separate summary of accounting policies, either apart from the notes to financial statements or as the first note. In some cases, it is acceptable to combine the description of an accounting policy with other data related to the policy. For example, disclosure of the accounting and funding policies with respect to pension costs may be combined with the other pension-related disclosures required by Statement of Financial Accounting Standards (SFAS) No. 87.

26.3 DISCLOSURE OF RELATED PARTY TRANSACTIONS

SFAS No. 57, *Related Party Disclosures* (Accounting Standards Section R36), requires disclosure in financial statements of material related party transactions (related parties are explicitly defined in Appendix B of SFAS No. 57 and in Chapter 0). That statement also requires disclosure of the nature of control relationships (with other entities) that could affect the operating results or financial position of the reporting entity, even though there were no transactions between the entities. AU Section 334, *Related Parties*, outlines specific auditing procedures that the auditor may consider in determining the existence of related parties, procedures intended to provide guidance for identifying material transactions with related parties, and procedures that should be considered in examining identified related party transactions. Auditing procedures regarding related party transactions are described in Chapter 8.

26.4 EARNINGS PER SHARE

SFAS No. 128, *Earnings Per Share* (Accounting Standards Section E11), specifies the computation, presentation, and disclosure requirements for earnings per share (EPS). SFAS No. 128 requires that entities with simple capital structures (those with only common stock outstanding) present basic EPS amounts for income from continuing operations and net income on the face of the income statement. All other entities are required to present both basic and diluted EPS for income from continuing operations and net income.

SFAS No. 128 is applicable to all entities with publicly held common stock or potential common stock. It also applies to an entity that has made a filing or is in the process of filing with a regulatory agency in preparation for the sale of securities in a public market. The statement does not apply to investment companies or to wholly owned subsidiaries that have not issued options or other potential common shares to employees or others. Entities not required to present EPS that choose to do so should do so in accordance with the requirements of the statement.

Auditing EPS information usually involves more than a simple recalculation of the arithmetic involved. The process may be viewed as consisting of the following three general steps:

1. Obtaining an understanding of the entity's capital structure
2. Determining that the required EPS amounts have been correctly calculated according to SFAS No. 128
3. Determining that the financial statements comply with the presentation and disclosure requirements of SFAS No. 128

Much of the understanding of the entity's capital structure is obtained in the course of auditing the debt and equity accounts. The auditor should review and document the conversion rights and terms of convertible securities and the exercise conditions of options or warrants when auditing the related debt or equity accounts. The terms of plans, contracts, and agreements for the issuance of stock to employees often contain provisions for contingent shares, restrictions on stock issued, and options, all of which may affect the EPS computations. Other agreements, such as for the sale or purchase of an affiliate, also may contain provisions that affect EPS. For purposes of computing EPS, an entity's capital structure often comprises more than the amounts presented in the equity section of the balance sheet. Consequently, the evidence needed to support the audit of the EPS computation and related disclosures may be gathered most efficiently at various stages of the audit and should be planned accordingly.

Because the computation of EPS includes the effect on EPS of securities that enable the holders to obtain common stock, assumptions must be made regarding the exercise, conversion, and issuance of securities, and prices to be used. SFAS No. 128 specifies how those assumptions are to be made, and also requires the use of specified methods to reflect the effect of certain securities. For example, the statement specifies the "if-converted" method for convertible securities and the "treasury stock" method for options and warrants. In the majority of situations, questions regarding the computation of EPS may be answered by reference to the statement, including its extensive appendices. Even though EPS has been the subject of exhaustive explanation, auditors may encounter transactions or events that have not been specifically addressed in the literature. In those cases, the auditor should ascertain that the provisions of the statement have been applied to the substance of the transactions.

26.5   COMPREHENSIVE INCOME

SFAS No. 130, *Reporting Comprehensive Income* (Accounting Standards Section C49), establishes standards for reporting and display of comprehensive income and its components (revenues, expenses, gains, and losses) in a full set of general-purpose financial statements.

SFAS No. 130 defines *comprehensive income* as it is defined in FASB Concepts Statement No. 6, that is, the change in equity of a business enterprise during a period from transactions and other events and circumstances from nonowner sources. Thus, comprehensive income includes net income. The term *other comprehensive income* refers to revenues, expenses, gains, and losses that, under generally accepted accounting principles (GAAP), are included in comprehensive income but excluded from net income. However, neither of those terms is required to be used in financial statements. Any equivalent term, such as *nonowner changes in equity* or *comprehensive loss*, may be used in the financial statements to refer to comprehensive income. The statement requires that entities (a) classify items of other comprehensive income by their nature in a financial statement and (b) display the accumulated balance of other comprehensive income separately in the equity section of the balance sheet.

The components of comprehensive income under SFAS No. 130 are those items that bypass the income statement and are reported in the balance sheet as a separate component of equity. Paragraph 39 of SFAS No. 130 describes those items, all of which relate to accounting under SFAS No. 52, *Foreign Currency Translation* (Accounting Standards Section F60), SFAS No. 80, *Accounting for Futures Contracts* (Accounting Standards Section F80), SFAS No. 87, *Employers' Accounting for Pensions* (Accounting Standards Section P16), and SFAS No. 115, *Accounting for Certain Investments in Debt and Equity Securities* (Accounting Standards Section I80).

SFAS No. 130 recognizes that there are other items that presently bypass the income statement and are reported as direct adjustments to paid-in capital, retained earnings, or other nonincome equity accounts. The statement provides that those items should not be included as components of comprehensive income. They include, for example, the direct reduction of shareholders' equity to recognize unearned compensation under APB Opinion No. 25, *Accounting for Stock Issued to Employees* (Accounting Standards Section C47), and to recognize unearned shares under employee stock ownership plans, taxes not payable in cash by an entity that has reorganized under SOP 90-7, *Financial Reporting by Entities in Reorganization Under the Bankruptcy Code,* and gains and losses resulting from contracts that are indexed to a company's shares and ultimately settled in cash (EITF Issue 94-7, *Accounting for Financial Instruments Indexed to, and Potentially Settled in, a Company's Own Stock*).

Audit evidence related to the various components of comprehensive income (e.g., unrealized holding gains or losses on available-for-sale securities) is obtained in the course of auditing the related balance sheet accounts (e.g., investments in available-for-sale securities). The auditor should ensure that the manner in which those components are displayed in the financial statements conforms with the requirements of SFAS No. 130.

26.6 SEGMENT INFORMATION

When a public entity issues a complete set of financial statements in conformity with GAAP, SFAS No. 14, *Financial Reporting for Segments of a Business Enterprise,* as amended by Statement Nos. 18, 21, 24, and 30 (Accounting Standards Section S20), requires that those statements include information regarding the entity's operations in different industries, its foreign operations and export sales, and its major customers.[1] The

---

[1] In June 1997, the FASB issued SFAS No. 131, *Disclosures about Segments of an Enterprise and Related Information,* which supersedes SFAS No. 14 and related amendments. For year-end disclosures, SFAS No. 131 is effective for years beginning after December 15, 1997, with earlier application encouraged. The statement's interim reporting disclosures would commence the first quarter immediately subsequent to the first year in which the entity provides year-end disclosures. The statement provides transition guidance. The SEC has stated its intent to conform Regulation S-K to SFAS No. 131. At the time of this writing, the Auditing Standards Board is considering guidance appropriate for auditing the disclosures required by SFAS No. 131.

following statement of the auditor's objective with respect to segment information is included in SAS No. 21, *Segment Information* (AU Section 435.03):

> The objective of auditing procedures applied to segment information is to provide the auditor with a reasonable basis for concluding whether the information is presented in conformity with FASB Statement No. 14 in relation to the financial statements taken as a whole. The auditor performing an audit of financial statements in accordance with generally accepted auditing standards considers segment information, as other informative disclosures, in relation to the financial statements taken as a whole, and is not required to apply auditing procedures that would be necessary to express a separate opinion on the segment information.

The preparation of segment information involves disaggregation of the financial statements and consequently may require the accumulation of information that would not otherwise be available from the accounting system. The auditor should consider the effect of segment information on the audit during the planning stage. This is necessary for both promoting audit efficiency and determining that the procedures used by the entity to develop the segment information are sufficient to enable the auditor to form a conclusion regarding the information. SAS No. 21 discusses the types of auditing procedures that the auditor should consider when financial statements include segment information. The nature and extent of the specific procedures depend on the number of industry and geographic segments in which the entity operates, the procedures used by the entity to accumulate the information, and the entity's operating structure. For example, an entity with several relatively autonomous divisions or subsidiaries, each operating in a different industry segment, may be able to accumulate most of the required information directly from the financial statements of the divisions or subsidiaries. Another entity that operates in the same industry segments, but whose operations are more integrated, may need to employ a number of additional procedures to disaggregate its financial statements. In the first instance, the auditor may be able to test the segment information by a few additional auditing procedures, while in the second instance, many additional audit tests may be required.

SFAS No. 21 suspended the segment reporting requirements of SFAS No. 14 (as well as the requirements of APB Opinion No. 15) for nonpublic entities. Consequently, most financial statements that include segment information are those of SEC registrants. The disclosure requirements of Regulation S-K covering the annual report to shareholders and Form 10-K are similar to those of SFAS No. 14, but include certain additional information. This additional information is not required to be audited, but entities often include parts of it in the notes to financial statements along with the information required by SFAS No. 14. In addition, entities often include segment information in a section of the report to shareholders that is outside of the basic financial statements and notes thereto. In these situations, the notes to financial statements should contain a cross-reference to the segment data. During the planning stage, the auditor should discuss the anticipated form and location of all segment information with entity management.

The auditor should read a draft of the annual report to determine whether all of the segment information included has been audited and covered by the audit report on the financial statements. If the annual report contains other segment data that is not required by SFAS No. 14 and has not been audited, such information should be presented in a manner that clearly distinguishes it from the information covered by the auditor's report. The auditor's report should not refer to segment information unless such information is materially misstated or omitted, there has been an accounting change with respect to the segment information that is material in relation to the financial statements taken as a whole, or a scope limitation has been placed on the auditor with respect to such information. A separate auditor's report should not be issued on the segment information unless the auditor has been engaged to report separately on such information and has issued the type of special report covered in SAS No. 62 (AU Section 623.11–.17) and SAS No. 21 (AU Section 435.18), as discussed in Chapter 29.

26.7 DISCLOSURE OF INFORMATION ABOUT FINANCIAL INSTRUMENTS

Several Statements of Financial Accounting Standards establish requirements for certain disclosures about financial instruments. Some of those requirements apply to off-balance-sheet financial instruments; others apply to both on- and off-balance-sheet financial instruments. The auditor's responsibilities with respect to those disclosures are similar to his or her responsibilities for all accounts, regardless of whether the financial instruments are on or off the entity's balance sheet. That is, audit assurance about the appropriateness of disclosures in this area requires that the auditor also obtain and evaluate evidence about the existence, completeness, accuracy, and valuation of financial instruments; the appropriateness of the accounting period in which transactions in those instruments were recorded or disclosed; and the existence of rights to or obligations for them. Accordingly, the auditing procedures discussed in Chapter 21, "Auditing Investments in Debt and Equity Securities and Related Income," should be considered in addition to those discussed in this section.

(a) Off-Balance-Sheet Risk and Concentrations of Credit Risk

SFAS No. 105, *Disclosure of Information about Financial Instruments with Off-Balance-Sheet Risk and Financial Instruments with Concentrations of Credit Risk* (Accounting Standards Section F25), establishes requirements for disclosure of such information. (The statement does not change any requirements for recognition, measurement, or classification of financial instruments in financial statements. These requirements are being addressed in separate phases of the FASB's financial instruments project.)

SFAS No. 105 requires disclosures about financial instruments that have off-balance-sheet credit or market risk. Off-balance-sheet risk is the risk that an entity may incur an accounting loss that exceeds the amount recognized in its financial statements. (The SFAS defines credit risk as "the possibility that a loss may occur from the failure of another party to perform according to the terms of a contract" and market risk as "the possibility that future changes in market prices may make a financial instrument less valuable or more onerous.") Examples of financial instruments with off-balance-sheet risk are commitments to lend, financial guarantees, options, recourse obligations on receivables sold, obligations to repurchase securities sold, commitments to purchase or sell other financial instruments at predetermined prices, futures contracts, interest rate and foreign currency swaps, and obligations arising from financial instruments sold short.

SFAS No. 105 also requires disclosures about concentrations of credit risk for all financial instruments—both on and off balance sheet. Concentration of credit risk can be viewed in several ways, for example, by region, by industry, or by type of issuer. An entity can have different types of concentrations for different classes of financial instruments. For example, an entity can have industry and type of issuer concentration in its common stock investments, and region and industry concentration in its convertible bond investments.

As amended by SFAS No. 119, *Disclosure about Derivative Financial Instruments and Fair Value of Financial Instruments* (Accounting Standards Section F25), the disclosures should be made by category of financial instruments either in the body of the financial statements or in the accompanying notes. ("Category of financial instruments" refers to a class of financial instrument, business activity, risk, or other category that is consistent with the entity's management of those instruments.) For each category of financial instruments with off-balance-sheet credit or market risk (distinguishing between those held or issued for trading purposes and those held or issued for purposes other than trading), the entity should disclose:

- The face or contract amount of the class of financial instruments (or, if none, the notional principal amount)
- The nature and terms, including at a minimum:
  - The credit and market risk of those instruments
  - The cash requirements of those instruments
  - The accounting policy relating to recognition of revenue and allocation of asset costs to current and future periods

Additional required disclosures relate to both off-balance-sheet credit risk and concentrations of credit risk and include:

- Information regarding the entity's policy of:
  - Requiring collateral or other security to support financial instruments subject to credit risk
  - The entity's access to that collateral or other security
  - The nature and a brief description of the collateral or other security supporting the financial instruments
- The amount of accounting loss the entity would incur if any party to the financial instrument failed to perform completely according to the terms of the contract and the collateral or other security, if any, proved to be of no value to the entity.

For concentrations of credit risk, the entity should also disclose information about the activity, region, or economic characteristic that identifies the concentrations.

Auditing procedures specifically designed to identify financial instruments with off-balance-sheet credit or market risk or concentrations of credit risk include:

- Reviewing the minutes of meetings of the board of directors and its executive or operating committees for information about material transactions authorized or discussed and for approval of overall corporate policy as to the entity's investment, financing, and hedge philosophy and guidelines

- Inquiring of management as to whether such transactions are occurring and, if so, how they are being recognized

- Reviewing, to the extent practicable, accounting records for large, unusual, or nonrecurring transactions that may expose the entity to significant credit or market risk

- Obtaining a representation from management that financial instruments with off-balance-sheet risk and financial instruments with concentrations of credit risk have been properly recorded and disclosed in the financial statements

(b) Fair Value

SFAS No. 107, *Disclosures about Fair Value of Financial Instruments*, as amended by SFAS No. 119, *Disclosure about Derivative Financial Instruments and Fair Value of Financial Instruments* (Accounting Standards Section F25), provides guidance on disclosures of fair value of financial instruments. Like SFAS No. 105, No. 107 applies to all types of entities, not just those in the financial services industry.

Financial instruments for which fair value disclosures are required include financial assets and liabilities both on and off the balance sheet. Examples include investments, loans receivable, current and long-term debt, repurchase agreements, interest rate and currency swap contracts, option contracts, foreign exchange contracts, letters of credit, and commitments to lend. The disclosures should distinguish between financial instruments held or issued for trading purposes and those held or issued for purposes other than trading.

Fair value information for derivative financial instruments should not be combined, aggregated, or netted with fair value information for nonderivative financial instruments. Also, the fair value information should be presented together with the related carrying amounts in the body of the financial statements, a single note to the financial statements, or a summary table in a form that makes it clear whether the amounts represent assets or liabilities.

If available, quoted market prices are to be used to determine fair values. Sources for quoted prices include the public exchange markets, dealer markets, and quotation services. If quoted prices are not available, fair values should be estimated using quoted prices of similar instruments or techniques such as present value of expected cash flows or option pricing models. The statement also requires disclosure of the methods and significant assumptions used to estimate fair values.

The fair value disclosures under SFAS No. 107, however, are required only if it is practicable to estimate those values. "Practicable" means that an estimate of fair value can be made without incurring excessive costs. Deciding whether costs are considered excessive will require exercise of judgment.

If it is not practicable to estimate fair value of a financial instrument or a class of financial instruments, the entity must disclose:

- Information pertinent to estimating the fair value (for example, the carrying amount, effective interest rate, and maturity)

- The reasons why it is not practicable to estimate fair value (that is, why estimation of values would require excessive costs)

Auditing procedures specifically designed to audit disclosures required by SFAS No. 107 include:

- Determining how the entity identifies financial instruments whose fair value needs to be disclosed under SFAS No. 107
- Obtaining a listing of financial instruments held or issued at year-end—both on and off the balance sheet—reconciling the on-balance-sheet instruments to the balance sheet and determining whether financial instruments identified through other auditing procedures have been included in the listing
- Identifying the method(s) the entity uses to estimate fair value and evaluating the reasonableness of any management determinations that it is not practicable to estimate fair value because of excessive costs
- For fair values obtained from external sources (as appropriate):
  - Comparing market prices with an independent published source
  - Confirming quotations from dealers and quotation services
  - Following procedures appropriate for using the work of a specialist for financial instruments valued using outside pricing services or other valuation specialists
- For estimates developed internally:
  - Reviewing the supporting documentation describing the methodology, underlying assumptions, factors, and input used and supporting calculations
  - Determining whether the valuation principles are acceptable and whether the assumptions are reasonable and reflect adjustments for differences in security characteristics such as credit risk and maturities
- Determining whether the disclosures are in accordance with SFAS No. 107 and SFAS No. 119
- Determining whether there have been any significant events subsequent to the balance sheet date that would materially affect fair values and would require disclosure
- Determining whether all appropriate items related to fair value disclosures have been included in the management representation letter, including support for management's decision not to disclose fair values when it was determined not to be practicable to estimate them

In addition to disclosing the fair value of financial instruments as required by SFAS No. 107, an entity may disclose voluntarily the fair value of other assets and liabilities not encompassed by that statement. An auditing interpretation of SAS No. 57, *Auditing Accounting Estimates* (AU Section 9342), indicates that the voluntary information may be audited only if the measurement and disclosure criteria used to prepare the fair value information are reasonable and competent persons using those criteria ordinarily would obtain materially similar measurements and disclosures. The interpretation provides reporting guidance when the audited disclosures constitute a complete balance sheet presentation and also when they do not. For voluntary disclosures that are not audited, the interpretation also provides reporting guidance when the disclosures are included in an auditor-submitted document and when they are included in a client-prepared document.

(c) Derivatives

SFAS No. 119, *Disclosure about Derivative Financial Instruments and Fair Value of Financial Instruments* (Accounting Standards Section F25), requires disclosures about derivative financial instruments—futures, forward, swap, and option contracts, and other financial instruments with similar characteristics. The statement requires disclosures about the amounts, nature, and terms of derivatives that are not subject to SFAS No. 105, which requires similar disclosures (see previous discussion of SFAS No. 105 in this chapter). SFAS No. 119 requires an entity to distinguish between derivatives that are held or issued for trading purposes and those that are held or issued for purposes other than trading.

Entities that hold or issue derivatives for trading purposes should disclose their average fair value and net trading gains and losses. Entities that hold or issue derivatives for purposes other than trading should disclose those purposes and how the derivatives are reported in the financial statements. For entities that hold or issue derivatives and account for them as hedges of anticipated transactions, the statement requires disclosure about the anticipated transactions, the classes of derivative financial instruments used to hedge those transactions, the amounts of hedging gains and losses deferred, and the transactions or other events that result in recognition of the deferred gains or losses in earnings. The statement encourages, but does not require, "quantitative information about market risks of derivative financial instruments, and also of other assets and liabilities, that is consistent with the way the entity manages or adjusts risks and that is useful for comparing the results of applying the entity's strategies to its objectives for holding or issuing the derivative financial instruments."

The auditor should be aware of the risks associated with derivatives and have a general understanding of their economics. It is not practical to develop a checklist of characteristics of every type of derivative. However, unfamiliar descriptions, nonstandard cash flows, unusual terms, or abnormal interest rates or pricing terms should cause the auditor to consider the presence of derivatives. Also, long-dated derivatives (e.g., those extending beyond ten years) may require careful evaluation.

When an entity engages in transactions involving derivatives, the auditor should:

- Identify the types of derivatives used
- Develop an understanding of the nature of each derivative and its underlying economic substance
- Understand the entity's strategy for entering into the transaction
- Identify the risks associated with each derivative and evaluate how those risks affect the entity's operations
- Understand the entity's controls over its transactions in derivatives

These procedures should be performed as part of the planning phase of the audit, considered in developing the audit program, and reconsidered during the course of the audit as additional information becomes available. The auditor also should consider the procedures noted in Chapter 21 [Section 21.4(f), Tests Related to Investments in Sophisticated Financial Instruments].

Many derivatives have significant off-balance-sheet risks. Auditing procedures specifically designed to identify derivatives with off-balance-sheet risk include:

- Reviewing the minutes of meetings of the board of directors and executive or operating committee for information about material transactions authorized or discussed or for approval of overall entity policy with respect to investment, financing, and hedging philosophy and guidelines

- Inquiring of management as to whether such transactions are occurring and, if so, how they are being recognized

- Reviewing, to the extent practicable, accounting records for large, unusual, or nonrecurring transactions that may expose the entity to significant credit or market risk

- Reviewing the methodology, underlying assumptions, and calculations used by management for valuing each type of derivative financial instrument, and determining whether they are appropriate

- Obtaining representation from management that derivatives have been properly recorded or disclosed in the financial statements

26.8   DISCLOSURE OF RISKS, UNCERTAINTIES, AND RELATED MATTERS

Among the matters that affect an entity's financial statements, and that need to be disclosed, are the significant risks and uncertainties it faces. Those risks and uncertainties can stem from such matters as the nature of the entity's operations, the use of estimates that are inherent in the accounting process, significant concentrations in certain aspects of the entity's operations, and contingencies such as the outcome of a pending lawsuit.

Uncertainties include, but are not limited to, the following:

- Contingencies covered by SFAS No. 5, *Accounting for Contingencies* (Accounting Standards Section C59)

- The possible inability of the entity to continue as a going concern for a reasonable period of time, as discussed in SAS No. 59, *The Auditor's Consideration of an Entity's Ability to Continue as a Going Concern* (AU Section 341)

- The possible nonrecoverability of the carrying amounts of long-lived assets, as discussed in SFAS No. 121, *Accounting for the Impairment of Long-Lived Assets and for Long-Lived Assets to Be Disposed Of* (Accounting Standards Section I08), which is discussed in Chapter 22 of this book

- Matters related to accounting estimates covered by AICPA Statement of Position (SOP) 94-6, *Disclosure of Certain Significant Risks and Uncertainties*

(a) Contingencies

A contingency is an existing condition, situation, or set of circumstances involving uncertainty as to possible gain (gain contingency) or loss (loss contingency) that will be resolved when one or more future events occur or fail to occur.

Contingencies that might result in gains, such as claims against others for patent infringement, usually are not recorded until realized. They should be adequately disclosed in the notes to the financial statements; however, misleading implications as to the likelihood of their realization should be avoided.

In many cases, the existence of a loss contingency results in a charge to income and the recording of a liability, for example, a probable loss resulting from the guarantee of the indebtedness of others or an obligation relating to a product warranty or defect. In other cases, such as a probable loss from uncollectible receivables, the existence of a loss contingency results in the write-down of an asset (often by means of an allowance account) and a charge to income. Still other loss contingencies result only in financial statement disclosure; an example would be litigation in which the likelihood of loss is "not probable." (Loss contingencies arising from litigation, claims, and assessments are discussed in detail in Chapter 27.) The following table summarizes the proper financial accounting and reporting for material loss contingencies.

| | Amount of Loss Can Be Reasonably Estimated | |
Likelihood of Occurrence	Yes	No
Probable	Accrue; consider need to disclose	Disclose
Reasonably possible	Disclose	Disclose
Remote	Not accrued or disclosed	

Paragraph 3 of SFAS No. 5 (Accounting Standards Section C59.104) defines the ranges of likelihood of occurrence, as follows:

- *Probable*. The future event or events are likely to occur.
- *Reasonably possible*. The chance of the future event or events occurring is more than remote but less than likely.
- *Remote*. The chance of the future event or events occurring is slight.

When a material loss contingency involves an *unasserted* claim or assessment, disclosure is not required if there is no evidence that the assertion of a claim is probable. If it is considered probable that the claim will be asserted and there is a reasonable possibility that the outcome will be unfavorable, disclosure is required.

The auditor's responsibilities with respect to loss contingencies involve identifying them and determining that they are appropriately recognized or disclosed; if they are, the auditor has no reporting responsibilities.[2] The auditor is not precluded, however,

---

[2] SAS No. 79, *Amendment to Statement on Auditing Standards No. 58*, Reports on Audited Financial Statements, eliminated the requirement that the auditor add an uncertainties explanatory paragraph to the auditor's report when certain criteria were met. [SAS No. 79 does not affect the provisions of SAS No. 59, *The Auditor's Consideration of an Entity's Ability to Continue as a Going Concern* (AU Section 341), which is discussed later in this chapter.]

from including an emphasis-of-a-matter paragraph in the auditor's report to emphasize a significant uncertainty that has been disclosed in the financial statements. (Emphasis-of-a-matter paragraphs in auditors' reports are discussed in Chapter 28.)

Auditing loss contingencies is one of the most difficult aspects of many audits, and the variety of conditions encountered makes it impossible to describe the auditor's task definitively. Following is a description of the kinds of procedures the auditor usually undertakes to identify material loss contingencies.

The auditor should be alert for possible contingent liabilities while performing tests for unrecorded liabilities, described in Chapter 23. For example, when inspecting the minute books, contracts, and other documents, the auditor should be alert for matters indicating contingencies to be investigated. When inquiring of management about the existence of unrecorded liabilities, the auditor also should consider the possibility of loss contingencies. Management's statement about loss contingencies should be included in the representation letter from management (discussed in Chapter 27).

An entity may have contingent liabilities for accounts receivable it has discounted, with recourse, with banks or other financial institutions. The auditor should be alert when performing other auditing procedures for indications of such transactions, for example, interest payments unrelated to recorded debt obligations, and should investigate them. An entity also may have guaranteed payment of the indebtedness of another entity, which may be an affiliate or a subsidiary or may be unrelated to the guarantor entity. The auditor should review the representation letter from management, corporate minutes, and contractual arrangements, and inquire of officials of the guarantor about such contingent liabilities.

Although it is customary to insure against liability for damages claimed by employees and the public, insurance policies usually do not cover unlimited liabilities and not all entities carry adequate insurance against all potential claims. Furthermore, unusual claims for damages may arise from alleged breach of contract, failure to deliver goods, antitrust violations, existence of foreign substances in an entity's product, violations of environmental laws, and other causes. The auditor should inquire about possible liabilities of that general character.[3] Possible sources of information include the entity's inside and outside attorneys, its risk manager, risk consultants, and insurance agents or brokers who provide insurance coverage.

Some claims may not be referred to the entity's counsel. For example, salespeople may claim commissions in excess of those paid or accrued, or employees who have been dismissed may claim salaries or other compensation for uncompleted terms of service. Often, those claims are handled as purely administrative matters and may not be referred to counsel unless they are substantial in amount. If the auditor learns of a possible material loss contingency from those types of claims, he or she should obtain the opinion of the entity's counsel with respect to the possible liability. (See Section 27.3, Lawyers' Letters.)

Occasionally, an entity disputes a claim, resorts to litigation, and has a judgment entered against it. If the case is appealed and a bond is given pending final decision, execution of the judgment may be stayed and the judgment not entered in the accounts. The auditor should obtain the opinion of the entity's counsel in these areas.

Auditors ordinarily perform additional procedures to obtain sufficient competent

---

[3] Environmental liabilities are discussed in Chapter 20.

evidential matter concerning litigation, claims, and assessments. Those procedures are discussed in Chapter 27 [Section 27.3(a), Auditing Procedures].

(b) Going Concern Uncertainties

One specific type of uncertainty the auditor should consider is the entity's continued existence as a "going concern." An entity is a going concern when it has the ability to continue in operation and meet its obligations. The concept that financial statements are prepared on the basis of a going concern is one of the basic tenets of financial accounting. Because the going concern assumption is so basic, the standard auditor's report does not make reference to it.

When the entity can continue in operation and meet its obligations only by selling substantial amounts of its assets outside the ordinary course of business or by its creditors' willingness to forgive or restructure its debt, such circumstances should raise doubts about whether the entity is a going concern. Doubts about the entity's continued existence also should raise questions about realizable value of assets, the order of payment of liabilities, the proper classification and carrying amounts of both, and the appropriateness of necessary financial statement disclosures. If the auditor concludes there is substantial doubt about the entity's ability to continue as a going concern for a reasonable period of time (not to exceed one year from the date of the financial statements), he or she should determine that this is appropriately disclosed in the financial statements and should include an explanatory paragraph in the auditor's report to reflect that conclusion. (Auditors' reports are discussed in Chapter 28.)

SAS No. 59 (AU Section 341) provides guidance to the auditor for meeting an explicit responsibility to evaluate whether there is substantial doubt about the entity's ability to continue as a going concern for a reasonable period of time. This is done through the following steps:

Step 1. Consider whether the results of procedures performed in planning, gathering evidence relative to the various audit objectives, and completing the audit identify conditions and events that, when considered in the aggregate, indicate there could be substantial doubt about the entity's ability to continue as a going concern for a reasonable period of time.

In a properly planned audit, it should not be necessary to design auditing procedures specifically directed at the going concern issue. The results of auditing procedures designed and performed to achieve other audit objectives should be sufficient for that purpose. For example, conditions and events that could raise doubts may be identified through some of the following procedures: analytical procedures; review of subsequent events; review of compliance with the terms of debt and loan agreements; reading of minutes of meetings of stockholders, board of directors, and important committees of the board; inquiry of the entity's lawyers about litigation, claims, and assessments; and confirmation with related and third parties of the details of arrangements to provide or maintain financial support.

In considering the evidence provided by those procedures, it may be necessary for the auditor to obtain additional information about conditions and events identified that could create substantial doubt about the entity's ability to continue as a going concern. Their significance will depend on the circumstances. SAS No. 59 (AU Section 341.06) gives the following examples of such conditions and events, some of which are interrelated:

- *Negative trends.* For example, recurring operating losses, working capital deficiencies, negative cash flows from operating activities, or adverse key financial ratios.

- *Other indications of possible financial difficulties.* For example, default on loan or similar agreements, arrearages in dividends, denial of usual trade credit from suppliers, restructuring of debt, noncompliance with statutory capital requirements, need to seek new sources or methods of financing or to dispose of substantial assets.

- *Internal matters.* For example, work stoppages or other labor difficulties, substantial dependence on the success of a particular project, uneconomic long-term commitments, need to significantly revise operations.

- *External matters that have occurred.* For example, legal proceedings, legislation, or similar matters that might jeopardize an entity's ability to operate; loss of a key franchise, license, or patent; loss of a principal customer or supplier; uninsured or underinsured catastrophe such as a drought, earthquake, or flood.

Step 2. If substantial doubt exists about the entity's ability to continue as a going concern for a reasonable period of time, obtain information about management's plans that are intended to mitigate the adverse effects of the conditions or events that gave rise to the doubt, and assess the likelihood that such plans can be effectively implemented.

Those plans might include plans to dispose of assets, reduce or delay expenditures, borrow money or restructure debt, or increase ownership equity. In evaluating those plans, the auditor should consider whether there is adequate evidence supporting management's ability to carry out the plans. For example, plans to dispose of assets could be difficult or impossible to accomplish if there are restrictive covenants in loan agreements limiting such disposals. When prospective financial information is particularly significant to management's plans, the auditor should request management to provide that information and should consider whether there is adequate support for the significant assumptions underlying it.

Step 3. After evaluating management's plans, conclude whether substantial doubt exists about the entity's ability to continue as a going concern for a reasonable period of time.

If the auditor concludes there *is* substantial doubt, he or she should then consider the adequacy of financial statement disclosure about the entity's possible inability to continue as a going concern *and include an explanatory paragraph* (following the opinion paragraph) in the audit report to reflect that conclusion. If the entity's disclosures with respect to its ability to continue as a going concern are inadequate, a departure from generally accepted accounting principles exists and would result in either a qualified or an adverse opinion. Auditors' reports in these circumstances are discussed further in Chapter 28.

Financial statement disclosures about the entity's ability to continue as a going concern might include the following information [as described in SAS No. 59 (AU Section 341.10)]:

- Pertinent conditions and events giving rise to the assessment of substantial doubt about the entity's ability to continue as a going concern for a reasonable period of time
- The possible effects of such conditions and events
- Management's evaluation of the significance of those conditions and events and any mitigating factors
- Possible discontinuance of operations
- Management's plans (including relevant prospective financial information)
- Information about the recoverability or classification of recorded asset amounts or the amounts or classification of liabilities

If, after considering management's plans, substantial doubt about the entity's ability to continue as a going concern is alleviated, the auditor should still consider whether the principal conditions and events that initially generated the doubt need to be disclosed. The consideration of disclosure should include the possible effects of those conditions and events and any mitigating factors, including management's plans.

(c) Operating in Bankruptcy or Liquidation

Entities that continue operations while in bankruptcy and prepare financial statements on a "going concern basis" also are subject to the requirements of SAS No. 59. In that situation, the financial statements ordinarily would include extensive disclosures about the entity's legal status, and the auditor's report would ordinarily contain an explanatory paragraph conveying the existence of substantial doubt about the entity's ability to continue as a going concern and referring the reader to the disclosures in the financial statements. If the entity is in liquidation, or if liquidation appears probable, a liquidation basis of accounting would be considered GAAP. If the liquidation basis of accounting has been properly applied and adequate disclosures made, the auditor's report should be unqualified, with the addition of explanatory language stating that the entity is being liquidated. An auditing interpretation (AU Section 9508.33–.38) provides reporting guidance in this situation.

Statement of Position (SOP) 90-7, *Financial Reporting by Entities in Reorganization Under the Bankruptcy Code*, provides detailed guidance on the accounting treatment of entities that enter into and emerge from bankruptcy. SOP 90-7 recommends that when an entity emerges from bankruptcy and meets specified criteria, it should adopt fresh-start reporting; in that situation, it should not present comparative financial statements in the first year after emerging from bankruptcy.

(d) Disclosures Required by SOP 94-6

SOP 94-6 requires the financial statements of all nongovernmental entities to include disclosures about the nature of the entity's operations and its use of estimates in the preparation of financial statements. In addition, if specified criteria are met, those entities also must include disclosures about significant estimates that are particularly sensitive to change in the near term and about the entity's current vulnerability due to certain concentrations. Meeting the SOP's materiality criterion for disclosure of a particular accounting estimate does not depend on the amount of the estimate that is reported in the financial statements, but rather on the "materiality of the effect that using a different estimate would have had on the financial statements."

The auditor's objective with regard to SOP 94-6 is to determine whether management has considered all risks and uncertainties and has applied appropriate judgment in determining which of those risks and uncertainties should be disclosed and how they should be disclosed. This ordinarily requires reviewing management's process for identifying and assessing the need to disclose various risks and uncertainties, obtaining (or preparing) a list of the entity's risks and uncertainties, determining that risks and uncertainties identified throughout the audit are on the list, and comparing the list with the requirements of SOP 94-6. The auditor should assess the appropriateness of the disclosures by considering the information on the list of risks and uncertainties along with the knowledge gained about the entity's business and the risks and uncertainties it faces. Representations about significant estimates and concentrations should be included in the management representation letter.

PART 4

Completing the Work and Reporting the Results

27

Completing the Audit

This chapter deals with auditing procedures and considerations that are part of the final phase of an audit but are not related to specific transaction cycles or accounts. The final phase occurs primarily after the balance sheet date. These procedures entail many subjective decisions requiring judgment and experience, and thus the senior members of the engagement team usually perform them.

The judgments made during this phase of an audit are often crucial to the ultimate outcome of the engagement. Accordingly, the procedures should reflect the auditor's assessment of the risks associated with the entity's business and the financial statements. The procedures covered in this chapter often bring to light matters that are of major concern in forming an opinion on the financial statements.

27.1 ANALYTICAL PROCEDURES

As noted in Chapter 15 (Section 15.3, Analytical Procedures), Statement on Auditing Standards (SAS) No. 56, *Analytical Procedures* (AU Section 329), requires the auditor to perform analytical procedures as an overall review of the financial statements at or near the end of the audit. The objective of analytical procedures used at this stage is to help the auditor assess the conclusions reached during the audit and form an opinion on the financial statements. The overall review generally includes reading the statements and notes, and considering (a) whether the information and explanations gathered in response to unusual or unexpected balances or relationships previously identified are adequate, and (b) whether there are unusual or unexpected balances or relationships that were not previously identified. The auditor may use a variety of analytical procedures (as described in Chapter 15) in making this overall review. Those procedures may provide added evidence that the financial statements are not materially misstated because of undetected errors or fraud, or they may indicate the need for additional auditing procedures before the report on the financial statements is issued.

27.2 READING MINUTES OF MEETINGS

Reading the minutes of meetings of the board of directors and its important committees enables the auditor to examine the board's approval of management's significant actions and to determine whether significant decisions that affect the financial statements or require disclosure in the notes have been appropriately reflected therein. Often the auditor reads minutes of meetings shortly after the meetings or during the early stage of the year-end fieldwork. This allows the auditor to amend the audit strategy, if necessary, for actions the board or a board committee has taken. For example, the board's authorizing the disposal of a segment of the business could significantly affect the audit strategy. The auditor should be satisfied that copies of minutes of all meetings held during the period have been provided, including meetings held after year-end but before the date of the audit report. If minutes were not prepared and approved for meetings held shortly before the date of the audit report, the auditor should inquire of the secretary of the board or the committee about actions taken. This inquiry should be documented in the working papers.

27.3 LAWYERS' LETTERS

Chapter 26 discussed accounting, reporting, and auditing aspects of loss contingencies. With respect to one particular group of loss contingencies—litigation, claims, and assessments—paragraph 4 of SAS No. 12, *Inquiry of a Client's Lawyer Concerning Litigation, Claims, and Assessments* (AU Section 337.04), requires the auditor to obtain evidential matter related to the following factors:

- The existence of a condition, situation, or set of circumstances indicating an uncertainty as to the possible loss to an entity arising from litigation, claims, and assessments
- The period in which the underlying cause for legal action occurred
- The probability of an unfavorable outcome
- The amount or range of potential loss

The term "litigation, claims, and assessments" includes both pending and threatened litigation, claims, and assessments and unasserted claims and assessments. The auditor needs to identify all material litigation, claims, and assessments and to obtain sufficient competent evidential matter about their recognition, measurement, and disclosure.

(a) Auditing Procedures

Management is responsible for adopting policies and procedures to identify, evaluate, and account for litigation, claims, and assessments. Accordingly, the auditor's procedures with respect to such matters should include:

- Asking management about its policies and procedures for identifying, evaluating, and accounting for litigation, claims, and assessments
- Near the completion of field work, obtaining from management a description and evaluation of litigation, claims, and assessments as of the balance sheet date and during the period from the balance sheet date to the date the information is furnished
- Examining documents related to litigation, claims, and assessments, including correspondence and invoices from lawyers
- Requesting management to send a letter of audit inquiry to lawyers who were consulted concerning litigation, claims, and assessments
- Obtaining assurance from management—preferably in the representation letter, discussed later in this chapter—that all contingencies, including litigation, claims, and assessments, required to be disclosed by Statement of Financial Accounting Standards (SFAS) No. 5 have been disclosed and that all unasserted claims that counsel has advised management are probable of assertion and must be disclosed in accordance with SFAS No. 5 have been disclosed.

Procedures undertaken for different purposes, for example, reading minutes, contracts, agreements, leases, and correspondence with taxing authorities, also may disclose the existence of litigation, claims, and assessments.

(b)   Inquiry of an Entity's Lawyer

The auditor can ascertain readily the existence of litigation, claims, and assessments when the accounts include provisions for losses. Also, while making routine audit inquiries and performing tests for unrecorded and contingent liabilities, the auditor may become aware of events that are likely to give or have given rise to litigation, claims, or assessments. Certain events, however, such as patent infringement or price fixing, may be more difficult to detect in an audit. As noted in SAS No. 54, *Illegal Acts by Clients* (AU Section 317.06), and as discussed in Chapter 4, many laws or regulations "relate more to an entity's operating aspects than to its financial and accounting aspects, and their financial statement effect is indirect. An auditor ordinarily does not have sufficient basis for recognizing possible violations of such laws and regulations."

At about the same time that SAS No. 12 was issued, the American Bar Association (ABA) issued a "Statement of Policy Regarding Lawyers' Responses to Auditors' Requests for Information," which is reproduced in Appendix C to SAS No. 12. These professional standards require the auditor, management, and lawyer all to become involved in determining which litigation, claims, and assessments need to be disclosed. Management is the primary source of information concerning litigation, claims, and assessments; the lawyer is expected to corroborate to the auditor the completeness of the information management supplied to the auditor and the lawyer regarding pending or threatened litigation, claims, and assessments.

Specifically, SAS No. 12 (AU Section 337.09) requires, among other things, the following to be included in management's letter of audit inquiry to the lawyer:

- A list prepared by management (or a request by management that the lawyer prepare a list) that describes and evaluates pending or threatened litigation, claims, and assessments with respect to which the lawyer has been engaged. When management prepares the list, the lawyer's response should state that the list is complete (or identify any omissions) and comment on management's evaluation.

- A list prepared by management (the lawyer will not prepare this list) that describes and evaluates unasserted claims, if any, that management considers to be probable of assertion, and that, if asserted, would have at least a reasonable possibility of an unfavorable outcome, with respect to which the lawyer has been engaged. The lawyer's response will not comment on the completeness of the list, but should comment on management's descriptions and evaluations.

Figure 27.1 illustrates a "lawyer's letter" based on SAS No. 12 and related interpretations. It is drafted on the assumption that management prepared the list of asserted claims as well as the list of unasserted claims. Various circumstances may necessitate changes in the format or content of the letter. For example, AU Section 9337.06–.07 provides wording for use when management prepares the list of pending or threatened litigation but represents that there are no unasserted claims and assessments. AU Section 9337.10–.14 provides wording for use when management requests the lawyer to prepare the list of pending or threatened litigation and also rep-

Figure 27.1 Illustrative Letter of Inquiry to Legal Counsel

[Entity's Letterhead]
[Date]

[Lawyer's Name and Address]

In connection with an audit of our financial statements at [balance sheet date] and for the [period] then ended, management of the Company has prepared, and furnished to our auditors [name and address of auditors], a description and evaluation of certain contingencies, including those set forth below involving matters with respect to which you have been engaged and to which you have devoted substantive attention on behalf of the Company in the form of legal consultation or representation. These contingencies are regarded by management of the Company as material for this purpose [management may indicate a materiality limit if an understanding has been reached with the auditor].

Pending or Threatened Litigation (excluding unasserted claims)

[Ordinarily the information would include the following: (1) the nature of the litigation, (2) the progress of the case to date, (3) how management is responding or intends to respond to the litigation (for example, to contest the case vigorously or to seek an out-of-court settlement), and (4) an evaluation of the likelihood of an unfavorable outcome and an estimate, if one can be made, of the amount or range of potential loss.] Please furnish to our auditors such explanation, if any, that you consider necessary to supplement the foregoing information, including an explanation of those matters as to which your views may differ from those stated and an identification of the omission of any pending or threatened litigation, claims, and assessments or a statement that the list of such matters is complete.

Unasserted Claims and Assessments (considered by management to be probable of assertion, and that, if asserted, would have at least a reasonable possibility of an unfavorable outcome)

[Ordinarily management's information would include the following: (1) the nature of the matter, (2) how management intends to respond if the claim is asserted, and (3) an evaluation of the likelihood of an unfavorable outcome and an estimate, if one can be made, of the amount or range of potential loss.] Please furnish to our auditors such explanation, if any, that you consider necessary to supplement the foregoing information, including an explanation of those matters as to which your views may differ from those stated.

We understand that whenever, in the course of performing legal services for us with respect to a matter recognized to involve an unasserted possible claim or assessment that may call for financial statement disclosure, if you have formed a professional conclusion that we should disclose or consider disclosure concerning such possible claim or assessment, as a matter of professional responsibility to us, you will so advise us and will consult with us concerning the question of such disclosure and the applicable requirements of Statement of Financial Accounting Standards No. 5. Please specifically confirm to our auditors that our understanding is correct.

Figure 27.1 *(Continued)*

Your response should include matters that existed as of [balance sheet date] and during the period from that date to the effective date of your response.

Please specifically identify the nature of and reasons for any limitation on your response.

Our auditors expect to have the audit completed about [expected completion date]. They would appreciate receiving your reply by that date with a specified effective date no earlier than [ordinarily two weeks before expected completion date].

[The auditor may request management to inquire about additional matters, for example, unpaid or unbilled charges or specified information on certain contractually assumed obligations of the entity, such as guarantees of indebtedness of others.]

Very truly yours,

[Name and Title of Entity Executive]

resents that there are no unasserted claims and assessments.[1] In addition, if the letter of audit inquiry does not specifically inform the lawyer of management's specific assurance to the auditor that all unasserted claims have been disclosed that the lawyer has advised management are probable of assertion, the auditor should include this information in a separate letter to the lawyer.

The lawyer should be informed in management's letter of audit inquiry of management's assurance to the auditor concerning unasserted claims and assessments. When management believes that there are no unasserted claims and assessments, the following would be substituted for the third paragraph of the illustrative letter (and the heading above that paragraph):

Unasserted Claims and Assessments

We have represented to our auditors that there are no unasserted possible claims that you have advised us are probable of assertion and must be disclosed in accordance with Statement of Financial Accounting Standards No. 5.

---

[1] If management requests the lawyer to prepare the list that describes and evaluates pending or threatened litigation, claims, and assessments, the following would be substituted for the first and second paragraphs of the illustrative letter:

In connection with an audit of our financial statements as of [balance sheet date] and for the [period] then ended, please furnish our auditors [name and address of auditors], with the information requested below concerning certain contingencies involving matters with respect to which you have devoted substantive attention on behalf of the Company in the form of legal consultation or representation. [When a materiality limit has been established based on an understanding between management and the auditor, the following sentence should be added: This request is limited to contingencies amounting to [$] individually or items involving lesser amounts that exceed [$] in the aggregate.]

Regarding pending or threatened litigation, claims, and assessments, please include in your response: (1) the nature of each matter, (2) the progress of each matter to date, (3) how the Company is responding or intends to respond (for example, to contest the case vigorously or seek an out-of-court settlement), and (4) an evaluation of the likelihood of an unfavorable outcome and an estimate, if one can be made, of the amount or range of potential loss.

If the lawyer has formed a professional conclusion that management should consider disclosure of an unasserted possible claim or assessment, the lawyer will, as a matter of professional responsibility to the client, consult with management concerning the applicable requirements of SFAS No. 5. While the lawyer will not comment on the completeness of management's list of unasserted claims, he or she will, at management's request, confirm to the auditor this professional responsibility to management. As SAS No. 12, paragraph 13, notes, "this approach with respect to unasserted claims and assessments is necessitated by the public interest in protecting the confidentiality of lawyer-client communications."

Inquiries generally should be sent to all lawyers who have devoted substantive attention to a matter on behalf of the entity in the form of legal consultation or representation. Management may not wish, however, to send a letter to a lawyer whose only relationship with the entity was representation in a case that was closed during the year or to lawyers handling routine matters such as collection of overdue accounts. If the auditor is satisfied either that the case is closed and other auditing procedures do not indicate the lawyer was involved in other matters, or that lawyers were involved in routine matters only, the auditor may accede to management's request.

If management wishes to limit the response to matters that are considered individually or collectively material to the presentation of the financial statements, materiality limits included in the letter should be stated both individually and in the aggregate. Any such materiality limits should be established based on an understanding between management and the auditor and should recognize the linkage between the materiality of items that the lawyer need not report (which represents detection risk) and the overall materiality thresholds relating to the engagement. In considering the circularization of several lawyers, the auditor should consider the appropriate limits of materiality both individually and in the aggregate for the separate lawyers, regardless of whether the letter of audit inquiry includes materiality limits. Materiality guidelines included in the letter should give appropriate consideration to the manner in which the lawyer will deal with related claims, that is, whether claims that appear to be related, such as product liability claims related to one product that have been filed in more than one federal district court, will be grouped for purposes of the lawyer's response.

If the lawyer disclaims responsibility for informing the auditor of any changes in the information reported to the auditor from the date of the response to the date of the auditor's report, it may be necessary to send a supplemental letter of audit inquiry. Factors to be considered in determining the need for a supplemental letter of audit inquiry include the length of time between the date of the response and the date of the auditor's report, the number and significance of matters included in the lawyer's response, the probability of more current developments related to matters included in the lawyer's response, and the reliability of the entity's policies and procedures for identifying, evaluating, and accounting for litigation, claims, and assessments. The auditor may determine that a supplemental letter of inquiry is not necessary, even though the lawyer's response is dated considerably earlier than the auditor's report. In those circumstances, the auditor ordinarily should arrange for an oral update and should document it in the working papers.

The illustrative letter of audit inquiry includes a "response date" that, combined with proper timing in mailing letters of audit inquiry, is intended to minimize the need for supplemental letters of audit inquiry. Letters of audit inquiry should be mailed at a date that provides the lawyer sufficient time to meet the response date (two weeks is ordinarily sufficient time). The response date should allow sufficient time prior to the date of the audit report for the auditor to evaluate the response and make supplemental inquiries, if necessary.

Acceptable responses from lawyers to letters of audit inquiry and the procedures outlined above and in SAS No. 12 usually will provide sufficient competent evidential matter to satisfy the auditor concerning the accounting for and reporting of litigation, claims, and assessments. The auditor also should investigate, however, to the extent deemed appropriate in the circumstances, any information gained in the course of the engagement that indicates there may be material litigation, claims, and assessments that management or the lawyer has not disclosed.

In evaluating responses from lawyers, the auditor should consider whether there is any reason to doubt their professional qualifications and reputation. If, as will often be the case, the auditor is familiar with the lawyer's professional reputation, there would be no need to make specific inquiries in this regard. An auditor who is not familiar with a lawyer representing the entity in what appears to be a significant case may wish to inquire as to the lawyer's professional background, reputation, and standing in the legal and financial community and to consider information available in such legal publications as the *Martindale–Hubbell Law Directory*. Once satisfied in this regard, the auditor can accept the lawyer's opinion regarding a legal matter, unless it appears to be unreasonable.

(i) Acceptable Limitations on the Scope of Lawyers' Responses. Several types of limitations on the scope of a lawyer's response to a letter of audit inquiry are acceptable. These limitations, which the lawyer may indicate in the response by either a direct statement or a reference to the ABA Statement of Policy, include:

- Limiting the response to matters to which the lawyer has devoted substantive attention on behalf of management in the form of legal consultation or representation

- When the letter of inquiry is addressed to a law firm, excluding matters that have been communicated to an individual member or employee of the firm by reason of that individual's serving in the capacity of director or officer of the entity

- Limiting the response to matters that are considered, individually or collectively, to be material to the entity's financial statements (see the previous discussion of the need to provide the lawyer with materiality guidelines)

- Disclaiming any undertaking to advise the auditor of changes in the status of litigation, claims, and assessments since the date the lawyer began internal review procedures for purposes of preparing the response

Both audit inquiry letters and lawyers' responses may include explanatory language intended to emphasize that the letters do not constitute a waiver of the attorney–client privilege or the attorney work product privilege. An auditing interpretation of Section 337 of SAS No. 1 (AU Section 9337.28–.30) clarifies that use of such language does not create an audit scope limitation.

(ii) Responses Resulting in Scope Limitations.   Responses that indicate or imply that the lawyer is withholding information, if not remedied, ordinarily should be considered an audit scope limitation [SAS No. 79, *Reports on Audited Financial Statements* (AU Section 508.22 ff)]. For example, the lawyer may state that the reply is limited because of the policy of the law firm or the impracticability of reviewing the files, or for reasons not given. Normally, such limitations would be considered significant, since the auditor usually cannot evaluate the effect of withheld information.

A response indicating that the newness of a case precludes evaluating it, requires further consideration and might not provide sufficient evidence to support an unqualified opinion. The following examples of actual language from lawyers' letters, if related to material items that are not resolved, may constitute limitations on the scope of the engagement, requiring modification of the scope paragraph of the audit report, a separate paragraph (preceding the opinion paragraph) describing the limitation, and a qualified opinion:

- The claim has been received by this office only recently, and is being investigated. At this time it is not possible to predict the outcome of the litigation.

- This suit for declaratory judgment by the plaintiff presents some risk for the Bank depending upon the values assigned to parcels of realty transferred to the Bank to reduce a preexisting debt owed by the plaintiff to the Bank. We have not been supplied with sufficient information to determine whether a deficiency existed which warranted the note and mortgage obtained from the plaintiff. At present, we can only assume that the Bank was justified in obtaining this obligation.

(iii) Responses Requiring Further Management and Auditor Consideration. Inherent uncertainties may preclude a lawyer from indicating whether an unfavorable outcome of material litigation, claims, or assessments is likely or from estimating the amount or range of potential loss. The lawyer may not be able to respond because the factors influencing the likelihood of an unfavorable outcome are not within the competence of lawyers to judge, historical experience of the entity in similar litigation or the experience of other entities may not be relevant or available, or the amount or range of possible loss may vary widely at different stages of litigation. In those circumstances, which do not constitute scope limitations, the auditor should discuss with management the need to disclose the uncertain outcome in a note to the financial statements. (If management declines to make the disclosure, the auditor would have to qualify the report because of inadequate disclosure or express an adverse opinion.)

Responses from lawyers that the auditor initially believes may require accrual or disclosure may in some instances be resolved to the extent that accrual or disclosure is not necessary. In some instances, information may have been withheld that management can persuade the lawyer to furnish. In other instances, management may authorize the lawyer to investigate the matter more thoroughly, which could lead to a change in the lawyer's evaluation. Occasionally, the apparent problem is the lawyer's choice of language and can be remedied by the lawyer's revising the letter.

Lawyers sometimes use language that is not sufficiently clear as to the likelihood of a favorable outcome. Examples of that kind of language are provided in an interpretation of SAS No. 12 (AU Section 9337.22), as follows:

- This action involves unique characteristics wherein authoritative legal precedents do not seem to exist. We believe that the plaintiff will have serious problems establishing the company's liability under the act; nevertheless, if the plaintiff is successful, the award may be substantial.

- It is our opinion that the company will be able to assert meritorious defenses to this action. (The term "meritorious defenses" indicates that the entity's defenses will not be summarily dismissed by the court; it does not necessarily indicate counsel's opinion that the entity will prevail.)

- We believe the action can be settled for less than the damages claimed.

- We are unable to express an opinion as to the merits of the litigation at this time. The company believes there is absolutely no merit to the litigation. (If the entity's counsel, with the benefit of all relevant information, is unable to conclude that the likelihood of an unfavorable outcome is "remote," it is unlikely that management would be able to form a judgment to that effect.)

- In our opinion, the company has a substantial chance of prevailing in this action. (A "substantial chance," a "reasonable opportunity," and similar terms indicate more uncertainty than an opinion that the entity will prevail.)

The interpretation states that an auditor who is uncertain about the meaning of a lawyer's evaluation should request clarification either in a follow-up letter or in a conference with the lawyer and management, which should be documented appropriately. If the lawyer is still unable to give, either in writing or orally, an unequivocal evaluation of the likelihood of an unfavorable outcome, management should disclose that circumstance in the notes to the financial statements.

(c) Inside Counsel

The duties of an inside counsel may vary from handling specialized litigation to acting as general counsel with supervisory authority in all legal matters, including the selection of outside counsel to represent or advise management on specific matters.

If inside counsel acts as general counsel, evidential matter gathered by and obtained from inside counsel may provide the necessary corroboration for the auditor. Letters of audit inquiry to outside counsel may be appropriate if inside general counsel has retained outside counsel to represent or advise management on certain matters. Information provided by inside counsel is not a substitute for information that outside counsel refuses to furnish.

(d) Changes or Resignations of Lawyers

The legal profession's Code of Professional Responsibility requires that, in some circumstances, lawyers must resign if a client has disregarded their advice concerning accounting for and reporting of litigation, claims, and assessments. The auditor should be alert for such circumstances and should ensure that he or she understands the reasons for the change or resignation of lawyers, and also should consider the implications for financial statement disclosures concerning litigation, claims, and assessments.

27.4 MANAGEMENT REPRESENTATIONS

The auditor is required by SAS No. 19, *Client Representations* (AU Section 333), to obtain a representation letter from management confirming that it is responsible for the financial statements and has made all pertinent information available to the auditor, and stating its belief in the accuracy and completeness of that information.[2] The representation letter provides written evidence that the auditor has made certain inquiries of management; ordinarily it documents oral responses given to the auditor, thus reducing the possibility of misunderstandings. A representation letter is one kind of competent evidence, but it is not a substitute for the application of auditing procedures that are necessary to provide the auditor with a reasonable basis for forming an opinion.

(a) Written Representations

The representation letter illustrated in Figure 27.2 incorporates the written representations that the auditor ordinarily should obtain. The letter should be tailored to the specific circumstances of the engagement and the nature and basis of presentation of the financial statements. For example, if the auditor is reporting on consolidated financial statements, the written representations obtained from the parent company's management should specify that they pertain to the consolidated financial statements. If comparative financial statements are presented, the representation letter should cover all years and periods presented. Representation letters in compliance audits (see Chapter 32) may cover matters relating to laws and regulations affecting the entity.

Written representations relating to management's knowledge or intent should be obtained when the auditor believes they are necessary to complement other auditing procedures. For example, even if the auditor has performed tests for unrecorded liabilities and has not detected any, written representation should be obtained to document that management has no knowledge of any liabilities that have not been recorded. Liabilities known to management but not accrued, through oversight, might be brought to the auditor's attention in this manner. Such a written representation, however, does not relieve the auditor of responsibility for planning the audit to identify material unrecorded liabilities. Information may be overlooked unintentionally or withheld intentionally from the auditor. Accordingly, the auditor should still perform all the usual tests to corroborate management's representations.

In some cases, evidential matter to corroborate management's plans or intentions is limited. For example, the auditor may not be able to obtain sufficient information through other auditing procedures to corroborate management's plan or intent to dis-

---

[2] At the time of this writing, a revision of SAS No. 19 is expected to be issued shortly. This section, including the illustrative letter in Figure 27.2, reflects the substance of the revised statement.

Figure 27.2   Illustrative Management Representation Letter

[The letter should be dated as of the date it is signed. That date should be no earlier than the date of the auditor's report and no later than the report release date.]

[Name of Auditors]
[Address]

Gentlemen:

In connection with your audit of the [consolidated] financial statements of [name of company] as of [date] and for the [period of audit] for the purpose of expressing an opinion as to whether such financial statements present fairly, in all material respects, the financial position, results of operations, and cash flows of [name of company] in conformity with generally accepted accounting principles [other comprehensive basis of accounting], we confirm, to the best of our knowledge and belief, as of __/__/__, the date of your report, the following representations made to you during your audit.

Certain representations in this letter are described as being limited to those matters that are material. Solely for the purpose of preparing this letter, the term "material," when used in this letter, means any items referred to in this letter, either individually or collectively in the aggregate, involving potential amounts of more than [$_____]. These amounts are not intended to represent the materiality threshold for financial reporting and disclosure purposes. Notwithstanding this, an item is considered material, regardless of size, if it involves an omission or misstatement of accounting information that, in the light of surrounding circumstances, makes it probable that the judgment of a reasonable person relying on the information would have been changed or influenced by the omission or misstatement.

- We are responsible for the fair presentation in the [consolidated] financial statements of financial position, results of operations, and cash flows in conformity with generally accepted accounting principles [or other comprehensive basis of accounting]. The financial statements and related notes include all disclosures necessary for a fair presentation of the financial position, results of operations, and cash flows of the company in conformity with generally accepted accounting principles [or other comprehensive basis of accounting] and disclosures otherwise required to be included therein by the laws and regulations to which the company is subject.

- We have made available to you all financial and accounting records and related data and all minutes of the meetings of shareholders, directors, and committees of directors [or summaries of actions of recent meetings for which minutes have not yet been prepared]. The most recent meetings held were: [state by group and date].

Figure 27.2   *(Continued)*

- There are no material transactions that have not been properly recorded in the accounting records underlying the financial statements.

- There has been no:

    Fraud involving management or those employees who have significant roles in the company's internal control.

    Fraud involving others that could have a material effect on the financial statements.

    Violations or possible violations of laws or regulations whose effects should be considered for disclosure in the financial statements or as a basis for recording a loss contingency.

    We understand the term "fraud" to mean those matters described in Statement on Auditing Standards No. 82.

- There have been no communications from regulatory agencies concerning noncompliance with or deficiencies in financial reporting practices that could have a material effect on the financial statements in the event of noncompliance.

- The company has complied with all aspects of debt and other contractual agreements that would have a material effect on the financial statements in the event of noncompliance.

- The company has satisfactory title to all owned assets. All liens, encumbrances, and security interests requiring disclosure in the financial statements have been properly disclosed.

- Provision, when material, has been made to reduce excess or obsolete inventories to their estimated net realizable value.

- There are no material liabilities or gain or loss contingencies that are required to be accrued or disclosed by Statement of Financial Accounting Standards No. 5 that have not been accrued or disclosed. There are no unasserted claims or assessments that our legal counsel has advised us are probable of assertion and must be disclosed in accordance with that Statement.

- Commitments for future purchases are for quantities not in excess of anticipated requirements and at prices that will not result in loss. Provision has been made for any material loss to be sustained in the fulfillment of, or from the inability to fulfill, any sales commitments.

- We have no plans or intentions that may materially affect the carrying value or classification of assets and liabilities.

Figure 27.2   *(Continued)*

- The following have been recorded or disclosed properly in the financial statements [if none, include under a separate item with the introduction "There are no . . ."]:

    Related party transactions and related amounts receivable or payable, including sales, purchases, loans, transfers, leasing arrangements, and guarantees. (We understand the term "related party" to include those entities described in Statement of Financial Accounting Standards No. 57.)

    Capital stock repurchase options or agreements or capital stock reserved for options, warrants, conversions, or other requirements.

    Arrangements with financial institutions involving compensating balances, arrangements involving restrictions on cash balances and lines of credit, or similar arrangements.

    Agreements to repurchase assets previously sold.

    Financial instruments with off-balance-sheet risk and financial instruments with concentrations of credit risk.

    Guarantees, whether written or oral, under which the company is contingently liable to a bank or other lending institution.

    Estimates for which both (a) it is at least reasonably possible that the estimates will change in the near future (i.e., within one year from the date of the financial statements) due to one or more future confirming events, and (b) the effect of the change would be material to the financial statements.

    Concentrations that make the company vulnerable to the risk of a near-term severe impact and for which it is at least reasonably possible that events that could cause the severe impact will occur in the near term. For the purpose of this letter, a "severe impact" is a significant financially disruptive effect on the normal functioning of the company.

[Add special-purpose representations that may be required in this letter in certain circumstances, e.g., a statement that a valuation allowance against deferred tax assets at the balance sheet date represents management's best estimate based on the weight of available evidence as prescribed in SFAS No. 109 or a positive statement that no such allowance is necessary.]

No events have occurred subsequent to the balance sheet date that would require adjustment to, or disclosure in, the financial statements.

_____

[Name and title of chief executive officer]

_____

[Name and title of chief financial officer]

continue a line of business. In that situation, the auditor should obtain a written representation from management to provide evidence of that plan or intent.

Figure 27.3 contains examples of situations that may suggest the need for modifications of the letter illustrated in Figure 27.2 or for special representations because they relate to management's knowledge or intent or because corroborating evidential matter is limited.

It would be unusual for the auditor to obtain a representation letter that did not include one or more modifications or special representations to cover individual entity circumstances. In addition, other matters may be applicable to entities in specialized industries; for example, it may be appropriate for management to acknowledge responsibility for important valuation accounts (such as loan loss reserves for a bank) or other industry-specific matters (such as revenue recognition in the software industry).

(i) Materiality.   Paragraph 5 of SAS No. 19 (AU Section 333.05) states that "management's representations may be limited to matters that are considered either individually or collectively material to the financial statements, provided management and the auditor have reached an understanding on the limits of materiality for this purpose." The authors believe that management should specify the agreed-on materiality limits in the representation letter (language for this purpose is included in the illustrative letter in Figure 27.2). The materiality limits may give recognition to different quantitative measures of materiality for various groups of accounts (e.g., amounts that affect assets, liabilities, shareholders' equity, or net income). Inclusion of a qualitative materiality criterion is advisable in all management representation letters, also illustrated in the letter in Figure 27.2.

(ii) Definitions.   Certain terms used in the letter in Figure 27.2 are described in the authoritative literature, for example, fraud [SAS No. 82 (AU Section 316.03–.05)], related party transactions [SFAS No. 57 (Accounting Standards Section R36.101)], and contingency [SFAS No. 5 (Accounting Standards Section C59.101)]. The auditor may wish to furnish the applicable literature to management and request acknowledgment in the representation letter that management has received it.

(iii) Dating and Signing.   The representation letter should be addressed to the auditor and should be dated no earlier than the date of the auditor's report (discussed later), but no later than the report release date. In any event, the letter should include a statement that management has made the representations as of the date of the auditor's report. If there is an inordinate delay in issuing the report, the auditor should consider asking management to update its written representations. An auditing interpretation of AU Section 333 (AU Section 9333.06) clarifies that the auditor should obtain written representations from current management on all periods covered in the auditor's report, even when current management was not present during the period under audit. Current management's inability or unwillingness to provide such representations would constitute a limitation on the scope of the audit sufficient to preclude expression of an unqualified opinion, as discussed below.

Representation letters ordinarily should be signed by both the chief executive and chief financial officers. Other members of management may sign the letter instead, however, if the auditor is satisfied that they are responsible for and knowledgeable

Figure 27.3   Management Representation Letter—Illustrative Situations Suggesting the Need for Modifications or Special Representations

1. Financial circumstances are strained and an assertion stating management's intentions and the entity's ability to continue as a going concern is considered relevant.
2. Management is required to justify a change in accounting.
3. Unusual considerations are involved in determining the application of the equity method of accounting for investments (e.g., level of ownership and ability to exercise significant influence).
4. Disclosure of interim financial information is required in the notes to the financial statements and separate representations have not been obtained previously during interim review procedures.
5. Unusual considerations are involved in determining the adequacy of collateral supporting receivables.
6. A decline in value of debt or equity securities classified as either available-for-sale or held-to-maturity is considered temporary.
7. Management intends to, and has the ability to, hold to maturity, debt securities classified as held-to-maturity.
8. Management has estimated the fair value of significant financial instruments that do not have readily determinable market value.
9. The recoverability of material expenditures (e.g., start-up costs or marketing costs) that have been deferred to future periods is uncertain.
10. Management plans to sell or abandon facilities or has estimated the effects of discontinuing certain operations.
11. There is a possibility that the value of specific significant long-lived assets may be impaired and the recovery of their carrying costs is uncertain.
12. The entity has the ability to refinance short-term debt on a long-term basis and management intends to either do so or not do so.
13. Percentage-of-completion accounting and the related cost estimates are significant in determining earnings.
14. Government contracts are a significant portion of the entity's business and are subject to not-yet-formalized change orders or price redeterminations that have been accounted for based on management's estimates.
15. Management intends to either continue to make or not make frequent amendments to its employee benefit plans, which may affect the amortization period of prior service cost, or has expressed a substantive commitment to increase benefits in the future, which may affect the amount of benefit obligations.
16. Employee layoffs that would otherwise lead to a curtailment of a benefit plan are intended to be temporary.
17. Management does not intend to compensate for the elimination of postretirement benefits by granting an increase in pension benefits.
18. Management is unable to determine the possibility of a withdrawal liability in a multiemployer benefit plan.
19. Management has the ability to implement and intends to implement the tax strategies used to support realization of a deferred tax asset, unless the need to do so is eliminated in future years.
20. An analysis of future taxable income includes assumptions for which management is responsible.
21. A valuation allowance against deferred tax assets at the balance sheet date represents management's best estimate based on the weight of available evidence as prescribed in SFAS No. 109 or management does not consider such an allowance necessary.
22. Management has a specific intention to reinvest the undistributed earnings of a foreign subsidiary.
23. Tax-exempt bonds issued have retained their tax-exempt status.

about the matters covered by the representations. A chief executive officer who does not participate in making accounting decisions may express an unwillingness to sign the standard representation letter. A separate letter indicating reliance on the chief financial officer's representations, and no contrary knowledge, would be acceptable.

(iv) Scope Limitations.   In rare instances, management may refuse to furnish a written representation that the auditor believes is essential or may refuse to sign the representation letter. SAS No. 19 (AU Section 333.11) notes that either refusal constitutes a limitation on the scope of the audit sufficient to preclude an unqualified opinion (AU Section 508.22 ff). An auditor should consider whether management's refusal to furnish a written representation affects the reliability of other management representations. Executives are expected to understand their legal and ethical responsibilities for financial statement representations. Thus, they also should understand that the representation letter only specifies some of those responsibilities but does not increase them. Refusal to sign the letter must be taken as a signal either of withheld evidence or of inadequately understood responsibilities; either destroys the basis for an unqualified opinion.

(v) Representations from Others.   In certain circumstances, the auditor may want to obtain representation letters from persons other than the entity's management. For example, an auditor of a subsidiary but not of its parent company (referred to as a "secondary auditor") may want to obtain representations from management or the auditor of the parent company regarding information that might require adjustment or disclosure in the subsidiary's financial statements.

Refusal by the parent company or principal auditor to furnish the written representations the secondary auditor believes are essential to the audit of the subsidiary constitutes a scope limitation, as described above. A representation letter from the parent company to a secondary auditor is illustrated in Figure 27.4.

(b)   Representations in Other than Audit Engagements

AICPA professional standards currently require CPAs to obtain written management representations when performing attestation services, including certain prospective financial information engagements, as discussed in Chapter 31. In addition, it is good practice to obtain written representations from management when performing other services, such as reviews of annual financial statements or limited reviews of interim financial information. Generally, the guidance for written audit representations can be modified appropriately for nonaudit services.

27.5   SUMMARIZING MISSTATEMENTS AND EVALUATING THE AUDIT FINDINGS

Auditors frequently maintain a summary of the audit differences they find in the course of the various procedures performed throughout the audit. The summary includes misstatements resulting from either errors or fraud, as defined in Chapter 4. Thus, misstatements include unintentional mistakes, unreasonable accounting estimates, intentional misrepresentations, and intentional or unintentional misapplica-

**Figure 27.4   Illustrative Representation Letter from Parent Company
to Secondary Auditor**

[Date—no earlier than the date of the
auditor's report but no later than the report
release date]

[Name of Auditors]
[Address]

Gentlemen:

We understand you will be reporting on your audit of the financial statements of [name of
subsidiary] as of [date] and for the [period of audit]. This is to advise you that, to the best
of our knowledge and belief, there are no related party transactions, including accounts
receivable or payable, sales, purchases, loans, transfers, leasing arrangements, and
guarantees, either recorded in the books and records of [name of parent company] or not
recorded in them (such as loan guarantees), that should be considered for possible
adjustment or disclosure in the financial statements of [name of subsidiary] as of [date]
and for the [period of audit], except as follows:

Amounts receivable [payable]
at [date]   _____

Guarantees, whether written
or oral, of amounts receivable
[payable] at [date]   _____

Sales [purchases] for the
[period of audit]   _____

Rental income [expense] for
the [period of audit]   _____

[Add other representations that may be required in this letter in certain circumstances.]

_____
[Name and title of chief financial officer of parent company]

tions of GAAP. Ordinarily, management makes adjustments for some items, leaving
only the unadjusted differences for the auditor to evaluate.[3] Normally the summary
includes items arising in the current year, but, as discussed below, it also may include
waived adjustments from prior years' audits that affect the current year's financial
statements.

The summary serves as the central means of evaluating whether the evidence the
auditor examined supports the conclusion that the financial statements are presented
fairly, in all material respects, in conformity with generally accepted accounting principles. The auditor should be sure that the items on the summary, either individually
or in the aggregate, do not cause the financial statements to be materially misstated.
If they do, either the financial statements will have to be revised by management, or

_____

[3] The auditor's responsibilities when a potential audit adjustment is or may be the result of fraud are
described in Chapter 4. The discussion here is limited to considering whether an audit adjustment is
necessary.

the auditor will have to express a qualified opinion or an adverse opinion because of departures from GAAP. Usually the auditor and management are able to reach agreement so that a qualified or an adverse opinion is not necessary.

As part of evaluating the audit findings, the auditor makes final materiality judgments to assess whether unadjusted misstatements disclosed by the audit make the financial statements materially misleading; and whether audit risk relating to the individual audit objectives has been limited to an acceptably low level for each account balance and class of transactions. As a result of changes in circumstances, final materiality judgments may be based on materiality thresholds that are lower than those that formed the basis for preliminary materiality judgments. The lower materiality thresholds may cause the assessments of the risk of material misstatement to be higher than those used in planning substantive tests. In response to those higher assessments, the auditor may need to consider whether additional substantive tests are required.

(a)   Categories of Misstatements to Be Evaluated

Authoritative auditing literature addresses the auditor's consideration of misstatements. SAS No. 39, *Audit Sampling* (AU Section 350.30), requires the auditor to consider "projected misstatement results for all audit sampling applications and all known misstatements from nonsampling applications" in the aggregate in evaluating whether the financial statements as a whole may be materially misstated. Projected misstatement is discussed in Chapter 16. SAS No. 47, *Audit Risk and Materiality in Conducting an Audit* (AU Section 312.34), expands on this concept by stating that "the auditor should aggregate misstatements that the entity has not corrected in a way that enables him or her to consider whether, in relation to individual amounts, subtotals, or totals in the financial statements, they materially misstate the financial statements taken as a whole." With regard to the amounts to be aggregated, SAS No. 47 states:

> The aggregation of misstatements should include the auditor's best estimate of the total misstatements in the account balances or classes of transactions that he or she has examined (hereafter referred to as likely misstatement), not just the amount of misstatements specifically identified (hereafter referred to as known misstatement). . . . Projected misstatement [from audit sampling, if used], along with the results of other substantive tests, contributes to the auditor's assessment of likely misstatement in the balance or class. (para. 35)

As defined in SAS No. 47, likely misstatement includes unreasonable differences between accounting estimates as determined by management and the amounts supported by audit evidence. SAS No. 47 states:

> Since no one accounting estimate can be considered accurate with certainty, the auditor recognizes that a difference between an estimated amount best supported by the audit evidence and the estimated amount included in the financial statements may be reasonable, and such difference would not be considered to be a likely misstatement. However, if the auditor believes the estimated amount included in the financial statements is unreasonable, he or she should treat the difference between that estimate and the closest reasonable estimate as a likely misstatement and aggregate it with other likely misstatements. (para. 36)

The auditor also should consider the likelihood of undetected misstatements, which could cause the financial statements to be misstated. Undetected misstatements may result from sampling risk; from not examining items or accumulating misstatements that fall below an established materiality threshold; or from materiality limits provided to lawyers, below which a response is not required (see discussion earlier in this chapter).

(b)   Preparing and Using the Summary

The exact form of the summary used to aggregate misstatements, and even what it is called, varies in practice. Its complexity depends on the complexity of the engagement (e.g., extensive subsidiary operations may require a more complex format) and circumstances (e.g., if significant misstatements are expected or many accounts are considered potentially troublesome, a more structured, formal format may be required). Additionally, professional standards may require specific documentation.

The summary is typically a multiple-column worksheet on which the auditor records the nature of misstatements identified, for example, descriptions of known misstatements from nonsampling procedures and projected misstatements from sampling procedures in the inventory accounts. The amount in question is then "spread" to show its impact on assets, liabilities and owners' equity, and income, such as a failure to record on a timely basis $10,000 of inventory received before year-end that might result in a $10,000 understatement of assets and a $10,000 understatement of liabilities.

A single document that summarizes and accumulates misstatements identified in all the accounts makes it easier for the auditor to evaluate the overall audit findings. For example, a review of the summary may reveal that individually immaterial misstatements taken together have a material impact on income or some other financial statement element. The summary is helpful in comparing the results of auditing procedures with materiality at the account level, for major groups of accounts (such as current assets), and for the financial statements as a whole. Figure 27.5 illustrates a summary of adjustments.

(c)   Aggregating and Netting Misstatements

The issue of aggregating and netting misstated amounts in the process of finalizing the audit opinion is complicated and somewhat controversial. The controversy centers around the appropriateness of netting or offsetting certain misstatements.

In aggregating misstatements affecting the income statement or balance sheet, likely misstatements relating to each line item are considered together to determine whether the line item is not materially misstated. The more "cushion" that exists between the total of likely misstatements and a larger amount that the auditor considers "material" for the line item, the higher the auditor's level of assurance that the item is not materially misstated.

One technique used in practice is to aggregate misstatements within groupings of financial statement components and to assess materiality at that level and at each successively higher logical subdivision of the financial statements. For example, misstatements found in cash and short-term liquid assets might be aggregated to determine whether the sum of those assets, which enters into the computation of the

Figure 27.5 Summary of Adjustments

Client: PSR Corporation
Period: 12/31/X0
Subject: Summary of Unadjusted Differences

W/P Reference	Description	Assets Current	Assets Noncurrent	Liabilities Current	Liabilities Noncurrent	Equity	Known Misstatements(1)	Projected(2)	Estimated(3)	Total	Operating Activities	Investing Activities	Financing Activities
		BALANCE SHEET IMPACT (DR<CR>)					**INCOME STATEMENT IMPACT (DR<CR>)**				**CASH FLOWS STAT. IMPACT**		
41.2	Checks to vendors issued in 19X0 but recorded in 19X1	(4,000)		4,000							(4,000)		
53.2	Additional provision for uncollectible accounts	(39,000)							39,000	39,000			
53.25	Sales invoice pricing misstatements (underbillings)	34,000						(34,000)		(34,000)			
55.2	Physical inventory count adjustments	38,000					(38,000)			(38,000)			
55.2	Inventory pricing misstatements	76,000						(76,000)		(76,000)			
71.2	Unrecorded liabilities adjustments (invoices received after cutoff date)	43,000		(63,000)			20,000			20,000			
72.25	Warranty accruals understatement			(50,000)					50,000	50,000			
93.1	Dividends paid treated as operating rather than as financing activities										15,000		(15,000)
Total Pretax Misstatements		**$148,000**	**$0**	**($109,000)**	**$0**	**($39,000)**	**($18,000)**	**($110,000)**	**$89,000**	**($39,000)**	**$11,000**		**($15,000)**
Tax Effects and Misstatements:													
Estimated tax impact of unadjusted misstatements				(14,000)		14,000	6,000	38,000	(30,000)	14,000			
Total After Tax Misstatements		**$148,000**	**$0**	**($123,000)**	**$0**	**($25,000)**	**($12,000)**	**($72,000)**	**$59,000**	**($25,000)**			
Balance Sheet Amounts:		11,193,000	22,438,000	5,780,000	10,354,000	17,497,000							
Percentage of Misstatements to Balance Sheet Amounts		1.32%	0.00%	-2.13%	0.00%	-0.14%							
Cash Flows Statement Totals											3,214,000	614,000	728,000
Percentage of Misstatements to Cash Flows Statement Totals											0.34%	0.00%	-2.06%

Pretax Income 3,671,000
Percentage of Pretax Misstatements to Pretax Income -1.06%
After Tax Income 2,569,000
Percentage of After Tax Misstatements to After Tax Income -0.97%

1 Misstatements specifically identified in nonsampling applications.
2 Misstatements relating to the application of audit sampling techniques (includes known misstatements identified in samples examined).
3 Misstatements determined by the difference between the entity's accounting estimate and the closest reasonable amount supported by the audit evidence.

"quick ratio," is reasonable. Other current assets such as accounts receivable might then be added and another assessment made at the current asset level. Finally, these results would be combined with a similar series of aggregations for noncurrent assets to evaluate reported assets in total. The auditor's ultimate objective, however, is to obtain reasonable assurance that the financial statements as a whole—not individual line items or groupings of line items—are not materially misstated.

The way items are added together or offset against each other can significantly affect evaluations of materiality. Some items or events are more significant than others, implying that they should be evaluated individually while others may be evaluated in groups. For example, many auditors consider it inappropriate to aggregate or offset an individually immaterial overstatement of cash with a misstatement in an unrelated account. The inherent risk associated with the cash account, as well as the potential for determining its value precisely, often precludes an auditor from treating misstatements of cash in the same manner as misstatements in other accounts. Immaterial inventory misstatements and immaterial receivable misstatements, however, often are offset in determining whether the financial statements as a whole may be materially misstated.

Netting separate items to determine the amount to be compared with materiality raises several questions. Is it acceptable, for example, to net the effect of an error against the effect of a change in accounting principle? Clearly, the answer is no. Accounting Principles Board Opinion No. 20, paragraph 38 (Accounting Standards Section A06.133), requires that materiality be considered for the separate effects of each accounting change. Also, netting individually material items to obtain an immaterial total would result in inadequate financial statement disclosure. It is acceptable, however, to net immaterial misstatements in a particular component of financial statements or in related accounts.

(d) Quantitative Aspects of Materiality Judgments

The question of how large a "difference" must be before it is material has never been definitively answered in the accounting and auditing literature. Many auditors have developed rules of thumb for setting materiality thresholds, such as some percentage of one or more financial statement totals. Net income is a commonly cited base for assessing materiality, but there are others, such as total assets, equity, or revenues, as well as trends in each of these. As long as investors continue to pay attention to net income in their investment assessments, however, an audit standard of materiality based on net income (or the trend of net income) is likely to be widely used.

A commonly used figure for materiality is 5 percent of the chosen base. That is, if the item is within 5 percent of what it might otherwise be, the difference may be immaterial. Obviously, any rule of thumb, such as 5 percent, must be used with a great deal of caution and careful judgment. Qualitative considerations, as discussed below, can render such a range too broad. Most studies of the subject have generally concluded that a single dollar amount or percentage is not appropriate in all situations. Five to ten percent of net income is frequently used, but is affected in individual cases by nonquantitative criteria. In addition, many auditors assign greater significance to differences that change the entity's trend of earnings than to those that do not.

Having established that there may be more than one level of materiality—for example, one level for income statement effects and a higher level in absolute terms for balance sheet effects—the auditor should recognize that a misstatement that affects both statements should be compared with the smaller materiality level in determining whether the misstatement requires correction or can be "waived" as immaterial. For instance, a misstated accrual may not materially affect the balance sheet, but may materially affect reported expenses and consequently net income. In that situation, the lower income statement threshold would determine materiality. Misclassifications that affect only balance sheet accounts would be material if they exceeded the balance sheet materiality threshold.

(e) Qualitative Considerations in Evaluating Misstatements

The types of misstatements found may influence the auditor's evaluation of the audit results. Paragraph 34 of SAS No. 82 (AU Section 316.34) states that the auditor should consider whether misstatements may be indicative of fraud. Because fraud is intentional, its implications for the audit extend beyond the direct monetary effect, and the auditor should consider those implications in evaluating the audit results. Chapter 4 discusses actions the auditor should take, including disclosures, when fraud may have a material effect on the financial statements.

In many cases, known misstatements in an account discovered by applying either sampling or nonsampling procedures are corrected in the accounts and entail no further consideration. Misstatements that arise from projecting the results of a sample to the population are more difficult to deal with. While the summary of adjustments should include projected misstatements, correcting the financial statements for them is difficult in practice, since sampling does not help identify all of the specific components, such as the individual accounts receivable, that may be misstated. Additionally, according to sampling theory, the projected misstatement is not the "true" misstatement, but only a presumably close approximation. Therefore, correcting the financial statements for nonspecific "projected" misstatements may create a risk that actual misstatements will be introduced into the financial statements. Sample results may be used, however, to identify aspects of an account (e.g., inventory) that deserve special attention by management, such as repricing or recounting. If such procedures are performed, the auditor will need to adjust the projected misstatement amount based on the results of the procedures.

Evaluating some types of misstatements involves distinguishing between "hard" and "soft" misstatements and properly characterizing the "soft" ones. A mathematical mistake, omission of a segment of inventory from the total inventory, or an accounting principle misapplication, whether discovered by sampling or nonsampling procedures, may be referred to as a "hard" misstatement. In these cases, the auditor knows there is a problem and can calculate the misstatement. If potential misstatements are based on judgments or estimates that cannot be calculated precisely but must be estimated, they are described as "soft."

Accounting and auditing are not exact sciences, and much judgment often goes into developing the account balances presented in the financial statements. The auditor must evaluate accounts, such as the allowance for uncollectible accounts receivable and liability for product warranties, that are based on estimates and are not subject to absolute determination. (The auditor's responsibility to evaluate management's estimates is discussed in Section 15.4, Testing Accounting Judgments and Estimates.) Using methods that are appropriate in the circumstances but are not exactly the same ones management used, the auditor may develop an estimate that differs from management's. The auditor should develop such estimates carefully and compare them with management's estimates to determine whether management's estimates are reasonable. Those considered unreasonable should be included with other likely misstatements and evaluated, and those deemed to be reasonable should be excluded from likely misstatement.

Sometimes the auditor may not be able to arrive at a single estimated amount, but may establish a range of "reasonableness"; if management's estimate falls within that range, no misstatement should be included on the summary. If management's estimate falls outside that range, the auditor should enter an item representing the difference between management's estimate and the nearest point in the range. For example, if management established a product warranty liability for $150,000 and the auditor, by analyzing past trends and the experience of other entities in similar circumstances, established a reasonable range of product warranty liability of between $200,000 and $300,000, the auditor might include on the summary $50,000 ($200,000 − $150,000) for possible adjustment by management. This would be a "soft" misstatement; only if the auditor knew the liability must exceed $200,000 could the difference in estimates be called a "hard" or "known" misstatement.

The Commission on Auditors' Responsibilities (also known as the Cohen Commission), in its 1978 *Report, Conclusions, and Recommendations*, noted that "the auditor may make many separate evaluations of the appropriateness of accounting principles selected and estimates made by management. On viewing the financial statements as a whole, the auditor may find that most or all of the selections or estimates made by management had the effect of increasing (or decreasing) earnings and that the overall result is a misleading picture of the entity's earning power or liquidity" (p. 21). SAS No. 47, *Audit Risk and Materiality in Conducting an Audit* (AU Section 312.36), addresses that possibility and suggests that "the auditor should also consider whether the difference between estimates best supported by the audit evidence and the estimates included in the financial statements, which are individually reasonable, indicates a possible bias on the part of the entity's management. For example, if each accounting estimate included in the financial statements was individually reasonable, but the effect of the difference between each estimate and the estimate best supported by the audit evidence was to increase income, the auditor should reconsider the estimates taken as a whole."

Other qualitative factors also may influence the auditor's response to likely misstatements in the financial statements. These factors may warrant consideration that goes beyond the quantitative significance of the misstatements. Following are examples of factors that may cause the auditor greater concern and prompt other reactions than the quantitative amounts themselves might indicate:

- *Business conditions*: In a weak economy or in an entity with a weak financial condition, for instance, materiality thresholds sometimes are lowered since the entity's future may rest on investors' and creditors' evaluations of the current financial position and recent trends.

- *Contractual arrangements*: Debt covenants, buy-sell agreements, and union contracts may be geared to various financial statement elements or relationships (such as the current ratio).

- *Cause of the misstatement*: Misapplications of GAAP (e.g., recording a purchase of a business as a pooling of interests or failing to accrue vacation pay or product warranties) may have possible long-term effects the auditor should assess, since correcting the misstatement later may erode investors' confidence in the entity's financial reporting.

- *Situations in which the "investor-based" materiality rule is difficult to apply*: For entities such as privately owned companies, trusts, and others, the auditor may need to consider who are the likely users of the financial statements and their interests, and designate a materiality level appropriate for their needs. Special user needs may tighten customary materiality standards.

- *Susceptibility of an account to misstatement*: Misstatements in the cash and capital accounts are generally unexpected and may warrant further investigation if discovered. The susceptibility of cash and other liquid assets to misuse or misappropriation should naturally heighten auditor concern about likely misstatements in these accounts.

- *Trends in financial statement components*: While it may be unrealistic to use a materiality standard as tight as a small fraction of the yearly change in net income or other financial statement components, longer-range trends or averages of balances or components (e.g., "normal income") may serve as useful signals to which users react. Consequently, auditors should be sensitive to departures from trends or normal expectations. Additionally, in an entity with a stable earnings history, smaller variations in cash flow, income, or other financial statement components may have more impact than in a less stable business environment where wider fluctuations are more common.

(f) Treatment of Prior-Year Waived Adjustments

An issue that often arises in assessing materiality is the treatment in the current year of prior-year waived adjustments. For example, the auditor may have waived a known overstatement of $10,000 in ending inventory and income in 19X1, caused perhaps by errors in pricing the inventory, on the grounds that the misstatement was not material. The overstatement of the 19X1 ending inventory and income will flow through to 19X2 income as an overstatement of cost of sales and an understatement of income. The issue in this case is this: In considering misstatements affecting income in the 19X2 financial statements, should the auditor include the $10,000 understatement of 19X2 income caused by the waived adjustment of the 19X1 misstatement?

Some auditors believe that prior-year waived adjustments should be ignored in considering likely misstatements in the current year; in effect, the "correct" beginning 19X2 inventory in the above example is the 19X1 ending inventory, with the misstatement in it. Since it was waived, those auditors treat the misstatement as not existing after 19X1 and consider that 19X2 starts with a "clean slate." Other auditors believe that the reversal in 19X2 of the 19X1 misstatement should be considered in assessing likely misstatements in 19X2.

The issue becomes even more complex when unadjusted misstatements, instead of reversing in the following year as in the above example, build up. Assume that the auditor determines that the estimated warranty liability at the end of 19X1 and warranty expense for 19X1 are understated by $15,000 because management made an unreasonable estimate. The auditor waived the adjustment because the amount was not material to either the balance sheet or the income statement. In the course of the audit of the 19X2 financial statements, the auditor determines that the estimated warranty liability at December 31, 19X2, is understated by $35,000—an additional $20,000. In assessing the materiality of the misstatement, the auditor may determine that neither the $35,000 cumulative misstatement on the balance sheet nor the $20,000 impact on current-year income is material and again waive the adjustment. This may continue for several years. At some point, the accumulated misstatement on the balance sheet will become material, and an adjustment will be necessary if the financial statements are to be presented fairly in conformity with GAAP. The resulting adjustment may be so large that it will produce a material misstatement in that year's income statement.

SAS No. 47 provides only the broadest guidance on this topic, stating merely that "if the auditor believes that there is an unacceptably high risk that the current period's financial statements may be materially misstated when those prior-period likely misstatements that affect the current period's financial statements are considered along with likely misstatements arising in the current period, the auditor should include in aggregate likely misstatement the effect on the current period's financial statements of those prior-period likely misstatements" (AU Section 312.37). It does not, however, state how the auditor should include the effect in likely misstatement, and accordingly does not resolve the issues discussed here.

The auditor should plan properly to ensure that sufficient auditing procedures are performed in the various accounts so that appropriate audit conclusions can be reached. If there has been a buildup of misstatements in an account from prior years, the auditor may have to do more work to refine the estimate of the present misstatement in the account. More audit work also may be necessary to prevent a materially misstated balance from going undetected. Of course, assessing at the planning stage whether an immaterially misstated account balance from prior years will no longer be misstated, remain similarly misstated, or become misstated in the opposite direction in the current period is difficult. Thus, the auditor's experience with the entity, assessment of the possible level of misstatement in the account, and the nature of the account all influence testing for the current period.

(g)   Disposition of Items on the Summary of Audit Differences

As the engagement progresses, the auditor should assess whether the items that have been accumulated on the summary of audit differences present a risk of material misstatement of the financial statements. Occasionally, the auditor will conclude after reviewing the summary that one or more financial statement components are materially misstated or cause the income statement or balance sheet in the aggregate to be materially misstated. The auditor then needs to discuss the items in question with the entity's management, who should be strongly encouraged to correct all misstatements currently. Management may be able to produce further evidence to justify the initial treatment of some items or may agree to record some of the discovered misstatements in the accounts and disclose more about the nature of and assumptions used in creating subjectively developed estimates that may be in dispute. Early communication is important; the earlier potential misstatements are identified and communicated, the more likely management will be receptive to correcting them. The discussions continue until enough items are resolved so that the auditor can conclude that the remaining items do not adversely affect the fair presentation of the financial statements.

The auditor should determine the reason for misstatements and inquire about management's plans to correct them currently, or in the future, and to prevent their recurrence. Depending on the size and complexity of an entity, the auditor may have to take up each item on the summary with several levels of management. The first consultation, of course, is with the individual directly responsible, who should supply all the facts. Additional conferences may include a supervisor and sometimes a plant or division controller. Often the deciding conference includes top management—the chief financial officer and chief executive. If discussions reach that level, two subjects should be probed: how to resolve the current problems so that an unqualified opinion can be given, and how to prevent similar problems from growing to such magnitude in the future. In these conferences, auditors should be careful not to allow factors such as pressing deadlines, heated arguments, or management dissatisfaction to influence them or to compromise their professional objectivity. Diplomacy, tact, and an attitude of constructive assistance are obviously important in such situations. Early and thorough consideration of potential problems is the best way to avoid actual problems that may lead to qualified or adverse opinions. In some situations, however, such opinions may be the only appropriate response to management's unwillingness to correct material financial statement misstatements.

As the engagement nears completion, the auditor should assess whether the misstatements management has not corrected and that remain on the summary are material, either individually or when aggregated with other misstatements. If so, at least enough of them should be adjusted to eliminate the material misstatement. At the final stage of the engagement, the auditor should assess the risk that the financial statements may be materially misstated when the items remaining on the summary are combined with audit differences that were not detected (as noted earlier). If the auditor decides that there is an unacceptable risk that the financial statements may be materially misstated because of undetected audit differences, one or both of the following actions should be considered:

1. Request management to record adjustments for misstatements reflected on the summary in order to increase the allowance for undetected audit differences.

2. Reconsider the adequacy of auditing procedures performed (i.e., whether audit detection risk is at an acceptable level), identifying any areas where the scope of work may not be sufficient and, if necessary, extending substantive tests—either or both analytical procedures and tests of details—to gain additional evidential matter about the likelihood of undetected misstatements.

27.6   WORKING PAPER REVIEW

Paragraph 11 of SAS No. 22, *Planning and Supervision* (AU Section 311.13), states that "the work performed by each assistant should be reviewed to determine whether it was adequately performed and to evaluate whether the results are consistent with the conclusions to be presented in the auditor's report."

(a)   Key Engagement Matters

To facilitate the review process, the audit personnel in charge of field work should document significant matters relating to the engagement and bring them to the attention of the partner in charge of the engagement. Key engagement matters include, but are not limited to, the following:

1. Significant questions involving accounting principles and auditing procedures, or failure to comply with regulatory requirements, even when the person in charge of the fieldwork is satisfied that the matter has been disposed of properly

2. Uncompleted audit steps or unresolved questions

3. Matters of significance noted in the previous year's engagement and their disposition

4. Resolved or unresolved disagreements with management on accounting and auditing matters

5. Any information, not otherwise obvious, that should be considered in evaluating the results of the audit or in discussing the financial statements with management

It is desirable to address significant matters in one section of the working papers. Those matters may be summarized in the lead working paper file, with cross-references to the related working papers that contain the details.

(b)   Types of Reviews

Generally, two types of reviews of working papers and procedures are performed on audit engagements:

- A review of the completed working papers by the person in charge of the field work to evaluate the audit results and ascertain that all appropriate auditing procedures have been applied.

- A review of the auditing procedures performed and the conclusions reached, by an individual who did not participate in the field work. This review provides an objective assessment of the procedures applied during the field work and their results, which form the basis of the audit opinion.

The person in charge of the field work is responsible for reviewing all completed working papers to determine that:

1. All appropriate auditing procedures have been completed and the nature and extent of the work performed have been documented adequately in the working papers

2. The requirements of the audit program were adhered to

3. The working papers are relevant, clearly presented, orderly, and self-explanatory

4. All exceptions have been appropriately cleared and documented

The second review is the responsibility of the partner, who exercises overall supervision but usually does not perform the detailed auditing procedures. Depending on the structure of the audit team, the partner may delegate a portion of the review to a manager who was not involved in preparing the working papers. The partner ordinarily would then focus primarily on the key engagement matters and any areas in which there is a high risk of material misstatement, taking into consideration the dollar amounts involved, the complexity of the problems, and the entity's internal control.

The purpose of the review of the audit program and working papers is to ensure that the procedures used are adequate and appropriate, that they have been performed properly, that they generated sufficient evidence to support the auditor's conclusions, that the conclusions reached are objective and logical, and that there is a properly documented basis for an informed opinion. The reviewer must evaluate the completeness of the audit program—including changes made to reflect changes in audit strategy in the course of the audit—in light of the results of the tests, the quality of the work performed by engagement team members, the quality of management's judgments and decisions, and the adequacy of both the work performed and its documentation by the team members. The exacting but inconclusive nature of most audit tasks makes it imperative that another qualified professional review every piece of work for completeness and logic. Whatever other purposes the review may have, its primary purpose must be to ensure that the logic of the audit is complete and properly documented. The logic calls for evidence in the working papers that the entity's internal control was understood, inherent risks were identified, and control risk was assessed, and, if appropriate, tests of controls were performed; the risk assessment activities were translated into a program of substantive tests; the results of those tests either corroborated the assertions embodied in the financial statements or led to a rational exploration of differences; and the results support each item in the financial statements.

The reviewer should be satisfied that the working papers have been integrated with the final financial statements. That is, the reviewer should ascertain that each account analysis in the working papers agrees with the corresponding amount shown on the trial balance, and that those amounts are reconcilable to the amounts shown on the financial statements. Amounts or other data appearing on the financial statements but not reflected on the trial balance (e.g., footnote or supplementary information) also must be agreed to the related working papers.

Regardless of what duties the partner delegates to a manager, the partner should review the auditor's report, related financial statements, and, where applicable, the entire text of the published report. The partner should consider each of the key engagement matters and ensure that the decision reached as to its disposition is appropriate.

(c) Review by a Concurring Review Partner

Many accounting firms require that all financial statements be reviewed by a concurring (sometimes referred to as a second) review partner before the audit report is released. Other firms limit this requirement to audits of specified entities, for example, entities in specialized industries and publicly owned entities.[4] In this review, the concurring review partner should be particularly concerned that matters of importance have been dealt with appropriately and that the financial statements and audit report comply with professional standards and firm policies. The concurring review partner should discuss with the partner in charge of the engagement questions regarding the consistent application of GAAP, auditing standards, or auditing procedures. The concurring review partner also may consider it advisable to review certain working papers. If a concurring review is required, the auditor's report should not be signed until all questions raised by the concurring review partner have been disposed of properly.

(d) Consultation on Critical Issues

As noted in Chapter 3, consultation is one aspect of quality control that CPA firms are required by Statement of Quality Control Standards No. 2 to consider in establishing systems of quality control. Accordingly, accounting firms often have policies requiring consultation on significant matters arising during an audit. Generally, the policies specify certain senior partners or partners with specific functional or industry expertise to act as consultants in specified circumstances, such as when there is an issue about the integrity of management, when management requests variations from standard forms of reporting, or when there is a difference of opinion on an accounting matter. Because the need for consultation must be determined in light of the circumstances of a particular engagement, most firms assign responsibility for determining that appropriate consultation has been undertaken to the engagement partner. Among the factors that may be relevant to such a determination are:

- The materiality of the matter
- The experience of senior engagement personnel in a particular industry or functional area
- Whether generally accepted accounting principles or generally accepted auditing standards in the area:
    1. Are based on an authoritative pronouncement that is subject to varying interpretations
    2. Are based on varied interpretations of prevailing practice
    3. Have yet to be developed
    4. Are under active consideration by an authoritative body
    5. Are not covered by the firm's policy or interpretation

Accounting firms may specify certain circumstances in which consultation is required; for example:

- An engagement partner (after discussion with the concurring review partner, if one has been assigned) believes the financial statements should reflect a de-

---

[4] As indicated in Chapter 3, concurring reviews are required on SEC engagements if the auditor is a member of the SEC Practice Section of the AICPA Division for CPA Firms.

parture from an authoritative pronouncement covered by Rule 203 (ET Section 203.01) of the AICPA's Code of Professional Conduct to make them not misleading. (The appropriate reporting in this situation is discussed in Chapter 28.)

- Management believes that a treatment specified in a lower category in the hierarchy of established accounting principles (described in Chapter 28) better presents the substance of a transaction than a treatment in a higher category that appears equally appropriate in the circumstances.

- The engagement partner believes that the application of a firm accounting policy might be inappropriate in the circumstances.

- The engagement partner believes that the application of a firm auditing policy might be inappropriate in the circumstances or lead to ineffective or significantly inefficient auditing procedures.

Whatever the circumstances in which consultation on accounting and auditing matters occurs, those consulted must have all the facts necessary to make an informed decision. The Public Oversight Board of the AICPA's SEC Practice Section has recommended that

> The concurring partner, whose participation in an audit is a membership requirement of the SEC Practice Section, should be responsible for assuring that those consulted on accounting matters are aware of all of the relevant facts and circumstances, including an understanding of the financial statements in whose context the accounting policy is being considered. The concurring and consulting partners should know enough about the client to ensure that all of the relevant facts and circumstances are marshaled, and also possess the increased detachment that comes from not having to face the client on an ongoing basis.[5]

(e) Aids for Reviewers

The review process is so critical that accounting firms are constantly seeking ways to help reviewers by providing aids such as engagement control checklists, standardized procedures, and policy bulletins. In providing such aids to the reviewer, accounting firms must try to guard against routinized performance of a highly judgmental task. The quality of the review, and therefore of the audit, rests on the professional diligence and sense of responsibility of the reviewer. Although guided and supported by aids such as those mentioned above, the reviewer cannot and should not be relieved of the responsibility for understanding all that is needed to form an appropriate opinion on the financial statements.

(f) Timing of the Review Process

For the sake of both audit efficiency and good client relations, potentially material issues must be raised at the earliest possible stage. More time for consideration by the partner on the engagement and management is thus available than if the review is postponed until the final stages of the audit when the report deadline is near.

The real substance of an audit is planning it intelligently and logically, executing it

---

[5] Public Oversight Board, *In the Public Interest: A Special Report* (Stamford, CT: Public Oversight Board, 1993).

diligently and perceptively, and supervising it so that the review is continuous and active. If an audit is properly planned, executed, and supervised, the working paper review becomes the final control over a result already accomplished—a means of determining that all items of significance have been considered in reaching an audit conclusion.

In practice, the review process rarely works as smoothly as it does in theory. There are delays by entity personnel, unexpected auditing or accounting problems, a staff member who falls ill or cannot complete the assignment on time, and innumerable other possible complications. Increasing public pressure for the fastest possible release of significant information causes deadlines to be drawn constantly tighter. The risk of oversight or misjudgment is greatest under the pressure of a deadline. Experienced auditors learn to resist those problems and pressures, and make sure they review an integrated set of financial statements supported by coherent working papers before committing themselves, explicitly or implicitly, to an opinion on the financial statements or to approving release of information drawn from them.

(g) Documentation of Significant Review Findings

During the various working paper reviews, reviewers generate what are commonly referred to as "review notes." Review notes are temporary notations of matters that have to be resolved or questions that have to be answered. Those questions often involve the appropriateness of accounting principles, auditing procedures used, or compliance with regulatory requirements, and call for further investigation. Some auditors require that the review notes become part of the audit working papers and that a clear and precise record be maintained of how such questions were resolved, including, among other things, such matters as the following (if applicable):

- The additional auditing procedures performed
- The individuals with whom the matter was discussed
- The conclusions arrived at and supporting rationale

Other auditors, including the authors, believe that matters identified in review notes should be adequately disposed of by changes or additions to appropriate working papers on a timely basis before the working papers are filed and the review notes should be destroyed.

27.7 SUBSEQUENT EVENTS

(a) Types of Subsequent Events

Section 560 of SAS No. 1 (AU Section 560.01–.09) defines subsequent events as events or transactions that "occur subsequent to the balance-sheet date, but prior to the issuance of the financial statements and auditor's report, that have a material effect on the financial statements and therefore require adjustment or disclosure in the statements."[6] Subsequent events that occur after the balance sheet date but before the is-

---

[6] The distinction between the discovery of subsequent events before the financial statements are issued and the later discovery of facts that existed at the date of the auditor's report, is significant. The latter is discussed in Chapter 28.

suance of the financial statements and the auditor's report fall into two categories: those that require adjustment of account balances (and consequently are reflected on the face of the financial statements) and those that should not be recorded but should be disclosed in the financial statements.

The first category of subsequent event is succinctly described in SAS No. 1 (AU Section 560.03), as follows:

> Those events that provide additional evidence with respect to conditions that existed at the date of the balance sheet and affect the estimates inherent in the process of preparing financial statements. All information that becomes available prior to the issuance of the financial statements should be used by management in its evaluation of the conditions on which the estimates were based. The financial statements should be adjusted for any changes in estimates resulting from the use of such evidence.

The second type of subsequent event is one that provides evidence about conditions that did not exist at the balance sheet date but arose afterwards. These events should be reflected in the financial statements of the year in which they occurred, and should not result in adjustment of the statements of the year being reported on. Some of these events, however, may be significant enough that, if they are not disclosed, the prior-year financial statements would be misleading. They include all transactions and other events and circumstances having significant financial impact. Some examples given in SAS No. 1 are issuance of debt or stock, acquisition of a business, and casualty losses.

Occasionally, an event of that type may be so significant that the auditor's report should call attention to it in an explanatory paragraph. Sometimes adequate disclosure can be made only by means of pro forma data giving effect to the event as if it had occurred at the balance sheet date; major acquisitions, mergers, and recapitalizations are examples.

Section 560 of SAS No. 1 illustrates the distinction between events that reveal or clarify conditions existing at the balance sheet date and those that represent new conditions. The illustration used is a receivable found to be uncollectible after year-end because of a customer's bankruptcy subsequent to that date. This event is in the first category (requiring adjustment of the gross receivable and possibly recalculation of bad debt expense and the allowance for uncollectible accounts) because the debtor's poor financial condition existed at the balance sheet date. A similar receivable found to be uncollectible because of a disaster occurring to the debtor after the balance sheet date is a new condition and falls in the second category, requiring disclosure in the notes to the financial statements rather than adjustment of the accounts. The SAS notes that making the distinction requires "the exercise of judgment and knowledge of the facts and circumstances" (AU Section 560.04).

The distinction is often a fine one and the judgment difficult to make. For example, deteriorating market conditions subsequent to year-end could be a new condition that merely requires disclosure, or it could be evidence of a condition that was inherent in the inventory at year-end, which calls for adjusting it to net realizable value. Similarly, a subsequent event that reveals that estimated expenses are insufficient because of conditions occurring after the balance sheet date should be disclosed. On the other hand, if the reason for the insufficiency is newly discovered evidence of conditions that existed at the balance sheet date, that evidence should be reflected in the expense and related asset or liability accounts on the face of the statements.

There is a third type of subsequent event—one occurring after year-end that requires neither adjustment nor disclosure in the financial statements. Events that do not affect the interpretation of financial statements should not be disclosed because describing them in the notes could cause misleading or confusing inferences. Since every event may have a financial impact, it is often extremely difficult to distinguish between events that should and those that should not be disclosed in the financial statements. Strikes, changes in customers or management, and new contracts and agreements are examples of events that ordinarily should not be disclosed in the financial statements, although management may have a responsibility to make public disclosure apart from the financial statements. If the events occur before the annual report to shareholders is printed, the president's letter often is used as a convenient method of communication.

(b)   Auditor's Responsibility for Subsequent Events

The auditor's responsibility for subsequent events depends on whether they occurred before or after the date of the auditor's report (discussed below). The auditor's responsibility for events occurring in the period between the entity's year-end and the audit report date (called the subsequent period) is defined in Section 560 of SAS No. 1. Auditors have no responsibility to seek any additional evidence in the period (typically a rather short time) between the date of the auditor's report and the date the financial statements and auditor's report are issued. Nevertheless, while auditors have no responsibility to seek additional evidence during that period, they do have a responsibility not to ignore information that comes to their attention.

(c)   Auditing Procedures in the Subsequent Period

Paragraphs 10–12 of Section 560 of SAS No. 1 (AU Section 560.10–.12) define the auditor's responsibility to determine whether relevant subsequent events have occurred and discuss auditing procedures performed in the subsequent period. That work generally falls into two major categories—procedures performed for the purpose of keeping current with respect to events occurring in the subsequent period, and completion of auditing procedures performed for other purposes.

The latter category consists of substantive tests that involve reviewing transactions occurring in the subsequent period as part of the audit of year-end account balances. These procedures, which have been discussed earlier in this book, include tests of the entity's cash cutoffs and sales and purchase cutoffs, and reviews of collections and payments after year-end. As previously noted, however, the auditor has no responsibility to carry out any auditing procedures for the period after the report date.

The procedures for keeping current with respect to events occurring in the subsequent period are specified in AU Section 560.12 and may be summarized as follows:

1. Read all available information relating to the entity's financial and accounting matters: interim financial statements; minutes of meetings of stockholders, directors, and any appropriate committees; pertinent performance and other management reports, and the like. An auditor who understands the entity knows which areas are sensitive or volatile and what information about them is likely to be available.

2. Make inquiries—the more specific the better—about such things as financing activities, unusual entries or adjustments in the accounts, and potential problems discovered during the audit. An auditor who has developed a close working relationship with the entity's management can make those inquiries easily and expeditiously.

3. Inquire of the entity's legal counsel concerning litigation, claims, and assessments. Obtain a letter of representation from management describing subsequent events or disclaiming knowledge of any such events.

In addition, as part of the subsequent-period review, the auditor may compare the latest available interim financial statements with the financial statements being reported on, as well as make other comparisons considered appropriate in the circumstances.

It is sometimes necessary in the subsequent period to perform analytical procedures or other substantive tests in a recognized problem area. Usually, their purpose is to decide whether management has measured the impact of a subsequent event reasonably, for example, the impact of a decision to discontinue a line of business made subsequent to year-end. Sometimes, however, tests are required to satisfy the auditor that a possible subsequent event did not occur; an example is tests of the net realizable value of inventories due to changed market conditions subsequent to year-end.

(d) Dating the Report

SAS No. 1 (AU Section 530.01) states that the auditor's report generally should be dated the date when the audit field work is complete, that is, when the auditor has completed substantially all the tests of the accounting records and all other auditing procedures considered necessary in the circumstances of the particular engagement. Matters that may require follow-up with management, particularly if performed off the entity's premises, generally do not affect the date of the auditor's report.

The date of the auditor's report establishes the end of the subsequent period—the period during which an auditor has responsibility for events occurring after the entity's year-end—unless the auditor agrees or is required to perform additional procedures, as, for example, in filings with the SEC under the Securities Act of 1933, discussed later in this chapter. The higher levels of responsibility that auditors are now being held to, the increased demands of users for reliable financial information, and the fact that the report date signifies the end of the period of the auditor's responsibility for that information have all imparted greater significance to the date of the auditor's report.

The report date is seldom the last day the auditors are on the entity's premises. Ancillary matters often require the engagement team's presence after the completion of field work. For example, various regulatory reports, covenant letters, and communications to management may have to be prepared or completed. Separate audits may be required for employee benefit plans or related foundations.

A report date about 25 to 45 days after the end of the fiscal year is common for publicly held commercial and manufacturing companies; 15 to 20 days is usual for commercial banks. It then may take several weeks for the published annual report containing the financial statements to be prepared, printed, and mailed, but the auditor's report carries the date on which agreement on the financial statements was reached (unless new information is incorporated in the statements—see the discussion under Dual Dating, below).

(i) Audit Planning Considerations.   If an audit report must be issued within two or three weeks of year-end, the amount of auditing that can take place after year-end is obviously limited. Thus, much of the auditor's work essentially must be completed by year-end. This usually requires that the entity have effective internal control and always requires careful planning by the auditor. As indicated in Chapter 15 [Section 15.2(b), Timing of Tests of Details], there are several strategies under which an auditor can perform substantive tests before the balance sheet date and have a reasonable basis for "rolling forward" conclusions from those tests to the balance sheet date.

Many entities, however, cannot or do not choose to seek such early publication of their financial statements. Also, depending on the control risk assessment, the auditor may find it necessary to perform much of the substantive testing after the balance sheet date, or problems may be encountered in making necessary valuations, estimates, and judgments. It may take 8 to 12 weeks, or even longer, for the audit to be completed. During that time, the auditor must "keep current" with respect to the entity so as to have a basis for an opinion that subsequent events are properly reflected or disclosed in the financial statements.

(ii) Dual Dating.   As described earlier, subsequent events that occur after the date of the auditor's report but before the report is issued and that come to the auditor's attention may require adjustment or disclosure in the financial statements. If such an event is disclosed, the auditor can either redate the report as of the date of that event or use "dual dating." In practice, unless the time period is very short, dual dating is more common because of the additional work (discussed above) necessary for the extended period if the report is redated.

An auditor may be required or requested to reissue a report after it was first issued. If the auditor is aware of subsequent events that occurred after the date of the original report, several alternatives are possible. For events that require adjustment of the previously issued financial statements, the report should be dual dated. For events that require disclosure only, the auditor may dual date the report, or the disclosure may be included in an additional (usually the last) note to the financial statements that is labeled "unaudited." When dual dating is used, it usually appears as "January 25, 19X2, except as to Note __, for which the date is March 1, 19X2."

(e)   The Securities Act of 1933

Auditors' SEC practice is dealt with in entire volumes and is beyond the scope of this work. As mentioned in SAS No. 37, *Filings Under Federal Securities Statutes* (AU Section 711.02), "the accountant's responsibility, generally [when reporting on financial statements included in a filing with the SEC], is in substance no different from that involved in other types of reporting." A critical consideration in a 1933 Act filing, however, is that the independent auditor's responsibility with respect to subsequent events extends *to the effective date* of the registration statement and does not terminate at the date of the audit report. This situation results from Section 11(a) of the 1933 Act, which provides for substantial liabilities to those involved in the preparation of a registration statement found to contain untrue statements or material omissions. As pointed out in SAS No. 37 (AU Section 711.10), "To sustain the burden of proof that he has made a 'reasonable investigation,' . . . as required under the Securities Act of 1933, an auditor should extend his procedures with respect to subsequent events from the date of his audit report up to the effective date or as close thereto as is reasonable and practicable in the circumstances."

(i) Subsequent Event Procedures for Keeping Current.   The procedures already discussed for keeping current with respect to subsequent events through the date of the auditor's report should be extended to the effective date of the registration statement. In addition, the auditor generally should read the entire prospectus and other pertinent sections of the registration statement.

(ii) Letters for Underwriters.   The procedures for keeping current that were discussed above are separate and distinct from any procedures that may be required by underwriters in connection with a 1933 Act filing, even though frequently they may be performed at the same time. Letters for underwriters, commonly called "comfort letters," are the subject of SAS No. 72, *Letters for Underwriters and Certain Other Requesting Parties*, as amended by SAS No. 76 (AU Section 634), and are discussed in Chapter 30.

27.8   ADMINISTRATIVE WRAP-UP

After the audit has been completed and the working papers have been reviewed and filed, there are both technical and administrative loose ends to wrap up. Special reports, tax returns, and similar matters are likely to have due dates that act as a professional discipline, but it is easy to let administrative matters slide. Tight administrative controls are necessary to prevent that from happening.

Time analyses must be completed and budget variances analyzed. Billings must be prepared and processed. The audit program should be revised in preliminary preparation for the next year's engagement. Ideally, the next year's engagement should be planned with management as part of the current wrapping-up process. On many well-organized engagements, the end of one engagement constitutes the beginning of the next.

Finally, the auditor is required by various Statements on Auditing Standards, including SAS No. 61, *Communication With Audit Committees* (AU Section 380), to communicate certain matters to the audit committee, or to determine that management has reported them appropriately. Those communications are discussed in Chapter 4.

28

Reporting on Audited Financial Statements

28.1 THE REPORTING FRAMEWORK: CATEGORIES OF ACCOUNTANTS' REPORTS

An accountant's report is the formal externally focused result of all the effort that goes into an engagement. There also are many other results—for example, the direct and indirect impact of an audit on an entity's control, accountability, and public reporting practices and the informal communication that also may occur. Guidance on preparing accountants' reports can be found in Statements on Auditing Standards (SASs), Statements on Standards for Accounting and Review Services (SSARSs), and Statements on Standards for Attestation Engagements (SSAEs), which roughly correspond to the broad types of engagements—audits of financial statements and other financial information, compilations and reviews of financial statements, and attest engagements.

The authoritative literature is not precise in differentiating the different types of possible engagements. Conceptually, any engagement in which an accountant expresses a conclusion about the reliability of information that is the responsibility of another party is an attest engagement, with audits and reviews being subsets of attest engagements. (Compilations are not attest engagements, since the accountant does not express a conclusion when performing a compilation.) Historically, however, the authoritative literature applicable to audits was developed before the profession delineated the concept of attest engagements. When performance and reporting guidance for attest engagements that clearly are not audits (such as *reviews* of interim financial information) was needed, it was incorporated into the authoritative auditing literature—the only available vehicle at the time. Moreover, it was not transferred to the attest literature when that literature was developed. As a result, the line between audits and attest engagements in the professional literature is unclear.

In recent years, "business assurance" and "assurance function" have come to be used as umbrella terms to describe the services that accountants perform in audits, reviews, and attest engagements, that is, engagements in which the accountant expresses an opinion about the reliability of specified information. When performing those services, accountants are said to be providers of assurance. The previous chapters of this book and the specialized industry chapters that follow discuss how audits of financial statements are performed. This chapter and Chapters 29 through 31 discuss how accountants report on the conclusions they have reached in audit and other engagements that provide assurance (and also in engagements to compile financial statements, which do not provide assurance).

This chapter discusses reports on audits of financial statements prepared in conformity with generally accepted accounting principles; those reports—referred to as audit reports or auditors' reports—are covered by the SASs. Chapter 29 discusses reports on other types of audit engagements, for example, reports on financial statements prepared on a non-GAAP basis of accounting and reports on parts of a financial statement. Those reports also are covered by the SASs. Chapter 30 discusses reporting on engagements to compile financial statements and to review financial statements, both of which are covered by the SSARSs. Chapter 30 also discusses other nonaudit assurance services—for example, reviews of interim financial information and agreed-upon procedures engagements such as those that result in specific assurances to underwriters—that are covered by the SASs. Chapter 31 discusses the performance and reporting guidance on attest engagements that are covered by the SSAEs. Those engagements encompass certain types of assurance services that do not involve audits, reviews, or other services that are covered by the SASs or SSARSs.

28.2 AUDITORS' REPORTS: STANDARD REPORTS

This chapter covers the standard auditor's report (often called an unqualified or "clean" report or opinion), matters that require explicit attention in issuing an auditor's report, and variations from the standard report. Those variations fall into two categories: *explanatory language* in the standard report that does not qualify the auditor's opinion, and *departures* from the standard report to express other than an unqualified opinion. The three types of departures from unqualified opinions—qualified opinions, adverse opinions, and disclaimers of opinion—what each conveys, and the circumstances in which each is appropriate are examined in detail, with illustrations. The chapter also includes a discussion of the auditor's responsibilities after the report date.

The auditor's report that appears in Figure 28.1 indicates the wording of the standard report prescribed by SAS No. 58, *Reports on Audited Financial Statements* (AU Section 508).

(a) Organization and Wording

The following paragraphs explain the language used in the standard report and its organization.

(i) Title.   The title should include the word "independent," as in the phrase "Independent Auditor's Report." This is intended to remind the reader of the credibility an audit adds to the financial statements because of the auditor's independence.

(ii) Introductory Paragraph.   The opening paragraph of the report identifies the financial statements that were audited and states that management is responsible for them.[1] The auditor's responsibility is to give an opinion on those statements based on the results of the audit. The phrase "we have audited" implies that the auditor is providing the highest level of assurance that can be given. (Lower levels of assurance can be provided in other types of engagements, such as "reviews.") The introductory paragraph also specifies the dates of and periods covered by the financial statements that were audited.

It is important that the reader of the document in which the financial statements appear know precisely what is covered by the auditor's report and, by inference, what is

---

[1] Many publicly traded entities include reports by management in their financial statements. Those reports usually contain a statement of management's responsibility for the financial statements. An auditing interpretation of SAS No. 58 (AU Section 9508.51) indicates that the statement about management's responsibility for the financial statements that appears in the introductory paragraph of the auditor's standard report should not be further elaborated on nor should it refer to a management report. Such modifications of the auditor's report might lead to unwarranted assumptions that the auditor was providing assurance about representations made by management about its responsibility for financial reporting, internal control, and other matters that might be discussed in the management report.

Figure 28.1 Sample Report of Independent Accountant

Report of Independent Accountants

To the Shareowners of AT&T Corp.:

We have audited the consolidated balance sheets of AT&T Corp. and subsidiaries (AT&T) at December 31, 1996 and 1995, and the related consolidated statements of income, changes in shareowners' equity and cash flows for the years ended December 31, 1996, 1995 and 1994. These financial statements are the responsibility of AT&T's management. Our responsibility is to express an opinion on these financial statements based on our audits.

We conducted our audits in accordance with generally accepted auditing standards. Those standards require that we plan and perform the audit to obtain reasonable assurance about whether the financial statements are free of material misstatement. An audit includes examining, on a test basis, evidence supporting the amounts and disclosures in the financial statements. An audit also includes assessing the accounting principles used and significant estimates made by management, as well as evaluating the overall financial statement presentation. We believe that our audits provide a reasonable basis for our opinion.

In our opinion, the financial statements referred to above present fairly, in all material respects, the consolidated financial position of AT&T at December 31, 1996 and 1995, and the consolidated results of their operations and their cash flows for the years ended December 31, 1996, 1995 and 1994, in conformity with generally accepted accounting principles.

Coopers & Lybrand LLP

Coopers & Lybrand L.L.P.
1301 Avenue of the Americas
New York, New York
January 22, 1997

---

not. Since an annual report or prospectus contains much more than the financial statements, the reader must be told specifically what has been audited (the financial statements and the related notes that are, as stated on each page of the body of the financial statements, an "integral part of the financial statements") and what, by implication, has not been audited, such as the letter from the president and chairman of the board, financial ratios, and information about stock prices. Sometimes there will be a reference to the page numbers containing information covered by the auditor's report.

(iii) Scope Paragraph. The scope paragraph describes the auditor's basis for forming the opinion on the financial statements. Telling the reader that the audit was conducted in accordance with generally accepted auditing standards is the equivalent of saying that the auditor has complied with the standards established by the auditing profession for performing an audit. The auditor's objective in performing an audit is to obtain enough evidence to enable him or her to provide *reasonable,* but not absolute, assurance that the financial statements do not contain material misstatements. (A misstatement is considered material if it is probable that the judgment of a reasonable person relying on the financial statements would have been changed or influenced by the misstatement. Materiality is discussed further in Chapter 6.)

The scope paragraph includes a thumbnail sketch of what an audit entails. It notes that evidence about the accounting measurements and disclosures in the financial statements was obtained only on a test basis. To do otherwise would be economically prohibitive and would entail costs that society as a whole would not be willing to pay. The report specifically states that assessing the entity's accounting principles, the estimates that are part of the financial statements, and the overall financial statement presentation are key elements of an audit. Last, the auditor explicitly states that the evidence obtained and evaluated in the course of the audit was sufficient to support the opinion given.

(iv) Opinion Paragraph. The opinion paragraph of the auditor's report—usually the third, and final, paragraph—states the conclusions the auditor has reached from the work performed. The auditor's opinion represents a judgment made after evaluating evidence about the assertions implicit in the financial statements; the phrase "in our opinion" is intended to convey this element of judgment, as opposed to a statement of fact. (As discussed later, in some cases the auditor may be unable to form an opinion.)

The conclusion the auditor reaches in most audits of financial statements is that the financial statements "present fairly . . . in conformity with generally accepted accounting principles."[2] The opinion illustrated here is technically called an unqualified opinion—that is, it is not qualified by any exceptions. A less technical term for an unqualified opinion is a "clean" opinion. Although authoritative AICPA literature describes other types of opinions (qualified opinions, adverse opinions, and disclaimers of opinion), the usual expectation is that the auditor will be able to render a positive, unqualified opinion. Anything less is usually undesirable, and often unacceptable either to the entity or to regulatory bodies. Users of financial statements are best served if the entity's financial statements do "present fairly . . . in conformity with generally accepted accounting principles." Thus, auditors have a responsibility to both the public and their clients to assist them in receiving an unqualified opinion by seeking to improve their financial reporting practices, when that may be necessary.

(b) History of the Standard Report

The wording of the auditor's report went through several changes before the present-day report was adopted in 1988. In the early 1920s, a typical audit report (covering a single year) was worded as follows:

---

[2] Note that the illustrative opinion is about the financial statements, not about individual account balances. The auditor may express an opinion about specific accounts, discussed in Chapter 29, rather than about the financial statements taken as a whole.

We have audited the accounts and records of the XYZ Company for the fiscal year ended March 31, 1920, and hereby Certify that, in our opinion, the annexed Balance Sheet correctly reflects the financial condition of the Company at March 31, 1920, subject to the liability for Federal Income and Profits Taxes accrued at that date.

It should be noted that this report refers to an audit of the "accounts and records" as opposed to the financial statements and that the auditors "certified" the balance sheet as being "correct." By the early 1930s, the accounting profession had come to the realization that it would be unwise to continue to use the word "certify" or similar words in the audit opinion. The word "certify" gives the reader the incorrect impression that the contents of the audited financial statements are subject to precise measurements and that the auditor could guarantee the exactness of the data in those statements.

Changes to the report in the 1930s deleted the word "certify" and introduced two new concepts: consistency of application of accepted accounting principles and fair presentation. Also, the scope paragraph of the report clarified the extent of the examination and included a specific reference to the review of internal control.

The SEC stated in 1941 that the auditor must indicate whether the examination was made in accordance with "generally accepted auditing standards" and whether all procedures that were deemed necessary were carried out. As a result, the AICPA promptly initiated a change in the wording of the audit report. The 1941 audit report follows:

We have examined the balance sheet of the XYZ Company as of February 28, 1941, and the statements of income and surplus for the fiscal year then ended, have reviewed the system of internal control and the accounting procedures of the company and, without making a detailed audit of the transactions, have examined or tested accounting records of the company and other supporting evidence, by methods and to the extent we deemed appropriate. Our examination was made in accordance with generally accepted auditing standards applicable in the circumstances and included all procedures which we considered necessary.

In our opinion, the accompanying balance sheet and related statements of income and surplus present fairly the position of the XYZ Company at February 28, 1941, and the results of its operations for the fiscal year, in conformity with generally accepted accounting principles applied on a basis consistent with that of the preceding year.

In 1944, further modifications were made, such as deleting mention of some of the specific procedures carried out by the auditor. This change was based on the recognition that "generally accepted auditing standards" encompassed the stated auditing procedures, therefore making the enumeration redundant. Minor modifications were made in 1948, and for the next 40 years the report read essentially as follows:

We have examined the balance sheet of X Company as of December 31, 19XX, and the related statements of income and retained earnings and changes in financial position for the year then ended. Our examination was made in accordance with generally accepted auditing standards and, accordingly, included such tests of the accounting records and such other auditing procedures as we considered necessary in the circumstances.

In our opinion, the financial statements referred to above present fairly the financial position of X Company at December 31, 19XX, and the results of its operations and the changes in its financial position for the year then ended, in conformity with generally accepted accounting principles applied on a basis consistent with that of the preceding year.

(c) The Meaning of Fair Presentation in Conformity with GAAP

The first standard of reporting states:

> The report shall state whether the financial statements are presented in accordance with generally accepted accounting principles.

Generally accepted accounting principles provide a consistent frame of reference against which each of management's assertions that are implicit in the financial statements can be evaluated. Obviously, an auditor must be thoroughly familiar with generally accepted accounting principles to comply responsibly with this standard.

Despite acknowledged deficiencies in generally accepted accounting principles, aggravated by some misunderstanding by nonaccountants, the phrase is generally understood by practitioners and many users of the report as well. SAS No. 69, *The Meaning of* Present Fairly in Conformity With Generally Accepted Accounting Principles *in the Independent Auditor's Report* (AU Section 411), defines generally accepted accounting principles as "a technical term that encompasses the conventions, rules, and procedures necessary to define accepted accounting practice at a particular time." The Commission on Auditors' Responsibilities (Cohen Commission) noted that generally accepted accounting principles

> Are not limited to the principles in pronouncements of authoritative bodies such as the Financial Accounting Standards Board (FASB). They also include practices that have achieved acceptance through common usage as well as principles in nonauthoritative pronouncements of bodies of recognized stature such as the Accounting Standards Division of the American Institute of Certified Public Accountants. Too narrow a view of the scope of those principles by auditors and preparers has contributed to the criticism of both generally accepted accounting principles and auditors. (p. 15)

SAS No. 69 also suggests that in addition to the accounting principles covered by Rule 203 of the AICPA Code of Professional Conduct [FASB Statements, FASB Interpretations, APB Opinions, AICPA Accounting Research Bulletins, and Statements and Interpretations of the Governmental Accounting Standards Board (GASB)], there are other possible sources of GAAP. These other sources include AICPA industry audit and accounting guides and Statements of Position, FASB and GASB Technical Bulletins, AICPA Accounting Interpretations, prevalent industry accounting practices, and other accounting literature, such as APB Statements, AICPA Issues Papers and Practice Bulletins, FASB and GASB Concepts Statements, and Statements of the International Accounting Standards Committee, as well as accounting textbooks, handbooks, and articles.

SAS No. 69 also specifies that a consensus of the FASB's Emerging Issues Task Force is a source of established accounting principles; that for SEC registrants, SEC rules and interpretive releases should be viewed as having the same level of authority as pronouncements covered by Rule 203 of the AICPA Code of Professional Conduct;

and that the relative standing of FASB and GASB pronouncements depends on the type of entity under consideration. The SAS contains a chart, reproduced as Figure 28.2, that summarizes the sources of accounting principles, commonly referred to as the GAAP hierarchy. (The summary excludes SEC rules and interpretive releases.)

The SAS notes that, in addition to SEC rules and interpretive releases, the staff of the SEC's Division of Corporation Finance and the Office of the Chief Accountant is-

Figure 28.2   GAAP Hierarchy Summary

	Nongovernmental Entities	*State and Local Governments*
Established Accounting Principles	FASB Statements and Interpretations, APB Opinions, and AICPA Accounting Research Bulletins	GASB Statements and Interpretations, plus AICPA and FASB pronouncements if made applicable to state and local governments by a GASB Statement or Interpretation
	FASB Technical Bulletins, AICPA industry audit and accounting guides, and AICPA Statements of Position	GASB Technical Bulletins, and the following pronouncements if specifically made applicable to state and local governments by the AICPA: AICPA industry audit and accounting guides and AICPA Statements of Position
	Consensus positions of the FASB Emerging Issues Task Force and AICPA Practice Bulletins	Consensus positions of the GASB Emerging Issues Task Force[b] and AICPA Practice Bulletins if specifically made applicable to state and local governments by the AICPA
	AICPA accounting interpretations, "Qs and As" published by the FASB staff, as well as industry practices widely recognized and prevalent	"Qs and As" published by the GASB staff, as well as industry practices widely recognized and prevalent
Other Accounting Literature[a]	Other accounting literature, including FASB Concepts Statements; APB Statements; AICPA Issues Papers; International Accounting Standards Committee Statements; GASB Statements, Interpretations, and Technical Bulletins; pronouncements of other professional associations or regulatory agencies; AICPA *Technical Practice Aids;* and accounting textbooks, handbooks, and articles	Other accounting literature, including GASB Concepts Statements; pronouncements in the ["Established Accounting Principles"] categories . . . of the hierarchy for nongovernmental entities when not specifically made applicable to state and local governments; APB Statements; FASB Concepts Statements; AICPA Issues Papers; International Accounting Standards Committee Statements; pronouncements of other professional associations or regulatory agencies; AICPA *Technical Practice Aids;* and accounting textbooks, handbooks, and articles

[a] In the absence of established accounting principles, the auditor may consider other accounting literature, depending on its relevance in the circumstances.

[b] As of the date of this Statement, the GASB had not organized such a group.

Source: Statement on Auditing Standards No. 69, *The Meaning of* Present Fairly in Conformity With Generally Accepted Accounting Principles *in the Independent Auditor's Report.* Copyright © 1992 by the American Institute of Certified Public Accountants, Inc.

sue Staff Accounting Bulletins (SABs) that "represent practices followed by the staff in administering SEC disclosure requirements." Of note is the emergence in the last few years of a new source of established accounting principles, namely, observations of "the SEC observer" (in reality, the Chief Accountant of the SEC) at meetings of the Emerging Issues Task Force—observations that also represent practices followed by the SEC staff in administering SEC accounting and financial reporting requirements. These observations have come to be known colloquially as "turbo-SABs," since they have much the same effect as SABs.

SAS No. 69 also notes that

> Because of developments such as new legislation or the evolution of a new type of business transaction, there sometimes are no established accounting principles for reporting a specific transaction or event. In those instances, it may be possible to report the event or transaction on the basis of its substance by selecting an accounting principle that appears appropriate when applied in a manner similar to the application of an established principle to an analogous transaction or event.

There have been efforts to expand the first reporting standard to require auditors to report on "fairness" separately from GAAP. The reason for these attempts is a belief in some quarters that it is possible to prepare financial statements that conform with GAAP but that nevertheless are not presented fairly and may in fact be misleading. Unfortunately, there has been some basis for that view in the past, principally because some preparers and auditors took a much narrower view of what constitutes GAAP than was explained earlier. SAS No. 69 (AU Section 411) clarified the situation by setting forth what the term "generally accepted accounting principles" encompassed (essentially, what was described earlier), and by noting that the auditor's judgment concerning the fairness of financial statement presentation should be applied within that frame of reference. Clearly, "fairness" is too loose a term to be practical or useful unless it is defined within a specific frame of reference, that is, GAAP. Some auditors believe that the word "fairly" should be removed from the auditor's opinion; that proposal has met strong resistance, particularly from the SEC.

SAS No. 69 also enumerates the various judgments that the auditor must make before rendering an unqualified opinion. The auditor's positive opinion about fair presentation in conformity with generally accepted accounting principles implies a belief that the financial statements have the following qualities:

1. The accounting principles selected and applied have general acceptance.
2. The accounting principles are appropriate in the circumstances.
3. The financial statements, including the related notes, are informative on matters that may affect their use, understanding, and interpretation.
4. The information presented in the financial statements is classified and summarized in a reasonable manner, that is, neither too detailed nor too condensed.
5. The financial statements reflect the underlying events and transactions in a manner that presents financial position, results of operations, and cash flows stated within a range of acceptable limits—that is, limits that are reasonable and practicable to attain in financial statements. [SAS No. 69 (AU Section 411.04)]

The standard to which the auditor has been held in determining whether the accounting principles selected and applied are "appropriate in the circumstances" has been whether the particular principle falls within the range of acceptable practice. Some auditors and others believe that auditors should be assigned the responsibility of communicating their views—at least to the entity's audit committee of the board of directors, if not directly to financial statement users—about the *appropriateness*, not just the *acceptability*, of the accounting principles used or proposed to be adopted by the entity, the clarity of its financial disclosures, and the degree of aggressiveness or conservatism of the entity's accounting principles and estimates.[3]

(d) Routine Variations in the Standard Report

Routine variations in the wording of the standard report include the party or parties to whom it is addressed, the identification of the statements reported on, the period(s) covered, and the date of the report. An auditor should not alter the standard report unless there are problems or unusual conditions to be highlighted—and then the alterations should follow the carefully drawn rules referred to in the following sections of this chapter—because any departure from the standard wording is usually regarded as some sort of warning to the reader.

(i) Addressing the Report. The report may be addressed to the entity itself or to its board of directors or stockholders. The authors believe that auditors have a responsibility to the owners of a business entity and therefore that the report should be addressed to the stockholders, board of directors and stockholders, partners, or proprietor. The authors also believe that reports generally should not be addressed solely to the board of directors, unless the entity is closely held. An auditor's ultimate responsibility is to the stockholders rather than to the entity or its management.

Sometimes an auditor is retained to audit the financial statements of a nonclient entity on behalf of a client. In that case, the report should be addressed to the client and not to the entity being audited or its directors or stockholders (but see the discussion about confidentiality in Chapter 3, concerning the necessity for making sure that all involved parties understand the auditor's responsibility).

(ii) Identifying the Statements. The statements should be clearly identified, usually in the introductory paragraph. The exact name of the entity should be used and the statements audited should be enumerated. Generally, these are the balance sheet, the statement of income and retained earnings, and the statement of cash flows. If any other statements are covered by the report, they also should be enumerated; for example, some entities present a separate statement of changes in stockholders' equity accounts. Sometimes it is more convenient to refer to an accompanying list or table of contents that enumerates the statements, in which case the first sentence of the scope paragraph would read as follows, "We have audited the financial statements of X Company listed in the accompanying table of contents." The enumeration of the statements need not be repeated in the opinion paragraph.

---

[3] Advisory Panel on Auditor Independence, *Strengthening the Professionalism of the Independent Auditor: Report to the Public Oversight Board of the SEC Practice Section, AICPA*, Stamford, CT: Public Oversight Board, 1994, p. 19.

(iii) Periods Covered.   The periods reported on should also be specified. In annual reports it is common to report on two years for comparative purposes. Entities whose securities are registered with the SEC are, however, required to present audited comparative income statements and statements of cash flows for three years and balance sheets for two years. A continuing auditor should update his or her report on the individual financial statements of the one or more prior periods presented on a comparative basis with those of the current period by referring to those statements in the introductory and opinion paragraphs.[4]

(iv) Dating the Report.   Inevitably, an auditor's report is issued on a date later than the end of the period being reported on because it takes time to close the books, prepare financial statements, and complete final auditing procedures. The selection of the appropriate date is discussed in Chapter 27.

Reports filed with the SEC also are required to indicate the city and state where issued. This information may be included in reports for non-SEC entities as well.

28.3 EXPLANATORY LANGUAGE ADDED TO THE STANDARD REPORT

There are several circumstances that while not affecting the auditor's unqualified opinion may require that the auditor add an explanatory paragraph (or other explanatory language) to the standard report. Those circumstances are discussed in the following paragraphs.

(a) Opinion Based in Part on Report of Another Auditor

Chapter 7 discusses audit planning considerations when part of an engagement is carried out by another auditor. The auditor who serves as the principal auditor may decide not to refer to that circumstance in the report, thus assuming responsibility for the work of the other auditor. If the principal auditor does refer to the work of the other auditor, the standard report is expanded to indicate the division of responsibility and the magnitude of the portion of the financial statements audited by the other auditor. Normally, this is done by noting the percentage or dollar amount of total assets and total revenues audited by the other auditor. Sometimes, other appropriate criteria, such as the percentage of net income, may be used. The other auditor usually is not named. When other auditors are named, their express permission must be obtained and their reports must be presented together with that of the principal auditor.

---

[4] SAS No. 58 states in a footnote to paragraph 74 (AU Section 508.65)

> An updated report on prior-period financial statements should be distinguished from a reissuance of a previous report . . . since in issuing an updated report the continuing auditor considers information that he has become aware of during his audit of the current-period financial statements . . . and because an updated report is issued in conjunction with the auditor's report on the current-period financial statements.

See also the discussion later in this chapter, "Different Reports on Comparative Financial Statements Presented."

If the other auditor's report contains explanatory language or a departure from an unqualified opinion (see the later discussion), the principal auditor should decide whether the cause of the explanatory language or departure is of such a nature and significance, in relation to the financial statements the principal auditor is reporting on, that it requires explanatory language or a departure from an unqualified opinion in the principal auditor's report. If the subject of the explanatory language or departure is not material to the overall financial statements, and if the other auditor's report is not presented, the principal auditor need not refer to the explanatory language or departure. If the other auditor's report is presented, the principal auditor may wish to make reference to the explanatory language or departure and its disposition.

An example of an unqualified report (on comparative financial statements) in which the work of another auditor has been used and is referred to follows[5]:

> We have audited the consolidated balance sheets of ABC Company as of December 31, 19X2 and 19X1, and the related consolidated statements of income, retained earnings, and cash flows for the years then ended. These financial statements are the responsibility of the Company's management. Our responsibility is to express an opinion on these financial statements based on our audits. We did not audit the financial statements of B Company, a wholly-owned subsidiary, which statements reflect total assets of $_____ and $_____ as of December 31, 19X2 and 19X1, respectively, and total revenues of $_____ and $_____ for the years then ended. Those statements were audited by other auditors whose report has been furnished to us, and our opinion, insofar as it relates to the amounts included for B Company, is based solely on the report of the other auditors.
>
> We conducted our audits in accordance with generally accepted auditing standards. Those standards require that we plan and perform the audit to obtain reasonable assurance about whether the financial statements are free of material misstatement. An audit includes examining, on a test basis, evidence supporting the amounts and disclosures in the financial statements. An audit also includes assessing the accounting principles used and significant estimates made by management, as well as evaluating the overall financial statement presentation. We believe that our audits and the report of other auditors provide a reasonable basis for our opinion.
>
> In our opinion, based on our audits and the report of other auditors, the consolidated financial statements referred to above present fairly, in all material respects, the financial position of ABC Company as of December 31, 19X2 and 19X1, and the results of its operations and its cash flows for the years then ended in conformity with generally accepted accounting principles.

The disclosure is lengthy and somewhat awkward and much expanded from reporting practice of some years ago when it was customary only to state that part of the engagement had been carried out by other auditors. Employing more than one auditor is an acceptable practice, but often results in divided responsibility and risk of misunderstanding or omission. The practice is sometimes followed, however, to take advantage of specialized expertise or when the principal auditor is not located in areas where subsidiaries are located. Chapter 7 includes a discussion of additional procedures the principal auditor may follow when the work of other auditors is used.

[5] SAS No. 58 (AU Section 508.08) specifies that a title that includes the word "independent" is one of the basic elements of the standard audit report. The illustrative standard reports in AU Section 508 use the title "Independent Auditor's Report." This and subsequent illustrative audit reports present only the body of the report and omit the title, as well as the date of the report and signature of the auditor's firm.

Also as discussed in Chapter 7, an auditor may obtain and use a report by another auditor on internal control at a service organization that is used by the entity to execute or record certain transactions or to process certain data. The auditor's report on the financial statements should not refer to the report of the auditor who reported on the service organization's internal control. As stated in AU Section 324.24, "The service [organization's] auditor's report is used in the audit, but the service [organization's] auditor is not responsible for examining a portion of the financial statements. . . . Thus, there cannot be a meaningful indication of a division of responsibility for the financial statements."

(b) Departures from a Promulgated Accounting Principle with Which an Auditor Agrees

Since 1964, members of the AICPA have been expected to treat departures from accounting principles promulgated in the Opinions of the APB and in the predecessor Accounting Research Bulletins as departures from GAAP, leading to a qualified or an adverse opinion. That expectation is now incorporated in Rule 203 of the AICPA Code of Professional Conduct and the related interpretations; it also applies to the pronouncements of the FASB and the GASB. It is covered by SAS No. 58 (AU Section 508.14–.15).

In rare and unusual circumstances, a departure from an accounting principle promulgated by the APB, the FASB, or the GASB may be required to present a particular transaction or other event or circumstance in a manner that is not misleading. If the auditor and entity management agree that a certain treatment that departs from such a promulgated principle is required in order to make the statements not misleading, it is permissible for the financial statements to reflect the departure, provided the departure and its effect are disclosed both in a note to the financial statements and in the auditor's report. The reason for believing that the departure from a promulgated standard is justified should be stated, and the auditor should express an unqualified opinion.

Although the kind of "unusual circumstances" referred to herein might conceivably exist in which the literal application of a pronouncement covered by Rule 203 would have the effect of making the financial statements misleading, instances of this kind arise only very rarely. Consequently, this type of opinion modification is rare and a recent example of it could not be located. The best-known example of that circumstance dates back to a report on an entity's financial statements for the year ended December 31, 1973. An explanatory paragraph therein read as follows:

> In October, 1973, the Company extinguished a substantial amount of debt through a direct exchange of new equity securities. Application of Opinion No. 26 of the Accounting Principles Board to this exchange requires that the excess of the debt extinguished over the present value of the new securities should be recognized as a gain in the period in which the extinguishment occurred. While it is not practicable to determine the present value of the new equity securities issued, such value is at least $2,000,000 less than the face amount of the debt extinguished. It is the opinion of the Company's Management, an opinion with which we agree, that no realization of a gain occurred in this exchange (Note 1), and therefore, no recognition of the excess of the debt extinguished over the present value of the new securities has been made in these financial statements.

Note 1 read (in part) as follows:

Extinguishment of Debt: In October, 1973, the Company issued 50,000 shares of 6% Prior Preferred Shares, par value $100, in exchange for the outstanding $5,000,000 of 6% senior subordinated notes. It also issued 18,040 shares of convertible $6 Serial Preference Shares, Series A, stated value $100 a share, in exchange for $1,300,000 and $504,000 of outstanding 6% convertible subordinated debentures and 5 3/4% convertible subordinated debentures, respectively. The Company expensed the unamortized balance (approximately $148,000) of the deferred financing costs associated with the issuance of each of the three classes of subordinated debt to the extent that such unamortized balances were allocable to the debt so extinguished.

Opinion No. 26 of the Accounting Principles Board of the American Institute of CPA's states that the excess of the carrying amount of the extinguished debt over the present value of the new securities issued should be recognized as a gain in the statement of operations of the period in which the extinguishment occurred. While it is not practicable to determine the present value of the new equity securities issued, such value is at least $2,000,000 less than the face amount of the debt extinguished. However, the terms and provisions of these new equity securities [which included a mandatory redemption provision] are substantially similar to those of the debt securities extinguished, both on the basis of the Company's continuing operations and in the event of liquidation. It is the opinion of the management, therefore, that no gain as a result of this exchange has been realized or should be recognized in the financial statements.

The auditors believed that the financial statements were presented fairly in conformity with GAAP, which would not have been the case if APB Opinion No. 26 had been followed. In this instance, the auditors did not, in the opinion paragraph, qualify the opinion as a result of the described departure from a promulgated accounting principle.

(c) Predecessor Auditor's Report Presented versus Not Presented

When comparative financial statements are presented and the prior year's statements were audited by another auditor, the successor auditor and the entity have two options concerning the auditor's report. Under the first option, the entity could make arrangements with the predecessor auditor to reissue and present the report on the financial statements of the prior period, provided the predecessor auditor performs the procedures described in paragraph 80 of SAS No. 58 (AU Section 508.71).

That paragraph requires that before reissuing (and presenting) a previously issued report, a predecessor auditor should consider whether the previous opinion is still appropriate. To do that,

A predecessor auditor should (a) read the financial statements of the current period, (b) compare the prior-period financial statements that he reported on with the financial statements to be presented for comparative purposes, and (c) obtain a letter of representations from the successor auditor.

The predecessor auditor also should read "other information" that may accompany the financial statements, as discussed in the following section. The predecessor auditor should not refer in the reissued report to the report of the successor auditor. The successor auditor should report only on the current year's financial statements.

Under the second option, the predecessor auditor's report is not presented.[6] In this case, pursuant to paragraph 83 of SAS No. 58 (AU Section 508.74),

> The successor auditor should indicate in the introductory paragraph of his report (a) that the financial statements of the prior period were audited by another auditor, (b) the date of his report, (c) the type of report issued by the predecessor auditor, and (d) if the report was other than a standard report, the substantive reasons therefor.

An example of a successor auditor's report when the predecessor auditor's report is not presented follows:

> We have audited the balance sheet of ABC Company as of December 31, 19X2, and the related statements of income, retained earnings, and cash flows for the year then ended. These financial statements are the responsibility of the Company's management. Our responsibility is to express an opinion on these financial statements based on our audit. The financial statements of ABC Company as of December 31, 19X1, were audited by other auditors whose report dated March 31, 19X2, expressed an unqualified opinion on those statements.
>
> [*Same second paragraph as the standard report*]
>
> In our opinion, the 19X2 financial statements referred to above present fairly, in all material respects, the financial position of ABC Company as of December 31, 19X2, and the results of its operations and its cash flows for the year then ended in conformity with generally accepted accounting principles.

If the predecessor auditor's report was other than a standard report, the successor auditor should describe the nature of and reasons for any explanatory paragraphs or opinion qualifications.

(d)   Material Inconsistency Between Financial Statements and Other Information Reported by Management

An entity may publish a document, such as an annual report, that contains information in addition to audited financial statements and the auditor's report. That information, which is referred to in professional pronouncements [SAS No. 8, *Other Information in Documents Containing Audited Financial Statements* (AU Section 550)] as "other information," includes such items as a ten-year financial summary and an analysis of financial data in the president's letter. It also includes management's discussion and analysis of operations (for the three most recent years) and of changes in financial position and liquidity (during the two most recent years), as required of entities whose securities are registered with the SEC. In addition, an auditing interpretation (AU Section 9550.01–.06) indicates that statements made in a report by management on the entity's internal control are "other information" covered by SAS No. 8.

---

[6] SEC proxy Rule 14c–3 permits the separate report of the predecessor auditor to be omitted in the annual report to securityholders, provided the registrant has obtained a reissued report from the predecessor auditor. The separate report of the predecessor auditor is, however, required in filings with the Commission.

The auditor has no responsibility to corroborate "other information," but SAS No. 8 specifies that the auditor does have a responsibility to read it and consider whether it is materially inconsistent with information appearing in the financial statements. If it is, the auditor should determine whether the financial statements, the auditor's report, or both should be revised. If the auditor concludes that they do not require revision, he or she should request the entity to revise the other information. If the other information is not revised to eliminate the inconsistency, the auditor should consider whether to withhold the audit report, withdraw from the engagement, or include an explanatory paragraph describing the inconsistency.[7] The auditor's opinion would still be unqualified, since the deficiency would not be in the audited financial statements. Such instances are, as might be expected, extremely rare, since even management that is prone to "puffery" of its accomplishments is likely to retreat in the face of the possibility of an explanatory comment in the auditor's report.

The auditor also has a responsibility to take action if, on reading the other information, he or she determines (on the basis of knowledge obtained in the course of the audit) that there is a material misstatement of fact that is not related to information in the audited financial statements. Beyond suggesting that the auditor consult others, including legal counsel, and notify the entity's management, the authoritative literature provides scant guidance; nor does the literature require the auditor to disclose the misstatement.

The Cohen Commission recommended (page 69) that the auditor be required to read the other information to ensure that it is not inconsistent with *anything* the auditor knows, as a result of the audit, about the entity and its operations and that the auditor modify the report to describe the misstatement if management does not correct it. At the date of this writing, no professional standard-setting body has acted on this recommendation.

(e) Supplementary Information Required by FASB or GASB Pronouncements

Supplementary information required by the FASB or the GASB differs from other types of information outside the basic financial statements. This is because the FASB or the GASB considers the information an essential part of the financial reporting of certain entities and has, therefore, established guidelines for the measurement and presentation of the information. For this reason, the AICPA has established limited procedures to be applied by the auditor to this information. The limited procedures, found in AU Section 558, *Required Supplementary Information*, can be summarized as follows:

- Inquire of management as to any significant assumptions or interpretations underlying the measurement or presentation, whether the methods of measurement and presentation are within guidelines prescribed by the FASB or the GASB, whether the assumptions or methods have changed from those used in the prior period, and the reasons for any such changes.

---

[7] As discussed in Chapter 29, an explanatory paragraph also is required if selected quarterly financial data required by SEC Regulation S-K has been omitted by the entity or has not been reviewed by the auditor.

- Compare the information for consistency with the audited financial statements, other knowledge obtained during the audit of the financial statements, and management's responses to the specific inquiries.

- Consider whether specific written representations on the information should be obtained from management.

- Make additional inquiries based on the results of the foregoing if the auditor believes that the measurement or presentation of the information may be inappropriate.

At the time of this writing, the only supplementary information required by the FASB or the GASB is oil and gas reserve information (SFAS No. 69, *Disclosures about Oil and Gas Producing Activities*) and ten-year historical trend pension information by public employee retirement systems and state and local governmental employers (GASB Statement No. 5, *Disclosure of Pension Information by Public Employee Retirement Systems and State and Local Government Employers*).

AU Section 558 specifies reporting guidelines, based on the performance of the limited procedures listed above, for FASB- or GASB-required information. If the information is presented in a note to the financial statements, it should be marked as "unaudited" or the auditor should expand the standard audit report to disclaim an opinion on the information. If the information appears outside the financial statements and the entity indicates that the auditor has performed procedures and does not also indicate that the auditor does not express an opinion on the information, the auditor should disclaim an opinion on the information. [If the required information has been audited, the auditor should follow the reporting guidance in SAS No. 42, *Reporting on Condensed Financial Statements and Selected Financial Data* (AU Section 552)]. In addition, AU Section 558.08 provides only for exception reporting; that is, the auditor is required to report, in an additional explanatory paragraph, (a) deficiencies in or the omission of such information, (b) an inability to complete the prescribed limited procedures, or (c) the inability to remove substantial doubts about whether the supplementary information conforms to prescribed guidelines.

(f) Going Concern Uncertainties

Chapter 26 discusses the auditor's performance and reporting responsibilities with respect to going concern uncertainties. If, based on the guidance suggested in Chapter 26, the auditor believes that there is substantial doubt about the entity's ability to continue as a going concern for a reasonable period of time (not to exceed one year from the date of the financial statements), he or she should determine that this is appropriately disclosed in the financial statements and should include an explanatory paragraph in the auditor's report (following the opinion paragraph) to reflect that conclusion. This is the only type of uncertainty for which an explanatory paragraph is required. If the entity's disclosures with respect to its ability to continue as a going concern are inadequate, a departure from generally accepted accounting principles exists and would result in either a qualified or an adverse opinion, as explained later in this chapter.

An example of an explanatory paragraph from SAS No. 59 (AU Section 341.13) follows:

The accompanying financial statements have been prepared assuming that the Company will continue as a going concern. As discussed in Note X to the financial statements, the Company has suffered recurring losses from operations and has a net capital deficiency that raise substantial doubt about its ability to continue as a going concern. Management's plans in regard to these matters are also described in Note X. The financial statements do not include any adjustments that might result from the outcome of this uncertainty.

SAS No. 64 amended SAS No. 59 (AU Section 341.12–.13) to clarify that the auditor's conclusion about the entity's ability to continue as a going concern should be expressed using the phrase "substantial doubt about its ability to continue as a going concern" or similar wording that includes both of the terms, "substantial doubt" and "going concern." SAS No. 77 prohibits the auditor from using conditional language—such as "If the company is unable to obtain financing, there may be substantial doubt . . ."—in the auditor's conclusion about the entity's ability to continue as a going concern in the explanatory paragraph (AU Section 341.13).

SAS No. 59 (AU Section 341.16) provides the following guidance when substantial doubt that formerly existed no longer exists and *comparative financial statements* are presented:

> If substantial doubt about the entity's ability to continue as a going concern for a reasonable period of time existed at the date of prior period financial statements that are presented on a comparative basis, and that doubt has been removed in the current period, the explanatory paragraph included in the auditor's report (following the opinion paragraph) on the financial statements of the prior period should not be repeated.

An auditor may be asked to *reissue* a report on financial statements and eliminate the going concern explanatory paragraph that appeared in the original report after the conditions that gave rise to substantial doubt about the entity's ability to continue as a going concern have been resolved. An interpretation of SAS No. 59 (AU Section 9341) describes factors the auditor should consider in determining whether to reissue the report without the going concern explanatory paragraph.

SAS No. 59 (AU Section 341.04) notes that

> The auditor is not responsible for predicting future conditions or events. The fact that the entity may cease to exist as a going concern subsequent to receiving a report from the auditor that does not refer to substantial doubt, even within one year following the date of the financial statements, does not, in itself, indicate inadequate performance by the auditor. Accordingly, the absence of reference to substantial doubt in an auditor's report should not be viewed as providing assurance as to an entity's ability to continue as a going concern.

(g) Lack of Consistency

The second standard of reporting is:

> The report shall identify those circumstances in which . . . [generally accepted accounting] principles have not been consistently observed in the current period in relation to the preceding period.[8]

---

[8] Until 1988, generally accepted auditing standards required a reference to consistency in the auditor's report. That requirement was eliminated by SAS No. 58, which requires the auditor to report only a *lack* of consistency in the application of GAAP.

The consistency standard requires an auditor to inform readers in the report if GAAP have not been applied consistently from period to period; consistency within a period and between periods is presumed unless otherwise disclosed. The objective is to ensure that changes in accounting principles that materially affect the comparability of financial statements between periods are highlighted in the auditor's report as well as in the financial statements.

Of course, factors other than consistent application of accounting principles also affect the comparability of financial statements between periods. For example, changed conditions that necessitate changes in accounting and changed conditions that are unrelated to accounting may exist. The effect of those other factors normally requires disclosure in the financial statements (covered by the third standard of reporting[9]), but not explanatory language in the auditor's report. In requiring other effects on comparability to be disclosed only under the more general third standard, the profession has singled out the consistency of accounting principles for separate attention. The reason for the different treatment lies in the nature of alternative accounting principles: Alternatives that are considered generally accepted may in some cases be substituted one for another, thus changing accounting results without any change in the underlying economic substance—a sound and sometimes necessary practice that is obviously susceptible to abuse.

Changes in accounting principles occur fairly often. Entities from time to time change managements, operating philosophies, or judgments about which accounting principles are most appropriate for the entity. Also, authoritative FASB and GASB pronouncements may change the way that various transactions or other events and circumstances are to be measured or reported.

Any significant change in accounting principle or method of applying a principle must be referred to in the auditor's report in an explanatory paragraph (following the opinion paragraph). That paragraph should identify the change and refer to the note in the financial statements that discusses the change. An example of an appropriate explanatory paragraph would be[10]

> As discussed in Note X to the financial statements, the Company changed its method of computing depreciation in 19X7.

The auditor's concurrence with a change is implicit unless he or she takes exception to it in the opinion.

Accounting Principles Board Opinion No. 20, *Accounting Changes* (Accounting Standards Sections A06 and A35), provides standards for accounting for and disclosing ac-

---

[9] The third standard of reporting states, "Informative disclosures in the financial statements are to be regarded as reasonably adequate unless otherwise stated in the report" (AU Section 150.02).

[10] SAS No. 58 (AU Section 508.18) notes that

> The addition of this explanatory paragraph in the auditor's report is required in reports on financial statements of subsequent years as long as the year of the change is presented and reported on. However, if the accounting change is accounted for by retroactive restatement of the financial statements affected, the additional paragraph is required only in the year of the change since, in subsequent years, all periods presented will be comparable.

An explanatory paragraph is also not required when a change in accounting principle that does not require a cumulative effect adjustment is made at the beginning of the earliest year presented and reported on.

counting changes in financial statements. Section 420, "Consistency of Application of Generally Accepted Accounting Principles," of SAS No. 1 (AU Section 420) provides guidelines for determining which accounting changes affect consistency and, therefore, require an explanatory paragraph in the auditor's report.

(i) Identifying Changes in Accounting Principles. Both APB Opinion No. 20 and SAS No. 1 distinguish changes in accounting principles from changes in accounting estimates or changes in the reporting entity. The three kinds of changes, called collectively "accounting changes," are further distinguished from other factors affecting the comparability of financial statements between periods, including errors in previously issued statements, changes in statement classification, initial adoption of an accounting principle to recognize an event occurring for the first time, and adoption or modification of an accounting principle necessitated by transactions that are clearly different in substance from previous transactions. Of all classes mentioned, only changes in accounting principles and, sometimes, changes in the reporting entity require an explanatory paragraph in an auditor's report under the second standard of reporting. Of course, the others may have to be either disclosed or commented on under the third standard of reporting.

(ii) Justification for Changes in Accounting Principles. An important advance in disclosure standards was the requirement in APB Opinion No. 20 (Accounting Standards Section A06), issued in 1971, that a change in accounting principle be justified by a clear explanation by management of why the newly adopted principle is preferable and that the justification be disclosed in the financial statements. Requiring that changes in accounting principles be justified was a significant step toward expecting issuers of financial statements to explain the "why" of their accounting as well as the "what." It should be noted, however, that while Opinion No. 20 prescribes that a note to the financial statements explain clearly why a newly adopted accounting principle is preferable, the authoritative literature of the profession does not explicitly require the auditor to be satisfied as to that preferability. The authoritative literature requires only that the auditor determine that a reasonable justification of preferability was properly disclosed. The SEC, however, requires the auditor to submit a "preferability letter" stating that the auditor is satisfied with the justification provided by management when an accounting change has been made. An illustrative preferability letter is shown in Chapter 29.

(iii) Correction of Errors. There are two types of corrections of errors. Both are accounted for as prior-period adjustments, and previous periods' statements are retroactively restated. The first type, which requires an explanatory paragraph following the auditor's opinion, involves a change from an accounting principle that is not generally accepted to one that is, including the correction of a mistake in applying a principle.

The second type of error correction involves errors in previously issued financial statements resulting from mathematical mistakes, oversight, or misuse of facts that existed at the time the financial statements were originally prepared, and does not involve the consistency standard. A correction of an error of this type should be reported in a note to the financial statements but need not be recognized in the auditor's report. The auditor may, however, include an explanatory paragraph to emphasize the revision. An example of such a paragraph when there has been a correction of an error resulting from an oversight is:

> As more fully described in note A of notes to statements of consolidated earnings (loss), certain errors resulting in overstatements of previously reported year-end inventories as of April 28, 19X7, April 29, 19X6 and April 30, 19X5 were discovered by management of the Company during the course of determining year-end inventory as of May 3, 19X8. Accordingly, the consolidated balance sheet as of April 28, 19X7 and the statements of consolidated earnings (loss), consolidated stockholders' equity, and consolidated cash flows for each of the three years then ended have been restated to reflect corrections to previously reported year-end inventories and the related tax effect.

If the auditor had previously reported on the financial statements containing the error, he or she should refer to Section 6(a), Discovery of Information After the Report Date.

(h) Emphasis of a Matter

The foregoing discussion of explanatory language added to the standard report covered situations in which such language is required. Although it does not occur often, sometimes the auditor wishes to emphasize a matter regarding the financial statements, even though he or she is expressing an unqualified opinion. Examples of matters the auditor may wish to emphasize are:

- That the entity is a component of a larger entity
- That the entity has had significant transactions with related parties
- Unusually important subsequent events
- Accounting matters other than those involving a change or changes in accounting principles, affecting comparability of the financial statements with those of the preceding period

Such explanatory language should be presented in a separate paragraph of the auditor's report. Professional standards do not specify where in the auditor's report the emphasis paragraph should appear. The opinion paragraph should not refer to the explanatory paragraph.

28.4 DEPARTURES FROM UNQUALIFIED OPINIONS

The fourth standard of reporting (AU Section 150.02) reads as follows:

> The report shall either contain an expression of opinion regarding the financial statements, taken as a whole, or an assertion to the effect that an opinion cannot be expressed. When an overall opinion cannot be expressed, the reasons therefor should be stated. In all cases where an auditor's name is associated with financial statements, the report should contain a clear-cut indication of the character of the auditor's work and the degree of responsibility, if any, the auditor is taking.

The standardized language of the unqualified report fosters precision in meeting this standard. The professional literature, both at the time of publication of the fourth standard of reporting and since then, has attempted to provide similar precision in describing departures from the standard report. Authoritative pronouncements on the fourth standard of reporting, including SAS No. 58, are set forth in AU Section 500 of *AICPA Professional Standards*.

There are two kinds of problems to overcome in achieving adequate precision and clarity of communication. First is the problem of trying to find a limited number of precisely defined qualifying or limiting phrases that will cover all possible situations. For professional auditors who have studied and understand the meaning and usage of the common qualifying phrases that have been developed, the effort has been largely successful. New conditions keep appearing, however, and when they do, a period of uncertainty ensues while auditors experiment and decide whether the new conditions can be covered by an existing type of qualification or a new phrase is required.

The second problem is communicating to the public the meaning of the qualifying phrases and the distinctions between them. The meaning of a highly stylized phrase can be understood and agreed on by practitioners, but it is useless unless it is equally recognized and understood by most readers. SAS No. 58 (AU Section 508.21) calls for explaining all departures from an unqualified opinion in one or more separate paragraphs preceding the opinion paragraph. Doing so clearly highlights the departures and provides an unmistakable place for full description, improving both disclosure and communication.

SAS No. 58 classifies departures from the standard unqualified report, sometimes referred to as a "clean" opinion, as qualified opinions, adverse opinions, and disclaimers of opinion. These departures are discussed in the following paragraphs.

(a) Qualified Opinions

There are two basic reasons for qualifying an opinion: limitations on the scope of the audit and departures from GAAP.

(i) Scope Limitations.   An audit can be limited by circumstances beyond the entity's control that preclude the auditor from employing the auditing procedures that would otherwise be considered necessary, or it can be limited by client-imposed restrictions.

(1) Circumstances Precluding Necessary Auditing Procedures.   Sometimes an auditor is not able to carry out procedures that customarily are considered necessary in the circumstances as a basis for rendering an unqualified opinion. In most instances, the auditor is able to design and perform alternative procedures that provide sufficient assurance that the relevant audit objectives have been achieved. The most common instances in which the auditor might not be able to perform alternative procedures are when conditions make it impracticable or impossible to confirm accounts receivable or observe inventories. Other examples of such scope limitations involve noncontrolling investments in affiliated entities, when the auditor is unable to either (1) obtain audited financial statements of an investee or apply auditing procedures to unaudited financial statements of an investee, or (2) examine sufficient evidence that

unrealized profits and losses resulting from transactions between the investor and the investee have been eliminated.

If an auditor cannot obtain satisfaction by means of alternative auditing procedures when circumstances preclude conventional procedures, the auditor should describe the problem and modify the standard report. If the auditor decides to express a qualified opinion (rather than disclaim an opinion), the problem should be described in a separate paragraph and referred to in both the scope paragraph and the opinion paragraph.

A scope limitation should always be described entirely within the auditor's report, in contrast to the treatment of qualifications related to information presented in the financial statements, which are usually described in a note to the statements and only referred to in the report. That is because a qualification based on a scope limitation arises from the auditor's activities and limitations on them, not from the financial statements themselves, which are the representations of management.

The qualification itself should be stated in terms of the scope limitation. SAS No. 58 (AU Section 508.26) presents an example regarding an investment in a foreign affiliate (the example assumes that the effects of the scope limitation do not cause the auditor to conclude that a disclaimer of opinion is appropriate).

[*Same first paragraph as the standard report*]

Except as discussed in the following paragraph, we conducted our audits in accordance with generally accepted auditing standards. Those standards require that we plan and perform the audit to obtain reasonable assurance about whether the financial statements are free of material misstatement. An audit includes examining, on a test basis, evidence supporting the amounts and disclosures in the financial statements. An audit also includes assessing the accounting principles used and significant estimates made by management, as well as evaluating the overall financial statement presentation. We believe that our audits provide a reasonable basis for our opinion.

We were unable to obtain audited financial statements supporting the Company's investment in a foreign affiliate stated at $_____ and $_____ at December 31, 19X2 and 19X1, respectively, or its equity in earnings of that affiliate of $_____ and $_____, which is included in net income for the years then ended as described in Note X to the financial statements; nor were we able to satisfy ourselves as to the carrying value of the investment in the foreign affiliate or the equity in its earnings by other auditing procedures.

In our opinion, except for the effects of such adjustments, if any, as might have been determined to be necessary had we been able to examine evidence regarding the foreign affiliate investment and earnings, the financial statements referred to in the first paragraph above present fairly, in all material respects, the financial position of X Company as of December 31, 19X2 and 19X1, and the results of its operations and its cash flows for the years then ended in conformity with generally accepted accounting principles.

(2) *Client-Imposed Restrictions.* The most common client-imposed restrictions are limitations preventing observation of physical inventories, confirmation of accounts receivable, or examination of a significant subsidiary. Usually, if scope is limited by client-imposed restrictions, an auditor should disclaim an opinion (see later discussion) because management's election to limit the auditor's scope implies also an election to limit the auditor's responsibility. On rare occasions, if a client-imposed scope limitation applies to an isolated transaction or a single account, a qualified opinion may be acceptable.

(ii) Departures from GAAP. The standard report makes the positive assertion that the financial statements are presented in conformity with generally accepted accounting principles; thus, any departures from GAAP must be noted as "exceptions" to that assertion. Such departures are rare in practice because most entities believe that an auditor's opinion qualified because of a departure from GAAP carries intolerable implications, and so they use accounting principles that are generally accepted. Also, only rarely are such qualified opinions acceptable in SEC filings. Nevertheless, instances of departures sometimes occur; the most common ones are described and examples presented in the following paragraphs.

(1) Departures from Measurement Principles. SAS No. 58 (AU Section 508.39) gives the following example of an auditor's report that is qualified because of the use of an accounting principle that is at variance with GAAP:

[*Same first and second paragraphs as the standard report*]

The Company has excluded, from property and debt in the accompanying balance sheets, certain lease obligations that, in our opinion, should be capitalized in order to conform with generally accepted accounting principles. If these lease obligations were capitalized, property would be increased by $_____ and $_____, long-term debt by $_____ and $_____, and retained earnings by $_____ and $_____ as of December 31, 19X2 and 19X1, respectively. Additionally, net income would be increased (decreased) by $_____ and $_____ and earnings per share would be increased (decreased) by $_____ and $_____, respectively, for the years then ended.

In our opinion, except for the effects of not capitalizing certain lease obligations as discussed in the preceding paragraph, the financial statements referred to above present fairly, in all material respects, the financial position of X Company as of December 31, 19X2 and 19X1, and the results of its operations and its cash flows for the years then ended in conformity with generally accepted accounting principles.

If the pertinent facts are disclosed in the notes to the financial statements, the separate paragraph preceding the opinion paragraph would read as follows:

As more fully described in Note X to the financial statements, the Company has excluded certain lease obligations from property and debt in the accompanying balance sheets. In our opinion, generally accepted accounting principles require that such obligations be included in the balance sheets.

(2) Departures from Disclosure Principles. Under the third standard of reporting (AU Section 150.02),

Informative disclosures in the financial statements are to be regarded as reasonably adequate unless otherwise stated in the report.

SAS No. 32, *Adequacy of Disclosure in Financial Statements* (AU Section 431), is general about what constitutes informative disclosures. Some specific disclosures required in financial statements are contained in various pronouncements that constitute GAAP, for example, Statements of the FASB and the GASB, Opinions of the Accounting Principles Board, Accounting Research Bulletins, and AICPA Statements of Position. Specific industry disclosures often are called for in AICPA industry audit and accounting guides. Those pronouncements, however, cover only the topics addressed, and not the vast area of financial information on which no pronouncement has been issued.

The intent of the third standard of reporting is to establish that issuers of financial statements and auditors have a responsibility to ensure that disclosures are adequate, regardless of whether a requirement, convention, or precedent covers the matter. Some issuers of financial statements, however, take the approach of "no rule, no disclosure." Court cases and items appearing in the press indicate that a disclosure policy based on this attitude is dangerous, not to mention its not being in the public interest. Deciding what should be disclosed beyond what is specifically required in authoritative pronouncements, however, requires a balancing of diverse interests. On one hand, management may believe that certain disclosures are likely to result in a competitive disadvantage or other detriment to the entity or its stockholders. On the other hand, directors, management, auditors, and their legal counsel need to consider the possibility that a detrimental disclosure not made may be a basis for litigation in the wake of subsequent difficulties, even if the cause of the difficulties is completely unrelated to the undisclosed matter.

Disclosure is never a substitute for the proper recognition and measurement of transactions and other events and circumstances in conformity with GAAP. In practice, a temptation on the part of issuers and auditors sometimes exists to resolve a difficult problem by presenting information in a footnote rather than by adjusting the financial statements. For example, a contingency that is likely to occur and for which an estimate of loss is known must be accrued in the financial statements according to GAAP; mere disclosure of such an item is not an acceptable alternative. (Recognition, measurement, and disclosure principles for contingencies and other types of uncertainties are discussed in Chapter 26.)

An auditor who believes that disclosures in the financial statements are inadequate is required to so state and to make the necessary disclosures in the auditor's report, if it is practicable to do so and unless the omission from the auditor's report is recognized as appropriate in a specific SAS. Since most entities choose to make the necessary disclosures rather than to have them appear in the auditor's report, this type of disclosure in an auditor's report is extremely rare. SAS No. 58 (AU Section 508.42) contains the following example of a report qualified for inadequate disclosure:

[*Same first and second paragraphs as the standard report*]

The Company's financial statements do not disclose [*describe the nature of the omitted disclosures*]. In our opinion, disclosure of this information is required by generally accepted accounting principles.

In our opinion, except for the omission of the information discussed in the preceding paragraph, . . .

There are two exceptions to the requirement that, when informative disclosures are omitted from the financial statements, the auditor should make the necessary disclosures in the auditor's report. The two exceptions, specifically sanctioned in the SASs (AU Sections 435.10 and 508.44), pertain to omitted segment information that is required by GAAP and to the statement of cash flows. The auditor should qualify the report if an entity declines to present the necessary segment information or a statement of cash flows, but the auditor is not required to provide the omitted segment information or to prepare the statement of cash flows and include it in the report.

An example of a report qualified because of the absence of a statement of cash flows follows:

> We have audited the accompanying balance sheets of X Company as of December 31, 19X2 and 19X1, and the related statements of income and retained earnings for the years then ended. These financial statements are the responsibility of the Company's management. Our responsibility is to express an opinion on these financial statements based on our audit.
>
> [*Same second paragraph as the standard report*]
>
> The Company declined to present a statement of cash flows for the years ended December 31, 19X2 and 19X1. Presentation of such statement summarizing the Company's operating, investing, and financing activities is required by generally accepted accounting principles.
>
> In our opinion, except that the omission of a statement of cash flows results in an incomplete presentation as explained in the preceding paragraph, the financial statements referred to above present fairly, in all material respects, the financial position of X Company as of December 31, 19X2 and 19X1, and the results of its operations for the years then ended in conformity with generally accepted accounting principles.

(3) Departures Related to Accounting Changes. SAS No. 58 requires the auditor to evaluate a change in accounting principle to be satisfied that (a) the newly adopted accounting principle is GAAP, (b) the method of accounting for the effect of the change is in conformity with GAAP, and (c) management's justification for the change is reasonable. APB Opinion No. 20, paragraph 16 (Accounting Standards Section A06.112), states:

> The presumption that an entity should not change an accounting principle may be overcome only if the entity justifies the use of an alternative acceptable accounting principle on the basis that it is preferable.

If management has not provided reasonable justification for the change, or if the change does not meet both of the other conditions mentioned above, the auditor should express a qualified opinion or, if the effect of the change is sufficiently material, express an adverse opinion on the financial statements.

AU Section 508.52 contains an example of a report qualified because management has not provided reasonable justification for a change in accounting principles:

> [*Same first and second paragraphs as the standard report*]
>
> As disclosed in Note X to the financial statements, the Company adopted, in 19X2, the first-in, first-out method of accounting for its inventories, whereas it previously used the

last-in, first-out method. Although use of the first-in, first-out method is in conformity with generally accepted accounting principles, in our opinion the Company has not provided reasonable justification for making this change as required by generally accepted accounting principles.[11]

In our opinion, except for the change in accounting principle discussed in the preceding paragraph, the financial statements referred to above present fairly, in all material respects, the financial position of X Company as of December 31, 19X2 and 19X1, and the results of its operations and its cash flows for the years then ended in conformity with generally accepted accounting principles.

Accounting changes that result in qualified or adverse opinions should also trigger similar opinions in future years as long as the change continues to have a material effect on either the financial statements of subsequent years or the financial statements of the year of the change when presented for comparative purposes. For example, as indicated by SAS No. 58 (AU Section 508.54–.57):

- If the financial statements for the year of such change are presented and reported on with a subsequent year's financial statements, the auditor's report should disclose his reservations with respect to the statements for the year of change.
- If an entity has adopted an accounting principle that is not a generally accepted accounting principle, its continued use might have a material effect on the statements of a subsequent year on which the auditor is reporting. In this situation, the independent auditor should express either a qualified opinion or an adverse opinion, depending on the materiality of the departure in relation to the statements of the subsequent year.
- If an entity accounts for the effect of a change prospectively when generally accepted accounting principles require restatement or the inclusion of the cumulative effect of the change in the year of change, a subsequent year's financial statements could improperly include a charge or credit that is material to those statements. This situation also requires that the auditor express a qualified or an adverse opinion.
- If management has not provided reasonable justification for a change in accounting principles, the auditor's opinion should . . . continue to express his exception with respect to the financial statements for the year of change as long as they are presented and reported on. However, the auditor's exception relates to the accounting change and does not affect the status of a newly adopted principle as a generally accepted accounting principle. Accordingly, while expressing an exception for the year of change, the independent auditor's opinion regarding the subsequent years' statements need not express an exception to the use of the newly adopted principle.

(b) Adverse Opinions

An adverse opinion expresses a belief that financial statements are not presented fairly in conformity with generally accepted accounting principles or otherwise do not

---

[11] Because this paragraph contains all of the information required in an explanatory paragraph on consistency, a separate explanatory paragraph (following the opinion paragraph) is not necessary in this instance.

present fairly what they purport to present. It is required when an auditor believes that one or more departures from GAAP are sufficiently material to make the statements as a whole misleading. The auditor cannot sidestep an adverse opinion by disclaiming an opinion.

When an adverse opinion is issued, the opinion paragraph should include a reference to a separate paragraph in the auditor's report that discloses all the reasons for the adverse opinion, including any reservations the auditor may have regarding fair presentation in conformity with GAAP other than those that gave rise to the adverse opinion. The separate paragraph (or paragraphs, if appropriate) should also disclose the effects of the departures from GAAP on the financial statements, or state that such a determination is not possible.

Adverse opinions are rare. It is obviously better for all concerned to correct the conditions before such an opinion is issued, and it is usually within the entity's power to correct them. Adverse opinions are sometimes issued on financial statements showing appraised values of property. Occasionally, an adverse opinion is issued on the financial statements of a regulated company that are prepared in accordance with a basis of accounting prescribed by a governmental agency and are presented other than in filings with the agency. In that situation, AU Section 544 indicates that the auditor generally should issue either a qualified or an adverse opinion, depending on the materiality of the departures from GAAP, and also, in an additional paragraph of the report, express an opinion on whether the financial statements are presented in conformity with the prescribed basis of accounting.

An example of an adverse opinion, taken from SAS No. 58 (AU Section 508.60), follows:

[*Same first and second paragraphs as the standard report*]

As discussed in Note X to the financial statements, the Company carries its property, plant and equipment accounts at appraisal values, and provides depreciation on the basis of such values. Further, the Company does not provide for income taxes with respect to differences between financial income and taxable income arising because of the use, for income tax purposes, of the installment method of reporting gross profit from certain types of sales. Generally accepted accounting principles require that property, plant and equipment be stated at an amount not in excess of cost, reduced by depreciation based on such amount, and that deferred income taxes be provided.

Because of the departures from generally accepted accounting principles identified above, as of December 31, 19X2 and 19X1, inventories have been increased $_____ and $_____ by inclusion in manufacturing overhead of depreciation in excess of that based on cost; property, plant and equipment, less accumulated depreciation, is carried at $_____ and $_____ in excess of an amount based on the cost to the Company; and deferred income taxes of $_____ and $_____ have not been recorded; resulting in an increase of $_____ and $_____ in retained earnings and in appraisal surplus of $_____ and $_____, respectively. For the years ended December 31, 19X2 and 19X1, cost of goods sold has been increased $_____ and $_____, respectively, because of the effects of the depreciation accounting referred to above and deferred income taxes of $_____ and $_____ have not been provided, resulting in an increase in net income of $_____ and $_____, respectively.

In our opinion, because of the effects of the matters discussed in the preceding paragraphs, the financial statements referred to above do not present fairly, in conformity with generally accepted accounting principles, the financial position of X Company as of December 31, 19X2 and 19X1, or the results of its operations or its cash flows for the years then ended.

(c) Disclaimers of Opinion

If an auditor does not have enough evidence to form an opinion, the appropriate form of report is a disclaimer of opinion. A disclaimer can result from an inability to obtain sufficient competent evidential matter because the scope of the audit was seriously limited. In addition, while SAS No. 59 indicates that the addition of an explanatory paragraph to the auditor's report serves adequately to inform financial statement users when the auditor has significant doubt about the entity's ability to continue as a going concern, an auditor nevertheless may decide to decline to express an opinion in that situation.

SAS No. 58 (AU Section 508.62) states that the reasons for a disclaimer must be given in a separate paragraph of the report. The auditor also is required to disclose in a separate paragraph any reservations about fair presentation in conformity with GAAP. It would be misleading for an auditor to issue a disclaimer if a basis for an adverse or a qualified opinion existed. Adverse opinions and disclaimers of opinion are never interchangeable, nor can an auditor's report contain both an adverse opinion and a disclaimer of opinion. A report may, however, contain an opinion that is qualified for more than one reason. For example, an opinion may be qualified because of a scope limitation and because of a departure from GAAP.

An example of a report (AU Section 508.63) disclaiming an opinion resulting from a scope limitation follows:

We were engaged to audit the accompanying balance sheets of X Company as of December 31, 19X2 and 19X1, and the related statements of income, retained earnings, and cash flows for the years then ended. These financial statements are the responsibility of the Company's management.

[*Second paragraph of standard report should be omitted*]

The Company did not make a count of its physical inventory in 19X2 or 19X1, stated in the accompanying financial statements at $_____ as of December 31, 19X2, and at $_____ as of December 31, 19X1. Further, evidence supporting the cost of property and equipment acquired prior to December 31, 19X1, is no longer available. The Company's records do not permit the application of other auditing procedures to inventories or property and equipment.

Since the Company did not take physical inventories and we were not able to apply other auditing procedures to satisfy ourselves as to inventory quantities and the cost of property and equipment, the scope of our work was not sufficient to enable us to express, and we do not express, an opinion on these financial statements.

Note that, as required in a footnote to AU Section 508.63,

The wording in the first paragraph of the auditor's standard report is changed in a disclaimer of opinion because of a scope limitation. The first sentence now states that "we were engaged to audit" rather than "we have audited" since, because of the scope limitation, the auditor was not able to perform an audit in accordance with generally accepted auditing standards. In addition, the last sentence of the first paragraph is also deleted, because of the scope limitation, to eliminate the reference to the auditor's responsibility to express an opinion.

The most frequently encountered examples of disclaimers because of scope limitations arise in initial engagements for new clients. In those circumstances, an auditor may begin work well after the beginning of the year under audit. If the opening inventory has a material effect on income for the year (as it usually does in most manufacturing and commercial entities), an auditor must gather evidence on which to base an opinion on the opening inventory in order to issue an unqualified opinion. If this is not possible, which often occurs, the auditor should, in the authors' opinion, disclaim an opinion on the income statement and statement of cash flows. When the auditor is able to form an opinion on the opening inventory—which ordinarily happens when another reputable auditor is succeeded—there is no need to cover the point in the report. (Chapter 19 discusses appropriate auditing procedures in this situation.)

As an alternative, the auditor could be asked to report on the balance sheet only. Such an engagement does not involve a scope limitation if the auditor's access to information is not limited and if the auditor applies all procedures appropriate in the circumstances. If an income statement and statement of cash flows accompany the balance sheet, a disclaimer on them will be required.

While an auditor must stand ready to serve a client in any way appropriate, limited reporting engagements in which only a balance sheet is presented may not best meet the entity's needs. Engagements likely to lead to a disclaimer on the income statement and statement of cash flows when a full set of financial statements is presented (other than when the auditor is appointed after year-end) should be approached reluctantly because of the risk that incorrect inferences about the auditor's responsibilities will be drawn by the entity's management and other users. Consideration should be given to whether an entity's needs can be better served by a review of financial statements performed in accordance with SSARS No. 1 or by designing a special engagement in which responsibilities can be spelled out explicitly. Reports on special engagements are discussed in Chapter 30.

(d) Piecemeal Opinions

Piecemeal opinions (opinions on certain identified financial statement items) are prohibited by SAS No. 58. A piecemeal opinion is the complement of a qualified opinion: A qualified opinion gives an opinion on the financial statements as a whole and makes exceptions for certain items, whereas a piecemeal opinion disclaims or is adverse on the financial statements as a whole and gives an opinion on certain items. In the past, piecemeal opinions were not uncommon, but they presented so many problems that they are now prohibited.

SAS No. 58 (AU Section 508.64) states as a reason that "piecemeal opinions tend to overshadow or contradict a disclaimer of opinion or an adverse opinion." In addition, piecemeal opinions took specific items out of the context of the financial statements as a whole, thus implying a greater degree of precision about those items under conditions that usually entailed a lesser degree of certainty. Also, the defect in the financial statements as a whole that caused the disclaimer or adverse opinion tended to destroy or call into question the interrelated, corroborative nature of accounts on which the audit logic depended. When all of these deficiencies were balanced against the limited usefulness of piecemeal opinions, the profession was well advised to abandon them.

e)   Adverse Opinions Versus Disclaimers

There is a fundamental difference between departures from GAAP, which affect the quality of the financial statements, and scope limitations, which affect the sufficiency and competence of audit evidence. Departures from GAAP call for a qualified opinion because of the auditor's reservations about the quality of the financial statements. If departures from GAAP become so great as to make the financial statements useless, an adverse opinion is called for. On the other hand, scope limitations affect the degree of assurance contained in the opinion, whether the limitations are imposed by the client or the result of circumstances, and call for a qualification in both the scope and opinion paragraphs. If scope limitations are so pervasive that the auditor cannot form an opinion, a disclaimer of opinion may be called for. The following tabulation helps keep in perspective the distinctions among qualified opinions, adverse opinions, and disclaimers of opinion.

	Degree of Materiality or Pervasiveness	
Condition	*Less*	*More*
Departures from GAAP	Qualified opinion	Adverse opinion
Scope limitations	Qualified opinion	Disclaimer of opinion

(f)   Distinguishing Among Situations Involving Scope Limitations, Uncertainties, and Departures from GAAP

Distinguishing between situations that require disclosures in the financial statements because of an uncertainty and those that require departures from an unqualified opinion because of a scope limitation or a departure from GAAP can sometimes be difficult.
    SAS No. 58, as amended by SAS No. 79 (AU Sections 508.29 and 508.31), notes that:

> A matter involving an uncertainty is one that is expected to be resolved at a future date, at which time conclusive evidential matter concerning its outcome would be expected to become available. . . . A qualification or disclaimer of opinion because of a scope limitation is appropriate if sufficient evidential matter related to an uncertainty does or did exist but was not available to the auditor for reasons such as management's record retention policies or a restriction imposed by management.

Departures from generally accepted accounting principles involving uncertainties usually involve inadequate disclosure of the uncertainty, the use of inappropriate accounting principles in making accounting estimates, or unreasonable accounting estimates themselves. These situations would require a qualified or an adverse opinion because of a departure from GAAP.

To distinguish among the various types of auditors' reports that are possible in situations involving uncertainties, consider the following example. As discussed in Chapter 27, SAS No. 12, *Inquiry of a Client's Lawyer Concerning Litigation, Claims, and Assessments* (AU Section 337), requires the auditor to obtain corroborating evidence from the entity's legal counsel about the completeness of the information supplied by management regarding pending or threatened litigation, claims, and assessments. If the entity refuses to request its lawyer to communicate with the auditor, or if the lawyer refuses to furnish information concerning the likelihood of an unfavorable outcome of material litigation, claims, or assessments, an audit scope limitation exists that would, depending on the potential materiality of the unresolved items, lead to a scope qualification or a disclaimer of opinion, along with a separate explanatory paragraph preceding the opinion or disclaimer. If the lawyer is unable to respond concerning the likelihood of an unfavorable outcome of the uncertainty or the amount or range of potential loss, an uncertainty exists that would need to be disclosed in the notes to the financial statements but would not require modification of the auditor's report. If, however, after both the entity and the lawyer acknowledge the uncertainty, the entity refuses to make the appropriate disclosures, a qualified or an adverse opinion because of a GAAP departure (along with a separate explanatory paragraph preceding the opinion paragraph) would be required. In practice, distinguishing among these three situations is not always easy.

Concern has been expressed that auditors sometimes have issued unqualified opinions, with appropriate disclosures in the financial statements, describing the existence of an uncertainty, in situations that require a qualified or an adverse opinion because of a departure from GAAP. Those situations usually involve uncertainties facing management about market or other business conditions that are inappropriately treated in auditors' reports as uncertainties about the likelihood of occurrence of future events. The presence of uncertainties in the economic environment in which an entity typically conducts business does not negate management's responsibility to make accounting estimates as a basis for the application of accounting principles. Management's unwillingness to make reasonable estimates in those situations indicates a possible departure from GAAP, which would require either a qualified or an adverse opinion. The auditor's inability to reach a conclusion about an accounting measurement or estimate made by management may indicate a scope limitation, which would require either a qualified opinion or a disclaimer.

(g) Different Reports on Comparative Financial Statements Presented

An auditor may express a qualified or an adverse opinion, disclaim an opinion, or include an explanatory paragraph with respect to one or more financial statements of one or more periods presented and issue a different report on the other financial statements presented. Following is an example of a report (AU Section 508.67) on comparative financial statements, consisting of a standard report on the current-year financial statements with a disclaimer of opinion on the prior-year statements of income, retained earnings, and cash flows:

[*Same first paragraph as the standard report*]

Except as explained in the following paragraph, we conducted our audits in accordance with generally accepted auditing standards. Those standards require that we plan and perform our audit to obtain reasonable assurance about whether the financial statements are free of material misstatement. An audit includes examining, on a test basis, evidence supporting the amounts and disclosures in the financial statements. An audit also includes assessing the accounting principles used and significant estimates made by management, as well as evaluating the overall financial statement presentation. We believe that our audits provide a reasonable basis for our opinion.

We did not observe the taking of the physical inventory as of December 31, 19X0, since that date was prior to our appointment as auditors for the Company, and we were unable to satisfy ourselves regarding inventory quantities by means of other auditing procedures. Inventory amounts as of December 31, 19X0, enter into the determination of net income and cash flows for the year ended December 31, 19X1.

Because of the matter discussed in the preceding paragraph, the scope of our work was not sufficient to enable us to express, and we do not express, an opinion on the results of operations and cash flows for the year ended December 31, 19X1.

In our opinion, the balance sheets of ABC Company as of December 31, 19X2 and 19X1, and the related statements of income, retained earnings, and cash flows for the year ended December 31, 19X2, present fairly, in all material respects, the financial position of ABC Company as of December 31, 19X2 and 19X1, and the results of its operations and its cash flows for the year ended December 31, 19X2, in conformity with generally accepted accounting principles.

SAS No. 58 also provides guidance when an auditor becomes aware, during the current audit, of circumstances or events that affect the financial statements of a prior period. For example, the subsequent restatement of prior-period financial statements on which the auditor had issued a qualified or an adverse opinion would cause the auditor to express an unqualified opinion in an updated report on the financial statements of the prior period. In these circumstances, SAS No. 58 (AU Section 508.69) requires that all the substantive reasons for the different opinion be disclosed in a separate explanatory paragraph(s) preceding the opinion paragraph of the report.

According to SAS No. 58 (AU Section 508.69), the explanatory paragraph should include:

(a) the date of the auditor's previous report, (b) the type of opinion previously expressed, (c) the circumstances or events that caused the auditor to express a different opinion, and (d) that the auditor's updated opinion on the financial statements of the prior period is different from his previous opinion on those statements.

28.5 SUMMARY: PRINCIPAL VARIATIONS FROM STANDARD REPORTS

Figure 28.3 summarizes the principal causes of variations from the standard, unqualified report and how they affect the report. In deciding whether a variation from the standard, unqualified report is appropriate, the auditor considers the materiality of the condition or circumstance in question. A materiality test must be applied in determining not only whether to depart from a standard, unqualified opinion but also whether the appropriate variation is to include explanatory language or to issue a qualified opinion on the one hand, or to issue an adverse opinion or a disclaimer of

Figure 28.3   Summary of Principal Variations from Standard Reports

Type of Variation	Report Treatment
Situations Requiring Unqualified Opinions *with Explanatory Language*	
Opinion based in part on report of another auditor	Add explanatory language in the introductory and opinion paragraphs
Departure from an authoritative pronouncement with which the auditor agrees	Add an explanatory paragraph describing and justifying the departure
Predecessor auditor's reports on prior year's comparative statements not presented	Add explanatory language in the introductory paragraph
Material inconsistency between financial statements and other information reported by management	Add an explanatory paragraph describing the inconsistency (The auditor also should consider withholding the audit report or withdrawing from the engagement)
Exceptions regarding supplementary information required by FASB or GASB	Add an explanatory paragraph describing the circumstances
Existence of substantial doubt about the entity's ability to continue as a going concern	Add an explanatory paragraph after the opinion paragraph (disclaimer of opinion is permissible but not required)
Lack of consistency in application of accounting principles	Add an explanatory paragraph after the opinion paragraph
Auditor wishes to emphasize a matter	Add an explanatory paragraph
Situations Requiring Departures *from Unqualified Opinions*	
Scope limitation	Qualify the scope paragraph ("except as"); describe the scope limitation in a separate paragraph preceding the opinion paragraph; qualify the opinion ("except for") or disclaim an opinion, depending on circumstances and materiality
Departure from GAAP	Describe the departure in a separate paragraph preceding the opinion paragraph; qualify the opinion ("except for") or give an adverse opinion, depending on materiality

opinion on the other. As noted earlier, a departure from GAAP that is sufficiently material could lead to an adverse opinion, and scope limitations that are sufficiently material could lead to a disclaimer of opinion.

Authoritative auditing literature provides scant guidance for deciding whether the effects of a particular condition or circumstance are sufficiently material to require a qualified opinion or either an adverse opinion or a disclaimer. Paragraph 50 of SAS No. 58 (AU Section 508.36) suggests several factors to be considered in determining the materiality of the effects of a departure from GAAP, namely, the dollar magnitude of the effects, the significance of an item to a particular entity, the pervasiveness of the misstatement, and the impact of the misstatement on the financial statements taken as a whole. There is no guidance in the authoritative literature concerning scope limitations.

28.6 RESPONSIBILITIES AFTER THE REPORT DATE

(a) Discovery of Information After the Report Date

Chapter 27 discusses an auditor's responsibility to obtain knowledge about subsequent events up to certain dates. Clearly, the auditor is not obligated to "keep current" indefinitely; as explained in Chapter 27, the responsibility ends with the issuance of the financial statements and the auditor's report, with the exception of a 1933 Act filing with the SEC. In that situation, the responsibility extends to the effective date of the registration statement.

After the financial statements and audit report have been issued, however, an auditor may become aware of information that relates to the financial statements previously reported on, but which was not known at the date of the report, and which would have been investigated had it been known. The auditor should determine whether the information is reliable and whether the facts existed at the date of the report. If the new information refers to a condition that did not exist at the date of the audit report, or if it refers to final resolutions of contingencies or other matters disclosed in the financial statements or the auditor's report, the auditor has no further obligation.

The new information may, however, be found to be reliable and relate to facts existing at the date of the audit report that might have affected the auditor's report if the auditor had been aware of them and they had not been reflected in the financial statements. For example, the auditor may learn on April 14, 19X7, after the financial statements for 19X6 were issued, that a large receivable on the December 31, 19X6, balance sheet believed at that date to be collectible was in fact uncollectible because the customer had declared bankruptcy on December 5, 19X6. In those circumstances, the auditor is obligated to pursue the matter. According to an auditing interpretation (AU Section 9561.01), that obligation exists even if the auditor has resigned or has been discharged.

While the distinction between the two kinds of new information is conceptually clear, in practice it is often difficult to tell, at least initially, whether the new information refers to a new condition or a preexisting one. The new information is often fragmentary, hearsay, or otherwise suspect, and may come from inside or outside the entity. Regardless of its source, the auditor ordinarily should discuss the information with management and request that it make any necessary investigations. There may be situations in which the auditor may find it desirable to seek the advice of legal counsel. The auditor also should determine if there are persons relying on, or likely to rely on, the financial statements who would consider the new information important.

SAS No. 1 (AU Section 561) provides guidance to the auditor on subsequent steps to be taken. If the entity's management cooperates and the information is found to be reliable and to have existed at the date of the auditor's report, and if it is likely that the financial statements are still being relied on, management should be advised to disclose the newly discovered facts and their effect on the financial statements by issuing revised financial statements and auditor's report. The reasons for the revisions should be described in a note to the financial statements and referred to in the auditor's report. An auditor's report accompanying revised financial statements would read (in part) as follows, "In our opinion, the financial statements referred to above, revised as described in Note X, present fairly. . . ." If financial statements for a subsequent period are about to be issued, the revision may be incorporated in those statements, as long as disclosure of the revision is not thereby unduly delayed. The auditor's report on the comparative financial statements need not refer to the revision provided there is appropriate disclosure. The auditor may, however, include an explanatory paragraph to emphasize the revision.

Sometimes, determining the effect on the financial statements requires prolonged investigation, or the information is so significant that no delay is tolerable. In those circumstances, the entity should notify all persons likely to be relying on the financial statements of the problem under investigation. Usually, that would include stockholders, banks, and, for publicly held entities, the SEC, stock exchanges, and regulatory agencies.

If the entity's management refuses to make the appropriate disclosures, the auditor should obtain the advice of legal counsel and should notify each member of the entity's board of directors of that refusal and of the subsequent steps the auditor will take to prevent future reliance on the audit report. Unless the auditor's counsel recommends otherwise, the auditor should notify the entity that the auditor's report is no longer to be associated with the financial statements. In addition, the auditor should notify the SEC, stock exchanges, and any other regulatory agencies involved of the situation and the withdrawal of the report and request that steps be taken to accomplish the necessary public disclosure (usually this notification is made public at once). The auditor should also notify in writing any others who are known to be currently relying or who are likely to rely on the financial statements and the related auditor's report. The public disclosure following notification of the SEC is intended to take care of all unknown interested parties.

The disclosures made by the auditor to regulatory agencies and other parties should, if possible, describe the information and its effect on the financial statements and the auditor's report. The description should be precise and factual and should avoid references to conduct, motives, and the like. SAS No. 1 (AU Section 561.09) describes the appropriate disclosure if precise and factual information is not available, as follows:

> If the client has not cooperated and as a result the auditor is unable to conduct a satisfactory investigation of the information, his disclosure need not detail the specific information but can merely indicate that information has come to his attention which his client has not cooperated in attempting to substantiate and that, if the information is true, the auditor believes that his report must no longer be relied upon or be associated with the financial statements. No such disclosure should be made unless the auditor believes that the financial statements are likely to be misleading and that his report should not be relied on.

(b) Consideration of Omitted Procedures After the Report Date

The auditor may, subsequent to issuing an audit report, conclude that one or more auditing procedures considered necessary in the circumstances were omitted during the audit. For example, as part of its internal quality review program, a CPA firm may discover that no physical inspection was performed of a significant quantity of an entity's inventory stored at a remote location. The actions to be taken by the auditor in this and similar situations vary depending on the circumstances, and the auditor should be guided by the advice of legal counsel. SAS No. 46, *Consideration of Omitted Procedures After the Report Date* (AU Section 390), provides guidance in this area.

The auditor should, as a first step, assess the importance of the omitted procedure in relation to his or her ability to support the previously issued opinion. On further investigation (such as, for example, review of working papers and inquiry of members of the engagement team), the auditor may decide that other procedures that were performed compensated adequately for the omitted procedure. In this instance, the auditor usually does not take any further steps. If, however, the auditor concludes that the omission of the auditing procedure significantly impairs his or her ability to support the previously issued opinion and believes there are persons currently relying or likely to rely on the report, additional procedures necessary to provide an adequate basis for the opinion issued should be performed promptly. Those procedures may be the omitted procedure or appropriate alternatives designed to compensate adequately for it.

The performance of those procedures may disclose facts that existed at the date of the audit report that would have affected the opinion rendered had the auditor been aware of them at the time. In such circumstances, the auditor should follow the steps outlined in the preceding section of this chapter.

Situations may arise, however, when because of the passage of time or other reasons, the auditor is unable to perform the previously omitted or alternative procedures. In such instances, the auditor should seek the advice of legal counsel before deciding on the appropriate course of action. In any event, strong consideration should be given to notifying the entity regarding the problem and the proposed action.

29

Other Reporting Situations Related to Audits

In the current business environment, accountants in public practice are engaged to provide a variety of services that extend beyond financial statement audits. The demand for these services resulted from the public's experience with traditional audit services. This chapter discusses a number of services that are closely related to financial statement audits and are covered by the Statements on Auditing Standards. Other services that have evolved over the years have moved further from an audit base and cannot be described as audit related. Those services are covered in Chapters 30 and 31.

The professional standards discussed in Chapter 3 apply with equal rigor to all work performed by a CPA—the only exception is the practical irrelevance of some of them in specific situations. AU Section 150.06 states, for example, that the "ten generally accepted standards, to the extent that they are relevant in the circumstances, apply to all other services covered by Statements on Auditing Standards unless the Statement specifies otherwise." The general standards—adequate training and proficiency, independence of mental attitude, and due professional care in the performance of the work—are all clearly applicable in every professional effort. Of the standards of field work, the first and third—planning and supervision of field work and sufficiency and competency of evidential matter as a basis for an opinion—also apply universally. The second standard—a sufficient understanding of internal control—is generally, though not universally, applicable. Whenever a professional report involves business activities, the auditor should obtain an understanding of the applicable controls to make adequate professional judgments. Some reports, however, such as those on an entity's compliance with aspects of contractual agreements, do not necessarily involve its internal control. The standards of reporting are more specific and therefore cannot be as universally applied. The first standard—adherence to generally accepted accounting principles (GAAP)—obviously applies only to financial statements that purport to present financial position, results of operations, and cash flows, and to items derived from those statements. The second standard, consistency, applies whenever a report addresses conformity with GAAP or an other comprehensive basis of accounting. The third and fourth standards—adequacy of informative disclosures and the requirement for a clear-cut indication of the degree of responsibility the auditor is taking—while stated in terms of financial statements, should be viewed as generally applicable to every report the auditor issues.

29.1   REPORTS ON NON-GAAP FINANCIAL STATEMENTS

Statement of Financial Accounting Concepts (SFAC) No. 1, *Objectives of Financial Reporting by Business Enterprises* (Accounting Standards Section CON1), issued by the Financial Accounting Standards Board (FASB), states that "information about enterprise earnings and its components measured by accrual accounting generally provides a better indication of enterprise performance than information about current cash receipts and payments" (para. 44). Stated another way, the accrual basis is generally necessary to measure financial position and results of operations in conformity with GAAP. Other comprehensive bases of accounting, such as the cash or modified accrual basis, the income tax basis, and statutory bases that meet reporting requirements of a governmental regulatory agency, ordinarily do not accomplish that objective.

There are some entities, however, that believe they do not need financial statements based on GAAP, that non-GAAP financial statements would be more informative in a particular situation, or that the extra effort and cost to prepare accrual basis statements are not worthwhile. Typical of entities that believe they are better served by a non-GAAP comprehensive basis of accounting are some not-for-profit entities, certain nonpublic entities, regulated companies that must file financial statements based on accounting principles prescribed by a government regulatory agency, and entities formed for special purposes, such as certain partnerships and joint ventures. A report containing an unqualified opinion on financial statements prepared in accordance with a comprehensive basis of accounting other than GAAP is a useful, practical alternative for entities that prepare statements on such a basis and wish an audit.

(a) Definition

Statement on Auditing Standards (SAS) No. 62, *Special Reports* (AU Section 623), defines a comprehensive basis of accounting other than GAAP as one of the following:

- A basis of accounting that the reporting entity uses to comply with the requirements or financial reporting provisions of a governmental regulatory agency to whose jurisdiction the entity is subject.

- A basis of accounting that the reporting entity uses or expects to use to file its income tax return for the period covered by the financial statements.

- The cash receipts and disbursements basis of accounting, and modifications of the cash basis having substantial support, such as recording depreciation on fixed assets or accruing income taxes.

- A definite set of criteria having substantial support that is applied to all material items appearing in financial statements, such as the price-level basis of accounting.

(b) Forms of Reporting

The key element of a report on a comprehensive basis of accounting other than GAAP is a paragraph stating the basis of presentation and that it is a comprehensive basis of accounting other than GAAP. The paragraph also refers to a note to the financial statements that describes the basis of presentation and how it differs from GAAP. (These differences need not be quantified, however.) The financial statements should be titled using terms that are not generally associated with financial statements intended to present financial position, results of operations, or cash flows in conformity with GAAP. For example, "statement of assets and liabilities arising from cash transactions" should be used instead of "balance sheet."

Financial statements may be prepared in conformity with the requirements or financial reporting provisions of a governmental regulatory agency solely for filing with that agency or with other agencies to whose jurisdiction the entity is subject. In that situation, the auditor should include a paragraph that restricts the use of the report to those within the entity and the regulatory agency or agencies. The fact that by law or regulation the auditor's report may be made a matter of public record is not relevant. Furthermore, AU Section 544 provides reporting guidance when a regulated company issues to the public the same financial statements that it files with the appropriate regulatory agency (where the basis of accounting complies with the regulatory agency's requirements but differs from GAAP). In this situation, the auditor's report on the financial statements ordinarily should contain either a qualified or an adverse opinion, as appropriate, because of the departures from GAAP. If supplementary data is presented in conformity with GAAP, an adverse opinion can be accompanied by an opinion on that data.

In all other situations, if the financial statements do not meet the definition of a presentation in conformity with a comprehensive basis of accounting other than GAAP, the auditor should issue the standard form of report (see Chapter 28), modified, as appropriate, for the departures from GAAP.

Illustrations of reports on financial statements prepared in accordance with a comprehensive basis of accounting other than GAAP can be found in AU Section 623.08. One example, that of a report on financial statements prepared on the entity's income tax basis, follows:[1]

> We have audited the accompanying statements of assets, liabilities, and capital— income tax basis of ABC Partnership as of December 31, 19X2 and 19X1, and the related statements of revenue and expenses—income tax basis and of changes in partners' capital accounts—income tax basis for the years then ended. These financial statements are the responsibility of the Partnership's management. Our responsibility is to express an opinion on these financial statements based on our audits.

> We conducted our audits in accordance with generally accepted auditing standards. Those standards require that we plan and perform the audit to obtain reasonable assurance about whether the financial statements are free of material misstatement. An audit includes examining, on a test basis, evidence supporting the amounts and disclosures in the financial statements. An audit also includes assessing the accounting principles used and significant estimates made by management, as well as evaluating the overall financial statement presentation. We believe that our audits provide a reasonable basis for our opinion.

> As described in Note X, these financial statements were prepared on the basis of accounting the Partnership uses for income tax purposes, which is a comprehensive basis of accounting other than generally accepted accounting principles.

> In our opinion, the financial statements referred to above present fairly, in all material respects, the assets, liabilities, and capital of ABC Partnership as of December 31, 19X2 and 19X1, and its revenue and expenses and changes in partners' capital accounts for the years then ended, on the basis of accounting described in Note X.

Printed forms or schedules designed for filing with various bodies sometimes prescribe the wording of the auditor's report. The prescribed wording may call for statements by the auditor that do not conform with relevant professional reporting standards. In those instances, the auditor should either reword the prescribed report language or replace it with a separate report on the financial information presented in the prescribed forms or schedules.[2]

---

[1] SAS No. 58 (AU Section 508.08) specifies that a title that includes the word "independent" is one of the basic elements of the standard audit report. The illustrative standard reports in AU Section 508 use the title "Independent Auditor's Report." This and subsequent illustrative audit reports present only the body of the report and omit the title, as well as the date of the report and signature of the auditor's firm.

[2] Guidance on compilation reports issued by an accountant on financial statements included in prescribed forms is provided in SSARS No. 3, *Compilation Reports on Financial Statements Included in Certain Prescribed Forms* (AR Section 300).

29.2 REPORTS ON PARTS OF A FINANCIAL STATEMENT

An auditor may be engaged to audit and express an opinion on one or more specified elements, accounts, or items of a financial statement.[3] Elements, accounts, or items of a financial statement constitute accounting information that is part of, but significantly less than, a financial statement. In the authors' opinion, such information encompasses accounting information contained in the entity's accounts that supports the elements, accounts, or items presented in the financial statements. Although accounting information generally is expressed in monetary amounts (or percentages derived therefrom), it also may include quantitative information derived from accounting records that is not expressed in monetary terms.

The audit might be performed as a separate engagement or, more commonly, in conjunction with an audit of financial statements taken as a whole. For example, the report might be on the amount of sales for the purpose of computing rentals, royalties, a profit participation, or the adequacy of a provision for income taxes in financial statements. AU Section 623 provides guidance on these kinds of engagements.

(a) Applicability of GAAP

The auditor's report should not address GAAP unless the elements, accounts, or items the auditor is reporting on are prepared in conformity with GAAP. For example, GAAP normally would not be applicable to items prepared in accordance with the provisions of a contract or agreement.

(b) Materiality

Since the auditor expresses an opinion on each specified element, account, or item of a financial statement covered by the report, the measurement of materiality should be related to each individual element, account, or item rather than to the aggregate thereof or to the financial statements taken as a whole. Thus, an audit of only specified parts of a set of financial statements is usually more extensive than an audit of those same parts if they are included in a full set of audited financial statements. Items that are interrelated with those the auditor has been engaged to express an opinion on also should be considered. Examples of interrelated financial statement elements are sales and receivables, inventories and payables, and property, plant, and equipment and depreciation.

(c) Forms of Reporting

As noted in Chapter 28, piecemeal opinions are not permitted, since they are considered to overshadow or contradict a disclaimer of opinion or an adverse opinion. Thus, the auditor should be careful to avoid expressing an opinion on specified elements, ac-

---

[3] In a different type of engagement, discussed in Chapter 30, an accountant may be engaged to apply agreed-upon procedures to specified elements, accounts, or items of a financial statement. An accountant also may be asked to provide a review of one or more specified elements, accounts, or items of a financial statement. For that type of engagement, the auditor should refer to the attestation standards (AT Section 100) and Chapter 31 of this book.

counts, or items of a financial statement that is tantamount to a piecemeal opinion, if the audit of the financial statements as a whole resulted in an adverse opinion or a disclaimer. That generally would not be a concern if the report did not cover a major portion of the financial statement elements, accounts, or items and did not accompany the entity's financial statements.

If the specified elements, accounts, or items are prepared in accordance with the requirements or financial reporting provisions of a contract or agreement that results in a presentation not in conformity with GAAP or other comprehensive basis of accounting, the auditor's report should contain a paragraph restricting use of the report to those within the entity and parties to the contract or agreement. Such a restriction is necessary because the basis of presentation is determined by reference to a document that generally would not be available to other third parties. As previously discussed, a similar paragraph restricting use is required if the presentation is prepared on a basis prescribed by a governmental regulatory agency solely for filing with that agency.

The form of report depends on the purpose of the audit and the elements, accounts, or items audited. Although the form of report varies, there are characteristics common to all reports on specified elements, accounts, or items. An illustration of a report of this type follows:

Report Relating to Royalties

We have audited the accompanying schedule of royalties applicable to engine production of the Q Division of XYZ Corporation for the year ended December 31, 19X2, under the terms of a license agreement dated May 14, 19XX, between ABC Company and XYZ Corporation. This schedule is the responsibility of XYZ Corporation's management. Our responsibility is to express an opinion on this schedule based on our audit.

We conducted our audit in accordance with generally accepted auditing standards. Those standards require that we plan and perform the audit to obtain reasonable assurance about whether the schedule of royalties is free of material misstatement. An audit includes examining, on a test basis, evidence supporting the amounts and disclosures in the schedule. An audit also includes assessing the accounting principles used and significant estimates made by management, as well as evaluating the overall schedule presentation. We believe that our audit provides a reasonable basis for our opinion.

In our opinion, the schedule of royalties referred to above presents fairly, in all material respects, the number of engines produced by the Q Division of XYZ Corporation during the year ended December 31, 19X2, and the amount of royalties applicable thereto, under the license agreement referred to above.

This report is intended solely for the information and use of the boards of directors and managements of XYZ Corporation and ABC Company and should not be used for any other purpose.

Another type of report on specified elements, accounts, or items is one on income tax provisions. Evaluating the reasonableness of a provision for income taxes requires broad knowledge of an entity's business transactions and of the content of many individual accounts. For that reason, a report on the adequacy of a provision for income taxes in financial statements should not be issued unless the auditor has audited the complete financial statements in which the provision appears. Similarly, the auditor should have audited the complete financial statements before issuing an opinion on a specified element, account, or item based on an entity's net income or equity. An illustrative report on an entity's provision for income taxes follows:

Report on Federal and State Income Taxes Included in Financial Statements

We have audited, in accordance with generally accepted auditing standards, the financial statements of XYZ Company, Inc., for the year ended June 30, 19X2, and have issued our report thereon dated August 15, 19X2. We have also audited the current and deferred provision for the Company's federal and state income taxes for the year ended June 30, 19X2, included in those financial statements, and the related asset and liability tax accounts as of June 30, 19X2. This income tax information is the responsibility of the Company's management. Our responsibility is to express an opinion on it based on our audit.

We conducted our audit of the income tax information in accordance with generally accepted auditing standards. Those standards require that we plan and perform the audit to obtain reasonable assurance about whether the federal and state income tax accounts are free of material misstatement. An audit includes examining, on a test basis, evidence supporting the amounts and disclosures related to the federal and state income tax accounts. An audit also includes assessing the accounting principles used and significant estimates made by management, as well as evaluating the overall presentation of the federal and state income tax accounts. We believe that our audit provides a reasonable basis for our opinion.

In our opinion, the Company has paid or, in all material respects, made adequate provision in the financial statements referred to above for the payment of all federal and state income taxes and for related deferred income taxes that could be reasonably estimated at the time of our audit of the financial statements of XYZ Company, Inc., for the year ended June 30, 19X2.

Other examples of reports on specified elements, accounts, or items are presented in AU Section 623.18.

29.3 REPORTS ON COMPLIANCE WITH ASPECTS OF CONTRACTUAL AGREEMENTS OR REGULATORY REQUIREMENTS, OR ON RELATED SPECIAL-PURPOSE PRESENTATIONS

Determining an entity's compliance with contractual agreements or regulatory requirements is integral to an audit of financial statements. If noncompliance with contracts or statutes could have a direct and material effect on an entity's financial statements, the auditor should determine the extent of compliance with them. For example, an auditor should determine that the entity has adhered to restrictive covenants in a long-term bond agreement, since a violation of those covenants could make the entire issue due and payable at the lender's option and require the debt to be classified as a current rather than a long-term liability. Entities may be required by a contractual agreement or regulatory agency to furnish a report on compliance with aspects of the agreement or regulatory requirements. For example, a loan agreement may call for assurance from an independent auditor that the borrower has complied with covenants in the agreement relating to accounting or auditing matters, or a state regulatory agency may require assurance that the entity has complied with certain accounting provisions specified by the agency. This section discusses engagements where the auditor has been requested to provide explicit assurance about the entity's compliance with contractual agreements or regulatory requirements.

AU Section 623 provides guidance on reports on compliance with aspects of contractual agreements or regulatory requirements related to audited financial statements. Reports of this type should be issued only if the auditor has audited the financial statements to which the contractual agreement or regulatory requirements relate. The report usually contains negative assurance relative to the applicable covenants of the agreement or the applicable regulatory requirements, and specifies that the negative assurance is being given in connection with the audit of the financial statements. The report also should state that the audit of the financial statements was not directed primarily toward obtaining knowledge about compliance. Furthermore, since the matters the auditor is reporting on are set forth in a document that generally would not be publicly available, the auditor's report should contain a paragraph restricting distribution to those within the entity and the parties to the contract or agreement or for filing with any applicable regulatory agency. The report on compliance may be given in a separate report or in two or three paragraphs following the opinion paragraph of the auditor's report accompanying the financial statements. An example of a separate report on compliance is presented below.

Report on Compliance with Contractual Provisions

We have audited, in accordance with generally accepted auditing standards, the balance sheet of XYZ Company as of December 31, 19X2, and the related statements of income, retained earnings, and cash flows for the year then ended, and have issued our report thereon dated February 16, 19X3.

In connection with our audit, nothing came to our attention that caused us to believe that the Company failed to comply with the terms, covenants, provisions, or conditions of sections XX to XX, inclusive, of the Indenture dated July 21, 19X0, with ABC Bank insofar as they relate to accounting matters. However, our audit was not directed primarily toward obtaining knowledge of such noncompliance.

This report is intended solely for the information and use of the boards of directors and managements of XYZ Company and ABC Bank and should not be used for any other purpose.

An auditor also may be engaged to provide assurance on compliance with contractual agreements or regulatory requirements relating to matters that have not been subjected to the auditing procedures applied in the audit of the financial statements. In those circumstances, the auditor should follow the guidance in the attestation standards, which are discussed in Chapter 31. When an auditor is engaged by a governmental entity or other recipient of governmental financial assistance to test compliance with the *Government Auditing Standards* (Yellow Book) issued by the Comptroller General of the United States, he or she should follow the performance and reporting guidance contained in SAS No. 74 (as amended by SAS No. 75), *Compliance Auditing Considerations in Audits of Governmental Entities and Recipients of Governmental Financial Assistance* (AU Section 801), which is discussed in Chapter 32.

Finally, an auditor may be engaged to audit and express an opinion on special-purpose financial statements prepared to comply with a contractual agreement or regulatory provisions. Those presentations typically are prepared on a basis of accounting that results in either (1) an incomplete presentation of an entity's historical financial position or results of operations (although the presentation is otherwise in conformity with GAAP or an other comprehensive basis of accounting), or (2) a presentation that is not in conformity with GAAP or an other comprehensive basis of accounting. Illustrations of reports on these types of financial presentations are provided in AU Section 623.

29.4   REPORTS ON INFORMATION ACCOMPANYING BASIC FINANCIAL STATEMENTS

Information such as additional details or explanations of items in the basic financial statements, historical summaries of items extracted from the basic financial statements, and other material, some of which may be from sources outside the accounting system or outside the entity, may be presented in a document, such as an annual report, that also includes basic audited financial statements. That information is not considered necessary for the fair presentation of financial position, results of operations, or cash flows in conformity with GAAP.

Such additional information, often referred to as "other information," may be included in a *client-prepared document* such as the annual report to shareholders. Alternatively, additional information could be included in an *auditor-submitted document*. For example, the auditor could present the client with a document bound in the CPA's own cover and including not only the basic financial statements and auditor's report, but also a detailed schedule of cost of goods sold or general and administrative expenses.

(a)   Additional Information in Client-Prepared Documents

The auditor's responsibility for other information included in a client-prepared document is set forth in SAS No. 8 (AU Section 550) and is discussed in Chapter 28. That chapter also discusses a specific type of other information for which AU Section 558 prescribes additional performance and exception-reporting responsibilities. That type of information is supplementary information *required* by FASB or GASB pronouncements. Some entities may *voluntarily* include in documents containing audited financial statements, certain supplementary information that is required by the FASB or the GASB to be presented by other entities. In that situation, the additional responsibilities set forth in AU Section 558 do *not* apply, provided it is clear that the information is not covered by the auditor's report. This may be accomplished by a statement by the entity that the auditor has not applied any procedures to the information or by the auditor's including in the report a disclaimer on the information.

(b)   Additional Information in Auditor-Submitted Documents

The auditor may be requested to include a variety of material in addition to the basic financial statements in a document submitted to the client. For example, the document might include details of the items composing financial statement captions, statistical data, consolidating data, explanatory comments, financial analyses, possibly some operational data, and occasionally a description of the auditing procedures applied to specific items in the financial statements. The additional financial statement caption details, analytical comments, and audit scope explanations might be combined under appropriate account headings, or these subjects might be separated and presented in different sections of the document.

The auditor has a responsibility to report—by a disclaimer or otherwise—on all information in a document containing audited financial statements that is submitted to the client. The auditor is not obligated, however, to apply auditing procedures to information presented outside the basic financial statements in such a document; in that event, the auditor should disclaim an opinion on the additional information and mark it as unaudited or reference it to the auditor's disclaimer of opinion. Alternatively, the auditor may choose to modify or redirect certain of the procedures applied in the audit so as to be able to express an opinion on the accompanying information rather than disclaim an opinion on it. SAS No. 29, *Reporting on Information Accompanying the Basic Financial Statements in Auditor-Submitted Documents* (AU Section 551), contains reporting guidelines, as well as examples, for reporting on such information.

The auditor's report on the accompanying information may be either added to the standard report on the basic financial statements or presented separately. In either case, the report should:

- State that the audit has been conducted for the purpose of forming an opinion on the basic financial statements taken as a whole
- Identify the accompanying information
- State that the accompanying information is presented for purposes of additional analysis and is not a required part of the basic financial statements
- Include either an opinion on whether the accompanying information is fairly stated in all material respects in relation to the basic financial statements taken as a whole or a disclaimer of opinion, depending on whether the information has been subjected to the auditing procedures applied in the audit of the basic financial statements (The auditor may express an opinion on a portion of the accompanying information and disclaim an opinion on the remainder)

For purposes of reporting in this manner, the measurement of materiality is the same as in forming an opinion on the basic financial statements taken as a whole. Accordingly, the auditor need not apply procedures as extensive as would be necessary to express an opinion on a separate presentation of the information, as would be true for a report on parts of a financial statement, as described earlier in this chapter.

(c)   Consolidating Information

The auditor may be requested to submit to the entity consolidating or combining financial statements with the basic consolidated financial statements. The consolidating or combining financial statements usually are presented in tabular form showing the accounts for each of the subsidiaries entering into the consolidated financial statements, together with the necessary eliminations and reclassifications. Usually the auditor is not engaged to report on each of the consolidated subsidiaries separately and thus does not specifically audit each subsidiary. When those statements are presented as supplementary data to the consolidated financial statements, they should be labeled clearly as supplementary information and the auditor's report should make clear the limits of responsibility taken for the individual subsidiary amounts. In this instance, the paragraph in the auditor's report relating to the consolidating information might read as follows, based on the guidance in SAS No. 29 (AU Section 551.18):

> Our audit was conducted for the purpose of forming an opinion on the consolidated financial statements taken as a whole. The consolidating information is presented for purposes of additional analysis of the consolidated financial statements rather than to present the financial position, results of operations, and cash flows of the individual companies. The consolidating information has been subjected to the auditing procedures applied in the audit of the consolidated financial statements and, in our opinion, is fairly stated in all material respects in relation to the consolidated financial statements taken as a whole.

If the auditor is asked to audit the consolidating or combining financial statements, his or her report should cover each of the components presented—referring to the components by name or collectively—as well as the consolidated financial statements. Audit judgments about materiality should be made in relation to the individual components on which the auditor is reporting.

(d) Condensed Financial Statements and Selected Financial Data

Condensed financial statements derived from audited financial statements may be included by a *public* entity in a client-prepared document, for example, an SEC filing on Form 10-Q in which condensed balance sheets are presented as of March 31, 19X1, and December 31, 19X0, with condensed statements of income and cash flows for the three-month periods ended March 31, 19X1 and 19X0. In that case, the auditor should report on the condensed financial statements of each period in a manner appropriate for the type of service provided in that period. SAS No. 42, *Reporting on Condensed Financial Statements and Selected Financial Data* (AU Section 552), provides the following example of such reporting in filings on Form 10-Q:

> We have reviewed the condensed consolidated balance sheet of ABC Company and subsidiaries as of March 31, 19X1, and the related condensed consolidated statements of income and cash flows for the three-month periods ended March 31, 19X1 and 19X0. These financial statements are the responsibility of the company's management.
>
> We conducted our review in accordance with standards established by the American Institute of Certified Public Accountants. A review of interim financial information consists principally of applying analytical procedures to financial data and making inquiries of persons responsible for financial and accounting matters. It is substantially less in scope than an audit conducted in accordance with generally accepted auditing standards, the objective of which is the expression of an opinion regarding the financial statements taken as a whole. Accordingly, we do not express such an opinion.
>
> Based on our review, we are not aware of any material modifications that should be made to the condensed consolidated financial statements referred to above for them to be in conformity with generally accepted accounting principles.

We have previously audited, in accordance with generally accepted auditing standards, the consolidated balance sheet as of December 31, 19X0, and the related consolidated statements of income, retained earnings, and cash flows for the year then ended (not presented herein); and in our report dated February 15, 19X1, we expressed an unqualified opinion on those consolidated financial statements. In our opinion, the information set forth in the accompanying condensed consolidated balance sheet as of December 31, 19X0, is fairly stated, in all material respects, in relation to the consolidated balance sheet from which it has been derived. (para. .08)

If, in a client-prepared document containing condensed financial statements identified as being derived from audited financial statements, a *nonpublic* entity names its auditor without including the audited financial statements, the auditor should request entity management to remove the auditor's name from the document. If management does not comply, the auditor ordinarily should express an adverse opinion on the condensed financial statements because of inadequate disclosure and should request management to include the report in the document. The auditor's report should not provide the disclosure. This requirement is intended to discourage nonpublic entities from substituting condensed financial statements for complete audited financial statements in a client-prepared document.

An auditor also may be engaged to report on selected financial data included in a client-prepared document that contains audited financial statements (or, for a public entity, that incorporates such statements by reference to information filed with a regulatory agency). The auditor's report should be limited to data derived from the audited financial statements. As in a report on condensed financial statements, it is appropriate to use wording indicating that the information is fairly stated in all material respects in relation to the financial statements from which it has been derived. AU Section 552.10 contains the following example of an auditor's report on selected financial data for a five-year period in a client-prepared document that includes audited financial statements:

We have audited the consolidated balance sheets of ABC Company and subsidiaries as of December 31, 19X5 and 19X4, and the related consolidated statements of income, retained earnings, and cash flows for each of the three years in the period ended December 31, 19X5. These financial statements are the responsibility of the Company's management. Our responsibility is to express an opinion on these financial statements based on our audits.

[*Standard scope paragraph*]

In our opinion, the consolidated financial statements referred to above present fairly, in all material respects, the financial position of the ABC Company and subsidiaries as of December 31, 19X5 and 19X4, and the results of their operations and their cash flows for each of the three years in the period ended December 31, 19X5, in conformity with generally accepted accounting principles.

We have also previously audited, in accordance with generally accepted auditing standards, the consolidated balance sheets as of December 31, 19X3, 19X2, and 19X1, and the related statements of income, retained earnings, and cash flows for the years ended December 31, 19X2 and 19X1 (none of which are presented herein); and we expressed unqualified opinions on those consolidated financial statements.

In our opinion, the information set forth in the selected financial data for each of the five years in the period ended December 31, 19X5, appearing on page xx, is fairly stated, in all material respects, in relation to the consolidated financial statements from which it has been derived.

29.5 REPORTS ON FINANCIAL STATEMENTS PREPARED FOR USE IN OTHER COUNTRIES

An auditor may be engaged to report on the financial statements of a U.S. entity (i.e., an entity that is organized or domiciled in the United States) that have been prepared in conformity with accounting principles generally accepted in another country. For example, the financial statements of a U.S. entity may be prepared for inclusion in the consolidated financial statements of a foreign parent company. SAS No. 51, *Reporting on Financial Statements Prepared for Use in Other Countries* (AU Section 534), provides performance and reporting standards for such engagements.

When auditing the financial statements of a U.S. entity prepared in conformity with accounting principles generally accepted in another country, the auditor should comply with both the general and field work standards of U.S. generally accepted auditing standards. The auditor also should comply with the general and field work standards of the other country, if asked to apply the auditing standards of that country. In engagements of this nature, the auditor should have an adequate understanding of the accounting principles generally accepted in the other country. The auditor usually can obtain this knowledge by reading the professional literature or statutes describing accounting principles generally accepted in the particular country. Similar considerations apply when a U.S. auditor reports on the financial statements of a U.S. entity presented in conformity with International Accounting Standards for general use only outside of the United States and performs the audit in accordance with International Standards on Auditing.

Illustrations of various reports on financial statements prepared for use in other countries are provided in AU Section 534.

29.6 REPORTS ON THE PROCESSING OF TRANSACTIONS BY A SERVICE ORGANIZATION

Service organizations may record transactions, process related data, or even execute and account for transactions on behalf of others. Organizations that provide such services include trust departments of banks (which invest and hold securities for others), computer service centers (which process data for others), and securities depositories (which hold and account for securities for others). A service organization may seek a special-purpose report from an auditor on the policies and procedures placed in operation surrounding the processing of those transactions or on both the policies and procedures placed in operation and tests of their operating effectiveness. SAS No. 70, *Reports on the Processing of Transactions by Service Organizations* (AU Section 324), provides guidance on the responsibilities of an auditor who issues these types of special reports. These reports are intended to be used by auditors of the entities whose transactions are executed or processed by the service organization (see the discussion in Chapter 12).

29.7 OPINIONS ON ACCOUNTING PRINCIPLES

An auditor often is requested to give a formal opinion on an accepted or preferred method of accounting, either for a hypothetical situation or for a specific proposed or completed transaction. Notable examples of this type of opinion are reports required by the SEC when an entity changes an accounting principle and pooling-of-interests accounting letters issued before the closing of a business combination.

(a) Preferability Letters

Paragraph 16 of Accounting Principles Board (APB) Opinion No. 20, *Accounting Changes* (Accounting Standards Section A06.112), requires entity management to justify a change to an alternative accounting principle on the basis that it is preferable. The SEC requires entities subject to its reporting regulations that make a discretionary accounting change to obtain concurrence from their independent auditors that the change is to a principle that is preferable in the circumstances.[4] The auditor's concurrence is required to be set forth in a "preferability letter" accompanying the first Form 10-Q filed after the discretionary accounting change. The requirements are also applicable to Form 10-K if a discretionary accounting change is made in the fourth quarter of an entity's fiscal year. Furthermore, as discussed in Chapter 4, the auditor should determine that the audit committee is informed about the initial selection of and changes in all significant accounting policies and their application.

A preferability letter is not required when a change is made in response to adoption of an FASB standard or other officially established accounting principle. The SEC staff also does not require the issuance of a preferability letter upon the adoption of FASB Technical Bulletins and AICPA Statements of Position and audit and accounting guides that have been cleared by the FASB, and consensus positions of the FASB Emerging Issues Task Force. (See the discussion on the GAAP hierarchy in Chapter 28.)

The auditor's evaluation of the justification for a discretionary accounting change depends on the facts and circumstances of the specific situation. Possible justifications for discretionary accounting changes include:

- Change to the preferred method where preferability among alternatives is expressed in Accounting Standards Executive Committee Practice Bulletins that have been cleared by the FASB
- Change to the method of accounting prevalent in a particular industry
- Change to reflect new circumstances (such as a change in depreciation methods to reflect the introduction of new types of equipment or new production processes)
- Change where preferability is based solely on elements of business judgment and business planning that do not fit into the aforementioned categories

The auditor should review carefully the reasonableness of management's justifica-

---

[4] Paragraph 29 of APB Opinion No. 20 (Accounting Standards Section A06.125) provides for a one-time exemption for accounting changes when an entity makes an initial public offering of its shares; in that situation, the entity is allowed to restate retroactively financial statements for all prior periods presented. The SEC also permits first-time registrants to change their accounting methods without filing a preferability letter.

tion for a change. This requires considering the entity's business as well as industry conditions, and relevant recent history of the entity. If the justification for the change is based on a desire to conform with industry practice, the auditor should corroborate management's position that the new accounting method is prevalent in the industry. Citing one or two instances of its use in a large industry would not necessarily indicate that the new method is prevalent in the industry.

The SEC has indicated that the auditor may rely, and express that reliance in the preferability letter, on management's determination of the elements of business judgment and business planning that affected the decision to make the accounting change. Examples of this may include management's expectations of the effect of general economic trends on the entity, and planned changes in products or marketing methods to meet expected changes in demand. Although the auditor's judgments should not replace management's judgments, the auditor should be satisfied that management's justification for the change is reasonable.

The staff of the SEC has indicated informally that a preferability letter also is required if a change in accounting is described in a document filed with the Commission, even if the effect of the change is not material in the current period. For example, a preferability letter would be required if a change in accounting was described in management's discussion and analysis but, because of immateriality, was not disclosed in the financial statements.

An example of an auditor's preferability letter for filing with the SEC on an accounting change follows:

> We are providing this letter to you for inclusion as an exhibit to your Form 10-Q filing pursuant to Item 601 of Regulation S-K.
>
> We have read management's justification for the change in accounting from the _____ method to the _____ method contained in the Company's Form 10-Q for the quarter ended _____ . Based on our reading of the data and discussions with Company officials of the business judgment and business planning factors relating to the change, we believe management's justification to be reasonable. Accordingly (in reliance on management's determination as regards elements of business judgment and business planning), we concur that the newly adopted accounting principle described above is preferable in the Company's circumstances to the method previously applied. [Note: The phrase in parentheses should be deleted if the auditor is not relying on management's determination in that regard in deciding whether he or she concurs with the preferability of the accounting change.]
>
> We have not audited any financial statements of ABC Corp. as of any date or for any period subsequent to _____ , nor have we audited the application of the change in accounting principle disclosed in Form 10-Q of ABC Corp. for the three months ended _____ ; accordingly, our comments are subject to revision on completion of an audit of the financial statements that include the accounting change.

If the letter is to be filed with Form 10-K, the form references should be changed and the third paragraph omitted.

(b) Pooling Letters

An auditor may be asked to furnish a pooling-of-interests accounting letter as a condition precedent to the closing of a business combination. In these instances, the client of the auditor furnishing the letter is either the target, the issuing company, or, where a holding company is formed to effect the business combination, one of the pooled entities. The auditor may be asked to issue such a letter to one or both entities that are parties to the combination.

The letter addresses whether a proposed business combination is in compliance with the pooling requirements of APB Opinion No. 16, *Business Combinations* (Accounting Standards Section B50), the related published interpretations of the AICPA and FASB, and the published rules and regulations of the SEC. The auditor should design and perform sufficient procedures to determine whether the contemplated transaction meets each of the requirements for pooling-of-interests accounting.

The pooling-of-interests accounting letter usually is issued at or near the consummation date. If the auditor's client is the issuing company, the letter ordinarily should address whether both the issuing company and the target are "poolable." If the auditor's client is the target, the letter ordinarily should address only whether the target is poolable.

(c)   Reports on the Application of Accounting Principles

An accountant (the "reporting accountant") may be asked by a nonaudit client (the "requestor") to give an opinion on the appropriate accounting for recording a hypothetical, proposed, or consummated transaction. The requestor may be, among others, an investment banker that has created a new type of financial product and wants to include an opinion from the reporting accountant (sometimes called a "generic letter") in its promotional material, an investment banker representing another accountant's client that is contemplating a specific transaction, or another accountant's (the "continuing accountant") client seeking a "second opinion" on a proposed or consummated transaction. The requestor may have a good reason for seeking the advice of a CPA other than its own auditor, perhaps based on a belief that its auditor lacks the expertise to evaluate the appropriate accounting for a new financial product. Or the requestor may be "opinion shopping," seeking an opinion that can be used to intimidate its auditor to accede to its preferences.

The profession has long been concerned with opinion shopping and has tried to prevent it. SAS No. 50, *Reports on the Application of Accounting Principles* (AU Section 625), specifies standards, for both performance and reporting, that should be followed by the reporting accountant when providing advice (either written or oral) on accounting matters or on the appropriate type of opinion on an entity's financial statements. If the advice sought is other than on a hypothetical transaction, the performance standards require that the reporting accountant seek permission from the requestor to consult with the continuing accountant and ask the requestor to authorize the continuing accountant to respond fully to the reporting accountant's inquiries. That requirement serves two purposes. The first, not explicitly stated in SAS No. 50, is to discourage opinion shopping. The second is to provide the reporting accountant with information that the continuing accountant may have and that otherwise might not be available.

A written report giving advice on accounting matters or on the appropriate type of opinion usually would contain the items described in AU Section 625.08. Section 625.09 illustrates the format that might be used for such a report, as follows:

Introduction

We have been engaged to report on the appropriate application of generally accepted accounting principles to the specific (hypothetical) transaction described below. This report is being issued to the ABC Company (XYZ Intermediaries) for assistance in evaluating accounting principles for the described specific (hypothetical) transaction. Our engagement has been conducted in accordance with standards established by the American Institute of Certified Public Accountants.

Description of Transaction

The facts, circumstances, and assumptions relevant to the specific (hypothetical) transaction as provided to us by the management of the ABC Company (XYZ Intermediaries) are as follows:

Appropriate Accounting Principles

[*Text discussing principles*]

Concluding Comments

The ultimate responsibility for the decision on the appropriate application of generally accepted accounting principles for an actual transaction rests with the preparers of financial statements, who should consult with their continuing accountants. Our judgment on the appropriate application of generally accepted accounting principles for the described specific (hypothetical) transaction is based solely on the facts provided to us as described above; should these facts and circumstances differ, our conclusion may change.

As discussed in Chapter 4, if an entity's auditor is aware that its management has consulted with other accountants (i.e., reporting accountants) about the application of accounting principles to a specific transaction or the rendering of an opinion on the entity's financial statements, the auditor should communicate his or her views about the subject of the consultation to the audit committee.

AU Section 625 is not applicable when the independent accountant (1) also is engaged to report on financial statements, (2) assists in litigation involving accounting matters or provides expert testimony in connection with such litigation, (3) provides professional advice to another accountant in public practice, or (4) prepares a communication or position paper for the purpose of presenting views on an issue not related to a specific transaction or specific entity's financial statements.

29.8 AUDITORS' CONSENTS

Section 11(a) of the Securities Act of 1933 imposes civil liability on a registrant's management personnel, underwriters, legal counsel, independent auditors, and all other parties involved if a 1933 Act registration statement is found to contain untrue statements or material omissions. Damages generally are limited to the excess of the purchase price (not exceeding the public offering price) over the later value of the security. Under Section 11(b)(3)(B), however, officers, directors, and underwriters may not be liable with respect to information included in any part of the registration statement that is purported to be included "on the authority of an expert." Because of the protection afforded to officers, directors, and underwriters by this provision, lawyers for the registrant and the underwriters usually request the insertion of language in the registration statement to specify that the audited financial statements and supporting schedules are included in reliance on the report of the independent auditors as "experts." There is no regulatory requirement for the inclusion of an experts section; however, if the independent auditors are referred to as experts, Section 7 of the Act requires their written consent to such reference.

The auditor should read the wording in the registration statement referring to the independent auditors as experts to ensure that it does not impute responsibility for financial data he or she does not intend to, or should not, assume. The expertising declaration should be limited to financial statements and supporting schedules covered by the auditor's report. (If the auditor's report departs in any manner from a standard report, it is advisable to make reference to that fact.) The expertising language is usually similar to the following:

Experts

The consolidated balance sheets as of December 31, 19X6 and 19X5 and the consolidated statements of income, retained earnings, and cash flows for each of the three years in the period ended December 31, 19X6, included [or incorporated by reference] in this prospectus, have been included [or incorporated] herein in reliance on the report of ABC, independent auditors, given on the authority of that firm as experts in accounting and auditing.

Consents in 1933 Act filings typically are worded as follows:

Consent of Independent Accountants

We consent to the inclusion in this registration statement on Form S-1 (File No. 2-0000) of our report dated February 7, 19X7, on our audits of the financial statements and financial statement schedules of XYZ Company. We also consent to the reference to our firm under the caption "Experts."

The auditors' consent should be dated, signed manually, and included in Part II of the 1933 Act registration statement. The consent is usually dated as of, or a few days prior to, the filing date of the registration statement. Any changes in the financial data covered by the auditors' report that occur between the initial 1933 Act filing and the filing of an amendment necessitate the inclusion in the amendment of a new manually signed consent as of a more current date. While technically not required, it is not uncommon for a registrant's counsel to request that the auditor manually sign a new consent every time an amendment is filed regardless of whether the financial information has changed.

A manually signed auditors' consent is required to be included in a document filed under the Securities Exchange Act of 1934 in certain situations, including when:

- The auditors' report in the document is being incorporated by reference into a currently effective 1933 Act registration statement
- The auditors' report included in a document filed under another of the acts administered by the SEC is being incorporated by reference

- Audited financial information previously included in a 1934 Act filing is being amended

A consent is not required in a document filed under the 1934 Act when financial information is being incorporated by reference from another 1934 Act filing or when financial statements are incorporated by reference in Form 10-K from the annual report to shareholders. In all such instances, however, the auditor must manually sign at least one copy of his or her report when it is filed with the SEC.

In certain circumstances, a client may propose to refer to the independent auditors as experts in a document that is not filed with the SEC—such as a bond offering document filed with a state agency—and may request the auditors to consent to that reference. An auditor should not consent to be named, or referred to, as an expert in an offering document in connection with securities offerings other than those registered under the 1933 Act unless the term "expert" is defined. If the term "expert" is defined under applicable state law, the auditor may agree to be named as an expert in an offering document in an intrastate securities offering. The auditor also may agree to be named as an expert, as that term is used by the Office of Thrift Supervision (OTS), in securities offering documents subject to the jurisdiction of the OTS. This is because the term "expert" typically is undefined outside the context of the 1933 Act, and the auditor's responsibility, as a result of the use of that term, also would be undefined.

In other instances, when a client wishes to refer to the auditors' role in a non-1933 Act offering document, the caption "Independent Auditors" should be used in the title of that section of the document instead of the caption "Experts," and the auditors should not be referred to as experts anywhere in the document. The following language may be used to describe the auditors' role:

> The financial statements as of December 31, 19XX and for the year then ended, included in this offering circular, have been audited by ABC, independent auditors, as stated in their report(s) appearing herein.

An auditing interpretation of AU Section 711 states that it usually is not necessary for the auditor to provide a consent when his or her report is included in a non-1933 Act offering document. A consent may be provided, however, if requested, and the following illustrative language is presented in the interpretation:

Consent of Independent Accountants

> We agree to the inclusion in this offering circular of our report, dated February 5, 19XX, on our audit of the financial statements of XYZ Company.

29.9 REAUDITS

It is becoming more common for a successor auditor to be asked to audit and report on financial statements that previously were audited and reported on by another auditor. This situation, commonly referred to as a reaudit, usually arises in connection with an underwriting when the underwriter desires that the audit reports covering all of the audited financial statements presented in the offering document be signed by the same auditor.

An interpretation to AU Section 315 (AU Section 9315.08–.18) clarifies the responsibilities of a successor auditor in a reaudit engagement. In addition to the usual communications between a successor auditor and the predecessor auditor, the successor auditor should stress to the predecessor auditor that the purpose of his or her additional inquiries is to obtain information about whether to accept the engagement to reaudit. The successor auditor should plan the engagement to obtain sufficient evidence to have a basis for expressing an opinion on the financial statements. The audit work performed and the conclusions reached in a reaudit are solely the responsibility of the successor auditor. Consequently, the successor should not issue a report that reflects divided responsibility for the reaudit.

The successor auditor should request working papers for the period or periods under reaudit and for the period prior to the reaudit period from the predecessor auditor. The successor auditor in a reaudit should always make, or observe, some physical counts of inventory at a date subsequent to the reaudit and apply appropriate tests of intervening transactions. If the successor auditor has audited the current year, the results of that audit should be taken into consideration in planning the reaudit and also may provide evidence that is useful in performing the reaudit.

30

Reporting on Nonaudit Services

The increased sophistication of our society and of the business environment, coupled with a better understanding by the public of certified public accountants' skills and experience, has created a demand for a variety of services far beyond audits of financial statements and audit-related services. The work accountants in public practice may be asked to perform, the diversity of resulting reports and letters that may be issued, and the reporting problems these create are virtually infinite. Standard setters have tried to keep pace with this explosion in the demand for diverse services. Their efforts are reflected in the Statements on Standards for Accounting and Review Services, the Statements on Standards for Attestation Engagements, and certain Statements on Auditing Standards. These statements address a number of nonaudit and attest services—among them compilations and reviews, interim reviews, engagements to perform agreed-upon procedures, letters for underwriters, attestation reports in general, reporting on an entity's internal control over financial reporting, compliance attestation, and reporting on pro forma financial information and prospective financial information. Nonaudit services commonly encountered in practice are described in this chapter and attestation engagements are covered in depth in Chapter 31.

Some of the issues addressed in this chapter arise because nonaudit services do not require obtaining sufficient competent evidence to provide the relatively high level of assurance an audit opinion demands. In discussing nonaudit services, both the professional literature and this chapter refer to a person who provides those services and issues a report as an "accountant," a "certified public accountant" (CPA), or a "practitioner." The term "auditor" is reserved for a person who undertakes to perform an audit in accordance with generally accepted auditing standards (GAAS) and expresses an opinion based on the results of that audit.

30.1 NONAUDITS, COMPILATIONS, AND REVIEWS

(a) Direct Association with Financial Data

A practitioner is directly involved with financial data whenever he or she is engaged to perform an audit, an audit-related service, a review, or a compilation. The level of assurance provided by these services ranges from no assurance on compiled statements, to limited or moderate assurance on reviews, to high assurance on audits and audit-related services. Also, as discussed in a later section of this chapter, the practitioner is directly involved with financial data when he or she is engaged to apply agreed-upon procedures to specified elements, accounts, or items of a financial statement. In this type of engagement, the practitioner's assurance is limited to findings based on the specified procedures and does not extend to the financial statement taken as a whole. For each of these types of engagements, there is a standard reporting format that conveys the appropriate level of assurance. Reporting on audited financial statements was discussed extensively in Chapter 28, and various audit-related reports were described in Chapter 29. Reporting on compilations, reviews, and engagements to apply agreed-upon procedures to specified elements, accounts, or items of a financial statement is discussed in this chapter.

(b) Indirect Association with Financial Data

Practitioners may be indirectly associated with financial data by virtue of special services provided to clients. These services range from merely typing or reproducing financial statements, as an accommodation to a client, that the practitioner has not
otherwise prepared or assisted in preparing, to various types of accounting services,
such as preparing a trial balance or assisting in adjusting the accounts. When a practitioner is indirectly associated with financial data, he or she needs to be aware that
third parties may infer an unwarranted level of assurance based on knowledge of the
practitioner's involvement. Because of this, the profession has provided guidance in
some areas where a practitioner may be indirectly associated with financial data.

A form of indirect association with financial statements of a nonpublic entity[1] that
was permitted at one time, but now is generally prohibited, is referred to as a "plain
paper" engagement. This is an engagement to prepare and submit to the entity's
management, for its use only, financial statements without any accompanying report
or other indication of a direct association of the CPA and without meeting the requirements for a compilation service (discussed below). Particularly when financial
statements have been generated by computer, it may be difficult to determine who
generated them. In 1989, the Accounting and Review Services Committee of the
AICPA decided to continue the prohibition of plain paper engagements and rejected
a proposal to allow CPAs to submit interim financial statements to nonpublic entities
without issuing a compilation, review, or other report. That committee readdressed
the subject beginning in 1995 and in 1997 reaffirmed that CPAs should not be permitted to issue plain paper financial statements.

(c) Unwarranted Association

An accountant may become aware that his or her name is to be included in a client-
prepared, written communication containing financial statements that have not been
audited, reviewed, or compiled. In that event, the accountant should make sure that
either (a) the name is not included in the communication or (b) the financial statements are accompanied by a notation that the accountant has not audited, reviewed,
or compiled them and thus does not assume any responsibility or express an opinion
on them. If the entity does not comply, the accountant should advise its management
that consent to use his or her name is not given. The accountant also should consider
what other actions might be appropriate, including consulting with an attorney.

On the other hand, if an accountant is identified by a financial reporting service as
being an entity's independent auditor in association with condensed financial data
produced by the reporting service, the accountant is not deemed to be associated, because neither the accountant nor the entity has the ability to require the reporting
service to withhold what is, in fact, public information.

---

[1] SSARS No. 1 defines "nonpublic entity" in paragraph 4 (AR Section 100.04) as follows: "A nonpublic entity is any entity other than (a) one whose securities trade in a public market either on a stock exchange
(domestic or foreign) or in the over-the-counter market, including securities quoted only locally or region-
ally, (b) one that makes a filing with a regulatory agency in preparation for the sale of any class of its securities in a public market, or (c) a subsidiary, corporate joint venture, or other entity controlled by an entity covered by (a) or (b)."

(d) Personal Financial Statements in a Financial Plan

Financial statements used solely to assist in developing a personal financial plan frequently omit disclosures required by GAAP or contain departures from GAAP or from an established comprehensive basis of accounting other than GAAP. For this reason, if the accountant establishes an understanding with the client that the financial statements will be used solely to assist the client and the client's advisors in developing the client's personal goals and objectives, personal financial statements included in written personal financial plans prepared by an accountant are exempt from the requirements of SSARS No. 1, *Compilation and Review of Financial Statements* (AR Section 100). SSARS No. 6, *Reporting on Personal Financial Statements Included in Written Personal Financial Plans* (AR Section 600.04–.05), specifies the content of a report on financial statements contained in a personal financial plan. The SSARS contains the following illustrative report:

> The accompanying Statement of Financial Condition of X, as of December 31, 19XX, was prepared solely to help you develop your personal financial plan. Accordingly, it may be incomplete or contain other departures from generally accepted accounting principles and should not be used to obtain credit or for any purposes other than developing your financial plan. We have not audited, reviewed, or compiled the statement.

An interpretation of SSARS No. 6 (AR Section 9600.01–.03) clarifies what activities are encompassed by the term "developing the client's financial goals and objectives." The interpretation states that developing personal financial goals and objectives extends to written personal financial plans containing unaudited personal financial statements to be used in implementing the plan by the client or the client's advisors. This includes, for example, use of the plan by an insurance broker who might identify specific insurance products, an investment advisor who might recommend specific investments, or an attorney who might draft a will or trust documents.

(e) Compilations of Financial Statements

Financial statements are considered unaudited if the accountant has not applied auditing procedures that are sufficient to permit the expression of an opinion on them, as described in Chapter 28.

The Accounting and Review Services Committee has established a level of professional service for nonpublic entities called a compilation. This service involves presenting information, consisting of management's representations in the form of financial statements, without expressing any assurance on them. The accountant is not required to make inquiries or perform other procedures to corroborate or review the information supplied by management. The accountant does, however, have certain other duties and responsibilities, specified in SSARS No. 1 (AR Section 100), because of this direct association with the financial statements.

(i) Compilation Procedures. At the outset, the accountant should establish an understanding, preferably in writing, with the client as to the nature and limitations of the service to be performed, and the type of report to be rendered. Before beginning the work, the accountant should have or acquire a knowledge of the accounting principles and practices of the entity's industry and a general understanding of the nature of its business transactions, the form of its accounting records, the qualifications of its accounting personnel, the accounting basis used, and the form and content of the financial statements.[2] The accountant should read the financial statements to see if they are free from obvious material errors, such as arithmetical or clerical mistakes, misapplication of accounting principles, and inadequate disclosures.

The accountant should discuss with management any items of concern that arise from performing the foregoing procedures. Management should be asked to revise the financial statements, as appropriate; if management does not comply, the accountant should modify the report. At the extreme, the accountant should withdraw from the engagement if modifying the report is not adequate to communicate the deficiencies.

(ii) Form of Reporting.   The accountant's report on a compilation engagement explicitly disclaims an opinion and gives no other form of assurance about the financial statements. The standard form of compilation report follows:

> We have compiled the accompanying balance sheet of XYZ Company as of December 31, 19XX, and the related statements of income, retained earnings, and cash flows for the year then ended, in accordance with Statements on Standards for Accounting and Review Services issued by the American Institute of Certified Public Accountants.
>
> A compilation is limited to presenting in the form of financial statements information that is the representation of management (owners). We have not audited or reviewed the accompanying financial statements and, accordingly, do not express an opinion or any other form of assurance on them.

The accountant's report should be dated as of the date the compilation was completed. Each page of the compiled financial statements should include a reference such as "See Accountant's Compilation Report." If substantially all disclosures are omitted, the accountant's report should highlight this fact to alert users of the financial statements.[3]

(f) Reviews of Financial Statements

A review of financial statements, as described in SSARS No. 1 (AR Section 100), involves inquiry and analytical procedures intended to provide the accountant with a reasonable basis for expressing limited assurance that there are no material modifications that should be made to the financial statements in order for them to be in conformity with GAAP or some other comprehensive basis of accounting.[4] Paragraph 4 of

---

[2] SSARS No. 4, *Communications Between Predecessor and Successor Accountants* (AR Section 400), provides guidance to a successor accountant who decides to inquire of a predecessor regarding acceptance of an engagement and to facilitate the conduct of that engagement.

[3] SSARS No. 3, *Compilation Reports on Financial Statements Included in Certain Prescribed Forms* (AR Section 300), provides additional guidance for accountants who are asked to compile financial statements included in a prescribed form that calls for departures from GAAP.

[4] Comprehensive bases of accounting other than GAAP are described and discussed in Chapter 29. Hereafter, reference to GAAP in this section of the chapter includes, where applicable, other comprehensive bases of accounting.

SSARS No. 1 (AR Section 100.04) compares a review with a compilation and an audit, as follows:

> The objective of a review differs significantly from the objective of a compilation. The inquiry and analytical procedures performed in a review should provide the accountant with a reasonable basis for expressing limited assurance that there are no material modifications that should be made to the financial statements. No expression of assurance is contemplated in a compilation.
>
> The objective of a review also differs significantly from the objective of an audit of financial statements in accordance with generally accepted auditing standards. The objective of an audit is to provide a reasonable basis for expressing an opinion regarding the financial statements taken as a whole. A review does not provide a basis for the expression of such an opinion because a review does not contemplate obtaining an understanding of . . . internal control . . . or assessing control risk, tests of accounting records and of responses to inquiries by obtaining corroborating evidential matter through inspection, observation or confirmation, and certain other procedures ordinarily performed during an audit. A review may bring to the accountant's attention significant matters affecting the financial statements, but it does not provide assurance that the accountant will become aware of all significant matters that would be disclosed in an audit.

Reviews may be performed only for nonpublic entities and for public companies that do not have their annual financial statements audited. Some states have established securities laws that permit public companies to raise a limited amount of capital with financial statements that have been reviewed, rather than audited. At the federal level, entities with "small offerings" also may be exempt from the requirement to have their financial statements audited.

(i) Review Procedures.   In a review engagement, either the accountant or management prepares the financial statements from the entity's records. As with a compilation engagement, the accountant should have or acquire a knowledge of the entity's industry and business. If management prepares the financial statements, the accountant should ascertain that they are supported by formal accounting records.

The accountant ordinarily should inquire about:

- The entity's accounting principles, practices, and methods of applying them
- Procedures for recording, classifying, and summarizing transactions and accumulating information for financial statement disclosures
- Actions taken at meetings (such as of stockholders or the board of directors) that could affect the financial statements
- Whether the financial statements have been prepared in conformity with GAAP consistently applied
- Changes in business activities or accounting principles and practices
- Subsequent events that could have a material effect on the financial statements
- Matters on which questions have arisen during the conduct of the review

Some accountants may find it helpful in making inquiries to use a checklist covering the general areas to ensure that important questions are not overlooked.

Analytical procedures should be designed and performed to identify relationships between account balances, and other fluctuations that appear unusual because they do not conform to a predictable pattern (e.g., changes in sales and in accounts receivable and expenses that ordinarily fluctuate with sales). The accountant also should make comparisons with prior-period financial statements and with budgets and forecasts, if any.

If other accountants have been engaged to audit or review the financial statements of significant components of the reporting entity, its subsidiaries, or other investees, the principal accountant should obtain reports from the other accountants as a basis, in part, for his or her report on the review of the reporting entity's financial statements. The accountant also should obtain a representation letter from management to confirm the oral representations made in the course of the review. That letter also serves as a means of reducing the possibility of misunderstanding and of documenting some of the more important inquiries.

Based on the results of the review, the accountant should consider whether the financial statements appear to conform with GAAP. Material departures from GAAP should cause the accountant to modify the standard review report, unless the financial statements are revised. If modifying the report is not adequate to indicate the deficiencies in the financial statements taken as a whole, the accountant may have to withdraw from the engagement.

(ii) Form of Reporting. The accountant's report on reviewed financial statements expresses limited assurance. The opinion is in the form of "negative assurance" that the accountant is not aware of any material modifications that should be made to the financial statements in order for them to be in conformity with GAAP. The standard form of review report follows:

> We have reviewed the accompanying balance sheet of XYZ Company as of December 31, 19XX, and the related statements of income, retained earnings, and cash flows for the year then ended, in accordance with Statements on Standards for Accounting and Review Services issued by the American Institute of Certified Public Accountants. All information included in these financial statements is the representation of the management (owners) of XYZ Company.

> A review consists principally of inquiries of company personnel and analytical procedures applied to financial data. It is substantially less in scope than an audit in accordance with generally accepted auditing standards, the objective of which is the expression of an opinion regarding the financial statements taken as a whole. Accordingly, we do not express such an opinion.

> Based on our review, we are not aware of any material modifications that should be made to the accompanying financial statements in order for them to be in conformity with generally accepted accounting principles.

The accountant's report should be dated as of the date the review was completed. Each page of the reviewed financial statements should include a reference such as "See Accountant's Review Report."[5]

---

[5] SSARS No. 2, *Reporting on Comparative Financial Statements* (AR Section 200), provides guidance for reporting on comparative financial statements of a nonpublic entity when financial statements of one or more periods presented have been compiled or reviewed.

(g)   Reporting When the Accountant Is Not Independent

Lack of independence precludes an accountant from issuing a review report. The accountant may, however, issue a report on a compilation engagement for a nonpublic entity with respect to which the accountant is not independent, provided the report includes language specifically stating the lack of independence. The reason for the lack of independence should not be described.

30.2   INTERIM REVIEWS

A public accountant may be requested to perform a preissuance review of interim financial information of a public entity for a number of reasons. The entity's management may wish to include a representation that the information has been reviewed in a document issued to shareholders or third parties or in Form 10-Q, a quarterly report required to be submitted to the SEC pursuant to Section 13 or 15(d) of the Securities Exchange Act of 1934. Such representation also may be included or incorporated by reference in a registration statement.

Larger, more widely traded companies meeting specified criteria are required by Item 302(a) of SEC Regulation S-K to include selected quarterly financial data in their annual reports or other documents filed with the SEC that contain audited financial statements. The selected quarterly financial data is required to be reviewed, on either a preissuance or retrospective basis. Other entities may voluntarily include similar information in documents containing audited financial statements. In the latter instance, the interim financial information may or may not have been reviewed. It is unlikely that an entity not required to include that information would do so without having it reviewed, since that would give rise to an expansion of the auditor's report. [See the discussion in Section 2(e)(ii), Interim Financial Information Presented in Annual Reports to Shareholders.]

An entity that includes quarterly financial information with its audited annual financial statements may want its accountants to review the information on a timely basis throughout the year, rather than retrospectively at year-end. In the authors' view, there are a number of tangible benefits to this approach:

- A preissuance review helps bring accounting problems to light on a timely basis, thereby avoiding year-end "surprises" that result in adjustments and restatements of previous interim information.
- Timely involvement by an entity's independent accountants can help improve the quality of the process that produces interim reports.
- Interim financial reporting generally includes more estimates than annual reporting, and a preissuance review can contribute to the quality of these estimates.
- The incremental costs associated with performing the reviews can be reduced substantially if the reviews are coordinated with the audit work, since certain auditing procedures may be performed concurrently with the interim review procedures. For example, abstracts of minutes of meetings of the board of directors read in connection with interim reviews may be carried forward for the audit

working papers. The audit and interim review programs should be coordinated to make efficient use of all information obtained.

- A preissuance review may preclude the need to publish quarterly financial information at year-end that differs from amounts previously reported during the year.

The National Commission on Fraudulent Financial Reporting (Treadway Commission) recommended that "the SEC should require independent public accountants to review quarterly financial data of all public companies before release to the public" (p. 53). At the time of this writing, the SEC has issued for comment a concept release entitled "Securities Act Concepts and Their Effects on Capital Formation." The release, which was based on the recommendations of an advisory committee established by the Commission, considered but did not recommend mandating interim reviews for quarterly reports filed on Form 10-Q. The advisory committee concluded that adequate incentives exist, such as the scope of procedures performed by outside directors and underwriters in fulfilling their due diligence responsibilities, to effectively increase the involvement of auditors in interim periods without requiring preissuance reviews.

(a) Objective of Reviews of Interim Financial Information

A review of interim financial information is intended to provide the accountant with a basis for reporting whether he or she is aware of material modifications that should be made to such information in order for it to conform with GAAP. The accountant does this by applying a knowledge of financial reporting practices to significant accounting matters that come to his or her attention through inquiries and analytical procedures.

(b) Nature of Reviews

SAS No. 71, *Interim Financial Information* (AU Section 722), sets forth the procedures established by the profession for a review of interim financial information. Those procedures are similar to the procedures discussed earlier in this chapter relating to review engagements conducted under the SSARSs. In order to select the inquiries and analytical procedures to be performed and to assess the nature and likelihood of material misstatements, the accountant needs sufficient knowledge of an entity's internal control as it relates to both annual and interim information. An accountant who has not previously audited the entity's annual financial statements and does not have the requisite knowledge of internal control should perform procedures to acquire that knowledge. SAS No. 71 also establishes requirements for communicating errors, fraud, and illegal acts that the accountant becomes aware of in performing an interim review.

If an accountant, as a result of assisting the entity in preparing its interim financial information or performing any review procedures, becomes aware of a probable material misstatement in interim financial information filed or to be filed with a regulatory agency, he or she should discuss the matter with the appropriate level of management as soon as practicable. If management does not respond appropriately, the accountant should inform the audit committee or others with equivalent authority. If there is still no appropriate response, the accountant should consider whether to resign from the interim engagement and whether to remain as the entity's auditor or to stand for reelection to audit the entity's financial statements.

(c) Timing of Reviews

The timing of procedures to be performed depends largely on whether the accountant has been engaged to perform a preissuance (or "timely") review of the interim financial information or a retrospective review.

While adequate planning by the accountant is essential to the timely completion of a preissuance review, the most critical element is the entity's interim reporting system. It must permit the preparation of reliable interim financial information; otherwise, the scope of the accountant's engagement may be restricted. In addition, the entity's interim financial controls should be adequate so that a preissuance review is not unduly expensive or time-consuming.

On the other hand, if a review is done retrospectively, there must be sufficient documentation, including the rationale for conclusions reached during the year, available for the accountant's purpose. For example, the accountant may review the entity's documentation in deciding whether an adjustment arising in a later quarter of the year is a change in estimate or correction of an error.

(d) Extent of Reviews

The extent to which the accountant makes inquiries and performs analytical procedures on the financial information to be reported on depends on a number of considerations. First, the accountant needs a knowledge of the entity's accounting and reporting practices, as well as its controls, as a practical basis for the inquiry and other procedures. The accountant ordinarily acquires this knowledge as a result of having audited the previous annual financial statements. Knowledge of deficiencies in an entity's controls, accounting changes, and changes in the nature or volume of the entity's business activities; the issuance of new accounting pronouncements; and questions raised during the review all may prompt the accountant to make more extensive inquiries or to employ other procedures to assess interim financial information.

If there appear to be deficiencies in the entity's controls that prevent the preparation of interim financial information in conformity with GAAP, and, as a result, the accountant cannot effectively apply his or her knowledge of financial reporting practices to the interim financial information, the accountant should consider whether there is a restriction on the scope of the engagement sufficient to preclude completing the review. Furthermore, the accountant should inform senior management and the board of directors (or its audit committee) of these circumstances.

There are also a number of practical considerations that affect the extent of review procedures. Examples are selecting locations to be visited if the accounting records are maintained at multiple locations, and acquiring the appropriate level of knowledge when there has been a change in auditors and the current accountant does not have an audit base. The accountant should consider such matters in determining the review strategy.

(e) Reporting Standards

An accountant may address a report on interim financial information to the entity, its board of directors, or its stockholders. The report should be dated as of the date the review was completed and is similar to a review report conducted under the SSARSs, as discussed earlier in this chapter. Each page of the interim financial information should be marked as "unaudited." The standard form of interim review report presented in AU Section 722.28 follows[6]:

> We have reviewed the accompanying [*describe the statements or information reviewed*] of ABC Company and consolidated subsidiaries as of September 30, 19X1, and for the three-month and nine-month periods then ended. These financial statements (information) are (is) the responsibility of the company's management.
>
> We conducted our review in accordance with standards established by the American Institute of Certified Public Accountants. A review of interim financial information consists principally of applying analytical procedures to financial data and making inquiries of persons responsible for financial and accounting matters. It is substantially less in scope than an audit conducted in accordance with generally accepted auditing standards, the objective of which is the expression of an opinion regarding the financial statements taken as a whole. Accordingly, we do not express such an opinion.
>
> Based on our review, we are not aware of any material modifications that should be made to the accompanying financial statements (information) for them (it) to be in conformity with generally accepted accounting principles.

When an accountant requires reports from other accountants as a basis, in part, for a report on a review of consolidated interim financial information, the accountant should refer in the report to the reports of the other accountants if there is a division of responsibility for performance of the review.

(i) Modifications to the Standard Review Report. The accountant should modify the standard review report only if the interim financial information departs from GAAP. Such departures include inadequate disclosure, as well as changes in accounting principles that are not in conformity with GAAP. For example, the existence of an uncertainty, substantial doubt about the entity's ability to continue as a going concern, or a lack of consistency in the application of GAAP would not cause the accountant to modify the standard review report as long as such matters were adequately disclosed in the interim financial information. The accountant may wish, however, to emphasize such matters in a separate paragraph of the report.

(ii) Interim Financial Information Presented in Annual Reports to Shareholders. Selected quarterly financial data may be presented in a note to the audited financial statements or as supplementary information outside the audited financial statements. If such information is presented in a note to the audited financial statements, the information should be marked as "unaudited." If it is included in an annual report to shareholders, either voluntarily or as required by Item 302(a) of SEC

---

[6] SAS No. 71 (AU Section 722.27) specifies that the accountant's review report on the interim financial information should have a title that includes the word "independent"; the illustrative report in AU Section 722.28 uses the title "Independent Accountant's Report."

Regulation S-K, there is a presumption in the absence of an indication to the contrary that the data has been reviewed in accordance with the established professional standards previously discussed. Because of this presumption, if an accountant has reviewed the data, the audit report on the annual financial statements ordinarily need not be modified, nor does the accountant have to report separately on the review.

The auditor's report on the annual financial statements should be expanded if the selected quarterly financial data required by Item 302(a) of Regulation S-K is omitted or if interim financial data presented (a) is not appropriately marked as "unaudited," (b) has not been reviewed, (c) does not appear to be presented in conformity with GAAP, or (d) includes an indication that a review was made but fails to state that "the review is substantially less in scope than an audit conducted in accordance with generally accepted auditing standards, the objective of which is an expression of opinion regarding the financial statements taken as a whole, and accordingly, no such opinion is expressed" (AU Section 722.42).[7]

(iii) SEC Filings.   If management includes a representation in a Form 10-Q that an accountant has reviewed interim financial information set forth in that document, the accountant should request that the review report be included. An example of such a report is presented in Section 29.4(d), Condensed Financial Statements and Selected Financial Data.

An accountant's report based on a review of interim financial information also may be presented or incorporated by reference in a registration statement. In that event, the accountant's responsibility and liability, if any, under the 1933 Act extend primarily to the financial statements covered by the audit report. As a consequence, the accountant's interim review report is not considered to be "expertized" in the same manner as the audit report, and the "keeping current" requirements do not apply to interim review reports. The discussion in the registration statement (prospectus) should clarify the accountant's responsibility in this regard. Suitable wording for this purpose is included in paragraph 9 of SAS No. 37, *Filings Under Federal Securities Statutes* (AU Section 711.09).

30.3 ENGAGEMENTS TO PERFORM AGREED-UPON PROCEDURES

Agreed-upon procedures engagements traditionally entailed the application of limited procedures to elements, accounts, or items of a financial statement. Today, such engagements are found in a variety of situations and are covered by a number of professional pronouncements. Agreed-upon procedures engagements that fall under Statements on Auditing Standards are discussed below; those that are covered by Statements on Standards for Attestation Engagements are discussed in Chapter 31.

SAS No. 75, *Engagements to Apply Agreed-Upon Procedures to Specified Elements, Accounts,*

---

[7] Under its present rules, it is unlikely the SEC would accept any expansion of the auditor's report in this regard. A possible exception might be if the auditor could not review the selected quarterly financial data in the annual report because the entity's system for preparing interim financial information did not provide an adequate basis for making such a review. In that case, however, there is a possibility that the entity might be in violation of the "accounting standards" provisions of the Foreign Corrupt Practices Act, as discussed in Chapter 9.

or Items of a Financial Statement (AU Section 622), applies when an accountant is asked to apply agreed-upon procedures to one or more specified elements, accounts, or items of a financial statement that are not sufficient to allow expressing an opinion on them. Even though the scope of the engagement is limited, the accountant may accept such an engagement provided the parties involved have a clear understanding of, and take responsibility for the sufficiency of, the procedures to be performed. There are a number of ways the accountant can obtain satisfaction that all parties involved know and agree on what is to be done. They range from meeting with the parties involved to discuss the procedures to be applied, to supplying a draft of the report to such parties with a request for comments before the report is issued. Use of the accountant's report should be restricted to the named parties involved.

Elements, accounts, or items of a financial statement constitute accounting information that is part of, but significantly less than, a financial statement. In the authors' view, agreed-upon procedures can be applied to all financial information in the entity's accounting records that is subject to its financial controls. For example, such an engagement could apply to an inspection of travel and expense reports that affect various general ledger accounts and financial statement captions for evidence of designated approvals and supporting documentation for a certain period.

The accountant should present the results of applying agreed-upon procedures to specific subject matter in the form of findings. The accountant should not provide negative assurance about whether the specified elements, accounts, or items of a financial statement are fairly stated in relation to established or stated criteria such as GAAP. An illustration of a report presented in SAS No. 75 (AU Section 622.34) follows[8]:

> We have performed the procedures enumerated below, which were agreed to by [*list specified users*], solely to assist you with respect to [*refer to the specified elements, accounts, or items of a financial statement for an identified entity and the character of the engagement*]. This engagement to apply agreed-upon procedures was performed in accordance with standards established by the American Institute of Certified Public Accountants. The sufficiency of the procedures is solely the responsibility of the specified users of the report. Consequently, we make no representation regarding the sufficiency of the procedures described below either for the purpose for which this report has been requested or for any other purpose.
>
> [*Include paragraphs to enumerate procedures and findings.*]
>
> We were not engaged to, and did not, perform an audit, the objective of which would be the expression of an opinion on the specified elements, accounts, or items. Accordingly, we do not express such an opinion. Had we performed additional procedures, other matters might have come to our attention that would have been reported to you.
>
> This report is intended solely for the use of the specified users listed above and should not be used by those who have not agreed to the procedures and taken responsibility for the sufficiency of the procedures for their purposes.

Engagements to perform agreed-upon procedures may arise in connection with an

---

[8] SAS No. 75 (AU Section 622.33) specifies that a title that includes the word "independent" is one of the elements of an accountant's report on applying agreed-upon procedures; the illustrative report in AU Section 622.34 uses the title "Independent Accountant's Report on Applying Agreed-Upon Procedures."

entity (the user organization) that uses a service organization to record and process its transactions, or to record and process transactions and also execute them and maintain the related accountability. Such engagements are covered by SAS No. 70, *Reports on the Processing of Transactions by Service Organizations* (AU Section 324). In obtaining an understanding of the relationship of the service organization to the entity's internal control, the user organization's auditor may determine that information in the entity's possession—such as user's manuals, system overviews, technical manuals, service auditors' reports, reports by the entity's or service organization's internal auditors, and reports by regulatory authorities—may not be sufficient to plan the audit. In that case, the user organization's auditor might contact the service organization, through the user organization, to ask the service organization's auditor to perform specific procedures to supply the necessary information. Additionally, the service organization's auditor may be requested to apply substantive procedures to the entity's transactions or assets at the service organization and to report on applying the agreed-upon procedures.

Another situation in which a report on agreed-upon procedures may be issued arises in connection with a request for a letter for underwriters (also known as a "comfort letter") by parties to whom accountants, under professional standards, cannot provide such a letter, as well as when commenting in a comfort letter on information outside of the audited financial statements. AU Section 634 discusses the use of a report on agreed-upon procedures in those circumstances, as discussed in greater depth in the next section of this chapter. An interpretation of AU Section 634 discusses performing specified procedures and reporting on the results of those procedures, at the request of the board of directors, with respect to various information contained in SEC Form 10-K, such as tables, statistics, and other financial information. This would occur when, in reviewing the Form 10-K, directors seek the involvement of the registrant's independent auditors to help them in the discharge of their governance responsibilities.

Finally, SAS No. 74, *Compliance Auditing Considerations in Audits of Governmental Entities and Recipients of Governmental Financial Assistance* (AU Section 801), covers agreed-upon procedures applied to determine whether an entity's activities related to governmental grants and programs are in compliance with laws and regulations. This topic is discussed in Chapter 32.

An accountant should not agree to perform procedures that are primarily subjective or judgmental in nature, or that are so general that they are not by themselves sufficient to indicate the work actually performed. For example, terms of uncertain meaning such as "review," "check," "test," or "read" should not be used in describing the procedures. Acceptable procedures, for example, would be "confirm," "compare," "recalculate," or "inquire." In reporting findings, the accountant should similarly avoid vague or ambiguous language.

30.4 LETTERS FOR UNDERWRITERS

The SEC's requirements for disclosures to be made in prospectuses and registration statements are complicated and periodically undergo significant changes. Accordingly, all parties to an SEC filing go to great lengths to ensure that the contents of those filings comply with the applicable requirements. In particular, as part of their "due diligence" duties, underwriters have had a long-standing practice of seeking specific assurance from lawyers and accountants that the SEC rules and regulations have been complied with. A common practice for underwriters is to seek "comfort" from an auditor on financial information in registration statements that is not covered by the auditor's report and on events subsequent to the report date.

As public expectations have grown and been reflected in legal and other attacks on those associated with disclosures, underwriters and their counsel have sought to obtain more and more "comfort" from accountants, which is expressed in a letter called a comfort letter. (Some lawyers still use the phrase common in earlier, more austere times: "cold comfort" letter.) Since the comfort letter (formally called "a letter for underwriters") is a significant communication that underwriters use to establish that they have made a reasonable investigation under the securities laws, accountants should be especially careful not to assume unwarranted responsibility, either explicitly or implicitly.

SAS No. 72 (as amended by SAS No. 76), *Letters for Underwriters and Certain Other Requesting Parties* (AU Section 634), provides guidelines intended to minimize misunderstandings in connection with comfort letters. The importance attached to comfort letters is reflected in the length and details of the numerous paragraphs in the statement. It covers the kinds of matters that properly may be commented on by accountants in comfort letters and how the matters should be phrased, suggests forms of letters and how to prepare them, and recommends ways of reducing or avoiding misunderstandings about responsibility. Accountants who are asked to prepare letters for underwriters should become thoroughly familiar with AU Section 634.

Comfort letters are required not by the SEC but by the underwriters as part of meeting their due diligence responsibilities; the letters are not "filed" with the SEC. Underwriting agreements usually set forth the requirement for and scope of a comfort letter. As soon as an underwriting is planned, the accountant, underwriter, and entity management meet to discuss the comfort letter. All parties usually recognize their respective objectives and welcome such a conference. The underwriter wants to have as much comfort as possible, and management is concerned with avoiding unnecessary problems and delays in the underwriting. The accountant should determine whether he or she can provide the comfort called for by the underwriting agreement. An accountant who understands the entity in the breadth and depth presumed throughout this book usually can benefit both the underwriter and the entity by clarifying what is possible and what is not possible. An early conference often results in timely recognition of desirable clarifying changes both in the registration statement itself and in the underwriting agreement.

The accountant should obtain a copy of the underwriting agreement as soon as it is in draft form. After reading the draft agreement, the accountant may wish to prepare a draft of the comfort letter. The purpose of the draft letter is to inform all parties what they may expect and to provide an opportunity to discuss and change contemplated procedures. This approach contributes toward a smooth execution of the subsequent steps in the underwriting.

Preparing and reviewing the comfort letter also gives the accountant the opportunity to emphasize that responsibility for the sufficiency of procedures carried out in the comfort review is the underwriter's, not the accountant's. This is generally the first step taken by the accountant to preclude allegations that the underwriter relied on the accountant for the sufficiency of the procedures if they subsequently appear to have been insufficient. An accountant should take great care to make clear to all the parties involved that a CPA may advise on procedures but may not assume responsibility for their adequacy or sufficiency in a given set of circumstances.

The assistance provided by accountants through comfort letters is subject to limitations. Independent accountants can comment only on matters to which their professional expertise is substantially relevant. Another limitation is that procedures short of an audit, such as those contemplated in a comfort letter, provide accountants with a basis for expressing, at the most, negative assurance (see below).

(a) Applicability

Accountants may provide a comfort letter to underwriters or to other parties with a statutory due diligence defense under Section 11 of the Securities Act of 1933 (the Act) in connection with financial statements and financial statement schedules included in registration statements filed with the SEC under the Act. A comfort letter may be addressed to parties with a statutory due diligence defense under Section 11 of the Act other than underwriters only when an attorney for the requesting party issues a written opinion to the accountant stating that such party has a due diligence defense. If the requesting party cannot provide such a letter, it must provide a representation letter stating that its review process is or will be substantially consistent with the due diligence review process that it would perform if securities were being registered pursuant to the Act.

Accountants also may issue a comfort letter to a broker-dealer or other financial intermediary in connection with foreign offerings, transactions that are exempt from the registration requirements of Section 5 of the Act, and offerings of securities issued or backed by governmental, municipal, banking, tax-exempt, or other entities that are exempt from registration under the Act. The representation letter previously described also should be provided in these situations. Finally, a comfort letter may be issued in connection with acquisitions in which there is an exchange of stock, provided that the comfort letter is requested by the buyer or seller, or both, and the representation letter described above is provided.

If any other party requests a comfort letter, it cannot be provided. The accountants, instead, should provide that party with a report on agreed-upon procedures, as discussed in the previous section of this chapter. For example, if a party such as a bank provided financing in a transaction, accountants could provide an agreed-upon procedures report but not a comfort letter.

(b) Other Accountants

There may be situations in which more than one accountant is involved in the audit of the financial statements and in which the reports of more than one accountant appear in the registration statement. The comfort letters of the other accountants reporting on significant units should contain statements similar to those contained in the comfort letter prepared by the principal accountants, including statements about their independence (see below). The principal accountants should state in their comfort letter that reading letters of the other accountants was one of the procedures performed and that the other procedures that they performed relate solely to the companies they audited and to the consolidated financial statements.

(c) Dating and Addressing the Letter

A comfort letter usually is requested at or shortly before the "effective date" of the registration statement (the date on which the registration statement becomes effective). Underwriting agreements generally specify the date, often referred to as the "cutoff date," through which procedures specified in the letter are to be performed (perhaps five business days before the effective date). The letter should make it clear that the period between the cutoff date and the date of the letter is not covered by the procedures and disclosures set forth in the letter. The comfort letter usually is updated to a new cutoff date at or shortly before the "closing date" (the date the securities are to be delivered to the underwriter in exchange for the proceeds of the offering) or to several closing dates and different managing underwriters, as might happen when securities are issued under a "shelf registration."[9]

The letter should not be addressed or given to any parties other than the client and the named underwriters, broker-dealer, financial intermediary, or buyer or seller. The appropriate addressee is the intermediary who negotiated the agreement with the client, and with whom the accountants will deal in discussions regarding the scope and sufficiency of the letter.

(d) Contents of the Letter

The following subjects may be covered in a comfort letter: the independence of the accountants; whether the audited financial statements and financial statement schedules in the registration statement comply as to form in all material respects with the applicable accounting requirements of the Act and the related published rules and regulations; unaudited financial statements, condensed interim financial information, capsule financial information, pro forma financial information, financial forecasts, and changes in selected financial statement items during a period after the latest financial statements included in the filing; tables, statistics, and other financial information included in the registration statement; and negative assurance as to whether certain included financial information outside of the financial statements complies as to form in all material respects with Regulation S-K. Since there is no way of anticipating other matters that would be of interest to an underwriter, accountants should not make a general statement in the letter that, as a result of carrying out the specified procedures, nothing else came to their attention that would be of interest to the underwriter. The following paragraphs illustrate a typical comfort letter. They need not be presented in the same order in an actual letter.

(i) Introductory Paragraph.   A typical introductory paragraph is as follows:

> June 30, 19X6
>
> (Addressee)
>
> We have audited the consolidated balance sheets of X Company (the company) and subsidiaries as of December 31, 19X6 and 19X5, and the consolidated statements of income,

---

[9] Rule 415 of the 1933 Act permits, in certain circumstances, the registration of securities to be offered on a delayed or continuous basis over an extended period of time—known as a shelf registration.

retained earnings, and cash flows for each of the three years in the period ended December 31, 19X6, and the related financial statement schedules included in the registration statement (No. ___) on Form ___ filed by the company under the Securities Act of 1933 (the Act); our reports with respect thereto are also included in that registration statement. The registration statement, as amended as of [date], is herein referred to as the registration statement.

The underwriter may request the accountants to repeat in the comfort letter their report on the audited financial statements included in the registration statement. Because of the special significance of the date of the accountants' report, the accountants should not repeat their opinion.

The underwriter also may request the accountants to give negative assurance on the accountants' report. Because accountants have a statutory responsibility with respect to their opinion as of the effective date of a registration statement, and because the additional significance, if any, of negative assurance is unclear and such assurance may be misunderstood, accountants should not give such negative assurance. Accountants may refer in the introductory paragraph to the fact that they have issued reports on other financial information: condensed financial statements that are derived from audited financial statements, selected financial data, interim financial information, pro forma financial information, or a financial forecast.

(ii) Independence.   It is customary in conjunction with SEC filings to make an assertion about independence, substantially as follows:

> We are independent certified public accountants with respect to X Company, within the meaning of the Act and the applicable published rules and regulations thereunder.

In a non-SEC filing, the assertion about independence would be substantially as follows:

> We are independent certified public accountants with respect to X Company, under Rule 101 of the AICPA's *Code of Professional Conduct* and its interpretations and rulings.

When the accountants report on a predecessor company rather than the registrant named in the registration statement and are no longer associated and therefore do not need to be independent currently, the assertion begins along the following lines:

> As of [date of the predecessor accountants' report] and during the period covered by the financial statements on which we reported, we were independent certified public accountants with respect to X Company, within the meaning of the Act and the applicable published rules and regulations thereunder.

(iii) Compliance with SEC Requirements.   It is also customary to require comfort on compliance as to form with SEC requirements, which may be expressed as follows:

> In our opinion, the consolidated financial statements and schedules audited by us and included in the registration statement comply as to form in all material respects with the applicable accounting requirements of the Act and the related published rules and regulations.

In the rare case of a material departure from the published requirements, the paragraph should include the phrase "except as disclosed in the registration statement," if applicable, and the departure should be disclosed in the letter. Normally, a departure would not be considered unless representatives of the SEC had agreed to it in advance; in that event, the agreement should be mentioned in the comfort letter.

Comfort on conformity with SEC requirements is limited to negative assurance when the financial statements or financial statement schedules have not been audited.

(iv) Commenting on Unaudited Financial Information.   Comments in a comfort letter on financial information other than audited financial statements often relate to unaudited condensed interim financial information; capsule financial information; pro forma financial information; financial forecasts; and changes in capital stock, increases in long-term debt, and decreases in other specified financial statement items. In all instances, terms of uncertain meaning, such as "general review," "limited review," "check," or "test," should not be used to describe the work unless the procedures comprehended by these terms are defined in the letter. Guidance for commenting on these matters and illustrative comments follow.

(1) Internal Control. Accountants should not comment in a comfort letter on unaudited financial information of the type enumerated in the preceding paragraph unless they have obtained knowledge of an entity's internal control as it relates to the preparation of both annual and interim financial information. Sufficient knowledge ordinarily would have been acquired by accountants who audited an entity's financial statements for one or more periods. If the accountants have not acquired sufficient knowledge of the entity's internal control, they should perform procedures to obtain that knowledge.

(2) Disclaiming an Opinion on Unaudited Information. When accountants are asked to comment on unaudited condensed interim financial information, capsule financial information, or pro forma financial information based on the performance of agreed-upon procedures, the comments should be accompanied by a disclaimer of opinion on the overall presentation. The following is an example of how this might be done in a letter when commenting on unaudited condensed interim financial statements:

> We have not audited any financial statements of the company as of any date or for any period subsequent to December 31, 19X6; although we have conducted an audit for the year ended December 31, 19X6, the purpose (and therefore the scope) of the audit was to enable us to express our opinion on the consolidated financial statements as of December 31, 19X6, and for the year ended, but not on the financial statements for any interim period within that year. Therefore, we are unable to and do not express any opinion on the unaudited condensed consolidated balance sheet as of March 31, 19X7, and the unaudited condensed consolidated statements of income, retained earnings, and cash flows for the three-month periods ended March 31, 19X7 and 19X6, included in the registration statement, or on the financial position, results of operations, or cash flows as of any date or for any period subsequent to December 31, 19X6.

(3) Enumerating Procedures. The limited procedures carried out by the accountants, which should have been agreed on in advance, as previously discussed, should be set

forth in the letter. To avoid any misunderstanding about the responsibility for the sufficiency of the agreed-upon procedures for the underwriter's purposes, the accountants should not state, or imply, that they have applied procedures that they determined to be necessary or sufficient for the underwriter's purposes. The following is an example of describing the agreed-upon procedures performed on unaudited financial statements:

> For purposes of this letter, we have read the 19X7 minutes of the meetings of the stockholders, the board of directors, and [*include other appropriate committees, if any*] of the company and its subsidiaries as set forth in the minute books at June 23, 19X7, officials of the company having advised us that the minutes of all such meetings through that date were set forth therein; and we have carried out other procedures to June 23, 19X7, as follows (our work did not extend to the period from June 24, 19X7, to June 28, 19X7, inclusive):
>
> a. With respect to the three-month periods ended March 31, 19X7 and 19X6, we have:
>
>> (i) Performed the procedures specified by the American Institute of Certified Public Accountants for a review of interim financial information as described in SAS No. 71, *Interim Financial Information*, on the unaudited condensed consolidated balance sheet as of March 31, 19X7, and unaudited condensed consolidated statements of income, retained earnings, and cash flows for the three-month periods ended March 31, 19X7 and 19X6, included in the registration statement.
>>
>> (ii) Inquired of certain officials of the company who have responsibility for financial and accounting matters whether the unaudited consolidated condensed financial statements referred to in a(i) comply as to form in all material respects with the applicable accounting requirements of the Act and the related published rules and regulations.
>
> b. With respect to the period from April 1, 19X7, to May 31, 19X7, we have:
>
>> (i) Read the unaudited consolidated financial statements of the company and subsidiaries for April and May of both 19X6 and 19X7 furnished us by the company, officials of the company having advised us that no such financial statements as of any date or for any period subsequent to May 31, 19X7, were available.
>>
>> (ii) Inquired of certain officials of the company who have responsibility for financial and accounting matters whether the unaudited consolidated financial statements referred to in b(i) are stated on a basis substantially consistent with that of the audited financial statements included in the registration statement.
>
> The foregoing procedures do not constitute an audit conducted in accordance with generally accepted auditing standards. Also, they would not necessarily reveal matters of significance with respect to the comments in the following paragraph. [See the paragraph illustrated below under "Negative Assurance" for the "following paragraph" referred to.] Accordingly, we make no representations regarding the sufficiency of the foregoing procedures for your purposes.

(4) Negative Assurance. Accountants may give negative assurance on unaudited condensed interim financial information or capsule financial information only when they have, among other requirements, conducted a review in accordance with SAS No. 71, *Interim Financial Information* (AU Section 722). Otherwise, accountants are limited to reporting on procedures performed and findings obtained.

Similarly, accountants cannot give negative assurance in a comfort letter on pro forma financial information,[10] the application of pro forma adjustments to historical amounts, the compilation of pro forma financial information, or whether the pro forma financial information complies as to form in all material respects with the applicable accounting requirements of Rule 11-02 of Regulation S-X, unless they have performed an audit of the annual financial statements or SAS No. 71 review of the interim financial statements to which the pro forma adjustments were applied.

Furthermore, accountants may not provide negative assurance on the results of procedures performed or with respect to compliance of a financial forecast with Rule 11-03 of Regulation S-X unless they have performed an examination of the forecast in accordance with AT Section 200, *Financial Forecasts and Projections*.

The following is an example of how negative assurance on unaudited condensed interim financial statements may be expressed, assuming the accountants performed a review of that information:

> Nothing came to our attention as a result of the foregoing procedures, however, that caused us to believe that:
>
> > (i) Any material modifications should be made to the unaudited condensed consolidated financial statements described in [*cite paragraph number*] for them to be in conformity with generally accepted accounting principles.
> >
> > (ii) The unaudited condensed consolidated financial statements described in [*cite paragraph number*] do not comply as to form in all material respects with the applicable accounting requirements of the Act and related published rules and regulations.

(5) Subsequent Changes. Comments regarding subsequent changes typically relate to whether there has been any change in capital stock, increase in long-term debt, or decreases in other specified financial statement items during the "change period" (period between the date of the latest financial statements and the cutoff date). Comments on the occurrence of these changes should be based solely on the limited procedures performed and limited to changes not disclosed in the registration statement. Additionally, comments on subsequent changes should not refer to "adverse changes" since that term does not have a clearly understood universal meaning.

Negative assurance may be given as to subsequent changes in specified financial statement items as of a date less than 135 days from the end of the most recent period for which an audit or SAS No. 71 interim review was performed. Otherwise, accountants may not provide negative assurance and are limited to reporting procedures performed and findings obtained. Wording describing procedures performed and expressing negative assurance with respect to subsequent changes might be as follows:

> Nothing came to our attention as a result of the foregoing procedures, however, that caused us to believe that:
>
> > (i) At May 31, 19X7, there was any change in capital stock, increase in long-term debt, or decrease in consolidated net current assets or stockholders' equity of the consolidated companies as compared with amounts shown in the March 31, 19X7 unaudited condensed consolidated balance sheet included in the registration statement, or (ii)

---

[10] Pro forma financial information is defined and discussed in Chapter 31.

for the period from April 1, 19X7, to May 31, 19X7, there were any decreases, as compared with the corresponding period in the preceding year, in consolidated net sales or in the total or per-share amounts of income before extraordinary items or of net income, except in all instances for changes, increases, or decreases that the registration statement discloses have occurred or may occur.

As mentioned in [*cite paragraph number*], company officials have advised us that no consolidated financial statements as of any date or for any period subsequent to May 31, 19X7, are available; accordingly, the procedures carried out by us with respect to changes in financial statement items after May 31, 19X7, have, of necessity, been even more limited than those with respect to the periods referred to in [*cite paragraph number*]. We have inquired of certain company officials who have responsibility for financial and accounting matters regarding whether (a) at June 23, 19X7, there was any change in capital stock, any increase in long-term debt, or any decreases in consolidated net current assets or stockholders' equity of the consolidated companies as compared with amounts shown on the March 31, 19X7, unaudited condensed consolidated balance sheet included in the registration statement or (b) for the period from April 1, 19X7, to June 23, 19X7, there were any decreases, as compared with the corresponding period in the preceding year, in consolidated net sales or in the total or per-share amounts of income before extraordinary items or of net income. On the basis of these inquiries and our reading of the minutes as described in [*cite paragraph number*], nothing came to our attention that caused us to believe that there was any such change, increase, or decrease, except in all instances for changes, increases, or decreases that the registration statement discloses have occurred or may occur.

(v) Tables, Statistics, and Other Financial Information. The underwriting agreement may call for a comfort letter that includes comments on tables, statistics, and other financial information appearing in the registration statement. Accountants should refrain from commenting on matters to which their competence as independent accountants has little relevance. It is appropriate for an accountant to comment on information expressed in dollars or in percentages derived from dollar amounts and on other quantitative information that has been obtained from accounting records that are subject to internal control over the entity's accounting system or that have been derived directly from such accounting records by analysis or computation. Accountants should not comment on matters involving the exercise of management's business judgment, like explanations of the reasons for changes in income or operating ratios, or on information not subjected to internal control over the accounting system, like square footage of facilities, number of employees, and backlog information. The procedures followed by accountants in support of comments on tables, statistics, and other financial information should be set out clearly in the letter and agreed on in advance. The procedures set forth in the letter also should be accompanied by a disclaimer of responsibility for their sufficiency for the underwriter's purposes.

The expression "present fairly" should not be used in comments concerning tables, statistics, and other financial information. As discussed more fully in Chapter 28, "present fairly" is meaningful only in relation to a specific frame of reference, which, for an accountant, usually is conformity with generally accepted accounting principles. Without that qualifying phrase, "present fairly" is too broad and imprecise and is likely to give rise to misunderstandings.

The comfort letter should state that the accountants make no representations regarding any matter of legal interpretation. Since accountants are not in a position to make any representations about the completeness or adequacy of disclosures or about the adequacy of procedures followed, the letter should so state.

Provided that certain conditions are met, accountants may comment as to whether certain financial information is in conformity with the disclosure requirements of Regulation S-K. Accountants are limited, however, to giving negative assurance or reporting procedures and findings, since this information is not given in the form of financial statements and generally has not been audited.

(vi) Concluding Paragraph.   To avoid the possibility of misunderstanding about the purpose and intended use of the comfort letter, it is customary to conclude the letter with a paragraph along the following lines:

> This letter is solely for the information of the addressees and to assist the underwriters in conducting and documenting their investigation of the affairs of the company in connection with the offering of the securities covered by the registration statement, and it is not to be used, circulated, quoted, or otherwise referred to within or without the underwriting group for any other purpose, including but not limited to the registration, purchase, or sale of securities, nor is it to be filed with or referred to in whole or in part in the registration statement or any other document, except that reference may be made to it in the underwriting agreement or in any list of closing documents pertaining to the offering of the securities covered by the registration statement.

(e) Subsequently Discovered Matters

When matters that may require mention in the final comfort letter were not mentioned in the draft letter furnished to the underwriter (such as changes, increases, or decreases in specified items not disclosed in the registration statement), the accountants should discuss them with management to consider whether disclosure should be made in the registration statement. If disclosure is not to be made, the accountants should inform management that the matters will be mentioned in the comfort letter and suggest that the underwriter be informed promptly. It is recommended that the accountants be present when management and the underwriter discuss such matters.

31

Attestation Engagements

Accountants in public practice frequently are engaged to express opinions about various representations unrelated to an audit or a review of historical financial statements or to apply agreed-upon procedures to those representations. These engagements are attest services and are covered by Statements on Standards for Attestation Engagements (SSAEs). The SSAEs were developed to establish a framework for addressing attest services in a wide variety of professional service engagements whose subject matter is not related to financial statements. The standards set boundaries around the types of attest services a CPA in the practice of public accounting (referred to hereafter as a practitioner) may perform. Those standards, and related interpretations, are the subject of this chapter.[1]

31.1 ATTESTATION STANDARDS

(a) Definitions

SSAE No. 1, *Attestation Standards* (AT Section 100.01), defines an attest engagement as "one in which a practitioner is engaged to issue or does issue a written communication that expresses a conclusion about the reliability of a written assertion that is the responsibility of another party." The definition uses the term "practitioner" to refer to certified public accountants in the practice of public accounting as well as full- or part-time non-CPA employees of a public accounting firm. Thus, an employee of a CPA firm who is not a CPA, such as a staff associate or a non-CPA management consultant, is required to comply with the provisions of SSAE No. 1 if the engagement meets the definition of an attest engagement.

(b) Services Covered by the Attestation Standards

Attest engagements might include reporting on an assertion regarding:

- An entity's internal control over financial reporting
- Compliance with laws and regulations
- Descriptions of computer software products to be marketed
- Investment performance statistics
- Antitrust case data
- Insurance claims data
- Labor data for union contract negotiation
- Audience and circulation data for broadcasters and publishers
- Occupancy, enrollment, and attendance data for universities
- Cost justification for a utility rate increase
- Productivity indicators
- Pension plan obligations of a target company in a buy-sell agreement

[1] Agreed-upon procedures engagements can relate to historical or prospective financial information or to nonfinancial data. Agreed-upon procedures engagements that relate to historical financial information are governed by Statements on Auditing Standards and were discussed in Chapter 30. Other agreed-upon procedures engagements meet the definition of attest engagements and are discussed in this chapter.

Engagements to report on pro forma financial information and prospective financial information are also attest engagements.

By contrast, the following professional services typically provided by practitioners are *not* attest engagements:

- Consulting engagements in which the practitioner provides advice or recommendations to management

- Engagements in which the practitioner is engaged to advocate an entity's position—for example, concerning tax matters being reviewed by the Internal Revenue Service

- Tax engagements in which a practitioner prepares tax returns or provides tax advice

- Engagements in which the practitioner compiles financial statements, because he or she is not required to examine or review evidence supporting the information furnished by the entity and does not express any conclusion on its reliability

- Engagements in which the practitioner's role is solely to assist management—such as preparing information other than financial statements

- Engagements in which a practitioner is engaged to testify as an expert witness in accounting, auditing, taxation, or other matters, given certain stipulated facts

- Engagements in which a practitioner provides an expert opinion on certain points of principle, such as the application of tax laws or accounting standards, given specific facts provided by another party (In this type of engagement, the expert opinion must not express a conclusion about the reliability of the facts provided by the other party)

- Engagements in which a practitioner is engaged to determine the error rate in insurance claims processing under contracts

- Engagements in which a practitioner makes actuarial determinations of costs of benefit plans or insurance programs

- Engagements to report on prospective oil and gas reserve information; determination of proved, probable, and possible reserves; and appraisals of oil and gas property

The distinguishing characteristic of the above services that are not attest engagements is that the services involve providing advice, recommendations, or assistance to an entity on the basis of a practitioner's experience and expertise in a particular area. They do not require the practitioner to express a conclusion about an assertion.

(c) Standards for Attestation Engagements

The introduction to SSAE No. 1 describes the eleven attestation standards as "a natural extension of the ten generally accepted auditing standards. Like the auditing standards, the attestation standards deal with the need for technical competence, independence in mental attitude, due professional care, adequate planning and supervision, sufficient evidence, and appropriate reporting; however, they are much broader in scope." The attestation standards need to be broader in scope than the ten generally accepted auditing standards because of the distinction between an audit engagement and an attest engagement. In its most basic form, auditing is concerned only with an entity's historical financial statements measured against a set of criteria known as generally accepted accounting principles or an other comprehensive basis of accounting. Because of the range of services that might qualify as an attest engagement, however, it is not possible to establish a single set of criteria that would be appropriate for all assertions. In one instance, the attestor may be asked to express a conclusion as to the conformity of audit software with stated criteria, and in another instance, the conclusion may relate to whether management's assumptions provide a reasonable basis for a financial forecast.

In adopting SSAE No. 1, the AICPA pointed out that the attestation standards did not supersede any existing standards. That is, the practitioner should look to Statements on Auditing Standards or Statements on Standards for Accounting and Review Services for guidance before looking to the attestation standards.

In practice, this frequently creates a dilemma—caused less by the attestation standards than by the auditing standards. Auditing standards were interpreted over the years in ways that broadened their original scope. When the ten generally accepted auditing standards were developed, the drafters undoubtedly had in mind a set of standards that would serve the attest function as it applied to historical financial statements. However, over time, the standards were interpreted broadly to include services that were not originally contemplated and that fall more logically under the umbrella of attestation. Figure 31.1 shows the eleven attestation standards and compares them with the ten auditing standards.

Some of the attestation standards are analogous to the auditing standards and related interpretations. For example, the third attestation standard of reporting, "The report shall state all of the practitioner's significant reservations about the engagement and the presentation of the assertion," is little different from the following statement from Statement on Auditing Standards (AU Section 508.37): "When the auditor expresses a qualified opinion, he should disclose . . . all of the substantive reasons that have led him to conclude that there has been a departure from generally accepted accounting principles."

Other attestation standards, however, are based on concepts that differ from their counterparts in an auditing environment. These concepts are explained in the remainder of this section of the chapter.

(i) Independence in Attest Engagements.   SSAE No. 1 notes that "practitioners performing an attest service should not only be independent in fact, but also should avoid situations that may impair the appearance of independence." If a particular attestation engagement will result in a report for unrestricted distribution, the independence rules applicable to audit services (where distribution of the independent accountant's report is not restricted) apply. If, however, the attestation report states that its use is to be restricted to identified parties, and the practitioner reasonably expects that the report will be restricted to these parties, more limited independence rules apply. Chapter 3 discusses in detail matters relating to independence, including an interpretation (ET Section 101.13) under Rule 101 dealing with independence and attest engagements.

(ii) Need for Reasonable Criteria.   AT Section 100.12 states that "the attest function should be performed only when it can be effective and useful. Practitioners should have a reasonable basis for believing that a meaningful conclusion can be provided on an assertion." This means that the assertion cannot be so subjective that it is meaningless or possibly misleading. To meet this condition, *reasonable criteria* should exist that competent persons could use to reach substantially similar estimates or measurements, although not necessarily the same conclusion. For example, attesting to a software product characterized as the "best" or attesting to the competence of management would not meet this condition for an attest function, since it is unlikely that reasonable criteria exist against which "best" and "competent" can be consistently measured. This condition applies equally to providing positive and negative assurance (discussed later).

Figure 31.1   Attestation Standards Compared with Generally Accepted Auditing Standards

Attestation Standards	*Generally Accepted Auditing Standards*
General Standards	
1. The engagement shall be performed by a practitioner or practitioners having adequate technical training and proficiency in the attest function.	1. The audit is to be performed by a person or persons having adequate technical training and proficiency as an auditor.
2. The engagement shall be performed by a practitioner or practitioners having adequate knowledge in the subject matter of the assertion.	
3. The practitioner shall perform an engagement only if he or she has reason to believe that the following two conditions exist:	
• The assertion is capable of evaluation against reasonable criteria that either have been established by a recognized body or are stated in the presentation of the assertion in a sufficiently clear and comprehensive manner for a knowledgeable reader to be able to understand them.	
• The assertion is capable of reasonably consistent estimation or measurement using such criteria.	
4. In all matters related to the engagement, an independence in mental attitude shall be maintained by the practitioner or practitioners.	2. In all matters relating to the assignment, an independence in mental attitude is to be maintained by the auditor or auditors.
5. Due professional care shall be exercised in the performance of the engagement.	3. Due professional care is to be exercised in the planning and performance of the audit and the preparation of the report.

Figure 31.1 *(Continued)*

Attestation Standards	*Generally Accepted Auditing Standards*

Standards of Field Work

1. The work shall be adequately planned and assistants, if any, shall be properly supervised.

    1. The work is to be adequately planned and assistants, if any, are to be properly supervised.

    2. A sufficient understanding of internal control is to be obtained to plan the audit and to determine the nature, timing, and extent of tests to be performed.

2. Sufficient evidence shall be obtained to provide a reasonable basis for the conclusion that is expressed in the report.

    3. Sufficient competent evidential matter is to be obtained through inspection, observation, inquiries, and confirmations to afford a reasonable basis for an opinion regarding the financial statements under audit.

Standards of Reporting

1. The report shall identify the assertion being reported on and state the character of the engagement.

2. The report shall state the practitioner's conclusion about whether the assertion is presented in conformity with the established or stated criteria against which it was measured.

    1. The report shall state whether the financial statements are presented in accordance with generally accepted accounting principles.

    2. The report shall identify those circumstances in which such principles have not been consistently observed in the current period in relation to the preceding period.

    3. Informative disclosures in the financial statements are to be regarded as reasonably adequate unless otherwise stated in the report.

3. The report shall state all of the practitioner's significant reservations about the engagement and the presentation of the assertion.

4. The report on an engagement to evaluate an assertion that has been prepared in conformity with agreed-upon criteria or on an engagement to apply agreed-upon procedures should contain a statement limiting its use to the parties who have agreed upon such criteria or procedures.

    4. The report shall either contain an expression of opinion regarding the financial statements, taken as a whole, or an assertion to the effect that an opinion cannot be expressed. When an overall opinion cannot be expressed, the reasons therefor should be stated. In all cases where an auditor's name is associated with financial statements, the report should contain a clear-cut indication of the character of the auditor's work, if any, and the degree of responsibility the auditor is taking.

Source: Adapted from Statement on Standards for Attestation Engagements, *Attestation Standards* (AT Section 100.82). Copyright © 1986 by the American Institute of Certified Public Accountants, Inc.

SSAE No. 1 (AT Section 100.15) defines reasonable criteria as "those that yield useful information." They may be criteria established by AICPA committees, regulatory agencies, or other bodies composed of experts that follow due process and represent the public interest. These are referred to as *established criteria*; they need only be referred to in the presentation of the assertion.

The absence of established criteria for estimating or measuring an assertion, however, does not prevent a practitioner from accepting an attest engagement. The main consideration is whether the criteria used are reasonable. Other criteria, such as standards prepared by an industry association or a similar group that does not follow due process or does not as clearly represent the public interest should be viewed more critically by the practitioner in deciding whether they pass the "reasonableness" test. Criteria of this type should be stated in the presentation of the assertion in a sufficiently clear and comprehensive manner for a knowledgeable reader to be able to understand them, as indicated by the third general attestation standard. (These are referred to as *stated criteria*.) The authors believe that stated criteria are not limited to those that have been published. Reasonable criteria that are stated in the presentation of the assertion may be able to be developed by the assertor, often with the help of a practitioner who is knowledgeable about the subject matter of the assertion. If those criteria are stated with sufficient clarity in the assertion so that users will be able to understand them, an attest report based on such criteria would be suitable for general use.

Still other criteria against which assertions may be evaluated may have been established (or agreed to) by specified users but may be reasonable only when reporting to those users because other potential users do not have the knowledge of the criteria or their context to understand them. (An example would be criteria set forth in a purchase agreement between the contracting parties.) These criteria are not deemed to be "reasonable" for an attest report prepared for general use. (These are referred to as *agreed-upon criteria*.)

(iii) Engagement Planning and Performance.   The practitioner should establish an understanding with the client, preferably in writing, regarding the services to be performed. Planning an attest engagement involves developing an overall strategy and designing a program of procedures that is consistent with the level of assurance to be provided. When planning those procedures, the practitioner considers a number of factors, including the nature and complexity of the assertions, the criteria against which the assertions will be evaluated, preliminary judgments about materiality, the anticipated level of attestation risk related to the assertions, and the level of assurance that the practitioner has been engaged to provide in the attest report.

Attestation risk, which is similar to the concept of audit risk as described in SAS No. 47, *Audit Risk and Materiality in Conducting an Audit* (AU Section 312), is the risk that the practitioner may unknowingly fail to appropriately modify his or her attest report on an assertion that is materially misstated. The level of attestation risk the practitioner is willing to accept varies inversely with the level of assurance he or she plans to provide on the presentation of assertions. In an attest engagement designed to provide the highest level of assurance (an examination), the practitioner should plan and perform procedures to generate sufficient evidence to limit attestation risk to an appropriately low level for the high level of assurance to be given. Those procedures generally involve search and verification (for example, inspection, confirmation, and observation) as well as internal inquiries and comparisons of internal information. In a limited assurance engagement (a review), the practitioner's objective is to accumulate sufficient evidence to limit attestation risk to a moderate level. This ordinarily can be achieved by internal inquiries and analytical procedures alone.

(d) Reports on Attest Engagements

A report for general distribution on an attest service may be based on either an examination or a review. The high level of assurance provided in a report on an examination is referred to as positive assurance; in a report on a review, the moderate level of assurance expressed is in the form of negative assurance. When expressing positive assurance, the practitioner states a conclusion about whether the assertions are presented in conformity with established or stated criteria. In providing negative assurance, the practitioner states only whether information has come to his or her atten tion that indicates the assertions are not presented in conformity with those criteria.

Reports expressing positive assurance based on an examination or negative assurance based on a review may be issued for general distribution, provided the assertions on which the auditor provides assurance are based on established or stated criteria. Examination and review reports also may be based on specified criteria agreed upon by the assertor and the user(s); in that event, use of the report is limited to those parties, because other parties may not understand the criteria or the assurance expressed in the report. For example, the assertion may be based on contractual terms known only by the specified users who participated in negotiating the contract.

When the presentation of assertions has been prepared in conformity with specified criteria agreed to by the assertor and the user, the report should contain:

1. A statement limiting use of the report to the specified parties

2. An indication, when applicable, that the presentation of assertions differs materially from what would have been presented if criteria for the presentation of such assertions for general distribution had been followed [For example, financial information prepared in accordance with criteria specified in a contract may differ materially from information prepared in conformity with generally accepted accounting principles (GAAP)]

A practitioner also may perform attest services based on the application of agreed-upon procedures; the reports on those services also are restricted to the parties that agreed to the procedures. The report in an agreed-upon procedures engagement should be in the form of a summary of findings. Management's assertion regarding the subject matter of the agreed-upon procedures, which may be in the form of a schedule, should accompany the practitioner's report.

An overview of each of the three attest services (including examples of reports) follows.

(i) Examination. When expressing a positive opinion, the practitioner should state clearly whether, in his or her opinion, the presentation of assertions is in conformity with established or stated criteria. Examination reports may provide qualified assurance, disclaim any assurance, or contain an adverse opinion. In addition, they may emphasize certain matters relating to the attest engagement or the presentation of assertions. The following is an illustrative examination report that expresses an unqualified opinion on a presentation of assertions:

> We have examined the accompanying Statement of Investment Performance Statistics of XYZ Fund for the year ended December 31, 19X1. Our examination was made in accordance with standards established by the American Institute of Certified Public Accountants and, accordingly, included such procedures as we considered necessary in the circumstances.
>
> [*Additional paragraph(s) may be added to emphasize certain matters relating to the attest engagement or the presentation of assertions.*]
>
> In our opinion, the Statement of Investment Performance Statistics referred to above presents the investment performance of XYZ Fund for the year ended December 31, 19X1, in conformity with the measurement and disclosure criteria set forth in Note 1.

(ii) Review. In providing negative assurance, the practitioner's conclusion should state whether any information came to his or her attention on the basis of the work performed that indicates the assertions are not presented in all material respects in conformity with established or stated criteria. The following illustrative review report expresses negative assurance where no exceptions have been found:

> We have reviewed the accompanying Statement of Investment Performance Statistics of XYZ Fund for the year ended December 31, 19X1. Our review was conducted in accordance with standards established by the American Institute of Certified Public Accountants.
>
> A review is substantially less in scope than an examination, the objective of which is the expression of an opinion on the Statement of Investment Performance Statistics. Accordingly, we do not express such an opinion.
>
> [*Additional paragraph(s) may be added to emphasize certain matters relating to the attest engagement or the presentation of assertions.*]
>
> Based on our review, nothing came to our attention that caused us to believe that the accompanying Statement of Investment Performance Statistics is not presented in conformity with the measurement and disclosure criteria set forth in Note 1.

(iii) Agreed-Upon Procedures. A practitioner may be engaged to perform specific procedures to assist specified users (including the client) in evaluating an assertion. In this type of engagement, the practitioner and the users agree on the attest procedures to be performed. The users also take responsibility for the adequacy of the procedures specified (and, therefore, the amount of assurance provided) for their purposes. In an agreed-upon procedures engagement, the practitioner does not provide either positive or negative assurance. Instead, the report consists of a list of the specific procedures performed on the subject matter of the assertion and a summary of findings. The report should indicate clearly that it is intended solely for the use of the specified users.

Following is an illustrative agreed-upon procedures report:

We have performed the procedures enumerated below, which were agreed to by the audit committees and managements of ABC Inc. and XYZ Fund, solely to assist you in evaluating the accompanying Statement of Investment Performance Statistics of XYZ Fund (prepared in accordance with the criteria specified therein) for the year ended December 31, 19X1. This agreed-upon procedures engagement was performed in accordance with standards established by the American Institute of Certified Public Accountants. The sufficiency of these procedures is solely the responsibility of the specified users of the report.

Consequently, we make no representation regarding the sufficiency of the procedures described below either for the purpose for which this report has been requested or for any other purpose.

[Include paragraphs to enumerate procedures and findings.]

We were not engaged to, and did not, perform an examination, the objective of which would be the expression of an opinion on the accompanying Statement of Investment Performance Statistics of XYZ Fund. Accordingly, we do not express such an opinion Had we performed additional procedures, other matters might have come to our attention that would have been reported to you.

This report is intended solely for the use of the audit committees and managements of ABC Inc. and XYZ Fund, and should not be used by those who have not agreed to the procedures and taken responsibility for the sufficiency of the procedures for their purposes.

(e) Interpretations of Attestation Standards

Four interpretations of SSAE No. 1 have been issued.

(i) Defense Industry Questionnaire.

"Defense Industry Questionnaire on Business Ethics and Conduct" (AT Section 9100.01–.32) provides guidance for engagements to express a conclusion about the appropriateness of management's responses to a defense industry questionnaire covering certain principles of business ethics and conduct. The interpretation contains guidance for this type of engagement, illustrative procedures that a practitioner may apply, and illustrative reports.

The questions in the questionnaire and accompanying responses constitute the written assertions of the defense contractor.

The practitioner's procedures are designed to obtain evidence that the defense contractor has designed and placed in operation policies and programs that conform to the criteria in the questionnaire in a manner that supports the responses to the questions, and that those policies and programs operated during the period covered by the defense contractor's assertions. The practitioner does not, however, provide assurance about the effectiveness of those policies and programs in ensuring compliance with the contractor's code of business ethics and conduct or about whether the contractor and its employees have complied with federal procurement laws.

(ii) Matters Relating to Solvency.

Lenders and others, as a condition to the closing of certain secured financings in connection with leveraged buyouts, recapitalizations, and certain other transactions, sometimes have requested written assurance from an accountant regarding the prospective borrower's solvency and related matters. "Responding to Requests for Reports on Matters Relating to Solvency" (AT Section 9100.33–.46) discusses requests for assurance on such matters.

The lenders are concerned that the financing not be considered a fraudulent conveyance under the Federal Bankruptcy Code and related state statutes. That would occur if the borrower was rendered insolvent as a result of the financing transaction, had unreasonably small capital after the transaction, or did not have the ability to pay its debts as they matured. From the perspective of the attestation standards, matters relating to solvency are subject to varying interpretations of the Federal Bankruptcy Code and various state fraudulent conveyance and transfer statutes and, as such, do not provide the accountant with reasonable criteria to evaluate the assertion under the general attestation standards. For that reason, the interpretation prohibits practitioners from providing any form of assurance with respect to matters relating to solvency through examination, review, or agreed-upon procedures engagements. The interpretation also discusses various other professional services that may be useful in connection with a financing and that an accountant may provide under professional standards.

(iii) Litigation Services.   "Applicability of Attestation Standards to Litigation Services" (AT Section 9100.47–.55) clarifies that the attestation standards apply to only those litigation services in which the practitioner (1) expresses a written conclusion about the reliability of a written assertion that is the responsibility of another party and the conclusion and assertion are for the use of others who do not have the opportunity to analyze and challenge the practitioner's work, or (2) is specifically engaged, in connection with litigation services, to perform work in accordance with the attestation standards.

Lastly, the interpretation specifies that a practitioner may provide an expert opinion or consulting advice about matters relating to solvency, in connection with formal legal or regulatory proceedings, since when giving expert testimony concerning solvency each party to the dispute has the opportunity to analyze and challenge the legal definition, the interpretation, and the criteria the practitioner uses to evaluate matters related to solvency.

(iv) Regulator Access to Working Papers.   Third party access to working papers is discussed in Chapter 3. "Providing Access to or Photocopies of Working Papers to a Regulator" (AT Section 9100.56–.59) clarifies that the guidance on this subject pertaining to audit working papers in AU Section 9339.01–.15 is applicable to an attestation engagement. The interpretation also includes illustrative letters to a regulator for both an attest examination engagement and an attest agreed-upon procedures engagement.

31.2   REPORTING ON AN ENTITY'S INTERNAL CONTROL OVER FINANCIAL REPORTING

SSAE No. 2 (as amended by SSAE No. 6), *Reporting on an Entity's Internal Control Over Financial Reporting* (AT Section 400), provides guidance on examining and reporting on management's written assertion about the effectiveness of an entity's internal control over financial reporting. SSAE No. 2 also permits a practitioner to perform agreed-upon procedures relating to that assertion, but it does not permit accepting an engagement to review and report on that assertion.

(a) Attestation Procedures in Examination Engagements

In order to form an opinion about management's assertion regarding the effectiveness of the entity's internal control over financial reporting, the practitioner should develop an overall strategy for the engagement, obtain an understanding of the entity's internal control, evaluate the design effectiveness of the controls, and test and evaluate their operating effectiveness. When evaluating the design effectiveness of a specific control, the practitioner should consider whether it is suitably designed to prevent or detect material misstatements on a timely basis. When evaluating operating effectiveness, the practitioner should consider how the control was applied, the consistency with which it was applied, and by whom it was applied. The nature and extent of the attestation procedures vary from entity to entity and are influenced by factors such as the extent to which the entity's internal auditors monitor the performance of controls and whether they are appropriately documented.

Management may perform tests of the operating effectiveness of certain controls and provide the results to the practitioner. The practitioner may consider the results of such tests and, if he or she intends to take these results into effect in planning the engagement, should corroborate the results of management's tests. However, additional evidence obtained through personal knowledge, observation, reperformance, and inspection generally is necessary to support the practitioner's opinion.

(b) Reporting on Examination Engagements

The practitioner may not report directly on the entity's internal control; the report is on management's assertion about internal control. Management's assertion may be as of a point in time or apply to a period of time, although the guidance in the attestation standards is geared to point-in-time reporting.

As indicated earlier in this chapter, for a practitioner to examine and report on management's assertion, reasonable criteria must exist against which the assertion can be evaluated. SSAE No. 2 notes that the report, *Internal Control—Integrated Framework*, authored by Coopers & Lybrand L.L.P. and published by the Committee of Sponsoring Organizations of the Treadway Commission (COSO), provides reasonable criteria for effective internal control.[2] The COSO Report provides integrated guidance on internal control, including a definition, description of its components, and criteria as to what constitutes an effective system. It also includes implementation guidelines for designing, evaluating, and monitoring internal control systems.

Management's written assertion may be presented either in a separate report that will accompany the practitioner's report or in a representation letter to the practitioner. The former approach is necessary for the practitioner to consent to the use of his or her report in a general use document; under the latter approach, the practitioner should restrict the use of his or her report to management and others within the entity and, if applicable, to specified regulatory agencies.

---

[2] SSAE No. 2 also provides guidance for reporting on assertions about the effectiveness of internal control based on criteria other than those established in the COSO Report.

An example of a report by management that contains an assertion about an entity's internal control at a point in time, based on the COSO Report, follows:

Report on Internal Control

XYZ Company maintains internal control over financial reporting that is designed to provide reasonable assurance to the Company's management and board of directors regarding the preparation of reliable published financial statements. The controls contain self-monitoring mechanisms, and actions are taken to correct deficiencies as they are identified. Even effective controls, no matter how well designed, have inherent limitations—including the possibility of their circumvention or overriding—and therefore can provide only reasonable assurance with respect to financial statement preparation. Further, because of changes in conditions, internal control effectiveness may vary over time.

The Company assessed its internal control as of December 31, 19XX, in relation to criteria for effective internal control over financial reporting described in *Internal Control—Integrated Framework* issued by the Committee of Sponsoring Organizations of the Treadway Commission. The Company believes that, based on those criteria, it maintained effective internal control over financial reporting as of December 31, 19XX.

A practitioner's attestation report on the assertion in the above management report might read as follows:

Independent Accountant's Report

We have examined management's assertion that XYZ Company maintained effective internal control over financial reporting as of December 31, 19XX, included in the accompanying Report on Internal Control.

Our examination was made in accordance with standards established by the American Institute of Certified Public Accountants and, accordingly, included obtaining an understanding of internal control over financial reporting, testing, and evaluating the design and operating effectiveness of the controls, and such other procedures as we considered necessary in the circumstances. We believe that our examination provides a reasonable basis for our opinion.

Because of inherent limitations in internal control, errors or fraud may occur and not be detected. Also, projections of any evaluation of internal control over financial reporting to future periods are subject to the risk that the controls may become inadequate because of changes in conditions, or that the degree of compliance with controls may deteriorate.

In our opinion, management's assertion that XYZ Company maintained effective internal control over financial reporting as of December 31, 19XX, is fairly stated, in all material respects, based upon criteria established in *Internal Control—Integrated Framework* issued by the Committee of Sponsoring Organizations of the Treadway Commission (COSO).

(c)   Material Weakness

The existence of a material weakness would preclude an assertion that the entity's internal control was effective. "Material weakness" is defined by SAS No. 60, *Communication of Internal Control Related Matters Noted in an Audit* (AU Section 325), as "a reportable condition in which the design or operation of one or more of the internal control components does not reduce to a relatively low level the risk that errors or . . . [fraud] in amounts that would be material in relation to the financial statements being audited may occur and not be detected within a timely period by employees in the normal course of performing their assigned functions."

If a material weakness in internal control exists, and management appropriately modifies its assertion in light of that weakness, the opinion paragraph of the attestation report should include a reference to the material weakness mentioned in the assertion and an explanatory paragraph should be added, following the opinion paragraph, describing the weakness. If management disagrees with the practitioner about the existence of a material weakness, and does not include a discussion of the material weakness in its assertion and appropriately modify the assertion as to effectiveness, the practitioner should express an adverse opinion on management's assertion.

(d) Related Issues

(i) Foreign Corrupt Practices Act   As discussed in Chapter 9, the Foreign Corrupt Practices Act (FCPA) includes provisions regarding internal control for entities subject to the Securities Exchange Act of 1934. Compliance with those provisions is a legal determination. Consequently, a practitioner's attestation report on an examination should not indicate whether an entity is in compliance with the FCPA provisions.

(ii) Report by Management on Internal Control in Communications to Various Parties.   If a management report on internal control is included in a document containing audited financial statements and the auditor has not been engaged to examine and report on management's assertion, the auditor may, but is not required to, add an explanatory paragraph to the audit report on the financial statements, disclaiming responsibility for an opinion on management's assertion. If the report by management includes or is accompanied by a statement that uses the auditor's name, the auditor should consider whether such use indicates or implies that the auditor's involvement is greater than is supported by the facts.

(iii) Other Internal Control Services.   A practitioner may be engaged to provide other types of attest services in connection with an entity's internal control, for example, performing agreed-upon procedures, discussed earlier in this chapter, relating to management's assertion about the effectiveness of the entity's internal control. A practitioner also may be engaged to provide a wide range of consulting services to evaluate and make recommendations for improvements in internal control.

31.3 COMPLIANCE ATTESTATION

SSAE No. 3, *Compliance Attestation* (AT Section 500), was developed to meet a growing need for broad guidance on attesting to assertions about entities' compliance with specified requirements of laws and regulations. The Auditing Standards Board's objective in promulgating a "generic" attestation statement on compliance was to preclude the need for separate statements covering individual laws and regulatory requirements. SSAE No. 3 provides guidance to a practitioner who is engaged to report on management's assertion about either an entity's compliance with requirements of specified laws, regulations, rules, contracts, or grants, or the effectiveness of an entity's internal control over compliance with specified requirements. The specified requirements may be either financial or nonfinancial in nature. The statement permits either an agreed-upon procedures or examination engagement to be performed. For example, a practitioner might be engaged to perform agreed-upon procedures to test management's assertion about the entity's compliance with specified requirements or the effectiveness of the entity's internal control over compliance.

SSAE No. 3 also discusses factors that affect the appropriateness of accepting either agreed-upon procedures or examination engagements and sets forth the conditions necessary for a practitioner to be able to perform each type of engagement. Other matters addressed are the responsibilities of management, the elements of an agreed-upon procedures engagement as contrasted with an examination engagement, and the reporting requirements, as well as the form of report that should be used, for each of the different services.

(a)   Agreed-Upon Procedures Engagements

In an agreed-upon procedures engagement, the practitioner is required to perform only those procedures that have been agreed to by the users of the report. Before performing those procedures, however, the practitioner should obtain an understanding of the compliance requirements specified in management's assertion.

The practitioner's report should enumerate the procedures performed and related findings and should not provide negative assurance about whether management's assertion is fairly stated. The report should contain a statement of restrictions on the use of the report because it is intended to be used solely by the specified users.

The agreed-upon procedures enumerated in the practitioner's report should be performed entirely by the practitioner. Internal auditors, however, may perform and report separately on procedures that they have carried out. The practitioner then may agree to perform procedures on the work performed by the internal auditors.

(b)   Examination Engagements

Management could present its assertion in a separate report to accompany the practitioner's report or only in a representation letter to the practitioner. If management presents its assertion only in a representation letter, the practitioner should modify the report to refer to management's assertion and add a paragraph that limits the distribution of the report to specified parties.

If the examination discloses material noncompliance with the specified requirements and management discloses the noncompliance and appropriately modifies its assertion, the practitioner should refer to the noncompliance in the opinion paragraph and add an explanatory paragraph after the opinion paragraph that emphasizes the noncompliance. If management does not disclose the material noncompliance and modify its assertion, the practitioner should express either a qualified or an adverse opinion on management's assertion, depending on the significance of the noncompliance to the entity and its pervasiveness.

Other report modifications might relate to a restriction on the scope of the engagement or to the practitioner's decision to refer to the report of another practitioner as the basis, in part, for his or her report.

31.4 PRO FORMA FINANCIAL INFORMATION

Pro forma financial information presents the significant effects on historical financial information of "what might have been," had a consummated or proposed transaction or event occurred at an earlier date. It is commonly used to show the effects of:

- Business combinations
- Changes in capitalization
- Dispositions of a significant portion of a business
- Changes in the form of a business organization or in its status as an autonomous entity
- Proposed sales of securities and the application of the proceeds

Pro forma financial information sometimes is included in prospectuses, proxy statements, and other public documents, and more often in less widely circulated, special-purpose documents. It is frequently the only way to illustrate the effects of a particular contemplated transaction. A particular business decision may be impossible to describe intelligibly without the use of pro forma data.

An SSAE, *Reporting on Pro Forma Financial Information* (AT Section 300), provides guidance to a practitioner who is engaged to examine or review and to report on pro forma financial information. Although this SSAE provides standards only for examinations and reviews of pro forma financial information, practitioners may apply agreed-upon procedures to such information in accordance with SSAE No. 4, *Agreed-Upon Procedures Engagements* (AT Section 600), provided the resulting report is restricted to the parties that agreed to the procedures.

AT Section 300 does not address circumstances in which, for purposes of a more meaningful presentation, a transaction consummated after the balance sheet date is reflected in historical financial statements, such as a revision of debt maturities or of earnings per share calculations for a stock split, or in which GAAP require the presentation of pro forma financial information in the financial statements or accompanying notes. It also does not cover pro forma financial information that the practitioner is not engaged to report on and that is presented outside the basic financial statements, but within the same document. AU Sections 550 and 711 describe the practitioner's responsibilities in those circumstances.

(a) Components of Pro Forma Financial Information

Pro forma financial information includes historical financial information and pro forma adjustments that are applied to the historical data to show the effect of the proposed transaction or event. The historical information, adjustments, and resulting pro forma amounts commonly are presented in columnar form.

Pro forma adjustments are based on assumptions reflecting, to the best of management's knowledge and belief, the conditions it expects would have existed and the course of action it would have taken had the proposed transaction or event occurred at an earlier date. Assumptions typically included in a presentation of pro forma financial information are:

- Bank borrowings and related interest rates
- Fixed asset purchases and disposals
- Business combinations and divestitures, including cash layouts and proceeds, respectively

(b) Criteria for Reporting

There are three conditions that must be met for a practitioner to examine or review, and report on, pro forma financial information.

1. The document containing the pro forma financial information should include (or incorporate by reference) complete historical financial statements of the entity or entities for the most recent year available. When pro forma financial information is presented for an interim period, the document should include historical financial information for that interim period. This facilitates comparisons of the effects of the proposed transaction or event with historical results. If pro forma financial information is presented in connection with a proposed business combination, appropriate historical financial information for the significant constituents of the combined entity should be included in the document.

2. The historical financial statements on which the pro forma financial information is based should have been audited or reviewed. The level of assurance that may be provided on the pro forma financial information as of a particular date or for a particular period cannot exceed the level of assurance provided on the related historical financial information. For example, if the underlying historical financial statements of the entity have been audited at year-end and reviewed at an interim date, the practitioner may perform an examination or a review of the year-end pro forma financial information, but is limited to performing a review of the interim pro forma financial information.

3. The practitioner should have an appropriate level of knowledge of the accounting and financial reporting practices of the entity or entities. This knowledge may have been obtained in an audit or a review of the historical financial statements; if not, the practitioner should design and perform procedures to obtain it. These procedures may include inquiry of management and review of another practitioner's working papers, particularly those dealing with financial reporting practices.

(c) Presentation of Pro Forma Financial Information

The presentation should:

- Label the pro forma financial information to distinguish it from the historical financial information

- Describe the transaction or event that is reflected in the pro forma financial information, along with the source of the historical financial information on which it is based

- Disclose the significant assumptions used in developing the pro forma adjustments, together with any significant uncertainties about those assumptions

- Include a statement to the effect that the pro forma financial information should be read in conjunction with the related historical financial information and that it is not necessarily indicative of the results that would have been attained had the transaction or event actually taken place earlier (Article 11 of Regulation S-X provides further guidance with respect to the presentation of pro forma financial information in SEC filings)

(d) Performance and Reporting Standards

The pro forma adjustments and the accompanying pro forma financial information constitute the presentation of the assertions. As in other attest engagements, two levels of assurance may be provided—positive assurance based on an examination or negative assurance based on a review. As noted earlier, examination procedures generally encompass a combination of inspection, confirmation, and observation, and review procedures generally include inquiry and analytical procedures.

The objective of examination procedures applied to pro forma financial information is to limit attestation risk to an appropriately low level to allow the practitioner to provide positive assurance about whether:

- Management's assumptions provide a reasonable basis for presenting the significant effects directly attributable to the underlying transaction or event

- The related pro forma adjustments give appropriate effect to those assumptions

- The pro forma column reflects the proper application of the adjustments to the historical financial statements

In a review, the procedures should be sufficient to limit attestation risk to a moderate level, so that the practitioner can provide negative assurance with respect to the same three items stated above.

Ordinarily, assurance that the pro forma adjustments "give appropriate effect" to management's assumptions means that pro forma adjustments are included for all significant effects directly attributable to the transaction or event and that the pro forma adjustments are consistent with each other and with the data used to develop them.

The practitioner's report should be dated as of the completion of the appropriate procedures. The report may be combined with the report on the historical financial information or may be separate. If the reports are combined and the date of completion of the procedures on the pro forma financial information is after the date of completion of the field work on the historical financial information, the combined report should be dual dated. (See Chapter 27 for an explanation of dual dating.)

(i) Examination Report. An example of a report on an examination of pro forma financial information based on AT Section 300.16 follows:

We have examined the pro forma adjustments reflecting the transaction described in Note 1 and the application of those adjustments to the historical amounts in the accompanying pro forma condensed balance sheet of X Company as of December 31, 19X1, and the pro forma condensed statement of income for the year then ended. The historical condensed financial statements are derived from the historical financial statements of X Company, which were audited by us, and of Y Company, which were audited by other accountants, appearing elsewhere herein. Such pro forma adjustments are based upon management's assumptions described in Note 2. Our examination was made in accordance with standards established by the American Institute of Certified Public Accountants and, accordingly, included such procedures as we considered necessary in the circumstances.

The objective of this pro forma financial information is to show what the significant effects on the historical financial information might have been had the transaction occurred at an earlier date. However, the pro forma condensed financial statements are not necessarily indicative of the results of operations or related effects on financial position that would have been attained had the above-mentioned transaction [or event] actually occurred earlier.

[Additional paragraph(s) may be added to emphasize certain matters relating to the attest engagement.]

In our opinion, management's assumptions provide a reasonable basis for presenting the significant effects directly attributable to the above-mentioned transaction described in Note 1, the related pro forma adjustments give appropriate effect to those assumptions, and the pro forma column reflects the proper application of those adjustments to the historical financial statement amounts in the pro forma condensed balance sheet as of December 31, 19X1, and the pro forma condensed statement of income for the year then ended.

Like an audit report on historical financial statements, an examination report on pro forma financial information may be modified to describe circumstances such as scope limitations, uncertainties about the assumptions, reservations about the propriety of the assumptions, or the conformity of the presentation with those assumptions. Examples of such reports are included in AT Section 300.

(ii) Review Report. As discussed earlier, a practitioner's review report on pro forma financial information expresses negative assurance with respect to the assumptions underlying the proposed transaction or event and how it might have affected the historical data. An example of a report on a review of pro forma financial information based on AT Section 300.17 follows:

We have reviewed the pro forma adjustments reflecting the transaction described in Note 1 and the application of those adjustments to the historical amounts in the accompanying pro forma condensed balance sheet of X Company as of March 31, 19X2, and the pro forma condensed statement of income for the three months then ended. These historical condensed financial statements are derived from the historical unaudited financial statements of X Company, which were reviewed by us, and of Y Company, which were reviewed by other accountants, appearing elsewhere herein. Such pro forma adjustments are based upon management's assumptions described in Note 2. Our review was conducted in accordance with standards established by the American Institute of Certified Public Accountants.

A review is substantially less in scope than an examination, the objective of which is the expression of an opinion on management's assumptions, the pro forma adjustments and the application of those adjustments to historical financial information. Accordingly, we do not express such an opinion.

[*Same paragraph as second paragraph of examination report*]

[*Additional paragraph(s) may be added to emphasize certain matters relating to the attest engagement.*]

Based on our review, nothing came to our attention that caused us to believe that management's assumptions do not provide a reasonable basis for presenting the significant effects directly attributable to the above-mentioned transaction described in Note 1, that the related pro forma adjustments do not give appropriate effect to those assumptions, or that the pro forma column does not reflect the proper application of those adjustments to the historical financial statement amounts in the pro forma condensed balance sheet as of March 31, 19X2, and the pro forma condensed statement of income for the three months then ended.

31.5 PROSPECTIVE FINANCIAL INFORMATION

The usefulness of prospective financial information has become widely recognized, and such information is in demand by the financial community, including investors and potential investors. Prospective financial information is used in a wide variety of situations, ranging from public offerings of bonds or other securities and arrangements for bank or similar financing, to computer spreadsheet software programs designed to facilitate the preparation of various internal financial analyses, including short-range plans (budgets), long-range plans, cash flow studies, capital improvement decisions, and other plans.

Prospective financial information is any financial information about the future. The information may be presented as complete prospective financial statements or limited to one or more elements, items, or accounts. To qualify as *prospective financial statements*, the presentation must meet specific criteria (discussed later). Other, more limited presentations of prospective financial information are referred to as *partial presentations*. The two types of prospective financial information are discussed separately in this chapter.

Although in many instances it is easy to determine what does not fall under the definition of prospective financial information, in others an answer may not be readily apparent. Carried to an extreme, almost any financial presentation arguably could be deemed to contain prospective financial information, since many amounts contained in historical financial statements are estimates calculated on the basis of assumptions about future events.

For practical purposes, presentations that contain dollar amounts based on assumptions of future events in each of a number of future years generally fall under the definition of prospective financial information. On the other hand, financial information based on historical values, such as annual depreciation expense or scheduled principal payments of debt, would not be considered prospective financial information. Also, information based on assumptions of future events that is used only in determining current values typically would not be considered prospective financial information. Thus, future cash streams that are projected to future periods and then discounted to their present values usually would not be considered prospective financial information, nor would actuarial calculations of current pension obligations.

To fill the need for guidance on the preparation and presentation of prospective financial information, the AICPA developed the following materials:

1. An SSAE on *Financial Forecasts and Projections* (AT Section 200). This SSAE applies when a practitioner reports on or submits to the client or others prospective financial information that he or she assisted in assembling and reasonably expects to be used by a third party. The statement specifies the procedures to be performed and the reports to be issued and sets forth minimum presentation guidelines for prospective financial statements.

2. AICPA *Guide for Prospective Financial Information* (hereinafter referred to as the Guide), which is a companion document to the SSAE. It includes all the standards set forth in the SSAE and provides additional explanatory and illustrative material to aid in applying the statement. It also includes guidance for entities that issue prospective financial statements, and guidance on presentations for internal use only, as well as on partial presentations.

(a) Prospective Financial Statements

Prospective financial statements are either financial forecasts or financial projections that present expected financial position, results of operations, and cash flows, and include summaries of significant assumptions and accounting policies.

Financial forecasts are prospective financial statements that present, to the best of the responsible party's[3] knowledge and belief, an entity's expected financial position, results of operations, and cash flows. A financial forecast is based on management's assumptions reflecting *conditions it expects to exist* and the *course of action it expects to take*. A financial forecast may be expressed in specific monetary amounts as a single-point estimate of forecasted results or as a range. In the latter instance, management selects key assumptions to form a range within which it reasonably expects the item or items subject to the assumptions to actually fall. For example, forecasted financial statements that present expected results for a proposed apartment complex may contain a range showing the sensitivity of the forecast to variations in occupancy rates. The range must not be selected in a biased or misleading manner, for example, a range in which one end is significantly less expected than the other.

Financial projections are prospective financial statements that present, to the best of management's knowledge and belief, given one or more *hypothetical assumptions*, an entity's expected financial position, results of operations, and cash flows. A financial projection is sometimes prepared to present one or more hypothetical courses of action for evaluation, as in response to a question such as, "What would happen if . . .?" A financial projection is based on management's assumptions reflecting conditions it expects would exist and the course of action it expects would be taken, given one or more hypothetical assumptions. For instance, a financial projection of an entity's results of operations and cash flows may be based on assumptions about

---

[3] See the discussion later on "Responsibility for Prospective Financial Statements." Generally, the responsible party is management, and this section uses the word "management" to mean the responsible party.

the construction of an additional plant facility. A projection, like a forecast, may contain a range.

Commonly presented prospective financial statements include:

- Forecasts in feasibility studies. These studies may cover hospitals, sports complexes, homes for the elderly, and real estate ventures, among others. Generally, they involve various types of capital expenditures.

- Forecasts or projections relating to new or expanded projects or operations or existing operations of an entity over specified future periods. The prospective financial statements may be, for example, forecasts of target companies the client is considering acquiring, forecasts of the client entity for purposes of conducting discussions with lenders, forecasts prepared on behalf of creditors (for example, in troubled financial situations, such as bankruptcies), or forecasts for the client entity in contemplation of a refinancing or eliminating a line of business.

- Forecasts filed in connection with applications for government assistance grants.

- Rate studies for municipalities and public utilities reported in financial statement format.

- Forecasts, including the actuarial components thereof, of insurance companies. Such forecasts may be filed, for example, with insurance commissions of states in which an insurance company wishes to be licensed to do business.

- Forecasts or projections of future results of a syndicated tax-oriented investment. Syndicated projects may involve real estate, oil and gas, alternative fuel programs, research and development programs, farming transactions, and equipment leases.

- Forecasts prepared in connection with a revenue bond issue.

A practitioner may be engaged to prepare a financial analysis of a potential project. Such an engagement includes obtaining the information, making appropriate assumptions, and assembling the presentation. For example, management may wish to analyze prospective data before making a decision, but may lack the expertise to formulate appropriate assumptions and assemble the data. Such an analysis is not, and should not be characterized as, a forecast or a projection and would not be appropriate for general use, because management does not take responsibility for the assumptions and presentation. The requirements of AT Section 200 and the Guide do not apply to a practitioner preparing a financial analysis.

Presentations of prospective financial statements may take the form of complete financial statements (the details of which may be summarized) or may be more limited, as long as they include, at a minimum, all of the following items that are applicable[4]:

1. Sales or gross revenues
2. Gross profit or cost of sales

---

[4] An applicable item is one that would be presented for historical financial statements. For example, earnings per share would not be an applicable item for a nonpublic entity, since earnings per share are not required to be presented in historical financial statements of such entities.

3. Unusual or infrequently occurring items

4. Provision for income taxes

5. Discontinued operations or extraordinary items

6. Income from continuing operations

7. Net income

8. Appropriate earnings per share information

9. Significant changes in financial position[5]

10. A description of what management intends the prospective financial statements to present, a statement that the assumptions are based on information about circumstances and conditions existing at the time the prospective information was prepared, and a caveat that the prospective results may not be achieved

11. Summary of significant assumptions

12. Summary of significant accounting policies

Items one through nine represent the minimum items that constitute prospective financial statements. A presentation that omits one or more of these applicable items would be considered a partial presentation, unless the omitted item was derivable from the information presented. Partial presentations, which ordinarily are not appropriate for general use, are discussed later in the chapter. Items ten through twelve should accompany all prospective financial statement presentations. A presentation that omits one of the latter items would not be a partial presentation but a deficient presentation, because of the lack of required disclosures.

Prospective financial statements usually should be prepared on a basis consistent with the accounting principles expected to be used in the historical financial statements covering the prospective period. Sometimes, however, the special purpose of the presentation requires that it be prepared based on a comprehensive basis of accounting other than GAAP. In that event, the use of a different basis of accounting should be disclosed.

(b)   Uses of Prospective Financial Statements

Prospective financial statements may be for either general use or limited use. *General use* refers to use of the statements by persons with whom management is not negotiating directly, such as in a debt or equity offering statement. Because recipients of prospective financial statements distributed for general use do not have the opportunity to communicate directly with management, the most useful presentation for them is one that portrays, to the best of management's knowledge and belief, the expected results. Thus, only a financial forecast is appropriate for general use.

Limited use refers to use of prospective financial statements by management only or by management and parties with whom management is negotiating directly. Examples include use in negotiations for financing, submission to a regulatory agency, and

---

[5] When the prospective financial statements take the form of basic financial statements, this requirement is met by presenting a statement of cash flows and related disclosures in accordance with SFAS No. 95, *Statement of Cash Flows* (Accounting Standards Section C25).

use within the entity. Such third-party recipients of prospective financial statements can address questions to and negotiate terms directly with management. Any type of prospective financial statements that would be useful in the particular circumstances normally would be appropriate for limited use. Thus, the presentation may be either a financial forecast or a financial projection.

(c)   Responsibility for Prospective Financial Statements

As indicated earlier, the party responsible for prospective financial statements usually is the entity's management. In certain circumstances, the responsible party may be a party outside the entity being reported on (for example, a party considering acquiring the entity).

The party responsible for the prospective financial statements, including the underlying assumptions, cannot guarantee the achievement of the financial results set forth in them, because achievability depends on many factors that are outside its control. However, that party may influence the operations of an entity through planning, organizing, controlling, and directing its activities, and therefore is in a position to develop reasonable or appropriate assumptions.

At times, the party responsible for the prospective financial statements may wish to enlist the assistance of outside parties in preparing the statements. For example, a practitioner may provide this assistance by helping the party identify key factors, develop assumptions, gather information, or assemble the statements. Such activities ordinarily would not affect the practitioner's independence in examining the prospective financial statements.[6] Regardless of the extent of the practitioner's participation, however, he or she is not responsible for the assumptions. The practitioner may assist in the formulation of assumptions, but management or another party is responsible for evaluating the assumptions, making key decisions, and adopting and presenting the assumptions as its own.

(d)   Services on Prospective Financial Statements

There are three services practitioners may undertake with respect to prospective financial statements—compilation, examination, and application of agreed-upon procedures. (Professional standards do not permit practitioners to review prospective financial statements.)

Examinations of and the application of agreed-upon procedures to prospective financial statements are substantially the same as those services for other attest engagements. A compilation of prospective financial statements is not an attest engagement, because it does not result in the expression of a conclusion on the reliability of the assertions contained in the financial statements. Compilation services involve a practitioner's expertise as an accountant, not as an attestor, and for this reason still can be a valuable professional service.

---

[6] The SEC staff has expressed concern about a practitioner's independence regarding prospective financial statements or historical financial statements covering the forecast period when a practitioner has assisted in preparing the prospective financial statements. Accordingly, the practitioner should consider the issue of independence if he or she is requested to assist in preparing prospective financial statements for an SEC registrant or for an entity that may become an SEC registrant during the forecast period.

(i) Compilation. A compilation of prospective financial statements (a financial forecast or projection) involves:

- Assembling the prospective data, to the extent necessary, based on the responsible party's assumptions
- Performing the compilation procedures required by professional standards
- Reading the prospective data and the underlying assumptions and considering whether they appear to be presented in conformity with AICPA presentation guidelines and are not obviously inappropriate

Assembling data refers to the manual or computer processing of mathematical or other clerical functions related to the presentation of the prospective financial statements. For instance, working with management in obtaining information, developing assumptions, and participating in preparing the prospective financial statements ordinarily would meet the definition of assembling data. On the other hand, merely reproducing and collating such statements or allowing the responsible party to use the practitioner's computer processing hardware or software generally would not constitute assembly.

In a compilation, the practitioner does not provide any assurance on the prospective data or the underlying assumptions. Consequently, the practitioner's procedures are limited, consisting principally of obtaining background knowledge of the industry and the entity, making inquiries, reading the data, and confirming with the responsible party the latter's responsibility for the assumptions.

(ii) Examination. An examination of a financial forecast or projection is the highest level of service offered by a practitioner with regard to prospective financial statements. An examination involves evaluating the:

- Preparation of the forecast or projection
- Support underlying the assumptions
- Presentation for conformity with AICPA presentation guidelines

In examining a projection, the practitioner need not obtain support for the hypothetical assumptions, but should consider whether they are consistent with the purpose of the presentation.

The practitioner's objective in examining a forecast or projection is to accumulate sufficient evidence to limit attestation risk to an appropriately low level. Thus, he or she should select the appropriate combination of available procedures to identify inherent risks and assess control risk, and thereby restrict detection risk to a level that can support his or her opinion on the prospective financial statements.

(iii) Applying Agreed-Upon Procedures. When a practitioner applies agreed-upon procedures to a financial forecast or projection, specified users of the forecast or projection participate in establishing the nature and scope of the engagement and take responsibility for the adequacy of the procedures to be performed. Generally, those procedures may be as limited or extensive as the specified users desire, as long as the users take responsibility for the adequacy of the procedures. Mere reading of the prospective financial statements, however, is not in itself a sufficient procedure. Consistent with other attest engagements involving the application of agreed-upon procedures, distribution of the practitioner's report when agreed-upon procedures are applied to a financial forecast or projection is restricted to the specified users. The report enumerates the procedures performed and states the practitioner's findings; it may not express any form of negative assurance on the financial statements taken as a whole.

(e) Reporting on Prospective Financial Statements

AT Section 200 and the Guide provide guidance for reports on compilations, examinations, and engagements to apply agreed-upon procedures.

(i) Standard Compilation Report.   An example of a standard report on a compilation of a forecast that does not contain a range follows:

> We have compiled the accompanying forecasted balance sheet of XYZ Company as of December 31, 19XX, and the related statements of income, retained earnings, and cash flows for the year then ended, in accordance with standards established by the American Institute of Certified Public Accountants.
>
> A compilation is limited to presenting in the form of a forecast information that is the representation of management and does not include evaluation of the support for the assumptions underlying the forecast. We have not examined the forecast and, accordingly, do not express an opinion or any other form of assurance on the accompanying statements or assumptions. Furthermore, there will usually be differences between the forecasted and actual results, because events and circumstances frequently do not occur as expected, and those differences may be material. We have no responsibility to update this report for events and circumstances occurring after the date of this report.

For a projection, the practitioner's report would include a separate paragraph describing the limitations on the usefulness of the presentation and its inappropriateness for general use.

A practitioner may compile prospective financial statements for an entity with respect to which he or she is not independent. In such circumstances, the practitioner may issue the standard compilation report, but should specifically disclose the fact that he or she is not independent, without describing the reason for the lack of independence.

(ii) Modifications to the Standard Compilation Report.   In some circumstances, a practitioner may wish to expand the report to emphasize a matter regarding the prospective financial statements. Such information may be presented in a separate paragraph of the report. For instance, an emphasis-of-a-matter paragraph may be used to bring to the reader's attention conditions that could significantly affect the prospective results, such as the impact that the repeal of a current regulation would have on the entity's sales. In emphasizing such a matter, however, the practitioner should ensure that he or she does not appear to be expressing assurance or expanding the degree of responsibility being taken with respect to the information. For example, the practitioner should not include statements in a compilation report about the mathematical accuracy of the statements or their conformity with presentation guidelines.

A practitioner may be asked to compile prospective financial statements that contain presentation deficiencies or omit disclosures other than those relating to significant assumptions. The practitioner may accept such engagements provided the deficiency or omission in the prospective financial statements is clearly indicated in the report and is not, to his or her knowledge, undertaken with the intention of misleading those who might reasonably be expected to use such statements.

(iii) Standard Examination Report.   An example of a standard report on an examination of a forecast that does not contain a range follows:

> We have examined the accompanying forecasted balance sheet of XYZ Company as of December 31, 19XX, and the related statements of income, retained earnings, and cash flows for the year then ended. Our examination was made in accordance with standards for an examination of a forecast established by the American Institute of Certified Public Accountants and, accordingly, included such procedures as we considered necessary to evaluate both the assumptions used by management and the preparation and presentation of the forecast.
>
> In our opinion, the accompanying forecast is presented in conformity with guidelines for presentation of a forecast established by the American Institute of Certified Public Accountants, and the underlying assumptions provide a reasonable basis for management's forecast. However, there will usually be differences between the forecasted and actual results, because events and circumstances frequently do not occur as expected, and those differences may be material. We have no responsibility to update this report for events and circumstances occurring after the date of this report.

In examining a projection, the practitioner's opinion regarding the assumptions should be predicated on the hypothetical assumptions; that is, the practitioner should express an opinion on whether the assumptions provide a reasonable basis for the projection given the hypothetical assumptions. The report also should describe the limitations on the usefulness of the presentation. An example that meets these requirements follows:

> [*Additional separate paragraph*]
>
> The accompanying projection and this report were prepared for the DEF National Bank for the purpose of negotiating a loan to expand XYZ Company's plant and should not be used for any other purpose.
>
> [*Opinion paragraph*]
>
> In our opinion, the accompanying projection is presented in conformity with guidelines for presentation of a projection established by the American Institute of Certified Public Accountants, and the underlying assumptions provide a reasonable basis for management's projection assuming the granting of the requested loan for the purpose of expanding XYZ Company's plant as described in the summary of significant assumptions. However, even if the loan is granted and the plant is expanded, there will usually be differences between the projected and actual results, because events and circumstances fre-

quently do not occur as expected, and those differences may be material. We have no responsibility to update this report for events and circumstances occurring after the date of this report.

(iv) Modifications to the Standard Examination Report. The following circumstances require the practitioner to modify the report:

- If the prospective financial statements depart from AICPA presentation guidelines, the practitioner should issue a qualified or an adverse opinion. If the departure is the failure to disclose assumptions that appear to be significant, however, the practitioner should issue an adverse opinion.

- If the practitioner believes that one or more significant assumptions do not provide a reasonable basis for the forecast, or a reasonable basis for the projection given the hypothetical assumptions, an adverse opinion should be issued.

- If the examination is affected by conditions that preclude application of one or more procedures considered necessary in the circumstances, the practitioner should disclaim an opinion and describe the scope limitation in the report. If the practitioner also believes there are material departures from the presentation guidelines, those departures should be described in the report.

The circumstances described below, although not necessarily resulting in modifications to the practitioner's opinion, would result in adding explanatory language to the standard examination report.

- As discussed earlier, in some circumstances the practitioner may wish to emphasize a matter regarding the prospective financial statements, but nevertheless intends to issue an unqualified opinion. The practitioner may present other information and explanatory comments or other informative material in a separate paragraph of the report.

- More than one practitioner may be involved in the examination, and the principal practitioner may decide to refer to the report of another practitioner as a basis, in part, for his or her own opinion. In that event, the principal practitioner should disclose that fact in stating the scope of the examination and should refer to the report of the other practitioner in expressing the opinion. Such a reference indicates the division of responsibility for the performance of the examination.

- For comparative purposes, prospective financial statements may be included in a document that also contains historical financial statements or summarized financial statements derived from audited financial statements and a practitioner's report thereon. In such situations, the practitioner's report on the prospective financial statements should include a reference to the historical statements and the report on them.

- When the practitioner's examination of prospective financial statements is part of a larger engagement, for example, a financial feasibility study or business acquisition study, the report on the examination of the prospective financial statements can be expanded to describe the entire engagement.

(f)   Prospective Financial Statements for Internal Use Only and Partial Presentations

The Guide includes guidance for performing and reporting on prospective financial statements for internal use only and on partial presentations.

(i) Internal Use Only.   A practitioner may be engaged to provide services on prospective financial statements that are restricted to internal use only. Examples are giving advice and assistance to a client on the tax consequences of future actions or on deciding whether to buy or lease an asset. In obtaining satisfaction that the prospective financial statements will be restricted to internal use, absent contrary information, the practitioner may rely on either the written or oral representation of the responsible party.

The practitioner may perform a compilation, an examination, or application of agreed-upon procedures in accordance with professional standards or may perform "other" services tailored to the particular engagement circumstances, such as merely assembling the statements. The practitioner need not report on such other services performed on prospective financial statements for internal use only. For example, a practitioner may submit computer-generated prospective financial statements without reporting on them, provided the statements are restricted to internal use only.

A practitioner may, however, elect to issue a report on other services performed on prospective financial statements for internal use only, provided the statements include a summary of significant assumptions. The report's form and content are flexible but typically would:

- Be addressed to the responsible party
- Identify the statements being reported on
- Describe the work performed and the degree of responsibility taken with respect to the prospective financial statements
- Include a caveat that the prospective results may not be achieved
- Indicate the restrictions as to the distribution of the prospective financial statements and report
- Be dated as of the date of the completion of the procedures

In addition, the practitioner's report on a financial projection for internal use only preferably would describe the limitations on the usefulness of the presentation.

An illustrative report follows that is appropriate for use when a practitioner has assembled a financial projection for internal use only:

> We have assembled, from information provided by management, the accompanying projected balance sheet and the related projected statements of income, retained earnings, and cash flows of XYZ Company as of December 31, 19XX, and for the year then ending. (This financial projection omits the summary of significant accounting policies.)[a]
>
> The accompanying projection and this report were prepared for [state special purpose, for example, "presentation to the Board of Directors of XYZ Company for its consideration as to whether to add a third operating shift"] and should not be used for any other purpose. We have not compiled or examined the financial projection and express no as-

surance of any kind on it. Further, even if [state hypothetical assumption, for example, "the third operating shift is added"] there will usually be differences between the projected and actual results, because events and circumstances frequently do not occur as expected, and those differences may be material. In accordance with the terms of our engagement, this report and the accompanying projection are restricted to internal use and may not be shown to any third party for any purpose.

_____

a This sentence would be included if applicable.

When prospective financial statements intended for internal use only are accompanied by a practitioner's written communication (for example, a transmittal letter), the communication should state that the prospective results may not be achieved and that the statements are for internal use only.

(ii) Partial Presentations. A partial presentation is a presentation of prospective financial information that excludes one or more of the items required to be included in prospective financial statements. A partial presentation may include either forecasted or projected information and may be either extracted from a presentation of prospective financial statements or prepared to satisfy a specific need. The following are examples of partial presentations:

- Sales forecasts
- Presentations of forecasted or projected capital expenditure programs
- Projections of financing needs
- Other presentations of specified elements, accounts, or items of prospective financial statements (for example, projected production costs) that might be part of the development of a full presentation of prospective financial statements
- Forecasts that present operating income, but not net income
- Forecasts or projections of taxable income that do not show significant changes in financial position
- Presentations that provide enough information to be translated into elements, accounts, or items of a financial forecast or projection. Examples include a forecast of sales units and unit selling prices, or a forecast of occupancy percentage, number of rooms, and average room rates for a hotel.

(1) Uses of Partial Presentations. Partial presentations may be appropriate in many "limited use" circumstances. For example, in analyzing whether to lease or buy a piece of equipment, or in evaluating the income tax implications of a given election, it may be necessary to assess the impact of a decision on one aspect of financial results rather than on the financial statements taken as a whole. Partial presentations ordinarily are not appropriate for general use. That is, a partial presentation ordinarily should not be distributed to third parties who will not be negotiating directly with the responsible party. For example, they should not be included in a debt or equity offering document.

(2) Preparation and Presentation. Much of the discussion of the preparation and presentation of prospective financial statements generally is also applicable to partial presentations. The Guide provides guidance on certain matters relating specifically to partial presentations, as follows:

1. If a partial presentation is prepared, but full prospective financial statements are not, the responsible party should consider key factors affecting elements, accounts, or items of prospective financial statements that are interrelated with those presented, for example, in a sales forecast whether productive capacity is sufficient to support forecasted sales.

2. Titles of partial presentations should be descriptive of the presentation and should disclose the limited nature of the presentation. The presentation should state whether it is of forecasted or projected information, but should not state that it is a "financial forecast" or a "financial projection."

3. Significant accounting principles and policies relevant to the presentation should be disclosed.

4. The concept of materiality should be related to the partial presentation taken as a whole.

5. Significant assumptions, such as those having a reasonable possibility of a variation that may significantly affect the prospective results, should be disclosed.

6. The introduction preceding the summary of assumptions should include a description of the purpose of the presentation and any limitations on the usefulness of the presentation.

(3) Services Relating to Partial Presentations. A practitioner may compile, examine, or apply agreed-upon procedures to a partial presentation. Performance of such engagements should be in accordance with the guidance for such services elsewhere in this chapter. Because of the limited nature of partial presentations, however, the practitioner may need to tailor the procedures. For instance, he or she may need to consider the impact that key factors affecting elements, accounts, or items that are not included in the presentation may have on elements, accounts, or items that are included, such as considering productive capacity in a sales forecast.

(4) Reporting. Reporting on partial presentations (both standard and modified reports) generally follows the same form as for full prospective financial statements. The Guide presents the various forms of the practitioner's report for the different services that may be performed on partial presentations, as well as some illustrative partial presentations.

32

Compliance Auditing

32.1   INTRODUCTION

Laws and governmental regulations play an integral part in an entity's operations, and failure to comply with them may affect its financial statements. Management is responsible for ensuring that the entity complies with applicable laws and regulations. To meet this responsibility, management identifies those laws and regulations and establishes controls designed to provide reasonable assurance of compliance. The auditor's responsibilities for testing and reporting on compliance with laws and governmental regulations varies according to the type of entity being audited and the terms of the engagement.

During the mid-1980s, Congress and the public began expressing concerns about increased reports of illegal acts and began questioning auditors' responsibility for detecting and reporting on these violations. Consequently, the Auditing Standards Board (ASB) issued two Statements on Auditing Standards (SASs): No. 53, *The Auditor's Responsibility to Detect and Report Errors and Irregularities*, and No. 54, *Illegal Acts by Clients*. Together they defined the auditor's responsibilities in this area under generally accepted auditing standards (GAAS). In February 1997, the ASB issued SAS No. 82, *Consideration of Fraud in a Financial Statement Audit*, which superseded SAS No. 53.

The responsibilities included in these SASs apply to *all* audits performed under GAAS. In addition to these requirements, an entity, particularly a governmental or nonprofit organization, may require an audit in accordance with government auditing standards issued by the Comptroller General of the United States, often referred to as the "Yellow Book"; the Single Audit Act, amended most recently in 1996; and Office of Management and Budget (OMB) Circular A-133, "Audits of States, Local Governments, and Non-Profit Organizations," revised in June 1997. In performing an audit in accordance with these requirements, the auditor assumes responsibilities beyond those encompassed by GAAS. Familiarity with each of these pronouncements—GAAS, generally accepted government auditing standards (GAGAS), the Single Audit Act, and OMB Circular A-133—is essential for the auditor to fully understand how the consideration of illegal acts affects the scope of such audits. This chapter discusses each of these sources of audit guidance regarding an entity's compliance with laws and regulations.

32.2   GENERALLY ACCEPTED AUDITING STANDARDS

The auditor's primary responsibilities with respect to compliance under GAAS are to provide reasonable assurance of detecting noncompliance with laws and regulations that could have a *direct and material* effect on financial statement amounts and to make the audit committee aware of any illegal acts that come to the auditor's attention. Specific audit responsibilities, which include the detection of errors, fraud, and illegal acts, are identified in SAS Nos. 54 and 82. These terms and responsibilities are discussed in Chapter 4.

SAS No. 82 (AU Section 316) states that "the auditor should specifically assess the risk of material misstatement of the financial statements due to fraud and should consider that assessment in designing the audit procedures to be performed" (para. 316.12). To ensure an effective risk assessment, the auditor should obtain an understanding of the entity's internal control. SAS No. 55, as amended by SAS No. 78, *Con-*

sideration of Internal Control in a Financial Statement Audit (AU Section 319), requires the auditor to obtain an understanding of internal control sufficient to plan the audit and to assess control risk for the assertions embodied in the financial statements. In assessing control risk with respect to compliance, the auditor should consider all five components of internal control, as outlined in SAS No. 78: the control environment, risk assessment, control activities, information and communication, and monitoring. This includes knowledge of an entity's controls designed to ensure compliance with laws and regulations that have a direct and material effect on the determination of financial statement amounts. Based on this assessment of internal control, the auditor designs substantive tests for compliance.

Audits conducted in accordance with GAAS ordinarily do not include procedures designed specifically to detect illegal acts that might have only an *indirect* effect on financial statements. However, these types of illegal acts may come to the auditor's attention through procedures performed to support the audit opinion, for example, reading minutes and reviewing management's policies for preventing illegal acts; inquiring of management and legal counsel concerning litigation, claims, and assessments; and obtaining periodic representations from management relative to compliance with laws and regulations. SAS No. 54 provides additional guidance with respect to detecting and reporting illegal acts.

Any illegal acts detected by an auditor should be brought to management's attention or, if management is involved, to the attention of the audit committee or its equivalent. SAS Nos. 54 and 82 do not require the auditor to issue a formal audit report on the client's compliance with laws and regulations. If the entity is an SEC registrant, additional reporting may be required pursuant to the Private Securities Litigation Reform Act of 1995.

32.3 SPECIAL CONSIDERATIONS IN PLANNING A GOVERNMENTAL AUDIT

For purposes of conducting an audit under GAGAS, the Single Audit Act, and OMB Circular A-133, a "governmental entity" includes federal, state, and local governments and nonprofit organizations that receive federal government funds. In developing the audit strategy for a governmental entity, the auditor should consider all the applicable performance and reporting requirements in combination. As previously discussed, there are four reference sources—GAAS, GAGAS, the Single Audit Act, and OMB Circular A-133. Each of these contains different requirements, which the auditor should understand when considering a governmental entity's compliance with laws and regulations. Because the provisions of these sources overlap, the ASB issued SAS No. 74, *Compliance Auditing Considerations in Audits of Governmental Entities and Recipients of Governmental Financial Assistance* (AU Section 801), to provide professional guidance for implementing these sources as they apply to compliance with laws and regulations.

Under GAAS, the method by which an auditor obtains an understanding of internal control and assesses control risk in auditing a governmental entity is similar to that used in audits of nongovernmental entities (explained in detail in Chapters 10–12). Because governmental entities typically are subject to more specific laws and regulations than are other business entities, however, the audit risk of failing to detect instances of noncompliance is correspondingly greater. Consequently, in planning an audit of a governmental entity, it is essential that the auditor design procedures to reduce the risk that the financial statements may be materially misstated due to noncompliance with laws and regulations to the appropriately low level required by professional standards. The auditor also should consider materiality not only in relation to the financial statements but also in relation to government-funded programs. Failure to consider this in the planning stages may cause a duplication of effort later in the audit.

As noted earlier, in assessing control risk relative to compliance with laws and regulations for a governmental entity, the auditor should consider controls in all five components of internal control. However, the following control environment factors are particularly relevant in planning a governmental audit:

- Management's awareness of relevant laws and regulations
- Policies regarding acceptable operating practices and codes of conduct
- Assignment of responsibility and delegation of authority over matters such as organizational goals and objectives, operating functions, and compliance with regulatory requirements

As discussed later in this chapter, GAGAS require that an audit be designed to provide reasonable assurance of detecting material noncompliance with applicable laws and regulations. In planning and conducting the necessary tests of compliance, the auditor should:

- Determine which laws and regulations could, if not complied with, have a direct and material effect on the financial statements
- Determine whether management has identified these laws and regulations
- Assess, for each significant law or regulation, the risk that material noncompliance could occur. This includes assessing the effectiveness of the design of controls the entity has placed in operation to ensure compliance with laws and regulations.
- Based on that assessment, design procedures to test compliance with laws and regulations to provide reasonable assurance that intentional or unintentional instances of noncompliance that could have a material effect on the financial statements have not occurred. These procedures may include considering knowledge obtained in prior year audits; inquiry of management, legal counsel, appropriate oversight organizations, and program administrators; reading relevant agreements; reviewing minutes of meetings of relevant legislative bodies; obtaining written representations from management; and reviewing other relevant information.

In addition to the usual requirements, the management representation letter for a governmental entity should include a statement that management acknowledges its responsibility for the entity's compliance with applicable laws and regulations, and a statement that management has identified and disclosed all laws and regulations having a direct and material effect on the determination of financial statement amounts.

SAS No. 74 provides general guidance for applying the provisions of SAS No. 54 to financial audits of governmental entities and for performing financial statement or single audits (discussed later) in accordance with government auditing standards and other federal audit requirements. This guidance incorporates the requirements of professional standards and government regulations as they relate to audits of governmental entities. In addition, SAS No. 74 requires the auditor to notify management or the audit committee if he or she became aware during an audit that the entity was subject to a legal, regulatory, or contractual audit requirement that was not covered by the terms of the engagement. For example, if the auditor was engaged only to conduct an audit in accordance with GAAS and became aware that the entity was also subject to the provisions of GAGAS, that fact should be communicated to the entity's management and audit committee.

32.4 GOVERNMENT AUDITING STANDARDS

Government auditing standards are established by the Comptroller General of the United States in *Government Auditing Standards* (the "Yellow Book"), which was revised most recently in 1994. GAGAS are applicable for audits of, among other entities, state and local governmental units; nonprofit organizations, such as universities and hospitals, that receive government aid or grants; and mortgage companies subject to the provisions of Housing and Urban Development (HUD) audit guides. Laws and regulations such as the Single Audit Act and OMB Circulars also require public accountants to follow government auditing standards for certain financial audits. These standards apply to primary recipients and subrecipients of federal awards, but do not apply to vendors unless specifically required by the contract between the parties. The distinction between a subrecipient and a vendor is that a subrecipient receives a federal award from a primary recipient to operate or administer a program or a program component, while a vendor provides goods and services related to the administrative support of a federal award.

The Yellow Book contains standards for two types of governmental audits, financial and performance. This chapter discusses only financial audits, because they are the type an independent auditor is more likely to perform. Although unique to the audit needs of governmental entities, GAGAS incorporate certain aspects of GAAS. Like GAAS, these standards are divided into three categories: general, field work, and reporting standards. Following is a summary of GAGAS.

(a) General Standards

The general standards cover four areas: qualifications (i.e., professional proficiency), independence, due professional care, and quality control.

The *qualifications* standard states that "the staff assigned to conduct the audit should collectively possess adequate professional proficiency for the tasks required." This standard imposes certain education and training requirements beyond those otherwise required. Specifically, the standard requires at least 80 hours of continuing education and training every two years for members of the engagement team. For members of the engagement team responsible for planning, directing, conducting substantial portions of the field work, and reporting on the audit, at least 24 of the 80 hours must be directly related to the governmental environment and/or governmental auditing.

The *independence* standard states that "in all matters relating to the audit work, the audit organization and the individual auditors, whether government or public, should be free from personal and external impairments to independence, should be organizationally independent, and should maintain an independent attitude and appearance." Personal impairments include official, professional, or financial relationships with an auditee; preconceived ideas toward individuals, groups, organizations, or objectives of a particular program; and biases induced by political or social convictions or any circumstances in which the auditor may not be impartial or may not be perceived as impartial. External impairments are factors external to the audit organization that may restrict the audit or interfere with an auditor's ability to form independent and objective opinions and conclusions, such as unreasonable restrictions on the time allowed to complete the audit; restrictions on funds or other resources provided to the audit organization that would adversely affect its ability to carry out its responsibilities; or external interference relative to the assignment, appointment, and promotion of audit personnel. Organizational independence requires the audit organization to be independent of the entities it audits. Neither GAAS or GAGAS preclude independent auditors from utilizing the work performed by internal auditors after it has been reviewed for adherence to professional standards. The independence standard is similar to that prescribed by GAAS for an audit of financial statements.

The standard regarding *due professional care* states, "Due professional care should be used in conducting the audit and in preparing related reports." This standard, which is substantially the same in both GAAS and GAGAS, identifies the need to use sound judgment in establishing the scope, selecting the methodology, and choosing tests and procedures for the audit.

The *quality control* standard states that "each audit organization conducting audits in accordance with these standards should have an appropriate internal quality control system in place and undergo an external quality control review" at least once every three years.

(b) Field Work Standards

The field work standards cover five topics: planning; irregularities, illegal acts, and other noncompliance; internal controls; working papers; and financial related audits. The Yellow Book incorporates SASs that are related to these topics, and in some cases prescribes additional responsibilities and guidance.

The *planning* standard requires that work be properly planned, and that auditors consider materiality, among other matters, in determining the nature, timing, and extent of auditing procedures. It also requires follow-up on known material findings and recommendations from previous audits.

The *irregularities, illegal acts, and other noncompliance* standard requires that audits be designed to provide reasonable assurance of detecting irregularities (which SAS No. 82 refers to as "fraud") that are material to the financial statements, material misstatements resulting from direct and material illegal acts, and material misstatements resulting from noncompliance with provisions of contracts or grant agreements. Auditors also should be aware of the possibility that indirect illegal acts may have occurred. This standard does not extend the auditor's responsibility beyond that established in SAS Nos. 54 and 82; however, entities subject to the provisions of GAGAS are likely to be subject to extensive laws and regulations.

The *internal controls* standard requires that the auditor obtain a sufficient understanding of internal control to plan the audit and determine the nature, timing, and extent of tests to be performed. This standard provides guidance in the following areas: control environment, safeguarding controls, controls over compliance with laws and regulations, and control risk assessment.

The *working papers* standard requires that a record of the auditor's work be retained in the form of working papers. This record should contain enough information for an experienced auditor, having no previous connection with the audit, to fully understand the content.

The *financial related audits* standard incorporates certain SASs into government auditing standards: SAS No. 62, *Special Reports* (relating to auditing specified elements, accounts, or items of a financial statement); SAS No. 70, SAS No. 74, SAS No. 75 (relating to the application of agreed-upon procedures to specified elements, accounts, or items of a financial statement), and Statement on Standards for Attestation Engagements (SSAE) Nos. 1, 2, and 3. According to GAGAS, examples of financial related audits include determining whether (1) financial information is presented in accordance with established or stated criteria, (2) the entity has adhered to specific financial compliance requirements, and (3) the entity's internal control over financial reporting and safeguarding assets is suitably designed and implemented to achieve relevant control objectives.

(c) Reporting Standards

For financial statement audits, GAGAS incorporate the four generally accepted standards of reporting, as found in AU Section 150. In addition, the following reporting standards are designed to satisfy the unique needs of governmental financial audits:

- Reporting on compliance with GAGAS
- Reporting on compliance with laws and regulations and internal controls
- Communication with the audit committee or other responsible individuals
- Privileged and confidential information
- Report distribution

Reporting on compliance with generally accepted government auditing standards requires that the auditor's report on the financial statements state that the audit was conducted in accordance with GAGAS as well as GAAS.

Reporting on compliance with laws and regulations and internal controls may be combined with the auditor's report on the financial statements or may be separate. Whether or not the two are combined, the auditor should describe the scope of testing of compliance with laws and regulations and internal controls and present the results of those tests and an introduction summarizing all audit findings. When the auditor reports on these matters separately, the report on the financial statements must refer to the reports on compliance and internal controls. In reporting on these matters, all instances of irregularities and illegal acts must be reported unless clearly inconsequential. Material noncompliance relative to contract agreements also must be reported.

Based on the assessment of internal controls or an assessment that the transactions and balances directly affected by laws and regulations are not material to the financial statements taken as a whole, the auditor may decide not to perform any tests of compliance with laws or regulations. In this instance, the report should be modified to indicate that the auditor did not test for compliance with laws and regulations.

The auditor is responsible for reporting material instances of noncompliance even if the resulting misstatements have been corrected in the financial statements. In those circumstances, the auditor may wish to include in the report a statement that the misstatements resulting from the instances of noncompliance have been corrected for purposes of financial statement presentation. The auditor is not required to disclose in the report instances of noncompliance that are inconsequential; however, such instances should be reported to the entity in a separate communication, preferably in writing. This separate communication, or management letter, should be referred to in the reports on compliance and internal controls.

The *communication with audit committees or other responsible individuals* standard requires the auditor to communicate information such as the auditor's responsibilities and internal control and compliance testing required by law.

The *privileged and confidential information* standard prohibits certain information from being disclosed generally. The audit report should, however, state the nature of the information omitted and the requirement that makes the omission necessary.

The *report distribution* standard requires written audit reports to be submitted to the appropriate officials of the auditee and to the appropriate officials of the organizations requiring or arranging for the audit.

(d) Reporting on HUD Audits

Although HUD program audits are subject to GAGAS, the U.S. Department of Housing and Urban Development's Office of Inspector General has developed a *Consolidated Audit Guide for Audits of HUD Programs* that sets forth specific requirements. Auditors are required to follow the provisions of this guide when auditing applicable HUD programs. At the time of this writing, HUD was in the process of revising this guide in response to changes in program regulations and experience in implementing the provisions of the guide.

32.5 HISTORY OF SINGLE AUDITS

Beginning in the mid-1960s, the number and dollar amounts of federally funded programs increased substantially. This increase accompanied a demand for responsible and effective management of government-funded programs and full accountability of those entrusted with public funds. During the 1960s and 1970s, a federal agency that issued a grant to a state or local government had the authority to establish its own audit guidelines. There was no oversight body or any other means of controlling the scope or number of required audits of a particular agency or other entity receiving federal awards, which often came from different agencies. As a result, the same controls and transactions often were tested more than once, frequently by different independent auditors, and sometimes even simultaneously. These duplicative audits caused organizational inefficiencies and led to increased audit costs.

In response to these concerns, Congress enacted the Single Audit Act of 1984 (the Act), which created a single, coordinated audit (often called a "single audit," "organization-wide audit," or "entity-wide audit") of all federal awards provided to state and local governments during a fiscal year. The Act emphasized audits of those federal award programs that the federal government had defined as major. The objectives of the Act were to:

- Promote the efficient and effective use of audit resources
- Improve state and local governments' financial management of federal financial assistance programs through more effective auditing
- Establish uniform requirements for audits of federal financial assistance provided to state and local governments
- Ensure that federal awards, to the greatest extent practicable, are audited in accordance with the requirements of the Single Audit Act

The Office of Management and Budget is the federal agency responsible for setting audit policy regarding the frequency and scope of audits of governmental entities. In an effort to facilitate the implementation of the Single Audit Act, the OMB issued Circular A-128, "Audits of State and Local Governments," in 1985. Together, Circular A-128 and the Act required: (1) an audit of the entity's general-purpose or basic financial statements, (2) the performance of additional audit tests for compliance with applicable laws and regulations related to grants received, and (3) tests of controls designed to ensure compliance with laws and regulations applicable to federal awards. Circular A-128 also prescribed the monitoring responsibilities for these requirements.

The Single Audit Act, as enacted in 1984, did not apply to institutions of higher education or other nonprofit agencies receiving federal funds. Consequently, the OMB issued Circular A-133, "Audits of Institutes of Higher Education and Other Non-Profit Institutions," in 1990. Circular A-133 extended requirements similar to those in the Act and Circular A-128 to institutions of higher education and nonprofit agencies receiving federal awards. To provide guidance to the auditor, the OMB issues compliance supplements describing compliance requirements that should be audited (see Section 6(c), Testing Compliance with Requirements of Major Federal Financial Assistance Programs). The AICPA also issues Statements of Position (SOPs) to provide auditors of governmental and nonprofit entities with a basic understanding of the work required and the reports that should be issued under GAGAS and the OMB Circulars.

32.6 SINGLE AUDIT ACT AMENDMENTS OF 1996 AND OMB CIRCULAR A-133

Amendments to the Single Audit Act in 1996 extended its provisions to institutions of higher education and other nonprofit entities. The 1996 amendments to the Act apply to nonfederal entities (defined as states, local governments, or nonprofit organizations) that expend $300,000 or more under federal awards in a fiscal year. In response to those amendments, the OMB revised its audit Circulars. OMB Circular A-133 was revised as of June 30, 1997 to include state and local governments. Titled "Audits of States, Local Governments, and Non-Profit Organizations," Circular A-133 now incorporates the amendments to the Single Audit Act and the requirements in Circular A-128, which consequently was rescinded. In addition, the OMB issued an updated provisional compliance supplement on June 30, 1997, consolidating the requirements for A-128 and A-133 audits and updating the compliance requirements that should be audited. At the time of this writing, the AICPA is revising the SOPs applicable to audits of governmental and nonprofit entities to conform to the revised Act and Circular A-133.

(a) Determination of a Major Program

Under the Single Audit Act, the auditor must report on whether the entity has complied with laws and regulations that have a material effect on each of its *major* federal programs. Before the Act was amended in 1996, the determination of a major program was based solely on dollar value; however, the 1996 amendments incorporate the auditor's risk assessment into the process of identifying a major program. Management is responsible for identifying the federal programs under which it receives funding, including funds received directly from federal agencies and federal funds passed through from other entities such as states, local governments, and nonprofit organizations. The OMB has created risk-based criteria to be used, in conjunction with specified dollar values, for identifying major programs. This process consists of four steps, which are described in detail in Circular A-133, subsection .520.

(b) Materiality and Risk Assessment Under the Single Audit Act

Under the Single Audit Act, the auditor must report on whether the entity has complied with laws and regulations that have a material effect on each major federal award program. The concept of materiality under the Act differs from that prescribed by GAAS. Under the Act, materiality is considered in relation to the individual major federal award program. Thus, a material amount pertaining to one program may not be considered material to another program of a different size or nature.

Risk assessment in an audit performed under GAGAS is similar to that under GAAS. Under the Single Audit Act, however, the auditor has responsibilities beyond those of GAAS and government auditing standards, namely, testing and reporting on the entity's compliance with the requirements of a particular program. Thus, in assessing risk in a compliance audit of a major federal program, the auditor also should consider the risk that he or she may fail to appropriately modify the opinion on compliance with such requirements. This risk has three aspects.

- Inherent risk—the risk that material noncompliance with requirements applicable to a federal program could occur assuming there were no related controls
- Control risk—the risk that material noncompliance in a federal program will not be prevented or detected on a timely basis by the entity's internal control
- Detection risk—the risk that the auditor's procedures will lead to the conclusion

that noncompliance that could be material to a federal program does not exist when in fact such noncompliance does exist

The following summarizes the requirements that pertain to each of those risks and explains how the requirements, taken together, provide a basis for the auditor's report on compliance.

(i) Inherent Risk. The auditor's identification of inherent risks is pervasive to the entire entity. In other words, the inherent risks that exist most likely would affect both the entity's ability to record financial transactions and its compliance with laws and regulations. Therefore, the identification of inherent risks for financial and compliance purposes sometimes may be combined.

(ii) Control Risk. Under the Single Audit Act the auditor is required to determine and report on whether the entity has controls to provide reasonable assurance that it is managing federal programs in compliance with applicable laws and regulations. The auditor should:

- Perform tests of controls to evaluate the effectiveness of the design and operation of the controls in preventing or detecting material noncompliance
- Examine the entity's controls for monitoring its subrecipients and obtaining and acting on subrecipients' audit reports
- Determine whether controls are in place to ensure that direct and indirect costs were computed and billed in accordance with requirements
- Document procedures employed to assess and test internal control

In planning a compliance audit, the auditor should obtain an understanding of each of the five components of the entity's internal control relative to each major federal program. Controls over federal programs may be separate from controls over other transactions entered into by the entity. For example, the controls in place to ensure eligibility for a program (such as student financial aid in a university) might be totally separate from those relating to the processing of financial transactions. The auditor's understanding should include knowledge about relevant control environment factors and the design of controls and records used in administering a federal program and whether they have been placed in operation. The understanding also should include knowledge about the design and extent of supervisory controls in place to ensure compliance with laws and regulations.

According to Circular A-133, audits of federal programs must be planned to achieve a low level of assessed control risk. If a low assessment is not possible, a reportable condition or material weakness should be reported. The auditor's determination of risk should be based on an overall evaluation of the risk of noncompliance occurring that could be material to the federal program. The following should be considered when assessing risk in a federal program:

- Internal control and compliance findings from the current and prior audits
- Oversight exercised by federal agencies and pass-through entities

- Inherent risks associated with the program
- Phase of the program (i.e., is it new or recently revised?)
- The existence of multiple program locations with limited oversight
- Implementation of new systems
- Experience and qualifications of key personnel

(iii) Detection Risk.   Circular A-133 requires that in an audit of an entity that has major federal award programs, a representative number of charges from each major program be selected for testing. The objective of these tests of compliance with requirements is to reduce detection risk. Just as in a financial statement audit, in a single audit the auditor determines how much substantive testing is necessary to reduce detection risk to an appropriately low level on the basis of the risk assessment activities.

(c) Testing Compliance with Requirements of Major Federal Financial Assistance Programs

The OMB issued a revised compliance supplement to its new Circular A-133 on June 30, 1997. This supplement provides a single source of information for auditors to understand the federal program objectives, procedures, and compliance requirements as well as audit objectives and suggested auditing procedures relative to these compliance requirements. The auditor should consult this supplement when considering the nature, timing, and extent of procedures to perform as a basis for expressing an opinion on compliance.

The A-133 compliance supplement describes 14 types of compliance requirements and related audit objectives and procedures to be considered in performing audits subject to Circular A-133. The 14 compliance requirements are as follows:

- *Activities allowed or unallowed*: Provides guidance on activities that can or cannot be funded under a specific program.
- *Allowable costs/cost principles*: Describes the cost accounting requirements associated with federal awards. These include OMB Circular A-21, "Cost Principles for Educational Institutions," Circular A-87, "Cost Principles for State, Local, and Indian Tribal Governments," Circular A-122, "Cost Principles for Nonprofit Organizations," and HHS CFR Title 45, Part 74, Appendix E, "Hospital Cost Principles for R&D."
- *Cash management*: Requires the adoption of procedures to minimize the time elapsing between the transfer of funds from the U.S. Treasury and disbursement by the grantee.
- *Davis–Bacon Act*: Requires that wages for "laborers and mechanics" employed by contractors of federally funded projects be paid in accordance with the prevailing local wage established by the Secretary of Labor.
- *Eligibility*: Specifies the criteria for determining the individuals, groups of indi-

viduals, or subrecipients that can participate in the program and the amounts of assistance for which they qualify.

- *Equipment and real property management*: Provides standards for the use and disposition of equipment and real property purchased with federal funds. These requirements cover records and inventory management.

- *Matching, level of effort, and earmarking*: Requires the auditor to determine whether the minimum amount (or percentage) of grantee contributions or matching funds was provided, specified service or expenditure levels were maintained, and minimum or maximum limits for specified purposes were met.

- *Period of availability of federal funds*: Requires that only those costs resulting from obligations incurred during the funding period for a federal award may be charged to the award.

- *Procurement and suspension and debarment*: Prohibits recipients of federal awards from contracting with parties that have been suspended or debarred by a federal agency.

- *Program income*: Requires that income generated from a federal program be recorded correctly and used as a deduction from outlays, as an addition to the project budget, or to meet matching requirements.

- *Real property acquisition and relocation assistance*: Requires that people displaced from their homes, businesses, or farms by a federal program be treated equitably and in accordance with the Uniform Relocation Assistance and Real Property Acquisition Policies Act of 1970.

- *Reporting*: Requires the use of standard reporting forms authorized by the OMB or the awarding agency and establishes due dates for report submission.

- *Subrecipient monitoring*: Requires entities to monitor the activities of subrecipients relative to their federal awards.

- *Special tests and provisions*: Requires the consideration of special provisions related to each federal program.

In addition to providing audit objectives and procedures for these 14 types of compliance requirements, the supplement also includes a description of the applicability of these requirements to each federal program covered by Circular A-133, internal control guidance to assist management in designing appropriate controls and to assist auditors in testing them, and guidance for auditing certain *cluster* programs and other programs not specifically covered by the supplement. (A cluster program is a grouping of closely related programs that share common compliance requirements.)

(d) Reporting Under the Single Audit Act

The reporting requirements of the Single Audit Act and OMB Circular A-133 are more extensive than those under GAAS and government auditing standards. In addition to the report required by GAAS on the financial statements and the reports required by government auditing standards on compliance with laws and regulations and internal controls, the auditor performing a single audit must issue reports specific to an entity's federal awards. The reporting requirements under the amended Single Audit Act and the revised Circular A-133 are as follows:

- *A report on the financial statements,* stating whether the financial statements are presented fairly in all material respects in conformity with GAAP and an opinion as to whether the schedule of expenditures of federal awards is presented fairly in all material respects in relation to the financial statements taken as a whole. The report on the financial statements submitted under Circular A-133 requires references to both GAAS and GAGAS and to the internal control and compliance reports required by GAGAS.

- *A report or reports on internal control related to the financial statements and major programs,* including the scope of internal control testing and the results of those tests, and referring to a separate schedule of findings, if applicable.

- *A report or reports on compliance with laws, regulations, and the provisions of contracts or grant agreements,* including an opinion as to whether the auditee complied with laws, regulations, and the provisions of contracts and grants that could have a direct and material effect on each of its major programs. If an auditor reports material findings of noncompliance relating to major programs on the part of an entity subject to the provisions of Circular A-133, the auditor is required to disclose, either in the report or in an attachment to it, the population size of transactions, the sample size of transactions tested, and the number of instances of noncompliance and dollar amounts.

- *A report on the schedule of federal awards.* The schedule lists total expenditures for each federal award as identified in the *Catalog of Federal Domestic Assistance* and describes the significant accounting policies used in preparing the schedule. The auditor's report on the schedule falls under the reporting guidelines of SAS No. 29, *Reporting on Information Accompanying the Basic Financial Statements in Auditor-Submitted Documents* (AU Section 551).

- *A schedule of findings and questioned costs,* including, but not limited to, the following: reportable conditions in internal control over major programs; material noncompliance with laws, regulations, and contract or grant provisions; known or likely questioned costs that are greater than $10,000; and known fraud affecting a federal award. If the auditor concludes that an illegal act has occurred or is likely to have occurred, before reporting information that would be available to the general public, he or she should communicate with counsel or with law enforcement or investigatory authorities to ensure that the information reported does not compromise ongoing investigative or legal proceedings.

Any restrictions on the scope of the audit (i.e., on the auditor's ability to perform all the procedures considered necessary in the circumstances) may require the auditor to qualify the opinion on compliance or disclaim an opinion. This decision depends on the auditor's judgment about the nature and magnitude of the potential effects of the scope limitation and their significance to each applicable major federal award program.

The auditor is precluded from issuing an unqualified opinion on compliance when the auditing procedures performed reveal instances of noncompliance that the auditor believes could have a material effect on a program. In these circumstances, the auditor should use professional judgment to determine whether a qualified or an adverse opinion is required.

In addition to these reporting requirements, Circular A-133 requires the preparation of a "data collection form" designed to provide summary information about the entity, its federal awards, and the audit results. The collection of this data is intended to serve as the basis for developing a government-wide database on federal awards administered by nonfederal government entities.

PART 5

Auditing Specialized Industries

Introduction to Part 5

The discussions of auditing concepts, principles, and procedures in Parts 1 through 4 of this book are presented principally within the framework of entities engaged in manufacturing, selling, and service activities. In contrast, the chapters in Part 5 deal with auditing a number of specific industries. While every industry has at least some characteristics that set it apart from other industries, those characteristics do not necessarily require unique audit strategies or procedures. In some industries, however, the risks, accounting principles, controls, transactions, and accounts are sufficiently different to require specialized knowledge on the part of an auditor. Seventeen such industries are covered in the chapters in Part 5.

The following chapters present detailed descriptions, as appropriate, of the business, economic, and regulatory environment and activities of organizations in the industry, the risks they typically face, unique accounting principles that have implications for auditing, typical transactions and key controls that are unique to the industry, and suggested auditing procedures. The relative emphasis given to each of those topics and the organization of the chapters vary by industry and were dictated by the nature of the industry and the environment in which it operates. The intent is to describe only the characteristics and auditing considerations that are unique to each industry. Accordingly, when reading any of the chapters in Part 5, the reader also should review the discussion of auditing standards and procedures in the first 32 chapters of the book; material from those chapters that is applicable to audits of specialized industries generally is not repeated in Part 5.

33

Auditing Banks and Savings Institutions

33.1 OVERVIEW OF THE INDUSTRY

Banks are primarily in the business of money brokerage. By accepting deposits and extending credit, banks act as conduits between those with funds to invest and borrowers. Bank loans and investment securities are earning assets, and the interest income they generate is the principal source of revenue for the banking industry.

Several different types of institutions within the banking industry[1] perform financial intermediary and service functions. Some of the typical activities of those institutions are listed below.

Type of Institution	*Typical Activities*
Commercial banks	Accept deposits, make loans, facilitate payments and collections, invest in securities, perform trust services, and provide financial services, such as discount brokerage and advisory services
Thrift institutions (savings and loan associations and savings banks)	Accept deposits, make mortgage and consumer loans, invest in securities, and provide other financial services
Trust companies	Manage funds and other assets, the beneficial interest in which remains with the owner and not the bank

While the differences among the activities of financial institutions were at one time fairly well pronounced, legislation and aggressive business development in recent years have blurred the traditional distinctions. As a result, the differences between banking institutions and others in the financial services industry, such as insurance companies and securities brokerage firms, are disappearing rapidly.

A bank may accept deposits in the form of demand deposits, which bear no or low interest, and time deposits, which ordinarily bear a higher rate of interest. Time deposits consist of savings accounts, certificates of deposit, negotiable orders of withdrawal (NOW) accounts, club accounts, and commercial and public fund time deposits. Bank earnings are generated principally by making loans to businesses and individuals and investing in U.S. government and municipal securities. Many banks also act in a fiduciary capacity by providing trust, investment management, and safekeeping services. Other income-producing activities include servicing mortgage loans for other entities; providing credit cards, safe deposit boxes, cashier checks, money orders, foreign currency exchange, travelers' checks, and savings bonds; and providing consulting services related to cash management, balance sheet financing, and personal equity management.

Commercial banks in the United States are either federal or state chartered. Federal-chartered banks must include "national" or "N.A." (national association) in

---

[1] As used in this chapter, the banking industry includes entities regulated by the various federal banking agencies—the Federal Deposit Insurance Corporation, the Board of Governors of the Federal Reserve System, the Office of the Comptroller of the Currency, and the Office of Thrift Supervision. This chapter does not discuss credit unions; credit unions are discussed in the AICPA audit and accounting guide, *Audits of Credit Unions.*

their name, are supervised by the Office of the Comptroller of the Currency, and are required to be members of the Federal Reserve System (FRS) and to have their deposits insured by the Federal Deposit Insurance Corporation (FDIC). State-chartered banks are supervised by the banking authorities of the chartering state, are required to obtain FDIC insurance coverage, and may elect to join the FRS. Commercial banks may be organized as unit banks, branch banks, or bank holding companies, depending on the laws of the state in which they operate. They also may engage in foreign operations using a foreign department, foreign offshore branches, an Edge Act Corporation, or a foreign subsidiary or affiliate.

A bank may hold assets that have been entrusted to it and for which it acts as agent or fiduciary for the customer. While the bank may have physical possession of the assets, they are not carried on its general ledger. Those assets, which are known as nonbank assets, may include a variety of items, such as marketable securities, real property, and other personal property. In some banks, the value of nonbank assets often approximates or exceeds the total assets shown in the bank's financial statements.

33.2 BANK REGULATION

Bank regulation is based on the philosophy that it is essential to the national interest that the banking system be sound, so as to merit complete and continued public confidence. As a result, banks are subject to strict governmental regulation and supervision.

(a) Bank Regulatory Agencies

There are four primary bank regulators, each with distinct but sometimes overlapping jurisdiction:

- *The Office of the Comptroller of the Currency.* The Comptroller of the Currency is the appointed official in the U.S. Treasury Department responsible for the chartering and supervision of national banks. (The *Office of Thrift Supervision* of the Treasury Department is the primary regulator for savings institutions.)

- *The Federal Reserve Board.* The Federal Reserve System (FRS) is the centralized banking system of the United States. It is guided by the Federal Reserve Board, which includes among its functions the examination and supervision of member banks.

- *The Federal Deposit Insurance Corporation.* The Federal Deposit Insurance Corporation examines state banks that are not members of the FRS. Sometimes these examinations are conducted simultaneously with those of state banking departments. The FDIC is the secondary regulator for federally insured institutions and oversees the Savings Association Insurance Fund (SAIF) in addition to the Bank Insurance Fund (BIF).

- *State Banking Authorities.* State banking authorities are responsible for and examine state banks that they have chartered. If a state bank is a member of the FRS, the examination is sometimes a joint state and federal examination. If a state bank is not a member of the FRS, the examination may be a joint state and FDIC examination.

The Securities and Exchange Commission (SEC) exerts significant influence over the financial reporting practices of publicly held bank holding companies. Historically, the SEC has deferred to the bank regulators on matters of disclosure by banks. Securities issued or guaranteed by a bank (as contrasted with a bank holding company) have been exempt from the registration provisions of the Securities Act of 1933 (the 1933 Act) since its adoption. In addition, few publicly held banks have been subject to the usual registration and reporting provisions of the Securities Exchange Act of 1934 (the 1934 Act) because they are subject to other regulatory agencies. Generally, the bank regulators must conform their regulations with those of the SEC, and thus there is a relatively high degree of consistency in reporting. Bank holding companies, however, do not come under the narrow exemption from the securities laws that was granted to banks. The SEC reviews registration statements filed by bank holding companies that offer securities pursuant to the 1933 Act and administers the registration, reporting, and insider trading provisions of the 1934 Act for bank holding companies with 500 or more shareholders and over $1 million in assets.

All of the authorities mentioned, except the SEC, are required to examine the banks under their regulation. There are significant differences between the scope of their examinations and the scope of an independent audit. The reports of those examiners are reviewed with the bank's board of directors. Independent auditors should request to attend those meetings and, at a minimum, obtain and review the reports, since the findings represent an important additional source of information for use in planning and performing a bank audit.

Banks are required by the various regulatory authorities to maintain certain standards of capital adequacy. Items included in capital for purposes of generally accepted accounting principles (GAAP) and for regulatory purposes differ. The primary difference is that goodwill is ineligible to satisfy regulatory capital requirements. In addition, the components of the several "tiers" of capital are specified in the regulations of various agencies.

The form and content of bank and bank holding company financial statements are based on GAAP, which, in turn, are influenced by the reporting requirements of the various applicable regulatory authorities and the SEC. Thus, the auditor of a bank should be familiar with the rules and regulations of the Comptroller of the Currency (for national banks) and of the FDIC (for state banks that are not members of the FRS), the regulations of the Board of Governors of the FRS (for state member banks), and the instructions to the annual report forms of the Board of Governors of the FRS applicable to bank holding companies. In addition, the regulations of the appropriate state banking authorities and of SEC Regulation S-X (particularly Article 9) and Guide 3 should be consulted.

(b) FIRREA

The Financial Institutions Reform, Recovery, and Enforcement Act (FIRREA) of 1989 changed the way in which the savings and loan sector is regulated. In addition to increasing regulators' enforcement powers, FIRREA expanded the population of those held accountable for regulatory violations to include institution-affiliated parties.

Institution-affiliated parties are defined to include accountants who are not otherwise participants in the affairs of a financial institution and who "knowingly or with reckless disregard participate in (a) any violation of any law or regulations; (b) any breach of fiduciary duty; or (c) any unsafe or unsound practice, which caused or is likely to cause more than a minimal financial loss to, or significant adverse effect on, the insured depository institution."

Regulations issued to implement FIRREA specify growth limitations, increased capital requirements, restrictions on permitted types of investments and loans, and the required divestiture of certain investments. Savings institutions may not invest in noninvestment-grade corporate debt securities and equity investments. In addition, for federal savings and loan associations, nonresidential real estate loans may not exceed 400 percent of capital.

(c) FDICIA

Many provisions of the Federal Deposit Insurance Corporation Improvement Act of 1991 (FDICIA) are amendments or additions to the Federal Deposit Insurance Act (FDIA). Major provisions affecting auditors of depository institutions are summarized below. Other provisions affect operational and consumer compliance aspects of depository institutions.

(i) Auditing Reforms. FDICIA added Section 36 to the FDIA to provide early identification of needed improvement in financial management at insured depository institutions. The implementing regulation of this provision applies to institutions with total assets of $500 million or more as of the beginning of the institution's fiscal year. The annual audit provision may be satisfied for consolidated subsidiaries by an independent audit of the holding company. Other provisions may be fulfilled by the holding company for subsidiaries having less than $5 billion in assets, or assets greater than $5 billion and a regulatory CAMELS (or comparable) rating of 1 or 2. (An institution's CAMELS rating relates to its capital adequacy, asset quality, management, earnings, liquidity, and sensitivity to various aspects of market risk.)

Management responsibilities under regulations implementing Section 36 include the following:

- *Annual reporting.* Each institution covered by the regulation must have an annual financial statement audit. Financial statements must be prepared in conformity with GAAP and any disclosure requirements regulators may establish. The financial statements must be accompanied by a written statement from management declaring its responsibility for financial statement preparation. Management also must report on its responsibility for and assessment of (a) the effectiveness of the institution's internal control over financial reporting and (b) the institution's compliance with laws and regulations relating to safety and soundness.
- *Communication with regulators.* Management must provide to federal and state regulators, within 15 days of receipt, a copy of any audit report, management letter, or other report from the institution's independent accountant. The institution also must notify regulators in writing of a change in auditors.
- *Communication with auditors.* Each institution must provide its independent ac-

countant with copies of the institution's most recent reports of condition and examination, any supervisory memorandum of understanding or written agreement with any federal or state regulatory agency, and a report of any action initiated or taken by federal or state banking regulators.

• *Audit committee.* Each institution must have an audit committee composed of outside directors independent of management. Audit committees of institutions with $3 billion or more in assets must include members with relevant banking or financial expertise, have access to their own outside counsel, and exclude large customers.

Provisions affecting independent accountants include the following:

• *Financial statement audits.* FDICIA requires that annual financial statement audits be performed in accordance with generally accepted auditing standards (GAAS).

• *Internal control attestation.* FDICIA also added Section 39 to the FDIA, which requires federal agencies to prescribe safety and soundness standards for the management and operation of insured depository institutions, including standards for internal control. Under Section 36, the independent accountant must examine and report on management's assertions about the institution's internal control over financial reporting, using the AICPA attestation standards. Management also is required to make a written assertion about compliance with laws and regulations governing loans to insiders and dividend restrictions, but that assertion need not be reported on by the independent accountant.

• *Other requirements.* Auditors must agree to provide related working papers, policies, and procedures to federal and state banking regulators on request. Auditors also must undergo a peer or quality review following guidelines acceptable to the FDIC and must notify regulators if services to the institution cease.

(ii) Accounting Reforms.   FDICIA added Section 37 to the FDIA to establish accounting objectives, standards, and requirements. Among other provisions, Section 37:

• Requires regulatory financial reporting to be uniform and consistent with GAAP, unless more stringent principles are considered necessary to reflect capital accurately, facilitate effective supervision, or permit prompt corrective action

• Instructs relevant regulatory agencies to develop both a method for supplemental disclosures of market values of assets and liabilities and regulations to ensure adequate reporting of off-balance-sheet transactions, including contingent assets and liabilities

• Promotes uniformity of capital and accounting standards among federal regulatory agencies

(iii) Prompt Corrective Action.   FDICIA added Section 38 to the FDIA, which focuses on changes in an institution's capital level. The regulation specifies five capital categories—well capitalized, adequately capitalized, undercapitalized, significantly undercapitalized, and critically undercapitalized. An institution is critically undercapitalized if its ratio of tangible equity to total assets is 2 percent or less, or if it otherwise fails to meet the critical capital level as defined. Institutions classified as undercapitalized or worse are subject to possible actions ranging from restriction or prohibition of certain activities to required submission of a capital plan for restoring an undercapitalized institution to an acceptable capital category. The plan must specify steps for becoming adequately capitalized, target capital levels for each year, how the institution intends to comply with other restrictions or requirements, and the types and levels of institution activities. Critically undercapitalized institutions are subject to regulatory seizure.

The regulation ties the five capital categories to three capital ratios—total risk-based capital, Tier I risk-based capital, and Tier I leverage capital—which are defined by the relevant regulatory agencies. Section 38 permits the agencies to reclassify an institution between certain capital categories if an institution's activities or condition is deemed to be unsafe or unsound. Noncompliance or expected noncompliance with the capital requirements may be a condition indicating substantial doubt about an entity's ability to continue as a going concern. Statement on Auditing Standards (SAS) No. 59, *The Auditor's Consideration of an Entity's Ability to Continue in Existence as a Going Concern* (AU Section 341), provides guidance in these circumstances.

(iv) Required Disclosures. The AICPA audit and accounting guide, *Banks and Savings Institutions*, requires institutions to disclose the following regulatory capital information in the notes to the financial statements:

- A description of regulatory capital requirements both (a) for capital adequacy purposes and (b) to meet the requirements established by the prompt corrective action provisions of Section 38 of the FDIA
- The material effects (actual or possible) of failure to comply with such requirements
- Whether the institution is in compliance with the regulatory capital requirements, including the following relating to quantitative measures:
  - Required and actual ratios and amounts of Tier I leverage capital, Tier I risk-based capital, and total risk-based capital, and (for savings institutions) tangible capital
  - Factors that may have a significant effect on capital adequacy, such as potentially volatile components of capital, qualitative factors, and regulatory requirements
- For each balance sheet date presented, the institution's prompt corrective action category as of its most recent notification
- As of the most recent balance sheet date, whether management believes the category has changed because of any events or conditions arising since notification
- As of the most recent balance sheet date presented, whether the institution either is not in compliance with the capital adequacy requirements or is considered less

than adequately capitalized under the prompt corrective action provisions, or both, and the possible material effects on financial statement amounts and disclosures

Examples of the above disclosures are presented in the audit and accounting guide.

(v) Auditing Impact.   Noncompliance with regulatory requirements, such as failure to meet minimum capital requirements or participation in impermissible activities or investments, exposes depository institutions to regulatory action and is an important consideration in the audits of troubled institutions, particularly in view of the prompt corrective action provisions of FDICIA. Events of noncompliance may be brought to the auditor's attention during the application of normal auditing procedures, during the review of regulatory examination reports, or as a result of regulatory actions. As noted earlier, actual or expected noncompliance with regulatory capital requirements is a condition, when considered with other factors, that could indicate substantial doubt about the entity's ability to continue as a going concern.

33.3   RISK FACTORS AND AUDIT REACTION

Several characteristics of the operations and business of banks are unique to the industry and require the auditor's consideration in assessing risks, determining the audit strategy, and performing auditing procedures. Some of the more important characteristics are:

- A bank's assets are highly negotiable and liquid. Thus, they are subject to greater risk of loss than are the assets of other businesses.
- Banks are subject to substantial regulatory reporting requirements that sometimes go beyond GAAP. Information needed to satisfy these reporting requirements must be anticipated in planning the audit.
- Banks typically process a significant volume of transactions, which requires comprehensive internal control over financial reporting and compliance with laws and regulations.
- The complexity and pervasiveness of a bank's internal control often make it effective and efficient for the auditor to perform tests of controls, thereby reducing by a significant extent the amount of substantive testing. These tests of controls should be performed in conjunction with the auditor's assessment of the bank's risk management function.
- Determining the need for and coordinating the work of different specialists who may be involved in the audit may be a complicated task.

(a)   Risk Factors

Banks are exposed to a variety of inherent risks that are unique to the industry. Increasingly, there has been more of a focus on management of these risks. In 1996, the Office of the Comptroller of the Currency (OCC) issued guidelines based on the nine risk categories noted below. The auditor should consider all of these risks, as well as the bank's risk management policies, procedures, and controls.

Credit risk is the risk to earnings or capital arising from an obligor's failure to meet the terms of any contract with a bank or otherwise to perform as agreed. Credit risk is the most recognizable risk associated with banking. The OCC's definition encompasses more than the traditional definition associated with lending activities. Credit risk also arises in conjunction with a broad range of banking activities where success depends on counterparty, issuer, or borrower performance. It arises any time bank funds are extended, committed, invested, or otherwise exposed through actual or implied contractual agreements, whether on or off the balance sheet.

Interest rate risk is the risk to earnings or capital arising from movements in interest rates. Interest rate risk arises from differences between the timing of rate changes and the timing of cash flows (repricing risk); from changing rate relationships among different yield curves affecting bank activities (basis risk); from changing rate relationships across the spectrum of maturities (yield curve risk); and from interest-related options embedded in bank products (options risk).

Banks assume interest rate risk as a basic function of accepting deposits and making loans, and derive income for undertaking this risk. Steps taken to neutralize interest rate exposure normally reduce earnings potential. Market interest rate fluctuations may affect management's intent and ability to hold securities and loans until maturity and may expose a bank to the risk of reduced net interest margin. Since banks must make investments and loans for extended periods, an inability to match these rate-sensitive assets with similarly rate-sensitive liabilities can cause the net interest margin to diminish or disappear entirely.

Liquidity risk is the risk to earnings or capital arising from a bank's inability to meet its obligations when they come due, without incurring unacceptable losses. Liquidity risk refers to banks' need to have funds available at all times to repay fully all maturing liabilities on a timely basis. Banks and bank holding companies act as financial intermediaries to assume liquidity risk by borrowing for shorter periods than those for which they lend. Banks must manage unplanned changes in funding sources and have the ability to recognize and address changes in market conditions that may affect how quickly assets can be liquidated.

Price risk is the risk to earnings or capital arising from changes in the value of portfolios of financial instruments. Price risk often is used interchangeably with market risk because price risk focuses on changes in market factors that affect the value of traded instruments.

Foreign exchange risk is the risk to earnings or capital arising from the movement of foreign exchange rates. Foreign exchange risk is known also as translation risk. These risks can arise in loans, deposits, and investments denominated in a foreign currency.

Transaction risk is the risk to earnings or capital arising from problems with service or product delivery. It also is referred to as operating risk and is a function of the institution's internal control, information systems, employee integrity, and operating processes.

Compliance risk is the risk to earnings or capital arising from violations of, or nonconformance with, laws, rules, regulations, prescribed practices, or ethical standards. Compliance risk exposes the institution to fines, civil money penalties, payment of damages, and voiding of contracts.

Strategic risk is the risk to earnings or capital arising from adverse business decisions or improper implementation of business decisions. This risk is a function of the compatibility of an entity's strategic goals, the strategies developed and resources to achieve those goals, and the quality of implementation.

Reputation risk is the risk to earnings or capital arising from negative public opinion. This affects the ability to establish new relationships or services or continue servicing existing relationships. This risk can expose the institution to litigation, financial loss, or damage to its reputation.

Banks may use derivatives (futures; forward, swap, and option contracts; and other similar financial contracts) for various purposes. One is as a financial management tool to alter various risks. Another is to make a market or trade in derivatives to earn income. Derivatives may mitigate or control risk exposures or may increase them. The complex nature of many of these contracts may make it difficult to distinguish between those that mitigate and those that increase those risks.

(b)   Interest Rate Sensitivity, Liquidity Management, and Capital Adequacy

Banks, in common with other financial institutions, are actively involved on a daily basis in various unrelated transactions affecting their asset and liability portfolios. Because of variations in both amounts and timing, these transactions cannot be matched perfectly in terms of interest sensitivities and maturities. Thus, the bank is left with an imbalance in its asset and liability positions that makes it sensitive to changes in interest rates.

Management attempts to control the spread, or gap, between asset and liability positions of different maturities in order to reduce interest rate risks to acceptable levels. The net interest rate sensitivity gap illustrated in Figure 33.1 indicates that, because of the projected imbalance, an increase in short-term interest rates could result in higher interest costs and a decrease in net interest income.

A concept closely related to interest rate sensitivity is liquidity management. Liquidity describes a bank's ability to meet financial obligations that arise during the normal course of business and is measured based on loan maturity. Figure 33.1 also indicates the bank's liquidity at each interval. If all liabilities due in one month or less were not refinanced, the bank would have to liquidate longer-term assets to cover the amount by which those liabilities exceeded assets convertible into cash in the same period.

In addition, as mentioned earlier, banks must maintain certain levels of capital as specified by regulatory authorities. The auditor should focus on the minimum ac-

Figure 33.1   Illustrative Interest Rate Sensitivity

	Projected Maturities (in millions)				
	1 Month or Less	*3 Months or Less*	*6 Months or less*	*1 Year or Less*	*More than 1 Year*
Interest-earning assets	$1,000	$1,400	$1,600	$1,700	$8,800
Interest-bearing liabilities	1,300	1,600	2,200	2,400	$7,000
Gap	($ 300)	($ 200)	($ 600)	($ 700)	$1,800

ceptable regulatory ratio of capital to risk-based assets and should determine whether those capital requirements are being met. From a regulatory standpoint, a bank's capital position could affect its ability to enter into mergers and acquisitions, since acquisitions can result in a dilution of capital.

(c) Planning Considerations

Unlike most other businesses, banks traditionally close their books daily and release their earnings results soon after year-end. Therefore, it is often important that the audit be completed quickly. Providing the necessary data on a timely basis requires extensive planning and coordination, which can be accomplished by establishing timetables that indicate when various phases of the year-end closing are to be completed. Sometimes a detailed checklist organized by department or activity is used as the control mechanism for the year-end audit. Such checklists identify the data that the auditor requires, the bank personnel responsible for preparing or providing it, when it is to be available, and the audit personnel responsible for that phase of the audit. The dates requested are based on the bank's clearance schedule and the related estimated audit time. These schedules must be monitored closely to identify problem areas on a timely basis and to ensure that all deadlines are met.

The audit program for a bank often provides for substantive tests to be performed throughout the year, with an update at year-end. This "continuous audit" approach has several benefits, including:

- Identification and resolution of issues prior to year-end
- The ability to review prior to year-end any regulatory and control matters identified by regulatory examiners at the time of their examination
- The opportunity to broaden audit personnel's understanding of the industry because one person may become involved in several areas of the bank
- Less disruption of the bank's operations because some of the work of the external auditor can be coordinated with that of the internal audit department throughout the year
- The ability to monitor the resolution of prior-year control deficiencies

The existence of an internal audit function is probably more prevalent in banking than in most other industries. If an internal audit function is objective, competent, and well supervised, the independent auditor's procedures often include assessment of the internal audit function for purposes of using the work of the internal auditors. Determining the way in which and the extent to which the internal audit function is to be utilized is part of developing the audit strategy. The internal auditors should participate in that process to ensure that everyone involved has a clear understanding of the work to be performed and its timing.

In addition, banks often have a separate credit review function that reviews loan quality, loan documentation, and credit administration controls. The auditor should ascertain to whom the credit review department reports and its annual scope. If the credit review function is independent of the chief lending officers and other loan department personnel, the auditor may be able to use the work performed by the credit reviewers, in much the same way as the work of the internal audit department is used.

Finally, a bank's trust department may be a *service organization*, as that term is used in SAS No. 70, *Reports on the Processing of Transactions by Service Organizations* (AU Section

324). The bank may be asked by an entity whose assets are held by the trust department or whose transactions are processed by the trust department to provide a report by the bank's auditor on the trust department's internal control. The auditor should ascertain the nature of the report on internal control that the bank has been asked to provide and plan the engagement to obtain sufficient evidence to issue the appropriate opinion. SAS No. 70 provides performance and reporting guidance in this area.

(d) Analytical Procedures

Banks generate considerable analytical information for regulators and others that may be useful to the auditor in the planning stage. The auditor should become familiar with the types of analytical information contained in management's monthly financial reports to the board of directors, regulators, and others, as this information often proves to be a valuable audit tool for identifying trends and unusual events. In addition, banks often capture historical data throughout the year so that they can prepare a statement of condition on the basis of average daily balances. Such statements are issued as supplementary information to the year-end balance sheet. Wherever possible, the auditor should use average daily figures to develop ratios that may be useful for performing analytical procedures. In addition, there are commercial services that provide specific data that is useful in comparing an entity's operations with those of its local and national peer groups within the industry. Figure 33.2 presents some significant ratios used in the banking industry.

(e) Materiality

Assessing materiality in the banking industry has several unique aspects. Two income statement line items, net interest income and net income, and the accounts included in the capital adequacy computations are focal points in assessing materiality. The illustrative financial statements of a bank contained in the AICPA audit guide, *Banks and Savings Institutions*, and the federal bank regulatory authorities' capital adequacy requirements indicate the accounts that are included in those items.

33.4 TYPICAL TRANSACTIONS, CONTROLS, AND AUDIT TESTS

(a) Operations

(i) Deposits.   One of the primary objectives of a bank is to obtain deposits, which it in turn lends to customers and invests in other earning assets. The deposit function, while not in itself revenue-producing (except for fees for various services), is important since it provides the funds for producing revenue through the lending and investment cycles.

Generally, demand deposit operations are automated, and tellers handle a large variety of micro-encoded (MICR) documents. Daily transactions involving demand deposits, savings deposits and withdrawals, installment loan payments, mortgage loan payments, teller cash tickets, and official checks, as well as departmental debits and credits, flow together from the tellers in individual branches into a central proof department.

Savings department operations parallel those of demand deposits; they include procedures for opening accounts and posting deposit and withdrawal transactions.

Figure 33.2   Selected Ratios Used in the Banking Industry

Ratio	Significance
Securities divided by total assets	Indication of earning asset mix
Securities by type divided by total securities	Measure of investment portfolio mix
Net loans divided by total assets	Indication of earning asset mix
Net loans divided by total deposits	Indication of funding sources for loan base
Loans by type divided by total loans	Measure of loan portfolio mix and indication of lending strategy and risk
Loan delinquencies divided by respective type of loan outstanding	Measure of past-due loan risk
Loan loss valuation reserve divided by total loans net of unearned discount	Measure of loan portfolio risk coverage
Loan loss recoveries divided by previous year's charge-offs	Measure of charge-off policy and recovery experience
Nonperforming loans to total loans	Measure of impact of nonperforming loans on net income
Reduction in interest income on nonperforming loans, net of tax effect, to net income	Measure of impact of nonperforming loans on net income
Investment income divided by average total securities	Measure of investment portfolio yield
Loan income divided by average net loans	Measure of loan portfolio yield
Total interest paid divided by average total deposits	Measure of cost of funds
Net income divided by average total assets	Measure of return on assets
Net income divided by average capital	Measure of return on equity
Primary capital to assets	Measure of capital adequacy
Noninterest expense divided by net operating revenues (or net margin)	Measure of operating efficiency
Net interest income divided by average earning assets	Measure of return on earning assets

Savings operations comprise interest computations, payments, and maintaining records for certificate-type time accounts.

For both types of deposit transactions, the teller is responsible for verifying the account number and name, the account balance, and the validity of the customer's signature on the transaction ticket. Many computerized systems allow the teller to make immediate inquiry of a customer's account and recent activity. That capability facilitates the determination of the validity of customer transactions.

Auditing procedures in the area of deposits are not significantly different from procedures performed on comparable transactions and accounts in other industries. Because of the automated nature of bank accounting systems, most tests of deposit operations are directed toward controls over the completeness and accuracy of data input and updates to master files. Controls related to authorization, other than teller verification, generally operate on an after-the-fact basis, with the bank relying on third parties to corroborate that transactions in deposit accounts are authorized. The authorization controls that typically are tested are those relating to changes to master files, such as interest rates paid, service charge levels, and new types of accounts. In addition, specific emphasis should be placed on dormant-account activity, because of the higher risk of fraud involving these accounts.

Substantive tests should include review and tests of the institution's reconciliations of detail ledgers to general ledger balances, confirmation of significant "due to" (interbank clearing) accounts, and analytical tests of period-end interest accruals and of interest yields on deposit accounts. If control risk has been assessed at other than low, the auditor may consider confirming deposit balances. Guidance on the confirmation process is found in SAS No. 67, *The Confirmation Process* (AU Section 330).

(ii) Electronic Funds Transfer Systems. An electronic funds transfer system (EFTS) is a computer-based network designed to transfer funds electronically. EFTS was developed primarily in an effort to reduce check processing costs in view of the increased volume of transactions. The most commonly used adaptations of EFTS are direct deposit systems, automated clearinghouse systems, and automated teller machines.

A direct deposit system involves the direct deposit of payments into the recipient's account without the use of a check. The process begins when the recipient submits a standing authorization form to the paying organization. Subsequently, when a payment is due, the payer submits to its bank a magnetic tape containing transaction information, and the tape is processed through the bank's system. Transactions to be credited to an account at the payer's bank are extracted and held in a temporary file until the transaction date. Other transactions are captured on a master tape, which is sent to an automated clearinghouse (ACH), where the items are transmitted to the appropriate financial institution to be cleared.

A direct deposit system also may include preauthorized payment. In a preauthorized payment system, recurring payments are made directly by the payer's bank to the recipient's bank without the payer writing a check. The process begins when the payer provides the recipient with written authorization to debit an account at a particular bank. When a payment is due, the recipient produces a form containing the payer's account number and amount, and the recipient deposits these check facsimiles in the bank, which then processes the check facsimiles through the proof department and credits the recipient's account.

An automated clearinghouse is a centralized computer operation that receives, sends, and controls specific EFT messages between member banks and other ACHs. In a non-ACH system, a large part of the transfer of funds also is done electronically, but only after the checks or other paper documents have been micro-encoded, sorted, and read to a computer file. In an ACH system, the check is eliminated, and the payment is cleared through the ACH automatically. Inputs to and outputs from the ACH are in electronic form.

Automated teller machines (ATMs) are remote banking terminals that allow customers to make deposits, withdrawals, or transfers between accounts and to inquire as to current balances. Most ATMs process transactions by maintaining a separate file that records customers' available account balances as well as a running total of transactions processed during a given day (in order to avoid customer overdrafts or withdrawals over the bank's set limit). Each night, the ATM file is processed against the deposit applications to update the customers' account balances.

Controls in an EFTS consist of system software, such as that related to access, asset protection, and documentation, in addition to the controls that would be performed in a teller-based operation. As suggested earlier, frequently those computer controls are tested by the auditor.

(b)   Loans

The organization of the lending function depends on the size of the bank and the complexity of its lending activities. A separate department usually handles each of the numerous types of loans.

(i)   Types of Loans.   Loans are categorized by type of borrower, purpose, maturity, and risk. Categorization is necessary for accounting control, reporting to various supervisory authorities, and management information. Generally, loans are categorized as commercial, real estate, or consumer finance.

Commercial loans include:

- Demand loans, which have no fixed maturity and are payable on demand. Interest, earned daily, is billed to the borrower periodically, usually monthly. These are the most liquid loans in a bank's portfolio.

- Time loans, which usually are made for a 30- to 120-day period. Interest may be payable at maturity, billed monthly, or discounted from the proceeds of the loan.

- Term loans, which are obligations with maturities usually ranging from one to ten years. These loans provide intermediate or long-term financing.

- Factoring, which occurs when a lender purchases accounts receivable at a discount. The bank may purchase the receivables with or without recourse to the borrower.

- Assigned accounts receivable financing, which is the pledging of accounts receivable to the bank as collateral for a loan. The bank usually lends from 60 to 90 percent of the face amount of the receivables, depending on their quality.

- Lease financing, in which personal property is purchased by the bank and leased to a customer on a net-lease, full-payout basis.

Real estate loans include:

- Residential mortgage loans, which consist of conventional, Federal Housing Administration insured, and Veterans Administration partially guaranteed loans. These loans are collateralized by mortgage liens on real property.

- Commercial and construction mortgage loans, which generally carry terms of one to three years, are collateralized by liens on real property, and are used to finance real estate development projects such as the construction of single-family dwellings, apartments, industrial complexes, commercial buildings, and land development.

Consumer finance loans include:

- Installment loans, which frequently are discounted and generally are made to customers to finance the purchase of consumer goods and services.
- Home equity loans and lines of credit, which generally are collateralized by second mortgages on residential real estate.
- Credit card loans, which are utilized to consolidate a consumer's charge purchases from participating merchants into a single revolving charge account.
- Cash advance loans, which are lines of credit established by consumers and are drawn on by writing a special check or by drawing a check on a checking account in excess of the funds on deposit.

(ii) Loan Confirmations.   SAS No. 67, *The Confirmation Process* (AU Section 330), provides guidance about the confirmation process. It establishes a presumption that the auditor will request the confirmation of a bank's loans unless the following conditions are met:

- The use of confirmations would be ineffective
- The auditor's assessed level of control risk is low and the assessed level, in conjunction with any identified inherent risks and the evidence expected to be provided by analytical procedures or other substantive tests of details, is sufficient to reduce audit risk to an acceptably low level for the applicable financial statement assertions

(iii) Loan Policy and Enforcement.   In formulating policy, decisions should be made as to what percentage of deposits and capital should be invested in loans, what types of loans should be made, and the probable character, likely diversification, and anticipated volume of commercial, real estate, and consumer finance loans. Limits for each line of business should be established. Directors and management should decide whether the bank will grant formal lines of credit and should determine the requirements for annual or seasonal liquidations of debt, interest rates, and compensating balance requirements. The loan policy should prevent an overinvestment in loans and should result in an acceptable ratio of loans to deposits. If this ratio becomes too high, regulatory authorities may require an increase in the bank's capital. Once the loan policy has been formulated, it should be enforced. The effect on bank operations should be reviewed periodically, and the policy should be updated when necessary.

Generally, loans are approved by the board of directors or its designated committee. Large loans are approved directly by a formal resolution in the minutes of the board or committee. Many banks have a committee that reviews all loans over a stipulated amount on a frequent basis. In banks that do not have a separate credit review function, the internal audit department usually reviews loan documentation and quality. The auditor normally performs tests of controls in the areas of credit granting, loan approval, and documentation; typically those tests include reviewing the minutes of the loan committee (to ensure that approvals are appropriately documented) and examining credit files for compliance with bank policy.

(iv) Income Recognition.   Interest and fees charged by a commercial bank on its loan portfolios are generally its principal source of income. The major types of fees and costs are shown below. Statement of Financial Accounting Standards (SFAS) No. 91 (Accounting Standards Section L20) requires that *nonrefundable* fees and costs be deferred as an adjustment of loan yield using the interest method. As indicated below, most such fees and certain direct origination costs (or initial direct costs of leases) should be deferred and amortized over the life of the loan (or lease) as a yield adjustment.

Description	*Required Accounting*
Loan origination fees	Deferred as an adjustment of loan yield, generally using the interest method
Commitment fees	Deferred as an adjustment of loan yield, generally using the interest method for commitments that are integral to the lending process; recognized during the commitment period for commitments that are considered a separate service
Syndication fees	Cash basis unless a portion of the loan is retained by the manager and the yield is lower than other participants' yield
Direct loan origination costs (internal and external)	Deferred as an adjustment of loan yield, generally using the interest method

Other fees for services should be taken into income when the service has been performed. Such fees may include debt placement fees that are similar to underwriting fees of investment bankers and do not represent adjustments to interest rates.

The audit objectives for the various service fees charged by banks relate to the timing and amount of revenue recognition. Generally, the auditor performs tests directed at the proper recording of amortization. These tests may include tests of controls and analytical tests of the account balances.

(v) Loan Reviews.   The impact of loan collectibility on a bank's financial position has compelled banks to use an ongoing form of credit evaluation. Many banks have a loan evaluation function that reports directly to, or indirectly through, the internal audit function, which in turn reports to the examining/audit committee of the board. In addition, bank regulators, as part of their examination procedures, designate individual loans as either classified or nonclassified; classified loans, which warrant monitoring and a specific allowance, are further labeled as either loss, doubtful, substandard, or special mention.

Evaluating loans and determining the adequacy of the allowance for loan losses is a complex process. It requires the ability to evaluate relative risk in the lending area based on types and volumes of lending activity. The auditor who reviews loans must be aware of the internal system for grading loan quality, including the procedures used to identify and monitor past-due and nonperforming loans, and quantifying potential losses. Nonperforming loans, also referred to as nonaccrual loans, are loans on which interest payments are delinquent or collection of the principal has become doubtful and for which the bank has accordingly ceased accruing interest income. Federal supervisory agencies and the SEC have established regulatory reporting guidelines for nonaccrual loans. The bank's policies for classifying loans as nonaccrual and for charging loans off, either partially or in full, are critical considerations in the auditor's loan review. In addition, the auditor should be familiar with the regulator's classification of loans as included in its report on the bank (discussed earlier).

The existence of internal loan review and the structure, size, and complexity of the bank should be considered in determining the extent of the auditor's loan review. The ultimate quality of the loan review depends on the exercise of business judgment.

Some of the more significant factors affecting the evaluation of individual loans and the overall loan portfolio are:

- Types and volumes of lending activity
- Dynamic nature of lending markets
- Economic and other risk factors within the particular entity and industry
- Management's lending policies
- Competence of lending officers
- Controls over monitoring the loan portfolio and reporting on its status
- Internal loan review and credit administration functions
- Industry and portfolio concentrations
- Past collection records
- Policy on nonaccrual of interest
- Policy on charging off loans
- Policy on providing for loan losses

Loan collectibility often depends on the worth of the collateral, particularly when loans are in default. Consequently, the auditor may need to review the value of collateral on a liquidation basis rather than on a going concern basis. Not all secured loans are completely collateralized. Also, although collateral is pledged, its value may not be sufficient to cover the entire loan principal. The loan portion not secured is the same as an unsecured loan and is subject to the same collection risks. Therefore, loan grading is usually subjected to tests of controls directed at completeness and accuracy, and the adequacy of the current-year provision as well as the allowance for loan losses should be substantively tested through individual loan review and overall portfolio analysis.

SFAS No. 114, *Accounting by Creditors for Impairment of a Loan* (Accounting Standards Section I08) applies to loans that are individually and specifically evaluated for impairment, whether collateralized or not, except loans accounted for at fair value or at the lower of cost or fair value. SFAS No. 114 states that "a loan is impaired when, based on current information and events, it is probable that a creditor will be unable to collect all amounts due according to the contractual terms of the loan agreement" (para. 8). It requires impaired loans to be measured at the present value of expected future cash flows by discounting such cash flows using the loan's effective interest rate. Loans probable of foreclosure should be measured at the collateral's fair value. SFAS No. 114 amends SFAS No. 5, *Accounting for Contingencies*, to require a creditor to evaluate the collectibility of contractual interest and principal payments. In addition, SFAS No. 114 amends SFAS No. 15, *Accounting by Debtors and Creditors for Troubled Debt Restructurings*, to require a creditor to account for a troubled debt restructuring involving a modification of terms by discounting the loan's cash flows at the loan's original effective interest rate. SFAS No. 114 also amends SFAS No. 15 to eliminate insubstance foreclosure accounting for loans (that is, accounting for such loans as other real estate owned) unless the creditor receives physical possession of the debtor's assets.

(c) Investments

Normally, the funds management department of a bank is governed by a funds management committee or an assets and liabilities management committee. The committee usually consists of senior executive officers such as the president, executive vice president(s), and heads of related departments, for example, loans, investments, and deposits. Their responsibility is to plan and periodically evaluate portfolio decisions on loans, investments, deposits, and other sources of funds. Traditionally, banks have not been allowed to invest in equity securities; investment has been limited to debt instruments.

(i) Control Objectives and Auditing Procedures. The following major control objectives should be considered in assessing internal control relative to investments in securities:

- Purchases and sales of securities should be initiated only on the basis of appropriate authorization to ensure compliance with bank policies and with legal, regulatory, and liquidity requirements.

- All authorized security transactions should be recorded accurately and on a timely basis.

- Adequate asset protection controls should be maintained for securities located in the bank and in the possession of correspondents or other independent custodians.

- All income earned on securities should be recorded accurately and collected on a timely basis.

Auditing procedures for securities include both tests of controls and substantive tests; they do not differ significantly from the procedures applied to investments of entities in other industries.

In recessionary periods, depository institutions typically revise their investment strategies to earn higher yields, including the purchase of complex financial instruments. Certain rules and regulations may affect classification and valuation of institutions' investments. Auditors should be aware of these rules and regulations and of the risks involved in complex securities, and should assess management's expertise in monitoring, evaluating, and accounting for the securities; consider whether the institution has established appropriate controls over investments in high-risk securities and whether there is adequate oversight by the board of directors; and involve specialists, when necessary, in valuing and auditing these investments.

(ii) Available-for-Sale and Held-to-Maturity Securities. SFAS No. 115, *Accounting for Certain Investments in Debt and Equity Securities* (Accounting Standards Section 180), addresses the accounting and reporting for investments in equity securities that have readily determinable fair values and for all investments in debt securities. Those investments are required to be classified in one of three categories: held-to-maturity, available-for-sale, and trading.

Available-for-sale and held-to-maturity securities generally represent a very significant asset and source of income for banks. The primary goals of the investment department are to maximize its contribution to the bank's overall profitability while maintaining liquidity and stability. Investment strategies should complement other facets of the overall operating strategy.

To meet both liquidity and income objectives, the investment portfolio should be managed so that maturity schedules are balanced. To do this, management must anticipate deposit trends and the credit needs of loan customers, without exposing the bank to significant security losses in times of rising interest rates. Orderly spacing of investment maturities permits reemployment of proceeds at more favorable yields in times of rising interest rates. Although the credit risks inherent in the investment portfolio may be minimal, because of the general character of commercial bank investments, the exposure to market declines resulting from market yield fluctuations is always present.

Normally, debt securities are purchased at a premium or discount. Amortization of premiums and accretion of discounts should be accounted for using the interest method, which results in a constant rate of return based on the adjusted book value of the security. Held-to-maturity securities are recorded at amortized cost. Available-for-sale securities are carried at fair value; changes in fair value of those securities result in unrealized holding gains and losses, which are recorded as a separate component of stockholders' equity. Commercial banks often are affected by fluctuating loan and deposit levels that necessitate selling available-for-sale securities for liquidity purposes before they mature, which results in an early realization of the unrealized gain or loss that was deferred in stockholders' equity.

(iii) Trading Securities. Banks frequently purchase and hold debt securities for resale in the near term; in engaging in this activity, banks essentially act as dealers in securities. All securities purchased solely for resale should be classified as trading securities. Management should document its intention at the date of acquisition. Trading securities should be carried at fair value, with increases or decreases in unrealized gains or losses included in the income statement.

When acting as a dealer, a bank may, either alone or in concert with other commercial banks in a syndicate, purchase an issue of municipal general obligation securities directly from the municipality at an agreed-on price arrived at through competitive bidding. The bank then sells the municipal securities to institutional investors or on the open market. The markup in price is compensation for distributing the securities and assuming the risk of a change in market value during distribution.

(iv) Transfers and Servicing of Financial Assets.   Banks often enter into securitization and securities borrowing and lending transactions, repurchase (repo) and reverse repurchase (reverse repo) agreements, and dollar repurchase agreements (dollar rolls). SFAS No. 125, *Accounting for Transfers and Servicing of Financial Assets and Extinguishment of Liabilities* (Accounting Standards Section F35), provides guidance for determining whether those transactions and agreements, which involve transfers of financial assets such as cash, loans, securities, and other financial instruments, should be accounted for as sales or as secured borrowings with pledges of collateral.

The auditor should consider the nature of a bank's significant financial asset transfers and, if necessary, should read and evaluate the applicable transfer agreements to determine whether the transfers represent sales or financing arrangements. The auditor also should consider using a specialist knowledgeable in the Uniform Commercial Code and applicable bankruptcy laws to assist in determining whether transfers represent sales or financing arrangements.

The auditor also should consider confirming receivable and payable balances related to securities borrowing and lending, repo, reverse repo, and dollar roll agreements, and should review the accounting for and sufficiency of collateral obtained pursuant to the terms of those transactions.

Banks that service financial assets should recognize a servicing asset or liability for the servicing contracts unless certain criteria are met. Servicing assets and liabilities that are purchased should be recorded at fair value, and all servicing assets and liabilities should be amortized in proportion to, and over the period of, estimated net servicing income (or loss). Servicing assets and liabilities also should be assessed for impairment or increased obligation based on their fair value. The auditor should review the assumptions used in the impairment assessment process, considering their reasonableness and evaluating the effect of changes in assumptions on the recoverability of assets or increases in the fair value of liabilities.

(d) Federal Funds

Federal funds are funds that banks deposit at the Federal Reserve to meet their reserve requirements. A bank can lend excess reserves if it has met its daily reserve requirement, or it can borrow funds to meet its reserve requirement, at the federal funds rate of interest. Federal funds transactions can be secured or unsecured. Unsecured transactions typically have a maturity of one day (the selling bank sells funds one day and is repaid with interest the next). In a secured transaction, the purchasing bank places government securities in custody for the selling bank until the funds are repaid. These transactions are an important tool for managing liquidity.

Federal funds transactions can be either investing or financing transactions, depending on the side of the transaction in which the bank participates. The bank records federal funds sold as an investment and federal funds borrowed as a liability. Auditing procedures that normally would be applied to investments and to borrowed funds are also applicable to federal funds loaned or borrowed.

(e) Real Estate Owned

Generally, foreclosed assets make up the largest component of real estate owned by banks. Foreclosed assets are assets that are received by a bank for full or partial payment of a loan. These assets could include personal property (automobiles) or real property (homes, commercial real estate). SFAS Nos. 15 and 121 and Statement of Position 92-3 address the accounting and reporting requirements for foreclosed assets.

The auditor's primary concern is the asset's valuation, that is, determining that the foreclosed assets are not reported at amounts in excess of their net realizable value. Relevant auditing procedures usually include reviewing independent appraisals, comparing the carrying value of the assets with appraisal amounts, and testing gains and losses on sales of foreclosed assets.

(f) Fiduciary and Other Activities

The primary concern in the audit of nonbank assets is the bank's contingent liability from not properly fulfilling its responsibilities as a fiduciary party or agent of the customer. As part of an audit of a bank, the auditor should determine whether adequate trust operating procedures and controls have been designed and placed in operation. Consideration should be given to physically counting assets held in trust or testing the internal audit department's counts to obtain satisfaction about their safeguarding. Testing in this area usually comprises a combination of tests of controls and substantive tests, with significant emphasis on testing the bank's reconciliations of trust accounts.

The auditor also should determine the extent to which a bank has engaged in other off-balance-sheet activities that create commitments or contingencies, including innovative transactions involving derivatives, securities, and loans (e.g., swaps of cash flows or assets), that could affect the financial statements, including disclosures in the notes. Inquiries of management relating to such activities should be formalized in the representation letter normally obtained at year-end.

34

Auditing Employee Benefit Plans

Employee benefit plans comprise pension plans and health and welfare plans. They operate by investing contributions of sponsors and employees in income-producing assets, which, together with the income thereon, are intended to be used to pay benefits to plan participants. Pension plans provide benefits to retired employees or their beneficiaries. Health and welfare plans provide benefits to current employees and their dependents, to retired employees and their dependents, or to both. Those benefits may include:

- Medical, dental, visual, psychiatric, or long-term health care
- Life insurance
- Accidental death or dismemberment benefits
- Unemployment, disability, vacation, or holiday benefits
- Apprenticeships, tuition assistance, dependent care, housing subsidies, or legal services

Employee benefit plans may be funded (e.g., the employer may establish a trust to hold assets that will be used to pay all or part of the covered benefits) or they may be unfunded (i.e., benefits are paid from the general assets of the employer). Most pension plans are funded, but health and welfare plans are often unfunded. Some employee benefit plans are insured plans, meaning that all or a portion of the benefits are provided through insurance contracts entered into by the employer. In recent years, employee benefit plans have taken on increased importance and also have become more complex as a result of changes in legislation, concern over the costs involved, and heightened awareness of the significance of such plans on the part of participants, particularly in situations where plans are underfunded (i.e., the plan's net assets available for benefits are less than the promised benefits).

An employee benefit plan is established and maintained pursuant to a plan instrument that specifies the plan's provisions. In a defined benefit plan, benefits are determined in advance by a fixed formula that usually is related to the employee's compensation, years of service, or both. Actuarial calculations are used to establish the amount of contributions required to meet those benefits. In a defined contribution plan, amounts are contributed to the individual account of each participant, and benefits are based solely on the accumulated contributions and income thereon. The plan must provide for the allocation of plan earnings and losses, and, in some plans, forfeitures, to participants' accounts. Employee benefit plans may be single employer plans (i.e., sponsored by one entity) or multiemployer plans, which are sponsored by several entities under, for example, a collective bargaining agreement. Many defined contribution plans are contributory; that is, the participants bear part of the cost. Most defined benefit pension plans are noncontributory.

34.1 FINANCIAL STATEMENTS AND ACCOUNTING METHODS

Before 1975, relatively little attention was given to preparing financial statements for employee benefit plans, and those statements rarely were examined by independent auditors. Passage by Congress of the Employee Retirement Income Security Act of 1974 (ERISA) created a new era in benefit plan accounting, financial reporting, and audits; it also expanded significantly the government's involvement in the design, operations, and reporting of benefit plans. ERISA requires those plans to file an annual report (Form 5500) with government agencies, including, with a few exceptions (noted later), financial statements and certain supplemental schedules. In addition, depending on the number of plan participants, an audit of the statements and schedules may be required to be performed by an independent certified public accountant.

Generally, health and welfare plans are subject to the reporting and disclosure requirements of ERISA, including filing annual reports on Form 5500. However, health and welfare plans that are unfunded, fully insured, or a combination of the two are not required to submit financial statements with the annual filings. If a separate trust has been established to hold assets for payment of covered benefits *and* the plan has more than 100 participants, audited financial statements generally are required to be included in the annual filing with ERISA.

The absence, at the time ERISA was enacted, of authoritative accounting pronouncements addressing benefit plan accounting and financial reporting requirements, coupled with auditors' limited experience with benefit plans and the minimal guidance initially provided by ERISA, created serious problems for auditors. The Financial Accounting Standards Board (FASB) and the AICPA have since issued standards, and the Department of Labor (DOL) has issued regulations, providing guidance on accounting and reporting matters, prescribing minimum disclosures, and reducing the confusion regarding audits of plans.

Statement of Financial Accounting Standards (SFAS) No. 35, *Accounting and Reporting by Defined Benefit Pension Plans*, as amended by SFAS No. 110, *Reporting by Defined Benefit Pension Plans of Investment Contracts* (Accounting Standards Section Pe5), is the authoritative pronouncement on accounting principles and financial reporting standards for defined benefit pension plans; it reduced the options previously available to such plans. SFAS No. 35 applies both to plans covered by ERISA and to those that are not. Accounting and reporting guidance for defined contribution pension plans is set forth in the AICPA audit and accounting guide, *Audits of Employee Benefit Plans*, described below. Guidance for health and welfare benefit plans is contained in Statement of Position (SOP) 92-6, *Accounting and Reporting by Health and Welfare Benefit Plans*. SOP 94-4, *Reporting of Investment Contracts Held by Health and Welfare Benefit Plans and Defined Contribution Pension Plans*, adds to the literature. Although the discussion of nonpension benefit plans in this chapter is principally in the context of plans providing health care benefits, it applies also to plans that provide other types of benefits, with appropriate modification of auditing procedures to fit the engagement circumstances.

The AICPA audit and accounting guide entitled *Audits of Employee Benefit Plans* (the audit guide) was issued originally in 1983 and revised most recently in 1997. The audit guide is updated periodically to reflect additional accounting and auditing requirements, clarify requirements, and incorporate new professional standards; it discusses both defined benefit and defined contribution pension and health and welfare plans. The auditor of an employee benefit plan should be familiar with the provisions of the audit guide, the accounting pronouncements discussed above, and relevant government regulations, as well as the instructions to the ERISA reporting forms.[1]

The audit guide notes that the primary objective of an employee benefit plan's financial statements—both pension and health and welfare, both defined benefit and defined contribution—is to provide financial information that is useful in assessing the plan's present and future ability to pay benefits when they come due. This objective recognizes that plan financial statements should address the needs of plan participants, because the plans exist primarily for their benefit. Those needs entail principally assessing the performance of plan administrators and other fiduciaries in managing plan assets. Accordingly, the plan rather than the trust holding the assets is the reporting entity.

To accomplish that objective, a pension plan's annual financial statements should include:

- A statement of net assets available for benefits as of the end of the plan year
- A statement of changes in net assets available for benefits for the year then ended
- For a defined benefit plan, information regarding the actuarial present value of accumulated plan benefits as of either the beginning or end of the plan year
- For a defined benefit plan, information regarding the effects, if significant, of certain factors on the year-to-year change in the actuarial present value of accumulated plan benefits

A health and welfare plan's financial statements should include:

- A statement of net assets available for benefits as of the end of the plan year
- A statement of changes in net assets available for benefits for the year then ended
- For a defined benefit plan, information regarding the plan's benefit obligations as of the end of the plan year, presented as a separate statement or included on another financial statement
- For a defined benefit plan, information regarding the effects, if significant, of certain factors on the year-to-year change in the plan's benefit obligations, presented as a separate statement or included on one of the other financial statements

Information concerning benefit obligations is not applicable to defined contribution pension or health and welfare plans because under this type of plan the plan's obligation is limited to the amounts that have accumulated in each participant's account.

Under both SFAS No. 35 and SOP 92-6, plan benefits or benefit obligations of defined benefit plans and the related activity are excluded and separately presented

---

[1] For a more in-depth study of employee benefit plans, see Richard M. Steinberg, Ronald J. Murray, and Harold Dankner, *Pensions and Other Employee Benefits: A Financial Reporting and ERISA Compliance Guide*, 4th ed. (New York: John Wiley & Sons, 1993).

from the statement of net assets available for plan benefits and the statement of changes in net assets available for plan benefits, respectively.

Information about benefit obligations of defined benefit health and welfare plans should include the following:

- Claims payable and currently due
- Premiums due under insurance arrangements
- Claims incurred but not reported to the plan
- Accumulated eligibility credits for active participants
- Postretirement benefits for participants and their beneficiaries and covered dependents

The statement of net assets available for benefits should be presented in enough detail to allow users to identify which of the plan's resources are available for benefits. Generally, all assets (except certain contracts with insurance companies) are presented at fair value. Similarly, the statement of changes in net assets available for benefits should contain sufficient detail to enable significant changes in net assets during the year to be identified. Paragraph 15 of SFAS No. 35 specifies the minimum disclosure requirements for information regarding changes in net assets available for benefits under pension plans. The requirements are the same for health and welfare plans, under SOP 92-6. SFAS No. 102, *Statement of Cash Flows—Exemption of Certain Enterprises and Classification of Cash Flows from Certain Securities Acquired for Resale* (Accounting Standards Section Pe5), provides an exemption from presenting a statement of cash flows for defined benefit pension plans and certain other employee benefit plans. This statement formalized what generally had been followed in practice prior to its issuance.

Accumulated plan benefits of participants of defined benefit pension plans are required to be shown at the present value of the future benefit payments attributable under the plan's provisions to employees' service rendered to the date of the actuarial valuation (discussed further in Section 3, Auditing Benefit Information). Disclosure of the actuarial present value of accumulated plan benefits (which can be made in the financial statements or accompanying notes) should be segmented into at least the following categories:

- Vested benefits of participants currently receiving payments
- Other vested benefits
- Nonvested benefits

Current employees' accumulated contributions to a defined benefit pension plan as of the benefit valuation date (including interest, if any) also should be disclosed.

The actuarial benefit calculations as of the end of the most recent plan year may not be completed at the time the financial statements are prepared; accordingly, often the actuarial present value of accumulated plan benefits is presented as of the beginning of the year. In these circumstances, a comparative statement of net assets available for benefits as of the beginning and end of the current year, comparative statements of changes in net assets available for benefits for the preceding and current plan years, and information regarding changes in the actuarial present value of accumulated plan benefits also should be presented.

Information regarding the effects of certain factors on the change in the actuarial present value of accumulated plan benefits for a defined benefit pension plan may be presented either in the notes or in financial statement format. Effects of plan amendments, changes in the nature of a plan (e.g., a merger with another plan), and changes in actuarial assumptions, if significant, should be disclosed; significant effects of other factors also may be identified. If a statement format is used and only the required information is disclosed, an additional "other" category will be needed to balance the statement. If a note format is used, the actuarial present value of accumulated plan benefits as of the preceding benefit information date also should be disclosed. Illustrative financial statements and note disclosures for a defined benefit pension plan are set forth as an appendix to SFAS No. 35.

Disclosures for a defined contribution pension plan, which are similar to those for a defined benefit plan, are contained in the audit guide. However, if a defined contribution plan provides for participant-directed investment programs (for example, equity, debt, or employer securities), amounts relating to each of the individual programs should be disclosed as separate funds. The funds should be shown either in the financial statements in columnar form (along with nonparticipant-directed program amounts), in the related disclosures, or in separate financial statements. AICPA Practice Bulletin 12, *Reporting Separate Investment Fund Option Information of Defined-Contribution Pension Plans*, has been incorporated into the audit guide to clarify this requirement and present illustrations.

Similar to the accounting for accumulated benefits of defined benefit pension plans, benefit obligations of defined benefit health and welfare plans should be shown at the actuarial present value of the future benefit payments attributable to employees' service rendered. However, information regarding the effects of certain factors on the change in the actuarial present value of accumulated plan benefits for a defined benefit health and welfare benefit plan must be presented on the face of the financial statements and not in the notes. The audit guide specifies the additional financial statement disclosures that should be made by both defined benefit and defined contribution health and welfare plans.

SFAS No. 35 and SOP 92-6 require the use of the accrual method for financial reporting purposes; this conforms to ERISA reporting requirements. The DOL permits financial statements in the annual report to be prepared on a basis of accounting other than generally accepted accounting principles (GAAP) if the differences are described in a note.

34.2   AUDITING PLAN ASSETS, LIABILITIES, REVENUES, AND EXPENSES

The audit strategy for an employee benefit plan varies depending on the nature and operation of the plan as well as the scope of services to be performed (discussed below). If the plan's auditor is also the auditor of the sponsoring entity, many of the auditing procedures discussed below will be performed as part of the audit of the sponsor's statements; those procedures need not be repeated in auditing the plan. Auditing employers' accounting for employee benefits is discussed in Chapter 20.

In planning the audit, the auditor should obtain sufficient information to identify inherent risks and assess control risk. The auditor's understanding of internal control may need to encompass controls that are maintained by others, including controls over transactions initiated by plan participants for which there is no written documentation. The audit guide provides guidance in this area as well as a discussion of the use of a service organization's auditor's report on the service organization's internal control. Statement on Auditing Standards (SAS) No. 70, *Reports on the Processing of Transactions by Service Organizations* (AU Section 324), provides guidance for situations where a service organization, such as a bank trustee, executes, for instance, investment transactions and maintains the related accountability on behalf of the plan. In addition, the auditor may need to examine evidence that is not part of the plan's records (e.g., employer payroll records and actuarial reports). In single employer plans, this ordinarily presents no problem, since the employer is usually also the plan administrator.

(a) Scope of Services

The auditor of a benefit plan may be engaged to perform an audit in accordance with generally accepted auditing standards (full-scope audit) or may be instructed by the plan administrator to limit the scope of the audit with respect to investment information prepared and certified as to both completeness and accuracy by a qualified trustee or custodian, which includes banks, insurance companies, or similar institutions. This exemption is permitted under DOL reporting and disclosure regulations if the institution is regulated and supervised and is subject to periodic examination by a state or federal agency. If the scope of the audit has been restricted in this way, the plan auditor should compare information covered by the certification of the institution with related information in the financial statements and supplemental schedules. Also, the auditor should be satisfied that amounts reported by the institution as received from or disbursed at the discretion of the plan administrator have been determined in accordance with the terms of the plan. The scope limitation and the corresponding limitation on the auditor's work extend only to investment information that has been certified by a qualified institution. Investment information that has not been certified (for example, loan receivables from participants) as well as noninvestment information (for example, contributions and benefit payments) should be subject to normal auditing procedures, as described below.

Whether the auditor is engaged to perform a full-scope or limited-scope audit, the results of the auditor's identification of inherent risks and assessment of control risk for relevant financial statement assertions will largely determine the nature, extent, and timing of the substantive tests to be performed. Accordingly, the auditing procedures presented in this chapter are meant to serve only as a guide for developing an audit program for a benefit plan and will need to be tailored to meet the particular circumstances of the engagement. This is particularly true for health and welfare plans, which may provide a wide variety of different benefits, as indicated earlier. Certain procedures (e.g., testing census data, reviewing the actuary's report, and testing the accumulated postretirement benefit obligation) may be performed as part of the audit of the employer, in which case they need not be repeated.

(b) Contributions

(i) Accounting Principles. Revenue reported in the plan's financial statements should include all contributions (by both the employer and employees) applicable to the year under audit. All amounts due to the plan as of the plan year-end are shown as contributions receivable, and include those pursuant to formal commitments as well as to legal or contractual requirements. Normally, employer contributions under defined benefit plans subject to ERISA should comply with the minimum funding standards established by ERISA. An allowance should be provided for estimated uncollectible amounts, if appropriate.

(ii) Controls. A single employer plan should have controls to determine that contributions meet the authorized or required amounts and are appropriately recorded on a timely basis. Controls include ensuring that the records contain documentation (formal commitments, plan instruments, and an actuary's report) supporting the basis of contributions reported as revenue or receivables of the plan. Employer payroll and other personnel records should be compared with employee contributions as reported by the plan or reflected on trustee statements.

Employer contributions to a multiemployer plan are made on a self-assessed basis and represent the majority of plan receipts. Contributions generally are determined by the number of hours or days worked or gross earnings of the participant at a standard contribution rate and are reported on standard preprinted forms. The plan should have a procedure for establishing initial accountability over the reporting forms immediately on receipt (e.g., by document number or dollar or other control total). The forms should be controlled throughout processing, from the time of receipt of contributions to final posting to the participant's eligibility records and employer's contribution records.

The plan's controls should be adequate to allow missing or delinquent employer reports and contributions and employer overpayments or underpayments to be identified for follow-up. Procedures may include audits of the employer's records on a systematic or exception basis, periodic requests that participants report any discrepancies in hours worked or contributions reported on their behalf by the employer, or a reconciliation of employee status reports furnished by a union to employer contribution reports.

Generally, contributions are mailed directly to a bank for credit to the plan's account or are received at the plan's office; in the latter event, receipts should be under numerical or other control. Numerical sequence should be reviewed and related deposit of the cash in the bank should be ascertained. Contributions received should be deposited intact on a timely basis and should not be used for payment of plan expenses.

A cumulative record of the employers' contributions should be maintained because the plan is required to report annually on contributions made by employers. The total contributions should be reconciled periodically to participants' records and the cash receipts records.

(iii) Audit Objectives and Procedures. The audit objectives for revenue and contributions receivable include determining whether amounts received during the year and due at year-end have been authorized and are accurate and complete, and whether any needed allowance for uncollectible receivables has been established. In auditing contributions, consideration should be given to evidence of employers' formal commitments as well as legal or contractual requirements. Specific auditing procedures relating to contributions receivable depend on whether the plan is a single employer or multiemployer plan. Auditing procedures for both types of plans include obtaining explanations for significant fluctuations in contributions for the year.

Suggested auditing procedures for single employer plans are shown in Figure 34.1. In most cases, audit efficiency is enhanced if the auditing procedures for contributions are coordinated and performed simultaneously with procedures applicable to employer records, referred to in the audit guide as participants' data and discussed in Section 3, Auditing Benefit Information. The audit objectives applicable to participants' data (which includes demographic, payroll, and benefit data) entail determining whether covered employees are properly included in the employee eligibility records or contribution reports and whether accurate data for eligible employees has been provided to the plan and, if applicable, the actuary. Accordingly, procedures to achieve these objectives also are suggested in Figure 34.1.

Unlike in defined benefit pension plans, in which contributions are based on actuarially determined amounts related to ERISA funding and tax deductibility rules, contributions to defined contribution pension and health and welfare benefit plans usually are not actuarially calculated. (Contributions related to certain health and welfare benefit plans, however, do involve actuarial calculations.) Accordingly, the auditor needs to determine the basis for contributions (which may involve payroll or census data) and perform appropriate auditing procedures. Some of the auditing procedures shown in Figure 34.1 may not be applicable to auditing contributions to health and welfare plans or may need to be tailored to the basis for the calculations, particularly procedures related to employer records and actuary's report.

Auditing contributions to multiemployer plans is more complex than for single employer plans; thus the auditor may need to apply additional procedures to obtain the required assurance about reported contributions. The auditor should determine whether the plan maintains adequate records of the contributions of the various employers and of the cumulative benefit credits of the individual plan participants.

Auditing a multiemployer plan often involves performing tests of the plan's controls relating to employers' contribution reports (which usually accompany periodic payments under the terms of the plan) for the purpose of reviewing the total hours worked and dollars earned (or other basis used for determining contributions) and allocating benefit credits to individual plan participants. The auditor should inquire about the methods used by the plan administrator to compensate for missing or incomplete participants' data.

Specific auditing procedures might include those shown in Figure 34.2. The auditor of a multiemployer plan should be aware of any risks arising from economic difficulties experienced by participating entities, since such circumstances could affect the collectibility of contributions receivable.

As with a single employer plan, some of the auditing procedures shown in Figure 34.2 may not be applicable to contributions of health and welfare plans or may need to be tailored to the basis for the calculations.

Figure 34.1   Suggested Auditing Procedures for Contributions Received and Receivable in Financial Statements of Single Employer Pension Plans

Contribution Records

Trace contributions recorded in the plan's general ledger to the cash receipts records and to deposits shown by bank statements or trustee reports.

Review amounts received subsequent to the statement date for consistency with reported contributions receivable.

Review adequacy of the allowance for uncollectible amounts.

Confirm contributions recorded as received and receivable by direct correspondence with the employer or by comparison with employer records.

For contributory plans, confirm employee contributions directly with participants on a test basis, as appropriate.

Employer Records

Reconcile total gross earnings shown by employees' earnings records to total wages shown by the general ledger and payroll tax reports.

Compare payroll data (e.g., salary, hours worked, hiring date, sex, birth date) for a selected group of employees with the employees' earnings records, time records, and personnel files.

Compare payroll data with participants' data furnished to the actuary.

Ascertain the completeness and accuracy of the basic data [see discussion in Section 3(a), Pension Plans] used by the actuary (e.g., work force size, hours worked, and sex of employees), including tracing key data from the actuary's report (if shown therein) or confirming such data with the actuary. Normally, these procedures are performed on individual data as well as summary totals. If contributions are not based on actuarial determinations, as in most defined contribution plans, test the data (e.g., hours worked and covered compensation) used in calculating contributions.

Determine whether contributions received and accrued comply with the applicable provisions of the plan instrument and, where applicable, with the collective bargaining agreement.

Actuary's Report

For defined benefit plans, review the actuary's report for consistency with reported contributions for the year.

If the work of an actuary is used, follow the guidance in SAS No. 73, *Using the Work of a Specialist* (discussed later in this chapter).

Conformity with GAAP and ERISA

Review the criteria used by the plan in accruing employer contributions, to determine whether the criteria have been applied consistently and contribution amounts comply with GAAP and the provisions of ERISA.

Figure 34.2   Suggested Auditing Procedures for Contributions Received and Receivable in Financial Statements of Multiemployer Pension Plans

Contribution Records

Reconcile total cash receipts as shown by the cash receipts records for a selected period to (1) total amount credited to the general ledger contribution accounts, (2) total amount posted to employers' contribution records, and (3) deposits shown by the bank statements or trustee reports.

If employer contributions are deposited in a central bank account, test amounts transferred to other bank accounts.

Compare selected individual employer contribution payments as shown by the cash receipts records with (1) amount shown on the employers' contribution reports and (2) amount posted to the individual employer contribution record, and trace selected postings from the employers' contribution records to the cash receipts records and the employer's contribution report.

Test the arithmetical accuracy of a selected number of contribution reports and ascertain whether the correct contribution rate was used.

Review employers' contribution reports to test the accuracy of the postings to participants' records, and trace entries on the participants' records to the contribution reports on a test basis. For defined contribution plans, determine that the contribution allocation to individual accounts conforms with the plan instrument.

Reconcile total participants' credits posted to the records for a selected period to the total credits shown by employers' contribution reports.

Determine the reasonableness of contributions receivable at the statement date by comparison with collections received subsequent to the statement date; also, review the related employers' contribution reports to ascertain that the receipts apply to the year under audit. If the plan's records are held open after the year-end, ascertain that amounts received in the next year that pertain to the year under audit have been recorded properly as accounts receivable.

Ascertain, by tests considered appropriate in the circumstances, the nature and amount of any delinquent or unreported contributions.

Review the adequacy of the allowance for uncollectible amounts.

Confirm contributions recorded as received during the period under audit on a test basis, by direct correspondence with selected employers.

Employer Records

Perform the auditing procedures under "Employer Records" in Figure 34.1 for selected employers.

Compare employers' contribution data for a selected number of participants with data shown on the employees' earnings records, and trace selected employees' earnings records to employers' contribution reports to ascertain that they have been properly included in or excluded from the reports.

Figure 34.2 *(Continued)*

Actuary's Report

For defined benefit plans, review the actuary's report for consistency with the amount of contributions.

If the work of an actuary is used, follow the guidance in SAS No. 73, *Using the Work of a Specialist* (discussed later in this chapter).

Conformity with GAAP and ERISA

Review the criteria used in accruing employer contributions to determine whether the criteria have been applied consistently and contribution amounts comply with GAAP. For defined benefit plans (other than certain insured plans), money-purchase plans, and target benefit plans, determine that the contributions required to be made are in accordance with the provisions of ERISA.

(iv) Employer Records.   For all plans, examining employer records is necessary to enable the auditor to gain assurance about contributions reported. For a defined contribution plan, employer records are the source of hours worked, pay rates, or other data on which contributions are based. Similarly, employer records are the source of pertinent data used by the actuary in determining contribution amounts for a defined benefit plan. For both types of plans, the auditor needs assurance that the information used in the determination of contributions is complete and accurate.

In some circumstances, the auditor may be unable to examine employer records; in that event, he or she should attempt to perform appropriate alternative auditing procedures to obtain satisfaction that the information on which contributions and other actuarially determined amounts are based is reasonable. For a single employer plan, the auditor should attempt to obtain a report from the employer's auditor stating that the appropriate auditing procedures have been performed.

The auditor of a multiemployer plan likewise may attempt to obtain reports from the auditors of selected employers, stating that appropriate auditing procedures have been performed. Alternatively, if the plan or related union maintains a complete record of participants, the auditor may deem it appropriate to correspond directly with participants. Such correspondence, which should request the participant's confirmation of employer, hours, pay rates, and so on, may be administered by the auditor, or by the plan or union under the auditor's control. Other alternative procedures might be appropriate in particular circumstances.

In addition to reviewing reports obtained from other auditors, the plan auditor should obtain satisfaction as to the independence and professional reputation of the other auditors and perform other procedures considered appropriate in the circumstances, as described in AU Section 543.04.

(c)   Investments

(i) Accounting Principles.   All plan investments (which represent a plan's largest asset), including equity and debt securities, real estate, bank common or commingled trust funds, and most contracts with insurance companies (discussed later), should be stated at fair value as of the date of the financial statements. The fair value of an investment is the amount a plan could reasonably expect to receive for it in a sale between a willing buyer and a willing seller. The relative difficulty of determining fair value depends on the nature of the investments held. For securities traded in an active market, published market quotations should be used as the basis for the determination; the closing price on the financial statement date is usually the fair value. If a plan's investments include restricted securities, which cannot be offered to the public without first being registered, the board of trustees or the administrative committee must consider the effect of the restriction on determining fair value. Fair value should be adjusted to reflect brokerage commissions and other selling expenses if these are significant.

Various special procedures may be required to determine fair value of other investments without readily determinable values, such as securities of closely held corporations or real estate. If there is no active market for an investment but there is such a market for similar investments, selling prices in that market may be helpful in estimating fair value. If a market price is not available, expected cash flows discounted at an appropriate interest rate may aid in estimating fair value. The use of independent specialists qualified to estimate fair value may be necessary for certain investments.

Purchases and sales of securities should be reflected on a trade-date basis. Thus, if a plan's accounts are maintained on a settlement-date basis, they should be adjusted to a trade-date basis to reflect year-end transactions, unless the effect of the adjustment would not be material to the financial statements taken as a whole. Similarly, dividend income should be recorded on the ex-dividend date, rather than on the record or payment date. Income from other investments, such as interest and rent, should be recorded as earned, and appropriate accruals should be made.

Footnote disclosures for investments of benefit plans include, among other items, identification of individual investments that represent 5 percent or more of the net assets available for benefits. In addition, the notes also may need to reflect requirements of other authoritative standards, including SFAS No. 105, *Disclosure of Information about Financial Instruments with Off-Balance-Sheet Risk and Financial Instruments with Concentrations of Credit Risk*, as amended by SFAS No. 119, *Disclosure about Derivative Financial Instruments and Fair Value of Financial Instruments*, and SFAS No. 107, *Disclosures about Fair Value of Financial Instruments*, also as amended by SFAS No. 119 and as amended by SFAS No. 126. Chapters 2 and 4 of the audit guide discuss how those pronouncements apply to pension and health and welfare plans, respectively.

The DOL requires that realized and unrealized gains and losses reported on its Form 5500 (the annual report that plan administrators may file to satisfy ERISA's reporting requirements) must be determined using revalued cost, that is, the current value of plan assets at the beginning of the plan year. Previously, many plans used historical cost as the basis of calculating realized and unrealized gains and losses. Although not required by professional pronouncements, some plans also report realized and unrealized gains and losses in their GAAP financial statements. Because GAAP requires the use of historical cost in computing realized and unrealized gains and losses, a discrepancy may exist between the amounts reported in the financial statements and in Form 5500. ERISA regulations require that such discrepancies be reconciled in the notes to the financial statements.

(ii) Controls.   Controls over plan investments depend largely on the form of trustee arrangement and the physical location of the plan's records and investments. Controls should ensure that investment transactions are recorded at appropriate amounts and on a timely basis. That usually is accomplished by maintaining detailed subsidiary records that are reconciled regularly to the plan's general ledger. If securities are held by trustees who issue periodic reports to the plan but retain the documentation of transactions, the plan should either have procedures to ensure the accuracy of such reports or maintain its own transaction records.

To ensure that investment income and expense are recorded at appropriate amounts, the plan should have procedures for reviewing commissions and fees for reasonableness and for comparing interest and dividend income with reliable reference sources. Investments carried at fair value should be compared with quotation sources and appraisal reports. Valuation methods, including good-faith estimates, should be documented in plan committee minutes.

The plan's investment policy and criteria and the responsibility for custody of its securities should be established and authorized by the board of trustees. The trustees should abide by any restrictions that may be imposed by the trust agreement or by government regulations. If the plan administrator is directly responsible for investment decisions, significant transactions should be approved by the board of trustees or an appropriate committee. If investment decisions are made by a custodian who also acts as trustee, the plan's agreement with the custodian-trustee should be approved by such board or committee. The board or committee also should monitor investment performance.

Investments held by the plan should be adequately protected from loss and misappropriation by physical and other controls and should be counted or confirmed periodically.

(iii) Audit Objectives and Procedures.   Although the audit objectives and procedures parallel those used by other entities whose principal assets are investments, various adaptations are necessary because of the nature of benefit plan operations and the requirements of ERISA. Further, the audit of investments is significantly influenced by the nature of trustee arrangements, as discussed in Section 2(d), Custodial Relationships.

The audit objectives for investment transactions include determining that all investments are recorded and exist, are owned by the plan, and are free of liens or pledges; that all investment transactions (including income thereon) are recorded; and that the investments are properly valued in conformity with GAAP.

The audit strategy for investments (i.e., determining whether it is efficient to perform tests of controls) depends to a large degree on the volume and portfolio mix of a plan's investment transactions and the plan's internal control. Procedures that may be performed include:

- Determining that investment transactions were properly authorized by tracing transactions to minutes of meetings indicating approval
- Examining brokers' advices, cash records, and other supporting documentation for the historical cost or selling price, quantity, identification, and acquisition and disposal dates of investments

- Comparing recorded prices of purchases and sales with published market price ranges on the trade dates
- Recomputing realized gains and losses

The auditor should perform analytical procedures to determine the overall reasonableness of investment income, considering the composition of the plan's investment portfolio and changes therein during the year. Such procedures include comparing current income with the corresponding period of the prior year, referring to industry indices for investment companies or mutual funds with similar portfolios, and reading and analyzing reports prepared for the plan's investment committee that compare actual returns with expected returns. In addition, the auditor should observe the trend of investment values in relation to the portfolio mix; an investigation of fluctuations may uncover errors or other events that may require recognition in the plan's financial statements.

The auditor should test the existence of securities either by inspecting and counting them or by obtaining a confirmation from the custodian. To be able to rely on a confirmation, the auditor should be satisfied with the custodian's legal responsibility for assets held in trust, reputation, and financial resources. [See Section 2(d), Custodial Relationships, for further discussion.] The auditor should inspect deeds, title policies, insurance contracts, and leases covering real property. Loan and mortgage instruments also should be examined, and the balances and terms should be confirmed, with appropriate consideration of collectibility.

The auditor should test the fair value of investments and test the computation of the net change in fair value. Determining fair value of publicly traded securities presents no difficulty. The fair value of investments for which market quotations cannot be readily obtained should be determined by the plan's administrative committee for single employer plans or its board of trustees for multiemployer plans. The auditor is not an appraiser and is not expected to substitute his or her judgment for that of management; the auditor should only ascertain whether the procedures followed by management were adequate and the results obtained appear to be reasonable. The auditor is justified in expecting that the plan's administrative committee or board of trustees will have documented its judgment of fair value and that the documentation will be made available for his or her evaluation.

The auditor should review and test the various reports, analyses, computations, appraisals, and other sources used in determining fair value as of the statement date. Written representations from appropriate specialists may be used in considering the reasonableness of values reported by the plan. When using a specialist, the auditor should apply the procedures in SAS No. 73 (AU Section 336).

The auditor should determine that the plan's investments do not violate restrictions or limitations imposed by the plan instrument or policy on types of investments. (In addition, the auditor should inquire whether the plan's investments comply with the provisions of ERISA.) If approval of investment transactions by the board of trustees or administrative committee is required, the auditor should examine evidence of such approval and also should review transactions for evidence of liens, pledges, or other security interest in investments. The auditor should test interest and dividend income received and receivable by computation, reference to appropriate published sources, or review of cash receipts and related documentation. Such procedures should include tests for unrecorded amounts.

Detailed procedures and illustrative audit programs for investments of benefit plans are presented in Chapter 7 of the audit guide.

(iv) Funding Arrangements Used by Employee Benefit Plans.   As noted earlier in this chapter, most pension plans and some health and welfare plans are funded. Funding arrangements used include Voluntary Employees' Beneficiary Associations (VEBAs) for health and welfare benefits and separate trusts within qualified defined benefit pension plans [401(h) accounts]. If the plan is funded, the auditor should be familiar with the funding arrangements and apply appropriate auditing procedures to the plan's investments.

(d) Custodial Relationships

As noted previously, many plans use some form of trust arrangement for investments. The plan's auditor should be aware of such arrangements and consider their impact on the audit.

(i) Trust Arrangements.   Trust arrangements are either directed or discretionary. In a directed trust, the trustee acts as custodian of the plan's investments and is responsible for collecting the investment income; the plan directs the trustee as to investment transactions and usually maintains the investment records, together with the supporting documentation. Accordingly, the auditor may perform the normal auditing procedures, as discussed earlier, with respect to investments.

In a discretionary trust, the trustee has discretionary authority over investment decisions and generally exercises control over the investments. The trustee usually issues periodic reports to the plan, but retains the documentation supporting transactions. Although the plan may have controls to ensure the accuracy of such reports and may maintain its own records of transactions, the lack of supporting documentation, such as brokers' advices, normally requires the auditor to gain an understanding of the trustee's controls over the processing of investment transactions. If the trustee has engaged an independent auditor to prepare a report in accordance with SAS No. 70 on the processing of transactions, the plan auditor should obtain and read such report. To be adequate for the auditor's purposes in such circumstances, the report should address whether the policies and procedures over the discretionary trust transactions were designed appropriately and were operating effectively, referred to as a "Type II report." Ordinarily, the plan auditor does not review the trustee's auditor's working papers, but obtains satisfaction as to the independence and professional reputation of the trustee's auditor.

If a Type II report cannot be obtained, the audit guide states that in order to express an unqualified opinion on the plan's financial statements, the auditor should apply appropriate procedures at the trustee organization. The guide further specifies that the plan auditor may consider using the work of the trustee's independent auditor or internal auditors relevant to the trustee's internal control. Alternatively, the auditor may need to visit the trustee organization to assess its relevant policies and procedures. If the auditor is not able to apply appropriate auditing procedures, a scope limitation ordinarily results. (The DOL will not accept an ERISA filing with this type of scope limitation.)

(ii) Common or Commingled Trust Funds.   Bank common or commingled trust funds and insurance company pooled separate accounts contain assets of two or more plans that are pooled for investment purposes. In a common or commingled fund, a benefit plan acquires units of the fund, generally referred to as units of participation. Pooled separate accounts are similar to common and commingled funds, and a plan's share of pooled separate accounts also is determined on a participation-unit basis. Periodically (e.g., each month or quarter), the unit value is determined based on the fair values of the underlying assets. The amount of a plan's equity in a common or commingled fund or pooled separate account is determined by multiplying the unit value by the number of units held. Assets invested in a common or commingled fund are held in trust for the plan, while assets invested in a pooled separate account are the property of the insurance company, and the plan has specified rights thereto.

Investments in common and commingled funds and pooled separate accounts should be reported as separate line items in the statement of net assets available for benefits and the change in value should be similarly reported in the statement of changes in net assets available for benefits. The plan's financial statements should not otherwise report the proportionate share of the underlying investments and transactions of these funds and accounts. This method of accounting and reporting is consistent with DOL regulations.

If a plan holds investments in common or commingled funds, the auditor normally should apply the following procedures:

- Physically examine or confirm with the trustee the number of units of participation in the fund held by the plan.

- Examine supporting documents for selected plan transactions in units of participation.

- Review the financial statements of the common or commingled fund and relate the per-unit information reported therein to amounts reported by the plan, including fair value, purchase and redemption values, and income amounts; if the fund's financial statements have been audited by an independent auditor, the plan auditor should obtain a copy of the fund auditor's report. The plan auditor should be satisfied as to the independence and professional reputation of the fund auditor, in accordance with AU Section 543.04. If the financial statements of the common or commingled fund have not been audited by an independent auditor, the plan auditor should obtain a copy of an SAS No. 70 report, if available, relating to the common or commingled fund's activities and controls, or should apply appropriate auditing procedures at the bank, including assessing control risk relating to the income amounts and unit values of the common or commingled fund. The audit guide indicates that the auditor may consider using the work of the bank's independent auditor or internal auditors. (If the plan auditor is unable to apply these procedures, a scope limitation will result.)

Auditing procedures for insurance company pooled separate accounts are described later in this chapter.

(iii) Master Trusts.   Master trusts hold assets only of plans maintained by a single employer or members of a controlled group of entities. Each plan with assets in a master trust has an undivided interest in the assets of the trust, and ownership is represented by a proportionate dollar interest or units of participation.

With respect to the accounting and reporting for master trusts, the audit guide specifies that investments in master trusts should be presented as a single line item in the statement of net assets available for benefits. The notes to the financial statements should detail the investments in the master trust by general type, such as government securities, short-term securities, corporate bonds, mortgages, and real estate as of the date of each statement of net assets available for benefits presented. In addition, net appreciation or depreciation and income by investment type should be disclosed. DOL regulations also require a master trust to file more detailed financial information directly with the DOL.

Because of the significance of the master trust to the plan's financial statements, sufficient procedures, normally those described earlier for investments, should be applied to the financial records of the master trust to enable the auditor to form an opinion on the plan's financial statements. The auditor is not required, however, to issue an opinion on the financial statements of the master trust.

If the same auditor audits more than one individual plan with assets in a master trust, normally it is more efficient to first apply auditing procedures to the master trust and then determine how ownership is attributed to the individual plans. The auditor should review the trust agreement to obtain satisfaction that the accounting for the individual plan interests is consistent with the allocation method set forth in the agreement. If the accounting is not specified in the agreement, the auditor should determine that all administrators of the plans participating in the master trust agree with the method of allocation.

(e)   Contracts with Insurance Companies

Benefit plans may invest some or all of their assets with insurance companies under several types of arrangements. The funds invested may be held in separate accounts by the insurance company or commingled with the insurance company's general assets (often referred to as general accounts). Separate accounts generally pool the funds of several plans (pooled separate accounts), although they may be established separately for one plan (individual separate accounts).

(i) Accounting Principles.   Insurance contracts should be recognized and measured for financial statement purposes in the same manner as called for under ERISA, which depends on their classification. Generally, the various types of insurance contracts can be classified according to whether the payment to the insurance company is allocated currently to purchase immediate or deferred annuity contracts (allocated contracts) for individual participants or is accumulated in an unallocated fund (unallocated contracts) that is used to meet benefit payments directly when they come due or to purchase annuities for individual participants on retirement (or earlier termination of service if the participant's benefits are partially or fully vested).

Under an allocated contract, plan benefits are fully guaranteed on payment of the premiums to the insurance company. Examples of allocated contracts include individual life insurance or annuity contracts, group permanent insurance contracts, and deferred group annuity contracts. Under unallocated contracts, plan benefits are guaranteed only to the extent that funds are available. Deposit administration (DA) group annuity contracts and immediate participation guarantee (IPG) contracts are examples of unallocated contracts. Under ERISA, unallocated insurance contracts should be recognized in the plan's financial statements, and allocated contracts should be excluded because the insurance company has assumed responsibility for the plan benefits.

ERISA requires investments in separate accounts to be carried at fair value, but permits other insurance contracts to be valued at either fair value or amounts determined by the insurance company in accordance with the terms of the contract (referred to as "contract value"). Historically, contract value almost invariably was used in plan reporting of all contracts, since normally insurance companies do not report fair value to the plan. SFAS No. 35, which generally required defined benefit pension plans to report plan investments at fair value, also permitted this exception because of recognized complexities in estimating fair value. SFAS No. 35 concluded that such contracts should be presented in the same manner as in filings with governmental agencies pursuant to ERISA, along with appropriate disclosures. As practice developed, this exception was applied to all contracts with insurance companies, including guaranteed investment contracts (GICs).

SFAS No. 107 requires holders of investment contracts, including defined benefit plans, to disclose the fair value of those contracts. As a result, some investment contracts, such as GICs, were reported at contract value in plan financial statements, while SFAS No. 107 required disclosure of fair value in the accompanying notes. The FASB then concluded that it would be more appropriate for such investment contracts to be reported at fair value in plan financial statements. Accordingly, the Board issued SFAS No. 110, *Reporting by Defined Benefit Pension Plans of Investment Contracts*, which requires defined benefit pension plans to report all investment contracts, whether issued by an insurance enterprise or another entity, at fair value. SFAS No. 110 amended SFAS No. 35 to permit defined benefit pension plans to report at contract value only contracts that incorporate mortality or morbidity risk (as well as DA and IPG contracts entered into before March 20, 1990).

SOP 94-4, *Reporting of Investment Contracts Held by Health and Welfare Benefit Plans and Defined Contribution Pension Plans*, conformed reporting by those plans of investment contracts issued by insurance companies, banks, thrift institutions, and others to the reporting by defined benefit pension plans, as specified in SFAS No. 110. The SOP specifies that investment contracts with fully-benefit-responsive features (as defined in the SOP) be reported at contract value and other contracts at fair value. The SOP also provides guidance for determining the fair value of investment contracts held by all types of plans.

(ii) Controls. The control objectives and the controls applicable to insurance contracts are similar to those for investments in general. They should include procedures to ensure that premiums and interest are recorded appropriately and on a timely basis. This can be accomplished by comparing premium statements with contracts, recalculating interest, and reviewing current participant listings.

(iii) Audit Objectives and Procedures. The audit objectives applicable to plan assets held by an insurance company are establishing the physical existence of the assets represented by the contract, corroborating their reported value in conformity with GAAP, and determining compliance with the terms of the contract.

As with investments in securities, the auditor should perform analytical procedures to determine the reasonableness of income recorded by the plan on insurance contracts, including comparisons with industry indices or other publicly available insurance return information. Since not all assets represented by insurance contracts are included in a plan's financial statements, the auditor should review all insurance contracts to determine whether they should be reported as assets in the plan's financial statements. The auditor should correspond directly with the insurance company to confirm information such as that summarized in Figure 34.3. Additional procedures depend on the type of contracts, as discussed in the following sections.

(iv) Separate Accounts.   An individual separate account is operated similar to a bank discretionary trust fund. Sometimes such accounts are audited by independent auditors, in which event the plan auditor may review the other auditors' report. Otherwise, the auditing procedures are similar to those for discretionary trust funds [discussed in Section 2(d)(i), Trust Arrangements]. They include obtaining a copy of an SAS No. 70 report relating to the insurance company's separate-account controls or applying appropriate auditing procedures at the insurance company. The audit guide indicates that the auditor may consider using the work of the insurance company's independent auditor or internal auditors.

Pooled separate accounts are similar to bank commingled funds, and the additional auditing procedures are similar to those discussed in Section 2(d)(ii), Common or

Figure 34.3   Suggested Information to Be Confirmed with Insurance Companies Holding Benefit Plan Assets

---

The contract value of funds in a general account or the fair value of funds in a separate account at the plan's year-end and the basis for determining such values

Contributions (premium payments) made during the year, including the dates received by the insurance company

Interest and dividends, changes therein, and whether such amounts have been earned or credited during the year on an estimated or actual basis

Refunds and credits paid or payable by the insurance company during the year because of termination of plan members

Dividend or rate credit given by the insurance company

Annuities purchased and/or benefits paid or payable during the year from unallocated insurance contracts

Asset management fees, commissions, sales fees, premium taxes, and other expenses (sometimes collectively referred to as "retention") charged or chargeable by the insurance company during the year

Amounts of transfers among various funds and accounts

Special conditions applicable on termination of a contract

Commingled Trust Funds. They include auditing the balance of and transactions in the plan's units of participation in the pooled account and obtaining the report of an independent auditor on the financial statements of the pooled separate account, obtaining a copy of an SAS No. 70 report relating to the separate-account controls, or applying appropriate auditing procedures at the insurance company. The audit guide indicates that the auditor may consider using the work of the insurance company's independent auditor or internal auditors.

(v) Deposit Administration Group Annuity and Immediate Participation Guarantee Contracts. DA or IPG contracts are used to provide future benefits to current employees. Contributions are deposited with the insurance company and credited to an unallocated account. When an employee retires, the amount required to purchase an annuity to provide for retiree benefits is charged to the account, along with any incidental benefits disbursed directly from the account.

DA contracts provide interest on the account at a guaranteed rate, and dividends or rate credits (generally net of contract expenses) are determined solely at the discretion of the insurance company. IPG contracts provide interest based on the insurance company's actual investment income, so there is an "immediate participation" in the insurance company's investment performance. Expenses under an IPG contract are charged directly to the account.

The following auditing procedures, in addition to those previously set forth for contracts with insurance companies in general, should be considered if plan assets are invested pursuant to a DA or an IPG contract:

- For DA contracts, evaluate the reasonableness of the interest credited to the contract in relation to the guaranteed rate stipulated in the contract.

- For IPG contracts, consider the plan administrator's conclusion regarding the reasonableness of the investment income credited to the contract. Reference should be made to insurance yield data furnished to the plan by the insurance company. Generally, this evaluation is sufficient to satisfy the auditor as to the aggregate investment yield. If, however, the amount credited does not appear to be reasonable, the auditor should apply additional procedures, such as asking the insurance company about its compliance with the method of computing investment yield under the terms of the contract. If the auditor is still not satisfied with the reasonableness of the investment return credited to the plan, consideration should be given to requesting the plan administrator to contact the insurance company to arrange for its independent auditor to perform agreed-on procedures and issue a report. Those procedures would be applied to the insurer's determination of investment return in accordance with the terms of the contract.

- If benefits are paid directly from the fund, determine that benefit payments were made to eligible beneficiaries and in the correct amounts. The auditor should consider applying the procedures for auditing benefit payments set forth in Figure 34.4. If annuities are purchased for employees on retirement or earlier separation, determine that the purchases were made based on rates stipulated in the contract and on benefit levels set forth in the plan document.

- Determine whether expenses charged to the fund are in accordance with the insurance contract or are otherwise authorized by the plan.

Figure 34.4   Illustrative Procedures for Auditing Benefit Payments

Review, on a test basis, the approved applications for benefits or other documentation and ascertain that the current benefit amounts have been properly approved. Examine service provider statements or other evidence of service rendered.

Review, on a test basis, employees' eligibility for the payment of benefits and evaluate the plan's procedures for monitoring continuation of benefits.

Evaluate selected participants' or beneficiaries' eligibility for the payment of benefits by examining evidence of age and employment history; comparing employment dates, credited service, earnings, dependency status, and employee contribution records, if any, with payroll or other accounting records; and examine benefit election and dependent designation forms to determine the appropriateness of payment.

Recalculate, on a test basis, the benefit payments and ascertain whether an independent individual has reviewed the calculation.

Ascertain that long-outstanding checks are investigated.

On a test basis, examine canceled checks for, or confirm by direct correspondence with selected participants or beneficiaries, benefits recorded as paid during the period under audit. Compare signatures with those on applications for benefits or with other appropriate plan documents.

Ascertain that payments made to participants or beneficiaries over an unusually long number of years are still appropriate.

For defined contribution plans, trace the amount paid to the individual participants' account records.

(f) Deposits with and Receivables from Insurance Companies

Health and welfare plan payments to insurance companies may include deposits and stabilization reserves. Deposits should be reported as plan assets until such amounts are used to pay premiums. Premium stabilization reserves, which exist when premiums paid to an insurance company exceed the total of claims paid and other charges and are used to reduce future premium payments, also are reported as assets of the plan until such amounts are used to pay premiums.

Plans also may receive refunds (or dividends) on insurance arrangements. Often, experience rating refunds are not determined by the insurance company until some months after the end of the plan year. In such circumstances, the plan will record, as of the year-end, a receivable for amounts due from the insurance company.

The auditor generally should read the contract to determine whether amounts paid to insurance companies represent deposits—which are plan assets—or payments for the transfer of risk. When the plan's year-end does not coincide with the insurance company's year-end, the auditor should determine whether any refund can be reasonably measured and whether its payment is probable. If the amount of the refund cannot be reasonably measured, no asset should be recognized, and the nature of the refund should be disclosed in the notes to the financial statements.

(g) Other Assets

Generally, other assets are limited to plan assets used in operations (e.g., building, equipment, and furniture and fixtures), which should be presented at cost less accumulated depreciation. This conflicts with DOL regulations concerning ERISA annual reports prepared under "the alternative method" of compliance,[2] since the regulations do not distinguish between operating and other assets, and require assets to be stated at current value. Practice in ERISA filings under the alternative method, however, has been to state operating assets at cost less accumulated depreciation. Internal control and audit objectives and procedures for such assets are similar to those for other entities.

(h) Liabilities

Generally, the principal liabilities of a benefit plan are accrued expenses [discussed in Section 2(j), Administrative Expenses] and amounts owed for securities purchased [discussed in Section 2(c), Investments].

(i) Benefit Payments

Benefit payments to retired or other eligible participants, including expenditures to purchase allocated insurance contracts, represent the largest item of operating expenses of a benefit plan.

(i) Controls. The plan's controls should ensure that benefit payments are recorded on a timely basis and that they are determined and authorized in accordance with the plan document. Procedures should include use of signed applications, where applicable, for the commencement of pension and other postretirement benefit payments and for nonretirement benefits; applications should be controlled and carefully processed. An individual not involved in the original processing procedures should review applicants' eligibility and ascertain that benefits have been determined in conformity with payroll and personnel records and with the plan documents or insurance company records. The board of trustees (for a multiemployer plan) or administrative committee or its designee (for a single employer plan) should approve all applications for benefits. Control totals of monthly retirement benefits should be maintained.

Controls should be established to ensure that individuals receiving benefits are eligible for the continuation of such benefits. Procedures might include periodic comparisons, by an individual not involved in processing benefit applications, of endorsements on paid checks with signatures in personnel records or on benefit applications; sending greeting cards to pensioners, returnable to the plan in the event of nondelivery; reviewing obituary notices; and visiting pensioners.

---

[2] Annual reports may be prepared in accordance with ERISA or under an "alternative method" prescribed by the DOL. The alternative method is by far the more frequently used of the two.

(ii) Audit Objectives and Procedures.   The audit objectives applicable to benefit payments include determining that recipients are eligible beneficiaries, that payments were made in correct amounts pursuant to plan provisions, and that people no longer eligible for benefit payments are removed from the benefit records. Auditing procedures, including both tests of controls and substantive tests, that may be performed to achieve these audit objectives are set forth in Figure 34.4. The auditor also should compare benefit payments made by the plan in the current period with those made in the prior period and obtain explanations for significant fluctuations that may have an impact on other audit areas. Often, tests of controls are performed in auditing benefit payments.

Where benefit payments for all or a portion of the participant population are used by the actuary in developing costs as part of the computation of actuarial benefit information or the benefit obligation, the auditor may already have applied procedures to such data; those procedures would not need to be repeated.

Benefit payments often are made by a third-party administrator. In such situations, the auditor may need to obtain an understanding of the third party's internal control as it relates to benefit payments. This can be accomplished by obtaining a report from the third party's independent auditor in accordance with SAS No. 70, if such a report is available. If not, the auditor may need to apply auditing procedures at the service organization; the use of the third party's independent auditor or internal auditor to perform procedures may be appropriate.

(j)   Administrative Expenses

(i) Accounting Principles.   Plan administrative expenses should be recorded in the financial statements in conformity with GAAP. Commonly, in many single employer plans, the employer bears all administrative expenses of the plan; this fact should be disclosed.

(ii) Controls.   Controls over administrative expenses should ensure that such expenses are recorded at appropriate amounts and on a timely basis, are authorized by a responsible official or board, and are supported by documentation. Procedures to ensure that unauthorized or duplicate payments are detected on a timely basis are also necessary.

In multiemployer plans, although the trustees are responsible for approving all administrative expenses, responsibility for approving routine expenses usually is delegated to the administrator or other employees of the plan. Because of their fiduciary responsibility, the trustees should make certain that controls over administrative expenses are adequate. The board of trustees generally retains the authority to approve expenditures over a stated amount. Contract or professional administrators are paid according to various criteria (e.g., the number of participants covered by the plan or the number of employers' reports processed). Therefore, it is important that the plan's records provide the information necessary to determine the reasonableness of such payments.

(iii) Audit Objectives and Procedures.   The audit objectives for administrative expenses include determining whether the expenses are in accordance with agreements, properly approved, properly classified, and recorded in appropriate amounts. In accordance with these objectives, the auditor should review the terms of the plan agreement and minutes of the meetings of the board of trustees or administrative committee to determine whether administrative expenses were properly authorized. The auditor also should analyze the account and examine contracts, agreements, invoices, and other supporting documentation. If the plan uses a contract administrator, the propriety and reasonableness of the payments should be evaluated by testing the basis of the contract payment.

If one office functions as a service organization for several plans, the auditor should review the organization's allocation of administrative expenses not directly associated with a specific plan to ascertain that the allocation is based on an equitable method. The auditor also should determine that the method selected was approved by the board of trustees.

34.3 AUDITING BENEFIT INFORMATION

(a) Pension Plans

(i) Background and Requirements. SFAS No. 35 requires defined benefit pension plans to report specified actuarial benefit information to accomplish the primary objective of plan financial statements. The benefit information to be presented is the actuarial present value of accumulated plan benefits. Accumulated plan benefits are future benefit payments that are attributable, under the plan's provisions, to participants' service rendered prior to the benefit information date. Accumulated plan benefits comprise benefits expected to be paid to retired or terminated employees or their beneficiaries, beneficiaries of deceased employees, and present employees or their beneficiaries. They include nonvested benefits as well as vested benefits.

Accumulated plan benefits should be reported only to the extent that related assets are included in the financial statements. Thus, the actuarial present value of accumulated plan benefits should exclude benefits that are fully guaranteed by an insurance company and for which the related assets are not reflected in the financial statements.

Plan administrators of defined benefit plans use the services of actuaries in determining benefit information. The assumptions to be included by an actuary in the accumulated benefit calculations are prescribed by SFAS No. 35, which sets forth specific guidelines for determining accumulated plan benefits. The actuarial present value of accumulated plan benefits is determined by applying actuarial assumptions to the accumulated plan benefit amounts. The actuarial assumptions are used to adjust those amounts to reflect the time value of money (discounts for interest) and the probability of payment (decrements such as mortality, disability, withdrawal, and early retirement) between the benefit information date and the expected date of payment. The actuarial assumptions should be based on an ongoing plan and should reflect the best estimate of the plan's future experience with regard to those assumptions.

The benefits should be discounted at assumed rates of return that reflect the rates expected during the periods for which payment of benefits has been deferred. Those assumed rates should be consistent with the returns realistically achievable on the types of assets held by the plan, the plan's investment policy, and the rates of inflation assumed in estimating automatic cost-of-living adjustments. Expected rates on existing assets and those available in the marketplace, expected rates from the reinvestment of actual returns from those investments, and rates on investments expected to be held in the future all enter into the determination of the assumed rates. Thus, accumulated plan benefits generally are not discounted solely at rates of return on existing investments. To the extent that assumed rates of return are based on values of existing plan assets, however, the values used should be the same as those presented in the plan's financial statements. The rates of return may be adjusted to account for administrative expenses of the plan.

In lieu of the assumed rate of return, SFAS No. 35 allows plans to use assumptions inherent in the estimated cost, at the benefit information date, of obtaining a contract with an insurance company to provide participants with accumulated plan benefits, whether or not that is the intent. Thus, the settlement rate concept set forth in SFAS No. 87, *Employers' Accounting for Pensions* (Accounting Standards Section P16) (i.e., use of a rate that reflects the amounts at which the pension benefits could be effectively settled), is an acceptable alternative under SFAS No. 35. Since the use of a settlement rate by the plan eliminates the need for different valuations by the employer and the plan, use of a settlement rate by plans has become more common since the issuance of SFAS No. 87.

Financial statement disclosures should include a description of the methods and significant assumptions (e.g., assumed rates of return) used to calculate the actuarial present value of accumulated plan benefits. If administrative expenses expected to be paid by the plan are reflected by adjusting the assumed rates of return, that should be disclosed. Changes in the methods or assumptions also should be disclosed.

Financial statements of defined contribution plans normally present only the net assets currently available for plan benefits, since benefits to be paid are not determinable until payment. Such plans may disclose the vested portion of benefits credited to participants' accounts, which does not require actuarial calculations.

(ii) Audit Objectives and Procedures.   Auditing actuarial benefit information requires testing certain participants' data needed by the plan's actuary in addition to performing procedures relating to the use of the work of the actuary. The participants' data to be tested in a pension plan audit varies with the factors on which contributions and benefits are based. Such factors are identified in the plan document and may be related to demographic or census data, payroll or salary data, and benefit data. Generally, as discussed earlier, this testing is also relevant to auditing plan contributions. In addition, since benefit payments ultimately are based on the participants' data, the results of the testing discussed in Section 2(i), Benefit Payments, should be considered in auditing actuarial benefit information.

The principal audit objective for actuarially determined information is to obtain satisfaction as to the reasonableness of the information to be disclosed in the plan's financial statements. Many of the auditing procedures (described below) relating to use of the actuary's report are performed in auditing the pension cost reported in the employer's financial statements; if so, they need not be repeated at the plan level.

In determining the reasonableness of the actuarial information prepared by the actuary, the auditor needs to obtain and review sufficient competent evidential matter. Normally this is accomplished by reviewing the actuary's report. Guidance on using the work of a specialist is provided by SAS No. 73 (AU Section 336), which requires auditors to satisfy themselves as to the professional qualifications and reputation of the actuary and the actuary's experience in the type of work under consideration, which in this case is performing valuations in connection with employee benefit plans. Usually this can be done by determining that the actuary is a member of a recognized professional actuarial society (e.g., a Fellow of the Society of Actuaries or a member of the American Academy of Actuaries). Alternatively, the auditor might consider whether the actuary is an "enrolled actuary" under ERISA or might obtain competent professional advice on the actuary's qualifications from another actuary who is known by the auditor to be qualified.

The auditor may need to consult with the actuary when report items require clarification or explanation. Such consultation may be reduced substantially by ascertaining in advance that the actuary's report will contain all the information required by the auditor. Also, if the auditor becomes aware of changes in conditions that might affect the actuary's determinations, it would be appropriate, after discussing the matter with plan management, for the auditor to advise the actuary. Other auditing procedures with respect to using the work of an actuary are outlined in SAS No. 73.

Procedures that the auditor may find useful in implementing the requirements of SAS No. 73 are set forth in Figure 34.5. In following those procedures, the auditor should not rely on an actuary's conclusion as to the conformity of actuarially computed amounts with GAAP. Such a conclusion requires a knowledge of accounting principles, including the concept of materiality. Conversely, the auditor should refrain from making actuarial judgments.

SAS No. 73 indicates that the understanding among auditor, management, and actuary regarding the actuary's representations as to any relationship with management should preferably be documented. Some auditors believe that the actuary should be requested to set forth in writing the circumstances of any relationship with management. The auditor also may wish to ask the actuary to send him or her a copy of the actuary's report as well as to confirm certain other information not contained in the actuary's report. An illustrative letter requesting this information (and also requesting information as to any relationship with management) is presented in the audit guide.

The audit objectives applicable to defined contribution plans require the auditor to determine that net assets have been allocated to individual participant accounts in accordance with the plan document and that participant accounts agree in the aggregate with total net assets. These objectives are accomplished by performing auditing procedures such as:

- Reviewing the plan documents to understand the basis of allocation
- Testing the allocation of investment income, employer contributions, appreciation (depreciation), and other items to the accounts
- Testing individual employee contributions to the respective account for contributory plans
- Determining that the sum of the individual accounts agrees with the total net assets
- Confirming information with participants as appropriate

Figure 34.5   Suggested Auditing Procedures for Actuarially Determined Information

---

Determine whether the actuary is familiar with the current terms of the pension plan and has properly recognized them in the calculations. This may be accomplished by reviewing the actuary's report or, with management's consent, contacting the actuary directly.

Determine the professional reputation and qualifications of the actuary.

Determine whether the actuary is unrelated to plan management.

Review and test the employee data given to the actuary on which the actuarial calculations are based. Procedures outlined in Figure 34.1 under "Employer Records" should be used as a guide.

Determine whether the actuarial methods used by the actuary to determine pension costs and accumulated plan benefits are appropriate and whether the same methods were used in the prior period.

Consider whether each significant actuarial assumption used to determine the actuarial present value of accumulated plan benefits appears reasonable, and is intended to reflect the best estimate of the plan's future experience solely with respect to that individual assumption.

Ascertain that the value of pension fund assets used in actuarial calculations to determine pension costs is not unreasonable.

Determine whether the effect of any changes in actuarial methods and assumptions has been disclosed.

Determine whether the actuarially determined information contained in the plan financial statements agrees with the actuary's report.

Review the period from the date of the actuarial valuation to the fiscal year-end (and through the subsequent events period) to see whether any significant events (e.g., plant closings, changes in plan, and changes in market value of securities) have occurred that would materially affect amounts reflected or disclosed in the financial statements. If such events have occurred, consult with the actuary and obtain an estimate of the dollar effect of such amounts.

(b)   Health and Welfare Plans

Benefit obligations for defined benefit health and welfare plans consist of claims payable, claims incurred but not reported (IBNR), insurance premiums payable, accumulated eligibility credits, and postretirement benefit obligations.

(i) Accounting Principles.   Under SOP 92-6, all benefit obligations, including those incurred as of the balance sheet date (i.e., claims payable, claims incurred but not reported, and insurance premiums payable) are presented together. Benefit obligations may be presented either with net asset information in a statement of benefit obligations and net assets available for benefits, or in a separate statement. This form of presentation is intended to generally track the presentation of accumulated pension plan benefits required by SFAS No. 35.

(ii) Audit Objectives and Procedures.   The objective of auditing procedures applied to the benefit obligation is to provide the auditor with a reasonable basis for determining whether the benefit obligation and its components and changes therein have been determined in conformity with GAAP. It is generally efficient to perform this testing in conjunction with the testing of plan contributions. The results of tests of payments also should be considered. For actuarially determined amounts, the auditor should consider confirming information with the actuary, including the items in Figure 34.6. The auditor also should consider the procedures described earlier in connection with auditing actuarial information relating to pension plans.

(iii) Claims Payable and Claims Incurred But Not Reported.   Self-insured plans record obligations for claims payable (i.e., reported but not paid) and estimated claims incurred by participants but not reported.[3] Plans that enter into administrative service contracts with insurance companies or other third party administrators also have benefit obligations, since such arrangements are, in essence, self-insured arrangements. Plans that enter into insurance contracts with stop-loss or trigger point provisions also may be obligated for claims reported but not paid. The cost of IBNR claims should be measured at the present value of the estimated ultimate cost of settling the claims and included in the postretirement benefit obligation (see below).

Figure 34.6   Information That May Be Confirmed with Actuary

A description of the participant group covered

A brief description of the terms of the plan used in the actuary's calculations, including the benefit provisions

The number of participants and beneficiaries who are active, terminated with vested benefits, or retired under the plan

The present value of the plan's obligations, excluding amounts recorded elsewhere (e.g., claims incurred but not reported)

The date of the valuation of the benefit obligation and the date of the census data used; if applicable, a description of the basis used to project the data to the end of the year

Descriptions of the principal assumptions and methods used in calculating the benefit obligation and of any changes in assumptions or methods (for example, interest rates) and the effect of the change

The effects on the benefit obligation amounts caused by plan amendments

Knowledge of an intent on the part of the employer to fully or partially terminate the plan

If payable by the plan, the amount of unbilled or unpaid actuary's fees

---

[3] Most health and welfare benefit plans with more than 100 participants are not insured plans.

While the obligation for claims payable is determined from the plan records, the obligation for IBNR claims generally is determined by an actuary. The financial statements should disclose a description of the significant actuarial assumptions used to determine the plan's obligations, and any significant changes in assumptions between financial statement dates.

For insured health and welfare benefit plans, claims payable and IBNR claims are paid by the insurance company. Therefore, no obligation for claims is reflected in the benefit obligations of the plan because the risk of loss has been assumed by the insurance company [see Section 3(b)(iv), Premiums Due Under Insurance Arrangements].

The auditor should consider performing the following procedures to determine whether claims payable are reported in the proper period:

- Compare individual claim amounts with the detailed trial balance
- Review supporting documentation for individual claim amounts and determine whether the claims are eligible for payment
- Compare individual claim payments made after the date of the financial statements to determine whether all claims reported have been included in the detailed trial balance
- Perform a search of open claim files

The auditor normally should follow the guidance earlier in the chapter with respect to the obligation for IBNR claims determined by an actuary.

(iv) Premiums Due Under Insurance Arrangements. Group insurance contracts usually are written for a one-year period and may provide for annual renewal. The contract generally specifies, among other things, the schedule of benefits, eligibility rules, premium rate per eligible participant, and the dates premiums are due. Benefit obligations should include any premiums due but not paid.

If the insurance contract requires payment of additional premiums (for example, retrospective premiums) when the loss ratio exceeds a specified percentage, an obligation for the estimated additional premiums should be included in benefit obligations. Also, in some instances, the period covered by the insurance contract does not coincide with the plan's fiscal year-end, and an accrual or prepayment for the partial period needs to be calculated.

Experience ratings determined by the insurance company or by estimates may result in a premium deficit. Premium deficits should be included in benefit obligations if (a) it is probable that the deficit will be applied against the amounts of future premiums or future experience rating refunds, and (b) the amount can be reasonably estimated. If no obligation is included for a premium deficit because those conditions are not met, or if an exposure to loss exists in excess of the amount accrued, disclosure of the premium deficit should be made in the notes to the financial statements if it is reasonably possible that a loss or an additional loss has been incurred.

The auditor's objective is to determine whether the proper premium amounts have been paid to the insurance company and whether any unpaid premiums are properly recorded. Premiums generally are determined from the participants' eligibility records and the premium rates in insurance contracts. In testing premiums and the related liability, procedures that should be considered include:

- Comparing the number of eligible participants, as shown by the eligibility records, with the premium computation and tracing the applicable premium rates to the insurance contract
- Tracing participants listed in the premium computation list to the eligibility records
- Comparing premiums paid with prior-period payments, including payments subsequent to year-end, and investigating the reasons for significant changes
- Requesting confirmation from the insurance company of the total amount of premiums paid during the year, premiums payable, and, if appropriate, other obligations and assets of the plan at year-end
- If the arrangements with the insurance company include retrospective premium and experience rating adjustment provisions, determining whether amounts related to these provisions are properly included in the benefit obligation

(v) Accumulated Eligibility Credits.   Certain plans provide participants health benefits or insurance coverage during periods of unemployment. Under this type of plan, participants earn credit hours for health benefit or insurance coverage (accumulated eligibility credits) while employed that can be applied in the event of unemployment or other temporary layoffs. If such coverage is offered to participants, the plan should recognize an obligation for the amount expected to be paid for eligibility credits accumulated to date. For self-insured plans, the average cost of benefits per eligible participant would be applied to the accumulated eligibility credits to determine the obligation. For insured plans, the amount would be determined by applying current insurance premium rates to the accumulated eligibility credits. Whether a plan is insured or self-insured, the determination of the obligation for accumulated eligibility credits also should consider assumptions for mortality and expected employee turnover or other appropriate adjustments, and thus may require the use of an actuary.

The auditor should review and test the accrued obligation for adequacy and reasonableness. Such tests normally include comparison of employers' contributions with selected participant eligibility records, testing the arithmetical accuracy of the accumulated credits, and an overall review of the computation. Where these are actuarially determined amounts, the auditor ordinarily should consider the procedures normally applied in using the work of an actuary, including determining that the data used by the actuary (e.g., premium rate, number of eligible participants, average cost of benefits, accumulated eligibility credits) is accurate and that the actuary's assumptions are not unreasonable.

(vi) Postretirement Benefits.   Postretirement benefits are the largest part of a health and welfare plan's benefit obligation. Plans that provide benefits to retired employees and their dependents may be structured to provide benefits immediately upon termination of service or upon attainment of a specific age.

Plans that provide postretirement benefits must include an obligation for the present value of all future retirement benefits attributed to plan participant services rendered as of the measurement date, which is the end of the plan year or another date that is not more than three months prior to the plan year-end.[4] The calculation assumes that the plan will continue in effect and that all assumptions about future events will be fulfilled. The postretirement benefit obligation includes only the portion of retiree benefits that has already been earned by participants as of the measurement date.

Measurement of the postretirement benefit obligation for a health and welfare plan requires the use of explicit assumptions representing the best estimate of particular future events. The principal actuarial assumptions include the discount rate, the timing and amount of future benefit payments, salary progression rates, and the probability of payment (i.e., turnover, dependency status, mortality). Benefits covered by insurance contracts are excluded from the postretirement benefit obligation recorded by the plan. Chapter 20 discusses measurement of employers' postretirement health and welfare benefit obligations, including the assumptions used.

SOP 92-6 requires that the financial statements report the postretirement benefit obligation for:

* Current retirees, including their beneficiaries and covered dependents
* Active or terminated participants fully eligible to receive benefits
* Active participants not yet fully eligible to receive benefits

This information may be provided either in a separate statement or with other information in another financial statement. However, all the information should be located in one place.

Typically, the plan auditor will have performed procedures to test the reasonableness of the postretirement benefit information as part of the audit of the employer. If so, the procedures need not be repeated in auditing the plan.[5] Chapter 20 describes procedures used to test accrued pension costs and notes that procedures for postretirement health care benefit costs are similar.

SFAS No. 106 does not require participating employers of a multiemployer plan to recognize a postretirement benefit obligation. SOP 92-6, however, notes that this exception does not affect the accounting for the postretirement benefit obligation by multiemployer plans. Thus, the auditor of a multiemployer plan will need to test the reasonableness of the postretirement benefit information.

(vii) Nonenforcement Policy for Multiemployer Health and Welfare Plans.
Under ERISA, the DOL can reject a Form 5500 filing if it determines that there is a material qualification of the auditor's opinion. If the DOL rejects a filing, it may assess a penalty of up to $1,000 a day. Certain multiemployer health and welfare plans have questioned the usefulness of the postretirement benefit obligation to multiemployer plan trustees and participants in light of the administrative burdens and costs of compliance. They asked the DOL not to reject Forms 5500 for multiemployer

---

[4] If the measurement date is other than the plan's year-end date, paragraph 72 of SFAS No. 106 requires that the same measurement date be used consistently from year to year.

[5] Illustrative procedures for auditing postretirement benefits for a defined benefit plan are presented in Chapter 10 of Richard M. Steinberg, Ronald J. Murray, and Harold Dankner, *Pensions and Other Employee Benefits: A Financial Reporting and ERISA Compliance Guide*, 4th ed. (New York: John Wiley & Sons, 1993).

health and welfare plans that did not comply with the provisions of SOP 92-6. (SOP 92-6 had a delayed effective date for multiemployer plans.)

In March 1997, the DOL announced that it was considering whether to adopt a nonenforcement policy with respect to SOP 92-6 for multiemployer health and welfare plans. Pending its decision, the DOL decided it would not reject filings for 1996 and 1997 solely because the auditor expressed an adverse or a qualified opinion on the financial statements due to a failure to account for and report postretirement benefit obligations in accordance with the provisions of SOP 92-6.

34.4   AUDITING OTHER FINANCIAL STATEMENT DISCLOSURES

(a)   Requirements

Financial statement disclosures for employee benefit plans are specified in SFAS No. 35, SOP 92-6, and the audit guide. In addition to the disclosures already described, the following disclosures are required:

- Brief general description of the plan agreement, including vesting and benefit provisions.

- Description of significant plan amendments adopted during the year ending on the latest benefit information date; if amendments were adopted between the latest benefit information date and the date of the financial statements, disclosure should be made that the actuarial present value of accumulated plan benefits does not reflect those amendments.

- For pension plans, a brief description of the priority of participants' claims to the assets of the plan on plan termination and, for plans subject to ERISA, benefits guaranteed by the Pension Benefit Guaranty Corporation (PBGC), including a discussion of the application of the PBGC guarantee to any recent plan amendments.

- Funding policy and any changes in such policy; if a plan is contributory, the method of determining participants' contributions should be disclosed. Noncash contributions, if any, by the employer should be described. Plans subject to ERISA should disclose whether the minimum funding requirements of ERISA have been met. If a minimum funding waiver has been granted by the IRS or if a request for a waiver is pending, that should be disclosed.

- The federal income tax status of the plan, if a favorable letter of determination has not been obtained or maintained.

- Plan administrative expenses; if significant plan administrative costs are absorbed by the employer, that fact should be disclosed.

- Significant transactions in which the plan is involved jointly with the plan sponsor, the employer, or employee organizations.

- Unusual or infrequent events or transactions occurring after the latest benefit information date but before issuance of the financial statements that might significantly affect the usefulness of the financial statements in assessing the plan's present and future ability to pay benefits; for example, a plan amendment adopted after the latest benefit information date that significantly increased future benefits attributable to participants' services rendered before that date. If they are reasonably determinable, the effects of such events or transactions should be disclosed; if such effects are not quantified, an explanation of why they are not reasonably determinable should be provided.

- If the plan provides for participant-directed investment programs (e.g., equity, debt, or employer securities), information about the net assets and significant components of the changes in net assets for each investment fund option. (AICPA Practice Bulletin 12, which has been incorporated into the guide, provides detailed guidance with respect to this requirement.)

Notes to employee benefit plan financial statements prepared pursuant to ERISA reporting and disclosure requirements include some of the disclosures required by SFAS No. 35, SOP 92-6, and the audit guide, as well as additional ones. Disclosures required by ERISA but not explicitly by the professional accounting literature are:

- Description of material lease commitments and other commitments and contingent liabilities
- Description of any agreements and transactions with persons known to be parties in interest
- Information concerning whether a tax ruling or determination letter has been obtained
- Any other information required for a fair presentation

Compliance with ERISA calls for a description of any variances between GAAP and the principles followed in the financial statements, and an explanation of any differences between the financial statements and amounts reported on Form 5500.

The disclosure requirements described for financial statements prepared pursuant to ERISA reporting and disclosure requirements apply to both defined contribution and defined benefit plans. Disclosures prescribed by professional literature relating to the actuarial present value of accumulated plan benefits, minimum funding requirements, and PBGC plan termination provisions, however, do not apply to defined contribution plans.

(b) Auditing Procedures

The following is a summary, and is not all-inclusive, of the auditing procedures applicable to other financial statement disclosures for employee benefit plans. Several of these procedures may be performed in conjunction with the audit of the sponsoring employer; if so, they need not be repeated at the plan level.

- Read and abstract key portions (employee coverage or eligibility, vesting, benefit determination, priority of claims, and so on) of the plan document, noting changes or amendments in the plan. This should be performed annually in conjunction with the actuary's report, which normally summarizes changes in the plan.
- Read the minutes of meetings of the board of trustees or administrative committee for amendments adopted, funding policy changes, or other matters affecting the plan.

- Request an analysis (generally in the actuary's report) of the plan's compliance with minimum funding requirements.

- For pension plans, examine the tax determination letter and inquire about changes therein. Inquire about the existence of (a) significant plan transactions with the employer, (b) parties-in-interest transactions, and (c) material lease or other commitments.

34.5 OTHER AUDIT CONSIDERATIONS

(a) Subsequent Events

In common with audits of other entities, the auditor of an employee benefit plan should consider events subsequent to the date of the financial statements through the date of the auditor's report, to determine whether adjustment of or disclosure in the financial statements is required. Auditing procedures might include, but are not necessarily limited to, those shown in Figure 34.7, which is based on the audit guide. Since investments normally represent the major part of a plan's assets, the auditor should be alert for material changes in the market value of securities subsequent to the financial statement date, particularly if the opinion is dated near the end of the filing period permitted by ERISA. If the auditor becomes aware of any such material changes, consideration should be given to whether there is adequate disclosure in the financial statements. (AU Sections 560.05 and 560.07 contain further guidance.)

(b) Audit Requirements Relating to ERISA

Certain requirements of ERISA result in the modification of auditing procedures or the performance of additional procedures. Those features fall into three principal cat-

Figure 34.7   Suggested Auditing Procedures in the Subsequent Period

---

Review minutes of board of trustees' or administrative committee meetings held through the completion of field work.

If available, obtain interim financial statements of the plan for a period subsequent to the audit date, compare with the financial statements being audited, and investigate unusual fluctuations.

Inquire of and discuss with the plan administrator:

- Abnormal disposal or purchase of investments since year-end
- Amendments to plan and trust instruments and to insurance contracts
- Unusual terminations of participants, such as terminations arising from sale of a division or layoffs
- Changes in commitments or contingent liabilities of the plan

If there is a significant period of time between the date of the response of the plan's legal counsel and the date of completion of field work, obtain supplemental legal representations.

egories: plan compliance with ERISA, transactions prohibited by ERISA, and reporting and disclosure requirements of ERISA.

(i) Plan Compliance with ERISA.   The auditor should consider whether the terms of the plan relating to participation, vesting, joint and survivorship coverage, and other provisions comply with pertinent ERISA requirements. Normally, the auditor can use one of two approaches in this connection. If it can be determined that the plan is a qualified plan under the provisions of the Internal Revenue Code, the auditor may conclude that the plan complies with the provisions of ERISA. Ordinarily, the auditor may gain reasonable assurance that a plan is qualified under the Code by examining the tax qualification letter issued by the IRS covering the current plan provisions. Alternatively, the auditor can obtain satisfaction that the plan's provisions comply with ERISA by obtaining a letter from the plan's legal counsel stating that the plan's provisions comply with either ERISA or the Code. If the auditor of the plan also audits the financial statements of the employer, this work may be done in connection with the audit of the employer and need not be duplicated.

The above procedures for determining plan compliance with ERISA would be appropriate for the first year in which a plan has been amended or for a new plan. The plan qualification provisions of the Code have been subject to frequent change, and corresponding changes have been made to ERISA. Accordingly, plans have been required to be amended to conform to these changes, and qualification letters are usually obtained regarding the plan amendments, when the amendments are significant. In theory, if there are no plan amendments thereafter, little or no additional work related to plan compliance would be needed in subsequent years. In practice, however, a tax qualification letter or other evidence of plan compliance tends to carry less weight with the passage of time, since the IRS is concerned not only with the plan provisions themselves, but also with the manner in which the plan operates in accordance with those provisions. Therefore, in subsequent years, the auditor should be alert to changes in the manner in which plan provisions are applied.

(ii) Transactions Prohibited by ERISA.   Transactions prohibited by ERISA should be reported on a schedule of parties-in-interest transactions. That schedule need not include any transactions exempted from the prohibited transaction rules, but the notes to the financial statements should include a description of all agreements and transactions with parties in interest. AU Section 334 and SFAS No. 57 (Accounting Standards Section R36) offer useful guidance in this regard; however, the ERISA definition of parties in interest is somewhat broader than the definition of related parties in those pronouncements.

Prohibited transactions could give rise to significant receivables because a plan fiduciary is liable for losses to the plan resulting from a breach of fiduciary duties and for restoring to the plan profits made by the fiduciary through the use of the plan's assets. Accordingly, the auditor should apply procedures to ascertain whether there has been a breach of fiduciary duties or prohibited transactions have occurred and, if so, whether a receivable or other disclosure should be reflected in the financial statements. Procedures for accomplishing this include:

- Inquiring whether any activities or transactions that might be prohibited have occurred

- Obtaining from the plan administrator a list of all parties in interest (to use as a reference point during the audit), reviewing the administrator's procedures for identifying parties in interest, and examining related documentation to determine whether the list appears to be complete
- Ascertaining whether any prohibited transactions have been disclosed as a result of past IRS or other governmental examinations

Because the auditor frequently, as a result of the ordinary audit work, is familiar with significant transactions that might be prohibited, few, if any, additional procedures should be necessary in most instances. The audit guide contains guidance on the auditor's responsibility if he or she concludes that the plan has entered into a prohibited transaction.

(iii) Reporting and Disclosure Requirements of ERISA.   As part of the audit, the auditor usually considers whether the financial statements and supplementary schedules have been prepared in conformity with ERISA and the related DOL reporting and disclosure regulations. The auditor should read the financial information contained in the plan's Form 5500 and consider whether such information is materially inconsistent with information in the financial statements. The auditor need not be unduly concerned, however, about whether the other reporting and disclosure requirements of ERISA have been complied with, because penalties imposed for noncompliance are not likely to have an impact on the plan. Nonetheless, the auditor should be alert to instances of noncompliance with respect to such items so as to be in a position to advise plan management of the need to consider corrective action.

(iv) Supplemental Schedules.   The normal auditing procedures should be sufficient to permit the auditor to report on most of the information included in the supplemental schedules. The auditor may perform some additional procedures, however, with respect to certain schedules, such as the schedule of 5 percent reportable transactions.

(c) Other Considerations

(i) Bonding.   The auditor may inquire whether the plan maintains at least the required minimum amount of fidelity insurance in accordance with provisions of ERISA.

(ii) Transaction Approval.   The auditor should be aware of the collective bargaining agreement, declaration of trust, insurance contract, and other plan documents, and should be alert for any transactions that require the approval of the board of trustees (for a multiemployer plan) or administrative committee (for a single employer plan).

(iii) Potential Plan Termination.   When reading minutes of meetings of the board of trustees and administrative committee and performing other auditing procedures, the auditor should be alert for any evidence of a potential plan termination. In addition, the auditor may wish to inquire of the employer's management as to the possibility of a plan termination. If a plan termination is more than a remote possibility, the auditor should ensure that the situation is appropriately reflected or disclosed in the financial statements.

(iv) Letter of Representation and Legal Counsel Letters.   The auditor should obtain a letter of representation from management immediately before completing the field work, worded to fit the circumstances of the engagement. In addition to representations obtained in accordance with SAS No. 19, the letter normally should include representations related to compliance with ERISA, any potential plan termination, changes in plan provisions, parties-in-interest transactions, value of investments (including those stated at fair value as determined by the board of trustees or administrative committee), and other pertinent matters. The representation letter should be signed by officials of the plan, generally the plan administrator and the individual equivalent to the chief financial officer. If the sponsoring employer is the plan administrator, one or more officials responsible for administration of and accounting for the plan should sign the letter. In addition, the auditor should obtain a letter from the plan's legal counsel concerning litigation, claims, and assessments, in accordance with SAS No. 12 (AU Section 337).

34.6 AUDIT REPORTS

An auditor's report on plan financial statements is included for most plans as part of the annual report required to be filed under ERISA. This section discusses and illustrates standard reports and commonly encountered departures from standard reports.

(a) Standard Report

If the auditor has audited a plan's financial statements in accordance with generally accepted auditing standards and concludes that they have been prepared in conformity with GAAP, an unqualified report is appropriate. The audit guide contains illustrative auditors' reports covering various types of plans and various circumstances. An illustrative standard auditor's report covering defined benefit pension plan financial statements prepared in accordance with SFAS No. 35 is shown in Figure 34.8. In the illustration, it is assumed that the required information regarding the actuarial present value of accumulated plan benefits and the changes therein is presented in separate financial statements. Figure 34.8 assumes that the actuarial benefit information is presented as of the end of the plan year.

Under GAAP, if information regarding the actuarial present value of accumulated plan benefits is presented as of the beginning rather than the end of the year, prior-year statements of net assets available for benefits and of changes in net assets available for benefits are required. Further, under the alternative method of complying with ERISA's reporting and disclosure requirements, plans must present comparative statements of assets and liabilities (or net assets available for benefits). In that event, the auditor's report in Figure 34.8 would be modified.

(i) Reporting on Supplemental Schedules Required by ERISA.   Annual reports filed pursuant to ERISA are required to contain certain supplemental schedules that

Figure 34.8   Illustrative Unqualified Auditor's Report on a Defined Benefit Pension Plan Assuming End of Year Benefit Data

---

Independent Auditor's Report

We have audited the accompanying statements of net assets available for benefits and of accumulated plan benefits of XYZ Pension Plan as of December 31, 19X2 and 19X1, and the related statements of changes in net assets available for benefits and of changes in accumulated plan benefits for the year ended December 31, 19X2. These financial statements are the responsibility of the Plan's management. Our responsibility is to express an opinion on these financial statements based on our audit.

We conducted our audit in accordance with generally accepted auditing standards. Those standards require that we plan and perform the audit to obtain reasonable assurance about whether the financial statements are free of material misstatement. An audit includes examining, on a test basis, evidence supporting the amounts and disclosures in the financial statements. An audit also includes assessing the accounting principles used and significant estimates made by management, as well as evaluating the overall financial statement presentation. We believe that our audit provides a reasonable basis for our opinion.

In our opinion, the financial statements referred to above present fairly, in all material respects, the financial status of the Plan as of December 31, 19X2 and 19X1, and the changes in its financial status for the year ended December 31, 19X2 in conformity with generally accepted accounting principles.

Signature

City and State

Date

---

must be covered by the auditor's report. SAS No. 29, *Reporting on Information Accompanying the Basic Financial Statements in Auditor-Submitted Documents* (AU Section 551), provides reporting guidelines when the auditor submits to management or others a document that contains information in addition to the basic financial statements. In addition, the audit guide contains illustrations of report modifications that the auditor might consider necessary when the supplemental schedules do not contain all required information or contain information that is inaccurate or inconsistent with the financial statements.

(ii) Reporting Separate Investment Fund Information.   As noted earlier, required information on separate investment fund options may be presented on the face of the financial statements. In these circumstances, the auditor's standard report should include a fourth paragraph describing his or her responsibility with respect to that information. Figure 34.9 contains illustrative wording for such circumstances.

Figure 34.9   Report Wording for Use When Separate Investment Fund Information Is Presented on the Face of the Financial Statements

[Same first three paragraphs as the standard report]

Our audits were performed for the purpose of forming an opinion on the basic financial statements taken as a whole. The supplemental schedules of [*DOL required schedules*] are presented for the purpose of additional analysis and are not a required part of the basic financial statements but are supplementary information required by the Department for Labor's Rules and Regulations for Reporting and Disclosure under the Employee Retirement Income Security Act of 1974. The Fund Information in the [statement of net assets available for benefits and the] statement of changes in net assets available for benefits is presented for purposes of additional analysis rather than to present the [net assets available for plan benefits and] changes in net assets available for plan benefits of each fund. The supplemental schedules and Fund Information have been subjected to the auditing procedures applied in the audits of the basic financial statements and, in our opinion, are fairly stated in all material respects in relation to the basic financial statements taken as a whole.

Figure 34.10   Illustrative Auditor's Report—Audit Scope Restricted by Plan Administrator Regarding Information Certified by Bank or Insurance Company

Independent Auditor's Report

We were engaged to audit the financial statements and supplemental schedules of XYZ Pension Plan as of December 31, 19X2 and 19X1 and for the year ended December 31, 19X2, as listed in the accompanying index. These financial statements and schedules are the responsibility of the Plan's management.

As permitted by 29 CFR 2520.103–8 of the Department of Labor's Rules and Regulations for Reporting and Disclosure under the Employee Retirement Income Security Act of 1974, the plan administrator instructed us not to perform, and we did not perform, any auditing procedures with respect to the information summarized in Note X, which was certified by ABC Bank, the trustee of the Plan, except for comparing such information with the related information included in the financial statements and supplemental schedules. We have been informed by the plan administrator that the trustee holds the Plan's investment assets and executes investment transactions. The plan administrator has obtained a certification from the trustee as of and for the years ended December 31, 19X2 (and 19X1), that the information provided to the plan administrator by the trustee is complete and accurate.

Because of the significance of the information that we did not audit, we are unable to, and do not, express an opinion on the accompanying financial statements and schedules taken as a whole. The form and content of the information included in

(Continues)

Figure 34.10 *(Continued)*

the financial statements and schedules, other than that derived from the information certified by the trustee, have been audited by us in accordance with generally accepted auditing standards and, in our opinion, are presented in compliance with the Department of Labor's Rules and Regulations for Reporting and Disclosure under the Employee Retirement Income Security Act of 1974.

Signature

City and State

Date

(b) Departures from the Standard Report

(i) Limited-Scope Audit Pursuant to DOL Regulations. As discussed earlier, the auditor may be instructed by the plan administrator, as permitted under DOL reporting and disclosure regulations, to limit the scope of the audit with respect to investment information prepared and certified to by a qualified trustee or custodian. Such a scope limitation ordinarily would require the auditor to disclaim an opinion. The auditor's report in Figure 34.10 assumes that the plan administrator has restricted the audit scope in this way.

(ii) Scope Limitation Relating to Employer Records. SAS No. 79, paragraphs 22–24 (AU Sections 508.22–.24), provides guidance when the auditor is unable to examine employer records or to perform appropriate alternative auditing procedures, as discussed earlier in the chapter.

35

Auditing Engineering and Construction Companies

35.1 OVERVIEW OF THE INDUSTRY

The U.S. Standard Industrial Classification Code divides the construction industry into three main categories:

- *Building construction*—including single-family dwellings, apartment houses, some industrial plants, hospitals, office buildings, and warehouses
- *Nonbuilding construction*
  - Heavy construction—dams, large bridges, tunnels, refineries, and electric power plants
  - Highway and street construction
- *Specialty trade construction*—including plumbing, heating and air conditioning, painting, electrical work, masonry, and carpentry

Providers of engineering and architectural services are classified separately in the Standard Industrial Classification Code, but many of the economic and financial issues, as well as the accounting and the audit guidance, affecting the construction industry apply also to them. Accordingly, they are covered in this chapter.

The forms in which business is conducted in the engineering and construction (E&C) industry segments vary widely, from large-scale international corporations that perform a whole spectrum of services, including engineering, procurement, construction, management, and financing, to small, family-operated businesses. Although many companies engage in more than one type of activity, most develop an expertise in one in particular.

The E&C industry has become increasingly competitive as the number of large infrastructure projects has declined because of financing constraints imposed on various governmental agencies and other macroeconomic influences. Additionally, the increased use of fixed-price and turnkey contracts, which entail increased risks, has created an environment in which E&C contractors are compelled to reduce margins to unrealistic levels in order to gain new work. (In a turnkey contract, the contractor performs all, or nearly all, of the aspects of the project, including engineering, procurement, and construction, often for a single price. The owner has little involvement with day-to-day management of the project.) With fewer projects available and margins declining, many contractors have begun to compete in unfamiliar markets, resulting in an increase in the number of loss contracts and of bankruptcies.

The E&C industry is very sensitive to changes in economic conditions. During recessionary periods, construction budgets are generally the first to be cut back as resources are redirected to current operations. During those times, E&C companies are more likely to accept less-profitable, riskier contracts as a means of utilizing overhead and retaining experienced personnel. The impact of an economic downturn, however, is not immediately reflected in an E&C company's financial statements. The effect is postponed because contracts in process and extending over a period of years normally are completed during the downturn, providing revenues for the near future. However, as contracts in process near completion, new projects may not be added to the contractor's backlog at a rate that will sustain adequate funding levels to cover future costs. When this situation arises, E&C companies are generally in a better position than entities in other industries because they are able to react by reducing variable cost components. However, staff reductions can be detrimental over an extended period, as the loss of talented personnel may mean that the contractor will not be well positioned when economic conditions improve.

If an E&C company reaches a point where its backlog is insufficient to cover fixed costs, the company may sell assets, issue debt, or restructure equity. These actions also may affect its ability to bid on additional work. Also, project costs could be underestimated or potential cost savings overestimated in order to obtain contracts. This strategy could be deliberate in the hope of obtaining work and making up profits from change orders as the contract is performed. Unfortunately, such a strategy may become more costly because additional management time is necessary to negotiate such changes and the potential for disputes increases. Many E&C companies do not possess the systems and administrative expertise to negotiate significant change orders on a timely basis. Consequently, such changes may be disputed, and arbitration or litigation may become the only means of settling the disputes. Costs associated with change order activities, including the allocation of internal resources, may result in greater economic losses than gains from settlements. A company also may experience injury to its professional reputation from excessive change order activity, which may result in the loss of potential lucrative future projects.

Similar to the effect of a downturn, the effect of an economic recovery on the E&C industry generally lags that in other industries. The number and profitability of contracts, or lack thereof, included in an E&C company's backlog affect its performance for a time generally equivalent to the average contract life cycle.

Government regulations and policies have a significant effect on the operations, although generally not on the financial reporting requirements, of E&C companies. The industry is required to comply with local building codes and zoning ordinances and with regulations of several federal regulatory agencies, such as the Occupational Safety and Health Administration, the Equal Employment Opportunity Commission, and the Environmental Protection Agency. Constant changes in government regulations are the reason for the practice, common in the industry, of disclaiming responsibility, in contracts, for obtaining all government approvals, licenses, and permits required for a construction or design project. This responsibility must be borne by the owner of the project.

Lower interest rates beginning in 1993 initiated an upswing for the industry as the residential building market strengthened. Growth in the residential market, the liquidation of overvalued real estate assets by financial institutions, a trend toward real estate securitization, and the return of traditional lenders to the market led to an increase in commercial construction in the mid-1990s. Additional governmental regulation, some of which is the result of regional natural disasters, further increased the number of infrastructure projects. A move toward privatization of projects traditionally supported by governmental funds, including toll roads and bridges; deregulation of electrical power generation; and continuing environmental remediation efforts also have contributed to a recovery within the E&C industry.

Even with this resurgence, competition within the E&C industry remains high and margins are low. It is expected that activity will remain low by comparison with the past few decades. Higher salary, insurance, tax, and compliance costs continue to have a negative impact on margins. With the continuing increase in competition and high costs of domestic operations, many larger companies within the industry are exploring opportunities in foreign countries. The expansion into foreign countries by E&C

companies not accustomed to operating internationally presents significant financial and operating risks.

Some E&C companies also are gaining market share through mergers and acquisitions of smaller competitors or competitors with a defined market niche. This enables companies to pursue a strategy of comprehensive service, which may combine design, construction, financing, and procurement at a lower cost than could be obtained by contracting each function separately.

Almost all E&C companies are looking for ways to reduce costs and improve performance through programs such as total quality management and continuous process improvement or by outsourcing various aspects of administrative functions. Sharing risks and improving communications with their clients also have become a focus of many companies. Those companies have structured partnering agreements with their clients in an effort to avoid costly disputes and to become the preferred provider of E&C services.

35.2   ACCOUNTING FOR ENGINEERING AND CONSTRUCTION CONTRACTS

Accounting principles for the E&C industry are prescribed mainly in Accounting Research Bulletin (ARB) No. 45, *Long-Term Construction-Type Contracts* (Accounting Standards Section Co4); the AICPA audit and accounting guides, *Construction Contractors*, and *Audits of Federal Government Contractors*; and Statement of Position (SOP) 81-1, *Accounting for Performance of Construction-Type and Certain Production-Type Contracts*. The Financial Accounting Standards Board (FASB), in Statement of Financial Accounting Standards (SFAS) No. 56, paragraph 8 (Accounting Standards Section A06.112), has indicated that the specialized accounting principles in SOP 81-1 and the construction contractors guide have been designated as preferable for purposes of justifying a change in accounting principle for long-term construction-type contracts.

The primary focus for recognizing revenues, accumulating costs, and measuring income by companies in the E&C industry is the profit center, which is usually the individual contract. SOP 81-1 provides criteria to be used in determining the appropriate profit center, a process that sometimes is quite complex. In certain circumstances, if the criteria in SOP 81-1 are met, a group of contracts (known as combining) or a phase or segment of a single contract (known as segmenting) may be used as a profit center. The profit center can have a significant impact on the amount of profit and loss recorded in a period (discussed later). For the purposes of this chapter, the profit center will be a single contract.

There are two generally accepted methods of accounting for contract performance: the percentage-of-completion method and the completed-contract method. (The units-of-delivery method is a modification of the percentage-of-completion method.) Guidance for determining which method to use is contained in SOP 81-1 and is discussed in this section.

(a)   Percentage-of-Completion Method

Under this method, revenue and income are recognized based on actual performance under a contract for a given period. When the criteria for using it (discussed later) are present, recognizing revenue under the percentage-of-completion method is preferable because it better reflects the economic results of contract performance. It also better relates revenues to period costs and provides more useful information about the volume of a contractor's economic activity.

A key aspect of the percentage-of-completion method is determining how to measure progress toward completion. A number of methods are used to measure the extent of completion on a contract. Generally, they can be grouped into input measures (based on efforts devoted to a contract, like costs or hours of labor) and output measures (based on results achieved, like contract milestones or units produced). One commonly used input measure relates costs incurred to date to the estimated total cost to complete the contract and is referred to as the cost-to-cost method. The measure or measures adopted should be applied consistently to contracts with similar characteristics.

(b) Completed-Contract Method

Under the completed-contract method, revenues and costs are recognized when the contract is substantially completed. Practice varies with respect to determining when substantial completion has occurred. As a general rule, substantial completion is reached when the contractor's remaining costs and potential risks are insignificant. Factors to be considered in determining whether substantial completion has been achieved may include departure from the construction site, acceptance by the owner, and compliance with performance specifications. The specific criteria adopted should be used consistently for contracts with similar characteristics.

(c) Choosing the Preferable Alternative

The two methods of accounting for contract performance are not acceptable alternatives in the same circumstances. SOP 81-1 recommends using the percentage-of-completion method when:

- Reasonably dependable estimates can be made of the extent of progress toward completion and the amount of total contract revenues and costs
- There is a clear specification in the contract of the enforceable rights regarding goods and services to be provided, the price or its method of determination, and the method and terms of settlement
- There is the expectation that both parties can fulfill their contractual obligations

The completed-contract method is recommended only if:

- Financial position and results of operations under this method would not vary materially from those resulting from the use of the percentage-of-completion method (e.g., if the entity has primarily short-term contracts), or
- The percentage-of-completion method is inappropriate because "inherent hazards" beyond management's control make estimates of contract revenues and costs doubtful, or other criteria for using the percentage-of-completion method are not met

The SOP indicates that "inherent hazards" do not relate to doubtful estimates resulting from inadequate estimating procedures. Instead, those hazards relate to external factors or contract conditions that raise questions about contract estimates and about the ability of the contractor or owner to perform the contractual obligations. While inadequate estimating procedures may influence an entity's ability to prepare reasonably dependable estimates, the presumption is that contractors have the ability to make estimates that are sufficiently dependable to justify using the percentage-of-completion method of accounting. Persuasive evidence to the contrary is necessary to overcome that presumption. Regardless of the accounting method used, if an entity's estimation procedures are inadequate to produce reasonably dependable estimates, the auditor may need to qualify the opinion because of a scope limitation.

(d)   Provision for Anticipated Losses

Under either method of accounting, if at any time the estimated total cost exceeds the total contract price, indicating a loss on the contract, the entire loss ordinarily should be recognized. There are, however, some rare exceptions to this principle, such as in loss-type contracts that are, in substance, research and development arrangements. For example, a contract may be entered into with the intent of developing a prototype whose cost is to be shared by the contractor. If the prototype is successful, profitable contracts are expected to follow. The costs are appropriately treated as research and development costs, and thus should be expensed as incurred but should not be anticipated. In addition, SOP 81-1 provides criteria for combining related contracts with different profit margins in determining the need for a provision for losses. Provisions for losses should be shown separately as a liability or as a deduction from any related accumulated costs.

(e)   Capitalization of Interest Cost

Paragraph 9 of SFAS No. 34 (Accounting Standards Section I67.105a–b) requires capitalization of interest on assets that an entity constructs for its own use and assets intended for lease or sale that are constructed as "discrete projects." An asset being constructed by a contractor under a long-term contract qualifies as a discrete project, even though title to all materials and improvements acquired or constructed by the contractor generally rests with the owner. Thus, it is not appropriate to offset advance payments on one contract against costs of another or to apply the aggregate advance payments against the total accumulated costs on the balance sheet to determine the amount of interest to be capitalized. Instead, the determination should be made on an individual-contract basis.

Although SFAS No. 34 is applicable to construction contractors, capitalization of interest cost may not have a material effect on the financial statements because of the financing arrangements typical in the industry. Generally, a contractor's financing requirements are for working capital purposes, and working capital loans usually are tied to individual contract requirements and made for a short period (e.g., 30 to 60 days). In addition, the contractor often arranges for advance payments or for payments to vendors to be made only on receipt of billings from the owner, resulting in a small net asset balance.

The effects of not capitalizing interest are even less likely to be material when the percentage-of-completion method of accounting is followed. Under that method, income is recognized currently and thus may offset, in whole or in part, the effect of expensing interest currently. The effects are more likely to be material under the completed-contract method, since accumulated costs are carried in the balance sheet and income is not recognized until the project is completed. In determining whether capitalization of interest will have a material effect on the financial statements under the completed-contract method, the auditor also should consider the pattern of contract completion, since the effect on income is less likely to be material if the contractor completes a number of contracts annually.

(f) Deferred Tax Assets and Liabilities

The Tax Reform Act of 1986 and subsequent federal tax legislation have significantly narrowed the differences in accounting for E&C contracts for income tax purposes and financial accounting and reporting purposes under generally accepted accounting principles (GAAP). Substantially all long-term contracts must be accounted for under the percentage-of-completion method for federal income tax purposes. However, to the extent that there are differences between tax and GAAP accounting, they would be treated as temporary differences under SFAS No. 109, *Accounting for Income Taxes* (Accounting Standards Section I27). The deferred tax consequences of such differences must be appropriately measured and accounted for. Many E&C companies operate in multiple foreign jurisdictions and states and should assess the significance of deferred foreign, state, and local tax expenses.

Examples of sources of temporary differences between tax accounting and financial accounting and reporting unique to contractors include:

- For federal tax purposes, percentage of completion must be computed based on the following ratio: IRC 460 contract costs incurred through the end of the tax year divided by estimated total IRC 460 contract costs.

- Contract loss jobs are deferred for federal tax purposes.

- Special federal tax rules may exclude certain home builders from the required percentage-of-completion method of accounting. Other exemptions may apply to other residential contractors.

- A "look-back" interest recalculation on contracts completed during the year—the difference between the look-back interest receivable or payable for tax purposes through the contractor's year-end and the amount accrued by the contractor at year-end—may be necessary. [Under IRC Section 460(b), on completion of a contract, contractors are required to recalculate prior years' income using actual total contract price and contract costs. A contractor that over-reported contract income in a corporate tax return for a prior year is entitled to interest from the government on the resulting overpayment of tax. Conversely, a contractor that underreported contract income in a return for a prior year owes interest to the government on the underpayment of tax.]

Contractors, in common with entities in other industries, need to assess both positive and negative evidence to form a conclusion as to the realizability of deferred tax assets that may arise from temporary differences and the need for a valuation allowance.

Examples of negative evidence that contractors may consider are:

- Cumulative losses and losses on individual contracts
- Tax benefits expiring unused (net operating losses, capital losses, and tax credits)
- Losses expected to be incurred in the near future
- Brief carryforward/carryback periods

Examples of positive evidence that contractors may consider are:

- Profitable existing contracts
- Backlog of profitable contracts
- Strong earnings history
- Existence of appreciated property that can be sold

(g) Financial Statement Presentation

Contractors use either a classified or an unclassified balance sheet. The construction contractors guide states that classified balance sheets are preferable for entities with operating cycles of one year or less and that unclassified balance sheets are preferable if the operating cycle exceeds one year. The guide presents guidelines both for statement presentation in accordance with those alternatives and for appropriate disclosures. Most contractors present classified balance sheets and commonly consider the assets and liabilities arising from long-term contract activities as current, even though the operating cycle of such contracts may extend over several years.

35.3 ENGINEERING AND CONSTRUCTION CONTRACTS, INTERNAL CONTROL, AND TESTS OF CONTROLS

The significant cycles in an E&C company usually include contract revenues, contract costs (and related cycles), and contract evaluation and control, including estimating and bidding.

(a) Types of Contracts

The contract is the key document in E&C companies. A construction contract is usually extensive and contains all the technical, legal, and financial details associated with a project. An engineering contract may be similar or may be more conceptual in nature. Engineering contracts also may be in a format that merely describes the capabilities and experience of the professionals committed to the project and their respective billing rates.

As presented in the construction contractors guide, there are four basic types of contracts:

- *A fixed-price (lump-sum) contract* provides for a single price for the total amount of work to be performed on a project.

- *A unit-price contract* provides that a contractor will perform a specific project at a fixed price per unit of output.

- *A cost-plus contract* (referred to in the guide as a "cost-type" contract) provides for reimbursement of allowable or otherwise defined costs incurred, plus a fee for the contractor's services. Usually, the contract requires only that the contractor's best efforts be used to accomplish the scope of the work. Cost-plus contracts occur in a variety of forms; often they contain terms specifying reimbursable costs, overhead recovery percentages, and fees. Fees may be fixed or based on a percentage of reimbursable costs.

- *A time-and-materials contract* is similar to a cost-plus contract and generally provides for payments to the contractor on the basis of direct labor hours at fixed hourly rates (the rates cover the cost of indirect labor and indirect expenses, and profit) and cost of materials or other specified costs.

The guide notes that "all types of contracts may be modified by target penalties and incentives relating to factors such as completion dates, plant capacity on completion of the project, and underruns and overruns of estimated costs." Under cost-type contracts with the federal government, statutory limitations have been imposed on fees negotiated at the outset of the contract. In addition, the federal government has significant contractual rights not generally found in contracts between commercial enterprises. Among them is the right to renegotiate the aggregate annual profits earned from contracts with specified federal departments and agencies.

Many factors influence the type of contract that is negotiated. Risk is the primary consideration addressed in negotiating a contract; other factors that influence the terms of the contract are the nature of the project, techniques to be used, the need for specialized equipment or specific knowledge, industry practice, method of financing, pricing practice, and billing terms.

In conjunction with assessing the type of contract to negotiate, the E&C company must estimate the total cost of the project. The overall strategy for performing the contract must be considered, including, but not limited to, availability of materials, labor, and equipment; weather; financing and subcontracting; competition; and provisions for profit and risk. Although the physical variables may not be present for contracts that are strictly engineering in nature, many of the same issues must be considered for those contracts as well. Cost estimates should be prepared in detail; all costs for which the contractor has responsibility or risk should be included. The preparation of the estimate should be systematized, with detailed written systems and procedures and requirements for review and approval by appropriate parties. The more disciplines involved (e.g., engineers, architects, attorneys, insurance and tax experts, and procurement specialists), the more likely that all items will be evaluated properly.

(b) Revenue Cycle

The auditor should be concerned with the amount and timing of revenue based on accurate and timely job forecasts. The method of revenue recognition should conform to GAAP and be consistent with prior years.

To meet those key control objectives in the revenue cycle, E&C companies generally establish controls over the following activities:

- Documenting total estimated contract revenues
- Issuing, approving, and recording change orders, claims, and back charges
- Identifying jobs in loss positions
- Recognizing changes in contract terms and the impact of penalty provisions
- Segregating recoverable and nonrecoverable costs, especially on cost-plus and time-and-materials contracts
- Computing and reviewing forecasts used in estimating extent of completion and costs to complete
- Preparing and approving billings based on job forecasts
- Recording job revenues and billings

If the auditor determines that evidence of the effectiveness of those controls is likely to be available and efficient to obtain, he or she generally will plan to perform tests of controls as a basis for reducing substantive tests. The tests of controls will consist of inquiry, observation, examination of evidence, and, if appropriate, reperformance of the contractor's controls.

(c) Job-Cost and Related Cycles

Job or contract costs are an accumulation of purchases, internal cost allocations for equipment and overhead, payroll costs, and possibly material costs assigned from inventory. Some auditors treat these different costs as different transaction classes in the job-cost cycle. The most common transaction classes are:

- Vendor purchases and payments
- Subcontractor payments
- Payroll
- Internal allocation of equipment costs
- Indirect cost allocations

Generally, the different types of costs are accumulated from various journals into what is commonly referred to as the job-cost report. Total costs in the job-cost report at any time reconcile to the general ledger; the job-cost report is also equal to the aggregate of costs incurred for each separate contract. Within the contract the costs are further subdivided by the type of work performed and the project phase. For example, the job-cost report on a building contract might show total job costs of $250,000, part of which would be recorded under the description "concrete work on the foundation." By segregating those costs, contractors can determine if they are over or under budget on a particular segment of a contract, and this helps in preparing accurate job forecasts. Similar segregation is necessary for engineering projects where certain tasks may require different levels of knowledge and professional expertise, or may be associated with specific contract revenue amounts.

Another reason for segregating job costs is that some may be recoverable under a contract. Certain costs may be for additional work performed at the owner's request or may result from specification alterations and may serve as a basis for a claim or change order. In such cases, the auditor is concerned with proper accounting for the related revenues, including the timing of revenue recognition.

Controls are necessary to ensure that all job costs incurred are recognized in the proper period. Procedures also are needed to ensure that subsidiary cost records agree with the control accounts.

Key controls for vendor purchases and subcontracting costs include:

- Authorization of purchases, supported by purchase orders. (Bids generally are obtained for major purchases.)

- Approval of vendor invoices by job site or project personnel to ensure that goods or services have been received; comparing invoices with quantities received and purchase order prices.

- Coding of invoices by personnel familiar with the job. (Many companies indicate job-cost codes on the purchase order to avoid miscoding.) Recoverable and non-recoverable costs usually are assigned different account codes in the job-cost report.

- Comparing subcontractor invoices with the subcontract for terms, retentions, prices, and related data. Project personnel should review and approve the percentage of completion or billing milestone stated on subcontractor invoices, so that billings are made in accordance with work performance.

- Requiring subcontractors to submit performance bonds. Lien waivers normally are obtained from subcontractors on final payment.

- Recording anticipated costs of materials used based on reasonable estimates if vendor invoices have not been received at the end of an accounting period; review of the accrual by supervisory personnel. (Purchases of materials at the end of an accounting period that have not been used are considered inventory.)

- Approval of back charges, claims, and additional work before recording and payment.

Controls related to other parts of the job-cost cycle include:

- Proper accumulation and recording of payroll costs in the correct cost codes in the job-cost report.

- Maintaining records of equipment on the job. Charges to the job generally are made monthly based on those records and the contractor's rates for company-owned equipment.

- Periodic reviews of equipment rental rates to ensure that they reflect actual equipment costs. On cost-plus contracts, the rates are based on contract specifications.

- Recording materials taken from inventory (such as gravel used by a paving contractor) based on inventory cost records.

- Proper calculation of overhead cost allocations, based on rates that are updated and approved periodically.

Job-cost cycle controls often are tested as a basis for restricting substantive tests. This strategy allows the auditor to perform a significant amount of the work at an interim date and determine early in the audit whether the job-cost report can be used for testing job forecasts, whether cutoff problems exist that may require extensive payable searches or other substantive tests, and whether detailed records are being maintained and agreed to the general ledger. The objectives of tests of controls in the job-cost cycle do not differ from those in the purchasing cycles of manufacturing entities.

(d) Contract Evaluation and Control, and Costs to Complete

Contractors constantly monitor projects in process to ascertain the percentage of completion for billing and revenue recognition purposes and to determine whether the projects are over or under budget. Cost overruns might indicate significant problems requiring immediate resolution to avoid losses, large cash outlays, and potential litigation. Constant monitoring also allows the contractor to evaluate its staff and obtain data that may be useful in future bidding, estimating, and project control.

(i) Estimating and Bidding. The beginning stage of every contract is the estimating process and submitting a bid based on project specifications from the owner. A lack of controls over these activities can result in unprofitable contracts or inaccurate estimates of percentage of completion, leading to possible misstatements of the financial statements.

The contractor's controls usually include recalculating the clerical accuracy of estimates and reviewing bids to determine that they cover all contract specifications. Bids are broken down by contract area (e.g., concrete work, plumbing, and electrical) to permit later budget analysis, project administration, and documentation of claims.

Bids obtained from vendors or subcontractors generally are documented. Requiring performance bonds on subcontractors ensures performance of subcontracts. Unit costs used in bidding are obtained from recent job-cost records or current price quotations. Bids are approved by an appropriate official before they are submitted, especially on low-margin jobs and jobs where profit margins are expected to change. Finally, the contractor evaluates successful as well as unsuccessful bids to determine whether they were reasonable and competitive. In assessing those controls, the auditor should consider testing the documentation of project bids, the comparison of bids with actual results on completed jobs (to provide an indication of the contractor's estimating results and profit margins), and the bid review and approval process.

(ii) Job Forecasts. Controls generally exist to ensure that forecasts are reasonable, timely, and based on an acceptable and consistent method, such as cost to cost, efforts expended, or units of work performed. In larger companies, a separate forecasting department may evaluate projects, either at the job site, in a regional office, or in the home office. In smaller companies, the field project manager or even the company president or owner may do the forecasting.

In reviewing contracts, management evaluates each phase or major component of the project. Costs incurred to date are compared with budgeted amounts for each contract phase, and the job forecast is updated based on variances. The following are common controls over forecasting:

- Reviewing records of open purchase orders and commitments (to ensure that all remaining major costs are considered)
- Comparing actual costs with the final budget that was prepared from the bid
- Examining correspondence from the field staff and the project's owner. Field staff should submit progress reports to the forecasting department periodically if the two departments are separate
- Reviewing changes in contract terms, prices, claims, and penalties
- Approving forecasts by appropriate officials
- Updating forecasts on a timely basis
- Reviewing forecasts to determine that they are based on actual costs incurred or efforts expended to date
- Reviewing comparisons of costs to date with budgeted amounts and noting whether variances are explained and properly reflected in the forecasts
- Reviewing the reporting of quantities of physical work performed to ensure that actual unit costs incurred are accurate and that forecasted unit costs for remaining work are appropriate

(e) Other Controls

In addition to the previously mentioned cycles, the contractor should have controls over major equipment items, claims, change orders, accounting for joint ventures, and regional office or job site accounting. With the exception of job site accounting, the auditor seldom performs tests of controls in those areas; instead, substantive tests usually are performed.

(i) Regional Office or Job Site Accounting.   The contractor's internal control may be centralized in the home office or decentralized and located at regional offices or the various job sites. If the contractor uses regional office or job site accounting, the auditor should be concerned with and assess controls over significant account balances. If controls in the previously mentioned cycles are decentralized, the auditor should consider each location as a separate company or division. As discussed later, only controls over transactions that could have a material impact on the financial statements would be considered for testing.

Often the job site staff may be small and temporary, and segregation of duties, especially over cash, may be lacking. Similarly, regional office staff may be small or unsophisticated. As a result, management may consider using internal auditors to review accounting records maintained by regional offices or job site offices. It is a good practice to have internal auditors or home office personnel distribute payroll checks periodically. Usually, an official who does not control and reconcile the cash accounts is designated to approve purchases and disbursements, based on proper documentation.

Cash receipts from contract billings are directed either to the home office or into a regional or job site account maintained at a zero balance. Lockboxes or automatic transfer accounts may be utilized for that account. This method of cash management allows the company optimum utilization of its cash while reducing the opportunities for personnel at locations outside of the home office to manipulate liquid assets.

(ii) Job Site Visits. Job site visits are not required in all circumstances, but they can be helpful to the auditor in understanding a contractor's operations. In addition, such visits can provide invaluable firsthand information about the physical status of projects and operational problems. Job site visits usually are necessary when the auditor intends to assess control risk at the site at low or when the related accounts cannot be substantiated by other procedures.

While the level of accounting functions (and related controls) varies depending on the size of the project, one objective of a site visit, regardless of the size of the project, is obtaining information and supporting documentation to evaluate the reasonableness of the progress of the project to date. The auditor may perform such procedures as:

- Identifying uninstalled materials that should be excluded when measuring progress toward completion, and noting the physical security over such materials

- Discussing with the contractor's personnel who are familiar with the contract, the status of labor hours incurred to date and estimates to complete, including evaluating those estimates by observing the physical progress of the project (if the project is complex, such evaluations may be beyond the auditor's capabilities, and he or she should consider engaging the services of a specialist)

- Inspecting contractor-owned or rented equipment

- Discussing with the contractor's personnel who are familiar with the project, other information required to evaluate the project's status or that may affect the estimated total gross margin (such as problems encountered or operational inefficiencies)

35.4 RISK ASSESSMENT AND AUDIT STRATEGY

In auditing commercial entities, the auditor usually emphasizes procedures directed at the reasonableness of the opening and closing balance sheets. While procedures also are performed directly on income statement accounts, usually such procedures are limited. In the audit of a contractor's financial statements, however, the auditor's primary concern is ascertaining the reasonableness of the estimated total gross margin of each contract and the recognition and measurement of gross margin for the period. High inherent risk often is associated with management's judgments underlying estimates that affect not only the amount and timing of revenue and expense, but also the resultant balances in the various asset and liability accounts. In auditing the financial statements, the auditor should keep in mind how contract accounting affects key relationships between accounts. For example, depending on the accounting method used, the measurement of progress toward completion can affect the determination of revenues, cost of revenues, accounts receivable, unbilled receivables, retentions receivable, and inventory.

Another difference between the audit of a typical commercial entity and that of a contractor is the nature of audit evidence. In the audit of a commercial entity, evidence obtained to support management's assertions in the financial statements is typically factual. For example, revenues may be supported by shipping documents like bills of lading; cost of sales may be supported by suppliers' invoices. Such evidence may require limited evaluation on the part of the auditor.

In the audit of a contractor, the evidence that supports financial statement assertions is more varied and usually requires greater judgment on the part of the auditor. For example, to audit earned revenues and the cost of such revenues, the auditor should review the estimates of progress toward completion and estimated gross profit, both of which require judgments to determine that income recognized during the period under audit has been calculated properly based on total projected gross profit for the contract at completion and on the work performed to date. Furthermore, judgment is required to evaluate whether the method utilized to measure progress produces reliable and meaningful measurements of the work performed to date.

If a project is evaluated at year-end and an incorrect percentage of completion is determined, it can have a significant impact on revenue recognized in the financial statements for both the current and subsequent years. In addition, contracts with potential losses and cash flow or other problems may not be identified. Therefore, project evaluation and control is a significant risk area for the auditor.

The auditor should consider such additional risk factors as the reasonableness of projected completion dates and related risks of incurring penalties for liquidated damages or overruns in projected job overhead costs. The auditor also should consider the status of relations with the owner and the potential for disputes over whether unanticipated work performed should be considered as an unpriced change order or a claim.

One of the most common errors of auditor judgment is spending numerous hours testing job costs to date and then accepting blindly (or with little scrutiny) the percentage of completion (based on estimated costs to complete) used by the contractor in recognizing revenue. From an audit risk standpoint, procedures to gain assurance about percentage of completion can be as important as job-cost testing.

In comparison, the audit of an engineering service provider is driven by the types of agreements entered into by the entity. For example, services may be contracted for on an hourly basis. In this case, the relationship between revenue and time expended is direct, and minimal judgment is required in evaluating evidence. Engineering companies may contract in a manner similar to construction contractors, accepting lump-sum, unit-price, guaranteed maximum price, and other types of contracts. Generally, computer software systems employed by engineering companies calculate revenues based on a multiplier applied to direct labor hours. This situation accentuates the need for the auditor to understand the nature of the contracts involved. The auditor also needs to ensure that if the company recognizes revenues on a percentage-of-completion basis, the systems-derived revenue is recognized on that basis and any loss projects are recognized in the appropriate period.

In developing the audit strategy, the auditor may determine that evidence of the effectiveness of controls that affect significant account balances is available and that it would be efficient to obtain it. The auditor should consider testing those controls if doing so would be more efficient than performing substantive tests. For example, it may be more efficient to test controls over accumulating job costs to date than to perform substantive tests by examining numerous invoices and payrolls. On the other hand, the revenue cycle usually lends itself to the use of substantive tests because contract prices, billings, current and retention receivables, and special terms can be confirmed easily.

In smaller companies where there are few open contracts at year-end, the auditor may find it efficient to substantiate job forecasts. If there are numerous large contracts open, the auditor may choose to test controls in the forecasting cycle to determine if the forecasts are reliable for determining the percentage of completion at year-end and the possibility of loss contracts. If the auditor's tests indicate that the contractor's controls over project forecasting are effective and result in accurate forecasts, it should be possible to limit substantive testing, perhaps to comparing the percentage of completion (and related estimate of costs to complete) used in revenue forecasts with the most recently approved forecast.

Certain projects are so large that many of the controls are exercised at the job site rather than at the contractor's headquarters, as described earlier. In those cases, job site visits may be a necessary element of the planning process, and many key auditing procedures may have to be performed at the site. On medium-sized projects, only certain aspects of internal control may be located at the job site. Transactions such as direct labor and miscellaneous disbursements may be processed at the construction site, while material purchases may originate from the contractor's headquarters. Small projects may have few or no controls exercised at the site. Control activities typically performed at the job site include preparing and approving time sheets; payment subsequently is made at the contractor's headquarters.

While construction contractors typically have operated on a centralized basis with temporary job site offices established at project locations, engineering service providers tend to operate on a decentralized regional basis from a series of permanent satellite offices. Regional office visits to engineering company locations may be necessary to ensure that appropriate controls are in place and operating effectively.

In determining which job sites or offices to visit and when, the auditor should consider the usual risk and materiality factors. Job site and office visits should be planned well in advance. Since visits may entail travel to a remote location, the auditor should arrange for the appropriate contractor personnel to be present and should ensure that any necessary accounting or other information (if not available at the site) is gathered and brought to the site. Similarly, the auditor should ensure, before leaving the site, that all necessary procedures have been performed and the required documentation has been gathered.

35.5 SUBSTANTIVE TESTS

The amount and timing of income to be recognized on contracts depend primarily on the methods and bases used to account for the contracts. Thus, to form a conclusion on the reasonableness of income to be recognized, the auditor should first evaluate the method of accounting for each contract, using the previously discussed criteria for the percentage-of-completion and completed-contract methods, and determine whether it is appropriate.

Next, the auditor considers the revenues and costs associated with each contract. Based on information about total contract revenues and costs, the auditor should evaluate management's determination of the amount of income to be recognized (for contracts accounted for under the percentage-of-completion method) or the amount of loss to be recognized (for both completed-contract and percentage-of-completion methods). As discussed earlier, the critical factor in that determination is the method used to measure the level of contract completion.

To evaluate the method used to determine the level of completion, the auditor should consider obtaining and reviewing documentation of contract revenues and estimates of costs, and the extent of progress toward completion for a sample of contracts, and consulting, if necessary, with contract managers and production personnel and with engineers, architects, and other specialists. An excellent audit tool for reviewing and evaluating contract revenues and costs is a summary of contract data, as presented in Figures 35.1 and 35.2 (reproduced from the AICPA audit and accounting guide, *Construction Contractors*). This summary provides an overview of the status of the contracts, permits the auditor to analyze the relationship between costs and revenue by individual contract, and highlights areas where adjustments may be required. Figure 35.3 summarizes many of the substantive tests appropriate for evaluating the timing and amount of income recognized during the period and for substantiating the related balance sheet accounts.

(a)   Contract Revenue

Estimating contract revenue can be a complex process. Although the estimate is based largely on the terms of the contract, numerous factors subject to a variety of uncertainties must be considered throughout the life of a contract. The estimates are made for the purpose of recognizing revenue in the appropriate period under the percentage-of-completion method of accounting, and to determine whether a loss has been incurred under both the completed-contract and percentage-of-completion methods.

The principal factors the auditor considers in reviewing the contractor's estimate of total contract revenue are original contract price, change orders, claims, contract options, and additions. Those factors, together with related substantive tests, are discussed in this section.

(i) Original Contract Price.   The original contract price is the total amount expected to be realized from the contract. This amount may be fixed or variable, depending on the type of contract. Fixed-price and unit-price contracts usually contain a stated contract price for a defined amount of work; however, they also may have provisions for adjustments to the stated price. Typical adjustments are escalation clauses (changes based on prescribed economic indices); bonus or penalty adjustments associated with target cost, completion dates, or performance levels; and price redetermination based on periodic or retroactive assessments of target cost or performance levels.

The auditor should obtain a summary of the key contract provisions affecting revenues, along with management's current assessment of the amounts associated with price adjustments. The original stated contract price can be substantiated by comparing the data with the signed contract or by direct confirmation with the owner; escalation price adjustments can be recalculated using formulas set forth in the con-

Figure 35.1   XYZ Company, Inc.
Fixed-Price Contracts in Process
Summary of Original and Revised Contract Estimates
as of Balance Sheet Date

| Contract Identification | Original Contract Price | Original Estimate of Contract Costs | Original Estimate of Gross Profit | | Net Changes in Contract Price | Revised Contrast Price | Revised Estimate of Contract Costs | | | Revised Estimate of Gross Profit | | % of Completion Measured by |
			Amount	%			Costs to Date	Estimated Costs to Complete	Revised Total Costs	Amount	%	
	(1)	(2)	(2)	(2)	(3)		(4)	(5)				(6)
A	$100,000	$ 55,000	$45,000	45%	-0-	$100,000	$ 42,000	$ 18,000	$ 60,000	$ 40,000	40%	Cost to cost
B	130,000	110,000	20,000	15.4%	20,000	150,000	80,000	40,000	120,000	30,000	20%	Cu. yds. completed
C	175,000	125,000	50,000	28.6%	25,000	200,000	125,000	75,000	200,000	-0-	—	Labor hours
D	250,000	200,000	50,000	20%	150,000	400,000	270,000	330,000	600,000	(200,000)	—	Cost to cost

(1) Per original contract.
(2) Per original bid.
(3) Supported by change orders and/or claims meeting accounting criteria for inclusion.

(4) Per audit of contract costs.
(5) Per audit of estimated costs to complete.
(6) Reviewed for appropriateness and consistency.

Source: Reproduced from AICPA audit and accounting guide, *Construction Contractors* (1996), p. 70. Copyright © 1996 by the American Institute of Certified Public Accountants, Inc.

Figure 35.2 XYZ Company, Inc.
Fixed-Price Contracts in Process
Analysis of Contract Status as of Balance Sheet Date

	Per Contractor's Books and Records				Gross Profit to Date		Revised % Completed	Revised Earned Revenue to Date	Auditor's Adjustments		Adjusted Gross Profit					
									Revenue Adjustments	Provision for Projected Loss Adjustments	To Date		Prior Periods		Current Period	
Contract Identification	Contract Billings to Date	Costs Incurred to Date	% Completed	Revenue Earned to Date	Amount	%					Amount	%	Amount	%	Amount	%
	(1)	(2)	(3)	(4)			(5)	(6)	(7)	(7)	(8)	(8)	(9)	(9)	(8)	(8)
A	$ 80,000	$ 42,000	70%	$ 80,000	$38,000	47.5%	70%	$ 70,000	($ 10,000)(A)		$ 28,000	40%	$20,250	45%	$ 7,750	31%
B	82,500	80,000	65%	97,500	17,500	17.9%	67%	100,500	3,000 (B)		20,500	20%	8,500	18.9%	12,000	21.6%
C	150,000	125,000	55%	110,000	(15,000)	—	62.5%	125,000	15,000 (C)		-0-	—	28,600	28.6%	(28,600)	—
D	300,000	270,000	45%	300,000	30,000	10%	45%	180,000	(120,000)(A)	110,000(D)	(200,000)	—	—	—	(200,000)	—

(1) Per audit of contract billings.
(2) Per audit of contract costs.
(3) Management's estimate of completion.
(4) Per contract revenue accounts on books.
(5) Per auditor—based on review and analysis of costs, billings, management's estimate of completion, job-site visits, etc.
(6) Result of applying revised percentage of completion to revised contract price.
(7) Adjustments to be reviewed with and accepted by management.
(8) Should be compared with prior periods and with similar contracts.
(9) Per audit of prior periods.

(A) Adjustment necessary to reduce earned revenue and recognize excess billings.
(B) Adjustment necessary to increase recorded earned revenue and recognize unbilled revenue.
(C) Adjustment necessary to increase recorded earned revenue and reduce recorded excess billings in order to reflect projected "break-even" on contract. Remaining revenue ($75,000) now equals estimated costs to complete.
(D) Adjustment necessary to provide for balance of the total projected loss on contract. Remaining revenue ($220,000) now equals estimated costs to complete ($330,000) less provision for projected loss ($110,000).

Source: Reproduced from AICPA audit and accounting guide, Construction Contractors (1996), p. 71. Copyright © 1996 by the American Institute of Certified Public Accountants, Inc.

Figure 35.3   Contract Revenue Cycle

Audit Objectives	Earned Revenue	Accounts Receivable	Unbilled Revenues (costs in excess of billings)	Advance Billings (billings in excess of costs)	Substantive Tests
Accuracy of contract value, including all change orders	X				Confirm original contract price and subsequent change orders directly with the owner.
					Examine signed original contract and subsequent change orders.
Accuracy of measured progress toward completion, including reasonableness of method used	X				Review and test contractor's procedures, including estimates and calculations. See "Contract Costs" later in this chapter.
Accuracy of calculation of owner billings, including consistency with provisions of the contract		X	X	X	Agree cumulative amounts billed plus unbilled revenues (or less advance billings) at the balance sheet date to earned revenues recorded through the balance sheet date.
					Confirm amounts billed with the owner.
					Alternative procedures—review amounts billable by referring to contract terms and recalculating; examine subsequent cash receipts.
Accuracy and completeness of cash receipts		X			Confirm payments made with the owner.
					Alternative procedure—examine subsequent cash receipts.
Collectibility of amounts reflected as outstanding		X	X		Review owner's financial statements to ascertain owner's financial condition and ability to pay total contract price yet to be billed, as well as unpaid billings, and availability of financial resources obtained through a third party.
					Review third party's financial statements and related arrangements entered into with owner.
					Review owner's past payment performance.
					Examine subsequent cash receipts.
					Review bonding arrangements and lien rights.

tract or can be confirmed directly with the owner. Evaluating the likelihood of price redetermination and bonus or penalty adjustments requires a careful review of the contract and the contractor's past and projected performance, and also may entail consultation with engineers, architects, or other specialists to evaluate the probability of future outcomes.

Cost-plus contracts occur in a variety of forms. Generally, the contract includes provisions for reimbursement of defined costs (often a maximum amount of reimbursable costs is set forth in the contract), overhead recovery percentages, and payment of a fee (which may be fixed or a percentage of defined reimbursable costs). Bonus or penalty provisions similar to those in fixed-price contracts also may be included. If a cost-plus contract involves management services only, and all costs are fully reimbursable (i.e., there is no risk to the contractor), only the fee should be included in determining revenue. If, however, the contractor is responsible for purchasing and managing materials and hiring workers and subcontractors (i.e., costs on which the fee is based or for which the contractor is at risk, even though they are reimbursable), these costs are properly included in determining revenue. The auditor should determine that disallowed or disallowable costs have been charged off.

As with fixed-price contracts, the auditor should obtain a summary of key contract data affecting revenues under cost-plus contracts (e.g., reimbursable costs, percentages of cost recovery, and the fee) and corroborate that information by referring to signed contracts or by confirming it with the owner. Audit emphasis for cost-plus contracts is on accumulating contract costs that serve as the basis for calculating the fee and overhead recovery amounts. The auditor should ensure that the contractor adequately distinguishes reimbursable costs associated with the contract (i.e., costs that give rise to contract revenues) from costs that are not reimbursable. If the contract includes bonus or penalty provisions, auditing procedures similar to those described for fixed-price contracts also should be performed.

Time-and-materials contracts have characteristics of both fixed-price and cost-plus contracts. Accordingly, the auditor should consider the various auditing procedures described in the preceding paragraphs, depending on the particular contracts involved.

Engineering companies also may contract on an indefinite deliverable basis where an umbrella contract is signed but work is performed only when specific task orders are issued. This contracting method typically is used by governmental agencies and is generally similar to cost-plus contracting, but the contracts are for definite time periods, which may include option periods. These contracts may be found where government funding is a key element in the completion of a large contract that can be broken down into specific tasks covering specific periods. Compensation under such contracts may involve performance fees based on a periodic evaluation of the contractor's services by the contracting agency. Because these contracts usually are used by governmental agencies, they generally are subject to the Federal Acquisition Regulation and contract compliance may be audited by the Defense Contract Audit Agency.

(ii) Change Orders.   Change orders modify the original provisions of a contract and may or may not affect the original contract price and scheduled completion date; they may be initiated by the owner or the contractor. The accounting for change orders depends on the underlying circumstances, so each change order must be analyzed individually. The auditor should determine whether the contractor has adequate controls to ensure that all change orders have been identified. Often the work to be performed under a change order is defined, but the adjustment to the contract price is not specified. Under the percentage-of-completion method, if there is evidence that the additional costs will be recovered, total contract revenues and costs may be adjusted accordingly; alternatively, the related costs may be deferred (i.e., excluded from income determination) until the amount is known. Anticipated revenues in excess of costs related to unpriced change orders should not be recognized, however, until realization is assured beyond a reasonable doubt. If change orders have not been processed, have not been approved for scope and price, or are in dispute, the accounting described below for claims is appropriate.

Auditing procedures for change orders that have been approved by the owner and are not in dispute are no different from those for contract revenues and costs incurred to date. If the change orders have not been approved or are in dispute, the auditor should evaluate the existence and collectibility of the related additional revenues and the propriety of the underlying accumulated costs. The auditor may be able to confirm the amounts of unapproved change orders with owners. If not, the auditor should review and discuss the contract terms with the contractor's legal counsel and knowledgeable contractor personnel. It may be appropriate to obtain written representations from the contractor's legal counsel and management regarding contract disputes. Testing the underlying accumulated costs generally involves examining supporting documents, seeking evidence of owner authorization for incurring those costs (if appropriate), and evaluating whether the costs relate to work within or outside the scope of the contract.

(iii) Claims. Contractors often seek to recover amounts in excess of the agreed-upon contract price for unanticipated costs caused by others, such as errors in construction drawings or design, owner-caused delays, or disputed or unresolved change orders or change orders that have not been approved as to scope or price. These claims may take the form of legally filed documents or negotiations in process, which, if allowed, would result in increased revenues. Such anticipated revenues should be reflected in total contract revenues only if it is probable that the claims will be upheld and the amount can be reasonably estimated, and only to the extent that they do not exceed related costs incurred. SOP 81-1 (para. 65) specifies the conditions that will satisfy those requirements. The auditing procedures for claims are similar to those for change orders, described above.

To the extent that receivables include amounts related to unapproved change orders, claims, or similar items, the nature and status of the items and the portion, if any, expected to be collected after one year should be disclosed in the financial statements.

(iv) Contract Renegotiation and Termination. The federal government retains the right to terminate contracts at its convenience or to alter their scope significantly. Federal regulations govern the termination or material modification of government contracts so as to protect contractors that do business with the government.

Revenue recognition on terminated contracts can be complex. If the government and the contractor agree on the settlement payments, revenue recognition follows the normal method. If, on the other hand, litigation appears likely, revenue recognition should follow the guidelines established for claims. Additional guidance on accounting for renegotiated and terminated government contracts is provided in Chapter 11B of ARB No. 43 and in the audit and accounting guide, *Audits of Federal Government Contractors*.

(v) Contract Options. Some contracts may include options that, if exercised by the owner, effectively increase the scope of work and total contract revenue. Generally, if the change in scope and price is predetermined in the contract, the accounting for contract options should be the same as that for change orders; that is, the options become part of the profit center containing the related contract. The options should be considered a separate profit center (i.e., segmented) if the scope of work is significantly different from that specified in the original contract, or if the scope is similar but the revenue and cost relationships differ significantly or the price was negotiated without regard to the original contract. The auditor should evaluate the appropriateness of the decision to combine or segment, by considering the circumstances in light of the criteria in SOP 81-1 (paras. 39–42). The auditing procedures for contract options are similar to those for change orders, as described above.

(vi) Additions. Contract additions are agreements that increase the scope of work beyond that in the original contract. The criteria for determining whether additions should be segmented from the original contract or combined with it are the same as described in the preceding paragraph. The auditing procedures for additions are similar to those for change orders.

(b) Contract Costs

Contract costs consist of two elements, costs incurred to date and estimated costs to complete. Costs incurred to date are based on the actual costs incurred in conjunction with a contract and are relatively easy to substantiate. Estimated costs to complete are more difficult to substantiate, since they require projecting future costs.

(i) Costs Incurred to Date. Accumulating costs incurred to date is essentially no different from accumulating inventory costs, and related auditing procedures are basically the same as those used in connection with inventories of commercial and industrial entities. Generally, the elements of contract costs are governed by the authoritative pronouncements applicable to inventories. Costs not clearly related, either directly or indirectly, to a contract should be excluded from contract costs and reflected as costs of the period to which they relate. The following general principles apply to accounting for contract costs, as prescribed by SOP 81-1 (paras. 69–75):

- All direct costs, such as material, direct labor, and subcontract costs, should be included in contract costs.
- Indirect costs allocable to contracts include the costs of indirect labor, contract supervision, tools and equipment, supplies, quality control and inspection, insurance, repairs and maintenance, depreciation, and amortization. Methods of allocating indirect costs should be systematic and rational. Appropriate bases for

allocating costs include direct labor hours and direct labor cost. The method used should be tailored to the particular contract.

- General and administrative costs ordinarily should be charged to expense as incurred, but may be accounted for as contract costs under the completed-contract method of accounting.

- Generally, selling costs should be excluded from contract costs and charged to expense. Precontract costs (including estimating and bidding costs) that are incurred for a specific anticipated contract and that will result in no future benefits unless the contract is obtained should not be included in contract costs before receipt of the contract. Such costs otherwise may be deferred only if they can be directly associated with a specific anticipated contract and if their recoverability from that contract is probable; they should be included in contract costs on receipt of the anticipated contract. Costs related to anticipated contracts that were charged to expense as incurred because their recovery was not considered probable, however, should not be reinstated by a credit to income on the subsequent receipt of the contract.

- Interest costs capitalizable according to the criteria discussed earlier in this chapter should be included in contract costs.

The auditor should ascertain that all costs to date have been recorded. Usually the cutoff for costs is tested in the search for unrecorded liabilities. Inquiry of knowledgeable contractor personnel and review of job-cost reports and contract files may indicate unusual costs that should be recorded. Overhead costs that are allocated to contracts in accordance with GAAP should be reviewed for proper and consistent allocation methods.

Costs or units to date reported in the job-cost report often are audited through tests of controls, as noted earlier. If the costs are audited through substantive tests, the auditor should review and test vendor and subcontractor invoices for proper coding to the correct job and job category and should note that the costs are properly allocable to the job.

Labor costs (or hours) should be tested to ascertain that the costs are coded properly to the job and reflect all labor-related costs. Payroll audit tests should be performed to test the propriety of the costs, and equipment charges should be tested for reasonableness and consistency. Equipment rental rates may be compared with actual costs or "blue book" rates. Invoices should be examined to determine that costs assigned from inventory are based on actual costs and that overhead allocations are consistent, reasonable, and computed accurately (subject to contract limitations, if appropriate).

The auditor should consider comparing material, labor, and overhead costs incurred to date and estimates to complete the contract with costs on similar contracts completed during the year, reviewing estimates and procedures from the prior year, and inquiring about and observing the contractor's procedures. (It may be possible to test key controls over the estimating process.)

The auditor may review individual annual employee earnings records for reasonableness and recalculate the allocation of labor to individual contracts based on some common element (e.g., materials or contract price). The reported allocation should be compared with actual labor reported, and significant discrepancies should be investigated. Labor costs allocated to individual contracts should be reconciled to total payroll costs.

On cost-plus contracts, the auditor should determine that recoverable and nonrecoverable costs are segregated in the accounting records and that the records are adequate to withstand the scrutiny of owners' auditors, if required. The review of contract revenues should satisfy the auditor that nonrecoverable costs are not being billed. Year-end billings and job-cost reports should be examined to ensure that all recoverable costs have been billed on a timely basis and that the related revenues have been recognized. On cost-plus contracts with a guaranteed maximum price or fee ceiling, costs and fees recognized to date should be analyzed. The analysis should consider the stage of completion of the project and the remaining costs and fees to be earned.

(ii) Estimated Costs to Complete.   Periodically, the costs to complete a contract must be reestimated. Since revenue is fixed (unless contract provisions permit specified changes), a change in estimated costs requires recognizing a change in the ratio of revenue to cost for accounting purposes. Since costs commonly change, regular, conscientiously prepared estimates are essential. Preparing estimates of costs to complete is one of management's most difficult tasks, and evaluating them is correspondingly difficult for an auditor. An auditor who understands the contractor's operations and business conditions will be better able to understand the estimate of costs to complete. If the estimates are prepared diligently and responsibly and if communication between auditor and contractor is open and candid, an auditor can obtain reasonable assurance that the estimates are attainable. Guidance on auditing accounting estimates is contained in Statement on Auditing Standards No. 57.

Most contractors prepare estimates of costs to complete in a systematized manner, with detailed written policies and procedures, including review and approval by appropriate officials. The estimates generally include detailed analyses of original bills of material, with items still to be obtained included at current prices, unless purchase commitments at specified prices exist. Initial estimates of various kinds of labor are analyzed in detail and compared with experience to date. Judgment is needed in extrapolating current experience into the future, particularly with respect to labor rates, fringe benefits, and overhead costs. The smaller and more specific the items extrapolated, the smaller the risk of error. The more often a contract is examined and judgments are made, the more reliable the estimates are likely to be.

In evaluating the estimate of costs to complete, the auditor should:

- Review the contractor's procedures for preparing the estimates
- Test the compilation of the estimates by reviewing the underlying data, such as manning tables (schedules of the human resource requirements for completing specific jobs), labor and overhead rate schedules, bills of material, and schedules of material received and still to be received (open purchase orders)
- Perform analytical procedures, like comparing the details of the estimate of costs to complete with the details of the original cost estimate supporting the contract bid, or comparing evidence of physical completion (e.g., number of units completed) with the percentage of completion indicated by cost estimates
- Consult with the engineering and production supervisors who make the critical judgments entering into the estimates in order to understand the reasons for their judgments and the degree of confidence with which the judgments are made, and to determine that the estimating process adequately recognizes anticipated changes in future costs resulting from collective bargaining agree-

ments, known price changes, estimated inflation rates, and other similar events and circumstances

- Assess management's ability, based on past experience, to estimate with reasonable accuracy the eventual outcome of contracts in process

- Be alert for long-lasting jobs likely to have cost overruns, and ensure that the implications of delays have been considered in estimating costs to complete

- Be alert for the inclusion of reserves in estimated costs to complete and ascertain that the contractor's method of determining and including those reserves is consistently applied and is in conformity with the requirements of SFAS No. 5 for the accrual of loss contingencies

However well organized or carefully performed and documented estimates of costs to complete are, they can never be more than estimates. Errors in judgment are inevitable, but can be minimized if the estimates are made according to a well-established, well-controlled routine. When estimates are revised, the related effect on contract costs should be recorded in the period in which the facts underlying the revision became known. If a revision is the result of a mechanical or factual error in a previous estimate, however, it should be accounted for as a prior-period adjustment pursuant to APB Opinion No. 20, *Accounting Changes* (Accounting Standards Section A06).

(c) Contract Losses

Auditing procedures should be designed to ensure that potential contract losses are identified and properly accounted for; losses that meet the criteria for accrual under SFAS No. 5 should be recognized in the financial statements in the proper period and other loss contingencies should be disclosed properly.

In reviewing contract loss reserves, the auditor may consider the nature of the contract and the historical results of similar contracts. The auditor should review job correspondence files, including correspondence with the owner; the reasonableness of the specific contract estimate; the aging of accounts receivable, including long-outstanding retentions (see below); and accounts receivable billings and collections in relation to total contract revenue. Certain comparisons also may be helpful in assessing the existence and amount of estimated or contingent losses, like comparing total budgeted costs with final costs incurred on similar jobs in the past, revised budgets with original budgets, other contract factors with corresponding budgeted items (e.g., labor hours and material used), total costs incurred with budgeted amounts, and the contractor's bid with bids of competitors, if available. The auditor should be alert for overlooked change orders and claims that may ameliorate losses. The auditor also should consider the contractor's controls over the estimating process.

(d) Contract Billings

The amount of revenue recognized on a contract does not always coincide with the amount billed to the owner, especially for contracts accounted for on the completed-contract basis. Often billings (amount and timing) are prescribed as part of the terms of the contract. When billings to owners are more or less than the amount of revenue recognized, the following situations result:

- *Unbilled receivables*. Revenue has been recognized but cannot be billed because of the terms of the contract. Such amounts are recorded in the balance sheet as accounts receivable and should be separately disclosed on the face of the balance sheet or in a footnote, if material.

- *Billings in excess of revenue*. Owners generally are billed in accordance with the terms of the contract, and the excess of billings over revenue is recorded as a liability. (Progress payments may be received, as stipulated in the contract, without regard to stage of completion.)

Auditing procedures in connection with receivables generally are the same as those performed on audits of commercial and industrial entities, except that certain alternative procedures should be applied to unbilled receivables. The auditor should evaluate billing data based on accumulated cost information and the terms of the contract, ascertain that the unbilled amounts were billed subsequently, and assess the ultimate collectibility of the receivables.

A portion of amounts billed over the duration of a contract will not be paid until the contract has been completed to the owner's satisfaction. These amounts are referred to as retentions. While auditing procedures for retentions are basically the same as for accounts receivable, the auditor should be especially concerned with evaluating the collectibility of these amounts, since payment may not be due for several years and is subject to owner claims for rework or other costs.

(e) Contract Liabilities

Contract liabilities result from purchases of materials, work performed by subcontractors, equipment rentals, accruals of payroll and related fringe benefit costs, penalty accruals, and accrued losses on contracts. The auditor should be satisfied that all liabilities have been recorded and properly classified and disclosed. Amounts due subcontractors are sometimes confirmed because subcontractor invoices may be received late and because the confirmation procedure provides evidence that supports the amounts and terms of retentions payable and may identify claims and disputes with subcontractors. If subcontractors' payables are not confirmed, the auditor should consider the need to reconcile payable balances to subcontractors' statements. In addition, the auditor should consider confirming the terms of long-term purchase commitments.

The auditor should ask management about existing claims or disputes against the contractor that have not been recorded. Old outstanding payables also may indicate contract problems, such as inadequacies in the work performed or penalties. The auditor should determine the need to accrue costs on the related claims in accordance with SFAS No. 5.

Sometimes, contractors do not use the cost-to-cost method to compute the percentage of completion. When other methods are used, the costs expensed to date in the financial statements represent the estimated final costs multiplied by the percentage of completion. The difference between the actual costs incurred and the costs expensed is recorded as a liability for costs to be incurred (or as a deferred asset).

36

Auditing Gas, Electric, and Telecommunications Companies

36.1 OVERVIEW OF THE INDUSTRY

Historically, electric, gas, and telephone companies were granted monopoly status within a designated service area because those services were considered essential to the public welfare and an exclusive franchise achieved the economies of scale that characterized monopoly operations. With this monopoly status came governmental regulation of the operations and rates charged for these services. With advances in technology in the electric industry, comparable third-party access to gas transportation, and the opening of electric transmission systems, electric and gas utilities have seen their monopoly status change and are endeavoring to operate successfully in a more competitive, less regulated environment. Comparable forces also have been at work in the telecommunications industry.

Public utilities[1] are capital-intensive businesses. In the past, for example, it was not unusual for an electric utility to spend several billion dollars constructing a large generating station. More recently, however, due to the changing regulatory environment, utilities have been building smaller units with construction costs in the $500 million range. The investment by electric, gas, and telecommunications utilities in plant facilities necessary to transmit and distribute their services is also significant. As a result of these capital requirements, the plant account typically is the most significant asset of a utility and usually approximates the long-term debt and equity capital on the balance sheet.

Electric and gas utilities may be either investor owned or publicly owned (by either governmental agencies or customers). Ownership by stockholders is the predominant form of business. In certain areas, the federal, state, or local government provides utility services. Cooperative systems usually serve rural areas and are owned by their customers (members).

The divestiture of American Telephone and Telegraph Company (AT&T) in 1983 began a new era in telecommunications, accelerating the penetration of competition into the long distance market. The divestiture created seven Regional Bell Operating Companies (RBOCs), which provide local exchange services to most areas of the United States; AT&T and the other interexchange carriers primarily provide long distance service. Since 1983, AT&T's market share has declined to 60 percent or less of the total long distance market. The local telecommunications market continues to be served primarily by the RBOCs. This is changing, however, as a result of the Telecommunications Act of 1996 (the Act), which is contributing to the dissolution of the RBOCs' monopoly status. The Act recognized multiple sources of supply, rapidly evolving technologies, and growing demand for new or improved telecommunication services, and placed reliance on market forces to achieve reasonable prices and economic efficiency. That is expected to be achieved as competitive local exchange carriers and traditional long distance providers expand their presence into local markets.

(a) Electric Utilities

Electricity is produced by large generating plants, although recent technology is making it possible to operate smaller plants economically. Typically, except for hydro-

---

[1] The terms "public utility" and "utility" are used interchangeably in this chapter to refer to electric and gas service providers, regardless of their current regulatory status. Depending on context, providers of telecommunications services are referred to as utilities or as companies.

electric plants, a heat source such as coal, oil, gas, or nuclear fuel is consumed to produce electric power. The power is delivered throughout the utility's service area by its transmission system and is made available to individual customers via the utility's distribution system.

Electric power cannot be stored; it must be produced as it is needed. This places unusual capital requirements on the utility, which must have sufficient generating capacity to meet peak load requirements even though those requirements might exist only for short periods during a day or during certain times of the year. To alleviate this situation, utilities have engaged in demand-side management activities to influence customer use of electricity in order to affect electricity demand. These activities include load management (which involves shifting demand from peak to off-peak periods), energy conservation, new uses of electricity, and innovative rate structures. Some utility commissions allow utilities to earn a return on their demand-side management investments because of their reported cost savings and environmental benefits.

An electric utility also must have sufficient excess or reserve capacity to operate even if one or more of its largest generating units are unavailable. Utilities can reduce the need to build reserve plant capacity, however, by joining power pools, integrating their systems with those of neighboring utilities, and contracting with other utilities, independent power producers, and cogenerators to purchase needed capacity. Cogenerators are often major commercial or industrial customers who install generating facilities for their own use. These facilities generate electricity and a by-product, such as steam, which the cogenerator uses in its operations or production.

Current federal regulations provide an incentive to commercial and industrial customers to build their own generating facilities, since surplus electricity generated may be purchased by the local utility at the utility's avoided cost. Avoided cost is determined differently in each jurisdiction, but the goal is to determine the cost the utility would have incurred to generate the electricity or purchase it elsewhere. Even though the utility has the obligation to purchase electricity generated by cogenerators when offered, it also must build capacity sufficient to satisfy the needs of its entire service territory, which includes the cogenerator.

To the extent that electric utilities are still monopolies and regulated entities, they are one of the last remaining industries to be so. As a result, pressure has been placed on the industry to drive the cost of its service down to a market-based level rather than a regulatory-determined rate. The ability to compete in a competitive market requires a detailed understanding of the cost of providing all forms of service. Regulatory commissions in the past often found it politically expedient to allow utilities to earn a greater rate of return from their industrial customers so that residential rates could be kept lower. Given this cross-subsidy, it is not surprising that it is the industrial customers who are leading the charge to push competition from the wholesale to the retail level. Many electric utilities are not positioned to compete in an open market and, therefore, are in the midst of a restructuring, primarily along functional lines, namely, power generation, transmission, and distribution.

The generating sector of the electric utility industry in particular has become increasingly competitive, with independent and affiliated nonutility power developers providing a growing percentage of the nation's new capacity. The prices that utilities pay for nonutility-generated power under newer power purchase contracts are usually market-based, determined through a competitive bidding process or set administratively by state regulators. Because the marginal cost of power has dropped substantially over the past five to ten years, some of the older contracts have locked-in prices that are considerably above the current market price of electricity. Utilities burdened with these high-cost power purchase contracts are caught between trying to honor these contracts and reducing costs in order to stay competitive.

Regulators and legislators in many states have evaluated and considered significant restructurings of the utility regulatory processes, including market-based rates for utility services and other dramatic changes, such as retail choice, divestiture of generation assets, and divesting transmission assets or relinquishing operating control over them to independent system operators. Several states have already passed legislation that establishes a competitive market for the sale of power at the retail customer level.

The passage of federal legislation providing open wholesale transmission access has increased the pressure on utilities to provide retail transmission access. Under retail access, end users could shop for inexpensive power and have it transmitted to them over their former retail suppliers' lines. This causes concern to utilities, whose remaining customers would have to bear a greater portion of a utility's fixed costs. Also, the recovery of stranded costs that the utility will not be able to recoup under competitive market conditions is a key issue in the debate over transmitting electric energy directly to ultimate consumers. (Stranded costs are costs related to plant assets that are no longer usable and not fully depreciated, and are included in a utility's revenue requirements, i.e., prices.) Although the Federal Energy Regulatory Commission (FERC) is prohibited by law from ordering retail access, a number of states have already passed legislation making it available, and virtually all other states are considering doing so. A number of utilities, as well as industrial customer groups, have urged state and federal regulators and legislators to require retail access.

As an alternative, where retail access is not available, many municipalities currently served at retail by investor-owned utilities are considering forming municipal utilities of their own to buy less expensive power from the competitive wholesale market and use wholesale access to transmit the power. Stranded cost recovery is a key issue with respect to these "municipalization" efforts as well. It is also a major impediment to municipalization because if full recovery of stranded costs from departing customers is granted, those customers would be charged the market rate plus a stranded cost surcharge, and thus would not realize any savings in the competitive environment.

As the number of buyers and sellers in the power market has grown, new entities, called "marketers" or "brokers," have sprung up to bring buyers and sellers together. Many of these entities are affiliates of investor-owned utilities. As the market for electricity has become more liquid, a spot, or cash, market has developed and is increasing in size and sophistication. Many of these marketers offer derivative contracts, and the New York Mercantile Exchange has developed a futures contract for electricity. In addition, many utilities have formed their own commodity trading operations.

Electric utilities are increasingly interested in entering into the telecommunications market, as they recognize they have important assets that can be leveraged, including fiberoptic cable networks and microwave licenses and other equipment currently used for internal communications. They also have well-established customer bases and sophisticated customer information systems. Even without additional investment, many electric companies could develop new revenue streams, reduce costs, and provide value-added service to existing electric customers while enhancing shareholder value by diversification into communications.

Electric utilities are not exempt from the forces of globalization, and many of them are becoming multinational energy providers. Stiff competition in electric generation in the United States, privatization in developed countries, and the energy needs of developing countries are the driving forces behind international investment by U.S. utilities.

As competition increased in the industry, utilities looked for strategic merger partners to enhance their ability to survive and thrive in the new environment. Accordingly, the pace of utility mergers picked up significantly in the late 1980s and continued through the mid-1990s. Even the specter of having to register as a public utility holding company under the Public Utility Holding Company Act (PUHCA; discussed later) did not stop multistate mergers from proceeding.

Possible health effects related to radiation from electric and magnetic fields (EMF) are an environmental concern, which utilities are addressing through research and customer and employee communications. If EMF radiation is found to be hazardous, the cost of rectification could be enormous. Many utilities are already dealing with litigation costs related to real estate, siting, and personal injury suits.

Because of the nature of their operations, utilities are faced with other environmental exposures, such as disposition of materials containing polychlorinated biphenyl (PCB), the disposition of high- and low-level radioactive waste, decommissioning of nuclear plants, the reduction of sulfur dioxide emissions, remediation of residuals associated with manufactured gas plant sites, and asbestos removal. Such environmental issues have the potential to result in significant costs to the utilities industry. Guidance on accounting for such costs is provided in AICPA Statement of Position 96-1, *Environmental Remediation Liabilities*.

The Clean Air Act of 1990 contains provisions for the reduction of sulfur dioxide and nitrogen oxide emissions, which are thought to be primary sources of acid rain. The legislation focuses on emissions from electric utility coal- and oil-fired generating facilities. It is historic in its unprecedented cost—$4 to $9 billion a year—and in its reliance on market forces. The Clean Air Act allows affected generators substantial flexibility in selecting compliance approaches by creating an entirely new market for emission allowances. (An emission allowance is a license to emit one ton of sulfur dioxide during a calendar year.) Since this legislation mandates compliance on a system-wide basis, rather than on the basis of individual facilities, a utility can overcomply at one site and undercomply at another. Regulators, who must approve utilities' compliance expenditures before their costs can be included in rates, will scrutinize the allocation of these significant costs among jurisdictions. Furthermore, the regulators can be expected to examine the total cost of compliance to ensure that the most cost-effective approach was adopted. The Clean Air Act and other environmental laws such as the Clean Water Act have greatly increased environmental expenditures, which will affect utilities' competitive position relative to newer, more environmentally friendly, and nonregulated generators.

(b) Gas Utilities

While electric utilities are moving to separate the generation from the transmission and distribution of electricity, these functions traditionally have been performed by separate entities in the gas industry. The extraction of natural gas from the ground is a nonregulated operation. Historically, regulated gas pipelines purchased gas from the wellhead, transported it, and sold it to distributors at wholesale prices. Regulated gas distributors sold and delivered the gas to ultimate consumers at retail. A series of rules by FERC in the 1980s changed the structure of the natural gas industry. The rules now allow "open access transportation," enabling end users to purchase gas on the spot market directly from producers and have the pipelines transport it to them. As a result, the role of the pipeline companies has changed from wholesale supplier to transporter or "common carrier." Even some gas distribution companies now transport gas for some of their customers without taking title to it.

Another distinction between electric and gas utilities is that gas can be stored pending customers' use; therefore, gas utilities do not require significant reserve plant capacity. Even so, regulators have encouraged gas utilities to invest in demand-side management for its efficiency and environmental benefits. Gas distributors, however, are more susceptible to changes in competitive fuel prices. Many large gas customers have dual fuel capabilities that enable them to burn either oil or gas in the same boiler with minimal conversion time or cost. These customers are very sensitive to differences between the prices of gas and oil. Many gas companies have responded by obtaining approved rates (tariffs) that allow the price of gas to change with the price of oil. Many gas utilities also have been authorized to sell gas based on incentive rates that result in the sharing of fuel cost savings between the company's customers and shareholders. This can move a significant portion of a gas utility's business into the nonregulated arena, complicating the application of Statement of Financial Accounting Standards (SFAS) No. 71. (The criteria for applying SFAS No. 71 are described later in this chapter.)

The impact of deregulation has been felt in all areas of the natural gas industry, including producers, interstate pipelines, and local distribution companies (LDCs). Interstate pipelines have been directly affected through a series of regulatory orders issued by FERC designed to promote greater competition in wellhead and downstream gas markets through "open access transportation" and "unbundling of services" for all users of the U.S. natural gas transmission system. Although this has led to much greater flexibility in the number of users and choices in the natural gas market, it also has resulted in difficult transitional issues with which the industry has had to deal, such as the sharing among pipelines and their customers (including LDCs, industrials, and shippers) of take-or-pay liabilities and stranded investment or transition costs resulting from the unbundling of various services formerly provided almost solely by interstate pipelines. As part of the pipeline industry's transition to competitive markets, long-term, fixed-price, take-or-pay gas contracts were renegotiated, at terms significantly less favorable to gas utilities.

LDCs, while remaining under state rate-making regulation, also have felt the effect of deregulation as costs and issues flow downstream to be dealt with separately by each state commission. Unbundling has forced more responsibility for acquiring reasonably priced gas supplies on the LDCs. Many natural gas utilities and their regulators are considering using natural gas futures and various types of derivative instruments to reduce risks and lower costs. LDCs have been affected by industrial customers "bypassing" their systems and purchasing gas directly from producers or pipelines, potentially shrinking their customer base and limiting their ability to allocate and recover fixed and transition costs.

One result of increased competition within the industry, and the favor natural gas is enjoying compared with other forms of energy, has been a tremendous expansion in pipeline construction, particularly in the western (primarily California) and northeastern markets. A number of these expansions and new systems were approved based on greater assumptions of risk on the part of their owners, another aspect of competition endorsed by FERC. This may result in excess pipeline capacity, reducing the pipelines' ability to recover their investment. Potential transmission overcapacity, "bypass," and the impact of interfuel competition with other forms of energy are all issues of strategic importance to gas utilities and their regulators as competition increasingly pervades the natural gas industry.

Both LDCs and pipelines have been required to establish natural gas marketing operations to procure and sell gas supplies. These marketing operations have grown rapidly, and the entities' control environments generally have not kept pace with the rapid expansion of these activities. The natural gas spot market is highly volatile because of capacity constraints in certain parts of the nation's natural gas transmission grid. This volatility is limited to some extent by the use of underground gas storage and a sophisticated natural gas futures market. Derivative and futures transactions are used extensively to manage the risks associated with increases in natural gas spot prices.

As the LDCs' and pipelines' return on investment continues to be affected by competition, these entities are beginning to investigate investments in unregulated products and services, including investments in newly privatized foreign natural gas pipeline and distribution systems. Other investments include telecommunication services, home security services, and gas appliance sales and repairs. Regulators may require utilities to share some of the earnings from these services with their customers.

Natural gas utilities also are faced with substantial environmental remediation liabilities. From the late 1800s to the mid-1900s, coal was used to "manufacture" natural gas. Wastes (coal tar) created from this process and disposed of at former manufactured gas plants are subject to remediation methods prescribed by the EPA. In addition, PCBs and mercury that leaked from meters along pipelines' systems require remediation. Remediation costs generally are allowed to be recovered from the utility's customers.

(c) Telecommunications Companies

Telecommunications companies provide services through a sophisticated network of wiring, cables, satellites, and switching equipment. These companies, for example, transmit both local and long distance calls by routing them through central offices that contain the switching equipment used to direct calls. Local calls are processed by one or more central offices within a company's domain. Long distance calls may be routed indirectly, depending on the availability of circuits in a long distance company's network.

The telecommunications industry continues to undergo revolutionary changes caused by increased competition, new technology, changing market demands, and international requirements for fully integrated, global, state-of-the-art communication capability. These external forces are largely responsible for new organizational structures, shifts in customer focus, the creation of new regulatory frameworks, and increased business risks.

At the time of the AT&T divestiture, a system of local access and transport areas (LATAs) was implemented, with many states divided into multiple LATAs. Under this system, revenues from intra-LATA calls generally belong to the local telephone company, and revenues from inter-LATA calls, to the long distance carrier. The local telephone company, however, charges the long distance carrier an access fee to hook the carrier's long distance network into the local network. These access charges represent a significant expense to long distance companies and a substantial revenue source for the local telephone company.

A primary objective of the Telecommunications Act of 1996 was to increase competition in the local telecommunications market. The Act will change the geographic market segmentation and eventually will blur the divisions between local and long distance companies. Long distance carriers will enter local markets and offer intra-LATA service, while local telephone companies will be able to offer inter-LATA calls and compete with the long distance companies. However, before the local telephone companies begin to offer long distance services, they must complete a complex process that demonstrates that they have sufficiently opened their markets to competitors. Competitive local exchange carriers also are expanding their market coverage.

The Act also allows the RBOCs to diversify their lines of business, provided that they have adhered to certain requirements. For example, a company previously offering telephone service only can now expand into other areas of communication such as long distance, cable, manufacturing, and electronic publishing. These changes eventually will permit a consumer to have one company provide cable TV, telephone, Internet, pager, and cellular services instead of receiving these services from several separate companies.

36.2 REGULATORY ENVIRONMENT

The rate-making process determines the selling price of retail services provided by rate-regulated companies; it specifies the overall level of revenues, the rates that may be charged, and the various classes of users to which the different rates apply. Rate making also influences the application of accounting principles by a public utility, because the regulatory body often prescribes accounting methods for utilities under its jurisdiction, which may or may not conform with generally accepted accounting principles (GAAP) appropriate for nonregulated businesses.

(a) Rate-Making Process

The rates that a public utility charges its customers are a matter of administrative process and are subject to the scrutiny of interested parties and the approval of regulatory bodies. The public utility proposes rates to the federal, state, or municipal regulatory commission or authority having jurisdiction. These rates are designed to recover the utility's operating costs and provide a reasonable return on its investment. (Delays inherent in the regulatory process prevent cost increases, or decreases, from being recognized on a timely basis, a phenomenon known as regulatory lag. This is eliminated when forecast test years are the basis of the rate request.) The regulatory authority then reviews the rate proposal and allows interested parties such as consumer groups or major industrial customers to respond to, and often challenge, the proposal. After the regulator has considered the arguments of the utility and interested parties, it determines the amount of revenue the utility should be permitted to receive (usually less than the utility's original proposal) and approves tariffs that specify the rates to be charged to various classes of customers. The rates of publicly owned power agencies usually are set by their own governing boards, as empowered by statute or contract.

(b) Rate-Making Formula

Determining the amount of revenue a utility should be allowed to earn (the revenue requirement) can be summarized in the following equations:

$$\text{Revenue Requirement} = \text{Cost of Service}$$
$$\text{Cost of Service} = \text{Operating Expenses} + \text{Return on Investment}$$
$$\text{Return on Investment} = \text{Rate Base} \times \text{Rate of Return}$$

(i) Cost of Service.   Cost of service is the amount of revenue that will permit the utility to meet all expenses properly chargeable to current utility operations and incurred to provide utility services, plus provide a return on amounts invested in assets necessary to provide such services. Operating expenses include salaries, materials, fuel costs, supplies, miscellaneous expenses, income and other taxes, and depreciation of plant.

Developing the operating expenses component of cost of service begins with the utility's historical accounting records of operating costs incurred, recorded in accordance with the uniform system of accounts prescribed by the regulator. The utility selects a test period to be used in the rate application. Ideally, the test period selected should be as close as possible to the period for which the rates to be fixed will be operational; in most instances, the test period will not coincide with the utility's fiscal year. Normally, test-period costs are adjusted for anticipated or known changes in expenses during or after the test period, in a process called normalizing. For example, annualized union wage increases during the test period and any contracted future cost increases would be normalized in determining cost of service. In some jurisdictions, utilities have been allowed to use a projected future test period. In these instances, the utility applies for rates to go into effect at a future date and projects the cost of service at the effective date.

If a utility develops a cost-of-service study that is reasonable in relation to costs incurred (or to be incurred) and is able to justify those costs, and if the regulatory commission agrees that the costs are reasonable, the utility should receive adequate revenues to operate successfully. That means that if the utility is operated efficiently, it should provide adequate service and be able to attract additional capital as needed. Unexpected changes in cost or sales volume, however, may preclude the utility from achieving the results anticipated in the rate application.

The terms "above the line" and "below the line" are commonly used in rate making. The "line" is net operating income (i.e., operating revenues net of operating expenses, including income taxes on utility operations). Costs above the line are operating expenses that are part of the cost of service, are reflected in the revenue requirement, and are borne, in effect, by the utility's customers. Other revenues and expenses, referred to as nonoperating items (e.g., rental income from nonutility property, and nonutility investing activities), do not constitute utility operating income or expense and, therefore, are not part of the cost of service; they are shown below the line as other income or expenses and are borne, in effect, by the common shareholders.

(ii) Return on Investment.   Return on investment is the amount that should induce investors to invest in, or retain their investment in, a public utility. That amount is a function of the rate base and the rate of return.

(1) Rate Base.   The rate base represents a utility's total investment in facilities used and useful in providing service, generally measured at its original cost. This is the base to which the rate of return is applied to obtain the level of operating earnings (i.e., return) at which the utility should be able to operate successfully. The principal components of the rate base are as follows:

- *Plant-in-Service.* Plant-in-service includes the cost of facilities used and useful in providing service to the public, net of accumulated depreciation. (The inclusion of depreciation expense in cost of service provides a recovery of the investment; hence, accumulated depreciation is deducted from the rate base.)

- *Construction-Work-in-Progress (CWIP).* Although it appears that the "used and useful" principle would automatically eliminate CWIP from inclusion in the rate base since CWIP will not be used or useful until some time in the future, some commissions include all or part of CWIP in the rate base. In some cases, CWIP is included to allow a utility that has significant construction projects to remain financially viable. This is a complex issue since the inclusion of CWIP in the rate base requires current customers to finance the construction of a plant that generally is considered to benefit future customers.

  In most jurisdictions, CWIP is excluded from the rate base. From the utility's viewpoint, however, the investment in CWIP is no different from any other investment and, therefore, merits a return. This is recognized, in those jurisdictions in which CWIP is excluded from the rate base, by capitalizing, as a cost of construction, an estimated return commonly referred to as an allowance for funds used during construction (AFUDC). The effect of recording the AFUDC is to recognize that the utility has sacrificed the alternative use of the funds invested in CWIP and that the return on amounts invested in construction represents part of the cost of completed construction. While the utility industry tends to view the AFUDC from a return perspective, capitalizing the carrying costs of construction projects is a generally accepted accounting principle. Accounting for the AFUDC is explained later in this chapter.

- *Deferred Income Taxes.* Since the adoption of SFAS No. 109, *Accounting for Income Taxes* (Accounting Standards Section I27), utilities are required to record deferred tax liabilities and assets that previously were not recorded because of the interplay of rate regulation and SFAS No. 71 (discussed later). Net deferred tax liabilities generally are deducted from the rate base because the positive cash flow resulting from deferred taxes provides the utility with cost-free capital that is supplied by the customers. Not deducting deferred income tax liabilities would have the effect of providing the utility's investors with a return on a portion of the rate base for which they did not provide the capital. (The utilities and their regulators have to identify any deferred taxes that were not provided by customers, so that those amounts are not deducted from the rate base.) Mainly as a result of accelerated tax depreciation on utility plant, utilities generally have large deferred tax liabilities. These deferred tax liabilities also usually result in the recognition of regulatory assets. Regulatory assets are capitalized costs incurred by the utility that are probable of future recovery as a result of rate actions of a regulator.

- *Working Capital.* Regulators recognize that a utility cannot operate without continuously available funds and, therefore, permit an allowance for working capital to be included in the rate base. This allowance may represent a specified number of days of a utility's cash requirement; however, regulators may require utilities to submit a study to justify the amount of working capital claimed.

(2) Rate of Return.   The authorized rate of return is the return expressed as a percentage of the utility's rate base. It is based on the utility's cost of capital.[2] The authorized rate of return is not a guarantee of a certain level of earnings and often is not attained because of delays in the rate-making process (regulatory lag) and revenues and expenses that vary from expected levels (attrition). A utility's actual (realized) rate of return is the amount it earns expressed as a percentage of the rate base. In the landmark case *Bluefield Water Works and Improvement Company* v. *Public Service Commission of West Virginia*,[3] the U.S. Supreme Court discussed rate of return as follows:

> A public utility is entitled to such rates as will permit it to earn a return on the value of the property which it employs for the convenience of the public equal to that generally being made at the same time and in the same general part of the country on investments in other business undertakings which are attended by corresponding risks and uncertainty; but it has no constitutional right to profits such as are realized or anticipated in highly profitable enterprises or speculative ventures. The return should be reasonably sufficient to assure confidence in the financial soundness of the utility and should be adequate, under efficient and economical management, to maintain and support its credit and enable it to raise the money necessary for the proper discharge of its public duties.

In determining the authorized rate of return, an appropriate cost for each of the utility's various sources of capital—long-term debt, preferred stock, and common equity, including retained earnings—is identified. For long-term debt and preferred stock, the coupon interest rate, appropriately adjusted for premiums or discounts, or dividend rate is the cost of capital. Determining an appropriate cost of capital for common equity (including retained earnings) is usually more subjective.[4] The overall cost of capital is the weighted average return on all sources of capital.

---

[2] Cost of capital is calculated as a weighted average of the cost of the various components of the utility's capital structure—its debt, preferred stock, and common shareholders' equity. Most corporate and managerial finance textbooks discuss at considerable length the concept of the cost of capital, how to calculate it, and the factors that affect it.

[3] 3-262 U.S. 679, 692 (1923).

[4] Determining an appropriate rate (or rates) of return on common equity is discussed in most finance textbooks.

(iii) Performance-Based Regulation. As the electric and gas industries have become more competitive, performance-based regulation and flexible rates have been implemented to provide utilities an incentive to operate more efficiently and the flexibility to respond to competitive situations. Performance-based rate making is a mechanism that specifically provides the potential for a utility to earn a return for its shareholders above the return it could earn in a traditional regulated environment. Such plans usually permit the utility to retain at least a portion of any benefits that result from surpassing predetermined targets for certain activities or on an overall basis. Some plans target plant performance or fuel. Other plans, such as rate of return incentive plans and price cap plans, address overall performance.

Under rate of return incentive plans, the regulator sets a range for return on equity above and below a certain target return. If the utility exceeds the target but remains in the range, it is allowed to keep at least a part of the "excess" earnings. If the utility falls below the target, it is not allowed to ask for a rate increase as long as its return falls within the identified range. Under a price cap plan, the regulator sets a price range or cap on rates charged to customers. The caps are adjusted based on changes in an index such as the Consumer Price Index and on a productivity improvement index. This approach allows the utility the flexibility to freeze or decrease rates for various classes or customer segments to cope with competition, as long as the rates fall below the rate cap.

With or without performance-based regulation, regulators increasingly are allowing utilities pricing flexibility to offer competitive rates to attract or retain industry in their service areas. Attractive electric rates often are an integral part of a state or county package offered to a major employer for relocating to the area. These rates usually are limited to customers that prove they have competitive options that would allow them to leave the utility's system, such as cogeneration, independent power, or municipalization for electric customers, and the ability to switch to an alternate fuel or bypass the local distribution company to obtain gas from another source for gas customers. Sometimes the utility is allowed to recover at least part of the discount offered to industrial customers through rates charged to other customers. Often, however, the utility is not allowed such recovery and must compensate for the discount in efficiencies and cost reductions or let it be borne by the shareholders.

(c) Electric Utilities

The National Energy Policy Act of 1992 (EPAct) caused sweeping changes in the electric industry. Title VII of EPAct increased competition in electric generation by revising the Public Utility Holding Company Act so that it is no longer an impediment to the development of nonrate-based power plants, and by granting FERC broad authority to open up the electric utility transmission grid on a case-by-case basis. The EPAct also created a new class of power providers, exempt wholesale generators (EWGs), that are exempt from regulation by the Securities and Exchange Commission (SEC) under PUHCA. EWGs are allowed to own eligible generating facilities, including those located abroad. The law also includes a foreign utility exemption that allows EWGs to own foreign facilities that sell electricity at retail.

To implement the EPAct, FERC issued a policy statement on transmission pricing and a notice of proposed rule making on comparable open access and stranded investment. The pricing policy allows utilities some flexibility to use nontraditional pricing methodologies if adequate support is provided. The comparable proposed access rule would require utilities to unbundle their transmission and ancillary services and provide them to others under a tariff that the utilities would have to apply to themselves as well as to wholesale transmission transactions. Recognizing that ordering utilities to open their transmission systems to third parties could result in stranded investments, FERC proposed that utilities be allowed to recover all legitimate, prudent, and verifiable costs incurred to provide service to a wholesale requirements customer, a retail customer, or a newly created wholesale power sales customer that subsequently becomes an unbundled wholesale transmission services customer.

FERC also proposed that wholesale stranded costs be directly assignable to a departing customer and be computed on a revenues lost basis. A departing customer is a customer that chooses to purchase electricity from a third party (generator or broker) rather than the local utility. The local utility would be required to deliver that electricity and provide other related services, for which it would be compensated. In addition to the delivery service fee, the departing customer would be required to compensate the local utility for any stranded or unrecovered costs incurred by the local utility due to the departure. Revenues lost are the revenues that would have been received from the customer less the revenues that the utility expects to receive from the sale of electricity that would not otherwise have been available.

High-cost power purchase contracts signed under the Public Utilities Regulatory Policy Act of 1978 (PURPA) have become a contentious issue between utilities and nonutility generators (NUGs). Utilities generally believe that the passage of the EPAct has obviated the need for PURPA and that PURPA has become an impediment to the development of a competitive market in electric generation. NUGs and others involved in the competitive power sector disagree. Utilities typically seek remedies from their state commissions, FERC, the courts, and even Congress because of the conflicts they face between coping with competition and honoring high-cost contracts. At the time of this writing, Congress is considering proposed legislation that would repeal PURPA in its entirety. Whether this legislation would adequately protect existing power purchase contracts is in dispute. Many regulatory jurisdictions view these high-cost power contracts as stranded costs to be included in the fee charged a departing customer. Also, many utilities are buying out of these contracts to lower their overall power supply costs.

NUGs insist that if PURPA is repealed, it must be replaced by another measure that will ensure continued competition. At the time of this writing, there is substantial legislative activity aimed at comprehensively reforming the electric industry. This activity is focused on repeal of PURPA, total reform or repeal of the Public Utility Holding Company Act, and mandating wholesale and retail electric power competition. The telecommunications legislation passed in 1996 modified PUHCA to allow registered holding companies to enter the telecommunications market.

(d) Gas Utilities

To resolve the take-or-pay liabilities resulting from the move to open-access transportation on interstate pipelines and in response to various court actions, in the late

1980s FERC issued a series of regulations to provide for a cost-sharing approach among the various parties affected, including pipelines, industrials, and LDCs. FERC also encouraged state commissions to require LDCs to absorb a share of such costs passed to them by pipelines rather than directly passing through all such costs to their customers. Although most take-or-pay contracts were restructured in response to these initiatives, the recovery of these costs by pipelines and LDCs from their customers is still a significant issue for the industry.

In what was characterized as the final stage in the move to a competitive environment in the natural gas industry, in 1992 FERC issued a new series of orders (the "restructuring rules") designed to ensure comparability of transportation service so that both pipeline and nonpipeline gas sellers would "compete for gas purchasers on an equal footing" (FERC Order No. 636). These rules provide for, among other things, the unbundling and separate pricing of various services such as gathering (collecting gas from the various wells and delivering it to a common point on the pipeline), sales, and storage, and the recovery by the pipelines of various "transition costs" such as unrecovered purchase gas costs remaining from regulated gas sales activities, gas supply contract realignment costs, and stranded costs of facilities that cannot be directly allocated to customers of unbundled services. Costs, as well as operational issues, resulting from these FERC regulations are substantial, and significant litigation and regulatory proceedings have arisen in connection with the resolution of cost sharing among industry participants.

State commissions with jurisdiction over LDCs have become increasingly interested in promoting competition behind the "city gate." LDCs are implementing alternative forms of regulation, such as performance-based rates, to meet the ever-growing competition. In addition, many of the pipeline companies have "spun down" their gathering operations out of their regulated pipeline companies. This has caused gathering companies, once subject to FERC jurisdiction with respect to the rates charged, to become essentially unregulated. There are, however, many proceedings before FERC with respect to whether FERC continues to have jurisdiction over rates charged for gathering.

(e) Telecommunications Companies

In October 1990, the Federal Communications Commission (FCC) initiated a system of price caps for local exchange carriers (LECs). In effect, this is a modified form of regulation, which retains some aspects of traditional regulation in that it is tied to a rate of return measure and requires prospective refunds (i.e., sharing of earnings) if earnings exceed specified levels. However, the price cap rules are based on an incentive structure that is more closely tied to the general economy and on a competitive market model, rather than traditional regulatory measures. The FCC's Report and Order (in Docket No. 87-313) states that "LECs that can outperform the productivity level embedded in the annual adjustment mechanism are rewarded with the ability to retain reasonably higher earnings than would be available under the former regulatory system" (para. 2). The price cap rules are mandatory only for the RBOCs and GTE Corporation; smaller LECs have the option of continuing to use traditional rate of return regulation and most have chosen to do so.

The price cap mechanism has three elements: a measure of inflation, a productivity offset, and exogenous costs, that is, cost changes beyond the control of the carrier. The measure of inflation is the 45-day estimate of the gross domestic product price index (GDP-PI); it is adjusted by an allowance for exogenous costs. The productivity offset is designed to reflect the degree to which LEC operations are more efficient than the general economy. Identifying and justifying exogenous costs is complex and involves determining that a cost is outside the control of the carrier and that it is unique to carriers (i.e., not already reflected in the GDP-PI) and is not an ongoing industry occurrence.

36.3 ACCOUNTING PRINCIPLES FOR RATE-REGULATED ENTITIES

Significant sources of accounting principles particularly relevant to rate-regulated entities are listed below:

- SFAS No. 71, *Accounting for the Effects of Certain Types of Regulation* (Accounting Standards Section Re6)
- SFAS No. 90, *Accounting for Abandonments and Disallowances of Plant Costs* (Accounting Standards Section Re6)
- SFAS No. 92, *Accounting for Phase-in Plans* (Accounting Standards Section Re6)
- SFAS No. 101, *Regulated Enterprises—Accounting for the Discontinuation of Application of FASB Statement No. 71* (Accounting Standards Section Re6)
- SFAS No. 109, *Accounting for Income Taxes* (Accounting Standards Section I27)
- SFAS No. 121, *Accounting for the Impairment of Long-Lived Assets and for Long-Lived Assets to Be Disposed Of* (Accounting Standards Section I08)
- FASB Technical Bulletin No. 87-2, *Computation of a Loss on an Abandonment*
- SOP 96-1, *Environmental Remediation Liabilities*
- EITF Issue 89-13, *Accounting for the Cost of Asbestos Removal*
- EITF Issue 90-8, *Capitalization of Costs to Treat Environmental Contamination*
- EITF Issue 91-6, *Revenue Recognition of Long-Term Power Sales Contracts*
- EITF Issue 92-7, *Accounting by Rate-Regulated Utilities for the Effects of Certain Alternative Revenue Programs*
- EITF Issue 92-12, *Accounting for OPEB Costs by Rate Regulated Enterprises*
- EITF Issue 93-4, *Accounting for Regulatory Assets*
- EITF Issue 96-17, *Revenue Recognition under Long-Term, Power Sales Contracts That Contain Both Fixed and Variable Pricing Terms*
- EITF Issue 97-4, *Deregulation of the Pricing of Electricity—Issues Related to the Application of FASB Statements No. 71,* Accounting for the Effects of Certain Types of Regulation, *and No. 101,* Regulated Enterprises—Accounting for the Discontinuation of Application of FASB Statement No. 71
- Prescribed systems of accounts issued by FERC for electric and gas utilities and state regulatory commissions (for example, the Uniform System of Accounts or NARUC's System of Accounts) and by the FCC for telecommunications companies

These pronouncements incorporate the economic effects of the rate-making process that are not considered in other authoritative pronouncements. At the time of this writing, numerous telecommunications companies have discontinued the application of SFAS No. 71.

In addition, various SEC Staff Accounting Bulletins deal with disclosures and accounting by electric utility companies:

- SAB Topic 10-A, Financing by Electric Utility Companies Through Use of Construction Intermediaries
- SAB Topic 10-B, Estimated Future Costs Related to Spent Nuclear Fuel and Nuclear Electric Generating Plants
- SAB Topic 10-C, Jointly Owned Electric Utility Plants
- SAB Topic 10-D, Long-Term Contracts for Purchase of Electric Power
- SAB Topic 10-E, Classification of Charges for Abandonments and Disallowances
- SAB Topic 10-F, Presentation of Liabilities for Environmental Costs

(a) Interrelationship of Rate Making and Accounting

As part of the rate-making process, rate orders (from FERC, the FCC, or state commissions) often require rate-regulated entities to observe accounting practices that would differ from GAAP for nonregulated entities. An example is the accounting for research and development costs; while GAAP require their immediate recognition as a period expense, public utility commissions often require a utility to defer research and development costs and amortize them over the future periods in which compensating revenues will be provided through the rate-making process.

The Financial Accounting Standards Board (FASB) recognizes the economic effect of regulation on public utilities. SFAS No. 71 requires companies to capitalize costs if it is probable that they will be recovered in the future through the rate-making process. For example, a commission may permit excessive repair costs incurred in one period to be recovered in a future period through increased customer rates. For accounting purposes, the excessive repair costs should be deferred until the increased rates are effective and should be amortized as the revenues are collected. Similarly, if current rates are provided for costs that are expected to be incurred in the future, such as the costs of potential storm damage repairs, SFAS No. 71 requires recognition of those current additional receipts as liabilities. SFAS No. 71 applies to regulated operations of an entity that meet all of the following criteria:

- The entity's rates for regulated services or products are established by an independent third-party regulator or by its own governing board.
- The regulated rates are designed to recover the specific entity's costs of providing the regulated service or products.
- It is reasonable to assume that the rates can be charged to and collected from customers, in view of the demand for the regulated service or product and the level of competition. This criterion requires consideration of anticipated changes in levels of demand or competition during the recovery period for any capitalized cost.

As a result of applying SFAS No. 71, a utility may record such regulatory assets as deferred fuel costs, environmental remediation costs, postretirement and postemployment benefits costs, losses on debt extinguishment, and storm damage repair costs.

Changes in the regulatory environment shortly after the issuance of SFAS No. 71 complicated the assessment of entities' ability to meet the criteria of that statement. In 1988, the FASB issued SFAS No. 101, *Regulated Enterprises—Accounting for the Discontinuation of Application of FASB Statement No. 71* (Accounting Standards Section Re6). SFAS No. 101 specifies that an entity that ceases to meet the criteria for application of SFAS No. 71 should report that event in its general-purpose financial statements. Since SFAS No. 71 requires an entity to meet all three criteria, it is possible for an entity to continue to be regulated (and meet the first criterion) and not be able to meet one or both of the other two criteria for applying SFAS No. 71. As a result, the entity would continue to have its rates established by the regulator and would follow the regulator's accounting principles in financial statements filed with the regulator, but would not be able to recognize the impact of the regulator's actions in its general-purpose external financial statements. Many telecommunications companies, in particular, have ceased to follow regulatory accounting rules for external reporting, but are still required to maintain regulatory records.

Several regulatory practices and alternative forms of rate regulation (such as disallowances of plant costs and price caps) may raise questions about an entity's ability to continue to meet the second criterion of SFAS No. 71. When a regulator departs from the traditional rate-making model, the regulated entity must assess whether the new rate regulation is designed to recover the specific costs of providing the regulated services or products.

SFAS No. 71 is based on the premise that rate regulation, not the marketplace, sets the price of regulated services. In the increasingly competitive market, the entity must constantly assess whether it has the ability to collect rates established by the regulator or whether its rates are being driven down to the competitive market.

Because paragraph 6 of SFAS No. 71 requires that statement to be applied to separable portions of a regulated entity's operations, SFAS No. 101 also should be applied to separable portions of the entity's operations, such as customer class or a functional group of assets within a jurisdiction.

Under SFAS No. 101, the entity is required to eliminate all assets recognized solely due to the actions of the regulator, irrespective of the potential recoverability of the amounts. Such assets include embedded regulatory assets, such as depreciation differences whereby the regulator established a depreciation life for an asset in excess of its economic useful life. SFAS No. 101 also required regulatory assets and liabilities to be eliminated "unless the right to receive payment or the obligation to pay exists as a result of past events or transactions and regardless of future transactions." In Issue No. 97-4, the EITF considered when an entity should cease applying SFAS No. 71 to a separable portion of its business whose pricing is being deregulated. The consensus reached was that the appropriate time is when the entity can reasonably determine how the transition plan will affect the portion of the business being deregulated. The EITF further reached a consensus that the related regulatory assets and liabilities should be evaluated on the basis of the source of the cash flows that will realize or settle them. Finally, a consensus was reached that the "source of the cash flow" approach should be applied to all relevant recoveries of costs and settlements of obligations.

The carrying amounts of assets also must be evaluated for impairment following the guidance contained in SFAS No. 121, *Accounting for the Impairment of Long-Lived Assets and for Long-Lived Assets to Be Disposed Of.* SFAS No. 121 amends paragraph 9 of SFAS No. 71 to provide that a rate-regulated entity should charge a regulatory asset to earnings if and when that asset no longer meets the criteria for capitalization in paragraph 9(a) and (b) of SFAS No. 71. This requires an ongoing assessment of the probability of recovery of regulatory assets subsequent to their initial recognition. As previously noted, the significant changes taking place in the industry are focused on competition at both the wholesale and retail level. This has caused a reevaluation of the applicability of SFAS No. 71. At the time of this writing, this area is under scrutiny by both the SEC and FASB.

(b)   Abandoned Plant Losses and Disallowances

Rate-regulated entities, particularly electric utilities, sometimes terminate the construction of a plant because of economic or other considerations. In similar circumstances, a nonregulated entity would be required to immediately write off its investment in the plant. A rate-regulated entity may be able to recover the cost of the abandoned plant from its customers and, therefore, may not be required to write off its investment. The utility should write off the investment, however, when it becomes probable that the cost of the abandoned plant will not be recovered from customers. FASB Interpretation No. 14, *Reasonable Estimation of the Amount of a Loss* (Accounting Standards Section C59), provides guidance on estimating the amount of a loss, and Technical Bulletin 87-2, *Computation of a Loss on an Abandonment* (Accounting Standards Section Re6), provides guidance on computing the loss.

Generally, when it becomes probable that a utility will abandon an operating asset or an asset under construction, SFAS No. 90 requires the cost of the asset to be removed from CWIP or plant-in-service. Estimated termination charges are added to the recorded costs. The entity should determine the likely recovery of the total costs to be provided from future rates, as permitted by its rate regulator. Only the amounts probable of recovery may be deferred; the remainder is recognized as a loss.

If the regulator permits the utility to recover the costs of an abandoned plant over a period of time, the utility must consider whether it will be allowed to earn a return on the investment. The concept of return was described earlier in this chapter. If it is likely that recovery of cost plus a full return will be granted, SFAS No. 90 requires that the costs be reported as a separate new asset and amortized in the same manner as used for rate-making purposes.

Often the regulatory body does not allow the utility to earn a return on its investment in abandoned plant. If no return or a partial return is allowed, only the present value of the future revenues expected to be provided is reported as a separate new asset. Any excess of the total cost of the abandonment over the present value of the estimated future revenues is recorded as a loss. Disallowances of a portion of the costs of new facilities follow the same accounting.

Because of regulatory lag, these accounting decisions generally are made before final rate orders are issued. During that time, the investment in abandoned plant (deferred debit) represents a loss contingency. After a final rate order is issued, any adjustments to the calculations described above must be recorded. FASB Technical

Bulletin No. 87-2 provides examples of the calculations and implementation guidance.

(c) Phase-in Plans

The construction costs of electric utility plants escalated significantly in the 1970s and 1980s; consequently, the completion of a new facility and its addition to the rate base sometimes resulted in a significant increase in rates. To avoid placing a financial strain on individual customers, "phase-in plans" were developed to moderate the initial rate increase. The objective of such plans was to avoid "rate shock" by increasing rates gradually. This was done by deferring some of the rate increase to future years and providing the utility with a return on investment of deferred amounts. SFAS No. 92 allowed costs deferred under a phase-in plan to be capitalized as deferred charges, provided that substantial physical construction had been performed on the plant prior to January 1, 1988. In addition, the costs had to be deferred pursuant to a formal plan that specified the timing of recovery (not to exceed ten years) and limited the scheduled annual increases in rates each year in order to prohibit a back-end loading of the recovery. Costs deferred for plants on which substantial construction had not been completed prior to January 1, 1988 are not allowed to be capitalized for financial reporting purposes. Therefore, application of this standard in the future is highly unlikely.

(d) Group Method Depreciation

Many large telecommunications companies have adopted group method depreciation. Under group method depreciation, also known as composite depreciation, the economic lives of a number of plant assets are averaged and depreciation is computed on an entire class of assets as if it were an operating unit. The principal difference between the group method and other, more commonly used methods is in the treatment of normal retirements and the gain or loss recorded as a result of differences between the cash proceeds and the net book value of the asset sold or retired. Under the group method of depreciation, gains or losses on retirement of assets are charged to accumulated depreciation.

(e) Allowance for Funds Used During Construction

As described earlier, in those jurisdictions in which CWIP is excluded from the rate base, rate-regulated entities capitalize a return on their investment in CWIP. That return takes into account the cost of different funding sources. Unlike nonregulated entities, utilities are permitted by SFAS No. 71 to recognize an equity return (and thereby recognize current-period income) on CWIP. The FASB considers this practice to be acceptable because the cumulative AFUDC, including the equity return recognized while the plant is under construction, later becomes part of the cost of the plant for rate-making purposes. When construction is completed and the asset is placed in service, the total cost of the asset, including the AFUDC, is recognized in the rate base on which the utility is permitted to earn a current return. As a result, the utility recovers the total cost of the plant, including the AFUDC, through depreciation charges that are part of the cost of service to be recovered from customers over the estimated life of the plant. SFAS No. 90 added a restriction that the AFUDC may be capitalized only if its subsequent inclusion in allowable costs for rate-making purposes is probable, and further limited capitalization of the AFUDC to that recorded during construction or as part of a qualifying phase-in plan.

The AFUDC return is normally divided into two components. For electric and gas utilities, each of these is reported separately on the income statement. They are the interest component, or the allowance for borrowed funds, and the equity component, or the allowance for other funds.

Some rate regulators have recognized the significant financing burdens faced by a utility in financing its CWIP by permitting the utility to collect a current cash return on some of its CWIP. In this way, a utility earns a current cash return to compensate for the carrying cost (borrowings and equity capital) of financing CWIP. If a utility is allowed to earn a current return on a portion of its CWIP, it is not permitted to recognize any AFUDC on that portion of CWIP. From the utility's perspective, it is preferable to earn a current cash return on CWIP; the resulting cash flow can be used to pay the carrying charges on CWIP, thereby lessening the overall financing requirements. In general, utilities that are permitted to earn a current return on CWIP are considered to have a better quality of earnings than those that do not earn a current cash return. In some cases, state and federal regulators have elected differing treatments.

(f) Embedded Regulatory Assets

SFAS No. 101 states that a required adjustment must be made to depreciation upon discontinuing the application of SFAS No. 71 if there is a cumulative difference between recorded depreciation and depreciation computed using a generally accepted method of depreciation. Therefore, if a utility has followed a regulatory method of computing depreciation or of determining an asset's life, and there is a cumulative difference between the recorded accumulated depreciation and the accumulated depreciation that would have been recorded using lives appropriate under GAAP, SFAS No. 101 requires the difference to be written off when SFAS No. 71 is discontinued. The difference was created solely by the actions of the regulator and should be treated similar to a regulatory asset for purposes of applying SFAS No. 101, regardless of whether it had been quantified previously.

Many utilities may not have viewed underdepreciation of plant and equipment explicitly as a regulatory asset and, therefore, may not have identified or tracked the differences. GAAP do not require a regulated entity to disclose the impact of applying SFAS No. 71 or to disclose regulatory assets that earn a return. Nevertheless, pursuant to SFAS No. 101, it is necessary for companies to quantify the amount of underdepreciation, if any, for purposes of adjusting the plant balances.

Any underdepreciation of assets caused by rate regulation in the past should be distinguished from a change in the estimated remaining useful life of assets determined based on current technology and competition. Changes in the period of benefit of an asset should be accounted for prospectively by adjusting the remaining period of depreciation.

Utilities should determine the extent to which their regulatory depreciation methods have differed from GAAP methods and lives. If the differences are significant, utilities should consider disclosing them in the financial statements. If the differences have not been quantified, regulated entities should consider disclosing that (1) there are differences between regulatory and GAAP depreciable lives, and (2) the related amount has not been quantified. If appropriate, the utility should consider disclosing that quantification of the amount is in process.

(g) Alternative Revenue Programs

In Issue 92-7, *Accounting by Rate-Regulated Utilities for the Effects of Certain Alternative Revenue Programs*, the consensus of the EITF was that once specified events occur that permit billing of additional revenues due to weather abnormalities or to compensate the utility for demand-side management initiatives or reward the utility for achieving certain objectives, the regulated utility should recognize the additional revenues if all of the following conditions are met:

1. The program is established by an order from the utility's regulatory commission that allows for automatic adjustment of future rates. Verification of the adjustment to future rates by the regulator would not preclude the adjustment from being considered automatic.

2. The amount of additional revenues for the period is objectively determinable and is probable of recovery.

3. The additional revenues will be collected within 24 months following the end of the annual period in which they are recognized.

(h) OPEB Costs

In EITF Issue 92-12, *Accounting for OPEB Costs by Rate Regulated Enterprises*, the task force reached consensus on several issues. For continuing plans providing postretirement benefits other than pensions (OPEB plans), the task force reached a consensus that a regulatory asset related to costs covered by SFAS No. 106, *Employers' Accounting for Postretirement Benefits Other Than Pensions* (Accounting Standards Section P40), should not be recorded if the regulator continues to include OPEB costs in rates on a pay-as-you-go basis. For a continuing plan, a rate-regulated entity should recognize a regulatory asset for the difference between SFAS No. 106 costs and OPEB costs included in the entity's rates if the entity (1) determines that it is probable that future revenue in an amount at least equal to the deferred cost (regulatory asset) will be recovered in rates, and (2) meets all of the following criteria:

1. The rate-regulated entity's regulator has issued a rate order or a policy statement or generic order applicable to entities within the regulator's jurisdiction that allows for both the deferral of SFAS No. 106 costs and the subsequent inclusion of those deferred costs in the entity's rates.

2. The annual SFAS No. 106 costs (including amortization of the transition obligation) will be included in rates within approximately five years from the date of adoption of SFAS No. 106. The change to full accrual accounting may take

place in steps, but the period for deferring additional amounts should not exceed approximately five years.

3. The combined deferral recovery period authorized by the regulator for the regulatory asset should not exceed approximately 20 years from the date of adoption of SFAS No. 106. To the extent that the regulator imposes a deferral recovery period for SFAS No. 106 costs greater than approximately 20 years, any proportionate amount of such costs not recoverable within approximately 20 years should not be recognized as a regulatory asset.

4. The percentage increase in rates scheduled under the regulatory recovery plan for each future year should be no greater than the percentage increase in rates scheduled under the plan for each immediately preceding year. This criterion is similar to that required for phase-in plans in paragraph 5(d) of SFAS No. 92, *Regulated Enterprises—Accounting for Phase-in Plans*. The task force observed that recovery of the regulatory asset in rates on a straight-line basis would meet this criterion.

For discontinued plans (those that have no current service costs), the task force reached a consensus that a regulatory asset related to SFAS No. 106 costs should be recorded if it is probable that future revenue in an amount at least equal to any deferred SFAS No. 106 costs will be recovered in rates within approximately 20 years following the adoption of SFAS No. 106. Rate recovery during that period may continue on a pay-as-you-go basis.

The task force also reached a consensus that a rate-regulated entity should disclose in its financial statements the regulatory treatment of OPEB costs, the status of any pending regulatory action, the amount of any SFAS No. 106 costs deferred as a regulatory asset at the balance sheet date, and the period over which the deferred amounts are expected to be recovered in rates.

Additionally, the task force concluded in Issue 93-4 that if a rate-regulated entity initially fails to meet the regulatory asset recognition requirements of the consensus developed in Issue 92-12, but meets those requirements in a subsequent period, a regulatory asset for the cumulative difference between SFAS No. 106 costs and OPEB costs included in rates since the date of adoption of SFAS No. 106 should be recognized in the period the requirements are met. The task force also reached a consensus that a cost that does not meet the asset recognition criteria in paragraph 9 of SFAS No. 71 at the date the cost is incurred should be recognized as a regulatory asset when it does meet those criteria at a later date.

(i) Revenue Subject to Refund

Sometimes regulated entities are granted temporary rate increases by a regulatory authority subject to the condition that all or a portion of the additional revenues may be refundable to customers. If the rates finally authorized are lower than the temporary rates, usually the utility is required to refund the excess revenues. The provisions of SFAS No. 5, *Accounting for Contingencies*, determine whether a provision for estimated refunds should be accrued for this loss contingency. Generally, a utility records a liability to refund revenues previously collected from customers when it is probable that a refund will be due and the amount of the refund is reasonably determinable. In practice, these conditions often are met only when the regulator issues an order for a refund; however, in some circumstances, the conditions of SFAS No. 5 may be met before a formal rate order is issued. SFAS No. 71 does not permit any refunds to be recognized as prior-period adjustments; instead, refunds must be recognized in the accounting period in which the requirements of SFAS No. 5 are met. The utility is required to disclose the effect of the refund on net income of the current year and to indicate the years in which the refunded revenue was recognized.

(j)   Unbilled Revenues

Utilities normally divide meter reading for customers into several cycles each month. Likewise, they bill their customers on a cycle basis during each month, which allows the utilities to spread the workload of meter reading, billing, and collection more evenly. At a given time, therefore, a portion of the service utilized by customers is unbilled. If a utility's sales volume, or sales mix, and rate per unit of sales do not fluctuate significantly from year to year, the impact of unbilled revenues on annual income is immaterial. The Tax Reform Act of 1986 required utilities to report unbilled revenue as taxable income and, as a result, for financial reporting purposes most public utilities accrue unbilled revenues based on estimated unbilled usage at the end of a period. Some utilities determine their revenues for both financial reporting and rate-making purposes on a meters-read or bills-rendered basis and, therefore, do not accrue unbilled revenues. This practice is acceptable provided that it is consistent with the utility's rate making. Telecommunications companies typically accrue unbilled revenues based on prorated basic service charges plus actual unbilled calls and other charges.

(k)   Deferred Energy Costs

Since the mid-1960s, many electric and gas utilities have had energy adjustment clauses in their rate structures as a means of automatically passing through to their customers energy costs (fuel expense for internally generated power, purchased gas costs, and the energy component of the cost of purchased power) above or below the approved base cost per unit as identified in the utilities' rates. An energy adjustment clause enables a utility to recover cost increases sooner and provides greater assurance that actual costs of energy will be recovered from customers. If regulatory approval were required for each rate change, the delays resulting from the administrative proceedings would adversely affect the utility's earnings. Even with energy adjustment clauses, a lag usually exists between the time energy costs are incurred and when they are billed to customers.

The energy cost increases experienced as a result of the OPEC oil embargo in 1973–74 gave rise to the practice of deferring unbilled energy costs until related revenues were collected in subsequent periods. As customers are billed, the related deferred energy costs are written off. If actual costs are less than those provided for in the base rates, the difference is recognized as a deferred credit and refunded to customers. Energy adjustment clauses vary substantially among regulatory jurisdictions, and the auditor should become familiar with the operation of the energy clause of the individual utility and ascertain that it is being applied properly.

(l) Leases

SFAS No. 71 requires rate-regulated entities to report capital leases, as defined in SFAS No. 13, *Accounting for Leases* (Accounting Standards Section L10), as capital leases in their financial statements, even though in many cases those leases are treated as operating leases for rate determination purposes. Therefore, it is necessary for utilities to adjust the aggregate income statement charges resulting from capital lease accounting to reflect the accounting that would have resulted from operating lease treatment.

Generally, this requires that the excess of the expense under capital lease treatment over the expense under operating lease treatment be deferred in the early years of a lease. The deferred charge is reduced and eventually eliminated in the later years of the lease, when the operating lease method results in higher expenses than does the capital lease method. This accounting results in aggregate income statement charges being recognized in an amount approximately equal to the revenues provided to cover the rate-making determination of allowable expenses on an operating lease basis. Aside from this deferred charge, capital leases are presented on the balance sheet as required by SFAS No. 13.

(m) Purchased Power Contracts

The increasing number of independent power producers and nonutility generators and the growing significance of purchased power contracts as a source of utility system capacity have focused attention on the accounting and disclosure of purchased power contracts. Some of these contracts have characteristics similar to leases. In addition to the capital lease tests found in SFAS No. 13, *Accounting for Leases*, the entity should consider whether the purchaser has evaluated the arrangements and assessed the risks and rewards assumed and retained by the parties to the agreement in determining the accounting for long-term purchased power contracts.

(n) Long-Term Power Sales Contracts

Nonutility generators provide an increasing percentage of new electric generating capacity. In order to finance these plants, nonutility generators sign long-term contracts with the purchasing utility. The structure of the contracts varies significantly. EITF Issue 91-6, *Revenue Recognition of Long-Term Power Sales Contracts*, provides accounting guidance relative to revenue recognition for contracts entered into or modified after May 21, 1992. EITF Issue 91-6 specifically excludes those contracts that qualify for lease accounting. The consensus reached by the EITF is that revenues should be recognized as the lesser of (1) the amount billable under the contract or (2) an amount determined by the kilowatt hours (kwhs) made available during the period multiplied by the estimated average revenue per kwh over the term of the contract. EITF Issue 96-17, *Revenue Recognition Under Long-Term Power Sales Contracts That Contain Both Fixed and Variable Pricing Terms*, provides accounting guidance on how revenue should be recognized on long-term power contracts that contain separate, specified terms for both (1) the fixed or scheduled prices per kwh and (2) the variable prices per kwh (based on market prices, actual avoided costs, or formula-based pricing arrangements), where there is no form of adjustment that determines or limits the total revenues to be billed under the contract over its entire period. The EITF concluded that revenues during the fixed-price period should be recognized in accordance with EITF Issue 91-6, while revenues during the variable-pricing period should be recognized as billed in accordance with the provisions of the contract.

(o)   Deferrals of Gains and Losses

Nonregulated entities are required to record a gain or loss on reacquisition of debt under APB Opinion No. 26, *Early Extinguishment of Debt*, as amended by SFAS No. 4, *Reporting Gains and Losses from Extinguishment of Debt* (Accounting Standards Section D14), and SFAS No. 125, *Accounting for Transfers and Servicing of Financial Assets and Extinguishments of Liabilities* (Accounting Standards Section F35). The difference between the reacquisition price and net carrying amount of the extinguished debt is classified as an extraordinary item. Rate regulators, however, generally require that utilities amortize these gains and losses over the remaining life of the issue unless the commission with the primary rate jurisdiction specifically allows an alternative treatment. If, by rate order, future revenues are to be adjusted to compensate for the gain or loss on early extinguishment of debt, SFAS No. 71 requires that the utility capitalize the gain or loss and amortize it over the period during which it will be allowed for rate-making purposes. Amounts amortized would not be classified as extraordinary items. If the utility is not afforded regulatory treatment, it would follow GAAP for nonregulated entities, and the gain or loss would not be deferred and amortized, but would be recognized currently as an extraordinary item.

Rate regulators often permit utilities to defer and amortize certain unusual costs over a specified period. The accounting treatment should conform with the entity's rate-making procedures. Examples of such unusual costs are storm damage, abandonments of construction programs, and development of electronic data processing systems.

(p)   Income Taxes

In the past, the recognition of income tax expense under GAAP was generally consistent with rate-making policies. SFAS No. 109 removed many of the exceptions previously permitted rate-regulated entities. Thus, while the distinctions in financial reporting of income taxes between regulated and nonregulated entities are narrowing, the gap between financial reporting and rate making may expand. It is essential for the auditor to understand the rate regulator's policies and practices thoroughly with respect to recognizing deferred income taxes.

Historically, most public utilities used the flow-through method of accounting for certain temporary differences. Under this method, income tax expense was recognized on the basis of taxes paid or payable. A small number of differences were accorded deferred tax treatment (commonly called normalization, from a regulatory standpoint), primarily because of IRS regulations. Normalization generally results in higher operating expenses for utilities and, therefore, higher revenue requirements. SFAS No. 71 allowed flow-through accounting to be used for financial reporting if certain criteria were met.

With the required adoption of SFAS No. 109, utilities changed the way deferred taxes are calculated and use the liability method to record deferred taxes on temporary differences, regardless of their regulatory treatment. In addition, the definition of temporary differences encompasses the equity component of the AFUDC, which utilities historically recorded on a net-of-tax basis. SFAS No. 109 prohibits recording of net-of-tax amounts and requires that those amounts be grossed up.

Many regulators may continue to require flow-through accounting for income taxes for rate-making purposes. If flow-through accounting is prescribed by the regulator and deferred taxes not currently provided under that method meet the recovery criteria set forth in SFAS No. 71, the differences between the flow-through method and the liability method would be recorded as regulatory assets or liabilities on the balance sheet. In determining the amount of deferred taxes to be established, SFAS No. 109 focuses on the probable future revenue to be recovered through rates. SFAS No. 109 recognizes that the future revenues will include recovery of the tax expense generated on the revenues as well as the deferred tax liability. The tax-on-tax item is recorded as a regulatory asset on the balance sheet, with the offset to the deferred tax liability.

Excess deferred taxes created by a reduction in the enacted tax rate are removed from the deferred income tax liability; however, these changes generally are not recognized in the income statement. The average rate assumption method provision contained in the 1986 Tax Reform Act prohibits excess deferred taxes related to "protected" depreciation differences from being used to reduce customer rates more rapidly than over the life of the assets giving rise to the differences. In addition, the utility is likely to be held accountable for other deferred taxes collected from customers. Consequently, the excess deferred taxes generally become liabilities to customers.

An increase in the enacted tax rate probably would not result in an immediate provision for income taxes. An increase in the deferred tax liabilities would cause a need for higher rates in the future in order to satisfy the liability. If it is probable that the regulator would grant such higher rates, the charge resulting from the increase in deferred tax liabilities would be carried as a regulatory asset in the utility's balance sheet.

(q) Nuclear Decommissioning Disclosures

SAB Topic 10-B, Estimated Future Costs Related to Spent Nuclear Fuel and Nuclear Electric Generating Plants, provides guidance on what disclosures should be made concerning the estimated future costs to decommission nuclear generating plants. The SEC requires that the financial statement notes disclose the estimated costs of dismantling or decontaminating nuclear generating plants and whether provision for these costs is being made in current operations and recognized in rates. If such expected costs are not being provided for currently, utilities should disclose any difference between current and expected future costs and the potential impact on the financial statements or future operations.

In February 1994, the Edison Electric Institute, in a publication entitled *Accounting for Removal Costs Issue Paper*, recommended that electric utilities consider financial statement disclosure of the following information:

- A statement that nuclear plant decommissioning costs are accrued over the expected service life of the related plant
- The estimated cost to decommission in current-year dollars
- The expected timing and method of the decommissioning
- The accrual in the current period for decommissioning costs
- That the estimated decommissioning costs are provided for currently by expense provisions for decommissioning and that such costs are recognized in service rates
- The accumulated decommissioning costs accrued through the balance sheet date
- The balance of funds accumulated for decommissioning at the balance sheet date
- The classification in the income statement and the balance sheet of the decommissioning costs
- A statement disclosing how the earnings on the decommissioning fund and related credits are accounted for

At the time of this writing, the FASB has issued an exposure draft addressing the accounting issues relating to future closure costs. Those issues are:

- Determination of legal and/or constructive obligations for closure cost liabilities
- Recognition and measurement of the closure cost liability, and associated assumptions to be used
- Accounting for capitalized costs and their potential impairment
- Effects of funding and assurance provisions
- Impacts on rate-regulated enterprises
- The types of liabilities to be covered by the proposed standard

(r)   Financial Statement Presentation

The format of the financial statements of a public utility is often different from that of other entities. The financial statements reflect the capital-intensive nature of the utility's operations and are presented from the regulator's viewpoint. The primary sources and the primary uses of capital are presented first on the balance sheet; thus utility plant is the first asset classification and capitalization is the first grouping shown in the liabilities and equity section. Many utilities traditionally group long-term debt, except for the current portion, with preferred stock and common equity as total capitalization.

The focal point of the income statement is operating income. In theory, operating income is the return on the investment or rate base. Revenue and expense items that do not relate to utility operations are reported below the line, or after operating income. Income taxes on utility operations are considered operating expenses and are reported above the line. Interest and the related AFUDC are presented below the line.

36.4 RISK FACTORS AND AUDIT STRATEGY

In formulating the audit strategy for a rate-regulated entity, the auditor should consider inherent risk factors relating to the regulatory structure of the industry. The recovery of regulatory assets such as deferred energy costs, environmental cleanup costs, abandoned plant assets, and phase-in assets, and SFAS No. 109-related regulatory assets depends on the rate-making process. Particularly in the context of the increasingly competitive environment, the auditor should assess whether it is probable that those costs will not be recovered and should determine that they have been accounted for properly.[5] The disposition of revenue subject to refund also depends on the rate-making process. The auditor should evaluate the adequacy of the reserve pending resolution of a rate case.

Electric, gas, and telecommunications companies are under constant scrutiny by regulators, which affects the auditor's assessment of control risk. Both management and regulators require extensive, accurate, and timely financial and operating information for use in the rate-making process, in accessing the capital markets, and in complying with SEC reporting requirements. As a result, gas, electric, and telecommunications companies usually have mature, well-developed monitoring and application controls. In addition, they generally have mature internal audit departments that serve to enhance the control environment.

Typically, accounting information is generated by large, highly automated, and complex systems. Much of the accounting data is systems derived and incorporates many controls. Electric and gas utilities use magnetic tapes and other devices in industrial meters and electronic meter-reading devices that enable utility personnel to input usage directly on a tape that can be read by the system. Other amounts also are calculated by the system, such as deferred energy costs and nuclear fuel amortization. In telecommunications companies, sophisticated central office switches record customer usage. This information automatically updates the system.

Accordingly, it is generally efficient to assess control risk at low for the audit objectives of completeness, accuracy, and existence/occurrence for accounts that are part of the revenue and purchasing cycles and to perform tests of application controls in the audit of gas, electric, and telecommunications companies. The transactions and controls in those cycles that are specific to utilities are highlighted below.

36.5 TYPICAL TRANSACTIONS, CONTROLS, AND TESTS OF CONTROLS

(a) Revenue Cycle

In common with other service businesses, a public utility's revenue cycle is concerned with processing transactions that generate service revenues. The related accounts that are unique to or particularly significant in the utility industry are unbilled revenues, customer deposits, and deferred costs.

---

[5] All major telecommunications companies have discontinued the application of SFAS No. 71 and accordingly have written off their regulatory assets.

Tests of controls usually are directed at activities intended to ensure that:

- All service installations are authorized and accurately monitored
- All installations or terminations are recorded at the time of installation or discontinuance
- Billing records are set up on a timely basis for all completed service
- All usage is recorded on a regular and timely basis
- All usage is billed on a timely basis
- Bills are accurately calculated using the rates approved by the applicable regulatory commission for the particular customer class
- Customer deposits are safeguarded and recorded
- Cash receipts are safeguarded and recorded in the proper accounts
- Write-offs of customer accounts receivable are authorized and recorded
- Service order terms, credit terms, and prices are properly approved
- Revenues are recorded in the correct period
- Access charges received from interexchange carriers are recorded in the proper period

Tests of controls would include an appropriate combination of inquiring about and observation of the utility's monitoring and application controls, examining evidence that the controls are designed and operating effectively, and in some instances reperforming the controls.

The auditor should consider the controls in place that enable management to monitor the flow of data through the subsequent processes from the initial recording of new connections and services requested by customers to the recording of use of these services to the write-off of debtor balances. This should help management to minimize "leakage of revenue" along these processes. The billing process is critical as it is during this process that management ensures that all services rendered are billed in accordance with established tariffs or agreements on a timely basis. A key control in this area is determining that all customers are billed each month and that amounts billed are reasonable in light of customers' usage patterns. These and similar controls are designed to identify unbilled service and avoid understatement of income.

(b) Purchasing Cycle

The purchasing cycle encompasses several classes of transactions that may differ from those found in other commercial entities:

- Purchases or construction of utility plant
- Fuel purchases
- Purchases or sales of power
- Incurring and accounting for costs through a work-order system

(i) Purchases or Construction of Utility Plant.   Accounting for transactions related to additions to and sales of utility plant differs from the accounting for similar transactions in nonregulated entities because of several specialized industry practices (described earlier) involving a utility's plant accounts. Tests of controls ordinarily are directed to activities to ensure that:

- Additions to and disposals of property, plant, and equipment are authorized
- Overhead items are accumulated and distributed accurately in accordance with accounting policies governing the capitalization of overhead
- Completed construction is transferred to plant-in-service on a timely basis so that depreciation accruals begin at the appropriate time
- Depreciation rates and policies conform to those prescribed by regulatory authorities
- The cost and accumulated depreciation of property, plant, and equipment are accurately recorded
- Plant retirements are reported on a timely basis, and the original cost of retired property (together with the costs of removal less salvage value) is eliminated appropriately against accumulated depreciation
- Idle or abandoned assets are excluded from plant-in-service, as applicable

(ii) Fuel Purchases.   Coal, oil, and gas are commonly referred to as fossil fuels; consumption of these fuels is one of the principal operating costs of an electric utility. The cost of purchased gas is even more significant for a gas distribution utility. In addition, the use of deferred energy accounting, described earlier, may result in significant deferred energy costs. Accounting for the purchase and consumption of fossil fuel and purchased gas must be controlled effectively; the procedures are similar to those for purchasing and using inventories in general.

If a utility owns a nuclear generating station, the auditor should assess the controls over purchases of nuclear fuel and the amortization of its cost and other related expenditures (e.g., spent fuel storage and reprocessing costs). The amortization is calculated by a units-of-production method based on the estimated total usable heat content of the nuclear fuel and the heat content expended in a given period. As mentioned earlier, the amortization amount may be generated by the accounting system. Because of the lead time involved in procuring and processing nuclear fuel, industry practice is to capitalize the AFUDC on nuclear fuel while it is being processed from uranium ore to fabricated fuel assemblies available for service. Controls over buying, storing, using, and disposing of nuclear fuel are similar to those for plant assets generally.

(iii) Purchases or Sales of Power.   Electric utilities frequently buy and sell temporarily surplus energy or plant capacity. Most electric utilities enter into these agreements through interchanges (i.e., arrangements with neighboring utilities to exchange power to promote overall efficiency and reliability) that operate independently of the utilities and coordinate the production of electric power of member utilities to achieve maximum economy. Gas utilities occasionally enter into contractual agreements with neighboring utilities for the purchase or sale of surplus gas. Normally, both purchase and sale transactions with interchanges are subject to similar procedures.

(iv) Incurring and Accounting for Costs Through a Work-Order System.   The work-order system is an integral part of the accounting system of most public utilities. In a work-order system, costs of all types enter the system, are summarized, and are allocated to general ledger accounts according to a predetermined arrangement. The arrangement may be based on a study of the activities of a particular group of employees to determine which functional activities of the utility are benefited, or it may be the result of a management decision made at the time a special project is authorized. The allocations determine whether various charges are classified as capital items or expense items. The work-order system is of particular concern to the auditor since a substantial amount of costs flow through it before ultimately being charged to a general ledger account. In some utilities, all labor costs initially are charged to a work order (departmental work order) and subsequently are allocated to the appropriate general ledger (capital or expense) accounts. Many of the costs that enter the work-order system originate in other subsystems or feeder systems, such as materials and supplies, payroll, and miscellaneous purchase transactions.

Tests of controls over the work-order system are usually directed at activities to ensure that:

- Work orders are initiated on the basis of proper authorization
- All charges to work orders are reviewed for accuracy and approval
- Adequate records are maintained of all work-order charges
- The allocation of departmental work-order costs to the general ledger accounts is reasonable and has been documented appropriately
- Work orders are closed once the project is completed and the work-in-process is transferred to plant-in-service

As noted in the discussion of the revenue cycle, the tests of controls would involve inquiry, observation, examination of evidence, and, if appropriate, reperformance.

36.6 SUBSTANTIVE TESTS

Certain areas can be audited more efficiently and effectively by means of substantive testing. A number of those areas do not have any unique features that differentiate them from comparable accounts of entities in other industries. Thus, accounts receivable other than from customers of the utility's services; prepaid insurance, taxes, and interest; accounts payable and accrued liabilities; long-term debt; and the capital stock accounts are tested in the same way as in other industries and are not discussed here. Other accounts, however, are unique to utilities, and the substantive tests typically performed on them are described in this section.

(a) Allowance for Funds Used During Construction

Because of the capital-intensive nature of rate-regulated utilities, the AFUDC may be an important audit area. The auditor should understand how CWIP is treated for rate-making purposes. If the accrual of the AFUDC is appropriate based on the rate making, the auditor should ascertain that the AFUDC rate has been computed in a manner consistent with the rate regulator's prescribed method. Further, the auditor should determine that the AFUDC accrual has been applied only to appropriate CWIP and that it has been calculated and allocated properly.

(b) Regulatory Assets

Because regulatory assets are recognized only to the extent that it is probable that future revenues will be provided to recover them, the auditor must have a thorough understanding of the regulatory environment. If the regulator has already acted on the recoverability of the deferred cost, the auditor should review the rate order to ascertain that the asset exists. If the regulator has not yet acted on recovery of the deferred cost, significant judgment must be exercised to conclude that it is probable of recovery and, therefore, an asset. Although "probable" does not mean that recovery is certain, it implies a high expectation that the regulator will grant future recovery. In evaluating management's assertions concerning the probability of future recovery in the absence of regulatory action with respect to the specific cost, the auditor should consider the past experience of the utility in the regulatory jurisdiction, the experience of other utilities in the regulatory jurisdiction, the views of the utility's rate counsel, and other relevant evidence.

(c) Unbilled Revenues

If the auditor has performed tests of controls in the revenue cycle and has been able to assess control risk at low, substantive tests may be limited to a review of the reasonableness of the estimates used in the accrual and analytical procedures applied to the unbilled revenues. Analytical procedures may consist of comparing the unbilled revenues with the prior year and with billed services, taking into account changes in customer usage, and rates.

(d) Deferred Costs

Deferred costs are calculated monthly, based on data generated from both the revenue and purchasing cycles. In addition to assessing their recoverability (discussed earlier), the auditor should test controls over the calculation or review the calculation itself.

(e) Analytical Procedures

Because of the nature of the utility business, the analytical procedures most useful to an auditor of a public utility involve comparing financial information with information for prior years and considering relationships among current-year accounts. Information on which to perform analytical procedures often is readily available since utility management also uses analytics as a tool to judge performance. Examples of analytical procedures in an electric and gas utility audit are:

- Comparing base revenue per kwh or million cubic feet by class of customer with the prior-year amounts and considering the reasonableness of any changes against rate orders

- Comparing monthly sales volumes with corresponding months of prior years and reviewing any changes in light of changes in rates, temperature, and similar factors

- Relating energy adjustment clause revenues to energy costs in the current period

- Comparing fuel expense per kwh by type of generation or per million cubic feet with prior-year amounts. The percentage change may be related, for example, to the percentage change in oil cost per barrel. Changes in the mix of fuel use and in the cost of purchased energy may be reviewed for reasonableness. The total sources of energy (internal generation plus purchases) may be compared with uses of energy (sales, internal use, and losses)

- Relating the AFUDC as a percentage of the average CWIP balance to the rates used by the company to accrue the AFUDC for the year

- Relating depreciation expense as a percentage of plant to authorized rates

In a telecommunications company audit, analytical procedures such as the following may be performed:

- Comparing access charges with the related minutes of use
- Comparing revenues with the number of messages
- Comparing local service revenues with the number of access lines
- Relating depreciation expense as a percentage of plant to authorized rates
- Comparing maintenance expense with total telephone plant or with number of access lines

37

Auditing Government Contractors

37.1 OVERVIEW OF THE INDUSTRY

Various types of entities may enter into contracts with the federal government,[1] for example, aerospace or other manufacturers, professional services firms, health care intermediaries, or research universities. Most of their essential business processes are the same with respect to their government contracting activities as with respect to their private-sector business. It is not the nature of what a contractor does that presents unique auditing issues; rather, it is the contractor's relationship with its customer when the customer is the federal government.

That relationship is defined by regulations with which federal government contractors must comply. These regulations give rise to unique contingent liabilities and other issues that auditors must consider. For example, the government may have the right to reprice a contract, or may withhold or reduce contract payments for an extended period of time. Such contract rights held by the government have no counterpart in the private sector.

The regulations with which government contractors must comply are written by the government and enforced by an elaborate oversight network of government auditors and contract administrators. The regulations, and the laws on which they are based, are inherently political and are subject to frequent change by elected and appointed officials. Many rules are fundamentally opposite to prevailing business practice in the private sector. For example, in many cases, a government contractor is required to disclose every aspect of its pricing process, including proprietary information, to the government. Failure to do so may be punishable as a criminal offense. This contrasts with private-sector contracts, for which disclosure of pricing details is highly unusual. This chapter focuses on identifying the circumstances that can give rise to these requirements and the attendant risks that government contractors face.

37.2 LAWS AND REGULATIONS

In general, the method by which the government makes a purchase determines what regulations apply. When the government buys "off the shelf" or commercial products, it generally does so on commercial terms. The current regulatory trend is toward broadening the definition of a commercial product and relaxing regulations accordingly. When the government makes an award based on a sealed bid, no pricing regulations are invoked, and performance proceeds much as in the commercial sector. However, if the contract price is negotiated, full disclosure of data is required and the resulting contract will be highly regulated. Similarly, when the government buys a unique item, such as a submarine or a battle tank, from a sole source, the full range and intensity of regulation will apply. Cost-reimbursement contract billings and proposals for negotiation, even on fixed-price contracts, are subject to audit and extensive regulatory coverage. In all cases where the auditor is unfamiliar with the regula-

---

[1] The AICPA audit and accounting guide, *Audits of Federal Government Contractors*, and this chapter cover federal government contracts. The guidance in this chapter also may be relevant in auditing entities that enter into contracts with other governmental entities.

tions and their application, he or she may want to consult with a specialist. Some of the more important regulations are discussed next.

(a) Cost Principles

All negotiated government contracts exceeding $500,000 are covered by cost principles. The particular cost principles followed will depend on the nature of the contractor. Most for-profit contractors are covered by the cost principles in the Federal Acquisition Regulation (FAR). Not-for-profit organizations are covered by the cost principles in Office of Management and Budget (OMB) Circular A-122; research universities are covered by the cost principles in OMB Circular A-21. While all cost principles have much in common, there are important differences and the auditor should always understand which regulations apply to a contract.

(i) FAR.   The Federal Acquisition Regulation is the government's comprehensive procurement regulation and applies to all agencies. Agencies may supplement the FAR with additional regulations, but must follow the basic rules in the FAR. In addition to defining and discussing such concepts as direct and indirect costs, Part 31 of the FAR introduces the concept of allowability. This is a uniquely governmental concept and establishes that the government, as a matter of policy, will not reimburse a contractor for certain costs that are not reasonable, not allocable to the contract, or specifically prohibited by the contract.

Additionally, Part 31 of the FAR contains specific instructions on approximately 50 categories of cost, ranging from advertising costs to taxes. Some costs are expressly unallowable, such as most advertising, lobbying, entertainment, interest, and alcoholic beverage costs. Other costs are reimbursable, including many types of compensation, depreciation, and research and development costs. The inclusion of costs directly associated with unallowable costs is prohibited, such as travel costs incurred in support of lobbying activities. Many of these prohibitions are rooted in law, and charging unallowable costs to the government is considered a serious matter. The amounts of unallowable costs are usually small from a materiality perspective; generally, unallowable costs constitute only a little over 1 percent of contract costs. The potential ramifications from billing unallowable costs, such as fines, penalties, repricing, and in extreme cases suspension, are far out of proportion to the amounts of such costs. Most unallowable costs are legitimate business costs, and the FAR prohibition does not affect their deductibility for tax purposes.

(ii) OMB Circular A-122.   This regulation covers not-for-profit contractors, except for certain research institutions (approximately 30) that have had a long-standing relationship with the Department of Defense and which are covered by the FAR. The Circular provides principles to be applied in establishing the allowability of certain costs; it also establishes uniform rules for determining the costs of grants, contracts, and other agreements, and guidelines on whether costs are to be treated as direct or indirect.

(iii) OMB Circular A-21.   Circular A-21 applies to universities, many of which are major research contractors, since much of the funding for research activities is provided by the government. Some universities conduct government research totaling hundreds of millions of dollars. Their cost principles differ from those for other government contractors in that they are tailored to the accounting systems used by universities, whose primary reporting objective is accounting for resources received and used. The cost principles are used in determining the allowable costs of work performed by colleges and universities under sponsored agreements and also under subgrants, cost-reimbursement subcontracts, and other awards. Section F of the Circular provides for identification and assignment of indirect costs such as depreciation, operating and maintenance expenses, general and administrative expenses, departmental administration expenses, library expenses, and student administration and services.

(b) Cost Accounting Standards

All negotiated government contracts over $500,000 are covered by certain Cost Accounting Standards (CAS). In addition, contracts over $25 million, individually or cumulatively, are subject to additional standards and a requirement to disclose cost accounting practices. These regulations generally are considered by contractors to be the most onerous and inflexible of all contract regulations. While most of the requirements of CAS are consistent with good accounting practice, the administration of these rules often has been very time-consuming and expensive for contractors. In addition, the contract terms that implement CAS provide for the government to reprice contracts in certain circumstances, including when there has been a material change in a cost accounting practice. Basic CAS requirements include consistency, written procedures, records, and allocation practices for costs.

(c) Other Provisions of the FAR

The FAR contains 53 parts, including the text of all standard contract clauses and all forms used in the contracting process. The FAR provides comprehensive guidance on topics such as acquisition planning, contracting methods, socioeconomic programs, and contract management. Part 52 of the FAR discusses contract clauses that directly affect the amounts that the government remits to the contractor for work performed. The inadvertent omission from a contract of clauses mandated by legislation does not release the contractor from the associated compliance responsibility.

(i) Truth in Negotiations Act. The Truth in Negotiations Act (TINA) applies to the award of any negotiated contract expected to exceed $500,000, or the pricing of any contract change. It requires that the contractor or subcontractor submit cost or pricing data and certify that to the best of his or her knowledge the data was accurate, complete, and current as of the date of agreement on price. TINA also provides that any contract or change must contain a price reduction provision. Under this provision, the contract price may be adjusted to exclude any significant amount by which the price is determined to have been increased because the contractor or subcontractor furnished cost and pricing data that was inaccurate, incomplete, or noncurrent. These prohibited practices are called "defective pricing." For the purpose of making a determination of defective pricing, the government has the right to examine all books, records, documents, and other data related to the negotiation, pricing, or performance of the contract. The purpose of the Act is to put the government on a par with contractors when negotiating noncompetitive or sole-source contracts.

(ii) Limitation of Cost. Under the provisions of cost-reimbursement contracts, government contractors are entitled to be compensated for their allowable incurred costs. Contractors are not entitled to compensation, however, for overrun costs in excess of the contract price. The government enforces management of costs under these contracts through the "limitation of cost" clause in the contract. As the contractor's billings approach the contract price, the contractor must notify the government that an overrun is imminent. This must occur by the point at which funds are 75 percent expended. The government then may decide to increase the funding in the contract or stop funding the effort beyond the current contract. The contractor will not be entitled to compensation for costs in excess of the contract value unless the proper notifications have been made.

(iii) Unilateral Changes. Government contracts provide the government with the right to unilaterally change the scope of work. Unilateral changes may be made in response to technological advances, an urgent requirement, unanticipated funding limitations, or reduced contractor capability. The notion of unilateral change is unusual in a commercial contracting situation and results from the government's unique needs. The right to unilateral change increases a government contractor's risk.

If such a change results in an increase in cost or time required to perform the contract, the contractor can submit a request for equitable adjustment (REA) to the government contracting officer. The government ordinarily requires that the costs resulting from the change be segregated or identified apart from the basic contract costs. The contractor is required to "proceed diligently with performance of the contract, pending final resolution of any requests for relief, claim, appeal or action arising under the contract, and comply with any decision of the contracting officer" [FAR 52.243–1(e)].

(iv) Contract Termination. The government has the right to terminate contracts, in whole or in part, for its convenience or because of default by the contractor. Termination for convenience is treated as a contract change because the government has changed the scope of the contract. In this situation, the contractor is entitled to recover costs attributable to the termination. This not only includes costs incurred in connection with the termination, but also may include ongoing costs that cannot be discontinued. Profit will be paid on work actually accomplished but anticipated profit on work eliminated by the termination is not compensable. In addition, if the contractor would have incurred a loss had the contract been completed, a proportionate share of the loss is offset against the final termination settlement.

Termination for default occurs when the contractor fails to meet some term, condition, or requirement of the contract. The most common examples are late delivery or failure to meet specifications. Before terminating a contract on the grounds of default, the contracting officer must issue a "cure notice" that gives the contractor a stated period of time to correct the deficiency. If the contractor does not correct the deficiency within the stated time, the government has the right to terminate the contract and reprocure it from another source. In this case, the government has a right to be reimbursed for the additional costs incurred in connection with the reprocurement. The resolution of contract terminations, even when there is accord between the parties, can take as long as several years. Contractors are not entitled to interest when the government delays termination settlements.

(d) Oversight

One of the unique characteristics of government contracts is that the government contractually acquires audit rights that are unknown in the private sector. In addition, the complexity of the terms and conditions of government contracts requires significantly more administration than is the norm in the private sector. These factors give rise to a large oversight infrastructure that includes auditors, negotiators, pricing specialists, quality inspectors, and others. These contract overseers ensure compliance with regulations and create an added burden for contractors in maintaining an ongoing relationship with the oversight personnel. From the standpoint of the auditor, the existence of this oversight infrastructure creates both the opportunity and necessity to become familiar with the government activities and findings. During the planning phase, the auditor should review the contractor's correspondence with government contract administrators, regulatory authorities, and government auditors. The auditor also should review the CAS disclosure statement, as discussed later in this chapter, to become familiar with cost accounting practices.

The main body of oversight for defense contracts is the Defense Contract Management Command (DCMC). Other agencies administer their own contracts and may use auditors from their agencies, from the Defense Contract Audit Agency, or from the private sector.

37.3 ACCOUNTING PRINCIPLES AND PRACTICES

(a) Revenue Recognition

Statement of Position (SOP) 81-1, *Accounting for Performance of Construction-Type and Certain Production-Type Contracts*, provides guidance on the application of generally accepted accounting principles (GAAP) for long-term, construction-type and performance-type contracts generally, including government contracts. Government contracts, however, entail activities that often are far more complex than those under traditional construction contracts and may include contracts, such as those that are part of a program and are accounted for under the program method of accounting, that are not addressed by the SOP. Federal government contracts involve the development and production of military aircraft, weapons delivery systems, space exploration hardware, computer software, and the provision of services to support these acquisitions. Accounting for long-term contracts entails the recording of direct costs by job, with appropriate allocation methods for distributing indirect costs.

There are two general types of government contracts: cost reimbursement and fixed price. Typically, cost-reimbursement contracts include a profit in the form of a fixed fee, while profit on a fixed-price contract will depend on successful performance within estimated costs. In either case, payments for goods that have been delivered under short-term contracts must be made within 30 days after the government receives a contractor's invoice, as required by the Prompt Payment Act. There is no similar time limit for interim payments under long-term contracts; those payments generally are based on costs incurred. In the case of cost-reimbursement contracts, interim payments are made in accordance with the contract clause covering allowable costs and payments. That clause allows a contractor to bill allowable incurred costs plus a pro rata share of the fee (less a small retention) on a monthly basis. In the case of fixed-price contracts, interim payments are made under the clause covering progress payments. These payments are usually a percentage (such as 75 percent) of the allowable costs incurred and do not include profit; the profit portion is paid on delivery.

For short-term contracts, revenue should be recognized when the government has received and accepted the goods or services that have been delivered by the contractor. For both cost-reimbursement and fixed-price, long-term contracts, revenue is recognized based on costs incurred. Fees or profits are recognized pro rata for cost-reimbursement contracts, and are based on percentage of completion for fixed-price contracts. Most payments under government contracts are made promptly, and long-outstanding invoices should alert the auditor to question whether revenue should have been recognized.

(b) Contract Costs

Contract costs are accumulated in the same manner as inventory costs and are charged to operations as the related revenue is recognized. Contract costs include all direct costs that are identifiable and allocable to the contract, such as materials, direct labor, and subcontract costs. Practices vary with respect to indirect costs considered allocable to the contract, but usually such indirect costs include costs of indirect labor, contract supervision, tools and equipment, supplies, quality control and inspection, insurance, repairs and maintenance, and depreciation and amortization. Methods of allocating indirect costs should be systematic and rational. Most costs are capitalized as inventory, including general and administrative expenses. Typically, the government withholds a defined amount or percentage of the contract price, known as the retainage, until certain conditions have been satisfactorily met. Examples of such conditions are completion of overhead negotiations, disposal of government-owned materials, fulfillment of contract guarantees or warranties, and substantial completion of contract performance.

(c) Contract Cost Estimates

The estimate of costs to complete a contract is the most crucial factor in determining income earned in accounting for government contracts. Accounting practices should be in place that are systematic and consistent and that are correlated with the cost accounting system to provide a basis for periodically comparing actual and estimated costs. The estimate of total contract costs should reflect expected price and wage escalations, particularly for longer-term contracts. Contract cost estimates are affected by factors such as the current actual costs of performance; changes in costs of material to be purchased in the future and not covered by firm purchase orders; changes in labor costs, including fringe benefits, that may take place in the future; changes in indirect costs; recoverability of contractor-sponsored research and development expenses; fluctuations in total production activity as they affect allocation bases for various indirect costs; technical problems encountered in performing the contract; and specific contract provisions such as performance requirements, warranties, and damages. The determination of cost estimates is a complex process and involves the financial, engineering, manufacturing, and other areas. As contract modifications occur, and additional information is obtained, contract estimates must be reviewed and updated regularly over the term of contract performance.

(d) Provisions for Anticipated Losses

According to SOP 81-1, paragraph 85, when current estimates of total contract revenue and cost indicate a loss, a provision for the entire loss on the contract should be made in the period in which the indication of the loss is discovered. Factors that should be included in arriving at a projected loss on a contract include target penalties and rewards, nonreimbursable costs on cost-plus contracts, change orders, and potential repricing. The provision for loss should be accounted for in the income statement as additional contract cost rather than a reduction of revenue and should be recognized as a current liability on the balance sheet. When a contract provides for progress payments, recognition of a loss necessarily triggers reductions in progress payments, resulting in reduced cash flow for the contractor.

(e) Contract-Related Assets and Liabilities

As set forth in the AICPA audit and accounting guide, *Audits of Federal Government Contractors*, government contractors present classified balance sheets. In classifying assets and liabilities as current or noncurrent, contractors should follow Accounting Research Bulletin No. 43. Figure 37.1 lists typical assets and liabilities related to government contracts.

Figure 37.1 Contract-Related Assets and Liabilities

Assets	*Liabilities*
Accounts receivable on contracts (including retention fees)	Accounts payable on contracts (including retention fees)
Unbilled contract receivables	Accrued contract costs
Costs in excess of billings and estimated earnings	Billings in excess of costs and estimated earnings
Other deferred contract costs	Advance payments on contracts
Equipment and tools specifically purchased for, and expected to be used solely on, an individual contract or group of related contracts	Obligations (regardless of payment terms) for equipment and tools specifically purchased for, and expected to be used solely on, an individual contract or group of related contracts
	Provisions for losses on contracts

(f) Research and Development Activities

Contractors may engage in contract research and development (R&D) or in independent research and development activities. Independent research and development is an allowable cost under government contracts, although there are limits for very large contractors. Contract research under cost-reimbursement contracts normally poses few accounting problems. However, fixed-price R&D contracts almost always result in significant losses and generally have been prohibited within the Department of Defense. These contracts must be accounted for in accordance with SOP 81-1, and losses must be recognized in the period in which they first become evident. In certain limited cases, contractors may enter into fixed-price, best-efforts, cost-sharing arrangements with the government. For this limited category of R&D agreements, the AICPA audit and accounting guide on government contractors permits costs to be treated as R&D costs as defined in Statement of Financial Accounting Standards (SFAS) No. 2, if they meet stringent criteria outlined in the guide.

37.4 RISK FACTORS

(a) Repricing of Contracts

As discussed earlier, some government contracts are subject to repricing. This can occur through a number of mechanisms, which are discussed below.

(i) CAS. Government contracts containing the CAS clause, as set out in FAR paragraph 52.230–2, provide that any failure by a contractor or subcontractor to comply with the Cost Accounting Standards may result in a contract repricing, which will include recovery of any increased costs, with interest computed at the annual rate established by the Treasury Department. The risk of noncompliance extends to three years after the final contract payment.

Among other requirements, the Cost Accounting Standards call for consistency in accounting practices used in estimating, accumulating, and reporting contract cost data for contracts covered by CAS. For contractors that are subject to the disclosure requirement discussed in the following paragraph, CAS also require a cost impact statement for any change in cost accounting practices that increases costs to the government. CAS 331.20 (k) defines a cost accounting practice as "any disclosed or established accounting method or technique which is used for measurement of cost, assignment of cost to cost accounting periods, or allocation of cost to cost objectives."

Entities with greater than $25 million in government contracts covered by CAS must file disclosure statements containing details of the entity's cost accounting practices. The disclosure statement contains such information as accounting for direct and indirect costs, allocation of indirect costs, depreciation practices, accounting for pension costs, deferred compensation and insurance programs, and allocation of corporate or home-office costs to segments. This information constitutes the entity's cost accounting practices against which consistency in estimating, accumulating, and reporting practices on individual contracts is measured. The disclosure statement is reviewed by the government to determine that it is current, accurate, and complete and that disclosed practices comply with relevant Cost Accounting Standards. Any changes in accounting practices must be communicated to the government office responsible for approving the contractor's disclosure statement. If the contractor subsequently follows accounting practices that are not consistent with the disclosed practices, or fails to comply with required standards, it is a violation of the contract terms. The government will conduct an audit to determine whether there is a cost impact to the contract as a result of the violation and may reduce the contract price if the changed accounting practice is to the government's disadvantage.

(ii) Defective Pricing.   Defective pricing arises when a contractor has failed to comply with the Truth in Negotiations Act, which requires contractors to certify that, at the date of the agreement on contract price, current, accurate, and complete cost and pricing data was provided. The definition of cost and pricing data includes vendor quotes, labor rates, projected indirect cost rates, and other cost factors. TINA also has been interpreted to include projections of future events such as business volume, expected scrap, rework, the ability to negotiate lower prices on material purchases, and management decisions that affect future costs, such as decisions to automate, acquire businesses, change employee benefits, and change tax accounting methods. When it is determined that defective pricing has occurred, contract prices, including the profit or fee, are reduced to the amount that would have been negotiated if the cost or pricing information had been accurate and complete. If the potential amount of adjustment is material, it must be disclosed in accordance with SFAS No. 5. Circumstances leading to defective pricing situations are reviewed by the government to determine whether there was intent by the contractor to make a false statement or prepare a false claim by providing the defective data, in which case the government may take criminal and civil actions against the contractor.

(iii) Cost Audits.   A government contract may be subject to a number of different types of government audits depending on the type of contract: incurred cost audits, cost accounting standards compliance and adequacy reviews, terminated contract audits, claim audits, operational audits and functional reviews, or "should-cost" team reviews.

The purpose of the incurred cost audit is to determine the allowability of direct and indirect costs billed to the government on cost-reimbursement contracts. The focus of the cost accounting standards compliance and adequacy review is to determine whether the contractor is in compliance with standards promulgated by the Cost Accounting Standards Board (CASB). Terminated contract audits evaluate terminated contracts for reasonableness and for compliance with termination cost principles.

Claim audits are conducted to determine equitable adjustments and examine claims under the Contract Disputes Act of 1978. Operational audits and functional reviews entail evaluation of management and operational decisions made by a contractor that affect the nature and level of costs proposed and incurred on government contracts, and typically result in a report that recommends how to improve internal control and the economy and efficiency of contractor operations.

Finally, should-cost team reviews involve contract cost analysis by an integrated team of government procurement, contract administration, contract audit, and engineering representatives. The team conducts a coordinated, in-depth cost analysis at the contractor's plant for the purpose of facilitating the establishment of a fair and reasonable price for a contract in the environment and under conditions predicted for contract performance.

(iv) Most Favored Customer Provision.   The Federal Supply Schedule (FSS) Program is a simplified process of buying commonly used supplies in varying quantities while obtaining discounts associated with high-volume purchases. These indefinite delivery contracts are awarded competitively and require vendors to provide supplies and services at stated prices for given periods of time. The buying office publishes a schedule providing the information needed for other federal agencies to place orders with contractors. The FSS Program may cover contracts awarded to a single supplier or to more than one supplier for delivery of comparable commercial supplies and services.

FSS contracts contain a most favored customer provision. This provision requires that the contractor sell to the government at a price that is at least equal to the price offered to its most favored customers. Government auditors review sales data for FSS contractors to ensure that the government is receiving the lowest price. If the auditors find sales at a lower price than that offered the government, they may reprice all of the contractors' sales to the government. Clearly, if the contractor has substantial sales to the government in violation of the clause, the adjustment can be quite large.

(b)   Claims

As noted earlier, the government has the right to make unilateral changes to its contracts. This authority, coupled with a large established administrative and oversight infrastructure, virtually guarantees that there will be changes to government contracts. Changes are implemented through change orders, of which contract law recognizes two broad types—formal and constructive. A formal change order is a written document issued by the government stating that, pursuant to the changes clause in the contract, a specific change or changes are being made. Since the government acknowledges that a change is being made, only the amount of the equitable adjustment in terms of contract price or delivery schedule is likely to be disputed. All changes effected by formal change orders should be documented. Constructive change orders, in contrast, are subtle and difficult to identify, document, and quantify. Constructive change orders may be either written or oral directives or requests, and represent informal actions, failures to act, or omissions on the part of the government.

Many, perhaps most, change orders are executed, priced, and adjudicated in accordance with the provisions of the contract and never require the attention of the auditor. On occasion, the government and the contractor will not be able to agree on the pricing of a change, however, or perhaps even that a change has been authorized. The latter situation is more common with constructive change orders, which frequently result in disputes regarding the contractor's right or entitlement to equitable adjustments, because the government and the contractor often disagree that the informal act or omission constitutes a valid contract change.

When there is a disagreement about a change order, the contractor must resort to an REA or a claim. Resolution of such claims often requires years, because the government typically denies that the contractor is entitled to additional compensation.

The contractor must argue the case first to the contracting officer, then to a Board of Contract Appeals. This process often results in a finding of entitlement for the contractor, who, if successful, will be awarded interest for the period of the dispute. However, during the process of resolving a dispute, the contract, by law, must be performed. Thus, contractors will incur costs for which it may not be clear that they are entitled to reimbursement. The auditor should evaluate how much, if any, of a claim should be recognized as an account receivable from the government. Guidelines to assist in that evaluation are provided in the AICPA's government contractors audit and accounting guide.

(c) Suspension

A conviction of or indictment for fraud, or the disclosure of a serious ethical issue, may call into question the integrity of the contractor's control systems. This may subject the contractor to suspension from doing business with the government, or, possibly, debarment. Such actions will preclude not only the awarding of new contracts, but also extensions of existing contracts. Suspension or debarment can have an adverse impact on earnings or profit, and, if the majority of the contractor's business is with the government, can raise a going concern issue.

(d) Fraud, Waste, and Abuse

Throughout the 1980s and early 1990s, U.S. fiscal policy was dominated by large, intractable budget deficits. The reluctance of elected officials to tax more or spend less led to a search for alternative solutions. A popular solution during this period was to promise savings through the elimination of fraud, waste, and abuse in government procurement. In the early 1980s, Congress passed laws requiring the assignment of inspectors general in all government agencies to identify instances of fraud, waste, and abuse. The campaign against fraud, waste, and abuse also encouraged internal "whistleblowers" and *qui tam* lawsuits (discussed below).

Whistleblowers, in this context, are contractor employees who voluntarily disclose alleged cases of fraud, waste, or abuse against the government. An elaborate regulatory framework protects such employees from reprisal by their employers. Since whistleblowers are subject to protection under federal law, whistleblowing becomes attractive to employees facing separation or discipline. As disruptive as this may be to contractors, they usually are aware of the allegations of whistleblowers and are able to respond to them. It is obviously important to auditors to be aware of any such allegations.

In a *qui tam* lawsuit, an employee brings a lawsuit against a contractor on behalf of the government and, if successful, shares in the proceeds. Some of these lawsuits have resulted in multimillion dollar awards for the *qui tam* plaintiff. Additionally, *qui tam* investigations are carried out under seal, and contractors may know nothing about an ongoing investigation. Accordingly, it is important for contractors to take all available precautions against instances of fraud, waste, and abuse, such as the establishment of ethics programs, as discussed later.

(e) Subcontractors

Federal subcontractors may be subject to the same terms and conditions that apply to prime contractors. The prime contractor is responsible for administering any subcontracts, including performing audits of subcontract prices and compliance with contractual requirements such as CAS, cost and pricing data, and progress payment provisions. If a significant portion of a contract is undertaken by subcontractors, this poses a risk to the prime contractor, since subcontractors are often reluctant to allow prime contractors to review their books and records. At the prime contractor's request, the government may perform reviews in lieu of the prime contractor. Nonetheless, the prime contractor still remains liable for subcontractors' compliance with applicable procurement rules and regulations. The government has the right to reduce the prime contract price for subcontractor violations. Prime contractors should obtain indemnification from subcontractors for losses suffered as a result of subcontractors' failure to comply with procurement regulations.

37.5 INTERNAL CONTROL

The most important elements in a government contractor's internal control are described in this section.

(a) Codes of Ethics

Public concern about defense procurement irregularities during the 1980s led to the creation of the Defense Industry Initiatives on Business Ethics and Conduct. The Initiatives sought to promote ethical business conduct through the implementation of policies, procedures, and programs in such areas as codes of ethics, ethics training, internal reporting of alleged misconduct, internal oversight, attendance at Best Practices Forums, and accountability to the public. While not all contractors signed the Initiatives, many did. The programs established by these contractors are intended to provide reasonable assurance of compliance with the Initiatives.

Codes of ethics are effective only if they are fully understood and adhered to by all employees. Evidence of employee awareness of business ethics includes broad distribution of a written code, personnel orientation programs, group meetings, videotapes, and articles. When assessing control risk, the auditor should consider a contractor's code of ethics and the tone set by management, and should document the procedures management has instituted. This includes inquiring about employee infractions of the code of conduct and actions taken by management.

One of the principles of business ethics and conduct contained in the Initiatives concerns defense contractors' public accountability for their commitment to the Initiatives. That principle requires completion of a questionnaire on business ethics and conduct. The principle also requires the contractor's independent public accountant or similar organization to express a conclusion about the responses to the questionnaire. Auditors of defense contractors frequently are engaged to perform that service. Engagements to examine or review a defense contractor's responses are covered by an Interpretation of the Statements on Standards for Attestation Engagements.

(b) Estimating Process

As discussed previously, estimates are critical in income determination. It is important that estimates be prepared in a consistent manner, with adequate documentation and support for management pricing decisions. The most sensitive areas in the estimating process are forward pricing and indirect cost rates, which should be based on the most current financial data available. Estimates to complete individual jobs are important, particularly fixed-price contracts, as anticipated losses on contracts must be recognized when they first become evident. The auditor should understand and document the contractor's estimating practices, the knowledge and experience of management personnel who participate in or oversee the development of estimates, and the timeliness and reliability of estimate data.

(c) Contract Cost Accounting Practices

Cost information drives the entire financial reporting process for most contractors. It is used to evaluate the status and profitability of contracts, and to prepare customer billings. The contract cost records classify and summarize costs into categories such as direct materials, labor and labor-related costs, subcontract charges, equipment costs, and indirect costs. The control system also provides timely cost reports to management. While the recognition, distribution, and accumulation of contract costs are similar for both commercial and government contractors, the additional feature of the government environment calls for special attention on the part of both the contractor and the auditor.

Controls must be in place to monitor various aspects of a government contractor's cost accounting practices. The auditor should understand and document the procedures management uses to ensure that its cost accounting practices are in compliance with government regulations. Those regulations require that:

- Costs be accurately distributed to the contract or cost objective for which they are incurred
- Costs be reasonable and in accordance with specific contractual provisions
- The cost accounting system segregate unallowable costs or have the capability of delineating such costs and providing the details necessary to segregate them
- Cost allocation practices used to charge indirect costs to contracts be reasonable, reflect the beneficial or causal relationship between costs and cost objectives, and be in conformity with CAS, if applicable
- Costs incurred on all cost-reimbursement projects or contracts be reconcilable to the costs reflected in the general ledger and, ultimately, the financial statements

(d) Unallowable Costs

Expressly unallowable costs must be separately identified and excluded from billings to the government. The Department of Defense Authorization Act of 1986 requires all contractors to certify that no unallowable costs are included in proposal or reimbursement submissions. Signing such a certification subjects the contractor to civil and criminal penalties for failure to remove such costs from government billings or proposal submissions. Cost Accounting Standard 405 requires contractors to identify and account separately for unallowable costs. Such costs may be deeply embedded in the contractor's accounting system and difficult to delineate. The auditor should consider the contractor's knowledge and treatment of allowable and unallowable costs, as well as carefully evaluate the capability of the entity's internal control to delineate these costs. If the contractor's system allows an unallowable cost to be included in a government billing or proposal, the impact can be significant, even though the amount of the unallowable cost is small.

(e) Job Order Integrity

In addition to ascertaining that costs are accumulated properly, another key objective of internal control is the establishment of a job order costing system that ensures that costs are charged to the appropriate contracts. The job cost report must reconcile to the general ledger and must equal the aggregate of the costs incurred for each separate contract. The area most vulnerable to mischarging is labor. Accordingly, the payroll and the monthly or biweekly labor costs for a particular contract should be reconciled periodically and any discrepancies investigated. The auditor should determine whether these reconciliations are performed. Many contractors have major contracts for which the cost accumulation and reporting function is decentralized and performed at the various contract sites. The auditor should obtain reasonable assurance that uniform controls are in place at each site and should document this information. Depending on the control risk assessment, this may entail contract site visits.

(f) Contract Revenue Recognition Practices

Internal control over contract revenues should be designed to provide reliable information about the amount and timing of revenue recognition. For cost-reimbursement contracts, revenues are directly related to costs incurred. For some fixed-price contracts, revenues also may be a function of costs, as in negotiated contracts where cost or pricing data is submitted. For other contracts, such as sealed bid contracts, revenues may be independent of actual costs incurred. Compliance with cost principles and CAS often has a direct effect on revenue recognized, as does the process of estimating contract progress. Controls over revenue recognition should ensure that:

- Estimates of contract revenues and costs are updated periodically and are reported to and reviewed by appropriate levels of management; revenues are compared with contract terms for compliance; and revenues recognized on all contracts are reconciled to revenues reported in the financial statements

- Revenue recognition is based on current estimates of costs to be incurred and is compared with contract prices

- Change order and claim revenues are recognized in conformity with GAAP

- Management reporting of updated estimates provides sufficient information to determine whether a contract loss reserve is required

- Revenues flow through an "unbilled receivables account" until the government is billed, at which time the amount is transferred to billed accounts receivable

The auditor should understand whether the contractor's controls over revenue recognition meet these objectives. The auditor also should understand whether controls over billing ensure compliance with the procedures set forth in FAR Part 32 and that billing conforms to contract terms.

(g) Pending Contracts and Modifications

If a contractor has commenced work based on a pending award for which unofficial notification has been received, the contractor is at risk of not being reimbursed for costs incurred prior to receipt of the award. Similarly, if a contract has a modification pending, there is a risk that funding for the modification may not materialize. Because of those risks, it is generally not appropriate to recognize revenue on pending contracts or modifications. In addition, government regulations permit unsuccessful competitors to protest an award. The General Accounting Office (GAO) adjudicates these protests. During the course of a protest, work on an awarded contract normally is suspended. If the protest is sustained, the award may be canceled.

37.6 SUBSTANTIVE TESTS

(a) Timeliness of Government Audits

The Defense Contract Audit Agency (DCAA) or similar bodies audit government contracts. With respect to cost-reimbursement-type contracts, they perform tests of direct labor and direct material costs for allowability, and perform indirect cost audits. There is usually a lag between these audits and the establishment of final "pricing rates"—the rates, typically based on direct labor costs, that are used to apply indirect costs to contracts. If a cost-reimbursement contract in a given year has not been "closed out," or audited by the government, the pricing rate from the most recent closed out year must be applied. When a final rate has been determined by the DCAA (or negotiated with the contracting officer, as is the case for most large contractors), the cost-reimbursement contract may be settled and closed out. However, contract records must be retained for at least three years after the contract's final settlement.

For most contractors, particularly small contractors, the latest audited pricing rates are the basis for future pricing, or provisional, rates. These provisional rates, which also are referred to as "forward pricing rates," will be used for negotiating contracts and billing the government until the costs incurred are eventually audited. Then, any cost-reimbursement contracts will be settled. For large contractors, the provisional rates may be the subject of a separate audit and may be negotiated with a contracting officer. The difference between actual rates incurred and provisional rates is referred to as "cost in excess of provisional" and is included in unbilled accounts receivable. The auditor should evaluate whether this differential between actual and provisional rates is collectible, if the amount is material.

(b) Contracts in Progress

Auditing procedures should be geared toward the contractor's processes for recognizing revenue, accumulating costs, and measuring income for the most significant contracts in progress. Contracts should be selected for testing based on size and other factors, such as whether there are problems associated with the contract. Problems include actual or anticipated cost overruns, which are evident if the percentage of costs incurred exceeds the percentage of work completed. When auditing contract costs, the auditor should be satisfied that they do not include unallowable costs, that accounting methods used are in compliance with the CAS disclosure statement, and that costs are charged in accordance with the terms of individual contracts.

Specific auditing procedures for contracts in progress include comparing contract cost components with the job cost ledger, and the job cost ledger with the general ledger. The auditor should recalculate overhead and general and administrative rates, and compare each of these with the terms of individual contracts. Some contracts contain limits, or caps, on rates, and the auditor should ascertain that the fee or profit billed to date is consistent with contract performance. The overall status of contracts should be discussed with key personnel, including the contract administrator, program manager, business manager, engineers, and manufacturing personnel.

The following auditing procedures should be performed to assess estimates to complete:

- Evaluate the contractor's historical ability to estimate accurately
- Assess the thoroughness with which the estimate to complete is prepared
- Compare actual costs incurred with estimates of future costs to be incurred
- Compare incurred costs with costs bid in the contract
- Identify and assess the reasonableness of anticipated efficiencies
- Determine whether all overhead costs are included in the estimate to complete
- Determine that projections of future business volume are comparable to levels used to calculate current overhead rates
- Assess the reasonableness of the method used to estimate progress toward completion
- Review indirect cost pools for recoverability, logical groupings, and the presence of beneficial and causal relationships
- Determine that the method of calculating costs and the overhead application rate is consistent from year to year and from contract to contract

38

Auditing Governmental Units

38.1   OVERVIEW OF THE STATE AND LOCAL GOVERNMENTAL ENVIRONMENT

State and local governmental accounting and auditing are in a period of significant and rapid change, as evidenced by changing governmental accounting principles and major revisions in 1994 to *Government Auditing Standards* and to the AICPA's audit and accounting guide, *Audits of State and Local Governmental Units*. Increasing numbers of governmental units are preparing financial statements in conformity with generally accepted accounting principles (GAAP) and having them audited in accordance with generally accepted auditing standards (GAAS). The expanding use of financing vehicles by port, housing, development, and transportation authorities and similar entities also has broadened the field of governmental accounting and auditing. Increasing attention has been focused on the appropriate spending of federal funds and on the auditor's role in preventing or detecting misappropriations of taxpayers' dollars. Because of this, standards covering governmental financial reporting, disclosure, and testing have become more uniform.

Users of governmental financial statements are different from and represent a more diverse range of interests than users of a business entity's financial statements. In addition to investors, labor organizations, oversight agencies, policy makers, and operating management—all of which have counterparts in the commercial environment—governmental entities also provide information to senior levels of government (for such purposes as grant compliance or data analysis) and, most important, their constituencies, which are most directly affected by decisions about obtaining and using resources. The needs of this wide variety of users differ. Holders of bonds are interested in fiscal performance and soundness of financial condition. Resource providers, whether taxpayers, other governmental entities, or legislatures, wish to ensure that governmental units are expending those resources efficiently and in the manner prescribed by law. The objectives of bondholders and constituents may conflict; for example, a large fund balance is desirable to bondholders but not to constituents. Managements of governmental entities must strike a balance between the objectives of the two groups.

A characteristic of the governmental environment of particular significance to the auditor is the large number of regulations that govern expenditures at all levels. Probably the most pervasive regulations are those embodied in a governmental entity's budgetary system; budgets that set revenue and expenditure levels have a greater effect on the operations of governments than budgets do in most other organizations. In addition, a network of regulations is embodied in laws that must be complied with by department, program, or grant administrators at a particular level of government or at lower levels. Thus, a department cannot overspend its budget, and its expenditures must meet the requirements of contracts, awards, laws, and regulations that govern the allowability of costs charged to specific contracts or programs.

Auditing guidelines and regulations established by federal, state, and local governments do not supersede GAAS, but may prescribe additional requirements. Generally accepted government auditing standards (GAGAS) for federally assisted programs are set forth in *Government Auditing Standards,* popularly referred to as the "Yellow Book," first published by the U.S. General Accounting Office (GAO) in 1972 and most recently revised in 1994.

The AICPA has provided guidance to the auditor in its audit and accounting guide, *Audits of State and Local Governmental Units,* which includes examples of auditors' reports. In addition, when auditing a state or local governmental unit that receives federal financial assistance, the auditor must comply with the requirements of the Single Audit Act (the Act) as described in Circular A-133, "Audits of States, Local Governments, and Non-Profit Organizations," issued by the U.S. Office of Management and Budget (OMB).

Statement on Auditing Standards (SAS) No. 74, *Compliance Auditing Considerations in Audits of Governmental Entities and Recipients of Governmental Financial Assistance* (AU Section 801), which superseded SAS No. 68, explains the relationship among GAAS, the Yellow Book, and the Act. SAS No. 74 also requires auditors to design audits to provide reasonable assurance that the financial statements are free of material misstatements resulting from violations of laws and regulations that have a direct and material effect in determining financial statement amounts. SAS No. 74 thus clarifies that violations of such laws and regulations are covered by the provisions of SAS No. 54, *Illegal Acts by Clients*.

38.2 GOVERNMENTAL ACCOUNTING AND REPORTING PRINCIPLES

Governmental accounting and reporting principles are unique in several respects and reflect the fundamental differences between commercial entities and governmental units.

(a) Fund Accounting

The most notable distinction between governmental and commercial accounting is the concept of fund accounting and the presentation of financial statements by fund types and account groups. In the governmental environment, the entity being audited is not viewed as an integrated accounting unit; instead, each of the individual fund types encompassed by the entity is considered and shown (although not necessarily reported on) separately. Transactions involving more than one fund should be recorded using interfund receivable and payable accounts. Fund accounting is used by governments as a means of controlling and accounting for various types of restricted resources and related expenditures.

The three broad types of funds typically found in governmental accounting systems are governmental, in which the primary concern is accounting for service delivery and demonstrating compliance with resource restrictions; proprietary, in which the concern is cost recovery (through user charges or fees) or cost determination for specific activities; and fiduciary, which account for assets held by a government as trustee or agent. These types of funds have been further subdivided and defined by the Governmental Accounting Standards Board (GASB).

(i) Governmental Funds. Governmental funds and their purposes are as follows:

- *General Fund*: Accounts for all financial resources except those required to be accounted for in another fund.

- *Special Revenue Funds*: Account for the proceeds of specific revenue sources (other than from expendable trusts or for major capital projects) that are legally restricted to expenditures for specified purposes.

- *Capital Project Funds*: Account for financial resources to be used for the acquisition or construction of major capital facilities (other than those financed by proprietary funds and fiduciary funds).

- *Debt Service Funds*: Account for the accumulation of resources for and payment of general long-term debt principal and interest.

(ii) Proprietary Funds.   The two kinds of proprietary funds are:

- *Enterprise Funds*: Account for operations that are financed and managed similar to the operations of private business entities. The governing body may have decided that the costs (including depreciation) of providing goods or services to the general public on a continuing basis should be financed or recovered primarily through user charges, or that periodic determination of revenues earned, expenses incurred, and net income is appropriate for capital maintenance, public policy, management information, accountability, or other purposes.

- *Internal Service Funds*: Account for financing of goods or services provided by one department or agency to other departments or agencies of a governmental unit or to other governmental units on a cost-reimbursement basis.

(iii) Fiduciary Funds.   Also called trust and agency funds, fiduciary funds account for assets held by a governmental unit in a trustee capacity or as agent for individuals, private organizations, other governmental units, or other funds. Fiduciary funds include expendable trust funds, nonexpendable trust funds, pension trust funds, and agency funds.

(iv) Account Groups.   In addition to the three fund types, two account groups are used to establish accountability over fixed assets and long-term obligations. The general fixed assets account group reflects a governmental unit's fixed assets, except those used in enterprise, internal service, or nonexpendable trust fund activities and therefore recorded in those funds. Historically, governments have not recorded "infrastructure" assets such as streets, sidewalks, bridges, and storm drains on the theory that they were immovable and not subject to theft. There is a growing trend, however, to record these items both for better accountability and for more accurate service cost information. Similarly, depreciation on these assets normally is not recorded, but increasing concern over the deterioration of the nation's infrastructure has prompted renewed interest in doing so. Such records would be helpful, for example, in ensuring accountability and in developing indirect cost systems. A government's policy for recording fixed assets and related accounts should be disclosed.

Originally, the general long-term debt account group was established to account for all governmental debt not carried as a liability of another fund. Its use has expanded to include other noncurrent liabilities, such as lease commitments, claims and judgments, and compensated absences.

(b) Modified Accrual Basis of Accounting

Another distinguishing characteristic of governmental accounting is the use of a modified accrual basis of accounting for reporting purposes. For governmental funds and expendable trust funds, the accrual basis of accounting is modified to focus on a measurement of financial flows, that is, to show the increase or decrease in financial resources. Revenues and other financial resources (such as bond proceeds) are recognized in the accounting period in which they become available and measurable. Expenditures are recognized on the accrual basis, with certain exceptions, among them:

- Unmatured principal and interest on general long-term debt, which usually are recorded as expenditures in the year of payment
- Inventory, which usually is recorded as an expenditure when purchased
- Prepaid items, such as insurance, which usually are recorded as expenditures when paid

GASB Statement No. 11, *Measurement Focus and Basis of Accounting—Governmental Fund Operating Statements,* issued in 1990, applies to governmental and expendable trust fund operating statements. It requires the use of the flow of financial resources measurement focus and the accrual basis of accounting. This statement, which would revise many modified accrual concepts, was originally to be effective for financial statements for periods beginning after June 15, 1994 (with early application not permitted). GASB Statement No. 17, *Measurement Focus and Basis of Accounting—Governmental Fund Operating Statements: An Amendment of the Effective Dates of GASB Statement No. 11 and Related Statements,* issued in 1993, defers the effective date of Statement No. 11 to periods beginning approximately two years after an implementation standard for Statement No. 11 has been issued. At the time of this writing, no such standard had been issued.

(c) Encumbrances

Encumbrances are another unique aspect of governmental accounting. The GASB defines encumbrances as "commitments related to unperformed (executory) contracts for goods or services." Many governments' budgetary laws require that encumbrances be recorded in governmental funds for which an annual budget has been adopted; their purpose is to aid in budgetary control and accountability, and they are also useful for cash planning. Encumbrances outstanding at year-end are neither expenditures nor liabilities. In some governmental units, budget appropriations lapse at year-end, while in other units they are carried forward. If appropriations are carried forward, outstanding encumbrances should be recorded by reserving part of the fund balance as a reserve for encumbrances. If appropriations lapse but the governmental unit intends to honor the commitments, outstanding encumbrances should be disclosed either by a reservation of the fund balance or in a note to the financial statements. The unit's policy as to appropriations and encumbrances should be disclosed in the accounting policies footnote.

(d)   Standard Setting for Governmental Accounting

The GASB was established in 1984 under the auspices of the Financial Accounting Foundation for the purpose of establishing accounting principles for state and local governmental units. [The National Council on Governmental Accounting (NCGA) previously performed that function.] One of the GASB's first actions was to address the then-current status of governmental accounting principles and to adopt certain of the NCGA statements and interpretations as part of generally accepted accounting principles for governmental entities. Those statements and interpretations, as well as GASB statements, interpretations, and technical bulletins issued as of June 30, 1997, are included in the GASB's *Codification of Governmental Accounting and Financial Reporting Standards as of June 30, 1997.* GASB pronouncements issued after that date have not yet been included in the Codification. The AICPA has designated the GASB as the body to establish financial accounting principles for state and local governmental entities under Rules 202 and 203 of the AICPA Code of Professional Conduct.

In the agreement that established the GASB, a hierarchy of generally accepted accounting principles applicable to state and local governments was specified in which GASB pronouncements take precedence over Financial Accounting Standards Board (FASB) pronouncements. The agreement also provided that, if the GASB had not issued a pronouncement on a particular matter, governmental entities were to be guided by FASB pronouncements. In 1989, this agreement was changed, placing FASB pronouncements issued since the formation of the GASB at a lower level; effectively, such FASB pronouncements do not need to be followed.

Under the hierarchy established by SAS No. 69, *The Meaning of* Present Fairly in Conformity With Generally Accepted Accounting Principles *in the Independent Auditor's Report* (AU Section 411), FASB pronouncements are not a source of established accounting principles for state and local governments unless the GASB issues a standard incorporating them into GAAP for state and local governments. GASB Statement No. 20, *Proprietary Fund Accounting,* issued in 1993, allows governments to adopt all FASB pronouncements issued subsequent to 1989 for proprietary funds.

(e)   Financial Reporting

NCGA Statement No. 1 specifies that for fair presentation of financial position, results of operations, and cash flows for proprietary and similar trust funds in conformity with GAAP, a governmental unit should prepare and issue general-purpose financial statements, consisting of:

- Combined balance sheet—all fund types and account groups
- Combined statement of revenues, expenditures, and changes in fund balances— all governmental fund types and expendable trust funds
- Combined statement of revenues, expenditures, and changes in fund balances— budget and actual—general and special revenue fund types (and similar governmental funds for which annual budgets have been legally adopted)
- Combined statement of revenues, expenses, and changes in retained earnings/fund balances—all proprietary fund types and similar trust funds

- Combined statement of cash flows—all proprietary fund types and similar trust funds

The GASB also recommends that a governmental unit issue a comprehensive annual financial report (CAFR) containing an introductory section, a financial section, and a statistical section. The introductory section contains financial highlights and organizational information. The financial section consists of the financial statements listed above plus combining statements by fund type, individual fund and account group statements, detailed budgetary data, and schedules. The statistical section may indicate compliance with legal or contractual provisions, present historical trend data, or simply report information in greater detail.

In identifying other agencies (such as housing authorities, utility systems, or school boards) that should be included as part of the governmental entity, the auditor should be aware that defining the entity to be included in the general-purpose financial statements and CAFR is not always straightforward. GASB Statement No. 14, *The Financial Reporting Entity,* establishes standards for defining and reporting on the financial reporting entity. The financial reporting entity consists of (a) the primary government, (b) organizations for which the primary government is financially accountable, and (c) other organizations, the nature and significance of whose relationship with the primary government are such that exclusion would cause the reporting entity's financial statements to be misleading or incomplete. In addition, Statement No. 14 provides for discrete presentation of components as well as blending of component units, depending on the relationship with the primary government. This criterion causes the reporting entity to be defined broadly and results in the inclusion in the reporting entity's financial statements of governmental units that may be audited by auditors other than those of the primary government. This could result in financial statements in which all or the majority of the components of a fund type are not audited by the auditor who is expected to issue the opinion. The AICPA audit and accounting guide, *Audits of State and Local Governmental Units*, provides guidance in this situation.

38.3 RISK FACTORS AND AUDIT REACTION

This section discusses risk factors that are prevalent in the governmental environment and their audit implications.

(a) Types of Governmental Audits

Both the auditor and management of the governmental unit should understand the type and scope of the audit to be performed. The Yellow Book describes two types of governmental audits.

(i) Financial Audits.   Financial audits include financial statement audits and financial related audits.

- Financial statement audits are concerned with whether the financial statements present fairly the financial position, results of operations, and cash flows in conformity with generally accepted accounting principles. Financial statement audits also include audits of financial statements prepared in conformity with any of several other bases of accounting discussed in SAS No. 62, *Special Reports* (AU Section 623).

- Financial related audits are concerned with whether (1) financial information is presented in accordance with established or stated criteria, (2) the entity has adhered to specific financial compliance requirements, or (3) the entity's internal control over financial reporting and safeguarding assets is suitably designed and implemented to achieve the control objectives.

(ii) Performance Audits.   Performance audits include economy and efficiency audits and program audits.

- Economy and efficiency audits are concerned with (1) whether the entity is acquiring, protecting, and using its resources (such as personnel, property, and space) economically and efficiently, (2) the causes of inefficiencies or uneconomical practices, and (3) whether the entity has complied with laws and regulations concerning matters of economy and efficiency.
- Program audits are concerned with (1) the extent to which the desired results or benefits established by the legislature or other authorizing body are being achieved, (2) the effectiveness of organizations, programs, activities, or functions, and (3) whether the entity has complied with laws and regulations applicable to the program.

Performance audits traditionally have been performed by federal or state government auditors. If during the course of a financial audit, however, an independent auditor identifies an opportunity for improved economy or efficiency, he or she should consider communicating this to management.

(b) Single Audit Considerations

The auditor frequently is engaged to perform an audit of a governmental unit in accordance with OMB Circular A-133 and the Single Audit Act. Referred to as a "single audit," it requires that the auditor perform procedures beyond those required by GAAS and GAGAS, in terms of both their nature and extent. The requirements of the Act are covered in Chapter 32. For audit efficiency, the auditor should consider the requirements of Circular A-133 and the Act when planning the engagement. For instance, federal regulations specify criteria for selecting grant costs to be tested in a single audit. The Act also specifies that the auditor obtain an understanding of controls used in administering federal financial assistance. Early identification of the requirements of the Act can prevent unnecessary duplication of efforts.

(c) Risk Factors and Materiality Considerations

The auditor should be sensitive to certain elements of risk that are unique to formulating a strategy for a governmental audit. For example, the absence of a unified, consistent level of overall financial management in many governmental units suggests that the strength of management and the performance of specific departments or programs may vary widely.

The auditor also should be sensitive to the materiality implications of autonomous, decentralized, individual entities and programs. A single department, program, or grant that is discovered not to be in compliance with laws, regulations, or contract terms may generate publicity and attendant effects far out of proportion to the normal materiality considerations in a commercial or industrial environment. In this regard, the Yellow Book states, "In an audit of the financial statements of a government entity that receives government assistance, auditors may set lower materiality levels than in similar-type audits in the private sector because of the public accountability of the entity, the various legal and regulatory requirements, and the visibility and sensitivity of government programs, activities, and functions." Also, as noted earlier, SAS No. 74 requires auditors to design audits to provide reasonable assurance that the financial statements are free of material misstatements resulting from violations of laws and regulations that have a material effect in determining financial statement amounts. Therefore, the auditor should consider external pressures exerted by the political process and the nature of the governmental unit's constituency. Much can be learned about the expectations of those constituencies by reading newspapers and minutes of council and legislative proceedings, hearings, and investigations.

The auditor should consider the level of financial statements on which his or her opinion is to be expressed. If the auditor has been engaged to express an opinion on the combined, or general-purpose, financial statements, materiality should be determined separately for each fund type and account group, and the individual discrete component units should be presented in side-by-side columns. In this case, the fund type and account group and component unit columns are considered to be elements of the financial statements. If the auditor has been engaged to express an opinion on the individual fund statements, materiality should be established at that level. In addition, there are no working capital or income measurements in governmental accounting, so the auditor must look to other measures of materiality, such as total assets, liabilities, fund balances, revenues, and expenditures.

(d)   Overall Audit Strategy and Planning Considerations

As mentioned earlier, governmental accounting uses the modified accrual basis, which focuses on the measurement of financial flows as opposed to profit or loss. As a result, the balance sheet often does not include productive assets, such as inventory and fixed assets, that enter into the determination of income. In addition, receivables and payables on the balance sheet usually are not derived from the revenue and purchasing cycles, but are recorded as assets independently of those cycles. For these reasons, it is often more efficient to test the flow of transactions and the resulting operating accounts separately from the balance sheet accounts. For example, based on the inherent risks identified and the understanding of internal control, the auditor may decide to perform tests of controls directed at the authorization and accuracy of input of transactions and at the completeness and accuracy of accumulated data for the purchasing cycle. If those tests support an assessment of control risk at low, the auditor might restrict substantive testing of the operating accounts affected by the purchasing cycle to analytical procedures, but might perform detailed substantive tests to satisfy the audit objectives for accounts payable.

Computer software can be used to enhance the efficiency of governmental audits.

For example, governmental entities frequently combine the cash balances of their agencies in order to be able to invest in assets with higher yields than otherwise would be available or to facilitate the treasury function in other ways. Software can be used to test both the distribution of interest to the various agencies and the accuracy of the equity positions of the individual agencies in the pooled cash fund. Similarly, software may be used to test assessed tax rolls, including calculation of the tax on individual properties and its distribution to the appropriate governmental agencies or units.

(e) Management Representation Letter

In addition to the items applicable to audits of business entities generally, a governmental management representation letter should cover several areas that are specific to governmental units and activities, namely, the inclusion of all component units, the proper classification of fund types and account groups, and compliance with budgets, laws, and regulations and with grant requirements, and management's responsibility for identifying and disclosing to the auditor all laws and regulations that have a direct and material effect in determining financial statement amounts. Changes in government administrations may cause difficulty in obtaining representations from former officials, and their replacements may not be willing or able to provide representations about periods and events that occurred before they took office. This could lead to a scope limitation that would require a qualified opinion.

38.4 TYPICAL TRANSACTIONS

Many governmental units use the cash basis of accounting throughout the year, with budgetary controls for expenditures, and adjust their accounting to the modified accrual basis at year-end for financial statement presentation purposes. By contrast, most commercial enterprises use the full accrual basis of accounting, which provides a degree of control over both revenues and expenditures by permitting analysis of interim financial statements as well as the timely comparison of control accounts with their supporting detail. Because of these differences in bookkeeping methods, the auditor of a governmental entity often devotes more attention to the flow of transactions than to the resulting balance sheet accounts. He or she should therefore have a thorough understanding of the transaction cycles and of the laws and regulations that govern the entity's transactions.

(a) Budget Cycle

A government's budget is a financial plan that contains the legal authority to spend money and incur liabilities. The budgetary process and the role that budgets play in governments differ from comparable considerations in business enterprises. Because a government's budget has the force of law once it has been adopted, it has great significance to both the governmental unit and the auditor. NCGA Statement No. 1 recommends that annual budgets be adopted by every governmental unit (whether or not required by law or regulation). Budgetary control should be provided through the accounting system, and budgetary comparisons should be included in the appropriate financial statements.

The annual budget should be established in accordance with applicable legal requirements, which might include, for example, holding public budget hearings, publishing the proposed or final budget, and approval of the budget by a higher level of government or the citizenry. The budget must conform to any applicable revenue and expenditure limitation laws or regulations; supplemental appropriations and budgetary transfers also must be in accordance with governmental regulations and limitations.

The adopted budget and subsequent supplemental appropriations should be recorded in the accounting system as a means of controlling expenditures and permitting management to monitor compliance with the budget on an ongoing basis. Budgetary controls frequently provide for a review of the remaining appropriation before final approval is given for an expenditure. Encumbrance accounting, described earlier, also enhances budgetary control by reducing the remaining appropriation when purchase orders are issued.

Because the budget cycle is central to the operations of a governmental unit, the auditor usually places particular emphasis on the cycle when assessing control risk. That is, the auditor will seek evidence that controls, as they affect the budget cycle, have been properly designed and placed in operation, and are operating effectively.

(b) Revenue Cycle

Governmental revenues can be classified conveniently into seven types:

- Assessed taxes
- Self-assessed taxes
- Intergovernmental revenue
- Revenue received for governmental services
- Licenses, fees, permits, and fines
- Investment revenue
- Contributions and donations

The aspects of each type of revenue that are unique to governments are discussed in this section. Controls for cash receipts are similar to those in commercial and industrial enterprises.

(i) Assessed Taxes.   The primary sources of revenue in this category are real property and special assessment taxes, which are levied according to the various state and local tax regulations. Many municipalities assess, levy, and collect their own property taxes. Sometimes the assessing, billing, and collecting are performed by one governmental entity for a group of entities. In such cases, a portion of the funds is retained by the collecting entity and the remaining amounts are recorded as "additions to agency funds" for future distribution to the other governmental entities. In such instances, the collecting government acts as a "service organization" for the other governments. SAS No. 70, *Reports on the Processing of Transactions by Service Organizations* (AU Section 324), provides guidance on assessing internal control of service organizations and for entities whose transactions are processed by service organizations. The auditor should have a clear understanding of the controls over the tax assessing and collection process as well as controls over appealing and changing valuations.

(ii) Self-Assessed Taxes.   Revenue in this category is based on taxpayer assessments; the accurate determination and reporting of amounts due are the responsibility of individual taxpayers. Examples of self-assessed taxes are income, sales, excise, utility, and personal property taxes. As with assessed taxes, sometimes one governmental entity collects self-assessed taxes for a group of entities. The recording of taxes collected by this process is the same as for assessed taxes. Income taxes may present an audit problem because the source documents—the tax forms—may be covered by a confidentiality law that prevents the auditor from obtaining and testing them. In that event, the auditor may have to use the work of the governmental entity's internal auditors, which may involve testing their work or even designing specific procedures for them to follow. [SAS No. 65, *The Auditor's Consideration of the Internal Audit Function in an Audit of Financial Statements* (AU Section 332), provides guidance.] For other self-assessed taxes, such as sales taxes, the auditor should consider the existence of a master file of taxpayers and the government's procedures applied to the file, including examinations.

(iii) Intergovernmental Revenue.   Intergovernmental revenue received by state and local governments can take one of three forms:

- Entitlements and shared revenue, which are based on a legally established or predetermined amount
- Collections, which result from collections made by another governmental entity
- Expenditure reimbursement-type grants, which are received as partial or full reimbursement of expenditures that meet certain preestablished criteria

There are two audit concerns about intergovernmental revenue. The first is ascertaining whether completeness and accuracy controls have been designed and placed in operation. The second is determining that the governmental unit is in compliance with the terms of the law or regulation establishing the revenue. As discussed later in the chapter [Section 5(b), Contingent Liabilities from Grant Noncompliance], noncompliance with laws or regulations may cause accounts to be uncollectible or may require repayments.

(iv) Other Governmental Revenues.   Transactions involving revenues from services; licenses, fees, permits, and fines; investment revenue; and contributions and donations generally are recorded on the cash basis. Control objectives for such transactions relate principally to completeness of input.

(c) Purchasing Cycle

The purchasing cycle consists of two distinct parts (goods and services, and payroll). The auditor's primary concern for both is that transactions are properly authorized.

In a governmental unit, the objective of proper authorization of expenditures has implications beyond those in other entities. Proper authorization implies that the expenditure is part of a legally adopted budget, that the persons contracting for the goods or services and approving their payment are properly authorized to do so, that the goods or services have been received, and that all laws and regulations affecting the expenditure (e.g., a requirement to obtain competitive bids) have been complied with.

In obtaining an understanding of internal control and assessing control risk for the purchasing cycle, the auditor needs to be aware that some important controls may not be applied as part of financial transaction processing. For example, a payment made to or on behalf of an individual under a government grant may require the individual to meet certain criteria in order to be eligible to receive the payment. The determination of eligibility, which is an important part of the authorization and payment process, often is made by someone outside of the financial area, such as a program administrator. The auditor needs to be aware of this and consider it when assessing control risk.

A significant and unique control in government payroll systems is known as "position control." Governments budget specific numbers of people in prescribed employment categories or positions at specified salary levels. For example, a department may be assigned one manager, two assistant managers, and four clerks. A position master file, similar to the employee master file, is created and maintained, based on the budget. In obtaining an understanding of internal control and assessing control risk, the auditor should consider controls established to ensure that changes made to both of these files are properly authorized. The auditor generally performs tests to determine that the position master file and the employee master file match, that salaries conform with the budget, and that the positions and salaries are authorized by the budget.

Government payroll systems are often structured so that employees, once they are included in the employee master file, continue to receive paychecks unless some positive action is taken to remove them from that file. That is, the payroll system typically is not based on time reporting by employees. As a result, there is the possibility of phantom employees. In assessing control risk, the auditor should consider whether controls exist to ensure that only employees who are properly includable on the payroll are paid and that they are paid in accordance with required attendance.

Payroll costs (and related overhead charges) may be chargeable to grants and thus reimbursable. Controls often are established to ensure that work was actually performed on grants, and that payroll costs are appropriately classified and allocated to those grants. Under the single audit approach, discussed earlier, compliance with the terms of some grants is tested as part of the requirements of OMB Circular A-133. In addition, the auditor may wish to test whether payroll rates related to federal grants comply with applicable local ordinances. The union-scale requirements of the Davis–Bacon Act are also important for construction projects financed with federal grants.

38.5   SUBSTANTIVE TESTS

This section discusses those aspects of substantive tests that are unique to audits of governmental units and activities. Most audit objectives and procedures to meet them are, of course, similar to those for business enterprises and are not discussed here.

(a) Balance Sheet Accounts

(i) Receivables from Taxes.   Governmental fund-type revenue presently is recognized under the modified accrual basis of accounting, that is, when it becomes measurable and available. (This may change when GASB Statement No. 11 is implemented, as discussed earlier.) The concept of measurable and available has not been quantified for all sources of revenue. NCGA Interpretation No. 3, however, specifies that property taxes that are due as of the balance sheet date and are expected to be collected within 60 days of year-end should be recognized as revenues; other taxes that have been assessed are reported as deferred revenues. The auditor often tests the accuracy and collectibility of tax receivables by examining cash receipts after year-end; material receivables resulting from collections by other governmental units may be confirmed. Total property tax revenue typically is reconciled to the value of assessed property.

(ii) Due to and Due from Other Funds, and Other Interfund Accounts.   Most interfund account balances are liquidated before year-end; those that are not should be examined to support their treatment as loans rather than as equity contributions. A typical auditing procedure is to reconcile all funds to each other (total due to's should equal total due from's) and to determine that there is a reasonable purpose for the interfund balance (i.e., that it was created by a normal operating interfund activity). The auditor also should determine that the receivable balances can be considered current available resources in the governmental funds. Amounts that are not currently available should be reserved against.

(iii) Restricted Assets.   Revenue bond indentures frequently require that a specified amount of cash be restricted for debt service or system rehabilitation. Such restricted assets should equal the sum of payables from restricted assets and the equity reserved for the restricted purpose. The auditor should determine that the amount of the restriction has been determined properly in accordance with the regulating instrument.

(iv) General Fixed Assets Account Group.   The general fixed assets account group is used to provide accountability for capital assets, even though their cost is charged to expenditures of a governmental fund when incurred. This practice was not always followed in the past, with the result that cost records may not be currently available. When the governmental unit establishes fixed asset carrying amounts, the auditor should determine that the procedures for estimating cost are reasonable and consistent. The same is true for assets donated to governmental activities.

(v) Liabilities.   Governmental accounting systems sometimes do not distinguish between actual liabilities in the form of accounts payable and encumbrances. There is no need to make that distinction for budgetary reporting purposes since both are deductions from budgeted appropriations. The distinction is necessary for reporting under GAAP, however, because expenditures and encumbrances are reported differently, and the auditor should ensure that it is made. The auditor also should perform tests to determine whether the reserve for encumbrances is supported by authorized commitments.

Judgments payable, litigation claims, and unfunded pensions and other employee-related accruals should be evaluated to determine that they will be payable from expendable available financial resources. If so, they should be treated as liabilities of the appropriate governmental fund; if not, presently they are treated as liabilities in the general long-term debt account group.

(vi) Fund Equity.   Changes in aggregate fund balances normally should result only from differences between revenues and other financing sources, and expenditures and other financing uses reported on the operating statement, residual equity transfers as defined in NCGA Statement No. 1, and prior-period adjustments [Statement of Financial Accounting Standards No. 16, *Prior Period Adjustments* (Accounting Standards Section A35)]. It is not uncommon, however, for governmental entities erroneously to record operating items directly in equity accounts. Accordingly, the auditor should review activity in all fund equity accounts to ensure that all charges and credits that should go through the operating statement have in fact done so.

Reserves are established to identify the existence of assets that are not available to be spent currently or assets that have claims against them that are not liabilities at the date of the balance sheet, such as encumbrances. Designations of fund balances are the result of voluntary management decisions to earmark resources for specific future uses. Designated fund balances should be supported by specific plans approved by senior management and, if appropriate, a legislative body.

(vii) Contingent Liabilities from Grant Noncompliance.   As noted earlier, grants frequently specify conditions with which the recipient must comply. Although some of those conditions are nonfinancial, such as those that relate to environmental and employment practices, others are of a financial nature, for example, those that specify costs properly chargeable to a grant. If costs are disallowed or a grant is rescinded by the granting agency, a contingent liability could result. The auditor should consider whether instances of noncompliance should result in financial statement accruals or disclosures.

Conceptually, there can be no quantitative materiality guidelines for evaluating the extent of a contingent liability that could result from a grant violation. In many cases, an entire grant could legally or contractually be canceled as a result of a minor violation. As a practical matter, however, the act of noncompliance generally has to be very serious to cause the recipient to lose grant funds that are material in relation to the financial statements. That presumption may be tested by reviewing historical records of the grantor's acceptance of performance under similar grants and the effects of disallowed costs, or by discussion with the grantor agency.

(b) Comparisons of Budget and Actual and Other Operating Statements

As noted earlier, a combined statement of revenues, expenditures, and changes in fund balances—budget and actual—is required by NCGA Statement No. 1 for general and special revenue fund types and similar governmental funds for which annual budgets have been legally adopted. The auditor's responsibility for and approach to that statement are the same as for the other financial statements. In addition to the auditing procedures appropriate under GAAS and GAGAS, usually the auditor is subject to a regulatory requirement to test the governmental unit's compliance with statutory and other regulations by comparing budgeted with actual expenditures at the level of detail at which the budget is legally controlled. Actual expenditures reported on this and the other operating statements should be subjected to analytical procedures—budget to actual and current year to prior years—and explanations for variances sought.

The budget versus actual comparison should be made using the basis of accounting used to develop the budget. If the budget has been prepared on the modified accrual basis, it may contain GAAP exceptions. Sometimes budgets may be prepared on the cash basis or may include encumbrances. The basis used to prepare the budget should be disclosed and differences between it and GAAP should be reconciled on the face of the statement or in the notes. The auditor may wish to test the current-period encumbrances and the controls for reappropriating these amounts, if applicable to the particular governmental unit. As discussed earlier, encumbrances are a means of measuring total commitments made against a particular budgetary amount. The auditor may wish to expand the normal cutoff procedures to include encumbrances.

When a fund, program, or object of annual budgetary spending authority is exhausted, management should seek a budgetary amendment for further expenditures. Occasionally in such circumstances, management may attempt to override budgetary controls by miscoding expenditures. The auditor should assess the appropriateness of segregation of duties between the expenditure coding and approval functions, and should consider the need to test the coding of expenditures.

39

Auditing Health Care Organizations

39.1   OVERVIEW OF THE INDUSTRY

Health care is one of the fastest-growing industries in the United States. The system of health care delivery organizations is extensive, encompassing the following segments:

- Hospitals
- Nursing homes
- Health maintenance organizations (HMOs) and other providers of prepaid care
- Continuing care retirement communities (CCRCs) and assisted-living facilities
- Home health agencies
- Medical group practices
- Clinics
- Other ambulatory care organizations

Expenditures for health care represent approximately one-seventh of the national economy, approaching $1 trillion annually. The federal government is the major payor for health care services, principally through the Medicare and Medicaid programs. States also participate in the funding and administration of Medicaid programs and, in some cases, in special payments for uncompensated care. Most Americans receive health care coverage through their employers and various types of insurance programs—Blue Cross, HMOs, and a wide variety of other programs and private insurers. Insurers offer a variety of managed care plans—preferred provider organizations (PPOs) or networks, point-of-service (POS) plans, and HMOs. A PPO is a management organization that contracts with a network of providers who agree to deliver health care services to enrollees. POS plans are hybrids of HMOs and traditional indemnity plans. They provide financial incentives to members to use network providers, but allow out-of-network care with a higher co-payment. Managed care is growing significantly, with expansion recently into Medicare and Medicaid managed care programs as the federal and state governments attempt to control health care spending.

Responding to financial pressures, the health care industry continues to reexamine the delivery of health care services in order to find cost-effective ways to provide high-quality health care. Driving the reorganization of health care markets are several forces: payors' demands for cost containment, uncompensated care for services to indigent populations, reductions in government spending, an aging population, new diseases requiring costly treatments, and emerging and expensive new technologies.

As managed care becomes more prevalent, providers find it difficult to prosper as stand-alone organizations. To participate in a managed care environment, hospitals and physicians have joined networks that generally require direct contracting with payors, adopted new reimbursement arrangements such as capitation, and increased their ability to offer a wide array of essential services. Providers increasingly are sharing in the risk of treating patient populations through receiving predetermined, per-person monthly payments (capitation) that may not necessarily take into account the level of services delivered.

Providers have restructured their organizations internally and externally to adapt to the managed care environment. Hospitals, physicians, and carriers have created vertically integrated networks through physician hospital organizations (PHOs), integrated delivery networks, consolidations, joint ventures, acquisitions, and mergers. These types of arrangements afford providers numerous advantages such as increased bargaining power, the capacity to contract directly with payors, consolidation of costly services, a wide array of service offerings, a cost-effective way to manage administrative and information functions, and a prominent market presence to attract health care buyers. Contributing to the trend toward hospital mergers is a shift to outpatient care due to technological advancements, with a resulting growth in excess bed capacity. Large for-profit hospital systems have expanded by purchasing other for-profit as well as not-for-profit hospitals. Physicians also have joined together to form group practices and Independent Physicians Associations (IPAs), often contracting with managed care organizations. Under some forms of managed care, physicians are subject to the monitoring of plan administrators (physician profiling), practice in accordance with accepted guidelines (clinical pathways, practice guidelines), and receive capitated reimbursement as their predominant form of payment.

(a) Health Care Services

Services provided by health care providers are generally described by a six-level classification. Those levels indicate, but do not strictly define, the type of organization, the level of medical treatment involved, or the severity of or prognosis for the medical situation. The levels are:

- *Preventive*. Health education and prevention programs provided by business and other organizations, such as schools and family planning clinics
- *Primary*. Early detection and routine treatment of health problems, such as often are provided by physicians' offices, industrial and school health units, and hospital outpatient and emergency departments
- *Secondary*. Acute-care services, typically provided by medical personnel, through hospitals, using elaborate diagnostic and treatment procedures
- *Tertiary*. Highly technical services, such as for psychiatric and chronic diseases, provided through specialty facilities and teaching hospitals
- *Restorative*. Rehabilitative and follow-up care, typically provided by home health agencies, nursing homes, and halfway houses
- *Continuing*. Long-term, chronic care, typically provided by CCRCs, geriatric day care centers, and nursing homes

The types of providers of health care services have increased in recent years. In addition to hospitals, there are ambulatory surgery centers, freestanding specialty clinics, physician group practices, hospices, day care centers for the elderly, specialized home health agencies, rehabilitative care centers, nursing homes, CCRCs, and HMOs, among others.

Often, four or more parties may be involved in arranging health care services, including:

- The patient
- The physician
- A health care organization that provides institutional or other services (hospital, nursing home, ambulatory surgical center, etc.)
- A third-party payor (such as governmental agencies including Medicare, which provides medical insurance coverage for most patients over the age of 65, and Medicaid, which provides coverage for indigent patients, and commercial insurance companies such as Blue Cross, HMOs, etc.)

Self-pay and charity patients, who do not have access to third-party coverage for their health care service needs, also utilize such services.

(b) Hospital Segment

Hospitals are the largest segment of the health care industry measured by both dollars of revenue and the variety of professional services delivered. Accordingly, the emphasis in this chapter is on auditing hospitals, although many of the principles and practices discussed are applicable to other types of health care providers as well.

Patient care is the essential and principal function of hospitals. Hospitals often play other vital roles for the advancement of health care, however, including medical education and research. Many larger general hospitals have become total community health centers, providing a wide range of outpatient services in addition to traditional inpatient care. One characteristic of the growth of the health center concept has been the emergence of such diverse related organizations as real estate holding companies and medical management companies. These organizations are a response to changes in the reimbursement, regulatory, tax, operating, and financial environment facing hospital management.

Hospitals may be classified by type of ownership and mode of operation, as follows:

- *Government*. Hospitals operated by governmental agencies and providing specialized services to specific groups and their dependents, such as the military, veterans, government employees, the indigent, and the mentally ill.
- *Investor-owned (proprietary)*. Hospitals owned by individual proprietors or groups of proprietors or by the public through stock ownership. The objective of such hospitals is to operate for profit.
- *Voluntary not-for-profit*. Hospitals operated under the sponsorship of a community, religious denomination, or other not-for-profit entity. This is the largest category (in numbers of hospitals), comprising two major types—teaching hospitals and community hospitals.
- *Teaching hospitals*. Generally university-related hospitals (government or private), their health care service activities combine education, research, and a broad range of sophisticated patient services. Community hospitals affiliated with medical schools and offering intern and resident programs also are considered teaching hospitals.
- *Community hospitals*. Hospitals that traditionally are established to serve a specific area, such as a city, town, or county, and usually offer more limited services than teaching hospitals.

Hospitals also may be categorized by the type of care provided, as short-term (acute), general, long-term general, psychiatric, and other special care. The mode of a hospital's operation and the type of care occur in various combinations, such as government psychiatric or short-term pediatric.

(c) Laws and Regulations

The growth of the health care system has led to increased regulatory activities focusing on health care. The largest and most evident regulatory activity involves reimbursement by federal and state governments; this is covered in Section 1(d), Third-Party Reimbursement or Payment. Other regulatory activities are concerned in varying degrees with the availability and quality of health care.

A number of specific regulatory and statutory actions have a significant effect on the health care industry. Health care providers have serious concerns about the impact of regulations and legislation on their ability to maintain financially viable operations. Some of the significant regulatory issues affecting health care are as follows:

- *Reimbursement.* Providers rely on reimbursement from the government for medical services provided to Medicare and Medicaid beneficiaries, and for the reasonable costs associated with medical education and research programs. Maintaining adequate reimbursement levels under Medicare and Medicaid is a top priority for many providers. Significant federal regulations were issued in the 1980s to control or reduce payments to providers, including:
  - The creation of a prospective payment system for capital costs and the phasing out of cost-based reimbursement for health care capital expenditures.
  - The implementation of a Medicare Resource Based Relative Value Scale (RBRVS) in an effort to reform the payment mechanism for physicians. It is designed to decrease reimbursement to specialists in favor of primary care physicians in an effort to encourage more preventive care.
  - More recent reductions in graduate medical education payments and limitations on inflation increases in Medicare payments, which placed additional financial pressures on hospitals.
- *Anti-Trust.* Providers have responded to market forces through mergers with other providers and the creation of comprehensive full-service integrated delivery systems. Anti-trust regulations may hinder the integration and the restructuring of the health care delivery system.
- *Fraud and Abuse.* The government has undertaken significant efforts to reduce fraud and abuse in the health care system with new rules and guidelines affecting health care providers. For example, safe harbor rules were published in 1992 outlining 11 areas relating to referrals, investment, and payment methods in which health care providers can operate safely, without concern for infringement of Medicare fraud and abuse regulations. In 1995, the Health Care Financing Administration (HCFA) of the U.S. Department of Health and Human Services published regulations that provided additional guidance on fraud and abuse. In 1997, the Office of the Inspector General and other federal and state regulatory agencies increased compliance reviews of health care providers,

resulting in fines, penalties, or sanctions against providers found not to be in compliance.

- *IRS Scrutiny*. Under pressure to increase tax revenue and with public questioning of hospitals' charitable intent, the IRS has increased its scrutiny of the tax-exempt status of health care providers. The IRS's focus has broadened to include examination of physician relationships, senior executives' compensation, and adherence to a community benefit standard, with an ongoing focus on unrelated business income tax issues.

- *SEC Secondary Market Disclosure*. Tax-exempt organizations seeking access to capital markets are required to provide annually information similar to that found in official statements required by Rule 15c2-12 under the Securities Exchange Act of 1934.

(d) Third-Party Reimbursement or Payment

A major difference between health care organizations and commercial entities is that the recipient of health care services—the patient—in most cases does not pay directly for the services. Instead, payment is made by some other organization. The payment often is referred to as "reimbursement," and the other organization is referred to as a "third party." Typically, a hospital's most significant source of patient revenue is its reimbursement contracts with third parties. The third party may be Medicare (for patients who meet certain age requirements), Medicaid (for patients who meet certain poverty level requirements), or another governmental agency, a PPO, or a commercial insurance company such as Blue Cross or an HMO. In each case, there is an identifiable group of patients whose health care services are paid for, in whole or in part, by the third party. The amount of the reimbursement, as well as the eligible class of patients and other administrative matters, is covered by regulations (for governmental third parties) or contracts (for PPOs, Blue Cross plans, HMOs, and other commercial insurance companies).

The major third parties, in dollar volume, are the governmental agencies. Of these, the federal government is the largest. Federal involvement became a major element of reimbursement beginning with the enactment of the Social Security Act of 1965, which created the Medicare and Medicaid programs to reimburse health care institutions for their costs of providing services to the elderly and the indigent. Medicaid is a state-administered, third-party reimbursement program designed to underwrite health care costs of the medically indigent and those eligible for certain types of public welfare. Medicare is a third-party reimbursement program administered by the HCFA. Medicare underwrites the medical costs of persons 65 and over and some qualified persons under 65. "Part A" covers hospital services and "Part B" covers physicians' services.

State governments have long been involved in reimbursement for health care services, and their involvement has increased through participation in the Medicaid program. The continued growth of third-party expenditures for reimbursement has fostered a number of state-based cost control programs and, more recently, an increased focus on managed care for Medicare and Medicaid recipients.

Medicare and Medicaid third-party reimbursement or payment systems were created to be retrospective in nature, meaning that the amount to be paid was determined after the services had been performed. Through government initiatives to reduce federal spending and the evolution of managed care, the payment systems for hospitals are moving to prospective and capitation-type payment arrangements (discussed later). In prospective payment systems, the amount is determined before the services have been performed. Reimbursements or payments usually are based on a fixed amount per case, or coupled with a payment for certain of the hospital's costs of services performed for eligible patients or a percentage of the amounts charged by the hospital for such services. The relevant regulations or contracts contain specific provisions designed to ensure that only certain fixed payments, costs, or charges enter into the determination of the reimbursement or payment. There are also provisions to ensure that reimbursement or payment is made only for services to eligible patients. The difference between the hospital's established rates for services rendered and the amounts received or receivable from third-party payors is known as a contractual allowance or adjustment and is a deduction from gross patient revenues.

Prior to 1983, Medicare payments to hospitals generally were based on defined allowable costs. In 1983, the federal government adopted the Prospective Payment System (PPS), which is based on a predetermined and generally fixed payment rate for each Medicare inpatient discharge. The rate of inpatient payment depends on a medical classification system, called Diagnosis Related Groups (DRGs), which takes into account patient diagnosis, clinical, and other medical factors. Under this system, discharge diagnoses are classified into major diagnostic categories, which then are subdivided into specific types of health problems. Currently, there are approximately 470 DRG classifications. Incorporated into the system is the concept of relative value, which provides hospitals with greater reimbursement for care associated with more difficult diagnoses. For example, an admission with a more acute diagnosis, such as a heart attack, would be classified as a higher-paying DRG than a simpler diagnosis, such as pneumonia. Outpatient services are reimbursed through a similar classification system called CPT-4 codes, based on the service provided.

Hospitals seeking payment under Medicare's PPS for inpatient services are subject to utilization and quality reviews conducted by Peer Review Organizations (PROs). The PRO determines whether hospital services paid by Medicare are reasonable, necessary, and performed in the most economical settings consistent with quality care. The PRO also validates DRG assignments and reviews length of stay and services received by inpatients as well as outliers (patients with unusually long stays compared with the DRG average length of stay, or patients who have incurred extremely costly treatments relative to other patients in their DRG class). If the PRO deems the DRG to be improper or judges the admission to be unnecessary, it will change or deny payment for services rendered. In addition, the intermediary (the local entity under contract with Medicare to manage reimbursement—often Blue Cross) performs compliance reviews, desk audits, and other quality review functions.

Certain items continue to be reimbursed by Medicare outside the prospective payment amount. These costs include capital costs (depreciation, interest on debt incurred for capital additions or renovations, operating leases, rents, and other capital-related costs) under a 10-year transition that expires in 2002, costs of medical education programs (intern, resident, and nursing school programs), and certain outpatient services. Some hospital inpatient units, commonly called "exempt units," such as psychiatric and rehabilitation programs, also are specifically excluded from the PPS program. The reimbursement for such units by Medicare continues, but is limited to "target rates of allowable cost increases" as provided under the Tax Equity and Fiscal Responsibility Act (TEFRA) of 1981.

Medicare reimbursement for freestanding nursing homes and home health agencies is based on allowable costs incurred, subject to certain limitations. Medicare payments for covered physicians' services are determined on the basis of the lowest of customary charges, prevailing charges, or actual physician charges. Customary and prevailing charge limits are established on a periodic basis by the Medicare program. States use various methods to pay health care providers for covered services under their Medicaid programs. All state programs must be approved by the federal government.

Medicare, Medicaid, and certain Blue Cross programs require filing of a year-end cost report in order to settle on an annual basis with hospitals, nursing homes, and home health agencies for services provided to beneficiaries of these programs. Even hospitals included in the PPS system must use cost-reporting principles and cost-report forms to determine reimbursement for services not covered by predetermined and fixed payment rates.

Contrary to payment rates under PPS, which often are clearly quantified, hospitals also enter into capitation contracts with health care providers and health care purchasers (HMOs or PPOs) whereby the provider contracts to provide specific health care services for a fixed amount per member. The health care purchaser pays the capitation payment on a monthly basis, usually expressed as a "per member per month" (PMPM). Capitation is a significant change in traditional hospital or physician payment arrangements in that the provider earns revenue by agreeing to provide specific health care services, regardless of the amount of services that are provided during the period. The health care provider is at risk for services provided to plan members in excess of the agreed-upon capitation payment amounts. In this way, health care providers have accepted risk generally assumed by insurance companies in the past. This requires health care management to have expertise in the demographics and historical health care usage of members of the capitation agreement, as well as the associated costs of the services to be provided. Revenues received under capitation contracts are premium revenues and should not be classified as patient service revenues.

39.2 ACCOUNTING PRINCIPLES AND PRACTICES

As previously indicated, hospitals may be governmental entities, investor-owned businesses, or not-for-profit organizations. Statement on Auditing Standards (SAS) No. 69, *The Meaning of* Present Fairly in Conformity With Generally Accepted Accounting Principles *in the Independent Auditor's Report* (AU Section 411), establishes separate hierarchies of generally accepted accounting principles (GAAP) for governmental and nongovernmental entities. At the top of the GAAP hierarchy for governmental entities are pronouncements issued by the Governmental Accounting Standards Board; those pronouncements are not discussed further in this chapter. At the top of the GAAP hierarchy for nongovernmental entities are Financial Accounting Standards

Board Statements and Interpretations, Opinions of the Accounting Principles Board, and AICPA Accounting Research Bulletins.

Two pronouncements particularly affecting health care financial reporting include Statement of Financial Accounting Standards (SFAS) No. 117, *Financial Statements of Not-for-Profit Organizations* (Accounting Standards Section No5), which establishes standards for the form and content of the financial statements of not-for-profit organizations (defined in this chapter as nongovernmental entities), and SFAS No. 116, *Accounting for Contributions Received and Contributions Made* (Accounting Standards Sections C67 and No5), which establishes recognition, measurement, and disclosure standards for contributions received by all nongovernmental entities, including not-for-profit organizations. The AICPA audit and accounting guide, *Health Care Organizations*, issued in 1996, assists both governmental and nongovernmental providers of health care services in preparing financial statements in conformity with GAAP and assists auditors in auditing and reporting on those financial statements.

(a) Authoritative Pronouncements

SFAS No. 116 requires that contributions received be recognized at their fair value as revenues and, depending on the nature of the benefits received by the organization, as assets, decreases of liabilities, or expenses. Contributions received should be classified as unrestricted support or as temporarily or permanently restricted support. Unconditional promises to give with payments due in future periods (i.e., pledges) should be reported as restricted support unless the donor clearly intended the moneys to be used to support current-period activities. If restrictions are met in the same reporting period in which the contribution is received, they may be reported as unrestricted support. Contributed services should be recognized as revenues or gains only if they "create or enhance nonfinancial assets or require specialized skills, are provided by individuals possessing those skills, and would typically need to be purchased if not provided by donation." Thus, most contributed services received by health care organizations from auxiliaries are not recorded as revenues.

SFAS No. 117 provides that the financial statements of not-for-profit organizations focus on the entity as a whole, rather than report on fund groups. Not-for-profit organizations are required, at a minimum, to present a statement of financial position, a statement of activities, and a statement of cash flows. The minimum requirements for each financial statement are as follows:

- The statement of financial position must include (1) total assets, (2) total liabilities, (3) amounts for three classes of net assets (unrestricted, temporarily restricted, and permanently restricted), and (4) total net assets.

- The statement of activities must include expenses reported by function or natural classification and the amount of the increase or decrease in unrestricted, temporarily restricted, permanently restricted, and total net assets. If expenses are reported by natural classification, functional expenses must be disclosed. The AICPA audit and accounting guide provides guidance on the use of an intermediate measure of operations in the statement of activities.

- The statement of cash flows must include the net cash used by operating, investing, and financing activities as well as the changes in cash and cash equivalents and a reconciliation of the change in net assets to the change in cash used by operating activities.

There are a number of additional pronouncements that require consideration. SFAS No. 121, *Accounting for the Impairment of Long-Lived Assets and for Long-Lived Assets to Be Disposed Of* (Accounting Standards Section I08), requires that long-lived assets be evaluated to assess whether their carrying value is recoverable or whether an impairment loss should be recorded in the financial statements. This requirement is of particular importance to health care providers as inpatient utilization declines, mergers and restructurings occur, technology changes, and some health care providers experience recurring operating losses.

SFAS No. 124, *Accounting for Certain Investments Held by Not-for-Profit Organizations* (Accounting Standards Section No5), provides measurement and reporting guidance to not-for-profit organizations for investments in equity securities with readily determinable fair values and all investments in debt securities. It requires the reporting of those investments at fair value and accounting for realized and unrealized gains and losses and other investment income in the statement of activities. Unless specifically required by law or by donor restrictions, all income from investments, including realized and unrealized gains and losses, increases or decreases unrestricted net assets.

Still other pronouncements that often have an impact on health care providers include:

- SFAS No. 106, *Employers' Accounting for Postretirement Benefits*
- SFAS No. 112, *Employers' Accounting for Postemployment Benefits*
- SFAS No. 125, *Accounting for Transfers and Servicing of Financial Assets and Extinguishments of Liabilities*

The increasing use of capitation-type payment contractual arrangements, as discussed earlier, has significant accounting and auditing implications. The AICPA audit and accounting guide provides guidance with respect to capitation contracts. Revenue under capitation arrangements is recognized monthly, based on the monthly capitation payments. The costs of providing health care under capitation contracts are accrued as the services are provided, including estimates of costs incurred but not yet reported (IBNR). IBNR costs usually are estimated using one of two methods: the open referrals or the claims lag analysis method. Under capitation arrangements, health care providers may incur losses when the costs incurred to provide the contracted services exceed the contracted capitation payment amounts. If such a loss has been determined, the provider should accrue the loss in the current period.

(b) Revenue from Health Care Services

As previously noted, the majority of a health care organization's revenue usually is received from third-party payors. Such third-party payors, however, typically do not pay for services based on the organization's established rates for the services. The difference between the established charges and the payment rates is referred to as a contractual allowance or adjustment.

Gross patient service revenue and accounts receivable from patients normally are recorded on the accrual basis utilizing the health care organization's established rates. Provisions and related allowances for contractual adjustments, charity care, and uncollectible accounts also are recorded on an accrual basis in the period in which the related services are provided. These provisions are deducted from gross patient service revenue to determine net patient service revenue. Provisions for charity care and uncollectible accounts are recorded at the health care organization's established rates. Charity care is reported net in net patient service revenue, while bad debts are recorded as an operating expense.

(c) Third-Party Payor Considerations

As previously noted, Medicare, Medicaid, some Blue Cross plans, and certain other third-party payors retrospectively determine payments to health care organizations for services provided for their beneficiaries. Many such third-party payors pay periodic interim amounts based on estimates (usually based on established rates on a per case basis) until a final retrospective determination can be made. The third parties audit the cost reports, often resulting in cost disallowances and subsequent appeals, as well as compliance issues, which may take years to resolve. Final settlements may, and often do, have a significant impact on a health care organization's results of operations. Therefore, a reasonable estimate of the final settlement amount should be made in the period in which related services are provided, and adjusted in subsequent years based on additional information available. Auditing such estimates requires an understanding of the financial aspects of each significant third-party payment program. The auditor often needs to use the work of specialists in the audit of third-party settlements. In certain circumstances, the auditor may request that the analysis of third-party payors' settlements be maintained by the organization's attorney to maintain attorney–client privilege.

(d) Deferred Third-Party Reimbursement and Payment

Certain reimbursable costs under retrospective third-party reimbursement contracts differ from the amounts recorded for financial accounting purposes. Some of those differences are timing differences and should be treated similar to book/tax temporary differences, that is, as a current or noncurrent asset or liability based on the difference between the cost expended and the cost allowed to date. Some health care organizations have established deferred reimbursement charges and credits based on the estimated reimbursement effect of such timing differences. Examples of retrospective reimbursement timing differences include depreciation, interest during construction, and losses on advance refunding of debt. Under the Medicare PPS, deferred reimbursement charges and credits should be recorded only for timing differences related to amounts that are reimbursed based on cost, which to a great extent are applicable only to outpatient Medicare cost reimbursement, Medicare-excluded units, or specific state and commercial arrangements. As such, the deferred amounts involved are relatively immaterial to most providers' financial statements.

(e) Accounting for Contracts with Hospital-Based Physicians

Hospitals may have a number of different arrangements with physicians for services performed in the hospital. The nature of the arrangements governs the reporting of related revenues and expenses. In general, when an employee or contractual relationship exists between the hospital and physician covering normal hospital ancillary services (e.g., radiology, pathology, cardiology, and emergency room care), a charge is made by the hospital for the service, and the hospital records the revenue. If a physician's services are billed separately under the physician's name and collections are turned over to the physician, either gross or net of an administrative fee, neither the billings nor the payments to the physician should be recorded in the hospital's accounts. Under these arrangements, the hospital is merely performing an administrative service for the physician. Other issues related to physician contracts include medical education costs, which are reimbursable under arrangements with certain governmental payors, as well as federal and state regulations for hospital-based physician billings.

As health care organizations strive to provide a continuum of care, more hospitals are purchasing physician practices and are providing primary care services in hospital-based clinics. Issues of particular concern include goodwill, physician incentives, and Stark II regulations, which regulate the compensation and valuation of physician practices.

(f) Continuing Care Retirement Communities

Also referred to as residential care facilities, CCRCs provide the elderly a broad spectrum of services in a controlled environment, including residential facilities, meals, recreational activities, and nursing home care. The array of CCRC financial arrangements has resulted in a diversity of accounting practices. Accounting for those financial arrangements is covered in the audit and accounting guide, which addresses accounting in five areas:

- Refundable fees
- Fees repayable to residents from reoccupancy proceeds
- Nonrefundable fees
- Obligation to provide future services and use of facilities
- Initial direct cost of acquiring continuing care contracts

(g) Capitalization of Interest

SFAS No. 62, *Capitalization of Interest Cost in Situations Involving Certain Tax-Exempt Borrowings and Certain Gifts and Grants* (Accounting Standards Section I67), amends certain provisions of SFAS No. 34, *Capitalization of Interest Cost.* Under SFAS No. 62, interest income is required to be offset against interest costs when qualifying assets are acquired with the proceeds of tax-exempt borrowings that are externally restricted to either finance the acquisition of specified qualifying assets or service the related debt. The amount to be capitalized is the interest cost of the borrowing, less interest earned on investments acquired with the proceeds of the borrowing from the date of the borrowing until the assets are ready for use. SFAS No. 62 also excludes assets acquired with restricted gifts and grants from the interest capitalization requirement. The exclusion applies to the extent that such gifts and grants are restricted to acquisition of particular assets and to the extent that funds are available from the gifts and grants.

(h)   Financial Statement Presentation

With the exception of continuing care retirement facilities, health care organizations present classified balance sheets. Most balance sheet categories and classifications are similar to those in other not-for-profit organizations. Several items are unique, however, and should be specifically explained:

- "Assets whose use is limited" is an asset category used to segregate those assets (generally investments) whose use is limited by board designation, as in the case of funded depreciation; by bond indentures or loan covenants, such as debt service reserve funds and other trustee held funds; or by donors, such as temporarily or permanently restricted funds. The specific limitation should be clearly disclosed, particularly in the case of board designations.

- Anticipated final settlements from third-party payors may consist of estimated receivables from and payables to third-party payors that may require separation on the balance sheet, depending on the right of offset. Further, these amounts generally are classified as noncurrent assets and liabilities, as most often settlements take more than one year to resolve, particularly for rate adjustments and appeals; however, in certain circumstances, such amounts may be current in nature.

The financial statements of most not-for-profit health care organizations historically were segregated into general funds and restricted funds, based on board or legal restrictions. Health care organizations now report only separate net asset classes for unrestricted, temporarily restricted, and permanently restricted net assets, based solely on donor restrictions.

One acceptable format for a hospital's statement of activities includes the following major categories:

- Net patient service revenue, consisting of gross charges net of charity care, contractual, or other allowances.

- Other operating revenue from nonpatient-care services to patients and from sales to nonpatients and other activities, such as cafeteria operations, sales of supplies, sales of scrap, and parking lot revenue.

- Total operating revenue, which consists of patient service revenue, net of deductions, plus other operating revenue. Total operating revenue shows the amount the hospital generates through services that is available to cover expenses.

- Operating expenses, which may be reported by major functional classification (e.g., nursing, administration) or by natural classification (e.g., salaries, supplies). If natural classifications are used, the functional expense classification must be disclosed elsewhere in the financial statements. Certain expenses, such as rent expense, depreciation, and interest, must be reported separately on the statement of activities or in the notes to the financial statements.

- Nonoperating revenues not directly related to patient care or sales of related goods and services are reported after income or loss from hospital operations. This presentation segregates the results of recurring hospital operations from nonoperating income, much of which is of a nonrecurring nature. Significant categories of nonoperating revenues may include unrestricted contributions and investment income. Other, less significant categories, such as income from rental properties, are generally reported net of related expenses.

An alternative to the above grouping of revenues segregates revenue as follows:

- Revenue from providing health care services to patients or residents
- Revenue from agreeing to provide or arrange for such services (capitation revenue)
- Other revenue

Under this approach, revenue from providing health care services to patients or residents typically is shown net of deductions. Revenue from agreeing to provide or arrange for health care services under prepaid arrangements with HMOs and PPOs is labeled "premiums earned." For revenue from other sources, revenue resulting from activities that are major and central to ongoing operations ("operating") is distinguished from revenue resulting from peripheral or incidental activities ("nonoperating"). Thus, similar revenue could be classified differently by different health care organizations, depending on how such revenue was generated. SFAS No. 117 permits flexibility in the presentation of the statement of activities, provided there is a clear presentation of the change in net assets for each net asset class.

39.3 RISK FACTORS AND AUDIT REACTION

(a) Inherent Risks

Health care organizations operate in a competitive, rapidly changing industry, which is characterized by the following inherent risks:

- Governmental budgetary constraints, which affect a health care organization's Medicare and Medicaid revenues, as well as reduced payments from third-party payors
- Changing payment mechanisms, particularly capitated payment arrangements that involve providers assuming insurance risk for health care services
- Competition for physicians and patients, particularly in metropolitan areas where there are numerous health care organizations with overlapping or common service areas

- Changes in health care demand, particularly greatly reduced demand for inpatient services, coupled with increased competition from other market segments, which have resulted in an overcapacity of beds
- Reduced profitability and cash flow, which could affect the ability to meet debt service payments and debt covenants
- Increased board pressure on management to improve financial condition and operating results
- Limited availability and high cost of adequate insurance coverage, particularly medical malpractice coverage

Many of those risks are related to the third-party reimbursement structure. A key audit concern is billing procedures, which are complicated by the significant involvement of third parties, few of which pay the hospital's gross charges. For retrospective or cost-based reimbursement mechanisms, the auditor should be particularly concerned about the accuracy of cost reports and allocations of the statistics on which they are based. For prospective payment systems, the greatest risk is the denial of reimbursement by a third party because of unnecessary utilization of services, referred to as "utilization denial." The auditor should consider whether the hospital has adequate utilization review procedures to monitor denials. Since testing medical records to determine the medical necessity of services performed is beyond the technical expertise of auditors, past history of denials may provide guidance in determining the extent of risk in this area. This includes a review of the historical PRO review results as well as the health care provider's internal records. For capitation-based payment mechanisms, the auditor should focus on the hospital's ability to monitor and record each capitation arrangement for appropriate revenue recognition and for complete capture of all IBNR costs and any losses on contracts in the appropriate accounting period. As losses on capitation agreements relate to actual costs of services rather than charges, a determination of the provider's cost accounting system reliability also may be necessary.

(i) Tax-Exempt Status.   Not-for-profit hospitals are affected by the exempt-organization provisions of the federal income tax laws and regulations, which grant tax-exempt status to specified organizations that meet a variety of tests. For example, one of those tests, the not-for-profit test, requires that a hospital not be organized for purposes of providing net income for investor-owners. An issue that has arisen in this area is "excess benefit" (private inurement) transactions involving physicians whose practices were purchased by a hospital and who remain employees of the hospital. Hospitals can lose their tax-exempt status if they fail to meet the tests for tax exemption. Auditors of not-for-profit hospitals should be aware of the tax-exempt provisions of the law and ascertain that tax-exempt hospitals have obtained a determination of their tax-exempt status.

(ii) Sources of Long-Term Financing.   A major source of not-for-profit hospital financing has been tax-exempt debt. This has resulted from the increase in construction costs and the decline in traditional sources of hospital capital, such as philanthropy. Approximately three-fourths of all not-for-profit hospital debt issued since the late 1970s has been tax-exempt bonds, generally revenue bonds. In many jurisdictions, not-for-profit hospitals may not issue such bonds directly, but legislation usually permits revenue bonds to be issued through financing authorities, which then make the proceeds available for use by the hospitals. The tax-exempt bond issues usually require meeting certain financial covenants on a periodic basis, such as a debt service coverage ratio. Generally the bond agreement requires an annual auditor's report on the provider's compliance with the bond covenants. As hospitals experience reductions in profitability, compliance with these bond covenants may become difficult.

(iii) Medical Malpractice Claims. The cost of malpractice claims can be significant to health care organizations, which may be uninsured, insured with limits, self-insured through participation in captive insurance companies, or otherwise self-insured. The audit and accounting guide, which provides specific guidance for applying SFAS No. 5, covers the following topics: the ultimate cost of malpractice claims, estimating the amount of the loss, reported and unreported incidents, disclosure issues, discounting, claims-made policies, retrospectively rated premiums, captive insurance companies, and trust funds.

(b) Audit Strategy

In developing an audit strategy for a hospital engagement, the auditor should have an understanding of the hospital's patient mix, which is influenced by the geographical location of the hospital, the range of services it provides, and federal and state regulations. In particular, the audit strategy will vary depending on whether services are rendered on a charge-paying or a cost-reimbursement or capitated basis. In prospective payment systems like the Medicare DRG system, the auditor should be concerned with the procedures used to abstract patients' medical records and to assign each case to the proper DRG, since that assignment determines the revenue to be received. In capitation systems, the auditor should focus on the ability to estimate, through lag analysis or other methods, the total costs of services provided, including services that may be rendered by other providers through subcontracts. If, however, most of the hospital's services will be paid on a cost-reimbursement basis, which still exists among some payors or specific programs, the propriety of costs incurred is a primary audit concern. The accuracy of expense classifications and of statistics used to allocate indirect costs to service departments is also significant. In addition, the accuracy of departmental revenue classification is important in the cost apportionment process. If payment is made either directly by the patient or by third parties based on actual charges billed, auditing statistical data and departmental cost classification is deemphasized since that data does not affect revenue. If reimbursement is primarily on a capitated basis, the hospital's cost accounting system and method of determining IBNR are important to determine whether losses have been incurred in the current period.

Controls in the patient revenue cycle are often effective, and the auditor may, depending on efficiency considerations, plan to perform tests of controls in this area. In an effort to control costs and comply with various regulatory requirements, hospitals often have sophisticated expense budgeting systems. In addition, hospitals often have effective monitoring controls in place, typically budgetary reviews and analyses of ex-

penses reflected in the monthly financial statements, which help ensure that underlying expense data has been processed correctly, and management reviews of the
third-party reimbursement structure and of cost reports.

In situations where the organization has a sizable accounting staff, a sufficient volume of transactions, and a well-controlled information technology function, the auditor may determine that it would be efficient to perform tests of controls as a basis for
reducing substantive tests. On the other hand, tests of controls may not be efficient
for hospitals that typically have small accounting staffs and a general absence of segregation of duties and supervision. Performance of substantive tests before year-end
can be particularly appropriate and efficient for accounts receivable, the allowance for
uncollectible accounts, and fixed assets.

In planning a hospital audit, the auditor needs to understand the hospital's current
financial position and financial trends. Financial ratio and other comparative analysis may lead to a better understanding of the hospital's operations and problems than
could be obtained from reviewing raw data. For example, the knowledge that a hospital has 90 days of its revenue in uncollected accounts receivable in comparison to a national average of 65 days may be more meaningful and cause a different level of concern than the knowledge that the accounts receivable balance is $4 million. It is also
helpful to compare the hospital's operations and financial position with those of other
institutions. A variance from industry averages could point to problems. In making
comparisons with industry data, the auditor should ensure that the sources and compilation of data are consistent and relevant; for example, industry statistics used
should be for hospitals of similar size (measured by number of beds) and geographical location. Industry statistics are published frequently and considerable industry financial comparisons are provided by industry associations and others.

(c) Materiality

Materiality guidelines for hospital audits should be based on the specific circumstances of each hospital. For not-for-profit hospitals, the excess of revenues over expenses may be less important as a basis for materiality judgments, because they often
have access to alternative capital sources (e.g., contributions and grants) and do not
provide a return to investors. Parameters frequently used by the auditor in evaluating
materiality in hospital financial statements include net patient service revenue, current ratios, debt equity ratios, and debt coverage ratios; restricted or unrestricted net
assets; and specific line items.

(d) Single Audit Act and Related Audit Considerations

Health care organizations that receive financial assistance from a governmental
agency may be required to have their financial statements audited in accordance with
the provisions of the Single Audit Act and OMB Circular A-133, "Audits of States, Local Governments, and Non-Profit Organizations," or A-110, "Uniform Requirements
for Grants to Universities, Hospitals, and Other Non-Profit Organizations." Financial
assistance may take the form of grants, contracts, loans, loan guarantees, property,
cooperative agreements, subsidies, and insurance or direct appropriation. SAS No. 74,
Compliance Auditing Considerations in Audits of Governmental Entities and Recipients of Gov-

ernmental Financial Assistance, provides guidance for audits of certain entities that receive governmental financial assistance and explains the relationship between those
requirements and the requirements of *Government Auditing Standards*, issued by the
U.S. General Accounting Office. Additional guidance on audits in accordance with the
Single Audit Act is provided in the AICPA audit and accounting guide, *Audits of State
and Local Governmental Units*. Guidance for audits under OMB Circular A-133 is provided in SOP 92-9, *Audits of Not-for-Profit Organizations Receiving Federal Awards*. At the
time of this writing, the AICPA is revising SOP 92-9 to conform to the Single Audit
Act and Circular A-133.

39.4 AUDIT CONSIDERATIONS

The unique aspect of the health care industry from an audit perspective is the health
care delivery system—the revenue cycle. Auditing the other cycles is essentially the
same as in manufacturing or selling entities and thus is not emphasized in this
chapter.

(a) Patient Revenue Cycle

The major source of revenues in a hospital is services provided to patients. Revenue
is recorded, at the hospital's established rates, on the accrual basis at the time services are performed. Patient service revenues are recorded separately by source (such
as laboratory revenue), by payor, and by patient type (such as inpatient or outpatient).
The source of payment or payor classification for each patient is essential information
that should be captured by the accounting system. Hospitals generally bill inpatients
after completion of a patient's stay in the hospital, whereas most recurring providers
such as CCRCs and rehabilitation facilities bill monthly.

The actual amount received by the hospital will vary depending on contractual arrangements between the hospital and the patient or a third-party payor. Contracts
with third-party payors may or may not provide for reimbursement that coincides with
a hospital's standard uniform rate structure. Instead, amounts due may be based on
the hospital's costs, volume, intensity of service, and so forth. The various third-party
payors utilize different payment mechanisms. Some arrangements with third parties
provide hospitals with interim cash flow, based on DRG rates, until the final settlement can be calculated. Services rendered to private-paying patients are billed at the
established rates except that courtesy allowances may be granted to doctors, employees, or members of religious orders, and charity allowances may be granted as determined by patient needs and hospital policy. The established rates billed to self-pay patients may be limited by state law.

To understand the hospital's patient revenue cycle, the auditor should become familiar with the various functions and departments that may serve patients and also
should understand how those functions and departments relate to accounting for patient revenue. Auditing a hospital's patient revenue cycle is discussed in the context
of the following typical functions and departments involved in serving patients.

(i) Admitting/Registration Function.

A patient is admitted to the hospital ei-
ther in an emergency situation or based on a licensed physician's recommendation.

The first step in the admitting function is acquiring credit and insurance information about the patient. The auditor should review the procedures for gathering and recording this information to gain an understanding of the patient classification system. Accurate patient classification is essential for determining the accuracy of patient accounts receivable. Frequently a patient's classification is redetermined after the patient has been admitted or after insurance verification has been performed; the hospital should have controls to ensure that classification changes are monitored. For outpatient services, similar controls are in effect to obtain patient information and insurance documentation.

The next step in the admitting function is initiating accounting documents. The primary document that begins the revenue accounting cycle is generally the admissions form. The auditor needs evidence of the completeness and accuracy of admissions forms; generally this is obtained by comparing them with other records produced by the accounting system. In addition, hospitals typically have a quality assurance or utilization review department that maintains records of their review of compliance with applicable regulations and requirements mandated by law or by payors, as well as monitors the PRO review process.

Finally, the admitting function is responsible for the location, by bed, of all patients in the hospital. The rate charged is based on the patient's location, which encompasses both accommodations and intensity of care. For example, the rate for a private room is higher than that for a semiprivate room, and intensive care is more costly than routine care. The auditor is concerned about the accuracy of revenue based on patient location; relevant audit evidence can be obtained by comparing daily census reports with patients' accounting records.

(ii) Daily Hospital Service Charges.   Daily hospital charges for room, board, and general nursing care provided to patients are recorded as revenue on a per diem basis. Daily hospital service departments typically include routine or general care, intensive care, coronary care, and nursery. Routine care is categorized further by room accommodations, such as private or semiprivate. Many third-party contracts reimburse hospitals for daily hospital services based on patient-day statistics or on diagnosis categorization; accordingly, the auditor should test those statistics or diagnosis categorizations for completeness and accuracy. If the hospital has effective controls for accumulating the statistics, the auditor may test those controls; alternatively, the auditor may perform substantive tests of the statistics.

(iii) Ancillary Service Charges.   Diagnostic or therapeutic services other than room, board, and general nursing care are referred to as ancillary services and include use of operating rooms, recovery rooms, anesthesiology, and nuclear medicine facilities. Unlike daily hospital service charges, ancillary charges are generated for each instance of service provided instead of on a per diem basis. Ancillary services in a hospital are complex and numerous, geographically distributed, and often processed by manual or separate data processing systems. Controls over the complete and timely processing of ancillary service charges, the materiality of the ancillary revenue, and the differences in the systems and personnel utilized to generate and process revenues, are important audit considerations.

(iv) Outpatient Service Charges. Outpatient services may include emergency room treatment; laboratory, radiology, or other testing procedures; or clinic services. Other terms for some of these services are observation beds and same-day surgery.

Outpatient records may be processed by the admitting function from the emergency room, clinic, or other location in the hospital; the procedures are similar to those for inpatients. An assigned admission number generally identifies the patient as an outpatient or inpatient. Ancillary services are provided to outpatients on the same charge basis as is used for inpatients. Outpatient service charges are recorded separately because different third-party reimbursement arrangements may apply to inpatients and outpatients. Since the two revenue sources are similar, the auditor may test controls unique to the outpatient revenue cycle when testing controls over inpatient revenues; however, as the reimbursement is different, the auditor should test the contractual allowances for these services separately.

(v) Discharge and Billing Functions. Notification that a patient is leaving the hospital results in discontinuance of the daily hospital service charge. During the patient's stay, routine and ancillary charges are recorded in the individual's subsidiary ledger account as part of "in-house accounts receivable." After discharge, this account is transferred to a "suspense" file, sometimes referred to as a "discharged but not billed" file. The patient's account remains there for several days to ensure that all charges for services are recorded properly in the account. After the suspense period, billings are prepared for all hospital services, and the account is transferred to the "billed" accounts receivable file. In many instances, the hospital calculates and records the third-party contractual allowance for inpatient services at this time. Credit and collection procedures are then applied to the billed accounts receivable. To aid in these efforts and to provide a basis for assessing the allowance for uncollectible accounts, the billed accounts receivable file is classified by payor category (e.g., Medicare, Blue Cross, or private-paying), since collection procedures differ by payor. Additionally, aging analyses by payor classification, usually aged on discharge date, are needed to evaluate the probability of collection for each category. As many patients have a secondary payor (e.g., Medigap insurance, self-pay deductible), after reimbursement from the primary payor the balance of the account is transferred to a receivable from the secondary payor and appropriate collection procedures are then applied. Outpatient receivables are handled in a similar manner; however, the contractual adjustment typically is not recorded until the reimbursement has been received, due to the volume of transactions.

(vi) Substantive Tests of Accounts Receivable. Hospital receivables have several characteristics normally not found in receivables of commercial organizations. First, charges to patients for services received may be settled for an amount that differs from the full rate because of contractual arrangements with third-party payors or courtesy, charity, or other policy discounts. Since revenue initially is recorded at the hospital's standard gross charges, patient accounts, which are recorded gross, must be adjusted to their net realizable value through a contractual allowance. Typically, inpatient accounts are adjusted at the billing date, although some hospitals may adjust at time of discharge or remittance.

Payment may be made by a single third-party payor or a combination of payors (e.g., commercial insurance, Medicare, Medicaid, workers compensation, and the patient). Since a patient may have more than one insurer, it is possible for duplicate payments to be made on the patient's account, which results in credit balances in accounts receivable. The auditor should review the components of these credit balances and, if they are significant, consider reclassifying them. Since the hospital must refund duplicate payments, the auditor should determine that refund checks are for authorized credit balances and that they are payable to the proper payee. In addition, the auditor should review correspondence from the PRO to determine whether any significant disallowed services are recorded as receivables.

In most hospitals, accounts receivable are classified according to the patient's billing status, generally using the following categories:

- Inpatient
  - Admitted but not discharged (commonly referred to as "in-house patients")
  - Discharged but not billed (accounts awaiting final or "late" charges, or unbilled as a result of a backlog in billing procedures—which might indicate a control deficiency)
  - Discharged and billed
- Outpatient
  - Unbilled
  - Billed

These categories of inpatient and outpatient receivables may be expanded further to indicate private-paying status or third-party responsibility for payment.

The accuracy and existence of accounts receivable are tested predominantly by reviewing subsequent cash receipts, analysis of agings by payor, and comparison with prior experience. In addition, the auditor may review days revenue in accounts receivable by the subcategories noted above, which often will indicate whether there is a control deficiency in the medical records or billing departments. The completeness and accuracy of admitted-but-not-discharged patient receivables can be tested by comparing accounts with the daily census report. Although SAS No. 67, *The Confirmation Process*, applies to health care organizations, confirming balances with patients or third-party payors may not be effective since many receivables are recorded at an amount that will not be received from a single payor due to deductibles, or are recorded gross of contractual adjustments.

(vii) Third-Party Payors.   Almost every hospital receives reimbursement under some type of third-party arrangement. Although programs vary from state to state and plan to plan, many third-party programs require an annual report to determine the final settlement for the accounting period. The final settlement, less amounts paid by the program during the period, is the settlement due to or from the third-party payor. This annual third-party report is referred to as the statement of reimbursable cost, or the cost report. The auditor's review of the cost report for completeness and accuracy is an important procedure in determining that the settlement is proper and that it has been appropriately reflected in the financial statements. The balance sheet and activities statement accounts usually affected by this report include third-party settlements receivable or payable, and contractual adjustments.

The auditor should determine the mix of third-party payors and should consider the controls for billing in each classification. Auditing procedures tailored to the specific situation should be performed to substantiate the contractual allowances for each third-party payor. In addition, the auditor should ascertain that appropriate allowances have been deducted from patient accounts receivable for third-party payments that will be less than the full charge reflected in accounts receivable. Patient accounts billed to third parties may be disallowed in whole or in part and rebilled to patients. Accordingly, the auditor should evaluate the hospital's past experience with receivables disallowed by third parties to determine that probable losses have been adequately provided for. If significant amounts of patient accounts receivable are in cost-reimbursement payor classifications, the auditor should consider whether substantive tests of receivables would be the most efficient way of obtaining evidence of the realizable value of accounts receivable at year-end. The auditor should be alert to delays in these settlements and should take them into consideration in making his or her evaluation.

Although the Medicare DRG system does not use cost reporting for rate determination purposes, cost reports are still necessary to determine the reimbursement for pass-through costs (i.e., costs excluded from the DRG rates), outpatient services, and excluded units. The auditor should test the hospital's summarization of costs to determine the amounts due from Medicare for such costs.

Medicare requires hospitals to report annual statistical and financial data concerning costs incurred. The data required for the Medicare cost report is as follows:

- Expenses by cost center as recorded in the hospital's general ledger, which are then adjusted and reclassified to exclude nonallowable costs (the A Schedules)

- Overhead costs of nonrevenue-producing departments, allocated to revenue-producing departments, also known as the step-down (the B Schedules)

- The full cost of each revenue-producing department, apportioned between the relevant payor and all other payors based on utilization of days or charges for that department (the C Schedules)

- A summary and comparison of Medicare costs with interim payments received or receivable by the hospital (the E Schedules)

As a result of the timing of the year-end cost report filing and of audits by Medicare, one or more prior-year cost reports may be unsettled at any point in time. Each year the auditor should review the status of prior-year reimbursement reports to assess new information, including cash received or paid on the settlements, the results of third-party audits, or other changes that would affect the hospital's estimate of amounts due from or to third-party payors. These changes in estimates should be recorded in the year they are determined as a component of net patient service revenue. In some situations, these changes in estimates may be significant and may require separate disclosure in the financial statements to ensure that current-year operating results are not distorted.

As noted earlier, various third-party reimbursements are determined using numerous statistics, including patient-days. Substantive tests of statistics typically include reviews of the method of their accumulation, adequacy of supporting documentation, adherence to prescribed regulations, comparability with prior years, and reasonableness.

Hospitals generally maintain logs of billings to and remittances from third-party payors, with details of patient-days, departmental revenues, coinsurance, deductibles, and other data. The auditor should test the accuracy of the logs because the final settlement will be based on information contained in them. Normally, patient data recorded in the logs is tested by comparison with remittance advices and billing forms.

In addition, a hospital's reimbursement structure entails a number of uncertainties, including disallowed costs and cases, rate and volume adjustments, final settlements, and compliance reviews. Most hospitals maintain a reserve for these items in their third-party settlement receivable or payable. The auditor usually compares the amount of the reserve with the prior-year reserve, as well as reviews the actual liability history of disallowed costs, final settlements, and compliance reviews, to determine the appropriateness of the reserve.

(viii) Nonpatient Revenues.   Revenues from sources other than patient charges consist of earnings on invested funds, unrestricted gifts and grants, and net assets released from restrictions. Auditing procedures for material nonpatient revenues may include, but need not be limited to:

- Confirming investment activity with banks or an external trustee
- Reviewing data and documents underlying gifts, grants, and bequests, such as board minutes, correspondence, and acknowledgment receipts
- Reviewing research or grant documentation
- Confirming pledges and evaluating their collectibility

(b) Purchasing Cycle

(i) Payroll.   Hospital employees may be classified as professional and nonprofessional. Examples of professional staff are registered nurses and licensed nurses. Nonprofessional employees include orderlies, housekeeping and maintenance personnel, dietary staff, and administrative personnel. Controls over both professional and nonprofessional time are critical since salaries constitute a significant portion of hospital costs.

Generally, the same payroll auditing procedures used in other organizations of comparable size also apply to hospitals. Testing of total payroll costs should cover classification of costs by department, which is important for purposes of reimbursement and also for accurate expense reporting. The auditor typically reviews the appropriateness of the account distribution and traces amounts to the payroll register or distribution summaries. Those registers or summaries are tested for mathematical accuracy and then agreed to the appropriate general ledger accounts.

(ii) Supplies and Other Expenses.   Most hospital payables and disbursement processes are similar to those in other businesses. Hospital expenses typically are classified by departmental function (such as nursing services and laboratory services). Proper classification of costs by department is important for financial statement purposes as well as for cost-based reimbursement. The auditor should test the propriety of the general ledger account distribution by reference to purchasing documentation and perform other tests of the accounts payable/purchasing function.

(c) Inventories

While supplies and drugs may be significant expenses to hospitals, inventory amounts for supplies and drugs are usually insignificant to the balance sheet. Therefore, substantive tests for inventory, for both activities statement and balance sheet accounts, often are limited to fluctuation analysis, such as gross profit analysis, and inquiry. If the auditor determines that it is necessary to observe the inventory-taking, the procedures are generally no different from those followed for a commercial entity. The auditor should make adequate arrangements prior to the date of the inventory-taking to facilitate an accurate count, with appropriate consideration to obsolete inventory, given frequent changes in technology. It is necessary to ensure that all inventory is counted; this may take careful planning because items usually are not tagged and supplies may be located in several different areas of the hospital. Pharmacy inventories often are taken by an independent service, which issues a report on the results of the physical count. The auditor generally reviews the qualifications of the independent service team, discusses procedures utilized with the team leader, and makes independent test counts, as necessary.

(d) Fixed Assets and Intangibles

Auditing procedures for a hospital's property, plant, and equipment and intangible assets are typically the same as those for a commercial entity. Some hospital departments own and use expensive, highly specialized equipment, such as nuclear magnetic resonance devices. Department heads should, of course, be closely involved in capital budgeting and purchasing decisions, but that involvement should not extend to overriding controls that have been instituted for purchases generally. Audit considerations should include the possibility of bed overcapacity, resulting in a potential write-down under SFAS No. 121, as well as technologically obsolete equipment.

With the increase in mergers and acquisitions, goodwill and other intangible assets have become increasingly significant to a hospital's balance sheet. Consideration should be given to the valuation of intangible assets based on service line. For example, if the purchase of a physician's practice resulted in goodwill or a covenant-not-to-compete, consideration should be given to whether revenues from the practice will continue to justify the amortization period.

(e) Tests of Restricted Net Assets

For organizations that receive temporarily or permanently restricted contributions, the auditor should review:

- The instruments applicable to the contributions, to test classification of both the original contribution as well as subsequent earnings, including unrealized gains or losses recorded in compliance with SFAS No. 124, and compliance with their restricted purpose
- Transfers to unrestricted net assets, to test whether expenditures were made for their intended purpose
- Investment activity, including independent confirmation of investments held by trustees, to test the appropriate classification of changes in net assets
- Solicitation and collection procedures, to assess control over cash receipts

Classification of net assets is governed by SFAS No. 116 and is covered by the AICPA audit and accounting guide, *Health Care Organizations*.

(f) Analytical Procedures

Because of the numerous statistics maintained by hospitals for measuring patient care activities (such as patient-days, laboratory tests, pharmacy requisitions, and number of X-ray tests), and because hospitals usually record revenues and expenses on a departmental basis, analytical procedures often are used for testing revenues and expenses. For example, patient service revenues can be tested by use of patient-day statistics and applicable room rates. Departmental expenses usually relate to departmental revenue. Gross margins on pharmacy and supply items are fairly constant, because consistent markup percentages normally are used.

(g) Malpractice Insurance

Increased patient volume, more complex treatment methods, and a consumer-oriented legal climate have combined to increase malpractice cases against hospitals. As insurance costs continue to rise, many hospitals have changed their insurance practices and are seeking other ways of covering and limiting their exposure to litigation. Insurance coverages vary from complete self-insurance to insurance with large deductibles. Insurance coverage may be on a claims-made basis or on an occurrence basis. Insurance premiums may be retrospectively rated. Organizations may establish trust funds to cover a portion of their self-insurance program or may place their insurance coverage with a captive insurance company. Each of these variations in insurance coverage requires a different accounting treatment and is explained in the audit and accounting guide. As a basis for designing substantive tests, the auditor needs to understand the organization's insurance program and its procedures for identifying and accruing losses.

For hospitals with a self-insurance or modified self-insurance program, the auditor should perform detailed reviews of "incident" reports. ("Incident" for this purpose is defined as "an event that could expose the hospital to liability.") The hospital should have established procedures for reporting incidents; those procedures may include preparing a narrative report of all incidents, interviewing hospital staff, obtaining evaluations of independent insurance adjusters, and, if appropriate, referring to legal counsel.

The auditor should review case-by-case reports of the status and estimates of potential liability for asserted and unasserted claims and obtain and review the opinions of independent consultants. In addition, the auditor should inquire into the hospital's reporting and investigation procedures for identifying and estimating potential liability. Confirmation requests should be sent to the hospital's incident investigator and the insurance adjusters and investigators as well as to its attorneys. Such incidents also should be covered in management's representation letter.

Other forms of significant insurance claims or sources of litigation include workers compensation, health care insurance, and Equal Employment Opportunity Commission issues. Many hospitals are self-insured or have large deductibles for these risks. The auditor should test actual or potential liabilities related to these areas in a manner similar to malpractice incidents.

40

Auditing High Technology Companies

40.1 OVERVIEW OF THE INDUSTRY

Companies that incorporate new technologies in their products have experienced rapid growth and provided dramatic new product offerings to the world markets. Furthermore, application of new technologies creates significant improvements in productivity and quality of life for major segments of society. As a result, high technology companies are becoming one of the largest industries in the U.S. and world economies. Segments of the high technology industry include computers, electronics, semiconductors, software, communications, instrumentation, robotics, biotechnology, medical devices, and other applied sciences. These businesses and the products they offer are diverse, but they share the following common characteristics that result in their inclusion in the high technology category:

- Intensive research and development, which generally cause operating losses prior to product introduction
- A need to identify funding to sustain the company prior to product introduction, and thereafter for marketing and sales efforts and working capital
- Products that derive value from technology as opposed to the production process
- Significant competitive advantage and rapid growth of companies that are first or second to market
- Sudden emergence of rapid-growth niche markets
- Rapid growth in total market and individual company size
- Extensive use of resellers and third-party channels as a means of increasing distribution volume and minimizing selling and administrative costs
- Rapid entry into international markets
- High gross margins that shrink rapidly as competing products are introduced
- Extensive warranty and customer support commitments that result in high customer service costs
- Rapid product obsolescence caused by the introduction of competing products utilizing more advanced technologies
- Frequent instances of products that fail to meet customer expectations or have short life cycles, resulting in rapid downturns for individual companies or entire niche markets

In addition to providing the defining characteristics of high technology companies, these attributes are often the cause of the most significant audit issues in the industry. Such issues include premature revenue recognition; improper capitalization of research and development costs; unexpected inventory write-offs; and failure to appropriately account for sales discounts, return provisions, and vendor commitments. Furthermore, the rapid growth experienced by many high technology companies frequently results in companies outgrowing their accounting systems and controls.

These factors and the frequency of business failures in the high technology industry make it necessary for the auditor to exercise increased diligence in assessing risk—including the risk that the company will be unable to obtain sufficient funding to continue as a going concern—and determining the audit strategy and in performing substantive tests. This chapter discusses unique aspects of the high technology environment and the related audit implications.

40.2   RISK FACTORS, AUDIT REACTION, AND AUDITING PROCEDURES

The common characteristics of high technology companies cited previously can increase dramatically the inherent risks to which such companies are vulnerable, as well as control risk. Audit areas commonly affected by these increased risks include revenue recognition, inventory, field-service operations, warranty accruals, and research and development costs. The remainder of this chapter discusses how the auditor should identify and address such risks.

(a)   Revenue Recognition

Technology developed by a vendor often can be applied to a large number of different types of product at minimal incremental cost. Therefore, it is not uncommon for sales and management personnel to structure large numbers of transactions so that each is unique in some manner. Especially close to the end of an accounting period, vendors commonly offer large sales discounts and other concessions, such as product warranties, rights of return or exchange, acceptance clauses, or free services. These unique contractual arrangements make the determination of revenue recognition more difficult than in many other industries.

Several high technology companies have experienced business failures as a result of inadequate controls, including monitoring controls. In some of those instances, employees took advantage of the company's ineffective internal control to record revenue that should have been deferred according to the provisions of the related sales contracts. Such provisions may grant rights of return, exchange, or acceptance; extended payment terms; and the right to receive additional products or services in the future; or may specify other vendor obligations. In assessing the company's internal control, the auditor should determine that management has established and maintains sufficient controls to identify and properly account for such unique sales arrangements. This commonly necessitates a review of all material nonstandard sales contracts by appropriate personnel. Controls also are needed to ensure that accounting personnel are notified of commitments made by sales personnel that are not included in sales contracts.

The auditor should read significant sales contracts and examine the relevant facts and circumstances surrounding individual transactions in order to determine whether revenue has been recognized appropriately. Frequently, a company will not have detailed customer documentation setting forth the terms of a particular sale. In these circumstances, the auditor should give serious consideration to contacting customers directly through detailed confirmations that include the specific terms of sale as represented by the company.

The auditor should not consider revenue recognition in isolation from the collectibility of the related accounts receivable. In many cases, the ability of the vendor to collect receivables is the ultimate determinant of when revenue should be recognized. Significant receivable balances that remain uncollected long after the balance sheet date or days sales outstanding that are unusually high may call into question the appropriateness of the entity's revenue recognition policies.

(b) Field-Service Operations

Many high technology manufacturers have field-service operations that support equipment that has been delivered and installed. Revenues from field-service operations may be based on contracts or individual service calls, depending on the underlying service or maintenance agreement with the customer. The auditor should be alert to service and maintenance costs that should not be billed to customers because the customer is entitled to the services under warranty agreements.

Field-service operations tend to be geographically dispersed and characterized by a large volume of low-dollar-value transactions. The geographical dispersion often requires large amounts of test equipment and parts inventory at many locations. Controlling these operations requires effective procedures and management systems, which may not be fully developed. Internal audit participation in this area is often critical in attaining adequate audit coverage.

(c) Computer Software Sales

AICPA Statement of Position (SOP) 97-2, *Software Revenue Recognition,* addresses software revenue recognition principles. SOP 97-2 superseded SOP 91-1, which was applied by analogy to revenue recognition for high technology products other than software. It is expected that SOP 97-2 also will be applied to nonsoftware sales. In general, SOP 97-2 requires that revenue not be recognized until the product is delivered; however, the SOP also states that revenue may not be recognized even when delivery has occurred, unless all of the following conditions have been met:

- Evidence of an agreement has been obtained
- Collectibility of the related receivable is probable
- The vendor's fee is fixed or determinable
- No significant uncertainties exist about customer acceptance

The conditions listed above are general in nature, and recognition of revenue for each sale must be based on the individual facts and circumstances surrounding the transaction. The principal change in revenue recognition principles resulting from the issuance of SOP 97-2 is the requirement that revenue be allocated among all products and services specified in a software arrangement, including products that the vendor is obligated to deliver only if and when they are developed. Revenue allocation is to be based on vendor-specific, objective evidence, such as a price list, of the fair value of each product and service. If evidence of fair value does not exist, revenue from the entire arrangement must be deferred until all elements have been delivered or the evidence becomes available. SOP 97-2 may result in some companies deferring a significant amount of revenue that would have been recognized earlier under SOP 91-1. Some companies also may change the manner in which sales contracts are written.

There have been numerous instances of improper recognition of revenue relating to software sales through distribution channels such as government resellers, original equipment manufacturers (OEMs), value-added resellers (VARs), and distributors. Sales arrangements between a company and resellers often include return provisions and/or price protection guarantees similar to those in the retail industry. The auditor should evaluate such sales terms in determining whether the entity's revenue recognition policy is appropriate. It also becomes increasingly critical to "look through" the sale into the specific arrangements to assess whether the proceeds of the sale can be collected. Such information should include an assessment of the reseller's ability to sell product inventory to end-users and an evaluation of the potential exposure generated by price protection guarantees. Often, this involves the company establishing procedures to monitor inventory held by distributors and retailers to address the extent to which the products have been sold to end-users. When evaluating these types of risks, the auditor should focus on the entity's actual business practices as opposed to its stated policy. In addition, the auditor should evaluate resellers' financial viability.

(d) Bioscience and Technology

Bioscience and technology involve applying biological science and engineering in a variety of industries, including pharmaceuticals, health care, and agriculture. Bioscience and technology companies have the same attributes as other high technology companies but have even greater research and development costs. Bioscience companies often enter into corporate sponsorship or partnership arrangements, which typically give larger companies the right to manufacture and sell products in exchange for research and development funding and royalty payments.

Bioscience and technology revenues are derived from contractual development arrangements, royalty agreements, or product sales. Appropriate revenue recognition depends on the company's state of development. Therefore, the auditor needs to understand the research and production contracts, assess the achievement of contract milestones, and understand related product licensing and royalty arrangements. Revenue recognition methods should be reevaluated as the company moves out of the prototype and initial production phases into commercial production.

Classification of costs is another important accounting and tax issue for bioscience and technology companies. Substantial judgment is required to determine the appropriate accounting for patent costs, purchased and sponsored research and development, licensed technology, and organizational expenses. Accounting for such costs is discussed later in the chapter.

(e) Foreign Operations

High technology companies typically enter foreign markets early in their development. Because of the opportunities presented by large foreign markets, many high technology companies consider various aspects of globalization, including what countries to penetrate, market entry strategies, distribution channels, and form of investment (e.g., direct or joint venture). Often, sales begin with direct exports and then occur through a local distributor, with field-service technicians added to support the installed base. Eventually, a separate sales office and a branch or subsidiary may be established. Companies also may choose to manufacture or to conduct research and development (R&D) activities offshore.

Foreign operations create many statutory reporting, legal, and tax compliance issues that both management and the auditor need to recognize. Additionally, expenses of operating abroad may be higher than comparable domestic costs, particularly because of additional duty, freight, insurance, and administrative costs. The auditor should be aware that the costs of duty requirements are often significant and subject to review and audit by customs authorities on a retroactive basis.

Foreign markets also create foreign currency translation and transaction problems arising from translation of asset and liability positions and revenue and expense transactions in currencies other than the U.S. dollar. The response to foreign currency exposure by high technology companies is determined to some degree by their relative size: Smaller, newer entrants into foreign markets often quote prices in U.S. dollars, while larger, more sophisticated companies frequently manage their net exposure for individual currencies and sometimes hedge those exposures. The appropriate accounting for exposures and related hedges is set forth in Statement of Financial Accounting Standards (SFAS) No. 52, *Foreign Currency Translation* (Accounting Standards Section F60). Companies with operations in certain foreign countries also may be faced with restrictions on currency withdrawals, which, if material, should be disclosed.

(f) Maintenance and Service Agreements

High technology companies frequently enter into agreements with customers to provide product maintenance. These agreements typically run for one year. Generally, the revenue associated with these agreements should be recognized over the period of the agreement rather than at the time of billing or receipt of payment.

In some cases, companies provide maintenance and support services that are not billed separately but instead are "bundled" in the sales price of the related product. These services should be identified separately and recognized ratably over the period of service in accordance with SOP 97-2 and Financial Accounting Standards Board (FASB) Technical Bulletin No. 90-1, *Accounting for Separately Priced Extended Warranty and Product Maintenance Contracts*. If the fair value of these services cannot be identified separately, companies may have to defer the recognition of revenue from the bundled product until all elements have been delivered or the fair value becomes determinable. Similarly, revenues from maintenance contracts that provide for unspecified product enhancements or upgrades should be recognized over the term of the contract. In auditing maintenance agreements, it may be appropriate to contact customers to confirm the details of commitments made by sales representatives.

(g) Inventory

Inventory may be a significant asset of high technology companies. Because the products are subject to rapid obsolescence, inventory is another highly judgmental audit area. Usually, the most difficult aspects within inventory are obsolescence reserves, field-service inventory, direct materials valuation, and inventory on consignment.

(i) Obsolescence.   Frequently, new products are introduced that exceed the performance of existing products. This causes inventory to become obsolete rapidly, creating significant valuation issues. The auditor should be alert to increasing inventory levels that are not in line with realistic sales expectations. To assess inventory obsolescence, the auditor should consider the following factors:

- Current levels of inventory and backlog held by the company and its resellers
- Effect of the next product release on the marketability of existing products
- Impact of forthcoming product releases by competitors
- Forecasted future demand
- Pricing trends and the impact of price decreases required to obtain or maintain market share
- External and internal changes in technology and standards

The auditor should consider evaluating the reasonableness of sales forecasts and the accuracy of the existing backlog on both a price and volume basis to determine whether inventory is appropriately valued at the lower of cost or market as required by Accounting Research Bulletin No. 43. This evaluation should address raw materials, work in process, and finished goods. A common industry practice is the use of a formula-driven approach (e.g., all items that have not moved in six months), which translates overall judgments about obsolete inventory into a systematic methodology that provides a basis for comparison between periods. Usually, such a system is subject to adjustment in light of particular circumstances. Any formula-driven approach should consider future demand and be reviewed frequently to determine whether it continues to be realistic in an environment of rapid technological change. Finally, the auditor should be mindful of the potential for obsolete inventory when observing a physical inventory.

Some companies have implemented inventory systems that include materials requirement planning features. In such cases, companies and auditors may assess inventory obsolescence by comparing materials requirements for budgeted sales over the next six to 12 months with raw materials, components, and finished goods on hand on an individual-part basis. This often enables both management and the auditor to specifically identify inventory on hand that is in excess of budgeted requirements.

(ii) Field-Service Inventory. Many computer and electronics companies maintain quantities of inventory for servicing their products over a portion of or the entire product life cycle. As indicated earlier, this so-called field-service inventory tends to be geographically dispersed and is characterized by small quantities of inventory in multiple locations.

Methods of valuing field-service inventory vary because of the different operational practices employed by companies in the industry. Many companies carry field-service inventories as they would any other type of inventory, at historical cost with provisions for obsolescence and shrinkage. Other companies value field-service inventories as if they were depreciable assets. These methods need to be evaluated on a company by company basis to ensure that asset valuation and cost allocation are appropriate.

(iii) Direct Materials Valuation. Because the costs of raw materials in high technology products often decrease over time, generally that component of inventory is valued on the average cost or first-in, first-out basis; the use of last-in, first-out valuation is less common than in many other industries. Many high technology companies are assemblers of components and are therefore material-intensive; vertical integration tends to be fairly limited. Accordingly, audit tests should focus on procedures for acquiring materials, accounting for purchase price variances, the existence of and appropriate accounting for purchase commitments, and the proper treatment of volume discount arrangements with vendors.

(iv) Consigned Inventory.   When auditing consigned inventory held by others, it is important to physically observe the inventory or confirm its existence directly with the holders (see AU Section 331.14, "Inventories Held in Public Warehouses," for a more detailed description of procedures that should be considered in this area). In addition, the company's documentation, controls, and valuation methods need to be evaluated to determine the extent of testing.

(h)   Overhead Accounting

Rapid growth and a short product life cycle create significant expenditures for new plant and new products. Start-up costs associated with new plants and products generally should be expensed and not capitalized as part of inventory. Consistent measurement of these costs is difficult. In periods of fluctuating growth rates, excess capacity should be assessed and the related costs excluded from inventory. These assessments are also difficult, but they are necessary to ensure that inventory does not include costs that have no earning potential.

Because direct labor is a decreasing percentage of total costs in high technology products, allocating overhead to production based on direct labor may not be the most appropriate method to match overhead costs to specific products. The auditor should determine the reasonableness of overhead allocations based on the products' cost structures in order to assess the reasonableness of the carrying costs.

Certain products (e.g., semiconductors) are manufactured by methods for which a process cost accounting system is appropriate. In those instances, the auditor should ensure that valuation procedures for work-in-process inventories appropriately account for lost or spoiled units. Similarly, the auditor should ensure that the "yield" assumptions underlying the standard costs established for completed products are realistic and supported by actual experience. Essentially, this involves assessing whether the average number of usable products completed absorbs the total cost associated with the number of products started at each stage of the manufacturing process.

(i)   Warranty Accruals

Manufacturers of high technology equipment often promise to assume all or part of the cost of repairing or replacing defective products for a certain period of time following the sale. These warranties or guarantees represent future costs. Although the exact cost of repair, date of failure, and customer identity are unknown, an accrual in accordance with SFAS No. 5, *Accounting for Contingencies* (Accounting Standards Section C59), is made based on estimated future warranty claims. This estimate usually is based on warranty claim experience of the company or on available industry standards. The extent of these costs should be evaluated in conjunction with the entity's revenue recognition policies to determine whether the costs are significant enough to preclude revenue recognition.

(j) Research and Development Costs

SFAS No. 2, *Accounting for Research and Development Costs* (Accounting Standards Section R50), generally requires research and development costs to be expensed as incurred. Therefore, the auditor should be skeptical of any deferred research and development costs unless they relate to software development, as discussed below. High technology companies often incur research and development costs for which specific accounting treatment is required. Three of these instances are described below.

(i) Software Development Costs.   Software companies and other entities with products that have a software component are required by SFAS No. 86, *Accounting for the Costs of Computer Software to be Sold, Leased, or Otherwise Marketed* (Accounting Standards Section Co2), to capitalize costs related to producing the software. SFAS No. 86 requires capitalization of costs related to software development from the point of technological feasibility to the product release date. The auditor should keep in mind the very specific criteria for determining technological feasibility under SFAS No. 86 and also consider whether the capitalized costs are realizable through future sales of the product (i.e., the auditor should apply an impairment test).

In 1995, a software industry trade group requested that SFAS No. 86 be amended to require that software development costs be expensed as incurred. A primary reason cited for the request was that SFAS No. 86 has promoted inconsistent accounting practices across the industry. At the time of this writing, the FASB staff is researching this request to determine whether it should be added to the Board's agenda, and the requirements of SFAS No. 86 remain in effect. This request highlights the unique nature of capitalized intangible assets such as software.

(ii) Contracted Research and Development.   High technology companies sometimes perform research and development under contract on behalf of a third party. SFAS No. 68, *Research and Development Arrangements* (Accounting Standards Section R55), addresses the treatment for these types of contract research and development arrangements. The accounting is dependent on the specific provisions of the particular contract. In evaluating the propriety of accounting and disclosures in this area, the auditor should obtain an understanding of the facts and circumstances surrounding such arrangements, including any relationships among the contracting parties.

(iii) Acquired Technology.   High technology companies frequently acquire technology through direct purchases of licenses. When technology is acquired through a direct purchase or as part of a business acquisition, it may include specific in-process research and development with no alternative future uses. In these situations, an allocation of the purchase price should be made to the in-process technology in accordance with Accounting Principles Board (APB) Opinion No. 16, *Accounting for Business Combinations* (Accounting Standards Section B50). The amounts allocated should then be expensed immediately, as required by FASB Interpretation No. 4, *Applicability of*

SFAS No. 2 to Business Combinations Accounted for by the Purchase Method, and Emerging Issues Task Force (EITF) Issue No. 86-14, *Purchased Research and Development Projects in a Business Combination*. Completed technology may be capitalized at its appraised fair value in accordance with APB Opinion No. 16 and amortized over its estimated useful life. Careful consideration should be given to the allocation of a purchase price to technology assets and the reasonableness of their estimated useful lives.

(k) Intercompany Transactions and Taxes

Tax issues for high technology companies generally relate to foreign manufacturing, sales, service operations, and R&D activities. In the past, American companies operating abroad avoided much of the U.S. tax burden on foreign earnings by claiming credits for foreign taxes paid. The 1986 Tax Reform Act decreased the U.S. tax rate and added major administrative burdens to the use of foreign tax credits. As a result, accounting and record-keeping requirements affecting foreign subsidiaries increased significantly.

Intercompany prices may be structured to reduce foreign taxes on business income in high-tax nations. Companies can accomplish this by carefully analyzing their transfer pricing alternatives, management fees, interest, and royalties. The auditor should ascertain that all intercompany profits have been eliminated from inventory for financial reporting purposes. The auditor also should be alert to intercompany profits in self-constructed assets. Consolidating entries for eliminating intercompany profits should be made net of tax effects.

While in the past, technology often was licensed to related foreign entities at an arm's-length price set at the time of agreement, the 1986 Tax Reform Act imposed a "superroyalty" provision. Now, U.S. companies may be required to periodically revise their licensing agreements or intercompany pricing policies with foreign affiliates to reflect current returns from the technology abroad; foreign tax liabilities, however, may not be correspondingly decreased. The auditor should be aware of such periodic revisions to the tax code.

Because of numerous complex foreign tax issues, considerable judgment is needed to apply relevant regulations. The auditor and a tax specialist should work closely together in evaluating the tax provision.

41

Auditing Insurance Companies

41.1 OVERVIEW OF THE INDUSTRY

The primary purpose of insurance is to spread risks among people or entities that typically are exposed to similar risks. When an insurance policy is issued, the insured makes a payment in advance of the possible occurrence of an insured event, such as death (life insurance), illness (accident and health insurance), or financial catastrophe (property and liability, also known as property and casualty insurance). Property and liability and accident and health insurance companies generally do not know whether a claim will result if the policy is kept in force, when it will occur, or how much will be paid under the policy. Life insurance companies, in contrast, can be sure a claim will result, if the policy is kept in force, but do not know when it will occur. The fundamental difference between the insurance industry and other industries is that insurance companies accumulate cash first and pay claims and claims settlement costs in the future. In other industries, generally costs are incurred first and cash is received later, after an entity's products have been sold or services performed.

The U.S. insurance industry provides financial protection against catastrophic events such as death and property loss, as well as a large share of the nation's health, welfare, and other financial benefits, making it one of the most important financial services industries of the U.S. economy. As a result, the industry receives much attention from lawmakers, industry regulators, the Securities and Exchange Commission (SEC), and the public.

(a) Structure of the Industry

There are three main types of insurance companies: life, property and liability, and title. Companies are further divided into direct or primary writers and reinsurers.

Life insurance companies provide financial assistance at the time of death and also during a person's lifetime in the form of annuity, endowment, and accident and health insurance policies. Premiums are often level, even though the policy benefits and services provided by the insurance company (insurance protection, sales effort, premium collection costs, and claims) are not expected to occur evenly over the contract period.

The life insurance industry has changed substantially over the years. Interest-sensitive products such as universal life and investment-type contracts typically promise higher investment returns to policyholders than do traditional products. Premiums on interest-sensitive products are a significant portion of total life premiums and are expected to grow. The profitability of these new products has been challenged by competition, however, including competition from other industries.

Health insurers also have undergone major changes. For example, traditional insurance products are being supplemented or replaced with administrative services only (ASO) contracts and managed care programs such as health maintenance organizations (HMOs) and preferred provider organizations (PPOs). These plans attempt to minimize the effects of rising costs by establishing contracts with health care providers to provide reduced rates and incentives for more efficient care.

Property and liability insurance companies provide protection against damage to or loss of property caused by various perils, like fire and theft, or legal liability resulting from injuries to other people or damage to their property. Property and liability insurance companies also may issue accident and health insurance contracts. Premiums received on property and liability contracts are intended to cover expected claims costs resulting from insured events that occur during a fixed period of short duration. Life insurance companies and property and liability companies are quite similar in their major operations, underwriting procedures, claims processing, and investment activities.

Property and liability insurers, however, undergo what some analysts and other observers have identified as distinct underwriting cycles, which recur every several years. During periods of industry profitability, downward pressure on prices occurs as new companies enter the market and existing companies seek to maintain or expand their market share. This phase of the cycle often is characterized by a pricing and risk acceptance practice referred to as *cash flow underwriting*. Companies may be inclined to accept additional underwriting risk in profitable times in anticipation of investment earnings on premiums collected. Under the cycle theory, this underwriting trend eventually leads to depressed earnings as lower prices result in higher underwriting losses. Companies react by firming prices and being more selective in accepting risks, thus causing a turn in the cycle.

Title insurance companies issue title insurance contracts that indemnify real estate owners, buyers, and mortgage lenders against loss or damage arising from defects in, liens on, or challenges to their title to real estate. Title insurance contracts usually cover an extended period, such as the period of ownership. Similarly, mortgage guaranty insurance companies issue mortgage guaranty insurance contracts that guarantee lenders, such as banks and savings and loan associations, against nonpayment by mortgagors.

Most insurance companies are organized as either stock or mutual companies. A stock company is owned by stockholders and earns income for their benefit by performing services for policyholders. A mutual company is owned by the policyholders and operates for their benefit; most mutual policies issued are participating policies under which profits are distributed to the policyholders as policy dividends. Stock companies also may issue participating policies, which entitle policyholders to share in the company's earnings through dividend distributions. Other types of organizations are reciprocal exchanges, which consist of a group of "subscribers" that exchange insurance contracts through an attorney-in-fact, and fraternal benefit societies, which are similar to mutual insurance companies and provide life or health insurance to their members.

Insurance companies in the United States are licensed as either life or general insurance companies (property and liability and title companies). Usually companies that do business in both markets are holding companies with separate life and property and liability subsidiaries, or companies licensed in one field with a subsidiary that is licensed in the other.

The McCarran Ferguson Act provides certain antitrust immunities to the insurance industry that allow companies, through organizations such as the Insurance Services Office, to obtain industry data in order to prevent inadequate pricing of products. This practice, which often is associated with price fixing in other industries, is considered necessary for the insurance industry since insurers must bill and collect premiums before actual costs are known.

Many industry observers speculate that some form of federal oversight of the insurance industry will occur in the future. Areas believed most probable for a federal role are regulation of reinsurance (particularly with foreign reinsurers who assume risks in U.S. markets), prevention and prosecution of illegal acts and fraud, and solvency regulation.

(b) Reinsurance

Reinsurance is a means by which the original or primary insurer, also known as the ceding company or the reinsured, transfers all or a portion of its risk under an insurance policy or a group of policies to another insurance company, known as the assuming company or the reinsurer. The assuming company may in turn transfer all or part of the risk to one or more other companies. The policyholder continues to hold the original insurance policy and usually does not know that the policy has been reinsured. Company policy regarding reinsurance is based on the desire to limit losses, stabilize underwriting results, and protect surplus. Property and liability companies also use reinsurance to avoid concentration in a single geographical area and thus reduce the possibility of a large number of claims resulting from one event. In transferring all or part of a risk, an insurance company still maintains its liability to the insured. Thus, to the extent that an assuming company might be unable to meet its obligations, a contingent liability exists on the part of the ceding company.

(c) Securitization

The securitization of insurance risk is the transfer of such risk to an unrelated third party in the form of an investment or financial instrument. Stated differently, insurance risk securitization is the bundling together of insured exposures into an investment product and effectively selling shares in the risk pool created. While reinsurance markets traditionally have provided an efficient source of capital to absorb certain liquidity and catastrophe exposures on behalf of primary insurers, securitization potentially provides a deeper source of capital for insurers, as well as another type of investment vehicle for the capital markets. Securitized instruments can add capacity to fund more difficult catastrophic exposures—the type that the insurance and reinsurance marketplaces are not willing to accept—with the funds coming from outside the insurance industry.

There are currently two main categories of risk funding products. At one end of the spectrum are catastrophe products that essentially provide statutory capital when a loss occurs and are clearly financing in nature. An example of this is surplus notes, whereby an insurer sets up a "fund" through the sale of notes that are backed by receivables or government securities. The insurer has the ability to access these funds for various purposes, including catastrophic loss coverage. Investors are paid a premium over the treasury bill rate for the use of the funds; they assume the risk of loan default but no real insurance risk. From the insurer's perspective, this type of product provides liquidity and protection and enhancement of regulatory surplus at interest rates, and with higher limits, that are theoretically more competitive than traditional catastrophe reinsurance.

At the other end of the spectrum are catastrophe and high excess layer products that provide both statutory capital and underwriting benefit. These securitized products are structured using special purpose entities (SPEs) and reinsurance contracts that meet the risk transfer guidelines in Statement of Financial Accounting Standards (SFAS) No. 113, *Accounting and Reporting for Reinsurance of Short-Duration and Long-Duration Contracts* (Accounting Standards Section In6).

In contrast to the traditional reinsurance company, an SPE may issue securities, the proceeds of which are used to fund the reinsurance. One example of such a securitized insurance risk product is "Act of God" bonds issued to fund catastrophic loss coverage, in which payment of interest (and sometimes repayment of principal) is linked directly to losses arising from catastrophes and natural disasters. Securitized transactions are complex and require careful risk transfer analysis under SFAS No. 113. Further, SFAS No. 125, *Accounting for Transfers and Servicing of Financial Assets and Extinguishments of Liabilities* (Accounting Standards Section F35), contains guidance on SPE accounting.

(d)   Industry Code of Conduct

In response to a number of highly publicized instances of questionable insurance marketing practices, the American Council of Life Insurers (ACLI) has developed a Code of Life Insurance Ethical Market Conduct (the Code) consisting of six principles to which life insurance companies should adhere. To assess compliance with the Code, a Questionnaire for Assessment of Compliance with the Principles of Ethical Market Conduct (the Questionnaire) has been developed. The Questionnaire is designed to be completed by insurers annually, with a periodic (at least once every three years) certification by independent assessors.

This initiative is being led by an organization created by the ACLI known as the Insurance Marketplace Standards Association (IMSA). Reports will be filed with IMSA, which will grant membership to companies meeting certain requirements, including the completion of periodic independent assessments of the Questionnaire. IMSA has issued applications for independent assessors, and will accept reports only from IMSA-approved assessors. The AICPA's Insurance Companies Committee has organized a task force to work with IMSA to provide guidance to accountants on the certification service.

41.2   REGULATORY ENVIRONMENT

(a)   State Regulation and the NAIC

Insurance company operations are significantly affected by state regulatory requirements; consequently, the auditor must know the specific applicable state statutes. Statutes in all states provide for a state insurance department to supervise insurance companies and enforce compliance with the law. In addition, the National Association of Insurance Commissioners (NAIC) promulgates uniform rules and regulations for the industry. The NAIC has no legal status, however, and any rules it adopts must be passed as law in the individual states before they become binding.

While statutes vary by state, their main objective is the development and enforcement of measures designed to promote solvency, appropriate premium rates, fair dealing with policyholders, and uniform financial reporting. In the majority of states, insurance companies cannot be organized or sell policies without insurance department authorization. Each state has its own statutory requirements for minimum capitalization, solvency margins, and dividend restrictions. Those requirements also may vary depending on the type of company (life or property and liability, stock company or mutual company) and the type of business conducted (marine or casualty, life or accident and health insurance).

Investment restrictions also vary from state to state. Regulations specify how funds may be invested and valued. Values for stocks and bonds are published by the NAIC each January in a manual entitled *Valuations of Securities*.

To promote uniform financial reporting, the statutes provide for annual (and, in some states, quarterly) statements in prescribed form to be filed with the insurance departments, and for insurance companies to be examined by the insurance departments at stated intervals. The annual statement (generally referred to as the "convention blank") includes a balance sheet, summary of operations, surplus statement, statement of cash flows, many supporting exhibits and schedules, and supplemental questionnaires and reports; the data in those statements is extracted from the company's accounting and statistical records. It is essential for auditors to have a working knowledge of the statutory annual statement, since it is usually convenient to use its various schedules and exhibits as a basis for substantive tests of details and analytical procedures. Where applicable, the auditor should make reference to the NAIC's *Accounting Practices and Procedures Manuals* (life/health and property/casualty).

(b) Annual Audit Requirements

Before 1986, only a few states required audited financial statements to be filed by insurers. Today, virtually all states have solvency legislation in place that includes a requirement for companies to file audited financial statements annually. NAIC audit rules also require, among other things, that companies file reports received from independent auditors pointing out reportable conditions in their internal control, if any, noted during the audit, as well as material errors in the financial statements and failure by companies to meet minimum capital and surplus requirements. In addition, the NAIC rules mandate rotation of independent CPAs or the partner in charge of the engagement every seven years.

In addition, the NAIC has published a "Guide to Compliance with State Audit Requirements." This guide provides summaries and actual text of the individual state and NAIC audit rules, and is an excellent source for keeping track of the audit rules that affect insurance companies and their auditors.[1]

The NAIC instructions to the annual statement form for property/casualty insurance companies requires them to instruct their independent auditors to extend the auditing procedures applied to the basic financial statements to include tests of certain loss and loss adjustment expense data contained in Schedule P–Part 1. AICPA Statement of Position (SOP) 92-8, *Auditing Property/Casualty Insurance Entities' Statutory Financial Statements—Applying Certain Requirements of the NAIC Annual Statement Instructions*, provides guidance for applying such auditing procedures and for issuing reports that may be required. SOP 95-4, *Letters for State Insurance Regulators to Comply With the NAIC Model Audit Rule*, and a related 1997 AICPA Notice to Practitioners provide guidance on such letters.

---

[1] Further information can be obtained via the NAIC's website on the Internet at http://www.naic.org.

SOP 95-5, *Auditor's Reporting on Statutory Financial Statements of Insurance Enterprises*, contains guidance regarding how auditors should apply Statement on Auditing Standards (SAS) Nos. 58 and 62 (AU Sections 508 and 623, respectively) when issuing opinions on statutory financial statements of insurance companies.

An interpretation of SAS No. 62 entitled "Evaluation of Appropriateness of Informative Disclosures in Statutory-Basis Financial Statements of Insurance Enterprises" (AU Section 9623) requires that the independent auditor determine whether disclosures similar to those required in financial statements prepared in conformity with generally accepted accounting principles (GAAP) are appropriately included in the audited statutory-basis financial statements of insurance enterprises, including mutual life insurers, for the same or similar types of items, in order to prevent those financial statements from being misleading.

(c)   Statements of Actuarial Opinion

The extensive underwriting losses experienced by property and liability insurers in the mid-1980s raised many questions about the industry's loss reserve practices. States began to require companies to have their loss and loss adjustment expense liabilities examined by qualified loss reserve specialists. In 1990, the NAIC adopted an annual statement instruction requiring certification of loss reserves. Life insurers previously had been required to file statements of actuarial opinion with respect to their reserves and other actuarially determined liabilities.

The NAIC annual statement instructions and most state rules currently allow statements of actuarial opinion to be made by qualified loss reserve specialists or actuaries who are employed by or otherwise not independent of the companies whose reserves are being evaluated. Certain states are considering requiring independent certification of reserves, in some cases in addition to the annual certifications currently required.

Several states have adopted the NAIC's "valuation actuary" amendments to the Standard Valuation Law for life and health insurers. The amendments require opining actuaries to address in their reports whether a company's reserves, when considered together with assets held to support those reserves, are adequate to meet the company's policy and contract obligations, unless a company meets certain requirements for exemption. An accompanying NAIC model regulation, *Actuarial Opinion and Memorandum Regulation*, contains additional requirements, including that the actuary be appointed by the authority of the board of directors.

A Notice to Practitioners, *Auditors' Responsibilities Concerning Statement of Actuarial Opinion Required by Insurance Regulators*, provides guidance by the AICPA Insurance Companies Committee in the form of questions and answers concerning an auditor's responsibilities when the actuary rendering an actuarial opinion on the client's reserves (1) assumes responsibility for examination of the underlying data, or (2) states in the actuarial opinion that he or she relied on the auditor for the accuracy of the underlying data. The notice also contains guidance for auditors when providing assistance to independent actuaries in their examination of data underlying reserves and discusses circumstances where the actuary is an employee of the audit firm. It states that an auditor should not consent to actuaries expressing, in their statement of opinion, reliance on the auditor's work regarding the accuracy of data underlying a company's reserves.

(d) Risk-Based Capital Requirements

The NAIC has adopted risk-based capital (RBC) requirements for both life and property and casualty insurance companies. The concept of risk-based capital was developed to provide a mechanism that can be applied to an individual company to ascertain whether it has a minimum acceptable level of surplus. The RBC requirements are used as early warning tools by the NAIC and state insurance departments to identify companies that merit further regulatory action. RBC consists of a series of surplus-related formulas that contain a variety of weighting factors that are applied to financial balances or to levels of activity based on the perceived degree of certain risks, such as asset risk, credit risk, interest rate risk (life insurance companies only), underwriting risk, and other business risks, such as risks related to management, regulatory action, and contingencies.

The RBC formulas provide for four different levels of regulatory attention depending on the ratio of a company's total adjusted capital to its RBC. The "company action level" is triggered if a company's total adjusted capital is less than 2.0 times its RBC but greater than or equal to 1.5 times its RBC. At the company action level, a company must submit a plan to the regulatory authority that discusses proposed corrective actions to improve its capital position. The "regulatory action level" is triggered if a company's total adjusted capital is less than 1.5 times but greater than or equal to 1.0 times its RBC. At the regulatory action level, the regulatory authority will perform a special examination of a company and issue an order specifying corrective actions that must be followed. The "authorized control level" is triggered if a company's total adjusted capital is less than 1.0 times but greater than or equal to 0.7 times its RBC. At this level, the regulatory authority may take any action it deems necessary, including placing a company under regulatory control. The "mandatory control level" is triggered if a company's total adjusted capital is less than 0.7 times its RBC, and the regulatory authority is required to place such company under its control.

SOP 93-8, *The Auditor's Consideration of Regulatory Risk-Based Capital for Life Insurance Enterprises*, provides guidance on the auditor's responsibility relating to the RBC requirements for life insurance companies. The scope of SOP 93-8 was effectively extended to all insurance enterprises through revisions made to the AICPA's audit and accounting guide, *Audits of Property and Liability Insurance Companies*.

(e) Insurance Regulatory Information System Tests (Early Warning Tests)

Insurance companies' operating results are scrutinized through a series of tests prescribed by the regulatory authorities. These tests consist of a series of separate analytical financial ratios and relationships for both life and property and liability companies and are designed to measure normal levels of financial stability. To the extent that the results of a number of the tests do not fall within acceptable parameters, closer scrutiny may be considered necessary. This information generally is not made public.

(f) Statutory-Basis Accounting Practices

Statutory financial accounting is required by the state insurance departments and prescribed by the NAIC. Supplemented by minimum capital and surplus requirements of individual states and other financial regulations, these measures serve as one of the primary means by which regulators monitor industry solvency. Statutory accounting practices traditionally have been viewed as conservative. In recent years, however, certain financial regulations and statutory accounting rules—for instance, the use of surplus notes[2] and other transactions entered into by companies solely to increase surplus—have been perceived as loopholes and criticized by regulators and Congress as "accounting gimmicks." In addition, statutory accounting clearly does not provide in all cases for the establishment of economic-based allowances for losses in the value of assets, such as those required by GAAP.

In 1997, the NAIC's Codification of Statutory Accounting Principles Working Group released an exposure draft of a complete codification of statutory accounting. The overall objective of the codification is to promote uniformity of statutory accounting practices among the individual states. The statutory accounting guidance that follows in this section does not contemplate changes, if any, that may occur as a result of the adoption of the proposed codification.

In addition to following prescribed accounting policies and procedures, insurance companies can seek permission from state insurance departments for special accounting treatment for certain transactions for statutory reporting purposes. Such treatment is known as permitted accounting practices. Permitted accounting practices include practices not prescribed by state laws, regulations, and general administrative rules applicable to all insurance companies domiciled in a particular state; the NAIC annual statement instructions; the NAIC *Accounting Practices and Procedures Manual*; the *Securities Valuation Manual*; NAIC official proceedings; and the NAIC *Examiners' Handbook*. Permitted accounting practices are generally subject to a "negotiation process" between the regulator and insurer. On occasion, there may be formal communications regarding this negotiation process; sometimes these permitted practices are discussed in the regulatory examination report. Often, however, because of either the passage of time or the limited amount of statutory guidance regarding a topic, it may be difficult for insurers to assess whether an accounting practice is prescribed or permitted. To limit the potential for confusion in this area, insurers should design and implement a process to assist in this assessment.

SOP 94-1, *Inquiries of State Insurance Regulators*, requires the auditor to obtain sufficient competent evidential matter to corroborate management's assertion that permitted statutory accounting practices that are material to an insurance company's financial statements are permitted by the insurance department of the state of domicile. In addition, SOP 94-5, *Disclosures of Certain Matters in the Financial Statements of Insurance Enterprises*, requires insurance companies to disclose information about permitted statutory accounting practices in their financial statements.

One of the main purposes of statutory-basis financial statements is to provide information about the solvency of an insurance company and its ability to pay policyholders' claims. Assets that cannot be used to pay policy claims (like furniture and fixtures, automobiles, prepaid expenses, and agents' balances receivable over 90 days) are irrelevant to that purpose; therefore, they are deducted directly from surplus (i.e., they are "nonadmitted" assets).

---

[2] Surplus notes represent loans to insurers that, on meeting certain criteria, may qualify under statutory accounting practices to be accounted for as surplus (equity) rather than as a liability. Surplus notes typically bear interest and are repayable (without special consent) only upon certain conditions and from defined excess surplus funds available.

Statutory accounting starts with "ledger assets," which are account balances arising from cash and premium transactions. The ledger assets are adjusted for accruals and reserves (including unearned premiums and claims or benefit reserves), which are referred to as nonledger assets and liabilities since they are not under general ledger control. These nonledger accounts are controlled by a separate accounting system and are posted to the trial balance for financial reporting purposes. Nonadmitted assets are then deducted to arrive at net admitted assets on a statutory basis. Conservative assumptions generally dominate statutory accounting principles.

41.3 GENERALLY ACCEPTED ACCOUNTING PRINCIPLES

The purpose of GAAP for insurance companies is the same as for any other type of entity, but differs from the purpose of statutory accounting. GAAP-basis financial statements include assets that are not admitted for statutory accounting purposes, and they are based on more realistic assumptions regarding accounting estimates. This section of the chapter describes the major accounts that are unique to insurance companies and the differences between statutory and GAAP-basis accounting. First, however, it discusses the principal sources of GAAP that are unique to insurance companies.

(a) Authoritative Accounting Pronouncements

Specific pronouncements related to the insurance industry have been issued by the Financial Accounting Standards Board (FASB) in:

- SFAS No. 60, *Accounting and Reporting by Insurance Enterprises* (Accounting Standards Section In6)
- SFAS No. 61, *Accounting for Title Plant* (Accounting Standards Section Ti7)
- SFAS No. 97, *Accounting and Reporting by Insurance Enterprises for Certain Long-Duration Contracts and for Realized Gains and Losses from the Sale of Investments* (Accounting Standards Section In6)
- SFAS No. 113, *Accounting and Reporting for Reinsurance of Short-Duration and Long-Duration Contracts* (Accounting Standards Section In6)
- SFAS No. 120, *Accounting and Reporting by Mutual Life Insurance Enterprises and by Insurance Enterprises for Certain Long-Duration Participating Contracts* (Accounting Standards Section In6)

AICPA Accounting Standards Division Practice Bulletin 8, *Application of FASB Statement No. 97,* Accounting and Reporting by Insurance Enterprises for Certain Long-Duration Contracts and for Realized Gains and Losses from the Sale of Investments, *to Insurance Enterprises*, contains implementation guidance in the form of 15 questions and answers about SFAS No. 97. AICPA Accounting Standards Division Practice Bulletin 15, *Accounting by the Issuer of Surplus Notes*, provides guidance on accounting, financial statement presentation, and disclosure by issuers of surplus notes.

SOP 92-5, *Accounting for Foreign Property and Liability Reinsurance*, provides guidance on accounting for reinsurance assumed from foreign companies. In 1997, the Deposit Accounting Task Force of the Insurance Companies Committee of the AICPA exposed for comment a proposed SOP, *Deposit Accounting: Accounting for Insurance and Reinsurance Contracts That Do Not Transfer Insurance Risk*. The proposed SOP would provide guidance on how to account for insurance and reinsurance contracts that do not transfer insurance risk and would be effective for financial statements for fiscal years beginning after December 15, 1998.

Mutual life insurance companies are subject to the provisions of FASB Interpretation No. 40, *Application of Generally Accepted Accounting Principles to Mutual Life Insurance and Other Enterprises* (Accounting Standards Section In6), as amended by SFAS No. 120. These pronouncements remove the exemption for mutual life insurance companies from SFAS Nos. 60, 97, and 113, thus precluding statutory accounting practices from being considered GAAP for such insurers. SOP 95-1, *Accounting for Certain Insurance Activities of Mutual Life Insurance Enterprises*, also addresses accounting and reporting by mutual life insurance enterprises.

The FASB has published a special report, *A Primer on Accounting Models for Long-Duration Life Insurance Contacts under U.S. GAAP*. The special report illustrates and explains the operation of the accounting models for long-duration contracts underlying SFAS Nos. 60 and 97 and SOP 95-1.

The AICPA insurance industry audit and accounting guides, *Audits of Stock Life Insurance Companies* and *Audits of Property and Liability Insurance Companies*, contain specialized accounting principles and practices. At the time of this writing, the AICPA is developing a comprehensive revision of the industry audit guide, *Audits of Stock Life Insurance Companies*, which, among other things, will include guidance for both stock and mutual life insurance enterprises and incorporate the guidance of SFAS No. 120 and SOP 95-1.

The AICPA also has issued an exposure draft of an SOP, *Accounting by Insurance and Other Enterprises for Guaranty-Fund and Certain Other Insurance-Related Assessments*. The proposed SOP would provide guidance to insurance and other enterprises on accounting for guaranty-fund and certain other insurance-related assessments and would be effective for financial statements for fiscal years beginning after December 15, 1997.

The FASB Emerging Issues Task Force (EITF) has discussed three issues specifically applicable to the insurance industry: EITF Issue 92-9, *Accounting for the Present Value of Future Profits Resulting from the Acquisition of a Life Insurance Company*, EITF Issue 93-6, *Accounting for Multiple-Year Retrospectively Rated Contracts by Ceding and Assuming Enterprises*, and EITF Issue 93-14, *Accounting for Multiple-Year Retrospectively Rated Insurance Contracts by Insurance Enterprises and Other Enterprises*.

The form and content of financial statements of insurance companies subject to SEC regulation are governed by Article 7 of Regulation S-X.

(b) Premium Revenue

Premiums are consideration received from an insured in exchange for the insurance company's contractual obligation to assume risk, and are a major source of an insurance company's income. Premiums are considered to be of short or long duration, depending on the terms of the insurance contract. SFAS No. 60 (Accounting Standards Section In6.107) defines these terms as follows:

Short-Duration Contract. The contract provides insurance protection for a fixed period of short duration and enables the insurer to cancel the contract or to adjust the provisions of the contract at the end of any contract period, such as adjusting the amount of premiums charged or coverage provided.

Long-Duration Contract. The contract generally is not subject to unilateral changes in its provisions, such as a noncancelable or guaranteed renewable contract, and requires the performance of various functions and services (including insurance protection) for an extended period.

As stated in Accounting Standards Section In6.108, examples of short-duration contracts include most property and liability insurance contracts, most accident and health insurance contracts, and certain term life insurance contracts, like credit life insurance. Examples of long-duration contracts are whole-life contracts, guaranteed renewable term life contracts, endowment contracts, annuity contracts, universal life type contracts, and title insurance contracts.

Premiums from short-duration contracts should be recognized as revenue over the period of the contract in proportion to the amount of insurance protection provided. Premiums from long-duration contracts should be recognized as revenue when they are due, unless the product has been classified as an investment contract, limited-payment contract, or universal life contract as defined in SFAS No. 97, which sets forth the accounting treatment for products meeting that definition. Investment contracts that do not contain significant mortality or morbidity risk are not accounted for as insurance contracts but as interest-bearing financial instruments. Gross premiums in excess of net premiums on limited-payment contracts must be deferred and recognized over the benefit period. SFAS No. 97 requires use of the retrospective deposit method for universal life type products. Under that method, premiums are not reported as income; instead, they are credited to policyholder accounts, which are charged periodically for mortality and administrative and other expenses.

(c) Unearned Premiums

Unearned premiums represent deferred income from policies written. Normally, unearned premiums are computed from a file of policies currently in effect, known as a premium in force file, based on either a monthly or daily proration. A monthly proration assumes that all policies with an effective date in a certain month are written evenly throughout the month. When the daily pro rata method is used, the unearned premium is calculated by multiplying premiums in force by the unexpired number of days divided by the total number of days for which the policy is effective. Unearned premiums are calculated for both statutory and GAAP accounting purposes. The calculation applies mainly to property and liability insurance companies, although group accident and health policies issued by life insurance companies also typically have unearned premiums.

(d) Policy Acquisition Costs

Policy acquisition costs on new and renewal contracts (for example, commissions, premium taxes, underwriting and issue expenses, and inspection reports) are charged to operations as incurred for statutory reporting purposes. For products accounted for under SFAS No. 60, the entire premium is not earned when the policy acquisition costs are expended. Therefore, acquisition expenses that vary with and are related mainly to the production of new business should be deferred and amortized over the period of premium revenue recognition for GAAP reporting purposes. For universal life type products, deferred policy acquisition costs should be amortized at a constant rate based on the present value of the estimated gross profit for GAAP reporting purposes.

(e)   Valuation of Investments

For statutory reporting purposes, investments are carried at values specified by the NAIC. Generally, common stocks are carried at market value, preferred stocks at cost for life insurance companies and at market for property and liability companies, and bonds at amortized cost. For GAAP purposes, SFAS No. 115, *Accounting for Certain Investments in Debt and Equity Securities* (Accounting Standards Section I80), has a significant effect on insurance company GAAP-basis financial statements. It addresses accounting for and reporting on investments in debt securities and in equity securities that have a readily determinable fair value. Under SFAS No. 115, investment securities that are classified as "held-to-maturity" are carried at amortized cost only if the reporting entity has the positive ability and intent to hold the securities to maturity. "Trading" securities are bought principally for the purpose of selling them in the near term and are carried at fair value. Unrealized gains and losses on trading securities are included in earnings. "Available-for-sale" securities are those that are classified as neither trading nor held to maturity, and are reported at fair value. Unrealized gains and losses on available-for-sale securities are excluded from earnings and shown, net of income taxes, as a separate component of shareholders' equity. The majority of securities currently held by insurance companies are categorized as available-for-sale.

Investments in policy loans and mortgage loans are reported at the outstanding principal balance, and investments in real estate are stated at cost less accumulated depreciation. If a decline in the value of an investment carried at cost or amortized cost is considered to be other than temporary, the investment should be reduced to its net realizable value.

SFAS No. 119, *Disclosure about Derivative Financial Instruments and Fair Value of Financial Instruments* (Accounting Standards Section F25), also is significant for insurance company financial statements. It requires disclosure of information about the amounts, nature, and terms of derivative financial instruments.

(f)   Nonadmitted Assets

For statutory reporting purposes, nonadmitted assets include all assets recognized under GAAP that are not permitted to be reported as admitted assets in the statutory-basis annual statement and are charged directly to surplus. Nonadmitted assets, including receivables outstanding for more than 90 days, prepaid expenses, goodwill, and certain property, plant, and equipment, are restored to the balance sheet for GAAP purposes. The auditor should review receivables outstanding for more than 90 days for collectibility and evaluate the need for an allowance for uncollectible accounts. The auditor also should review prepaid expenses, goodwill, and property, plant, and equipment for propriety of capitalization.

(g)   Realized and Unrealized Investment Gains and Losses

Realized investment gains or losses are recognized in determining net income for GAAP reporting and for statutory reporting by property and liability companies. Realized gains and losses are reported in the income statement as a component of other income on a pretax basis. Life insurance companies record realized gains or losses directly in surplus for statutory purposes. Unrealized investment gains and losses are credited or charged directly to stockholders' equity in all instances, except for those associated with trading securities. Unrealized gains and losses associated with trading securities are recognized in income both for statutory reporting purposes and under GAAP.

(h)   Asset Valuation Reserve and Interest Maintenance Reserve

The NAIC requires life insurance companies to maintain an Asset Valuation Reserve (AVR). The AVR is computed in accordance with a prescribed formula and represents a provision for possible fluctuations in the value of bonds, equity securities, mortgage loans, real estate, and other investments. The AVR is recorded as a liability and charged directly to surplus. Similarly, changes in AVR are included in surplus.

The NAIC also requires life insurance companies to establish an Interest Maintenance Reserve (IMR), which represents realized capital gains and losses on fixed income investments, principally bonds and mortgage loans, attributable to interest rate changes. Such gains and losses are deferred and amortized to income over the expected lives of the investments sold. The IMR is recorded as a liability and charged directly to surplus. Similarly, changes in IMR are included in surplus.

Such reserves are not required in the statutory-basis financial statements of property and liability insurance companies. They also are not appropriate for GAAP-basis financial statements of insurance companies.

(i)   Investments in Subsidiaries

GAAP-basis financial statements for insurance companies should follow the requirements of SFAS No. 94, *Consolidation of All Majority-Owned Subsidiaries* (Accounting Standards Section C51), regarding the inclusion of subsidiaries for consolidation purposes. Investments in subsidiaries may not be consolidated under statutory-basis reporting requirements but must be accounted for, as prescribed by the NAIC, using methods similar to those for investments in common or preferred stocks. Generally, the carrying value of common stock of subsidiaries is established by the company based on the book value or equity of the subsidiary at the balance sheet date.

(j)   Income Taxes

The Tax Reform Act of 1984 established a single-base tax structure for life insurance companies. This structure embodies the tax rules applicable to corporations in general while retaining provisions that reflect the unique nature of the life insurance industry and its products.

The Tax Reform Act of 1986 (TRA 86) had a significant impact on property and casualty companies. TRA 86 required property and casualty and health insurers to recompute loss reserves and loss adjustment expense reserves for tax purposes as of January 1, 1987. In addition, the Revenue Reconciliation Act of 1990 required property and casualty insurers to accrue estimated salvage and subrogation recoverables. Since 1990, life insurance companies have been required to capitalize and amortize policy acquisition expenses for purposes of determining taxable income. The amount to be capitalized is determined using a "proxy method," which specifies percentages of net premiums to be considered as policy acquisition expenses. The capitalized amounts are amortized over a 120-month period (60-month period for small companies).

GAAP-basis financial statements for insurance companies should follow the requirements of SFAS No. 109, *Accounting for Income Taxes.* Under GAAP, companies must record deferred income taxes for specified differences between GAAP income and taxable income. For statutory reporting purposes, insurance companies do not provide for deferred income taxes.

(k) Policy Reserve (Future Policy Benefits) Valuation

Policy reserves represent the future guaranteed benefits of life insurance policies payable under the contract provisions of the policies. Policy reserves are actuarially computed to show the present value of future benefits reduced by the present value of future net premiums. Policy reserves are the largest liability on a life insurance company's balance sheet.

Statutory reserves for life insurance companies are calculated assuming conservative estimates for interest earned on premium revenue that is collected and invested and for mortality (probability of death or proportion of persons expected to die at particular ages per thousand persons). Published actuarial tables, sometimes modified to reflect a company's experience, are used by life insurance companies; approval of a state insurance department is required if the tables are modified. Morbidity tables that indicate the probability of incidence, by age, of becoming mentally or physically diseased or of becoming physically impaired are used for accident and health insurance. No assumption for withdrawals in the form of lapsed (or, for cash value life insurance policies, surrendered) policies is made in statutory reserve calculations, since statutory reserves usually are expected to equal or exceed cash surrender values.

Statutory reserves are subject to limitations and methods prescribed or permitted by regulatory authorities that are at variance with GAAP. Under GAAP, the interest assumption should reflect the current investment return, the mortality or morbidity assumptions should reflect recent experience, and a withdrawal assumption should be included. Other assumptions relating to guaranteed contract benefits and conversion privileges also should be considered. In addition, the assumptions should include a provision for adverse deviation in light of the long-term nature of life insurance and the inherent inability to predict the future with certainty. GAAP require that the original assumptions made at the time the product was sold continue to be used (i.e., to be "locked in") as long as reserves are sufficient to provide for future benefits and expenses. If a deficiency occurs, the assumptions are revised for loss recognition purposes, as discussed later. Revised assumptions may be applied to new sales as necessary.

(l)   Loss (or Claim) and Loss (or Claim) Adjustment Expense Reserves

Under both statutory and GAAP accounting practices, loss and claim reserves of property and casualty companies are recognized when incurred. Estimated liabilities are established for losses that have been reported, and additional estimates are made for losses that have been incurred but have not yet been reported (IBNR). SFAS No. 60 (Accounting Standards Section In6) neither prohibits nor requires discounting of estimated liabilities.

In establishing the estimated IBNR liability, a company accumulates its past reported losses by line of business and attempts to project the ultimate cost of settling all losses for a given year. Other factors that should be considered include changes in inflation rates, reinsurance programs, and lines or volume of business written.

Statutory and GAAP accounting methods also provide that costs associated with settling losses (loss adjustment expenses) should be accrued in the period when the related losses were incurred. These costs include amounts paid for outside services like claims adjusters and attorneys, and direct and indirect internal costs associated with settling claims. Under GAAP, estimates of recoveries on unsettled claims for salvage (an amount received by an insurance company from the sale of property on which a total loss has been paid to the insured) and subrogation (the statutory or legal right of an insurance company to recover amounts from a third party that is wholly or partially responsible for a loss the insurance company paid) should be deducted from the liability for unpaid claims. Under statutory accounting practices, netting of salvage and subrogation in loss reserves is permitted by most, but not all, states. Consequently, permission must be sought from the state insurance department if such a practice is followed in a state where it is not explicitly permitted. SOP 94-5, *Disclosures of Certain Matters in the Financial Statements of Insurance Enterprises*, prescribes disclosures relating to the liability for unpaid claims and claim adjustment expenses. In addition, insurance companies are required to disclose the reasons for the change in the provision for incurred claims and claim adjustment expenses attributable to insured events of prior fiscal years.

(m)   Earned But Unbilled Premiums

Some property and liability companies write a significant volume of business, such as workers' compensation, for which the initial payment is in the form of a deposit premium. After part or all of the policy period has passed, the insured's reported payroll is audited and a billing made to adjust the premium. When a company writes this type of business, the amount of additional premium receivable at the financial statement date should be estimated and recorded. Statutory accounting for earned but unbilled premiums varies by state.

41.4   RISK FACTORS AND AUDIT REACTION

To formulate the audit strategy for an insurance company, the auditor must understand the environment in which the company operates, including the products it offers and how long it has been involved in specific product lines; its underwriting policies and procedures; and its loss experience by product. In addition, the auditor should be aware of the regulatory constraints of the individual states where the company does business.

If a company has handled certain product lines for a considerable time, it usually has effective controls that the auditor can test. Tests of controls are often efficient because of the massive amounts of data typically processed by insurance companies. In addition, in many companies management reviews profit and loss analyses by line of business or product as a basis for reacting to decreases in premium revenue or increases in claims or benefit payments, which may call for changing product pricing, underwriting standards, or reinsurance. If such reviews are made, the auditor may consider it efficient to test them.

In developing the overall audit strategy, the auditor should fully utilize the statutory information the insurance company generates to comply with state regulations. Information like annual statements, RBC calculations, Early Warning Test results, and state examination reports are invaluable tools for assessing a company's financial position and operating results. Specifically, the auditor should understand the company's statutory minimum capital and surplus requirements, which depend on the types of business written and the state of domicile. In addition, many insurance companies have sophisticated management decision-making systems for assessing profitability and monitoring progress in meeting budgets and business plans. The auditor should obtain an understanding of management's objectives and methods of controlling the business as a basis for identifying the inherent risks associated with the company and its products and assessing control risk.

One of the most significant assets of an insurance company is its portfolio of bonds. If interest rates are high, there is a risk that the market value of bonds classified as held to maturity may be significantly lower than their amortized cost. If a company is faced with the prospect of a negative cash flow, this may affect its ability to hold the bonds to maturity. Accordingly, the auditor should assess the company's ability and intent to hold the bonds to maturity and consider the possibility that the carrying value of the bonds may have to be adjusted to market. In addition, the auditor, in conjunction with the actuaries, should assess the company's efforts to match asset and liability maturities. In some instances, duration mismatches may signal cash flow, liquidity, or valuation exposures.

Most companies rely heavily on reinsurance. Accordingly, the ceding company must assess and monitor the financial stability of its reinsurers. To the extent that procedures for accomplishing this are not in place, the auditor should consider the possibility of contingent liabilities from reinsurer failures. In addition, special consideration should be given to ensuring that reinsurance contracts meet the transfer of risk criteria in SFAS No. 113 and Chapters 22 and 24 of the NAIC *Accounting Practices and Procedures Manual.*

Assessing the adequacy of loss reserves is critical for an auditor of a property and liability company. The company establishes its loss reserves based on reported claim data and historical information plus considerations such as changes in its underwriting philosophy and mix of business, reductions or increases in retention for its own account (use of reinsurers), unusually large or nonrecurring losses, and dramatic increases in either inflation rates or current awards by juries or judges in liability cases. It is important for the auditor to assess the company's experience in these areas in light of the planned audit strategy.

41.5 TYPICAL TRANSACTIONS AND INTERNAL CONTROL

The flow of operations of a typical insurance company is as follows:

1. The company determines the appropriate premium, bills the insured, and collects the premium.
2. Some of the premium is used to pay immediate expenses, like commissions and operating costs.
3. Most of the premium is invested to pay claims in the future.
4. Investment income and proceeds from sales of investments are used to pay claims as incurred.
5. Profits, if any, are returned in part to the stockholders or policyholders as dividends.

Those operations may be viewed as falling into three major transaction cycles:

- The premium cycle
- The claim cycle
- The investment cycle

The investment cycle includes buying and selling investments and receiving investment income, net of related investment expenses. Auditing an insurance company's investment cycle is the same as in other businesses that maintain investment portfolios; thus it is not described in this chapter. The other two cycles, which are unique to the insurance industry, are discussed below.

(a) Premium Cycle

The premium cycle includes all phases of premium recognition, from application to expiration of the policy. They can be divided into four functions:

- Policy writing
- Policy underwriting
- Recording premiums
- Collecting premiums

The accounts related to the premium cycle are premium income, reinsurance ceded, commission expense, premiums receivable, ceded premiums payable, future policy benefits (policy reserves), and unearned premiums.

(i) Policy Writing.   The policy writing function consists of writing and issuing insurance policies. A policy is a contract between the insurer and the insured and contains all the terms and conditions agreed to. In a life insurance company, policies generally are prepared at the home office; a number is assigned to each policy. The initial premium usually is paid when the policy is delivered, although many companies encourage payment with the application. Close control must be kept over policies delivered but not paid for. As soon as a policy is issued, an in-force file is created; this is probably the most important file used by a life insurance company. It is a perpetual inventory of all policies issued and in force at a given time and is the source for preparing or calculating premium billings, commission payments, premium taxes, policyholder dividends, and the actuarial reserve liability. Once a policy has been issued, all information on the application, including age, gender, premium, and limits of coverage, is entered on this file. The policy is the source document for the master file.

In a property and liability insurance company, policy writing may be done by agents, at a branch, or at the home office. It may be completed before or after risk underwriting, depending on who writes the policy. If an agent writes a policy, the home or branch office underwrites the policy after it has been written, based on a copy or abstract of the policy called a "daily." An agent is a person who has a relationship with a particular insurance company and has the authority to bind the company on the coverage for the insured. In contrast, a broker has a relationship with various insurers and does not have the authority to bind a company but can only submit an application for coverage. If the branch or home office writes a policy, the company underwrites from the application sent by a salesperson.

The major control objective in the policy writing function is the prompt, complete, and accurate reporting of all policy writing transactions to the company or home office. This objective is achieved mainly by controlling blank policies issued to agents or employees, policies issued to agents and insureds after they have been written and recorded, and dailies processed at the home office. If, based on the understanding of internal control, the auditor expects to be able to assess control risk at low, the audit strategy generally is to perform tests of controls relating to the policy writing function.

(ii) Policy Underwriting.   Underwriting is the assumption of risk for designated loss or damage in exchange for a premium. It includes evaluating the acceptability of the risk, assessing the company's capacity to assume the entire risk (i.e., considering whether reinsurance is required), and determining the premium if the risk is accepted. In a life insurance company, applications require information about age, gender, occupation, health history, and any additional facts that might affect insurability. The information on the application, the medical and inspection report, and the company's own guidelines are used to rate the applicant as a standard, substandard, or uninsurable risk. Applicants subject to a higher than normal mortality are substandard risks. Some companies refuse to insure substandard risks, and others insure them at higher than normal rates. The premium charged is based on the insured's age and risk group and is determined by the underwriter, using company premium rate books. Normally the quality of the underwriting is not apparent until a substantial period of time has passed. The company's reinsurance limits must be considered in underwriting policies. Policies to be reinsured because they are in excess of company retention limits or are substandard risks must be coded when they are issued and reported to the reinsurance department for processing.

In a property and liability insurance company, evaluating the acceptability of risks involves reviewing the exposure and potential loss, which is based on information on the dailies and endorsements (amendments or changes to existing policies). Both individual company policies and state laws often specify procedures for investigating risks; for example, information about applicants for automobile insurance may be requested from the State Department of Motor Vehicles.

Premiums on policies written by the company are determined and premiums on policies written by agents are reviewed by referring to bureau or company rate manuals or applying underwriting expertise. For policies written by agents, cursory reviews are made in the field office and the dailies are recorded. Although the coverage can be canceled by the company after the underwriting has been completed, it is customary to record the policy before acceptance; if the policy is subsequently rejected, it is canceled and the records are adjusted.

In policy underwriting, the major control objective is the prompt, accurate, and complete recording of all risks that have been accepted in accordance with the company's predetermined standards and the documenting of all policy underwriting transactions. In obtaining an understanding of controls over policy underwriting, the auditor should consider whether premium, commission, and reinsurance rates coded on dailies or underwriting worksheets are accurate. Often the auditor examines policies to determine whether the risks accepted are within the company's established retention limits, reinsurance has been considered, and there is evidence of review by a supervisor in the underwriting department. The auditor also should determine whether the findings are consistent with the assumptions that will be used in auditing loss reserves. Past loss trends may not be a valid basis for predicting future losses if underwriting standards have changed, controls are ineffective, definitions of risk categories are revised, or reinsurance limits are changed.

(iii) Recording Premiums.   When a premium is received by a life insurance company, usually the amount is credited to either premium income, a policyholder account, or premium suspense. Premium suspense is a liability account used to record amounts that are intended as premiums but cannot be credited to income until a particular event occurs, like approval and issuance of the policy or allocation of amounts received to appropriate premium income or policyholder accounts.

When statutory-basis financial statements are prepared, uncollected premiums (premiums currently due but unpaid as of the statement date) and deferred premiums (premiums applicable to the current policy year but not yet due) must be calculated. The gross amount of uncollected and deferred premiums is used to adjust premium income from the cash to the accrual basis for the statutory summary of operations.

In property and liability companies, premium recording includes coding and processing transactions (dailies and endorsements) to produce the premiums written account, and maintaining statistical data to produce the premium in-force and premium earned accounts. Dailies and endorsements may be coded at the time the policy is underwritten or later.

Premiums written are premiums billed less premiums returned for endorsement or cancellation. If there are endorsements, the premiums written account includes a pro rata portion of the related original premium. The original premium amount is the premium for the full term of a policy for the current coverage at the latest premium rate shown in the policy or the endorsement.

The major control objective of the policy recording function is maintaining accurate records of the policies in force. That objective calls for controls to ensure the completeness and accuracy of input and updating of the in-force records. Entries to the policy master file are made mainly from the premium cycle, although in a life insurance company entries also are made from the claim cycle. The auditor should assess controls over all entries with financial statement significance.

The auditor often compares the information contained in the policy, such as policy number, name and address of policyholder, issue date and term of policy, plan code, mode of payment, face amount of insurance, and premium, to the in-force listing. In addition, the auditor usually considers tests of the company's controls designed to ensure that all risks are recorded.

(iv) Collecting Premiums. The premium collecting function includes billing, receiving cash, applying receipts to agents' balances, and paying commissions. In a life insurance company, insureds generally are billed directly, and they pay the company directly. An unpaid premium file is kept by either policy number or insured's name, rather than by agent, and commissions are paid directly to agents. Premiums may be paid monthly, quarterly, semiannually, or annually depending on the policyholder's preference or the company's marketing strategy.

In a property and liability insurance company, three basic methods are used for billing premiums:

- The company bills the agents, who, in turn, bill the insureds. The monthly statements to the agents usually include policy number, name of insured, effective date of policy, gross premium, commission rate, and amount of commission. The agents transmit the premiums, after deducting their commissions, to the company as they are collected.

- The unpaid premium file is kept by the agents, who bill the insureds, collect the premiums, and transmit the payments to the company after deducting their commissions. Agents transmit a monthly statement listing all transactions for which premiums are due. In general, these transactions have already been recorded by the company from dailies previously received or issued.

- Insureds are billed directly by the company and pay the company directly. The company then pays commissions to the agents, usually on a periodic basis.

The major control objectives of premium billing and collecting are to calculate receivables, commissions, and related accounts accurately; to determine that billing file data agrees with the in-force file data; to bill promptly; to investigate and resolve differences between company records and agents' records; and to ensure that all cash receipts are recorded promptly and accurately.

Usually tests of controls are performed on the premium billing and collection system, although substantive tests like confirmation of receivables and review of subsequent cash receipts from agents and insureds normally are also performed. In addition, the auditor often reviews specific transactions selected from throughout the period and tests the summarization and recording procedures, including recalculation of commissions to agents and brokers. Tests of controls relating to cash receipts and to the accuracy and authorization of cash disbursements, premium revenue, and commission general ledger entries arising from the premium cycle are no different than for any other type of business.

(b) Claim Cycle

The claim cycle encompasses disbursing benefits and recording paid and unpaid claims, and includes the following functions:

- Notification of the loss
- Verification of the loss
- Evaluation of the loss
- Settlement and recording of the loss

Claim expense and the related liability should be recorded when a loss is incurred. Because an insurance company cannot always determine the exact amount of claims incurred, the liability often must be estimated. The claim cycle is concerned with reported claims and their settlement, and the accumulation of statistical data to facilitate estimating and evaluating liabilities at the date of the financial statements. The financial statement accounts affected by the claim cycle are claims expense and reinsurance recoveries, future policy benefits, provision for outstanding claims, and reinsurance balances.

(i) Notification of the Loss.   Although loss reporting is not controlled directly by the insurance company, knowledge of its characteristics is necessary to enable the company to carry out other claim functions. A loss (or claim) report by a claimant is the company's first notification of a loss occurrence. The claimant may be the policyholder, a beneficiary named in a life insurance policy, or a third party entitled to benefits under the terms of the policy. A claimant contacts either the insurance company directly or the insured's agent or broker. This results in a written notice of loss, which becomes the original documentation of the claim.

The primary control objective relating to notification of losses is the prompt, accurate, and complete recording of all claims, since those records are the basis for determining the company's liability. The objective may be achieved by promptly creating a loss file and assigning a claim number to each claim reported, matching incoming correspondence with the claim, and following up on claims that have been open for a long time. Control over claim numbers is important to ensure that the company is aware of all reported claims and can identify them as either open or closed.

Audit tests include determining whether there are abnormal delays between reporting dates and dates claims are filed and abstracts prepared, and between dates claim notices are received at branches and dates they are received at the home office; testing the numerical sequence of claim numbers; examining documentation of the matching of claim notices to related dailies, policies, or applications; determining that loss abstracts have been authorized; and determining that all documents are included in the claim file.

(ii) Verification of the Loss.   The insurance company verifies a claim by obtaining evidence that a loss occurred and that it was covered under the terms of the policy, and determining that the policy was properly in force.

Death claims are generally easy to verify because the occurrence of the loss is definite. The company investigates whether the policy is in force and obtains proof of death, such as a physician's statement (death certificate), and any other evidence considered necessary to substantiate that the claim is valid and the loss was within the terms of the policy. The validity of a property or liability claim is determined by comparing the loss report with the record of insurance coverage in force. After the insurance coverage has been verified, an adjuster is assigned to investigate the loss and determine that it actually occurred and is valid.

The basic objective of verifying the claim is to ensure that only valid claims are included in the company's claim liability. Although the specific tests vary from company to company, they usually include examining documentation of verification that the policy was in force, of the existence of reinsurance, and of verification of the claim.

(iii) Evaluation of the Loss. The insurance company's liability under the terms of the policy may be clearly stated in the policy or may require an estimate based on the judgment of someone familiar with the details of the particular claim. Any amounts that may be recoverable from a reinsurance company are calculated, and the reinsurer is notified of the pending loss. Often the liability for a life insurance claim is clearly stated under the terms of the policy and, therefore, can be established easily. The occurrence and extent of property losses are not difficult to evaluate either, and usually the estimate of the company's liability is also easily determinable.

A claims adjuster estimates the amount or cost of the loss and the approximate amount of any potential salvage or subrogation, both of which reduce the loss ultimately paid by an insurance company. The policy limits and the existence of any deductible under the terms of the policy should be noted in the loss file. Both the ultimate cost of the loss and the loss adjustment expenses to be incurred in settling it are estimated. These expenses may include payments for the services of a claims adjuster, legal expenses, and other costs.

For certain liability losses, estimates of the ultimate cost of the loss to the company are highly subjective. Not only is there often a long reporting and settlement lag, but the extent of the loss may be difficult to determine and there may be the possibility of unknown injuries.

The major control objectives are prompt establishment of reasonable initial claim reserves in accordance with company policy, and prompt adjustment of reserves for changes in circumstances or knowledge of new facts. Tests of controls may include determining whether the company's policy for evaluating losses is documented, adjusters are adequately supervised to ensure that losses are estimated in accordance with company policy, there are procedures to ensure that incoming correspondence is matched promptly with the appropriate claim documents and that reserves are revised accordingly, and open claim files are reviewed periodically.

(iv) Settlement and Recording of the Loss. Losses incurred include paid and unpaid (outstanding loss reserve) portions, both of which are recorded. Details on losses incurred are maintained on a gross basis, before reinsurance, with reinsurance records maintained separately. Financial statements show losses on a net basis.

A claim may be settled by payment or by the decision not to pay. Once the claim has been settled, the loss file is reviewed to ensure that:

- The final payment or other settlement resulted in removal of any remaining amount from the outstanding loss reserve account.

- A release has been obtained from the claimant that the claim was settled satisfactorily.

- Reinsurers have been notified of their liability, and the receivable has been recorded properly.

- The policy is canceled if risks covered no longer exist.

- Statistical data has been updated properly.

- The loss file has been marked "closed" or "paid."

In liability insurance, many factors, including the incidence of litigation, the likelihood of a court settlement, the judgment of the court, the effects of inflation, and state laws (especially in workers' compensation cases) affect costs. Familiarity with the delay characteristics of loss types is important, because knowing what factors influence the final settlement of losses is necessary to evaluate the loss reserves required. After a final payment has been made, the policy generally stays in force. It should be annotated regarding the loss for future underwriting considerations.

The major control objectives are similar to those in any payment cycle, including prompt payment of valid claims, proper authorization for disbursements, and accurate recording of payments. These can be achieved by establishing procedures for approving disbursements, following up long-outstanding claims, and recording disbursements.

Audit tests in this cycle often include tests of the approval of documents before processing, tests of the completeness and accuracy of recording payments, tests of postings to ledger and nonledger accounts, tests of reinsurance recoveries, tests of salvage and subrogation recoveries, and comparison and reconciliation of accounting data with statistical data.

41.6 SUBSTANTIVE TESTS

This section describes accounts that are unique to the insurance industry and the procedures used in auditing them.

(a) Policy Reserves

The actuarial reserve liability of a life insurance company is computed based on the record of policies in force. This record is similar to a perpetual inventory. Moreover, the auditing procedures are analogous to those for the inventory of a commercial entity: reviewing appropriate sections or parts of policies, testing the application of the appropriate actuarial factors, and recalculating the extensions. Auditing the statutory actuarial liabilities of a life insurance company requires the ability to recognize the appropriate tables and rates used in connection with the various groupings of the units in the inventory. Therefore, the auditor should consider having a life insurance actuary assist in recalculating the reserves.

As indicated earlier, the auditor ordinarily tests the company's controls to ensure the completeness and accuracy of updating of the master file, or inventory of policies in force. In addition, the auditor performs substantive tests of the master file similar to those used in auditing any inventory. Those tests include recalculating extensions of reserve factors and comparing selected policies with the inventory listing. The auditor generally traces reserve factors used in the computation to the appropriate factor tables and compares the number of policies and face value of insurance with the exhibit of life insurance included in the statutory annual statement and with the policy master file. These tests, for both statutory and GAAP purposes, may be performed using audit software.

As already noted, the main difference in auditing policy reserves calculated in conformity with GAAP compared with statutory reserves relates to determining the reasonableness of the assumptions and the propriety of the actuarial factors used. If a complete inventory of policies in force is used in the GAAP reserve computation, the tests directed at completeness and accuracy are the same as those performed in auditing the statutory reserves. Often, however, companies use a model of their policy inventory to determine the GAAP reserves; in that event, the auditor should be satisfied that the model is appropriate.

In using models, the reserve factors derived for key plans are extended to other plans that logically can be placed in the same category. An appropriate model would include those plans, age groupings, and durations required to make the model sensitive to material changes in the plan and age distribution. At a minimum, the auditor should be satisfied that the model effectively reproduces the statutory results for insurance in force, premiums, expenses, and reserves. In most cases, the auditor considers it necessary to test the model under varying conditions to determine whether it is properly responsive. This testing often is done using audit software.

For many plans, the factors for statutory reserves are published. A company calculating GAAP reserves, however, should develop its own factors using its own historical data and based on assumptions that are reasonably conservative and include a provision for the risk of adverse deviation. The auditor should be satisfied as to the following:

- The reasonableness and appropriateness of the basic assumptions (interest, mortality, expenses, and withdrawals) underlying the calculations of the reserve factors, including the reasonableness of the provision for the risk of adverse deviation
- The appropriateness of the actuarial formulas
- The accuracy of the factors resulting from applying formulas to the assumptions

(b) Reported Losses

Determining whether loss or claim reserves are adequate is by far the most difficult aspect of auditing a property and liability insurance company. In many instances, the auditor needs actuarial assistance to determine the adequacy of the reserves. Some accounting firms employ actuarial consultants and also have developed software packages to calculate the reserve amounts under various methods. Auditing liability claim reserves is particularly difficult, because of the long period that elapses before claims are finally settled. SOP 92-4, *Auditing Insurance Entities' Loss Reserves*, contains comprehensive guidance for auditing loss reserves, including situations where a company employs or does not employ a qualified loss reserve specialist. It provides, among other things, that the absence of a qualified loss reserve specialist (other than one employed by the independent auditor) may be a reportable condition or material weakness.

The auditor should obtain listings of losses reported but unpaid and reinsurance recoverable thereon at the statement date, including estimates of unpaid loss adjustment expenses calculated on an individual-case basis. The auditor should test them for arithmetical accuracy and trace the totals to the financial statements. Claims processing should be reviewed to ensure that it is consistent with prior years and that year-end cutoff dates are appropriate.

If loss estimates are based on average costs, the auditor should review the methods used in determining them, including the logic applied, trends over a period of years, and whether the volume is sufficient to produce credible results. The auditor also should consider how reinsurance recoverables are treated in calculating average costs, particularly if there is a substantial amount of reinsurance as well as salvage and subrogation.

As part of tests performed in the claim cycle, the auditor should review the company's loss experience statistics for a number of years. Normally, a long development period is needed to determine with reasonable accuracy the actual settlement costs of liability claims. The difficulty of accurately estimating the costs of settling outstanding claims is further complicated by inflation and the litigious environment.

(c) Unreported Losses

The reserve for losses incurred but not yet reported (IBNR) provides for claims occurring before year-end but reported to the insurer in later periods. This requires estimating the number of such claims and the corresponding dollar amount required for final settlement. The methods used in these estimates are numerous and varied, as previously discussed, but generally they are based on past experience and should in all cases reflect the application of sound judgment.

Since IBNR claim reserves are based on estimates, the auditor needs to understand the company's estimating approach. Prior-year results in estimating IBNR reserves are a valuable guide to the effectiveness of the approach used. This type of comparison usually is made by means of a "runoff" that lists all payments on claims that were incurred but not reported as of the previous year-end. The total of this runoff and any remaining liability is compared with the IBNR reserve established at that time. In analyzing loss reserves, management must use judgment about past experience and trends. The auditor should be able to evaluate the methods used by the company's management, including whether they are consistent between years. In addition, benchmarking against other companies' experience with similar types and amounts of business may be useful in evaluating overall experience and trends.

It is also important, however, to consider the extent to which industry statistics can be used in making a projection. In particular, adjustments to industry statistics may be necessary to take into account:

- Changes in the mix of business written and related loss data in the current year
- Reserving policy—a change in claims department personnel or a decision by management to change its reserving or claim settling policy may cause an increase in the average loss reserve per case.

- Catastrophes like earthquakes or hurricanes
- Inflation—reserves should take into account increases in the expected costs of loss settlements caused by inflation.
- Long-tailed liabilities—the presence or absence of long-tailed liabilities—such as those related to asbestos, environmental, or product liabilities—could have a significant effect on loss statistics.
- Reinsurance—the presence or absence of reinsurance coverage or a change in the level or type of reinsurance also could have a significant effect on loss statistics.

The auditor should use all available statistical data in determining the reasonableness of the loss reserves. Regardless of the methods used by the company, the auditor should be satisfied that the information used for the loss reserve analysis agrees with actual experience and that the methods are reliable and valid. The auditor should review and test the data used in developing the percentages and ratios entering into the IBNR computation. Basically, the same methods and auditing procedures used in evaluating loss reserves (discussed earlier) are used in auditing loss adjustment expenses.

(d) Deferred Acquisition Costs

A life insurance company normally develops cost studies that segregate acquisition costs from costs attributable to maintaining policies. These cost studies also isolate development and other similar expenses so that it can be determined whether any of those costs should be deferred. These determinations require judgment on the part of both management and the auditor; they should give overriding consideration to future benefit, consistency, amortization period, and probability of recovery. If cost studies are not available, it is necessary to estimate acquisition costs, based on information used in determining the premiums to be charged. The audit of cost studies should be the same as for any other cost system.

Under GAAP, a premium deficiency must be recognized when it is probable and quantifiable. Thus, all or part of the unamortized balance of deferred acquisition costs of a life insurance company may have to be written off if the future revenue stream that the costs are to be amortized against becomes impaired. Through a procedure known as loss recognition or recoverability test, impairments in the revenue stream are identified by comparing actual with expected interest rates, mortality experience, and policy continuations as well as by reviewing the effects of rising expenses and general economic conditions. After future premiums have provided for all policy benefits and expenses, the remaining margins must be sufficient to amortize the deferred costs. Since GAAP do not allow losses on unprofitable business to be deferred, the present value of these losses should be written off in the year when they become evident. If the premium deficiency exceeds the deferred acquisition costs to be written off, a liability should be established for the excess amount.

Generally, acquisition costs to be deferred for property and liability insurance companies are determined by calculating ratios of acquisition costs to written premiums and applying those ratios to unearned premiums. Testing such ratios is relatively simple; however, the auditor should carefully evaluate whether the costs included in the calculations are proper and should ascertain that the expenses vary with and are directly related to the production of new business. In addition, the auditor should review the business groupings used by the company to determine whether the basis for deferral is reasonable and consistent, and whether deferring acquisition costs to future periods is justified in the light of prevailing operating conditions.

When premiums are established for a property and liability company, it is expected they will be sufficient to pay losses and expenses, including amortization of deferred acquisition expenses, and to provide a margin of profit over the contract period. There are circumstances, however, in which premiums are not sufficient to cover anticipated losses, loss expenses, deferred acquisition costs, and other costs subsequent to acquisition. Any such premium deficiencies should be determined by reasonable groupings of the business, consistent with the company's operations. If it is expected that losses and loss adjustment expenses, maintenance expenses, and unamortized deferred acquisition expenses will exceed the related unearned premiums, the expected premium deficiency should be provided for by writing off any unamortized deferred acquisition costs, and a liability should be established for any excess deficiency.

(e) Inquiries of Regulators

SOP 94-1, *Inquiries of State Insurance Regulators*, has significantly influenced the level of communications among regulators, insurers, and accountants relating to permitted accounting practices under statutory accounting. The guidance in SOP 94-1 consists of (1) guidance for evaluating the effect of the status of regulatory examinations on the financial reporting process, and (2) formalization of the communication process between insurers and regulatory authorities with respect to material permitted statutory accounting practices.

The auditor should review reports of examinations and communications between regulators and the insurance company and make inquiries of the regulators. Specifically, the auditor should:

- Request that management provide access to all reports of examinations and related correspondence, including correspondence relating to financial conditions.
- Read reports of examinations and related correspondence between regulators and the insurance company during the period under audit through the date of the auditor's report.
- Inquire of management and communicate with the regulators, with prior approval of the insurance company, when an examination is in process or a report on an examination has not been received by the insurance company regarding conclusions reached during the examination.

Auditors should exercise care in concluding that an accounting treatment is permitted, and should consider the adequacy of disclosures in the financial statements regarding such matters. The auditor should obtain sufficient competent evidential matter to corroborate management's assertion that statutory accounting practices that are material to an insurance company's financial statements are permitted by the state insurance department. Sufficient competent evidential matter consists of any one or a combination of:

- Written acknowledgment sent directly from the regulator to the auditor (This type of corroboration includes letters similar to attorneys' letters and responses to confirmations.)

- Written acknowledgment prepared by the regulator, but not sent directly to the auditor, such as a letter to the insurance company

- Direct oral communications between the regulator and the auditor, supported by a written memorandum (If the auditor, rather than the regulator, prepares the memorandum, the auditor should send such memorandum to the regulator to make sure it accurately reflects the communication.)

42

Auditing Investment Companies

42.1 OVERVIEW OF THE INDUSTRY

An investment company serves as a vehicle for investors with similar investment objectives to benefit from professional investment selection and management and diversification of investments without incurring the substantial costs that would be associated with smaller portfolio positions. The business of an investment company consists of selling its capital shares to the public; investing the proceeds, principally in securities, in a manner that seeks to achieve its established investment objectives; and distributing to its shareholders the net income from, and net gains realized on sales of, its investments.

There are many different categories of investment companies: management investment companies, unit investment trusts, collective trusts, investment partnerships, certain separate accounts of insurance companies, and offshore funds. Ownership in an investment company is represented by units of ownership, such as shares or a partnership interest, to which proportionate shares of net assets can be attributed.

The management investment company is the most dominant of the several types of investment companies. The discussion in this chapter is presented principally in terms of management investment companies registered with the Securities and Exchange Commission (SEC) under the Investment Company Act of 1940 (the 1940 Act), which predominate in the industry. However, the accounting principles and auditing procedures discussed herein generally apply to all types of investment companies. Within the management investment company classification, the two main types are open-end (i.e., mutual) funds and closed-end funds. Investors in mutual funds invest and disinvest directly with the fund on a continuous basis; that is, mutual funds generally issue and redeem their shares daily. Closed-end funds do not redeem capital shares on a continuous basis; instead, investors disinvest by selling capital shares to others, as with securities in general. Other types of investment companies generally issue or redeem their equity interests in accordance with their organizing document (i.e., partnership agreement or trust indenture). Management investment companies operate in an environment that is highly regulated by the SEC, extremely competitive, and subject to specialized tax treatment.

In the early 1980s, the investment company industry changed from one that was principally equity-oriented to one that also includes mutual funds that invest in debt and money market instruments. Since that time, mutual fund products have continued to develop in response to customer demand and the availability of innovative investment vehicles, such as international/global funds, high-yield (or "junk") bond funds, sector funds, tax-exempt funds, multiple portfolio series funds, and mortgage-backed security funds. Investment strategies utilizing options, futures, and forward contracts have been used to enhance yields and to hedge investment risk. In addition, closed-end funds with a variety of objectives, including foreign and domestic equity growth as well as fixed-income bond portfolios, have found increased favor with the investing public.

The conduit, or "pass-through," concept underlies the operations of the entire industry. By complying with specific SEC regulations and certain sections of the Internal Revenue Code (IRC) (described later), a management investment company can distribute as dividends to its shareholders, net investment income earned and capital gains realized, with no federal income taxes being assessed against the fund; the shareholder pays the appropriate tax and thus double taxation is avoided. Net investment income under generally accepted accounting principles (GAAP) comprises income from dividends and interest on an investment company's investments, plus all other income except realized and unrealized gains or losses from security and foreign currency transactions, minus operating expenses other than federal, state, and foreign income taxes on realized gains from security transactions. In addition, the eligibility of dividends for certain favorable corporate federal income tax considerations can be retained by the fund and passed through to its corporate shareholders. Failure of a fund to comply with SEC and Internal Revenue Service (IRS) regulations could subject it to the tax rules applicable to ordinary corporations.

The auditor should be aware of a number of specific tax and regulatory constraints on management investment companies. First, to qualify as a regulated investment company (RIC), discussed later, for tax purposes, an investment company must[1]:

- Be registered under the 1940 Act as a management investment company or unit investment trust, or have elected to be treated as a business development company. The investment company also must elect to be treated as a RIC.

- Meet several diversification-of-assets tests on a quarterly basis. These tests are particularly important for start-up funds, because certain requirements must be met at the end of the first quarter of a fund's initial year.

- Derive at least 90 percent of its "gross income" from dividends, interest, and gains from the sale or other disposition of securities, foreign currencies, or other qualifying income, including, but not limited to, gains from options, futures contracts, or forward contracts.

- Distribute to shareholders at least 90 percent of the fund's "net investment company taxable income."

While this is not a requirement to maintain RIC status, the IRC requires that a RIC must distribute to its shareholders by December 31 at least 98 percent of its capital gains income (for the 12-month period ended October 31) and 98 percent of its ordinary income (for the 12-month period ended December 31), or pay a nondeductible 4 percent federal excise tax on the undistributed amount.

Second, to qualify for exemption from taxes on net investment income and capital gains realized, a RIC must distribute 100 percent of such income annually to its shareholders. Other tax matters that must be considered include the following:

- For federal income tax purposes, net short-term capital gains are considered ordinary income to the extent that they exceed net long-term capital losses.

- Certain corporate actions, such as a return of capital, affect capital gain or loss determination.

- A fund may elect not to distribute long-term capital gains, but may retain them and record and pay a federal income tax liability thereon (in this situation, the shareholders of the RIC would receive a credit for the taxes paid by the fund).

---

[1] For tax years beginning on or before August 5, 1997, RICs also are required to derive less than 30 percent of their gross income from gains (disregarding losses) on the sale or disposition of securities held for less than three months.

- Capital gains need not be distributed if the fund has an equal or greater amount of capital loss carryovers available. Funds may carry capital losses forward for eight years.
- The SEC usually permits only two distributions of long-term capital gains in a tax year.

In addition to Subchapter M of the Internal Revenue Code, as amended (Sections 851 to 855 and Section 4982), the auditor of a management investment company should be familiar with the following federal regulations, which address all aspects of fund operations, including the contents of a fund prospectus, investment portfolio diversification, record keeping, advertising, and related party transactions, as well as financial statement reporting and disclosures:

- The Investment Company Act of 1940, as amended
- The Investment Advisors Act of 1940, as amended (the Advisors Act)
- The Securities Act of 1933 (the 1933 Act)
- The Securities Exchange Act of 1934 (the 1934 Act)
- Article 6 of Regulation S-X
- SEC's Codification of Financial Reporting Policies

The auditor also should be familiar with the guidance in the AICPA audit and accounting guide, *Audits of Investment Companies.*

The auditor should understand the differences among the following designations relating to mutual funds, some of which have been formulated by the regulatory and taxing authorities:

- *Regulated Investment Company.* An investment company that qualifies for special tax treatment provided by Subchapter M of the IRC by meeting the requirements of Subchapter M and following the conduit concept of passing its income to its shareholders.
- *Registered Investment Company.* An investment company that has filed a registration statement with the SEC in accordance with the requirements of the 1940 Act, which statement has been declared effective by the SEC.
- *Diversified Investment Company.* A management investment company having at least 75 percent of its total assets in cash and cash items (including receivables), government securities, securities of other investment companies, and other securities, with no more than 5 percent of its total assets in any one issuer, and not holding more than 10 percent of the voting securities of any one issuer (Section 5 of the 1940 Act).
- *Load Fund.* An open-end investment company that adds a sales charge (of up to 8-1/2 percent) to the net asset value in computing the offering price to provide for underwriters' and dealers' commissions.
- *No-Load Fund.* A mutual fund selling its shares to the public at net asset value without a sales charge.
- *12b-1 Plan Fund.* A load or no-load mutual fund that covers certain expenses of promoting the sale of fund shares through payments by the fund to an advisor,

distributor, or service organization under a Rule 12b-1 plan approved and adopted by the fund's directors and shareholders. A 12b-1 plan fund may include a contingent deferred sales load (CDSL), which is imposed under certain conditions when a shareholder redeems shares.

- *Series Fund.* A mutual fund offering several distinct portfolios from which an investor can choose. The assets of each series are segregated from the assets of the other series in the fund. While each portfolio of a series is considered a separate corporation (trust) for tax purposes, all portfolios of a series are considered as one registrant with the SEC. This treatment leads to many efficiencies, particularly in the registration process.

- *Multiclass Fund.* A mutual fund that offers multiple classes of shares, each of which represents interests in the same investment portfolio, with varying arrangements for distribution of its shares and provision of services to shareholders; for example, one class might have a front-end sales load and another class may have a 12b-1 fee arrangement and a CDSL. Before the SEC issued Rule 18f-3 of the 1940 Act, mutual funds offering multiple classes of shares had to obtain exemptive relief from various provisions of the 1940 Act. (Rule 18f-3 formalized the conditions under which multiple classes of shares could be sold without applying for an exemptive order.) Most funds, including those that originally had obtained exemptive orders, operate under Rule 18f-3.

- *Master/Feeder Funds.* Generally, a feeder fund is a mutual fund that holds shares of another mutual fund as its only investment security; however, in certain situations, feeder funds can invest in more than one master fund or in a master fund and directly in other securities. A master fund is a mutual fund that has as its investors one or more feeder funds. The master fund and the feeder funds must have the same investment objective. The master fund usually registers under the 1940 Act, while the feeder fund registers under the 1940 Act and the 1933 Act.

The operations of a mutual fund, including its portfolio management, the distribution of its shares, the maintenance and reliability of accounting records, and the issuance of financial reports are the responsibility of its officers and board. These functions sometimes are performed by fund employees ("internalized" funds); however, in the majority of funds such functions are provided by other organizations, usually under contract (managed funds). Because some of the organizations that provide such services are considered to have a conflict of interests, the 1940 Act provides for the board of an investment company to play a specific role in its management. The 1940 Act distinguishes between "interested" and "disinterested" persons [Section 2(a)(19) of the 1940 Act defines interested persons] and requires that the board of a management investment company consist of no more than 60 percent interested persons (50 percent if the investment company has a 12b-1 plan), and specifies certain actions that must be approved by a majority of the disinterested directors. Some of the responsibilities of both the entire board and the disinterested board members include approving the investment advisory contract, underwriting agreement, 12b-1 plan (if applicable), custodian arrangements, transfer agent contract, valuation procedures, and appointment of the independent accountants and the principal financial officer.

Organizations that typically provide services to funds are:

- *Investment Advisors (Managers)*. Managers generally provide investment advice, research services, and certain administrative services under a contract that provides for an annual fee, which usually is based on a specified percentage of average net assets (although some agreements provide for a fee based on gross investment income as well as average net assets).

- *Distributors*. Distributors, often referred to as principal underwriters, act as agents or principals and sell the fund's shares at net asset value with or without a sales charge (load), either as wholesalers through independent dealers or as retailers through their own sales networks. Some funds adopt distribution plans under Rule 12b-1 that use fund assets to pay for distribution expenses.

- *Transfer Agents*. Transfer agents issue, transfer, redeem, and account for the fund's capital shares under an agreement with the fund. In addition, transfer agents usually process the distribution of dividends and realized gains on securities, including any reinvestment of dividends by shareholders. The transfer agent function may be performed by a bank or a private company or by a related party, such as the investment advisor, distributor, or other affiliated company.

- *Custodians*. Custody of a fund's cash and portfolio securities usually is entrusted to a bank that has prescribed minimum aggregate capital, surplus, and undivided profits, and that is responsible for the receipt, delivery, safekeeping, and often the valuation of the securities. An investment company using a bank as custodian may allow the bank to deposit qualifying securities in a central securities depository, such as the Depository Trust Company (DTC). Most U.S. traded securities are held by this depository on behalf of the securities industry. With respect to global or international funds, the custodian typically has a sub-custodian network that holds foreign securities and receives cash dividends, interest income, and other distributions such as stock splits or dividends. However, because a foreign bank is not a bank as defined in the 1940 Act, a fund placing its securities with a foreign custodian or subcustodian is required to follow the procedures in Rule 17f-5 of the 1940 Act relating to implementing foreign custody arrangements.

Clearing organizations use "book entry" methods to record transfers of securities, thus obviating the need for physical movements of the securities. Custodians also may use the Federal Reserve Treasury book entry system as a depository for U.S. government and agency securities. Rule 17f-4 of the 1940 Act contains special rules applying to the use of book entry systems.

42.2 ACCOUNTING PRINCIPLES AND PRACTICES

Under the 1940 Act, management investment companies are required to maintain certain accounting records, including:

- Transaction journals that contain the details of investment activity, capital share activity, and related cash activity
- Securities ledger(s), which contain a detailed listing of securities held by the fund

- An order book, showing the details of orders for each purchase or sale of portfolio items

- Shareholder ledger(s) showing the number of shares owned by each shareholder

A mutual fund generally is required to calculate its net asset value per share on a daily basis. Net asset values are the basis for the purchase and redemption of fund shares by investors. The net asset value per share is computed by dividing the value of all the assets of the fund, less liabilities, by the number of shares outstanding at the end of the day. Closed-end investment companies are required to calculate their net asset value per share quarterly; however, most closed-end investment companies make their net asset value per share available to their shareholders on a daily or weekly basis. Because of these requirements, a management investment company must establish internal control over the accurate and timely calculation of its net asset value per share. In most instances, this means that controls must be in place to reflect in the records of the fund on a daily basis its investment transactions, shareholder transactions, and income and expense accruals, and that the investment portfolio must be valued accurately at current market values. If transactions are not recorded in a timely manner or the portfolio is inaccurately valued, the net asset value per share that is used to price the fund's subscriptions and redemptions of capital shares could be misstated.

(a) Valuation

A fund's assets are stated at current fair value. The valuation of securities according to the fund's policies, as described in its prospectus, constitutes one of the most significant procedures performed in determining the fund's net asset value per share. Valuation sources include prices reported by national stock exchanges, over-the-counter markets, brokers, specialized pricing services, and foreign exchanges; board valuations; and other specialized methods, such as matrix pricing. Matrix pricing is a technique for valuing securities based on an aggregate of factors and without exclusive reliance on quoted market prices.

Illiquid securities and restricted securities, which cannot be offered for public sale without first being registered under the 1933 Act, generally are valued in good faith by the board. The objective is to state the securities at the amount the owner could reasonably expect to receive for them in a current sale. A pricing agent usually furnishes prices daily for tax-exempt funds based on information about market transactions and quotations from recognized municipal securities dealers.

Money market funds usually seek to maintain a constant net asset value per share of $1. To accomplish this, most money market funds value their portfolio securities on the basis of amortized cost. Other money market funds use the penny-rounding method (rounding the net asset value per share to the nearest cent based on a share value of $1). Both of those methods are allowed by Rule 2a-7 of the 1940 Act. This rule places certain responsibilities on the board of a money market fund and requires the board to establish procedures designed to stabilize the net asset value of the fund's shares at a single value.

(b) Income Recognition

Dividend income is recorded on the ex-dividend date, that is, the date the security trades without the dividend attached to it. Dividends that are treated as a return of capital by the payor for tax purposes also would be treated by the payee as a return of capital for financial reporting purposes. Such dividends should be recorded as a reduction of the cost of the investment or, if the cost basis of the investment is zero, as a realized gain. Interest income is accrued daily as earned. Interest income on zero coupon, payment-in-kind (PIK), and step bonds is determined using the effective interest method. Amortization of premiums and accretion of discounts on bonds usually are determined using the effective interest method.

(c) Investment Transactions

Purchases and sales of investments are recorded on the trade date, that is, the date the transaction is entered into. Realized gains and losses on the sale of securities are determined using either the specific identification method or the average cost method. Since the average cost method is not acceptable for federal income tax purposes, most management investment companies use the specific identification method for both financial reporting and federal income tax purposes. The use of specific identification permits a fund to choose the particular lot of shares to be sold and thereby accomplish specified performance objectives (or manage the utilization of capital loss carryforwards).

In certain instances, affiliates, primarily investment advisors, have compensated funds for losses on certain of their investment holdings. This compensation usually takes one of the following forms: (1) a direct contribution of cash to the fund to offset the effect of a realized or unrealized loss, (2) the purchase by the affiliate of a security from the fund at a price in excess of the current market price, or (3) the advisor arranging for a credit enhancement either by issuing a nontransferable put option or obtaining a nontransferable letter of credit issued by a financial institution. In each instance, the fund should recognize a loss on the investment and a contribution of capital. If the contribution of capital is equal to the loss on the investment, there is no net effect on net asset value.

(d) Foreign Currency

Investment company transactions that are denominated in foreign currencies include, but are not necessarily restricted to, purchases and sales of investments, dividends, interest, accretion and amortization of discounts and premiums on debt securities, and the opening and closing of forward exchange contracts. Each of these transactions gives rise to either an asset, a liability, or a commitment in a foreign currency. All foreign currency transactions should be recorded in the functional currency using the spot exchange rate at the date of the transaction, that is, trade date with respect to purchases and sales, ex-dividend date with respect to dividends, and accrual date with respect to interest, accretion, and amortization. Investments in foreign securities (traded in foreign markets) should be valued using the foreign currency price of the security on the valuation day and then translated into the functional currency using the valuation day's spot exchange rate. The unrealized gain or loss between the original cost (translated on the trade date) and the market value (translated on the valuation date) is made up of two elements: (1) the movements in market price and (2) the movement in foreign currency. GAAP permit these elements to be combined, but they can be disclosed separately.

Forward exchange contracts are valued at the appropriate forward rate on the valuation date. Other foreign currency assets and liabilities should be translated into the functional currency using the valuation day's spot exchange rate. The difference between the functional currency amount originally recorded and the valuation day's functional currency amount is a foreign currency unrealized gain or loss. Upon settlement, this difference becomes a realized foreign currency gain or loss.

(e) Shareholder Distributions

Accumulated net investment income and realized gains (losses) on investments and foreign currency and their distributions are accumulated in separate accounts. The liability for distributions to shareholders is recorded on the ex-dividend date. Many management investment companies offer shareholders the right to reinvest distributions and receive additional shares of the fund. The issuance of additional shares in connection with the dividend reinvestment is accounted for on the valuation date (usually established at the time the dividend is declared) or, if no valuation date has been established, on the payable date.

Amounts distributed to shareholders of a RIC usually are based on the fund's federal taxable income and long-term capital gains, which, in many instances, differ from net investment income and realized gains reported in accordance with GAAP. Because of this, situations arise that create book return of capital (i.e., distributions in excess of book earnings) but not tax return of capital distributions. In situations where a book return of capital would be caused by temporary or permanent book–tax timing differences, amounts distributed in excess of GAAP-basis earnings attributable to such book–tax differences should be shown as distributions in excess of such earnings. Such excess distributions should not be deducted from paid-in capital unless they are caused by a permanent book–tax difference. Only payments that have been designated as a return of capital for tax purposes should be treated as a book return of capital. Periodically, reclassifications are required when a temporary timing difference turns into a permanent difference, for example, the expiration of a capital loss carryforward.

(f) Equalization

Income equalization, which is no longer very common and is becoming less so, is a practice that is unique to the investment company industry. It applies to mutual funds that do not pay dividends daily and is used to prevent a dilution (caused by the continuous sales and redemptions of capital shares) of the continuing shareholders' per-share equity in undistributed net investment income. The method involves applying a portion of the proceeds from sales and the costs of repurchases of capital shares to undistributed net investment income (which excludes all capital gains and losses); the portion is equivalent to the amount, on a per-share basis, of distributable net investment income on the date of the related transaction. Income equalization is based on the concept that the net asset value of each share sold or repurchased is composed of both undistributed net investment income and capital components.

(g)   Brokerage/Service and Expense Offset Arrangements

Some investment companies have entered into brokerage/service and expense offset arrangements. In brokerage/service arrangements, various expenses (such as printing, transfer agent, and legal fees) are paid with brokerage commission dollars. In expense offset arrangements, expenses are reduced by forgoing income; for example, the custodian reduces its fees if the fund maintains cash balances on deposit with it in a noninterest-bearing account. Investment companies are required to include in specific expense categories in the statement of operations amounts paid by others under these types of arrangements and to reflect a corresponding reduction in total expenses. The auditor should pay close attention to these types of arrangements, because they may be accounted for in ways that do not reflect accurately the underlying substance of the transaction.

(h)   Reporting

Reporting requirements for management investment companies include:

- Annual audited financial statements to shareholders
- Semiannual and annual reports to the SEC on Form N-SAR. The annual report must include a letter to the SEC from the auditor on the adequacy of the fund's internal control as of year-end. Multiclass funds operating under an exemptive order are required to include with their annual N-SAR filing an auditor's report, prepared in accordance with Statement on Auditing Standards (SAS) No. 70, on the adequacy of the design of the methodology used by the fund to calculate multiclass net assets and to allocate income, expenses, gains, and losses among its classes, and on tests of the effectiveness of that methodology. Multiclass funds operating under Rule 18f-3 are not required to include such a report in their annual N-SAR filings, since the SEC has concluded that the report on the fund's internal control already required to be included in the annual N-SAR covers the procedures for calculating multiple class net assets.
- Semiannual financial statements to shareholders (not required to be audited)
- Posteffective amendments to registration statements on Form N-1A, Parts A, B, and C
- Federal Tax Form 1120 RIC, if operating in a corporate or Massachusetts or Maryland business trust form
- Federal Form 8613 (Excise Tax), if a distributable amount exists
- Federal Form 1099 DIV to shareholders

The form and content of financial statements for SEC purposes are governed by Regulation S-X (primarily Article 6) and by the audit and accounting guide for investment companies. The requirements of Article 6 are generally more comprehensive than those of the guide, and encompass the following financial statements:

- Statement of assets and liabilities
- Statement of operations
- Statement of changes in net assets for the current and previous reporting periods (In certain circumstances, specified in Statements of Financial Accounting Standards Nos. 95 and 102, a statement of cash flows is required.)
- Investment portfolio

In addition, certain financial highlights are required to be presented.

Annual reports of master/feeder funds include the financial statements of the feeder fund and the master fund. The notes to the financial statements usually include a general description of the master/feeder structure, and the master's financial statements are referred to in the feeder's notes. In addition to the typical financial statement disclosures, the financial statements of multiclass funds generally disclose net assets, net asset value per share, and shares outstanding by class; class-specific expenses; shareholder transactions by class; distributions to shareholders by class; and financial highlights for each class of shares. The notes to the financial statements usually describe each class of shares and the methodology for allocating income and expenses among the classes.

Investment partnerships, many of which operate as hedge funds (i.e., seek to minimize market risks through the use of both long and short positions), that are exempt from registration under the 1940 Act are permitted under GAAP to include in their financial statements a condensed schedule of investments categorized by type of security, country or geographical region, and industry (each investment constituting more than 5 percent of net assets and all investments of one issuer aggregating more than 5 percent of net assets must be disclosed separately), rather than the detailed schedule of investments that is required of funds registered under the 1940 Act An investment in another investment company should be considered an investment for purposes of the disclosures described above. In addition, an investment partnership is required to disclose in its condensed schedule of investments or in a note thereto, each investment of an investment company that it owns in which its proportional share exceeds 5 percent of its net assets. In addition, all management fees received by the general partner, including amounts received as net income allocated from the limited partners' capital accounts to the general partner's capital account, are required to be reflected in the statement of operations or the statement of changes in partners' capital, and the method of computing such amounts must be disclosed in the notes to the financial statements.

42.3 RISK FACTORS AND AUDIT REACTION

(a) Processing Environment

Two areas of major concern in a management investment company audit relate to portfolio accounting (accounting for investments purchased and sold, investment valuation, income received, and other corporate actions) and shareholder accounting (which applies to mutual funds only and entails accounting for ownership, sales, redemptions, and payment of dividends, including dividend reinvestment). In determining the audit strategy for a management investment company, the auditor may be confronted with one of several different processing environments, ranging from a comprehensive in-house system to one principally provided by third-party organizations.

As described earlier, third-party organizations under contract to funds usually provide services involving bookkeeping, custody of cash and investments, maintenance of shareholder accounts, and pricing of certain portfolio investments. In most instances, the accounting system is computerized, particularly with respect to shareholder records. Many auditors believe that the latter function is the most critical for a mutual fund, since the number of its capital shares is not constant, as in an industrial corporation or closed-end fund, but contracts or expands daily. This "breathing capital structure" increases the inherent risks associated with capital accounts beyond those typically found in other corporations.

In determining the audit approach, the auditor should obtain an understanding of the fund's internal control and assess control risk as a basis for determining the substantive tests to be performed. If a fund has an in-house system that encompasses the record keeping for the fund's transactions and the maintenance of shareholder accounts, the auditor generally has ready access to the system and can, with minimal difficulty, carry out the procedures necessary to assess its effectiveness.

If accounting procedures and control activities are provided by a service organization, the auditor should obtain an understanding of the service organization's internal control and assess control risk associated with the service organization to the extent deemed necessary to plan the audit. Reports issued in accordance with SAS No. 70 on the policies and procedures placed in operation and tests of their effectiveness should enable the auditor to understand the internal control of the service organization and assess its effectiveness. In some instances, the service organization report addresses only the policies and procedures placed in operation by the service organization, but does not include tests of their effectiveness. The service organization report should be reviewed carefully, since it may enable the auditor to reduce or eliminate testing of the records maintained by the service organization. Since the date of the service organization report and the period covered by it may not coincide with the investment company's report date and period, the auditor may have to perform additional procedures to determine whether there have been significant changes at the service organization. If the service organization does not have an SAS No. 70 report available, the auditor may have to visit the service organization to assess the effectiveness of its internal control. If a pricing agent is relied on for quotations used in valuing investments, the auditor also should consider periodically visiting the pricing service's facilities to review the procedures used in obtaining daily quotations.

(b) Derivatives Transactions

Another area of concern is an investment company's use of derivative financial instruments. Many derivatives have significant off-balance-sheet risk, that is, the risk that accounting losses may be incurred that exceed amounts recognized in the financial statements. Investment companies may engage in derivatives transactions to improve their present performance at the expense of future results. The auditor should be aware of risks associated with derivatives transactions, and should pay particular attention to the company's disclosures of such transactions, as required by Statement of Financial Accounting Standards (SFAS) No. 119, *Disclosure about Derivative Financial Instruments and Fair Value of Financial Instruments* (Accounting Standards Section F25). Auditing procedures specifically designed to identify derivatives with off-balance-sheet risk include:

- Reviewing the investment company's prospectus and statement of additional information to determine what types of derivative transactions it is permitted to enter into

- Reviewing the minutes of meetings of the board of directors and executive or operating committee for information about material transactions authorized or discussed or for approval of overall entity policy with respect to investment, financing, and hedging philosophy and guidelines

- Inquiring of management as to whether such transactions are occurring and, if so, how they are being recognized

- Reviewing, to the extent practicable, accounting records for large, unusual, or nonrecurring transactions that may expose the entity to significant credit or market risk

- Reviewing the methodology, underlying assumptions, and calculations used by management for valuing each type of derivative financial instrument, and determining whether they are appropriate

- Obtaining representation from management that derivatives have been properly recorded or disclosed in the financial statements

Investment companies also are required, under SFAS No. 105, *Disclosure of Information about Financial Instruments with Off-Balance-Sheet Risk and Financial Instruments with Concentrations of Credit Risk* (Accounting Standards Section F25), to present disclosures about financial instruments that have off-balance-sheet credit or market risk.

42.4 TYPICAL TRANSACTIONS AND CONTROLS

As indicated earlier, investment companies engage in a number of transactions that are unique to the industry. Controls over investment companies' portfolio accounting, which may be established by the companies or provided for them by custodians and/or other third parties, generally relate to the following:

- The receipt and delivery of securities as authorized by responsible officials and the recording of cash paid and received

- Appropriate valuation of the portfolio of investments and proper recording of cost for financial reporting and tax purposes

- Safeguarding securities

- Ensuring compliance with restrictions on the company's investment objectives and policies (as stated in its prospectus)

- Ensuring the custody, pricing, and timely notification of corporate actions with respect to domestic and foreign securities

Investment companies have large volumes of cash receipts and cash disbursements, many of which are handled by wire. Controls are needed to ensure that such transactions are accompanied by sufficient information to allow amounts to be recorded in the proper customer's account. Because of the volume of these transactions, reconciliations are performed frequently, sometimes even daily. The auditor should review the reconciliations, including procedures for investigating and resolving differences. In general, controls applied to investment accounts, income from investments, accruals, and expenses are similar to those found in commercial and manufacturing entities, except that, as mentioned earlier, the prompt recording of transactions is of particular importance because of the need to ensure that the net asset value per share, which is used to value subscriptions and redemptions, is properly calculated.

Controls relating to an investment company's shareholder accounting, including those of the fund's transfer agent, also should be reviewed and, if called for by the audit strategy, tested. Since a fund's capital changes daily, specialized procedures are frequently found in this area. At a minimum, the auditor should gain an understanding of controls over processing:

- Sales of fund shares and related collections
- Redemptions of fund shares
- Payments of dividends in cash and additional shares
- Inactive or dormant accounts
- Cancellations of sales and repurchases
- Wire orders in federal funds
- Check writing and telephone redemptions
- Electronic funds transfers
- Pending or incomplete transactions (such as unidentified wire orders and incomplete purchase applications)
- Sales or redemptions for which processing is delayed beyond the normal trade date ("as of" trades)
- Incoming mail (i.e., ensuring that it is properly time and date stamped)
- Shareholder correspondence

Under Rule 17A(d)-13 of the 1934 Act, certain registered transfer agents are required to obtain a report by an independent accountant on their internal control. This report is prepared in accordance with the attestation standards (AT Section of *AICPA Professional Standards*) and its use usually is limited by the independent accountant to management of the transfer agent and the SEC. The criteria underlying this report are well established within Rule 17A(d)-13, and the auditor of an investment company may obtain some audit evidence from an unqualified report. Any qualifications in such a report should be considered by the auditor of the investment company in developing the audit strategy.

42.5 SUBSTANTIVE TESTS

Substantive tests for a management investment company generally can be grouped into five major financial statement areas: investments, income, expenses, taxes, and shareholders' equity. Because of specialized industry practices and regulatory requirements, many of the procedures are unique to management investment companies. The following discussion is limited to these industry practices and related auditing procedures.

(a) Investments

Investments represent the most significant asset in a management investment company's statement of assets and liabilities. The auditor's concerns about investments are related to custody, unsettled trades, valuation, recording of financial reporting and tax cost, and adherence to the fund's investment policies and restrictions. Tests of the accuracy of the fund's records are the same as for other industries and are not discussed here.

In connection with the audit of investments, the auditor is required by section 404.03 of the SEC's Codification of Financial Reporting Policies (Codification) to confirm with the custodian or brokers all portfolio positions held at the audit date and all open (unsettled) investment transactions. With the exception of certain situations described under Rules 17f-1 and 17f-2 of the 1940 Act, it generally is not necessary for the auditor to count securities held by the custodian unless the investment company requests it. All unsettled investment transactions should be confirmed with the appropriate brokers. Alternative auditing procedures should be employed to substantiate unconfirmed open transactions at the audit date. The confirmation procedures followed are detailed in the scope paragraph of the auditor's report. (See Figure 42.1 later in this chapter.)

Section 404.03 of the Codification also requires that values assigned to all investments be independently verified by the auditor. Auditors use several different means of obtaining prices to substantiate the values assigned to investments, depending on the type of fund under consideration. Some auditors have developed computer software packages that compare market prices obtained from an independent source with the security prices used by the fund. These packages also permit the auditor to recalculate the fund's extensions and footings. Other auditors purchase and use commercially available software packages designed to accomplish the same objectives. In all instances, the auditor should attempt to use a different source from the one that provided quotes to the fund. In instances where no source other than the one used by the fund is available to price a security, the auditor should consider the marketability and liquidity of the security. If it is determined that a security is illiquid and not readily marketable, it should be valued at fair value as determined in good faith by the board of the fund. The SEC has issued guidance (in sections 404.03 and 404.04 of the Codification) with respect to some of the factors to be considered in determining fair value.

For domestic publicly traded common and preferred stocks and corporate bonds, daily quotes from national stock exchanges are available to the auditor from several published sources. Daily quotes from international exchanges, which usually close earlier in the day than do the U.S. exchanges, generally are provided by a broker or pricing agent for foreign common and preferred stocks and bonds. If published sources are not available to verify these prices, the auditor should consider obtaining quotes from independent sources by using correspondent firms or foreign offices of the auditing firm, which should provide the quotes from local published or electronic financial sources. If the fund uses a computerized pricing service, the auditor should become familiar with the information provided by the service.

For thinly traded securities, it may be necessary for the auditor to obtain quotes from brokers that deal specifically in such securities. For corporate bonds without published quotes, generally the auditor should obtain quotes from several brokers in order to evaluate the reasonableness of the quotes used by the fund or should compare recent trade prices with broker-provided quotes.

The auditor should review the reasonableness of the procedures followed to identify and value illiquid and restricted securities. Disclosure of restricted securities must be made in the financial statements, together with certain other information required by sections 404.03 and 404.04 of the Codification.

The auditor can substantiate prices for tax-exempt funds, which usually are furnished by a pricing agent, by obtaining quotations from market-makers and comparing them with the furnished prices, comparing selected proceeds from sales during the period with the value used on the day preceding the sale, or obtaining a portfolio valuation from a second pricing service.

As discussed earlier, many money market funds value their securities at amortized cost, either based on exemptive orders granted by the SEC or as allowed by Rule 2a-7. If a fund follows an exemptive order, the auditor should review a copy of the order and ascertain that the fund has procedures in place for monitoring adherence to the conditions enumerated in the order. If a fund adopts Rule 2a-7, the auditor should review that rule and ascertain that the fund has procedures in place for ensuring that the conditions in the rule will be met. Among those conditions are that investments are to be limited to short-term, high-quality debt instruments, and a requirement that the fund's board determine that using either the amortized cost method or the penny-rounding pricing method (described earlier) is in the best interests of the fund and its shareholders, and ensure that a stable price per share is maintained.

Both exemptive orders permitting use of amortized cost valuation and Rule 2a-7 require a money market fund to price its portfolio periodically, using available market quotations, to determine whether the net asset value deviates from $1 per share. The auditor should review those pricing procedures and inquire whether, during the period under audit, a deviation occurred and, if so, what corrective action was taken by the board. The auditor also should obtain market quotations (usually given in yields) directly from a major market-maker at the audit date to determine the reasonableness of prices used by the fund. (The fund should be requested to price its portfolio at market at the audit date or a date close to the audit date.)

In addition to SEC and IRS restrictions on a fund's investments, which deal principally with diversification and classification, there are generally restrictions in the fund's prospectus relating to the quality of investments, geographical dispersion, type of security, and so on. The auditor should test the fund's controls over compliance with such restrictions and/or review the fund's portfolio for compliance with those restrictions.

(b) Investment Income and Realized Gains

The conduit concept underlying mutual funds increases the audit significance of the recording and classification of investment income and realized gains from sales of investments. Investment income usually is composed of dividends and interest earned. The auditor should determine that all income earned during the period has been recorded for financial reporting purposes. Investment vehicles such as convertible securities, "deep discount" bonds, PIK bonds, and "securitized" or "collateralized" obligations must be reviewed carefully to ensure the proper accounting and recording of income. With respect to dividends, the auditor usually substantiates domestic dividends and other corporate actions (such as stock splits and issuance of stock rights) by referring to published sources. Software packages are available that allow the auditor to compare recorded corporate actions with corresponding information from an independent source. (The same software packages also can be used to compare the market prices mentioned earlier.) In circumstances where control risk relating to recording dividend income has been assessed below the maximum or at low, the auditor may decide to perform analytical procedures instead of the substantive tests of details described above.

Pricing services are available for foreign securities; however, the auditor may wish to make arrangements, usually with correspondents, to identify corporate actions such as cash dividends, stock dividends or splits, and stock rights. The auditor also should review the federal taxability of such corporate actions, as well as the related foreign currency gains and losses, to assist fund management in determining investment company taxable income available for distribution.

In auditing investment sales and the related realized gains and losses, the auditor should test the classification of capital gains and losses for tax purposes.

The test of the classification of gains and losses should include a review for wash sales. A wash sale occurs when securities are sold (or otherwise disposed of) at a loss and, within a period beginning 30 days prior to the sale date and ending 30 days after that date (a 61-day period), the investment company has acquired (or has contracts to acquire) substantially identical securities. A loss sustained on such a sale (or other disposition) is not allowed by the IRS. Instead, for tax purposes the amount of loss is added to the basis of the "substantially identical" security. Determining the extent to which wash sales have occurred is necessary to enable a fund to properly distribute its investment company taxable income and long-term capital gains, to maintain its RIC status, and to avoid excise taxes.

(c) Accruals and Expenses

The auditor should determine that expenses incurred by the investment company are in accordance with the provisions of the investment advisory contract, prospectus, or other related agreements. Usually the auditor recalculates the management fee, which typically is the largest expense incurred by an investment company, and any other fees, such as administrative and 12b-1 fees, that are based on net assets of the fund. Other expenses, such as printing, transfer agent and custodial fees, and professional fees, should be reviewed for authorization by a fund officer and, if they are significant, should be traced to invoices and agreements. State income and franchise taxes should be recalculated, if significant. The auditor ordinarily analyzes changes in significant expense categories between the current and prior periods. As indicated earlier, the auditor should evaluate the appropriateness of the accounting for brokerage/service and expense offset arrangements.

The auditor should ascertain that management reviews expense accruals periodically and allocates expenses ratably over the year. The securities laws of the states ("Blue Sky" laws) in which an investment company's securities are sold generally limit certain investment company expenses. A more restrictive limitation may be provided for in the investment advisory contract or cited in the prospectus. In addition, during the start-up period of a new fund, the investment advisor may voluntarily limit the expenses of the fund by agreeing to reimburse the fund for certain expenses in excess of a specified percentage of the average value of the fund's net assets during the year. The auditor should review and recalculate such reimbursable amounts.

(d) Taxes

As described earlier, the consequences for a management investment company of not qualifying as a RIC are severe. The already complex investment company environment is made even more so because of the ever-changing tax law, as well as the need to apply tax rules to trading in options, futures, and forward contracts. Accordingly, the auditor should be satisfied that the fund is in compliance with all such requirements.

(e) Capital Accounts

Auditing capital or shareholders' accounts does not require any unusual considerations other than reviewing and testing the internal control of the transfer agent, as previously discussed, and testing the computations of the net asset value per share used in the daily purchase and sale transactions of a fund's shares.

To determine whether the fund followed the procedures specified in Rule 2a-4 of the 1940 Act in calculating the current net asset value of its outstanding shares for purposes of distributing and redeeming such shares, the auditor should obtain an understanding of and document internal control with respect to the calculation of net asset value per share and either perform tests of the controls over that process or select a number of days and review the fund's net asset value computations as shown on the price make-up sheets. The review should include:

- Comparing quantities and description of portfolio securities owned with data in the investment ledger
- Tracing quoted market prices to independent sources
- Testing the clerical accuracy of market value extensions and footings
- Reconciling amounts for other assets and liabilities to the general ledger accounts
- Reviewing the reasonableness of income and expense accruals
- Reconciling the number of the fund's shares outstanding to information received from the transfer agent

• Recalculating the net asset value per share

If the fund follows the practice of income equalization (described earlier), the auditor should test the breakdown between the undistributed net investment income and other capital components of the net asset value of shares for several days during the period under audit; often sampling is involved in this procedure.

(f) Financial Highlights and Investment Portfolio

There are two unique aspects of reporting on the financial statements of an investment company. The first involves the inclusion of a table showing financial highlights for the past five years. The other unique reporting feature for mutual funds is that every security position in the fund's portfolio is shown in the financial statements, including number of shares held, face amount, description, market or fair value, category (industry or similar grouping), and type of security. Each of these are covered by the auditor's report. Figure 42.1 shows the standard auditor's report for a single fund investment company. The same report, with appropriate wording changes, would be used for a series of funds.

Figure 42.1   Auditor's Standard Report

Independent Auditor's Report

We have audited the accompanying statement of assets and liabilities of XYZ Investment Company, including the schedule of portfolio investments, as of December 31, 19XX, and the related statement of operations for the year then ended, the statements of changes in net assets for each of the two years in the period then ended, and the financial highlights for each of the five years in the period then ended. These financial statements and financial highlights are the responsibility of the Company's management. Our responsibility is to express an opinion on these financial statements and financial highlights based on our audits.

We conducted our audits in accordance with generally accepted auditing standards. Those standards require that we plan and perform the audit to obtain reasonable assurance about whether the financial statements and financial highlights are free of material misstatement. An audit includes examining, on a test basis, evidence supporting the amounts and disclosures in the financial statements. Our procedures included confirmation of securities owned as of December 31, 19XX, by correspondence with the custodian and brokers, and other auditing procedures. An audit also includes assessing the accounting principles used and significant estimates made by management, as well as evaluating the overall financial statement presentation. We believe that our audits provide a reasonable basis for our opinion.

(Continues)

Figure 42.1 *(Continued)*

In our opinion, the financial statements and financial highlights referred to above present fairly, in all material respects, the financial position of XYZ Investment Company as of December 31, 19XX, the results of its operations for the year then ended, the changes in its net assets for each of the two years in the period then ended, and the financial highlights for each of the five years in the period then ended, in conformity with generally accepted accounting principles.

[Signature]

[Date]

43

Auditing Lodging Companies

43.1 OVERVIEW OF THE INDUSTRY

(a) Ownership and Operation

The structure of the lodging industry is complex because of the variety of methods by which lodging properties can be owned and operated. These methods can be combined in various ways.

(i) Forms of Ownership. Ownership can be held in the form of sole proprietorships, partnerships, limited liability companies, or corporations. Some owners engage individuals or entities to manage their hotels.[1] Other owners are owner/operators and operate their hotels themselves. Still others engage a lodging chain to operate their hotels under the chain's brand name.

Corporations include C-Corporations (C-Corps) and Real Estate Investment Trusts (REITs). A C-Corp is a legal, taxable entity chartered by a state and owned by stockholders. A C-Corp can be structured as a chain management company, an independent management company, a franchisor, an owner/operator, or an owner. The primary advantages of a C-Corp compared with a REIT are that a C-Corp is not subject to the strict ownership and income requirements that apply to a REIT and is not required to lease assets to a lessee. Except for REITs, it is uncommon for hotels to be leased from an owner, but there are situations involving older, smaller, or international hotels—often government owned—where leasing occurs.

REITs must comply with a series of ownership and income requirements that prevent them from operating hotels. As a result, REITs own the real estate but lease it to a lessee who operates the property. There are two types of REITs: equity REITs and mortgage REITs. Both equity and mortgage REITs raise equity through initial public offerings. Equity REITs utilize the proceeds from equity offerings for the development or acquisition of properties. Mortgage REITs utilize funds to make loans for new development or acquisition of properties. Mortgage REITs earn income by charging interest to borrowers and can participate in the profit from the sale of a property, while equity REITs derive income through rents received based on lease agreements with tenants (such as hotel operating companies). Mortgage REITs can choose either to lend 100 percent of the mortgage or to lend 50 percent and have a partner.

REITs are exempt from corporate income taxes if they meet certain income, ownership, and distribution requirements. The major provisions of the regulations governing REITs are as follows:

- A REIT must have a minimum of 100 shareholders.
- No more than 50 percent of the shares may be held by five or fewer shareholders.
- At least 75 percent of the REIT's assets must consist of real estate, cash, or government securities.

---

[1] The term "motel" historically was associated with smaller, roadside, lower-priced properties that attract leisure travelers who do not require extensive amenities. Over the years, the term "hotel" has evolved to encompass all types of lodging properties in all types of locations, including motel-type properties. For this reason, this chapter does not distinguish between hotels and motels but uses the term "hotel" to refer to all types of lodging properties.

- At least 95 percent of the REIT's gross income must be from rents, dispositions, interest, or dividends.

- At least 75 percent of the REIT's gross income must be from real property rents, interest from mortgages on real property, gains from sales of real property, or gains from sales of mortgage interests.

- Less than 30 percent of the REIT's gross income may come from the sale of real estate held for less than four years.

- At least 95 percent of the REIT's taxable income must be distributed to the shareholders.

REITs must access external capital sources in order to grow. To access those sources, REITs establish a line of credit with a lending institution and typically borrow 40 to 50 percent of the value of their hotel properties. A REIT generates additional cash flow for distribution to shareholders when hotel property revenues increase and additional properties are acquired that generate additional lease income. The tenants can be independent of the REIT, but sometimes are controlled by its board of directors or officers.

(ii) Management Companies.   There are two types of hotel management companies: independent and chain. Independent management companies run the day-to-day operations of individual hotels in accordance with standards defined by the hotel owner. Independent management companies can manage different hotel chains simultaneously. They are paid a management fee by the hotel owners that usually comprises a base fee plus an incentive fee, if the management company exceeds certain financial goals. Total fees typically range between 4 and 7 percent of revenue. In addition, independent management companies charge fees for accounting and other services. Independent management companies are not limited to managing hotels; they can, and often do, participate as owners.

Chain management companies, also referred to as "chains," "brands," or "systems," can own and operate hotels and provide franchise or license agreements to owners of hotel properties. For managing a hotel property, the chain management company receives a customary management fee from the hotel's owner. Chain management contracts can range from 30 days to 50 years, with overall fees ranging from 5 to 12 percent of total revenue. If, in addition to managing a hotel, a chain management company also participates in the ownership of the property by way of a financial investment, it receives its share of ownership profits over and above the management fees.

(iii) Affiliations and Independent Hotels.   One of the major decisions facing an owner is whether to operate independently or to affiliate with a hotel system; affiliation may be in the form of either a franchise organization or a membership organization. Approximately one-third of the hotel properties in the United States are independent hotels, unaffiliated with a national or regional hotel chain.

Franchise organizations grant franchise rights and provide hotel brand franchise services to hotel owner/operators in exchange for application, royalty, marketing, reservation, and other fees, which in total range from 4 to 13 percent of room revenue. Franchise agreement contracts typically range from 5 to 25 years.

Membership organizations are associations of independently owned and operated hotels. Some membership organizations consist of member hotels using the same name, while others are affiliations of independent hotels operating under different names. The governing body of a hotel membership organization is a not-for-profit entity with a board of directors representing member hotels. Members pay annual dues for services, which include a central reservation system, marketing assistance, and quality assurance. Sometimes members are charged additional fees, such as on a per reservation basis. In addition, some membership organizations provide education and training, design standards, central purchasing, and marketing and other promotional initiatives for properties in the membership organization.

Figure 43.1 summarizes the activities and revenues of the various types of lodging entities.

(b) Supply Segmentation

The lodging industry has three "service" or "supply" segments: full service, limited service, and luxury. These broad categories encompass all hotel brand names, price categories, and supply types, such as budget, economy, moderate, upscale, all-suite, conference centers, resorts, and extended-stay properties. Services and features provided at hotels are referred to as "amenities" and help determine the category in which a hotel belongs. Typically, the higher the level of amenities, the more full service and upscale the hotel is considered.

(i) Full Service. The full service segment is the largest segment of the hotel industry. Full service hotels offer food and beverage outlets and room service, meeting and catering facilities, and bell service. Full service hotels attract both business and leisure travelers and offer a broader range of price and amenity categories than do limited service hotels. Full service hotels generally are described as either resort, luxury, upscale, mid-price, convention, conference center, or all-suite.

(ii) Limited Service. Unlike full service hotels, limited service hotels offer few amenities. Most notably, limited service hotels usually have no meeting facilities or restaurants, although some do offer complimentary breakfast or a cocktail hour in the lobby. Because of the lack of an in-house restaurant, most limited service hotels are located next door to a full service restaurant, usually a local, regional, or national restaurant chain. Limited service categories include extended-stay, upscale limited service, moderate, and budget. They serve primarily price-sensitive business and leisure travelers.

(iii) Luxury. While luxury hotels are full service hotels, they are considered a different category because they offer the highest level of service and amenities. Luxury hotels capture both business and leisure guests as well as groups, and tend to be located in larger cities and vacation destinations.

(c) Recent History

The years from 1984 to 1992 were marked by heavy losses and low occupancy rates in the U.S. lodging industry. These conditions were the result of a sharp increase in new

Figure 43.1 Activities and Sources of Revenue by Type of Lodging Entity

Type of Entity	Sources of Income	Typical Income
Franchise organization	Application fees	$10,000 to $150,000 per application
	Royalty fees	3 to 12 percent of room revenue
	Purchasing services	Percentage of reduced cost to franchises
	Reservation connection fees	Monthly fee
	Reservation charges	$3 to $12 per room night or reservation
	National advertising support fees	Varies depending on type of hotel brand, number of properties, advertising initiatives, and sales volume
Chain management company	Base fees	2 to 5 percent of all revenue
	Incentive fees	10 percent of income before fixed charges, or a percentage of increases in annual earnings, or a percentage of cash provided by operations
	Accounting fees	$10,000 to $100,000 per year
	Technical service fees	Based on use of services
Independent management company	Base fees	1 to 5 percent of all revenue
	Incentive fees	10 percent of income before fixed charges, or a percentage of increases in annual earnings, or a percentage of cash provided by operations
	Accounting fees	$10,000 to $100,000 per year
	Technical service fees	Based on use of services
Owner/ operator	Profits from lodging operations	——
Owner	Profits from lodging operations	——
Equity REIT	Base rent from tenants	25 to 35 percent of a base level of revenue
	Rent escalations as revenue increases	50 to 75 percent of additional revenue
Mortgage REIT	Interest	Fixed or variable rate
	Participations	Percentage of revenue, or cash provided by operations, or by participation in the profit from sale of a property
Membership organization (not-for-profit entity)	Annual dues; reservation, marketing, advertising, and other fees	Varies depending on size of property, number of rooms, and use of services

hotel development and acquisition activity. Severe overleveraging occurred, with owners committing an average of 15 percent of total revenue to interest expense, up from only 6 percent in 1977. Debt leverage ratios increased from 65–70 percent to 75–80 percent.

The Tax Reform Act of 1986 phased out the extent to which passive investment losses could be offset against ordinary income, which made hotel investments less attractive to many investors. The loss of this capital source, together with concerns expressed by financial institutions, made hotel financing difficult starting in 1987. With declining hotel occupancy rates, increased competition from newer, limited service, economy hotels, and an economic recession, hoteliers discounted rates in an effort to stimulate business. As a result, between 1988 and 1992, hotel average daily rates did not keep pace with inflation. Finally, the Gulf War, combined with the many weak international economies, hurt travel to the United States and thus the U.S. hotel market.

As large balloon payments on hotel loans became due in the late 1980s and early 1990s, and with the industry suffering an overall downturn, many lenders were forced to foreclose on hotel assets and thus become reluctant and uneducated hotel owners. Other hotel owners and operators struggled to cover debt service and had no funds available for necessary improvements, new development, or acquisitions. As a result, relatively few new hotel rooms were added to the U.S. hotel supply between 1991 and 1993. In addition, new hotel properties became smaller, with the average number of rooms per property dropping from 121 in 1988 and 1989 to 74 rooms per property by 1993.

By the end of 1994, the industry had found solutions to many of its problems and entered a period of record profitability and near-record occupancy rates. The turnaround can be attributed to the following:

- Owners restructured debt, thereby lowering interest expense.
- Other expenses, such as management fees, payroll, food and beverage, marketing, and maintenance, were scaled down significantly.
- Property taxes were lowered through the appeal process.
- Most lenders had written off underperforming hotel assets.
- Troubled hotel assets had changed hands or been repositioned.
- New construction sharply declined.
- The industry began to benefit from the stronger economy, increasing consumer confidence, and the weak U.S. dollar.

Both debt and equity financing once again became available to the lodging industry. The increase in average daily rates exceeded inflation in 1993, and hotel occupancy rates across the nation improved. These factors, combined with the lack of growth in supply during the early 1990s, helped the lodging industry turn from its worst period in history to its most profitable.

(d) Laws and Regulations

Hotels are subject to the same regulations as other commercial buildings, for example, building codes and fire safety regulations. Because they serve food, hotels are required to obtain certain food handling permits and are subject to inspections by health departments. Certain jurisdictions require the posting of room rates and the completion of guest registration cards. In addition, hotels are subject to state regulations governing the sale of alcoholic beverages. The state regulates the time of day sales can be made and the age of drinkers and servers. In some cases, licenses to sell alcoholic beverages are restricted by number, and to obtain a license it may be necessary to purchase it from an existing holder.

(e) Uniform System of Accounts for Hotels

The industry has a long history of sharing financial information. In 1926, the Hotel Association of New York City published the first edition of the Uniform System of Accounts for Hotels, which currently is in its ninth edition. The book established a uniform accounting and financial reporting system for hotels. This system has been adopted by most major hotel companies around the world and it has standardized the presentation of financial data in the industry.

There are two main department classifications in a hotel: operating and overhead. The operating (revenue-producing) departments include rooms, food and beverage, telecommunications, and similar departments. The overhead departments include administrative and general, data processing, human resources, transportation, marketing, guest entertainment, energy costs, and property operation and maintenance.

43.2 RISK FACTORS

Several characteristics of the environment in which hotels operate present inherent risks that are unique to the lodging industry. Those inherent risks include the following:

- Hotels operate in a highly competitive market and require periodic renovation. If a hotel is not properly maintained, it will lose market share.

- Franchisors establish standards that franchisees must meet to obtain and maintain a franchise. The franchise name is important to a hotel because it attracts guests, and the central reservation system operated by the franchisor generates a substantial amount of the room revenue.

- The profitability of a hotel is sensitive to the characteristics of the area in which the hotel operates. A deteriorating area may adversely affect the hotel's operating results.

- The oversupply of hotel rooms built in the late 1970s and early 1980s led to a general decline in the values of hotel properties in the late 1980s and early 1990s. Even though a substantial number of hotels restructured their debt, the value of some properties may be less than their outstanding debt.

- Hotels have a substantial amount of fixed overhead, and a small drop in occupancy rates may mean the difference between making a profit or having a loss. Therefore, the opening of a new hotel in an area may have an adverse effect on an existing hotel.

- Management companies may seek to defer expenses or capitalize repairs to meet the minimum earnings requirement to earn incentive performance fees.

See Chapter 47, "Auditing Real Estate Companies," for a discussion of the structure of real estate entities and various audit and accounting issues connected with owning and operating a real estate company, which is essentially what a lodging company is.

The auditor should consider the current condition of the lodging industry in the local area by comparing the hotel's operating results with published ratios related to that area. If industry statistics are not available, the typical common size income statement illustrated in Figure 43.2 can be used as a guide for considering the reasonableness of the hotel's statement of operations.

43.3   REVENUE CYCLE

The principal differences between a hotel's transactions and internal control and those of other businesses are found in the revenue cycle. Room revenue is the most important source of income to a hotel. The front desk is the center of the hotel's operation and the place where the guest ledger, which summarizes and accumulates all charges to guests using the hotel facilities, is maintained. Some of the functions performed by front desk personnel are registering guests, recording room revenue, recording food and beverage and other guest charges, checking out guests, and settling guests' bills.

(a)   Room Revenue

Guests arriving at a hotel check in at the front desk, where the clerk checks the guest reservation for type of room and room rate. Most hotel guests make advance reservations; at that time the room rate is determined by the salesperson in the reservation department or the central reservation system. There are many different rates: corporate, group, special, and weekend, among others. Hotels use yield management systems to obtain the highest rate in periods of peak demand and to sell rooms at a discount rate during slow periods. Controls should be established in the reservation department and central reservation system over room rates that can be offered by the reservation clerks. A monitoring system should be in place to ensure that the reservation clerks adhere to the hotel's pricing policy.

For guests without a reservation, the front desk clerk checks the room listing (rack) for available rooms and for room rates, which are predetermined. The front desk clerk should not be able to deviate from the established rates without the approval of the front desk manager. The guest completes and signs a registration card. The guest name, address, room number, room rate, and method of payment are recorded in the guest folio, which serves as a basis to establish the guest accounts receivable ledger.

If the account is to be settled with a credit card, an imprint of the card is taken at registration and credit approval obtained from the charge card company for the estimated amount of the bill. If payment is to be in cash, an advance deposit usually is obtained to cover the estimated charges based on the length of stay.

Allowances are deductions from a particular department's revenue, generally resulting from disputes over telephone calls, room rate adjustments, or adjustments for overcharges or unsatisfactory service. Allowances are documented on an allowance voucher, which generally includes the date, guest's name and room number, the department that made the charge that is being adjusted, the amount of the allowance,

Figure 43.2   Typical Common Size Income Statement Following the Uniform System of Accounts for the Lodging Industry

	Limited Service	Full Service	Luxury
Revenue			
Rooms	95.4%	69.8%	64.3%
Food and Beverage	0.0	24.4	28.4
Telecommunications	2.0	2.5	2.9
Minor Operated Departments	1.0	2.1	3.1
Rentals and Other Income	1.6	1.2	1.3
Total	100.0	100.0	100.0
Departmental Expenses[1]			
Rooms	24.9	25.2	24.7
Food and Beverage	0.0	82.6	79.4
Telecommunications	72.0	54.2	50.3
Minor Operated Departments	0.7	1.4	2.3
Total[2]	25.9	40.6	42.2
Departmental Profit[2]	74.1	59.4	57.8
Undistributed Operating Expenses[2]			
Administrative and General	9.0	9.7	8.9
Marketing	4.5	5.3	5.9
Franchise Fees	2.0	1.6	1.0
Utilities	5.1	4.5	3.6
Property Operation and Maintenance	5.0	5.0	4.8
Total[2]	25.6	26.1	24.2
Gross Operating Profit[2]	48.5	33.3	33.6
Management Fees[2]	2.8	3.7	3.1
Income Before Fixed Charges[2]	45.7	29.6	30.5
Fixed Charges[2]			
Property Taxes	3.6	3.0	3.0
Insurance	1.0	0.7	0.5
Land and Building Rental	2.3	2.0	1.7
Equipment Rental	0.8	0.4	0.2
Interest	4.3	4.9	3.8
Depreciation and Amortization	5.3	4.5	3.8
Other Fixed Charges	0.3	0.8	0.8
Total[2]	17.6	16.3	13.8
Pretax Income[2]	28.1%	13.3%	16.7%

Notes

[1] As a percentage of appropriate departmental revenue

[2] As a percentage of total revenue

Source: Data adapted from Smith Travel Research, 1996, HOST data base.

and an explanation. A separate voucher should be prepared for each allowance. If the allowance voucher is for an adjustment of the room rate, it should be signed by the person authorized to approve the allowance as well as by the billing clerk who credits it to the guest's account. Usually, only a few allowances are granted each day. Since individuals working at the front desk have access to cash, it is important to ensure that allowances are properly approved. If adjustments are made before management's approval is obtained, management subsequently should review and approve them.

Computerized property management systems are available that eliminate the traditional manual room rack and automatically verify reservations and provide room and rate data at check-in. The electronic room rack displays the status, features, and location of all the rooms in the hotel. Electronic guest folios contain guest and room data that is immediately available; at check-out a detailed folio is printed. Once a guest folio account is opened, it cannot be closed by front desk personnel unless payment of charges is received or an allowance is authorized for the outstanding balance. Computerized management systems also include posting of telephone, food and beverage, and other charges; the night audit function (described below); posting of all room charges; and the transfer of accounts of checked out guests to the proper "city ledger" accounts, which contain receivables from credit card companies, travel agents, and direct-bill customers.

The individual guest folios constitute the accounts receivable guest ledger, which is used to account for all in-house guest charges. When a guest checks out, the folio is reviewed for accuracy. If the account is settled by credit card or is to be direct-billed, this is indicated on the folio; credit card slips are attached to the folio. At the end of each shift, the front desk clerk performs a "shift close" by printing out all activity and reconciling cash and credit card receipts to the revenue postings. This reconciliation, supported by all tape totals, miscellaneous vouchers, cash sheets, credit card receipts, and food and beverage charges, will be approved by a supervisor and included in the package to be sent to the night auditor. (It is common practice for hotels to reconcile and report their daily activity as of midnight.) Cash receipts are sent to the general cashier, who prepares the cash deposit.

In a fully integrated system, a computer-generated folio automatically summarizes all guest charges. It also produces summary reports for each shift, with totals for each type of settlement; the clerks reconcile these reports at the end of their shifts. Each night, the night auditor prints out a report, known as the "D Report," that summarizes all transactions from all sources for that day. This includes a breakdown of revenue by type and the offsetting settlement by type. The settlement can be either cash, credit card, guest ledger for in-house guests, or city ledger for guests who have checked out that day. The night auditor determines that there is detailed support for each type of revenue recorded and that the settlements posted also reconcile to the revenue recorded.

The following procedures are performed by the night auditor:

- Tracing the totals of the charges by department and agreeing the total to the revenue posted by type
- Reviewing the room rate variance report, which lists each room and the rate it was sold for, and comparing those rates with established rates
- Determining that all food, beverage, phone, and other charges have been posted to each guest's account

- Determining that the shift closes performed by the front desk clerks included the appropriate reconciliations
- Comparing the cash settlement per the D Report to the shift close cash sheets and the cash transmitted to the general cashier
- Agreeing the total of credit card charges to the daily summary total
- Determining that advance deposits were properly applied to the accounts of guests who checked in
- For guests who have checked out, ensuring that proper check-out procedures were performed and that the settlement of accounts (paid by cash or credit card) has been applied properly. The total of all credit card payments is the support for the transfer of guests' accounts out of the guest ledger and into the city ledger.
- Checking that the prior day's city ledger accounts receivable balance has been properly carried forward and is updated only by the current day's cash receipts and the transfer from the guest ledger

The final procedure is to determine that all the transactions posted during the day balance. Once all information is balanced, the night auditor closes out the day and forwards all information to the accounting department, where an employee, known as the income auditor, verifies the sales records of the previous day.

One of the major elements of internal control over room sales is the housekeeper's daily inspection and related report. The housekeeper's inspection report indicates the status of the rooms, for example, vacant, occupied, out of order, occupied but no baggage, or baggage but not occupied. The original of this report is sent to the accounting department so that a designated person, usually the income auditor, can make a daily comparison of rooms occupied with rooms reported as sold and investigate any discrepancies. A copy of this report is sent to the front desk to use in following up on problems. A room marked occupied but no baggage may indicate that a guest left the hotel without checking out. In fully computerized systems, the housekeeper can enter the status of the room through a terminal and the computer system will generate an exception report.

The income auditor is responsible for tracing sales of the various departments in the hotel to supporting documentation. This person also compares daily room revenue with the housekeeper's daily inspection report or reviews the exception report and follows up on all exceptions. After the daily audit has been completed, the income auditor summarizes room revenue in a report, called the daily report, which is submitted to the hotel's management.

Management typically uses a number of industry operating ratios to compare results from period to period and with published data for other hotels. Following are the major room ratios generally applied:

- Average daily rate (for occupied rooms): total guest room revenue for a given period divided by number of rooms occupied, excluding complimentary rooms
- Revenue per available room: total room revenue divided by total available rooms
- Occupancy rate: number of rooms occupied divided by number of available rooms

- Percentage of double-room occupancy rate: number of guests minus rooms occupied, divided by rooms occupied

(b) Restaurant Revenue

Hotels typically use a point-of-sale computerized system to control restaurant revenue. A waitperson activates the system only with a personal code or identification card. After taking an order, the waitperson enters it into a terminal connected to printers in the kitchen and service bar. The waitperson cannot void a transaction once it has been entered into the system. To void a transaction, the manager or designated person must insert an identification card or a key into the machine. No food or drinks are dispensed to the waitperson without the printed request in the kitchen or at the service bar.

The computer assigns check numbers and keeps the check open until the bill has been settled. The guest can pay cash, use a credit card, or charge it to the room bill. The waitperson takes the payment to the restaurant's cashier, who processes the payment. This system allows for an easy check of any unsettled accounts before the waitperson leaves, and it has the capability of easily accumulating information on volume of business by waitperson and detailed breakdowns of sales by menu item. It also allows the transfer of hotel guest charges directly to the guest folio maintained at the front desk.

At the end of each day, a sales report is printed and reviewed by the restaurant manager. Information relative to guest charges is sent to the front desk to be verified by the night auditor. The reports are sent to the income auditor for review and to record the revenue; cash is sent to the general cashier and the credit card slips are sent to the accounts receivable department for processing.

The following are the major restaurant operating ratios that are used to compare results from period to period and with published operating data for other restaurants:

- Average food and beverage check: average amount spent per customer in the restaurant, calculated by dividing total food and beverage sales by number of customers served
- Combined food and beverage sales per seat: food and beverage sales divided by the number of seats
- Average daily seat turnover: number of meals served divided by number of seats in the restaurant

(c) Bar and Cocktail Lounge Revenue

The bartender usually is responsible for the bar's cashiering function. Point-of-sale machines record both cash sales and credit sales. A complex analysis of bar income is helpful and, where the technology exists, sales should be analyzed by type, such as beer, spirits, and other drinks.

Sales are recorded through the point-of-sale system, similar to that described for restaurant revenue. Cash settlements are recorded through the cash key. For guest charges, a separate bar bill is made out, signed by the guest, and, after proper verification, recorded through the credit key. The signed bill is forwarded to the front office to be posted to the guest's account. Integrated systems can post these charges directly to guests' folios. The daily closing procedures are similar to those described for restaurant revenue.

(d) Banquet and Conference Revenue

Usually, banquet and meeting space is not blocked out until a contract has been signed. Contracts should be prenumbered and contain the name of the person or organization booking the event, the price, the number of guests guaranteed, the date of the event, the deposit paid, and other contractual matters, such as penalties for cancellation.

The banquet manager prepares detailed lists of forthcoming events, including the following:

- Weekly report of functions to be held, which is used for staffing purposes
- Daily report detailing the function's location, for example, the banquet room to be used, the type of function, the number of attendees, and the manager, assistant manager, or conference planner dealing with the function
- Banquet event orders, which are sent to personnel who deal with items such as special lighting, stages, microphones, tables, and linen

A prenumbered banquet or conference instruction sheet is prepared giving the following details: description of function, number attending, menu details and prices, other services to be provided and prices, and billing details.

Banquet and conference revenue is an area where the salesperson has certain discretion as to prices. For example, if a wedding is booked on a Sunday instead of Saturday, usually a discount is given. There should be established procedures in the banquet department as to pricing and who has the authority to approve discounts. The accounting department should be sent a copy of the instruction sheet for billing purposes.

When the function is over, the banquet department determines the food and beverages consumed and forwards the information to the accounting department, along with the total number of guests and any additional charges not listed on the instruction sheet. The accounting department analyzes details as to food, beverages, room rental charges, and items that are to be treated as "paid-outs" such as band or flowers, and prepares the banquet bill. The accounting department ensures that it has received all instruction sheets by accounting for their numerical sequence and comparing the sheets with the weekly report of functions. The accounting department also ascertains that all information relating to the function has been received and correctly priced by the banquet department. The cost of food and beverages as a ratio of sales should be compared with industry statistics for similar types of facilities.

(e) Other Revenue

Hotels usually have automated telephone systems that summarize daily telephone charges incurred by each guest and post them directly to the guest's folio through a telephone switch. Telephone bills should be reviewed by the accounting department to ensure that all telephone calls have been charged to guests or administrative departments. Every few months management should check the telephone call pricing rates to make sure they are current and that the hotel is in compliance with relevant regulations.

Other revenues come from various sources, for example, laundry, valet, gift shop, other shops, golf courses, hairdresser, parking, and room service. Each of these income departments should have appropriate controls over its operations. All guest charges should be added to the guest's bill; all other revenues should be summarized and given to the income auditor to be entered onto the daily report.

43.4 SUBSTANTIVE TESTS OF REVENUES AND RECEIVABLES

Depending on the auditor's risk assessment, the following substantive tests may be used in auditing a hotel's revenue.

- Room revenue
  - Review reconciliations of rooms occupied per the front desk to the housekeeper's daily inspection report or the exception report
  - Compare the room rate charged on the guest folio with that on the guest registration and room rack for a selected number of folios
  - Trace room charges to guest folios and compare with established rates
  - Trace cash receipts to the cashier's report and the cash receipts journal
- Restaurant and bar sales
  - Compare restaurant and bar revenue per the daily reports with the recap prepared by the restaurant or bar staff
  - Trace the posting of charge sales to the guest folios
  - Trace cash sales to the cash receipts journal
- Banquet and conference revenue
  - Determine that prices quoted in contracts agree to prices in the established price list
  - Trace the function reports to the banquet control sheet
  - Trace revenue to the daily report
- Sales of minor revenue departments
  - Trace daily totals of sales to the income records and daily report
  - Trace charges to individual guest folios

In auditing revenue deductions (allowances), the auditor may:

- Determine that adjustments (credits) made to guests' accounts in connection with overcharges, disputed charges, or rate changes were properly approved

- Review supporting documentation for propriety
- Trace credit postings to individual guest folios

As previously indicated, hotels have two accounts receivable ledgers: the guest ledger, which is maintained at the front desk, and the city ledger, which is maintained in the back office. The guest ledger usually is not material in dollar amount; the auditor should review it for unusual items and reconcile entries to the control account. The credit card receivables in the city ledger should be traced to payments received. Usually they are paid within a few days of submission to the credit card company. Based on materiality of the other city ledger receivables, the auditor should consider confirming the balances.

44

Auditing Mining Companies

44.1 OVERVIEW OF THE INDUSTRY

The principal difference between hard-rock mining companies and companies involved in oil and gas producing activities relates to the nature, timing, and extent of expenditures incurred for exploration, development, production, and processing of minerals. Generally in the mining industry, a period of as long as several years elapses between the time exploration costs are incurred to discover a commercially viable body of ore and the expenditure of development costs, which are usually substantial, to complete the project. Therefore, the economic benefits derived from a project are long term in nature and subject to the uncertainties inherent in the passage of time. In contrast, the costs related to exploring for deposits of oil and gas are expended over a relatively short time.

The mining industry is highly capital intensive. Substantial investments in property, plant, and equipment are required; usually they represent more than 50 percent of a mining company's total assets. The significant capital investments of mining companies and the related risks inherent in any long-term major project may affect the recoverability of capitalized costs. The auditor should be cognizant of these factors, among others, and should assess the risk that costs will not be recovered.

The operational stages in mining companies vary somewhat depending on the type of mineral, because of differences in geological, chemical, and economic factors. The basic operations common to mining companies are exploration, development, mining, milling, beneficiation and agglomeration, smelting, refining, and solvent extraction-electrowinning.

Exploration is the search for natural accumulations of minerals with economic value. Exploration for minerals is a specialized activity involving the use of complex geophysical and geochemical equipment and procedures. There is an element of financial risk in every decision to pursue exploration, and explorers generally seek to minimize the costs and increase the probability of success. As a result, before any field work begins, extensive studies are made concerning which types of minerals are to be sought and where they are most likely to occur. Market studies and forecasts, studies of geological maps and reports, and logistical evaluations are performed to provide information for use in determining the economic feasibility of a potential project.

Exploration can be divided into two phases, prospecting and geophysical analysis. Prospecting is the search for geological information over a broad area. It embraces such activities as geological mapping, analysis of rock types and structures, searches for direct manifestations of mineralization, taking samples of minerals found, and aeromagnetic surveys. Geophysical analysis is conducted in specific areas of interest localized during the prospecting phase. Rock and soil samples are examined, and the earth's crust is monitored directly for magnetic, gravitational, sonic, radioactive, and electrical data. Based on the analysis, targets for trenching, test pits, and exploratory drilling are identified. Drilling is particularly useful in evaluating the shape and character of a deposit. Analysis of samples is necessary to determine the grade of the deposit.

Once the grade and quantity of the deposit have been determined, a decision must be made regarding the technical feasibility and commercial viability of developing the deposit for mining activity. The value of a mineral deposit is determined by the intrinsic value of the minerals present and by the nature and location of their occurrence. In addition to the grade and quantity of the ore, such factors as the physical accessibility of the deposit, the estimated costs of production, and the value of joint products and by-products are key elements in the decision to develop a deposit for commercial exploitation.

The *development* stage of production involves planning and preparing for commercial operation. Development of surface mines is relatively straightforward. For open-pit mines, which are surface mines, the principal procedure is to remove sufficient overburden to expose the ore. For strip mines, an initial cut is made to expose the mineral to be mined. For underground mines, data resulting from exploratory drilling is evaluated as a basis for planning the shafts and tunnels that will provide access to the mineral deposit. Substantial capital investment in mineral rights, machinery and equipment, and related facilities generally is required in the development stage.

The goal at the *mining* stage of production is to break up the rock and ore to the extent necessary for loading and removal to the processing location. A variety of mining techniques exist to accomplish this. The drilling and blasting technique is utilized frequently; an alternative is the continuous mining method, in which a boring or tearing machine is mounted on a forward crawler to break the material away from the rock face.

After removal from the mine site, the ore is ready for *milling*. The first phase of the milling stage involves crushing and grinding the chunks of ore to reduce them to particle size. This is performed in several steps; water generally is used in the grinding process, and the end product of this phase is a slurry, or combination of finely ground ore and water.

The second milling procedure is concentration, which involves the separation of the mineral constituents from the rock. This usually is done using separation techniques such as flotation, and leaching and precipitation. Flotation is a process in which heavy metallic substances are made to cling to the bubbles of an oily froth and rise to the surface, from which they can easily be skimmed off. This process is used primarily for concentrations of ores that contain compounds of sulfur. Since most of the metal production in the United States comes from sulfide ores, flotation is the most commonly used concentration process in this country. Flotation is used not only to separate the desired mineral from the waste rock, but also to separate different minerals from each other. Leaching and precipitation are particularly important for concentrating oxide ores. Leaching is a process of extracting the metallic compound from the ore by selectively dissolving it in a suitable solvent, such as water, sulfuric acid, or hydrochloric acid. The metal is then removed from the solution using chemical or electrochemical precipitation techniques. Heap leaching, another method for recovery of various minerals, primarily gold and silver, from low-grade ore deposits, is a significant factor in gold production. Even though the recovery of the minerals in heap leach operations is often much lower than in other processes, heap leaching is nevertheless a cost-effective process.

Beneficiation and agglomeration relate to ferrous (iron) mining. Beneficiation is the dressing or processing of ore for the purpose of regulating the size of the desired product, removing unwanted constituents, and improving the quality, purity, or assay grade of the ore. Beneficiation techniques include crushing, screening, and washing, and also involve the use of gravity, magnetic, and flotation methods. Small particles of iron ore generally are subjected to an additional process called agglomeration. Agglomeration is a process in which the beneficiated particles are fused together into larger bits or pellets that are easier to handle.

Smelting is the process of separating the metal from impurities with which it may be chemically bound or physically mixed too closely to be removed by concentration. Most smelting is accomplished through fusion, which is the liquefaction of a metal under heat. In some cases, chemical processes are used instead of, or in combination with, heating techniques. Since metals occur in a variety of combinations with other elements, the smelting technique utilized depends on the characteristics of the concentrate. The principal phases of the smelting process include roasting, "true" smelting, and converting. Roasting is a heating process used primarily for sulfide ores as a means of driving out the sulfur. "True" smelting is the process of separating the metal from its chemical bonds by melting. Converting entails blowing oxygen-enriched air through molten metal, causing oxidation and removal of sulfur and other impurities from the metal.

Refining is the last step in isolating the metal. The primary methods utilized are fire refining and electrolytic refining. Fire refining is similar to smelting. The metal is kept in a molten state and treated with pine logs, hydrocarbon gas, or other substances to enable impurities to be removed. Fire refining generally does not allow the recovery of by-products. Electrolytic refining uses an electrical current to separate metals from a solution in such a way that by-products can be recovered. In electrolytic refining of copper, plates of impure copper (anodes) are suspended between thin plates of pure copper (cathodes), and both are then submerged in a solution of copper sulfate and sulfuric acid. When an electrical current is passed through the solution, pure copper from the anodes is deposited on the cathodes. Gold and silver are important by-products of the electrolytic refining of copper.

Solvent extraction-electrowinning (SX-EW) is a method often used in processing oxide ore, a less common type of ore found in the United States. The SX-EW process involves extracting metal from mined ore through leaching and then removing it from the solvent using electrochemical refining techniques. The final product of the SX-EW process is refined metal.

While almost all businesses face increased legislation and prosecution relating to environmental violations, mining companies, because of the nature of their operations, are particularly vulnerable to environmental liabilities. As a result, the area of contingent liabilities often is a focal point in the audit of a mining company. Two federal laws provide the primary basis for regulation of hazardous waste disposal and cleanup. They are the Resource Conservation and Recovery Act of 1976, referred to as RCRA, and the Comprehensive Environmental Response, Compensation and Liability Act of 1980, referred to as CERCLA and also known as Superfund. Both laws, which are administered by the Environmental Protection Agency (EPA) and by similar state agencies, established regulatory controls over the generation, transportation, and disposal of hazardous wastes.

Statement of Position (SOP) 96-1, *Environmental Remediation Liabilities*, provides accounting guidance for cleanup costs incurred under Superfund and other pollution control laws and regulations. SOP 96-1 is particularly relevant to auditing a mining company's accounting for and disclosure of environmental liabilities. It requires environmental remediation liabilities to be accrued when the criteria of Statement of Financial Accounting Standards (SFAS) No. 5, *Accounting for Contingencies*, are met, and includes benchmarks to aid in determining when such liabilities should be recognized. It provides guidance on the recognition, measurement, display, and disclosure of environmental remediation liabilities. The SOP also includes a nonauthoritative section on pollution control and environmental remediation liability laws and regulations.

The SOP provides guidance only on accounting for and auditing environmental *remediation* liabilities; it does not provide guidance on accounting for pollution control costs with respect to current operations, for costs of future site restoration or closure that are required upon the cessation of operations or sale of facilities, or for environmental remediation undertaken at the sole discretion of management. Also, it does not provide guidance on recognizing liabilities of insurance companies for unpaid environmental cleanup-related claims or address asset impairment issues.

44.2 ACCOUNTING PRINCIPLES AND PRACTICES

Accounting and reporting issues in the mining industry are discussed in AICPA Accounting Research Study No. 11, *Financial Reporting in the Extractive Industries* (1969). In 1976, the Financial Accounting Standards Board (FASB) issued a discussion memorandum, *Financial Accounting and Reporting in the Extractive Industries*, which analyzed issues relevant to the extractive industries. Neither of these attempts, however, culminated in the issuance of an authoritative pronouncement for mining companies. At present, therefore, the accounting practices prevalent among mining companies are the principal source of generally accepted accounting practices for the industry.

Exploration and development costs are major expenditures of mining companies, and auditors of such companies should have an understanding of the activities involved in those processes and the related accounting principles. The characterization of expenditures as either exploration, development, or production usually determines whether they are capitalized or expensed. For accounting purposes, it is useful to identify five basic phases of exploration and development: prospecting, property acquisition, geophysical analysis, development before production, and development during production.

(a) Exploration Costs

Prospecting usually begins with obtaining (or preparing) and studying topographical and geological maps. Prospecting costs, which generally are expensed as incurred, include options to lease or buy property; rights of access to lands for geophysical work; and salaries, equipment, and supplies for scouts, geologists, and geophysical crews.

Property acquisition includes both the purchase of property and the purchase or lease of mineral rights. Costs incurred to purchase property are capitalized; costs attributable to the purchase or lease of mineral rights are expensed as incurred until a commercial body of ore is identified, or they are deferred until it is determined whether a project is commercially feasible. Acquisition costs may include lease bonus and lease extension costs, lease brokers' commissions, abstract and recording fees, filing and patent fees and other legal expenses, and costs of land and lease departments.

Geophysical analysis is performed to discover specific deposits of minerals. Most companies expense the related costs (commonly referred to simply as exploration costs) as incurred. As indicated below, geophysical analysis costs incurred in the development stage of a project, once a commercially viable ore body has been established, are capitalized, along with other development costs.

(b) Development Costs

A body of ore reaches the development stage when the decision has been made to develop it for mining. Development costs include expenditures associated with drilling, removing overburden (waste rock), sinking shafts, driving tunnels, building roads and dikes, purchasing primary cleaning or processing equipment and equipment used in developing the mine, and constructing supporting facilities to house and care for the work force. In many respects, the expenditures in the development stage are similar to those incurred during exploration. As a result, it is sometimes difficult to distinguish the point at which exploration ends and development begins. For example, the sinking of shafts and driving of tunnels may begin in the exploration stage and continue into the development stage. In most instances, the transition from the exploration to the development stage is the same for both accounting and tax purposes.

Generally, all costs incurred during the development stage before production starts are capitalized; usually they are reduced by the proceeds from the sale of any production during the development period. Development ore (ore extracted in the process of gaining access to the body of ore) is normally incidental to the development process.

Development also takes place during the production stage. The accounting treatment of development costs incurred during the ongoing operation of a mine depends on the nature and purpose of the expenditures. Costs associated with expansion of capacity generally are capitalized; costs incurred to maintain production normally are included in production costs in the period in which they are incurred. In certain instances, the benefits of development activity will be realized in future periods, such as when the "block caving" and open-pit mining methods are used. In the block caving method, entire sections of a body of ore are collapsed intentionally to permit the mass removal of minerals; extraction may take place two to three years after access to the ore is gained and the block prepared. In an open-pit mine, there is typically an expected ratio of overburden to mineral-bearing ore over the life of the mine. The cost of stripping the overburden to gain access to the ore is expensed in those periods in which the actual ratio of overburden to ore approximates the expected ratio. In certain instances, however, extensive stripping is performed to remove the overburden in advance of the period in which the ore will be extracted. When the benefits of either development activity are to be realized in a future accounting period, the costs associated with the development activity should be deferred and amortized during the period in which the ore is extracted or the product produced. As discussed below, those assets should be reviewed for impairment whenever events or changes in circumstances indicate that the carrying amounts may not be recoverable.

(c) Determining the Start of the Production Phase

Determining when the production phase begins is important for accounting purposes because, in general, at that time development costs are no longer capitalized and revenue from the sale of ore is included in sales revenue rather than as a reduction of capitalized development costs. The point at which production is considered to begin is sometimes stipulated in loan agreements and may initiate debt payments. Determining the commencement of production is also significant for federal income tax purposes. The point at which a mine is considered to begin production is generally the same for both accounting and tax purposes.

SFAS No. 7, *Accounting and Reporting by Development Stage Enterprises* (Accounting Standards Section De4), states that "an enterprise shall be considered to be in the development stage if it is devoting substantially all of its efforts to establishing a new business" and "the planned principal operations have not commenced" or they "have commenced, but there has been no significant revenue therefrom." Although SFAS No. 7 specifically excludes mining companies from its application, the definition of a development stage enterprise may be helpful in defining the point at which a mine is considered to be in the production phase.

Mining companies usually follow one of three assumptions as to when the production phase begins.

1. When the value of the ore extracted is greater than the cost of extraction and milling
2. When both the mine and the mill produce on a regularly scheduled basis at the planned activity levels
3. When ore is extracted on a regular basis without regard to the milling capability

When the mine begins production, the capitalized property costs are recognized as costs of production through their amortization, generally on the unit-of-production method, over the expected productive life of the mine.

It is generally preferable to expense as incurred start-up costs of mill facilities, smelters, and refineries. Start-up costs are defined as costs incurred after operations have begun but before the facilities have reached anticipated productive capacity and an economically viable level of commercial production.

44.3 RISK FACTORS AND AUDIT REACTION

(a) Inherent Risks

Among the inherent risk factors in the mining industry are the very long time it generally takes to bring a mine from the exploration and development stages to the commercially viable production stage, the capital intensity of the industry, the significant use of riskier forms of capital—debt financing and joint ventures—to finance new projects, and financial pressures on the industry from various sources. From an audit standpoint, those risk factors may have an effect on the recoverability of capitalized costs carried on the balance sheet at large dollar amounts.

Auditing mining companies requires the auditor to evaluate many types of management judgments for which it is usually extremely difficult to obtain "hard" data. For example, for purposes of both auditing cost accumulations and their allocation to current production and assessing the recoverability of highly material capitalized costs through production and sales, the auditor must evaluate (1) the reasonableness of management judgments about proved and probable mineral reserves, (2) the metal content of those reserves, (3) estimated future production costs, (4) estimated future metal prices, (5) the lives of mining properties and equipment with economic lives and values that are determined largely by those prices, and (6) the dates when a mine passes from the exploration stage to the development stage and then to the production stage. These management judgments have a pervasive effect on the financial statements of mining companies. For example, as discussed later, the estimate of mineral reserves affects balances in the property, plant, and equipment accounts as well as the product inventory and cost of sales accounts.

SFAS No. 121, *Accounting for the Impairment of Long-Lived Assets and for Long-Lived Assets to Be Disposed Of* (Accounting Standards Section I08), requires that long-lived assets (for example, plant and equipment and capitalized development costs) and identifiable intangibles that are to be held and used by an entity be reviewed for impairment whenever events or changes in circumstances indicate that the carrying amounts may not be recoverable. Changes in circumstances that are common in the mining industry could include, among other things, declining metal prices, increasing environmental and operating costs, and reduced recoveries from mineral reserves.

If such indicators are present, the entity is required to estimate the future cash flows expected to result from the use of the assets and their eventual disposition. If the sum of the expected future cash flows (undiscounted and without interest charges) is less than the carrying amounts of the assets, the entity should recognize an impairment loss. If it is determined that an impairment loss must be recognized, the loss is measured by the excess of the asset's carrying amount over its fair value, or discounted cash flows if fair value is not available. After an impairment has been recognized, the reduced amount is the asset's new cost. Restoration of previously recognized impairment losses is prohibited.

Another area in which the auditor must evaluate management judgments in the absence of relatively reliable audit evidence involves a decision by management to shut down operations. Volatile metal prices may make active operations uneconomical from time to time, and, as a result, mining companies will shut down operations, either temporarily or permanently. A significant concern of the auditor when operations are temporarily shut down is the carrying value of the related assets. If a long-term diminution in the value of the assets has occurred, a write-down of the carrying value to fair value should be recorded. This decision is extremely judgmental and depends on projections of whether viable mining operations can ever be resumed.

Those projections are based on significant assumptions as to prices, production quantities, and costs; because most minerals are worldwide commodities, the projections must take into account global supply and demand factors. The auditor can corroborate management's assumptions as to prices by using independent price projections; assumptions relating to production quantities can be evaluated by comparing historical metal recoveries with projections and overall mine capacity; and cost assumptions can be evaluated based on historical and projected inflation rates and cost increases. A temporary shutdown of a mining company's facility may raise questions as to whether the company can continue as a going concern, and it may be necessary for the auditor to include an explanatory paragraph in the audit report, particularly if the facility represents a major part of the company's assets.

Valuation of product inventory also is affected by worldwide imbalances between supply and demand for certain metals. Companies sometimes produce larger quantities of a metal than can be absorbed by the market. In that situation, management may have to write the inventory down to its net realizable value; determining that value, however, may be difficult if there is no established market or only a thin market for the particular metal. The auditor should evaluate management's judgments about the value of its inventory. Furthermore, the valuation of the company's property, plant, and equipment accounts may be affected if imbalances persist for a long time.

Collectibility of receivables traditionally has not been a major concern in the industry, since sales historically have been to customers who are relatively strong financially. However, economic conditions are not static, and the auditor must be cognizant of the company's customers and the industries in which they operate. For instance, suppliers of copper may experience declining demand from end users in the construction industry who are negatively affected by a slump in residential and commercial real estate markets. In that economic environment, collectibility of receivables may become a troubling issue. Confronted with long-outstanding balances, the auditor should determine the extent (if any) to which assets have been impaired.

Additionally, in light of SFAS No. 105, *Disclosure of Information about Financial Instruments with Off-Balance-Sheet Risk and Financial Instruments with Concentrations of Credit Risk* (Accounting Standards Section F25), the auditor should determine the extent to which group concentrations of credit risk exist. SFAS No. 105 states that "group concentrations of credit risk exist if a number of counterparties are engaged in similar activities and have similar characteristics that would cause their ability to meet contractual obligations to be similarly affected by changes in economic or other conditions." In other words, concentrations of credit risk may exist where a producer sells a product (e.g., copper) to a small number of large customers who operate in one industry (e.g., construction). In situations where concentrations of credit risk exist, the auditor should ensure that the disclosure requirements of SFAS No. 105 are met.

Other risks unique to the mining industry relate to a company's compliance with governmental and other requirements concerning toxic waste, reclamation, and a wide range of other environmental matters such as land destruction and air and water pollution. Mining companies also are subject to regulations concerning occupational hazards to the health of their employees and public health considerations. The auditor should evaluate a mining company's potential legal exposure arising from failure to meet those requirements, compliance with required disclosures, and the impact of any noncompliance on the audit opinion. Typically, these matters are addressed in letters from the company's attorneys.

(b) Audit Strategy

In planning the audit of a mining company, occasionally the auditor may decide to use the services of surveyors, engineers, geologists, or other specialists that are independent of the company. The auditor also should be aware, in the planning stage, of the unusual difficulties often associated with physical counts of mineral products and metals, particularly considerations relating to the form or shape in which the inventory is stored and to determining the metal content of minerals in the various stages of production. Another consideration that is unique to the mining industry is the need to evaluate certain computations made for income tax purposes on the basis of individual mining properties, as discussed later in the chapter.

The audit strategy for mature mining companies generally calls for tests of controls and early substantive testing. Established mining companies usually have effective controls in all transaction cycles, and the auditor typically is able to obtain the evidence necessary to assess control risk at low. Controls to safeguard inventories of precious metals, while typically very effective, are particularly important to the auditor's assessment of control risk. For some accounts, the only substantive tests performed may be analytical procedures.

The expenditure cycle is particularly significant in the mining industry; each year management attempts to determine, based on market and other factors, its year-end inventory position. The audit strategy may depend largely on the inventory level expected at year-end and the company's method of costing inventory. If a company uses the last-in, first-out method and an inventory buildup is not expected, the auditor is not likely to encounter inventory costing problems. On the other hand, if a company uses another costing method or if an inventory buildup is expected, as may happen during an economic downturn, the risk of misstatement in costing out the inventory will likely increase and the auditor may plan to perform detailed substantive tests of inventory balances.

Management of new mining companies, often called "venture mining companies," is generally not as control conscious as management of mature companies. For venture mining companies, the auditor usually performs detailed substantive tests of account balances, with emphasis on capitalized costs, which typically represent a large proportion of a venture company's assets.

Audit strategy decisions are further affected by the degree of vertical integration of a company's operations. Companies that are not vertically integrated generally sell to only a few large customers; consequently, receivables can be substantively tested efficiently. In general, the greater the degree of vertical integration, the more likely the auditor is to plan to perform tests of controls, because of the larger number of individual transactions and customers.

While the usual materiality considerations apply to the mining industry, the auditor should note that the property, plant, and equipment accounts are likely to be relatively more significant than they are in many commercial and industrial entities because of the capital intensity of the industry. As explained later in this chapter, the auditor also is likely to find large materials and supplies inventories. Both of those areas may require audit attention beyond what is usual in other entities.

44.4 TYPICAL TRANSACTIONS, CONTROLS, AND AUDIT TESTS

(a) Revenue Cycle

Depending on the degree of vertical integration, mining companies may derive revenue from sales of minerals in the form of ore, concentrate, or finished metal; tolling; royalties; or mineral property conveyances. A company also may have gains and losses from commodity futures transactions.

(i) Sales of Minerals. Generally, minerals are not sold in the raw-ore stage because of the insignificant quantity of minerals relative to the total volume of waste rock. (There are, however, some exceptions, such as iron ore and coal.) The ore usually is milled at or near the mine site to produce a concentrate containing a significantly higher percentage of mineral content. For example, the metal content of copper concentrate typically is 25 to 30 percent, as opposed to between one-half and 1 percent for the raw ore. The concentrate frequently is sold to other processors; occasionally, mining companies exchange concentrate to reduce transportation costs. After the refining process, metallic minerals may be sold as finished metals, either in the form of products for remelting by final users (e.g., pig iron or cathode copper) or as finished products (e.g., copper rod or aluminum foil).

Sales of raw ore and concentrate entail determining metal content based initially on estimated weights, moisture content, and ore grade. Those estimates subsequently are revised, based on the actual metal content recovered from the raw ore or concentrate, if settlement is based on actual recoveries. Estimates generally are made by both the seller and the buyer; the difference is usually split, but sometimes an "umpire" is required to determine the metal content sold.

Sales prices often are based on the market price on a commodity exchange such as the COMEX (New York Commodity Exchange) or LME (London Metal Exchange) at the time of delivery. Sometimes a time other than delivery is used to set the price; for example, the average of daily COMEX prices for the two-week period subsequent to delivery of the minerals could be used. In those circumstances, it might be necessary to record revenue based on an estimate of the total sales value of the shipment at the point of sale and adjust the amount when the sales price has been determined.

If the planned audit strategy calls for tests of controls in a mining company's revenue cycle, the tests are similar for the most part to those performed in other industries. As noted earlier, some companies may sell to a small number of large customers; in that event, accounts receivable are easily tested using only substantive tests.

(ii) Tolling. Companies with smelters and refineries also may realize revenue from tolling, which is the processing of metal-bearing materials of other mining companies for a fee. The fee is based on numerous factors, including the weight and metal content of the materials processed. Normally, the processed minerals are returned to the original producer for subsequent sale. To supplement the recovery of fixed costs, companies with smelters and refineries frequently enter into tolling agreements when they have excess capacity.

(iii) Royalties. For a variety of reasons, companies may not wish to mine certain properties that they own. Mineral royalty agreements may be entered into that provide for royalties based on a percentage of the total value of the mineral or of gross revenue, to be paid when the minerals extracted from the property are sold.

(iv) Mineral Property Conveyances. A mining company also may enter into arrangements, often as a means of obtaining financing, to convey a portion of its mineral reserves to others. In addition to the more usual forms of conveyances (joint ventures—both incorporated and unincorporated—outright sales, and partnerships), these conveyances take the form of, for example, sales of minerals-in-place (i.e., in the ground), sales of fractional interests in undeveloped mining properties, conveyances with the right of return after a specified period (which are usually termed sales, but are accounted for as leases), bullion loans (loans that will be repaid from the proceeds of sales of gold), and any number of other possible combinations. The auditor should analyze such transactions carefully to determine their economic substance for purposes of evaluating the revenue recognition principles applied by the company.

(v) Recognizing Revenues.   Generally, revenue should be recognized only when all of the following conditions have been met:

- The product has been shipped and is no longer under physical control of the seller (and title to the product and the risk of ownership have already passed to the buyer).
- The quantity and quality of the product can be determined with reasonable accuracy.
- The selling price can be determined with reasonable accuracy.

Mining companies often encounter problems with the last two conditions because final quantities and prices may not be established at the time of delivery. Provisional invoices commonly are recorded using estimated quantities and prices that are adjusted when details of the deliveries are finalized. The auditor can ascertain that estimated quantities and prices are reasonable by comparing final invoices with the provisional invoices, paying particular attention to the trend of revisions.

(vi) Commodity Futures Transactions.   Mining companies usually have significant inventories of commodities that are traded in worldwide markets, and frequently enter into long-term forward sales contracts specifying sales prices based on market prices at time of delivery. To protect themselves from the risk of loss that could result from price declines, mining companies often "hedge" against price changes by entering into commodities-based futures, forwards, swaps, and option contracts. Companies sell contracts when they expect selling prices to decline or are satisfied with the current price and want to "lock in" the profit (or loss) on the sale of their inventory. To establish a hedge when it has or expects to have a commodity (e.g., copper) in inventory, a company sells a contract that commits it to deliver that commodity in the future at a fixed price. The company usually closes out the futures position before the delivery date by buying the contract back at the current market price.

As an example of a hedging transaction, assume the following facts:

- A mining company enters into a forward sales contract with a customer on March 14 to deliver 20,000 pounds of copper on June 3 of the same year at the COMEX spot market price per pound at that time.
- The company's cost to produce is 69 cents a pound, which is not expected to change.
- On March 14, the COMEX copper price for June delivery is 75 cents a pound.
- On June 3, when delivery on the sales contract is due, the COMEX spot price for June delivery is 65 cents a pound.

If the company wants to "lock in" its profit of 6 cents per pound (the 75-cent price on March 14 for June delivery minus the 69-cent production cost), it will hedge the sale. To do so, on March 14, the company enters into a June futures contract on the COMEX to sell 20,000 pounds of copper at 75 cents a pound. In June, the company will offset its position by buying a futures contract for 20,000 pounds on the COMEX at 65 cents a pound. In so doing, the company will realize a profit of 10 cents a pound on closing out the futures contract and a loss of 4 cents a pound (the 69-cent production cost less the 65-cent selling price) on the sales contract. By hedging the sales commitment, the company has locked in the profit of 6 cents a pound that was determinable on March 14, regardless of whether the price of copper for June delivery rises or falls between March 14 and June 3.

The accounting for commodity futures contracts depends on whether the contract qualifies as a hedge under SFAS No. 80, *Accounting for Futures Contracts* (Accounting Standards Section F80). For transactions that are hedged by the use of derivatives, SFAS No. 119, *Disclosure about Derivative Financial Instruments and Fair Value of Financial Instruments* (Accounting Standards Section F25), requires specific disclosures of derivative financial instruments, including those accounted for as hedges of anticipated transactions. To ensure that commodity futures and similar transactions are accounted for and disclosed in the financial statements appropriately, the auditor should understand the mining company's trading philosophy and internal control relating to hedging and derivatives trading. Controls include overall authorization, often by the board of directors, of the maximum hedged and risk positions, periodic reconciliations of positions, and confirmation of open positions. The auditor should understand, and in some situations may test, the company's controls for authorizing, processing, and recording trades and should determine that the inventory of open positions is adequately maintained and that adequate segregation of duties exists. Accounting Research Bulletin No. 43, Chapter 4 (Accounting Standards Section I78), requires the company to consider whether a write-down of inventory to lower of cost or market is necessary.

(b) Expenditure Cycle

The audit strategy for the expenditure cycle often calls for tests of controls as a basis for restricting substantive tests. Tests of controls usually are performed for payroll accounts in the mining industry and often are performed for purchases of materials and supplies, especially if the auditor expects inventory levels to be material at year-end. If purchase costs are expected to flow through to cost of sales by year-end, the auditor may perform a combination of analytical procedures of cost of sales and detailed substantive tests of the related quantities instead of performing tests of controls.

(i) Exploration and Development Costs.   Exploration and development activities and accounting for costs associated with them were discussed earlier. This section of the chapter covers controls and both tests of controls and substantive tests for exploration and development activities.

The auditor should determine whether the mining company has controls over acquiring exploration rights and maintaining title or mining rights to properties being explored. The auditor should review the company's procedures for accumulating exploration expenditures and allocating them to various properties, to determine that costs related to properties that have not demonstrated economically recoverable ore have not been capitalized or inappropriately allocated to other properties.

Additional auditing procedures may include reviewing management, engineering, and geological reports to establish that properties identified as successful are in fact successful. The auditor might want to discuss the company's accounting policy with its engineering and geological experts to make them aware of the policy and its ramifications. This may be helpful in determining whether accounting personnel receive the expert information necessary to implement the policy. As with any accounting policy, the auditor should determine whether the policy is applied consistently from period to period.

The auditor should understand the company's controls for accumulating and allocating development costs. Since the generally accepted practice is to capitalize all development costs related to a mining property, it is important for the auditor to examine evidence corroborating the identification of expenditures as development expenditures. Because similar expenditures may be classified as either exploration or development, the company should have procedures in place to ensure proper classification. For example, drilling costs usually must be apportioned among exploration, development, and production activities; this may be accomplished on the basis of feet drilled or hours of drill use. The auditor should review the bases of allocation and determine that they are appropriate.

For each project in which the company is involved, its engineering and geological staff generally develops a mine plan detailing the projected costs and revenues. The plan should reflect the input of industry experts and economists regarding the economic viability of the project. The auditor should review the plan to evaluate management's judgment about the economic viability of the project. Discussions should be held with senior management about its intention to continue to expend amounts for the project and ultimately to begin production. Significant projects should be subject to the board of directors' approval; the auditor should review the approval and also should evaluate the company's ability to obtain necessary financing for the project. Although these procedures are performed initially when a company begins capitalizing costs, annual updates are usually necessary to evaluate the carrying value of the costs.

The auditor should be aware of important decisions that affect accounting policies at the time a new mine makes the transition from the development stage to the production stage. Among them are the accounting treatment of ore processed during the development stage (development ore) and costs incurred to bring mill facilities, smelters, and refineries to commercial levels of production (start-up costs). The proceeds from the sale of development ore sold before completion of the development stage normally are credited against capitalized development expenditures. The auditor should review the company's procedures for identifying such proceeds to ensure that they are recorded properly. If the company's policy is to inventory development ore and record sales proceeds as sales, the auditor should review the company's procedures for identifying, controlling, and taking inventory of development ore quantities and related costs. Companies often capitalize costs incurred in excess of normal costs as development costs; in that event, the auditor should review the basis for determining normal costs to ensure that both production costs and development costs are stated properly.

(ii) Inventory. A mining company's inventory generally has two major components—metals and minerals, and materials and supplies that are used in mining operations.

(1) Metals and Minerals. Metal and mineral inventories usually comprise broken ore; crushed ore; concentrate; materials in process at concentrators, smelters, and refineries; metal; and joint and by-products. The usual practice of mining companies is not to recognize metal inventories for financial reporting purposes before the concentrate stage, that is, until the majority of the nonmineralized material has been removed from the ore. Thus, ore is not included in inventory until it has been processed through the concentrator and is ready for delivery to the smelter. This practice evolved because the amounts of broken ore before the concentrating process ordinarily are relatively small, and consequently the cost of that ore and of concentrate in process generally is not significant. Furthermore, the amount of broken ore and concentrate in process is relatively constant at the end of each month, and the concentrating process is quite rapid—usually a matter of hours. Companies that have significant quantities of broken ore that is measurable and quantifiable as to metal content often defer the costs of extracting the ore and expense them as the final product is produced. In the case of leach operations, generally the mineral content of the ore is estimated and costs are inventoried. Practice varies, however, and some companies do not inventory costs until the leached product is introduced into the electrochemical refinery cells.

Determining inventory quantities during the production process is often difficult. Broken ore, crushed ore, concentrate, and materials in process may be stored in various ways or enclosed in vessels or pipes. The auditor should consider the dimensions of piles or containers, density of the material, moisture content, and assay factors, and should ensure that measurement methods are applied consistently from period to period. The auditor also should review the various engineering formulas used, to determine that they are reasonable and comparable between periods. If production inventories are taken by surveying techniques, such as piles of concentrate, the auditor should observe the surveying as it occurs. In some circumstances, the auditor may want to discuss the surveying techniques with company personnel or to consider using the services of an independent surveyor. Quantities of production inventories on hand in enclosed vessels, pipes, or tanks should be compared with capacity factors of the various containers. Density, moisture, and assay factors should be examined for reasonableness and comparability between periods. The auditor may collect samples and have them tested for the various factors by an independent laboratory; in most circumstances, however, the mining company's laboratories may be used provided the source of the samples is not identified.

Examining the metallurgical balances reconciliation, which is prepared periodically by the company's technical staff, is a useful auditing procedure. That reconciliation may be performed for both ore and concentrate quantities; it reconciles opening amounts on hand to ending balances by accounting for additions and reductions during the period.

Processed metal is generally easier to measure than broken ore and concentrate because it is substantially uniform in purity and is cast into specific shapes and forms. The auditor should observe the counting or weighing of amounts on hand and also may want to obtain independent assays. In addition, the auditor should determine that the company has adequate procedures to ensure that scales are calibrated periodically, since it is seldom practicable for the auditor to test the accuracy of the scales independently.

With few exceptions, mining companies carry metal inventory at the lower of cost—determined on a last-in, first-out, first-in, first-out, or average basis—or market. Occasionally, mining companies value inventories of precious metals in finished and salable form at net realizable value, which approximates market but exceeds cost. Although this policy is acceptable, it rarely is applied, and then only if there is an assured market at quoted prices.

Product costs for mining companies usually reflect all normal and necessary expenditures associated with cost centers such as mines, concentrators, smelters, and refineries. Inventory costs comprise not only direct costs of production, but also an allocation of overhead, including mine and other plant administrative expenses. Depreciation, depletion, and amortization of capitalized exploration, acquisition, and development costs also should be included in inventory.

When production inventories are in the form of ore or concentrate, a primary audit concern with respect to valuation is determining the metal content of such inventories. The company normally has procedures in place to monitor the percentage recovery, assay, and moisture content factors used. The auditor should be satisfied that those factors are reasonable and consistent with current expectations of the company and independent assayers. Actual settlement assays agreed to by the seller and buyer during the year may provide evidence that current estimates are either reasonable or unreasonable. In the latter instance, the auditor may consider it appropriate to seek independent corroborative evidence.

If a company engages in tolling (described earlier), it may have significant production inventories on hand that belong to other mining companies. Usually, it is not possible to physically segregate inventories owned by others from similar inventories owned by the company. Memorandum records of tolling inventories should be maintained and reconciled periodically to physical counts. The auditor should review the reconciliations and ascertain that differences have been resolved satisfactorily.

(2) Materials and Supplies.   Materials and supplies usually constitute a substantial portion of the inventory of most mining companies, sometimes exceeding the value of metal inventories. This is because a lack of supplies or spare parts could cause the curtailment of operations. In addition to normal operating supplies, materials and supplies inventories often include such items as fuel and spare parts for trucks, locomotives, and other machinery. Occasionally, because of the significance of the cost of certain spare parts and the need to have them on hand to ensure the uninterrupted operation of production equipment, mining companies capitalize spare parts and treat them as equipment (accounting for them as "emergency spare parts" or "insurance spares") rather than inventory. These emergency spare parts are depreciated over the same period as the equipment with which they are associated. Most mining companies use perpetual inventory systems to account for materials and supplies because of their high unit value.

The auditor should understand the company's procedures for ordering, purchasing, issuing, and counting materials and supplies inventories. Because of the value of these parts, mining companies commonly have comprehensive cycle count procedures, the results of which are summarized and reported to upper-level operating management for scrutiny and review. The auditor should observe the cycle count procedures, perform test counts, and ascertain that book–physical differences are resolved and unusual trends and variations are adequately explained.

Materials and supplies inventories normally are valued at cost minus a reserve for surplus items and obsolescence. The auditor should understand the company's procedures for identifying surplus and obsolete items, parts for equipment that is no longer in use, and damaged or deteriorated items, and should obtain satisfaction that those procedures are operating as prescribed.

(iii) Property, Plant, and Equipment.   Because mining companies are capital intensive, the auditor should be particularly concerned with the controls over authorizing and recording capital expenditures. Auditing procedures in this area do not differ from those used in other industries; however, the importance of the controls may be greater because of the volume and high dollar value of transactions.

When operations are temporarily shut down, the related facilities usually are placed in a "standby mode" that provides for care and maintenance so that the assets will be retained in a reasonable condition that will facilitate resumption of operations. Care and maintenance costs usually are recorded as expenses in the period in which they are incurred. Examples of typical care and maintenance costs are security, preventive and protective maintenance, and depreciation.

(iv) Expenses.   Three expense accounts—depreciation, depletion and amortization, and royalties—are discussed in the following paragraphs because they ordinarily are significant to companies that engage in mining operations.

(1) Depreciation.   The principal difference between computing depreciation in the mining industry and in other industries is that useful lives of assets that are not readily movable from a mine site must not exceed the estimated life of the mine, which in turn is based on the remaining economically recoverable ore reserves. In some instances, this may require depreciating certain mining equipment over a period that is shorter than its physical life.

Depreciation charges are significant because of the highly capital-intensive nature of the industry. Moreover, those charges are affected by numerous factors, such as the physical environment, revisions of recoverable ore estimates, environmental regulations, and improved technology. Thus, the auditor should critically review the depreciation rates used for the various categories of fixed assets. The point at which depreciation begins is also of concern to the auditor; the appropriateness of dates selected should be evaluated. In many instances, depreciation charges on similar equipment with different intended uses may begin at different times. For example, depreciation of equipment used for exploration purposes may begin when it is purchased and use has begun, while depreciation of milling equipment may not begin until a certain level of commercial production has been attained.

(2) Depletion and Amortization.   Depletion of property acquisition, exploration, and development costs related to a body of ore is calculated in a manner similar to the

unit-of-production method of depreciation. The cost of the body of ore is divided by the estimated quantity of ore reserves or units of metal or mineral to arrive at a depletion charge per unit. The unit charge is multiplied by the number of units extracted to arrive at the depletion charge for the period. This computation requires a current estimate of economically recoverable mineral reserves at the end of the period; the auditor should be satisfied with this estimate.

It is often appropriate for different depletion calculations to be made for different types of capitalized exploration and development expenditures. The auditor should evaluate the categories utilized and determine their appropriateness. For instance, one factor to be considered is whether capitalized costs relate to gaining access to the total economically recoverable ore reserves of the mine or only to specific portions.

Usually, estimated quantities of economically recoverable mineral reserves are the basis for computing depletion and amortization under the unit-of-production method. Therefore, the auditor should be satisfied that the ore reserve information is computed properly, which requires that the ore reserve unit and ore reserve base be determined. The choice of the reserve unit is not a problem if there is only one product; if, however, as in many extractive operations, several products are recovered, a decision must be made whether to measure production on the basis of the major product or on the basis of an aggregation of all products. Generally, the reserve base is the company's total proved and probable ore reserve quantities; it is determined by specialists, such as geologists or mining engineers. Proved and probable reserves typically are used as the reserve base because of the degree of uncertainty surrounding estimates of possible reserves. The imprecise nature of reserve estimates makes it inevitable that the reserve base will be revised over time as additional data becomes available. Changes in the reserve base should be treated as changes in accounting estimates in accordance with Accounting Principles Board Opinion No. 20, *Accounting Changes* (Accounting Standards Section A06), and accounted for prospectively.

Under generally accepted auditing standards, the auditor may use the work of specialists in examining matters that are potentially material to the financial statements and that require special knowledge in areas other than accounting and auditing. Reviewing ore reserve data for purposes of calculating depreciation and depletion is a primary example of a circumstance in which the auditor may use estimates of ore reserve quantities provided by experts, such as geologists or mining engineers. Statement on Auditing Standards No. 73, *Using the Work of a Specialist* (AU Section 336), discusses the auditor's responsibilities and required procedures when using the work of a specialist.

(3) Royalties.   Because royalties commonly are a significant expense to a mining company, the auditor should substantiate periodic payments by reference to underlying royalty agreements and should agree quantities and values to recorded amounts. The auditor also should ensure that royalty costs based on production are included in production costs for purposes of valuing the inventory.

(v) Liabilities.   Mining companies usually are subject to various types of mineral taxes that must be accrued, including ad valorem, production, and gross proceeds taxes. In addition, as a result of environmental considerations, mining companies may incur significant costs for restoration, reclamation, and rehabilitation of mining facilities after the mining process has been completed. Those costs should be accrued during the revenue-producing period. As noted earlier, SOP 96-1, *Environmental Remediation Liabilities*, requires environmental remediation liabilities to be accrued when the criteria of SFAS No. 5, *Accounting for Contingencies*, are met.

The auditor should review the accruals for restoration, reclamation, rehabilitation, and remediation and ensure that estimated costs are reasonable and consistent with current expectations. Reading lease agreements and discussions with lawyers concerning environmental requirements, discussed earlier, may disclose the need for additional accruals.

(c)   Risks and Uncertainties

As indicated earlier, because of the nature of their operations, the financial statements of mining companies include account balances that reflect the use of many estimates that are subject to material change. SOP 94-6, *Disclosure of Certain Significant Risks and Uncertainties*, requires that the risks and uncertainties associated with estimating environmental reclamation and remediation liabilities, recoverability of long-lived assets, reserves, gold price and operating cost factors, unit-of-production depreciation rates, and inventories be disclosed in the financial statements if it is at least reasonably possible that the estimate will materially change over the next year. The auditor should ensure that all significant estimates are identified and evaluated by management as to risks and uncertainties involved.

(d)   Income Taxes

The most significant differences between financial reporting and U.S. income tax treatment for mining companies are mine development and exploration expenditures, impairment reserves, and percentage depletion.

For financial reporting purposes, mine development and exploration expenditures generally are capitalized and amortized over the life of the ore deposit; for tax purposes, a majority of those expenditures are likely to be currently deductible. Additions to impairment reserves are expensed currently for accounting purposes, but do not generate a tax deduction until the underlying property is abandoned, sold, or exchanged.

Percentage depletion is a statutory allowance designed to encourage mining and is, therefore, computed without regard to the cost or adjusted basis of the property. The excess of tax percentage depletion over the cost depletion expensed in the financial statements is usually the principal difference between financial and tax reporting for many mining companies. While an in-depth analysis of percentage depletion is beyond the scope of this book, there are certain concerns of which the auditor should be aware.

The deduction for tax depletion is a percentage of the gross income from a mining property, limited to 50 percent of the taxable income from the property. Because this computation is made for each mining property, the determination of revenues and costs for individual properties is significant to a mining company. The auditor should understand the company's procedures for accumulating the amounts necessary to compute percentage depletion. In particular, the auditor should understand the method of determining taxable income for each property and gross income from mining.

Areas of particular concern in determining taxable income from a property include the appropriate allocation of indirect costs, such as selling expenses, general and administrative overhead, state and local taxes, and interest costs if a borrowing is directly related to a specific property. In addition, the auditor should ensure that the computation is in accordance with current tax regulations; the assistance of a qualified tax specialist should be sought when necessary. These procedures should provide reasonable assurance that tax liabilities in excess of amounts accrued will not be assessed by the taxing authorities as a result of their review of percentage depletion deductions.

The determination of gross income from mining is based on the value of the mineral at the cutoff point (i.e., before application of nonmining processes). To the extent that minerals are sold to independent third parties at the cutoff point, the sales price generally determines gross income from mining. For an integrated mining company, gross income generally is determined under the proportionate profits method (which attributes an equal amount of profit to each dollar of mining and nonmining cost incurred), unless the company can establish the existence of a representative field or market price for an ore or mineral of similar kind and grade. The auditor should ensure that direct mining and nonmining costs are properly identified and that indirect costs (i.e., costs not directly identifiable with a particular mining or nonmining process) are reasonably apportioned.

Corporations are subject to an Alternative Minimum Tax (AMT), which is applicable if it exceeds the regular tax liability. It is common for mining companies to be in an AMT position, as noted below. The AMT taxes a much broader income base than the regular tax, although at a lower rate. To compute AMT liability, the corporation's regular taxable income is recomputed to reflect certain adjustments and preferences. The resulting amount, referred to as Alternative Minimum Taxable Income (AMTI), is multiplied by the corporate AMT rate to arrive at a Tentative Minimum Tax (TMT). The TMT is compared with the regular tax liability, and the greater of the two amounts must be paid.

The major impact of the AMT on mining companies lies in the rule that a deduction for percentage depletion that, combined with prior-year depletion deductions, is in excess of a mineral property's basis generally is not allowable for AMT purposes. In addition, exploration and development expenditures generally are amortized over ten years for AMT purposes. Consequently, many mining companies may find themselves subject to the AMT.

A credit for minimum tax paid (minimum tax credit, or MTC) is allowed to offset regular tax liability in future years. All AMT paid results in MTC. However, the MTC may not reduce the regular tax below the TMT for the taxable year in which the credit is utilized. An important issue for the mining industry relates to the interplay of percentage depletion and net operating loss carryforwards in calculating the MTC.

Since mining is a global industry, the impact of foreign taxes also must be considered. It is essential that the auditor obtain an understanding of the international tax aspects of a mining company's tax situation.

(e) Supplementary Financial Statement Information—Ore Reserves

SFAS No. 89, *Financial Reporting and Changing Prices* (Accounting Standards Section C28), eliminated the requirement that certain publicly traded companies meeting specified size criteria must disclose the effects of changing prices and supplemental disclosures of ore reserves. However, Item 102 of Securities and Exchange Commission Regulation S-K requires that publicly traded mining companies present information related to production, reserves, locations, developments, and the nature of the registrant's interest in properties. The auditor should ensure that the production and reserve information disclosed is consistent with data used by the registrant in calculating depreciation, depletion, and amortization, and, to the extent applicable, is consistent with information used in considering any property impairment.

45

Auditing Not-for-Profit Organizations

45.1 OVERVIEW OF THE INDUSTRY

The not-for-profit sector of the economy includes many diverse types of entities, including colleges and universities, voluntary health and welfare organizations, public and private foundations, museums and other cultural institutions, and associations, to name just a few. Such organizations may have little in common beyond a mission that excludes providing a return to owners and a set of accounting recognition, measurement, and reporting standards that reflect the absence of ownership interests and the existence of contributions by donors. This chapter discusses various aspects of auditing a not-for-profit organization. It does not cover hospitals, however, which may be organized for profit or not-for-profit purposes or which may be governmental units.

The business operations of not-for-profit organizations, and hence their accounting practices, differ from those of commercial entities in three significant respects. First, such organizations generally do not have owners. This should not affect the audit because the responsibility to report to the trustees, creditors, and other providers of resources does not differ significantly from the auditor's responsibility to the shareholders of a corporation. The second and most obvious difference between not-for-profit and commercial entities is that the receipts of the former may include contributions. Restrictions that donors may have placed on those contributions are the primary basis for the difference in accounting and reporting by not-for-profit organizations. Third, a not-for-profit's net assets may be subject to donor restrictions and other limitations, such as designations by the organization's trustees. The auditor should understand these restrictions and other limitations and test expenditures for compliance with them. Some of these limitations may not be significantly different from those placed on a commercial entity through its budgetary process; the limitations that differ most significantly are the result of donor-imposed restrictions that differentiate temporarily and permanently restricted net assets from unrestricted net assets.

Not-for-profit organizations differ from commercial entities in other ways as well.

- Service, not profit, is the objective of not-for-profit organizations. Not-for-profit organizations do not spend to produce revenues; instead, they spend to accomplish their mission or program. As a result, a primary objective of financial reporting is accounting for resources received and used rather than determining net income.

- In some ways, not-for-profit organizations are more stringently regulated and controlled than are for-profit entities. Not-for-profit operations may be affected by legal and contractual requirements in the form of federal and state statutes, grant stipulations, judicial decrees, charters, bylaws, trust agreements, or contracts with grantors and donors.

- Most not-for-profit organizations put a great deal of effort into establishing goals and budgets, which are then monitored closely.

- Under Internal Revenue Code Section 501, a variety of not-for-profit organizations may gain tax-exempt status; however, they may become subject to an income tax on income from for-profit activities not related to their exempt purpose.

45.2 ACCOUNTING PRINCIPLES

(a) Statements of Financial Accounting Standards No. 116 and No. 117

The differences listed above between for-profit and not-for-profit organizations do not suggest basic changes in the procedures applied in auditing not-for-profit organizations. They do, however, require refinements in the accounting principles used by such organizations. Current accounting principles for all not-for-profit organizations are discussed in the AICPA's audit and accounting guide, *Not-for-Profit Organizations* (the guide). Chapter 1 of the guide provides guidance for determining which accounting principles should be followed by not-for-profit entities; basically, principles that do not apply are those that result from specific exclusions or because not-for-profit organizations do not have transactions or circumstances covered by the pronouncement.

Statement of Financial Accounting Standards (SFAS) No. 116, *Accounting for Contributions Received and Contributions Made* (Accounting Standards Sections C67 and No5), and No. 117, *Financial Statements of Not-for-Profit Organizations* (Accounting Standards Sections C25 and No5), establish standards for accounting for contributions and collections and for reporting certain basic information in financial statements that are applicable to all not-for-profit organizations. The guide provides detailed guidance for implementing the provisions of SFAS Nos. 116 and 117. SFAS No. 124, *Accounting for Certain Investments Held by Not-for-Profit Organizations* (Accounting Standards Section No5), establishes measurement and disclosure standards for certain investments in equity securities and all investments in debt securities held by not-for-profit organizations.

SFAS No. 117 requires not-for-profit organizations to classify their net assets and their revenues, expenses, gains, and losses into three categories, based solely on the presence or absence of donor-imposed restrictions on contributions:

- Permanently restricted net assets, which result from contributions whose use is limited by donor-imposed stipulations that neither expire with the passage of time nor can be met or otherwise removed by the organization's actions

- Temporarily restricted net assets, which result from contributions whose use is limited by donor-imposed stipulations that either expire with the passage of time or can be met and removed by the organization's actions pursuant to those stipulations

- Unrestricted net assets, which result from contributions whose use is not limited by donor-imposed stipulations

SFAS No. 116 requires that contributions received be recognized at their fair value as revenues and, depending on the nature of the benefits received by the organization, as assets, decreases of liabilities, or expenses. Contributions received are classified as unrestricted support or as temporarily or permanently restricted support. Unconditional promises to give (often referred to as pledges before the issuance of SFAS No. 116) with payments due in the current period are reported as unrestricted support.

Unconditional promises to give with payments due in future periods are reported as temporarily restricted support unless the donor clearly intended the moneys to be used to support current-period activities. Conditional promises to give are not recognized in the financial statements until the condition is satisfied.

Although organizations must disclose certain information about their collections of works of art, historical treasures, and similar assets, they are not required to capitalize them or recognize contributed collection items as revenues or gains as long as the collections meet the following conditions:

- They are held for public exhibition, education, or research to further public service, rather than for financial gain
- They are protected, kept unencumbered, cared for, and preserved
- They are subject to an organizational policy that requires proceeds from sales of collection items to be used to acquire other collection items

Contributed services are recognized as revenues or gains only if they "create or enhance nonfinancial assets or require specialized skills, are provided by individuals possessing those skills, and would typically need to be purchased if not provided by donation."

SFAS No. 117 provides that the financial statements of not-for-profit organizations focus on the entity as a whole. Such organizations are required, at a minimum, to present a statement of financial position, a statement of activities, and a statement of cash flows. Voluntary health and welfare organizations also must prepare a statement of functional expenses that presents information about expenses by their natural classification in a matrix format. The minimum requirements for each financial statement are as follows:

- The statement of financial position must include (1) total assets, (2) total liabilities, (3) total net assets for each of the three classes of net assets (unrestricted, temporarily restricted, and permanently restricted), and (4) total net assets.
- The statement of activities must include expenses reported by function and the amount of the increase or decrease in unrestricted, temporarily restricted, permanently restricted, and total net assets.
- The statement of cash flows must include the net cash used by operating, investing, and financing activities as well as the changes in cash and cash equivalents and a reconciliation of the change in net assets to the change in cash used by operating activities.

SFAS No. 124 requires that investments in equity securities with readily determinable fair values and all investments in debt securities be reported at fair value, with gains and losses reported in the statement of activities. The statement provides guidance on how investment gains and losses and dividend, interest, and other investment income should be reported. It also specifies certain disclosures about all types of investments held by not-for-profit organizations and the return on investments.

(b) Governmental Entities

The guide (and, by implication, SFAS Nos. 116 and 117) applies to nongovernmental not-for-profit organizations (except those that are providers of health care services, which should follow the audit and accounting guide, *Health Care Organizations*). Those guides define governmental and nongovernmental organizations.

According to the guide, governmental organizations are "public corporations and bodies corporate and politic" and other organizations that have one or more of the following characteristics:

a. Popular election of officers or appointment (or approval) of a controlling majority of the members of the organization's governing body by officials or one or more state or local governments;

b. The potential for unilateral dissolution by a government with the net assets reverting to a government; or

c. The power to enact and enforce a tax levy. (para. 1.03)

Nongovernmental organizations are all organizations that do not meet the definition of governmental organizations.

Government Accounting Standards Board (GASB) pronouncements apply to governmental organizations generally. GASB Statement No. 29, *The Use of Not-for-Profit Accounting and Financial Reporting Principles by Governmental Entities*, provides that governmental entities that have applied the principles of the AICPA industry audit guide, *Audits of Voluntary Health and Welfare Organizations*, and Statement of Position (SOP) 78-10, *Accounting Principles and Reporting Practices for Certain Nonprofit Organizations* (modified by all applicable FASB pronouncements issued through November 30, 1989, and by most applicable GASB pronouncements), may continue to do so; they should not change their accounting and reporting to conform to SFAS Nos. 116 and 117. Alternatively, they may change to the current governmental financial reporting model described below.

GASB Statement No. 15, *Governmental College and University Accounting and Financial Reporting Models*, requires governmental colleges and universities to use one of two accounting and financial reporting models:

1. The "AICPA College Guide Model." This is the accounting and financial reporting guidance recognized by the 1973 AICPA industry audit guide, *Audits of Colleges and Universities*, as amended by SOP 74-8, *Financial Accounting and Reporting by Colleges and Universities*, and as modified by applicable FASB pronouncements issued through November 30, 1989 and all applicable GASB pronouncements.

2. The "Government Model." This model is the accounting and financial reporting standards established by National Council on Governmental Accounting (NCGA) Statement 1, *Governmental Accounting and Financial Reporting Principles*, as modified by subsequent NCGA and GASB pronouncements.

(c) Fund Accounting

Before the issuance of SFAS No. 117, the basis of accounting and reporting for most not-for-profit organizations was the principles of fund accounting. Basically, those principles called for the maintenance of the accounts in a series of self-balancing individual funds. Similar type fund groups were aggregated and reported as if they were individual entities in the financial statements. Fund accounting evolved to meet organizations' fiduciary duty to ensure that resources are used in accordance with the contributor's stipulations and the governing board's designations. Although those requirements still exist and fund accounting may be used internally to monitor those requirements, fund accounting is not an appropriate basis of accounting for general-purpose external financial reporting under SFAS No. 117. SFAS No. 117 does permit organizations to disaggregate information by individual funds or fund groups, however, as long as the required aggregated amounts for each of the three specified net asset classes are displayed appropriately.

As previously discussed, contributions received by a not-for-profit organization often are restricted by the donor for specific purposes and activities. For example, a not-for-profit organization may receive a gift that can be used only in a certain geographical area or for purchasing a specific asset. In accepting those resources, the organization also assumes the accompanying custodial obligations. The organization has the fiduciary duty to ensure that such resources are used in accordance with the contributor's stipulations and often is required to report on compliance with those stipulations. Fund accounting has been employed to monitor restricted or earmarked resources and to ensure and demonstrate the institution's compliance with legal and administrative requirements. As a result, although external financial statement reporting is now based on net asset classes, not-for-profit organizations often maintain their records by fund group. The auditor may be required to understand the basic principles of fund accounting and to "bridge" between the entity's underlying accounting records and the external financial reporting requirements. The guide provides assistance in making that "bridge."

As used in not-for-profit accounting, a fund is an accounting entity with a self-balancing set of accounts for recording assets, liabilities, the fund balance, and changes in the fund balance. Separate accounts are maintained for each fund to ensure that the limitations and restrictions on the use of resources are observed. While the fund concept involves separate accounting records, it does not necessarily entail physical segregation of resources. Fund accounting is basically a mechanism to assist in exercising control over the purpose of particular resources and amounts of those resources available for use. For reporting purposes, funds that have similar characteristics or common purposes may be combined into fund groups. The major fund groups include restricted and unrestricted current operating funds, loan funds, endowment and similar funds, annuity and life income funds, plant funds, and agency funds. The guide describes how information derived from an internal fund accounting system can be used to prepare external financial statements in conformity with GAAP.

45.3   RISK ASSESSMENT AND AUDIT STRATEGY

An auditor assigned to a not-for-profit engagement for the first time may find that its operations are very small and simplistic or very large and decentralized, that management relies on a great many disparate accounting and information systems, and that the financial statements arc complex. There are often more accounts to examine for a not-for-profit engagement than for a commercial engagement, primarily related to donor restrictions on contributions.

For certain types of transactions, such as those in the purchasing cycle, the auditor may find it most efficient to perform tests of controls in order to be able to assess control risk at low and thus to significantly restrict substantive tests. For other accounts, such as revenues from major gifts, the most efficient strategy may be to employ primarily substantive tests. The audit strategy should be reconsidered annually, because sources of revenue and types of expenditures may change dramatically as an organization adapts its operations to the marketplace.

Generally, the auditor's focus shifts with the size and complexity, rather than the type, of organization under audit. Hence, the audit of a large university, for example, is likely to resemble the audit of a large museum or charity (or of any large, decentralized corporation) more closely than the audit of a small college, and the audits of a small independent school and a smaller charitable or social organization are likely to be similar.

While operating costs of not-for-profit organizations have been rising, some of their traditional sources of revenue have been decreasing. With respect to colleges and universities, for example, the college-age population began to decline in the 1970s. State and municipal governments have fewer resources available for support. The federal government has cut back on research, training, and financial aid programs that in the past had provided support to education. In addition, various changes in the Internal Revenue Code and related regulations have affected not-for-profit organizations. Some changes, such as those that limit the benefits to certain donors from supporting not-for-profit organizations, have adversely affected contributions. (In reducing individuals' tax rates, the tax code has raised the effective cost of giving.) More detailed compliance regulations for the IRS information return Form 990 have increased the paperwork burden at many organizations.

Not-for-profit organizations have responded to these financial pressures in various ways, including cutting costs, retrenchment, seeking to attract new constituents, developing new sources of revenue, using more aggressive investment strategies, and issuing debt. Each of these responses increases the risks—both inherent and control risks—that should be recognized by independent, internal, and government auditors practicing in the not-for-profit industry.

Figure 45.1 summarizes many of those risks.

Materiality poses a unique problem in auditing not-for-profit organizations. SAS No. 47 (AU Section 312) requires the auditor to consider materiality for planning purposes in terms of the smallest aggregate level of misstatements that could be considered material to any one of the financial statements. Since even the largest organizations generally adopt a balanced budget, their operating margin is likely to be quite small. Hence, it may not be meaningful to emphasize net results of financial activities in making materiality judgments. Instead, many auditors consider materiality in terms of each of the various net asset classes, total net assets, or other measures, such as total expenditures and total unrestricted revenue. Obviously, such judgments must be made on a case-by-case basis. Expenditures that do not conform to donor restrictions may expose the organization to adverse publicity or legal penalties. Such situations should be disclosed to management and the board and considered for adjustment, no matter how small.

45.4 AUDITING THE REVENUE CYCLE

Classes of transactions in the revenue cycle that are unique and significant to not-for-profit organizations include the following:

- Contributions (which are classified depending on donor restrictions)

Figure 45.1   Risks in the Not-for-Profit Environment

Financial Pressure	Responses	Potential Risks
Increased costs or reduced revenues	Cutting costs	Reduced controls because of cutbacks in administrative staff
		Incentives to postpone accounting recognition of liabilities
		Use of restricted funds for expenses outside donor's original intent
	Retrenchment	Potential difficult judgments in the accounting treatment of excess facilities
Reduced sources of funds and increased competition for donor dollars	Aggressive investment strategies	Valuation of real estate, venture capital, and other investments for which market values may not be readily determinable
		Need to determine physical existence of borrowed or loaned securities by confirmation or observation
		Accounting for complex transactions involving derivatives
	Creation of unrelated affiliates and other new revenue sources; aggressive marketing strategies	Increased risk from operations outside management's traditional understanding and control
		Doubtful collectibility of receivables
		Valuation of investments in new business ventures
		Nonobservance of stipulations imposed by sponsors on use of funds
		Valuation of funds received under split-interest agreements
		Appraisal of value of gifts in kind
		Exposure to taxation of unrelated business income

Figure 45.1 *(Continued)*

Financial Pressure	*Responses*	*Potential Risks*
	Borrowings among and between net asset classes	Borrowing from restricted amounts, possibly contrary to donor's intent
		Inappropriate or illegal expenditures of endowment principal
	External debt	Possible noncompliance with covenants
		Responsibility to report to holders of publicly held debt
		Possible need to capitalize interest
Need to modernize facilities	Capital expenditures	Expenditures on new space while deferring maintenance on old space
		Assumption of role of general contractor without requisite expertise

- Investment income (which involves income allocation based on donor restrictions)
- Grants and contracts (which can have extensive compliance requirements)
- Revenues and other fees (such as association dues, tuition charged for educational programs, program admissions, and fees charged for services provided to program participants), some of which may be similar to revenue transactions of commercial entities
- Student loan programs of colleges and universities (which have extensive compliance requirements)

(a) Contributions

Some not-for-profit organizations have developed sophisticated means of soliciting support from individuals, foundations, corporations, and other sources. Most systems provide for recording promises to give, summarizing fund-raising performance, and comparing performance with campaign goals. The sophistication of those systems may highlight the need for the auditor to understand the solicitation process and its results. The auditor's objective, however, remains the same—determining that contributions are recorded completely and accurately and that management has a means of recognizing any restrictions placed by donors on the use of contributions.

Financial management may include separate systems for annual giving and other development activities. Comparing development department records with the accounting records may provide evidence that all gifts have been recorded. The auditor may compare amounts recorded for the current year with those contributed in the past and should review the terms of significant contributions to determine that restrictions in the gifts have been recorded properly. Trustees often acknowledge receipt of major contributions; the auditor should review minutes of their meetings for mention of specific gifts. A review of selected correspondence files may provide the auditor with information about the process by which contributions are solicited and used. Finally, the auditor should consider the use of correspondence, pledge cards, acknowledgments, and other documentation to obtain satisfaction that donor restrictions have been properly recognized and classified. Many not-for-profit organizations have a policy of rejecting gifts that carry onerous restrictions, such as institutional matching or support of particular political views. The auditor's review of correspondence files may reveal whether all organizational units within the institution are following such policies.

Accounting for contributions has certain features of which the auditor should be aware.

- *Promises to give* for which there is sufficient evidence in the form of verifiable documentation should be recorded as receivables at their fair value. The auditor should be particularly attentive to their collectibility and should consider confirming promises to give, especially to ascertain any changes in terms or restrictions.

- *Deferred giving programs* generate life income and annuity funds that are available only at the time specified in individual agreements. In addition, such receipts often are subject to a commitment to pay stipulated amounts (annuity funds) or a certain percentage return (life income funds) periodically to the donor or other designated individual. These and similar types of arrangements are commonly known as *split-interest agreements*. The guide provides extensive guidance on accounting for and auditing these agreements.

- Not-for-profit organizations may receive promises to give merchandise, services, real estate, and works of art. SFAS No. 116 and the guide provide guidance for the initial recognition and subsequent valuation of such contributions.

(b) Investments and Investment Income

Equity securities with a readily determinable market value and all debt securities should be valued at market for financial reporting purposes. The valuation of other investments should follow the guidance provided in the guide. Auditing procedures for investments include periodic determination of their physical existence and tests of market value. In testing investment income, the auditor should use procedures appropriate for investment companies, including tests of unit-value calculations for pooled investments and of the distribution of income from pooled investments to unrestricted, temporarily restricted, or permanently restricted net assets. Restricted securities and contributions limited to a particular type of investment should not enter into a general investment pool. The auditor also should be aware that donors may have placed restrictions on the use of investment income or gains associated with endowment funds. In addition, state law governs the use of donor restricted investment income and gains; the auditor should become familiar with those laws. SFAS No. 124 establishes standards for reporting gains and losses on investments in circumstances where their use is temporarily or permanently restricted by explicit donor stipulations or by law.

Organizations may hedge their fixed-income portfolios with financial futures or options and may seek to increase investment income through securities lending, repurchase agreements, and options trading. The auditor should review the relevant controls to ascertain that the organization maintains a traceable record of the physical existence of the related securities, and should determine that such transactions are properly collateralized, that the net proceeds from the transactions are recognized as capital or income transactions in the appropriate period, and that the arrangements (if material) are disclosed.

(c)   Grants and Contracts

Many programs of not-for-profit organizations may be conducted with the direct support of external sponsors. The restrictions frequently placed on expenditures by grant and contract sponsors may require special audit attention. Under many federally sponsored grants, revenues associated with direct costs of the projects are recognized when the related expenses are incurred, while reimbursement for indirect costs and employee benefits is recorded at predetermined rates that later are adjusted to reflect actual expenditures. The difference between actual and estimated overhead costs usually is not recognized as revenue or expense in the year in which the costs are incurred; instead, it is reflected as an adjustment in the overhead rate in the future.

Specific audit objectives in this area include ascertaining that:

- Payroll charges, materials, and other direct costs are summarized accurately and distributed to individual contracts or grant activities, and overhead is applied at current rates and on an appropriate basis
- Revenues are recorded completely and accurately, sponsors are billed on a timely basis, and adequate follow-up procedures exist for outstanding receivables
- All cash receipts are recorded accurately, and advance payments or letter-of-credit advances are applied to the proper accounts
- Procedures to monitor cost overruns are functioning

If such activity is significant, the auditor should examine grants and contracts to ascertain that contract charges, including indirect cost allowances, are recorded in accordance with contract provisions.

Federal grants and contracts impose particular administrative burdens on recipients. The auditor should review reports of government auditors and correspondence with sponsors to determine whether a contingent liability for disallowed costs should be recorded or disclosed in accordance with SFAS No. 5 (Accounting Standards Section C59).

(d)   Tuition Revenue and Related Fees

College and university applications for admission are first solicited and received from prospective students. Once students are admitted, their names and other data are entered on a master file from which billings are generated at the start of each school term. Normally, students must pay tuition and related fees in order to register. Accordingly, it would be unusual for a significant number of student accounts to be outstanding at the end of the fiscal year. Balances may exist with outside scholarship providers or other third parties, however, and the auditor should review them for collectibility. In addition, it is becoming increasingly common for students to pay a deposit in one fiscal year that is applied to tuition in the following period; the auditor should ascertain that tuition revenue is recognized in the proper period.

It is also common for colleges and universities, as well as some other not-for-profit organizations, to provide reductions in the amounts charged for goods and services, such as financial aid provided to students. The auditor should be aware that the appropriate classification and display of those reductions depends on the circumstances. If those reductions are given other than in exchange for services provided to the organization (for example, as part of a compensation package), the guide specifies that they should be reported as discounts and netted against revenues, unless the organization incurs incremental expense in providing such goods or services, in which case they should be reported as expenses. (Net revenue may be displayed as a single line item in a statement of activities. Alternatively, gross revenue may be displayed, with the related discount displayed immediately below the revenue.)

Tuition and other student revenues are usually a sensitive audit area because of the large transaction volume and the resulting need for effective controls. These controls should address the control objectives of completeness, accuracy, and authorization. Specifically, controls should ensure that all students enrolled are billed, that tuition billings to individual students are appropriate, that financial aid was authorized, and that appropriate fees for room, board, and other services were billed and allocated to the proper accounts. In addition, controls should be in place to ensure that cash receipts, scholarships, loans, and other credits are applied to the correct accounts and that all transactions are reflected accurately on individual students' records. Also, there should be follow-up procedures to collect outstanding balances.

In examining student revenues, the auditor may find the following analytical procedures effective:

- Comparing students who received grade reports with those who paid bills
- Comparing students registered at standard tuition rates with gross tuition revenue
- Comparing revenue recognized with budgets
- Testing tuition rates by comparing student status at the time of application (instate, out-of-state, full-time, part-time, and so on) with amounts charged

Continuing education revenues may not lend themselves to such analytical procedures.

The automation of most student revenue systems suggests that computer controls, especially those relating to maintenance of master files, may be of particular importance. Also, the auditor should be alert to the assignment of tuition, particularly for summer programs, to the proper fiscal year. Finally, in considering tuition revenues at a public institution, the auditor should recognize the distinction between funds received from day and other degree students (which may be subject to the appropriation process) and those received for nondegree, adult education courses (which often are not).

(e) Student Loans

Colleges and universities may make loans to students from both governmental and institutional loan funds. After loan funds have been applied for and received by the institution, loans are granted to individual qualifying students. For certain programs, a "needs analysis" must be performed on an individual-student basis to match the student's resources with aid that may be available from governmental programs. The loan recipient executes a note, and a loan receivable is created; after the recipient's graduation, collection procedures are put into effect for outstanding principal and interest balances. Annual reporting by the institution to the federal government on loan activity involving federal programs is required, and periodic independent audits of those programs are required to address compliance as well as the financial administration of the program.

Major audit concerns include policies and procedures for establishing loan collectibility allowances and maintaining accurate loan records. A major audit planning procedure involves coordinating tests of student loan accounts with government financial aid audits performed by the institution's independent auditors, or other auditors, to ensure that work is not duplicated.

45.5 AUDITING THE PURCHASING CYCLE

The purchasing cycle of a not-for-profit organization does not differ significantly from that of a for-profit entity. Both employ separate capital and operating budgets, both face certain limitations on the use of funds by operating divisions, and payrolls and other expenses of both are subject to various levels of management approval. Accounting for buildings and equipment has some special characteristics, however, including those related to donor restrictions, that the auditor should be aware of.

(a) Capital Assets

Potential audit concerns in the area of capital assets are as follows:

- There may be a question as to whether all capital assets have been recorded, particularly at decentralized organizations.
- The distinction between expense and capital items may not be observed consistently
- The acquisition of assets through external borrowing may subject the organization to restrictions on the use of related revenues and to other debt covenants
- Deferred maintenance may present a serious financial risk that may not be reflected in the financial statements

The auditor should review provisions of long-term external borrowing agreements to observe that all debt covenants have been met. The nature and extent of pledged assets and revenues should be disclosed in the financial statements. The auditor also should determine that SFAS No. 62, *Capitalization of Interest Cost in Situations Involving Certain Tax-Exempt Borrowings and Certain Gifts and Grants* (Accounting Standards Section I67), has been properly applied. That statement calls for the capitalization of interest during construction on fixed assets purchased with external debt, except that capitalized amounts are recorded net of income earned on unexpended construction funds financed with tax-exempt borrowings that are externally restricted to finance specified assets or to service the related debt.

(b)   Release of Donor Restrictions

Occasionally, the distinction between expenditures of restricted and unrestricted net assets is not clear. For example, donors may contribute funds for purposes for which unrestricted funds are also available. SFAS No. 116 requires that restricted net assets be used first when there are both unrestricted and temporarily restricted net assets available for the same purpose. The auditor should consider examining some expenditures to ensure that restrictions have been met and appropriate reclassifications from temporarily restricted to unrestricted net assets have been recognized.

45.6   INFORMATION TECHNOLOGY IN THE NOT-FOR-PROFIT ENVIRONMENT

Information technology (IT) considerations in many not-for-profit environments are similar to those encountered in for-profit environments. In some not-for-profit environments, however, IT operations may consist of two or more completely different computerized systems. For example, in some colleges and universities, what generally is referred to as "administrative computing" is the counterpart of financial data processing operations in most other entities. Administrative computing involves payroll, general ledger, and other accounting processing functions, as well as admissions and other university functions. The other aspect of university IT operations often is referred to as "academic computing." This is the component of university computer use involved in instruction and research. The auditor should, as one of the first steps in planning the audit of a university, determine how the two components interface.

In some not-for-profit environments, particularly in colleges and universities, it is not uncommon for data processing or computer science students to be employed as computer operators for the administrative system. While this is not necessarily an audit risk, there must be adequate separation of duties and supervision. In considering student accounts receivable, for example, the auditor should determine whether student operators have access to information that could be considered sensitive.

Another aspect of the university IT environment that demands special attention is the proliferation of personal and institutional computers. Most students own a personal computer and have access to one or more university computers; their use has become a key area of audit concern. The auditor should be alert to the need for computer controls to prevent and detect unauthorized access to computer files.

45.7 AUDITS OF FEDERAL AND STATE PROGRAMS

Grants from individual federal agencies such as the National Endowment for the Arts, the National Institutes of Health, the National Science Foundation, the Department of Defense, and the Department of Education have become significant sources of revenue for many not-for-profit organizations. Not-for-profit organizations that receive federal financial assistance may be required to have an audit performed in accordance with government auditing standards, and some states have similar requirements. Office of Management and Budget (OMB) Circular A-133 also prescribes audit requirements for not-for-profit organizations receiving federal awards. Those organizations are required to engage their independent auditors to study and evaluate their financial management systems relating to federal projects and to determine that their transactions comply with federal regulations. In these audits, the organization, rather than the individual grants, is considered the entity subject to audit.

Independent auditors of not-for-profit organizations that receive federal funds should add federally related procedures to the financial statement audit. The objective of those procedures is not to provide a basis for forming an opinion on the organization's financial statements. Rather, the auditor's objective is to determine whether:

- The organization has implemented and utilized appropriate financial and administrative systems and procedures to discharge management responsibilities effectively and to protect the federal interest
- The institution is in compliance with the uniform federal administrative requirements
- Financial reports submitted to federal agencies contain reliable financial data

In meeting that objective, the auditor determines that costs incurred under federal contracts:

- Are necessary and reasonable
- Conform with any limitation or exclusion in the award
- Are accounted for consistently and uniformly with other institutional activities
- Are net of "applicable credits"
- Are approved in advance, if required
- Are incurred in accordance with competitive procurement procedures
- Absorb indirect costs at the proper rate

Audits should be conducted and financial, internal control, and compliance reports should be issued in accordance with government regulations (as specified in *Government Auditing Standards*, often called the "Yellow Book," issued by the Comptroller General of the United States).

46

Auditing Oil and Gas Producing Activities

Statement of Financial Accounting Standards (SFAS) No. 19, *Financial Accounting and Reporting by Oil and Gas Producing Companies* (Accounting Standards Section Oi5.101), defines oil and gas producing activities as those that "involve the acquisition of mineral interests in properties, exploration (including prospecting), development, and production of crude oil, including condensate and natural gas liquids, and natural gas." This chapter covers those activities; it does not address the refining, marketing, and distribution of petroleum products.

46.1 OVERVIEW OF OIL AND GAS PRODUCING ACTIVITIES

The oil and gas industry is extremely complex, primarily because of (1) the risks involved in the exploration and production process (including low exploration success rates, volatility of oil and gas prices, and fluctuations in supply and demand for oil and natural gas), and (2) the variety of business strategies used to raise capital and share risks. The auditor's understanding of these areas is critical to the application of appropriate auditing procedures. In addition, the auditor should be generally familiar with the operating characteristics of entities involved in oil and gas producing activities. The AICPA *Guide for Audits of Entities with Oil and Gas Producing Activities* contains guidance for this industry. Additional guidance is provided in the fourth edition of *Petroleum Accounting: Principles, Procedures, & Issues* (1996, Denton: University of North Texas, Professional Development Institute).

(a) Oil and Gas Producing Operations

Oil and gas producing activities begin with the search for prospects—parcels of acreage that management thinks may contain formations of oil or gas that will be economically viable to produce. For the most likely prospects, the entity may contract with a geological and geophysical (G&G) company to conduct various tests to assess the types of subsurface formations and their depths. Based on the G&G studies, the entity evaluates the various prospects, rejecting some and accepting others as suitable for acquisition of lease rights. Prospecting may be done before or after obtaining lease rights.

Specialists called landmen may be used to obtain lease rights. A landman is in effect a lease broker who searches titles and negotiates with property owners. Although the landman may be part of the entity's staff, oil and gas companies often acquire lease rights to properties through independent landmen. Consideration for leasing the mineral rights usually includes a bonus (an immediate cash payment to the lessor), a delay rental paid to the lessor (subsequent to the payment of any bonus) for the privilege of deferring the commencement of drilling a well or the commencement of commercial production on the lease, and a royalty interest retained by the lessor (a specified percentage of subsequent production minus applicable taxes).

Once the leases have been obtained and the rights and obligations of all parties determined, exploratory drilling begins. Because drilling costs run to hundreds of thousands or millions of dollars, most entities reduce their capital commitment and related risks by seeking others to participate in joint venture arrangements. Participants in a joint venture are called joint interest owners; one owner, usually the entity that obtained the leases, acts as operator. The operator manages the venture and reports to the nonoperator participants. The operator pays the drilling costs of the venture and bills nonoperators for their share.

The operator acquires the necessary supplies and contracts with a drilling company for drilling the well. The drilling time may be a few days, several months, or even up to a year or longer depending on many factors, particularly well depth and location. When the hole reaches the desired depth, various instruments are lowered to "log the well" to detect the presence of oil or gas. The joint interest owners evaluate the drilling and logging results to determine whether sufficient oil or gas can be extracted to justify the cost of completing the well. If the evaluation is negative, the well is plugged and abandoned as a dry hole. If the evaluation indicates the presence of sufficient quantities of crude oil or natural gas (hydrocarbons), the well is completed and equipment is installed to extract and separate the hydrocarbons from any water produced from the underground reservoir. Completion costs may exceed the initial drilling costs.

To transport oil or gas from the well, a gathering line may be built to the nearest major pipeline; for crude oil, an alternative exists of storing the oil in tanks as it is produced and removing it later by truck to a crude oil pipeline or refinery. Gas may be sent first to a natural gas processing plant for removing natural gas liquids (NGLs), such as propane and butane, for sale. Removing the NGLs converts the "wet" gas to "dry" gas for sale.

In the United States, crude oil typically is sold "at the wellhead" on a spot basis at posted prices shown on an oil purchaser's posted price bulletin in effect at the time of sale. The bulletin may show price adjustments for the location and quality of the oil production. The oil purchaser may be a refiner, an oil pipeline company, or a crude oil broker. The oil purchaser issues a division order, which is signed by the seller(s), acknowledging who is to receive what share of the sales proceeds. Many oil division orders specify that the purchaser will send separate checks to each owner of an economic interest in the production.

Since the early 1990s, natural gas producers typically have sold their gas directly to "end users," such as manufacturers, to gas utilities (also called local distribution companies or LDCs), or to gas marketing companies selling to these markets. Producers pay fees to gas pipeline companies to transport the gas to their customers. In many cases, gathering systems are used and fees paid to move oil and gas from the wellheads to the pipelines. Transportation through a pipeline involves a pipeline company receiving a producer's quantity of gas measured by heat or energy content, expressed in million British thermal units (MMBtu), and delivering an equivalent quantity to the producer's customer at another location. Natural gas usually is sold on a spot basis at a negotiated price for the coming month's production. Some gas is sold under long-term contracts. If the joint venture operator sells the gas on behalf of the joint venture owners, the customer typically pays all proceeds to the operator. The operator then distributes the appropriate amounts to the other joint interest owners and the lessor(s).

Various factors determine the economic success or failure of oil and gas exploration activities. Those factors, some of which are discussed below, set the oil and gas industry apart from other capital-intensive industries.

Anticipated Success of Drilling. According to figures compiled by the American Petroleum Institute, only about 25 percent of the exploratory wells in areas with previously discovered reservoirs are successful (i.e., economically productive). For the exploratory wells drilled in new areas (outside fields of previously discovered reservoirs), the success rate approximates 15 percent.

Declining Production. Oil and gas reservoirs are depleting assets whose production declines over time. Annual U.S. production averages 11 percent of proven reserves. Oil and gas companies must find or acquire new reserves continually to maintain production levels.

Taxation. A substantial portion of revenues from the sale of crude oil and natural gas goes directly or indirectly to the federal and state governments in the form of production taxes, ad valorem taxes, and income taxes. After the various taxes, royalties to the landowner, and production costs have been deducted, the producer's income from the sale of crude oil and natural gas may be only a small percentage of gross revenues.

Product Price and Marketability. U.S. producers typically do not encounter problems selling the oil they produce since the U.S. produces only half of its crude oil needs. Crude oil prices are volatile; posted prices may change several times during a month. In contrast, roughly 90 percent of U.S. gas demand is met by domestic production and 10 percent by Canadian imports, and many U.S. gas wells produce below capacity due to limits in transportation capacity and demand. Demand for natural gas is seasonal; generally it is higher in the winter due to increased demands for space heating. Natural gas marketability and wellhead prices vary significantly in different areas of the United States. General indicators of oil and gas prices are the national benchmark prices of West Texas Intermediate crude oil and Southern Louisiana natural gas reflected in oil and gas futures contracts as published in daily newspapers. Oil and gas futures, options on such futures, and other oil and gas price derivative contracts may serve to hedge wellhead price risks.

Timing of Production. How quickly oil and gas are produced directly affects the payback period of an investment and its financial success or failure. The timing of production varies with the geological characteristics of the reservoir and the marketability of the product being produced. Reservoirs may contain the same gross producible reserves, yet the timing of production may cause significant differences in the present value of the future revenue stream.

Exploration Emphasis Outside the United States. The United States has become a mature area for oil exploration. It had 63 percent of the world's producing oil wells at the beginning of 1995, but produced only 10 percent of the world's oil and had less than 3 percent of the world's proven oil reserves. Increasingly, U.S. oil and gas companies are emphasizing exploration outside the country. Foreign exploration and production introduce many additional factors that have an impact on economic success, such as varying laws and regulations, currency fluctuations, nationalization risks, and marketing complexities.

Acreage and Drilling Costs. The costs of lease acreage and drilling are volatile and vary by area of the country and the world. Exploration success may create shortages of local acreage and drilling rigs, substantially raising their costs and limiting producers' profits from exploiting a new discovery by additional drilling in the area.

Technology Advancements. In recent years, advancements in G&G techniques and drilling methods have lowered the cost of exploration and production.

(b) Oil and Gas Ownership Interests

An oil or gas company typically acquires ownership of a prospect by obtaining a lease from the mineral owners. The lease is for a specified term (for example, three years) and usually includes a provision renewing the lease as long as oil or gas is commercially produced.

As previously indicated, often several oil and gas companies jointly will explore and develop a lease through a joint venture arrangement. Ownership is transferred to joint venture participants by means of an assignment. The lessee creates an "assignment of oil and gas lease," specifying the location of the lease, the lessor, that the assignment is subject to the royalty interest reserved by the lessor (and any prior assignments), and the amount of ownership interest assigned to the joint venture participants.

Leases and assignments are legal documents and generally are recorded with the appropriate governmental agency (for example, the Registry of Deeds in the county where the property is located). Before drilling begins, an attorney is engaged to perform a title search. If a well is successful, the attorney issues a division order title opinion to the oil purchaser and joint venture operator (and sometimes the gas purchaser), naming the owners of the oil and gas interests and the amount of the interest. Based on this, the purchaser or operator prepares division order instruments and forwards them to the appropriate oil and gas owner for signature. The purchaser or operator distributes monthly revenue to the owners based on the percentages in the division order. Often, the attorney's division order title opinion shows two interest percentages—the net revenue interest and the working interest—for each owner. The purchaser distributes revenue based on the net revenue interest, and the operator prepares monthly billings for operating cost based on the working interest.

A net revenue interest entitles the owner to share in the revenues generated by an oil or gas well; a working interest obligates the owner to pay a portion of the cost associated with drilling and operating a well. For example, if an oil company (the operator) leases mineral rights, granting a one-eighth royalty, and then obtains a joint venture participant who agrees to participate equally in drilling an exploratory well, the following situation exists:

	Net Revenue Interest	Working Interest
Lessor (royalty interest)	12.50%	0%
Lessees:		
Operator	43.75	50.00
Joint venture participant	43.75	50.00
Total	100.00%	100.00%

If the well costs $1 million to drill and complete and generates $100,000 of revenue during the first month of operation, the operator and the joint venture participant each would be entitled to $43,750 of revenue (a 43.75 percent net revenue interest) and would be obligated to pay $500,000 in drilling and completion costs (a 50 percent working interest). The lessor's royalty interest would be $12,500. The operator and the joint venture participant also would each pay 50 percent of any operating costs.

In practice, there may be numerous joint venture participants (working interest owners), as well as overriding royalty interest owners. An overriding royalty interest is similar to the lessor's royalty in that it entitles the owner to a percentage of revenues without obligation to pay the costs of drilling, completing, and operating the well. Overriding royalty interests (ORRIs) may be created (1) for geologists who generate the prospect, (2) for independent landmen as compensation for obtaining the lease from the owner, (3) for banks or other institutions lending money but negotiating an ORRI over and above a stated interest rate, (4) as part of "farmout" agreements (discussed later in this chapter), or (5) for a variety of other reasons.

(c) Raising Capital and Sharing Risks

In light of the high risks and significant capital requirements involved in exploring for oil and gas, funds are raised and risks are shared through a wide variety of techniques, some of which historically have been motivated by the availability of varying tax benefits to investors.

Many mature companies use the cash flow from existing oil and gas production to finance additional drilling activities. Banks are a traditional source of capital; however, banks typically lend no more than 50 percent of the estimated value of proved developed oil and gas properties. Sales of bonds or stock also are used to finance drilling activities. Consistent with other industries, the availability of such debt or equity funds varies significantly depending on the perceptions of the investment community.

Two other traditional methods of raising drilling capital and sharing risks have been used by oil and gas companies. As previously mentioned, an oil and gas company often can attract other exploration companies (and sometimes individuals or partnerships) to participate in a joint venture to explore leased acreage. Joint ventures allow oil and gas companies to spread limited funds among more exploration and development activities, reducing overall investment risk. For leases that are particularly promising, the other joint venture participants may even pay all of the drilling costs in return for less than 100 percent of the operating income from the well. Less common in the 1990s is the joint venture partnership whereby the oil and gas company forms a "drilling fund" structured as a limited or general partnership in which individual investors participate by funding substantial portions of the drilling costs. Changes in the tax laws disallowing offsetting of passive losses generated by limited partnerships against active income, accompanied by volatility of energy prices, have substantially reduced the use of limited partnerships. During the late 1970s and early 1980s, limited partnerships called "income funds" were popular for acquiring proved producing oil and gas properties.

During much of the 1980s the industry underwent a period of capital starvation, falling oil and gas prices, and significant loss of technical personnel. The late 1980s saw greater volatility of oil prices and seasonality of gas prices. Such price volatility has continued in the 1990s, significantly affecting the operating cash flows of oil and gas companies. Accordingly, finding sufficient capital at acceptable costs is a challenge for most oil and gas companies.

During periods when traditional financing sources are not available, the industry has developed more innovative methods of raising capital, including:

- *Mezzanine Financing.* Through pooled funds raised primarily from institutional sources, funds are loaned to operators for completion expenses, development drilling, and acreage acquisition (activities historically not funded by banks). The loans, which are collateralized by interests in the financed properties, typically are made at interest rates somewhat below market. The lower interest rate is compensated for by an equity interest in the properties, and accordingly the mezzanine financier may have a higher overall return, commensurate with the increased risk, than a bank would earn under traditional financing. Today, many banks also provide this type of investment banking service in addition to conventional financing.

- *Oil Field-Services Joint Ventures.* An operator holding relatively low-risk developmental drilling prospects may enter into a joint venture with a drilling contractor or other oil field-services vendors. The vendors provide services in exchange for an interest in the properties being developed and receive a return from future production from the wells drilled, with or without recourse to the operator.

- *Exchange Offers.* Also known as roll-ups, these transactions involve one entity's issuance of common stock, partnership units, or debt in exchange for several entities' limited partner interests, working interests, or other direct or indirect interests in oil and gas production. Through an exchange offer, numerous investors with small interests in existing production may reinvest cash flow more efficiently in new exploration and development ventures. The Securities and Exchange Commission (SEC) has prescribed rules for accounting for these transactions in Staff Accounting Bulletin (SAB) No. 47. The surviving entity may be a master limited partnership (MLP) for which the limited partner interests may be freely traded.

- *Production Payments.* An oil and gas company may receive funds that represent either (1) a loan to be repaid with interest from specified production or (2) the sale of a mineral interest whereby the company promises to deliver specified quantities of oil or gas from specified future production. Major gas purchasers and mezzanine financing companies are potential sources of such funds. Some production payments are treated as loans for income tax reporting, but as sales for financial reporting.

- *Net Profit Interests.* In this arrangement, the oil and gas company sells an interest in the net profits of specified producing properties. The company may sell a limited net profit interest that remains in effect until a specified time or when cumulative production reaches a specified amount. Alternatively, the company might sell an ORRI. Occasionally, special purpose entities are formed to acquire, with borrowed funds, net profit interests, ORRIs, or production payment interests (see above).

These financing methods are important to the auditor's understanding of an oil and gas company's business. Typically, they are accompanied by complex agreements, sharing ratios that change during the life of the project, and tax treatment that may differ from accounting treatment, all of which must be considered in assessing audit risk, as discussed later in the chapter.

46.2   ACCOUNTING PRINCIPLES AND PRACTICES

(a)   Successful Efforts and Full Cost Accounting

The following pronouncements set forth generally accepted accounting principles unique to oil and gas producing activities:

- SFAS No. 19, *Financial Accounting and Reporting by Oil and Gas Producing Companies* (Accounting Standards Section Oi5.101), which describes the "successful efforts" method of accounting

- SFAS No. 25, *Suspension of Certain Accounting Requirements for Oil and Gas Producing Companies* (Accounting Standards Section Oi5), which recognizes that other methods may be appropriate

- SFAS No. 69, *Disclosures about Oil and Gas Producing Activities* (Accounting Standards Section Oi5), which requires supplementary disclosures of oil and gas producing activities

- SEC Regulation S-X, Article 4, Section 10 (also referred to as S-X Rule 4-10), which prescribes two acceptable methods for public entities—either the successful efforts method described in SFAS No. 19 or a "full cost" method

As a result of these pronouncements, all publicly held (and many privately held) U.S. companies follow either the successful efforts method described in SFAS No. 19 or the full cost method described in S-X Rule 4-10 for oil and gas producing activities.

Additional guidance and interpretations are found in FASB Interpretations, SEC Staff Accounting Bulletins and Financial Reporting Releases, surveys of industry accounting practices, and petroleum accounting books and journals.

The primary differences between the successful efforts and full cost methods relate to capitalization rules and impairment rules. Under the successful efforts method, only those costs associated with the successful discovery of reserves are capitalized, while the costs of unsuccessful exploratory activities are charged directly to expense. Under the full cost method, all exploration efforts are treated as capital costs under the theory that the reserves found are the result of all costs incurred. For impairment of proved properties, SFAS No. 121, *Accounting for the Impairment of Long-Lived Assets to Be Disposed Of* (Accounting Standards Section Oi5.141A), applies to companies using the successful efforts method. The full cost accounting impairment test required by S-X Rule 4-10 effectively supersedes SFAS No. 121 for companies using the full cost method. Both the successful efforts and full cost methods are widely used, with the largest companies tending to use the successful efforts method.[1]

The following examples of accounting policy notes briefly describe each of the two methods prescribed in S-X Rule 4-10:

---

[1] SFAS No. 25, issued in 1979, allowed private companies to use other generally accepted methods of accounting for oil and gas producing activities. At that time, many private companies were using variations of the successful efforts and full cost methods. Currently, such variations are rare.

Oil and Gas Properties—Successful Efforts Method

The Company follows the successful efforts method of accounting for oil and gas producing activities. Under this method, exploration costs, including geological and geophysical costs, delay rentals on undeveloped leases, and exploratory dry hole costs are charged to expense as incurred. Drilling and development costs are capitalized on wells in progress, successful wells, and development dry holes. Lease acquisition costs are capitalized as incurred and are charged to expense when a property is abandoned or its value is substantially impaired, based on a property-by-property evaluation. [Impairment of lease acquisition costs may also be recognized on a group or aggregate basis.] Proved oil and gas properties are assessed for impairment on a field by field basis when circumstances indicate that the carrying amount of properties may not be recoverable. For fields where the Company estimates that its investment will not be recovered, the carrying value of the Company's interest in the field is reduced to the estimated fair value of the property.

Capitalized acquisition costs are depleted on the unit-of-production method based on estimated quantities of total proved reserves. Capitalized drilling and development costs are depleted on the unit-of-production method based on estimated quantities of proved developed reserves.

Gains and losses from sales of proved properties generally are included in the results of operations. Proceeds from sales of unproved properties in which the Company retains an economic interest generally are credited against property costs. No gain is recognized until all property costs have been fully recovered and the Company has no substantial commitment for future performance.

Oil and Gas Properties—Full Cost Method

The Company follows the full cost method of accounting for oil and gas producing activities whereby all costs, by country, of acquiring, exploring for, and developing oil and gas reserves are capitalized and charged against earnings, as set out below. Capitalized costs include lease acquisition costs, geological and geophysical costs, lease rentals and related charges applicable to nonproducing properties, costs of drilling both productive and nonproductive wells, and overhead charges applicable to acquisition, exploration, and development activity.

The capitalized costs for each cost center are amortized using the unit-of-production method based on estimated quantities of total proved reserves. [Amortization may also be computed using units of revenue produced. Also, as discussed below, certain capitalized costs may initially be excluded from the amortization computation.] The Company's calculation of amortization includes estimated future expenditures to be incurred in developing proved reserves and estimated dismantlement and abandonment costs, net of estimated salvage values. In the event the unamortized cost of oil and gas properties exceeds the sum of (a) the present value of future net revenues from proved reserves, computed using current prices and costs and a 10 percent annual discount factor, plus (b) the lower of cost or estimated fair value of unproved properties, plus (c) the cost of properties not being amortized, less (d) the income tax effects related to differences between the book and tax bases of the properties involved, the excess is charged to expense in the period during which such excess occurs.

Sales of oil and gas reserves in place and abandonments of properties are accounted for as a reduction of capitalized costs, with no gain or loss recognized, unless the reduction would significantly alter the relationship between capitalized costs and proved oil and gas reserves.

S-X Rule 4-10(i), on full cost accounting, provides for two alternative methods of determining when costs of investments in unproved properties and major development projects-in-progress should first be included in the costs being amortized over proved reserves: (1) immediate inclusion as incurred or (2) temporary exclusion of such costs until the related property or project has been evaluated. Examples of costs that relate directly to unevaluated properties include leasehold acquisition costs, delay rentals, geological and geophysical costs, exploratory drilling, and capitalized interest. The cost of drilling an exploratory dry hole (i.e., a well not finding proved reserves) should be included in the amortization base upon determination that the well is dry. Any proved reserves associated with the excluded costs of development projects in progress are excluded from the amortization calculation as well.

Unproved property costs must be assessed for impairment at least annually, and preferably quarterly, either (1) individually for each significant property with costs exceeding 10 percent of the net full cost pool or (2) in the aggregate for insignificant properties as discussed in S-X Rule 4-10(c)(1).

In computing amortization under both the full cost and successful efforts methods, S-X Rule 4-10 allows production and proved reserves to be expressed as equivalent physical units based on relative energy content, with gas converted to oil or vice versa. Approximately 5.6 to 5.8 thousand cubic feet (mcf) of gas have the same energy content as one barrel of oil. In practice, most companies use a general approximation that one barrel of oil contains six times as much energy as does one mcf of gas. For full cost accounting, Rule 4-10(i) also allows production and proved reserves to be expressed in units of revenue; amortization then is based on current gross revenues in relation to future gross revenues using current prices and prices contractually stipulated. SAB No. 85 expresses the SEC staff's belief that the units-of-revenue method may be more appropriate than the units-of-production method when oil and gas sales prices are disproportionate to the relative energy content. For example, if the price of oil was $15 per barrel when the price of gas was $1.50 per mcf, then the conversion ratio of 10 mcf to one barrel is disproportionate to the approximate 5.6 to 5.8 mcf to one barrel relative energy content.

(b) Accounting for Joint Operations

Accounting systems for oil and gas producing activities are similar to general business accounting systems. There are significant differences in the data gathering and reporting requirements, however, depending on whether the entity is an operator or a joint venture participant (nonoperator). The two major systems unique to oil and gas producing activities are the joint interest billing system and the revenue distribution system. The operator's joint interest billing system must calculate and record the operator's net cost as well as the costs to be billed to nonoperators. Likewise, the revenue distribution system should allocate revenue among venture participants; this entails first recording the amounts payable to the participants and later making the appropriate payments.

As previously mentioned, joint interest operations evolved because of the need to share the financial burden and risks of oil and gas producing activities. Joint operations typically take the form of a simple joint venture evidenced by a formal agreement, generally referred to as an exploration agreement, defining the geographical area involved and the cost-sharing arrangements, rights, and obligations of the joint venture participants and referencing a second agreement called the operating agreement. The operating agreement designates which party will act as operator of the venture and sets forth the related rights and responsibilities of the operator and nonoperators. The operating agreement includes an exhibit on joint venture accounting that establishes how the operator is to bill the nonoperators for joint venture expenditures and provides nonoperators with the right to conduct joint interest audits of the operator's accounting records for the joint venture. This exhibit usually is based on one of several standard forms developed by the Council of Petroleum Accountants Societies (COPAS) and often is referred to simply as the "COPAS Exhibit."

The following discusses accounting for joint operations, first from the operator's perspective and then from the nonoperators' perspective.

(i) Operator Accounting.   Before a joint venture undertakes a major capital project, such as drilling a well, the operator prepares an authorization for expenditure (AFE) itemizing the estimated costs to complete the project and listing the venture partners and their interests. While an AFE normally is required by the operating agreement, it is also useful as a capital budgeting tool and is used routinely for all major expenditures by oil and gas companies, even if no joint venture exists. As a well is drilled and completed, the operator's field supervisor or engineer at the well site prepares a daily drilling report, which is an abbreviated report of the current status and the drilling or completion activity of the past 24 hours. That report may be compared with another drilling report, prepared by the drilling contractor (also called a tour report). Some daily drilling reports indicate estimated cumulative costs incurred to date.

For shallow wells that are quickly and easily drilled, the AFE subsidiary ledger, combined with the daily drilling report, may provide the basis for the operator's estimate of costs incurred but not invoiced. For other wells, however, the engineering department prepares an estimate of cumulative costs incurred through year-end as a basis for recording the accrual and, if material, of commitments for future expenditures. Since the costs related to wells in progress typically would represent a large portion of an oil and gas company's accrued current liabilities, the auditor's review of the engineering estimates would be a significant part of the auditor's tests for unrecorded liabilities. An oil and gas company will have various other informational reports that can be made available to the auditor for substantiating the cost and status of a well: production reports, drilling contracts, drilling permits, and documents on field schematics, cementing, well completion, material usage, and well plugging and abandonment.

The operator receives charges, credits, and sometimes revenue for a particular property on a 100 percent ("8/8th's") basis and allocates amounts to the nonoperators based on ownership percentages set forth in the division order and maintained in joint interest and revenue distribution master files. One of two approaches generally is used to record these transactions. The first is for the operator to record in the appropriate cost category, such as intangible drilling costs, the full amount of each invoice or remittance as received, as if the operator owned 100 percent of the working interests. At the end of each month, the amounts owed to or from the nonoperators are removed (or cut back) from the operator's accounts utilizing contra or clearing accounts, and are recorded as receivables from (or payables to) the nonoperators. The second commonly used approach is to allocate amounts, when the transaction is recorded initially, to the joint interest receivable accounts and to the operator's appropriate asset, liability, expense, or revenue account.

Periodically, the operator furnishes the nonoperators with a summary billing (joint interest billing) that provides the allocation of all costs (or credits) spent in the current billing period on a property-by-property basis and the total amount owed by the nonoperator for the period. An invoice for each property accompanies the summary billing, providing a brief one-line description of the expenditure or credit under major expense categories for the property and the billing interest and amount owed by the nonoperator. The operator generally is not required to furnish copies of vendor invoices with joint interest billings, but these can be examined and copied during the nonoperators' joint interest audit of the billings.

(ii) Nonoperator Accounting.   The nonoperator's accounting for joint operations is basically the same as that followed by the operator. It is common for a company to act as an operator on some properties and a nonoperator on others. To be able to make comparisons and evaluations that include both types of properties, such companies should record items on a gross basis. A nonoperator should institute timely reviews, followed by timely joint interest audits, of the joint interest billings and any revenue distributions from the operator to determine whether the operator is complying with the joint operating agreement, is billing the nonoperator only authorized charges at the appropriate percentages, and is distributing the appropriate share of revenues.

(iii) Other Accounting Procedures.   The operating agreement's COPAS Exhibit usually permits the operator to charge the joint venture a monthly fixed fee to cover internal costs incurred in operating the joint venture. The COPAS Exhibit also may provide for reimbursement of the operator's actual costs not deemed covered by the fixed fee.

The parties in a joint operation may agree either to share costs in a proportion that is different from that used for sharing revenues, or to change the sharing percentages after a specific event takes place. Typically, that event is "payout," the point at which certain venturers have recovered their initial investment. All parties involved in joint operations encounter payout situations at some time. Controls should be designed to monitor payout status to ensure that all parties are satisfied that items have been properly allocated in accordance with the joint operating agreement.

(c)   Accounting for Gas Imbalances

Generally, the working interest owners of a gas well may take their share of production in kind. Owners may disagree about when and to whom gas is to be sold. If one or more owners cannot, or will not, sell their shares of current production, the remaining owners can sell the entire production as if it were their own and keep the revenues. In such cases, all owners have an understanding that a "gas imbalance" has been created that should be reversed or settled in the future.

The rights of producers related to such imbalances typically are governed by a gas balancing agreement (GBA) which is generally a component of the joint venture's operating agreement. Under the GBA, the owners that did not sell (i.e., the underproduced owners) are allowed to take and sell in the future an additional quantity of gas in excess of their proportionate share to eliminate the imbalance. However, the gas imbalance may grow substantially over several months or even years to the point where full reversal through disproportionate gas sales may not be possible. The GBA may provide for cash settlement, typically for imbalances remaining when gas production ceases.

The operator is responsible for maintaining accountability of gas imbalances and issues a monthly gas balance statement apprising each working interest owner of the difference between the cumulative gas sold and credited to the owner and its economic share, or true ownership, of gas produced for sale. The auditor may utilize these operator statements (perhaps in combination with confirmations or other procedures) to substantiate the quantities of gas reflected in the owner's recorded imbalance.

As explained in COPAS Bulletin No. 24, *Producer Gas Imbalances*, gas sales are accounted for using one of two methods—the entitlements method and the sales method. Under the entitlements method, each working interest owner recognizes gas revenues based on the proportionate share of gas production owned, not on revenues received. Overtakes are recorded as liabilities or deferred revenues, depending on the anticipated method of settlement. Undertakes are recorded as receivables. Collectibility of the receivables is dependent on the settlement terms for imbalances, the plans for settlement, and the adequacy of underlying reserves.

Under the sales method, each working interest owner recognizes gas revenues based on actual sales. This continues as long as an owner has not overproduced its reserves (i.e., has not sold more than its share of ultimate expected gross production). Once an owner reaches this point of overproduction on a well, a liability—not revenue—is recognized. Also at this point, an underproduced owner may recognize revenue and a receivable, recorded in the same way as under the entitlements method and subject to the collectibility considerations mentioned earlier.

Because production expenses are processed by the joint interest billing system and are therefore not affected by the allocation of gas sales among individual well owners, adjustments to production expenses may be necessary under the sales method to reasonably match expenses with revenues. Additionally, estimated oil and gas reserve quantities for companies utilizing the sales method should be adjusted to reflect gas imbalances. Such adjustments generally would not be necessary under the entitlements method.

Additional guidance on gas imbalance accounting is provided by Emerging Issues Task Force (EITF) Issue 90-22, which includes a discussion of the SEC's positions on gas balancing. EITF Issue 90-22 states that:

- All significant gas imbalances should be accounted for consistently (i.e., using either the entitlements or the sales accounting method).

- The method of accounting, as well as the amount of imbalances (units and value), should be disclosed. For SEC registrants, the effect of gas imbalances on operations, liquidity, and capital resources should be disclosed in Management's Discussion and Analysis.

- Receivables recorded using the entitlements method should be valued at the lower of (1) the price in effect at the time of production, (2) the current market price, or (3) the contract price, if there is a contract. (Guidance for gas imbalance liabilities is unclear but would seem to be the greater of the three values. However, when the "liability" is to be liquidated by reduced takes of future gas production, instead of paid in cash, the credit may be viewed as deferred revenue to be carried at the gas price received for the overtake that gave rise to the imbalance.)

- Under the sales method, liabilities recorded for overproduced positions with insufficient reserves to offset the imbalance should be valued at current market price unless a different price is specified in the contract, in which case the contract price may be used.

Gas balancing accounting issues also should be considered when companies purchase oil and gas properties, as it is not unusual for such acquisitions to include properties with significant imbalances. The need to record receivables or liabilities should be considered in recording the acquisition.

The following examples of accounting policy notes briefly describe the two methods of accounting for gas imbalances:

Entitlements Method

The Company accounts for oil and gas operations on the entitlements method, recording as revenue and operating expenses its pro rata share of production and associated operating costs from its oil and gas properties. For sales of natural gas which differ from the Company's pro rata ownership in a well, a receivable (for underproduced properties) or deferred revenue (for overproduced properties) is recorded. Receivables are carried at the lower of current market price or the market price at the time the imbalance occurred. Deferred revenue is carried at the gas price received for gas sold that gave rise to the imbalance.

Sales Method

Sales of natural gas applicable to the Company's interest in producing oil and gas leases are recorded as income when the gas is metered and title transferred pursuant to the gas sales contracts covering the Company's interest in natural gas reserves. During such times as the Company's sales of gas exceed its pro rata ownership in a well, such sales are recorded as income unless total sales from the well have exceeded the Company's share of estimated total gas reserves underlying the property at which time such excess is recorded as a liability.

The Company's method of recording natural gas sales allows for recognition of revenue which may be more or less than the Company's share of pro rata production from certain wells. At December 31, 19___, the Company estimates its balancing position to be approximately ___ mcf on underproduced properties and ___ mcf on overproduced properties. Such volumes have been reflected in the accompanying oil and gas reserve disclosures and the Standardized Measure of Discounted Net Cash Flows Relating to Proved Oil and Gas Reserve Quantities [i.e., special supplemental unaudited disclosures required under SFAS No. 69, discussed later in this chapter].

The Company's policy is to record lease operating expenses from all wells to correspond with the related recognition of revenue.

Alternatively, when balancing positions are not significant and matching of revenue and expenses would not be materially affected, the operating expense policy might indicate, "The Company's policy is to expense its pro rata share of lease operating costs from all wells as incurred. Such expenses relating to the Company's balancing positions on wells are not material."

46.3 RISK FACTORS AND AUDIT REACTION

International economic factors, OPEC politics, volatility in oil and gas prices, the demand for natural gas, interest rates, changes in the U.S. tax law, and changes in capital and credit market perceptions significantly affect industry economics and behavior. In addition, changing prices and demand affect the value of oil and gas reserves used as collateral for bank loans. As a result, companies may find it difficult at times to service their bank debt, pay trade accounts, and meet drilling commitments. Over the past decade, many oil and gas companies have sought to address such problems through property sales, mergers, settlement of trade debt with stock or leasehold interests, reducing overhead costs through salary cuts and personnel layoffs, bankruptcy protection, and debt restructuring.

The auditor should consider such inherent risks, both overall and at the account balance level. Specifically, the auditor should consider the following internal and external risk factors:

- *Liquidity and Financial Resources*. Risks relating to financing include the availability of adequate cash flow from internal and external sources, the impact on cash flow of volatile timing and pricing of oil and gas production, the ability to meet fixed commitments and debt service requirements, and the implications of evidence that may bring into question the entity's continued existence as a going concern.

- *Asset Realization*. The realization of assets is subject to the collectibility of joint interest receivables, the possible impairment of undeveloped properties resulting from declining leasehold values or the entity's inability to carry and develop properties, the potential impairment of producing properties as a result of volatility in the value of the related reserves, and consideration of the need to write down lease and well equipment inventory because of excess supply or obsolescence.

- *Product Marketability*. Production of gas wells may be suspended or curtailed because of such factors as (1) seasonal changes in demand, (2) management's response to low gas prices, and (3) pipeline restrictions. The auditor should ensure that nonproducing gas wells have been identified and should become aware of significant gas contract provisions.

- *Joint Interest Operations.* Joint ownership increases the likelihood of a nonoperator's exposure to a financially distressed operator. The auditor of the nonoperator may need to consider the extent and findings of joint interest audits, the adequacy of the operator's internal control, any conflicts of interest or related party transactions involving the operator, and the operator's ability to meet its financial and operating commitments. The auditor also may consider whether the operator is using funds and properties in accordance with agreements and whether the nonoperator has legal and unencumbered ownership of properties and production revenues.

- *Reliability of Reserve Estimates.* Estimates of future oil and gas production are inherently imprecise. Still, the reliability of reserve estimates depends primarily on the use of reputable and qualified petroleum engineers, and the availability, nature, completeness, and accuracy of the data needed to develop reserve estimates. The reliability of reserve estimates has a direct impact on the calculation of depreciation, depletion, and amortization (DD&A), gas imbalance liabilities, and ceiling and impairment tests (which are described later in this chapter and relate to the realization of the carrying values of assets).

- *Debt Compliance.* Complying with debt covenants may be difficult for oil and gas companies due to the volatility of oil and gas operations. Technical defaults require written waivers and close review by the auditor.

- *Variety and Complexity of Agreements.* The extensive use of innovative financing methods involving complex sharing and commitment terms that require accounting recognition or disclosure is common in the industry. Complying with the specific terms of partnership, joint venture, and operating agreements may be difficult. Contract terms otherwise regarded as inconsequential (e.g., dissolution, buyouts, and additional financing commitments) take on increased importance to both the company and its auditor in an industry downturn.

- *International Risks.* The trend in recent years toward international oil and gas exploration projects exposes companies to business and political risks not previously experienced. Evaluating such projects can be difficult due to the high rate of change in many of these environments and to limitations on the quality and timeliness of information received on the status of such projects. Auditors should evaluate these risk factors carefully as they have an impact on the realizability of oil and gas investments.

- *Environmental Issues.* Energy companies face significant environmental compliance issues related to their exploration and development of oil and gas properties. Such issues normally involve plugging or other means of remediation associated with those properties. Auditors should consider the potential existence of environmental liabilities and the appropriateness of the method used by the company to recognize such costs.

- *Derivatives.* In recent years, the use of derivatives such as options, futures, and swaps has increased significantly. Typically, such derivatives are employed to hedge sales prices of future oil and gas production, but also may be used to speculate on the future price movements of oil and gas. Auditors should understand the nature and underlying purpose of these instruments to effectively evaluate their accounting treatment. For derivatives designated as hedges, auditors should scrutinize the appropriateness of hedge accounting, particularly the effectiveness of the derivative as a hedge, as there are numerous factors that may have an impact on the correlation of price movement between the derivative and the hedged transaction.

- *Limited Insurance Coverage.* Oil and gas companies may, voluntarily or involuntarily, have limited insurance coverage, such as for a well blowout. The auditor should understand the company's risk management policies and consider their effect on the appropriateness of accrued losses and related disclosures.

- *Complex Income Tax Considerations.* The oil and gas industry is subject to very complex tax rules. As a result, income tax accruals of oil and gas companies are unusually complicated. Tax considerations affect the economics of many transactions in the industry to such an extent that they may become a determining factor in investment decisions. Virtually every oil and gas company is faced with a variety of transactions that either must or may be treated differently for tax purposes than for financial reporting purposes. Tax considerations include the immediate deductibility of intangible drilling costs, percentage depletion, tax credits for certain production, and alternative minimum tax issues. Additionally, as a result of the significant industry decline in the 1980s, many oil and gas companies may have net operating loss carryforwards and statutory depletion or tax credit carryforwards that must be evaluated for realizability under the provisions of SFAS No. 109, *Accounting for Income Taxes* (Accounting Standards Section I27). It is also necessary to maintain detailed accounting records to meet IRS and financial reporting requirements resulting from these complex tax regulations. The auditor needs an adequate understanding of the principal income tax considerations affecting oil and gas companies.

- *Related Party Transactions.* Related party transactions are often extensive and may result in possible conflicts of interest among investors, operators, and general partners.

Characteristically, smaller oil and gas companies do not have adequate segregation of duties, although senior management's knowledge of the industry and the company's operations may compensate for this weakness. As oil and gas companies grow, the increase in the number and location of properties requires the development of more comprehensive internal control. This includes the development of sophisticated accounting systems capable of tracking detailed drilling costs, revenue and operating expense information on a well-by-well basis, information needed by management to effectively monitor the operations of its properties, and detailed information necessary for income tax reporting purposes.

In determining the audit strategy for an entity with significant oil and gas producing activities, the auditor should consider the type of operations in which it engages. Such considerations include whether the entity is an operator or a nonoperator; whether its properties are offshore or onshore, or located in numerous countries; whether it manages limited partnerships; and whether it owns a small percentage of many properties or a larger percentage of a few properties. In addition, the audit strategy will be affected by the company's accounting method. In full cost accounting, there is a possibility of error in measuring depletion and in overall valuation relating to the ceiling test. Successful efforts companies have a large number of cost centers, requiring accurate records and depletion calculations.

46.4   TYPICAL TRANSACTIONS AND INTERNAL CONTROL

As previously noted, key transactions of property operators are the receipt and distribution of oil and gas revenues and the payment and rebilling of drilling and operating costs to joint interest partners. Accordingly, property owners' accounting systems are focused on those transactions. Due to the high volume of transactions typically processed by these systems, related controls (both monitoring and application controls) are critical to the reliability of the resulting accounting records and financial reporting. Testing the controls to support a control risk assessment that is below the maximum or at low typically will be an efficient audit strategy.

Typical controls in the industry are described below.

(a)   Lease Records and Master File Maintenance

Oil and gas companies generally maintain detailed title records supporting the allocation of ownership interests in operated properties. Typically, such ownership information also is input into lease master files, detailing the working interest and revenue allocation percentages of each interest owner. These master files are utilized on a monthly basis to process revenue checks and joint interest billings for distribution to all relevant parties. Controls should provide for accurate and timely updating of these master files, as well as prevent unauthorized access to, or alteration of, such master files. Segregation of duties and supervisory review and approval of all changes to master files are typical.

(b)   Revenue and Royalties Payable

Controls should ensure that the company receives all production revenues to which it is entitled and makes appropriate distributions to other joint interest partners. Controls generally will include comparison of revenue receipts to run tickets, gauge reports, or meter statements; month-to-month comparison of production volumes and prices, including investigation of variances; and regular comparison of revenue data to production data. Controls over revenues received for distribution may include monthly reconciliation of amounts received to amounts disbursed or transferred to suspense accounts. Controls over suspensed amounts should ensure that the amounts are reviewed regularly and released only upon proper authorization.

(c)   Determination of Royalties and Production Taxes

Traditionally, sales of produced crude oil and natural gas occurred at the point of production (i.e., "at the wellhead"), and payments of royalties and production-based taxes were based on the sales prices. Calculating royalties and production-based taxes has become complicated because of the numerous variations in the points at which oil and gas currently are sold. In addition to being sold at the point of production, produced crude oil and natural gas may be sold at a distant location such as a crude oil refinery or various points on a gas pipeline system. In addition, oil and gas may be sold under forward sales contracts at fixed prices or at prices tied to published price indices that vary from prices for sales at the wellhead. State and local tax regulations and lease provisions affecting royalties may be unclear as to whether or how sales prices should be adjusted for purposes of determining taxes or royalties. As a result, royalty owners and state agencies have asserted claims against oil and gas producing companies for underpayment of royalties and taxes, creating contingent liabilities for such companies.

(d)   Joint Interest Billings

An operator of oil and gas properties should have controls to ensure that costs are properly authorized and recorded, that gross costs are charged to the correct wells and projects (and as a result to the correct joint interest owners), and that accurate and timely joint interest statements are generated. Such controls should include review and approval of all such costs, including the appropriate approval for payment, coding of costs to the proper property, and the proper classification of expenditures. Such coding is particularly important in light of the complexities inherent in joint interest operations. Coding is also significant to financial reporting of exploration activities, particularly for successful efforts companies.

In a typical limited partnership, virtually all transactions affecting the partnership flow through the general partner's accounting system. Only isolated revenue and expenses flow directly to the limited partners. Auditors of both companies that act as general partners and the limited partnerships they manage often find it efficient to perform tests of controls relating to joint interest billings and revenue.

46.5   SUBSTANTIVE TESTS

The following discussion addresses the principal audit areas unique to oil and gas producing activities. The audit objectives and auditing procedures are not intended to be all-inclusive, nor are all of the procedures likely to be applicable to any one audit. The auditing procedures used on an engagement should be tailored to the specific accounting method followed and usually will be significantly affected by the control risk assessment.

(a)   Joint Interest Billings Receivable

As noted previously, oil and gas operators may have difficulty collecting joint interest billings when there is a downturn in the industry and nonoperators experience liquidity problems. In evaluating the collectibility of receivables, the operator often estimates the future net revenues that it can withhold from properties operated on behalf of nonpaying parties. The auditor should examine evidence that a valid claim exists against future revenues. If the operator projects recovery of amounts over a period of more than one year, classification between current and long-term assets should be considered.

When it becomes apparent that delinquent accounts are uncollectible, operators often contemplate charging them to the cost of oil and gas properties rather than to the allowance for uncollectible accounts, or current-period expense, as appropriate. Uncollectible receivables should be charged to the allowance account, or to current-period operations as bad debt expense, unless the operator has obtained, or will obtain, an assignment of the nonpaying party's interest in the properties. At a minimum, the portion of those uncollectible receivables realizable from future production may be capitalized as a cost of oil and gas properties. These capitalized costs would then be subject to the operator's normal accounting policy for the disposition of capitalized oil and gas property costs.

Audit objectives and related auditing procedures for joint interest receivables include:

Audit Objective	*Typical Auditing Procedures*
Joint interest receivables represent valid and accurate amounts owed to the company for authorized charges incurred on behalf of other participants in joint operations.	Confirm receivables and/or examine subsequent receipts of significant receivables.
	Examine third-party charges billed to others to determine that they have been charged to the proper well and are classified appropriately as to type of cost.
	Test ownership percentages used in billing by examining operating agreements, lease assignments, AFEs, title opinions, or division orders.
Joint interest receivables include all amounts due to the company relating to joint operations.	Obtain a list of all properties for which the company acts as operator.
	Determine that the company has recorded all costs incurred related to its operated properties, including amounts to be billed to others and its own pro rata share.
Joint interest receivable listings are compiled accurately and the totals are included properly in the financial statements.	Test the clerical accuracy of joint interest receivable listings.
Joint interest receivables are collectible and reduced to estimated realizable value when appropriate.	Review joint interest receivables for potential uncollectible accounts.
	Test the aging and amounts due.
	Review subsequent receipts. For receivables that are collateralized by the participant's interest in a well, examine the supporting assignments and reserve reports.

Audit Objective	*Typical Auditing Procedures*
Joint interest receivables are classified properly in the balance sheet (current versus long-term) and the appropriate disclosures of amounts due from related parties have been made.	Review reserve reports to determine timing of receipt, if collection is dependent on future revenues from production. Review disclosure of categories of joint interest receivables.

(b) Oil and Gas Property Costs

Oil and gas property costs typically represent the largest asset in the balance sheet and may be the most complex account to audit. The audit aspects of oil and gas property costs vary according to the method of accounting, although some issues, such as reliance on proved reserve estimates, interest capitalization, and expensing of workovers, are common to both methods. Under either full cost or successful efforts, the major audit issues relate to the following accounting areas: (1) determining which costs are capitalizable, (2) amortizing capitalized costs, (3) performing impairment tests, and (4) recording mineral conveyances. SFAS No. 19 and SEC S-X Rule 4-10 prescribe how a public company should make those determinations.

(i) Successful Efforts Issues.   Paragraph 19 of SFAS No. 19 requires the costs of dry exploratory wells to be charged to expense, while under paragraph 22 the costs of dry development wells are capitalized. Therefore, it is important that wells be classified properly. SFAS No. 19 (para. 274) defines a development well as "a well drilled within the proved area of an oil or gas reservoir to the depth of a stratigraphic horizon known to be productive." Generally, an exploratory well is any well other than a development well, a service well, or a stratigraphic test well.

Those definitions do not always coincide with definitions commonly used in the industry (e.g., the industry definition of a development well may be broader than the definition in SFAS No. 19). This results in two auditing problems. First, certain exploratory dry holes may be improperly classified as development wells, a situation that occurs primarily with stepout or delineation wells drilled at the edges of a producing reservoir. Second, there may be inconsistencies between the SFAS No. 69 disclosures and the drilling statistics found in Item 2 of Form 10-K (which usually is prepared by nonaccounting personnel). The auditor should examine the data (such as maps and reserve reports) supporting the classification of significant wells and discuss the classifications with appropriate company personnel. A company that reports a large number of unsuccessful development wells may not be classifying wells correctly, since development wells are generally successful.

The auditor should consider reviewing the status of wells, particularly gas wells, in which production has been suspended. The criteria under which management continues to carry as an asset the costs of wells where drilling is complete but the evaluation of the well is not complete, should be reviewed. Paragraph 34 of SFAS No. 19 identifies criteria that must be met for continued capitalization of those costs. The auditor should review budgets, AFEs, and other documentation supporting management's firm commitments and plans to further develop areas in which exploratory wells are located, as well as the company's ability to make appropriate future expenditures.

FASB Interpretation No. 36, *Accounting for Exploratory Wells in Progress at the End of a Period* (Accounting Standards Section Oi5), requires that the accumulated costs at year-end for an exploratory well that is determined to be a dry hole in the following year, but before the financial statements are issued, be charged to expense in the year in which they were incurred. Costs incurred in the subsequent year should be charged to expense in the period incurred. If the amount to be expensed in the subsequent year is deemed material, the auditor should consider whether disclosure as a subsequent event is appropriate.

In assessing impairment of unproved properties on an individual property basis under SFAS No. 19 (para. 28), the auditor should consider the nature of a company's activities. For example, if a company sells undeveloped leases (either to other oil and gas companies or to partnerships), impairment should be evaluated based on expected selling prices for the acreage rather than on drilling plans. The key audit issue is identifying management's intent with regard to each property and relating that intent, and the entity's ability to achieve it, to the impairment calculation. The auditor should be aware that most companies do not formally segregate undeveloped properties into two categories on their books (i.e., to be sold as an undeveloped lease or to be drilled); instead, the segregation occurs quarterly and at year-end when the company assesses impairment. The auditor should seek evidence from exploration personnel who are involved with the properties on a daily basis.

(ii) Full Cost Issues.   Capitalized costs for a company using the full cost method of accounting include internal labor and overhead costs directly related to acquisition, exploration, and development activities. Capitalization of internal costs is very subjective, however, and the portion of labor and overhead costs capitalized varies significantly from company to company. Whatever practice is adopted, it must be reasonable and applied consistently from year to year; audit evidence also should be available to support management's assertions about the level of labor and overhead capitalized.

For many full cost companies, the greatest risk that the financial statements will be materially misstated arises from the application of the full cost ceiling test. Under the ceiling test, for each cost center, the capitalized costs, less accumulated amortization and related deferred income taxes, may not exceed the sum of (1) the present value, discounted at 10 percent a year, of projected future after-tax cash flow from producing proved reserves, assuming that current prices and cost rates remain unchanged; (2) the lower of cost or fair value (net of related deferred taxes) of unproved properties included in costs being amortized; and (3) the cost (net of related deferred taxes) of unevaluated properties that are not being amortized (i.e., major development projects), which must be evaluated separately for impairment at least annually. The SEC staff has informally expressed the view that oil and gas companies should perform ceiling tests quarterly, based on spot prices and fixed and determinable contract prices as of the end of each quarter. This means that seasonally low gas prices at the end of a quarter may necessitate an irreversible write-off of capitalized costs, even though the impairment that has occurred seems temporary and related to seasonal factors.

If net capitalized costs in the full cost pool exceed the ceiling, a write-down may be avoided if consideration of subsequent events, such as price increases or additional reserves on properties owned at year-end becoming proved, eliminates the excess. Such subsequent events must occur before the audit report date and must relate to properties owned at year-end. The avoidance of a write-down must be adequately disclosed, but the subsequent events should not be considered in the disclosures required by SFAS No. 69 of proved reserves and related discounted future cash flows. SAB No. 47, Topic 12, Item D-3b, contains further details.

S-X Rule 4-10(i)(6) provides rules regarding mineral property conveyances requiring that sales of oil and gas properties be accounted for as an adjustment of capitalized costs, unless the adjustment would cause a significant alteration of the relationship between remaining capitalized costs and proved reserves attributable to the cost center. A significant alteration normally would not be expected to result from a sale involving less than 25 percent of the total reserve quantities of the cost center. Rule 4-10(i)(6) also limits the recognition of income from management fees from limited partnerships, and drilling or other contract services on properties in which the company owns an economic interest.

(iii) Proved Reserves.   Amortization, the full cost ceiling test, and proved property impairment assessment are all based on proved reserve estimates made by specialists, generally petroleum engineers. The auditor should follow the guidance on use of a specialist, as discussed later in this chapter [see Section 5(f), Supplementary Financial Disclosures].

(iv) Impairment of Oil and Gas Properties.   Proved oil and gas properties must be considered for impairment under the provisions of SFAS No. 121. SFAS No. 121 did not amend the impairment consideration requirements previously discussed with respect to unproved properties. Additionally, companies utilizing full cost accounting will continue to apply the full cost ceiling test prescribed by the SEC, which is often more restrictive than the provisions of SFAS No. 121.

Applying certain provisions of SFAS No. 121 to oil and gas companies requires judgment. Some of those provisions are discussed below:

- Long-lived assets must be assessed for impairment "whenever events or changes in circumstances indicate that the carrying amount of an asset may not be recoverable." Due to the volatility of prices and other industry factors, as well as the large number and wide dispersion of many oil and gas companies' properties, determining the events and circumstances warranting further assessment of impairment may be difficult. Factors such as declines in oil or natural gas prices, changes in estimated development or production costs, and significant downward revisions of reserve estimates should be considered. The use of the units-of-production method of amortization may lead to an impairment in the later stages of the life of a reservoir because of the increasing per unit production cost. An additional complicating factor is that public companies will be required to assess such impairment indicators quarterly.

- For purposes of assessing impairment, assets should be "grouped at the lowest level for which there are identifiable cash flows that are largely independent of the cash flows of other groups of assets." Accordingly, assessment of oil and gas properties typically is done on a field basis. Although reserves and net revenues can be estimated for individual wells, all wells in a field produce from a common reservoir, and therefore cash flows from one well generally are not independent of those generated by other wells in the field. This provision of SFAS No. 121 changed significantly the consideration of impairment for successful efforts companies, which previously evaluated the recoverability of total oil and gas properties generally based on undiscounted net cash flows on a worldwide basis. Accordingly, many successful efforts companies recorded write-downs of oil and gas properties upon implementation of the standard.

- Estimates of expected future cash flows must represent "the best estimate based on reasonable and supportable assumptions and projections." SFAS No. 121 allows the consideration of judgmental factors such as oil and gas price escalations and probable or possible reserve quantities, which were not considered under prior accounting standards.

- For properties for which impairment is indicated, judgment also is involved in the consideration of fair value. While valuation generally is based on the present value of estimated future cash flows, available information on purchases and sales of similar properties should be considered. Determining an appropriate interest rate for calculating the discounted cash flows, which under SFAS No. 121 is defined as a rate commensurate with the risks involved, also involves considerable judgment.

(v) Capitalization of Interest.   There are several issues involved in applying SFAS No. 34, *Capitalization of Interest Cost* (Accounting Standards Section I67), to successful efforts companies and to full cost companies that exclude unevaluated property costs from amortization. Undeveloped leases qualify for interest capitalization as long as exploration activities necessary to prepare the lease for its intended use are in progress. Qualifying activities include predrilling administrative and technical work, title opinion curative work, and obtaining drilling permits from regulatory agencies. For an unproved property covering a large number of acres, the auditor should review the circumstances and activity carefully to determine whether the work being done on a portion of the acreage allows interest capitalization on the entire block. If drilling activities are continuous, drilling costs qualify for interest capitalization until the property is capable of producing and delivering oil or gas.

Two related problems exist with regard to the capitalization period. The first concerns the temporary suspension of activities. If substantially all activities related to acquisition of an asset are suspended, interest capitalization should cease until they are resumed. For example, if a company determines that an exploration project is too expensive or risky to pursue without joint venture partners and suspends activities until joint venture partners are located, interest capitalization should cease. When activities resume, the project again qualifies for interest capitalization.

The second issue relates to the cessation of capitalization on completion of activities. Generally, when a well is completed, interest capitalization is suspended unless external factors (e.g., the failure of the pipeline company to complete construction) prevent the well from producing. If significant costs are required to hook up a well, capitalization should recommence when those activities begin and should cease again when the hookup is completed. Interest capitalization may cease sooner under the full cost method as a result of unevaluated properties being transferred into the amortization base on determining that proved reserves exist, even if production has not yet commenced.

(vi) Workover Costs.   Operations to restore or increase production from an already producing well are referred to as a "workover." The accounting for workover costs depends on whether the project is designed to increase the quantity of proved reserves assigned to the property. If it is, the workover costs should be treated as part of the capitalized costs of oil and gas properties. If, on the other hand, the workover project is designed to restore or maintain production or enhance the rate of production without significantly increasing proved reserves, the workover costs should be treated as lease operating expenses. Completion costs incurred within a geological formation to which proved developed nonproducing reserves previously have been assigned are considered to be development costs, not workover costs.

(vii) Mineral Conveyances.   Mineral interests in oil and gas properties are conveyed to others for a variety of reasons, including to spread risks, obtain financing, improve operating efficiency, and achieve tax benefits. A transaction may involve the transfer of all or part of the rights and responsibilities of operating a property (an operating or working interest); the transferor may or may not retain an interest in the oil and gas produced. Sometimes an interest in a property entitles the owner to a share of revenues from the property, but does not obligate the owner to pay the costs of operating the property (a nonoperating interest such as a royalty, ORRI, or net profit interest). A transaction may, on the other hand, involve transferring a nonoperating interest to another party and retaining the operating interest, or transferring part of an operating interest and retaining the remaining part. One example of a mineral conveyance is a farmout arrangement, in which the farmor (or holder of the lease right) allows another entity (as farmee) to earn a working interest in the lease in exchange for paying all costs of drilling and completing a well. Usually the farmor retains a small overriding royalty that is convertible to a stated working interest at payout.

SFAS No. 19 contains detailed guidance on how the various types of mineral conveyances should be accounted for under the successful efforts method of accounting. As previously mentioned, Rule 4-10(i)(6) generally prohibits income recognition in connection with sales or other conveyances of oil and gas properties under full cost accounting.

Typically, the auditor should examine individual mineral conveyances in detail to discern the true economic substance of the transaction. In auditing mineral conveyances, the auditor should remember that under the successful efforts method, while income recognition is possible when an economic interest is retained, it is not appropriate if the original cost has not been fully recovered. As noted, under the full cost method, income recognition has been virtually eliminated by Rule 4-10. Accordingly, the auditor should review carefully any income recognized from mineral conveyances. Special attention should be paid to situations in which income is recognized by sponsors of limited partnerships.

(viii) Audit Objectives and Related Auditing Procedures. Audit objectives and related auditing procedures for costs of oil and gas properties include:

Audit Objective	*Typical Auditing Procedures*
Oil and gas properties physically exist and the company has legal title or similar rights of ownership to the properties.	Examine drilling reports, AFEs, operating agreements, mineral leases, and assignments.
	Compare listing of producing wells with revenue records.
	Determine that delay rentals have been paid or that leases are currently under production.
Oil and gas properties recorded include all mineral interests owned by the company.	Reconcile data maintained by the land department (for undeveloped leases), exploration department (for wells in progress), and production department (for producing wells) to the general ledger and properties listed in the joint interest billing and division of interest master files.
	Perform a reasonableness test of the relationship of costs incurred, as recorded in the general ledger, to documentation about net wells and net acreage maintained outside the accounting department.
	Compare the listing of well activity with the AFE log.
Amortization is calculated properly.	Test the mathematical calculation of amortization.
	Assess the reasonableness of the proved reserve estimates, applying the procedures for use of a specialist.
Oil and gas property listings are compiled accurately and the totals are included properly in the financial statements.	Test the clerical accuracy of oil and gas property listings.
Oil and gas properties are properly stated at the lower of (1) cost, less accumulated DD&A, or (2) unimpaired value.	Examine canceled checks for lease bonus payments, and supporting documents for other direct acquisition costs.
	Determine that well costs incurred in the current year are supportable, recorded at the company's proper ownership percentage, and properly classified as to cost type.

Audit Objective	*Typical Auditing Procedures*

<table>
<tr><td></td><td>Determine well status (i.e., exploratory versus development).</td></tr>
<tr><td></td><td>Ascertain that internal costs capitalized are supportable and in compliance with the method of accounting followed.</td></tr>
<tr><td></td><td>Determine that interest cost capitalized during the current year relates to qualifying property on which qualifying activity has occurred.</td></tr>
<tr><td></td><td>Review the company's DD&A computations for accuracy, use of appropriate data, and conformity with GAAP and S-X Rule 4-10.</td></tr>
<tr><td></td><td>For full cost companies, review the ceiling test and analysis of unamortized property impairment for accuracy, use of appropriate data, and conformity with S-X Rule 4-10 and SAB No. 47.</td></tr>
<tr><td></td><td>For successful efforts companies, determine whether proved and unproved property costs have been impaired.</td></tr>
<tr><td>Sold, abandoned, or transferred properties have been identified and accounted for properly.</td><td>Examine supporting documentation (e.g., cash receipts, farmout agreement, or lease assignment) and determine that the disposition is properly recorded.</td></tr>
<tr><td></td><td>Recalculate the gain or loss, if applicable.</td></tr>
<tr><td></td><td>Compare wells with capitalized costs to revenue records.</td></tr>
<tr><td>Wells in progress at year-end are reflected appropriately in the financial statements.</td><td>Review results of drilling up to the date of financial statement issuance.</td></tr>
<tr><td></td><td>Determine that all costs incurred through year-end have been properly accrued.</td></tr>
<tr><td>Oil and gas properties are classified properly in the balance sheet and appropriate disclosures have been made.</td><td>Review financial statement classifications, possibly with the aid of a specialized disclosure checklist or other practice aid.</td></tr>
</table>

(c) Oil and Gas Revenues and Related Expenses

Except for companies with sophisticated computerized revenue systems (which record revenue on the accrual basis using monthly production data), revenues usually are accounted for initially on the cash basis; the remittance advice prepared by the purchaser is used as the source document. The cash basis often is used by smaller companies and companies that do not operate properties, because they either do not receive monthly production data from the field or lack the capability to accurately compute production and revenue by well from internal data.

For purposes of accrual basis reporting, a company using the cash basis must accrue unpaid production at least quarterly and at year-end. The accrual is composed of two parts, amounts related to the typical one- to two-month lag in collections for mature wells, and amounts held in suspense because of title problems on new wells. The auditor might employ analytical procedures that focus on the amount accrued, the proper inclusion of all operated and nonoperated properties, the use of appropriate production data and sales prices, and the proper accrual of related taxes and operating expenses. Accrued oil and gas sales also may be substantiated by comparison with subsequent receipts.

Generally, in the continental United States, oil remaining in storage tanks at period-end (i.e., inventory) is not recognized as inventory on the balance sheet. Accrued revenue typically is based either on the company's production and pricing records of recent monthly sales quantities or on recent cash remittances.

For companies involved in the marketing of natural gas, imbalances may arise between joint interest owners and with a gas pipeline. The pipeline gas imbalance is the difference between gas produced and delivered into pipelines for transport and gas taken by the company's purchaser. Such pipeline imbalances can be positive—creating a receivable or natural gas inventory, or negative—generally requiring the company to produce and deliver additional gas to the pipeline to cover the negative position. Typically, such negative pipeline imbalances are reflected as a liability to the pipeline, effectively deferring the recognition of revenue until the gas has been produced. Pipeline imbalances typically can be confirmed with the pipeline or agreed to a monthly statement provided by the pipeline. As a part of the changes resulting from the Federal Energy Regulatory Commission's Order 636, pipelines have instituted potentially significant penalties for such imbalances in excess of specified tolerance levels. Accordingly, production monitoring and control activities by gas producers have become increasingly important. Auditors should obtain support for the existence and realizability of gas inventories, including consideration of the impact of any such penalties for pipeline imbalance positions.

As previously noted, companies utilizing the sales method of accounting for gas imbalances must consider the need for deferral of revenue on individual wells when it is estimated that the company has produced more than its share of ultimate reserves. Similarly, an accrual or deferral of operating expenses may be warranted to properly match such expenses with gas sales revenues. Auditors should evaluate the procedures utilized by gas producers to ensure the completeness and accuracy of gas balancing information utilized in these analyses. An additional concern is ensuring that such information is current, particularly for nonoperated wells where producers typically rely on the well operator to supply gas balancing statements.

Audit objectives and related procedures for testing oil and gas revenues include:

Audit Objective	*Typical Auditing Procedures*
Recorded oil and gas revenues represent the company's proper ownership share of actual quantities produced and sold. Recorded oil and gas revenues do not in-	For selected wells or individual amounts recorded, agree recorded revenue and quantities sold to supporting remittance advices.

Audit Objective	*Typical Auditing Procedures*
clude amounts owned by others.	Compare recorded production with production reports.
	Test the accuracy of the master division of interest file. Agree ownership percentages to signed division orders.
All oil and gas produced and sold during the year is reflected in the accounting records.	In conjunction with the review of the company's year-end revenue accrual, determine that the appropriate number of months' revenue has been recorded for significant wells.
	Compare amounts recorded with remittance advices or production reports.
	Compare recorded revenue with amounts projected in the company's reserve report and with prior-year production.
	Investigate accounting for imbalances.
	Analyze monthly production revenue in total, or for significant wells, and investigate unusual fluctuations.
Oil and gas revenues are recorded at the proper price.	Compare unit sales prices by well with sales contracts or posted prices.
	Compare average unit prices by well or lease with prior-year prices and/or industry data.
	Investigate significant unusual fluctuations.

(d) Lease and Well Equipment Inventory

Declines in drilling activity may be accompanied by higher levels of inventory of tubular goods and wellhead equipment than are needed for planned drilling activities. It has become standard industry practice to classify tubular goods and wellhead equipment as inventory in the current assets section of a company's balance sheet. This inventory actually has two components. One is the portion of inventory that will be transferred to the company's oil and gas property accounts as it is used in drilling. The second component is the portion to be sold to joint interest partners at the time the goods are used in drilling activity. The accounting procedures called for in standard operating agreements allow new material to be transferred to the joint account at the manufacturer's prevailing base price. This component of inventory should be carried at the lower of cost or the amount that will be recovered from the joint interest partners. If the company has more than a one-year supply of inventory to be sold to joint venture partners, classification of the excess portion as a noncurrent asset should be considered (such classification does not mitigate the necessity to consider impairment).

If the company has more inventory on hand than can reasonably be used in its operations and consequently intends to sell the excess at current market prices, impairment should be considered. This may be done by comparing the carrying amount with market prices and, if appropriate, charging the excess to current-period earnings. In determining the impairment amount, it is acceptable to apply the lower of cost or market test to either individual items or inventory in the aggregate. The auditor also should consider observing the inventory, paying particular attention to the condition of the lease and well equipment.

(e) Analytical Procedures

Consistent with the nature of oil and gas exploration and production, for which results of operations are determined largely by production levels and product prices, analytical procedures are highly effective. Typical analytical procedures may include:

- Comparison of current-year production levels of oil and gas with those of prior years, giving consideration to new wells acquired or drilled and the anticipated production decline from existing wells, and review of monthly production levels, considering unusual variances and seasonal trends.
- Review of average oil and gas prices for the current year in relation to the prior year and current-year industry data.
- Review of average monthly prices, considering unusual variances and seasonal pricing patterns.
- Review of lease operating expenses in comparison to the prior year.
- Review of production tax expense, as a percentage of oil and gas sales for the current versus prior year for consistency.
- Review of DD&A in comparison to the prior year, including comparison of DD&A expense per equivalent unit of production.

Additionally, management's use of such analytical procedures on a monthly basis, combined with investigation and resolution of any unusual variances noted by such review, generally is a significant control supporting the reliability of the company's financial statements. The auditor should consider this monitoring control in assessing control risk.

(f) Supplementary Financial Disclosures

SFAS No. 69 details supplementary disclosures for the oil and gas industry, which are required only for public companies. Both public and nonpublic companies, however, must provide a description of the accounting method followed and net of disposing of capitalized costs. Supplementary disclosures required for financial statements filed with the SEC fall into three categories:

- Historical data relating to capitalized costs, costs incurred, and operations with regard to oil and gas producing activity
- Proved reserve quantities

- Standardized measure of discounted future net cash flows relating to proved oil and gas reserve quantities, also known as SMOG (standardized measure of oil and gas)

The supplementary disclosures are required of companies with significant oil and gas producing activities; significant is defined as 10 percent or more of revenue, operating results, or identifiable assets. The supplementary disclosures need not be audited, but must be labeled clearly as unaudited.

Because of the reliance placed on supplementary reserve information by financial statement users, and because certain audited information (i.e., amortization and impairment information) is derived directly from the reserve data, the auditor should have a basic understanding of how reserve data is developed and of the inherent risks associated with it. Proved oil and gas reserves are the estimated quantities of crude oil, natural gas, and natural gas liquids that have been demonstrated with reasonable certainty, based on geological and engineering data, to be recoverable in future years from known reservoirs under existing economic and operating conditions (i.e., using prices and costs in effect on the date of the estimate). Proved reserves are inherently imprecise because of the uncertainties and limitations of the data available.

For financial reporting purposes, SFAS No. 25 specifies that the definition of "proved reserves" is that developed by the Department of Energy and adopted by the SEC. In applying for credit and for other purposes, however, oil and gas companies often use proved reserve estimates based on the definition of proved reserves adopted by the Society of Petroleum Engineers (SPE) and Society of Petroleum Evaluation Engineers (SPEE), which is broader than the SEC definition.

Most large and many medium-sized companies have qualified engineers on their staff to prepare oil and gas reserve studies. Many companies use independent engineering consultants to determine, review, or "audit" reserve estimates. Usually, reserve studies are reviewed and updated at least annually to take into account new discoveries and adjustments of previous estimates.

Auditors of oil and gas companies generally use the reserve studies prepared by petroleum engineers. Because of the expertise required to estimate reserve quantities, however, the auditor typically does not have the necessary qualifications to fully evaluate an engineer's estimate. Therefore, as required by SAS No. 73, *Using the Work of a Specialist* (AU Section 336), the auditor ordinarily should be satisfied as to the reputation and independence of an outside engineer or the qualifications and experience of an in-house engineer who estimates reserve quantities. The auditor also should obtain an understanding of the engineer's methods and assumptions used in preparing the reserve estimates, should appropriately test the accounting data provided to the engineer, and should consider whether the engineer's report supports the related information in the financial statements.

Appropriate testing of the accounting data varies with the circumstances of the engagement. It may include (1) performing analytical procedures on summarized reserve information, (2) comparing reserve information with the current year's actual production and operating costs, and (3) testing the accuracy and completeness of selected properties' historical production, ownership interests, payout determinations, year-end prices, and cost rates.

In addition, if the SFAS No. 69 supplementary reserve information accompanies audited financial statements, AU Section 558, *Required Supplementary Information*, and interpretations thereof (AU Section 9558) require that the auditor:

- Inquire about management's understanding of the specific requirements for disclosure of supplementary oil and gas reserve information
- Inquire about the qualifications of the person who estimated the reserve quantity information
- Compare recent production with reserve estimates for significant properties and inquire about disproportionate ratios
- Compare reserve quantity information with information used for the amortization computation and inquire about differences
- Inquire about the methods used to calculate the SMOG disclosures
- Inquire about whether the methods and bases for estimating reserve information are documented and whether the information is current

An additional factor that the auditor should review for reasonableness is the projected development expenditures included in the reserve study and whether the company has sufficient financial resources to complete such development in the projected time frame.

If the auditor believes that the information is not presented appropriately, AU Section 558 requires additional inquiries. Because of the nature of estimates of oil and gas reserve information, however, the auditor may not be able to evaluate the responses to additional inquiries. If the auditor is unable to complete the prescribed procedures or has unresolved doubts about adherence to the guidelines for presenting the data, he or she should include an explanatory paragraph in the report on the related financial statements.

(g) Statement of Cash Flows

With respect to the reporting of cash flows, particular consideration should be given to the classification of activities between operating, investing, and financing activities. For example, exploration costs are related to investing activities; however, successful efforts companies have to add back the activities that have been expensed (such as dry hole costs) to net income in order to derive cash flow from operating activities. The purchase of equipment inventory may be reported both as an operating activity (to the extent that inventory will be sold to third parties) and as an investing activity (to the extent that inventory will be transferred to oil and gas properties upon completion of wells). Another issue is the presentation of changes in joint interest billings receivable or payable. For nonoperators, presentation as an operating activity appears appropriate; however, for operators, classification as a financing or investing activity may be appropriate under the assumption that the transaction spreads risk, or that the operator either lends funds to, or borrows funds from, nonoperators. Auditors should consider the substance of transactions to ensure that proper classification is achieved.

(h)   Disclosure of Risks and Uncertainties

Statement of Position (SOP) 94-6, *Disclosure of Certain Significant Risks and Uncertainties*, requires companies to disclose information regarding the nature of operations, accounting estimates (including those deemed to be significant estimates), and current vulnerability due to concentrations. Most significant to oil and gas companies is the consideration of significant estimates requiring disclosure. Any or all of the inherent risk factors mentioned previously might necessitate the use of estimates meeting the disclosure requirements of SOP 94-6. Disclosure is required if it is reasonably possible that an estimate will change in the near term and the effect of the change would be material to the financial statements. Because of the imprecise nature of oil and gas reserve estimation, and the potential significance of changes in such estimates to the financial statements, disclosure of reserve estimates normally would be expected. The existence of concentrations, such as significant revenue from a particular area, project, or purchaser, also should be considered for disclosure.

47

Auditing Real Estate Companies

OVERVIEW OF THE INDUSTRY

The boundaries of the real estate industry are difficult to define because many entities that engage in real estate transactions also derive substantial revenues from other sources. For the purposes of this chapter, a real estate company is one that derives its principal revenues from activities involving the control, ownership, or sale of land and buildings. This definition encompasses companies that engage in:

- Owning undeveloped land for wholesale or retail sale
- Land development
- Improving and selling real property as a primary product (e.g., a home builder)
- Acquiring and improving property to be held as an investment for the production of current income and for future appreciation

Many companies are involved in more than one of those activities and, in addition, derive revenues from a variety of ancillary services associated with real estate, such as financing, property management, insurance, subcontracting, and brokerage. In addition, a number of other types of businesses, such as brokerage, leasing, management, and financing, are closely associated with real estate ownership and operations.

(a) Organizational Forms

Companies in the real estate industry are organized under various legal forms, including sole proprietorships, limited partnerships, limited liability companies, general partnerships, corporations, joint ventures, and trusts. The form of organization is governed largely by the objectives of the business. For example, a contractor or builder normally selects the corporate form of organization to obtain the benefits of limited liability because of the business risks associated with this type of operation. Owners of an individual project may organize as a limited partnership to obtain the benefits of both limited liability for the passive investors and the pass-through of tax losses that may be deductible in certain situations.

Real estate is particularly sensitive to changes in economic conditions, and real estate companies usually avoid assembling large central staffs and making heavy capital investments, so that overhead can be reduced to a minimum during difficult economic times.

(i) Limited Partnerships.   The limited partnership form of organization is especially well suited to real estate ventures. It has many of the favorable tax attributes of a general partnership, but provides limited liability for the limited partners. These limited partners generally are responsible only for the capital that they have committed to the partnership, although in some instances they may be required to return cash previously withdrawn from the partnership. The limited partnership form enables the general partners, who are usually developers, to obtain equity from outside sources for real estate projects and may permit limited partners to sell their interests (e.g., the trading units in a master limited partnership), thus providing the limited partners with liquidity.

Investors in a limited partnership receive a share of the partnership losses, which they can use to offset taxable income from other sources in certain circumstances. Income from the sale of real estate results in a capital gain, which receives preferential tax treatment. Under the Tax Reform Act of 1986 (TRA 86), losses from an investment in a limited partnership are classified as passive losses that can offset only other passive income and may subject the investor to the alternative minimum tax.

(ii) Limited Liability Companies. Many states have passed legislation allowing for the formation of limited liability companies. These organizations provide members (shareholders) with the protection of a corporation but for tax purposes are treated as partnerships. The advantage of a limited liability company over a limited partnership is that it provides the shareholders who function as general partners with the same limited liability as those who function as limited partners. This type of organization eventually may become the preferred method of ownership of real estate.

(iii) Partnership Agreements. The partnership agreement is a significant document for real estate companies organized as partnerships. The agreement identifies the scope of activities in which the partnership may operate, sets forth the partnership's term of existence, defines the conditions under which the partnership may be terminated or dissolved before the stated termination date, and details the respective partners' rights and responsibilities. The agreement affects not only the accounting for the partnership, but also the profit recognized by the developer/general partner. The following provisions of a typical partnership agreement are of particular interest to the auditor:

- *Capital Contributions and Borrowings.* The agreement sets forth the total amount of the partner's investment and the payment schedule on which capital contributions are to be made. The amount and timing of contributions materially affect both the investor's return on the investment and the cost of the project. Normally, an investor is required to sign a promissory note for the capital contributions that are payable after the date of admission. Terms of default and remedies for the general partners are defined, and normally the use of all capital contributions is specified in the partnership agreement. Most agreements also grant the partnership the right to borrow money from other sources and establish certain requirements for and limitations on such borrowings.

- *Capital Accounts, Profits and Losses, Cash Flow, and Distributions.* The agreement states the accounting method (cash or accrual) and the fiscal year of the partnership (which is normally a calendar year). Cash flow and profits and losses normally are defined, and the method of allocation among partners is stated. In addition, the allocation of gain or loss and of the proceeds on a sale of the project and the distribution of proceeds from a refinancing are specified.

- *Rights and Responsibilities of Partners.* The agreement defines the rights and responsibilities of the limited partners. Limited partners usually have the right to call meetings, vote for amendments to the limited partnership agreement, and vote for removal or substitution of the general partners; participation in management by the limited partners usually is prohibited. In addition, the agreement sets forth the general partners' responsibilities for managing the partnership. These generally include the power to appoint the managing general partner and the right to acquire property and to execute a mortgage note, construction contract, management agreement, and other documents required in connection with the construction and operation of the project. In addition, the agreement generally specifies whether an audit or review of financial statements will be provided within a specified time frame. The most relevant provisions from the auditor's viewpoint relate to the general partners' right to pay or receive specified fees as compensation for organizing and developing the partnership and for managing the construction phase of the project. Also significant are the general partners' obligations to initiate and support rental operations. Usually the general partners and managing general partner do not receive any compensation for managing the affairs of the partnership in their capacity as general partners. They may, however, receive fees through related parties, such as management fees to affiliated management companies, for providing services other than those that are part of their role as general partners.

The specific terms of partnership agreements vary widely. The auditor should be familiar with the partnership agreement to determine whether the accounting principles applied by the partnership are in conformity with the agreement, and whether the general and limited partners have complied with the restrictive provisions of the agreement. The terms of the partnership agreement can significantly affect the amount and timing of the profit a developer/general partner may recognize on a transaction with the partnership.

(b)   Real Estate Investment Trusts

Real Estate Investment Trusts (REITs) are corporations that allow investors to purchase stock at a stated price per share. The stock may be listed on an exchange and actively traded, thus providing investors a means of liquidity. An investor generally receives a dividend each year, since the REIT rules require that 95 percent of earnings be distributed. Income from a REIT is considered portfolio income and thus cannot be used to offset passive losses.

A common type of entity that holds real estate is known as an Umbrella Partnership Real Estate Investment Trust (UPREIT). An UPREIT is an operating partnership that owns property and has a REIT as its sole general partner. The seller of property has an option to receive operating partnership interests (units) or shares in the REIT. If the seller receives units, in certain circumstances it may retain a portion of the tax benefits associated with ownership of the property.

(c)   Regulatory Framework

Real estate transactions have become increasingly subject to regulations. An auditor should be knowledgeable about those regulations and ensure that they are considered in planning the audit and for purposes of financial statement disclosures. Statement of Financial Accounting Standards (SFAS) No. 5, *Accounting for Contingencies* (Accounting Standards Section C59), provides guidance for determining whether accrual or disclosure is required with respect to pending or threatened litigation and possible assessments for noncompliance with federal, state, and local regulations.

Investments in real estate, generally in the form of an interest in a real estate limited partnership, may be subject to the same Securities and Exchange Commission (SEC) registration and reporting requirements as are other investments. A seller of a public or private investment should prepare a complete disclosure document (prospectus or offering memorandum) to ensure against future claims by buyers that disclosures were inadequate or misleading. If such disclosures are not presented, the auditor should be alert to possible claims by buyers for recision of a transaction and refund of the purchase price.

The Department of Housing and Urban Development (HUD) regulates the development and operation of all projects for which it insures the mortgages or provides rent subsidies. In addition, most agreements and documents governing the development, construction, and financing of such projects are required to be approved by HUD and, in most instances, must be filed on specified forms. State housing agencies impose similar restrictions and requirements.

The Interstate Land Sales Full Disclosure Act requires developers to make full disclosure in connection with the sale or lease of certain undeveloped subdivided land. Developers establish certain mechanisms to sell property that they have developed. One such mechanism is a common promotional plan, which is a plan undertaken by a single developer or a group of developers to offer for sale or lease lots that are contiguous or are designated as a common unit or by a common name. The Act makes it unlawful for a developer to sell or lease, by use of the mail or any other means of interstate commerce, any land offered as part of a common promotional plan unless the land is registered with the Office of Interstate Land Sales Registration; a printed property report must be furnished to prospective purchasers or lessees. Similarly, the Federal Trade Commission (FTC) has authority to act on unfair or deceptive trade practices with respect to real estate sales, particularly as related to marketing and selling activities of real estate companies.

Regulation Z of the Consumer Credit Protection Act (the truth in lending law) has a significant effect on real estate financing transactions, since many real estate purchases are made on credit. Regulation Z outlines requirements for both creditors and borrowers for the full disclosure of credit costs and is applicable to essentially all real estate transactions, regardless of amount, in which individual borrowers are involved in nonbusiness transactions.

47.2 ACCOUNTING PRINCIPLES AND PRACTICES

(a) Equity Investments

Joint ventures are common in the real estate industry; most are for single projects and are of limited life. Accounting for an investment in a real estate venture is governed by Accounting Principles Board (APB) Opinion No. 18, *The Equity Method of Accounting for Investments in Common Stock* (Accounting Standards Section I82), Statement of Position (SOP) 78-9, *Accounting for Investments in Real Estate Ventures*, SFAS No. 94, *Consolidation of All Majority-Owned Subsidiaries* (Accounting Standards Section C51), SEC Regulation S-X, and Emerging Issues Task Force (EITF) Issue 94-1, *Accounting for Tax Benefits Resulting from Investments in Affordable Housing Projects*. At the time of this writing, the Financial Accounting Standards Board (FASB) is studying the requirements for and application of consolidation and equity accounting, and the AICPA is considering issuing an SOP on *Accounting for Investors' Interests in Unconsolidated Real Estate Ventures* as well as possibly developing an SOP on time shares.

SFAS No. 94 requires consolidation of all majority-owned subsidiaries unless control is temporary or does not rest with the majority owner. Determining an investor's ability to exert control over an investment in a joint venture organized as a partnership is sometimes difficult. A partnership that is controlled by an investor, that is, one in which the investor has a majority voting interest, should be considered a subsidiary of the investor for reporting purposes; thus, it should be consolidated and intercompany profits and losses not yet realized in transactions with third parties should be eliminated. Since partnerships do not have voting stock, the condition that usually indicates control is ownership of a majority (over 50 percent) of the interest in profits and losses. Control also may exist with a lesser percentage of ownership, as specified by terms included in contracts, leases, partnership agreements, or court decrees that give the investor a majority voting interest. Alternatively, if major decisions—such as the right to replace general partners, approve the sale or refinancing of the principal assets, or approve the acquisition of principal assets—require approval by the limited partners, ownership of a majority of the interest in profits and losses may not in itself constitute control. A noncontrolling investor in a general partnership generally should account for the investment by the equity method, although SOP 78-9 notes that there are circumstances in which the cost method may be appropriate.

Real property owned by undivided interests (e.g., as tenants in common) is subject to joint control if decisions concerning financing, development, sale, or operation require the approval of two or more of the owners. Most real estate ventures in the form of undivided interests are subject to some level of joint control, and they should be presented in the same manner as investments in noncontrolled partnerships, as discussed above. Occasionally, in a joint venture in which the participants have undivided interests, approval of two or more of the owners is not required for major decisions, each investor is entitled only to its pro rata share of income and expenses, and the investors are severally liable only for the indebtedness each incurs in connection with its interest in the property. In those circumstances, the investment may be presented by recording the undivided interest in the assets, liabilities, revenues, and expenses of the venture, which sometimes is referred to as pro rata consolidation.

In practice, pro rata consolidation also is used in circumstances other than in the limited ones described above. An entity is not required to change its accounting for investments owned prior to the issuance of SOP 78-9 from pro rata consolidation if it followed that practice prior to the issuance of the SOP.

Investors may contribute, in exchange for an ownership interest in an entity, real estate that has a fair value in excess of its book value. SOP 78-9 indicates that generally an investor should not recognize any profit on the contribution and that the investor and investee should record the transaction at the historical cost of the real estate. If one investor contributes real estate and another investor contributes cash in proportion to their respective ownership interests, however, certain of those transactions may in essence be sales. The SEC staff has expressed [in Staff Accounting Bulletin (SAB) No. 48] the position that transfers by promoters and shareholders of nonmonetary assets to an entity in exchange for its stock usually should be recorded at the transferor's historical cost basis. SAB No. 97, however, clarified that when two or more businesses combine just prior to or contemporaneously with an initial public offering, the guidance in SAB No. 48 should not be followed. (The guidance in SAB No. 48 is intended to address the transfer of nonmonetary assets in exchange for a company's stock; it is not intended to modify the requirements of APB Opinion No. 16, *Business Combinations*. The SEC staff believes that the combination of two or more businesses should be accounted for in accordance with Opinion No. 16 and its interpretations.)

Venture agreements may designate different percentage allocations among the investors for profits and losses, cash distributions from operations, and distributions of cash proceeds from liquidation. To ascertain the economic substance of the investor's share of the venture net income or loss, such agreements should be analyzed to determine how an increase or a decrease in net assets of the venture will affect cash payments to the investor over the life of the venture and on its liquidation. Specified profit and loss allocation ratios alone should not be used to determine an investor's equity in venture earnings if the allocation of cash distributions and liquidating distributions is determined on a different basis. Often the investor's equity is determined by assuming the liquidation of all assets and liabilities at their book values and the distribution of the proceeds to the venture participants, the change in each participant's equity position during the year should equal its share of venture profit or loss on a GAAP basis.

EITF Issue 94-1 allows an election to account for investments in "affordable housing projects" held through a limited partnership by use of the effective interest method. Absent such an election, SOP 78-9 would continue to provide appropriate guidance. The EITF also provided additional guidance for use of the cost method of accounting for these investments.

(b) Real Estate Properties and Deferred Costs

A variety of costs are incurred in the acquisition, development, leasing, sale, or operation of a real estate development project. SFAS No. 67, *Accounting for Costs and Initial Rental Operations of Real Estate Projects* (Accounting Standards Section Re2), provides guidance on when costs should be capitalized, deferred, or expensed. After a determination is made to capitalize a cost, it is allocated to the specific parcels or components of a project that are benefited. Guidance for situations where specific identification is not practicable is provided by SFAS No. 67.

Property taxes and insurance costs incurred on real estate projects should be capitalized only during the period in which activities necessary to get the property ready for its intended use are in progress. Such costs incurred after the property is substantially complete and held available for occupancy should be charged to expense as incurred. Paragraph 22 of SFAS No. 67 states that "a real estate project shall be considered substantially completed and held available for occupancy upon completion of tenant improvements by the developer, but not later than one year from cessation of major construction activity."

SFAS No. 34, *Capitalization of Interest Cost* (Accounting Standards Section I67), generally requires capitalization of interest during construction and development. Assets qualifying for interest capitalization include real estate developments intended for sale or lease that are constructed as discrete projects. Land that is not undergoing activities necessary to prepare it for its intended use does not qualify for capitalization. When development activities are undertaken, however, expenditures to acquire land qualify for interest capitalization while the development activities are in process. If the resulting asset is a structure, the interest capitalized on land expenditures becomes part of the cost of the structure; if the resulting asset is developed land, the capitalized interest is part of the cost of the land. SFAS No. 34 provides guidance on determining the appropriate amount of interest to be capitalized.

Incremental revenue from incidental operations in excess of related incremental costs should be accounted for as a reduction of capitalized project costs. Incremental costs in excess of incremental revenue from incidental operations should be charged to expense as incurred, because the incidental operations did not increase the costs of developing the property for its intended use.

Estimates and cost allocations should be reviewed at the end of each financial reporting period until a project is substantially completed and available for sale. Costs should be revised and reallocated as necessary on the basis of current estimates. Revisions of estimates and cost allocations on projects for which sales revenue has not been recognized are not accounting changes as defined by APB Opinion No. 20, *Accounting Changes* (Accounting Standards Section A06), and their effects therefore should be accounted for as adjustments to capitalized costs.

(c)   Impairment and Valuation of Real Estate Assets

The recognition and measurement principles of SFAS No. 121, *Accounting for the Impairment of Long-Lived Assets and for Long-Lived Assets to Be Disposed Of* (Accounting Standards Section I08), apply to real estate held for development and sale, including property to be developed in the future as well as that currently under development. SFAS No. 121 requires management of an entity to review long-lived assets for impairment whenever events or changes in circumstances indicate that the carrying value of an asset may not be recoverable. The entity first must determine whether an impairment exists. If an impairment exists, it then must determine the amount of the impairment. Care must be exercised in determining the various assumptions used, as a small change in assumptions can lead to a large variation in results. The determination of impairment is required regardless of the type of financing (recourse vs. nonrecourse). Once property has been determined to be impaired and its carrying value written down, it subsequently cannot be written back up.

The valuation of loans collateralized by real estate should be made in accordance with the provisions of SFAS No. 114, as amended by SFAS No. 118 (Accounting Standards Section I08). SFAS No. 114 requires that impaired loans should be measured based on the present value of expected cash flows or, as a practical expedient, at the loan's observable market price or the fair value of the collateral.

Real estate held for investment should be carried at cost, less accumulated depreciation, unless it is probable that the unamortized cost will not be recovered through operations (or sale if the investor ultimately intends to dispose of the property). If the investor intends to operate the property, the need to recognize an impairment loss should be determined by comparing the property's undiscounted operating cash flows and residual value with its net carrying amount. If the undiscounted cash flows are insufficient to recover the carrying amount of the property and it is probable that operating cash flows will not increase to a level that would recover the carrying amount of the property over its remaining useful life, an impairment loss should be recognized.

Capitalized costs of abandoned real estate should be written off as current expenses or, if appropriate, should be charged to allowances established for that purpose. They should not be allocated to other components of a project or to other projects. Donations of land to municipalities or other governmental agencies for uses that will benefit a project are not abandonments. The costs of the donated land should be allocated to the various components of the project.

(d)   Leasing, Sale, and Operational Period

In addition to capitalized costs, project owners generally incur certain other preoccupancy costs not specifically identifiable with construction activity but necessary to make a project operational or to stimulate sales or rentals. Depending on the type of business in which a real estate company is engaged, such costs might include financing, tenant leasing, and selling costs. In general, such costs may be deferred and amortized in future periods if they are associated with future revenues and if their recovery is reasonably assured.

Financing or loan costs include loan fees, finders' fees, legal fees, commissions, document printing costs, and other costs and expenses directly related to financing. The accounting for financing costs applicable to construction loans is the same as that for construction-period interest. Costs applicable to permanent financing should be classified as deferred financing costs and amortized over the terms of the related mortgages, preferably using the interest method.

SFAS No. 67 provides criteria for deferring and expensing selling costs. Costs incurred to sell real estate projects (project costs) should be classified with and accounted for in the same manner as construction costs if both of the following tests are met:

- The costs are reasonably expected to be recovered from sales of the project or from incidental operations.
- The costs are incurred for tangible assets that are used directly throughout the selling period to aid in the sale of the project or for services that have been performed to obtain regulatory approval for sales.

Examples of selling costs that ordinarily meet these criteria are expenditures for model units and related furnishings, sales facilities, legal and other fees incurred to obtain regulatory approval for sales, and semipermanent signs.

Other costs incurred to sell real estate projects should be classified and accounted for as prepaid expenses if they do not meet the criteria for project costs and they are incurred prior to receipt or use of the related goods or services and are expected to benefit future periods. Expenditures for future advertising, brochures, and similar selling tools, and draws against future commissions are examples of selling costs that ordinarily meet those criteria. Certain prepaid expenses (e.g., sales commissions under the installment method) can be identified with specific future revenue and therefore should be charged to operations in the period in which the related sales revenue is recognized. Costs that do not meet the criteria for capitalization or deferral should be expensed as incurred.

SFAS No. 13, *Accounting for Leases*, paragraph 19 (Accounting Standards Section L10.115), governs accounting by lessors for "initial direct costs" of operating leases. Initial direct costs, as defined in paragraph 24 of SFAS No. 91, *Nonrefundable Fees and Costs Associated with Originating or Acquiring Loans and Initial Direct Costs of Leases* (Accounting Standards Section L10.411), are to be deferred and allocated over the lease term in proportion to the recognition of rental income, or they may be charged to expense as incurred if the effect is not materially different. Costs related to unsuccessful leasing activities should be expensed as incurred. SFAS No. 67 allows the deferral of certain leasing costs, such as model units and their furnishings, that are related to and recoverable from future rental operations. Such costs should be amortized over the lease term if they can be identified with a specific lease; otherwise, they should be amortized over the expected period of benefit.

(e) Profit Recognition on Sales of Real Estate

Accounting principles for recognizing real estate sales and profits are found in SFAS No. 66, *Accounting for Sales of Real Estate* (Accounting Standards Section Re1). The statement emphasizes that, after determining the economic substance of a transaction, the matters with the greatest impact on the timing of profit recognition are:

- The extent of the buyer's investment in the property acquired and the certainty of collection of the seller's receivables
- The continuing involvement of the seller with the property sold

SFAS No. 66 prescribes that revenue and profit be recognized at the time real estate is sold, provided that the amount of the revenue is measurable (which is a collectibility issue) and the earning process is complete or virtually complete (i.e., the seller has no obligations to perform activities subsequent to the sale in order to earn the revenue). In addition, the statement specifies that the economic substance, as opposed to the legal form, of the transaction determines the timing, amount, and designation of revenue. Because many real estate transactions are designed to maximize income tax benefits, and in some instances profits, the economic substance of a real estate transaction may differ in many aspects from its legal form.

Real estate sales differ from revenue transactions in many other industries in that consideration for a significant portion of the sales value is often a long-term, nonrecourse note receivable that usually is collateralized only by the property sold. Since the uncertainty about the collectibility of a receivable arising from the sale of real estate is usually greater than in other business transactions, SFAS No. 66 requires that, for profit to be recognized on the accrual basis, both a buyer's initial investment and subsequent payments on the note receivable must be adequate to demonstrate a commitment to pay for the property. If a buyer's initial down payment or continuing payments do not meet the requirements of accrual-basis profit recognition, the deposit, installment, reduced-profit, or cost recovery method should be used. Those methods are discussed in SFAS No. 66.

The requirements in SFAS No. 66 relating to the down payment and continuing investment are designed to satisfy the revenue measurement criterion for the recognition of revenue and profit. The second set of requirements relates to the criterion that the earning process be complete or virtually complete. After the date of sale, the seller may be obligated to arrange financing, develop or construct facilities on the property sold, manage the property, guarantee a return on investment, or provide leasing or other forms of support in operating the property. In general, SFAS No. 66 requires that the effect of the seller's continued involvement be evaluated. In some instances, such involvement may have little effect on the amount or timing of profit recognition; in other instances, recognition of all or part of the profit from the sale should be deferred until the seller's performance of required continuing obligations.

A sales agreement or contract should not be recorded as an accrual-basis sale if the seller's continued involvement results in the retention of the same kinds of risks as the retention of ownership would entail. For example, if a seller is obligated to operate the property subsequent to its sale and may suffer operating losses, a sale has not occurred. If the amount of the seller's loss resulting from continued involvement is limited by the terms of the sales agreement or by business considerations, profit recognized at the time of sale must be reduced by the maximum amount of exposure to loss. Profit may be recognized when realized if the agreement allows the seller to participate solely in future profit from the operation or resale of property with no risk of loss. SFAS No. 98, *Accounting for Leases* (Accounting Standards Section L10), however, provides that a sale leaseback transaction that includes any continuing involvement other than a normal leaseback during which the seller-lessee intends to actively use the property should be accounted for by the deposit method or as a financing.

If, under the terms of a real estate sales agreement, the seller is required to obtain or provide permanent financing on the property for the buyer, no sale should be recognized until such financing has been obtained. A sales agreement may require the seller to provide management or other services relating to the property after the sale, without compensation or with compensation in an amount less than prevailing rates. In these circumstances, the seller's profit on the sale should be reduced by the anticipated costs to be incurred for those services and by a reasonable profit, which will be brought back into income as the services are performed.

Agreements for the sale of undeveloped or partially developed land often include a requirement that the seller develop the property, provide off-site improvements, or construct facilities on the land. The accounting for the seller's performance of development and construction should be the same as the accounting for long-term construction contracts, namely, the percentage-of-completion basis should be used, unless the seller cannot reasonably estimate total cost and profit. In that case, the completed-contract method would be used. The same rate of profit should be used on the recognition of the land sale and the development and construction activity.

Profit also may be recognized by real estate lessors if a lease transaction meets the criteria in SFAS No. 13 for classification as a sales-type lease and the criteria in SFAS Nos. 66 and 98 for full and immediate profit recognition. Since a lease usually involves no down payment and SFAS No. 66 requires a minimum down payment, that requirement effectively prohibits sales-type leases of real estate.

(f) Accounting by Participating Mortgage Loan Borrowers

SOP 97-1, *Accounting by Participating Mortgage Loan Borrowers*, establishes the accounting by borrowers for a participating mortgage loan if the lender participates in increases in the market value of the mortgaged real estate project or in the results of operations of the mortgaged real estate project. SOP 97-1 applies to all borrowers in participating mortgage loan arrangements; it does not apply to participating leases, debt convertible at the option of the lender into equity ownership of the property, or participating loans resulting from troubled debt restructurings, or to creditors in participating mortgage loan arrangements.

SOP 97-1 requires:

- If the lender is entitled to participate in appreciation in the market value of the mortgaged real estate project, the borrower, at origination, should determine the fair value of the participation feature and should recognize a liability for that amount, with a corresponding charge to a debt-discount account, which should be amortized by the interest method, using the effective interest rate.

- The balance of the participation liability should be adjusted at the end of each reporting period to equal the fair value of the participation feature at that time. The corresponding charge or credit should be to the related debt-discount account, which should be amortized prospectively, using the effective interest rate.

The following disclosures should be made in the borrower's financial statements:

- The aggregate amount of participating mortgage obligations at the balance-sheet date, with the aggregate participation liabilities and related debt discounts disclosed separately
- Terms of the relevant participations by the lender

(g) Extinguishment of Debt

SFAS No. 125, *Accounting for Transfers and Servicing of Financial Assets and Extinguishments of Liabilities* (Accounting Standards Section F35), describes the circumstances in which an entity should consider its debt to be extinguished and thereby derecognized for financial reporting purposes; in describing these circumstances, the statement provides specific criteria that must be met for debt to be considered extinguished.

Repayment is the most common circumstance for extinguishment of debt and includes an entity's reacquisition of its debt in the open market, regardless of whether the securities are canceled or held as treasury bonds. Repayments of debt are considered extinguishments if the entity is relieved of its obligations with respect to the debt.

The accounting rules for extinguishing debt by third-party assumption are particularly important to entities that sell real estate. SFAS No. 125 specifically provides that when a nonrecourse mortgage is assumed by a third party in conjunction with the sale of an asset that serves as sole collateral for the mortgage, the legal release criterion has been met and the seller-debtor may consider the mortgage to be extinguished. In the event of a sale of property subject to a recourse mortgage, the transaction must be evaluated to determine whether the seller has been legally released from the primary repayment obligation. If the legal release criterion has not been met, the financial statements of the seller should continue to reflect the mortgage payable, and a "receivable" from the purchaser should be recorded for the mortgage payments to be made by the purchaser. According to SFAS No. 4, *Reporting Gains and Losses from Extinguishment of Debt* (Accounting Standards Section D14), gains and losses arising from an extinguishment of debt should be aggregated and, if material, classified as an extraordinary item, net of related income tax effect.

(h) Operating Rental Revenues

Most reporting on operating rental properties is directed to individual projects. Although not required, rental income often is shown on a gross basis, with a deduction for vacancies to arrive at net rental income. Presenting only the net amount reduces the usefulness of the information to management, investors, and lenders. Nonoperating and service income, such as payments for services, interest income, and assessments, are classified separately. Lease terms vary depending on the type of properties being leased and special terms that are agreed on in lease negotiations. Common types of charges to tenants include base rental income, percentage rents, expense rebillings, and common area charges.

Base rental income is the basic rental charge stated in a lease and is applicable to all types of property. Sometimes it is adjusted for prior-year increases in the consumer price index. A question frequently arises regarding the accounting for rent concessions given to a new tenant at the inception of a lease. Payment of a tenant's prior lease or lease cancellation charges should be deferred and amortized on a straight-line basis over the initial term of the new lease. Generally, lease income should be recognized on a straight-line basis unless there is an economic justification for using some other method. Accordingly, if the tenant is not required to pay rent during the initial months of a lease, it is appropriate to allocate the aggregate rental revenue related to the initial noncancelable lease term over that entire term.

Percentage rents are found principally in retail leases and call for additional amounts based on the lessee's sales activity. Because sales normally increase over time, the lessor is partially protected from the effects of inflation over the life of the lease. Leases usually contain definitions of the terms used (e.g., gross receipts) and state how the percentage rent is to be calculated. Terms can vary widely from lease to lease, and the auditor should understand the specific lease terms. Determining the accrual for percentage rents at the end of an accounting period can be difficult because tenants normally are not up-to-date in reporting their gross receipts and because sales reporting periods may be different from financial reporting periods. Therefore, a method of estimating the gross receipts expected by tenants for the period is needed. If the property has been in operation for a few years, historical data may be available to form a basis for an estimate. If not, it may be necessary to contact tenants for an estimate or to use industry data.

Rebilling increased expenses to tenants is common in most types of commercial properties. Some examples of expenses rebilled to tenants are real estate taxes, utility costs, and maintenance expenses. The types of expenses that may be rebilled are specified in the lease. Generally, the amount is based on a comparison of current expenses with base-year amounts, that is, amounts incurred during the first year of the lease. Terms vary from lease to lease, depending on the date the lease was negotiated and the negotiating ability of the parties involved. Rebilled expenses preferably should be reflected in the income statement as revenue rather than netted against the related expense, since the lessor is responsible for their incurrence and that presentation is likely to be more informative.

Determining revenue from rebilled expenses can be complex if one or more of the following situations exist:

- There are several leases that began at different dates and have different base years.

- Lease terms specify that only increases over a certain amount are to be rebilled after the base year.

- Different factors are used to determine each type of rebilled expense.

- Leases provide different bases for allocating costs, such as gross area, net rentable area, and gross occupied area.

- Base-year or current-year expenses are required to reflect pro forma amounts at some different (generally higher) level of occupancy.

Common area charges are made for common areas in shopping centers and, in some cases, in low-rise, multiple-use office buildings. Some examples of common areas are indoor and outdoor malls, parking areas, and lobbies. Normally, charges for areas used in common by tenants are based on an agreed-on amount per square foot as stated in the lease or on actual costs incurred. In some cases, percentage rents paid by a tenant may be reduced by the common area charges. Sometimes tenants agree to maintain the common areas adjacent to their space instead of paying these charges; many "anchor" tenants (tenants that rent a significant area, e.g., a major department store in a shopping mall) select this method.

47.3   AUDIT STRATEGY

The audit strategy for a real estate company depends largely on the volume of its transactions and its internal control. If, for example, a company is involved in the development and sale of only one or a few projects during the period under audit, it probably would be more efficient to emphasize substantive testing, even if controls appeared to be effective. Particularly for smaller companies, which generally have a limited number of transactions during a year, it is usually more efficient to perform substantive tests of transactions and account balances. Furthermore, many real estate companies are closely held by entrepreneurial builders who do not place a great deal of emphasis on controls. For such companies, a substantive testing approach may be the only feasible strategy.

Other real estate companies, particularly those that are large and publicly held, have adequate controls and transaction volumes to warrant an audit strategy based on the performance of tests of controls to reduce the assessed level of control risk to low. For example, tests of controls would be appropriate for a multilocation home builder that sells hundreds of units a year and has effective controls. The auditor also should consider the composition of the various account balances. If an account balance comprises a large number of items with relatively low individual values, such as a large number of houses produced by a builder, testing controls is generally more efficient because of the impracticability of substantiating a large dollar amount of the total. The procedures for the closing and legal recording of a sale of a residence are standardized within a state, as are the documents that the auditor would examine. In addition, applying the principles in SFAS No. 66 to the sale of residences is seldom complicated unless exceptionally small down payments are received. Even in that instance, it would seem inefficient to substantiate a multitude of individual sales transactions; instead, tests of controls coupled with year-end cutoff procedures would be more practical.

Historically, HUD has been closely associated with real estate projects through its mortgage insurance and rent subsidies programs. State governments, through housing finance agencies, have been increasing their involvement in the housing industry, primarily as lenders but in some instances as developers or insurers. The activities of HUD, however, are limited to insuring mortgages on residential real estate and in some cases rent subsidies. It neither plans nor builds housing and it does not loan funds directly to mortgagors. The mortgagor, general contractor, and subcontractor all agree to abide by the rules and regulations prescribed by HUD.

HUD Handbook 4470.2, Rev. 1, *Cost Certification Guide for Mortgagors and Contractors of HUD-Insured Multifamily Projects* (April 1994), and Handbook IG 4200.1A, *Audit Guide for Auditing Development Cost of HUD Insured Multifamily Projects for Use by Independent Public Accountants* (March 1978), are the two primary sources for cost certification rules. Auditors often are requested to provide a special report to satisfy the requirements of HUD or the state. The specific reporting rules are complex and are found in the applicable federal or state publications. HUD Handbook 2000.04, Rev. 2, *Consolidated Audit Guide for Audits of HUD Programs* (August 1997), and the Public and Indian Housing Compliance Supplement were issued to reflect changes that have taken place in program regulations, HUD Handbooks, and AICPA reporting formats. In September 1995, the AICPA issued a "Non-Authoritative Practice Aid" to assist practitioners in their reporting to HUD as a result of the 1994 revision to *Government Auditing Standards*. The auditor should be familiar with those rules and reports and should take them into consideration in planning the engagement.

47.4 SUBSTANTIVE TESTS

The transaction cycles, typical controls, and tests of those controls in real estate companies do not differ significantly from those in commercial and industrial companies and accordingly are not discussed further here. The remainder of this chapter discusses substantive tests that are of particular importance in auditing real estate companies.

(a) Developer's Receivables

Individual accounts and notes receivable of a developer may be material to the entity, and their collectibility may depend on the economic conditions of a myriad of entities or their limited partners. Collectibility may be further complicated by the developer's role as general partner of the debtor entity. Accordingly, for material receivables, the auditor should review the financial position of the debtor entity in evaluating the collectibility of amounts due from general and limited partners. If the receivables are without recourse, the auditor should evaluate the realizable value of the underlying collateral property or its ability to generate sufficient cash to realize the receivable, and determine whether the receivables should be discounted in accordance with APB Opinion No. 21, *Interest on Receivables and Payables* (Accounting Standards Section I69).

The auditor also must address related party transactions and the required disclosures. Reviewing the sales contracts, partnership agreements, offering documents, and construction and management operating contracts assists in determining whether the financial statement disclosures comply with SFAS No. 57, *Related Party Disclosures* (Accounting Standards Section R36). The auditor should be particularly sensitive to transactions between the entity and related parties and should ensure that such transactions are not prohibited by contracts or agreements.

(b) Property Acquisition and Development Costs

The following objectives are of particular significance in auditing capitalized acquisition and development costs:

- Determine whether the cost capitalization and allocation policies conform with GAAP and are appropriate in the circumstances
- Determine whether costs are charged to cost of sales on a systematic, rational, and timely basis
- Ascertain that projects to which costs have been charged physically exist
- Obtain satisfaction about the recoverability of capitalized costs

In testing acquisition and development costs, the auditor should examine documentation that is appropriate to each particular type of cost. Figure 47.1 suggests the appropriate documents for the major types of capitalized costs.

(c) Real Estate Sales

Except for retail lot sales, sales transactions usually occur infrequently and involve large sums of money. Sales of land, apartment complexes, shopping centers, office buildings, and other large projects often are complex transactions, which usually require an audit approach that emphasizes substantive testing. The objective of the audit of sales transactions is to determine that the proper amount of revenue has been recognized in the appropriate period and that the proper charge to cost of sales has been made, all in accordance with the pertinent authoritative accounting pronouncements (as discussed earlier in this chapter). Emphasis should be placed on the method of revenue recognition, the adequacy of the down payment and continuing payments on any notes received, and the nature of any continuing responsibilities of the seller. The economic substance of a real estate sale often varies from its legal form, and close attention must be paid to the sales agreements and related documents, including, but not limited to, agreements of sale, notes receivable, escrow instructions, management agreements, lease agreements, partnership agreements, and construction contracts. All of those documents could contain provisions affecting the timing and amount of revenue recognition in sales transactions. The auditor also should be aware of the possibility of related party transactions and should apply procedures necessary to identify related parties.

If revenue from sales of real estate has been recognized using the installment method, the entity should have controls in place to ensure that the appropriate

Figure 47.1   Evidential Matter for Real Estate Acquisition and Development Costs

Type of Cost	Documents to Be Examined (If Applicable)	Information Derived
Vacant land	Deed	Ownership
	Purchase contract	Price
	Title policy	Restrictions
	Mortgage	Financing terms
Developed property	Deed	Ownership
	Purchase contract	Price
	Title policy	Restrictions
	Mortgage	Financing terms
	Closing statement	Prorations of costs
	Security agreement	Security interest
	Insurance policies	Coverage and value
	Certificates of occupancy	Legal occupancy
Land improvements	Contracts	Price, performance
	Subcontracts	Price, performance
	Vendor invoices	Costs billed to date
	Insurance policies	Coverage and value
Structures and equipment	Construction loan	Construction financing
	Construction contract	Price, performance
	Subcontracts	Price, performance
	Vendor invoices	Costs billed to date
	Permanent loan (mortgage)	Financing terms
	Insurance policies	Coverage and value
Indirect project costs	Vendor invoices	Costs billed to date
	Company-prepared analyses indicating cost allocations	Reasonableness of cost allocations
Property taxes and insurance costs	Vendor invoices	Costs billed to date
	Real estate bills	Applicable amount and period
Legal fees, recording fees, survey fees, appraisal fees, and similar charges associated with real estate properties	Vendor invoices and billings	Costs associated with acquisition of properties

amount of deferred (unrealized) profit is recognized as earned in the proper period. Either through testing those controls or through substantive tests, the auditor should obtain evidence that the amount of revenue recognized in the current period from current- and prior-period sales is appropriate.

(d) Operating Rental Revenues

Following is an efficient approach to testing base rentals:

- Obtain a rent roll for one month during the year.
- Examine selected leases to ascertain the correctness of the rental income.

- Annualize the rental income of the month tested and compare the result with the amount recorded in the general ledger.
- Investigate significant variations between recorded revenues and the computed amounts and obtain documentation to support reasons for the differences.

That approach may be applied to all types of rental operations; however, if the number of tenants is large, such as in apartment buildings, and the desired audit coverage cannot be achieved without examining a significant number of leases, additional or alternative procedures may be needed. Possible procedures include:

- Testing rental revenues according to type of unit (appropriate for properties that have standard rents) by:
  - Determining total possible rental revenues to be collected, using full occupancy at current rents
  - Deducting amounts for vacancies, based on vacancy rates shown in rent rolls
  - Obtaining documentation to support the reasons for significant variations between recorded revenues and the computed amount
- Testing rental revenues by:
  - Tracing rents received to cash records
  - Tracing cash receipts records to bank statements and the general ledger
- Confirming lease terms (should be performed in conjunction with auditing rents receivable and security deposits)
- Obtaining the rent rolls and examining apartments indicated as vacant to ascertain that they are in fact vacant

The following procedures may be used in auditing percentage rents:

- Obtain an analysis, by tenant, detailing the activity in percentage rentals and showing accruals at the beginning of the period, collections, income for the period, and accruals at the end of the period
- Select several tenants for detailed testing of percentage rentals by:
  - Examining sales reports in support of receipts for the period
  - Testing the accuracy of percentage rental computations
  - Tracing percentage rental rates and minimum rents to leases on file
  - Reviewing tenants' sales reports and obtaining explanations for significant fluctuations between months or periods
- Review the reasonableness of the estimate of year-end sales and test the computation of rents accrued; compare estimates with prior-period amounts
- Review procedures and results of percentage rent audits performed by company personnel
- Examine subsequent receipts of sales reports and percentage rents

Income from rebilled expenses is often an increasing part of total property income; therefore, it should receive appropriate audit attention. As with percentage rents, determining the accrual for rebilled expenses as of the close of a period is complex because lease periods may be different from reporting periods. Therefore, amounts to be rebilled may be determined on the basis of estimated expenses. One possibility is to use budgeted expenses as a basis for rebilling, if they are determined to be reasonable.

Procedures to consider in auditing rebilled expenses are as follows:

- Obtain an analysis of rebilled expenses showing beginning accruals, receipts, rebillings for the current year, and ending accruals
- Select several tenants for testing by:
  - Examining leases to ascertain which expenses are to be rebilled, the base year, and the base amount that should be used in the current-year computation
  - Testing the company's computation to see if it is in accordance with lease provisions
- Recalculate and review the reasonableness of management estimates used to determine rebillable amounts
- If the company bills on an interim basis, determine whether accrued income is recorded properly at year-end
- Review past-due amounts to determine whether any disputes exist between the company and the tenant; consider whether adjustments of the accruals are necessary

In most cases, income from common area charges is not significant in relation to total property income, and no special auditing procedures are performed. If considered significant, these accounts may be tested in connection with tests of lease rental income. If common area charges are based on actual expenses incurred, audit tests are similar to those performed in connection with expense billings.

(e) Depreciation Expense

Depreciation is a substantial noncash expense for real estate companies that lease property. Depreciation on a project begins when the property or a phase is substantially complete and available for occupancy (as defined in SFAS No. 67). Documents such as the certificate of occupancy and contractor invoices can assist the auditor in determining when it is appropriate to begin recording depreciation. In reviewing the reasonableness of the calculations, the auditor can compare useful lives with tax guidelines, real estate literature, or engineering studies. The auditor also should review the depreciation methods used for consistency.

48

Auditing Retail Companies

Retailing is the selling of goods to the ultimate consumer, usually in small quantities. Retailers vary greatly in size, format, geographical base, product mix, sophistication, and type of customer. Although there are many ways to categorize retailers (for example, by type of customer or product line), one of the most useful ways for purposes of understanding their business processes is to classify them according to whether they are store-based or direct response retailers. Store-based retailers include department stores, supermarkets, warehouse stores, home centers, outlets, and drug stores—any retailer that sells merchandise from a physical location where consumers come to purchase products. Direct response retailers include catalog merchants, cable television home shopping services, and computer-based shopping services. These retailers do not have face-to-face contact with their customers. Many retailers operate in a combination of these formats.

48.1   ACCOUNTING PRINCIPLES AND PRACTICES

(a)   Inventory

One of the primary areas of focus for a retail entity is merchandise inventory. Several inventory accounting methods are used in the retail industry.

(i)   Cost Method.   The cost method tracks sales and costs by specific stock keeping units (SKUs). This method can be burdensome without a computer system because individual cost records must be kept for each item. Historically, this method was practical only for retail operations that carried a limited number of SKUs, such as jewelry stores, furniture dealers, and consumer electronics and appliance retailers. However, as computer systems became more sophisticated, the cost method has become increasingly practical even for retailers with many SKUs. Accounting control under the cost method is based on a cumulative record of cost figures.

(ii)   Gross Profit Method.   The gross profit method, used by some retailers (often drug and convenience store chains), is an estimating technique in which cost of goods sold is calculated using an estimated cost percentage that is computed as 1 – the estimated gross profit percentage. There are two ways of estimating the cost percentage. One is to count a representative sample of items that are valued at both cost and retail; the inventory at cost is divided by the inventory at retail to compute the cost percentage. The other way of estimating the cost percentage is to use gross profit registers to record all sales at both cost and retail. (The use of gross profit registers requires that all store inventory be cost coded.) To arrive at the amount of inventory on hand, the retailer first determines the cost of goods available for sale by adding the cost of beginning inventory to the cost of current-period purchases. Then, sales for the period are multiplied by the estimated cost percentage to arrive at estimated cost of goods sold. The difference between the two calculations is the estimated inventory on hand. When retailers use the gross profit method, it is important that physical inventories be taken at or near year-end to adjust the book inventory to actual.

The gross profit method is particularly useful in estimating cost of goods sold and inventory for interim reporting purposes. There are, however, a number of disadvantages to its use:

1. The estimated gross profit may be distorted because the mix of products actually sold during the period may be different from the mix used to calculate the estimated gross profit percentage.

2. The estimated gross profit percentage can be changed to manipulate gross profits and distort interim results.

3. The amount of inventory shrinkage (discussed later in the chapter) cannot be determined because part of it may be caused by an inaccurate gross profit percentage.

Gross profit cannot be determined accurately until a complete physical inventory at cost is taken at the end of the period and appropriate adjustments to book ending inventories are made.

(iii) Retail Method. The retail method is the method most commonly used by store-based retailers. It was developed in response to the difficulty of costing individual items. In the retail method, purchases and sales are recorded at retail prices, price changes are recognized at retail prices, an estimated value for ending inventory is calculated at retail, and then ending inventory is converted from retail price to cost. The retail method requires that all changes in selling prices be accounted for.

The retail method is an averaging method used with reasonably homogeneous inventory groupings, in which the retailer establishes the relationship, generally by department, between goods available for sale at cost and at retail. Using this relationship, the retailer derives a cost multiplier, which is used to convert the period-end inventory from retail to cost. Because this is an averaging method, consistency in gross profit percentages within a department is important to avoid skewing the cost multiplier as a result of changes in the departmental item mix. Proper treatment of markups and markdowns will result in inventory stated at the lower of cost or market, which is required regardless of the accounting method used.

The retail method has several advantages, including providing periodic inventory and cost of goods sold calculations without a physical inventory. When physical inventories are taken, they can be priced at retail only. Because the retail method is a perpetual method, it can be compared with physical counts and the amounts of shortages can be determined.

Figure 48.1 illustrates the calculation of ending inventory at the lower of cost or market using the retail method.

(iv) Last-in, First-out Methods. Last-in, first-out (LIFO) methods match the most recent costs of purchases against current revenues. LIFO methods, including retail LIFO, typically used by retailers are dollar value LIFO methods. When retail LIFO is used in connection with the retail method of valuing inventories, inventory increments or decrements are measured in retail dollars. (Other dollar value LIFO methods measure increments or decrements at cost.) LIFO typically is chosen by retailers because of tax benefits obtained during periods of price and inventory level increases. If LIFO is adopted for tax purposes, it also must be used for financial reporting purposes. There are disadvantages to the LIFO method, including a significantly increased record-keeping burden and reduced earnings and inventory values in periods of rising prices. Alternatively, deflation or lower inventory levels can increase taxable income.

Figure 48.1   Retail Method Calculation

Calculation	Cost	Retail	Description
Total merchandise handled			Components of total merchandise handled:
Opening inventory	$60,000	$100,000	• Opening inventory at cost and retail
Purchases	30,000	50,000	• Purchases at cost and retail (cost includes invoice cost, freight-in, and additional capitalized costs)
Markups, net of markup cancellations of $3,000		10,000	• Markups net of any markup cancellations
Total merchandise handled	$90,000	$160,000	
Cumulative markon percentage	43.75%		Cumulative markon divided by retail total of merchandise handled: ($160,000 − $90,000) ÷ $160,000
Cost multiplier	56.25%		Complement of the cumulative markon percentage: 100% − 43.75% = 56.25% Can be calculated by dividing total cost by total retail: ($90,000 ÷ $160,000)
Inventory reductions			Components of inventory reductions:
Sales, net		$28,000	• Sales
Sales discounts		1,120	• Sales discounts
Markdowns, net of markdown cancellations of $2,000		3,920	• Markdowns taken and markdown cancellations to restore temporary price reductions
Shrinkage		560	• Estimated value of book inventory in excess of actual physical inventory
Total of inventory reductions		$33,600	
Ending inventory at retail		$126,400	Difference between total merchandise handled (at retail) and total inventory reductions (at retail): $160,000 − $33,600 = $126,400
Ending inventory at lower of cost or market	$71,100		Conversion of retail price of inventory to lower of cost or market. Product of multiplying ending retail inventory by cost multiplier: 56.25% × $126,400 = $71,100

(v) Stock Ledger.   The stock ledger is the primary record used to record and value inventories. The ledger may be maintained by merchandise classification, by department, or by line item. When the retail method is used, the stock ledger accumulates data related to purchases, sales and returns, markups and markdowns (and markup and markdown cancellations), discounts, and shrinkage. Beginning inventories and purchases are recorded at both cost and retail.

Stock ledgers may be abbreviated or detailed. Generally, they consist of three sections: (1) merchandise costs, (2) retail prices, and (3) closing inventory at cost and retail, and gross margin for the period. Regardless of its form, the ledger's purpose is to capture all sales and inventory transactions for the period. The amounts in the stock ledger are used to determine the results of operations for the period. Controls to ensure that all information in the stock ledger required for proper inventory valuation is completely and accurately recorded are discussed later in the chapter.

(vi) Transfers.   Retailers often transfer merchandise from one department or store to another. These transfers should be recorded in the stock ledger as a reduction of one department's inventory and an increase of the other's. Determining the appropriate cost and retail amounts of transfers can be difficult. Controls over transfers may include use of prenumbered transfer forms and accounting for their numerical sequence. These procedures help ensure accountability and complete and accurate posting in the stock ledger. Retailers may use current selling prices to record transfers and then reduce the transfers to cost using an average markon for the transferring department.

(vii) Physical Inventories.   Retailers take physical inventories to determine the accuracy of the inventory records, as well as how effectively inventory is safeguarded against theft, damage, and other types of shrinkage. Physical inventories also help identify obsolete inventory. A major concern in physical inventory taking is ensuring that there is a proper cutoff for both receipts and shipments.

Retailers often use an outside inventory counting service to perform the physical inventory. The service usually transmits the inventory information electronically (usually on machine-readable tape) in such a way that it can be loaded directly onto the retailer's system and can interface with the appropriate data files. Generally, totals of retail dollars (and sometimes costs) or total units counted are supplied to the store manager at the conclusion of the inventory.

(viii) Shrinkage.   Shrinkage is the excess of book inventory over physical inventory. For example, if the book inventory indicates that a department should have on hand $100,000 worth of merchandise, and the physical inventory indicates that it actually has only $98,000, the department records $2,000 in shrinkage.

Shrinkage is caused by employee theft, shoplifting, breakage, and errors in record keeping and in recording sales, and by unrecorded markdowns (known as "paper shrink"). Shrinkage often is expressed as a percentage of net sales and can be evaluated only in the context of industry segment averages as well as the store's own operating conditions and historical results. Shrinkage rates can vary significantly from one retailer to another, as well as between stores and merchandise departments.

(b) Leases

Leases represent another area with significant accounting implications for retailers. Many retailers lease multiple locations for their operations and have leased departments within their stores. Each lease must be evaluated for proper classification in accordance with the terms of Statement of Financial Accounting Standards (SFAS) No. 13, *Accounting for Leases*, as amended (Accounting Standards Section L10). This process is complicated by leases that involve only a portion of a building, land and building, or equipment as well as real estate. Fair market values for older real estate may not be readily available.

Minimum lease payments must be determined. Contingent rentals (i.e., increases or decreases due to changes in the factors on which lease payments are based, such as sales volume) should be excluded from minimum lease payments. The minimum lease term may include option periods for which renewal appears reasonably assured (for example, because of the existence of significant lessee-owned leasehold improvements that cannot be recovered during the stated initial lease term, or a guarantee of the lessor's debt by the lessee). The minimum lease term and the amortization period for leasehold improvements should be consistent.

If the lessor reimburses certain expenses of the lessee, such as moving expenses, the lessee should recognize these expenses immediately and amortize the benefit of the reimbursement over the term of the lease. Construction allowances should not be offset against leasehold improvements, but should be deferred and amortized as a reduction of expense over the lease term. Leases assumed in connection with the acquisition of a retail entity may include rental rates more favorable than those currently available in the market. The appraised present value of this favorable spread may result in recording an intangible asset known as a "beneficial leasehold," which should be amortized on a straight-line basis over the remaining lease term.

Retailers may lease space from a shopping center or other landlord. In these circumstances, the premises generally need to be customized, or "finished out," to the retailer's specifications. In many cases, the landlord will pay for all or part of that construction or renovation, either directly or by reimbursing the retailer. In either case, FASB Technical Bulletin No. 88-1 requires that the retailer capitalize the full amount of the construction costs and amortize them over the shorter of their estimated useful life or the term of the lease. The payment or reimbursement by the landlord should be recorded as a deferred lease incentive to be offset against rent expense over the life of the lease on a straight-line basis. The retailer should not include the reimbursement as income.

Competitive pressures often lead a retailer to renovate or remodel a store long before the lease expires or the estimated useful life of the leasehold improvements and fixtures is reached. When this happens, the retailer should write off the unamortized or undepreciated cost of the leasehold improvements and fixtures that are replaced. Frequently, detailed records may not exist, and it may be necessary to estimate the undepreciated balance of discarded fixtures by estimating their net book value.

Rent escalations, "rent holidays," upfront cash, and contingent rentals are typical in the retail industry. Rent holidays (e.g., first three months of occupancy at no cost to the lessor) or upfront cash may be given as an incentive to enter a leasing agreement. Scheduled rent escalations typically help the lessor offset the anticipated impact of inflation. Contingent rentals generally are based on sales volumes and can vary from period to period. Contingent rentals usually are clearly defined in the leasing agreement, so accrual generally is not difficult. Other lease-related accruals may include base rents, common area maintenance (CAM) charges not included in the base rent amounts, property taxes, insurance, contingent rentals, and utilities. CAM charges and property taxes may be difficult to estimate accurately until the related bill arrives from the lessor. The typical practice is to accrue an amount based on the prior-year charges, allowing for anticipated increases based on historical experience. Generally, rent expense should be recognized on a straight-line basis over the life of the lease (including renewal options when it is apparent that they will be exercised), irrespective of the timing of the actual payments. In the case of rent holidays, deferred rent income is recorded during the period of the rent holiday and amortized over the lease term against rent expense (based on actual payments) on a straight-line basis. As contingent rentals generally cannot be estimated accurately over the life of the lease, they are excluded from the calculation of straight-line lease expense and are recognized as they accrue.

(c) Asset Impairment

SFAS No. 121, *Accounting for the Impairment of Long-Lived Assets and for Long-Lived Assets to Be Disposed Of* (Accounting Standards Section I08), requires entities to evaluate the recoverability of long-lived assets in certain circumstances, including changes in market conditions because of an increase in competition. This statement has a direct impact on retailers, especially those with multiple locations and significant investments in real estate or leasehold improvements. The requirement to evaluate cash flows at the lowest level possible requires judgments as to appropriate groupings of cash flows (individual store level or stores grouped by geographical location or product lines).

(d) 52-53 Week Year

Rather than using a fiscal period that ends at a calendar month-end, many retailers use fiscal years that end on the same day of the week; for example, the Saturday closest to January 31. This results in a fiscal year that ends on a different date each year, but the fiscal year is divided into periods that end on the same day and have the same number of weeks, except when the year has a fifty-third week. Publicly held companies use the 4-5-4 method (13 weeks in each quarter) for quarterly reporting purposes. These methods allow comparability of operating results with prior periods.

(e) Preopening Costs

Many types of costs are incurred in connection with opening a new store, such as employee training, preopening rent, advertising, utilities, and security costs. These costs may be deferred if they are incremental, specifically identifiable, and directly associated with a store that has not yet opened. Alternatively, they may be expensed as incurred. If deferred, they should be amortized over a period, generally 12 months, commencing with the store opening. The accounting policy followed should be reasonable in the circumstances and consistently applied. For publicly held companies, it generally is not considered preferable to change from a policy of expensing preopening costs to one that allows for deferral of those costs.

(f)   Store Closing Reserves

Strategic store closings have become part of the normal operations of retailers; accordingly, the charges that are recorded as a result of closing a store generally are included in income from operations. [Certain store closings, however, may qualify for treatment as a disposal of a segment under Accounting Principles Board (APB) Opinion No. 30 (Accounting Standards Section I13).] Landlords and retailers increasingly are entering into lease modification arrangements as a result of store closures. Guidance on accounting for these types of transactions can be found in Emerging Issues Task Force (EITF) Issue 95-17, *Accounting for Modifications to an Operating Lease*. Some retailers disclose their store closing accounting policies.

Once a decision has been made to close a store, the retailer should consider establishing a reserve in accordance with SFAS No. 121, *Accounting for the Impairment of Long-Lived Assets and for Long-Lived Assets to Be Disposed Of* (Accounting Standards Section I08), and/or EITF Issue 94-3, *Liability Recognition for Certain Employee Termination Benefits and Other Costs to Exit an Activity (including Certain Costs Incurred in a Restructuring)*, for the costs it expects to incur in closing the store. Those costs may include:

- Expected future rental costs, net of anticipated future sublease rental income (or cost of lease cancellation)
- Costs to return premises to the physical condition required under the lease
- Reduction of fixed assets and supplies to net realizable value
- Write-off of leasehold improvements
- Estimated payroll costs incurred to close the store

In general, future estimated operating losses of stores to be closed should not be accrued at the time a decision to close is made; instead, the losses should be recorded when incurred. Also, costs associated with relocating inventory, equipment, or personnel to other continuing locations should not be accrued. Further, it is not appropriate to offset a loss of a closed store against the operations of a new store location.

Store closures may be part of a restructuring or exit plan. The nature and timing of expense and liability recognition for costs associated with a restructuring, such as employee termination benefits, should be evaluated in accordance with guidelines established under APB Opinion No. 30, SFAS No. 5, and recent EITF concensuses, including Issue 94-3. The SEC staff has indicated that inventory markdowns associated with a restructuring should be classified as a component of cost of goods sold in the income statement.

(g)   Slotting Fees

Manufacturers typically make payments to retailers, primarily supermarkets, for shelf space in their stores. These fees, referred to as slotting fees, should be deferred and amortized over the period during which the retailer has obligations to the manufacturer to hold open shelf space or make purchases. Slotting fees should be recognized immediately only if the retailer has no future obligations.

(h) Discounts and Rebates

Vendor discounts or rebates, such as free goods, off-invoice allowances, and cash rebates, should be accounted for as a reduction of the purchase price of the related merchandise. This treatment results in the discounts or rebates increasing income as they are earned, that is, as the merchandise is sold. These discounts and rebates differ from discounts for prompt payment; the latter usually are recognized in the income statement as a component of cost of goods sold at the time of payment.

(i) Advertising

Statement of Position (SOP) 93-7, *Reporting on Advertising Costs*, requires that costs of advertising be expensed as incurred or when the advertising first takes place, except for direct-response advertising, which should be capitalized if (1) its primary purpose is to attract customers who could be shown to have responded specifically to the advertising, and (2) the advertising results in probable future economic benefits that can be substantiated by verifiable historical patterns of operating results.

In cooperative (co-op) advertising, often called vendor-paid advertising, the manufacturer whose products are being promoted shares the retailer's advertising costs. The arrangement usually is negotiated by the buyer as part of the purchase, with agreed-upon terms indicated on the purchase order or in a separate written agreement. In the more common co-op advertising arrangements:

- The vendor or distributor provides ads for release to newspapers. The retailer may pay for part of the newspaper space or not, depending on the agreement.
- The retailer receives an advertising allowance, usually based on a percentage of vendor-product sales.
- The manufacturer pays all or part of the cost of an ad, upon receipt of a tear sheet of the ad from the retailer as proof of performance.

The auditor should ascertain the nature of all such arrangements and should determine that the costs associated with them are recorded completely and accurately at the end of each accounting period.

(j) Commissions

Retail operations that sell high-ticket items such as furniture, appliances, furs, jewelry, and men's and women's clothing generally compensate salespeople on a commission basis. The commission paid generally is based on a percentage of sales, with the amount of the percentage varying according to the type of merchandise, length of employment, or store policy. There may be a base minimum amount of sales that the salesperson must achieve before receiving a commission.

Commission arrangements vary from store to store, and from department to department within a store. For example, commissions may be:

- Accrued at the time the sale is recorded, whether or not the merchandise is delivered

- Recorded only when the merchandise has been delivered and accepted by the customer

- Recorded only after payments have been received

However, generally accepted accounting principles require that commission expense, if material, be recorded in the same period as the related revenue. Moreover, sales returns and allowances may or may not result in deductions from commissions payable.

(k) Separately Priced Service Contracts

Many retailers offer service contracts concurrent with the sale of products such as appliances, computer hardware, and electronic equipment. Such contracts cover a stated period and are generally noncancelable unless the product is returned. Service contracts are often highly profitable since the cost of fulfilling them is usually minor, and thus they are often an integral part of the retailer's marketing and pricing strategy. FASB Technical Policy Bulletin No. 90-1 requires that revenues from separately priced extended warranty and product maintenance contracts be deferred and recognized in income on a straight-line basis over the contract period, except in circumstances in which sufficient historical evidence indicates that the costs of performing services under the contract are incurred on other than a straight-line basis. In these circumstances, revenue should be recognized over the contract period in proportion to the costs expected to be incurred in performing services under the contract. A loss should be recognized if the sum of expected costs of providing services under the contract exceeds related unearned revenue.

(l) Consignment Inventory

Inventory held on consignment and the related liability to the vendor typically are not recorded until an item is sold. However, the amounts of consignment inventory held should be considered for disclosure in the financial statements. Inventory on consignment should be counted and compared with vendor and perpetual records. A liability should be recognized for inventory that cannot be identified at the time of physical count (consignment shrinkage).

(m) Layaways

Layaway sales may be recognized in income and cost of goods sold at the time of the initial transaction based on historical experience with sales that are completed. Alternatively, deposits may be recorded as liabilities and sales deferred until full payment is received. Abandoned layaway deposits should not be recorded as revenue but must be treated according to state and local escheat laws.

(n)   Area Franchise Fees

SFAS No. 45, *Accounting for Franchise Fee Revenue* (Accounting Standards Section Fr3), provides that franchisors generally can recognize area franchise fees as revenue when all material services and conditions relating to the contract have been substantially performed. If obligations exist, such as training, site location, store setup, and so on, fees should be recognized in proportion to fulfillment of the obligations. Franchisees may amortize franchise fees over the term of the franchise agreement. The franchisee's financial statements should disclose the amortization method and terms.

(o)   Credit Card Sales

Retailers often issue proprietary (in-house) credit cards to customers or accept third-party credit cards. Customers are billed for proprietary credit card sales on a cyclical basis throughout the month. Normally, customers are encouraged to send their payments directly to a bank lockbox. Most retailers allow customers to make payment at the store, and these payments are forwarded directly to the store cashier and included with the daily deposit.

In third-party credit sales, the retailer is paid by the third party. Third-party issuers charge retailers for the servicing of these transactions and normally deduct the charges before remitting payment to the retailer. These charges usually are either a percentage of sales or a fixed charge per transaction. The timely processing of third-party charges is critical to the retailer's cash flow.

48.2   RISK FACTORS AND AUDIT REACTION

Certain characteristics of the retail industry influence the design and structure of accounting systems and controls or present risks that the auditor should consider. These characteristics include:

- Competition, in the form of frequent new entrants into a retailer's market, competing common and new products, and discounting (Competitors may be larger and better financed)
- Changing technology, resulting in improved marketing techniques or new accounting and inventory management systems
- High volume of low-value transactions, which is traditionally a major factor in the design of accounting and control systems
- A primary focus of retailers and their auditors on inventory, including costing and valuation
- Continual opening and closing of locations by retail chains
- Dependence on a large number of clerical level employees to serve customers
- Multiple locations, creating real estate and internal control issues
- A need for reliable and timely information to protect retailers' profit margin
- Real estate issues involving locations, leases, real estate taxes, construction, and financing

Retailers often have risk management programs—including worker's compensation, group medical, and general liability insurance plans—that include elements of self-insurance risk. Each area of self-insurance risk must be identified and analyzed to develop adequate loss accruals for these risks, including incurred-but-not-reported claims. The auditor may need specialized knowledge if significant self-insurance exposure exists.

Retailers may have environmental risks, for example, if gasoline is sold at the retailer's site and underground storage tanks are used. The auditor should identify these environmental risks through inquiry, observation, and review of available documentation relating to compliance with applicable environmental laws and regulations. Any resulting contingencies should be evaluated for accrual and disclosure in accordance with applicable standards, including SFAS No. 5, SEC Staff Accounting Bulletin No. 92, and SOP 96-1, *Environmental Remediation Liabilities*.

(a)   Financial Ratios and Performance Indicators

Financial ratios and performance indicators provide interested parties, such as investors and creditors, with important information about a retailer's overall performance. Such ratios and performance indicators also can identify risks that the auditor should consider. Listed below are some of the more significant ratios and performance indicators in the retail industry.

Gross margin percentage

Probably the most important operating ratio, this is based on the difference between sales and cost of merchandise sold. Even small changes in gross margin percentages can have a major impact on net income.

Changes, particularly reductions, in gross margin percentages may reflect:

- Inventory obsolescence, resulting in the need for additional price markdowns
- Deterioration of store locations
- Reduced sales levels
- Increased shrinkage due to spoilage or theft
- A change in the sales mix
- A change in pricing strategy

Comparable store sales percentage

This indicates the percentage change in sales for stores that have been open during both periods being compared. Stores with higher than average increases may have better merchandise mixes or better locations. Below-average increases (or decreases) may reflect:

- Sales not properly recorded
- Unsuccessful or improperly reported merchandise offerings

- Inadequate or poorly trained sales staff
- Low inventory turnover
- Deterioration of a store location

Shrinkage as a percentage of sales	An increase in this percentage usually is caused by inadequate controls over the completeness and accuracy of processing transactions and accumulating data, or by actual theft or breakage. A review of inventory shrinkage statistics by department and by store, for example, also may indicate that inventory cutoff problems exist or that an accurate physical inventory was not taken.
Sales per square foot	This ratio indicates how productively the store is using selling space. Lower than expected sales per square foot may reflect: • Inappropriate inventory levels • Poor management or inadequate staff • Poor store or department location
Sales per employee hour; payroll as a percent of sales; payroll per square foot	These percentages indicate the productivity level of store and department employees. Lower percentages may reflect: • An inadequate investment in labor-saving technology • An inadequately staffed store or department • Possible inventory shrinkage

48.3 TYPICAL TRANSACTIONS, CONTROLS, AND AUDIT TESTS

(a) Information Technology

The retail industry uses sophisticated technology in many aspects of operations. For example, consumers can "pay at the pump" for gasoline purchases and can receive "trigger" coupons on merchandise closely related to their grocery purchases. Most retail stores use point-of-sale (POS) technology, which enables them to scan merchandise at checkout, thereby increasing the accuracy and speed of transactions, and building a valuable data base on customers' purchasing habits.

In POS technology, the retailer's computer contains a file that recognizes items as they are scanned and provides the appropriate prices to the terminal (cash register), which then summarizes the purchase. The retailer can change the price in the file, and the new price will be transmitted to all locations immediately. This technology is useful mainly in grocery stores and was developed to automatically update shelf prices. An additional benefit of this technology is inventory management. Merchants can use this information to automatically determine what merchandise needs to be ordered and to track sales and adjust future purchases accordingly. Furthermore, some POS systems, primarily in grocery stores, summarize purchase information and sell it to manufacturers for target marketing purposes.

Electronic Data Interchange (EDI) has become the preferred way of exchanging information between retailers and suppliers, thereby eliminating traditional paper trails. EDI can be used for purchase orders, invoices, and payment remittances. It enables the information to be interfaced into existing systems, such as accounts payable, thereby eliminating the need for the data entry function. Many retailers are requiring the use of EDI by their suppliers.

The disappearing paper trails present challenges and opportunities for management of entities that use sophisticated electronic information systems and for the auditors of those entities. Management must design controls to include appropriate reconciliation and review procedures in order to ensure the validity of information captured by those systems. For example, sales transactions in a store may be captured at the register and electronically transmitted to a direct interface with the sales accounts in the general ledger. Controls should include reconciliation of cash deposits and other daily activity to credits posted to sales accounts as part of the sales audit function (described later). Merchandise management systems update perpetual inventory balances when a receiving report is entered into the system that can be matched to a purchase order previously entered. If a proper match is not made by the system, the receiving report is rejected, even though the inventory and related payable should be recorded. Controls should include review and investigation of edit reports that list these rejected receiving reports. Cycle counts should be made and reconciled to perpetual inventory balances. The frequency of the physical counts will depend on the accuracy of the perpetual records. The additional information available from merchandise management systems can be useful to the auditor in identifying departmental unit (also referred to as stock keeping unit, or SKU) profit margins and slow-moving or obsolete inventories.

Technology also has led to a variety of ways of paying for retail purchases, including credit cards, checks, and debit cards. Checks normally are verified, within seconds, through a number of check verification services. Debit cards instantly commit the funds from a customer's available balance; the money is transferred automatically to the merchant's bank account the same day.

(b) Revenue Cycle

Sales and related collections typically consist of a large volume of small individual transactions. A broad range of transaction types can be involved, including cash sales, layaways, CODs, house account sales, and third-party or bank card sales. Supporting documentation for these transactions is typically voluminous and can consist of register tapes, sales invoices, layaway and COD records, merchandise credit and refund slips, and cash receipts.

(i) Cash/Credit/Layaway Sales.   For many retailers, cash sales are a significant portion of total daily sales transactions. Because of the sheer volume of these typically small transactions, in-store cash controls are very important. Typical controls include counting of each cash drawer prior to opening; supervisory approval for voids, overrings, and returns; and close-out procedures (balancing or reconciliation of the cash drawer to sales activity for the day). Cash deposits typically are made daily, either by individual stores or by the central office.

Credit sales typically fall into two categories: house and third party (bank cards). House sales are based on credit terms granted and managed by the retailer. These receivables are owned by the retailer. Third-party sales are based on credit granted and receivables owned by a bank or other financial institution. Credit terms range from 30-day accounts to revolving credit plans; the latter generally provide for periodic finance charges. Controls typically found related to house credit include credit limit approval procedures, periodic reconciliation of detail subsidiary ledgers to related general ledger control accounts, and analysis of uncollectible accounts (aging of accounts receivable).

Although generally not found in larger department stores, layaways are typical in discount and specialty stores and usually apply to all merchandise types sold. Layaways are treated as a type of deposit sale, with the merchandise released only after full payment for the goods has been received. Generally, a deposit is required to place merchandise on layaway, with a commitment to pay the remaining balance over a specified period of time (generally 90 days or less). The merchandise is set aside for the "layaway period" and if the customer does not make the required payments during the specified time, it is returned to stock. Various refund policies exist, in which the customer may receive full to no credit toward future purchases. Very rarely is the cash deposit or periodic payments refunded when a layaway transaction is canceled by the customer.

Similar to other deposit sales, revenue generally is recognized for layaway sales either when the full purchase price has been received (similar to a cash sale) or at the time of the first payment (similar to a credit sale). When recognition of the sale is deferred, all deposits and payments are recorded as liabilities. Layaway items typically are segregated from other inventories. Detailed records should be maintained similar to accounts receivable for each layaway item.

(ii) Controls over Sales.   The high volume of sales transactions in a retail business increases the risk of errors. This risk can be compounded as the number of individuals involved in executing transactions increases. To minimize this risk, retailers generally establish controls over sales that include the compilation and verification of daily sales data prior to recording. Those controls often are referred to as the sales audit process.

The details of a retailer's sales audit process vary depending on the nature of its business and the volume of daily transactions. The process should include compilation of departmental gross and net sales and reconciliation of total sales and cash register totals to supporting documentation and cash receipt listings/deposit slips (e.g., preparation of a daily or weekly "store report"). Other controls may include review and testing of supporting documentation to determine the accuracy, completeness, and occurrence of sales, and reconciliation of nonsales revenues and cash collections (e.g., delivery and handling charges) and of leased department transactions.

Specific controls over sales transactions vary. As in other industries, a retailer usually has controls in place that help ensure that all transactions are processed accurately and in a timely fashion. These controls may include procedures to ensure that all cash register transactions are reported daily (e.g., comparison of the prior day's ending register readings to the current day's beginning readings, and issuance and control of sequentially numbered sales books when manual sales slips are used).

(iii) Substantive Tests.   The primary substantive test of sales is a store-by-store (or department-by-department) analysis of net sales for the current period compared with previous periods and other stores or departments. Other common analytical tests of sales include considering the reasonableness of sales per square foot, and comparing gross margins from period to period and investigating unexpected variances. Substantive tests of accounts receivable might include confirmation of significant individual accounts receivable balances and analytical analysis of the allowance for doubtful accounts.

(c) Purchasing Cycle

Open to buy (OTB) is a methodology used to determine whether inventory levels are adequate to meet expected sales volumes. OTB is a management tool for monitoring and controlling purchases and related inventory levels based on projected and actual sales activity. Properly implemented, OTB can alert management to when purchase orders should be initiated through projections of when merchandise will be received and goods will be sold.

Data used in OTB consists of planned, projected, and actual results of operations on a consolidated or departmental basis. OTB planned data comprises planned beginning and ending inventories (for both retail outlets and warehouse), planned receipts and sales (or shipments in the case of warehouse inventories), and anticipated adjustments (markups/markdowns and returns to vendors) for a number of months or periods. The planned data initially comes from the merchandise planning system. During the year, ending inventory for future months is projected by adding actual amounts on order, actual past-due orders, and actual receipts, less planned sales and adjustments, to actual beginning inventories as of the most recent month-end. At the end of each month or period, actual ending inventories are determined using actual data. OTB for the most recent month-end is calculated as the difference between planned and actual inventories. OTB for any future month- or period-end is calculated as the difference between planned and projected inventories.

Some of the more important controls over OTB are those associated with the issuance of purchase orders. At a minimum, these controls should include review and approval by someone other than buyers and comparison of the OTB report with related actual purchase orders to ensure that excess quantities are not ordered. Other related controls are the same as in other industries that maintain inventories.

(d) Inventory Cycle

(i) Price Adjustments.   Price adjustments (markups, markdowns, and markup and markdown cancellations) occur often in retail businesses. The most frequently used and significant type of price change is the markdown. The amount and frequency of markdowns depend on the type of retail operation (i.e., department store versus specialty or discount store). Typically, a department store will begin with a higher initial markon and maintain the higher sales price for a longer period of time than will a specialty or discount retailer. Markdowns reduce inventory in the retail stock ledger (described earlier) to recognize the reduction of retail value originally recorded in the ledger. Sales of marked down merchandise reduce inventory at the marked down prices.

Retailers should have procedures for the implementation and summarization of all price changes, which should be recorded on price change reports on a timely basis. Price change reports should be reviewed for completeness and accuracy prior to processing. Both buyers and merchandise managers should be required to approve price changes.

(ii) Retail Method. As noted above, the retail method was developed in response to difficulties encountered in costing individual items. The retail method should be tested periodically by comparison with physical inventories and, if necessary, book amounts should be adjusted. Other controls over the accuracy of inventories are discussed above in connection with the OTB methodology.

(iii) Substantive Tests. Inventory generally is a retailer's most significant asset and often presents significant inherent risk. The audit strategy for retail inventories emphasizes two objectives—existence and valuation. Valuation includes both determining cost and pricing the inventory at the lower of cost or market.

A retailer may physically count all locations at year-end or cycle count throughout the year. Physical counts may be made by internal personnel or by outside independent counting services. The retailer should stop merchandise flow for a period before a physical inventory in order to ensure that an accurate cutoff can be achieved. If goods are received near or on the day of the physical count, they should be segregated and clearly labeled as after-inventory merchandise. The corresponding receiving documents also should indicate that the merchandise was not counted in the physical inventory. The auditor should be familiar with the retailer's cutoff procedures in connection with a physical inventory. Unusual book-to-physical adjustments are often the result of poor cutoff for merchandise receipts and shipments.

The auditor should observe physical counts at some locations, even if an outside service is used. The number of locations visited is a matter of auditor judgment based on factors such as knowledge of the retailer and past experience with the accuracy of counts, the quality of the inventory records and procedures, and the use of outside services or internal auditors. Sufficient test counts should be made and recorded and appropriate cutoff information obtained. If the retailer uses cycle counts, the auditor should test some counts during the year and ensure that inventory roll-forward procedures are adequate for any locations not counted at year-end. If an outside counting service is used, direct confirmation of counts made by the service may be appropriate.

Obsolescence is a major concern of retailers. If excess inventory accumulates, it may have to be discounted or it may not be sold. Obsolete inventory can be signaled in a number of ways, including high ending inventory balances, low inventory turnover rate, dust on merchandise at stores, out-of-code product at stores, and reports of slow-moving items by store personnel.

If a retailer uses the cost method for valuation, costs typically can be vouched directly to applicable vendor invoices. Cost should include the cost of the merchandise and freight-in. In addition, some retailers may include other costs related to bringing inventory to a salable condition and location, such as buying costs, warehouse and distribution costs, occupancy costs, and insurance. These additional capitalized costs should be analyzed for appropriateness and consistency with prior years.

If the retail method is used, the auditor should determine that the retailer has appropriate procedures and records in effect to ensure proper application of that method, including entry of all purchases into the stock ledger at both cost and retail, and capturing of all other transactions, such as sales, price changes, returns to vendors, and goods removed from stock. In addition, the auditor should determine that the different types of merchandise included in a particular group or departmental cost calculation were reasonably similar in terms of margin and turnover so as not to distort the calculations of inventory cost; the auditor also should determine that a reasonable number of departmental cost multiplier calculations were made. Finally, the recorded provision for inventory shrinkage should be reviewed for reasonableness.

If a retailer has multiple locations with similar types of inventory, store-by-store comparisons are effective analytical substantive tests, including period-to-period and location-to-location balance comparisons and inventory per square foot calculations. Comparison of gross margins between similar departments in multiple locations and gross margin fluctuations among periods within a department are useful tools in analyzing the lower of cost or market valuation. If a cost method of valuation is used, analysis of excess, slow-moving, or obsolete inventory is needed to ensure that appropriate reserves have been recorded. This may include analysis of markdowns taken subsequent to year-end or analysis of quantities and prices of subsequent sales of various types of merchandise included in ending inventory.

(e) Payroll Cycle

Incentive compensation for retail sales is most often in the form of commissions, which typically are used in combination with a base salary. As a result, a salesperson's compensation depends, at least in part, on sales made. As discussed earlier, issues that may arise when commissions are paid relate to the salesperson not earning a commission because of returns, uncollectible credit sales, and advances against future commissions. Commissions typically are paid in the period following a sales transaction. Thus, the commission generally has been paid by the time a return is made or an account is determined to be uncollectible, which typically results in a reduction of future commissions.

Substantive tests of commissions include recalculating selected salespersons' commissions based on related sales and comparing the amounts with the payroll summary. Overall appropriateness of commission expense can be determined by comparing commissions as a percentage of related sales with established policies on commission percentages.

(f) Leasing Cycle

The existence of leases can be determined through inquiry of company personnel, review of minutes, and analysis of rental expense. Lease agreements should be reviewed and tested to determine that they have been properly classified in accordance with the provisions of SFAS No. 13 and related amendments and interpretations. Rental expense should be analytically tested based on the provisions of all leases. If the retailer leases portions of a store to independent operators, the auditor should review the agreements covering these leased departments for the impact on the retailer in terms of rental income, payroll expense, insurance arrangements, and similar matters.

The auditor should examine lease agreements to identify the lease expiration dates or any special clauses that may require a penalty for early termination or may obligate the lessee to make physical changes to the premises. In addition, the auditor should pay special attention to management's estimate of potential future sublease income and compare the estimates with formal sublease agreements, if available. If no agreements exist, the auditor should determine whether management's estimate of future rentals is reasonable in light of market conditions.

Contingent rentals and CAM charges (discussed earlier) are common in the retail industry. During an initial engagement, the auditor should obtain a schedule of leases containing these provisions and compare it with year-end accruals for these types of charges. Once completeness of accruals has been established, future lease-related accruals may be analytically reviewed in comparison with prior years, adjusted for known changes in locations or lease terms.

(g)   Arrangements with Vendors

The auditor should inquire as to arrangements with vendors, such as long-term supply arrangements and rebates and allowances. Issues related to long-term supply arrangements may include disclosures of purchase commitments or concentration of supplier relationships under SOP 94-6, *Disclosure of Certain Risks and Uncertainties*. In some circumstances, purchase commitments may exist for quantities in excess of amounts that can be sold above cost, requiring a loss accrual relating to the commitments or cancellation penalties.

Rebates and allowances due from vendors are common in the retail industry and can significantly affect cost of goods sold. These arrangements generally are based on volume purchased and often are not documented adequately in writing between the vendor and the retailer. Rebates and allowances should be the subject of specific inquiry by the auditor. The auditor should be aware that these arrangements may involve cash payments from vendors to retailers that may not be recorded properly by the retailers.

If the retailer has cooperative advertising arrangements with vendors, the auditor should understand the terms of the agreements, ensure that the costs associated with the arrangements have been recorded completely and accurately, review an aged trial balance of vendor receivables, and consider the collectibility of such amounts.

If the retailer has employees who are paid by vendors, for example, cosmetics demonstrators in a department store whose salaries are paid by the cosmetics manufacturers, controls are needed to ensure that the employees are not paid by both the vendor and the retailer. The auditor should understand the arrangements in effect and determine that they have been adhered to and that duplicate payments have not been made.

49

Auditing Securities and Commodities Broker-Dealers

49.1 OVERVIEW OF THE INDUSTRY

The securities industry has been shaped most significantly by the 1929 stock market crash and events that followed it. After the crash, broker-dealers (also referred to as securities firms or simply firms) were given exclusive franchise to two areas previously dominated by banks—underwriting and the financing of customer securities transactions. It was thought—whether rightly or wrongly—that lending to finance speculative stock market investments was a prime cause of bank failures in the crash. As a result, this activity was forbidden to banks and fell to securities firms; the balance sheets of many broker-dealers today still show large balances resulting from such lending activities. Since 1975, when commission rates were deregulated, brokers typically have focused more on the revenues that can be generated from holding customer balances, as well as other revenue sources such as proprietary trading and investment banking fees, than on the transaction fees (commissions) themselves.

Commissions—and, to a lesser extent, transaction costs—have been on a downward trend for the past 20 years. Competition from discount brokerage firms has lowered retail commission rates, and institutional commission rates have been extremely thin for years. In the 1980s, firms serving institutional markets began offering soft-dollar arrangements to their customers. (A soft-dollar arrangement is a form of discounting in which the broker provides services, such as research, to a customer in return for the customer providing a given level of commission business to the broker.) Although some large, prestigious firms long resisted this practice, claiming that they provided other, intangible benefits to their customers, competition has forced almost all institutional brokers into providing soft-dollar arrangements.

Costs, particularly on the production side, have been slower to decline. Compensation to sales personnel still takes an unusually large percentage of total sales dollars, relative to other industries. In "full-service" retail firms, compensation is usually a percentage of transaction revenues. Discount brokerage firms, often associated with mutual fund groups, usually compensate their brokers on a salary plus bonus basis. Institutional sales personnel, as well as investment bankers, generally are compensated on an incentive basis, although typically not in a way that is directly linked to transaction volume.

Costs associated with clearing securities transactions have proven more tractable. Compensation, once substantially higher than in other industries, has been reduced. Increased automation has reduced the need for skilled clerical personnel, and consolidation and higher transaction volumes have reduced per trade costs. Transaction volume has skyrocketed in the past 25 years. In 1972, the average daily New York Stock Exchange (NYSE) volume was 22 million shares; by 1997, it was over 500 million shares daily. Retrenchment and cost-containment measures have become the rule, not the exception. Common buzzwords are downsizing, right-sizing, reengineering, and outsourcing. Outsourcing of operations finds its fullest expression in the practice of correspondent clearing, discussed later. Several firms have been quite successful in developing this business, often clearing for dozens or even hundreds of other firms. Geography is also a factor, as securities firms are no longer concentrated in lower Manhattan, but have dispersed to other, often lower-cost, locations.

The move to consolidation has been fitful but continual. In the late 1970s and early 1980s, the "financial supermarket" became popular. The idea was to provide an outlet for the products of various financial services entities. The results were less than satisfactory. The freewheeling, entrepreneurial cultures of securities firms coexisted poorly with the structured, bureaucratic cultures of other financial services industries. This type of consolidation continues today, but for different reasons and with different expectations, as firms, in efforts to drive down transaction costs in order to remain competitive, are increasing in size and seeking to obtain additional capital, mainly through mergers. Securities firms also have focused on the potential effects of deregulation that would remove the barriers that prevent banks from engaging in securities-related activities.

Banks are formidable competitors to securities firms, even without changes in the legal and regulatory framework.[1] The sizable fees that securities firms earn from investment banking activities, and the profits derived from trading activities, ensure that banks will continue to enter these arenas. In addition, as restrictions on the types of securities that banks may underwrite ease, the securities industry faces competition in what traditionally has been one of its most profitable lines of business. Capital requirements for banks give them a competitive advantage, because they can leverage their vast capital bases. If banks were permitted to engage in the activities now exclusively reserved to brokers and dealers, their considerable retail know-how, lower sales costs, and large capital bases would make them even more formidable competitors to securities firms.

At the time of this writing, major revisions to the Glass–Steagall Act, the federal statute that limits the securities activities of banks and the affiliation between banking and securities firms, and the Bank Holding Company Act, the federal statute that limits the activities of companies that control banks, are under consideration by Congress to modernize the U.S. financial services marketplace. One proposal would eliminate the separation of banking and general commercial activities altogether, while another would modify the relationship more modestly. Still another proposal supports giving holding companies' securities and insurance affiliates powers and expanding nonbanking powers to include activities that are "financial in nature."

The need for more capital is typically the most significant issue that broker-dealers face. International expansion, skyrocketing technology costs, and the competition for skilled industry resources all place extraordinary demands on capital. While securities firms finance their current assets through current liabilities (generally, collateralized financing), they usually rely almost exclusively on equity financing otherwise. Debt financing, known as subordinated lending, typically is not especially attractive to lenders.[2]

As much as the trend toward consolidation continues, the industry remains remarkably open to new and smaller firms. There are few barriers to entering new busi-

---

[1] Banks engage in securities transactions that are forbidden to the banks themselves through *Section 20* subsidiaries, special-purpose broker-dealers that are limited in the amount of revenue they can earn from underwriting and dealing in bank "ineligible" securities (i.e., those securities that a bank is not permitted to deal in or underwrite itself). That limit was increased from the original 5 percent in 1987, to 25 percent in 1997.

[2] This is due to provisions that the net capital rules require in debt instruments if they are to be considered "good" capital for regulatory purposes (*see* footnote 7). These provisions essentially prohibit lenders from withdrawing funds when the financial health of a firm starts to deteriorate. If a firm fails, a subordinated lender cannot be paid until after customers have been made whole.

nesses, and boutique firms, often started by successful producers from larger firms, offer specialized services, such as hedge funds.[3]

Transactions in emerging markets have caught the investing public's attention, and broker-dealers have rushed to develop execution, clearing, and settlement mechanisms in these markets. In comparison with the highly automated U.S. markets, clearing mechanisms in these markets are often crude. In addition, they can expose firms to considerable risk. For example, in U.S. markets, the simultaneous exchange of money for securities is presumed, so that a broker faces little exposure if a trade fails to clear midstream. However, in overseas markets, money and securities may move hours, or in some cases even days, apart, exposing the broker to substantial counterparty risk if a trade fails midstream.

After the 1929 crash, the next large-scale disruption to the industry occurred in the 1960s. In the paperwork and financial crisis experienced by many firms in the late 1960s, investor confidence was reduced drastically. As a result of having poor controls, or for other reasons, firms were found to have been using customer-owned securities to obtain collateralized financing, or to have used customers' cash left on deposit to finance speculative investments. In response, Congress created the Securities Investor Protection Corporation (SIPC) to insure customers' funds and securities held by securities firms up to a specified amount. The Securities and Exchange Commission (SEC) then established additional rules to improve the protection of investors' property, particularly Rule 15c3-3. That rule, commonly referred to as the "customer protection rule," prescribed standards for the protection of customers' property. At the same time, the SEC tightened and standardized its capital and financial reporting rules. Similar rules subsequently were developed by the Commodity Futures Trading Commission (CFTC) for firms engaged in commodities brokerage. The CFTC is discussed later in the chapter.

In the late 1970s and early 1980s, the repurchase (repo) agreement market developed.[4] In the early days of that market, there existed what was known as a "trust me" repo, so called because the borrower did not transfer legal title to the collateral to the lender.[5] Lenders suffered substantial losses when several government dealers folded. In response, Congress passed the Government Securities Act of 1986 (GSA), which regulates a previously unregulated area of the financial markets. The GSA is discussed later in the chapter.

After the 1987 stock market crash, various changes were made to address failings in execution and clearing mechanisms that became apparent on October 19 of that year, or "Black Monday," as the day has been referred to. For example, the National Association of Securities Dealers (NASD), sensitive to the charge that market-makers often failed to answer their phones, imposed more stringent requirements on its members to continue to make markets even when it is difficult to do so. Exchanges,

---

[3] Hedge funds are investment companies formed for high net worth individuals. Some hedge funds are organized as registered broker-dealers, because of the favorable regulatory treatment they receive by operating in that form. This chapter does not address hedge funds, except to the extent that they share features with other types of broker-dealers.

[4] In most cases, repurchase agreements are a form of collateralized financing. In some cases, they are sales with off-balance sheet commitments to repurchase.

[5] This form of custody still exists in a modified form known as the "hold-in-custody" (HIC) repo. HIC repos give the counterparty greater legal protection than "trust me" repos did.

clearinghouses, and many firms revisited and in many cases upgraded their execution and settlement capacities to ensure that they could handle sharp spikes in volume.

In the late 1980s, indictments and allegations of securities law violations involving insider trading, accommodation and accumulation transactions (i.e., "parking"), and practices that favor a securities firm or its employees over customers (e.g., "front running") created a concern among management, auditors, and lawyers over corporate responsibility and supervision of employees. This concern resulted in heightened surveillance efforts on the part of the SEC and various self-regulatory organizations, as well as increased internal audits and compliance reviews, and a new focus on codes of ethics and conflict-of-interest policies.

In the early 1990s, the SEC began looking at the relationship between securities firms and their owners, and the extent to which transactions with parent and associated firms could place a securities firm at risk. This led to the issuance of provisional "risk assessment rules," which require a broker-dealer to report to the SEC on the activities of those termed "materially associated persons" (MAPs), and to an interest in financial relationships between securities firms and their MAPs that could pose risk to the firms. These rules are discussed and MAPs are defined later in the chapter.

The bankruptcy of Orange County, California, and numerous other highly publicized losses related to financial instruments, further focused attention of regulators, other government authorities, and end-users on derivative securities. Derivative securities—financial instruments whose values are derived directly from the values of other, related instuments—are discussed later in the chapter.

49.2   LAWS AND REGULATIONS

The securities industry is one of the most highly regulated industries in the United States. Industry spokespersons maintain that it is grossly overregulated and overaudited. Regulators, on the other hand, maintain that, unlike banks in the 1930s and savings and loan institutions in the 1980s, the industry has never experienced significant customer losses or government bailouts. They attribute that to the efficacy of regulation.

While auditors are always concerned with an entity's compliance with laws and regulations, in auditing securities firms, they are subject to specific regulatory testing and reporting requirements. The primary testing requirements relate to the net capital and customer protection rules. Certain other audit and reporting requirements also are detailed here.

(a)   Net Capital (SEC Rule 15c3-1)

SEC Rule 15c3-1 under the Securities Exchange Act of 1934 prescribes net capital requirements for broker-dealers.[6] It was amended in 1975 to establish a uniform and comprehensive net capital standard for the industry—a standard that was adopted by

---

[6] The provisions of this rule require a registered broker-dealer to be in compliance with the Rule *at all times*. Although the Rule does not require daily computations of net capital, broker-dealers are required to maintain controls sufficient to ensure that they are continuously in compliance.

all the national securities exchanges. (Previously, many firms, in addition to complying with the SEC's net capital rule, were required to be in compliance with separate net capital rules of the various national securities and commodities exchanges of which they were members.)

As defined, net capital comprises the net worth of a firm plus approved[7] subordinated liabilities, less deductions for (a) assets that are essentially not readily convertible into cash, (b) percentages ("haircuts") of the various components of a firm's trading and investment accounts, and (c) percentages of market-value amounts of certain other open or unsettled securities and commodities transactions with customers and other broker-dealers.

The capital requirement may be computed under one of two methods. Under the first method, broker-dealers must maintain a maximum specified ratio of aggregate indebtedness to net capital. (Aggregate indebtedness generally comprises all liabilities pertaining to a firm's customer business.) Under this method, the broker-dealer must maintain a minimum dollar amount of net capital. If the ratio of aggregate indebtedness to net capital exceeds 10 to 1, a firm may no longer expand its business[8]; if the ratio exceeds 12 to 1, it must contract its business; and if the ratio exceeds 15 to 1, the firm must discontinue operations.[9]

The alternative method of computation, used by most firms, is designed to measure a firm's net capital in relation to its customer balances.[10] Under the alternative net capital rule, a broker-dealer must maintain a minimum dollar amount of net capital and cease to expand its business if net capital falls below 5 percent of aggregate debits (i.e., debit balances associated with customer transactions). The firm must contract its business if net capital falls below 4 percent of aggregate debits, and cease operations if net capital falls below 2 percent.

(b) Customer Protection (SEC Rule 15c3-3)

The problems encountered in the early 1970s in connection with the first liquidations of broker-dealers under the Securities Investor Protection Act and the desire for more timely clearing of transactions between securities firms led to the design of additional financial responsibility regulations. To ensure the protection of customers' assets held by securities firms, SEC Rule 15c3-3 was adopted. It includes the following:

- *Weekly Computation of Reserve Formula.* Securities firms must perform weekly calculations, known as the computation of the reserve requirement pursuant to Rule 15c3-3, that account for all debit and credit cash balances attributable to

---

[7] Subordinated debt cannot be considered "good" regulatory capital until the firm's designated self-regulatory organization (DSRO) has approved its use. The DSRO generally seeks to ensure that the terms of the debt agreement meet the requirements for subordinated debt set forth in Rule 15c3-1.

[8] Broker-dealers who violate any of the net capital thresholds have an affirmative obligation to notify the SEC once they become aware of the violation.

[9] Sometimes lenders or insurers impose stricter net capital requirements than those imposed by SEC Rule 15c3-1. An auditor needs to be aware of any such requirements.

[10] The customer balances on which the computation is made are the aggregate debits computed under Rule 15c3-3. (Aggregate debits are collateralized, customer-related assets, such as margin loans receivable.)

customers (as defined in the Rule).[11] All customers' cash balances are considered to be fungible, and the total debit (receivable) balances are subtracted from the total credit balances attributable to customers. If the result of this computation is a net credit balance, the firm must deposit that amount of cash or cash equivalents in a "special reserve bank account" for the exclusive benefit of customers. Such amounts must remain in the reserve account until another computation is performed that results in such deposits no longer being needed. If the formula results in a net debit balance, no deposit is required. In determining the amounts to be included in the formula, a firm may use either specific identification of customer versus firm transactions or any other rational and systematic method of allocation.[12]

• *Possession or Control Requirement.* Securities firms must maintain a system for identifying all customer securities that are fully paid for or are held as excess collateral[13] in connection with margin transactions. Further, firms must develop systems for issuing instructions to segregate these securities and promptly "reduce them" to the firm's possession or control.[14] If the securities are not in the broker's possession or control, the Rule specifies various time periods, considering the business environment, after which the firm must take prescribed actions. For example, customers' fully paid or excess margin securities may be reported as "fail to receive" for 30 days or less; older fails are required to be "bought in" by the broker-dealer to protect customers. Firms that neither clear transactions for customers nor carry customer accounts are exempted from these requirements.

(c) Financial Reporting and Annual Audit Requirements (SEC Rule 17a-5)

In the mid-1970s, the SEC adopted a streamlined uniform regulatory report, still in use, to be filed periodically by all broker-dealers. Known as the Financial and Operational Combined Uniform Single Report (FOCUS Report), it is required by the NYSE, NASD, and other self-regulatory organizations. Regulatory reporting for securities broker-dealers, as well as annual auditing requirements, are stipulated by SEC

---

[11] The logic on which the computation is based is that a firm is not risking one customer's money by lending it to another customer in a margin lending transaction, since the mechanics of margining ensure that the customer loan is fully collateralized. This requirement is designed to prevent the use of customers' money to finance speculative firm trading.

[12] In all but the smallest firms, automated allocation procedures are used to perform this task. While the Rule permits any systematic method to be used, the auditor needs to be aware of what strategy has been programmed into the system to accomplish the allocation.

[13] That is, the value of securities in excess of what is needed to adequately collateralize a margin loan receivable. The Rule defines that amount as 40 percent of the margin loan receivable. Thus, a broker-dealer may hypothecate securities held to the extent of 140 percent of the customer debit balance; securities in excess of that amount are considered to be excess margin securities and must be "locked up."

[14] Possession is rare today as few securities exist in physical form. A control location is one in which the broker has unrestricted access to the security—for example, a U.S. depository. A bank loan (i.e., securities pledged as collateral for a bank loan) would not be a good control location since a broker can obtain the securities only by repaying the loan.

Rule 17a-5. As discussed later, the CFTC has prescribed similar reporting requirements for commodities brokers.

(i) Regulatory Reporting.   Every broker-dealer registered under Section 15 of the 1934 Act must periodically file the FOCUS Report with the SEC on Form X17A-5 or, if certain conditions exist, with a DSRO (i.e., either a national securities exchange or a registered national securities association) that transmits the information to the SEC. Part I of the FOCUS Report is filed monthly (either 10 business days or, for NYSE firms, 17 business days after month-end) by broker-dealers that carry customer accounts or clear transactions for customers. Part I is a one-page summary of 26 key indicators designed to highlight the broker-dealer's financial and operating condition.

All broker-dealers must file either Part II or Part IIA of the FOCUS Report at the end of each calendar quarter. Part II is a comprehensive set of financial statements, comprising a statement of financial condition, statements of income and of changes in subordinated liabilities and stockholders' equity or partners' or sole proprietor's capital, and supplementary schedules, including the reserve formula (Rule 15c3-3) and net capital (Rule 15c3-1) computations, and possession or control (Rule 15c3-3) information. Part II is intended to be generally consistent with similar financial statements prepared in conformity with generally accepted accounting principles (GAAP). Part IIA is an abbreviated version of Part II and is used by broker-dealers that do not carry customer accounts or clear transactions for customers, or that are registered solely to sell shares of investment companies and do not clear transactions entered into on their own behalf. Part II or IIA must be filed 17 business days after the end of the reporting period.

(ii) Audited Financial Statements.   Every broker-dealer registered under Section 15 of the 1934 Act must file, pursuant to paragraph (d) of Rule 17a-5, audited financial statements (either calendar- or fiscal-year) within 60 *calendar* days following year-end. The broker-dealer may adopt a fiscal year-end for purposes of this rule that differs from its fiscal year-end for tax or other financial reporting purposes; however, once a year-end has been established, it cannot be changed without SEC approval.

The annual audit report is required to include the following financial statements and supplementary schedules, all of which must be prepared in conformity with GAAP:

- Statement of financial condition
- Statement of income (loss)
- Statement of changes in liabilities subordinated to the claims of general creditors
- Statement of changes in stockholders' equity, partners' capital, or sole proprietor's capital
- Statement of cash flows
- Supplementary schedules:
  - Computation of net capital under SEC Rule 15c3-1
  - Computation of reserve requirements under SEC Rule 15c3-3

- Information relating to possession or control requirements under SEC Rule 15c3-3

- A reconciliation of the computation of net capital under Rule 15c3-1 and the computation of the reserve requirement under Rule 15c3-3 to the corresponding computations included in the unaudited FOCUS Report as of the same date, if these computations differ materially. If no material differences exist, a statement to that effect is required.[15]

In conjunction with an audit performed in accordance with the requirements specified by Rule 17a-5, the independent accountant also must prepare a separate report on internal control. That report must comment on any material inadequacies existing at the date of the audit in the accounting system, the internal accounting control procedures, the procedures for safeguarding securities, and the practices and procedures reviewed as specified in items (i)-(iv) of Rule 17a-5 [paragraph (g)], described below. The term "material inadequacy" is defined in the rule as:

> Any condition which has contributed substantially to or, if appropriate corrective action is not taken, could reasonably be expected to (i) inhibit a broker or dealer from promptly completing securities transactions or promptly discharging his responsibilities to customers, other broker-dealers or creditors; (ii) result in material financial loss; (iii) result in material misstatements of the broker-dealer's financial statements; or (iv) result in violations of the Commission's record-keeping or financial responsibility rules to an extent that could reasonably be expected to result in the conditions described in parts (i), (ii), or (iii) of this subparagraph.[16]

If the audit did not disclose any material inadequacies, the independent accountant's report on internal control should so state. Comments on material inadequacies must be submitted with the broker-dealer's audited financial statements and must, if applicable, indicate corrective action taken or proposed by the broker-dealer.[17]

In adopting the FOCUS Report, the SEC amended Rule 17a-5 to eliminate previously prescribed auditing procedures. It replaced those procedures with language that permits auditors to exercise professional judgment in establishing the nature, timing,

---

[15] The statement should be included on the schedules computing the reserve requirement under Rule 15c3-3 and net capital under Rule 15c3-1, and should be worded as follows: There are no [material] differences between this [computation of net capital] [reserve required pursuant to Rule 15c3-3] and the corresponding computation prepared by the Company and included in its unaudited FOCUS filing as of the same date.

[16] The portion of Release No. 34-11935 in which the amendments to Rule 17a-5 are summarized, under the caption "Accountants' Reports," includes language to the effect that determining a material inadequacy generally requires (1) completion of auditing procedures in the particular area, (2) appropriate review at the decision-making level by both management and the independent accountant, and (3) possible consultation with counsel. Consequently, there could be a reasonable period of time between the date a potential condition considered to be a material inadequacy is first identified and the date such determination is finally made.

[17] Upon being notified by the auditor that a material inadequacy exists, a broker-dealer is required to give notice of such condition to the SEC by facsimile. A copy of that notice must be furnished to the auditor. If the auditor fails to receive that notice from the broker-dealer within 24 hours or disagrees with the statements contained in the notice, the auditor must report the material inadequacy to the SEC and the DSRO within 24 hours, as set forth in Rule 17a-11.

and extent of auditing procedures to be applied. Pursuant to Rule 17a-5 [paragraph (g)]:

> The scope of the audit and review of the accounting system, the internal control and procedures for safeguarding securities shall be sufficient to provide reasonable assurance that any material inadequacies existing at the date of the examination . . . would be disclosed. Additionally, as specific objectives, the audit shall include reviews of the practices and procedures followed by the client:
>
> (i) in making the periodic computations of aggregate indebtedness and net capital under Rule 17a-3(a)(11) and the reserve required by Rule 15c3-3(e);
>
> (ii) in making the quarterly securities examinations, counts, verifications and comparisons and the recordation of differences required by Rule 17a-13;
>
> (iii) in complying with the requirement for prompt payment for securities of Section 4(c)[18] of Regulation T of the Federal Reserve Bank; and
>
> (iv) in obtaining and maintaining physical possession or control of all fully paid and excess margin securities of customers as required by Rule 15c3-3.

Annual audited financial statements are treated by the SEC as public documents. To achieve some degree of confidentiality, however, a firm may file two sets of financial statements. The set that is to be treated as a public document is required to contain the broker-dealer's statement of financial condition, the related notes, and the auditor's report thereon and the auditor's report on internal control. The second, complete set of financial statements, including the statement of operations, and supporting schedules, and the auditor's report thereon, should be marked "Confidential."

Rule 17a-5 also prescribes requirements for obtaining filing extensions as well as for written notification to the SEC of the appointment and termination of auditors. In addition to providing audited financial statements to regulatory organizations, SEC Rule 17a-5 requires that broker-dealers, within specified time frames, furnish their customers with semiannual statements of financial condition, the year-end copy of which must be audited, together with appropriate footnotes.

(d) Government Securities Act of 1986

Congress passed the GSA primarily to establish capital adequacy, record-keeping, and financial disclosure guidelines for government securities dealers, who, before its enactment, were largely unregulated. The capital requirements of the GSA essentially track relevant regulations previously applicable to securities firms, most notably Rule 15c3-1, with certain variations to enable the regulators to better monitor the risks that are more common to government securities dealers. The most significant variation relates to the required haircut calculations for a government securities dealer's inventory. In recognition of the unique characteristics of government securities, haircuts have been designed to measure market risk and credit risk as well as the broker-dealer's liquidity.

The GSA is administered by the U.S. Treasury Department and monitored by the

---

[18] The requirement relates to procedures for cash accounts, not margin accounts. Typically, however, auditors review the procedures for margin accounts as well, although they are not required to do so by Rule 17a-5.

SEC. A government securities dealer that is required to adhere to the GSA is subject to annual audits of its financial statements and must make quarterly unaudited filings with the regulators. If a government securities dealer is subject to other regulations as a securities broker-dealer (e.g., Rules 15c3-1 and 17a-5), the dealer is exempted from the requirements of the GSA (because of the similarities of the rules).

(e) Commodity Futures Trading Commission

Regulation 1.10 of the CFTC requires futures commission merchants (FCMs) to file quarterly and annual financial reports (on Form 1-FR) similar to those required in the FOCUS Report filed with the SEC by securities broker-dealers. Regulation 1.10 allows FCMs who also are registered securities broker-dealers to satisfy this requirement by filing a copy of their FOCUS Report, described earlier, with the CFTC in lieu of Form 1-FR. Also similar to the SEC requirements for securities broker-dealers, CFTC Regulation 1.16 requires auditors to examine and report on the annual financial statements; to review and report on an FCM's accounting systems, internal control procedures, and procedures for safeguarding customer and firm assets; and to report material inadequacies.

(f) Other Rules and Regulations

Other SEC rules under the 1934 Act pertain to broker-dealers, particularly Rules 8c-1 and 15c2-1, 17a-3, 17a-4, 17a-11, and 17a-13. Rules 8c-1 and 15c2-1 deal with fraudulent practices and hypothecation of customers' securities; Rule 17a-3, with records required to be maintained; Rule 17a-4, with record retention; Rule 17a-11, with notification concerning violations of SEC rules; and Rule 17a-13, with quarterly security counts, verifications, and comparisons. Broker-dealers are also subject to pertinent regulations of the Federal Reserve Bank—Regulation T, which governs the amount of credit that broker-dealers may extend to customers; Regulation U, concerning the amount of credit that banks may grant to customers for the purpose of buying securities on margin; and Regulation X, which specifies conditions borrowers must meet when obtaining credit for the purpose of purchasing or carrying securities. The rules and regulations of the pertinent national stock exchanges or NASD are also relevant to audits of broker-dealers. The auditor of a broker-dealer should be aware of all the above regulations. The auditor should review the report on the most recent examination by the broker-dealer's DSRO as part of the process of evaluating the firm's compliance with regulatory requirements.

The SEC's risk-assessment rules (17h-1T and 17h-2T) require that broker-dealers maintain and preserve records and other financial information and that they report, on a quarterly basis, certain information to the SEC regarding the financial activities of MAPs. MAPs are affiliates or other associated persons that could have a material impact on the financial or operational condition of a broker-dealer. Broker-dealers who clear customer accounts and have less than $250,000 in capital, including subordinated debt, as well as broker-dealers who do not clear customer accounts and are exempt from Rule 15c3-3, and have less than $20,000,000 in capital, including subordinated debt, are exempt from these rules. Although auditors are not required to report on compliance with these rules, auditors should inquire as to broker-dealers' procedures for complying with the rules as part of the other procedures performed on regulatory matters.

49.3   ACCOUNTING PRINCIPLES AND PRACTICES

GAAP for broker-dealers are somewhat unique, especially the pervasiveness of their use of mark-to-market accounting. In other respects, GAAP are the same for broker-dealers as for entities in other industries.

A broker-dealer accounts for financial instruments in which it has an economic interest at fair value, including those (such as futures, forwards, swaps, and options) that are not recorded on the statement of financial condition at their contracted settlement amounts. Most other assets and liabilities are recorded at historical costs or at contract values. The fair value of a financial instrument is the price at which a willing buyer and a willing seller would enter into an exchange. Fair value usually is determined for accounting purposes using the end-of-the-day price in the principal market in which the instrument trades. [Market prices are discussed further in Section 6(f), Firm Inventory Accounts.]

In an effort to handle the numerous complex financial instruments being introduced into the market, the Financial Accounting Standards Board issued SFAS No. 105, *Disclosures of Information about Financial Instruments with Off-Balance-Sheet Risk and Financial Instruments with Concentrations of Credit Risk* (Accounting Standards Section F25). Because of the extent of a typical broker-dealer's dealings in financial instruments, disclosures under SFAS No. 105 tend to be extensive for broker-dealers. SFAS No. 107, *Disclosures about Fair Value of Financial Instruments* (Accounting Standards Section F25), extended fair value disclosure practices for some instruments by requiring all entities to disclose fair value of financial instruments, both assets and liabilities recognized and unrecognized in the statement of financial position, for which it is practicable to estimate fair value. If estimating fair value is not practicable, disclosure of descriptive information pertinent to estimating the value of a financial instrument is required. Because most financial instruments that a broker-dealer holds are carried at fair value or at amounts that approximate fair value, disclosures under SFAS No. 107 are usually minimal for most broker-dealers.

SFAS No. 119, *Disclosure about Derivative Financial Instruments and Fair Value of Financial Instruments* (Accounting Standards Section F25), requires disclosures about amounts, nature, and terms of derivatives that are not subject to SFAS No. 105 and do not result in off-balance-sheet risk of accounting loss. It also encourages, but does not require, quantitative information about market risks of derivatives, and also of other assets and liabilities, that is consistent with the way the entity manages or adjusts those risks. The SEC requires certain disclosures of derivatives and other financial instruments beyond those required under GAAP.

SFAS No. 125, *Accounting for Transfers and Servicing of Financial Assets and Extinguishments of Liabilities* (Accounting Standards Section F35), provides accounting and reporting standards for transfers and servicing of financial assets and extinguishments of liabilities, including standards for distinguishing transfers of financial assets that are sales from transfers that are secured borrowings. Transfers of financial assets by broker-dealers are discussed in Section 6(m), Secured Borrowings.

49.4 RISK FACTORS AND AUDIT REACTION

As a result of high capital leverage, inherent risks are high for broker-dealers. On the other hand, well-developed clearing and settlement mechanisms (at least in domestic markets) make control risk related to securities clearance low in many cases. The degree of risk associated with a particular firm depends on a number of factors, including:

- The "tone" set by top management (e.g., management's risk philosophy, focus on controls, exercise of oversight and supervision, and emphasis placed on profitability)
- The types of financial instruments the firm trades
- The markets in which a firm clears (domestic, net settlement markets pose fewer control problems than emerging markets)
- The effectiveness of the firm's internal control and internal reports to alert management to adverse situations that may expose the firm to losses
- The effectiveness of the compliance and internal audit functions

The securities industry is unusual in the degree to which the details of transactions are substantiated with counterparties, which usually is done on the date of the transaction. If the transaction is being executed on behalf of a customer, it is confirmed with the customer as well.

A further level of control is achieved by the fact that most securities transactions involve the simultaneous (or nearly so) exchange of securities for cash. (This is not necessarily the case in foreign and emerging markets, however.) As a result, most balances on a broker-dealer's balance sheet are collateralized, and for most such balances there are well-developed mechanisms for monitoring the adequacy of the collateral.

Finally, the regulatory environment has an effect on internal control, since it specifies certain procedures that must be performed regularly. The most significant of these, from an auditor's standpoint, is SEC Rule 17a-13, which requires a broker-dealer quarterly to account for (by means of count or confirmation) securities positions for which it has custodial responsibility.[19]

As discussed earlier, SEC Rule 17a-5 requires that broker-dealers' auditors, as part of the annual audit, report that they have found no material inadequacies in internal control and in the procedures for complying with specific rules dealing with net capital, customer protection, and timely cash collections. Auditors also are required to report on the net capital and reserve formula computations performed at year-end. Accordingly, usually some testing of controls is necessary even if the auditor otherwise would not elect to do so. However, the extent of tests of controls considered necessary for regulatory reporting purposes is subject to auditor judgment; often the net capital and reserve formula computations are tested substantively, rather than by tests of controls over the process, for efficiency reasons.

---

[19] This may be less significant than in the past. Few securities today are held by broker-dealers in physical form. Most are held in book-entry form at depositories, which are often reconciled daily by brokers.

The volatility and risk factors in the industry, and the level of activity in various accounts, affect the auditor's decision to perform interim substantive tests, such as confirming various balances. In many, if not most, cases, the short reporting time frame (60 days from year-end), combined with a typically low control risk assessment, will suggest interim substantiation of account balances and stock record positions. On the other hand, because most assets and liabilities are presented at market value, auditing procedures directed at the valuation objective often will be deferred until year-end.

Rule 17a-5, paragraph (h)(1), requires auditors to be "mindful" of the need to consider synchronizing the application of certain auditing procedures and performing tests in certain areas simultaneously. Typically, stock record substantiation and customer confirmation procedures are performed as of a single month-end. (This is not always the case, however, and careful consideration of the risks involved may allow the auditor to perform tests as of different month-ends.) When performing tests at a single date, the auditor should consider that the reporting capabilities of various stock record subsystems may not always allow for perfect synchronization. For example, a customer subsystem may provide for month-end reporting, while a fail subsystem may report on Fridays. In designing tests, the auditor needs to consider the possibility of deliberate misstatement through use of this lack of synchronization.

Recognizing the operating risks they face, many broker-dealers have established risk analysis departments and devised specialized computerized "exposure reports" to highlight exposure areas. Exposure reports typically identify exposure in repo transactions (discussed earlier) and stock loan transactions, trading limit violations, and aged suspense and receivable accounts. Furthermore, many firms have sophisticated credit functions and internal audit procedures to address risk analysis. The auditor should consider the effect of those controls on the audit strategy by ascertaining the completeness and accuracy of the exposure reports, the thoroughness of management's review of them, and management's responsiveness to adverse exposures reflected by the reports and to recommendations for improvements noted in internal audit reports.

Several types of transactions typically entered into by securities firms have inherent risks that are unique to the industry. A pervasive risk inherent in many financial products is that a liquid market may not exist for them. For example, "private-label," mortgage-backed securities may be traded actively by their sponsor but have a limited market otherwise. Another risk, from both a business and a regulatory viewpoint, is an undue concentration in securities of a single issuer.

Broker-dealers are subject to a unique risk resulting from regulations governing use of customers' securities as collateral for financing arrangements, such as bank loans. As noted earlier, Rule 15c3-3 prohibits broker-dealers from utilizing customers' fully paid or excess margin securities as collateral for customers' bank loans. In addition, under Regulation U, the required ratios of the value of collateral to the amount of loans differ between loans for purposes of financing customer-related activity and loans on behalf of the firm. Thus firms must maintain separate records for customer and firm loans and related collateral.

The inherent risks associated with repo transactions relate essentially to the creditworthiness of counterparties. Because repo transactions are intended to be fully collateralized, they are not considered customers' securities for purposes of the customer protection rule. There is, however, risk involved in these transactions, and regulations have been issued governing them. Among other things, these rules require broker-dealers to obtain repo agreements specifying the contract terms; to maintain certain records; and to confirm repos with the counterparty to the transactions. The auditor should be alert to the procedures for complying with those rules and for evaluating the credit risks assumed by the business. The auditor also should review collateral valuation procedures.

Another type of transaction securities firms may engage in is risk arbitrage, in which a firm invests in securities that generally are involved in mergers or tender offers. In a merger, the acquirer's stock generally declines in value while the acquiree's increases in value. A risk arbitrageur who believes a merger will go through, will buy the acquiree's shares and sell short the acquirer's shares. This is, as its name suggests, a high-risk endeavor. Some firms establish control over this activity by permitting investments only in response to announced deals. Firms that engage in this activity typically limit the exposure that an arbitrageur can accept with regard to a single deal.

The inherent risks unique to underwriting securities include the possibility that underwriters may be required to purchase unsold securities positions offered pursuant to a "firm-commitment" underwriting. (Some underwritings are done on a "best-efforts" basis, which, as its name implies, leaves the underwriter with no risk.) A firm-commitment underwriting results in the need to finance the securities, assume the market risk of ownership, and take haircuts pursuant to Rule 15c3-1. It is not uncommon for the results of failed underwritings to appear in a broker-dealer's inventory, and usually once or twice in a decade there is a major underwriting debacle on Wall Street that leaves billions in unsold securities sitting in firms' inventories. Lawsuits are the other major risk in underwritings. Lawsuits may be initiated by purchasers of the securities under Section 11 of the Securities Act of 1933, under which all persons (including underwriters) connected with a registration statement have responsibility for material misstatements contained therein.

Because there are few barriers to entry in the securities business, and even fewer means for a firm to distinguish itself from its peers, margins on most traditional products have been driven to minimum levels. Typically, only low-cost firms can effectively deal with the clearing of these products, and a few firms have made a business clearing such instruments for others on a large-scale basis. The majority of firms, however, strive toward product differentiation. In a process referred to as "financial engineering," products termed, generically, "derivative products" are created. A derivative product is a complex financial instrument built from simpler, more commonplace instruments, or one whose value is tied directly to price movements in an underlying instrument. An example of the former is the collateralized mortgage obligation (CMO), which is generally a package of ordinary mortgage-backed, pass-through securities, such as those guaranteed by the Government National Mortgage Association, referred to as GNMAs. An example of the latter is the interest-rate swap, which hedges interest-rate movements for a buyer or seller by tracking changes in interest-rate movements in differing markets.

The essence of marketing certain derivative products is to produce instruments that collectively are more valuable than the sum of their parts. The risk to a securities firm is that it may create an attractive derivative instrument for a customer only to be left with another derivative instrument in inventory that has high risk and is undesirable. The least marketable of these instruments have acquired the epithet *toxic waste*. Many firms view the production of these "waste" products as a necessary evil in the process of producing derivatives, and price their products accordingly.

Dealing in derivative instruments poses significant control risk if the risk profile of a firm's inventory is poorly understood. Large firms often rely on complex mathematical models to create and price derivative instruments. The accountants and risk managers charged with monitoring the pricing and risk in a firm's inventory of derivatives are often at a disadvantage to the firm's traders, since they often do not have sophisticated tools to enable them to effectively challenge traders' prices.

In July 1993, the Group of Thirty, an international association of bankers and former government officials, published a study entitled *Derivatives: Practices and Principles*. This study includes recommendations for the management of derivatives. In August 1994, the Derivatives Product Group (DPG) was formed at the suggestion of the Chairman of the SEC. The DPG, comprising members from several large securities firms, was organized to promote monitoring and reporting of risks relating to derivatives product trading. In March 1995, the DPG published *Framework for Voluntary Oversight*, which contains guidelines for monitoring and benchmarking controls related to over-the-counter (OTC) derivatives.

49.5 TYPICAL TRANSACTIONS

As part of assessing control risk, an auditor may perform tests of controls within a firm's major transaction cycles. Although the specific transaction cycles for which this strategy is used depend on the complexity of a particular broker-dealer's operations and the diversity of its product line, two cycles are significant to most firms in the industry: the trading cycle and the financing cycle. This section also describes the underwriting cycle. Although it is usually more efficient to test transactions and balances in this cycle substantively, an understanding of the mechanics of underwriting may be helpful in designing tests of such balances.

Many broker-dealers have state-of-the-art computer systems capable of handling large transaction volumes, new types of financial instruments, and acquisitions of other firms. These systems also include sophisticated computer controls that are applied within a firm's data center and which often enable the auditor to reduce substantive tests considerably. Audit software designed to assist in performing audit tests has not kept pace, however, and general audit software packages cannot address efficiently the numerous hardware platforms, complex processing environments, and multiplicity of products that characterize the industry. As a result, auditors typically develop audit programs tailored to each firm for confirming customers' accounts and performing other auditing procedures. Testing compliance with regulations has proven particularly intractable for generalized audit software, and auditors typically use a combination of testing controls and substantive testing in this area.

(a) Trading Cycle

The trading cycle is concerned with the processing of transactions that generate commissions or trading revenues of a firm. Firms enter into transactions either on their own behalf or on behalf of customers. When a firm acts on its own behalf, it acts as principal in purchasing or selling for its own account. Generally, the purpose of such activities is to make a market in the securities (trading activity) or to invest in securities (investing activity). In executing such trades, a broker-dealer acts as a dealer. In its dealings with customers, it may act as a dealer (i.e., sell from inventory) or as a broker (i.e., act solely as the customers' agent in executing transactions). Exchange-traded securities are brokered, while OTC securities trades are done on a principal (dealer) basis. A hybrid transaction is the "riskless trade," in which a broker-dealer simultaneously executes offsetting OTC trades on a principal basis, without taking the securities into inventory. Brokered and riskless trade revenues are derived from commissions; dealer trade revenues are from trading profits.

The trading cycle encompasses controls over the processing of transactions from the inception of orders to their final disposition in the general ledger. The processing of trades is similar for most domestic securities; however, each type of transaction has certain distinctive features. These features relate to the time required for a transaction to settle (corporate securities transactions generally settle in three business days, while commercial paper, listed options, government securities, and commodity futures transactions generally settle on the same or the next day), the mode of clearance (broker-to-broker or through the agency of a clearing organization), or the terminology used. Nevertheless, the controls and audit objectives for the different types of transactions are the same.

To demonstrate the flow of a transaction in this cycle, a corporate equity securities transaction is illustrated. If the trading transaction is entered into on behalf of the firm, the trading decision is made in the firm's trading department; if the transaction is on behalf of a customer, the order is transmitted by the customer to a registered representative or salesperson. Buy or sell orders are then submitted by the firm to the floor of an exchange for execution.[20] (For securities not listed on an exchange, the transaction is executed directly with a firm that makes a market in the particular security being traded.) Once the order has been executed, a confirmation is sent back to the firm, which then processes the order through its internal processing system, using in-house or service organization computer facilities.

Between the time a transaction is executed and the time it settles, the firm performs several comparisons with information generated by the clearing facilities of the exchanges or other brokers with whom it has dealt, to ensure the correctness of the executed trades. During this time, the firm also submits trade confirmations to customers or, for transactions executed on its own behalf, to firm traders to ensure agreement with their records.

Comparisons and confirmations are important controls that the auditor may test to obtain evidence of their effectiveness in meeting control objectives relating to completeness, accuracy, and authorization of securities and commodities transactions. For example, a control deficiency might be identified by the existence of an unusually large number of unresolved differences relating to clearinghouse comparisons or of

---

[20] Most NYSE transactions are executed automatically through its automated execution service, Super-DOT. Few transactions are executed on the floor. A firm may execute floor transactions through its own floor brokers, or it may use the services of a "two-dollar broker." A two-dollar broker, who may be an employee of another member firm or a freelancer, charges execution fees, known as "floor brokerage," to the transacting broker. Similarly, smaller firms may not have an automated SuperDOT interface and will pay floor brokerage to another firm to execute transactions through its SuperDOT program.

significant differences related to confirmations with other broker-dealers. Most securities and commodities transactions entered into by broker-dealers are with third parties, usually settle in a short time, and are confirmed by third parties on a regular basis. Accordingly, the existence of aged transactions could be an indication of ineffective controls.

On the settlement date, the firm records the transaction in its general ledger. The detailed customer and firm inventory records are updated as part of this process, and the stock record also is updated to reflect the transaction. A stock record is a detailed listing, by security position, of all securities attributable to customers, other brokers, and the firm. One side of the stock record indicates ownership of the security (e.g., customer or proprietary), and the other side shows its location (e.g., depository, vault, at the transfer agent, failed to receive from another broker-dealer, or pledged as collateral for a bank loan or stock loan). The ownership side of the stock record is called the long side and the location side is known as the short side. For each security issue, the record must be in balance (i.e., the longs must equal the shorts).

Most securities transactions are settled on a "continuous net settlement" basis, in which a firm settles the net monetary effect of all settling transactions with the clearinghouse and the net position effect, by security, with the depository. As part of the settlement process, a firm must maintain records of amounts payable and receivable from the clearing organizations and other brokers, as well as of the related securities to be received or delivered. These balances, referred to as fails, are an unavoidable consequence of securities trading. A fail occurs when securities are not received or delivered on the settlement date, and a firm has an open position with another firm or with a clearing organization. When a firm fails to receive securities, its general ledger shows a payable for the contract value of the securities, and the stock record shows a short position for the number of shares not received. Conversely, when a firm fails to deliver, it has a debit balance in its general ledger for the amount receivable from the sale of the securities; the stock record shows a long position on behalf of the firm to which the securities are deliverable. Unsettled agency transactions do not appear on a broker-dealer's balance sheet (except for accrued commission income); only failed agency transactions appear.[21]

In addition to applying procedures to these positions to ensure that amounts receivable and payable are complete and accurate and that pertinent regulatory requirements are being met, many firms have instituted sophisticated procedures for these positions as part of their cash management systems. In all businesses, attention must be given to the collection of outstanding receivables as a means of providing operating funds. In the securities industry, the focus is on obtaining securities that a firm is failing to receive so that they may in turn be delivered, thereby freeing cash to be used in operating the business.

For commodity futures activity, the equivalent of the stock ledger commonly is referred to as the point balance. Detailed ledgers, including money balances, are maintained for each customer's domestic and foreign transactions, and for firm transactions, with the net offsetting balance representing the position with the commodity clearing organization. Commodity futures clearing organizations settle unrealized

---

[21] For firms, such as government securities brokers, that deal in transactions that occur in large denominations, this phenomenon can result in large, random fluctuations in the daily total footings of a broker's balance sheet.

gains or losses daily (sometimes twice daily) with member firms. The daily payment is reconciled through the point balance, and the unrealized gain or loss is included in a customer's account balance in the general ledger.

As noted previously, one of the exclusive franchises granted to securities firms is the right to extend credit to customers to purchase securities.[22] Such loans are referred to as "margin loans." Margin loans must be collateralized by securities held in the borrower's customer account.[23] Firms have margin departments that compute collateral adequacy daily[24] and issue "margin calls" when there is a deficiency. Although the auditor need not be an expert in margining, he or she needs to ensure that proper controls exist over the computation of margin and collection of margin calls.

Control objectives for the trading cycle include ensuring that:

- Orders are executed and processed based on proper authorizations

- Executed orders are recorded and summarized completely and accurately

- Transactions are compared with information received from clearing organizations and other broker-dealers, and discrepancies are identified and resolved

- All transactions are accurately recorded in the general ledger, stock record or commodities ledger, and detailed firm, customer, and fail accounts

- Securities are received and delivered appropriately, and related receipt and payment of cash are recorded completely and accurately

- Securities in-house and at depositories are under control

- Credit extended to customers is within prescribed guidelines, and open balances are collected

- Regulatory requirements with respect to extending credit, executing transactions, and monitoring open positions are complied with

(b) Financing Cycle

In common with other profit-oriented businesses, securities firms require permanent financing. For corporations, permanent financing generally is provided through the sale of common and preferred stock; for partnerships or sole proprietorships, it is provided through contributions to capital.[25] Permanent financing also may be provided through subordinated lending agreements under which funds or securities are provided to a firm for its use in financing operations. Subordinated lending arrangements are evidenced by formal agreements and are entered into for defined periods of time. The claims of these lenders, in the event of liquidation of a broker-dealer, are subordinated to the claims of the firm's customers and general creditors. Subordinated

---

[22] Under Federal Reserve Bank Regulation T, a broker-dealer may extend credit for other purposes. Such loans, which are not subject to the same conditions as loans for the purchase of securities, are called non-purpose loans.

[23] Federal Reserve and NYSE regulations limit the extent of lending, respectively, for the purchase of securities (initial margin) and on a continuing basis (maintenance margin). Commodities regulations permit much higher leverage by a customer.

[24] This procedure is usually highly automated.

[25] Few large firms currently operate as partnerships.

loans, which must be approved in writing by the DSRO (a national stock exchange or NASD) to be acceptable to the SEC, may be treated as capital for computing net capital pursuant to SEC Rule 15c3-1. Since permanent financing is obtained at regular, planned intervals and is not used to fund day-to-day operations, these financing activities are audited as part of capital.

In addition to permanent financing, individual transactions entered into by a securities firm require financing of some kind. The financing may be provided by several sources. For example, fails to receive may be considered as a means of financing fails to deliver. In addition, certain trading strategies on the part of firms and their customers that generate short positions may be considered as financing certain customer and firm long positions. Financing through fail transactions is audited as part of the trading cycle. Financing also may be obtained from customer credit (cash) balances left on deposit for reinvestment. For many firms, this represents an inexpensive source of financing. The customer protection rule (Rule 15c3-3) limits the extent to which such balances can be used. Basically, a broker-dealer can use customer credit balances to finance fully collateralized customer margin receivables. (Other customer credit balances must be locked up in a special reserve bank account.)

Three major sources of external financing in the securities industry are bank loans, stock lending, and repurchase agreements. Bank loans normally are obtained on a short-term basis to meet day-to-day operating needs and may be collateralized by securities or commodities. The market value of such collateral is governed by Regulation U of the Federal Reserve Bank. Pursuant to this regulation, firms are required to maintain prescribed ratios of collateral to loan balances based on whether the loan is on behalf of the firm or its customers. This collateral also must be accounted for separately by loan type and may not be commingled. Since firms are required, pursuant to Rule 15c3-3, to maintain possession or control of customers' fully paid or excess margin securities, only "marginable" securities in customers' margin accounts may be used to collateralize bank loans obtained on behalf of customers. The interest rate charged for bank loans is based on the "broker call" loan rate, which approximates the prime lending rate.

Securities lending is used by broker-dealers to meet delivery commitments that otherwise cannot be met, typically because the firm or one of its customers has sold a security it does not own ("sold short"). In a stock loan transaction, there is a simultaneous exchange of a specific security for cash collateral. (Letters of credit may be used instead of cash.) The lending broker pays interest (rebate) to the borrowing broker. The rebate rate is negotiated on an individual-transaction basis.[26] As part of their daily procedures, firms mark their stock-lending and borrowing transactions to market, a process whereby contract value is compared with current market value and the cash collateral is increased or decreased to maintain the agreed-on relationship between the value of the securities and cash collateral.

Because of the prevalence of stock-lending transactions in the securities industry, many firms act as intermediaries by locating dealers willing to lend securities to other

---

[26] Stock loan rebate rates are lower than broker call rates. (For hard-to-borrow securities, they may be zero.) In addition, the exchange of cash collateral for securities approximates the value of the securities. (Banks typically lend only a percentage of value.) Both of these conditions reflect the fact that credit risk is not built into the pricing of stock loan transactions.

dealers. The income that such firms earn on these transactions is the difference between what they pay to the borrowers of securities and what they charge the providers. These arrangements are known as conduits.

Government securities dealers act as market-makers in government securities and other money market instruments. Since those dealers maintain inventories to be sold to customers, they may hold positions that they either cannot dispose of immediately or have purchased for purposes of speculation. These positions require some form of outside financing, because they may equal many times a firm's permanent financing. Firms that deal extensively in these types of securities use repurchase agreements to finance the inventories.

In a repurchase agreement, a dealer sells to an investor who has funds to invest overnight, a specified amount of securities in exchange for cash, which is deposited in the dealer's bank account. Concurrently, the dealer agrees to repurchase the securities from the investor at a specified date at a slightly higher price, the difference in prices representing the interest to be earned by the overnight investor.

As in securities-lending transactions, many firms act as intermediaries by investing in reverse repurchase transactions. These transactions are called "matched book repos"; firms entering into them earn income on the spread between the interest paid on the repurchase agreement and the interest earned on the reverse repurchase agreement.[27] A firm engaging in repurchase transactions should mark the securities underlying the transactions to market on a daily basis and make calls for additional collateral in the event of significant market fluctuations. Under FASB Interpretation No. 41, *Offsetting of Amounts Related to Certain Repurchase and Reverse Repurchase Agreements* (Accounting Standards Section B10), certain amounts recognized as payables under repurchase agreements may be offset against amounts recognized as receivables under reverse repurchase agreements and reported as a net amount in the statement of financial position, provided that certain conditions are met, such as the transactions having the same counterparty and same explicit settlement date, and the existence of a master netting agreement.

The auditor should note the terms of repurchase agreements vis-à-vis the terms of reverse repurchase agreements or inventory positions.[28] To the extent that repurchase agreements expire before the maturities of the inventory positions or reverse repurchase agreements, the firm may be required to refinance those positions. Depending on prevailing interest rates, financing may be at higher rates than the related investments and could result in a loss to the firm.

Control objectives in the financing cycle include ensuring that:

- Management oversees financing activities
- Stock-lending and repurchase agreements are obtained for each customer with whom the firm conducts such business[29]

---

[27] Often, spreads are only a few basis points.

[28] This is known as temporal matching.

[29] Agreements, particularly those with banks, may name other parties whose securities, held in custody, are actually being lent. Firms should have a mechanism to determine with whom the risk of counterparty loss actually resides, and credit monitoring controls.

- The amount of loans and the value of collateral pledged are authorized and are recorded completely and accurately

- Interest paid and collected is completely and accurately recorded

- Open stock-lending and repurchase transactions are marked to market and additional collateral is obtained, as appropriate

- Credit checks and continued credit surveillance are performed

- The collectibility of stock-lending receivables is evaluated

- Financial statement disclosures are appropriate

(c) Underwriting Cycle

Many firms offer investment banking or underwriting services to assist corporations and state and local governments in raising funds, primarily through the private or public sale of securities.

Generally, securities offered to the public must be registered with the SEC pursuant to the Securities Act of 1933. Securities offered pursuant to a private placement are exempt from SEC registration, although they may be required (as may publicly offered corporate securities) to be registered with the states in which they are offered. In a private placement, the securities are offered to a limited number of investors and generally are restricted as to resale.[30] Private placements are less costly and burdensome than public offerings. Bonds offered to the public by state and local governments, commonly referred to as "municipal underwritings," are also exempt from SEC registration, although the Municipal Securities Rulemaking Board (MSRB), as well as the SEC, supervises firms conducting business in these securities.

As noted earlier, firms may underwrite securities on either a firm-commitment or a best-efforts basis. If securities are underwritten on a firm-commitment basis, the underwriter agrees to purchase the security issue from the issuer at a specified price and then sells the securities to the public at a higher price. When an underwriting is undertaken on a best-efforts basis, the underwriter agrees to sell as much of the security issue as possible. Investment bankers generally prefer the best-efforts basis for securities of emerging companies that do not have proven performance records. Most private placements are underwritten on a best-efforts basis.

Underwritings are costly to complete and require a capital commitment on the part of the underwriting firm, which must purchase any unsold securities and take haircuts pursuant to Rule 15c3-1 on these securities as well as on underwriting commitments and "when-issued" transactions (described below). Also, in computing regulatory net capital, an underwriting firm is required to deduct from capital certain good-faith deposits and receivables attributable to underwritings. As a result, firms that engage in this activity often form underwriting syndicates to sell the securities. An underwriting syndicate normally comprises one or two firms that act as managers and a number of other firms that participate in underwriting the securities.[31] Under-

---

[30] So-called Rule 144A offerings fall somewhere between public and private offerings. They allow unregistered securities to be freely traded among investors meeting certain characteristics.

[31] A third group, the selling group, participates in the sale of the securities but does not commit to take down any unsold securities or otherwise share in any liabilities. As a result, selling group compensation is lower.

writing syndicates are formed on an individual offering basis. In large firms, a high-level commitment committee comprising senior management usually determines whether to participate in an offering.

Before the securities are sold to the public, a due diligence meeting is held between the issuer of the securities and the broker-dealers that intend to manage and participate in the underwriting. At this meeting, financial and other information that relates to the company and the securities to be issued is reviewed. Such information is included in the registration statement. Another purpose of this meeting is to reach a preliminary understanding concerning the general terms of the formal underwriting agreement between the issuer and the underwriters.

Shortly after this meeting, an underwriting agreement is executed between the issuer and the manager of the underwriting syndicate. The agreement specifies the terms of the transaction, including the underwriting spread, which is the difference between the price at which the securities are to be sold and the proceeds to be received by the issuer. (Before the formal agreement, which is usually effective on the date the registration statement is completed, the manager and the issuer operate pursuant to a letter of intent.) The manager, in turn, executes agreements with the underwriting participants for their respective portions of the underwriting commitment.[32]

The manager has the authority to retain a portion of the securities, usually for sale to large institutions such as banks and insurance companies. It is more efficient for the manager to handle sales of this nature directly; in addition, it eliminates the inconvenience of institutional purchasers having to purchase several smaller blocks from various members of the underwriting syndicate. These transactions are termed "group sales" and constitute what is commonly referred to as the "pot."

The newly issued securities may begin trading in the open market in a stock exchange or in the OTC market in what is commonly referred to as the aftermarket. Practical problems may occur for the underwriting syndicate if the securities trade in the aftermarket at a price below that at which they are being sold by the underwriters. In that event, the underwriting agreement may require the manager to stabilize the price by entering a bid for the securities at or close to the offering price. This practice is permissible under the Securities Exchange Act of 1934, but it must be carried out within strict guidelines. Any securities purchased by the underwriter in this fashion are taken into inventory to be sold at a future date.

On the other hand, if the securities sell in the open market at a price above the offering price, investor demand for the offering may be so great that the underwriters may oversell the position by committing to sell to customers more shares than are being offered, that is, by assuming a short position for the excess. If all the customers honored their commitments, the manager of the underwriting would have to purchase shares on the open market to meet the syndicate's commitments; the resulting gain or loss (usually there is a loss) would be allocated to those members of the syndicate that had oversold positions.

In addition to performing the preceding tasks, broker-dealers that function as managers in an underwriting maintain the books and records for the underwriting and account for sold and unsold securities positions for the entire underwriting. They

---

[32] Normally, there are no formal written agreements between the manager and the selling group, which functions as agent for the underwriters.

also maintain detailed income and expense accounts so that the profit or loss on the underwriting can be distributed to the participants on termination of the underwriting syndicate. All participants also maintain records to the extent of their involvement in the underwriting.

For services performed in connection with the underwriting, the manager receives a management fee, which is deducted from the underwriting spread. Members of the selling group also receive a fee for their services, called the selling concession, which is a percentage of the underwriting spread. The selling concession also is deducted from the underwriting spread. The remaining portion of the underwriting spread minus related expenses is allocated to the other members of the underwriting syndicate based on their respective participations.

Transactions in securities that have not been issued because the underwriting has not been completed are considered to be when-issued transactions. When-issued transactions are contracts to purchase or sell securities when, and if, they are issued. These transactions are not recorded in a firm's asset and liability accounts, but are accounted for separately in subsidiary records and in the detailed customer accounts.

49.6 SUBSTANTIVE TESTS OF BALANCES

Based on the inherent risks identified and the assessment of control risk, the auditor plans the nature, timing, and extent of substantive tests. The discussion in this section is limited to accounts unique to the securities and commodities industry. As noted previously, broker-dealers' internal control often permits interim testing of account balances. In particular, also as noted earlier, tests of the stock record often are performed as of a month-end near year-end.

(a) Special Reserve Bank Account

The auditor should confirm the existence of the special reserve bank account, which is required to be maintained in an amount equivalent to the excess credit balance, pursuant to the Rule 15c3-3 computation, attributable to a firm's customers. Similarly, CFTC Regulations 1.20 and 30.7 require segregation of commodity futures or commodity option customer funds. Such funds may be deposited in a bank account (or with a clearing organization or another FCM). The auditor should determine that the special account is subject to a written agreement specifying that, in the event of liquidation, the balance is to be used solely to satisfy customers' claims.[33]

(b) Receivables from and Payables to Brokers and Dealers and Clearing Organizations

Receivable balances consist of unsettled trades with other firms for which the expected settlement date has passed (referred to as fails to deliver), floor brokerage fees receivable, and receivables from clearing organizations. As noted earlier, fails to deliver result from sales of securities (either as principal or as agent on behalf of customers) to another broker-dealer in which the selling broker-dealer cannot deliver the

---

[33] Although these accounts are "for the exclusive benefit of customers," they are broker-dealer assets.

securities to the buying broker-dealer by the settlement date. These transactions appear as long positions on the stock record and as receivables in the general ledger. They are stated at the contract amount.

Auditing procedures for fail-to-deliver balances may include confirmation with the other parties to the transactions. Additionally, the auditor should review the aging of these balances and consider whether monetary balances are fully collateralized by the market values of the securities. The auditor also may wish to review the subsequent collection ("cleanup") of these balances.[34]

Normally, the auditor confirms floor brokerage fee balances with the firms from which they are receivable. In addition, the auditor should review the aging of the receivables and, in certain circumstances, examine subsequent collections.[35]

When buying or selling regulated commodities, FCMs deal directly with the clearing organizations of futures exchanges. When dealing in nonregulated commodities, such as forward contracts, FCMs deal directly with other counterparties. A forward contract is a transaction that will settle on a specified later date and at a specific price; however, unlike futures contracts, for which quantity and delivery date are fixed by a futures exchange, the quantity and delivery date of forward contracts are negotiated by the contracting parties. In addition, forward contracts, unlike futures contracts, usually do not require margin payments, nor are they guaranteed by a clearing organization; therefore, there is greater counterparty risk than with a futures contract. FCMs measure gain or loss on these transactions daily by comparing the current day's value of the contract with the amount specified in the contract. (Unlike futures, however, for which there is daily settlement of gains and losses, gains and losses on forward transactions typically are not settled until expiration of the contract.) If the current day's value is different from the contract value, the difference generally is recorded as an unrealized gain or loss, and as a receivable or payable, as appropriate.[36]

Receivables from or payables to FCMs associated with forward contracts, as well as the existence and terms of the forward contracts, may be confirmed with the counterparties. Since confirming these transactions sometimes can be difficult, the auditor should consider procedures such as reviewing settlement of open forward contracts subsequent to year-end. In addition, the auditor should test the FCM's methodology for the daily valuation of forward contracts, which could involve complex calculations and the exercise of judgment. Furthermore, the auditor should understand the broker-dealer's procedures for assessing the financial viability of the counterparty to determine whether collectibility appears to be a concern.

Receivables from clearing organizations represent the net amount by which secu-

---

[34] Before engaging in an extensive confirmation effort, the auditor should consider the composition of these balances. Often, they are open only a day or two before being cleaned up, are fully (or nearly) collateralized, and may be with reputable counterparties. These conditions should be considered, as they may limit the need to confirm the balances.

[35] Floor brokerage usually is settled through the applicable securities exchange's settlement mechanisms. In designing tests, the auditor may want to take into account the mechanism by which these receivables and payables are settled.

[36] Prices for most such instruments can be obtained from pricing services or directly from the bid/ask screens posted by interdealer brokers in many markets. However, it is often difficult to obtain these prices on a historical basis. The auditor should consider the availability of historical price information in establishing the timing and logistics of the testing of pricing.

rities that a firm fails to deliver exceed its fail-to-receive positions. These balances should be confirmed with the clearing organizations.

Payables to brokers and dealers include payables arising from fails to receive and net payables to clearing organizations. A firm has exposure on fails to receive if the market value of the securities increases and the delivering broker-dealer does not deliver them. At this point, a firm may have to purchase the securities in the marketplace, and a loss will be recognized in the amount of the appreciation on the securities.

Payables should be confirmed with the other broker-dealers. The auditor also should review the aging of the fails to receive and the relationship of market value of the securities to the monetary balance contract value of each fail. For FCMs, payables to broker-dealers relate primarily to a mark to market on forward contracts. This amount represents the FCM's market risk with respect to the forward contracts based on the current value of the commodity versus the forward contract prices. The auditor should confirm the existence and terms of the forward contracts with the counterparty and review the calculation of the mark to market on the contracts and the creditworthiness of the counterparty.

Payables to clearing organizations represent net amounts due for securities that a firm fails to receive in excess of its fail-to-deliver positions. Payables to clearing organizations for commodities represent the amount due for the day's change in margin requirements resulting from a mark-to-market loss on the underlying futures contract. These balances are confirmed with the clearing organizations. Additionally, if appropriate, the auditor should review the aging of the individual positions and the relationship of market value of the securities to the monetary balance or contract value of each fail.

(c) Omnibus Accounts

In a practice known as correspondent clearing, broker-dealers may perform clearing functions for other firms, such as processing trade information, comparing executed transactions with records of other broker-dealers and clearing organizations, and accounting for open positions with other broker-dealers and clearing organizations. The net effect of all transactions with clearing organizations and other broker-dealers is contained in an "omnibus account" of the introducing broker-dealer (i.e., the broker doing the trades, either for the firm or on behalf of customers). Omnibus clearing arrangements provide for clearing brokers to perform the mechanical aspects of settling trades (thus allowing introducing brokers to reduce or eliminate their "back office"), but for introducing brokers to maintain their own customer and securities records. If the clearing organization clears transactions on behalf of introducing brokers on a "fully disclosed basis," the introducing broker-dealer's customers' accounts are recorded by the clearing firm. The clearing firm treats those accounts as if they were its own accounts and is responsible for ensuring that they are collateralized and maintained in compliance with the appropriate regulatory requirements.

In auditing an introducing broker-dealer, the auditor should confirm balances in the omnibus account and should review the clearing agreement and evaluate the firm's procedures for ascertaining the clearing firm's compliance with the clearing agreement. In addition, the auditor should assess, by reference to the clearing agreement, any risks or exposure assumed by the introducing broker-dealer with respect to executed transactions or open positions maintained by the clearing firm on the introducing broker-dealer's behalf.[37] The auditor also should obtain and review the clearing broker-dealer's auditor's report on internal control.

The auditor of a clearing firm should confirm the balances in the omnibus accounts and assess the firm's procedures for ensuring compliance with clearing agreements. The open positions with other broker-dealers, clearing organizations, and customers' accounts should be tested in connection with the previously described auditing procedures applicable to those accounts.

(d)   Deposits with Clearing Organizations

Clearing organizations function as adjuncts to securities exchanges to facilitate the settlement of transactions; their growth has enhanced the ability of broker-dealers to process increasing numbers of transactions. Examples of clearing organizations are the National Securities Clearing Corporation, which clears transactions executed on the New York and American Stock Exchanges; the Stock Clearing Corporation of Philadelphia, which serves as an adjunct to the Philadelphia Stock Exchange; and the Options Clearing Corporation, which clears all listed options transactions.

Clearing organizations net individual transactions in the same security to arrive at one position for each security to be delivered or received between a clearing organization and a firm, and one net monetary balance to be received or paid. Money is received or paid daily. These receivables from and payables to clearing organizations should be reconciled daily. The reconciliations are key controls and thus the auditor usually tests them to obtain evidence that they are operating effectively throughout the year and that any unreconciled items are appropriately disposed of at year-end.

Deposits, which may be in cash or securities, with clearing organizations are made to collateralize open positions at those organizations. (The types of securities suitable for this purpose are defined by each clearing organization and generally comprise U.S. Treasury bills.) The auditor usually confirms deposits with clearing organizations as to type and amount. If securities are on deposit, their market values should be substantiated by reference to independent pricing sources.

Deposits with the clearing organizations of regulated futures exchanges differ from those with securities exchanges. Futures transactions represent legally binding contracts between a firm or its customers (as either buyer or seller) and a futures exchange clearing organization (rather than the counterparty to the transaction). Such contracts obligate the trading parties to buy or sell a standardized quantity of a commodity at a specific future date and price. Since the clearing organization guarantees performance on the contract, it requires a margin deposit. Margin rates vary based on the specific commodity traded. On the date the transaction is entered into, the clearing organization requires an "initial margin" deposit, and the contract is marked to market daily, with any difference resulting in a "variation margin" payable or receivable. All margin amounts are determined at the close of the applicable exchange's

---

[37] Although firms that introduce transactions on a fully disclosed basis generally have no risk once the trade has been executed, many clearing agreements hold the introducing broker liable for certain losses arising out of introduced accounts. The auditor should consider confirming with the clearing broker that no such liabilities exist at the reporting date.

business day and are settled on the following day (some exchanges have intraday settlements).

Deposits made with clearing organizations of regulated futures exchanges may consist of cash, certain obligations of the U.S. government, or letters of credit, as determined by the various exchanges. These deposits are segregated between customers' and firm deposits and are accounted for separately. Auditing procedures should include tests of the separate identification of customers' and firm margin amounts.

(e)   Receivables from and Payables to Customers

Receivables from customers comprise debit balances in customers' accounts, which include all accounts resulting from normal securities and commodities transactions other than with other broker-dealers or with persons whose securities or funds either are part of the net capital of the broker-dealer or are subordinated to claims of general creditors. Receivables from customers may include receivables from a firm's employees but may not include balances owed by partners, officers, directors, stockholders, or certain other "noncustomers" as defined by the regulators.

Customers' debit balances arise from the purchase of securities, either in a cash account or on margin, for which the firm has not been fully paid. These receivables are collateralized by the customers' securities held by the firm, which may be used by the firm to obtain financing.

In purchases of commodities, customers' debit balances arise when an initial or variation margin deposit is due. These receivables usually are satisfied within one or two business days. Generally, the margin requirements of an FCM are in excess of the requirements of the applicable exchange. The use of the FCM's margin requirements, and daily variation margin calls, allows FCMs to reduce their risk with respect to commodity customers' debit balances. The auditor should confirm customers' account balances and securities and commodities positions. Consideration also should be given to confirming accounts closed during the year and accounts with zero balances.

The relationships between debit balances and the value of securities in each account should be reviewed. Based on this review, the auditor should assess the reasonableness of the firm's allowance for uncollectible accounts. The auditor should evaluate the firm's procedures to ensure the adequacy of margin in customers' accounts and the issuance of calls for additional margin, and should review the firm's procedures for compliance with Regulation T of the Federal Reserve Bank.

Payables to customers comprise credit balances in securities customers' accounts that are owed in connection with sales of securities, or open trade equity and securities or other collateral on deposit for commodities customers' accounts. These balances are audited as part of the customer account confirmation process.

(f)   Firm Inventory Accounts

Firm inventory accounts include securities that are owned by the firm; they are classified as either trading or investment accounts. Trading accounts contain securities purchased for resale to customers or other brokers and are a firm's stock-in-trade. Investment securities are intended to be held for longer periods than are securities in trading accounts and are purchased with the expectation of capital gain.

For financial statement purposes, firm inventory accounts should be classified into marketable securities and securities that are not readily marketable. Securities in firm inventory accounts are valued at current market value for financial statement purposes. Unrealized appreciation and depreciation in values are included in determining net income; as a result, deferred taxes should be computed, if appropriate, on gains and losses in investment accounts.[38] The auditor should reconcile the securities in the firm investment accounts to the stock record. In addition, the market values of the securities should be substantiated by reference to financial journals or other independent sources, which may best be accomplished on the reporting date.

Market values may not be available for all securities positions. For example, market quotations for some bonds issued by municipalities are not readily available. For those bonds, values are determined by management, based on various factors such as the rating of the bond, its coupon rate, the prime lending rate, unique redemption provisions of the bond, and its maturity date. In addition, firms may hold other securities for which there are no quoted market prices, or for which the quoted market prices are not reflective of what the firm could obtain for the securities in a sale. These may include securities purchased in a merchant banking transaction that cannot be sold or offered because of a restriction, or that are pending registration pursuant to the Securities Act of 1933. In these instances, management of the broker-dealer should value the securities based on the earnings records of the companies in conjunction with other factors, such as book values, yields, and current market conditions.

In evaluating the market value assigned a security, the auditor should be mindful that in certain situations the total market value of the security may not be readily realizable, for example, in the case of a thinly traded or restricted security. It is permissible under GAAP for a broker-dealer to value a financial instrument at a value lower than that which is quoted. The notes to the financial statements should disclose the following when financial instruments are valued by a broker-dealer at lower than quoted market prices:

- Description of the financial instrument
- Total value of the financial instrument as measured by the quoted market price
- Total value reported in the statement of financial condition
- The methods and significant assumptions used to value the instrument at lower than quoted market price

Firm inventory trading accounts also include spot commodities, that is, physical commodity, futures, and forward contracts, and options owned by the firm. Commodities, like securities, are valued at current market value for financial statement purposes. While the auditor, by reference to financial journals, can substantiate market values for spot commodities and futures contracts that are traded on exchanges,

---

[38] Some firms may be phasing in the inclusion of unrealized gains on trading positions in taxable income, in accordance with recent tax law changes.

market values of forward contracts and options (and nonregulated spot commodities and futures contracts) are determined by FCMs, using calculations that are often complex. Such calculations, which involve a certain degree of subjectivity, consider factors such as current interest rates, period of time until settlement, volatility, transportation costs with respect to commodities purchased in foreign markets, and closing time of foreign markets. The FCM attempts to determine what the commodity would be worth in the normal course of business at the FCM's location. The auditor should review the FCM's assumptions and substantiate the calculation, or use a recognized pricing model to review the FCM's calculation.

Securities sold but not yet purchased (short sales) generally consist of securities that a firm sold but did not have in its inventory, securities sold that are "covered" by call options, and securities that are arbitraged against proprietary long positions.[39]

Hedging short securities positions with call options is a trading strategy utilized by many firms. In its most basic form, it is used by a firm in an attempt to protect itself from price increases by fixing the price at which it will be able to buy securities through exercise of call options. In reviewing these positions, the auditor should ascertain the exercise price of the options relative to the market value of the short securities. In addition, the auditor should determine that the options have not expired. In recent years, many complex trading strategies involving options have gained wide acceptance. In applying auditing procedures in this area, the auditor should obtain an understanding of the transactions, evaluate the risk to the firm, and determine that the firm has given appropriate recognition to regulatory considerations, especially the charges that enter into the computation of net capital under SEC Rule 15c3-1.

(g) Arbitrage Transactions

Securities firms may engage in "classic (riskless) arbitrage" and "risk arbitrage" transactions. In classic arbitrage transactions, the investor purchases and sells similar securities in a like market. Convertible and when-issued securities are the principal trading instruments in this form of transaction. In risk arbitrage transactions (described earlier), the firm invests in securities that are generally the subject of mergers or tender offers. The auditor should understand the nature and purpose of arbitrage transactions entered into by the firm. In addition, the auditor should determine that the appropriate haircut is taken pursuant to Rule 15c3-1.

Commodities firms also engage in a type of arbitrage transaction. In these transactions, the FCM or customer purchases one commodity contract and concurrently sells another contract for the same commodity. These types of transactions have increased through global trading of commodities as traders seek price variations in the same commodity on a global basis. For example, an FCM can purchase a forward contract for gold in London and sell a gold futures contract for a like amount on the Commodity Exchange in New York. The auditor should ensure that the commodity purchased is deliverable against the commodity sold and that the costs of delivery and similar costs are considered in the valuation process.

---

[39] Firms may go "short against the box," i.e., have long positions that offset short sales. These are not offset for financial statement purposes.

(h) Securities Positions

The auditor should review the stock record as a basis for auditing all securities positions, both long and short. For example, the auditor should determine that securities related to fails to receive or fails to deliver are confirmed in connection with the fail confirmations, that securities at clearing organizations and depositories are confirmed, that securities positions attributable to customers are confirmed in connection with the audit of customers' accounts, and that securities held in the firm's custody are counted. In addition, the auditor should review the mathematical accuracy of the stock record and ensure that any out-of-balance conditions are appropriately resolved.

Pursuant to SEC Rule 17a-5, the auditor should determine that the firm has complied with all other provisions of Rule 17a-13. Specifically, on a quarterly basis, the firm is required to count or confirm all securities positions in its possession or control. (Some firms may cycle count their positions, i.e., verify them on an ongoing basis throughout a quarter.) These generally are considered to be securities in the broker-dealer's vault, securities at custodians or depositories, fails to deliver, stock loans, and securities in transfer. Accordingly, it is customary for the auditor to count securities in the physical possession of the broker-dealer or observe and test the count performed by the broker-dealer's personnel. In the latter instance, the auditor should ensure that the broker-dealer's procedures result in a complete and accurate count. In addition, the auditor should perform some independent test counts.[40]

The auditor should ensure that all securities are counted, including those for which the broker-dealer exercises custodial and fiduciary responsibility. In that regard, customers may leave their fully paid securities with the broker-dealer to be held on their behalf. Those securities may be in the names of the individual customers or in the broker-dealer's "street name" (i.e., the name of a nominee of a broker-dealer). Typically, securities registered in customers' names are located in areas of the broker-dealer's stock record identified as "safekeeping."[41] Customers' fully paid securities registered in street name are typically at a depository and identified in the stock record in a location designated as "free." Such designation indicates that the securities have not been pledged as collateral for a loan.

The auditor should evaluate the procedures for recording and summarizing count differences and determine that those differences are resolved appropriately. The auditor also should determine the cause and disposition of unresolved differences and their impact on the financial statements and other regulatory reports.

The observation of the broker-dealer's count can be made either at interim or at

---

[40] Not that long ago, the "vault count" was a major part of an audit of a securities firm. Often these counts lasted for days, employed dozens of counters and test counters, and resulted in hundreds or even thousands of differences between the count and the stock record. With virtually all domestic securities now held in book-entry form, a vault today may be closet-sized, the count of its contents may take only a few hours, and there may be no differences at all.

[41] Safekeeping accounts are unusual. Most securities firms have found it unprofitable to maintain stock-record locations for these positions and, if customers refused to allow them to be reregistered in street name, returned them to their owners. In some foreign countries, however (e.g., Brazil), street name accounts do not exist and all securities are held in customers' names. This may require substantial additional reconciliation procedures for a U.S. broker-dealer.

year-end, depending on the auditor's assessment of control risk. Also, as part of auditing the securities positions, the auditor should determine the nature and value of securities held by transfer agents, securities in transit, and securities held at branch offices. Appropriate tests should be performed based on the materiality of those securities in relation to the financial statements of the firm and on the controls applied to them.

Most positions are held at depositories and custodial organizations. The positions reported by these organizations should be reconciled with the broker-dealer's stock record daily. Auditors should confirm positions directly with these organizations and test the firm's reconciliations as of the date selected for confirmation.

FCMs maintain a physical commodity inventory similar to a stock record. Generally, physical commodities are represented by warehouse receipts, which are negotiable instruments. These warehouse receipts, which may be held in an FCM's vault or by a custodian, are numbered and state the commodity type and quantity. The inventory record should include this information for each warehouse receipt and indicate the location of the receipt and ownership (firm or customer) of the physical commodity. In testing the accuracy of the inventory record, the auditor should examine the warehouse receipts in the FCM's possession and confirm those held by custodians.

In addition to a physical commodity inventory, FCMs prepare a "point balance," which is a listing by commodity type of all open futures contracts. This report shows the contract price, the current market value, and the gain or loss caused by the difference. This difference should be the balance of the amounts due from, or to, the respective futures exchange clearing organization. While the CFTC requires this report monthly, most FCMs prepare it daily to facilitate their reconciliations with clearing organizations.

(i) Suspense and Error Accounts

The auditor should determine the composition of securities and cash balances in suspense accounts. Generally, suspense items are attributable to transactions that cannot be readily identified as to the appropriate customer, broker-dealer, or firm account. Thus they are "suspensed" until the necessary research is performed to determine their disposition. As a rule, balances should remain in suspense accounts for only a short time.

In reviewing suspense balances, the auditor should determine their appropriate resolution and their impact on the financial statements and on other auditing procedures.[42] For example, balances in suspense accounts that are resolved against customers' accounts may, if material, cause the auditor to amend the confirmations sent to customers. The auditor also should review the broker-dealer's procedures for the timely resolution of suspense balances and determine their impact on SEC Rule 15c3-1 and Rule 15c3-3 computations.

Error accounts contain cash or securities balances, as well as profit and loss amounts, that are attributable to errors on the part of a broker-dealer, usually in processing orders on behalf of the firm or its customers. For example, if as the result of

---

[42] A short suspense difference, for example, exposes the firm to risk equal to the value of the difference until it is located. Auditors need to evaluate unresolved differences.

an incorrectly prepared order ticket, 100 shares of ABC Company were purchased on behalf of a customer instead of 100 shares of XYZ Company, the ABC shares would be placed into an error account until they were sold. Any profit or loss realized on the subsequent sale, as well as any profit or loss incurred in connection with the purchase of the XYZ shares, also would be placed into the appropriate "error" profit and loss account. (In many firms, securities positions attributable to errors are recorded in the proprietary trading accounts, and the profit or loss resulting from the liquidation of those positions is included as trading profit or loss.)

The auditor should assess the controls over error accounts as a basis for determining the nature, timing, and extent of auditing procedures. The auditor also should determine that management performs sufficient review and follow-up procedures to ensure that appropriate corrective action is taken on a timely basis.

(j) Dividends Receivable and Payable

Cash or stock dividends receivable should be reviewed as to completeness and as to age and collectibility. The auditor should review the broker-dealer's procedures for recording dividends payable. Based on this review, the materiality of the individual balances, and the assessment of control risk, the auditor may decide to test the accuracy of these balances.

Many firms record dividends receivable and payable on the payable date rather than on the record date. The auditor should review the amount of dividends receivable and payable attributable to record dates and payable dates that straddle the balance sheet date to ascertain the materiality of those amounts, and consider their impact on the financial statements. The auditor also should review procedures for recording unclaimed dividends to ascertain the broker-dealer's compliance with the pertinent state escheat laws.

(k) Exchange Memberships

Exchange memberships are either owned by the broker-dealer or contributed to the firm under a subordinated lending agreement. The carrying value of exchange memberships owned by the firm for financial statement purposes is cost. Exchange memberships contributed for the use of the broker-dealer and subordinated to claims of general creditors should be carried at market value, with an offsetting amount shown as a liability subordinated to claims of general creditors. Generally, a valuation reserve is not established unless a reduction in market value is considered to be other than temporary.

The ownership of exchange memberships and their current market values (usually the last price of a membership sold) may be confirmed directly with the exchanges. The propriety of considering exchange memberships as assets of the broker-dealer should be evaluated by reference to partnership agreements or other documents.

(l) Bank Loans

Bank loans are obtained by securities firms as a means of financing customer and firm positions. Loan balances, as well as the related collateral, should be confirmed with banks.[43] If formal lending arrangements exist, such as those for compensating balances and commitment fees, the auditor should confirm those arrangements. In addition, the collateral (customer or firm securities) should be reviewed to determine the firm's compliance with SEC Rule 15c3-3 and Regulation U of the Federal Reserve Bank.

(m) Secured Borrowings

Broker-dealers enter into securities borrowing and lending transactions, repurchase (repo) and reverse repurchase (reverse repo or resale) agreements, and dollar repurchase agreements (also called "dollar rolls"). SFAS No. 125, *Accounting for Transfers and Servicing of Financial Assets and Extinguishment of Liabilities* (Accounting Standards Section F35), provides guidance for determining whether those transactions and agreements, which involve transfers of financial assets, should be accounted for as sales or as secured borrowings with pledge of collateral.

Regardless of the accounting treatment, broker-dealers document securities-lending transactions as loans of securities in which the borrower provides collateral in the form of cash, other securities, or standby letters of credit. Repo and reverse repo agreements typically are documented as agreements to sell and repurchase the same securities. Dollar rolls are documented as agreements to sell and repurchase substantially the same, but not identical, securities.

The auditor should consider the controls over all transactions and agreements involving transfers of financial assets. The auditor also should determine whether there are adequate procedures for ensuring that appropriate collateral is obtained. Furthermore, the auditor should review the relationships of the monetary balances arising from transactions and agreements involving transfers of financial assets to the value of related collateral to determine whether any material discrepancies exist.

The auditor should confirm balances related to borrowing and lending, repo, reverse repo, and dollar roll agreements with the relevant counterparties, as well as the terms of the agreements and the related collateral (and its location), and should focus on the relationship of amounts owed to the collateral received, as part of assessing collectibility and any required charges to income. The auditor also should determine that the transactions are properly accounted for under SFAS No. 125 and that the appropriate capital charges are taken in accordance with Rule 15c3-1.

In examining balances arising from transfers of financial assets, the auditor should be cognizant of the credit risks associated with the related transactions and should determine that the broker-dealer is diligent in obtaining the necessary collateral. In addition, for reverse repo agreements that are matched with repo agreements, the auditor should ascertain whether any exposure exists with respect to repo agreements that expire before the maturities of the related reverse repo agreements, in which case the auditor also should determine the broker-dealer's ability to refinance these positions.

---

[43] Some loan agreements may provide an agreement to pledge collateral in which the broker agrees to collateralize the loan daily but does not transfer the collateral to the lender. In such situations, the lender is likely to be able to confirm only that the broker advised it of securities pledged as collateral.

(n) Subordinated Liabilities

Subordinated liabilities are borrowings, pursuant to formal lending agreements, that are subordinated to the claims of general creditors. Typically, a subordinated lender provides cash in return for the firm's formal agreement to pay a stipulated interest rate. A subordinated agreement also could take the form of a secured demand note, under which the lender provides the firm with securities or other collateral that may be used by the firm to borrow funds to finance operations. In a secured demand note transaction, the firm records a receivable for the amount of the subordinated loan, which should be less than the value of the securities that serve as collateral. The auditor should ascertain whether subordination agreements have been approved by the appropriate regulatory bodies, whether the balances of the liabilities are stated fairly, and whether the value of the related collateral is accurately computed. This may be confirmed directly. The auditor also should confirm the expiration dates of the agreements, the extent of the amount subordinated, any limit as to that amount, and the exact nature of the liability to the subordinating party.

Subordinated debt is considered capital for regulatory purposes, as long as it has been so approved by the firm's designated self-regulatory organization. For financial reporting purposes, it is a liability.

(o) Open Contractual Commitments

Contractual commitments that normally are not recorded in the statement of financial condition include, among other items, underwriting commitments, swaps, when-issued contracts, endorsements of puts and calls, futures and forward contracts, and commitments in foreign currencies. The auditor may wish to confirm those contractual commitments (other than endorsed puts and calls, the holders of which are unknown). In many cases, the commitments of customers will appear in the accounts of the customers and will be confirmed when the accounts are confirmed. In other cases, information concerning purchases and sales of securities on a when-issued or when-distributed basis may not appear in the accounts of customers or in the stock record but instead may be maintained in a subsidiary record (such as tickets in an open contract file). In such cases, the open contracts may be confirmed in the same manner as are other accounts.

A swap is a contractual agreement in which two counterparties exchange cash flows. Broker-dealers enter into swap transactions to deal, to take proprietary positions, to effect economic hedges of instruments in other trading portfolios, or to execute arbitrage strategies. Swaps entered into by dealers should be carried at fair value, with resultant gains and losses reported currently in income. Fair value generally is considered to be the value that could be realized through termination or assignment of the swap. Although there is no standard for determining the fair value of a swap, common valuation methodologies would incorporate a comparison of the terms of the swap to the current treasury security yield curve and swap-to-treasury spread quotations, or to the current swap yield curve. The swap yield curve is derived from quoted swap rates. Dealer bid and offer quotes are generally available for basic interest rate swaps reflecting investment-grade counterparties. Factors that could influence the pricing of an individual swap include the counterparty's credit standing and the complexity of the swap. When those factors differ from the basic factors underlying the quote, an adjustment to the quoted rate should be considered.

In connection with the mark to market of swap contracts, unrealized gains should be recorded as assets and unrealized losses as liabilities on the statement of financial condition. In accordance with FASB Interpretation No. 39, *Offsetting of Amounts Related to Certain Contracts* (Accounting Standards Section B10), unrealized gains and unrealized losses arising from contracts executed with the same counterparty under a master netting arrangement may be offset.

Disclosure of the underlying notional principal amounts associated with swap contracts is required by SFAS No. 105, *Disclosures of Information about Financial Instruments with Off-Balance-Sheet Risk and Financial Instruments with Concentrations of Credit Risk* (Accounting Standards Section F25).

(p) Soft-Dollar Arrangements and Order Flow Payments

The term "soft dollars" is used to describe an arrangement in which a broker-dealer provides services (often, research) to a customer in return for trade order flow from that customer. This generates commission income for the broker-dealer. These agreements are generally oral, and the value of the services to be provided typically is based on a percentage of commission income. Soft-dollar customers are typically institutional investors or money managers. Soft-dollar services may be either generated internally by the broker-dealer or purchased by the broker-dealer from a third party.[44]

At the date of the statement of financial condition, the broker-dealer should analyze both the commission income generated from soft-dollar customers and the services provided to the soft-dollar customers. This analysis determines whether a liability should be accrued for services due to customers based on the commission income generated or whether any soft-dollar expenses have been prepaid and need to be deferred. The realizability of any prepaid expenses should be evaluated at the audit date.

It is common in over-the-counter markets (less so in listed markets) for firms that make markets to pay customers to direct order flow to the firms. Auditors should inquire of management as to the existence of any such arrangements and ensure that any obligations have been properly accounted for.

(q) Underwriting Agreements

The auditor should review underwriting agreements to ascertain the terms and amounts of open contractual commitments. In measuring the amounts of those commitments, the auditor should determine the underwriter's liability for unsold positions. That liability may be either divided—meaning that each participant in the underwriting syndicate is responsible for purchasing a specified maximum number of shares of stock or principal amount of bonds—or undivided—in which case each participant is liable for a designated percentage of unsold securities. The auditor also

---

[44] Certain types of customers (asset managers) are limited in the types of services that they may receive as soft-dollar payments. The SEC's safe harbor rules lay out the types of services that applicable customers may receive. Other types of customers can, and do, receive a wide variety of services.

should confirm when-issued transactions with the customers that committed to purchase those securities. If the amounts are material, the broker-dealer should consider the need to disclose those transactions in a note to the financial statements. The auditor may review the subsequent settlement of those transactions.

With respect to private-placement transactions, the auditor should review with management the agreements between the broker-dealer and the companies issuing the securities to ascertain whether the broker-dealer has any obligations that require disclosure in the financial statements.

Generally, good-faith deposits are required in connection with the purchase of new issues of securities. When a firm acts on behalf of a syndicate, each member's share of the good-faith deposit is given to the manager. As part of the audit of the managing underwriter, the good-faith deposit may be confirmed with the issuer, and the liability for participants' deposits may be confirmed with the participants. In auditing a participant, the auditor may confirm the good-faith deposit with the managing underwriter. The auditor should review the aging of good-faith deposits to ascertain that the appropriate capital deductions have been taken pursuant to Rule 15c3-1.

There is customarily a lag between the time an underwriting is completed and the time all expenses are accounted for and the profit or loss allocable to the participants is distributed. In an attempt to expedite this settlement process, Rule 15c3-1 imposes capital charges for receivables relating to underwritings. In performing substantive tests of those balances, the auditor should focus particularly on any unusually old balances. In auditing the accounts of the managing underwriter, the auditor should consider the adequacy of procedures for recording revenues and expenses pertaining to these items, including necessary accruals. In an audit of a participant in an underwriting, the auditor should review agings of receivables and, as appropriate, examine subsequent collections. Also, the auditor should review the receivable balances in light of Rule 15c3-1 to ascertain that the appropriate capital deductions have been taken.

To obtain additional assurance as to the completeness and accuracy of the firm's records of underwriting commitments, the auditor may review for a selected period the "tombstone" advertisements that appear in newspapers and financial journals announcing the offering of securities. The auditor's purpose in this review is to determine that the broker-dealer has recorded the commitments pertaining to the offerings in which its name appears as manager or participant. Tombstone advertisements, however, are not necessarily published for each underwriting.

As part of the evaluation of litigation, the auditor should ascertain the existence of any lawsuits or pending claims resulting from underwriting activities and determine their impact on the financial statements. Specifically, the auditor should determine whether the participants in an underwriting syndicate are jointly or severally liable for legal claims arising in connection with the underwriting. Generally, if the participants are severally liable, each participant is liable only to the extent that it is responsible for the claims, that is, they relate to its portion of the securities underwritten. If the participants are jointly liable, each participant is responsible for all claims to the extent that they are not satisfied by the other participants of the syndicate. The auditor should ensure that representation has been obtained from legal counsel involved in each underwriting as to the status of actual or pending litigation and, if possible, an estimate of the potential liability and assessment of the possibility of an adverse outcome.

In addition to their underwriting activities, many firms provide corporate finance services in which they advise businesses in connection with mergers and acquisitions and with corporate reorganizations, assist in tender offers for securities, and provide various types of investment advisory services. The auditor should review the receivables resulting from fees attributable to those activities and perform appropriate substantive tests, such as confirming the balances or examining underlying agreements, letters of arrangement, and so forth; reviewing the aging and subsequent collection of the balances; and ascertaining that income as well as any related expenses are recorded in the proper accounting period.

(r) Interest, Dividends, and Rebates

The income statement classification of interest, dividends, and rebate income and expense varies, because certain transactions are entered into as financings while others are entered into as part of trading strategies. When stock loan and repurchase transactions are entered into for the purpose of financing positions, the rebate or interest expense should be reflected in the income statement as an expense separate from trading gains or losses.

As noted earlier, broker-dealers sometimes enter into matched stock borrowing and lending transactions as a finder or conduit, or enter into repurchase and reverse repurchase agreements as a part of a matched book trading strategy. Further, complex trading strategies often involve numerous long and short positions in different products, so that those positions reflect a trading position that is different from their individual components. While the SEC requires public companies to report such amounts gross, there is diversity in practice among private companies, and income and expense resulting from those activities may be reflected net in the income statement. The auditor should ensure that the income statement classification of interest, dividends, and rebates is consistent and conforms with the firm's policy for such accounts and with SEC requirements, where applicable.

(s) Derivatives

The value of a derivative financial instrument generally is linked to an underlying security, commodity, or index. Derivatives can be entered into in exchange for no cash payment (e.g., swaps and forwards) or for a cash payment that is small in relation to the potential risks and rewards associated with them (e.g., margin deposits on futures contracts and premiums for option contracts). SFAS No. 119, *Disclosure about Derivative Financial Instruments and Fair Value of Financial Instruments,* covers the disclosure requirements for derivative financial instruments. The SEC requires certain disclosures of derivatives and other financial instruments beyond those required under GAAP.

For all firms engaged in transactions involving derivatives, the auditor should:

- Identify the types of derivatives used
- Develop an understanding of the nature of each derivative and its underlying economic substance
- Understand management's strategy for entering into the transaction
- Assess the risks associated with each derivative and evaluate how those risks affect the firm's operations

These procedures should be performed as part of the planning phase of the audit, considered in developing the audit strategy, and reconsidered during the course of the audit as additional information becomes available.

Many derivatives have significant off-balance-sheet risks. Auditing procedures designed to identify derivatives with off-balance-sheet risk include:

- Reviewing the minutes of the board of directors and executive or operating committee meetings for information about material transactions authorized or discussed, or for approval of overall firm policy as to investment, financing, and hedging philosophy and guidelines

- Inquiring of management as to whether such transactions are occurring and, if so, where they are being given recognition

- Reviewing, to the extent practicable, accounting records for large, unusual, or nonrecurring transactions that may involve exposure to significant credit or market risk

- Obtaining representation from management that derivatives have been properly recorded or disclosed in the financial statements

Derivatives without readily determinable market prices are valued in good faith by management. In general, the auditor should review all information considered by the board of directors and management to determine whether the procedures followed in estimating the value are reasonable.

(t)   Supplementary Information Under Rule 17a-5

The auditor should perform auditing procedures with respect to the computation of net capital under SEC Rule 15c3-1, the computation of reserve requirements pursuant to Rule 15c3-3, and the information relating to possession or control requirements under Rule 15c3-3, all prepared as of the date of the financial statements. Those procedures may include reperforming the calculations, reasonableness tests, and analytical procedures directed at significant items in the determination of the various computations. The nature, timing, and extent of those auditing procedures are based largely on the auditor's assessment of control risk. Furthermore, in applying auditing procedures to these schedules, the auditor should consider that such information is not a part of the basic financial statements prepared in conformity with GAAP, but is supplementary information required by Rule 17a-5, and that the schedules must be considered in relation to the basic financial statements taken as a whole.

(u)   Other Areas

For many broker-dealers, fixed assets, depreciation, prepaid assets, and expenses may not be material in relation to net assets, and the auditor can use analytical procedures to test the reasonableness of account balances. The management representation letter should include industry-specific items, including those concerning compliance with regulatory requirements. An illustrative representation letter is presented in the AICPA audit and accounting guide for brokers and dealers.

Index

Note: **Boldface** numbers represent chapters; lightface numbers represent page numbers; and an *n* following a page number represents a footnote.